**AA**

# 3 MILE
# ROAD
# ATLAS
## — OF —
# BRITAIN

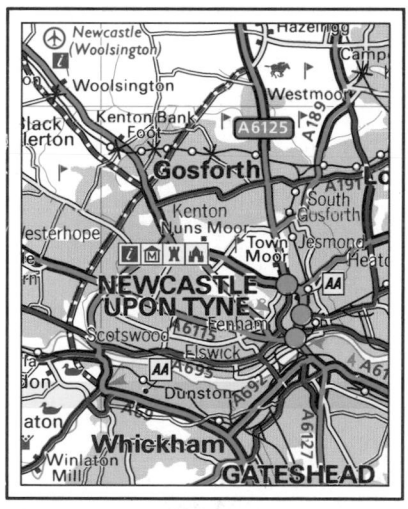

1:200,000
Approximately 3 miles to 1 inch

**6th edition October 1989**
5th edition October 1988
4th edition October 1987
3rd edition October 1986
Reprinted December 1986
Reprinted March 1987
2nd edition September 1985
Reprinted April 1986
1st edition February 1985

Published by The Automobile Association, Fanum House, Basingstoke, Hampshire RG21 2EA. ISBN 07495 0000X

Printed by Graficromo SA, Spain.

The contents of this book are believed correct at the time of printing. Nevertheless, the publisher can accept no responsibility for errors or omissions, or for changes in the details given.

Mapping produced by the Cartographic Department of The Automobile Association. This atlas has been compiled and produced from the Automaps database utilising electronic and computer technology.

The London section is based on Ordnance Survey maps with the permission of the Controller of Her Majesty's Stationery Office. Crown copyright.

Every effort has been made to ensure that the contents of our new database are correct. However, if there are any errors or omissions, please write to the Cartographic Editor, Publishing Division, The Automobile Association, Fanum House, Basingstoke, Hampshire RG21 2EA.

A CIP catalogue record for this book is available from the British Library.

# CONTENTS

## INTRODUCTION

This atlas begins with a unique index to the landscape features of Britain. Listed here are mountains, glens and valleys, waterfalls, caves, heaths and moors, forests, lakes and reservoirs, rivers and canals, bays, cliffs and headlands, and islands of England, Scotland and Wales – a total of approximately 8000 entries. Also in the index are National Parks, Areas of Outstanding Natural Beauty and National Scenic Areas.

Each entry in the index is followed by the National Grid reference, to enable you to find its exact position. An explanation of how to use the National Grid is given on page 78.

Throughout the index, a selection of landscape features is described and illustrated, including all the National Parks and all National Scenic Areas. Acknowledgements are due to the staff of both Countryside Commissions and the two National Trusts, for England and Wales, and for Scotland.

## THE 3 MILE ROAD ATLAS

At the scale of approximately 3 miles to 1 inch, this atlas offers superb clarity and detail. The atlas includes local radio maps, a detailed London street map, 61 town plans with area plan and street index, and 12 town plans marked out for tourists. It is preceded by 10 pages of route planning maps, designed to help you plan long distance journeys quickly and easily – for a full explanation of how to use the maps, start reading at page 66.

# National Parks

*The 1949 Act of Parliament proposing the setting up of National Parks was the culmination of over half a century of pressure for greater access to, and more protection for, areas 'of beautiful and relatively wild country'. It was intended to create 12, but the Sussex Downs and Norfolk Broads schemes were later rejected.*
*When designated, the parks faced almost constant threats from various 'special interest' groups. They still do, but much of Britain's finest scenery is now protected and is available for us to explore. Hopefully, by continuing to visit National Parks, we will persuade governments to maintain that protection.*

# Brecon Beacons

Grid ref: 33 SO02

*There is a significant difference between the Beacons and the Peak District National Park inaugurated exactly six years earlier. Where the Peak District includes much private land previously inaccessible to the public, the Beacons have an extensive acreage of common land which has long attracted visitors wishing to escape, however briefly, from the industrialised towns and valleys immediately to the south. Today, with motorways from the Midlands and London creating easy access, the English are also discovering this lovely Welsh landscape.*

Historically the Beacons formed a barrier between the two countries, and they halted the spread of industrialisation when South Wales was swallowed up in the 19th century. Sheep farming remained the industry of the mountains – and what mountains they are! South of the lovely market town of Brecon, at the heart of the Park, stands Pen-y-Fan – the highest peak south of the Snowdon range. To the west is the Black Mountain, still remarkably remote. To the east lie (confusingly) the Black Mountains which run north from Abergavenny to Hay-on-Wye, where bookshops almost equal the numbers of sheep in other parts of the Park.

It is a truism that the character of a landscape is largely determined by what lies beneath it. The dramatic northern ranges are of sandstone, but to the south they give way to limestone and millstone grit. On one 200 ft outcrop of limestone at the far west of the Park stands the medieval ruin of Carreg Cennen Castle. Beneath it is a cave possibly once used as a dungeon, but more spectacular are the great caves carved out of the limestone by the rivers of the south. Some are dangerous to enter but the best known, Dan-yr-Ogof, is well-lit and safe for visitors. Beautiful waterfalls result from rivers like the Afon Mellte passing over millstone grit. People rarely equal nature but one of their better creations is the Monmouthshire and Brecon Canal which shares the valley of the Usk and is a joy in any season.

The motorist is fortunate in that the A40 runs from end to end of the Beacons, giving a sort of overview, while several roads run like fingers into the Beacons pointing out different aspects of their beauty. Drive, for example, from Hay over the road between Hay Bluff and Twympa, and on down the Vale of Ewyas. The views alone justify the nerve tingling occasioned by the narrow (one car's width) route. Make the journey in the evening as the sun sets, halt at Llanthony Priory and stand, surrounded by the velvet blackness of the mountains, under the canopy of stars and absorb the mystic air of peace and timelessness. The Brecon Beacons are full of such places.
*A WATERFALL ON THE AFON MELLTE Caves and waterfalls abound in the limestone and millstone grit of the southern parts of the Park.*

# Dartmoor

Grid ref: 8 SX58

*Daniel Defoe, who had quite a lot to say about the Brecons (and little complimentary!) makes no reference to Dartmoor – proof that the roads which now cross it were no more than dangerous tracks in his day. It remains, without question, the wildest part of southern Britain, with barely a modern settlement on its 95,000 acres. Yet, 3000 years ago, when the climate was very different, Bronze Age people escaped from the mosquito-ridden lowlands to the moor. Here they built and here the evidence remains – the National Trust alone has more than 100 hut circles on the land it owns on Dartmoor.*

The moor is quite literally crossed by two roads, the B3357 and B3212, which intersect at Two Bridges. The B3357 leaves that most civilised of greystone towns, Tavistock, climbing to enter the moor at Merrivale, a good place to explore prehistoric remains. After crossing the West Dart at Two Bridges it runs parallel to the river before meeting it again at Dartmeet, where the East Dart arrives to create a sort of log jam. Steep gradients are encountered at this point, and after Dartmeet the road leaves the moor, becoming one of a series of typically narrow, high-banked Devon lanes.

The B3212 is the major east–west route over the moor, hardly less crowded now than before the A38 was widened almost to motorway proportions in an attempt to handle the bulk of the summer traffic. The problem is that it is one of those roads which retain their appeal however often they are driven. Within two or three miles of leaving Exeter there are glimpses of the distant moor and beyond Steps Bridge rise the magnificent beech and oak woods of the Teign Valley. Moretonhampstead is a busy place set at the real entrance to the moor. Through

*BRONZE AGE REMAINS AT GRIMSPOUND More than 20 hut circles and several cattle pens can be seen at this site.*

*DARTMOOR PONIES graze on the open moorland near the market town of Tavistock at the western edge of the National Park.*

a series of sharp bends and sharper climbs and dips, the road reaches the top of the moor, passing the bleak Warren House Inn named after one of the many artificial mounds built for rabbit rearing in the Middle Ages. Past Postbridge with its pretty clapper bridge and by the conifers marking the edge of Bellever Wood it leads on to Two Bridges where the meeting with the B3357 seems to attract parked cars at almost any season. The last part of the journey takes the B3212 past Princetown and the prison before the road dips steeply, seeming to gather pace as it heads down towards Yelverton.

Some of the very best of Dartmoor is under the control of the Ministry of Defence, and firing ranges cover 78 per cent of the true 'wilderness area'. But it is possible to find solitude just a few yards from the roadside, and to find challenges and deep satisfaction from a day spent following the centuries-old tracks.

Dartmoor occupies a unique place in the affections of those who love wild country. Their presence in large numbers each year helps the effort to retain land for the public.

# Exmoor
### Grid ref: 19 SS74

*'Exmoor is the high country of the winds, which are to the falcons and the hawks; clothed by whortleberry bushes and lichens and ferns and mossed trees in the goyals (valleys), which are to the foxes, the badgers, and the red deer; served by rain clouds and drained by rock-littered streams, which are to the otters.' So wrote Henry Williamson in* Tarka the Otter *and if we add a comment on the wild ponies we have an evocative description of the moor's infinitely varied scenery. Here are bogs and rivers, cliffs and combes; here is magnificent moorland – but sadly only two-thirds of what was present when the Park was established.*

This is no new problem for Exmoor. Unlike most of the other Parks, it has been under pressure from farming interests since the early 1800s when a Shropshire ironmaster, John Knight, purchased much of the old Royal Forest and proceeded to reclaim a large proportion of the water-logged moors for agricultural use. The Exmoor we visit, with its small high-banked fields, owes its present form to the Knight family. Unfortunately, their successful example led generations of farmers to 'nibble' at the Park until 1976 when official action had to be taken to halt the loss of irreplaceable moorland.

The obvious route through the moor is along the A39, which enters Exmoor at Dunster then proceeds close by the coast to Porlock and Lynton before leaving at Blackmoor Gate.

Alternatively, drive up from Tiverton along the A396, beside the Exe, deserting it at Exebridge and taking the B3222, which soon has the River Barle for company, to Dulverton and the edge of Exmoor. Dulverton is the administrative

*LORNA DOONE FARM (left) is one of a number of sites associated with R D Blackmore, whose* Lorna Doone *was based on Exmoor.*

*DOONE VALLEY (below left) The entrance to Hoccombe Combe off Badgworthy Valley resembles the hideout described by Blackmore.*

centre for the Park but don't expect a dull place. It is a bustling, lively town particularly on market day when the talk is of country life. A place worth exploring before setting out along the B3223, at first beside the steeply wooded banks of the Barle and then up on to the open moor. Easily reached diversions are Winsford Hill with its reminders of our past, the Wambarrows and the Caratacus Stone, or that 'prehistoric' monument, Tarr Steps.

Withypool and Exford are at the centre of Exmoor, close to the road and very prettily thatched. Simonsbath was the creation of the Knight family and their headquarters. They built the church, planted the wood and were responsible for improving the roads over the moor. At this point the B3223 turns north for Lynton but the B3358 continues into the north-west corner of the moor through The Chains, one of the bleakest parts of Exmoor. Beyond Challacombe the road reaches Blackmoor Gate and the A39.

Full of 'honeypots' but even more of highlights, Exmoor continually surprises those who claim to know it well and it is arguably the best of the Parks 'out of season'.

*SELWORTHY, arguably one of Britain's most attractive villages, is situated near the coast. It provides a contrast to the wild, bleak moorland to the south.*

# Lake District

Grid ref: 87 SD39

*The largest and the most popular of the National Parks, the Lake District suffers more from over-visiting but a little less from threats to its acreage than any other. It has possessed a special appeal since the Romantic movement began here with the writings of William Wordsworth, and people began to consider the aesthetics of land as opposed to its commercial value. A moving and simple expression of the depth of feeling the Lakes arouse occurred in 1902 when the National Trust appealed on behalf of Brandelhow Woods. Among the subscriptions received was this: 'I am a working man and cannot afford more than 2s but I once saw Derwentwater and can never forget it.' All who visit this unique blend of water, mountains, fells and valleys will echo that comment.*

Even more than in the other National Parks, it is advisable to plan one's travels in favour of walking. This is not just because the true spirit of the Lakes is to be found away from roads, for they carry a good deal of traffic and, in summer, may be congested. For those who are exploring by car the following route will at least provide a flavour of the variety of the National Park area.

Start from Penrith and follow the A592 to Ullswater. If a walk is possible then a visit to Aira Force will indicate the power of the waters which have shaped so much of the Lakeland scenery. Aira, like many of the places on the route, is owned by the National Trust which manages the Hartsop estate around tiny Brothers Water. The road up Kirkstone Pass cowers under Rough Edge which, still dusted with snow late in spring, can look more like chalk than volcanic rock. Past the inn the road drops into Troutbeck where Townend is a unique survival, a yeoman's house which remained in one family for nearly three hundred years and reflects their taste and interests. Try to avoid visiting it on a dull day – there is no electricity!

Cross Windermere by the ferry to reach Near Sawrey. Here, Hill Top belongs, nominally, to the National Trust, but children of all ages *know* that it is the home of Jemima Puddleduck, Tom Kitten and other magical creations of Beatrix Potter. After Sawrey follow the B5285 through Hawkshead towards Coniston. Take the road on the east side of the lake and marvel at the view of the Old Man of Coniston reflected in the waters of the lake. This road is never far from the water's edge and it passes through a series of splendid woods in which several interesting nature trails have been laid out.

Return on the other bank through Coniston to Skelwith Bridge and then up Great Langdale if only to reflect that here was a Neolithic factory producing axes and exporting them to settlements as far away as Hampshire.

At this point the alternatives are almost limitless. Will it be the adventure of Wrynose and Hard Knott Passes, the tourist attractions of Ambleside and Grasmere, or past the chill deadness of Thirlmere to Keswick and Derwentwater? Does a drive round beautiful Bassenthwaite and back to Keswick in the lee of mighty Skiddaw appeal more? Whatever the choice, pleasure is assured even on those true Lakeland days of endlessly sweeping rain.

THE LADY OF THE LAKE, ULLSWATER *(above) Several of the larger lakes are served by steamers which enable vistors to admire the scenery from new viewpoints.*

*TARN HOWS (below) From these conifer-surrounded lakes good views of the high Lakeland peaks can be obtained. Only limited planting of conifers has been allowed in the Lake District.*

# Northumberland

Grid ref: 102 NY89

*Northumberland National Park encompasses the last part of the Pennine Way in its 50-mile length. With so much outstanding coastal scenery in the region it may seem strange that the Park is entirely landlocked, but one explanation is that the marvellous hill country was and still is more threatened than the coast. In particular, the rounded, peat-covered Cheviots and the moors above Hadrian's Wall were seen as needing protection. Linked in an imaginative scheme they have in their midst the contrasting presence of military ranges and forests. The Ministry of Defence uses a large area around Redesdale, while the Forestry Commission has made extensive plantings of conifers.*

This National Park is an area of great and wild beauty allied to remarkable remoteness. Perhaps the bloody history of the area contributes to a sense of unease which can occur when the motorist halts the car and ventures on to the hills. In the south are reminders of Roman occupation and in the north of the Park, memories of violent Border struggles. This is not a comfortable place but a challenge and, for those who get to know it, one which yields great satisfaction.

*THE ROMAN FORT AT
HOUSESTEADS (left), situated in the south of
the National Park, is one of the 17 forts
constructed on Hadrian's Wall. It was once known
as Borcovicium and was built to house up to
1,000 infantrymen. Relics found during
excavations at the site can be seen in the museum.*

*HADRIAN'S WALL (below) runs for 73 miles
across northern England and was built to keep the
Scottish tribes at bay. Some of the best preserved
parts are situated within the National Park.*

Northumberland is not the easiest of National Parks to explore by car because there is no north to south road. The obvious road for the 'Roman' south is the B6318 which marks the lower boundary of the Park. It can hardly be said to be undiscovered and is usually very busy during the holiday season. The A68, which cuts almost exactly through the narrow waist of the Park, is the major route from Newcastle to the Lowland towns and a popular alternative to the A1 to Edinburgh.

A better road for the leisurely traveller is the unclassified road which enters the Park at Alwinton and follows the line of the River Coquet to end about a mile short of Coquet Head. Another unclassified road, from Wooler along the Harthope valley, ends at Langleeford close to The Cheviot, at 2674 ft the highest of the Border hills. A walk to either Coquet Head or The Cheviot (or both) will provide the visitor with a very good insight into the 'heart' of the Park.

# North York Moors

Grid ref: 90 SE69

*Unlike the Northumberland National Park, with its artificial boundaries, the North York Moors Park is clearly defined – a vast lake of moorland set on a high plateau. Granted its proximity to towns like Middlesbrough and York, seaside resorts like Whitby and Scarborough and its nearness to several excellent roads, the Park remains gratifyingly quiet. From that general comment it is necessary to omit the spectacular coast around the resorts, with certain 'honeypots' like Robin Hood's Bay being particularly busy.*

The North York Moors are under less pressure from outside influences than most of the other Parks but erosion of the cliffs by the sea is an ever-present threat, and improved agricultural techniques are leading to the loss of some of the beautiful and colourful moorland.

Another major contrast with the Northumberland Park are the roads which make access to the moors easy and route planning simple. To the south is the A170 which runs from Thirsk to Scarborough following the line of the boundary. Almost immediately on entering the Park, the road climbs Sutton Bank with its steep gradient and famous hairpin bend. The welcoming market town of Helmsley makes a fine centre for exploring the Park. Close by is Rievaulx, one of the most attractive of all ruined abbeys; in remarkably beautiful surroundings on a bend of the River Rye, a gem of a river, it is best appreciated from the Terrace high above.

Running like fingers north from the A170 into the heart of the moors are five dales. All have advocates of their charms

although Farndale is the most visited due to its marvellous spring display of daffodils. In autumn the dales are, if anything, even more colourful. The best way through the moorlands is the unclassified road from Hutton-le-Hole to Rosedale Abbey and onwards to Danby and the valley of the Esk.

The main route to the north of the Park is the A169 which runs from Pickering to Whitby. It passes several fine moors including Lockton and Goathland and close to one of the Park's more controversial landmarks - the Early Warning Station on Fylingdales Moor. The Early Warning Station is so outlandish as to possess some charm, like a huge folly.

The A171 is the major road along the east and north of the Park. To reach the glorious coastal scenery it is necessary to leave the road which turns inland at Whitby, towards Guisborough. Slightly bleaker moors than before are characteristic of this area.

The Cleveland Way footpath runs along the coast and is a good way to explore it. Classic, longstanding resorts, stretches of designated 'Heritage Coast' and some of England's highest cliffs (at Boulby) are among the attractions to be seen.

The western boundary of the Park is formed, in part, by several roads, some unclassified but perfectly good. For example, leave the A19 at Over Silton and head for Kepwick, Cowesby, Boltby and Thirlby – small villages under the Hambleton Hills and all on the edge of this lovely and still quite secret Park.

*HUTTON-LE-HOLE (above) is a pretty, stone-built village in the south of the Park. Its attractions include the Rydale Folk Museum.*

*SUTTON BANK (below) is well known for the steep gradients and hairpin bend as the A170 climbs to its highest point on the Hambleton Hills.*

# Peak District

Grid ref: 74 SK07

*Historically, it is entirely appropriate that the Peak District should have been the first of the National Parks. It was here that the fight for greater access to the moorland of the High Peak had been waged with people prepared to go to prison for the right to walk on Kinder Scout. The National Parks and Access to the Countryside Act of 1949 was the outcome of the struggle, leading to the setting up of all our National Parks. The Peak retains one advantage over all the others: it is run by a financially independent board. As a result it has shown flexibility and flair, introducing a variety of innovative moves which other Parks at home and abroad have copied.*

The Peak District Park is really two in one, but the joy is that both are easily accessible and can even be discovered in one day by the determined traveller. The contrast between the Dark Peak and the White Peak is very marked. The White Peak (even the name is gentle) has the softer, more rounded landscape with lovely, ash-lined and world famous valleys. The authentic voice is the sound of streams bubbling over the limestone rocks – not the wailing wind, fragmenting the call of the curlew on the peat bogs of the Dark Peak. For many, toughened by years of living in harsh conditions in the industrial towns which surround the Peak, the Dark Peak was, and remains, the ideal challenge, the perfect escape to a freedom denied them in their everyday lives. Others, seeking less dominating scenery, make gratefully for the unfailing beauty of the White Peak. And many love both with equal fierceness!

The motorist is very well treated in the Peak District although some parts are just not accessible by car. With the Pennine Way starting in the Park, walking is naturally the major alternative but cycling along special paths is increasingly popular. The greatest danger the Park faces is from over-visiting, but the authority continuously devises ways of dealing with the problems of visitor flow, including exceptionally well signposted routes for motorists in the White Peak.

The A515 is the road for the White Peak passing close to most of the main beauty spots – Dovedale, the valley of the Manifold, Tissington and the fascinating,

*WINNATS PASS This spectacular limestone gorge near Castleton was known as 'Windy Gates' by the Romans. In the mid-18th century a young couple on their way to Peak Forest to be married were robbed and murdered at this lonely site by five miners who, themselves, all met strange deaths.*

evocative Arbor Low. The A6 runs across the Park through or near Bakewell, Haddon Hall, Chatsworth House, Ashford-in-the-Water and Monsal Dale. At least a hint of the grandeur of the Dark Peak can be obtained by taking the A57 up Snake Pass (with a diversion up the unclassified road beside Ladybower Reservoir). To the left is the Kinder massif, to the right Hope Woodlands and then Bleaklow Hill. From Glossop drive south to Chapel-en-le-Frith and then take the A625 to Castleton.

Edale, the show caverns like Blue John, Lyme Park over in the less visited west side of the Park and the country park of Longshaw overlooking the Derwent in the east . . . The rivers Wye, Dove, Manifold, Derwent and Ashop and the quiet, unchanging villages linked by drystone walls . . . All these attractions and much more make some think that this National Park is 'first amongst equals'.

# Pembrokeshire Coast
## Grid ref: 30 SM81

*The smallest Park and, remarkably for an island, the only one which is primarily devoted to the coastline. It has, in St David's, the smallest city in Britain and, in Tenby, the largest town within the boundaries of any National Park. For good measure it is the narrowest Park and the only one to be fragmented. Like all coastlines, Pembroke faces threats from erosion by the sea, oil pollution from tankers (including those which visit Milford Haven), and from tourist pressures. But the glory of the magnificent coast, with its mighty, wave-battered cliffs, is undiminished. Between the cliffs are small, sheltered bays, while offshore are islands, the haunt of seals and literally thousands of seabirds.*

Pembroke is divided culturally and physically. South of a line drawn between Newgale and Amroth, a line marked by a series of castles, is the land known as 'Little England beyond Wales'. Historically it might be argued that this should have been 'Little Normandy' since it was the Normans who conquered and held the more fertile land around Pembroke. The Welsh retreated, with their language and culture, towards St David's Head and the mountains. Physically the division runs along the edge of the old red sandstone and limestone deposits of the south, and the very old Pre-Cambrian and Ordovician rocks of the north. The types of rock help to determine the variety of coastline which is the Park's greatest asset. The coast is not always easily accessible by car and a walk is often necessary.

Not all the roads are classified but it is not difficult to chart a route from Amroth in the east, through Saundersfoot and into Tenby, which has the happy knack of seeming to absorb large numbers of visitors and still remain utterly charming. After a diversion to Manorbier to see the brooding castle, it is possible to study the

*TENBY This attractive resort, set on a rocky promontory, has a picturesque harbour. Parts of the town wall date from the 13th century.*

*ST DAVID'S HEAD is situated at the far western tip of the Pembrokeshire Park. Neolithic, Iron Age and Celtic remains have been found.*

problems of unplanned development at Freshwater East before visiting Stackpole Quay where sandstone and limestone meet to gladden the geologist's heart. If the military permit, St Govan's Chapel, set in a cleft in the cliffs, is an always moving sight. The spectacular sand dunes of Freshwater West complete an introduction to the south Pembroke coast.

Dale is a remote village in a landscape reminiscent of Ireland while the whole of the peninsula by Marloes is a pleasure with fine clifftop views and memorable sunsets. Broad Haven and Solva are remarkably picturesque harbour villages and St David's is still a place of pilgrimage for many. The B4329 is the road from which to explore the wildest part of the Park, north-east from Haverfordwest.

And should the visitor seek something completely different there remains 'the inner sanctuary' – the region of the rivers by Carew Newton and Cresswell, an enclosed, dark area of muddy inlets, piping waders and a sense of timelessness rarely equalled anywhere in Britain. This, too, is Pembroke National Park; as legend has it 'the land of magic and enchantment'.

# Snowdonia

### Grid ref: 69 SH65

*A large and varied Park which offers much more than just the mountain from which it takes its name. The magnificent mountain ranges are, of course, climbed and enjoyed by large numbers of visitors each year. Indeed, one of the greatest problems the Park faces is the over-visiting of some areas, but the Park authority is now taking steps to remedy the position.*

For those who seek solitude in the National Parks, Snowdon has marvellous moorlands. Wild, still untamed country like the 700 acres of rough grazing on Cregennan, the National Trust's holding close under Cader Idris, or, more easily reached, the great moors which lie on either side of the B4407. Here, just below the road, the Conwy river begins to assert itself, swollen by the waters squeezing from the sodden peat. This has always been called 'the swampy place', and anyone venturing a few feet from a car parked by the road will discover why. The moor must look today as it has for centuries, during which the people of North Wales have fiercely defended their land and culture from a series of would-be invaders.

As a complete contrast to the stark beauty of the moors, Snowdon can offer some of the most attractive coastal scenery in Britain. Northwards from the estuary of the Dyfi there are miles of sandy beaches overlooking wide sweeping bays and backed by outstandingly beautiful views

inland towards the mountains.

Motorists have a choice when considering how to explore Snowdonia. They may select the main roads which cross the heart of the region, take to the more demanding unclassified roads into less visited territory or combine the two. Telford's A5 is the main road into the north of the Park. Branching left from it is a series of roads leading to exciting places. Already mentioned is the B4407 which can be linked to the B4406 by a distinctly challenging unclassified road to provide a cameo of the area. The A4086 down or, better, up the Pass of Llanberis and the A498 to Beddgelert skirt Snowdon; they present dramatic but very different views of the mountain. It is easy to follow virtually the whole of the coastline of the Park along the A496 and A493. The A494 from Dolgellau to Bala then the A4212 to Trawsfynydd and the never dull unclassified road back past Pennant Lliw to Bala completes a tour of the central area.

One major road is left; it provides the

*VIEW FROM MOEL HEBOG with the village of Beddgelert and the Snowdonia mountains. The name Beddgelert is explained in the legend of Llywelyn and his dog Gelert. The dog's 'grave' can be seen in the village.*

best overview of Snowdonia. Indeed, the A470 must rank high on any list of memorable roads in Britain. Starting on the edge of the Park at Llandudno it follows the valley of the Conwy up to Betws-y-Coed. It goes through the mountains to the Ffestiniogs where the influence of people is at its most marked, then past Trawsfynydd with its power station and lake. A long run downhill follows, touching the forest of Coed-y-Brenin and then Ganllwyd with its lovely waterfall. The road leaves the Park at Mallwyd on its way through the heart of Wales. Even without a visit to several near at hand diversions, the variety of scenery, beautiful and rugged, along the A470, explains the lure which draws visitors again and again to Snowdonia.

# Yorkshire Dales

## Grid ref: 88 SD96

*A land of green and fertile dales and high, heather clad fells stretching to infinity. A land for walking, where there are a thousand miles of paths and the authority has negotiated access to hundreds of acres of moorland. But a land visited in summer by cars, whose occupants can journey along a well-established network of roads. For much of the wildest country in our National Parks, increased accessibility has encouraged brief visits as well as careful, leisurely exploration.*

Not that the Dales are exclusively wild country. Nor are the high moors entirely deserted. Indeed, it is certain that no previous generations of the Swaledale sheep which roam the fells have witnessed a comparable invasion by man.

What makes the Yorkshire Dales so attractive? There is a completeness about them, a sense of homogeneity rarely matched elsewhere. The architecture, based on native sandstone, has a uniformity which creates harmony. Even those who over the centuries have invaded the area have contributed much in a manner that enhances the whole.

One of the greatest contributions came from the monasteries which, for four centuries, owned and developed large areas of the Dales. They cleared the land, began the practice of enclosing it with dry-stone walls, developed the sheep industry and laid the framework of the road system.

The development of that system ensures that the Yorkshire Dales are exceptionally accessible to the motorist, with roads ranging from trunk to terrifying. Most of the major roads run east–west and it is necessary to use unclassified roads for the exploration of what lies between them.

The B6270 is the road for Swaledale but also for Arkengarthdale, along which an unclassified road runs up to Tan Hill Inn (the highest in England) then turns back to consciously pretty Keld and the B6270. From nearby Thwaite another unclassified road leads past Butter Tubs to Hardraw Force and Hawes, at the head of Wensleydale. Hawes is an ideal centre for exploring the Dales and the A684, which runs clean through the Park, is a good road for the motorist with only limited time.

One of the finest, and certainly the highest, of all roads in the Dales runs from Hawes over Fleet Moss and down historic Langstrothdale to Buckden where it joins the B6160. This is a very different road, following the Wharfe to Bolton Abbey. Wharfedale is the 'White Peak' of the Dales, softer than the other valleys. At Bolton the road joins the A65 which skirts the southern boundary of the Park. It can be deserted at Settle for the B6479 and an exploration of Ribblesdale. From Ribble Head, the B6255 leads back to Hawes but by turning left it is possible to go down to Ingleton and up another exciting road to Deepdale, unspoilt Dent Dale and then back to the B6255 and Hawes . . . But what of that spectacular road from busy Malham to Arncliffe in delightful Litton Dale? What of high hills like Pen-y-Ghent; villages like Aysgarth and Appletreewick? It is possible to 'do' some of our National Parks in a day – but not the Yorkshire Dales.

*SWALEDALE FROM HUNT HOUSE (above) Swaledale runs west from Richmond towards Great Shunner Fell.*

*LIMESTONE PAVEMENT AT MALHAM COVE (below) Spectacular views attract visitors to Malham.*

# Areas of Outstanding Natural Beauty

*National Parks concentrate, by statute, on 'wild country', a definition which excludes much fine scenery. There are almost 40 Areas of Outstanding Natural Beauty in England and Wales, covering over 7500 square miles of land of high quality. Indeed, a glance at the list of AONBs may well lead to the conclusion that they include most of our best-loved countryside.*

No one who studies a list of Areas of Outstanding Natural Beauty can fail to be impressed by the sheer variety of the landscape the areas cover. It might not inspire a William Wordsworth, but it is landscape which John Constable would recognise and paint, and Edward Thomas appreciate and write about, more tranquil than dramatic as a rule.

It will be seen that the majority of AONBs are sited below a line drawn from the Lleyn Peninsula to the Wash. The wildest of our country is the concern of the National Parks and the bulk of it is found in the north. Much of the landscape of

Wales, the Midlands and the south and east of England which has attracted designation as AONBs is no less enjoyable, and it faces the same problems of over-visiting, agricultural and industrial encroachment and, additionally, pressure for housing development.

In addition to AONBs, the Countryside Commission, which designates them, has introduced heritage coasts. The comparatively small amount of coastline protected by National Parks has already been mentioned and concern for the future of some of the finest led to the decision to give it a special status. Already 38 outstanding lengths of coastline have been identified in England and Wales, and the Countryside Commission is contributing to the cost of their management. These are in addition to the stretches of coastline given protection by AONBs; together, the two schemes should ensure the preservation of considerable stretches of beautiful but threatened coastline in England and Wales.

What follows is a brief summary of the features of a limited number of Areas of Outstanding Natural Beauty in England and Wales, selected to represent the variety they include:

**Arnside and Silverdale** Interesting limestone formations and flora at Arnside and important bird life on the salt marshes of Silverdale. Tremendous views from Arnside Knott (NT) over Morecambe Bay and the Cumbrian Hills. Increasingly popular for sailing and birdwatching holidays.

**Cannock Chase** Once a Royal Forest, now valued for its wildlife.

**Chichester Harbour** Extensive mudflats and salt marshes; home to thousands of wintering waders and wildfowl. Heavy concentration of dark-bellied race of brent goose. Still changing East Head has many rare plant species.

**Clwydian Range** A series of round-topped hills dividing Wales from England. Extensive views into Wales from Offa's Dyke Path, which runs the length of the range. Iron Age hill-forts.

**Cotswolds** One of the largest AONBs and, justifiably, one of the most popular. Picturebook villages full of superbly maintained and architecturally perfect houses, built of warm Cotswold stone, with the wealth of the wool trade. A wide range of habitats, including ancient woodlands and limestone grasslands, creates a paradise for a staggering diversity of wildlife. Excellent range of leisure facilities including country and farm parks. The 100-mile Cotswold Way, along the north-west edge, is ideal for walkers who want attractive, not-too-strenuous hiking.

*THE TROUGH OF BOWLAND NEAR BLAZE MOSS Attractive wooded streams as well as wild and lonely moorland can be found in this Lancashire AONB.*

**Dedham Vale** Inextricably linked with Constable and remarkably little changed in appearance since he painted the mills along the slow, winding Stour.

**Dorset** With Cranborne Chase and West Wiltshire Downs it covers a beautiful tract of central southern England. Includes historic downlands full of reminders of past settlers, rich arable land and lovely coasts, some of which are heavily visited in summer.

**Forest of Bowland** One of the wildest AONBs, with high fells and good walking. The unclassified road from Newton towards Lancaster through the Trough of Bowland is one of the very best, scenically, to be found in England.

**Gower** The first AONB to be designated. A complete limestone peninsula to the west of Swansea but largely untouched by urbanisation, although the holiday industry has scarred some areas with unsuitable building. A land of remarkable contrasts – salt marshes, sweeping sandy bays and dizzying cliffs surrounding rough central uplands.

**High Weald** Historic Wealden country of attractive villages and towns in a lovely rural setting. One of five AONBs – the others are Sussex Downs, East Hampshire, Surrey Hills and Kent Downs – which give hope of protection to the ceaselessly threatened countryside of the south-east of England.

**Scilly Isles** Granite islands, many of them uninhabited and a paradise for birds and flowers. Their beauty and gentle climate attract summer tourists.

**Lleyn** Almost untouched by the 20th century, utterly different from the country through which the visitor passes to reach it. A patchwork of fields edged by narrow high-banked lanes, high cliffs, sweeping bays and unsurpassed sunsets.

**Malvern Hills** Ancient rocks forming a ridge dividing the plains of Hereford and Worcester. Some natural woods, grassland, good walks and views. Administered with particular reference to its potential for recreation.

*CASWELL BAY is typical of the wide sandy beaches backed by limestone cliffs on the Gower Peninsula.*

**Norfolk Coast** Extends along the remote and threatened (by the sea) coastline. Some of the finest nature reserves in Europe are here, as are flint-walled villages, sea-saltings and quiet inlets under vast skies.

*HEREFORD BEACON, an Iron Age hill-fort, is one of the attractions of the Malvern Hills.*

**Quantock Hills** Low hills with deep wooded combes and open heathland. Forest trails; interpretation centre for wildlife.

**Solway Coast** There is easy access for walkers and birdwatchers, but a lack of holiday facilities preserves this as one of the most tranquil parts of the coast. Comparable to the Norfolk coast, but with views – north to Scottish, south to English mountains.

| AREAS OF OUTSTANDING NATURAL BEAUTY (ENGLAND AND WALES) | A | | D | | H | | M | | S | |
|---|---|---|---|---|---|---|---|---|---|---|
| | Anglesey | SH 37 | Dedham Vale | TM 03 | High Weald | TQ 43 | Malvern Hills | SO 74 | Scilly Isles | SV 91 |
| | Arnside & Silverdale | SD 47 | Dorset | 11 | | | Mendip Hills | ST 55 | Shropshire Hills | |
| | | | | | | | | | Solway Coast | NY 26 |
| | | | | | I | | | | South Devon | SX 54–7 |
| | | | E | | Isle of Wight | SZ 48 | | | | SX 95 |
| | C | | East Devon | SY 08 | | | Norfolk Coast | TF 64–71 | South Hampshire | SU 39 |
| | Cannock Chase | SJ 91 | | –SY 39 | | | | TG 33 | Coast | |
| | Chichester Harbour | SU 70 | East Hampshire | SU 62 | K | | North Devon | SS 22-19 | Suffolk Coast & | TM 33 |
| | | | | | Kent Downs | TQ 95 | | SS 54 | Heaths | –TM 58 |
| | Chilterns | SU 78 | | | | | North Wessex Downs | | Surrey Hills | |
| | | –SP 80 | F | | L | | | | Sussex Downs | |
| | Clwydian Range | SJ 16 | Forest of Bowland | SD 65 | Lincolnshire Wolds | TF 28 | Northumberland Coast | NU 05 | | |
| | Cornwall | | | | | | | –NU 20 | | |
| | Cotswolds | ST 89-37 | | | Lleyn | SH 23 | | | W | |
| | | SP 12 | G | | | | | | Wye Valley | SO 50 |
| | Cranbourne Chase & West Wilts Downs | SU91 & ST 93 | Gower | SS 48 | | | Q | | | |
| | | | | | | | Quantock Hills | ST 13 | | |

# National Scenic Areas – Scotland

*The Countryside Commission for Scotland has identified 40 areas of national scenic significance, covering almost one-eighth of the land. National Scenic Areas in Scotland approximate, very roughly, to National Parks in England and Wales. They are in almost exclusively 'wild country' – as is the case in England and Wales – and conservation is given higher priority than recreation.*

The Countryside Commission for Scotland was set up in 1967, as an agent of central government, to help in the provision of facilities for the enjoyment of the countryside. It was also given responsibilities for the conservation and enhancement of Scotland's natural beauty.

The Countryside Commission for Scotland has drawn a distinction between land where recreational uses have precedence and land where conservation is paramount. Interestingly, this has not happened in England and Wales, where recreation is not necessarily an objective of designation in Areas of Outstanding Natural Beauty. The parks system proposed by the Countryside Commission for Scotland makes specific provision for recreation areas to ease the pressure on farming and forestry interests in 'regional parks' – somewhat similar to AONBs in England and Wales.

At the same time the Commission recognised that there were areas in Scotland of outstanding scenic importance in national and even international terms, which, largely due to their geographical situation, were not under great recreational pressure. In 1978 they identified 40 of these 'National Scenic Areas' which are now protected against a variety of developments considered likely to have a significantly ad-

verse effect on scenic interest in the area. As in England and Wales, the Countryside Commission for Scotland and planning authorities can make land management agreements with private landowners. Where land uses are modified, payment may be made in recognition of the public benefit secured by the agreement.

How were the National Scenic Areas identified and where are they? The choice was based on the subjective judgement of a group of assessors who sought to identify scenery containing a range of beautiful features. In the opinion of the Commission 'this means that richly diverse landscapes which combine prominent landforms, coastline, sea and freshwater lochs, rivers, woodlands, and moorlands with some admixture of cultivated land are generally the most prized'. The Commission concluded that 'outstanding examples of such scenery are most frequently found north of or on the Highland Boundary Fault'. They felt that, in the main, the more managed landscapes of the south and east lacked the diversity of form found in Highland Scotland but they did include some areas in the Southern Uplands.

The result of the Countryside Commission for Scotland's deliberations was a list of areas situated largely in the more remote parts of Scotland, excluding large towns

*LOCH DUICH AND THE KINTAIL MOUNTAINS Between the rivers Croe and Shiel, which run south-east from Loch Duich, are the mountains known as the Five Sisters of Kintail. The highest of these peaks, Sgurr Fhuaran, reaches over 3,500 feet in height.*

and, for the most part, not faced with recreational problems. In this respect they differ from the National Parks set up south of the border, but in most other respects there are strong similarities. The idea of National Parks was, incidentally, rejected by the Countryside Commission as being inappropriate for a comparatively small country like Scotland.

In a splendidly magisterial comment, the Commission has said it 'does not wish to see land in Scotland managed as though it were a museum'. The complete list of National Scenic Areas contains 12.8 per cent of Scotland's unequalled scenic beauty, which the Countryside Commission for Scotland have rightly termed part of her national heritage.

In the following list there are brief descriptions of the outstanding features of each area including some which are of general interest. That is to say, although they lie within the area selected, they were not necessarily considered by the Commission when the area was designated.

**SHETLAND ISLANDS:** a number of predominantely coastal areas on Shetland; the islands of Foula and Fair Isle with its bird observatory; the red sandstone cliffs of Muckle Roe.

**ORKNEY ISLANDS:** Hoy and the famous 450 ft sheer stack of the Old Man of Hoy; 1040 ft St John's Head; the port of Stromness with its internationally recognised arts centre; many reminders of the ancient inhabitants of Orkney.

**HIGHLAND REGION:** by far the largest acreage covered by National Scenic Areas – Wester Ross alone exceeds the total of Strathclyde, the next largest Region – including 16 Areas, some of which fall into more than one Region. This is the list:

**Kyle of Tongue:** beautiful coastal scenery at the mouth of the Kyle; moorland running into deserted sandy beaches; surprisingly lush woodland; towering mountains in massive Ben Hope and elegant Ben Loyal.

**North-West Sutherland:** noted for the great trio of quartzite mountains, Foinaven, Arkle and Ben Stack; some heavily 'fjorded' coastline; the island of Handa, an RSPB reserve.

**Assynt-Coigach:** an area of truly spectacular scenery. Dramatically shaped sandstone mountains, some 'clad' with scree of different rock forms, rising steeply from moorland; sea lochs, bays, rivers and tiny hamlets behind which lie unexpectedly grassy fields; a ruined castle; Inverpolly, the second largest National Nature Re-

serve in Britain, with access by road; the delightfully named Summer Isles of Achiltibuie – the Commission seem justified when they call this 'a landscape unparalleled in Britain'.

**Wester Ross:** a vast area, wonderfully varied; six great mountain ranges are included; Loch Maree with its many islands; low-lying areas of semi-natural woodland that soften the otherwise bleak and uncompromising mountain landscape; Inverewe, one of the finest sub-tropical gardens in Britain.

**Trotternish:** small area in north of Skye; includes the 'fantastical' and eerie basalt formations of the Quiraing: 'kilt rocks'; spectacular waterfalls; crofting settlements.

**Cuillin Hills:** contains the twin mountain ranges, the pink granite Red Cuillin and the toothlike gabbro of the Black Cuillin; waterfalls; folk museum; classic mountain views.

**The Small Isles:** Rhum, Eigg, Muck and Canna – four very different landscapes in a tiny area; huge granite cliffs; pasture; sand dunes; caves; National Nature Reserve on Rhum.

*THE BAY OF LAIG (below left) on the remote north-west coast of Eigg in the Small Isles. Nearby the famous 'singing' sands of Camas Sgiotaig squeak when walked upon.*

*THE PASS OF GLEN COE (below right) runs from Loch Leven up towards Rannoch Moor. The glen is famous for the Glen Coe Massacre (1692), as well as for its magnificent scenery.*

**Morar, Moidart and Ardnamurchan:** long, narrow stretch on coastland backed by mountains; splendid variety of landscapes; heavily indented fjord coastline; steeply wooded, almost 'Devonian' scenery at Loch Moidart; remote, difficult to reach but a truly romantic area.

**Loch Shiel:** the fjord-like Loch Shiel; remote Glen Hurich and its river; towering mountains; woodland; information centre at Glenfinnan; walking country – there are no roads other than Forestry Commission roads suitable for walking.

**Knoydart:** two deep sea lochs, Loch Hourn and Loch Nevis, flank landscape of unmatched remoteness; archetypal sea lochs, but very different. Hourn is dark, fjord-like, thrusting between towering mountains; Nevis is more open; inland is classic moorland without roads.

**Kintail:** perhaps the most 'touristy' of the Highlands NSAs, but justifiably so. Marvellously varied mountain peaks; rushing rivers; lowland pasture; magic castle; information centres; all easily accessible.

**Glen Affric:** generally considered the finest of all glens; attractive, high mountains to the north; forest and woodland – substantial relict area of native Caledonian pine forest; moorland; wild but not bleak; road into heart of area.

**Glen Strathfarrar:** affected by hydroelectric schemes, but remains attractive; River Farrer bordered by natural pinewoods; tranquil Loch Beannacharan; exciting Culligran Falls; road access through centre of area.

*MORAR SANDS are passed as you follow the road to Mallaig. They form part of the remote coastal NSA of Morar, Moidart and Ardnamurchan.*

*QUEEN'S VIEW, LOCH TUMMEL This site provides a place to look down the 5-mile long loch and on to the mountain Schiehallion beyond.*

**Dornoch Firth:** unusual for east coast firth – narrow and winding; last undeveloped east coast estuary; great range of landscape; woodlands (birch, oak and conifers); farming and crofting communities; forest walks; sandy shores, small bays; inland loch; delightful area, long known to golfers.

**Ben Nevis and Glen Coe:** spreads over three regions; important and intricate geological structure; hills varied – smooth, jagged, bare or heather clad; glens enclose moors, meadows, arable and forest land; Glen Nevis vies with Affric for beauty, by turns pastoral, Himalayan and Alpine; fjord-like Loch Leven; river and waterfalls in Glen Etive; infinite wasteland of Rannoch Moor; visitor centre. Glen Coe is covered in Glens and Valleys, page 26.

**Cairngorm Mountains:** bleak and bare, the largest tract of upland over 3000 ft in Britain. World famous salmon river Spey; heather-dominated moorland; Caledonian pine forest with outstanding flora and fauna; excellent visitor centre.

**WESTERN ISLES:** several areas and islands are included, giving examples of various landscapes; ragged hills; blanket bog; dizzy granite cliffs on St Kilda; crofting; flower-rich pasture of South Uist Machair.

**GRAMPIAN REGION:** possesses only one NSA, Deeside and Lochnagar; river and mountain dominated landscape; pine and birch woods; dramatic river scenery; heather-clad mountain slopes – one of the most managed landscapes in the list, an example of what mankind and nature may jointly achieve.

**TAYSIDE REGION:** there are four NSAs, all including land which has been

adversely affected by man, but all justifying inclusion by the natural beauty of their landscape.

**Loch Tummel:** picturesque landscape; mountains; rivers; woods; infinitely gentler than areas to the north and west.

**Loch Rannoch and Glen Lyon:** man-made Loch of Dunalastair is very unlikely landscape for the area – a shallow, reed fringed 'lake'; Loch Rannoch is wide and light, bounded by woods of great variety.

**River Tay (Dunkeld):** compact area centred on ancient cathedral city of Dunkeld; charm lies in combination of water and heavily wooded hills; sinuous River Tay, tumbling River Braan; Hermitage Gorge, an example of helping nature.

**River Earn** (Comrie to St Fillans): well proportioned landscape where highland and lowland meet; River Earn, by turns fast and slow, flows through good quality farmland; well planned woodland; robust hills.

**STRATHCLYDE REGION:** second largest Region in terms of acreage. Primarily coastal, it includes areas, like Lomond, of great tourist attraction.

**Loch na Keal,** Isle of Mull: distinct phases in landscape of lochs; rough grazing; attractive bays; bold cliffs; gentle meadows; Fingal's Cave on Staffa, one of many islands.

**Lynn of Lorn:** includes the island of Lismore, so enclosed as to appear part of the mainland; limestone soil supporting impressive range of flora; exceptional views; fine houses.

**Scarba, Lunga and the Garvellachs:** distinctive islands, presenting different faces to each aspect; forbidding cliffs; flower-strewn meadows; tidal races; oldest chapel in Scotland.

*THE RIVER TAY This famous salmon river flows over 160 miles from Loch Tay to the coastal estuary at Perth. Some of its most beautiful stretches are near Dunkeld and Aberfeldy.*

**Jura:** uncompromising inner area with the elegant Paps rising from moor and peat-bogs; varied coastline of bays and sharp cliffs; tide race; sub-tropical southern corner.

**Knapdale:** fingers of sea, heavily wooded glens and burns slice the surface; extensive Forestry Commission presence; historical and religious importance.

**Kyles of Bute:** the inverted 'Y' formed by the narrow waters of the Kyles of Bute, including well wooded hills; mudflats; moorland; easily reached from holiday resort of Rothesay.

**North Arran:** scenically the outstanding mountains of the region; highland massif sweeping down to northern coast.

**Loch Lomond:** largest water area in Britain; splendidly mixed scenery along highland boundary fault. Beautiful, but busy.

**CENTRAL REGION:** one area, the Trossachs, bringing highland scenery within reach of Glasgow. A marvellous and satisfying mix of mountain, woodland and water. Deservedly popular.

**BORDERS REGION:** two areas, both centred around the Tweed.

**Upper Tweeddale:** narrow, steepsided valley flanked by high hills; scenery is enlivened by good architecture.

**Eildon and Leaderfoot:** the Eildon Hills with renowned viewpoints; the Tweed now wider, graceful; well cultivated landscape; much of historical and architectural interest.

**DUMFRIES AND GALLOWAY REGION:** three areas along the Solway Firth. A complete contrast to almost all the other NSAs.

**Nith Estuary:** the granite summit of Criffel overlooks the area; saltings and extensive mudflats with backdrop of woods and pastoral land; each tide produces fresh visual delights.

**East Stewartry Coast:** contrast of small-scale shoreline landscape with wide sand and mudflats; charming villages.

**Fleet Valley:** a mixture of estuary and upland landscape linked by cultivated land; village is focal point.

| NATIONAL SCENIC AREAS (SCOTLAND) | A | | E | | K | | N | | T | |
|---|---|---|---|---|---|---|---|---|---|---|
| | Assynt – Coigach | NB 22 & NC 10 | East Stewartry Coast | NX 85 | Kintail | NG 92 | Nith Estuary | NX 96 | Trossachs | NN 40 |
| | | | Eildon & Leaderfoot | NT 53 | Knapdale | NR 76 | North Arran | NR 93 | Trotternish | NG 46 |
| | | | | | Knoydart | NG 70 | North West Sutherland | NC 25 | | |
| | B | | | | Kyle of Tongue | NC 55 | | | U | |
| | Ben Nevis & Glen Coe | NM 17 & NN 25 | F | | Kyles of Bute | NS 07 | R | | Upper Tweeddale | NT 13 |
| | | | Fleet Valley | NX 55 | | | River Earn | NN 91 | | |
| | | | | | L | | River Tay | NO 03 | W | |
| | C | | | | Loch Lomond | NS 39 | | | Wester Ross | NG 97 |
| | Cairngorm Mountains | NH 90 | G | | Loch na Keal (Mull) | NM 43 | S | | | |
| | Cuillin Hills | NG 42 | Glen Affric | NG 12 | Loch Rannoch & Glen Lyon | NN 55 | St Kilda (not in atlas) | NF 09 | | |
| | | | Glen Strathfarrar | NH 33 | Loch Shiel | NM 87 | Scarba, Lunga & Garvellachs | NM 60 | | |
| | D | | | | Loch Tummel | NN 85 | | | | |
| | Deeside & Lochnagar | NO 19 | H | | Lynn of Lorn | NM 83 | Shetland (incl Foula & Fair Isle) | | | |
| | Dornoch Firth | NH 88 | Hoy & West Mainland (Orkney) | ND 29 | | | Small Isles | NM 39 | | |
| | | | | | M | | South Lewis, Harris & Nth Uist | NG 09 | | |
| | | | J | | Morar, Moidart & Ardnamurcham | NM 79/ 77/56 | South Uist Machair | NF 72 | | |
| | | | Jura | NR 57 | | | | | | |

# Mountains

*The mystery of the Black Mountain; Cadair Idris, the 'honeypot'; Sugar Loaf the accessible; the beauty of Scottish Torridon, arguably the most important of British ranges; Coniston Old Man and Pen-y-Ghent, representatives of the (sometimes scorned) English mountains. Each justifiably included, yet each could be replaced by several splendid alternatives in Scotland alone.*

## Brecon Beacons

Pen-y-Fan is the highest mountain in the Beacons at just over 2900 ft, and it forms part of the range from which the National Park takes its name. A recurring problem in the Beacons is caused by the two mountain ranges, one called the Black Mountain and the other the Black Mountains. Once they have been visited the problem recedes, for they are utterly dissimilar. Different again is the Sugar Loaf in the east of the Park.

The Black Mountain is formed, as are most of the mountains of Brecon, of Old Red Sandstone. It is a fascinating, remarkably remote and somehow frightening range where Celtic legend mingles with fact. From the south, treeless moorland rises to summits like Bannau Brycheiniog, the highest point of Fan Foel which gives vast views to those other great ranges, Cader Idris (see page 21) and Mynydd Preseli. Semi-circular *cwms*, gouged out by Ice Age glaciers and holding lakes like Llyn-y-fan Fawr, lie beneath the summit. Bannau Sir Gaer, the red cliff which forms the north-west face of Fan Foel encompasses a smaller lake, Llyn-y-fan Fach. The dark, mysterious waters harbour a beautiful fairy, a member of the Fair Community (*Tylwyth Teg*). She met, courted and married a local farmer by whom she had three sons. When he broke a pledge never to touch her with cold iron (some versions say strike her in anger), she returned to the lake taking her dowry of

*BLACK MOUNTAIN (top) A twisting road climbs through the undulating moorland of the Black Mountain, on the Dyfed/Powys border.*

*A PATH UP SUGAR LOAF This cone-shaped mountain, north-west of Abergavenny, can be approached just off the A40.*

cattle with her. Some have it that she returned and taught her three sons herbal remedies, and that they and their descendants all became physicians, the last of whom was still practising in 1881.

Pen-y-Fan, too, has a lake of its own, nestling below it. The mountain is again of red sandstone, its northern face steep, its southern gentler, less dramatic. The views encompass even larger areas than those from Fan Foel, and on a fine day it is possible to see Somerset and Devon over the Bristol Channel. Pen-y-Fan is one of five flat-topped mountains in the central part of the National Park; Corn-Du and Cribyn are its major companions.

The Sugar Loaf is very different. A cone-shaped mountain, it dominates the greener, softer landscape around Abergavenny. The south-facing surfaces are covered in bracken and small shrubs. Access to the top is by a good path from the car park, or by more direct but considerably harder routes up the mountain.

It is not possible to take cars to, or near, the summits of any of the mountains but the Beacons are well served by roads, and the car park on Sugar Loaf gives superb views from its height of 1100 ft. It is signposted off the A40. To reach Llyn-y-fan Fach it is necessary to drive to Llanddeusant off the A4069. The road on from the village ends about 2½ miles from the lake and there is another walk which leads to the top of the escarpment and around Fan Foel. At Libanus, south of Brecon on the A470, there is a (very) minor road which can be taken towards Pen-y-Fan.

## Cader Idris

Why does Cader Idris dominate the landscape of Snowdonia so much? More than Snowdon or any of its satellites, Cader Idris looms and lives in the memory of those who have seen it. Not for reasons of size – Snowdon is distinctly higher – but because its great bulk, crouching over the Mawddach Estuary, has majesty coupled with an appearance of gentleness. The appearance is deceptive and those who wish to climb the mountain by any one of three paths must go prepared for a struggle.

For the motorist, Cader Idris is a useful mountain as it can be circled by car. From

Dolgellau, the A487 turns past the north-eastern end, the B4405 continues beside Tal-y-llyn Lake and the railway of the same name, then gives way to the A493 at Bryncrug. The return to Dolgellau, via Arthog, is full of good things, including the views over the Mawddach Estuary.

Best of all, if nerves and car survive, is the very steep, twisting road leading up from Arthog to the Cregennen Lakes. On quiet days, and especially in the morning or evening, there are few more ravishingly beautiful lakes than the Cregennen twins. The views from them stretch across the estuary to encompass Cardigan Bay and the Lleyn Peninsula (see page 56); behind and above rises the steep, glacier scarred mass of the mountain.

After skirting the lakes, the road improves as it continues towards Dolgellau – the route from Dolgellau is an alternative to driving the Arthog section. A car park is provided by the National Trust, who own the lakes and 700 acres in this wild upland. Three miles from Creggenen is another car park; nearby, the Pony Path, one of the northern walks to the summit, begins.

*THE CREGENNEN LAKES It is worth the climb just to see these beautiful lakes, but in addition there are magnificent views of Cader Idris and, in the opposite direction, the coast of Barmouth.*

This, with the overused and worn Fox's Path, converges on the frost-shattered volcanic ridge called Penygadair. Here is the triangulation point, and here the high point of Cader Idris at 2930 ft. The views are enormous and include English hills and Irish mountains. Immediately below and to the north is Llyn y Gadair, a dark oval of a lake, ringed by raven- and buzzard-haunted cliffs; to the south is Llyn Cau, reputedly bottomless and home to a monster. Like many *cwms*, Llyn Cau looks a little like a water-filled bomb crater, with debris scattered over its slopes.

Considering the wildness of the area, Cader Idris has a remarkable wildlife, including alpine flower species like rose-root and the rose-coloured purple saxifrage. Around the wetter areas the marsh fritillary feeds on devil's bit scabious and, occasionally, a red kite may drift over the mountain.

| | | | | | | | | | | | |
|---|---|---|---|---|---|---|---|---|---|---|---|
| Beinn Dearg Mhor | NH 0379 | Beinn Liath Mhor | NG 9652 | Beinn nan | NN 1440 | Ben Aden | NM 8998 | Ben More | NN 4324 | Betsom's Hill | TQ 4356 |
| Beinn Dorain | NN 3237 | Beinn Luibhean | NN 2407 | Aigheanan | | Ben Alder | NN 4972 | Ben More, Assynt | NC 3120 | Bidean nam Bian | NN 1454 |
| Beinn Dronaig | NH 0338 | Beinn Maol | NN 1352 | Beinn nan Imirean | NN 4130 | Ben Arthur | NN 2505 | Ben Nevis | NN 1671 | Bidein a' Choire | NH 0441 |
| Beinn Dubhcraig | NN 3025 | Chaluim | | Beinn Narnain | NN 2706 | Ben Avon | NJ 1302 | Ben Oss | NN 2825 | Sheasgaich | |
| Beinn Eibhinn | NN 4473 | Beinn Mhanach | NN 3741 | Beinn Odhar | NN 3333 | Ben Chonzie | NN 7730 | Ben Resipol | NM 7665 | Bidein a' Ghlas | NH 0684 |
| Beinn Eighe | NG 9659 | Beinn Mheadhoin | NJ 0201 | Beinn Odhar | NM 8477 | Ben Cruachan | NN 0630 | Ben Rinnes | NJ 2535 | Thuill | |
| Beinn Enaglair | NH 2280 | Beinn | NN 8875 | Bheag | | Ben Donich | NN 2104 | Ben Sgritheall | NG 8312 | Bink Moss | NY 8724 |
| Beinn Eunaich | NN 1332 | Mheadhonach | | Beinn Sgulaird | NN 0546 | Ben Gulabin | NO 1072 | Ben Stack | NB 2842 | Binnein an Fhidleir | NN 2110 |
| Beinn Fhada | NH 0119 | Beinn Mhic | NN 2250 | Beinn Spionnaidh | NC 3657 | Ben Hee | NC 4233 | Ben Starav | NN1242 | Binnein Beag | NH 2267 |
| Beinn Fhionnlaidh | NN 0949 | Chasgaig | | Beinn Tarsuinn | NR 9541 | Ben Hope | NC 4750 | Ben Tee | NN 2497 | Binnein Mor | NN 2166 |
| Beinn Fhionnlaidh | NH 1128 | Beinn Mhic | NN 2035 | Beinn Tarsuinn | NH 0372 | Ben Kilbreck | NC 5829 | Ben Tirran | NO 3774 | Birks Fell | SD 9187 |
| Beinn Ghlas | NN 6240 | Mhonaidh | | Beinn Teallach | NN 3685 | Ben Lawers | NN 6341 | Ben Vane | NN 2709 | Birkscairn Hill | NT 2733 |
| Beinn Heasgarnich | NN 4138 | Beinn Mholach | NN 5865 | Beinn Tharsuinn | NH 0543 | Ben Ledi | NN 5609 | Ben Vane | NN 5313 | Bla Bheinn | NG 5321 |
| Beinn Iaruinn | NN 2990 | Beinn na Caillich | NG 7906 | Beinn Trilleachan | NN 0843 | Ben Liath Mhor | NH 2272 | Ben Vorlich | NN 2912 | Black Down | SU 9129 |
| Beinn Ime | NN 2508 | Beinn na Caorach | NG 8712 | Beinn Tulaichean | NN 4119 | Ben Lomond | NN 3602 | Ben Vorlich | NN 6219 | Black Fell | NY 6444 |
| Beinn Iutharn | NO 0479 | Beinn na | NG 8512 | Beinn Udlaidh | NN 2833 | Ben Loyal | NC 5748 | Ben Vrackie | NN 9563 | Black Hill | SE 0704 |
| Mhor | | h'Eaglaise | | Beinn Udlamain | NN 5774 | Ben Lui | NN 2626 | Ben Vuirich | NN 9969 | Black Law | NT 2227 |
| Beinn Lair | NG 9873 | Beinn na Lap | NN 3769 | Bellbeaver Rigg | NY 7635 | Ben Macdui | NN 9899 | Ben Wyvis | NH 4668 | Black Mountain | SN 71 |
| Beinn Leoid | NC 3229 | Beinn nam Fuaran | NN 3638 | Bell Craig | NT 1812 | Ben More | NM 5232 | Bencleuch | NN 9000 | Black Mountains | SO 22 |

## The Old Man of Coniston

Without doubt the best view of Coniston Old Man is from the road on the east side of the lake. Volcanic slopes appear to rise steeply out of the small town of Coniston, reaching a slight peak at the end of a long ridge. Often the mountain is reflected in the lake, producing a memorable picture.

The view from the top is, in some respects, even more marvellous. From the cairn, set just a few feet below the summit, there are immense views to the east, with the long, narrow lake spread out in the foreground but far below. Sometimes the shape of the little steamer *Gondola* can be seen, puffing smoke, with a herringbone of bow wave spreading out towards the shore. Glinting in the distance are the waters of Tarn Hows and Windermere. South is more water – the silvery mass of Morecambe Bay lying beyond Ulverston over a patchwork of fields and woods. The whole of the northern prospect is a vast jumble of mountains, bubbling up to the sky and defying identification by any but the most experienced of map readers. Dow Crag dominates the western foreground, its scree slopes tumbling down to Goat's Water, forever trapped in a corrie between the side walls of the Crag and the Old Man (Goat's Water can't actually be seen from the cairn, but comes into view a little lower down).

The route to the top of the Old Man, following the ancient Walna Scar Road past Boo Tarn and Goat Fell, is not the shortest but is probably the best and most attractive. It must be stressed that fell walking is never to be undertaken lightly and that conditions on mountains can change with frightening rapidity. Please take every precaution, especially if children or older people are involved.

The bare landscape around the upper levels of mountains like the Old Man is relatively recent. As in other areas (see Grimes Graves, page 34), Neolithic people were responsible for the clearing of large areas of forest up to about 2000 ft above sea level. On the evidence of pollen records this clearing began about 3000 BC.

A different sort of clearing has affected the slopes around Coniston Old Man in recent centuries. This has been brought about by the over-grazing of good grassland by sheep. The result has been the spread of the virtually inedible mat-grass – very obvious on Walna Scar side.

Reference to any large-scale map will confirm that the evidence of Bronze Age settlers in the Lake District is extensive. It includes an important circle close to Boo Tarn where, in addition to cremation urns, one of the earliest fragments of woven cloth was discovered.

*CONISTON OLD MAN, with its cone-shaped outline, is one of the highest mountains in south Cumbria. It reaches over 2,600 ft.*

No description of Coniston and the Old Man can avoid reference to John Ruskin. Ruskin's home for the last 30 years of his life, Brantwood, is on the east shore of the lake. Over it looms the Old Man. Could one conceive of a better place to consider, as he wrote, 'the dependence of architecture on the inspiration of Nature'?

## Pen-y-Ghent

It is common practice to refer to the outline of Pen-y-Ghent as leonine and there are those who believe that the Golden Lion Inn at Horton-in-Ribblesdale is so named for that reason. Certainly, the classic, and much photographed, views of the 2273 ft mountain are from Dale Head and Horton-in-Ribblesdale.

Pen-y-Ghent is one of three flat-topped peaks around Ribble Head – Great Whernside and Ingleborough are the others – lying on the Craven Uplands. Their dramatic outlines are formed from limestone, overlaid by shales and capped by millstone grit. Over the centuries the shales have eroded at a faster rate than the limestone, creating the pronounced steps to be seen particularly on the south flank of Pen-y-Ghent. The change from limestone to shale is clearly visible in the exposed sides of the mountain, the rock colour switching from grey to brown quite suddenly, while the first plateau is littered with pieces of shale and grit which have broken from the upper levels.

Connoisseurs invariably place Pen-y-Ghent high on their list of beautiful mountains, comparing it, without detriment, to some of the Scottish peaks. The Pennine Way takes a steep, but not too difficult route to the bare, wind-swept summit which has some fine and extensive views on every side. Cars can be parked in Horton-in-Ribblesdale and a walk can be taken along this part of the Pennine Way past Hull Pot and Hunt Pot, two examples of the great holes which have been created in the limestone by centuries of water action. Hull Pot is about two miles from Horton, a huge gaping hole some 300 ft long, 60 ft wide and the same in depth. After heavy rain it can fill to overflowing but the water usually soaks away to re-emerge above Horton. Hunt Pot is very narrow but deep and it absorbs one of the

streams flowing off the mountain to disgorge it north of the village.

Alternatively, the marvellous hill road between Stainforth and Halton Gill in Upper Littondale passes within a mile of the summit, and the Pennine Way can be joined near Dale Head. The constant tramping of the paths leading to the top has created a problem with erosion, and walkers are urged to use any boardwalks and causeways laid out by the National Park authorities.

For botanists, both amateur and professional, the plant life of the mountain is exciting, with unusual species recorded, including maritime plants like sea campion and thrift. Two relatively localised species – purple and yellow mountain saxifrage – add interest and colour during spring and summer. Bird life is not plentiful, although the meadow pipit maintains a constant presence as does the golden plover, and it is possible to see the occasional ring-ouzel in summer. A rarity which is still sometimes found on Pen-y-Ghent is the Scotch argus, a butterfly now restricted almost entirely to Scotland.

*PEN-Y-GHENT One of the 'classic' views of this characteristically shaped mountain can be seen from the churchyard at Horton-in-Ribblesdale.*

# Torridon Range

In 1960 the National Trust for Scotland commissioned a report from W H Murray, their adviser on mountain properties. Murray investigated 52 regions for what he termed 'impairment' and calculated that only six were unspoilt. Five were in the Western Highlands, and Torridon was one of them. Murray's survey, a classic of its type, clearly influenced the Countryside Commission for Scotland when it was preparing its proposals for National Scenic Areas (page 16) some years later – many of his comments were included in its notes explaining the choice of specific areas.

Classification is always fraught with difficulties, especially with landscape – who can 'grade' the relative merits of the Cairngorms and the Cotswolds? But Murray made one assertion in his report which has often been quoted: 'Glen Torridon,' he wrote, 'its loch and the mountains on either side exhibit more beauty than any other district of Scotland'. At the time that was written, Torridon did not belong to the Trust, but it was obviously delighted to be offered 14,000 acres in 1967, with additions a little later.

Lengthy descriptions of it occur in all the best books on the Highlands: what is it about the Torridon area that makes it so attractive to visitor and writer alike? 'The last great wilderness', Torridon has all the elements of a classic upland landscape – stark, dramatic mountains set off by splendid lochs around which pine and oak woods have developed, softening and relieving outlines. Perhaps part of the pleasure is brought about by the scale of Torridon; there is a grandeur here, but one is never completely overpowered by it.

The mountains are not remarkably high for Scotland, being in the region of 3000 ft, yet Beinn Alligin, Beinn Dearg, Beinn Eighe and Liathach appear higher because they rise very steeply from the moorland on their lower slopes. To quote Murray again 'Liathach (is) the most soaring mountain in the North'.

In geological terms the mountains contain certain differences in their rock formations. Beinn Alligin, Beinn Dearg and Liathach were formed of red-brown Torridonian sandstone some 750 million years ago while Beinn Eighe has an outer covering of younger Cambrian rock. All these mountains have tops containing white quartzite which, at its deepest, on Beinn Eighe, creates a strong impression of a permanent snow cap. The quartzite also contains fossils of some of the earliest animals on earth – worms up to half an inch in diameter. In other ways there are strong similarities between the mountains. Both Liathach and Beinn Eighe actually consist of a series of peaks, seven and nine respectively, with the highest of Liathach's, Spidean a' Coire Leith, at 3456 ft and Rhuard-stac Mor on Beinn Eighe standing 3313 ft above sea level. Beinn Alligin is slightly lower at 3232 ft.

The Torridon region has only really been opened up in a big way to visitors since the 1960s. Visitor Centres with leaflets describing walks, 'proper' roads, even National Nature Reserves – Beinn Eighe was the first in Britain, in 1951 – make some feel that the essential wildness is in danger of being 'caged' and put on display as in a zoo or museum. Whatever the validity of that argument, which raises the conflict between conservation and recreation, the fact is that many visitors will now feel able to discover an area they might have hesitated to enter 20 years ago.

One example is Beinn Eighe National

| | | | | | | | | | | |
|---|---|---|---|---|---|---|---|---|---|---|
| Chapelfell Top | NY 8734 | Coran of Portmark | NX 5093 | Creag Mac | NN 5425 | Crinkle Crags | NY 2404 | Diffwys | SH 6623 | Dun Law | NS 9713 |
| Chapelgill Hill | NT 0630 | Corrie Habbie | NJ 2828 | Ranaich | | Croft Head | NT 1505 | Ditchling Beacon | TQ 3313 | Dun Rig | NT 2531 |
| Cheviot The | NT 9020 | Corserine | NX 4987 | Creag Meaghaidh | NN 4187 | Cross Fell | NY 6834 | Dodd The | NY 7837 | Dungeon Hill | NX 4685 |
| Chno Dearg | NN 3774 | Crag Hill | NY 1920 | Creag Mhor | NN 3936 | Cruach Ardrain | NN 4021 | Dodd Fell Hill | SD 8384 | Dunkery Beacon | ST 8941 |
| Chwarel y Fan | SO 2529 | Craig an Loch | NN 7380 | Creag Mhor | NN 6949 | Cruach Innse | NN 2876 | Dollar Law | NT 1827 | Dunstable Down | TL 0019 |
| Cir Mhor | NR 9743 | Craig Cwm Silyn | SH 5250 | Creag Mhor | NJ 0504 | Cuillin Hills | NG 42 | Dollywaggon Pike | NY 3413 | | |
| Ciste Dhubh | NH 0616 | Craignan | NX 4583 | Creag nan Damh | NG 9411 | Cul Beag | NC 1408 | Dow Crag | SD 2697 | | |
| Clath Leathad | NN 2449 | Craig-y-llyn | SH 6611 | Creag nan Gabhar | NO 1584 | Cul Mor | NC 1611 | Driesh | NO 2773 | E | |
| Cleeve Cloud | SO 9924 | Cramalt Craig | NS 1624 | Creag Pitridh | NN 4881 | Culardoch | NO 1998 | Drosgl | SH 6668 | Earncraig Hill | NS 9701 |
| Clisham | NB 1507 | Cramalt Craig | NT 1624 | Creag Rainich | NH 0975 | Culter Fell | NT 0539 | Druim Fiaclach | NM 7979 | East Mount | NS 8710 |
| Clough Head | NY 3322 | Cranstacke | NC 3555 | Creag Toll a' Choin | NH 1335 | Curley Wee | NX 4576 | Druim Garbh | NM 8868 | Lowther | |
| Cnicht | SH 6447 | Creach Bheinn | NM 8757 | Creag Uchdag | NN 7032 | Cushat Law | NT 9213 | Druim nan Cnamh | NH 1307 | Eididh nan Clach | NH 2584 |
| Cold Fell | NY 6055 | Creach Bheinn | NN 0242 | Creagan na Beinne | NN 7436 | Cyrniau Nôd | SH 9827 | Druim Shionnach | NH 0708 | Geala | |
| Comb Fell | NT 9118 | Creag a' Choir Aird | NH 0825 | Creigiau Gleision | SH 7261 | | | Druim Tasuinn | NM 8772 | Eildon Hills | NT 53 |
| Comb Law | NS 9407 | Creag a' Mhaim | NH 0807 | Crib-goch | SH 6255 | | | Drum | SH 7069 | Elidir Fawr | SH 6161 |
| Cona Mheall | NH 2781 | Creag an Dail | NO 1598 | Cribin Fawr | SH 7915 | **D** | | Drumaldrace | SD 8786 | Erie Hill | NT 1218 |
| Conachraig | NO 2886 | Bheag | | Cribin | SO 0221 | Dale Head | NY 2215 | Drumelzier Law | NT 1431 | Esk Pike | NY 2307 |
| Conival | NC 3019 | Creag Leacach | NO 1775 | Crib-y-ddysgl | SH 6155 | Derry Cairngorm | NO 0198 | Drygarn Fawr | SN 8658 | Ettrick Pen | NS 1908 |
| Cook's Cairn | NJ 3027 | Creag Liath | NC 2815 | Criffel | NX 9662 | Devils Point The | NN 9695 | Dun da Ghaoithe | NM 6736 | | |

Nature Reserve, 10,500 acres of outstanding moorland and mountain scenery on the northern slopes of the range. It became a reserve mainly because it includes a relic of the old Caledonian pine forest, the vast natural forest which once sprawled over three million acres of Scotland. There are trails to both the pine forest and the mountain. Above the tree line is a typical upland scene – rough, stony moraine slopes where heathers struggle to remain upright and juniper adopts a prostrate form. Cuckoos, surprisingly common on Highland uplands, feed on the caterpillars of the northern eggar moth, and other, fiercer predators are present – though only the lucky will get a glimpse of a pine marten or wildcat. Below there are views of Loch Maree which is of a classic beauty, full of small pine-clad islands, backed by the wildly beautiful mountain of Slioch and dark green forest, and azaleas and rhododendrons in the spring.

*LOCH TORRIDON AND THE TORRIDON RANGE seen from the coastal road between Kenmore and Shieldaig.*

*BEINN EIGHE The mountain consists of several peaks, the highest reaching over 3,300 ft.*

There is a deer museum and a visitor centre run by the National Trust for Scotland at Torridon village. The Trust leaflet suggests a number of walks graded in degrees of difficulty, but care should be exercised on even the shortest of strolls in regions like this, if only by ensuring that clothing and footwear can stand up to roughish ground and weather conditions.

Three miles from the centre, at Coire Mhic Nobuill bridge, there are walks through pine woods to see the splendid, craggy eastern face of Beinn Alligin. Another diversion is to the deep corrie, Coire Mhic Fhearchair, on the western slopes of Beinn Eighe, which contains a rock shape known as the Triple B ·ttress, a quite fantastic and impressive mass of grey quartzite which seems to spring out of the sandstone. On all these paths the walker is conscious of Liathach, its stepped escarpment a constantly impressive presence.

For the motorist, the improvement in the roads around Torridon is particularly welcome, with a choice of good roads from Kinlochewe. The A832 leads past the Beinn Eighe reserve and along the shores of Loch Maree; the views north over the loch are almost as dramatic as those from higher up the slopes of the mountain.

The road to the south of Liathach, the A896, turns away at Torridon village but the road on to Lower Diabaig, past Coire Mhic Nobuill, becomes an exciting single-track switchback beyond Inveralligin. Scrambling along the slopes of Beinn Alligin, the road allows passengers – if not drivers – splendid views of the mountain and, across Loch Torridon, some of the best scenery in all Scotland.

| | | | | | |
|---|---|---|---|---|---|
| Hopegill Head | NY 1822 | Meall Uaine | NO 1167 | Place Fell | NY 4017 |

**I**
Ill Bell, Kentmere NY 4307
Ingleborough Hill SD 7474
Innerdownie NN 9603
Iron Crag SY 1212

**J**
James's Hill NY 9232
Jeffries Corse NT 2749

**K**
Killhope Law NY 7837
Kilnshaw Chimney NY 3908
Kinder Scout SK 0789
King's Seat Hill NS 9399
Kirk Fell West NY 1910
Kirriereoch Hill NX 4187
Kirrireoch Hill NX 4287
Knock Fell NY 7230
Knott NY 2933
Knoutberry Haw SD 7391

**L**
Ladhair Bheinn NG 8204
Lamachan Hill NX 4377
Larg Hill NX 4275
Leathad an NN 8285
  Toabhain
Leith Hill TQ 1343
Leum Uilleim NN 3364
Liatach NG 9458
Lingmell NY 2008
Little Fell NY 7822
Little Scoat Fell NY 1511
Llechog SH 6056
Loch Craig Head NT 1617
Loch Fell NT 1704
Lochnagar NO 2487
Lonscale Fell NY 2827
Lousie Wood Law NS 9315
Lovely Seat SD 8795
Lowther Hill NS 8910
Luinne Bhein NG 8600
Lurg Mhor NH 0640

**M**
Maesglasau SH 8215
Mam na Gualainn NN 1162
Mam Sodhail NH 1225
Manod Mawr SH 7244
  South
Maol Chean-Dearg NG 9249
Maol Chinn-Dearg NH 0308
Mayar NO 2473
Meal a' Bhuiridh NN 2550
Meal nan NN 5839
  Tarmachan
Meall a' NH 1073
  Chrasgaidh
Meall a' Choire NN 6143
  Leith
Meall a' NJ 9911
  Bhuachaille
Meall a' Ghuibhais NG 9763
Meall a' Phubuill NN 0285
Meall an Fhudair NN 2719
Meall an NN 5423
  t' Seallaidh
Meall Buidhe NN 4245
Meall Buidhe NN 4949
Meall Chuaich NH 7187
Meall Coire nan NN 1795
  Saobhaidh
Meall Corranaich NN 6141
Meall Dearg NN 1658
Meall Dubh NH 2407
Meall Dubhag NN 8895
Meall Garbh NN 6443
Meall Ghaordie NN 5139
Meall Glas NN 4332
Meall Gorm NN 2269
Meall Greigh NN 6743
Meall Horn NC 3544
Meall Luaidhe NN 5843
Meall na Fearna NN 6518
Meall na h'Aisre NH 5100
Meall na Leitreach NN 6470
Meall na Teanga NN 2292
Meall nan NH 2582
  Ceapraichean
Meall nan Eun NN 1944
Meall nan Subh NN 4639
Meall nan NN 8054
  Tairneachan

Meall Uaine NO 1167
Meallach Mor NN 7790
Meallan Liath NC 3539
  Coire Mhic Dhugail
Meallan nan Uan NH 2654
Meaul NX 5091
Meikle Millyea NX 5182
Meldon Hill NY 7729
Melmerby Fell NY 6537
Merrick NX 4285
Mickle Fell NY 8024
Middle Hill NT 1529
Middlehope Moor NY 8642
Milk Hill SU 1064
Mill Down NX 5183
Millfore NX 4775
Moel Eilio SH 5557
Moel Fammau SJ 1662
Moel Fferna SJ 1139
Moel Hebog SH 5647
Moel Lefn SH 5548
Moel Llyfnant SH 8035
Moel Nant yr Ogof SH 6758
Moel Pemamnen SH 7148
Moel Poethion SJ 0830
Moel Siabod SH 7054
Moel Sych SJ 0631
Moel SH 6534
  Ysgyfarnogod
Moel y Cerrig- SH 9224
  duon
Moel y Cynghorion SH 5856
Moelwyn Bach SH 6643
Moelwyn Mawr SH 6545
Moel-yr-hydd SH 6745
Moll Cleuch Dod NT 1518
Mon Ameanach NO 1770
Monadh Mor NN 9394
Moorbrock Hill NX 6298
Morrone NO 1388
Morven NJ 3704
Morwisg NH 1050
Mnunt Battock NO 5584
Mount Keen NO 4086
Mullach Choire an NN 5081
  lubhair
Mullach Clach a' NN 8892
  Bhlair
Mullach Coire NH 0573
  Mhic Fhearchair
Mullach Fraoch- NH 0917
  Choire
Mullach Nan NN 1266
  Coirean
Mullwharcher NX 4586
Murton Fell NY 7524
Mynydd Mawr SH 5354
Mynydd Moel SH 7213
Mynydd Tal-y- SH 5351
  mignedd

**N**
Na Gruagaichean NN 2065
Nonnau Sir Gaer SN 8121

**O**
Oeann na NN 4716
  Baintighearna
Old Man of SD 2797
  Coniston
Oliver Hill SK 0267

**P**
Pen Allt-mawr SO 2024
Pen-aran, Aran SH 8624
  Benllyn
Pen Cerrig-calch SO 2122
Pen Llithrig y SH 7262
  Wrâch
Pen Pumlumon SN 8187
  Arwystli
Pen Pumlumon SN 7886
  Fawr
Pen Punlumon SN 8087
  Llygadbychan
Pen y Boncyn SH 9528
  trefeilw
Pen y Craig-y-llyn SN 9003
Pen-y-Fan SO 0121
Pen y Garn Fawr SO 2830
Pen-y-Ghent SD 8373
Pen yr Allt-uchaf SH 8719
Pen yr Helgi-du SH 6963
Pen-yr-oleu-wen SH 6561
Pike o' Blisco NY 2704
Pillar Fell NY 1712
Pilot Hill SU 3960
Pilsden Pen ST 4101

Place Fell NY 4017
Plover Hill SD 8575
Post Gwyn SJ 0429
Pykestone Hill NT 1731

**Q**
Queensberry NX 9899

**R**
Raise NY 3417
Randygill Top NY 6800
Red Pike NY 1615
Red Pike NY 1610
Rest Dodd NY 4313
Rhinog Fach SH 6627
Rhinog Fawr SH 6529
Rhobell Fawr SH 7825
Rhôs Dringarth SN 9621
Robinson NY 2016
Rogan's Seat NY 9102
Roisbheinn NM 7577
Round Hill NY 7436
Ruadh-Stac Beag NG 9761
Ruadh Stac Mhor NH 0275

**S**
Saddle The NG 9313
Sail Charbh NC 2029
Sail Mhor NH 0388
Saileag NH 0114
Sails SD 8096
St Boniface Down SZ 5678
Scafell NY 2006
Scafell Pike NY 2107
Scar Crags NY 2020
Scaw'd Law NS 9203
Schihallion NN 7154
Seana Braigh NH 2887
Seat Sandal NY 3411
Seatallan NY 1408
Sgairneach Mhor NN 5972
Sgiath Chuil NN 4631
Sgor Craobh a' NM 8975
  Chaoruinn
Sgor Gaibhre NN 4467
Sgor Gaoith NN 9098
Sgor Mor NO 0091
Sgor Mor NO 1182
Sgor na h-Ulaidh NN 1151
Sgor nam NN 1458
  Fiannaidh
Sgorr Dhonvill NN 0455
Sgorr nan Lochan NG 9653
  Uaine
Sgorr Ruadh NG 9550
Sguman Coinntich NG 9730
Sgurr a' Bhealaich NG 0314
  Dheirg
Sgurr a' Choire- NG 8901
  Bheithe
Sgurr a' Choire NH 2543
  Ghlais
Sgurr a' Mhaim NN 1666
Sgurr a' Mhuillin NH 2655
Sgurr NG 7941
  a' Chadrachain
Sgurr a' NH 0844
  Chaorachain
Sgurr a' NG 4423
  Ghreadaidh
Sgurr a' NG 9806
  Mhaoraich
Sgurr Alasdair NG 4520
Sgurr an Airgid NG 9422
Sgurr an Doire NH 0109
  Leathain
Sgurr an Fhuarain NM 9897
Sgurr an Lochain NG 0010
Sgurr Ban NH 0574
Sgurr Breac NH 1571
Sgurr Choinnich NH 0744
Sgurr Choinnich NN 2271
  Mor
Sgurr Coire NG 7901
  Choinnichean
Sgurr Dearg NG4421
Sgurr Dhomhnuill NM 8867
Sgurr Dubh NG 9755
Sgurr Dubh Mor NG 4520
Sgurr Eilde Mor NN 2365
Sgurr Fhuaran NG 9716
Sgurr Fhuar-Thuill NH 2343
Sgurr Innse NN 2974
Sgurr Mhic NG 9117
  Bharraich
Sgurr Mhic NG 4521
  Coinnich
Sgurr Mhurlagain NN 0194

Sgurr Mor NM 9698
Sgurr Mor NH 2071
Sgurr na NG 4422
  Banachdich
Sgurr na Cicho NM 9096
Sgurr na Ciste NG 9814
  Duibhe
Sgurr na Diollaid NH 2836
Sgurr na Feartaig NH 0545
Sgurr na h'Aide NM 8893
Sgurr na Lapaich NH 1635
Sgurr na Ruaidhe NH 2842
Sgurr nan NH 0848
  Ceannaichean
Sgurr nan NH 0523
  Ceathreamhnan
Sgurr nan Clach NH 1871
  Geala
Sgurr nan NM 9088
  Coireachan
Sgurr nan NM 9395
  Coireachan
Sgurr nan NH 1213
  Conbhairean
Sgurr nan Each NH 1869
Sgurr nan Eag NG 4519
Sgurr nan Eugallt NG 9304
Sgurr nan Gillean NG 4725
Sgurr nan Utha NM 8883
Sgurr Thuilm NG 4324
Shallow on NX 4090
  Minnoch
Sheffield Pike NY 3618
Shirburn Hill SU 7295
Skiddaw NY 2629
Slioch NH 0069
Snaefell SC 3988
Snowdon SH 6155
Spidean a' Choire NG 9258
  Leith
Spidean Coinich NC 2027
Spidean Mialach NN 0604
Sron a' Choire NN 2294
  Ghairbh
Steeple, Little NY 1511
  Scoat Fell
Stob a Choin NN 4116
Stub a' Choire NN 3173
  Mheadhoin
Stob a' Choire NN 2546
  Odhair

Stob an Aonaich NN 5369
  Mhoir
Stob Ban NN 1465
Stob Ban NN 2672
Stob Binnein NN 4322
Stob Chabhar NN 2345
Stob Choire NN 2673
  Clairigh
Stob Coir'an NN 1644
  Albannaich
Stob Coire a' NN 1866
  Chairn
Stob Coire a' NM 0172
  Chearcaill
Stob Coire an NN 2472
  Laoigh
Stob Coire Easain NN 3073
Stob Coire NN 3574
  Sgriodain
Stob Daimh NN 0930
Stob Dubh NN 1648
Stob Law NT 2333
Stob Poite Coire NN 4288
  Ardair
Stony Cove Pike NY 4210
Streap NM 9486
St. Sunday Crag NY 3613
Stuc a' Chroin NN 6117
Stuchd an Lochain NN 4844
Stybarrow Dod NY 3418
Sugar Loaf SO 2716
Swarth Fell SD 7596
Swatte Fell NT 1111
Swirl How NY 2700

**T**
Tal y Fan SH 7272
Talla Cleuch Head NT 1321
Tan Hill SU 0864
Tarfessock NX 4089
Tarmangie Hill NN 9401
Tarn Crag NY 4807
Tarren y Gesail SH 7105
Tarrenhendre SH 6803
Tigh Mor na NH 1315
  Seilge
Tinto NS 9534
Toll Creagach NH 1928
Tolmount NO 2180
Tom a' Choinich NH 1627
Tom Buidhe NO 2178
Torridon NG 9055

Trum y Ddysgl SH 5451
Trum y Sarn SH 9931
Tryfan SH 6659
Tumpa The SO 2234
Tyrau Mawr SH 6713

**U**
Ullscarf NY 2912
Under Saddle NT 1412
  Yoke

**V**
Viewing Hill NY 7833

**W**
Waen-rydd SO 0620
Walbury Hill SU 3761
Waun Fach SO 2129
Waun-oer SH 7814
Wedden Law NX 9302
Wendover Woods SP 8908
Wether Hill NY 4516
Wetherlam NY 2801
Whernside SD 7381
White Coombe NS 1615
White Mossy Hill NY 8205
Whitehope Law NT 3344
Whitehope Hts NT 0913
Whiteside NY 1721
Wild Boar Fell SD 7599
Wind Fell NT 1706
Windlestraw Law NT 3743
Windy Gyle NT 8515
Windy Standard NS 6201

**Y**
Y Dduallt SH 8127
Y Garn SH 7023
Y Garn SH 6359
Y Llethr SH 6623
Y Lliwedd SH 6253
Y Wyddfa SH 6054
Yarlside SD 6898
Yewbarrow NY 1708
Yockenthwaite SD 9081
  Moor
Yr Aran SH 6051
Yr Elen SH 6765
Ysgafell Wen SH 6648

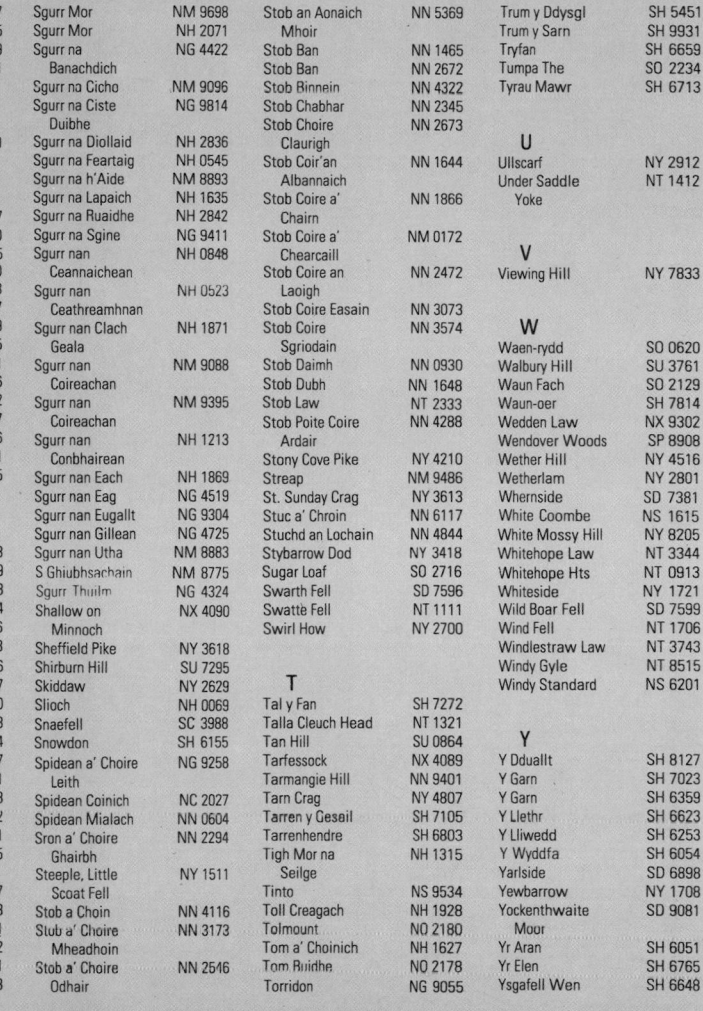

*A SKI RACE ON CAIRNGORM Skiing has become a popular sport in the Cairngorms, where a number of the peaks reach over 4,000 feet.*

# Glens and Valleys

*There is a wonderful range and variety to be considered under the blanket heading of Glens and Valleys. Simply contrast Glencoe with the Vale of Pewsey or the Vale of Ewyas. Splendid and challenging, soft and welcoming or beautiful and uplifting – the choice is this, and much more.*

## Churnet Valley

There is a belief in the minds of many that Staffordshire is a county of drab pottery towns. Once valleys like the Churnet have been discovered the idea will be entirely dispelled.

The valley of the Churnet is remarkable for many reasons. It is most attractive and it offers enjoyment for the industrial archaeologist, marvellous nature reserves for the naturalist and splendid and easy walking. A further blessing of the valley is that it does not attract the flood of visitors with which some of neighbouring Derbyshire's 'honeypots' struggle.

Throughout its journey to join the Dove, the River Churnet twists, turns and wanders at will in a shallow valley it once almost certainly filled more deeply. Nowadays, the river's flow is controlled from the Tittesworth Reservoir above Leek. At Leek it powers the waterwheel of the Brindley Mill, an outstanding example of what a small museum trust can achieve. A little further downstream, but in a far more rural setting, are the twin mills at Cheddleton, pressed between the river and the Caldon Canal.

Two excellent nature reserves lie in the valley of the Churnet. One is Coombes Valley, owned by the RSPB, a woodland reserve around one of the streams which feed the river. The other is the National Trust's Hawksmoor nature reserve with four nature trails which cover a range of terrain, some of it a little difficult, including farm and woodland, the river and the old railway and canal.

Between Oakamoor and Alton, the track of the old Churnet Valley railway has been converted to a footpath. Although walking is easy, the scenery, particularly in spring and autumn, is delightful and pleasingly wild.

## Glen Coe

The name Glen Coe is one, like the Battle of Hastings, with which every child is familiar. Here was one of the greatest betrayals – 'murder under trust' were the words used in a parliamentary enquiry – ever perpetrated. Cold-blooded, ruthless murder by men abusing the hospitality extended to them. As with most legends there is much truth in the story but it has to be said that of 150 intended male victims, only 38 were killed and that in the annals of Scottish history there are many bloody and treacherous incidents.

The image of Glen Coe as a place under a perpetual cloak of gloom seems to have arisen out of the desire to 'promote' the legend, yet the darkest thoughts in the vicinity of the Glen must surely be experienced on grim Rannoch Moor. The sudden descent, by the A82, from that

*GLEN COE Even well below the peaks, the wild nature of the Glen can be appreciated.*

**A**

| Name | Ref | Name | Ref | Name | Ref | Name | Ref | Name | Ref | Name | Ref |
|---|---|---|---|---|---|---|---|---|---|---|---|
| Abernethy Glen | NO 1814 | Biggin Dale | SK 1457 | Coilessan Glen | NN 2401 | Cwm Cadian | SH 7405 | Cwm Dulais | SN 6204 | Cwm Llech | SN 9233 |
| Achamy Glen | NC 5702 | Bilsdale | SE 5691 | Coire a' Bhaile | NO 1162 | Cwm Callan | SO 0614 | Cwm Du | SN 7306 | Cwm Llefrith | SH 5547 |
| Airedale | SE 0145 | Birk Dale | NY 8301 | Coire Chuaich | NN 7186 | Cwm Camlais | SN 9528 | Cwm Du | SO 2502 | Cwm Lluest | SS 9199 |
| Alport Dale | SK 1391 | Bishopdale | SD 9885 | Coire Dhomhain | NN 6074 | Cwm Canol | SJ 1134 | Cwm Du | SH 5355 | Cwm Llusog | SH 9328 |
| Alva Glen | NS 8898 | Blackmoor Vale | ST 7315 | Coire Laire | NN 3175 | Cwm Carn Fechan | SS 8991 | Cwm Dwfnant | SN 9042 | Cwm Llwydd | SH 8723 |
| An Caoran Beag | NH 0713 | Boredale | NY 4217 | Coire nan Grabhar | NM 5336 | Cwm Carw Fechan | SS 8991 | Cwm Dwr | SN 8431 | Cwm Llwydo | SH 8208 |
| An Caorann Mór | NH 0813 | Borland Glen | NN 9906 | Colne Valley | TL 8628 | Cwm Cathan | SN 6409 | Cwm Dwygo | SJ 0424 | Cwm Llwyd | SH 9700 |
| An Gleann | NR 1858 | Borrowby Dale | NZ 7816 | Cona Ghleann | NS 2898 | Cwm Cathan | SN 6409 | Cwm Dyffryn | SS 7990 | Cwm Llygoed | SH 9119 |
| Annandale | NY 1085 | Borrowdale | NY 2516 | Cona Glen | NM 9472 | Cwm Cerdin | SS 8488 | Cwm Dyfolog | SS 9789 | Cwm Mabws | SN 5568 |
| Ape Dale | SO 4889 | Borrowdale | NY 5603 | Conagleann | NH 5820 | Cwm Cesig | SS 9694 | Cwm Dyli | SH 6454 | Cwm Maelwg | SS 8087 |
| Apedale | SE 0194 | Borough Valley | SS 4845 | Conie Glen | NR 6911 | Cwm Ceulan | SN 7090 | Cwm Ednaut | SH 8500 | Cwm Maen | SJ 1031 |
| Appin of Dull | NN 7948 | Bradwell Dale | SK 1780 | Conies Dale | SK 1280 | Cwm Ceunant | SH 6263 | Cwm Egnant | SN 9338 | Gwynedd | |
| Arkengarthdale | NZ 0002 | Bramley Dale | SK 2372 | Coombe Valley | SS 2111 | Cwm Ciprwth | SH 5247 | Cwm Eigiau | SH 7063 | Cwm Main | SH 9841 |
| Ashwood Dale | SK 0772 | Bransdale | SE 6296 | Coplow Dale | SK 1579 | Cwm Cleisfer | SO 1418 | Cwm Einion | SN 7094 | Cwm Mawan | SN 8935 |
| Auch Gleann | NN 3336 | Brede Level | TQ 8417 | Coquetdale | NU 0101 | Cwm Clorad | SH 6855 | Cwm Erchan | SN 9434 | Cwm Meillionen | SH 5648 |
| Auchie Glen | NX 1332 | Brindley Valley | SK 0014 | Corb Glen | NN 0008 | Cwm Clydach | SN 6804 | Cwm Esgyll | SH 8818 | Cwm Merddog | SO 1806 |
|  |  | Brompton Dale | SE 9383 | Cormonachan Glen | NS 1897 | Cwm Clydach | SO 0496 | Cwm Faf | SO 0013 | Cwm Moch | SH 6636 |
|  |  |  |  | Corrachaive Glen | NS 0980 | Cwm Clydach | SN 9127 | Cwm Farteg | SS 8291 | Cwm Nantcol | SH 6326 |
|  |  |  |  | Corve Dale | SO 5488 | Cwm Clydach | SO 2112 | Cwm Ffrwd | SO 2505 | Cwm Nant-y-felin | SO 1424 |
|  |  |  |  | Cotton Dale | TA 0276 | Cwm Cneifio | SH 6258 | Cwm Ffynnon | SJ 0930 | Cwm Nant-y-glo | SS 8189 |
| **B** |  |  |  | Coverdale | SE 0582 | Cwm Cnyw | SO 2200 | Cwm Garw | SS 9089 | Cwm Nant-y-meichiaid | SJ 1316 |
| Back Dale | SK 0972 | **C** |  | Crake Dale | SE 9868 | Cwm Coch | SH 6361 | Cwm Gast | SH 8509 |  |  |
| Baldersdale | NY 9218 | Caenlochan Glen | NO 1876 | Crookdale | NY 5306 | Cwm Coedycerrig | SO 2921 | Cwm Gloywfa | SJ 0629 | Cwm Nant-y-moel | SS 9293 |
| Ballaglass Glen | SC 4689 | Cama Choire | NN 6878 | Crossaig Glen | NR 8251 | Cwm Cothi | ST 0998 | Cwm Gwaun | SN 0034 | Cwm Newynydd | SN 8621 |
| Ballochray Glen | NR 7451 | Camp Dale | TA 0577 | Cruaidh Ghleann | NR 4153 | Cwm Crai | SN 8925 | Cwm Gwenîfrud | SS 7997 | Cwm Nofydd | ST 1483 |
| Ballymichael Glen | NR 9331 | Canness Glen | NO 2076 | Cruaidh Ghleann | NR 5890 | Cwm Cregan | SS 8497 | Cwm Gwenffrwd | SO 2517 | Cwm Oergwm | SO 0420 |
| Balnabraid Glen | NR 7415 | Cans Dale | TA 0674 | Culm Valley | ST 1013 | Cwm Crew | SO 0018 | Cwm Gwerin | SN 8888 | Cwm Ogwr Fach | SS 9586 |
| Bannerdale | NY 4215 | Caol Ghleann | NS 0693 | Cumyffynnon | SH 8824 | Cwm Croesor | SH 6445 | Cwm Gwernfelen | SN 7933 | Cwm Ogwr Fawr | SS 9391 |
| Bannisdale | NY 5103 | Carron Glen | NS 7784 | Cunning Dale | SK 0773 | Cwm Croes | SH 8825 | Cwm Gwrelych | SN 9005 | Cwm Orci | SS 9598 |
| Barbondale | SD 6583 | Carrs The | SE 9879 | Currarie Glen | NX 0678 | Cwm Cwareli | SO 0521 | Cwm Gwyn | SH 9629 | Cwm Padest | SN 8620 |
| Bargaly Glen | NX 4667 | Cates Dale | SK 1765 | Cwm Afan | SS 8395 | Cwm Cwy | SO 0922 | Cwm Haffes | SN 8317 | Cwm Pedol | SN 7016 |
| Barr Glen | NR 6937 | Cawdale | NY 4817 | Cwm Afon | SO 2607 | Cwm Cynfal | SH 7241 | Cwm Hesgyn | SH 8841 | Cwm Pelenna | SS 7996 |
| Baysdale | NZ 6307 | Cefn Cwm Llurch | SO 0122 | Cwm Amarch | SH 7110 | Cwm Cynffig | SS 8386 | Cwm Hirnant | SH 9531 | Cwm Penanner | SH 9046 |
| Bealach á Chasain | NG 9014 | Chee Dale | SK 1273 | Cwm Banw | SO 2223 | Cwm Cynllwyd | SH 9025 | Cwm Hirnant | SJ 0523 | Cwm Penmachno | SH 7547 |
| Bee Dale | SE 9586 | Churnet Valley | SK 0642 | Cwm Bargoed | SO 0901 | Cwm Cynwyn | SO 0321 | Cwm Iân | SS 9594 | Cwm Pennant | SH 5347 |
| Benlister Glen | NR 9931 | Clachaig Glen | NR 6940 | Cwm Beusych | SO 2521 | Cwm Cywarch | SH 8617 | Cwm Iau | SO 3023 | Cwm Pennant | SJ 0325 |
| Benmore Glen | NN 4124 | Clauchan Glen | NR 9430 | Cwm Big | SO 2003 | Cwm Dâr | SS 9495 | Cwm Lasgarn | SO 2804 | Cwm Pennant | SJ 0335 |
| Beresford Dale | SK 1259 | Cleann Choinneachain | NG 9922 | C. Blaenpelenna | SS 8197 | Cwm Ddu | SH 8823 | Cwm Lickey | ST 2698 | Cwm Pen-y-gelli | SH 9118 |
| Bernice Glen | NS 1291 | Clydesdale | NS 8346 | Cwm Bychan | SH 6431 | Cwm Dimbath | SS 9589 | Cwm Llanwenarth | SO 2512 | Cwm Perfedd | SH 6361 |
| Bickleigh Vale | SX 5261 | Cockers Dale | SE 2330 |  |  |  |  |  |  |  |  |

place of true desolation into the broad valley of the shiny, tumbling River Coe is often a considerable relief. True, on dark Highland days when the highest peaks are masked and rain sweeps over the valley, Glen Coe can be a sad place.

Glen Coe has an excellent range of facilities for the tourist, including information centres, camp sites, a museum and several good nature trails for those wishing to explore some of its wilder aspects. Nor is it necessary to climb the highest peaks to experience that wildness. Indeed, some of the peaks, like Buachaille Etive Mor, at the head of the valley, are only for the most expert climber.

But in spring and summer when alpine flowers make their miraculous appearance

*MILLER'S DALE FROM MONSAL HEAD Gentle wooded slopes contrast with limestone cliffs in this part of Derbyshire.*

on the heights and the pink flowerheads of mountain everlasting fleck the lower ground; when there is just the possibility of a sighting of a peregrine or even an eagle, then Glen Coe, always imposing, becomes memorable.

## Heddon Valley and Valley of Rocks

Two for the price of one, but difficult to resist as they are so close and so remarkably different. It cannot be claimed that either are undiscovered British beauty spots and the toll road which connects them carries a considerable quantity of traffic during the summer, but if that is borne in mind a visit can be a joy.

The Valley of the Rocks is almost certainly a relic of the Ice Age, abandoned

when the ice retreated and the waters of the Lyn adopted their present course. The valley runs parallel to the sea and the high, ragged granite rocks which stand on the seaward side have acquired whimsical names – Ragged Jack, Devil's Cheesewring and Castle Rocks, at 800 ft one of the highest cliff faces in Britain.

By contrast, Heddon Valley is a typically heavily wooded Exmoor combe through which a small river falls at the end of its short journey to the sea. Paths on either side of the Heddon 'escort' it as it rushes and tumbles down the valley. Deep, well protected and invariably several degrees warmer than the surrounding country, the valley has an interesting plant and insect life.

## Monsal Dale

Most people probably see Monsal Dale first from the marvellous viewpoint at Monsal Head. Some 200 ft below runs the Wye, emerging from spectacular limestone country to continue its journey through one of the loveliest villages, Ashford in the Water, before visiting Bakewell, then on to join the Derwent. Below, too, is the viaduct which so infuriated Ruskin when it was built. That same Ruskin who could foolishly dismiss the 'wide acreage of field or moor above' as 'wholly without interest', could at least recognise the joy to be found in the 'clefts' and 'dingles'. There are few more remarkable examples of the effects of water on limestone than are to be found by following the Monsal Trail over the viaduct and up Monsal Dale to Miller's Dale, Chee Dale and thence to the breathtaking cliffs of Chee Tor.

| | | | | | | | | | | |
|---|---|---|---|---|---|---|---|---|---|---|
| Cwm Philip | SS 8287 | Cwmdwyfor | SH 5451 | Duffryn Edeirnion | SJ 0743 | Garrachra Glen | NS 0990 | Gleann a' | NR 3166 | Gleann Beag | NO 1273 |
| Cwm Prysor | SH 7436 | Cwmdwythurch | SH 5657 | Duffryn Meifod | SJ 1513 | Garsdale | SD 7389 | Chardaidh | | Gleann Beag | NO 1273 |
| Cwm Ratgoed | SH 7711 | Cwmglas Mawr | SH 6156 | Dunnerdale | SD 2093 | Garwick Glen | SC 4381 | Gleann a' Chilleine | NN 7237 | Gleann Beag | NH 3283 |
| Cwm Rheidol | SN 7178 | Cwmheisian | SH 7427 | Dunrobin Glen | NC 8003 | Given Dale | SE 8784 | Gleann a' Choilich | NH 1026 | Gleann | NR 6391 |
| Cwm Rhiwarth | SJ 0328 | Cwm-pen-Uydan | SJ 0432 | Dyffryn Crawnon | SO 1117 | Glac Gille Gun | NR 4075 | Gleann a' Chroin | NN 6214 | Bhaidseachan | |
| Cwm Rhyd-y-gau | SN 8805 | Cwm-y-burch | ST 1690 | Dyffryn Tywi | SN 6322 | Cheann | | Gleann a' | NN 7971 | Gleann Bianasdail | NH 0267 |
| Cwm Saerbren | SS 9397 | Cwm-y-Dolau | SH 8423 | | | Glaisdale | NZ 7503 | Chrombaidh | | Gleann Bun an | NR 2946 |
| Cwm Sawdale | SN 7620 | Cwm-y-fforch | SS 9499 | | | Glasgwm | SJ 0421 | Gleann a' Phuill | NG 1843 | Easa | |
| Fechan | | Cwm-y-ffosp | SS 9492 | E | | Glean an t-Slugain | NO 1494 | Gleann Airigh | NR 6392 | Gleann Cailliche | NN 3742 |
| Cwm Selsig | SS 9197 | Cwm-yr-Allt-lwyd | SH 7829 | East Allen Dale | NY 8352 | Glean Ardbhair | NC 1733 | Mhic-cearra | | Gleann | NM 9888 |
| Cwm Sian Llwyd | SJ 0032 | | | East Baldwin | SC 3682 | Glean Cia-aig | NN 1890 | Gleann Airigh na | NM 4722 | Camgharaidh | |
| Cwm Sorgwm | SO 1627 | | | East Dale | SE 9433 | Glean Da-Eig | NN 6045 | Searsain | | Gleann | NN 1704 |
| Cwm Sychan | SO 2404 | D | | Ebbw Vale | ST 2198 | Glean Dà-ghob | NN 6945 | Gleann Airigh | NR 9195 | Canachadan | |
| Cwm Sychbant | SS 8390 | Dam Dale | SK 1178 | Elloughton Dale | SE 9528 | Glean Donn | NM 8784 | Gleann Amaind | NR 2155 | Gleann Casaig | NN 5410 |
| Cwm Taf | SO 0013 | Danby Dale | NZ 6905 | Ely Valley | ST 0579 | Glean Easan | NR 9448 | Gleann an | NR 3344 | Gleann Choillean | NN 3435 |
| Cwm Tafolog | SH 8910 | Darley Dale | SK 2663 | Ennerdale | NY 1214 | Biorach | | Dobhrain | | Gleann | NR 4460 |
| Cwm Teigl | SH 7243 | Deep Dale | SK 0971 | Esk Dale | NZ 8005 | Glean Goibhre | NH 4248 | Gleann an Dubh | NN 6416 | Choireadail | |
| Cwm Terwyn | SH 8718 | Deep Dale | SK 1669 | Eskdale | NY 1500 | Glean Kyllachy | NH 7424 | Choirein | | Gleann Chomhraig | NN 7895 |
| Cwm Tirmynach | SH 9042 | Deep Dale | SE 9235 | Eskdale | NY 3090 | Glean Laoigh | NC 1609 | Gleann an Dubh | NM 8568 | Gleann Chomraidh | NN 4854 |
| Cwm Treweryn | SN 9125 | Deep Dale | SE 8155 | Exe Valley | ST 9221 | Glean Laragain | NN 1179 | Choirein | | Gleann Cinn-locha | NR 7879 |
| Cwm Trusgl | SH 5449 | Deep Dale | SE 9190 | | | Glean Mazeran | NH 7221 | Gleann an Fhiodh | NN 0755 | Gleann Coille Chill | NM 4546 |
| Cwm Tryfan | SH 6759 | Deepdale | NY 3520 | | | Glean na Ciche | NH 1217 | Gleann an Lochain | NM 9070 | a' Mhoraire | |
| Cwm Tyleri | SO 2207 | Deepdale | NY 3812 | F | | Glean na Gaoithe | NC 0812 | Duibh | | Gleann Coire | NR 4358 |
| Cwm Wernden | SS 8090 | Dent Dale | SD 7186 | Farndale | SE 6697 | Glean na Speireig | NH 5064 | Gleann an Lochain | NM 8892 | Liunndrein | |
| Cwm Wyre | SN 5569 | Derwent Dale | SK 1790 | Fathan Glinne | NN 4917 | Glean Sleibhte- | NM 6529 | Eanaiche | | Gleann Cosaidh | NG 9302 |
| Cwm y Fuwch | SS 9490 | Dhoon Glen | SC 4586 | Fin Glen | NN 8802 | coire | | Gleann an Oba | NH 6778 | Gleann Crotha | NN 5021 |
| Cwm y Garn | SS 8089 | Dimmings Dale | SK 0443 | Fin Glen | NS 5881 | Glean Torr- | NG 5330 | Gleann an t-Siob | NR 5073 | Gleann Cul an | NM 8588 |
| Cwm y Garn | SS 8089 | Dirrie More | NH 2375 | Fin Glen | NN 6344 | mhichaig | | Gleann ant-Suidhe | NR 9635 | Staca | |
| Cwm y Glyn | ST 2699 | Dove Dale | SK 1452 | Fin Glen | NN 6622 | Gleann a' Chadha | NH 2687 | Gleann Aoistail | NR 6187 | Gleann Culanach | NS 2698 |
| Cwm yr Aethnen | SH 9529 | Dovedale | NY 3811 | Findhu Glen | NN 7215 | Dheirg | | Gleann Astaile | NR 4871 | Gleann dà Leirg | NR 8478 |
| Cwm yr Argoed | SS 8294 | Doveholes Dale | SK 0877 | Fionn Ghleann | NN 1254 | Gleann a' Chaiginn | NM 6126 | Gleann Aurigh an | NR 3670 | Gleann Daimh | NN 4446 |
| Cwm yr Argoed | SS 8704 | Dovey Valley | SN 7401 | Fionn Ghleann | NN 3122 | Mhoir | | t-Sluic | | Gleann Diomhan | NR 9346 |
| Cwm yr Eithin | SJ 0430 | Druidale | SC 3688 | Fionn Leirg | NN 2139 | Gleann a' Chàm | NN 0586 | Gleann Ballach | NH 6401 | Gleann Diridh | NN 8774 |
| Cwm yr Hafod | SH 9620 | Drynain Glen | NS 1689 | Fionnglean | NH 0518 | Dhoire | | Gleann Ballach | NH 6402 | Gleann Doire | NM 4834 |
| Cwm yr Hom | SO 2427 | Dubh Chleann | NO 0697 | Flax Dale | SE 8686 | Gleann a' Chaolais | NN 0457 | Gleann Bàn | NN 1700 | Dhubhaig | |
| Cwm yr Wuin | SH 7120 | Dubh Ghleann | NO 0697 | Fusedale | NY 4418 | Gleann a' | NM 9588 | Gleann Bàn | NS 1282 | Gleann Domhain | NM 8509 |
| Cwm Ysgiach | SN 6203 | Dubh Gleann | NO 0697 | | | Chaorainn | | Gleann Beag or | NN 1706 | Gleann | NN 1577 |
| Cwmbrwynog | SH 5956 | Duffryn Ardudwy | SH 6022 | G | | Gleann a' Chapuill | NR 3872 | Hell's Glen | | Domhanaidh | |
| Cwmclogwyn | SH 5954 | Duffryn Dysynni | SH 6105 | Ganton Dale | TA 0075 | Bhain | | Gleann Beag | NG 8317 | Gleann Dorch | NR 5884 |

## Vale of Ewyas

Here is one of the most beautiful valleys in Wales – if not the entire British Isles – accessible via the road from Llanfihangel Crucorney to Hay Bluff.

For much of its route the road runs beside the lovely little Afon Honddu, which rises on the bare moors below Hay Bluff but soon gathers trees around it as it descends the valley. On the left of the road leaving Llanfihangel Crucorney are wooded slopes, on the right the first of many splendid views, in this instance to Graig, standing sentinel over Cwymoy's little church. Then, as the valley narrows, the road reaches the historic remains of Llanthony Priory. Nowadays many of those who walk the Offa's Dyke Path, which passes close to Llanthony, turn aside to visit the priory remains, and others, attracted by the chance to explore the paths which cover the surrounding hills, use Llanthony as a centre.

Beyond the priory the already narrow road closes in further, climbing to Capel-y-ffin where there is a monastery built in mock Gothic style for a 19th-century Anglican sect.

Rising still more steeply, the road suddenly emerges from the tree line and on to the moors. Here there are marvellous views back down the valley towards England. Over Gospel Pass the road seems to squeeze between Twympa and Hay Bluff before revealing even more spectacular views into Wales over a steeply descending green valley on the left.

In the 12th century the Welsh chronicler Giraldus wrote of monks returning to Llanthony to be 'restored to health for which they yearn', and sitting in the cloisters beholding 'the tops of the mountains touching the heavens'. The red-tinged sandstone mountains still touch the heavens and few can fail to feel restored after the pleasure of a visit to the Vale of Ewyas.

*VIEW FROM GOSPEL PASS About a mile from the England/Wales border, at the head of the Vale of Ewyas, Gospel Pass overlooks the Wye Valley and the small town of Hay-on-Wye.*

| | |
|---|---|
| Glen Eagles | NN 9307 |
| Glen Effock | NO 4377 |
| Glen Einig | NH 3598 |
| Glen Elchaig | NG 9627 |
| Glen Ernan | NJ 3112 |
| Glen Errochty | NN 7663 |
| Glen Esk | NO 4778 |
| Glen Etive | NN 1549 |
| Glen Etive | NN 1550 |
| Glen Eynort | NG 3828 |
| Glen Ey | NO 0985 |
| Glen Falloch | NN 3622 |
| Glen Farg | NO 1513 |
| Glen Feardar | NO 1996 |
| Glen Feardar | NO 1996 |
| Glen Fender | NN 9068 |
| Glen Fenzie | NJ 3201 |
| Glen Feochan | NM 8924 |
| Glen Feshie | NN 8494 |
| Glen Fiag | NC 4524 |
| Glen Fiddich | NJ 3234 |
| Glen Finart | NS 1790 |
| Glen Fincastle | NN 8661 |
| Glen Finglas | NN 5011 |
| Glen Finlet | NO 2267 |
| Glen Finnan | NM 9183 |
| Glen Forsa | NM 6138 |
| Glen Forslan | NM 7773 |
| Glen Fruin | NS 2888 |
| Glen Fyne | NS 1172 |
| Glen Fyne | NN 2216 |
| Glen Gairn | NO 3498 |
| Glen Gallain | NM 8418 |
| Glen Galmadale | NM 8654 |
| Glen Ganisdale | NR 6496 |
| Glen Garry | NH 1801 |
| Glen Garr | NO 0137 |
| Glen Garvan | NM 9675 |
| Glen Gelder | NO 2491 |
| Glen Geusachan | NN 9694 |
| Glen Geusachan | NN 9694 |
| Glen Gheallaidh | NJ 1338 |
| Glen Girnaig | NN 9366 |
| Glen Girnock | NO 3193 |
| Glen Girnock | NO 3193 |
| Glen Glass | NH 5568 |
| Glen Gloy | NN 2689 |
| Glen Fintaig | NN 2688 |
| Glen Gluitanen | NM 7976 |
| Glen Golach | NR 3044 |
| Glen Golly | NC 4243 |
| Glen Gorm | NM 4353 |
| Glen Gour | NM 9364 |
| Glen Graigag | NR 9534 |
| Glen Grenaugh | SC 3170 |
| Glen Grudie | NG 9666 |
| Glen Grundale | NR 6289 |
| Glen Guirdil | NG 3200 |
| Glen Gyle | NN 3713 |
| Glen Gyle | NN 3713 |
| Glen Gynack | NH 7402 |
| Glen Harris | NM 3596 |
| Glen Haultin | NG 4451 |
| Glen Helen | SC 3084 |
| Glen Hervie | NR 7411 |
| Glen Heysdal | NG 3044 |
| Glen Hinnisdal | NG 4057 |
| Glen Hurich | NM 8469 |
| Glen Ionadal | NG 1942 |
| Glen Iorsa | NR 9238 |
| Glen Isla | NO 1864 |
| Glen Isla | NO 1961 |
| Glen Kendrum | NN 5623 |
| Glen Kerran | NR 7113 |
| Glen Kingie | NN 0497 |
| Glen Kinglas | NN 2109 |
| Glen Kinglass | NN 1335 |
| Glen Kin | NS 1279 |
| Glen Labisdale | NF 7823 |
| Glen Laft | NJ 4319 |
| Glen Laudale | NM 7258 |
| Glen Lealt | NR 6693 |
| Glen Lean | NS 0982 |
| Glen Lednock | NN 7426 |
| Glen Lee | NO 3881 |
| Glen Leidle | NM 5224 |
| Glen Liadale | NF 8230 |
| Glen Libidil | NM 6622 |
| Glen Liever | NM 9008 |
| Glen Ling | NG 9533 |
| Glen Liver | NN 0835 |
| Glen Livet | NJ 2027 |
| Glen Lochan | NN 8435 |
| Glen Lochay | NN 4936 |
| Glen Lochsie | NO 0572 |
| Glen Lochy | NN 2831 |
| Glen Lochy | NJ 1222 |
| Glen Loch | NN 9873 |
| Glen Logan | NR 4262 |
| Glen Logie | NO 3168 |
| Glen Loin | NN 3006 |
| Glen Loin | NJ 1409 |
| Glen Lonan | NM 9427 |
| Glen Lorgasdal | NG 2338 |
| Glen Loth | NC 9412 |
| Glen Loyne | NH 1404 |
| Glen Loy | NN 1084 |
| Glen Loy | NN 1084 |
| Glen Luibeg | NN 0293 |
| Glen Luibeg | NO 0293 |
| Glen Lui | NO 0592 |
| Glen Lussa | NR 7326 |
| Glen Luss | NS 3293 |
| Glen Lyon | NN 5445 |
| Glen Macduff | NN 8803 |
| Glen Machrie | NR 3451 |
| Glen Mallie | NN 0787 |
| Glen Mallochan | NS 3195 |
| Glen Markie | NH 5407 |
| Glen Markie | NN 5897 |
| Glen Mark | NO 3684 |
| Glen Massan | NS 1186 |
| Glen Maye | SC 2379 |
| Glen Meavaig | NB 0908 |
| Glen Moidart | NM 7573 |
| Glen Mona | SC 4688 |
| Glen Mooar | SC 2478 |
| Glen More | NS 0268 |
| Glen More | NM 6230 |
| Glen More | NG 8818 |
| Glen More | NH 9809 |
| Glen Moriston | NH 3113 |
| Glen Moy | NO 3963 |
| Glen Muick | NO 3188 |
| Glen Nant | NN 0120 |
| Glen Neil | NS 0672 |
| Glen Nevis | NN 1468 |
| Glen Noe | NN 0733 |
| Glen of Drumtochty | NO 7079 |
| Glen of Kinpauch | NN 8906 |
| Glen of Noth | NJ 5030 |
| Glen of Rait | NO 2127 |
| Glen of Trool | NX 4079 |
| Glen Ogilvy | NO 3743 |
| Glen Ogil | NO 4465 |
| Glen Ogle | NN 5725 |
| Glen Ollisdal | NG 2139 |
| Glen Orchy | NN 2433 |
| Glen Ormidale | NR 9834 |
| Glen Orrin | NH 3649 |
| Glen Osdale | NG 2344 |
| Glen Ose | NG 3241 |
| Glen Ouharity | NO 2861 |
| Glen Ouoich | NH 0107 |
| Glen Ouoich | NO 0893 |
| Glen Oykel | NC 3108 |
| Glen Pean | NM 9490 |
| Glen Prosen | NO 3067 |
| Glen Quaich | NN 8439 |
| Glen Quoich | NO 0892 |
| Glen Remuil | NR 6312 |
| Glen Rinnes | NJ 2834 |
| Glen Risdale | NM 8018 |
| Glen Rosa | NR 9838 |
| Glen Roy | NN 3189 |
| Glen Roy | SC 4183 |
| Glen Rushen | SC 2477 |
| Glen Sanda | NM 8047 |
| Glen Sannox | NR 9944 |
| Glen Sassunn | NN 6554 |
| Glen Scaddle | NM 9567 |
| Glen Scaftigill | NR 9039 |
| Glen Sgionie | NN 4316 |
| Glen Shee | NN 9734 |
| Glen Shee | NO 1459 |
| Glen Shee | NO 1463 |
| Glen Shellesder | NG 3301 |
| Glen Shellish | NS 1094 |
| Glen Sherup | NN 9503 |
| Glen Shervie | NN 8135 |
| Glen Shieldaig | NG 8251 |
| Glen Shiel | NH 0311 |
| Glen Shira | NN 1314 |
| Glen Shirra | NN 5391 |
| Glen Shurig | NR 9936 |
| Glen Sletdale | NC 9112 |
| Glen Sligachan | NG 4927 |
| Glen Spean | NN 3580 |
| Glen Stockadale | NX 0161 |
| Glen Stockdale | NM 9448 |
| Glen Strae | NN 1631 |
| Glen Striddle | NS 3295 |
| Glen Suardal | NG 2451 |
| Glen Suardal | NG 6320 |
| Glen Suie | NJ 2826 |
| Glen Taitney | NO 2365 |
| Glen Tanar | NO 4594 |
| Glen Tanar | NO 4594 |
| Glen Tarbert | NM 8660 |
| Glen Tarff | NH 3902 |
| Glen Tarken | NN 6626 |
| Glen Tarsan | NS 0785 |
| Glen Tennet | NO 5183 |
| Glen Tig | NX 1482 |
| Glen Tilt | NN 9273 |
| Glen Torridon | NG 9356 |
| Glen Tromie | NN 7694 |
| Glen Truim | NN 6789 |
| Glen Truim | NN 6790 |
| Glen Tulchan | NJ 1036 |
| Glen Tungadal | NG 4238 |
| Glen Turret | NR 7929 |
| Glen Turret | NN 3392 |
| Glen Tye | NN 8401 |
| Glen Uig | NM 6776 |
| Glen Uig | NO 3163 |
| Glen Uig | NG 4163 |
| Glen Ulladale | NB 0714 |
| Glen Ure | NN 0547 |
| Glen Urquhart | NH 4530 |
| Glen Usinish | NF 8333 |
| Glen Vale | NO 1805 |
| Glen Valtos | NB 0734 |
| Glen Varragill | NG 4736 |
| Glen Vidigill | NG 3936 |
| Glen Vorlich | NN 6321 |
| Glencoyne | NY 3718 |
| Glendaruel | NR 9985 |
| Glenesslin | NX 8284 |
| Glenhoul Glen | NX 6188 |
| Glenn Fender | NN 8938 |
| Glenridding | NY 3717 |
| Glens of Foudland | NJ 6034 |
| Glyn Corrwg | SS 8697 |
| Glyn Toroll | SN 9723 |
| Golden Valley | ST 4692 |
| Golden Valley | SO 8802 |
| Gonachan Glen | NS 6385 |
| Goyt Valley | SK 0177 |
| Gratton Dale | SK 2060 |
| Great Fryup Dale | NZ 7304 |
| Great Langdale | NY 3006 |
| Great Rocks Dale | SK 1073 |
| Grey Valley | SO 4032 |
| Griffe Grange Valley | SK 2556 |
| Grimsworth Dean | SD 9830 |
| Grisedale | SD 7792 |
| Grisedale | NY 3715 |
| Grize Dale | SD 5148 |
| Groudle Glen | SC 4178 |

## H

| | |
|---|---|
| Hall Dale | SK 2864 |
| Hay Dale | SK 1276 |
| Heck Dale | SE 8686 |
| Heddon Valley | SS 6549 |
| High Dales | SE 9493 |
| High Dale | SK 1571 |
| Hope Dale | SO 4988 |
| Hope Valley | SK 1783 |
| Horseshoe Dale | SK 0970 |

## I

| | |
|---|---|
| Inverchaolain Glen | NS 1076 |
| Inverlochlarig Glen | NN 4319 |
| Invervegain Glen | NS 0879 |
| Ishag Glen | NN 4018 |

## K

| | |
|---|---|
| Kildonan Glen | NF 7527 |
| Kilmory Glen | NG 3602 |
| Kingsdale | SD 6976 |
| Kinloch Glen | NG 3800 |
| Kippenrait Glen | NS 7999 |
| Kirk Dale | SK 1868 |
| Kirk Dale | SE 6687 |
| Kirk Dale | SE 8984 |
| Kirkbean Glen | NX 9759 |
| Kirkton Glen | NN 5322 |
| Kyle of Sutherland | NH 5795 |
| Kylerhea Glen | NG 7720 |

## L

| | |
|---|---|
| Lady Clough | SK 1091 |
| Laing Dale | TA 0476 |
| Lairig Arnan | NN 2918 |
| Lairig Eilde | NN 1754 |
| Lairig Gartain | NN 1954 |
| Lairig Ghru | NN 9798 |
| Lairig Leacach | NN 2873 |
| Lampeter Vale | SN 1615 |
| Langdale | NY 6502 |
| Langstrothdale | SD 9078 |
| Lathhill Dale | SK 1865 |
| Lauderdale | NT 5544 |
| Laxey Glen | SC 4286 |
| Liddesdale | NY 4887 |
| Lin Dale | SK 1551 |
| Linkins Glen | NX 7655 |
| Little Dale | SD 7681 |
| Little Langdale | NY 3003 |
| Little Sled Dale | NY 8201 |
| Litton Dale | SK 1574 |
| Littondale | SD 9172 |
| Liundale | NR 5479 |
| Llyfnant Valley | SN 7297 |
| Llynfi Valley | SS 8788 |
| Long Dale | SK 1361 |
| Long Dale | SK 1860 |
| Long Dale | SE 8360 |
| Longdendale | SK 0498 |
| Longsleddale | NY 4902 |
| Lorton Vale | NY 1526 |
| Low Dales | SE 9591 |
| Lower Glen Astle | NR 2845 |
| Luddenden Dean | SE 0328 |
| Lunedale | NY 9221 |
| Lyth Valley | SD 4787 |

## M

| | |
|---|---|
| Mall Dale | SK 1453 |
| Mallerstang Common | NY 7800 |
| Marshwood Vale | SY 4097 |
| Matlock Dale | SK 2958 |
| Meon Valley | SU 6015 |
| Mickleden | NY 2606 |
| Middleton Dale | SK 2175 |
| Mill Glen | NS 9198 |
| Miller's Dale | SK 1573 |
| Monachyle Glen | NN 4722 |
| Monamore Glen | NS 0029 |
| Monk's Dale | SK 1374 |
| Monsal Dale | SK 1771 |
| Mosedale | NY 1810 |
| Mosedale | NY 2402 |
| Mosedale | NY 4909 |
| Mosedale | NY 1318 |

## N

| | |
|---|---|
| Nant Colwyn | SH 5749 |
| Nant Ffraneon | SH 6362 |
| Nant yr Eira | SH 9706 |
| Nantgwynant | SH 6250 |
| Netherby Dale | SE 9083 |
| Newton Dale | SE 8191 |
| Nidd Valley | SE 2059 |
| Nidderdale | SE 1073 |
| Nithsdale | NX 8792 |
| North Dale | TA 0475 |
| North Glen Dale | NF 8016 |
| North Glen Sannox | NR 9946 |

## O

| | |
|---|---|
| Ogmore Valley | SS 9184 |
| Olchon Valley | SO 2931 |
| Open Dale | SE 8060 |
| Over Dale | SK 1880 |
| Ox Dale | SE 8884 |
| Oxendale | NY 2705 |

## P

| | |
|---|---|
| Pass of Brander | NN 0528 |
| Perry Dale | SK 1080 |
| Peter Dale | SK 1275 |
| Petta Dale | HU 4157 |
| Pevensey Levels | TQ 6307 |
| Pin Dale | SK 1582 |
| Port Soderick Glen | SC 3472 |

## R

| | |
|---|---|
| Ramps Gill | NY 4315 |
| Raydale | SD 9085 |
| Redesdale | NY 8397 |
| Rhondda Fach | ST 0195 |
| Rhonddà Fawr | SS 9992 |
| Rhymney Valley | ST 1493 |
| Ribblesdale | SD 8163 |
| Riccal Dale | SE 6287 |
| Riggindale | NY 4511 |
| Rosedale | SE 7196 |
| Ross The | NR 9628 |
| Rother Levels | TQ 9125 |
| Rye Dale | SE 5883 |

## S

| | |
|---|---|
| Saddell Glen | NR 7733 |
| Sairdon Dale | SE 9484 |
| St John's in the Vale | NY 3122 |
| Salachan Glen | NM 9852 |
| Sand Dale | SE 8785 |
| Savary Glen | NM 6447 |
| Sean Ghleann | NR 7561 |
| Seive Dale | SE 8688 |
| Severn Valley | SO 7192 |
| Shirley Moor | TQ 9332 |
| Sirhony Valley | ST 1797 |
| Sleadale | NG 3229 |
| Sled Dale | NY 8400 |
| Sleddale | SD 8587 |
| Sma' Glen | NN 8930 |
| Snever Dale | SE 8687 |
| South Dale | TA 0775 |
| Sow Dale | TF 3466 |
| Srath a' Bhathaich | NG 8847 |
| Srath a Chraisg | NC 5324 |
| Srath a' Ghlinne | NN 6816 |
| Srath Ach' a' Bhathaich | NH 7095 |
| Srath an Eilich | NN 6496 |
| Srath an Lòin | NC 4416 |
| Srath Ascaig | NG 8633 |
| Srath Beag | NG 5722 |
| Srath Beag | NC 3853 |
| Srath Bhata | NR 4152 |
| Srath Carnaig | NH 7098 |
| Srath Chrombuill | NH 1264 |
| Srath Coille na Fearna | NC 3750 |
| Srath Creag nain Fitheach | NM 4841 |
| Srath Dionard | NC 3353 |
| Srath Dubh-uisge | NN 2915 |
| Srath Duilleach | NH 0328 |
| Srath Luacrach | NR 3970 |
| Srath Luib na Seilich | NC 3241 |
| Srath Lungard | NG 9164 |
| Srath Maol Chaluim | NG 7347 |
| Srath Mór | NG 5624 |
| Srath na Crèitheach | NG 5022 |
| Srath na Fritne | NC 8227 |
| Srath na Seilge | NC 1818 |
| Srath nan Caran | NC 3036 |
| Srath nan Lòn | NC 2301 |
| Srath nan Lùb | NS 0691 |
| Srath Nimhe | NH 2090 |
| Srath Shuardail | NM 7346 |
| Stain Dale | SE 8690 |
| Stank Glen | NN 5710 |
| Storridge Valley | SS 5545 |
| Strath of Kildonan *(or Strath Ullie)* | NC 9219 |
| Strath Allan | NN 8308 |
| Strath Ardle | NO 0955 |
| Strath Avon | NJ 1525 |
| Strath Beag | NH 1087 |
| Strath Beg | NC 8531 |
| Strath Blane | NS 5380 |
| Strath Bogie | NJ 5237 |
| Strath Bran | NH 2461 |
| Strath Brora | NC 7408 |
| Strath Carron | NH 5192 |
| Strath Chailleach | NC 2466 |
| Strath Croe | NG 9621 |
| Strath Dearn | NH 8028 |
| Strath Dores | NH 6036 |
| Strath Eachaig | NS 1484 |
| Strath Errick | NH 5320 |
| Strath Fillan | NN 3528 |
| Strath Finella | NO 6879 |
| Strath Fleet | NC 7102 |
| Strath Grudie | NC 5205 |
| Strath Halladale | NC 8953 |
| Strath Isla | NJ 4251 |
| Strath Kanaird | NC 1501 |
| Strath Lunndaidh | NC 7800 |
| Strath Mashie | NN 5892 |
| Strath Mashie | NN 5892 |
| Strath More | NH 1882 |
| Strath More | NC 4544 |
| Strath More | NO 4757 |
| Strath Mulzie | NH 3193 |
| Strath na Sealga | NH 0780 |
| Strath Nairn | NH 6629 |
| Strath Naver | NC 7045 |
| Strath Nethy | NJ 0207 |
| Strath of Appin | NM 9445 |
| Strath of Orchy | NN 1627 |
| Strath Oykel | NC 4200 |
| Strath Peffer | NH 5159 |
| Strath Rannoch | NH 3972 |
| Strath Rory | NH 6777 |
| Strath Rusdale | NH 5776 |
| Strath Sgitheach | NH 5263 |
| Strath Shinary | NC 2461 |
| Strath Skinsdale | NC 7616 |
| Strath Spey | NH 7800 |
| Strath Spey | NJ 1436 |
| Strath Stack | NC 2740 |
| Strath Stack | NC 2740 |
| Strath Suadal | NG 6221 |
| Strath Tay | NO 0042 |
| Strath Tirry | NC 5319 |
| Strath Tollaidh | NH 6999 |
| Strath Vagastie | NC 5430 |
| Strath Vaich | NH 3572 |
| Strathconon | NH 3856 |
| Strath Cuileannach | NH 4293 |
| Strathdearn | NH 7733 |
| Strathglass | NH 3734 |
| Strathgryfe | NS 3370 |
| Strathjarrar | NH 3139 |
| Strathyre | NN 5618 |
| Streens | NH 8639 |
| Strine Dale | SD 9506 |
| Strone Glen | NR 6409 |
| Sulby Glen | SC 3891 |
| Sunning Dale | SE 9573 |
| Swair Dale | SE 8689 |
| Swaledale | SE 0198 |
| Swansea Valley | SN 7304 |

## T

| | |
|---|---|
| Taddington Dale | SK 1671 |
| Taff Vale | ST 0892 |
| Tanat Valley | SJ 0924 |
| Teanchoisin Glen | NR 7440 |
| Teesdale | NY 9325 |
| Teviotdale | NT 5620 |
| Thornton Dale | SE 8586 |
| Tideswell Dale | SK 1574 |
| Toadsmoor Valley | SO 8804 |
| Tog Dale | TA 0368 |
| Torris Dale | NR 7837 |
| Traeth Mawr | SH 5940 |
| Trent Valley | SJ 9329 |
| Trouts Dale | SE 9287 |
| Tusdale | NG 3525 |

## U

| | |
|---|---|
| Uldale | SD 7496 |

## V

| | |
|---|---|
| Vale of Ewyas | SO 2827 |
| Vale of Belvoir | SK 8039 |
| Vale of Berkeley | ST 6899 |
| Vale of Catmose | SK 8608 |
| Vale of Clwyd | SJ 0768 |
| Vale of Conwy | SH 7767 |
| Vale of Edale | SK 1285 |
| Vale of Evesham | SP 0441 |
| Vale of Ffestiniog | SH 6640 |
| Vale of Glamorgan | ST 0072 |
| Vale of Gloucester | SO 8118 |
| Vale of Llangollen | SJ 2641 |
| Vale of Mawgan or Lanherne | SW 8765 |
| Vale of Neath | SN 8303 |
| Vale of Pewsey | SU 1159 |
| Vale of Taunton Deane | ST 1926 |
| Vale of White Horse | SU 3191 |
| Valley of Rocks | SS 7049 |
| Valley of Stones | SY 5987 |

## W

| | |
|---|---|
| Wad Dale | SE 9572 |
| Wasdale | NY 1808 |
| Weardale | NY 9038 |
| Well Vale | TF 4373 |
| Welton Dale | SE 9628 |
| Wensley Dale | SK 2520 |
| Wensleydale | SD 9988 |
| West Allen Dale | NY 7852 |
| West Baldwin | SC 3582 |
| West Dale | TA 0374 |
| West Stones Dale | NY 8803 |
| Westerdale | NZ 6606 |
| Wharfdale | SE 0753 |
| Wharfedale | SD 9768 |
| Whicham Valley | SD 1583 |
| Whisper Dales | SE 9592 |
| White Glen | NO 2371 |
| Whitekeld Dale | SE 8253 |
| Whitsun Dale | NY 8503 |
| Widdale | SD 8388 |
| Willdale | NY 4817 |
| Wolfscote Dale | SK 1357 |
| Woo Dale | SK 0973 |
| Woodlands Valley | SK 1588 |
| Wye Valley | SO 5112 |
| Wye Dale | SK 1072 |
| Wye Valley | SN 9668 |
| Wylye Valley | SU 0038 |

# Waterfalls

*We all have a vision of what constitutes 'a waterfall'. Some would, with justification, include the stepped waterfalls which tumble in a series of miniature cascades through villages like Aysgarth in Yorkshire. The dramatic, romantic falls included in this section have been chosen for their wide appeal.*

## Falls of Measach

If it were not in so remote a part of the country, Corrieshalloch Gorge would surely attract vast numbers of visitors each year. Through it flows the dramatic River Droma and it possesses a flora and fauna of exceptional richness. The gorge is narrow, never more than 100 ft wide and up to 200 ft deep in places – a true box canyon. The river, flowing towards Loch Broom and finding itself constrained by the walls of the gorge, gathers force and hurtles, in an impressive display of white water strength, 150 ft over a ledge to the floor of the gorge.

The conditions created in the gorge are ideal for many plants including ferns, mosses and liverworts. Hazel, birch, larch, bird cherry and rowan form a thick woodland which, in turn, shelters a wide variety of birds.

The waterfall can be seen from two vantage points; one is a small observation platform giving a good general view of both it and the gorge, the other a suspension bridge above the falls.

*FALLS OF MEASACH*

## Grey Mare's Tail

High in the bleak, grassy fell land some eight miles from Moffat, the National Trust for Scotland have a car park and information display. From the park a short trail leads to one of the most familiar waterfalls in Britain—the Grey Mare's Tail.

Named after the grey mare in Robert Burns' poem *Tam O'Shanter*, the delicate, feathery strands of water which represent her tail drift down against a green clad, almost treeless background. Above, and out of sight, is Loch Skeen, a reminder of a glacial past when water which was trapped as ice first carved out a valley, then threw up a barrier to contain the waters of the Tail Burn. Across the end of the valley flowed the glacier of Moffat Water, at once more powerful and grinding over a softer rock. Inevitably, the effect was to lower the main valley more than its tributary. When the ice retreated a 'hanging' valley was created and the burn could escape only by plunging 200 ft from the upper to the lower level.

The wildlife of the area is quite fascinating and remarkably varied. Trees may be missing, but birds, animals and, in particular, plants, are not. Sheep have long grazed the grass and heather moors around the waterfall, and in its immediate vicinity a herd of feral goats have, by their close cropping, created an almost alpine carpet of grass. Conditions around the waterfall have, in fact, proved very acceptable to alpine plants and the area is covered throughout the spring and summer with an exciting variety of flowers. Wrens whirl and scold among the rocks of the falls, grey wagtails and dippers use them for perches and the common gull breeds on the quiet waters of the loch.

## Hardrow Force

In the Yorkshire Dales there are numerous waterfalls. Hardrow has been chosen because it is a record breaker – the highest unbroken fall in Great Britain.

Different rock strata often create waterfalls and Hardrow Force (sometimes spelled Hardraw) is an example. Hard limestone overlays soft shale to produce a jutting ledge which brings about the 'spout' effect, where the flow is projected clear of the rocks leaving space behind the curtain of water. This is exactly what happens at Hardrow with a drop of 100 ft. The Romantic movement, and particularly Wordsworth, were responsible for 'discovering' Hardrow. He wrote appreciatively of 'the contrast between the falling water and that which is apparently at rest, or rather settling gradually into quiet in the pool below'. Others will look no further than the exciting spectacle of glittering water forming a mask over the central section of the natural amphitheatre – the setting for Hardrow Force.

## High Force

More than thirty years ago the artist Sidney Jones lamented the popularity of High Force as a 'beauty spot' noting how much better it was when 'the wireless' had announced bad weather. His words are still true for, though the crowds thin, the falls become more dramatic after rain.

The popular route to the falls is by a well signposted path leading down from the hotel beside the B6277. Here, among mainly coniferous woodland and as if to confirm that it has recovered from the indignity imposed upon it by the building of the Cow Green Reservoir further along the valley, the River Tees defiantly hurls itself over 70 ft whinstone cliffs.

An alternative way to the falls would be to join the Pennine Way at Middleton in Teesdale. This is, perhaps, the easiest section of the whole of that most difficult of walks, but to have tackled any part of it is an experience! From here the Way follows the route of the Tees, heading upstream to enter a long, narrow limestone gorge

down which the river, still smarting from man-imposed constraints higher up, rushes, grumbling. Three miles above Middleton the path passes Low Force and a further two miles along the valley lies High Force.

HARDROW FORCE (above)

## Pistyll Rhaeadr

Although close to the English border, the Berwyn Mountains are relatively unexplored. Few roads run into them, and those that do are narrow and difficult. Certainly the road which leads from Llanrhaeadr-ym-Mochnant towards Pistyll Rhaeadr comes into this category. But, unlike most of the other roads, it is frequently heavy with traffic making for the highest waterfall in England or Wales.

The name Pistyll Rhaeadr is an example of the preciseness of the Welsh language in description. It means waterfall cataract and it aptly sums up the twin character of the falls. Formed about 10,000 years ago it consists of two distinct phases. First, the Afon Disgynfa appears in a small nick in the cliff, plunging steeply for over 100ft then, collected in a rock filled pot, gathers itself for a second fall of some 120 ft under a natural arch to a pool by a footbridge. The effect, particularly after rain, is both dramatic and inspiring and the fall is, not surprisingly, one of the 'Seven Wonders of Wales'.

PISTYLL RHAEADR (below)

# Caves

*Whole books could be devoted to the infinite variety of limestone landscape alone. Certainly, in any selection of caves, it would be easy to include only those carved out of it. But that would have led to the omission of awesome sea caves, and of those fashioned by people . . .*

## Cresswell Crags

Palaeolithic communities have left few relics, but one of the best sites is at Cresswell Crags.

In a narrow gorge, carved out of grey limestone cliffs, are a series of caves and fissures which gave protection to early Stone Age man. Under layers of earth, stone axes and arrow heads have been found, but the most important discoveries at Cresswell have been the bones of animals. Here is fascinating evidence of the animals which inhabited Britain after the Ice Age – wolves, mammoths and woolly rhinoceros. An interpretive centre explains the relationship between men and animals.

## Dan-yr-Ogof and Ogof-Ffynnon-Ddu

For the caver, the Brecon Beacons contains some of the largest and most challenging cave systems, comparable to those of North Yorkshire. The majority of these caves are inaccessible to all but the most expert, but, at Dan-yr-Ogof, close to the Craig-y-Nos Country Park, there is the opportunity to study a limestone cave system in complete safety.

The caves at Dan-yr-Ogof were first discovered in 1912 and, at that time, they were flooded and could only be explored by boat. Over the years they have been developed into the largest cave system in Western Europe open to visitors. Beautifully and imaginatively lit, Dan-yr-Ogof has won several awards from tourist bodies.

Inside the caves the visitor is able to walk through light, dry passages into vast caverns where stalactites and stalagmites have been, and still are, developing over thousands of years. The largest of the caves is known as Cathedral Cave, and its dimensions justify the description. It is 160 ft long and 70 ft high and was formed, as are all limestone caves, by a combination of mechanical and chemical action. The waters from a river flowing into a fault in the limestone rock create a solution of calcium carbonate which the river then leaches out over a period of many centuries.

Across the valley of the Tawe there is another cave system which attracts a great deal of attention from scientists as well as cavers. Open only by permit, *Ogof-Ffynnon-Ddu* – 'the cave of the black spring' – is unique in two ways. It is the largest and deepest cave system in Britain, with more than 20 miles of passages running hun-

*STALACTITES IN TREAK CLIFF CAVERN The caverns around Castleton are also known for their 'Blue John' stone.*

*DAN-YR-OGOF CAVES These spectacular limestone caves are open to visitors. Other local caves are only accessible to expert cavers.*

dreds of feet below the surface, and the only subterranean National Nature Reserve. For those who prefer to stay above ground there are interesting plants to be seen in the limestone 'pavement'.

## Dolaucothi

One of the only three known gold mines in the whole of the Roman Empire is situated on the side of a heavily wooded hill in a remote region of Wales.

It is probable that the first deposits of gold were found in the gravel bed of the River Cothi. From midway through the first century AD until about AD 200, the invaders, using slaves to hew the mine shafts, struggled to extract sufficient gold to justify the degree of expertise which they applied to the project. The very fact that they built a fort, presumably to protect their finds and their engineers, suggests that, at least initially, they were successful.

Eventually, first the fort and then the Romans departed, leaving the workings and the land to return to a natural state for over 1800 years. Interest revived in the late 19th century and a number of limited

companies were formed. For more than 40 years attempts were made to re-establish the mines as a viable concern, but in 1938 they closed and abandoned.

The mine is only a small part of a large estate which had been in the hands of one family since the time of Henry VII. During the war it was transferred to the National Trust who have managed the (largely farming) estate ever since.

In recent years the Trust have improved visitor facilities to the mine, laying out trails around parts of the estate, including one which gives an insight into the extent of the original Roman workings. In 1986 a new information centre was opened with an exhibition concentrating on the early 20th-century efforts to work the mine. Guided tours take place during the summer months which penetrate a little way into the caves.

*ROMAN GOLD MINE AT DOLAUCOTHI, NEAR PUMSAINT*
*Many of the shafts were dug by Roman slaves, though further mining took place during the late 19th century.*

## Fingal's Cave

Fingal's Cave is one of several similar 'structures' formed of basalt lava on the island of Staffa. The astonishingly precise geometric patterns of the basalt columns in Fingal's Cave are echoed, to a remarkable degree, in the formations of the Giant's Causeway in Northern Ireland. The link is compounded by the legend of Fionn mac Cumhaill, after whom the cave is named, and who is credited with the building of the causeway.

Staffa itself is largely composed of symmetrical basalt columns formed by the cooling, at different rates, of a mass of molten lava. There are three distinct phases to be observed in this cooling process. The top of the island (and of the cave) consists of a rather unstructured crust, resulting from a relatively rapid rate of cooling. The middle section cooled less quickly and contracted as it cooled. That process produced a series of hexagonal cracks in the top surface which extended down into the mass and produced the

elegant columns at the entrance to Fingal's Cave. The shorter, broader columns which form the 'causeway' – and which are closest in appearance to the Ulster formation – cooled at a slower rate, from below.

Fascinating as that may be from a geological standpoint, it pales beside the interest the island aroused in the 19th-century Romantics, who were continually making fresh discoveries of pleasing natural phenomena.

Yet Staffa and its caves were hardly known until the naturalist Sir Joseph Banks waxed lyrical about Fingal's Cave in 1772. 'Compared to this,' he wrote, 'what are the cathedrals and palaces built by men!' His comment opened a flood gate, until it sometimes appears that every 19th-century man and woman – Queen Victoria included – of 'sensibility' must have visited the cave. Mendelssohn composed an overture around it, Turner painted it and poets honoured it. It is indeed impressive – over 200 ft deep, 70 ft high and 40 ft wide at the entrance – and has a romantic grandeur – the sea really *does* make music about it.

## Grimes Graves

It is difficult to envisage two more distinct landscapes than those of Great Langdale in Cumbria and the Norfolk Brecklands, but in Neolithic times both possessed 'axe factories'. The light, sandy soil of the Brecklands was rich in flints and, at the site we know as Grimes Graves, Neolithic men dug for them, using deer antlers as a primitive form of pick.

Some of the first tools were fashioned here, and in addition to being used for cutting down the local forest in preparation for farming, were 'exported' to sites on Salisbury Plain, probably along the Ridgeway.

As they worked, the prehistoric miners filled in old shafts (some of which are believed to have been up to 40 ft deep) with spoil from the new. After the site was abandoned subsidence completed the work, almost obliterating it. Today however, the excavated shafts can be descended, and visitors are, for a moment, transported back 4000 years into the past.

## Smoo Cave

A few miles to the east of Cape Wrath, on Scotland's far north coast, is the crofting centre of Durness. Close by is Smoo Cave, a fascinating example of a limestone chamber produced by the joint action of marine erosion and an underground river.

What makes Smoo Cave particularly exciting is the waterfall formed by the river, the Allt Smoo, plunging 80 ft down an open shaft to a pool within the huge, cathedral-like cave. The size of the main chamber has been estimated as 200 ft long by 120 ft wide and over 100 ft high. Where light strikes the walls from above or near the cave entrance, moss, liverworts and ferns grow freely. The cave itself is at the end of a cleft in the limestone – the name comes from the Norse, *smuga*, for a cleft – and it is almost certain that, at some time in the past, the limestone 'roof' extended much further towards the sea.

The river rises in Loch Meadaidh, flows off the moors and enters the cave through what is probably a fault in the limestone.

There is a belief that it was the Devil who created the shaft when he was cornered by a local with an account to settle, and made a rapid exit. The river makes its descent through not one, but three chambers – two of them inaccessible without potholing equipment and expertise – and emerges from the boulder-strewn cave entrance on a short journey to the sea.

*GRIMES GRAVES At this prehistoric 'axe factory' some of the old shafts have been cleared enabling visitors to see their original extent. Over 800 pits are thought to have been dug.*

*PORTH-YR-OGOF CAVE At this limestone cave near Ystradfellte in the Brecon Beacons the Afon Mellte disappears underground. Many other caves, streams and waterfalls can be seen.*

# Heaths and Moors

*Variety is the constant theme of Britain's moors. Studland, Dunwich and Tregaron offer striking examples of wildlife habitats which have virtually vanished elsewhere. Bodmin is a moor surrounded by major roads, which remains remarkably unknown. Wheeldale has a Roman road, and Abergwesyn a drover's way.*

## Bodmin Moor

Bodmin Moor was once well populated, probably prosperous. Now it stands, touched by a little industry, but largely an empty, unfriendly expanse of moor through which the traveller to Cornish holiday resorts must pass.

Yet, thousands of years ago, the same seeker after sun might have paused on the moor, for it seems almost certain that Bodmin was both warmer and considerably more hospitable during the time of the Neolithic and Bronze Age people. We have evidence that villages were established, farming developed and religious ceremonies performed on the moor: there are enclosures, field boundaries, hut circles and standing stones. The granite blocks of the Stripple Stones and King Arthur's Hall; the prehistoric burial chamber of Trethevy Quoit; even the Arthurian legends surrounding Dozmary Pool – all reveal, if only through a tantalising mist, that people were active here in the past.

But climate and habits changed, and men deserted the moor until, in the Middle Ages, a growing population brought farming back to the edges and along the rivers of the moor. In the 18th century its mineral wealth was attacked and copper mines prospered. The stacks of their engine houses survive – less obtrusive than the spoil heaps of the china clay industry which continue to dominate parts of the moor.

Regardless of people's activities, the plant and bird life thrives in an area with a high average rainfall. Plants, in particular, have colonised the bogs which have formed over the centuries, lying on the granite which is at the heart of Bodmin. Cotton-grass and mare's-tail, bog-moss and bog-asphodel are common here, as is the insect-eating sundew.

In places the granite has thrust out of the moor and, from Brown Willy, the tallest tor at 1375 ft, the view extends to both sides of Cornwall.

## Dunwich Heath

Much of Britain's fascination lies in its wonderful juxtaposition of periods. The little village of Dunwich is all that remains of a town which was the capital of 7th-century Saxon East Anglia but has succumbed to the endless pounding of the sea. Next to it lies the heath, once an extensive medieval sheep grazing area. To the south is a creation of the 20th century, Minsmere bird reserve; while looming on the horizon, Sizewell nuclear power station suggests the shape of the future.

The 214 acres of Dunwich Heath stand on top of low, crumbling, sandy cliffs above a long pebble beach used all year by

*TRETHEVY QUOIT (left) This prehistoric burial chamber at St Cleer is just one sign of the past occupation of the moorland near Bodmin.*

*SILVER STUDDED BLUE One of the butterflies found on Dunwich Heath. It feeds on heather, and can be seen in flight between June and August. Males are blue, females brown.*

| A | | Barningham Moor | NZ 00 | Bodmin Moor | SX 17/27 | Burnhope Moor | NY 83 | Cotherstone Moor | NY 91 | Downham Moor | SD 74 |
|---|---|---|---|---|---|---|---|---|---|---|---|
| Abney Moor | SK 17 | Barnsfield Heath | SU 10 | Bowes Moor | NY 91 | Butterton Moor | SK 05 | Cowpe Moor | SD 81 | Downholme Moor | SE 19 |
| Agra Moor | SE 18 | Baysdale Moor | NZ 60 | Bradfield Moors | SK 29 | | | Cragdale Moor | SD 98 | Dunwich Heath | TM 46 |
| Alport Moor | SK 19 | Beamsley Moor | SE 15 | Bradwell Moor | SK 18 | C | | Cragdale Moor | SD 98 | | |
| Alston Moor | NY 73 | Beaulieu Heath | SU 30 | Braidley Moor | SE 08 | Calderbergh Moor | SE 18 | Craven Moor | SE 06 | | |
| Anglezarke Moor | SD 61 | Beeley Moor | SK 26 | Braithwaite Moor | SE 18 | Canford Heath | SU 09 | Culloden Muir | NH 74 | E | |
| Appletreewick | SE 06 | Bell House Moor | SD 92 | Bramham Moor | SE 44 | Cardinham Moor | SX 17 | | | Earswick Moor | SE 65 |
| Moor | | Bellerby Moor | SE 09 | Brampton East | SK 27 | Carle Moor | SE 17 | | | East Bolton Moor | SE 09 |
| Arden Great Moor | SE 59 | Bewerley Moor | SE 16 | Moor | | Carlton Moor | SE 08 | D | | East Moor | SX 27 |
| Arkengarthdale | NY 90 | Big Moor | SK 27 | Brandwood Moor | SD 82 | Carr & Craggs | SD 82 | Dallow Moor | SE 16 | East Moor | SK 26/27 |
| Moor | | Bilsdale West | SE 59 | Bransdale Moor | SE 69 | Moor | | Dallowgill Moor | SE 17 | East Moors | SE 69 |
| Arkleside Moor | SE 07 | Moor | | Breadsall Moor | SK 34 | Castleshaw Moor | SD 91 | Danby High Moor | NZ 60 | Edale Moor | SK 18 |
| Axe Edge Moor | SK 07 | Bingley Moor | SE 14 | Brent Moor | SX 66 | Caton Moor | SD 56 | Danby Low Moor | NZ 71 | Egton High Moor | NZ 70 |
| | | Black Ashop Moor | SK 09 | Bretterham Heath | TL 98 | Caudale Moor | NY 41 | Dartmoor | SX 58/68 | Ellerton Moor | SE 09 |
| B | | Black Moor | SD 93 | Bridgham Heath | TL 98 | Chelburn Moor | SD 91 | Darwen Moor | SD 61 | Elslack Moor | SD 94 |
| Baildon Moor | SE 14 | Black Moor | SE 59 | Brown Moor | SE 66 | Clegg Moor | SD 91 | Davistow Moor | SX 18 | Embsay Moor | SD 95 |
| Bamford Moor | SK 28 | Blake Moor | SD 92 | Brownsey Moor | SD 99 | Coldharbour Moor | SK 09 | Dean Moor | SX 66 | Emmott Moor | SD 93 |
| Banshaw Moor | SE 03 | Bleakedgate Moor | SD 91 | Buckton Moor | SD 90 | Colsterdale Moor | SE 18 | Dean Moor | NY 02 | Erringden Moor | SD 92 |
| Barden Moor | SE 05 | Bleasdale Moor | SD 54 | Burbage Moor | SK 28 | Commondale | NZ 61 | Dearden Moor | SD 82 | Exmoor | SS 74/84 |
| Bardon Moor | SE 19 | Blubberhouses | SE 15 | Burley Moor | SE 14 | Moor | | Deerplay Moor | SD 82 | Eyam Moor | SK 27 |
| Barley Moor | SD 74 | Moor | | Burn Moor | SD 84 | Conistone Moor | SE 07 | Denton Moor | SE 15 | | |
| | | | | Burn Moor | SD 66 | | | Derwent Moors | SK 28 | | |

hardy sea fishermen. It is true heath, colonised by great clumps of gorse, sweeps of bracken and, in the more protected area away from the cliffs, by silver birch.

The National Trust, which owns the heath, has a waymarked walk which gives an introduction to the extensive wildlife of the area. Where Minsmere is, arguably, at its best in winter, Dunwich attracts many species in summer, including the evening flying nightjar. For many birdwatchers, the finest music is heard in the boom of the bittern at Minsmere and the churr of the nightjar on Dunwich.

## Purbeck Heath

Taken together, the heaths of the Isle of Purbeck, including Studland, Godlingston and Middlebere, represent almost the 'last stand' of a once extensive habitat. Threatened from the east by the encroachment of the holiday industry, from behind by farming interests and from within by the oil lobby, the heaths are protected by three major agencies – the RSPB, the Nature Conservancy Council and the National Trust.

Within the heaths are rare species under constant threat of extinction and, for the visitor, there is a very special 'feel' – something quite unique about the area. The views are distinctive: purple heather splashed with bright yellow gorse, stretching to calm lagoons and inlets mirroring the sky, and all round, at any season, the plant and animal life for which the reserves are famous.

Throughout the summer months, the insect population is evident as butterflies, moths and, over the water, dragonflies flutter or dart. The heaths are home to all six species of British reptiles and that means exercising caution, for the adder

*PURBECK HEATH Heathers, gorse and birch are common on the drier parts of the heath. A number of rare insects, reptiles and birds (including the Dartford warbler) live in this habitat.*

breeds here in some numbers. Signs give a reminder of the dangers.

The most famous bird of the area is also one of the shyest: the Dartford Warbler clings to existence here and on a few other sites in the south-east, struggling against loss of habitat and its own vulnerability to heath fire or winter cold. In the winter, ducks and waders use the sheltered waters for resting and feeding.

Four heathers cover the heath; the most distinctive is the very localised Dorset heath, its pink flowers carried on spikes, not clusters. The rather attractive parasitic dodder threads itself over the heather in high summer. In the damper places, the aromatic bog-myrtle of spring gives way to the long-leaved sundew in June.

## Tregaron and Abergwesyn

One of the last great bogs outside Scotland, Tregaron Bog was formed when the Teifi was trapped by rocky debris deposited at the end of the Ice Age. It formed a shallow lake, at the sides of which plant and organic materials were deposited. Material built up steadily, rotted, raised the level and gradually created a peat-based bog.

Now one of the most important of wetland sites, Tregaron is a National Nature Reserve and permits are required for the centre. But it is possible to walk part of an abandoned railway track beside the bog, and the opportunities for quiet

| F | | H | | Hollingworthhall | SJ 99 | Kirk Gill Moor | SD 97 | M | | N | |
|---|---|---|---|---|---|---|---|---|---|---|---|
| Faggergill Moor | NY 90 | Hallam Moors | SK 28 | Moor | | Kirkby Malzeard | SE 17 | Malham Moor | SD 96 | Nether Moor | SK 18 |
| Farndale Moor | NZ 60 | Hannah Moor | NX 91 | Holne Moor | SX 67 | Moor | | Marrick Moor | NZ 00 | North Moor | SD 97 |
| Flat Moor | SE 16 | Hardcastle Moor | SE 16 | Holt Heath | SU 00 | Kirkby Moor | SD 28 | Marston Moor | SE 45 | North Moor | SE 07 |
| Forest Moor | SE 25 | Harden Moor | SD 81 | Hope Moor | NZ 00 | Knowl Moor | SD 81 | Masham Moor | SE 17 | North Yorkshire | NZ 50 |
| Fountains Earth | SE 17 | Harden Moor | SE 03 | Horse Head Moor | SD 87 | | | Masham Moor | SE 17 | Moors | –NZ 90 |
| Moor | | Harden Moor | SK 19 | Houndkirk Moor | SK 28 | | | Matley Heath | SU 30 | | |
| Foxup Moor | SD 87 | Harford Moor | SX 66 | Howden Moors | SK 19 | L | | Melbecks Moor | NY 90 | | |
| Fylingdales Moor | SE 99 | Harkerside Moor | SE 09 | Hunderthwaite | NY 91 | Langbar Moor | SE 15 | Mellor Moor | SJ 98 | O | |
| | | Hauxwell Moor | SE 19 | Moor | | Langsett Moors | SK 19 | Melmerby Moor | SE 08 | Oakworth Moor | SD 93 |
| | | Hawksworth Moor | SE 14 | Hurst Moor | NZ 00 | Lee Moor | SX 56 | Meltham Moor | SE 00 | Offerton Moor | SK 28 |
| G | | Hawnby Moor | SE 59 | | | Leyburn Moor | SE 09 | Mickleton Moor | NY 92 | Old Moor | SK 18 |
| Galyle Moor | SD 78 | Haworth Moor | SE 03 | | | Lindley Moor | SE 25 | Middle Moor | SD 97 | Osmotherley Moor | SE 49 |
| Gayles Moor | NZ 00 | Haxby Moor | SE 66 | I | | Little Howden | SK 19 | Middlebere Heath | SY 98 | Oswaldtwistle | SD 72 |
| Gisborough Moor | NZ 61 | Hazelwood Moor | SE 05 | Ickornshaw Moor | SD 94 | Moor | | Middleham High | SE 09 | Moor | |
| Glaisdale Moor | NZ 70 | Heald Moor | SD 82 | Ilkley Moor | SE 14 | Little Moor | SE 49 | Moor | | Ot Moor | SP 51 |
| Glusburn Moor | SD 94 | Heathfield Moor | SE 16 | Illton Moor | SE 17 | Lockton High Moor | SE 89 | Middleham Low | SE 09 | Ovenden Moor | SE 03 |
| Goathland Moor | SE 89 | Hebden Moor | SE 06 | In Moor | SE 07 | Lockton Low Moor | SE 89 | Moor | | Oxenhope Moor | SE 03 |
| Godlingston Heath | SZ 08 | Helmsley Moor | SE 59 | Inchfield Moor | SD 92 | Lodge Moor | SE 07 | Midhope Moors | SK 19 | | |
| Gouthwaite Moor | SE 06 | Heptonstall Moor | SD 93 | | | Longstone Moor | SK 17 | Morton Moor | SE 14 | | |
| Grasmoor | NY 12 | Heyshaw Moor | SE 16 | | | Longworth Moor | SD 61 | Moscar Moor | SK 28 | P | |
| Grassington Moor | SE 06 | High Ash Head | SE 17 | K | | Low House Moor | SD 91 | Moss Moor | SD 91 | Park Moor | SJ 98 |
| Gratton Moor | SK 16 | Moor | | Keighley Moor | SE 03 | Ludworth Moor | SJ 99 | Mossdale Moor | SD 89 | Pateley Moor | SE 16 |
| Grewelthorpe | SE 17 | High Bradley Moor | SE 05 | Kelbrook Moor | SD 94 | Lune Moor | NY 82 | Moxby Moor | SE 56 | Paythorne Moor | SD 85 |
| Moor | | High Moor | SX 18 | Kepwick Moor | SE 49 | | | | | Peaknaze Moor | SK 09 |
| Grindon Moor | SK 05 | High Moor | SE 99 | Kexwith Moor | NZ 00 | | | | | Penn Moor | SX 66 |
| Grinton Moor | SE 09 | Hipswell Moor | SE 19 | Kildale Moor | NZ 60 | | | | | Pikenaze Moor | SE 10 |
| Guiseley Moor | SE 14 | Holcombe Moor | SD 71 | Kilnsey Moor | SD 96 | | | | | Pock Stones Moor | SE 16 |

*THE MOUNTAIN PASS AT ABERGWESYN Crossing the southern end of the Cambrian Mountains, the road winds past forestry plantations and open moorland.*

moor, now owned by the National Trust.

If possible, complete a memorable tour by forking left to Beulah and Newbridge on Wye. Then, at Rhayader, take another marvellous mountain road to Cwmystwyth and back along the B4343 past Tregaron Bog. It is long and sometimes difficult, but endlessly exciting: a journey through the 'Desert of Wales' and into its very heart.

## Wheeldale Moor

For much of its journey over the moors to Goathland, the A169 runs parallel to the remains of one of the most remarkable roads in England. On Wheeldale Moor is the marvellously preserved length of Roman road known as Wade's Causeway. It retains the clear character of a paved road, with well defined kerbstones and culverts edging the heavy foundation stones.

Opinions vary as to the original route, its length, and even its age. Almost certainly the road started from Malton, and it probably ran to the Esk Valley or to the signal stations which were known to have been set up on the coast. But this theory conflicts with evidence suggesting that the road is older than the 4th century AD when the stations were operating. The name comes from the tradition that it was built by a local giant called Wade.

Today the Roman soldiers of 2000 years ago have been replaced by walkers from the Wheeldale Lodge Youth Hostel at Hunt House, and by sheep, trotting easily between the glorious purple oceans of heather which spread to the horizon.

A minor road south of Egton Bridge meets the causeway about a mile below the Youth Hostel. There is a further section of the road close to the Roman camp near Cropton.

observation are almost limitless – and breathtakingly exciting.

Willow and birch harbour sedge warblers and reed buntings. Water-rail step stealthily and often unseen through cotton-sedge. Over the cover of sphagnum moss the polecat hunts for reptiles, and the occasional red kite visits the area, as do hen harriers in winter. Otters and merlins, sundews and crowberry – this is a wonderland with, in the distance, the heights of the Cambrian Mountains.

The mountain road from Tregaron to Abergwesyn is high, narrow and difficult in bad weather, but it justifies the effort. Climbing steeply out of Tregaron, the road (once described by Leslie Thomas as 'wonderful, exultant') begins a switchback progress over unbelievably wild country Wild, but with signs of efforts to tame it, in stone walls and Forestry Commission plantings on distant hills. Historical country too: for centuries drovers and their livestock began a great trek from Tregaron to the markets of south-east England over these mountains.

Water is never far from the road. Streams bounce off the hills and the Afon Irfon accompanies it for the last part of the journey to Abergwesyn. Close to the point where the river joins the road is the start of 16,500 acres of the bleakest part of the

# Forests and Woods

*Border, Glen More and the Queen Elizabeth Forest are examples of modern Forest Parks. All have been enlarged or developed comparatively recently on upland sites where little but trees could be grown. The New Forest and Savernake, by contrast, have existed for centuries.*

## Border – Kielder Forest

Imagine turning an acre of grass by hand, carefully creating 1750 turves. Into each, a single seedling is inserted and the turf is replaced, grass down. That is how, in 1923, the planting of the Border Forest began. As the seedlings were of Sitka and Norway Spruce, the old adage of 'from small acorns...' is not entirely appropriate, but how the forest has grown! The largest forest in Britain, surrounding the largest man-made lake in Western Europe.

Part of the fascination of the Border Forest – Kielder, by which name it is commonly known, is only one of several forests making up the whole – lies in its history. For centuries, the Borders were heavily wooded with deciduous trees: oak, alder, birch and rowan. But people began to clear the trees to allow flocks of sheep to roam on the hills. Slowly, aided by roe deer, cattle and the harsh weather, which restricted new growth, the sheep began to reduce even the available grass and the area deteriorated into a bleak, boggy wilderness. Until 1923.

There are still many who would argue that the forest is another form of wilderness, dark and arid. The sight of millions of trees of similar age and size, stretching away across hill and valley, has limited appeal for those who love the small-scale beauty of a mixed broad-leaved wood. But it is impossible to deny the effect that sheer size has on the senses – visitors can hardly remain unimpressed as they drive along the exciting toll road through the heart of the forest.

The Border Forest is increasingly managed to allow the public to take advantage of leisure facilities. At the centre is Kielder Castle, headquarters of the Forestry Commission staff; close by is an excellent information centre. The needs of disabled visitors have received particular attention at Kielder, both in planning buildings and trails and providing facilities for courses, many involving activities on the expanse of Kielder Water.

Kielder Water is immense and arguments have been had over its construction, but it adds another element to the forest and has certainly been welcomed by many plant and animal species, who are rapidly colonising it.

The natural history of the forest is very much what one might expect. Goldcrest, siskin and crossbill live in heavily wooded areas, and red squirrels in older trees. Rabbits, foxes and badgers are common; roe deer are increasing after suffering a decline some years ago. The short-eared owl and the black grouse thrive in this environment. Red grouse and mountain hare live on the moors, while the plants of the boggy areas are probably more varied than those of the forest.

The Border Forest is not conventionally 'beautiful', but this new and exciting environment has a grandeur that will remain in the memory.

## Glen More Forest Park

Glen More is different from other major forest parks in this section – it contains more moors than woods. However, many will be content to explore the woods around the information centre at Loch Morlich and leave the moors to the hardier visitor.

Loch Morlich is over a thousand feet above sea level and retains a definite chill even in summer. The sandy shores are surrounded by rowan, alder and birch thickets, willow and juniper. There are many footpaths and waymarked trails, some concentrating on specific habitats like rivers, shore or forest, which branch out from the centre.

The River Trail provides a relatively easy introduction to the birdlife of the area. Along a three-mile route it should prove possible to see the localised capercaillie, crested tit and crossbill. Crossbills or crested tits may occur quite close to the start of the walk, but capercaillie will probably only be seen at the far point of the route, and early or late in the day. In the evening you may also hear the wing clapping of a long-eared owl or its rather muted, reflective hooting.

The Pinewood Trail leads to Ryvoan where there is a 300-acre remnant of the Caledonian pine forest. The range of tree species in the forest can be assessed from any of the main paths: Sitka, Douglas, larch, alder, juniper and Scots pine. It is possible to follow paths going above the tree line to Castle Hill, offering views over the whole of the Spey Valley. Easier by far is the road from the loch which ends under Cairn Gorm with a choice of car parks, two or which have excellent viewpoints. On the moors is a reindeer herd and sometimes an eagle can be seen.

Even without these, Glen More is a delightful place to visit. Perhaps because, though large, it is smaller than the other forest parks, and has an intimacy of scale that does not oppress the visitor. Maybe it helps that most of the trails never stray far from the loch or road; and that there is a touch more landscaping about it than some of its fellows. Whatever the reasons – the Glen More Forest Park is generally agreed to be delightful.

| A | | | | B | | | | | | | |
|---|---|---|---|---|---|---|---|---|---|---|---|
| Abbeyford Woods | SX 59 | Ardcanny Wood | NJ 24 | B | | Bawtry Forest | SK 69 | Birkshaw Forest | NY 17 | Bog of Shannon | NH 65 |
| Aberhethy Forest | NH 91 | Ardcastle Forest | NR 99 | Bad na Bàighe | NC 24 | Beddgelert Forest | SH 55 | Birnam Wood | NO 03 | Wood | |
| Aber-pergwm | SN 80 | Ardgarten Forest | NN 20 | Forest | | Bedgebury Forest | TQ 73 | Bishop Wood | SE 53 | Bogallan Wood | NH 65 |
| Wood | | Ardgoil Forest | NS 29 | Badby Wood | SP 58 | Beecraigs Wood | NT 07 | Bishop's Wood | SJ 73 | Bogbuie Wood | NH 65 |
| Abinger Forest | TQ 14 | Ardmolich Wood | NM 77 | Badnage Wood | SO 44 | Beinneun Forest | NH 20 | Black Andrew | NT 42 | Bohally Wood | NN 75 |
| Achaglachgach | NR 86 | Ardross Forest | NH 57 | Bagley Wood | SP 50 | Bellever Forest | SX 67 | Wood | | Bolton Muir Wood | NT 56 |
| Forest | | Arecleoch Forest | NX 17 | Bagot Forest | SK 02 | Bellton Wood | NH 65 | Black Dog Wood | ST 84 | Boothroyd Wood | SE 11 |
| Achfary Forest | NC 23 | Argyll Forest | NS 19/ | Balblair Wood | NH 54 | Benmore Forest | NS 18 | Black Dog Woods | ST 84 | Border | NY 68 |
| Achnashellach | NH 04 | | NN 20 | (Balblair) | | Bennachie Forest | NJ 62 | Black Wood | SU 54 | Borgie Forest | NC 65 |
| Forest | | Asham Wood | ST 74 | Balblair Wood (Nr | NH 79 | Bentley Wood | SU 22 | Black Wood | NH 54 | Botany Bay Wood | SJ 79 |
| Achray Forest | NN 50 | Ashclyst Forest | SY 09 | Bonar Bridge) | | Benton Wood | SN 00 | Black Wood | NN 59 | Botley Wood | SU 51 |
| Alfpuddle Heath | SY 89 | Ashdown Forest | TQ 43 | Balblair Wood (Nr | NH 79 | Bere Wood | SY 89 | Blackcraig Forest | NO 15 | Bourton Woods | SP 13 |
| Alice Holt Forest | SU 84 | Asknish Forest | NR 99 | Golspie) | | Bickleigh Wood | SS 91 | Blackcraig Wood | NX 46 | Bowmont Forest | NT 72 |
| Allean Forest | NN 86 | Assich Forest | NH 84 | Baldruim Wood | NH 78 | Bickley Forest | SE 99 | Blackhall Forest | NO 69 | Box Hill | TQ 15 |
| Alltcailleach | NO 39 | Auchenrodden | NY 18 | Balker Wood | NX 16 | Bicton Wood | SX 36 | Blackmuir Wood | NH 45 | Bracken Wood | SK 26 |
| Forest | | Forest | | Ballechin Wood | NN 95 | Big Wood | SJ 80 | Blairadam Forest | NT 19 | Bradley Wood | SU 45 |
| Altyre Woods | NJ 05 | Auchmore Wood | NH 45 | Ballochbuie Forest | NO 29 | Big Wood | NT 42 | Blakeridge Wood | SO 39 | Braemore Wood | NC 50 |
| Alves Wood | NJ 16 | Aultmorehill Wood | NJ 45 | Balnacoul Wood | NJ 35 | Bilberry Wood | SJ 36 | Blanchdown Wood | SX 47 | Brafferton Spring | SE 47 |
| Amat Forest | NH 48 | Austy Wood | SP 16 | Baluain Wood | NN 86 | Bin Forest The | NJ 44 | Bledlow Great | SP 70 | Wood | |
| Ampfield Wood | SU 42 | Aversley Wood | TL 18 | Balvraid Wood | NH 79 | Binning Wood | NT 68 | Wood | | Brahan Wood | NH 55 |
| Angley Forest | TQ 73 | | | Barcaldine Forest | NM 94 | Binsted Wood | SU 90 | Blengdale Forest | NY 00 | Brampton Wood | SP 78 |
| | | | | Baron Wood | NY 54 | Bintree Wood | TG 02 | Boblainy Forest | NH 43 | Brampton Wood | SP 17 |

## New Forest

A first view of the New Forest can be a disappointment. A large heathland, dotted with Scots pine – can this be a forest? Yes, and there can be no disputing that this is one of the last great unchanged areas of Britain, steadfastly resisting attempts to encroach. There have been losses, but much of the forest would be recognisable to a traveller from an earlier time.

'Forest' is used here in the old sense of a place set aside for deer to roam and be hunted. The New (it acquired the name in 1079) Forest was created by Neolithic man destroying trees to produce crops. When the soil was exhausted, it was abandoned and later settlers maintained the heathland habitat by grazing their stock on it. By the time the Crown attempted to assert control over the land, it had acquired common rights of such antiquity that even kings were forced to compromise. These ancient rights remain: the Court of Verderers still protects the interests of commoners, and their animals, including the New Forest ponies, still graze the commons and heaths.

Within the 145 square miles of the National Forest Park are a number of

*RHINEFIELD, NEW FOREST Many ornamental species were planted in parts of the New Forest in the 19th century.*

*QUEEN ELIZABETH FOREST PARK AND BEN LOMOND Peaceful wooded lochs add to the beauty of this large forest.*

towns, villages, commons, heaths, bogs and grassland, as well as managed and semi-natural woodland. The variety is such that it is almost impossible to select any area and say that it truly represents the forest. The Forestry Commission has laid out trails; there are ornamental drives and nature walks, and there are roads through the forest from which the motorist can obtain at least an impression of this historic place.

## Queen Elizabeth Forest

Like most of the major forests developed on upland country (see Border page 38 and Glen More page 38), Queen Elizabeth is conscious of its recreational possibilities. Situated as it is, within easy reach of both Glasgow and Edinburgh, it attracts thousands of visitors each week, anxious to escape for a few hours to a different environment. The park, while maintaining its prime objective – the commercial production of timber – has made great strides in the provision of recreational facilities.

The Queen Elizabeth Forest Park covers 65 square miles of some of the best and most varied scenery in central Scotland. Included in it is one complete National

Scenic Area (the Trossachs) and part of another (Loch Lomond). It covers both highland and lowland landscapes; the mountains of Ben Venue and Ben Lomond; no less than six lochs – Achray, Ard, Chon, Drunkie, Lomond and Vennacher; and more than 170 miles of footpaths. To complete a remarkable statistical analysis, it consists of three forests – Achray, Loch Ard and Rowardennan.

There is a fine information centre, the David Marshall Lodge, just north of Aberfoyle. There is an AA viewpoint, with the usual engraved plaque to identify the marvellous views from the lodge. Several paths, including a waterfall trail, begin here, and the seven-mile Achray Forest drive starts a couple of miles north of the lodge, off the A821, itself an exciting, twisting road over the Duke's Pass.

There is a six-mile walk – full of delights – to Loch Chon from Aberfoyle, passing Loch Ard, through part of Loch Ard Forest and by streams and lochans. The loch can also be reached by car along the B829, another exciting road, which continues on to Inverslaid, overlooking Loch Lomond. By following the West Highland Way from here, it is possible to walk to Rowardennan (described under Loch Lomond, page 43).

The wildlife of this region is varied because of the mix of highland and lowland scenery. In addition to the vast conifer and smaller broad-leaved plantations, there is open moorland around Ben Venue. Here, crossleaved heath is common, bog myrtle signals the damper ground and birds include red grouse.

The lochs contains a wide range of wildfowl, both resident and visiting. Land birds include birds of prey from golden eagles to sparrowhawks, and in addition to the moorland birds most of the smaller birds typical of conifer forests have been recorded here. Roe and red deer and most of the hunting mammals including otter and wildcat have been observed within the forest park.

The chances of seeing these mammals are slight, but the park is so large and so diverse, that, even if disappointed in a specific quest, anyone who visits it is likely to find something to please.

## Savernake Forest

'Forest' originally meant a place for deer, and this applied to Savernake. The scale is small, the woods dotted among land which is open and well farmed. At the time of Magna Carta, its size was considerably reduced, and it was never a heavily wooded area: its prime role was to support the herds of deer which roamed it. Over the centuries it was rented for various uses then partially enclosed in the 17th century. In the early 18th century, ambitious plans for landscaping were put in hand and 'Capability' Brown has been mentioned in connection with the Grand Avenue and other walks. It is possible to drive along the Grand Avenue, now a rather informal but most attractive grouping of tall trees interspersed with young growth.

Savernake is a lovely, gentle, enticing place. On sunny days especially, there is an overwhelming temptation to linger. Perhaps some folk memory tells us that this is what Savernake should be like – full of tall, old trees and alive with the sounds of birds and insects.

Sadly, there is a problem hidden in that image; many of the finest beech and oak trees are nearing the end of their lives. It will take an imaginative programme of replanting to ensure that future generations will be able to enjoy a similar scene. Not necessarily the same, for there has always been change, and several of the trees we see were planted after a Navy Surveyor reported in 1675 that only three or four trees in the forest were fit for use.

Because of its age Savernake has a varied and settled wildlife. Much may be glimpsed, or sensed, by anyone walking the two-mile Forest Trail from the Posterne Hill picnic site. Spring primroses give way to rosebay willow herb and summer orchids. The oak is particularly renowned for its capacity to act as host to a remarkable number of insect species and many can be seen on and around the trees.

*OLD BEECH TREES IN SAVERNAKE FOREST This view shows the typical bare nature of the woodland floor under the dense shade of the beeches. Many of the large oaks and beeches in the forest are now nearing the end of their lives.*

| | |
|---|---|
| Glenrigh Forest | NN 06 |
| Glentress Forest | NT 24 |
| Glentrool Forest | NX 38 |
| Gorsley Wood | TR 15 |
| Gorthy Wood | NN 92 |
| Grange Wood | NX 74 |
| Great Bookham Common | TQ 15 |
| Great Bradley Wood | ST 74 |
| Great Haldon | SX 88 |
| Great Pen Wood | SU 46 |
| Great Wood (Nr *Henley*) | SU 78 |
| Great Wood | SU 08 |
| Great Wood | TL 20 |
| Great Wood | TG 12 |
| Great Wood | TG 14 |
| Great Wood | NY 22 |
| Green Wood | NX 56 |
| Greenfield Wood | SU 79 |
| Greno Wood | SK 39 |
| Greystoke Forest | NY 33 |
| Grizedale Forest | SD 39 |
| Gruids Wood | NC 50 |
| Guisborough Woods | NZ 61 |
| Guiting Wood | SP 02 |
| Gwydyr Forest | SH 75 |
| Gypt Forest | SJ 97 |

## H

| | |
|---|---|
| Hafren Forest | SN 88 |
| Hagley Wood | SO 98 |
| Hailey Wood | ST 90 |
| Halfway Forest | SN 83 |
| Haltham Wood | SK 26 |
| Halvana Plantation | SX 27 |
| Hamsterley Forest | NZ 02 |
| Happendon Wood | NS 83 |
| Harewood Forest | SU 34 |
| Harwood Dale Forest | SE 99 |
| Harwood Forest | NY 99 |
| Hatfield Forest | TL 52 |
| Haugh Wood | SO 53 |
| Haugham Wood | SK 38 |
| Hawley Common | SU 85 |
| Hay Wood | SO 62 |
| Hay Wood | SP 27 |
| Haye Park Wood | SO 47 |
| Hazel Head Wood | SE 59 |
| Hazel Wood | SE 43 |
| Hazelborough Wood | SP 64 |
| Headley Heath | TQ 15 |
| Hempstead Wood | TL 64 |
| Hemsted Forest | TQ 83 |
| Hendale Wood | TA 10 |
| Hens Wood | SU 26 |
| Hensol Forest | ST 07 |
| Hepburn Wood | NU 02 |
| Hespin Wood | NY 36 |
| High Wood | SE 90 |
| High Wood | NZ 96 |
| High Wood | NT 67 |
| Highall Wood | SK 26 |
| Highnam Woods | SO 71 |
| Hindhead Common | SU 83 |
| Hitch Wood | TL 12 |
| Hockering Wood | TG 01 |
| Hockley Woods | TQ 89 |
| Hodgemoor Woods | SU 99 |
| Holme Wood | NY 12 |
| Holmwood Common | TQ 14 |
| Holsworthy | SS 30 |
| Hopesike Woods | NY 36 |
| Hopetown Wood | NT 07 |
| Hopwas Hays Wood | SK 10 |
| Horner Wood | SS 84 |
| Hornshurst Wood | TQ 53 |
| Horsford Woods | TG 11 |
| Houghton Forest | SU 91 |
| Hovingham High Wood | SE 67 |
| Howell Wood | SE 40 |
| Howgill Wood | NY 13 |
| Hugset Wood | SE 30 |
| Hundred Acre Wood | TG 14 |
| Hurn Forest | SZ 19 |
| Hurt Wood | TQ 04 |
| Hustyn Wood | SX 06 |
| Hutton Lowcross Woods | NZ 51 |
| Hutton Mulgrave Wood | NZ 80 |

## I

| | |
|---|---|
| Inchnacardoch Forest | NH 30 |
| Inchvuilt Wood | NH 23 |
| Inshriach Forest | NN 80 |
| Inverinan Forest | NM 91 |
| Inverliever Forest | NM 91 |
| Inverwick Forest | NH 31 |
| Irfon Forest | SN 85 |

## J

| | |
|---|---|
| Joyden's Wood | TQ 47 |

## K

| | |
|---|---|
| Kemback Wood | NO 41 |
| Ken Hill Wood | TF 63 |
| Kerrow Wood | NH 33 |
| Kerry Wood | NG 87 |
| Kershope Forest | NY 58 |
| Kidland Forest | NT 91 |
| Kielder Forest | NY 68 |
| Killiegowan Wood | NX 55 |
| Kilmory Forest | NR 88 |
| Kilsture Forest (Nr *Sorbie*) | NX 44 |
| Kilsture Forest (Nr *Wigtown*) | NX 46 |
| Kindrogan Wood | NO 06 |
| King's Forest The | TL 87 |
| King's Wood | TR 05 |
| King's Wood | SO 41 |
| King's Wood | SK 58 |
| Kings Wood | SJ 83 |
| Kingstone Wood | SK 02 |
| Kinlea Wood | NH 54 |
| Kinneil Wood | NS 98 |
| Kinrive Wood | NH 67 |
| Kinveachy Forest | NH 81 |
| Kirkhill Forest | NJ 81 |
| Kirroughtree Forest | NX 47 |
| Klauchope Forest | NT 60 |
| Knapdale Forest | NR 79 |
| Knockman Wood | NX 46 |
| Kyle Forest | NS 41 |

## L

| | |
|---|---|
| Lael Forest | NH 18 |
| Laggan Wood | NN 72 |
| Laiken Forest | NH 95 |
| Langdale Forest | SE 99 |
| Langley Wood | SU 22 |
| Lasgarn Wood | SO 20 |
| Laughton Forest | SK 89 |
| Laurieston Forest | NX 66 |
| Leanachan Forest | NN 17 |
| Leapmoor Forest | NS 27 |
| Legsby Wood | TF 18 |
| Leigh Woods | ST 57 |
| Leithenwater Forest | NT 34 |
| Leithope Forest | NT 70 |
| Lidcombe Wood | SP 03 |
| Linley Big Wood | SO 38 |
| Little Park Wood | NX 46 |
| Llaneglwys Wood | SO 03 |
| Llantrisant Forest | ST 08 |
| Loch Ard Forest | NN 40 |
| Loch Eck Forest | NS 19 |
| Loch Ericht Forest | NN 58 |
| Lochletter Wood | NH 42 |
| Logierait Wood | NN 95 |
| Long Mendip Wood | ST 45 |
| Long Wood | SN 65 |
| Longart Forest | NH 46 |
| Longbeech Wood | TQ 95 |
| Lordship Wood | TQ 72 |
| Lossie Wood | NJ 26 |
| Ludshott Common | SU 83 |
| Lunan Wood | NJ 36 |

## M

| | |
|---|---|
| Mabie Forest (NE *Stranraer*) | NY 07 |
| Mabie Forest (SE *Stranraer*) | NY 07 |
| Mabie Forest (SW *Stranraer*) | NX 97 |
| Macclesfield Forest | SJ 97 |
| Maer Hills | SJ 73 |
| Maikle Wood | NH 79 |
| Mainshill Wood | NS 83 |
| Manby Wood | SE 90 |
| Markshall Wood | TL 82 |
| Maulden Wood | TL 03 |
| Mausoleum Woods | TA 11 |
| Melkinthorpe Wood | NY 52 |
| Mellfield Wood | TL 96 |
| Melton Wood | SE 50 |
| Mereworth Woods | TQ 65 |
| Messengermire Wood | NY 23 |
| Micheldever Wood | SU 53 |
| Midmar Forest | NJ 60 |
| Mildenhall Woods | TL 77 |
| Milkwellburn Wood | NZ 15 |
| Miltonrigg Wood | NY 56 |
| Minard Forest | NR 99 |
| Mintlyn Wood | TF 61 |
| Minwear Wood | SN 01 |
| Miterdale Forest | NY 10 |
| Mochrum Wood | NS 21 |
| Monaughty Forest | NJ 15 |
| Monks Wood | TL 18 |
| Montcoffer Wood | NJ 66 |
| Montreathmont Forest | NO 55 |
| Morangie Forest | NH 78 |
| Morkery Wood | SK 91 |
| Morralee Wood | NY 86 |
| Morton Wood | NX 89 |
| Moy Wood | NH 45 |
| Muirton Wood | NH 45 |
| Muirward Wood | NO 12 |
| Mulgrave Woods | NZ 81 |
| Mynydd Du Forest | SO 22 |

## N

| | |
|---|---|
| Naver Forest | NC 64 |
| Nevis Forest | NN 17 |
| New House Wood | SO 23 |
| Newball Wood | TF 07 |
| Newborough Forest | SH 46 |
| Newcastleton Forest | NY 58 |
| Newent Woods | SO 72 |
| New Forest | SU 20 |
| Newlands of Fleenas Wood | NH 94 |
| Newmore Wood | NH 67 |
| Newpark Wood | NZ 09 |
| Newton Wood | TL 22 |
| Newtyle Forest | NJ 05 |
| New Forest | SU 20/30 |
| Nobottle Wood | SP 66 |
| Nocton Wood | TF 06 |
| Norridge Wood | ST 84 |
| North Wood | NZ 12 |
| Northpark Wood | TQ 01 |

## O

| | |
|---|---|
| Oaken Wood | TQ 75 |
| Oakhill Wood | SU 35 |
| Oakley Wood | ST 90 |
| Ockeridge Wood | SO 76 |
| Odell Great Wood | SP 95 |
| Ogmore Forest | ST 98 |
| Oldpark Wood | NZ 18 |
| Old Wood | SK 97 |
| Owston Wood | SK 70 |
| Oxhey Wood | TQ 19 |
| Oxpasture Wood | TQ 63 |

## P

| | |
|---|---|
| Pamber Forest | SU 66 |
| Pantmaenog Forest | SN 03 |
| Park Wood (Nr *Bassenthwaite*) | NY23 |
| Park Wood (Nr *Blindcrake*) | NY 13 |
| Park Wood | SO 28 |
| Park Wood | TQ 08 |
| Park Wood | SJ 50 |
| Park Wood | NY 24 |
| Park Woods | SS 58 |
| Parkhurst Forest | SZ 49 |
| Parnholt Wood | SU 32 |
| Pembrey Forest | SN 30 |
| Pencelly Forest | SN 13 |
| Penllergaer Forest | SN 60 |
| Penllyn Forest | SH 93 |
| Penn Wood | SU 99 |
| Penninghame Forest | NX 36 |
| Penwardine Wood | SO 37 |
| Petts Wood | TQ 46 |
| Pettypool Wood | SJ 67 |
| Pitfichie Forest | NJ 61 |
| Pitmedden Forest | NO 21 |
| Pitmiddle Wood | NO 23 |
| Portclair Forest | NH 31 |
| Potterhanworth Wood | TF 06 |
| Potton Wood | TL 25 |
| Prae Wood | TL 10 |
| Pressmennan Wood | NT 67 |
| Puddletown Forest | SY 79 |

## Q

| | |
|---|---|
| Quantock Forest | ST 13 |
| Quarry Wood | NJ 16 |
| Queen Elizabeth Forest | SU 71 |
| Queen Elizabeth Forest | NS 49/ NN 30 |
| Queen's Wood | SO 62 |

## R

| | |
|---|---|
| Raasay Forest | NG 53 |
| Radnor Forest | SO 16 |
| Raemore Wood | NC 50 |
| Rannoch Forest | NN 45/55 |
| Ratagan Forest | NG 92 |
| Raydon Great Wood | TM 04 |
| Redesdale Forest | NT 70 |
| Rendlesham Forest | TM 34 |
| Rendlesham Forest | TM 35 |
| Rewell Wood | SU 90 |
| Rhindbuckie Wood | NO 79 |
| Ribbesford Woods | SO 77 |
| Riccal Dale Wood | SE 68 |
| Ringwood Forest | SU 10 |
| Robin Wood | SK 32 |
| Ros Hill Wood | NU 02 |
| Rosarie Forest | NJ 34 |
| Roseisle Forest | NJ 16 |
| Rossal Wood | NC 40 |
| Roughilly Wood | NJ 56 |
| Rowardennan Forest | NS 39 |
| Rowberrow Warren | ST 45 |
| Wood | TL 14 |
| Roxton Wood | TA 11 |
| Rumster Forest | ND 23 |
| Ruskich Wood | NH 42 |
| Ruttle Wood | NH 44 |

## S

| | |
|---|---|
| Saddell Wood | NR 73 |
| St Clement Wood | SW 84 |
| St Gwynno Forest | ST 09 |
| St Helen's Wood | SK 25 |
| St Leonard's Forest | TQ 23 |
| Salcey Forest | SP 85 |
| Salen Forest | NM 54 |
| Saltoun Forest | NT 46 |
| Sandall Beat Wood | SE 60 |
| Sandford Woods | SU 55 |
| Sandy Warren | TL 14 |
| Savernake Forest | SU 26 |
| Sawmill Wood | NZ 14 |
| Scabba Wood | SE 50 |
| Scalderskew Wood | NY 00 |
| Scootmore Forest | NJ 13 |
| Scotsburn Wood | NH 77 |
| Selborne Common | SU 73 |
| Selm Muir Wood | NT 06 |
| Senwick Wood | NX 64 |
| Shambellie Wood | NX 96 |
| Shardlowe's Wood | TL 73 |
| Sheerhatch Wood | TL 14 |
| Sherwood Forest | SK 55 –SK 67 |
| Shewglie wood | NH 42 |
| Shin Forest | NH 59 |
| Shirralds Wood | NJ 46 |
| Shobdon Hill Wood | SO 36 |
| Shouldham Warren | TF 61 |
| Shrawley Wood | SO 86 |
| Silk Wood | ST 88 |
| Sillyearn Wood | NJ 55 |
| Silverhill Wood | NY 37 |
| Skelbo Wood | NH 79 |
| Slackbraes Wood | NY 37 |
| Slaley Forest | NZ 95 |
| Slattadale Forest | NG 87 |
| Sleepieshill Wood | NJ 26 |
| Slorach's Wood | NJ 35 |
| Smallacoombe Downs | SX 27 |
| Snipes Dene Wood | NZ 15 |
| Sotby Wood | TF 17 |
| South Laggan Forest | NN 29 |
| Southey Wood | TF 10 |
| Southleigh Forest | SU 70 |
| Southrey Wood | TF 16 |
| Sowerby Wood | NY 35 |
| Spadeadam Forest | NY 67 |
| Speymouth Forest | NJ 35 |
| Stainfield Wood | TF 17 |
| Stang The | NZ 00 |
| Stanley Wood | NZ 14 |
| Stanstead Forest | SU 71 |
| Stanstead Great Wood | TL 84 |
| Stapleford Wood | SK 85 |
| Stockhill Plantation | ST 55 |
| Stoke Woods | SS 99 |
| Stokepark Wood | SP 84 |
| Straan Wood | NJ 13 |
| Strathconon Wood | NH 35 |
| Strathellen Wood | NG 83 |
| Strathgarve Forest | NH 46 |
| Strathlachan Forest | NS 09 |
| Strathord Forest | NO 03 |
| Strathy Forest | NC 86 |
| Strathyre Forest | NN 51 |
| Strelitz Wood | NO 13 |
| Struie Wood | NH 68 |
| Stype Wood | SU 36 |
| Swaffham Heath | TF 70 |
| Swannacott Wood | SX 29 |
| Swarland Wood | NU 10 |
| Symonshyde Great Wood | TL 11 |
| Sywell Wood | SP 86 |

## T

| | |
|---|---|
| Tackley Wood | SP 42 |
| Taf Fechan Forest | SO 01 |
| Talybont Forest | SO 01 |
| Tarlogie Wood | NH 78 |
| Teign Valley Woods | SX 78 |
| Teindland Forest | NJ 25 |
| Temple Wood | TF 02 |
| Tentsmuir Forest | NO 42 |
| Thetford Warren | TL 88 |
| Thornden Wood | TR 16 |
| Threestoneburn Wood | NT 91 |
| Thrunton Wood | NU 00 |
| Tiddesley Wood | SO 94 |
| Tighnabruaich Forest | NR 96 |
| Tinnisburn Forest | NY 48 |
| Tintern Forest | SO 50 |
| Todlaw Wood | NJ 65 |
| Tomfarclas Wood | NJ 23 |
| Torlum Wood | NN 81 |
| Tornagrain Wood | NH 75 |
| Tornashean Forest | NJ 31 |
| Torrachilty Wood | NH 45 |
| Torrie Forest | NN 60 |
| Tothill Wood | SK 48 |
| Townhead Wood | NS 82 |
| Trickley Wood | NU 02 |
| Tubney Wood | SP 40 |
| Tummel Forest | NN 76 |
| Tunman Wood | SK 86 |
| Tunstall Forest | TM 35 |
| Twemlows Big Wood | SJ 53 |
| Twigmoor Wood | SE 90 |
| Twyford Wood | SK 92 |
| Twyi Forest | SN 85 |

## U

| | |
|---|---|
| Uffmoor Wood | SO 98 |
| Upcott Wood | SS 40 |
| Upper and Lower Vert Wood | TQ 51 |
| Upper Tomraich Wood | NH 03 |

## V

| | |
|---|---|
| Valley Wood | SS 69 |
| Vernditch Chase | SU 02 |

## W

| | |
|---|---|
| Wadworth Wood | SK 59 |
| Walton Wood | NY 56 |
| Warden Warren | TL 14 |
| Wardley Wood | SP 89 |
| Wareham Forest | SY 89 |
| Wark Forest | NY 77 |
| Warleigh Wood | ST 76 |
| Warren Heath | SU 75 |
| Waterhouses Wood | NZ 14 |
| Waterperry Wood | SP 60 |
| Waveney Forest | TG 40 |
| Weardale Forest | NY 84 |
| Webb's Wood | SU 08 |
| Weldrake Wood | SE 64 |
| Wellington Wood | SO 44 |
| Wendover Woods | SP 80 |
| Wentwood | SO 49 |
| Wepham Wood | TQ 00 |
| West & East Harling Heath | TL 98 |
| West Bilney Warren | TF 61 |
| West Blean Wood | TR 16 |
| West Haigh Wood | SE 40 |
| West Walk | SU 51 |
| West Wood | SU 16 |
| West Wood | SU 42 |
| West Wood | SP 96 |
| West Wood | SE 90 |
| Westdean Woods | SU 81 |
| Wester Culbo Wood | NH 65 |
| Westonhill Wood | SO 34 |
| Westridge Wood | ST 79 |
| Wharncliffe Wood | SK 39 |
| Wharton Wood | SK 89 |
| Whippendell Wood | TQ 09 |
| Whippendell Wood | TQ 09 |
| Whitcliffe Wood | SO 47 |
| White Hills Wood | TF 62 |
| Whiteash Hill Wood | NJ 35 |
| Whitehaugh Forest | NJ 52 |
| Whitewell Wood | SK 57 |
| Whittlewood Forest | SP 74 |
| Willingham Forest | TF 19 |
| Willingham Woods | TF 18 |
| Wilmington Wood | TQ 50 |
| Windsor Forest | SU 97 |
| Winterfold Forest | TQ 04 |
| Wisley Common | TQ 05 |
| Wisley Down | SX 18 |
| Witherdon Wood | SX 49 |
| Withington Woods | SP 01 |
| Wolford Wood | SP 23 |
| Wombwell Wood | SE 30 |
| Wood of Arndilly | NJ 24 |
| Wood of Conerock | NJ 24 |
| Wood of Delgaty | NJ 75 |
| Wood of Easter Clune | NO 69 |
| Wood of Mulderie | NJ 35 |
| Wood of Ordiequish | NJ 35 |
| Woods of Garmaddie | NO 29 |
| Woods of Knockfrink | NJ 13 |
| Woolmer Forest | SU 83 |
| Worth Forest | TQ 33 |
| Wychwood Forest | SP 31 |
| Wyddle Forest | SE 98 |
| Wykeham Forest | SE 98 |
| Wyre Forest | SO 77 |
| Wythop Woods | NY 22 |

## Y

| | |
|---|---|
| Yair Hill Forest | NT 43 |
| Yarner Wood | SX 77 |
| Yateley Heath Wood | SU 85 |

# Lakes and Reservoirs

*Forbidding Wast Water and welcoming Loch Lomond; tranquil Loch of Lowes and Loe Pool, one easily 'explored' from the car, the other definitely not; Elan Valley and Rutland Water, examples of the very different approach of the 19th and 20th centuries to reservoir building; Loch Leven, historically and ecologically important – a fascinating combination.*

## Elan Valley

However much the arguments may rage as to the siting and building of reservoirs – and nowhere have they raged more fiercely than in Wales – the fact remains that plants and animals have not hesitated to take advantage of the opportunities presented by them. In many areas, humans too have profited by the provision of recreational facilities even if, as in the Elan Valley, limited to walking and driving.

The valley was, until the end of the last century, home to the River Elan and little else, but the growing demand for water from the developing industrial towns, in this instance Birmingham, saw the building of a village and then four reservoirs. Caban-coch, completed in 1904, was the first, followed by Garreg-ddu, Pen-y-garreg and Craig Goch. All the lakes are long, narrow and, in the case of the first three, attractively wooded.

The magnificent, multi-arched dam between Pen-y-garreg and Craig Goch marks the change to open moorland in dramatic fashion. Trees crowd almost to the outfall of Craig Goch, and up the narrow slopes flanking it, but give way instantly to a typical moorland scene of yellows, browns, greens and purples across which clouds create ever-changing patterns of light. The amount of water pouring over the dam after rain can be very spectacular, producing a roar like a miniature Niagara.

One of the pleasures of the Elan Valley

*PEN-Y-GARREG DAM AND CRAIG GOCH RESERVOIR, in the Elan Valley. Note the contrast between the wooded lower reservoir and the bare moorland beyond.*

lakes is the ease with which they can be enjoyed by car. After leaving Rhayader on the B4518, the road passes Elan village before turning along the top of Caban Coch and the east bank of Garreg Ddu. In the pleasantly wooded section between it and Pen-y-garreg, the road switches to the west bank for the two remaining lakes. The journey may be through a man-made and controlled landscape but it is a continual pleasure. At the head of Craig Goch there is a choice of routes. The Elan may be followed along an old drovers' road towards Cwmystwyth (see also Moors, page 35) and Devil's Bridge, or it is possible to return to Rhayader.

Although not strictly part of the Elan Valley, the more recent Claerwen Reservoir can be visited by taking a left fork at Caban Coch. The road ends at the dam, but it is possible to walk along the east bank using a reasonable track. From the head of Claerwen there are some wonderful walks. One, well defined but not easy, continues to Ffairrhos; another, definitely not for beginners, turns back to the Elan Valley. Climbing in places to 1700 ft, both tracks pass close to small lakes, and both give more than a hint of the true wildness of this area.

It is, let it be stressed, quite possible to walk in the Elan valley with safety. There are places where cars may be left, and the road, or a track, used to absorb the beauty of the lakes in more leisurely fashion.

Birds have always shown a readiness to adopt man's structures, and the Elan Lakes are no exception. Goosander throughout the year, and goldeneye in the winter are examples of species which can be seen here because of the building of the reservoirs.

## Loch Leven

Loch Leven is known for its trout fishing – international competitions are frequently held here – and its birds: thousands of pink-footed and greylag geese each winter. The presence of both is due, in part, to the influence of mankind, also responsible for the loss of other species.

The loch is unusual in that it was

| A | | | | | | | |
|---|---|---|---|---|---|---|---|
| Abberton Res | TL 9718 | Ardsley Res | SE 2924 | Bar Mere | SJ 5347 | Birkenburn Res | NS 6780 | Blue Pool | SY 9383 | Burnhope Res | NY 8438 |
| Abbeystead Res | SD 5553 | Argal Res | SW 7632 | Barbrook Res | SK 2777 | Bishop Loch | NS 6866 | Boddington Res | SP 4953 | Burnmoor Tarn | NY 1804 |
| Achridigill Loch | NC 8661 | Arlington Res | TQ 5307 | Barcraigs Res | NS 3857 | Black Esk Res | NY 2096 | Bogton Loch | NS 4605 | Burntfen Broad | TG 3318 |
| Acreknowe Res | NT 4910 | Arnfield Res | SK 0197 | Bardowie Loch | NS 5773 | Black Lake | SU 8644 | Bolam Lake | NZ 0881 | Burrator Res | SX 5568 |
| Afton Res | NS 6304 | Arnot Res | NO 2002 | Barean Loch | NX 8655 | Black Loch | NX 1161 | Bolder Mere | TQ 0758 | Burton Mill Pond | SU 9717 |
| Agden Res | SK 2592 | Arrow Valley Lake | SP 0667 | Bargatton Loch | NX 6961 | Black Loch | NX 2765 | Bomere Pool | SJ 4908 | Busbie Muir Res | NS 2446 |
| Akermoor Loch | NT 4020 | Asgog Loch | NR 9470 | Barhapple Loch | NX 2559 | Black Loch | NX 3054 | Bonaly Res | NT 2066 | Butterley Res | SK 4051 |
| Aldenham Res | TQ 1695 | Ashgrove Loch | NS 2744 | Barnacre Res | SD 5247 | Black Loch | NS 4951 | Booth Wood Res | SE 0216 | Butterley Res | SE 0410 |
| Aled Isef Res | SH 9159 | Ashworth Moor Res | SD 8215 | Barns Fold Res | SD 5741 | Black Loch | NS 8670 | Boretree Tarn | SD 3587 | Buttermere | NY 1815 |
| Alemoor Loch | NT 3914 | Aucha Lochy | NR 7222 | Barnshean Loch | NS 3711 | Black Lochs | NM 9231 | Bosherston, Fish Ponds | SR 9794 | |
| Alkmund Park Pool | SJ 4716 | Auchendores Res | NS 3572 | Barr Loch | NS 3557 | Black Moss Res | SE 0308 | | |
| Alston Res | SD 6036 | Auchintaple Loch | NO 1964 | Barrow Res | ST 5367 | Blackbrook Res | SK 4517 | Bosley Res | SJ 9266 | C |
| Alton Water | TM 1436 | Auckenreoch Loch | NX 8171 | Barscobe Loch | NX 6681 | Blackmill Loch | NR 9495 | Bottoms Res | SK 0296 | Càm Loch | NM 9009 |
| Alwen Res | SH 9454 | Audenshaw Res | SJ 9196 | Bartley Res | SP 0081 | Blackmoorfoot Res | SE 0912 | Bough Beech Res | TQ 4948 | Caban-coch Res | SN 9163 |
| Am Fiar-loch | NH 2446 | Avon Dam Res | SX 6765 | Barton Broad | TG 3621 | Blackpark Lake | TQ 0083 | Bracebridge Pool | SP 0998 | Calder Dam | NS 2965 |
| Ampton Water | TL 8770 | | | Bassenthwaite | NY 2129 | Blackroot Pool | SP 1097 | Braeroddach Loch | NJK 4800 | Calf Hey Res | SD 7522 |
| An Caol-loch | NC 5544 | | | Bayfield Loch | NH 8271 | Blackton Res | NY 9418 | Branxholme Easter Loch | NT 4311 | Cally Lake | NX 6055 |
| An Dubh-loch | NG 7350 | B | | Beacons Res | SN 9818 | Blackwater Res | NN 2560 | | | Cam Loch | NR 8287 |
| An Gead Loch | NH 1038 | Backwater Res | NO 2560 | Bear Wood Lake | SU 7768 | Blagdan Lake | SX 3796 | Braydon Pond | ST 9987 | Cameron Res | NO 4711 |
| An Glas-loch | NC 4931 | Baddiley Mere Res | SJ 5950 | Beaver Dyke Res | SE 2254 | Blagdon Lake | ST 5159 | Brent Res | TQ 2187 | Camphill Res | NS 2655 |
| An Gorm-loch | NH 2244 | Baddinsgill Res | NT 1255 | Belmont Res | SD 6716 | Blake Mere | SJ 4133 | Broadlands Lake | SU 3516 | Camps Res | NT 0022 |
| Angle Tarn | NY 2407 | Baitings Res | SE 0018 | Belston Loch | NS 4716 | Blakestone Edge Res | SD 9718 | Broadstone Res | SE 1906 | Can Loch | NC 2113 |
| Angle Tarn | NY 4114 | Bakethin Res | NY 6391 | Belvide Res | SJ 8610 | | | Broomhead Res | SK 2695 | Cannop Ponds | SO 6010 |
| Anglezarke Res | SD 6116 | Bala Lake | SH 9033 | Bennan Loch | NS 5250 | Blarloch Mór | NC 2849 | Broomlee Lough | NY 7969 | Cant Clough Res | SD 8930 |
| Angram Res | SE 0476 | Balderhead Res | NY 9118 | Berrington Pool | SO 5063 | Blatherwycke Lake | SP 9796 | Brother Loch | NS 5052 | Cantref Res | SN 9915 |
| Antermony Loch | NS 6676 | Balgavies Loch | NO 5350 | Bossborough Res | TQ 1268 | Blea Tarn Res | SD 4958 | Brothers Water | NY 4012 | Caol Loch | ND 0248 |
| Appleton Res | SJ 6084 | Balgray Res | NS 5157 | Betton Pool | SJ 5107 | Blea Tarn | NY 2904 | Brownhill Res | SE 1106 | Caol-loch Mór | NC 7844 |
| Aqualate Mere | SJ 7720 | Ballo Res | NO 2204 | Bewl Bridge Res | TQ 6732 | Blea Tarn | NY 2914 | Budworth Mere | SJ 6576 | Caol-loch | NC 9261 |
| Ardingly Res | TQ 3329 | Ballochling Loch | NX 4594 | Bhlaraidh Res | NH 3518 | Blea Water | NY 4410 | Bugeilyn | SN 8292 | Caol-loch | NC 8554 |
| Ardleigh Res | TM 0328 | Banbury Res | TQ 3691 | Big Mere | SJ 5545 | Blelham Tarn | NY 3600 | Burncrooks Res | NS 4879 | Caol-loch | NC 8554 |
| | | | | Birkdale Tarn | NY 8501 | Blithfield Res | SK 0523 | Burnfoot Res | NS 4544 | Caplaw Dam | NS 4358 |

*THE VIEW ALONG LOCH LEVEN FROM CRAIG RANNOCH Many people visit Loch Leven for its bird life, but the scenery alone is worth seeing.*

reduced in size in the 1830s, following work to control the outflow of water for industrial use. The effect of this was to allow a substantial acreage to be reclaimed for farming. The crops growing on this rich soil provided geese with an excellent food source on which they could feed before returning to their traditional roosting places, the estuaries of the east coast. Three hundred acres at Vane Farm are now an RSPB reserve and are deliberately managed to supply autumn and winter food in the form of potato and barley gleanings.

But rich soil ultimately produces rich water and this is happening in Loch Leven. Nutrients are encouraging algal growth which is altering the balance of species. Most of the ducks which are another feature of the loch have not been affected by the loss of pondweed and other submerged plants, although pochard numbers have certainly decreased and the numbers of swans and coots are markedly down.

There remains a very great deal for the visitor to see and enjoy. The RSPB have converted an old farm building into an information centre, and there are observation points and a nature trail. In addition to the duck – at least 500 pairs of tufted duck – geese and whooper swan populations, other waterside and woodland species are always present, depending on the season. The woodland, mostly birch scrub, is

being improved and a good show of spring flowers brightens it.

Loch Leven has historical connections, and on one of its six islands are the ruins of the 15th-century castle from which Mary Queen of Scots made a famous escape in 1568. An earlier ruin, the 9th-century priory, stands on the biggest of the islands, St Serf's. On the shore of the loch is Kinross House, with its lovely grounds occasionally open to the public.

## Loch Lomond

A frequent comment about Loch Lomond is that it is two lakes in one. Broad and open in the south, it narrows dramatically at its northern end, becoming more like a highland fjord loch. And that is precisely what it is, for a fault runs across the loch and through the island of Inchcailloch where the changes in rock formation are clearly visible. Even the water changes: at the northern end of the loch it is acidic and at the south, alkaline. This is not unknown with lakes, though it is more

common with rivers – for example the Severn – which rise among acid rocks in peaty soil and run into agricultural areas where they can leach out nutrients. In fact this is very much what happens in Loch Lomond where the northern streams come off the mountains and the southern comes from farmland.

Until the Ice Age, Loch Lomond was a sea loch, but the land at the southern end rose as the weight of ice was lifted, blocking the entrance to the Firth of Clyde and creating the largest freshwater lake in Britain. The range of conditions and habitats make Loch Lomond one of the most important sites in Britain for wildlife.

Inchcailloch is a National Nature Reserve, easily reached by boat, where examples of this diversity can be studied by following the well-planned nature trail. A total of 300 plants and ferns have been recorded on the island and it is claimed that almost a quarter of the entire range of British flowering plants occur around Loch Lomond. The woodland trees on the island are sessile oak, the oak of the uplands of Britain.

The birds of the island are typical of woodland species, but the full range of species around the loch is a staggering 220. From divers to sparrows almost every family is represented, and the list contains some exciting rarities. Spring visitors invariably include osprey returning from Africa; red- and black-throated divers, merganser and snow bunting appear in summer; winter brings many thousands of geese and whooper swan to the River Endrick; and both migration seasons see numerous waders, while residents include the localised capercaillie.

The fish of the loch are what would be expected, a mixture of game and coarse fish, with one notable exception – the rare powan, a sort of salmon which resembles a herring.

The Forestry Commission has over 20 miles of woodland with many paths in the area, and broadleaved trees are particularly well represented, with other good ex-

| | | | | | | | | | | | |
|---|---|---|---|---|---|---|---|---|---|---|---|
| Carlhurlie Res | NO 3904 | Clar Loch Mór | NB 9914 | Coldwell Res | SD 9036 | Creoch Loch | NS 5915 | Deer Hill Res | SE 0711 | Dubh Loch Beag | NC 3216 |
| Carlingwark Loch | NX 7661 | Clar Loch Mór | NC 1707 | Cole Mere | SJ 4333 | Crom Loch | NH 3982 | Deil's Craig Dam | NS 5578 | Dubh Loch Mór | NM 9438 |
| Carman Res | NS 3778 | Clar Lochan | NH 2594 | College Res | SW 7633 | Crombie Res | NO 5240 | Delph Res | SD 6915 | Dubh Loch Mór | NC 3118 |
| Carno Res | SO 1613 | Clar Lochan | TQ 1363 | Colliford Lake | SX 1772 | Crookfoot Res | NZ 4331 | Den of Ogil Res | NO 4361 | Dubh Lochan | NN 2753 |
| Carr Mill Dam | SJ 5298 | Clar-loch Mór | NC 6458 | Colt Crag Res | NY 9378 | Cropston Res | SK 5410 | Denton Res | SK 8733 | Dubh Lochan | NO 0999 |
| Carriston Res | NO 3203 | Clattercote Res | SP 4548 | Comber Mere | SJ 5844 | Crosby Marina | SJ 3197 | Derclach Loch | NX 4498 | Dubh Loch | NM 9303 |
| Carron Valley Res | NS 6983 | Clatteringshaws | NX 5476 | Combs Res | SK 0379 | Crose Mere | SJ 4330 | Dernaglar Loch | NX 2658 | Dubh Loch | NR 7680 |
| Carsebreck Loch | NN 8609 | Loch | | Commore Dam | NS 4654 | Cross Lochs The | NC 8746 | Derwent Res | SK 1790 | Dubh Loch | NG 8470 |
| Carsfad Loch | NX 6086 | Clatto Res | NO 3607 | Compensation Res | NS 2572 | Crosswood Res | NT 0557 | Derwent Res | NZ 0052 | Dubh Loch | NG 9876 |
| Castle Carrock Res | NY 5454 | Clatto Res | NO 3634 | Coniston Water | SD 3094 | Crowdy Res | SX 1483 | Derwent Water | NY 2620 | Dubh Loch | NO 2382 |
| Castle Loch | NX 2853 | Clatworthy Res | ST 0431 | Coombe Pool | SP 3979 | Cruachan Res | NN 0828 | Devoke Water | SD 1597 | Dubh-loch na | NC 5050 |
| Castle Semple | NS 3659 | Clawbridge Res | SD 8228 | Cop Mere | SJ 8029 | Crummock Water | NY 1619 | Dewy Broad | TG 3216 | Creige Riabhaich | |
| Loch | | Clearburn Loch | NT 3415 | Corby Loch | NJ 9214 | Cullaloe Res | NT 1887 | Digley Res | SE 1007 | Duddingston Loch | NT 2872 |
| Castlehill Res | NN 9903 | Clearwen Res | SN 8565 | Corsehouse Res | NS 4850 | Culter Waterhead | NT 0327 | Dinas Res | SN 7482 | Dulyn Res | SH 7066 |
| Castleshaw Res | SD 9909 | Clough Bottom | SD 8426 | Corsoch Loch | NX 7575 | Res | | Dingle Res | SD 6914 | Dundreggan Res | NH 3515 |
| Catcleugh Res | NT 7303 | Res | | Coul Res | NO 2603 | Curra Lochain | NS 1599 | Dog Kennel Pond | SK 4096 | Dun's Dish | NO 6460 |
| Cauldshiels Loch | NT 5132 | Cloverley Pool | SJ 6136 | Covenham Res | TF 3495 | Cwm Lliedi Res | SN 5103 | Dolwen Res | SH 9770 | Duns Mere | SU 4560 |
| Ceann Loch | NN 2895 | Clugston Loch | NX 3457 | Cow Green Res | NY 8030 | Cwmtillery Res | SO 2207 | Donald Rose Res | NO 3303 | Dunside Res | NS 7437 |
| Chapel Mere | SJ 5451 | Clumber Lake | SK 6374 | Cowgill Upper Res | NT 0027 | | | Donolly Res | NT 5768 | Dunviden Lochs | NC 7450 |
| Chard Res | ST 3309 | Clunas Res | NH 8545 | Cowm Res | SD 8819 | | | Dornell Loch | NX 7065 | Dunwan Dam | NS 5549 |
| Chasewater | SK 0307 | Coaf Res | NS 2550 | Cowpe Res | SD 8420 | **D** | | Dove Stone Res | SE 0103 | Dunalastair Water | NN 6958 |
| Cheddar Res | ST 4453 | Coate Water | SU 1782 | Crag Lough | NY 7668 | Daer Res | NS 9707 | Dowdeswell Res | SO 9919 | Dupplin Lake | NN 0320 |
| Chelburn Res | SD 9518 | Cobbinshaw Res | NT 0158 | Craig Goch Res | SN 8969 | Daff Res | NS 2371 | Dowry Res | SD 9811 | Durleigh Res | ST 2636 |
| Chelker Res | SE 0551 | Cochno Loch | NS 4976 | Craigallian Loch | NS 5378 | Daill Res | NR 8189 | Dozmary Pool | SX 1974 | | |
| Chelmarsh Res | SO 7387 | Cockshoot Broad | TG 3415 | Craigendunton Res | NS 5245 | Dale Dike Res | SK 2391 | Draycote Water | SP 4670 | | |
| Chew Res | SE 0301 | Coedty Res | SH 7566 | Craigluscar Res | NT 0690 | Damflask Res | SK 2790 | Drayton Res | SP 5664 | **E** | |
| Chew Valley Lake | ST 5760 | Cogra Moss | NY 0919 | Craigmaddie Res | NS 5675 | Darwell Res | TQ 7121 | Drift Res | SW 4329 | Earlsburn Res | NS 7089 |
| Chum Clough Res | SD 7838 | Coire Lochan | NH 1227 | Cran Loch | NH 9459 | Daventry Res | SP 5763 | Drumbowie Res | NS 7881 | Earnsdale Res | SD 6722 |
| Claerwen Res | SN 8565 | Coire Loch | NC 3639 | Cransley Res | SP 8277 | Dean Clough Res | SD 7133 | Drumlamford Loch | NX 2877 | Easèdale Tarn | NY 3008 |
| Clàr Loch Cnoc | NC 2041 | Cold Hiendley Res | SE 3614 | Cray Res | SN 8821 | Dean Head Res | SE 0230 | Drumore Loch | NO 1660 | Easrlstoun Loch | NX 6183 |
| Thormaid | | Coldingham Loch | NT 8968 | Cregennen Lakes | SH 6614 | Deanhead Res | SE 0315 | Dub Lochain | NG 8909 | Eccleston Mere | SJ 4894 |

LOCH LOMOND *There are many types of scenery and habitats at Loch Lomond, which is the largest freshwater lake in Britain.*

## Loch of Lowes

The Scottish Wildlife Trust purchased this delightful loch in 1969 and almost at once received a bonus in the form of nesting ospreys. As at Loch Garten, these birds are on 'public display' and can be seen from the Trust's observation hide. The loch is very different from the Loe Pool (below) because much of the varied wildlife it supports can be studied either from, or close to, a car parked in one of several lay-bys along the south shore.

Part of the explanation for the loch's importance lies in its geographical position. This leads to a mixture of Lowland and Highland species hardly equalled elsewhere in Scotland. For example, the waters of the loch contain many plants which occur in nutrient-poor highland waters and others which prefer nutrient-rich lowland waters. 'Lowland' geese like greylags replace the 'highland' osprey in winter while the broad-leaved woodland is home to both resident and summer visiting lowland birds. A fascinating loch for all seasons.

## Loe Pool

When the National Trust was given the Loe Pool and its protective surrounding woodland, it was the donor's wish that it should remain a place of peace, an escape from the crowds who flock to much of the south Cornwall coast in summer. So four small car parks are carefully sited among trees, paths surround the lake and, as a deliberate policy, there is no waymarked trail or information centre. The Loe is a place visitors are encouraged to discover for themselves, including wheelchair users for whom a specially adapted bird hide has been provided.

Not that most visitors will need much encouragement. This is the largest freshwater lake in Cornwall, formed when the longshore drift created a sand and shingle

amples of sessile oak, chestnut, rowan, birch, beech and, by the water edges, alder and willow carr.

The A82 is the most popular route, twisting along the west shore of the loch, but the road to Rowardennan leads to picnic and camping sites and to the area where many walks begin, either along the shore or up Ben Lomond. The West Highland Way, one of the best and most

imaginative of long distance paths – from Glasgow to Fort William using the old military roads – runs along the east shore and can be 'sampled' by the least athletic of motorists, strolling a short way towards Rob Roy's Cave.

bar across the mouth of the River Cober about 600 or 700 years ago. The result, a lake some 10 feet above sea level, left the port of Helston with two problems – no outlet to the sea, and frequent floodings. One proved insoluble, the other was eventually solved by the cutting of a permanent culvert.

The beauty of the Loe is in marked contrast to the surrounding landscape. Woods of oak and sycamore, underpinned by rhododendron, are full of summer bird song while, on the water, coot and moorhen, swan and mallard shepherd their young past white water-lilies. Most freshwater duck species occur on the Loe, which attracts many waders, terns and an occasional rarity like the spoonbill.

In the height of the summer season, it is possible to find tranquillity around the Loe Pool. Out of season, it is simply one of the most delightful places in which to walk, relax and observe nature anywhere in the south of England.

## Rutland Water

Rutland Water caters primarily for general recreational purposes – sailing and fishing are both of considerable importance in the management of the lake. It is the second largest man-made lake in Britain and one of the largest in Europe, covering over 3000 acres, of which some 350 form the Rutland Water Nature Reserve at the west end of the lake.

The reserve is typical of what is happening at the 'new breed' of reservoirs to which Rutland belongs: planning and consultation have led to the preservation of old wildlife habitats and the provision of new. Already – it was only completed in 1979 – Rutland's edges are softening, and attractive woodlands, well carpeted with flowers, are developing. Migrating birds are a feature of spring and autumn, and flocks of wildfowl and several maritime species have already discovered it. Rutland Water even has its 'own' species: the ruddy duck, an escapee, has settled here and is steadily increasing its numbers.

## Wast Water

Because Wast Water is detached from the main grouping of the Lakes, it is often missed by visitors. Wast Water is a very distinctive place. It lacks the immediate charm of some of its softer brethren, although it has nothing of the deadness of Thirlmere. It is an austere lake and it can be forbidding, but it has a scale and a grandeur which draws people to it again and again.

The road which follows its northern shoreline from Nether Wasdale to Wasdale

*LOE POOL resulted from the laying down of a sand and shingle bar across the mouth of the River Cober. The lake surface is about 10ft above sea level, and the sea can just be seen at the right of the picture.*

Head allows the motorist an opportunity to appreciate the scenery of the lake in a way matched only by the lovely road that runs along the east bank of Coniston (see page 22).

Do not be deceived by the green of the woods or even, depending on the time of year, the sprinkling of flowers in them. At Wasdale Hall, the marvellous view up the length of the lake will dispel any cosy thoughts. The jumbled mass of rocks which form Long and Goat Crags stretch up to Middle Fell and the eye seems to glance off them, to be focussed on the distant, classic view of three peaks. These are the three peaks represented on the logo of the Lake District National Park – Kirk Fell, Great Gable and Lingmell. Seen in summer they are impressive but, when framed in clear blue, touched by snow, and reflected in the still, mirror-like surface of the lake, they show a stark simplicity of line that is literally breathtaking.

Continue along the road, past the steep-sided valley of the Nether Beck to the car park of Overbeck. This is a good point from which to study the south side of the lake and, in particular, the huge scree slopes. Grey, splashed with orange rust beneath black volcanic caps, the screes would be the major feature of many landscapes. But demanding attention in this one is Scafell Pike, the highest mountain in England as Wast Water is the deepest lake, towering over Lingmell.

The final section of the road, under Yewbarrow, is past small green fields, edged by drystone walls. But there are few trees at this end of the lake and the nearness of the rough peaks and fells can induce an enclosed feeling, lightened by a glance back down the line of the lake.

For the walker, there are paths at Wasdale Head, including routes into the mountains. None is easy and all should be approached with caution. The waymarked trails laid out by the Cumbria Trust for Nature Conservation at Netherwasdale are an excellent introduction to the wildlife of the valley.

| | | | | | | | | | | | |
|---|---|---|---|---|---|---|---|---|---|---|---|
| Hurworth Burn Res | NZ 4033 | Kilantringan Loch | NX 0979 | Lake The | SP 6716 | Lluest-wen Res | SN 9401 | Llyn Cwmorthin | SH 6746 | Llyn Llagi | SH 6448 |
| Hury Res | NY 9619 | Kilbirnie Loch | NS 3354 | Lake Vyrnwy | SH 9921 | Llwyn-on Res | SO 0011 | L. Cwmystradllyn | SH 5644 | Llyn Llech Owen | SN 5615 |
| | | Kilchoan Lochs | NM 7914 | Lamaload Res | SJ 9775 | Llyn Alaw | SH 3986 | L. Cwm-y-ffynnon | SH 6456 | Llyn Lliwbran | SH 8725 |
| | | Kilconquhar Loch | NO 4801 | Laneshaw Res | SD 9441 | Llyn Alaw | SH 9157 | Llyn Cyfynwy | SJ 2154 | Llyn Llydw | SH 6254 |
| **I** | | Killington Res | SD 5991 | Langold Lake | SK 5786 | Llyn Alwen | SH 8956 | Llyn Cynwch | SH 7320 | L. Llygad Rheidol | SN 7987 |
| Ingbirchworth Res | SE 2105 | Killypole Loch | NR 6417 | Langsett Res | SE 2000 | Llyn Anafon | SH 6969 | Llyn Dinan | SH 3177 | Llyn Llygeirian | SH 3489 |
| Island Barn Res | TQ 1467 | Kilmannan Res | NS 4978 | Leez Lodge Lakes | TL 7018 | Llyn Arenig Fach | SH 8241 | Llyn Dinas | SH 6149 | Llyn Llywenan | SH 3481 |
| Isle Pool | SJ 4617 | Kinder Res | SK 0588 | Leighton Res | SE 1578 | Llyn Arenig Fawr | SH 8438 | Llyn Du | SO 0096 | Llyn Mawr | SO 0097 |
| | | King George VI Res | TQ 0473 | Leperstone Res | NS 3571 | Llyn Berwyn | SN 7456 | Llyn Dwythwch | SH 5758 | Llyn Morwynion | SH 7342 |
| | | King George's Res | TQ 3796 | Levers Water | SD 2799 | L. Blaenmelindwr | SN 7183 | Llyn Ebyr | SN 9788 | Llyn Nantlle Uchaf | SH 5153 |
| **J** | | Kinghorn Loch | NT 2587 | Light Hazzles Res | SD 9620 | Llyn Bochlwyd | SH 6559 | Llyn Edno | SH 6649 | Llyn Newydd | SH 7247 |
| Jackhouse Res | SD 7425 | King's Mere | SU 8164 | Lilly Loch | NS 8266 | Llyn Bodgynydd | SH 7659 | Llyn Egnant | SN 7967 | Llyn Ogwen | SH 6560 |
| Jacks Key Res | SD 7020 | Kingside Loch | NT 3413 | Lily Broad | TG 4514 | Llyn Bodlyn | SH 6423 | Llyn Eiddew-mawr | SH 6433 | Llyn Padarn | SH 5761 |
| Jaw Res | NS 4975 | Kirriereoch Loch | NX 3686 | Lily Mere | SD 6091 | Llyn Bowydd | SH 7246 | Llyn Eiddwen | SN 6066 | Llyn Pen-rhaiadr | SN 7593 |
| Jennetts Res | SS 4424 | Knapps Loch | NS 3668 | Linacre Res | SK 3372 | Llyn Bran | SH 9659 | Llyn Eigiau Res | SH 7265 | Llyn Penrhyn | SH 3176 |
| Johnston Loch | NS 6968 | Kneppmull Pond | TQ 1521 | Lindley Wood Res | SE 2149 | Llyn Brenig | SH 9755 | Llyn Elsi Res | SH 7855 | Llyn Peris | SH 5959 |
| Jumbles Res | SD 7314 | Knight Res | TQ 1167 | Lindores Loch | NO 2616 | Llyn Brianne Res | SN 8049 | Llyn Fach | SN 9003 | L. Plas-y-mynydd | SN 7492 |
| | | Knipton Res | SK 8130 | Linfern Loch | NX 3697 | Llyn Caer-Euni | SN 9840 | Llyn Fawr | SN 9103 | Llyn Rhosrtrydd | SN 7075 |
| | | Knockendon Res | NS 2452 | Linlithgow Loch | NT 0077 | Llyn Cau | SH 7112 | L. Ffynnon-y-gwas | SH 5955 | Llyn Stwlan | SH 6644 |
| **K** | | Knocksting Loch | NX 6988 | Linshiels Lake | NT 8904 | Llyn Celyn | SH 8540 | Llyn Frongoch | SN 7275 | Llyn Syfydrin | SN 7284 |
| Kaim Dam | NS 3462 | Knypersley Res | SJ 8955 | Little Denny Res | NS 7981 | Llyn Clywedog | SN 8988 | Llyn Fyrddon-Fawr | SN 8070 | Llyn Tecwyn Uchaf | SH 6438 |
| Keighley Moor Res | SD 9839 | Kype Res | NS 7338 | Little Langdale Tarn | NY 3003 | Llyn Coch-Lwyad | SH 9211 | Llyn Geirionydd | SH 7660 | Llyn Teifi | SN 7867 |
| Kendoon Lock | NX 6090 | | | Little Loch Skiach | NN 9546 | Llyn Conach | SN 7393 | Llyn Glandwgan | SN 7075 | Llyn Traffwll | SH 3276 |
| Kenfig Pool | SS 7981 | | | Little Sea | SZ 0284 | Llyn Conglog | SH 6747 | Llyn Gwyddior | SH 9307 | Llyn Trawsfynydd | SH 6936 |
| Kennick Res | SX 6684 | **L** | | Llan Bwch-llyn Lake | SO 1146 | Llyn Conwy | SH 7846 | Llyn Gwynant | SH 6451 | Llyn Tryweryn | SH 7838 |
| Kentmere Res | NY 4408 | Ladybower Res | SK 1986 | | | Llyn Coron | SH 3770 | Llyn Gynon | SN 7964 | Llyn-y-fan Fach | SN 8021 |
| Kerse Loch | NS 4214 | Lake of Menteith | NN 5700 | Llandegfedd Res | ST 3299 | Llyn Cowlyd Res | SH 7262 | Llyn Helyg | SJ 1177 | Llyn-y-fan Fawr | SN 8321 |
| Kettleton Burn | NS 8900 | Lake The | SU 9631 | Llangorse Lake | SO 1326 | Llyn Crafnant Res | SH 7461 | Llyn Hîr | SN 7867 | Llyn y Garn | SH 7637 |
| Kielder Water | NY 6788 | Lake The | TQ 2752 | Llangynidr Res | SO 1514 | Llyn Craigypistyll | SN 7285 | Llyn Hywel | SH 6626 | Llyn y Manod | SH 7144 |
| | | Lake The | ST 1879 | Llanishen Res | ST 1881 | Llyn Cwellyn | SH 5655 | Llyn Idwal | SH 6459 | Llyn y Parc | SH 7958 |
| | | | | | | Llyn Cwm-mynach | SH 6723 | Llyn Irddyn | SH 6322 | Llyn y Tarw | SO 0197 |

46

| | |
|---|---|
| Loch Inshore | NC 3269 |
| Loch Insh | NH 8304 |
| Loch Iubhair | NN 4226 |
| Loch Katrine | NN 3813 |
| Loch Keisgarg | NC 2667 |
| Loch Kemp | NH 4616 |
| Loch Kennard | NO 9045 |
| Loch Ken | NX 6475 |
| Loch Kernsary | NG 8880 |
| Loch Killin | NH 5210 |
| Loch Kindardochy | NN 7755 |
| Loch Kindar | NX 9664 |
| Loch Kinnabus | NR 3042 |
| Loch Kinord | NO 4499 |
| Loch Knockie | NH 4513 |
| Loch Laggan | NN 4483 |
| Loch Laggan | NS 6292 |
| Loch Laicheard | NC 1846 |
| Loch Laide | NH 5435 |
| Loch Laidon | NN 3854 |
| Loch Lànnsaidh | NH 7394 |
| Loch Laoigh | NH 7395 |
| Loch Laro | NH 6099 |
| Loch Laya | NM 6463 |
| Loch Leacann | NM 9903 |
| Loch Leachd | NM 9504 |
| Loch Leathan | NR 8798 |
| Loch Leathan | NG 5051 |
| Loch Leathed a' Bhaile Fhoghair | NC 0527 |
| Loch Lednock Res | NN 7129 |
| Loch Lee | NO 4279 |
| Loch Lèir | NC 9545 |
| Loch Leitir Easaidh | NC 1626 |
| Loch Leven | NO 1401 |
| Loch Liath | NH 3319 |
| Loch Libo | NS 4355 |
| Loch Linne | NR 7991 |
| Loch Li | NH 2270 |
| Loch Liuravay | NG 4858 |
| Loch Lochy | NN 1884 |
| Loch Loch | NN 9874 |
| Loch Loh na h-Uanha | NC 1210 |
| Loch Iol-ghaoith | NC 3530 |
| Loch Lomond | NN 3215 |
| Loch Lonachan | NG 6219 |
| Loch Loyal | NC 6247 |
| Loch Loyne | NH 1105 |
| Loch Loy | NH 9358 |
| Loch Lubnaig | NN 5813 |
| Loch Lucy | NC 8739 |
| Loch Luiehart | NH 3661 |
| Loch Lundie | NG 8031 |
| Loch Lundie | NG 8049 |
| Loch Lundie | NH 2903 |
| Loch Lunndaidh | NC 7800 |
| Loch Lurgainn | NC 1108 |
| Loch Lyon | NN 4141 |
| Loch ma Stac | NH 3421 |
| Loch Maberry | NX 2874 |
| Loch Macaterick | NX 4391 |
| Loch Magharaidh | NH 4576 |
| Loch Mahaick | NN 7006 |
| Loch Mallachie | NH 9617 |
| Loch Mannoch | NX 6660 |
| Loch Maovally | NC 5160 |
| Loch Maree | NG 9371 |
| Loch Mare | NC 3237 |
| Loch Marie | NH 5375 |
| Loch Meadaidh | NC 4064 |
| Loch Meadie | ND 0848 |
| Loch Meadie | NC 5041 |
| Loch Meadie | NC 7560 |
| Loch Meala | NC 7856 |
| Loch Meall a' Bhuirich | NC 3512 |
| Loch Meallbrodden | NN 9125 |
| Loch Meall Dheirgidh | NH 4893 |
| Loch Mealt | NG 5065 |
| Loch Meig | NH 3655 |
| Loch Meiklie | NH 4330 |
| Loch Melldalloch | NR 9374 |
| Loch Merkland | NC 3831 |
| Loch Mhairc | NN 8879 |
| Loch Mhaolach-coire | NC 2719 |
| Loch Mhic Ghille-chaoil | NH 9202 |
| Loch Mhic Mhàirtein | NM 7803 |
| Loch Mhic'ille Riabhaich | NG 9084 |
| Loch Mhoicean | NH 0731 |
| Loch Mhor | NH 5319 |
| Loch Mhuilich | NH 1243 |
| Loch Middle | NX 3974 |
| Loch Migdale | NH 6391 |
| Loch Minnoch | NX 5385 |
| Loch Moan | NX 3485 |
| Loch Móine Sheilg | NG 9189 |
| Loch Monaghan | NN 5355 |
| Loch Monar | NH 0842 |
| Loch Monzievaird | NN 8423 |
| Loch Mór a' Chraisg | NC 2260 |
| Loch Mór Bad an Ducharaich | NH 0086 |
| Loch Mór na Caorach | NC 7654 |
| Loch Moraig | NN 9066 |
| Loch Morar | NM 6991 |
| Loch More | ND 0745 |
| Loch Morlich | NH 9609 |
| Loch Mór | NG 1448 |
| Loch Mor | NH 1535 |
| Loch Moy | NH 7734 |
| Loch Muck | NS 5100 |
| Loch Mudle | NM 5466 |
| Loch Muick | NO 2882 |
| Loch Muigh-bhlàraidh | NH 6383 |
| Loch Mullardoch | NH 0929 |
| Loch na Bairness | NM 6575 |
| Loch na Bà | NG 9089 |
| Loch na Beinne Baine | NH 2819 |
| Loch na Beinne Moire | NH 3226 |
| Loch na Beinne Reidhe | NC 2121 |
| Loch na Béisle | NC 0012 |
| Loch na Béiste | NG 8894 |
| Loch na Bo | NJ 2860 |
| Loch na Caillich | NC 5108 |
| Loch na Caoidhe | NH 2246 |
| Loch na Caorach | NC 9158 |
| Loch na Claise Móire | NC 3805 |
| Loch na Claise Càrnaich | NC 2752 |
| Loch na Claise Carraich | NG 9087 |
| Loch na Claise Feàrna | NC 2046 |
| Loch na Claise Luúchraich | NC 2249 |
| Loch na Claise | NC 0330 |
| Loch na Cloiche | NC 9747 |
| Loch na Coireig | NH 0593 |
| Loch na Craige gràinde | NR 7682 |
| Loch na Craige | NO 8845 |
| Loch na Creige Duibha | NM 7685 |
| Loch na Creige Duibhe | NC 2836 |
| Loch na Creige Maolaich | NM 9401 |
| Loch na Creige | NG 7457 |
| Loch na Curra | NH 2363 |
| Loch na Curra | NG 8280 |
| Loch na Doire Duinne | NG 8596 |
| Loch na Faic | NC 3907 |
| Loch na Faoilinn | NR 8188 |
| Loch na Féithe Mùgaig | NG 8574 |
| Loch na Fuaralachd | NC 6016 |
| Loch na Fuaralaich | NC 4806 |
| Loch na Gabhalach Nodha | NH 3685 |
| Loch na Gaineimh | NC 7630 |
| Loch na Gaineimh | NC 6912 |
| Loch na Gainimh | NC 2061 |
| Loch na Gainimh | NC 2656 |
| Loch na Gainimh | NC 1718 |
| Loch na Gainmhich | NC 2428 |
| Loch na Gainmhich | NC 3065 |
| Loch na Garbhe Uidhe | NC 1624 |
| Loch na Glaic | NC 7513 |
| Loch na Glas-choille | NC 5530 |
| Loch na h-Airigh Sléibhe | NC 1843 |
| Loch na h-Ath | NC 2341 |
| Loch na h-Eaglaise Beag | NC 8559 |
| Loch na h-Eaglaise Mór | NC 8660 |
| Loch na h-Earrainn | NR 7378 |
| Loch na h-Innse Fraoich | NC 1626 |
| Loch na h-Oidhche | NG 8965 |
| Loch na h-Onaich | NG 9231 |
| Loch na h-Uamha | NG 7766 |
| Loch na h-Uamhaidh Beag | NG 7991 |
| Loch na h-Uamhaidh Móire | NG 7991 |
| Loch na h-Uidhe Doimhne | NC 0628 |
| Loch na h-Uidhe | NG 9387 |
| Loch na h-Uidhe | NH 0493 |
| Loch na Keal | NM 43 |
| Loch na Lairige | NH 5601 |
| Loch na Iap | NN 3971 |
| Loch na Larach | NC 2158 |
| Loch na Leirsdein | NH 3723 |
| Loch na Leitire | NG 8432 |
| Loch na Leitreach | NH 0127 |
| Loch na Lochain | NG 8113 |
| Loch na Mnatha | NC 1944 |
| Loch na Mòine Beag | NH 1962 |
| Loch na Mòiné Buige | NG 9283 |
| Loch na Mòine Mór | NH 1863 |
| Loch na Mòine | NG 9278 |
| Loch na Mucnaich | NC 3238 |
| Loch na Ruighe Duibhe | NH 3823 |
| Loch na Sailm | NM 8714 |
| Loch na Sealga | NH 0383 |
| Loch na Seilge | NC 2543 |
| Loch na Seilge | NC 3644 |
| Loch na Seilge | NC 9258 |
| Loch na Seilg | NC 4950 |
| Loch na Sgeallaig | NN 3665 |
| Loch na Sguabaidh | NG 5523 |
| Loch na Smeoraich | NG 8430 |
| Loch na Sreinge | NM 9216 |
| Loch na Sròne Luime | NC 3421 |
| Loch na Crèitheach | NG 5120 |
| Loch na Doireanach | NG 6310 |
| Loch na Saobhaidhe | NC 6501 |
| Loch na Saobhaidhe | NC 8047 |
| Loch na Thull | NC 2550 |
| Loch na Totaig | NB 9715 |
| Loch na Tuadh | NC 3147 |
| Loch na h-Uamhaig | NG 8162 |
| Loch nam Bò Uidhre | NC 8457 |
| Loch nam Brac | NC 1747 |
| Loch nam Brathain | NH 3921 |
| Loch nam Breac Buidge | NC 6556 |
| Loch nam Breac Beag | NC 8160 |
| Loch nam Breac Dearga | NH 4522 |
| Loch nam Breac Mór | NC 8160 |
| Loch nam Breac | NC 6649 |
| Loch nam Breac | NC 8247 |
| Loch nam Faoileag | NH 4932 |
| Loch nam Fear | ND 0243 |
| Loch nam Fiadh | NH 3164 |
| Loch nam Meallan Liatha | NC 2220 |
| Loch nam Meur | NH 3923 |
| Loch nam Meur | NH 3925 |
| Loch nam Paitean | NM 7273 |
| Loch nam Buainichean | NG 8573 |
| Loch nan Amaichean | NH 4176 |
| Loch nan Badan Boga | NH 0992 |
| Loch nan Bonnach | NH 4848 |
| Loch nan Caorach | NC 2927 |
| Loch nan Cèard Mor | NM 9102 |
| Loch nan Clach Dubha | NG 9278 |
| Loch nan Clachan Geala | NG 8595 |
| Loch nan Clachar Geala | ND 0058 |
| Loch nan Clach | NM 7846 |
| Loch nan Clach | NC 7652 |
| Loch nan Clar | NC 7535 |
| Loch nan Cuaran | NC 2923 |
| Loch nan Daihthean | NG 8782 |
| Loch nan Druidean | NH 4671 |
| Loch nan Druimnean | NM 8414 |
| Loch nan Ealachan | NC 1709 |
| Loch nan Ealachan | NC 2939 |
| Loch nan Ealachan | NC 6751 |
| Loch nan Eilean | NM 9403 |
| Loch nan Eun | NH 4509 |
| Loch nan Eun | NG 7048 |
| Loch nan Eun | NG 9526 |
| Loch nan Eun | NH 3120 |
| Loch nan Eun | NH 4648 |
| Loch nan Eun | NG 7791 |
| Loch nan Eun | NH 1581 |
| Loch nan Eun | NO 0678 |
| Loch nan Eun | NO 2385 |
| Loch nan Gabhar | NM 9663 |
| Loch nan Gad | NR 7857 |
| Loch nan Gall | NC 8657 |
| Loch nan Gillean | NG 8332 |
| Loch nan Lann | NH 4413 |
| Loch nan Liagh | NG 8081 |
| Loch nan Lùb | NC 0730 |
| Loch nan Sgaraig | NC 3424 |
| Loch nan Spréidh | NH 3893 |
| Loch nan Torran | NR 7568 |
| Loch nan Uamh | NG 6308 |
| Loch nan Uan | NC 5629 |
| Loch nan Uidhean Beaga | NC 0927 |
| Loch Nant | NN 0024 |
| Loch nar Ealachan | NC 5444 |
| Loch Naver | NC 6136 |
| Loch Naw | NW 9963 |
| Loch Neaty | NH 4336 |
| Loch Neil | NM 8927 |
| Loch Neldricken | NX 4482 |
| Loch Ness | NH 3809 |
| Loch Nevis | NM 79 |
| Loch Niarsco | NG 3947 |
| Loch Noir | NJ 0945 |
| Loch o' th' Lowes | NS 6014 |
| Loch Ob an Lochain | NH 1598 |
| Loch Ochiltree | NX 3174 |
| Loch of Aboyne | NO 5399 |
| Loch of Blairs | NJ 0255 |
| Loch of Bushta | ND 1972 |
| Loch of Butterstone | NO 0645 |
| Loch of Clunie | NO 1144 |
| Loch of Craiglush | NO 0444 |
| Loch of Drumellie | NO 1444 |
| Loch of Forfar | NO 4450 |
| Loch of Fyntalloch | NX 3174 |
| Loch of Killimster | ND 3055 |
| Loch of Lintrathen | NO 2754 |
| Loch of Lowes | NO 0544 |
| Loch of Mey | ND 2773 |
| Loch of Skene | NJ 7807 |
| Loch of Strathbeg | NK 0758 |
| Loch of the Lowes | NT 2319 |
| Loch of Toftingall | ND 1852 |
| Loch of Wester | ND 3259 |
| Loch of Winless | ND 2954 |
| Loch of Yarrows | ND 3043 |
| Loch Oich | NH 3100 |
| Loch Olgihey | ND 0857 |
| Loch Ordie | NO 0350 |
| Loch Ore | NT 1695 |
| Loch Ospisdale | NH 7388 |
| Loch Ossian | NN 3968 |
| Loch Oss | NN 3025 |
| Loch Park | NJ 3543 |
| Loch Pattack | NN 5378 |
| Loch Pityoulish | NH 9213 |
| Loch Poll an Droighinn | NC 0528 |
| Loch Poll Dhaidh | NC 0729 |
| Loch Poll | NC 1030 |
| Loch Poulary | NH 1201 |
| Loch Preas nan Aighean | NC 1127 |
| Loch Preas nan Sgiathanach | NC 6809 |
| Loch Prille | NH 2881 |
| Loch Quoich | NM 9399 |
| Loch Raa | NC 0111 |
| Loch Racadal | NR 7665 |
| Loch Rangag | ND 1741 |
| Loch Rannoch | NN 5157 |
| Loch Ravag | NG 3744 |
| Loch Ree | NX 1069 |
| Loch Reidh | NH 1887 |
| Loch Restil | NN 2207 |
| Loch Riabhachain | NH 3630 |
| Loch Riecawr | NX 4393 |
| Loch Rifa-gil | NC 7448 |
| Loch Righ Guidh | NH 3820 |
| Loch Rimsdale | NC 7335 |
| Loch Roan | NX 7469 |
| Loch Romain | NR 8253 |
| Loch Ronald | NX 2664 |
| Loch Rosail | NC 7140 |
| Loch Ruard | ND 1443 |
| Loch Rumsdale | NC 9641 |
| Loch Rusky | NN 6103 |
| Loch Ruthver | NH 6127 |
| Loch Sail an Ruathair | NC 3314 |
| Loch Sainn | NC 9352 |
| Loch Saird | NC 9451 |
| Loch Salachaidh | NC 7503 |
| Loch Sand | ND 0940 |
| Loch Saorach | ND 0160 |
| Loch Sarclet | ND 3442 |
| Loch Saugh | NO 6778 |
| Loch Scalloch | NX 2889 |
| Loch Scammadale | NM 8920 |
| Loch Scarmclate | ND 1859 |
| Loch Scye | ND 0055 |
| Loch Sealbhanach | NH 2331 |
| Loch Searrach | NG 9386 |
| Loch Seil | NM 8020 |
| Loch Sgamhain | NH 0952 |
| Loch Sgeireach | NH 2373 |
| Loch Sgeireach | NC 4611 |
| Loch Sguadaig | NN 3687 |
| Loch Sguod | NG 8187 |
| Loch Shandra | NO 2162 |
| Loch Sheilah | NH 6778 |
| Loch Sheosdal | NG 4169 |
| Loch Shiel | NG 9418 |
| Loch Shiel | NM 6868 |
| Loch Shin | NC 3724 |
| Loch Shurrery | ND 0455 |
| Loch Sionascaig | NC 1113 |
| Loch Skae | NX 7183 |
| Loch Skeen | NT 1716 |
| Loch Skerray | NC 6660 |
| Loch Skerrow | NX 6068 |
| Loch Skiach | NN 9547 |
| Loch Slaim | NC 6253 |
| Loch Sleadale | NG 3429 |
| Loch Sletill | NC 9547 |
| Loch Slochy | NX 4292 |
| Loch Sloy | NN 2812 |
| Loch Sonachan | NM 9324 |
| Loch Spallander Res | NS 3908 |
| Loch Spey | NN 4293 |
| Loch Spynie | NJ 2366 |
| Loch Srùban Móra | NH 3824 |
| Loch Stack | NC 2942 |
| Loch Staing | NC 5740 |
| Loch Staonsaid | NC 3947 |
| Loch Stemster | ND 1842 |
| Loch Stephan | NC 6955 |
| Loch Strath nan Aisinnin | NC 3232 |
| Loch Strathy | NC 7747 |
| Loch Syre | NC 6644 |
| Loch Talaheel | NC 9548 |
| Loch Tarbhaidh | NC 6335 |
| Loch Tarff | NH 4209 |
| Loch Tarsan | NS 0784 |
| Loch Tay | NN 5833 |
| Loch Teàrnait | NM 7447 |
| Loch Tholldhoire | NG 8977 |
| Loch Thom | NS 2572 |
| Loch Thormaid | ND 0060 |
| Loch Tigh na Creige | NC 6109 |
| Loch Tilt | NN 9982 |
| Loch Tinker | NN 4406 |
| Loch Tolaidh | NG 8478 |
| Loch Toll a' Mhadaidh | NG 9881 |
| Loch Toll an Lochain | NH 0783 |
| Loch Toll an Lochain | NH 1471 |
| Loch Toll Lochain | NH 2348 |
| Loch Tor na h-Eigin | NC 1230 |
| Loch Torr na Ceardaich | NC 9751 |
| Loch Tralaig | NM 8816 |
| Loch Treig | NN 3169 |
| Loch Tromlee | NN 0425 |
| Loch Trool | NX 4179 |
| Loch Truderscaig | NC 7132 |
| Loch Tuill Bhearnach | NH 1634 |
| Loch Tuim Ghlais | NC 9752 |
| Loch Tulla | NN 2942 |
| Loch Tummel | NN 8159 |
| Loch Turret Res | NN 8027 |
| Loch Uanagan | NH 3607 |
| Loch Uidh na Geádaig | NC 1425 |
| Loch Uidh na h-Iarna | NC 1630 |
| Loch Uisge | NM 8055 |
| Loch Ulagadale | NR 7346 |
| Loch Ulbhach Coire | NC 3737 |
| Loch Unapool | NC 2231 |
| Loch Urigill | NC 2409 |
| Loch Urr | NX 7684 |
| Loch Usgaig | NC 0411 |
| Loch Ussie | NH 5057 |
| Loch Vaa | NH 9117 |
| Loch Vaich | NH 3477 |
| Loch Valigan | NN 9769 |
| Loch Valley | NX 4481 |
| Loch Vatachan | NC 0110 |
| Loch Venachar | NN 5705 |
| Loch Veyatie | NC 1813 |
| Loch Voil | NN 5019 |
| Loch Vrotachan | NO 1278 |
| Loch Walton | NS 6686 |
| Loch Watenan | ND 3141 |
| Loch Watston | NN 7100 |
| Loch Watten | ND 2256 |
| Loch Wharral | NO 3574 |
| Loch Whinyeon | NX 6260 |
| Loch Yucal | NC 2036 |
| Locha an Ais | NC 1809 |
| Locha Na h-Earba | NN 4883 |
| Lochaber Loch | NX 9270 |
| Lochain a' Mheadhoin | NM 6994 |
| Lochain Meallan a' Chuail | NC 3529 |
| Lochain nan Cnaimh | NS 1697 |
| Lochan a' Bhruic | NM 9210 |
| Lochan a' Chairn | NH 5184 |
| Lochan a' Choire | NN 4388 |
| Lochan a' Choire | NC 4613 |
| Lochan a' Mhuilinn | NM 7074 |
| Lochan a' Dhealaich | NC 3838 |
| Lochan a' Chlaidheimh | NN 4060 |
| Lochan a' Chneamh | NM 6988 |
| Lochan a' Chreachain | NN 3644 |
| Lochan a' Mhadaidh Riabhaich | NM 5565 |
| Lochan a' Mhuilinn | NN 8435 |
| Lochan a' Bhrodainn | NM 8387 |
| Lochan Airigh Leathaid | NC 9939 |
| Lochan an Ais | 1809 |
| Lochan an Bad an Losguinn | NH 1503 |
| Lochan an Eoin Ruadha | NH 6132 |
| Lochan an Láir | NN 0743 |
| Lochan an t-Sagairt | NG 7437 |
| Lochan an Tairt | NH 4433 |
| Lochan An Tuirc | NN 4280 |
| Lochan Badan Glasliath | NH 2691 |
| Lochan Bealach Cornaidh | NC 2028 |
| Lochan Beannach Beag | NG 9477 |
| Lochan Beannach Mór | NG 9377 |
| Lochan Beinn Chaorach | NN 3151 |
| Lochan Beinn Damhain | NN 2917 |
| Lochan Blar nan Lochan | NM 9749 |
| Lochan Breaclaich | NN 6231 |
| Lochan Carn a' Chuilinn | NH 4303 |
| Lochan Coire na Mèinne | NN 3952 |
| Lochan Croc nan Làir | ND 0345 |
| Lochan Dearg Uillt | NH 4103 |
| Lochan Dearg | NC 0907 |
| Lochan Dearg | NC 1509 |
| Lochan Dhonnachaidh | NM 7060 |
| Lochan Druin na Fearna | NG 8270 |
| Lochan Dubh Cùl na h-Amaite | NC 7514 |
| Lochan Dubh Cùl na Beinne | NC 9854 |
| Lochan Dubh nan Geodh | ND 0547 |
| Lochan Dubh | NN 0616 |
| Lochan Dubh | NM 9039 |
| Lochan Dubh | NM 8970 |
| Lochan Dubh | NN 0695 |
| Lochan Dubh | NC 7412 |
| Lochan Ealach Beag | NC 9649 |
| Lochan Ealach Mór | NC 9648 |

# Rivers and Canals

*The Dee and the Itchen, so dissimilar, but both great fishing rivers; the Wye and the Tamar, sinuously acting as the boundaries between countries and counties respectively; the Wey, river and canal, and the Llangollen and Stratford canals, moving through (and over) very different yet equally beautiful countryside.*

## Dee (Royal Deeside)

The Pools of Dee rise high in the Lairig Ghru between Braeriach and Ben Macdui, and the river gathers a host of tributaries before reaching Linn of Dee. Here is a perfect example of one of the typical Dee landscapes; a narrow, steep cleft through which the water rushes in an exciting torrent.

The castle at Braemar is the first representative of another of the Dee's typical landscapes. Historically there are connections with royalty stretching back to the 10th century, but it is Balmoral which has conferred great social cachet on 'Royal Deeside'. The present castle, used and beloved by royalty since the 1850s, was built by Queen Victoria and Prince Albert on an earlier site.

The Queen further influenced the landscape by her purchase of the Lochnagar Estate. The controlled felling of broadleaved trees, allied to sensible conifer planting, both policies which she im-plemented, was copied by other owners, producing the superb mixed woods we see along the Dee today.

In addition to royalty, the clans have long been established along the banks of the river. Homes like that of the Gordons at Aboyne and the 13th-century castle of the Irvines at Drum add to the mixture of natural and man-made landscape.

*THE OLD BRIDGE OF DEE AND BALMORAL FOREST Snow covers valley and peaks in this winter view near Braemar.*

| A | | Arnol | NB 3045 | Bank | TL 5368 | Bran | NH 1958 | Calder (*Lancs*) | SD 5346 | Chelmer & | TL 7908 |
|---|---|---|---|---|---|---|---|---|---|---|---|
| Add | NR 8192 | Arrow (*Here & W*) | SO 4058 | Barle | SS 8829 | Brant | SK 9356 | Calder (*Lancs*) | SD 7833 | Blackwater Navigation | |
| Adur | TQ 2118 | Arun | TQ 0422 | Barrisdale | NG 8803 | Brathay | NY 2802 | Calder (*Strath*) | NS 3162 | Cherwell (*Nhants*) | SP 4947 |
| Affric (*Highld*) | NH 0920 | Ash | TL 4216 | Basingstoke Canal | SU 7251 | Bray | SS 6932 | Calder (*W Yorks*) | SE 2620 | Cherwell (*Oxon*) | SP 5212 |
| Aire | SE 3630 | Ashby Canal | SK 3801 | Beauly | NH 4641 | Breamish | NT 9615 | Calder & Hebble | SE 1322 | Chess | TQ 0695 |
| Aire & Calder Nav | SE 7322 | Ashop | SK 1389 | Bellart | NM 4448 | Brede | TQ 8217 | Caldron Canal | SJ 9849 | Chesterfield Canal | SK 6582 |
| Alde | TM 2967 | Ashton Canal | SJ 8798 | Beult | TQ 7747 | Brent | TM 0145 | Cale | ST 7422 | Chet | TM 3799 |
| Allen (*Corn*) | SX 0678 | Attadale | NG 9337 | Birmingham Canal | SO 9791 | Bridgewater Canal | SJ 5581 | Caledonian Canal | NN1277 | Churn | SP 0108 |
| Allen (*Dorset*) | SU 0006 | Avan | SS 8195 | Birmingham & | SP 2097 | Bridgewater & | ST 0331 | Cam or Rhee | TL 2643 | Churnet | SK 0147 |
| Almond (*Tayside*) | NO 0228 | Avon (*Avon*) | ST 6966 | Frazeley Canal | | Taunton Canal | | Cam (*Cambs*) | TL 5268 | Claw | SX 3498 |
| Aln | NU 1214 | Avon (*Central*) | NS 8773 | Blackwater | TL 8322 | Brit | SY 4795 | Cam (*Essex*) | TL 5233 | Clun | SO 3976 |
| Alne | SP 1562 | Avon (*Devon*) | SX 7157 | Bladnoch | NX 3657 | Brittle | NG 4022 | Camel | SX 0168 | Clwyd | SK 0276 |
| Alness | NH 6273 | Avon (*Grampn*) | NJ 1614 | Bleng | NY 0804 | Brock | SD 5140 | Can | TL 6807 | Clyde (*Strath*) | NS 9933 |
| Alport | SK 1292 | Avon (*Warw*) | SP 2659 | Blithe | SK 0424 | Broom | NH 1881 | Cannich | NH 2833 | Clyst | SX 9998 |
| Alt | SD 3105 | Avon (*Wilts*) | SV 1301 | Blyth (*Northum*) | NZ 1877 | Brora | NC 6613 | Carey | SX 3687 | Clywedog | SJ 0962 |
| Alun | SM 7627 | Awe | NN 0229 | Blyth (*Suff*) | TM 4376 | Brue (*Somer*) | ST 6032 | Caron (*Highld*) | NG 9442 | Cocker | NY 1228 |
| Alwin | NT 9110 | Axe (*Devon*) | ST 3303 | Blythe (*Warw*) | SP 2184 | Brue (*Dorset*) | ST 4044 | Carron (*Central*) | NS 7684 | Coiltie | NH 4426 |
| Alyn | SJ 3656 | Axe (*Somer*) | ST 4647 | Bogie | NJ 5234 | Bude Canal | SS2005 | Carron (*Highld*) | NH 4489 | Cole (*Glos*) | SU 2195 |
| Amber | SK 3463 | Ayr | NS 5826 | Bollin | SJ 7785 | Bure | TG 2521 | Cary | ST 4530 | Cole (*W Mids*) | SP 1587 |
| Anker | SK 2305 | | | Borgie | NC 6655 | | | Cassley | NC 4012 | Coll | NB 4540 |
| Annan (*D & G*) | NY 1176 | | | Bourne | SU 2038 | | | Ceiriog | SJ 2237 | Coln | SP 1305 |
| Ant | TG 3617 | **B** | | Bovey | SX 7583 | **C** | | Char | SY 3996 | Colne | TL 9327 |
| Apple Cross | NG 7246 | Ba | NN 2648 | Braan | NN 9438 | Calder | NN 6698 | Chater | SK 8303 | Conder | SD 4958 |
| Ardle | NO 1054 | Bain | TF 2473 | Brain | TL 7918 | Calder (*Cumb*) | NY 0609 | Chelmer | TL 6520 | Conon (*Highld*) | NG 4163 |

## Itchen

Around AD 1200, the Bishop of Winchester built a reservoir at Alresford to control the water supply to local mills and to provide additional water for the Itchen. This made the river navigable between Alresford and the sea at Southampton; how long it remained so is not known. With the revival of interest in water transport in the 18th century, the Itchen was re-opened and survived as a waterway until 1869. Old Alresford Pond can still be seen beside the B3046, which runs along the embankment built to create the reservoir.

The Itchen rises in unpromising circumstances in marshy fields near Cheriton, flowing though water-meadows at Titchborne, before it is joined by the Alre (pronounced 'arl') close to Itchen Stoke. From here to Winchester there isn't a false note as it passes Ovington, Itchen Abbas, Avington, Easton and the Worthys. Below Winchester the river is less impressive, but nowhere in Britain is that middle section surpassed.

A perfect chalk stream, the Itchen is managed so as to produce ideal conditions for the trout for which it is famous. A good site from which to study the beauty of a chalk river is the footbridge at Ovington, where there is a short riverside path.

## Llangollen Canal

A great deal of the Llangollen canal is of interest, but it is the last section of 10 or so miles that best represents the attraction of canals – a pleasing combination of industrial architecture and scenic beauty.

Why this should be so is an interesting question in itself. The Bearley Aqueduct on the Stratford Canal (page 51) is almost as great an achievement as Telford's Pontcysyllte Aqueduct on the Llangollen, and few would deny that the Brecon and Abergavenny is as beautiful as the Llangollen; yet it is the Llangollen which has caught the public imagination.

*LLANGOLLEN CANAL*

Having clung to the English side of the valley, the canal makes a dramatic entrance into Wales at Chirk, crossing the River Ceiriog on a lofty aqueduct. It immediately tunnels through a hill before turning north and then west through the Vale of Llangollen; and on its way it is carried over the River Dee on 'the stream in the sky', as Scott described Pontcysyllte Aqueduct.

Above the canal as it completes its journey, soar the limestone cliffs of Creigiau Eglwyseg. Along the way, the naturalist will see much to confirm the view that nature is always ready to add to man's works – even those of Thomas Telford.

## Wandle

Rising in the Surrey hills and near South Croydon, the Wandle travels a mere nine miles before spilling into the Thames at Wandsworth. Yet this relatively short and narrow river has a fascinating industrial history.

Thirteen Wandle mills were listed in Domesday Book; by the early 17th century there were two dozen, and the total had reached 90 by the middle of the 19th century – the Wandle's heyday – before the water level fell and steam power arrived. Corn, gunpowder, leather processing, copper and iron works, fabrics, peppermint, lavender, and even snuff – were either processed, made, powered or distilled by mills on the Wandle.

William Morris, the Victorian artist and designer, set up print mills and workshops on the Wandle at Merton in 1881, where he produced his famous hand-woven tapestries, carpets and windows of painted glass.

The growth of interest in industrial archaeology and in conservation has led to a great improvement in the condition of the Wandle in recent years. A 'trail' traces the main industrial developments; watercress again grows in the upper reaches and trout have been re-introduced into the river at Carshalton. Mallard and moorhen thrive, and kingfishers have returned to the river – a cheering example of what can be achieved in situations as unpromising as the Wandle's had become after years of neglect.

## Stratford-upon-Avon Canal

The restoration of the 13-mile long southern section of the Stratford-upon-Avon canal began in 1961 and the canal was re-opened in 1964. The project, run and organised with great energy, was carried out by volunteers, some of them a 'captive' bunch, from a local prison. The commitment and hard work of these volunteers confirmed that similar projects could be successful. Not only that, it had cost less than half the estimated cost of closure. The movement to repair many neglected canals and restore them to working order had received a vitally important boost and inspiration.

For nearly 20 years, the Inland Waterways Association had campaigned for the restoration of derelict canals. As a result of this first success, many schemes – some wildly over-optimistic – have been floated by enthusiasts fired by visits to the Stratford Canal. Success has not been without further difficulties – maintenance of the canal has presented problems, and there has been debate over who should manage it in future.

But for those who use the canal, or walk the rough, overgrown towpath, little of this matters. This delightful stretch of waterway passes through some of the loveliest Midlands scenery. Once clear of Stratford the canal climbs the 11 Wilmcote locks and passes Mary Arden's cottage. On the route there are three aqueducts and a further series of locks – no less than 36 were repaired during work on the canal. At Lapworth the canal has a link with the Grand Union Canal (the cause of its original lack of success) before climbing towards Birmingham.

The industrial architecture of the canal is fascinating: the various sections were constructed under different engineers, who provided individual solutions to problems. Examples are unique barrel vaulted lock houses, iron footbridges that divide to allow towing ropes to pass, and the 500 ft long red-brick Bearley Aqueduct crossing the Alne valley, where boats make a remarkable sight above the countryside.

*THE RIVER TAMAR forms the boundary between Devon and Cornwall for much of its length.*

## Tamar

It is said that the Tamar prevented the Romans entering Cornwall, so leaving it to develop its Celtic heritage. The river still divides Cornwall from Devon most effectively and, shortly after it rises near Youlstone, with only a brief remission at Bridgerule, the Tamar is the official boundary between the counties.

At first it avoids people and their habitations, preferring to gather tributaries, as if building its strength for its journey to the sea at Plymouth. After Launceston it begins to essay some loops, and when it has passed under the 16th-century, six-arched bridge at Gunnislake. the river executes a series of contortions which put even the Wye (page 53) to shame.

The Tamar is tidal from Morwellham, a port of significance long before the local copper mines were at their peak in the early 19th century. However, as they declined, so did Morwellham. Nowadays, the old port has been restored as a museum, as has the last of the Tamar's working barges, the *Shamrock*, which lies at Cotehele Quay, just below the small manor house, Cotehele House (NT).

| | | | | | | | | | | | |
|---|---|---|---|---|---|---|---|---|---|---|---|
| Glyme | SP 4418 | Helford | SW 7526 | Isis (Berks) | SP 4302 | Killin | NH 5308 | Lee Navigation | TQ 3587 | Lowther | NY 5120 |
| Gour | NM 9364 | Helmsdale | NC 8925 | Isla (Grampn) | NJ 4046 | Kingie | NN 0197 | Leeds & Liverpool | SD 5407 | Loxley | SK 2989 |
| Gowy | SJ 4864 | Hepste | SN 9612 | Isla (Tays) | NO 2357 | Kirkaig | NC 0918 | Canal | | Loy | NN 1183 |
| Grand Union Canal | SP 9220 | Hertford | TA 0281 | Isle | ST 3722 | Knaik | NN 8012 | | SD 9553 | Loyne | HH 0706 |
| | TQ 0586 | Hindburn | SD 6366 | Itchen (Hants) | SU 4616 | Kym | TL 1066 | Len | TQ 8054 | Lugg (Here & W) | SO 5251 |
| | SP 3964 | Hinnisdal | NG 4158 | Itchen (Warw) | SP 4062 | | | Leven (Fife) | NO 2601 | Lugg (Powys) | SO 3264 |
| (Leicester Section) | SP 6692 | Hiz | TL 1833 | Ithon | SO 1066 | | | Leven (Highld) | NN 2160 | Luineag | NH 9209 |
| Grand Western C. | SS 9712 | Hodder | SD 7050 | Ivel | TL 1938 | | | Leven (N Yorks) | NZ 4906 | Lune (Durham) | NY 8720 |
| Granta | TL 5051 | Hope | NC 4760 | | | Lael | NH 2184 | Leven (Strath) | NS 3976 | Lune (Lancs) | SD 6075 |
| Great Ouse (Bucks) | SP 8646 | Huddersfield | SE 1518 | | | Laggan | NR 3156 | Lew | SS 5301 | Lydden | ST 7208 |
| Great Ouse (Camb) | TL 5996 | Broad Canal | | K | | Lair | NG 9850 | Liever | NM 8907 | Lyne | NY 4871 |
| Great Ouse (Leics) | SP 5936 | Hull | TA 0646 | Kannaird | NC 1702 | Lambourn | SU 4370 | Ling | NG 9834 | Lynher | SX 3663 |
| Greta (Cumbr) | NY 2924 | Humber | TA 2119 | Keekle | NY 0118 | Lancaster Canal | SD 4853 | Livet | NJ 2523 | Lyon | NN 6147 |
| Greta (Durham) | NZ 0511 | Hurich | NM 8267 | Keer | SD 5472 | Lark | TL 6476 | Liza | NY 1313 | Lyvennet | NY 6122 |
| Greta (Lancs) | SD 6271 | | | Kelvin | NS 6775 | Laver | SE 2072 | Llangollen Canal | SJ 5446 | | |
| Grudie (Highld) | NG 9665 | | | Kenn (Avon) | ST 4269 | Laxay | NB 3022 | Loanan | NC 2418 | | |
| Gryfe | NS 3666 | I | | Kenn (Devon) | SX 9385 | Laxdale | NB 3835 | Lochay | NN 5037 | M | |
| Gwash | SK 8906 | Idle | SK 7497 | Kennet | SU 5366 | Laxford | NC 2545 | Lochy (Highld) | NN 1379 | Macclesfield C. | SJ 9067 |
| | | Inny | SX 2383 | Kennet & Avon | SU 4366 | Lea | TL 1614 | Lochy (Strath) | NN 2629 | Mallie | NN 0687 |
| H | | Inver | NC 1123 | Canal (Berks) | | Leach | SP 1708 | Loddon | SU 7568 | Manchester Ship | SJ 4978 |
| | | Irt | NY 1000 | | ST 8660 | Leadon | SO 7628 | Lodon | SO 6152 | Canal | |
| Hamble | SU 5214 | Irthing | NY 6469 | Kennett (Cambs) | TL 6969 | Leam | SP 4568 | Lossie (Grampn) | NJ 1044 | Manifold | SK 1054 |
| Hart | SU 7659 | Irvine | NS 4737 | Kent (Cumbr) | SD 5086 | Lea or Lee | TL 3700 | Lossie (Grampn) | NJ 2564 | Mashie | NN 5787 |
| Haultin | NG 4451 | Irwell | SD 7913 | Kerry | NG 8271 | Lednock | NN 7625 | Lostock | SD 5119 | Maun | SK 6166 |
| Hayle | SW 5632 | Isbourne | SP 0334 | Kiachnish | NN 0969 | Leen | SK 5450 | Loughor | SN 6007 | Mease | SK 2711 |

## Wey

The Wey is both river and canal. It rises in Hampshire and Surrey – the streams merge at Tilford – and flows through Godalming and Guildford before meeting the Thames below Shepperton Lock. In 1653 the river was made navigable from the Thames to Guildford and it was extended to Godalming in 1760. The project proved financially viable until the coming of the railway to Guildford in the mid-19th century. The canal continued to be used commercially until the early 1980s, by which time it had been developed, under the management of the National Trust, for recreational use.

The Wey is a river of surprising beauty and, given its closeness to so many urban centres, it is remarkably unfrequented. It is possible to take a narrow boat along it on a summer Sunday and meet very few people, while, close by, the M25 and A3 hum with heavy traffic. The towpath, like the canal, is invariably uncrowded, used only by occasional anglers and walkers.

Geese and cattle still feed by it almost to the centre of Godalming, on the old common meadowlands. Rural scenes reminiscent of quiet Suffolk rivers stretch away from the towpath leading to Guildford, with more cattle feeding contentedly in alder and osier-edged water meadows. The centre of Guildford is busy, but the Wey heads on into a section which includes one of Surrey's finest houses, Sutton Place. There are canalside pubs, locks with attractive cottages, even some light but unobtrusive industry, as it pursues a less direct route through peaceful country. Occasionally, urban civilisation reasserts itself, but the canal soon returns to its rural wanderings, before passing under the M25 and on to a quiet ending at the Thames.

THE WEY NAVIGATION AT GODALMING (above) provides a quiet retreat for boating.

THE WYE VALLEY AT TINTERN The roofless ruins of this Cistercian abbey are set on meadowland within a bend of the River Wye.

## River Wye

Those who know the Welsh Border Wye believe it to be unsurpassed for beauty, whether grand or gentle, a river to inspire poets and common folk alike. Why does the river have such an effect on all who are acquainted with it?

It could hardly have a more dramatic start, rising on Plynlimon, that dark and boggy wilderness which is also the birthplace of the Severn. Usefully, it joins the A44 to Llangurig then the A470 to Rhayader, Newbridge and Builth Wells. Kilvert saw 'a beautiful enchantment' in Builth, although not everyone will agree with that. Now the river begins to widen and experiment with the sinuous loops for which it is famous. At Llyswen it parts company with the A470 and heads north, sliding round Hay and beginning an exploration of the Herefordshire plain, now in company with the A438 to Hereford. Suddenly the river begins a tortuous series of loops, as if trying to escape from the small roads which now run alongside it, now rise high above it, presenting classic views of the heavily wooded river far below – miniature versions of the high viewpoint at Symonds Yat, but without the tourists.

Ross-on-Wye is passed, high on its sandstone ridge, a lovely sight, with the spire of St Mary's elegant by day and night. Then the Wye enters its most famous stretch, passing Symonds Yat; here it has cut its way deeply through a variety of rock surfaces, leaving almost sheer cliffs covered in woods which in their autumn colours are unsurpassed in Britain.

After this display of exuberance the Wye re-enters Wales and straightens until it has passed Monmouth, collecting both the River Monnow and the A466 to accompany it on the final phase of its journey to Chepstow. Narrower now, the river hurries down to Tintern Abbey, proof, if it were needed, of the Cistercians' eye for a dramatically beautiful site. Below Tintern the river widens, makes a few last elegant sweeps, passes Chepstow and is united, after a joint journey of over 300 miles,

with the Severn – which rose just two miles from it on Plynlimon!

Good roads are rarely far from the river, and the Wye Valley and Lower Wye Valley Walks cover much of its length, throughout which there are many opportunities to study its wildlife. Because the Wye changes its character from acid to alkaline, the wildlife is particularly rich and varied. The broadleaved trees are the obvious feature, recognised from hundreds of photographs of the Wye's woods in glowing colours, and the smaller plant life and bird and butterfly populations are also notable.

## Helford River

One of England's shorter waterways, the Helford River, rises near Helston in Cornwall and flows eastwards for a mile or so until it reaches the little fishing village of Gweek. Here it immediately widens into Gweek Drive, and cuts deeply through a 'drowned valley' – the technical term for its estuary – on its journey to the sea. In a five-mile stretch from Gweek to Rosemullion Head and Nare Point, there are numerous small coves, wooded inlets on either side of the river and creeks such as Frenchman's Creek, made famous by the novelist Daphne du Maurier. Add to this the towering cliffs and a National Trust garden, and the visitor begins to realise why the Helford River is so renowned for beauty as well as natural history and maritime interest.

The garden is Glendurgan, designed around one of the many streams that feed the estuary; it has the added advantage of closeness to the Gulf Stream, so is able to support a great number of rare, tender and exotic shrubs and other plants. Other attractions are a maze, water gardens, and superb views. Glendurgan's valley runs down to the tiny, enchanting hamlet of Durgan, once a fishing village, and also owned by the National Trust.

The Helford estuary also has oysters, seals, and – in the inlets – a variety of waders, such as the greenshank. It is a paradise for the birdwatcher, the angler, the yachtsman and the naturalist.

*THE HELFORD RIVER on the Lizard peninsula is one of England's shortest rivers. It is very popular with anglers, yachtsmen and naturalists.*

| | | | | | | | | | |
|---|---|---|---|---|---|---|---|---|---|
| Sow | SJ 8628 | Swere | SP 4733 | Test | SU 3637 | Trent & Mersey C. | SJ 7165 | **V** | |
| Sowe | SP 3777 | Swift | SP 5283 | Teviot | NT 6424 | | SK 4229 | Ver | TL 1209 |
| Spean | NN 2481 | | | Thames (Berks) | SU 5985 | Trent or Piddle | SY 8392 | | |
| Spey (Grampn) | NJ 3050 | | | Thames or Isis | SP 4302 | Tromie | NN 7694 | | |
| Spey (Highld) | NN 5094 | **T** | | Thet | TL 9584 | Trothy | SO 4314 | **W** | |
| Spey (Highld) | NH 9315 | Taff | ST 1578 | Thrushel | SX 4789 | Truim | NN 6485 | Waldon | SS 3610 |
| Sprint | NY 4903 | Tale | ST 0702 | Thurne | TG 4017 | Tud | TG 0812 | Wampool | NY 2454 |
| Staff & Worc C. | SO 8898 | Tamar | SX 3682 | Thurso | ND 1065 | Tummel (Tays) | NN 7459 | Wandle | TQ 2866 |
| | SO 8273 | Tame (Gtr Manch) | SJ 9092 | Tiddy | SX 3064 | Turret | NN 3394 | Wansbeck | NZ 1285 |
| Stainforth & Keadby Canal – see | | Tame (Staffs) | SK 1807 | Til (Beds) | TL 0268 | Tweed (Borders) | NT 0722 | Washburn | SE 1458 |
| Sheffield & South Yorkshire | | Tame Valley Canal | SP 0393 | Till (Lincs) | SK 9077 | Tweed (Borders) | NT 4235 | Waveney | TM 2381 |
| Stiffkey | TF 9233 | Tarbert | NM 9259 | Till (Northumb) | NT 9533 | Tyne (Lothian) | NT 5474 | Waver | NY 1850 |
| Stinchar | NX 2291 | Tarff | NH 3805 | Tillingham | TQ 8720 | Tyne (Tyne & Wear) | NZ 0361 | Wear | NZ 1134 |
| Stort | TL 4829 | Tavy | SX 4765 | Tilt | NN 9575 | | | Weaver | SJ 5877 |
| Stour (Dorset) | ST 7619 | Taw | SS 6614 | Tirry | NC 5318 | | | Welland | SP 8894 |
| Stour (Essex) | TL 9233 | Tawe | SS 6799 | Tone | ST 3227 | | | Wenning | SD 7167 |
| Stour (Here & W) | SO 8278 | Tay (Tays) | NO 1138 | Torne | SE 6502 | | | Wensum | TG 0518 |
| Stour (Kent) | TR 2763 | Tees (Cumbr) | NY 7334 | Torridge | SS 5509 | **U** | | Went | SE 5917 |
| Stour (Warw) | SP 2249 | Tees (N Yorks) | NZ 2711 | Torridon | NG 9255 | Ugie | NK 0849 | West Allen | NY 7854 |
| Stourbridge Canal | SO 8785 | Teign | SX 7689 | Toscaig | NG 7337 | Union Canal | NS 9875 | Wey (Hants) | SU 7742 |
| Strae | NN 1833 | Teith | NN 6306 | Tove | SP 7746 | Ure (N Yorks) | SE 4662 | Wharfe | SE 0262 |
| Stratford-upon-Avon Canal | SP 1663 | Teme (Here & W) | SO 7067 | Traligill | NC 2621 | Ure & Ripon Canal | SE 3269 | Wheelock | SJ 7063 |
| | | Teme (Powys) | SO 3073 | Trent (Lincs) | SE 8619 | Urie | NJ 6629 | Whitelake | ST 5340 |
| Strathy | NC 8051 | Ter | TL 7714 | Trent (Notts) | SK 6239 | Usk | SO 2515 | Windrush | SP 1817 |
| Swale | SE 2796 | Tern | SJ 7037 | Trent (Staffs) | SJ 9231 | | | Winster | SD 4185 |

| | |
|---|---|
| Wiske | SE 3497 |
| Wissey | TF 8401 |
| Witham (Lincs) | SK 9328 |
| Wolf | SX 4290 |
| Worcester & Birmingham C. | SP 0484 |
| Worfe | SO 7698 |
| Worth | SE 0137 |
| Wreake | SK 6616 |
| Wye (Derbs) | SK 2069 |
| Wye (Here & W) | SO 3045 |
| Wylye | SU 0536 |
| Wyre | SD 4341 |
| Wyrley & Essington Canal | SK 0102 |
| | |
| **Y** | |
| Yar | SZ 6186 |
| Yare | TG 1108 |
| Yarrow | SD 5117 |
| Yarty | ST 2505 |
| Yealm | SX 6056 |
| Yeo (Devon) | SS 7306 |
| Yeo (Somer) | ST 5223 |
| Ythan | NJ 8636 |

# Bays and Headlands

*Included here are some of the most popular bays and headlands in Britain – Beachy Head, the Lizard and Rhossili – with St Abb's and St David's representing the 'saints' who gave their names to so many headlands around our coastline. Also described are the unique environments of the Lleyn, Dungeness and remote, timeless Sandwell Bay.*

## Beachy Head

Beachy Head has been called a vast self-destruct area. Certainly, the sea is committing vandalism here virtually unchecked and at a considerable pace – about 18 in a year. The Iron Age fort of Belle Tout, near the old lighthouse, was once over a mile inland, and is now perilously close to the edge of the high cliffs. In geological time, it isn't long since the sea first broke through the chalk ridge connecting England and France, creating the English Channel.

Beachy Head is very popular with both motorists and walkers. A road leaves the A259 at East Dean, rejoining it nearer Eastbourne and passing several car parks on the way which can be crowded in summer. There is an extensive area of open grassland behind the cliff edges where visitors can stroll without feeling too crowded. The cliffs are largely unfenced and sheer, falling 534 ft at their highest point to a rocky foreshore. This is not the place for sufferers from vertigo.

The South Downs Way begins at Eastbourne with a choice of routes, one of which is over Beachy Head. The modern lighthouse at the base of the cliffs is said to throw its light 16 miles into the Channel. After passing the old granite lighthouse, built in 1831 and also named Belle Tout, the South Downs Way heads past the eight cliffs which form the so-called Seven Sisters and down to sea level at Birling Gap.

Sea-lavender, knapweed and wild carrot grow right up to the cliff edges on Beachy Head and the area has some rare chalk-loving plants like the burnt orchid. This is an excellent place for finding a variety of orchids throughout the summer.

In spring Beachy Head is on the migration route of returning summer birds like warblers and swallows. Below the cliffs, terns and ringed plover nest while gulls and jackdaws practice aerobatics on the breeze for much of the year – the breeze which so attracted Richard Jefferies when he lived in the area. 'Windswept and washed with air' he said of Beachy Head, and that perfectly describes it today, a century later.

*BEACHY HEAD Wild carrot and knapweed clothe the cliff tops.*

| A | | B | | | | | | | | | |
|---|---|---|---|---|---|---|---|---|---|---|---|
| Abbey Head | NX 7443 | Babbacombe Bay | SX 9366 | Bay of Quendale | HY 3712 | Blakeney Point | TF 9946 | Brough Head | ND 3763 | Cape Wrath | NC 2574 |
| Aberdaron Bay | SH 1725 | Badcall Bay | NC 1641 | Bay of Skail | HY 2319 | Blue Anchor Bay | ST 0144 | Brough Head | HY 2328 | Carleon Cove | SW 7215 |
| Aberffraw Bay | SH 3567 | Badentarbat Bay | NC 0108 | Beachley Point | ST 5490 | Blue Head | NH 8166 | Brough Ness | ND 4482 | Carlingheugh Bay | NO 6742 |
| Aberlady Bay | NT 4581 | Baggy Point | SS 4140 | Beachy Head | TV 5995 | Blue Point | NX 3902 | Brown Head | NR 8925 | Carlyon Bay | SX 0552 |
| Aire Point | SW 3528 | Bàgh nan Gunnaichean | NG 4573 | Beacon Cove | SW 8466 | Boddin Point | NO 7153 | Bruernish Point | NF 7300 | Carmel Head | SH 2993 |
| Aldeburgh Bay | TM 4755 | Balcary Point | NX 8249 | Beacon Point | NY 4445 | Bolt Head | SX 7236 | Buchan Ness | NK 1342 | Carn Gloose | SW 3531 |
| Allonby Bay | NY 0641 | Balephetrish Bay | NM 0047 | Beacon Point | NZ 3189 | Bolt Tail | SX 6639 | Buddon Ness | NO 5430 | Carn Naun Point | SW 4741 |
| Alness Bay | NH 6467 | Balgowan Point | NX 1242 | Beadnell Bay | NU 2327 | Bonne Nuit Bay | Jersey | Bude Bay | SS 1706 | Carradale Point | NR 8136 |
| Alness Point | NH 6567 | Ballantrae Bay | NX 0783 | Beer Head | SY 2287 | Booby's Bay | SW 8575 | Budle Bay | NU 1636 | Carreg Ddu | SH 2742 |
| Alnmouth Bay | NU 2510 | Ballard Point | SZ 0481 | Belcroute Bay | Jersey | Botallack Head | SW 3633 | Bull Bay | SH 4394 | Carregwastad Point | SM 9240 |
| Alturlie Point | NH 7149 | Balnakeil Bay | NC 3869 | Belhaven Bay | NT 6579 | Botany Bay | TR 3971 | Bull Point | SS 4646 | |  |
| Alum Bay | SZ 3085 | Banff Bay | NJ 6964 | Belle Greve Bay | Guernsey | Bouley Bay | Jersey | Burghhead Bay | NJ 0867 | Carsaig Bay | NR 7387 |
| Angle Bay | SM 8802 | Barafundle Bay | SR 9995 | Belle Hougue Point | Jersey | Bovisand Bay | SX 4850 | Burrow Head | NX 4534 | Castle Point | NU 1441 |
| Annat Bay | NH 0397 | Bard Head | HU 5135 | Bellochantry Bay | NR 6532 | Bow Head | HY 4552 | Butt of Lewis | NB 5166 | Caswell Bay | SS 5987 |
| Anstey's Cove | SX 9364 | Barmouth Bay | SH 5914 | Belvoir Bay | Herm | Bowleaze Cove | SY 7081 | | | Cawsand Bay | SX 4450 |
| Anvil Point | SZ 0276 | Barns Ness | NT 7277 | Benacre Ness | TM 5384 | Boyndie Bay | NJ 6765 | | | Cayton Bay | TA 0684 |
| Ardlamont Point | NR 9963 | Barnstaple or Bideford Bay | SS 4133 | Bennan Head | NR 9920 | Bracelet Bay | SS 6387 | C | | Cellar Head | NB 5656 |
| Ardmore Point | NR 4750 | Barrisdale Bay | NG 8605 | Bennane Head | NX 0986 | Bracklesham Bay | SZ 8095 | Caerbwdi Bay | SM 7624 | Cemaes Bay | SH 3694 |
| Ardmore Point | NM 4759 | Barsalloch Point | NX 3441 | Berry Head | SX 9456 | Bradda Head | SC 1869 | Caerfai Bay | SM 7524 | Cemaes Head | SN 1350 |
| Ardmore Point | NG 2159 | Basset's Cove | SW 6344 | Berryl's Point | SW 8467 | Brancaster Bay | TF 7646 | Cailleach Head | NG 9898 | Chanonry Point | NH 7455 |
| Ardmore Point | NC 7766 | Bat's Head | SY 7980 | Bervie Bay | NO 8372 | Brandy Cove | SS 5887 | Cailliness Point | NX 1535 | Chapel Point | SX 0243 |
| Ardmucknish Bay | NM 8937 | Battery Point | ST 4677 | Bigbury Bay | SX 6343 | Breaksea Point | ST 0265 | Cairn Head | NX 4838 | Chapel Point | TF 5673 |
| Ardnacross Bay | NR 7724 | Baulk Head | SW 6522 | Bill of Portland | SY 6768 | Brean Down | ST 2859 | Cairnbulg Point | NK 0365 | Chapel Point | NT 7475 |
| Ardnave Point | NR 2974 | Bay of Cruden | NK 0934 | Binnel Bay | SZ 5175 | Bridgwater Bay | ST 2648 | Calgary Bay | NM 3751 | Chapel Porth | SW 6949 |
| Ardscalpsie Point | NS 0457 | Bay of Holland | HY 6422 | Binnol Point | SZ 5275 | Bridlington Bay | TA 2065 | Calgary Point | NM 1052 | Chichester Harbour | SU 7500 |
| Ardvachar Point | NF 7446 | Bay of Laig | NM 4688 | Black Head | SW 0347 | Briga Head | ND 1875 | Caliach Point | NM 3454 | Chicken Head | NB 4929 |
| Armadale Bay | NC 7965 | Bay of Lopness | HY 7443 | Black Head | SW 7716 | Brighouse Bay | NX 6345 | Cambeak | SX 1296 | Christchurch Bay | SZ 2191 |
| Atherfield Point | SZ 4579 | Bay of Pierowall | HY 4448 | Black Head | NW 9856 | Brighstone bay | SZ 4280 | Cambuscurrie Bay | NH 7285 | Church Bay | SH 2989 |
| Auchencairn Bay | NX 8151 | | | Black Nore | ST 4476 | Brims Ness | ND 0471 | Cammachmore Bay | NO 9295 | Church Cove | SW 6620 |
| Auliston Point | NM 5458 | | | Blackstone Point | SS 6048 | Broadford Bay | NG 6523 | Cape Cornwall | SW 3531 | | |
| | | | | | | Brodick Bay | NS 0136 | | | | |

## Dungeness

No one would claim that this is a place of conventional beauty, but it attracts visitors by the thousand each year. Perhaps some arrive to study the great blocks of the 'A' and 'B' nuclear power stations; the lighthouses, the desolate shingle beach; even the MOD firing ranges. But the most numerous visitors are the migrating birds for which Dungeness is world famous, and the humans who come to the RSPB's bird reserve to study them.

Dungeness in winter months has to be one of the least hospitable parts of all Britain's coastline. Fierce, spray-laden winds drive over the surface of the dripping shingle, turning instantly to cutting rain and snow. Or the wind drops and the cold, heavy, blanket of fog, which makes this an area of great danger to shipping, comes almost instantly to obliterate everyting but a few feet of featureless stones, dotted with sad jetsam.

The plant life of the shingle is restricted although it does have a good lichen flora: several species have adopted a prostrate form in order to survive. Between May and June a rarity yellow flowering Nottingham catchfly, can sometimes be found on the shingle.

The buildings are functional: the power stations, a few habitations, mostly made from railway carriages, and the modern lighthouse, with some aesthetic appeal.

The birds love it all: the lighthouse for the guidance it gives them; the gravel pits, gorse and bramble for shelter; the warm sea water flowing round the power stations. In autumn and spring the migrants use Dungeness as a landmark and in winter great numbers rest and recover within the reserve or offshore.

In autumn, as swifts and swallows depart, the winter hordes of starlings, redwings, and fieldfares arrive. During winter several birds of prey appear – rough-legged buzzards and hen harriers amongst them – and ducks gather in large numbers on the lakes. The spring is the

*BIRLING GAP, just along the coast from Beachy Head, used to be a favourite landing site for smugglers. Nearby are the Seven Sisters Cliffs.*

time of greatest excitement as all the familiar summer migrants begin to return. In their numbers will be some who are merely pausing on our shores as they return to other countries – birds like bluethroats and insects such as the clouded yellow butterfly which stubbornly refuses to colonise Britain in other than very small numbers and never survives the winter.

Some bird species, including magpies, crows and pigeons, have made their home at Dungeness, adapting their normal habitats to suit the area. Common gulls, little terns and black redstarts (on the 'cliffs' of the power station) all nest here in small numbers.

This is the largest expanse of shingle beach in Britain, possibly in Europe: flat, bleak and at first sight unwelcoming, with a few concrete roads leading to it. But for naturalists, like birds, it is a magnet, and always fascinating.

## Lizard Point

This comparatively low, broad, grass-topped peninsula jutting into the English Channel, culminates in the most southerly point in England – the first sight of land for many returning seamen. The beam of its lighthouse can be seen 21 miles away, and Cornwall's first lighthouse was built on this site in 1619 against strong opposition from the locals who foresaw an end to picking riches from wrecked ships.

It is said that it was from Pen Olver that the Spanish Armada was first sighted in 1588. More than three centuries later Marconi used the same cliff for experiments in radio transmissions, speaking to the Isle of

*POLPEOR COVE AND LIZARD POINT (left) Small coves and grass-topped cliffs are typical of the Lizard.*

*KYNANCE COVE (below) exposes the serpentine rocks of the Lizard. The rock was much prized for ornaments.*

Wight from Pen Olver a month before he achieved his historic radio contact with America. A mile west of Mullion village stands the memorial to his labours, built by the Marconi Company, and given to the National Trust in 1937.

The Trust owns over 1100 acres of the Lizard, including Kynance Cove, with its richly coloured serpentine cliffs and fantastically shaped rocks. Serpentine was used for making ornaments, highly polished to show its subtle tints and patterns to best advantage.

Wild flowers rare elsewhere in Britain are found at the Lizard: its climate is ideal for the Hottentot fig, and the Cornish heath grows better here than in other parts of the county. A Victorian naturalist claimed that wherever he chose to lay his hat on these flower-laden cliffs, it would cover twelve different plants, and there seems no reason to doubt this.

## Lleyn Peninsula

Some of the most westerly reaches of Wales – Dale, Marloes, St David's, Anglesey and the Lleyn – bear a strong resemblance to an Irish or Scottish landscape. Even more remarkable is the strong and abiding Celtic tradition of the people. They think in Welsh, they express themselves in Welsh, and they struggle, with the grave and innate courtesy of the true Celt, to speak the alien English tongue simply to accommodate the visitor to their beautiful land.

For the Lleyn *is* a separate land, particularly west of the A497. The roads here are narrow, they twist and turn, often between high hedges, and they frequently admit of no signposting – or none that the English will understand. One is reminded of the classic advice 'if I was going there, I wouldn't start from here'.

In that spirit, let us meander around the Lleyn which, although remote, has a fas-

cinating history. Eighteen hundred feet above sea level on Yr Eifl are the remarkably well preserved remains of Tre'r Ceiri, a five-acre fortified site of an Iron Age settlement containing some 150 stone walled houses. Possibly because of the extensive views, ensuring early warning of any potential attack, the settlement survived well into Roman times.

In the 19th century the delightful Porth Dinllaen was proposed as the major ferry port for Irish ferries. In the event, Holyhead was selected, leaving the little harbour unspoilt – but not before what is now the A497 had been built to Pwllheli.

One of the more unexpected of the National Trust's smaller manor houses is Plas-yn-Rhiw, basically Tudor but a charming mixture of styles, with a delightful small garden. It lies beneath Mynydd Rhiw and there is, from the garden, a stupendous view across the popular holiday beach of Porth Neigwl. Like the beach at Rhossili (below), Porth Neigwl Bay has a grimmer side – Hell's Mouth is its other name, acquired when sailing boats were regularly driven ashore here – but the view extends over Mynydd Cilan and into the vast sweep of Cardigan Bay.

Masked from Plas-yn-Rhiw is Porth Ysgo, quieter, but hardly less attractive than Neigwl. Not far along the coast is Aberdaron, a resort, but in a limited way, unlike Pwllheli. Aberdaron is just like a fishing village in the west of Ireland. North is Porth Oer, where the sand granules allegedly squeak when they are trodden on; called the 'whistling sands' they are attractive even without a whistle.

West of Aberdaron are a series of tiny roads, one of which leads (given fortunate map reading) to the Coastguard Lookout at Braich y Pwyll on Mynydd Mawr. From here, if good fortune continues, it is possible to see Bardsey Island against a setting sun and watch choughs playing on the evening breezes. This is a land of Celtic magic to which the most cynical Anglo-Saxon cannot fail to respond.

## Rhossili and Worms Head

A few yards from the car park at Rhossili it is possible to look over the great sweep of sandy beach which runs for three miles towards Burry Holms. In the opposite direction is the spectacular Worms Head; parallel with the beach is Rhossili Down and linking this almost unequalled 'package' of sea, sand and cliff are several paths including a nature trail. Here, no more than 16 miles from the centre of Swansea, is the chance to walk on beautiful beaches, explore ancient downland with historic connections, and visit an important national nature reserve – all in a day.

*Wurm* is 'dragon' in Old English and, from certain angles, this knife-edged, hump-backed ridge can look like a sea-monster straining to escape from the restraining influence of the Gower Peninsula. The path from the car park leads over the clifftop, drops down to the causeway (a route over rocks uncovered by the sea for about five hours at low tide) and continues on to the 200 ft high headland.

In summer it is possible to watch kittiwakes, fulmars, razorbills, guillemots and a few puffins nesting or flying off the sheer cliff faces. In winter look for the yellow-legged purple sandpiper among the turnstones. Large 'rafts' of common scoters can also be seen off Worms Head during the winter.

The beach in summer can look as delightful and innocent as the beaches of all our childhood imaginings. Only the stark black ribs of the *Helvetia*, clearly visible from the cliffs, or the remains of the *City of Bristol* nearer Burry Holms, point to a less idyllic mood.

The summit of whalebacked Rhossili Down, the Beacon, is also the highest point on the Gower at 632 ft. A major feature of the Downs is Sweyne's Howes, a Neolithic burial site of about 2500 BC. A Viking, 'Sweyne' is said to have given his name to Swansea.

From Rhossili village the paths offer alternatives of coast, country or a combination of both – part of Rhossili's continuing appeal to visitors. The Down, two miles of the beach and Worms Head are all owned by the National Trust.

*RHOSSILI DOWN AND WORMS HEAD at the far western tip of the Gower Peninsula.*

| Name | Ref |
|---|---|
| Mount's Bay | SW 5127 |
| Mull Head | HY 4955 |
| Mull of Kintyre | NR 5906 |
| Mumbles Head | SS 6387 |
| Munlochy Bay | NH 6752 |
| **N** | |
| Nare Head | SW 9136 |
| Nare Point | SW 8025 |
| Nash Point | SS 9168 |
| Navax Point | SW 5943 |
| Naze The | TM 2623 |
| Needles The | SZ 2984 |
| Needs Ore Point | SZ 4297 |
| Ness Cove | SX 9371 |
| Ness Head | ND 3866 |
| Ness of Duncansby | ND 3873 |
| Ness Point or North Cheek | NZ 9506 |
| Nettlestone Point | SZ 6291 |
| Newbiggin Bay | NZ 3187 |
| Newhall Point | NH 7067 |
| Newport Bay | SN 0340 |
| Newquay Bay | SW 8162 |
| Newton Point | SS 8376 |
| Newtown Bay | SZ 4192 |
| Newtrain Bay | SW 8875 |
| Niarbyl Bay | SC 2175 |
| Nigg Bay | NJ 9604 |

| Name | Ref |
|---|---|
| Nigg Bay | NH 7771 |
| Noirmont Point | Jersey |
| North Bay | TA 0489 |
| North Foreland | TR 4069 |
| North Haven | NK 1138 |
| North Sutor | NH 8168 |
| Noss Head | ND 3854 |
| Noup Head | HY 3950 |
| Noup The | HU 6318 |
| **O** | |
| Ockle Bay | NM 5571 |
| Oisgill Bay | NG 1349 |
| Old Peak or South Cheek | NZ 9702 |
| Old Town Bay | SV 9109 |
| Onchan Head | SC 4077 |
| Ord Point | ND 0617 |
| Orford Ness | TM 4549 |
| Otter Cove | SY 0479 |
| Oxwich Bay | SS 5186 |
| Oxwich Point | SS 5185 |
| **P** | |
| Padstow Bay | SW 9179 |
| Pagham Harbour | SZ 8796 |
| Palm Bay | TR 3771 |
| Park Head | SW 8470 |
| Peaked Tor Cove | SX 9262 |

| Name | Ref |
|---|---|
| Pease Bay | NT 7971 |
| Pegwell Bay | TR 3563 |
| Pelistry Bay | SV 9311 |
| Pen Olver | SW 7111 |
| Penarth Head | ST 1971 |
| Penberth Cove | SW 4022 |
| Pencarrow Head | SX 1550 |
| Pencarrow Point | SX 1397 |
| Pendeen Watch | SW 3735 |
| Pendennis Point | SW 8231 |
| Pendour Cove | SW 4439 |
| Pendower Coves | SW 3522 |
| Penhale Point | SW 7559 |
| Penhallic Point | SX 0487 |
| Peninnis Head | SV 9109 |
| Penlee Point | SW 4726 |
| Penlee Point | SX 4448 |
| Pennyhole Bay | TM 2526 |
| Pentire Point | SW 9280 |
| Pentire Point East | SW 7861 |
| Pentire Point West | SW 7761 |
| Pentle Bay | SV 9021 |
| Pen-ychain | SH 4335 |
| Perelle Bay | Guernsey |
| Peterhead Bay | NK 1345 |
| Pettycur Bay | NT 2585 |
| Pevensey Bay | TQ 6603 |
| Pezeries Point | Guernsey |
| Pine Haven | SW 9981 |
| Plat Rocque Point | Jersey |
| Pleinmont Point | Guernsey |

| Name | Ref |
|---|---|
| Plémont Point | Jersey |
| Point de la Moye | Guernsey |
| Point Lynas | SH 4793 |
| Point of Ardnamurchan | NM 4167 |
| Point of Ayr | SJ 1285 |
| Point of Ayre | NX 4605 |
| Point of Ayre | HY 5903 |
| Point of Fethaland | HU 3795 |
| Point of Knap | NR 6972 |
| Point of Sleat | NG 5699 |
| Point of Stoer | NC 0235 |
| Point Robert | Sark |
| Poldhu Cove | SW 6619 |
| Polliwilline Bay | NR 7409 |
| Polpeor Cove | SW 6911 |
| Polpry Cove | SW 3529 |
| Polridmouth | SX 1050 |
| Polurrian Cove | SW 6618 |
| Poole Bay | SZ 0887 |
| Popton Point | SM 8903 |
| Pordenack Point | SW 3424 |
| Porlock Bay | SS 8748 |
| Port Cornaa | SC 4787 |
| Port Eynon Point | SS 4784 |
| Port Isaac Bay | SX 0082 |
| Port Mooar | SC 4890 |
| Port Quin Bay | SW 9580 |
| Port Soderick | SC 3472 |
| Portelet Bay | Guernsey |
| Portelet Bay | Jersey |

| Name | Ref |
|---|---|
| Porth Ceiriad | SH 3124 |
| Porth Conger | SV 8808 |
| Porth Cressa | SV 9009 |
| Porth Curno | SW 3822 |
| Porth Dinllaen | SH 2841 |
| Porth Eilean | SH 4793 |
| Porth Hellick Point | SV 9210 |
| Porth Iago | SH 1631 |
| Porth Joke | SW 7760 |
| Porth Loe | SW 3621 |
| Porth Mear | SW 8471 |
| Porth Morran | SV 9217 |
| Porth Nanven | SW 3530 |
| Porth Nefyn | SH 2940 |
| Porth Neigwl | SH 2626 |
| Porth Penrhyn Mawr | SH 2883 |
| Porth Trecastell | SH 3370 |
| Porth Tywyn Mawr | SH 2885 |
| Porth Wen | SH 4094 |
| Porth y Nant | SH 3444 |
| Porth Ychen | SH 2036 |
| Porth Ysgaden | SH 2137 |
| Porth Ysgo | SH 2620 |
| Portheras Cove | SW 3835 |
| Porthluney Cove | SW 9741 |
| Porthmellin Head | SW 8632 |
| Porthor | SH 1630 |
| Porthstinian | SM 7224 |
| Portland Harbour | SY 6876 |
| Portling Bay | NX 8854 |

| Name | Ref |
|---|---|
| Portsmouth Harbour | SU 6202 |
| Prawle Point | SX 7735 |
| Predannack Head | SW 6816 |
| Priest's Cove | SW 3531 |
| Proth Clais | SM 7423 |
| Prussia Cove | SW 5628 |
| Pwllderi | SM 8838 |
| Pwllddu Bay | SS 5786 |
| Pwllddu Head | SS 5786 |
| **Q** | |
| Quarry Head | NJ 9065 |
| Quinish Point | NM 4057 |
| **R** | |
| Rame Head | SX 4148 |
| Rams Ness | HU 6087 |
| Ramsey Bay | SC 4695 |
| Rattray Head | NK 1057 |
| Readymoney Cove | SX 1151 |
| Red Head | NO 7047 |
| Red Point | NC 9365 |
| Red Wharf Bay | SH 5481 |
| Redhythe Point | NJ 5767 |
| Reed Point | NT 7772 |
| Reeth Bay | SZ 5075 |
| Renish Point | NG 0481 |
| Rerwick Head | HY 5411 |

## Sandwood Bay

Only a little south of Cape Wrath, Sandwood Bay is by far the most remote of the bays and headlands featured here. Remote not just by reason of its position in the far north of Scotland but because it is about four miles from the nearest road. The path, from Blairmore, should be tackled wearing sturdy shoes, for the route, through boggy land, can be both rough and wet. The effort will be justified; this is, by any criteria, one of the most beautiful bays in Scotland, if not the whole of Britain.

From the freshwater loch, a stream runs through the marram-clad dunes (avoid the small quicksands), picking its way past rocks rich in semi-precious stones. The colours of the sea are incredibly deep – greens, blues and whites – and the waves are capable of changing in moments, rolling gently and distantly in over sand tinged with pink, or pouring up the beach, stretching out for the dunes, snarling and pounding angrily around the red Torridon rocks. At the south of the bay there is a stack, Am Buachaille ('the herdsman') – perfectly named, gathering in the waves at the end of their thousands of miles of freedom.

There is a haunting quality about Sandwood Bay, perhaps because such beauty is observed by so few – although legend has it that this is a place known to mermaids.

*SANDWOOD BAY This remote bay in north Scotland is about four miles from a road. The stack, Am Buachaille, can be seen in the distance.*

*ST ABB'S HEAD, on Scotland's eastern coast, is an important site for sea birds. Many flowers and butterflies are also found in the area.*

## St Abb's Head

It would be difficult to imagine two sites as different as Dungeness (page 55) and St Abb's, but wryneck and bluethroat are examples of species which have been recorded at both places in recent years. The birds of St Abb's are mainly sea birds, breeding in their thousands on the highest cliffs on the east coast of Scotland, secure from man and other predators.

Each year, more than 170 species are recorded around the headland, with 15,000 pairs of kittiwakes alone. St Abb's is now a national nature reserve, jointly managed by the Scottish Wildlife Trust and the National Trust for Scotland, which owns much of the headland. In addition, the offshore waters, which support two rarities – leopard-spotted goby and cup coral – have been declared part of a volun-

| | | | | | | | | | | |
|---|---|---|---|---|---|---|---|---|---|---|
| Rest Bay | SS 7978 | Rubha Fàsachd | NM 1652 | Runswick Bay | NZ 8115 | St. John's Head | HY 1803 | Sauchar Point | NT 4999 | Sorel Point | Jersey |
| Rhoscolyn Head | SH 2674 | Rubha Hunish | NG 4076 | Rushy Bay | SV 8713 | St. Lawrence Bay | TL 9605 | Scabbacombe | SX 9251 | Sotherness Point | NX 9754 |
| Rhossili Bay | SS 4090 | Rubha Mór | NM 2464 | Rye Bay | TQ 9517 | St. Magnus Bay | HU 1570 | Head | | Souter Head | NJ 9601 |
| Rickets Head | SM 8518 | Rubha na Faing | NR 1553 | | | St. Margaret's Bay | TR 3744 | Scapa Bay | HY 4307 | Souter Point | NZ 4162 |
| Ringstead Bay | SY 7581 | Rubha na Faing | NM 6477 | | | St. Martin's Point | Guernsey | Schooner Point | NM 3098 | South Bay | TA 0487 |
| Rinns Point | NR 1751 | Moire | | **S** | | St. Mary's Bay | SX 9355 | Sconce Point | SZ 3389 | South Foreland | TR 3643 |
| Rinsey Head | SW 5826 | Rubha na Fearn | NG 7261 | St. Abb's Head | NT 9169 | St. Mary's Well | ST 1767 | Scope Head | HU 5145 | South Head | ND 3749 |
| Robin Hood's Bay | NZ 9504 | Rubha na h-Aiseig | NG 4476 | St. Agnes Head | SW 6951 | Bay | | Scotstown Head | NK 1151 | South Nesting Bay | HU 4956 |
| Rockham Bay | SS 4546 | Rubha na | NG 5311 | St. Alkhelm's or | SY 9675 | St. Mildred's Bay | TR 3270 | Scourie Bay | NC 1445 | Southward Well | SV 8812 |
| Rocquaine bay | Guernsey | h'Easgainne | | St. Alban's Head | | St. Ouen's Bay | Jersey | Scurdie Ness | NO 7356 | Point | |
| Ronachan Point | NR 7455 | Rubha na | NM 4027 | St. Andrews Bay | NO 5318 | St. Tudwal's Road | SH 3328 | Scurrival Point | NF 6909 | Spear Head | ND 0971 |
| Ronez Point | Jersey | h-Uamha | | St. Ann's Head | SM 8002 | Sacquoy Head | HY 3835 | Seaford Bay | TV 4798 | Spey Bay | NJ 3866 |
| Rora Head | ND 1799 | )Rubha na' Leac | NG 5938 | St. Anthony Head | SW 8431 | Saint's Bay | Guernsey | Sealky Head | ND 3852 | Spur Ness | HY 6032 |
| Rosemullion Head | SW 7927 | Rubha na Ridire | NM 7340 | St. Aubin's Bay | Jersey | Sales Point | TM 0209 | Selker Bay | SD 0788 | Spurn Head | TA 3910 |
| Ross Bay | NX 6544 | Rubha na Stròine | NM 3642 | St. Audrie's Bay | ST 1043 | Saligo Bay | NR 2066 | Selsey Bill | SZ 8592 | Stackhouse Cove | SW 5428 |
| Rossall Point | SD 3147 | Rubha na Traille | NR 5162 | St. Austell Bay | SX 0650 | Saline Bay | Guernsey | Selwicks Bay | TA 2570 | Stackpole Head | SR 9994 |
| Royal Bay of | Jersey | Rubha nam | NM 3690 | St. Bees Head | NX 9413 | Saltom Bay | NX 9515 | Shandwich Bay | NH 8674 | Staffin Bay | NG 4869 |
| Grouville | | Mierleach | | St. Brelade's Bay | Jersey | Saltwick Bay | NZ 9110 | Sharkham Point | SX 9354 | Stanger Head | HY 5142 |
| Rozel Bay | Jersey | Rubha nan Ceare | NM 3125 | St. Brides Bay | SM 8118 | Sand Bay | ST 3264 | Shell Ness | TR 0567 | Stansore Point | SZ 4698 |
| Rubh' a' Chaoil | NM 3346 | Rubha nan Clach | NG 3033 | St. Brides Haven | SM 8011 | Sand Point | ST 3165 | Shian Bay | NR 5287 | Starehole Bay | SX 7236 |
| Rubh' an Dunain | NG 3816 | Rubha nan Leacan | NR 3140 | St. Catharine's | NK 0428 | Sandaig Bay | NG 7101 | Shipload Bay | SS 2427 | Start Bay | SX 8442 |
| Rubh' Ardalanish | NM 3516 | Rubha nan Maol | NM 3316 | Dub | | Sandend Bay | NJ 5566 | Shoebury Ness | TQ 9383 | Start Point | SX 0485 |
| Rubh' Arisaig | NM 6184 | Móra | | St. Catherine's | Jersey | Sandford Bay | NK 1243 | Siccar Point | NT 8170 | Start Point | SX 8237 |
| Rubha' a' Geodha | NR 4399 | Rubha Port na | NM 4298 | Bay | | Sandown Bay | SZ 6183 | Silversands Bay | NT 2085 | Start Point | HY 7843 |
| Rubha a' Mhail | NR 4279 | Caranean | | St. Catherine's | SZ 4975 | Sandside bay | NC 9665 | Sinclair's Bay | ND 3656 | Stattic Point | NG 9796 |
| Rubha Aird | NM 5772 | Rubha Reidh | NG 7391 | Point | | Sandwich Bay | TR 3759 | Skatie Shore | NO 8987 | Steeple Point | SS 1911 |
| Druimnich | | Rubha Shamhnan | NG 3704 | St. Clement's Bay | Jersey | Sandwood Bay | NC 2165 | Skelda Ness | HU 3040 | Stepper Point | SW 9178 |
| Rubha Bhiosd | NL 9648 | Insir | | St. David's Head | SM 7228 | Sandy Bay | SY 0379 | Sker Point | SS 7879 | Stert Point | ST 2847 |
| Rubha Chraiginis | NL 9245 | Rubha Suisnish | NG 5815 | St. Govan's Head | SR 9792 | Sandy Bay | SS 8276 | Skipness Point | NR 9157 | Stokes Bay | SZ 5898 |
| Rubha Dubh | NR 3991 | Rue Point | NX 4003 | St. Ives Bay | SW 5540 | Sanna Bay | NM 4368 | Soar Mill Cove | SX 6937 | Stonehaven Bay | NO 8786 |
| Rubha Dubh | NM 0948 | Rumps Point | SW 9381 | St. Ives Head | SW 5241 | Santon Head | SC 3370 | Sole Bay | TM 5176 | Strandburg Ness | HU 6792 |

tary marine nature reserve, Scotland's first. Action is now under way to create several national marine reserves, starting with Lundy (page 62), and including St Abb's.

The natural delights of St Abb's may be enjoyed by following a trail laid out around the reserve. The walk is easy, and can be completed in about 1½ hours. The main car park is off the B6438, and there is a smaller car park, near the lighthouse, for elderly or disabled people.

St Abb's village was only founded in 1832, but it takes its name from a daughter of the royal house of Northumbria, who founded a convent on Kirk Hill in the 7th century. A few mounds mark the remains. The lighthouse on the cliffs stands on a single-storey building – the height of the cliffs is sufficient without the need for a tower. Mire Loch was created in 1900 when a stream was dammed, and several common water birds, including ducks, grebes, and moorhens – joined in winter by goldeneye and teal – have established themselves on it.

The rocks which form St Abb's Head are volcanic. Unlike the grey, sedimentary rock on either side, they fall sheer to the sea, an advantage for breeding species like razorbills and guillemots, which prefer a straight drop into the sea for their young.

Because of this, St Abb's is a nationally important site for ledge-breeding species, but it attracts many waders, including purple sandpipers who feed along the rocky coast just north of the village. At Kirk Hill, wheatears have taken over rabbit burrows, while gannets can be seen from St Abb's Headland, passing to and from the Bass Rock.

Part of the attraction of St Abb's is the delightful plant life it supports. Because some parts have never been grazed and others are unimproved grassland, there is a fine variety of plants in the area. Thrift, sea-campion, Scots lovage and roseroot thrive in those areas which have avoided man's efforts, tormentil and heath bed-straw grow in the turf of the acid soils, with rockrose and wild thyme on the alkaline slopes away from the cliffs. The localised northern brown argus breeds here, as do many more common species of butterfly.

## St David's Head

It is necessary to leave the car at Whitesand Bay before exploring St David's Head on foot. Whitesand is one of those great sandy bays beloved of surfers who can be watched, in summer, sweeping in with the waves. For most of the year there is more fun watching sanderling skittering in and out ahead of the waves and the occasional red-legged chough performing aerobatics towards St David's Head.

This is an historic area with a whole host of reminders of the distant past. Just north of the bay is the site of St Patrick's Chapel, from where the saint is said to have departed for Ireland. Within each of the fields in the stone-walled outlines of an Iron Age field system there is a large rock, seeming to act as a marker. On the headland is a fortification called the Warrior's Dyke, while a burial chamber with a 13 ft long capstone is a reminder of Neolithic times.

St David's Head is renowned for both its views and its sunsets. Carnllidi, the highest point at 600 ft, is an ideal place from which to watch the sun go down behind the group of small islands called the Bishops and Clerks. Nearer at hand is Ramsey Island, home of the 6th-century Saint Justinian. He it was who allegedly severed Ramsey from the mainland with one mighty blow of an axe. Sea birds have taken advantage of the seclusion of the island to take over its steep cliffs, while seals play round visiting boats.

*ST DAVID'S HEAD, with its cliffs and large sandy bays, is well known for spectacular sunsets.*

| | | | | | | | | | | | |
|---|---|---|---|---|---|---|---|---|---|---|---|
| Strathy Point | NC 8269 | Tor Bay | SX 9160 | **W** | | Woodspring Bay | ST 3566 | Worms Head | SS 3887 | **Z** | |
| Strom Ness | HY 7651 | Torness Point | NT 7475 | Warden Point | TQ 0272 | Woody Bay | SS 6749 | Wringcliff Bay | SS 7049 | Zennor Head | SW 4439 |
| Strumble Head | SM 8942 | Torrisdale Bay | NC 6862 | Wash The | TF 53 | Worbarrow Bay | SY 8680 | Wyke The | TA 1082 | Zone Point | SW 8530 |
| Studland Bay | SZ 0482 | Towan Head | SW 7962 | Watch House | ST 0465 | Worbarrow Tout | SY 8679 | Wylfa Head | SH 3594 | | |
| Sumburgh Head | HY 4007 | Toward Point | NS 1367 | Point | | | | | | | |
| Summerhouse | SS 9966 | Tower Point | SM 7810 | Watergate Bay | SW 8365 | | | | | | |
| Point | | Traeth Bychan | SH 5184 | Wats Ness | HU 1750 | | | | | | |
| Sunderland Point | SD 4255 | Trecco Bay | SS 8376 | Welshmans Bay | SM 7904 | | | | | | |
| Sutors of Cromarty | NH 8166 | Trefusis Point | SW 8133 | Wembury Bay | SX 5147 | | | | | | |
| Swanage Bay | SZ 0379 | Trelong Bay | NO 8778 | Wembury Point | SX 5048 | | | | | | |
| Swansea Bay | SS 6589 | Treshnish Point | NM 3348 | West Angle Bay | SM 8403 | | | | | | |
| | | Trevase Head | SW 8576 | West Bay | SY 4690 | | | | | | |
| | | Trevaunance Cove | SW 7251 | West Point | SH 4252 | | | | | | |
| **T** | | Trevelgue Head | SW 8263 | Westdale Bay | SM 7905 | | | | | | |
| Talisker Bay | NG 3130 | Trevellas Porth | SW 7252 | Westgate Bay | TR 3170 | | | | | | |
| Talland Bay | SX 2251 | Trewavas Head | SW 5926 | Weston Bay | ST 3060 | | | | | | |
| Tang Head | ND 3560 | Troup Head | NJ 8267 | Weymouth Bay | SY 6979 | | | | | | |
| Tarbat Ness | NH 9487 | Turnberry Bay | NS 1906 | White Ness | TR 3971 | | | | | | |
| Tees Bay | NZ 5528 | | | Whiten Head | NC 5068 | | | | | | |
| Thirl The | ND 1872 | | | Whiteness Head | NH 8058 | | | | | | |
| Thorness Bay | SZ 4694 | **U** | | Whitesand Bay | SW 3527 | | | | | | |
| Thornwick Bay | TA 2372 | Udale Bay | NH 7166 | Whitesand Bay | SM 7327 | | | | | | |
| Thorpe Ness | TM 4760 | | | Whiteshell Point | SS 5986 | | | | | | |
| Three cliff Bay | SS 5387 | | | Whitford Point | SS 4496 | | | | | | |
| Thurso Bay | ND 1169 | **V** | | Whiting Bay | NS 0526 | | | | | | |
| Tianavaig Bay | NG 5138 | Varley Head | SW 9881 | Whitmore Bay | ST 1166 | | | | | | |
| Tintagel Head | SX 0489 | Vaternish Point | NG 2367 | Whitsand Bay | SX 3851 | | | | | | |
| Tiumpan Head | NB 5737 | Vazon Bay | Guernsey | Whitstable Bay | TR 0866 | | | | | | |
| Todhead Point | NO 8776 | Vellan Head | SW 6614 | Wick Bay | ND 3750 | | | | | | |
| Toe Head | NF 9594 | Veryan Bay | SW 9739 | Wigtown Bay | NX 4555 | | | | | | |
| Tolsta Head | NB 5647 | Vig Bay | NG 3762 | Windbury Point | SS 3027 | | | | | | |

*FLAMBOROUGH HEAD on the east coast near Bridlington.*

# Islands

*An island for saints, a luxuriant northern garden and a pirate's base . . . islands have been places of shelter for centuries, and they still are. Birds feature prominently – on Handa, Havergate and Skomer. On the Farnes the birds co-exist with seals, and on Lundy, with people – weather permitting.*

## Farne Islands

At low water there are 28 islands, reduced to 15 at high tide. The Farnes are part of the Whin Sill, a formation of 100 ft-thick dolerite rock that stretches from High Force on the River Tees, through the counties of Durham and Northumberland, until it reaches the coast at the vertical cliff of Cullernose Point and extends out into the North Sea.

Some of the islands are tall 'stack' cliffs – seabird sanctuaries such as the Pinnacle's and The Stack. Others are barely above the surface of the waves, and yet more lie largely beneath the water, emerging only at low tide.

One of the largest islands, and that closest to the mainland is the Inner Farne, where the two Northumbrian saints, Aidan and Cuthbert, lived at different times in the 7th century. Aidan, when Bishop of nearby Holy Island, used the island solely as a retreat for prayer and meditation, but Cuthbert lived there for 12 years, and was responsible for the protection of the charming eider ducks, still known as St Cuthbert's chicks. On the Inner Farne, visitors can see the ruins of two medieval chapels and an early 16th-century pele tower, said to house 'St Cuthbert's Well'.

The Inner Farne has a lighthouse, but the most famous light in this group of islands must be the Longstone, where Grace Darling and her family lived. She died of consumption only four years after her dramatic rescue, with her father, of survivors of the wrecked *Forfarshire*.

Today, the Farne Islands are in the care of the National Trust, and in the breeding season there is necessarily restricted access. Eighteen species of seabird live here – as well as the eider there are cormorants, shags, oystercatchers, puffins, four species of tern, guillemots and fulmars. Grey seals have greatly increased here in recent years, and present a problem in that they threaten the fragile soil cap of some of the lower islands. Rabbit colonies survive on certain of the islands, a relic of the days when the lighthouse keepers kept rabbits as food.

*LINDISFARNE CASTLE, ON HOLY ISLAND, was built as a harbour defence in the 16th century.*

## Gigha Island

In not much more than 40 years, the garden at Achamore on Gigha has become one of the finest and best known in Britain, and among Gigha's other delights is its quiet air of peace and prosperity. Almost certainly one of the earliest of the islands to be colonised, Gigha has the same fertile soil as nearby Kintyre, and has never suffered from depopulation.

Formed of a ridge of epidiorite bordered by sandy loam, it can be viewed in its entirety by climbing Creag Bhan, the highest point at 331 ft. Much of the uncultivated area of Gigha is pretty rough and

| A | | B | | | | C | | | | | |
|---|---|---|---|---|---|---|---|---|---|---|---|
| A' Chleit | NC 0220 | Bac Beag | NM 2337 | Black Islands | NF 7202 | **C** | | Carn Iar | NB 9602 | Corr Eilean | NR 6775 |
| A' Chuli | NM 6511 | (Treshnish Isles) | | Boreray | NA 1505 | Càiream | NG 1690 | Carna | NM 6258 | Corregan | SV 8405 |
| (Garvellachs) | | Bach Island | NM 7726 | Boreray (North | NF 8581 | Cairn na Burgh | NM 3044 | Carradale Point | NR 8136 | Craigean | NB 1632 |
| Ailsa Craig | NX 0199 | Baker's Island | SU 6903 | Uist) | | Beag (Treshnish Isles) | | Carrey Rhoson | SM 6625 | Craiglerth | NT 5587 |
| Aird Orasay | NB 1331 | Baleshare | NF 7860 | Bottle Island | NB 9501 | Cairn na Burgh | NM 3044 | Carsaig Island | NR 7389 | Cramand Island | NT 1978 |
| Alderney | | Balhepburn Island | NO 1720 | Bound Skerry (Out | HU 7071 | Mor (Treshnish Isles) | | Carter's or Gull Rocks | SW 7559 | Craro Island | NR 6247 |
| Am Balg | NC 1866 | Balta | HP 6608 | Skerries) | | Càrn nan Sgeir | NC 0101 | Causamul | NF 6670 | Creag Island | NM 8337 |
| Am Fraoch Eilean | NR 4662 | Bardsey Island | SH 1121 | Boursa Island | NC 8067 | Calavey | NF 8654 | Cava | ND 3299 | Crowlin Islands | NG 6934 |
| Am Fraoch-eilean | NM 6783 | (Ynys Enlli) | | Brechon | | Calbha Beag | NC 1536 | Ceann (Monach | NF 6162 | Cùl Campay | NB 1443 |
| An Garbh eilean | NM 6783 | Barlocco Isle | NX 5748 | Bressay | HU 5040 | Calbha Mór | NC 1636 | Islands) | | Cùl Eilean | NC 1233 |
| An Garbh-eilean | NG 8036 | Barra | NF 60 | Bridgemarsh | TQ 8996 | Caldey Island | SS 1396 | Ceannamhór | NC 1439 | | |
| An Garbh-eilean | NC 3373 | Bass Rock | NT 6087 | Island | | Calf of Eday | HY 5839 | Ceann Ear | NF 6462 | | |
| An Glas-eilean | NM 6376 | Bearasay | NB 1242 | Brisons The | SW 3431 | Calf of Flotta | ND 3896 | (Monach Islands) | | **D** | |
| An Glas-eilean | NM 6682 | Belnahna | NM 7112 | Brosdale Island | NR 4962 | Calf of Man | SC 1565 | Cheynies | HU 3438 | Daaey | HU 6094 |
| Anglesey (Yns | SH 47 | Benbecula | NF 85 | Brother Isle | HU 4281 | Calvary (Loch | NF 7728 | Cindery Island | TM 0915 | Damsay | HY 3913 |
| Môn) | | Bernera Island | NM 7939 | Brough Head | HY 2328 | Eynort) | | Clett | NG 2258 | Darnet Fort | TQ 8070 |
| Annet | SV 8608 | (Lismore) | | Brownsea Island | SZ 0287 | Calvay (Loch | NF 8117 | Cliasay Beg | NF 9270 | Daufraich | SM 6623 |
| Ardminish Point | NR 6649 | Berneray | NF 9181 | Brownsman | NU 2337 | Boisdale) | | Cliasay More | NF 9370 | Deadmans Island | TQ 8972 |
| Ardwall Island | NX 5749 | Bhatarsaidh | NB 4023 | Bruray (Out | HU 6972 | Calvay (Sound of | NF 8012 | Cliatasay | NB 1333 | Deasker | NF 6466 |
| Arran, Island of | NR 91 | (Barkin Isles) | | Skerries) | | Eriskay) | | Cobmarsh Island | TM 0012 | Denny Island | ST 4580 |
| | —NR 94 | Big Harcar | NU 2338 | Bruse Holm | HU 5263 | Calve Island | NM 5254 | Coiresa | NM 7400 | Direg | NF 8343 |
| Asparagus | SW 6813 | Big Scare | NX 2533 | Bryher | SV 8714 | Campay | NB 1442 | Coll, Isle of | NM 15 | Drake's Island | SX 4652 |
| Island | | Bigga | HU 4479 | Burgh Island | SX 6443 | Canna | NG 2405 | Colonsay | NR 3894 | Dubh Eilean | NR 3388 |
| Auskerry | HY 6716 | Bihdalein Island | NB 1741 | Burnt Islands | NS 0175 | Canvey Island | TQ 7883 | Colsay | HU 3618 | Dubh Sgeirean | NC 1754 |
| | | Birnbeck Island | ST 3062 | (Kyles of Bute) | | Cara Island | NR 6343 | Coomb Island | NC 6664 | Dubh Sgeir | NM 7625 |
| | | Biruaslum | NL 6096 | Burntwick Island | TQ 8572 | Carbh Eilean | NG 6153 | Copinsay | HY 6162 | Dùn-aarin | NG 0280 |
| | | Black Holm | HY 5902 | Burray | ND 4796 | Cardigan Island | SN 1551 | Coppay | NF 9393 | Dùn Chonnuill | NM 6812 |
| | | Black Islands | NG 7529 | Burry Holms | SS 3992 | Carminish Islands | NG 0185 | Coquet Island | NU 2904 | (Garvellachs) | |
| | | | | Burwick Holm | HU 3840 | Carn Deas | NB 9602 | Corn Holm | HY 5901 | | |
| | | | | Bute, Island of | NS 06 | | | | | | |

Creag Bhan is no exception. The views of the island, of Jura and Kintyre and, far away, of Ireland are worth the struggle.

Naturalists will make a visit to the north of the island, where the twin bays – West and East Tarbert – nip the land close to the road. Great Northern, black- and red-throated divers all occur in the waters off Gigha, the first two frequently, and it is sometimes possible to see them from the road, swimming in the bays.

In addition to the large colony of gulls on Eilean Garbh – connected to the island by a narrow strip of sand – there are cormorants, shags and guillemots. The pink rocks are splashed with yellow lichen – and white guano – while thrift adds its colour throughout the summer. Rabbits are the only land-based mammals but grey seals are usually to be seen playing around the shore or basking on rocks.

The long history of Gigha can be studied by exploring the ruins of St Catan's chapel and its surroundings. Around the 13th-century chapel are carved tombstones of 14th-century origin. With them are the graves of those who have lived and died here during more recent times. Nearby is an ogham stone, a standing stone inscribed with a form of gaelic 'shorthand', believed to commemorate an Irish warrior of some 15 centuries ago – an apt expression of continuity in this spot overlooking the Sound of Gigha.

Continuity of a different sort is being ensured at the Achamore Garden. Created as recently as 1945 by the late Sir James Horlick, it already has the appearance of a mature garden. This has been achieved by a combination of transplanting large plants from Sir James' existing garden in Ascot, and by the situation of the garden – warmed by the Gulf Stream, sheltered by the Gigha ridge – which admirably suit the rhododendrons and azaleas forming the nucleus of the garden. The inspired decision to give the collection – not the garden – to the National Trust for Scotland has meant that young plants can be raised here and transferred to other gardens of the Trust, lessening the risk of natural disaster.

## Handa Island

Handa has a remarkable history and an equally remarkable plant and bird life. Until the potato famine of 1848 several families lived here, surviving on a diet of potatoes, fish, and birds' eggs. As on St Kilda, they operated a daily 'parliament', where the men met on equal terms to decide the work load. For several centuries Handa was a burial ground for people from the mainland, supposedly as protection against scavenging wolves.

The rock formation of the mainland hereabouts is of Lewisian gneiss, but Handa is formed of an outcrop of Torridonian sandstone, the rock of Sandwood Bay (page 58), a few miles to the north. Handa, an RSPB reserve, is less than a mile from Tarbet, from which boats depart for the small white-sand beach on the island. The north and west of the island have 300 ft cliffs rising sheer from the sea in a series of horizontal layers – ideal for

*A STACK ON HANDA ISLAND This small island, off north-west Scotland, is famous for its bird life.*

ledge-nesting auks. An impressive feature is Great Stack – undercut by the action of the sea, it now rests on three pillars, and it is possible, in good weather, to sail under the Stack, usually watched by interested grey seals.

The interior of Handa is pasture, heather and bog with several lochans. There are a few scattered pine and alder trees, but it is the 216 plant and over 100 moss species which are of significance – those and the birds. Red-throated divers nest on the lochans, and the numbers of Arctic and Great skuas are increasing. Tens of thousands of guillemots, razorbills, fulmar and kittiwake nest on the cliffs, 'real' rock doves, the type from which the Trafalgar Square hybrids are descended, live in Handa's caves, and waders feed and breed on its beaches.

## Havergate Island

Like Handa, Havergate is an RSPB reserve, but it is totally dissimilar, geographically and physically. Almost all they have in common are shelduck.

A few hundred yards downstream from Orford, Havergate marks the point where the River Alde becomes the Ore, to the confusion of many. Lying behind the long, narrow strip of Orford beach, it is a fascinating combination of the work of nature and man. Orford beach has only been created in the last 500 years, and the levels of the many lagoons on the island are artificially controlled to provide the correct depth of water for different species of birds. The most famous of these is the avocet: persecuted for its eggs and feathers, it deserted Britain in the mid-19th century, returning to Havergate in 1947. It's interesting to speculate whether today the Society would be able to maintain the secrecy with which this exciting return was surrounded in the 1940s and 50s.

Within Havergate's 300 acres, large numbers of ducks and waders rest, feed and rear their young. Each of the rather

quaintly-named lagoons – one is named Cuckolds – has its own observation hide, and all are linked by clearly defined walkways. The deepest lagoon attracts goldeneye and red-breasted merganser, while the shallow lakes are home to both wintering and summer avocets. The overwintering of birds here is a comparatively new development – for some years avocets have spent the winter on the Tamar – which may be influencing the increasing numbers of breeding birds. Hen harriers, black- and bar-tailed godwits are regular winter visitors. Short-eared owls breed on Havergate as do several tern species.

## Lundy

This small, isolated granite island, just three miles long and half a mile across at its widest point, has been inhabited since prehistoric times. After the Norman Conquest the island was owned by the Norman Marisco family until the 13th century, and the ruins of their castle remain today. Pirates used it as a headquarters in Elizabethan times, and one owner in the 18th century, an MP, used convicts meant for Australia to build his roads and walls.

Sika deer, Lundy ponies – now a recognised breed – and Soay sheep were introduced by Martin Coles Harman who bought Lundy in 1925. When, a few years later, the Post Office withdrew its services from the island, Harman produced his own stamps which are still in use today. The earlier issues are much sought-after by collectors. The National Trust acquired Lundy in 1968.

Lundy is Norse for 'puffin isle', and although there are few puffins now, many other seabirds nest in great numbers on the steep cliffs. Ravens and peregrine falcons are resident on the island, but a most exciting development is in the decision to establish Britain's first marine nature reserve around the island. In these relatively warm waters sea anemones and corals flourish along with other marine life usually associated with warmer climates.

Ships make the journey to Lundy several times a week; but landing is often impossible, as gales and rough seas can spring up so quickly in the uncertain waters of the Bristol Channel.

*THE ISLE OF RHUM, as it can be seen from the Bay of Laig on Eigg.*

## Rhum

Like most other part of the Highlands and Islands, the 'Small Islands' – Canna, Rhum, Eigg and Muck – suffered appallingly in the Clearances. The history of Rhum followed a depressingly familiar pattern for much of the last two centuries but here, at least, there is a happy ending.

| | | | | | | | | | | | |
|---|---|---|---|---|---|---|---|---|---|---|---|
| Eilean Mhic Mhaolmhoire | NR 4548 | Eilean Mór (*Jura*) | NM 6701 | Eilean na Saille | NC 1753 | Eilean nan Gobhar | NM 6979 | Eilean Shona | NM 6573 | **F** | |
| | | Eilean Mór Laxey | NB 3320 | Eilean nam Bairneach | NM 7279 | Eilean nan Gobhar Mór | NG 7631 | Eilean Thinngarstaig | NB 2702 | Faihore | NF 9367 |
| Eilean Mhie Chiarain | NM 7211 | Eilean Mór (*Loch Boisdale*) | NF 7718 | Eilean nam Beathach | NM 7820 | Eilean nan Leoc | NR 6875 | Eilean Thòraidh | NB 4220 | Fair Isle | HZ 2071 |
| Eilean Mhogh-Sgeir | NG 9007 | Eilean Mor (*Lochbuie*) | NM 6124 | Eilean nam Fearnnag | NB 1433 | Eilean nan Ron | NR 3386 | Eilean Tigh | NG 6053 | Fara | ND 3295 |
| Eilean Mhugaig | NR 3589 | Eilean Mór (*Loch Fyne*) | NR 8883 | Eilean nam Freumha | NM 7820 | Eilean Nan Ron | NC 6365 | Eilean Tighe (*Flannan Isles*) | NA 7246 | Faray | HY 5336 |
| Eilean Mhuire (*Shaint Islands*) | NG 4398 | Eilean Mor (*Loch Sunart*) | NM 7560 | Eilean nam Gamhna | NM 8130 | Eilean nan Trom | NM 7279 | | | Farne Islands | NU 2337 |
| Eilean Mòineseach | NC 0617 | Eilean Mór (*Ross of Mull*) | NM 3416 | | | Eilean nan Uan | NR 3488 | Eilean Tioram | NG 8310 | Fawley Island | TQ 9665 |
| Eilean Molach | NA 9932 | Eilean Mullagrach | NB 9511 | Eilean nam Muc | NM 2819 | Eilean nan Uan | NR 6877 | Eilean Tioram | NG 8726 | Ferramas | NF 9369 |
| Eilean Mór | NR 6675 | Eilean Mundre | NN 0859 | Eilean nan Ban | NM 3024 | Eilean nan Uan (*Stornoway*) | NB 4630 | Eilean Traighe | NR 7372 | Fetlar | HU 6291 |
| Eilean Mor | NG 2248 | Eilean Musdile | NM 7835 | Eilean nan Cabar | NM 6883 | | | Eilean Traighe | NR 7457 | Fiaray | NF 7010 |
| Eilean Mor | NG 3557 | Eilean na Bà | NG 6937 | Eilean nan Caorach | NR 3644 | Eilean on Tighe (*Shaint Islands*) | NG 4297 | Eilean Trosdam | NB 2132 | Fidra | NT 5186 |
| Eilean Mór | NG 7558 | Eilean na Bearachd | NM 1439 | | | Eilean Ona | NM 7602 | Eileanan a' Ghille-bheid | NG 1796 | Finsbay Island | NG 0985 |
| Eilean Mór | NC 0517 | | | Eilean nan Coarach | NM 9046 | Eilean Orasaidh | NB 4121 | | | Fiola an Droma | NM 7009 |
| Eilean Mòr a' Bhàigh | NB 2600 | Eilean na Beithe | NR 9270 | Eilean nan Coinein | NR 5468 | Eilean Orasaigh (*Barkin Isles*) | NB 4024 | Eileanan Dubha | NC 1851 | Fiola Meadhonach | NM 7109 |
| Eilean Mór (*Ardnamuschan*) | NM 5861 | Eilean na Beitheiche | NM 62146 | Eilean nan Coinean | NR 7186 | Eilean Ornsay | NM 2255 | Eileanan Glasa | NM 5945 | Fish Holm | HU 4774 |
| Eilean Mór (*Coll*) | NM 2764 | Eilean na Cille | NR 7597 | Eilean nan Coinean | NR 7796 | Eilean Port a' Choit | NC 2148 | Eileanan Iasgaich | NF 7818 | Fladda | NM 7212 |
| Eilean Mór (*Dunstaffnage Bay*) | NM 8834 | Eilean na Cloiche | NM 8338 | Eilean nan Each | NM 3981 | Eilean Quidnish | NG 0986 | Elizabeth Castle | | Fladda (*Treshnish Isles*) | NM 2943 |
| | | Eilean na Crèadha | NG 7631 | Eilean nan Each | NF 8751 | Eilean Rairidh | NC 1635 | Ensay | NF 9786 | | |
| Eilean Mór (*Flannan Isles*) | NA 7246 | Eilean na Creiche | NM 3838 | Eilean na Eildean | NM 6158 | Eilean Ramsay | NM 8845 | Eorsa | NM 4837 | Fladday | NA 9915 |
| Eilean Mór (*Great Bernera*) | NB 1738 | Eilean na Sgaite | NG 1992 | Eilean nan Gabhar | NM 5367 | Eilean Ràrsaidh | NG 8111 | Erisgeir | NM 3832 | Flat Holm | ST 2264 |
| | | Eilean na h-Airde | NG 5211 | Eilean nan Gabhar | NM 7900 | Eilean Riabhach | NC 1440 | Eriska | NM 9042 | Floday | NB 1033 |
| Eilean Mor (*Islay*) | NR 2169 | Eilean na h-Aiteig | NC 1958 | Eilean nan Gamhna | NM 8338 | Eilean Righ | NM 8001 | Eriskay | NF 7910 | Floday | NB 1241 |
| | | Eilean na Rainich | NC 1439 | | | Eilean Rosaidh | NB 4120 | Erraid | NM 2919 | Flodda (*Berbecula*) | NF 8455 |
| | | | | | | Eilean Rubha an Ridire | NM 7240 | Eughlam | NB 1639 | Flodday (*Barra*) | NF 7502 |
| | | | | | | | | Eunay Mór | NB 1336 | Flodday (*Loch Maddy*) | NF 9469 |
| | | | | | | | | Eynhallow | HY 3529 | Flodday (Nr Sandray) | NL 6192 |

Part of the tragedy of the islands is that the majority of those involved in creating it were not the evil men they have sometimes been painted. When the McLeans of Coll purchased Rhum at the end of the 17th century crofting was just possible. But the growth of the population produced too much of a strain on the limited quantity of land which could sustain crops. By 1826, poverty was rife and 350 of the islanders agreed to emigrate to Canada. The decision to introduce sheep might have worked but 8000 of them proved beyond the capabilities of the land which became further degraded.

This was the period of the sporting estate and the Marquis of Salisbury, the next owner, developed schemes to improve the rivers, stocking them with salmon and trout – only to find that the results were still disappointing. Red deer were more successful but, by the 1880s, after various owners had been defeated by the 'wet desert', Rhum passed to the Lancashire milling magnate, John Bullough. His son built Kinloch Castle, an Edwardian fantasy in pink Arran sandstone and now, in part, an hotel worth visiting.

At one time a journalist labelled Rhum under the Bullough family 'the forbidden island'; today, however, its owners, the Nature Conservancy Council, welcome visitors.

What does Rhum offer? The geology is fascinating, a ridge of gabbro peaks on a Torridonian sandstone base, creating some weird shapes for the walker to struggle over. Care must be taken, for the weather is notoriously unreliable and the terrain horrendously difficult, but the rewards are magnificent views.

On the Rhum Cuillins feral goats may be found. Slightly less adventurous are the red deer, now so successfully managed that the Rhum method of culling one-sixth of the herd each year, is being employed all over Scotland. Highland cattle and Rhum ponies – much admired by Dr Johnson, whose opinion of the area generally was not high – contribute to a unique environ-

*ST MICHAEL'S MOUNT rises to 250ft from the waters of Mount's Bay at Penzance. Its castle dates from the 11th century.*

ment, intensively studied and reported, to the advantage of many other Scottish sites.

The two most successful experiments on Rhum have involved plants and birds. The NCC decided to restore the natural woodlands and their planting policy has been remarkably effective, with some trees, oak for example, showing exceptional growth rates. But the most spectacular of the NCC's successes has been the re-introduction of the white-tailed or sea eagle. Missing as a British species since 1908, it is now re-established on Rhum and showing signs of colonising neighbouring areas like Skye.

## Skomer Island

The windswept island of Skomer was selected for designation as one of the first marine nature reserves in Britain, as its underwater scenery rivals that of the island in beauty and abundant plant and animal life.

Skomer is a high rocky plateau, its steep grassy slopes strewn with boulders and surrounded by cliffs. It is less accessible than its sister island, Skokholm, and supports an internationally famous nature reserve with a vast colony of seabirds. Ful-

mars, razorbills, guillemots, kittiwakes and many others nest on the cliffs, while beneath the turf are the nests of the tunnelling storm petrels, puffins and Manx shearwaters.

The island has a large variety of rodents, but perhaps the most fascinating is the Skomer vole – a strain of the bank vole to be found on the mainland, but lighter in colour and larger, with a differently-shaped skull. There are no predatory mammals on the island so the animal population can only be threatened from the air – by peregrine falcons among others. Grey seals play in the many rocky bays and inlets, as indeed they do everywhere along this fascinating stretch of Pembrokeshire coastline.

Maritime plants thrive on the island and in the sea surrounding it. Skomer also has areas of heath and moorland plants, which cope well with the winds that continually batter these lonely heights.

Skomer can be visited in summer but sailings must be arranged in advance (a way of controlling the numbers of visitors). Landing is subject to calm weather.

# 3 MILE
# ROAD
# ATLAS
## — OF —
# BRITAIN

1:200,000
Approximately 3 miles to 1 inch

# Route Planning

The *3 Mile Road Atlas of Britain* has been specially designed by AA experts to make the exploration and navigation of Britain's roads as easy and pleasurable as possilbe.

The route planning maps on this and the following pages can be used to help with journey planning. If you know the name of the village or town of your destination but not its location, look the name up in the index at the back of this atlas. Next to the name will be the atlas page number on which it appears and its National Grid reference. (An explanation of the National Grid is given on page 78) Once you have located the place, note the name of the nearest large conurbation to it shown on the route planning maps. By locating the nearest marked conurbation to your start point, it is then possible to plot a basic route between the two large places. More detailed routes can be planned by consulting the main atlas. A special feature of these maps is that a key to the atlas pages is superimposed –making at-a-glance place location much easier.

As a general rule, motorways are the quickest and most efficient means of travelling across the country; primary routes are usually the next-best thing. The shortest route is not necessarily the quickest, whereas motorways and primary routes usually avoid the centres of towns, other roads may lead you into a maze of side streets and an endless succession of traffic lights, one-way systems etc. Radio stations often give invaluable information about road conditions in areas that you may be passing through; maps of the areas covered by BBC and Independent local radio stations can be found on pages 76 and 77

## Legend

| | |
|---|---|
| Motorway | |
| Motorway under construction | |
| Primary route single carriageway | |
| Primary route dual carriageway | |
| Other A roads | |
| Motorway junction | ③ |
| Motorway junction with limited entries or exits. | ❼ |

Scale 16 miles to 1 inch

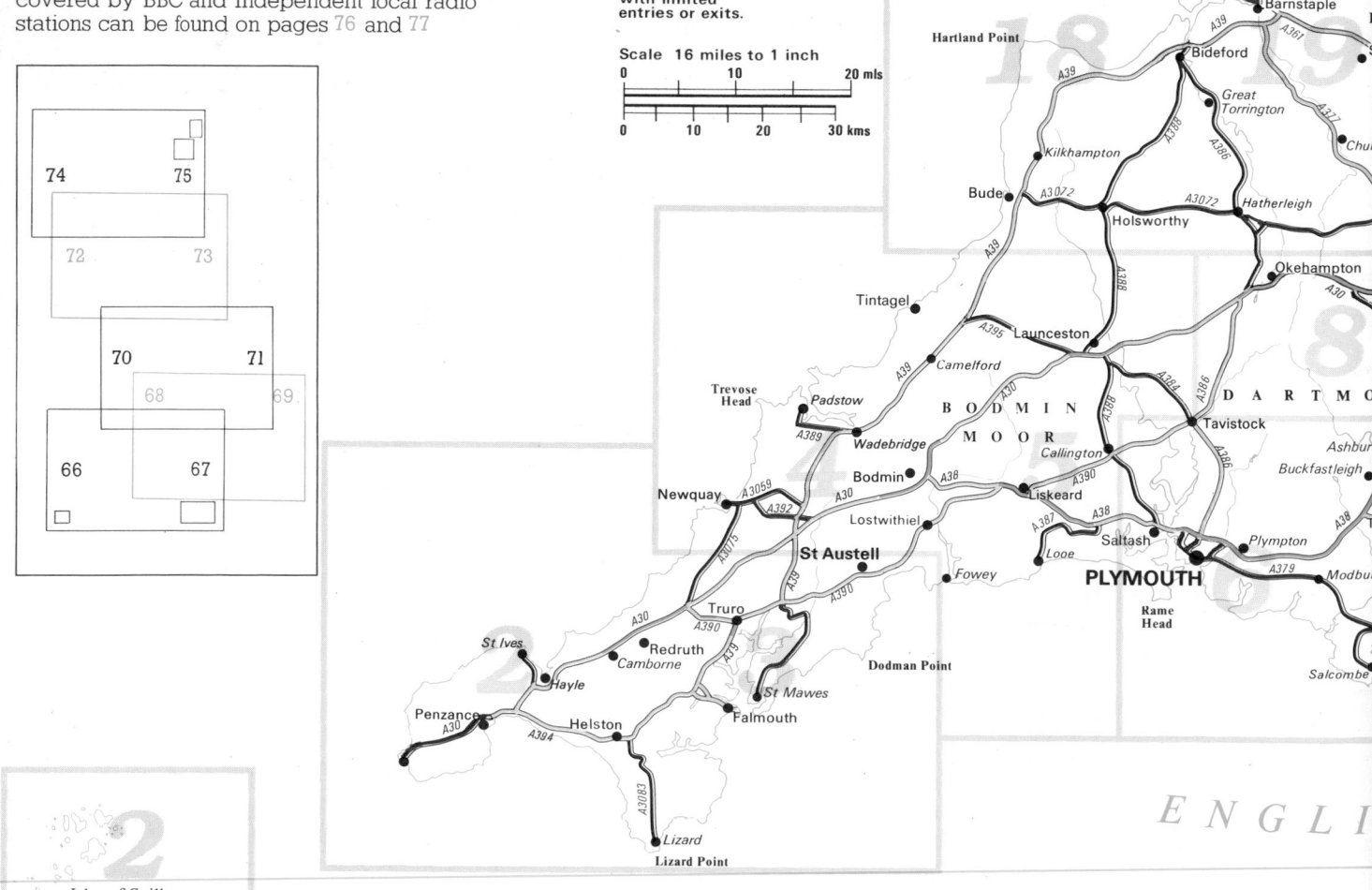

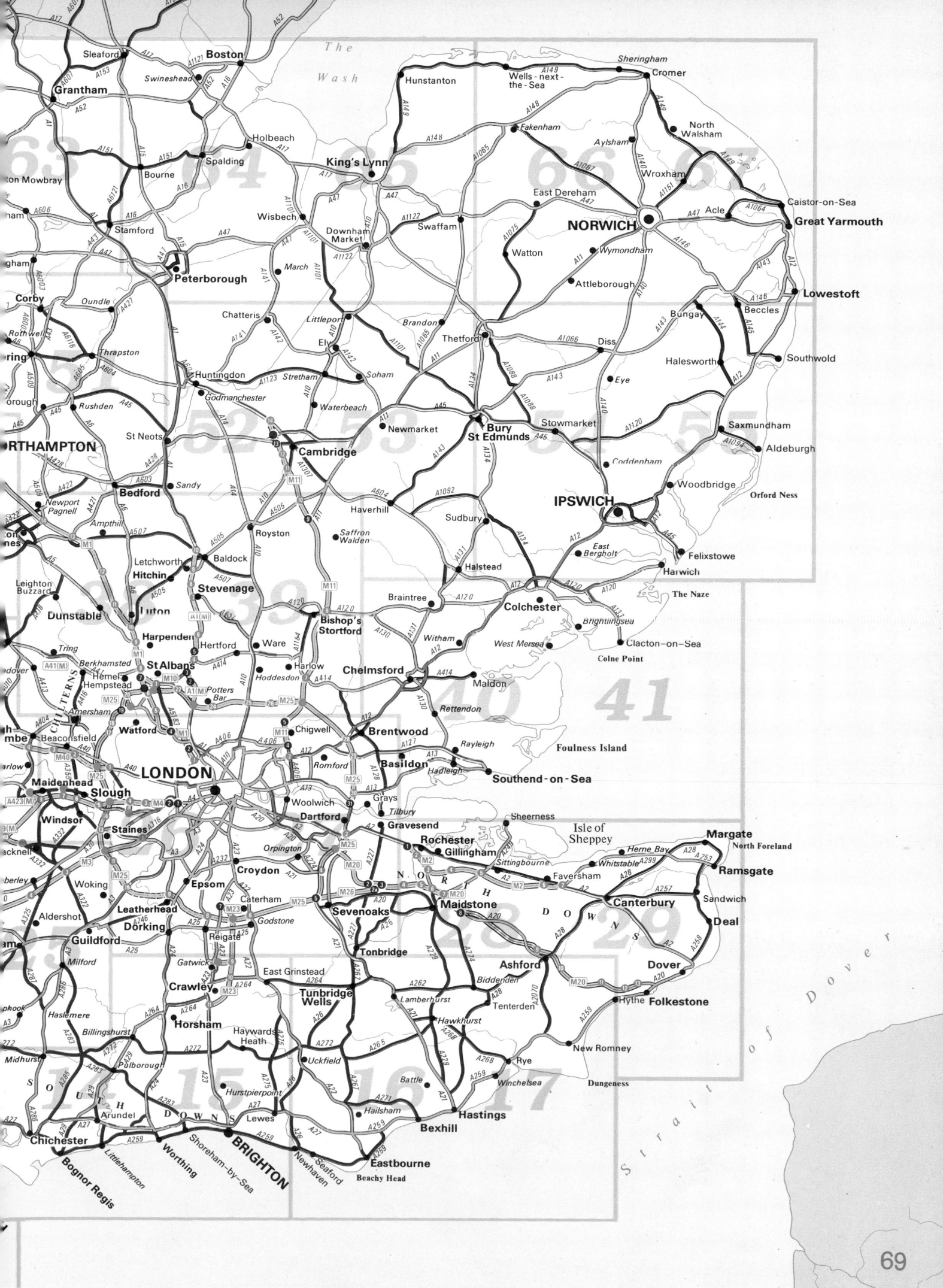

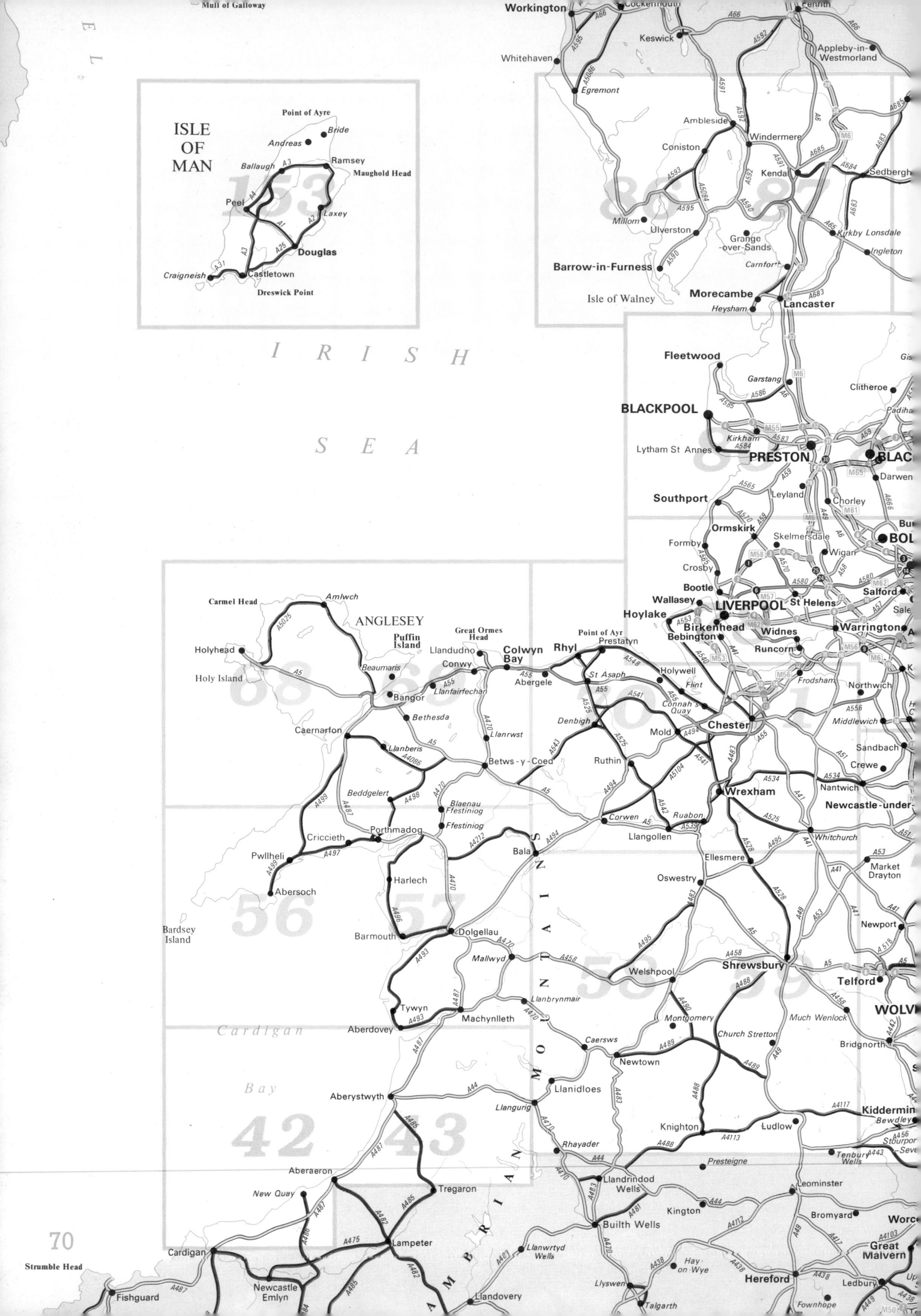

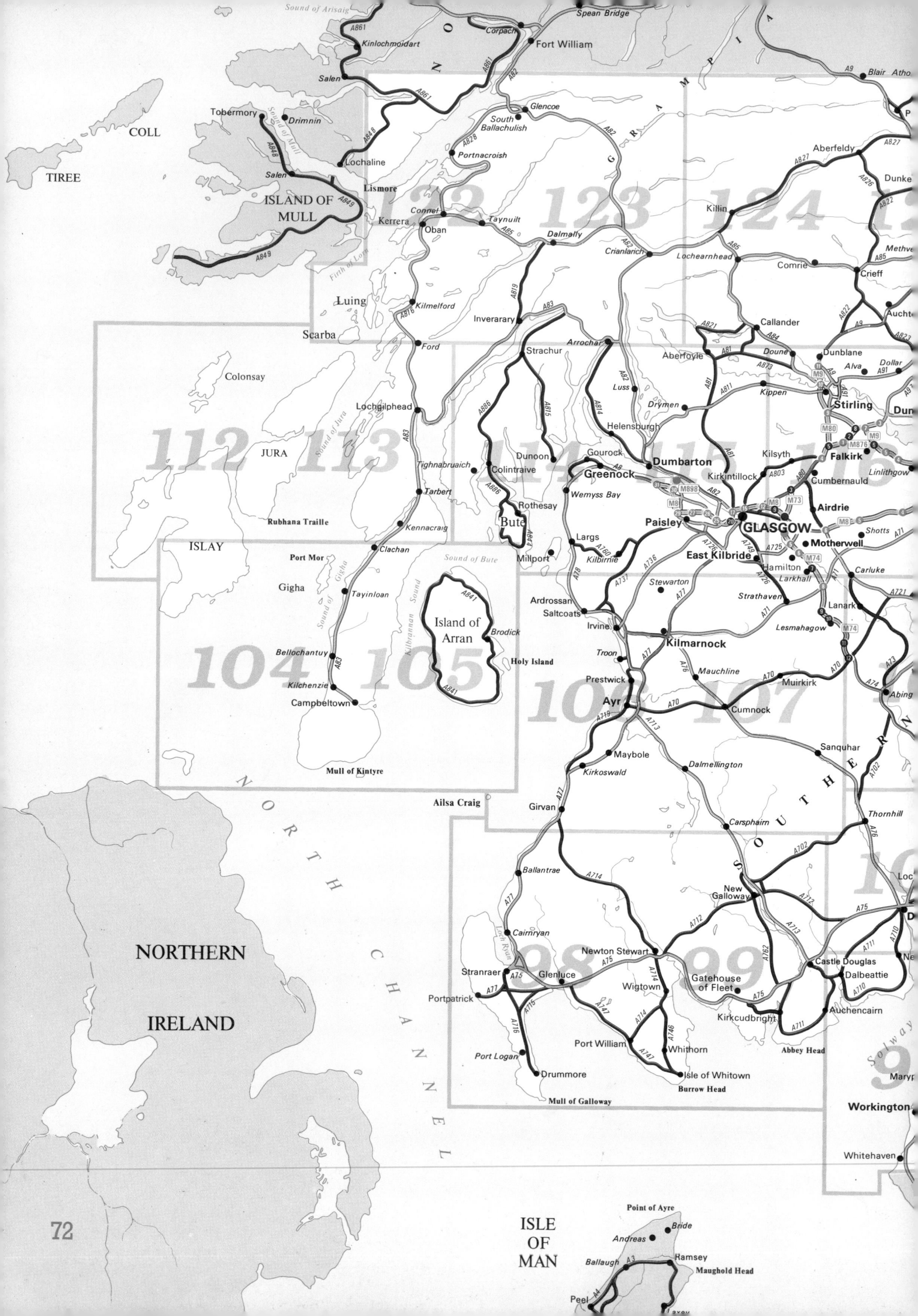

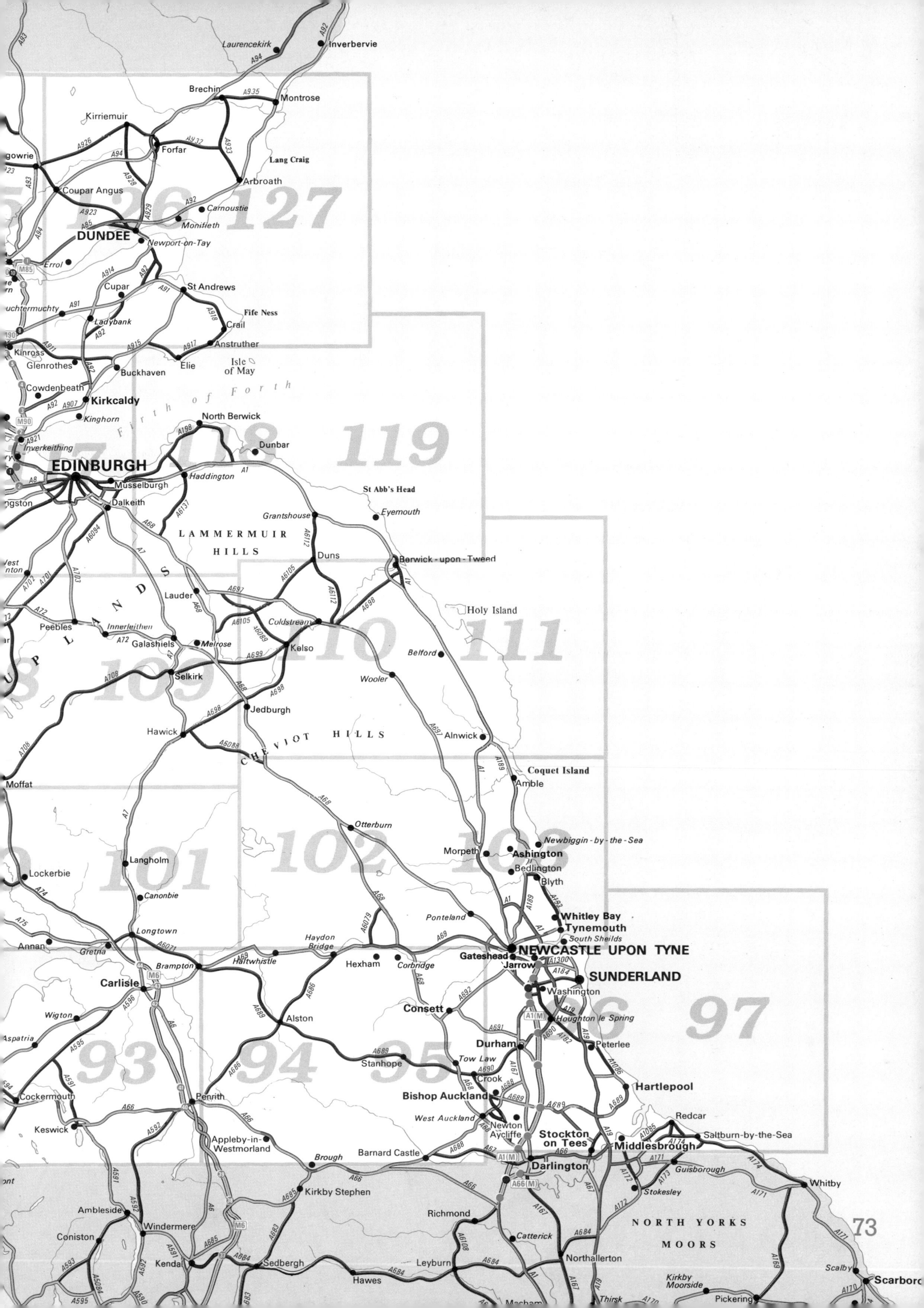

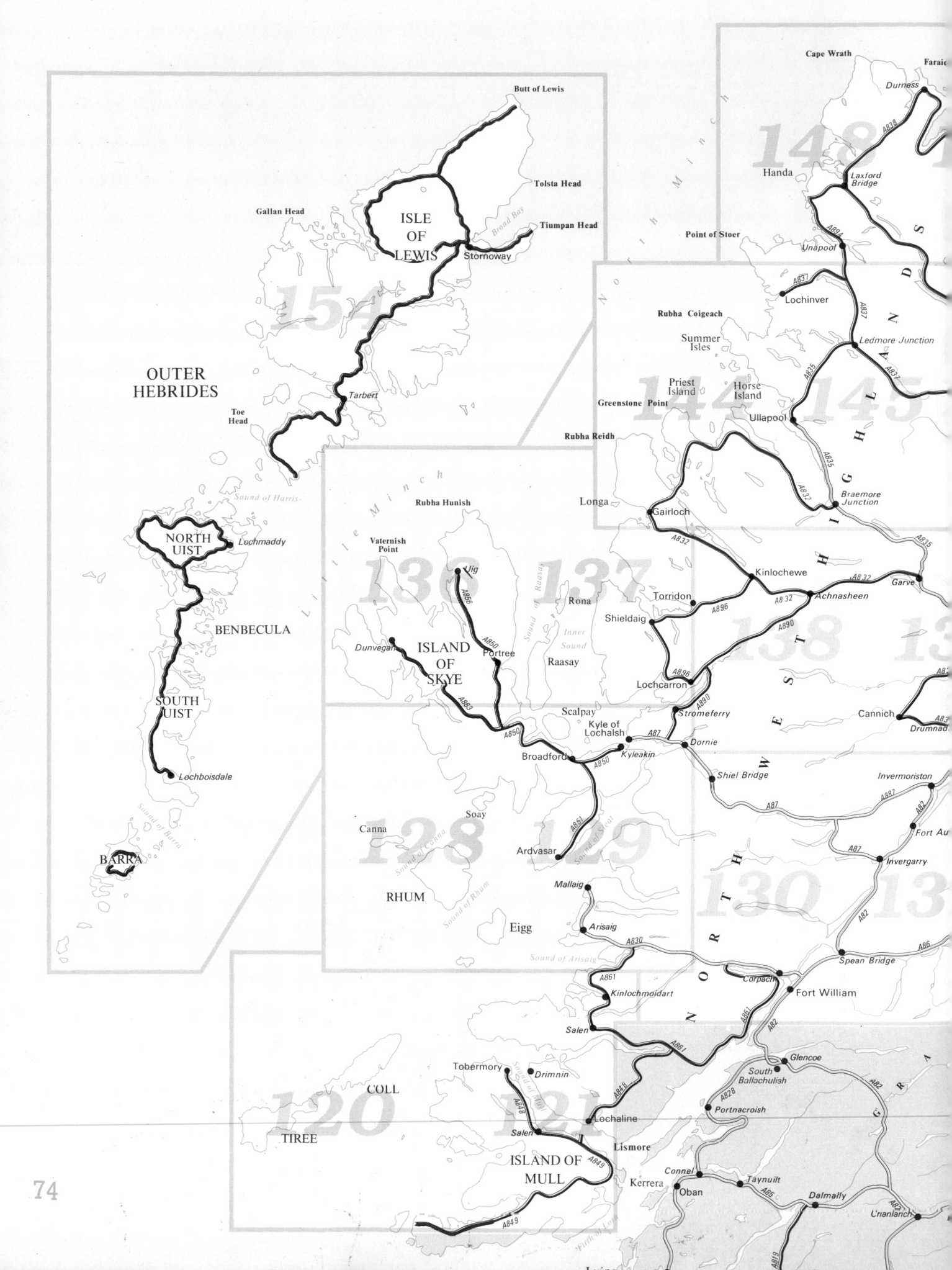

Butt of Lewis

Tolsta Head

Gallan Head

ISLE
OF
LEWIS

Tiumpan Head

*Broad Bay*

Stornoway

*154*

OUTER
HEBRIDES

Tarbert

Toe
Head

*Sound of Harris*

Rubha Coigeach

Summer
Isles

Priest
Island

Horse
Island

Greenstone Point

Ullapool

Rubha Reidh

*144*

*145*

Longa

Braemore
Junction

NORTH
UIST

*Lochmaddy*

Gairloch

A832

A815

BENBECULA

*Little Minch*

Rubha Hunish

Vaternish
Point

Uig

*136*

*137*

Rona

Kinlochewe

A8 32

Garve

Dunvegan

ISLAND
OF
SKYE

A850

Portree

Raasay

Torridon

A896

Achnasheen

A890

*138*

*13*

Shieldaig

SOUTH
UIST

*Lochboisdale*

A863

Scalpay

Lochcarron

A896

A890

Cannich

A83

Drumnad

*Sound of Barra*

A850

Kyle of
Lochalsh

A87

Stromeferry

BARRA

Broadford

A850

Kyleakin

Dornie

Shiel Bridge

Invermoriston

A887

Fort Au

Soay

A851

A87

Invergarry

Canna

*128*

*129*

Ardvasar

*Sound of Sleat*

*130*

*13*

RHUM

Eigg

Mallaig

Arisaig

A830

*Sound of Arisaig*

Spean Bridge

A86

A861

Kinlochmoidart

Corpach

Fort William

Salen

A861

A82

COLL

Tobermory

*Drimnin*

Glencoe

South
Ballachulish

A828

Portnacroish

A84 ?

Lochaline

*120*

*121*

A848

TIREE

Salen

Lismore

ISLAND OF
MULL

A949

*Connel*

Taynuilt

Kerrera

Oban

A85

Dalmally

Crianlarich

Cape Wrath

Faraid

Durness

A838

*148*

Handa

Laxford
Bridge

Point of Stoer

A894

Unapool

A837

Lochinver

A837

Ledmore Junction

A835

A837

A832

A815

A896

*North Minch*

*North Minch*

*Sound of Raasay*

*Inner
Sound*

*Sound of Canna*

*Sound of Rhum*

A84 8

*Firth of L*

*Luing*

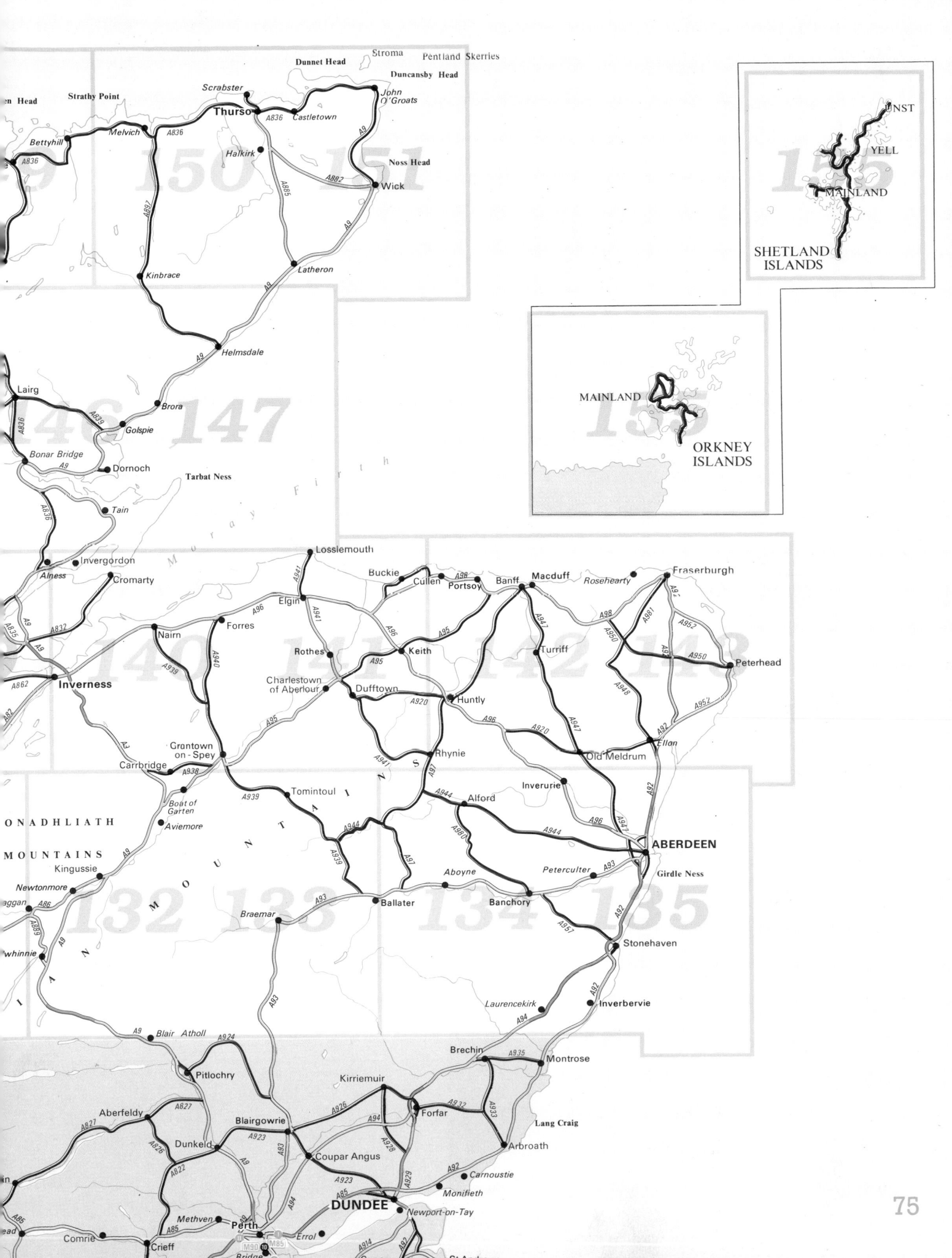

# Local Radio Broadcasting

All BBC & IBA local radio stations, including three of the BBC national networks, give up-to-date information on road and weather conditions. Stations marked * broadcast regular travel bulletins provided by AA Roadwatch, the AA's broadcasting service.

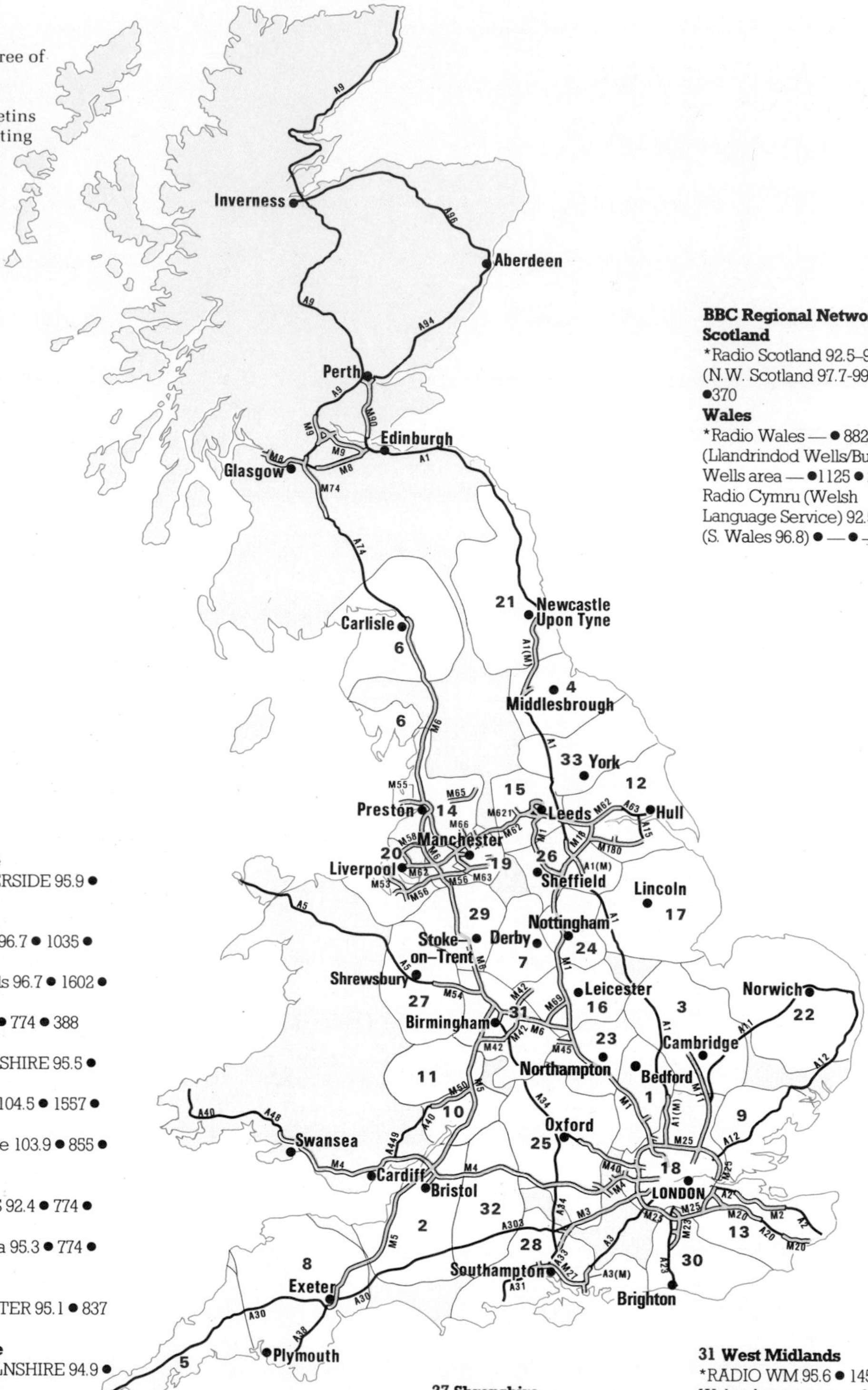

## BBC Local Radio Stations

**1 Bedfordshire**
*RADIO BEDFORDSHIRE
95.5 ● 630 ● 476
Bedford 95.5 ● 1161 ● 258
Luton & Dunstable 103.8 ● 630
● 476

**2 Bristol**
RADIO BRISTOL 95.5 ● 1548 ●
194
Bristol 94.9 ● 1548 ● 194
Bath 104.6 ● 1548 ● 194
Central Somerset 95.5 ● 1323 ●
227

**3 Cambridgeshire**
RADIO CAMBRIDGESHIRE
96.0 ● 1026 ● 292
Peterborough and
N Cambridgeshire 95.7 ● 1449
● 207

**4 Cleveland**
*RADIO CLEVELAND 95.0 ●
1548 ● 194
Whitby area 95.8 ● 1548 ● 194

**5 Cornwall**
RADIO CORNWALL
East Cornwall 95.2 ● 657 ● 457
West Cornwall 103.9 ● 630 ●
476
Isles of Scilly area 96.0 ● 630 ●
476

**6 Cumbria**
RADIO CUMBRIA
N. Cumbria 95.6 ● 756 ● 397
Whitehaven area 95.6 ● 1458 ●
206
RADIO FURNESS
S. Cumbria 96.1 ● 837 ● 358
Kendal 95.2 ● 837 ● 358
Windermere 104.2 ● 837 ● 358

**7 Derby**
RADIO DERBY 104.5 ● 1116 ●
269
Derby only 94.2 ● 1116 ● 269
Bakewell/Matlock area 95.3 ●
— ● —

**8 Devon**
RADIO DEVON
Exeter & Devon 95.8 ● 990 ●
303
Torbay area 103.4 ● 1458 ● 206
Plymouth area 103.4 ● 855 ●
351
Barnstaple area 94.8 ● 801 ●
375
N Devon 103.4 ● 801 ● 375
Okehampton area 96.0 ● 801 ●
375

**9 Essex**
*BBC ESSEX 103.5 ● 765 ● 392
N E Essex 103.5 ● 729 ● 412
S E Essex 95.3 ● 1530 ● 196

**10 Gloucestershire**
RADIO GLOUCESTER 104 7 ●
603 ● 498
Stroud area 95.0 — ● —

**11 Hereford & Worcester**
RADIO HEREFORD &
WORCESTER
Hereford 94.7 ● 819 ● 366
Worcester 104.0 ● 738 ● 407

**12 Humberside**
RADIO HUMBERSIDE 95.9 ●
1485 ● 202

**13 Kent**
*RADIO KENT 96.7 ● 1035 ●
290
Tunbridge Wells 96.7 ● 1602 ●
187
East Kent 104.2 ● 774 ● 388

**14 Lancashire**
RADIO LANCASHIRE 95.5 ●
855 ● 351
Lancaster area 104.5 ● 1557 ●
193
South Lancashire 103.9 ● 855 ●
351

**15 Leeds**
*RADIO LEEDS 92.4 ● 774 ●
388
Ilkley/Otley area 95.3 ● 774 ●
388

**16 Leicester**
RADIO LEICESTER 95.1 ● 837
● 358

**17 Lincolnshire**
RADIO LINCOLNSHIRE 94.9 ●
1368 ● 219

**18 London**
*GREATER LONDON RADIO
94.9 ● 1458 ● 206

**19 Manchester**
*GREATER MANCHESTER
RADIO 95.1 ● 1458 ● 206

**20 Merseyside**
*RADIO MERSEYSIDE 95.8 ●
1485 ● 202

**21 Newcastle**
*RADIO NEWCASTLE 95.4 ●
1458 ● 206
NE Northumberland 96.0 ●
1458 ● 206
Newcastle & Gateshead 104.4
● 1458 ● 206

**22 Norfolk**
*RADIO NORFOLK
E Norfolk 95.1 ● 855 ● 351
W Norfolk 104.4 ● 873 ● 344

**23 Northampton**
RADIO NORTHAMPTON
104.2 ● 1107 ● 271
Corby area 103.6 ● 1107 ● 271

**24 Nottingham**
*RADIO NOTTINGHAM 103.8
● 1521 ● 197
Central Nottinghamshire 95.5 ●
1584 ● 189

**25 Oxford**
RADIO OXFORD 95.2 ● 1485 ●
202

**26 Sheffield**
RADIO SHEFFIELD 104.1 ●
1035 ● 290
Sheffield area 88.6 ● 1035 ● 290

**27 Shropshire**
*RADIO SHROPSHIRE 96.0 ●
1584 ● 189

**28 Solent**
RADIO SOLENT 96.1 ● 999 ●
300
Bournemouth area 96.1 ● 1359
● 221

**29 Stoke-on-Trent**
*RADIO STOKE-ON-TRENT
94.6 ● 1503 ● 200

**30 Sussex**
RADIO SUSSEX
Brighton/Worthing area 95.3 ●
1485 ● 202
East Sussex, including Eastern
West Sussex 104.5 ● 1161 ● 258
Reigate/Crawley/Horsham
area 104.0 ● 1368 ● 219
Newhaven — FM frequency
to be announced

**31 West Midlands**
*RADIO WM 95.6 ● 1458 ● 206
Wolverhampton area 95.6 ●
828 ● 362

**32 Wiltshire**
WILTSHIRE SOUND
North Wilts 103.6 ● 1368 ● 219
Salisbury 103.5 ● — ● —
West Wilts ● 104.3 ● 1332 ● 225

**33 York**
*RADIO YORK 103.7 ● 666 ●
450
Scarborough area 95.5 ● 1260
● 238
Central N Yorkshire 104.3 ●
666 ● 450

## BBC Regional Networks
**Scotland**
*Radio Scotland 92.5–94.7
(N.W. Scotland 97.7-99.3) ● 810
●370
**Wales**
*Radio Wales — ● 882 ●340
(Llandrindod Wells/Builth
Wells area — ●1125 ● 267)
Radio Cymru (Welsh
Language Service) 92.5-94.5
(S. Wales 96.8) ● — ● —

## Channel Islands
RADIO GUERNSEY 93.2 ●
1116 ● 269
RADIO JERSEY 88.8 ● 1026 ●
292

# Independent Local Radio Stations

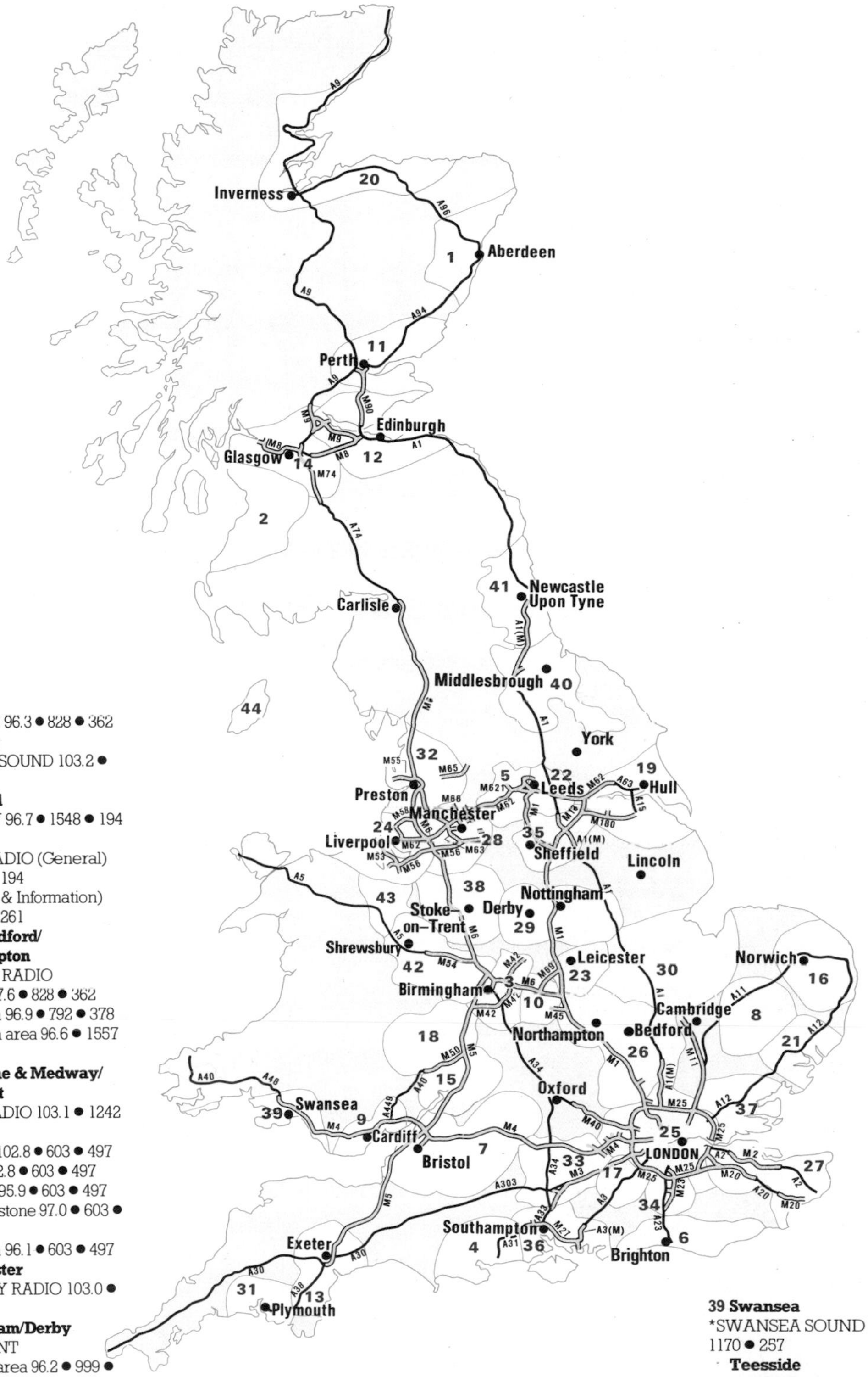

**1 Aberdeen**
*NORTHSOUND RADIO 96.9
● 1035 ● 290
**2 Ayr**
*WEST SOUND 96.7 ● 1035 ●
290
Girvan area 97.5 ● 1035 ● 290
**3 Birmingham**
BRMB RADIO ● 96.4 ● 1152 ●
261
**4 Bournemouth**
2CR (Two Counties Radio) 97.2
● 828 ● 362
**5 Bradford/Halifax**
**& Huddersfield**
PENNINE RADIO
Bradford area 97.5 ● 1278 ● 235
Halifax/Huddersfield area
102.5 ● 1530 ● 196
**6 Brighton**
SOUTHERN SOUND 103.5 ●
1323 ● 227
Hastings 97.5 ● — ● —
Eastbourne 102.4 ● — ● —
Newhaven 96.9 ● — ● —
**7 Bristol**
GWR RADIO
Avon & N Somerset 96.3 ● 1260
● 238
Bath area 103.0 ● 1260 ● 238
Swindon area 97.2 ● 1161 ● 258
W Wiltshire 102.2 ● 936 ● 321
**8 Bury St Edmunds**
SAXON RADIO 96.4 ● 1251 ●
240
**9 Cardiff/Newport**
*RED DRAGON RADIO
Cardiff 103.2 ● 1359 ● 221
Newport 97.4 ● 1305 ● 230
**10 Coventry**
MERCIA SOUND 97.0 ● 1359 ●
220
**11 Dundee/Perth**
*RADIO TAY
Dundee area 102.8 ● 1161 ●
258
Perth area 96.4 ● 1584 ● 189
**12 Edinburgh**
*RADIO FORTH 97.3 ● 1548 ●
194
**13 Exeter/Torbay**
*DEVONAIR RADIO
Exeter area 97.0 ● 666 ● 450
Torbay area 96.4 ● 954 ● 314
**14 Glasgow**
*RADIO CLYDE 102.5 ● 1152 ●
261
**15 Gloucester & Cheltenham**
SEVERN SOUND 102.4 ● 774 ●
388
Stroud area 103.0 ● — ● —
**16 Great Yarmouth &**
**Norwich**
RADIO BROADLAND 102.4 ●
1152 ● 260
**17 Guildford**
*COUNTY SOUND 96.4 ● 1476
● 203
**18 Hereford/Worcester**
*RADIO WYVERN
Hereford area 97.6 ● 954 ● 314
Worcester area 102.8 ● 1530 ●
196
**19 Humberside**
VIKING RADIO 96.9 ● 1161 ●
258
**20 Inverness**
MORAY FIRTH RADIO 97.4 ●
1107 ● 271
**21 Ipswich**
RADIO ORWELL 97.1 ● 1170 ●
257

**22 Leeds**
RADIO AIRE 96.3 ● 828 ● 362
**23 Leicester**
LEICESTER SOUND 103.2 ●
1260 ● 238
**24 Liverpool**
RADIO CITY 96.7 ● 1548 ● 194
**25 London**
CAPITAL RADIO (General)
95.8 ● 1548 ● 194
*LBC (News & Information)
97.3 ● 1152 ● 261
**26 Luton/Bedford/**
**Northampton**
*CHILTERN RADIO
Luton area 97.6 ● 828 ● 362
Bedford area 96.9 ● 792 ● 378
Northampton area 96.6 ● 1557
● 193
**27 Maidstone & Medway/**
**East Kent**
INVICTA RADIO 103.1 ● 1242
● 242
Canterbury 102.8 ● 603 ● 497
East Kent 102.8 ● 603 ● 497
Thanet area 95.9 ● 603 ● 497
Dover/Folkestone 97.0 ● 603 ●
497
Ashford area 96.1 ● 603 ● 497
**28 Manchester**
PICCADILLY RADIO 103.0 ●
1152 ● 261
**29 Nottingham/Derby**
RADIO TRENT
Nottingham area 96.2 ● 999 ●
301
Derby area 102.8 ● 945 ● 317
**30 Peterborough**
*HEREWARD RADIO 102.7 ●
1332 ● 225
**31 Plymouth**
*PLYMOUTH SOUND 97.0 ●
1152 ● 261
Tavistock area 96.6 ● — ● —
**32 Preston & Blackpool**
RED ROSE RADIO 97.4 ● 999 ●
301
**33 Reading/Basingstoke &**
**Andover**
*RADIO 210
Reading & E Berkshire 97.0 ●
1431 ● 225
W Berkshire & N Hampshire
102.9 ● — ● —

**34 Reigate & Crawley**
*RADIO MERCURY 102.7 ●
1521 ● 197
Horsham area 97.5 ● — ● —
**35 Sheffield/Rotherham/**
**Barnsley/Doncaster**
RADIO HALLAM
Sheffield area 97.4 ● 1548 ● 194
Rotherham area 96.1 ● 1548 ●
194
Barnsley area 102.9 ● 1305 ●
230
Doncaster area 103.4 ● 990 ●
303
**36 Southampton/Portsmouth/**
**Winchester**
OCEAN SOUND

Ocean Sound West
Southampton, S W Hampshire
and Isle of Wight 103.2 ● 1557
● 193
Ocean Sound North
Winchester area 96.7 ● — ● —
Ocean Sound East
Portsmouth, S E Hampshire
and Chichester area 97.5 ●
1170 ● 257
**37 Southend/Chelmsford**
*ESSEX RADIO
Southend area 96.3 ● 1431 ●
210
Chelmsford area 102.6 ● 1359 ●
220
**38 Stoke-on-Trent**
SIGNAL RADIO 102.6 ● 1170 ●
257

**39 Swansea**
*SWANSEA SOUND 96.4 ●
1170 ● 257
**Teesside**
TFM RADIO 96.6 ● 1170 ● 257
**41 Tyne & Wear**
METRO RADIO 97.1 ● 1152 ●
261
**42 Wolverhampton & Black**
**Country/Shrewsbury**
**&Telford**
BEACON RADIO
Wolverhampton & Black
Country 97.2 ● 990 ● 303
Shrewsbury & Telford area
103.1 ● — ● —
**43 Wrexham & Deeside**
*MARCHER SOUND 103.4 ●
1260 ● 238
**44 Isle of Man**
MANX RADIO (not run by
IBA)
97.3/89.0 ● 1368 ● 219

# The National Grid

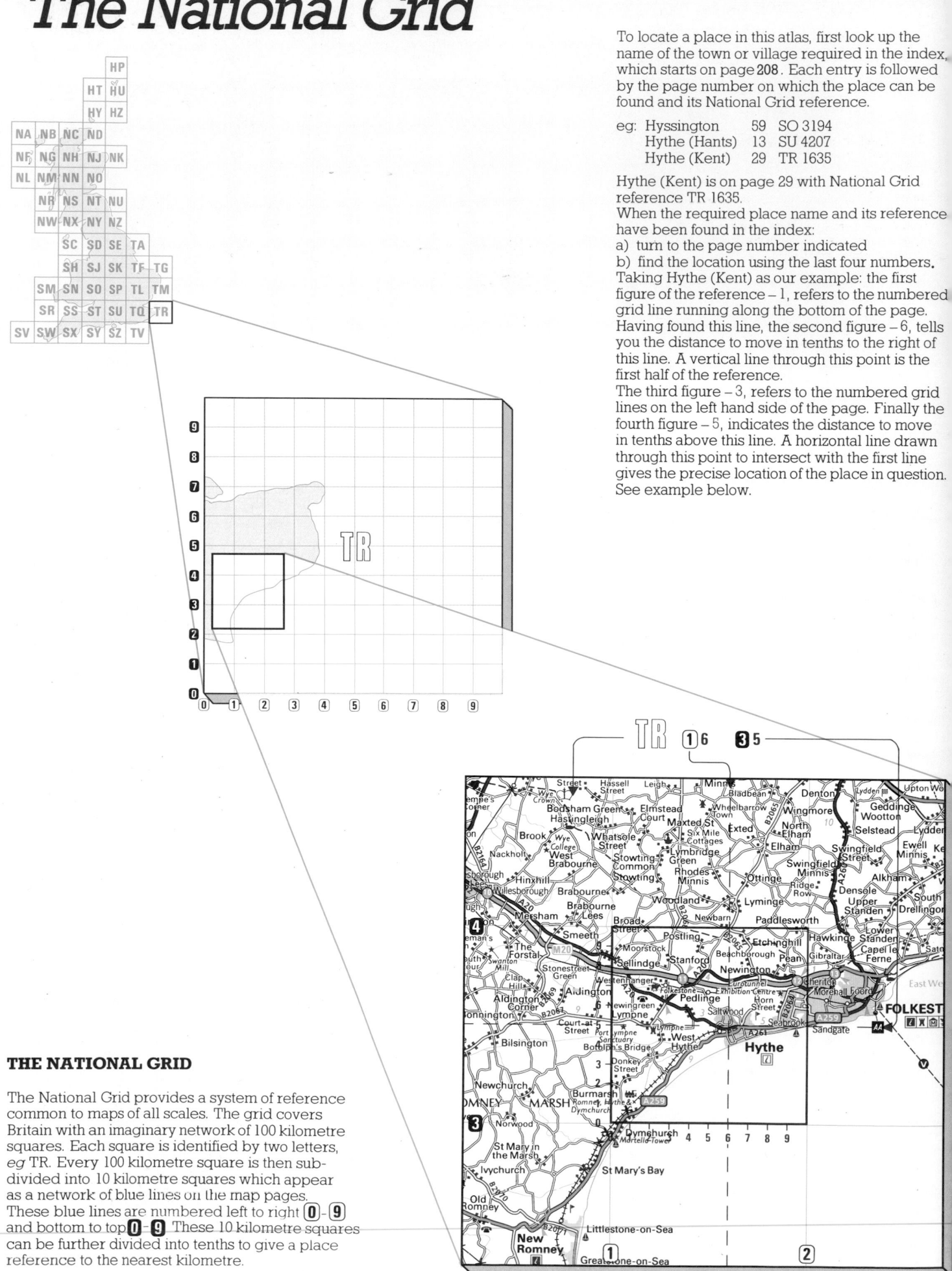

To locate a place in this atlas, first look up the name of the town or village required in the index, which starts on page 208. Each entry is followed by the page number on which the place can be found and its National Grid reference.

eg: Hyssington     59   SO 3194
    Hythe (Hants)   13   SU 4207
    Hythe (Kent)    29   TR 1635

Hythe (Kent) is on page 29 with National Grid reference TR 1635.
When the required place name and its reference have been found in the index:
a) turn to the page number indicated
b) find the location using the last four numbers.
Taking Hythe (Kent) as our example: the first figure of the reference – 1, refers to the numbered grid line running along the bottom of the page. Having found this line, the second figure – 6, tells you the distance to move in tenths to the right of this line. A vertical line through this point is the first half of the reference.
The third figure – 3, refers to the numbered grid lines on the left hand side of the page. Finally the fourth figure – 5, indicates the distance to move in tenths above this line. A horizontal line drawn through this point to intersect with the first line gives the precise location of the place in question. See example below.

## THE NATIONAL GRID

The National Grid provides a system of reference common to maps of all scales. The grid covers Britain with an imaginary network of 100 kilometre squares. Each square is identified by two letters, eg TR. Every 100 kilometre square is then sub-divided into 10 kilometre squares which appear as a network of blue lines on the map pages. These blue lines are numbered left to right 0-9 and bottom to top 0-9. These 10 kilometre squares can be further divided into tenths to give a place reference to the nearest kilometre.

# Mileage Chart

The distances between towns on the mileage chart are given to the nearest mile, and are measured along the normal AA recommended routes. It should be noted that AA recommended routes do not necessarily follow the shortest distances between places but are based on the quickest travelling time, making maximum use of motorways or dual carriageway roads.

Aberdeen
468 Aberystwyth
605 222 Barnstaple
431 122 178 Birmingham
611 290 206 185 Brighton
515 132 100 88 170 Bristol
473 218 269 101 121 172 Cambridge
534 116 138 108 205 47 207 Cardiff
232 235 372 198 378 282 280 302 Carlisle
521 48 200 170 268 110 270 68 288 Carmarthen
526 288 292 171 112 195 47 230 313 293 Colchester
597 214 95 170 118 62 182 129 364 192 208 Dorchester
631 323 278 206 78 210 122 245 398 308 113 206 Dover
126 335 472 298 478 381 343 401 99 398 396 463 466 Edinburgh
588 206 40 162 172 84 252 121 355 183 275 54 250 455 Exeter
159 445 581 407 587 491 470 511 209 498 522 573 608 133 565 Fort William
146 334 471 297 477 381 359 401 98 387 412 463 497 46 454 102 Glasgow
480 110 126 54 157 36 124 66 247 128 172 118 198 347 110 457 346 Gloucester
568 226 176 143 45 106 92 141 335 204 103 98 101 435 148 545 434 102 Guildford
482 79 144 55 188 54 156 58 249 85 203 136 229 349 127 458 348 31 133 Hereford
462 106 327 153 333 237 249 205 229 154 319 319 353 328 310 438 328 202 290 158 Holyhead
360 228 322 135 283 231 144 251 173 314 196 313 266 231 305 382 272 197 241 198 222 Hull
106 493 630 456 636 540 518 560 257 546 571 622 656 157 613 65 172 505 593 507 487 431 Inverness
284 190 327 153 333 237 253 257 51 243 318 319 353 151 310 260 150 202 290 204 184 165 309 Kendal
336 174 310 115 264 220 149 240 123 226 201 302 271 206 294 333 222 185 221 187 167 61 381 72 Leeds
397 198 272 94 216 182 95 202 185 264 148 265 218 268 256 394 284 147 175 149 205 48 442 177 73 Lincoln
358 111 275 101 281 185 217 205 125 159 267 267 302 225 259 334 224 150 238 118 104 130 383 80 75 142 Liverpool
593 285 234 168 50 166 85 201 361 264 76 162 45 428 206 570 460 154 57 185 316 228 619 316 233 180 264 Maidstone
352 131 263 89 269 172 161 192 119 184 214 254 289 219 246 329 218 138 226 140 124 99 377 74 44 85 35 251 Manchester
277 224 359 172 321 268 200 288 96 296 253 350 323 147 342 281 195 234 278 236 237 87 308 85 63 125 145 285 114 Middlesbrough
237 273 388 202 350 298 230 318 57 326 283 380 353 108 372 241 152 264 308 265 267 142 268 100 93 154 175 315 144 39 Newcastle-upon-Tyne
481 172 208 55 133 112 56 163 248 225 118 157 153 347 192 457 347 93 90 110 203 153 506 203 133 88 151 116 138 190 220 Northampton
498 280 330 163 168 233 63 269 286 331 58 244 170 369 313 495 385 187 160 218 306 152 543 278 174 104 243 132 186 226 255 118 Norwich
403 160 236 54 196 146 87 165 190 228 140 228 217 273 219 489 289 111 153 113 176 93 448 163 73 35 109 179 70 130 160 66 119 Nottingham
497 159 171 62 110 74 101 109 264 172 124 117 150 364 154 473 363 50 67 81 219 189 522 219 169 124 167 106 155 226 256 40 143 102 Oxford
701 318 111 275 287 196 365 234 468 296 388 168 364 568 112 678 567 222 262 240 423 418 726 423 406 368 371 320 359 455 485 304 426 332 267 Penzance
87 381 518 344 524 428 406 447 145 434 459 510 544 42 501 103 59 393 481 395 375 276 114 197 269 330 271 506 265 193 153 394 431 336 410 614 Perth
630 247 59 203 215 125 293 162 397 225 317 97 293 496 45 606 496 151 191 169 352 346 655 352 335 297 300 249 287 383 413 233 355 261 196 78 543 Plymouth
321 147 284 110 290 194 211 213 89 200 275 276 310 188 267 298 188 159 247 161 140 123 347 44 69 135 37 272 32 106 138 160 236 118 176 380 234 309 Preston
549 185 119 123 87 54 140 100 316 162 166 40 164 416 91 526 415 75 62 106 271 254 574 271 234 189 219 120 207 291 321 105 202 167 64 205 462 134 228 Salisbury
377 163 272 86 234 182 124 202 164 264 176 264 265 247 256 373 263 148 192 149 157 67 422 122 35 48 77 217 37 104 134 104 149 44 140 369 310 297 80 205 Sheffield
411 75 222 48 228 131 144 110 178 117 213 248 278 205 388 277 97 185 52 105 163 436 133 117 123 65 210 69 187 216 97 206 85 114 318 324 246 90 166 114 Shrewsbury
575 226 143 129 64 78 132 141 343 203 158 55 156 442 109 552 442 101 48 132 298 256 600 297 237 215 246 112 233 294 323 107 194 169 67 224 488 152 254 24 207 192 Southampton
388 110 220 46 285 130 130 150 155 212 212 212 247 255 204 364 254 95 184 97 125 129 413 110 93 90 58 209 46 163 193 96 173 91 125 286 191 78 36 191 Stoke-on-Trent
240 343 489 305 485 389 368 409 107 395 420 471 506 132 463 188 85 354 443 356 336 280 265 318 231 292 232 468 227 203 161 355 393 298 371 575 313 504 196 424 271 286 452 Stranraer
556 173 51 130 157 51 220 89 323 151 243 46 229 423 34 533 422 77 127 95 278 273 581 278 261 223 226 185 214 310 340 159 281 187 122 147 469 75 235 70 224 173 94 171 430 Taunton
323 201 316 129 277 225 157 245 117 253 210 307 280 193 299 327 216 191 235 193 194 37 375 90 24 81 102 242 71 50 87 147 182 87 183 412 263 340 95 248 61 144 250 120 225 267 York
546 237 217 120 60 120 61 155 313 217 61 130 80 413 200 522 412 105 30 136 268 218 571 268 199 145 216 38 204 256 285 68 115 131 57 313 459 241 225 88 169 163 80 161 420 168 212 LONDON

# Map Pages

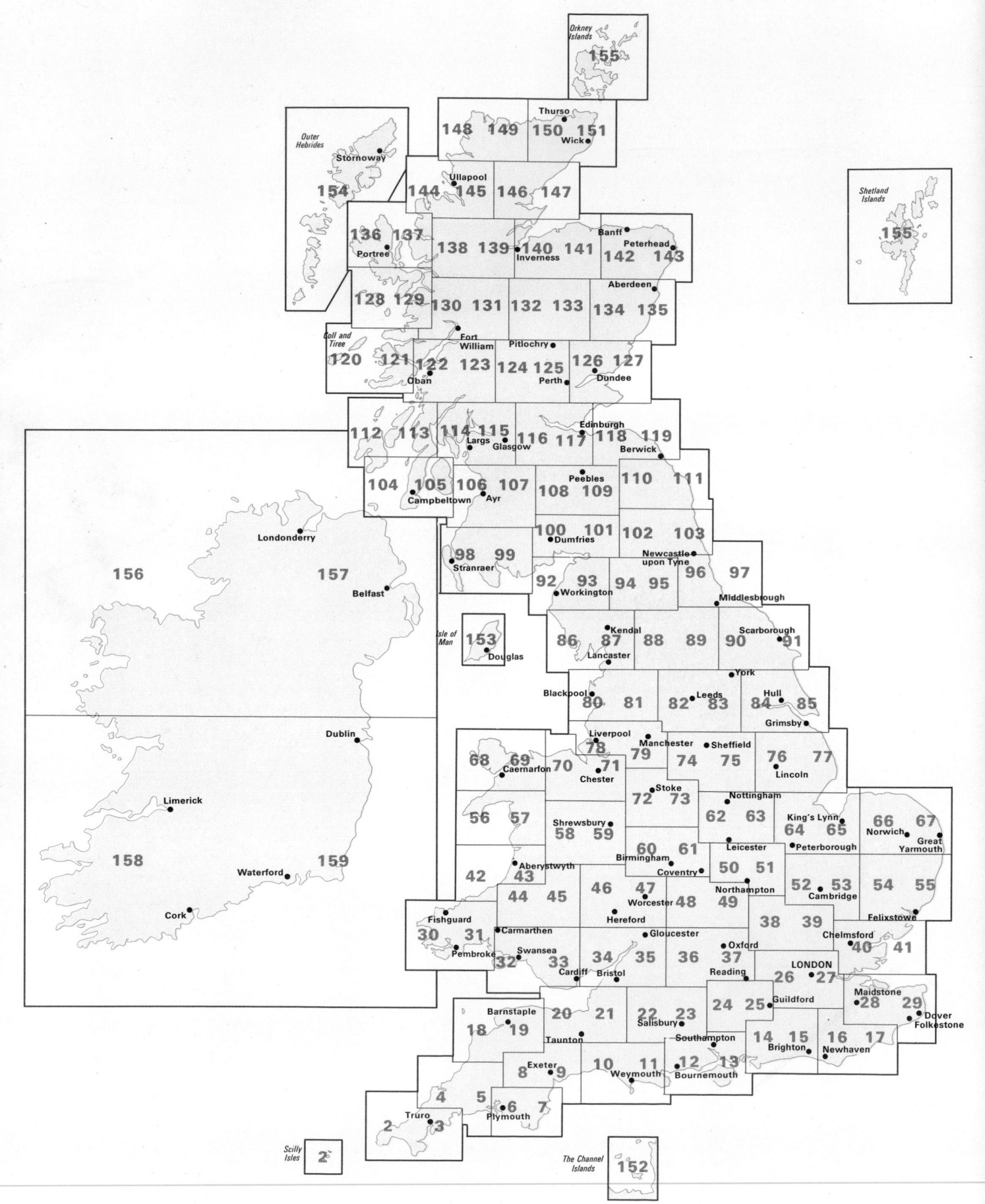

# Map Symbols

## MOTORING INFORMATION : VERKEHRSINFORMATIONEN : INFORMATIONS ROUTIERES

Motorway with number
Autobahn mit Nummer
Autoroute avec numéro

Motorway junction with and without number
Anschlußstelle mit/ohne Nummer
Echangeur avec/sans numéro

Motorway junction with limited access
Anschlußstelle mit beschränkter Auf- bzw. Abfahrt
Echangeur partiel

Motorway service area
Tanken und Rasten
Aire de Service

Motorway and junction under construction
Autobahn und Anschlußstelle im Bau
Autoroute et échangeur en construction

Primary route single/dual carriageway
Hauptverbindungsstraße 1 Fahrspur/2 Fahrspuren
Route principale 1 voie/2 voies

Other A road single/dual carriageway
Andere Straße der Klasse A 1 Fahrspur/2 Fahrspuren
Autre route catégorie A 1 voie/2 voies

B road single/dual carriageway
Straße der Klasse B 1 Fahrspur/2 Fahrspuren
Route catégorie B 1 voie/2 voies

Unclassified road, single/dual carriageway
Nicht klassifizierte Straße 1 Fahrspur/2 Fahrspuren
Route non classifiée 1 voie/ 2 voies

Road under construction
Straße im Bau
Route en construction

Narrow primary, other A or B road with passing places (Scotland)
enge Hauptverbindungsstraße, 'A' bzw. 'B' Straße mit Ausweichstellen (in Schottland)
Route principale étroite/autre route catégorie A ou B étroite avec places d'évitement (en Ecosse)

Road tunnel
Straßentunnel
Tunnel routier

Steep gradient (arrows point downhill)
Steigung/Gefälle (Pfeile weisen bergab)
Montée/Descente (à la flèche dirigée vers le bas)

Road toll
Straße mit Gebühr
Route à péage

Distance in miles between symbols
Entfernungen in Meilen zwischen Zeichen
Distance en milles entre symboles

Vehicle ferry – Great Britain
Autofähre – Inland
Bac pour automobiles en Grande Bretagne

Vehicle ferry – Continental
Autofähre – Ausland
Bac pour automobile – à l'étranger

Hovercraft ferry
Luftkissenfähre
Aéroglisseur

Airport
Flughafen
Aéroport

Heliport
Hubschrauberlandungsplatz
Héliport

Railway line/in tunnel
Bahnlinie/im Tunnel
Voie ferrée/sous tunnel

Railway station and level crossing
Bahnhof und Bahnübergang
Gare et passage à niveau

AA Centre – full services
AA-Hauptdienststelle
Centre AA principal

AA Road Service Centre – limited services
AA-Straßendienststelle – beschränkte Dienstleistungen
Centre-service routier auxiliare

AA Port Services – open as season demands
AA-Hafendienststelle – Öffnungszeiten von Jahreszeit abhängig
AA Centre-service de port – heures d'ouvertures varient selon la saison

AA and RAC telephones
AA bzw. RAC-Telefon
Téléphone AA et RAC

BT telephone in isolated places
Öffentliche Telefonzelle in abgelegenen Gebieten
Téléphone PTT aux endroits isolés

Urban area/village
Stadtgebiet/Dorf
Agglomération/Village

Spot height in metres
Höhenangabe in Meters
Altitude en mètres

River, canal, lake
Fluss, Kanal, See
Fleuve, canal, lac

Sandy beach
Sandstrand
Plage de sable

National boundary
Landesgrenze
Frontière nationale

Page overlap and number
Hinweiszahlen für die Anschlußkarten
Suite à la page indiquée

## TOURIST INFORMATION : FREMDENVERKEHR : RENSEIGNEMENTS TOURISTIQUES

Tourist Information Centre
Informationsbüro
Syndicat d'initiative

Tourist Information Centre (summer only)
Informationsbüro (nur im Sommer)
Syndicat d'initiative (seulement en été)

Abbey, cathedral or priory
Abtei, Dom, Kloster
Abbaye, cathédrale, prieuré

Ruined abbey, cathedral or priory
Abtei-, Dom-, Klosterruine
Abbaye, cathédrale, prieuré en ruines

Castle
Schloss/Burg
Château

Historic house
Historisches Gebäude
Edifice d'intérêt historique

Museum or art gallery
Museum/Kunstgalerie
Musée/galerie d'art

Industrial interest
Von industriellem Interesse
De l'intérêt industriel

Garden
Gartenanlage
Jardin

Arboretum
Arboretum
Arborétum

Country park
Park auf dem Lande
Parc promenade

Theme park
Freizeitpark
Parc d'attractions

Zoo
Tiergarten
Zoo

Wildlife collection – mammals
Tierpark – Säugetiere
Réserve d'animaux sauvages/mammifères

Wildlife collection – birds
Tierpark – Vögel
Réserve Ornithologique

Aquarium
Aquarium
Aquarium

Nature reserve
Naturschutzgebiet
Réserve naturelle

Nature trail
Naturlehrpfad
Sentier de découverte de la nature

Forest drive
Waldstraße
Route forestière

Long distance footpath
Fernwanderweg
Sentier de grande randonnée

Hill fort
Prähistorische Festungsanlage
Colline fortifiée

Roman antiquity
Überreste aus der Römerzeit
Antiquités romaines

Prehistoric monument
Prähistorisches Monument
Monument préhistorique

Battle site with year
Schlachtfeld mit Datum
Champ de bataille et Date

Preserved railway/steam centre
Museumbahn/Dampflokomotivmuseum
Chemin de fer touristique/musée de la vapeur

Cave
Höhle
Grotte

Windmill
Windmühle
Moulin à vent

AA viewpoint
AA-Aussichtspunkt
AA-Panorama

Picnic site
Picknickplatz
Lieu pour pique-nique

Golf course
Golfplatz
Golf

County cricket ground
wichtiger Kricketspielplatz
Terrain de cricket important

Horse racing
Pferderennbahn
Hippodrome

Show jumping/equestrian circuit
Reit-und Springturnier
Saut d'obstacles/circuit equestre

Motor racing circuit
Autorennen
Courses automobiles

Gliding centre
Segelflugplatz
Centre de vol à voile

Coastal launching site
Slipanlage für Boote
Air de mise à l'eau

Ski slope – natural
Skigelände
Piste de ski

Ski slope – artificial
Skigelände – künstlich
Piste de ski artificielle

Other places of interest
Weitere Sehenswürdigkeiten
Autres curiosités

Boxed symbols indicate attractions within urban areas
Das Einrahmen eines Zeichens bedeutet: die Sehenswürdigkeit befindet sich in einem Stadtgebiet
Dans le cas où le symbole est dans une case, la curiosité se trouve dans une localité

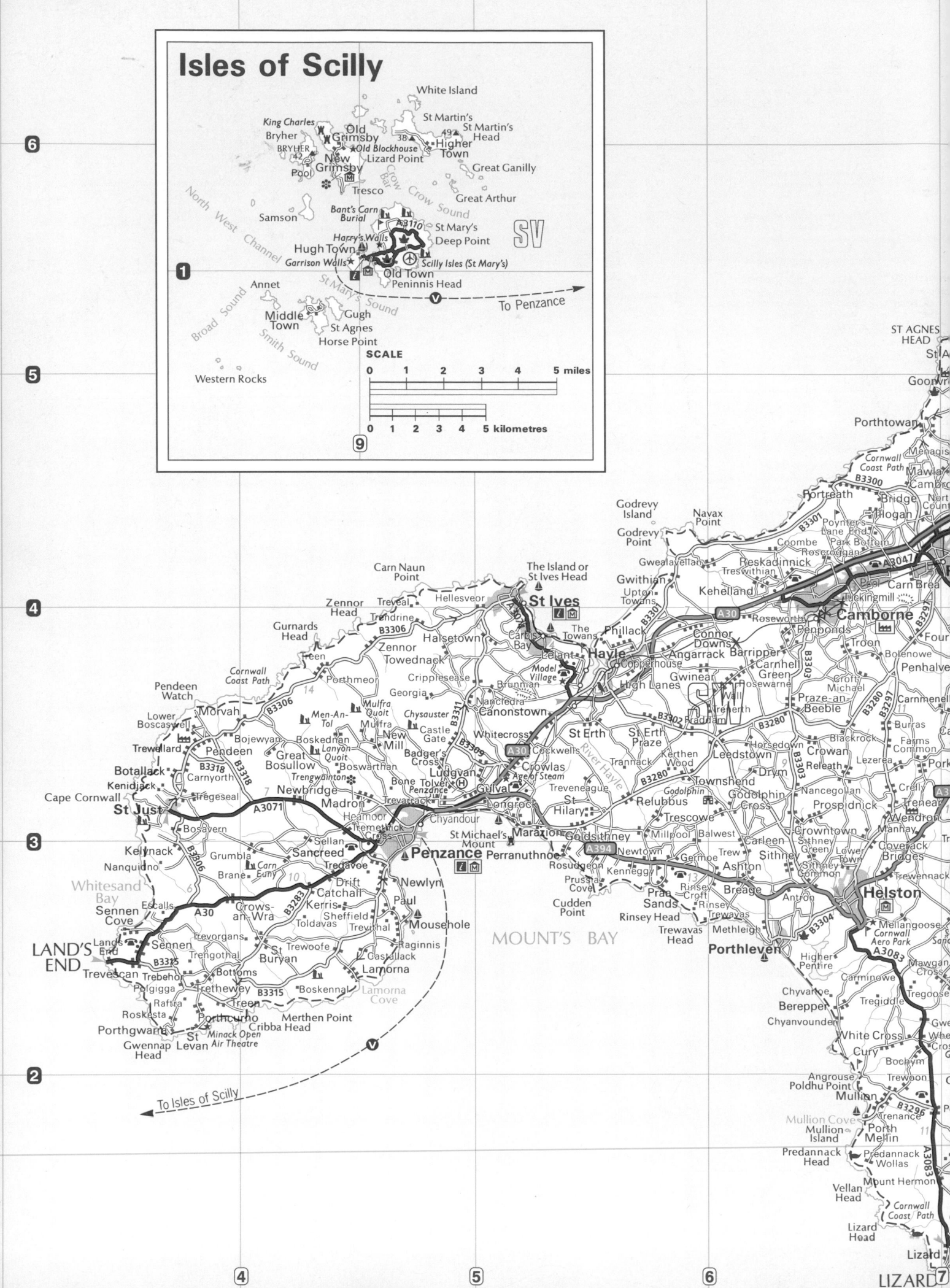

## Isles of Scilly

White Island

King Charles
Bryher
Old Grimsby
St Martin's
St Martin's
Head
BRYHER
38
497
Old Blockhouse
Higher
Town
42
New
Grimsby
Lizard Point
Pool
Great Ganilly
Tresco
Crow Bay
Crow Sound
Great Arthur

North West Channel
Samson
Bant's Carn
Burial
A3110
St Mary's
Deep Point

Harry's Walls
Hugh Town
Garrison Walls
Scilly Isles (St Mary's)
Old Town
Peninnis Head
St Mary's Sound
To Penzance

Annet
Broad Sound
Middle
Town
Gugh
St Agnes
Horse Point
Smith Sound

**SV**

Western Rocks

ST AGNES
HEAD
St A
Goonvr

**SCALE**

0   1   2   3   4   5 miles

0   1   2   3   4   5 kilometres

**9**

Godrevy
Island
Navax
Point
Godrevy
Point
Gwealavellan
Reskadinnick
Treswithian
Menagis
B3300
Portreath
Bridge
Camb
Poynter's
Lane End
Nort
Coun
Coombe
Roscroggan
A3047
Pool
Carn Brea
Gwithian
Upton
Towns
Kehelland
Illogan
Tuckingmill

Carn Naun
Point
The Island or
St Ives Head
St Ives
A30
Roseworthy
Camborne

Zennor
Head
Treveal
Hellesveor
Carbis
Bay
The Towans
Phillack
Connor
Downs
Penponds
Troon
Bolenowe
Four

Gurnards
Head
B3306
Trendrine
Halsetown
Lelant
Hayle
Copperhouse
Angarrack
Barripper
Carnhell
Green
Praze-an-
Beeble
Penhalve

Cornwall
Coast Path
Treen
Zennor
Towednack
Cripplesease
Model
Village
High Lanes
Gwinear
Rosewarne
Croft
Michael
B3280
B3297
Carnmenel

Pendeen
Watch
14
Porthmeor
Georgia
Brunnian
B3302
Gwealfa
Treneith
Pradaam
Blackrock
Burras
Car

Lower
Boscaswell
Morvah
B3306
Men-An-
Tol
Mulfra
Quoit
Chysauster
Nancledra
Canonstown
Whitecross
Ludgvan
Trannack
Leedstown
Horsedown
Crowan
Lezerea
Pork

Trewellard
Pendeen
Bojewyan
Boskednan
Mulfra
New
Mill
Castle
Gate
Boswarthen
Age of Steam
Cockwells
Kerthen
Wood
Drym
B3303
Releath

Botallack
Great
Bosullow
Lanyon
Quoit
Badger's
Cross
Crowlas
Treveneague
St
Hilary
Relubbus
Townshend
Godolphin
Cross
Nancegollan
Crell

Kenidjack
B3318
Carnyorth
Trengwainton
Bone Tolver
Gulval
Longrock
Trescowe
Prospidnick
Treneai
Wendro

Cape Cornwall
Tregeseal
7
Newbridge
Madron
Penzance
Trevarrack
Marazion
Goldsithney
Millpool
Balwest
Carleen
Crowntown
Manhay

St Just
A3071
Heamoor
Tremethick
Cross
Chyandour
St Michael's
Mount
Newtown
Germoe
Trew
Ashton
Sithney
Green
Lower
Town
Coverack
Bridges

Bosavern
Sellan
Perranuthnoe
Rosudgeon
A394
Breage
Anton
Trewennack

Kelynack
Grumbla
Sancreed
Tredavoe
Perranuthnoe
Prussia
Cove
Kenneggy
Praa
Sands
Rinsey
Croft
Sithney
Common

Nanquidno
Brane
Carn
Euny
Drift
Newlyn
Cudden
Point
Rinsey
Head
Trewavas
Methleigh
Helston
B3304

Whitesand
Bay
Escalls
A30
Crows-
an-Wra
Catchall
Kerris
Paul
Mousehole
Rinsey
Trewavas
Head
Porthleven
Mellangoose
Cornwall
Aero Park
Tregoose

Sennen
Cove
Sennen
Trevorgans
Toldavas
Trevithal
Raginnis
MOUNT'S BAY
Higher
Pentire
A3083
Mawgan
Cross

LAND'S
END
Land's
End
B3315
Trengothal
St
Buryan
Trewoofe
Castallack
Lamorna
Carminowe
Chyvarloe
Tregiddle
Gwe
Wher
Cros

Trevescan
Trebehor
Bottoms
Boskennal
Lamorna
Cove
Berepper
Chyanvounder
White Cross
Cury
Bochym

Polgigga
Trethewey
Treen
Merthen Point
Cribba Head
Angrouse
Poldhu Point
Trewoon
Trenance
A3083

Raftra
Porthcurno
Poldhu Point
Mullion
B3296
Pe

Porthgwarra
St
Gwennap
Levan
Head
Minack Open
Air Theatre
Mullion Cove
Mullion
Island
Porth
Mellin

To Isles of Scilly
Predannack
Head
Predannack
Wollas
Mount Hermon

Vellan
Head
Cornwall
Coast Path

Lizard
Head
Lizard

LIZARD
POINT

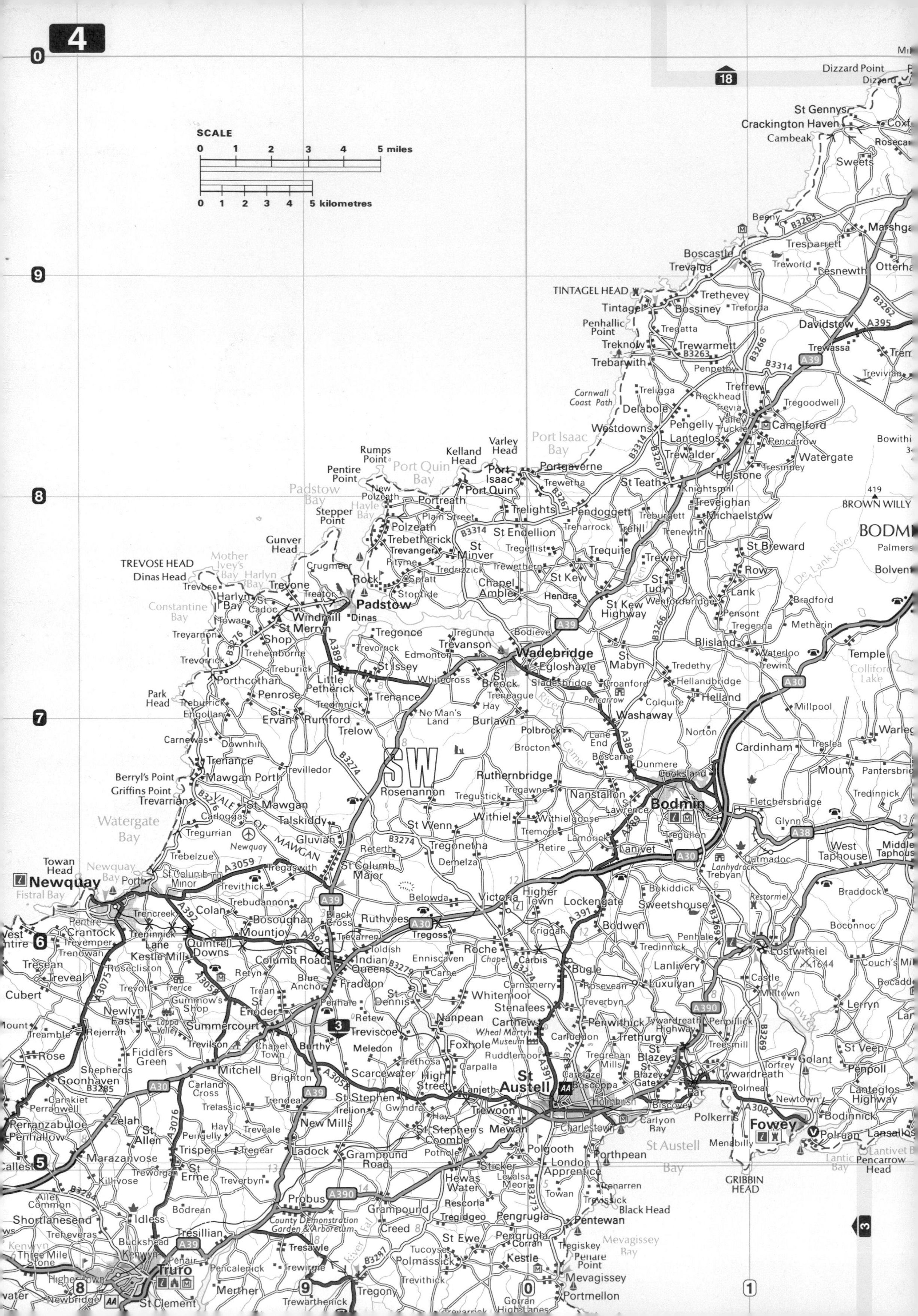

0

**SCALE**

0 1 2 3 4 5 miles

0 1 2 3 4 5 kilometres

9

8

7

6

5

18

Dizzard Point
Dizzard
St Gennys
Crackington Haven
Cambeak
Coxf
Rosecar
Sweets
Marshga
Tresparrett
B3263
Beeny
Boscastle
Trevalga
Treworld
Lesnewth
Otterha
15
TINTAGEL HEAD
Tintagel
Bossiney
Treforda
Trethevey
Tregatta
Davidstow
A395
Penhallic Point
Tregatta
Trewarmett
B3266
Trewassa
Trem
Treknow
Penpethy
B3314
A39
Trevivian
Trebarwith
Treligga
Trefrew
Cornwall Coast Path
Rockhead
Trevia
Tregoodwell
Delabole
Pengelly Valley Truckle
Camelford
Westdowns
Lanteglos
Pencarrow
Watergate
Trewalder
Tresinney
Helstone
419
BROWN WILLY
Bowithi
3
Port Isaac Bay
Portgaverne
Knightsmill
Treveighan
Michaelstow
St Breward
BODM
Palmers
Bolven
Rumps Point
Varley Head
Kelland Head
Port Isaac
Trewetha
Port Quin Bay
B3267
Trelights
St Teath
Pendoggett
Treburgett
Trehll
Tenewth
St Tudy
Row
Lank
Bradford
Temple
Collifor
Lake
Pentire Point
Port Quin
Port Quin
Portreath
Plain Street
B3314
St Endellion
Tregellist
Treharrock
Trequite
Trewen
Pensont
Tregenna
Metherin
Padstow Bay
New Polzeath
Hayle Bay
Polzeath
Trebetherick
Trevanger
St Minver
Tredrizzick
Trewethern
St Kew
St Kew Highway
Hendra
Westfordbridge
Helland
Blisland
Waterloo
Trewint
Stepper Point
Gunver Head
Crugmeer
Pityme
Splatt
Stoptide
Chapel Amble
Tregennis
Bodieve
A39
St Mabyn
Tredethy
Hellandbridge
Colquite
Helland
A30
Millpool
Mother Ivey's Bay
Harlyn Bay
Rock
Dinas
Wadebridge
Egloshayle
Sladesbridge
Croanford
Pencarrow
Washaway
Norton
TREVOSE HEAD
Dinas Head
Trevose
Harlyn
St Cadoc
Treator
Trevone
Padstow
Windmill
Tregonce
Trevanson
St Breock
Treneague Hay
Brocton
Boscarne
Dunmere
Cooksland
Cardinham
Treslea
Mount
Pantersbri
Treyarnon
St Merryn
Shop
Trehemborne
Treburick
Tredinnick
Little Petherick
Trenance
No Man's Land
Burlawn
Polbrock
Lane End
A389
Fletchersbridge
Tredinnick
Porthcothan
Penrose
St Issey
Whitecross
SW
Ruthernbridge
Tregawne
Nanstallon
Bodmin
Glynn
A38
West Taphouse
Middle Taphous
Park Head
Treburrick
Engollan
St Ervan
Rumford
Trelow
B3274
Rosenannon
Tregustick
Withiel
Withielgoose
Tremore
Lamorick
Retire
Lawrence
Tregullon
Lanivet
A30
Lanhydrock
Trebyan
Cutmadoc
Braddock
Boconnoc
Carnewas
Downhill
Trenance
Trevilledor
Mawgan Porth
VALE OF MAWGAN
St Mawgan
Talskiddy
Gluvian
B3274
Tregonetha
Demelza
Reterth
St Wenn
Higher Town
Lockengate
Bodwen
Sweetshouse
Penhale
Tredinnick
Berry's Point
Griffins Point
Trevarrian
Carloggas
Tregurrian
Trebelzue
Newquay
St Columb Major
Victoria
Belowda
Criggan
B3269
Lostwithiel
1644
Couch's
Bocadd
Watergate Bay
Towan Head
Newquay Bay
Porth
St Columb Minor
Trevithick
Tregaswith
A3059
St Columb Minor
A39
Black Cross
Ruthvoes
Tregoss
Roche
Bugle
Lanlivery
Luxulyan
A390
Castle
Restormel
Newquay
Fistral Bay
Pentire
Crantock
Treninnick
Lane
Trevemper
Trenowah
Colan
Bosoughan
Mountjoy
Trevarren
A3058
Toldish
Indian Queens
Enniscaven
Carne
Carbis
Carnsmerry
Treverbyn
Rosevean
Tredinnick
Tywardreath Highway
Penpillick
Treesmill
Golant
St Veep
Lar
Kestle Mill
Quintrell Downs
St Columb Road
B3279
Fraddon
Blue Anchor
Roche
Chapel
Whitemoor
Stenalees
Penwithick
Carluddon
Tregrehan Mills
St Blazey
Tywardreath
Lantic
Penpoll
West ntire
Tresean
Treveal
Cubert
Trevowah
Rejerrah
Newlyn East
Gummow's Shop
Lappa Valley
Trerice
Retyn
Troan
St Enoder
Summercourt
Chapel Town
Burthy
Treviscoe
Meledon
St Dennis
Nanpean
Foxhole
Ruddlemoor
Carpalla
Trethosa
Wheal Martyn Museum
Carlyon Bay
Charlestown
Par
Polmear
Tywardreath
Newtown
Lanteglos Highway
Bodinnick
Mount
Treamble
Rose
Fiddlers Green
Trevilson
Mitchell
Brighton
B3275
Scarcewater
High Street
A3058
St Stephen
Trendea
Trelion
Trewoon
Gwindra
St Austell
AA
Holmbush
Biscovey
A390
Fowey
Polruan
Goonhaven
Carnkiet
B3285
Perranwell
Carland Cross
Trelassick
A30
A39
New Mills
Trevaile
St Stephen's Coombe
Pothole
St Stephen's Mewan
Polgooth
Porthpean
St Austell Bay
Menabilly
GRIBBIN HEAD
Rerranzabuloe
Penhallow
Zelah
St Allen
Hay
Pengelly
Tregear
Ladock
Grampound Road
Hewas Water
Sticker
London Apprentice
Towan
callest
Marazanvose
Trispen
St Erme
Treworgan
Killivose
Trewarthenick
Trispen
Bodrean
Probus
A390
Grampound
Creed
Rescorla
Tregidgeo
Pengrugla
Pengrugla
Pentewan
Allet Common
Idless
Tresillian
County Demonstration Garden & Arboretum
River Fal
St Ewe
Tucoyse
Corran
Tregiskey
Mevagissey Bay
Shortlanesend
Treneveras
Buckshead
A39
Tresawle
B3287
Polmassick
Trevithick
Penare Point
Three Mile Stone
Kenwyn
Penair
Pencalenick
Trewirgie
Kestle
Penare
water
Newbridge
Truro
AA
St Clement
Merther
Tregony
Gorran High Lanes
Mevagissey
Portmellon
3
1

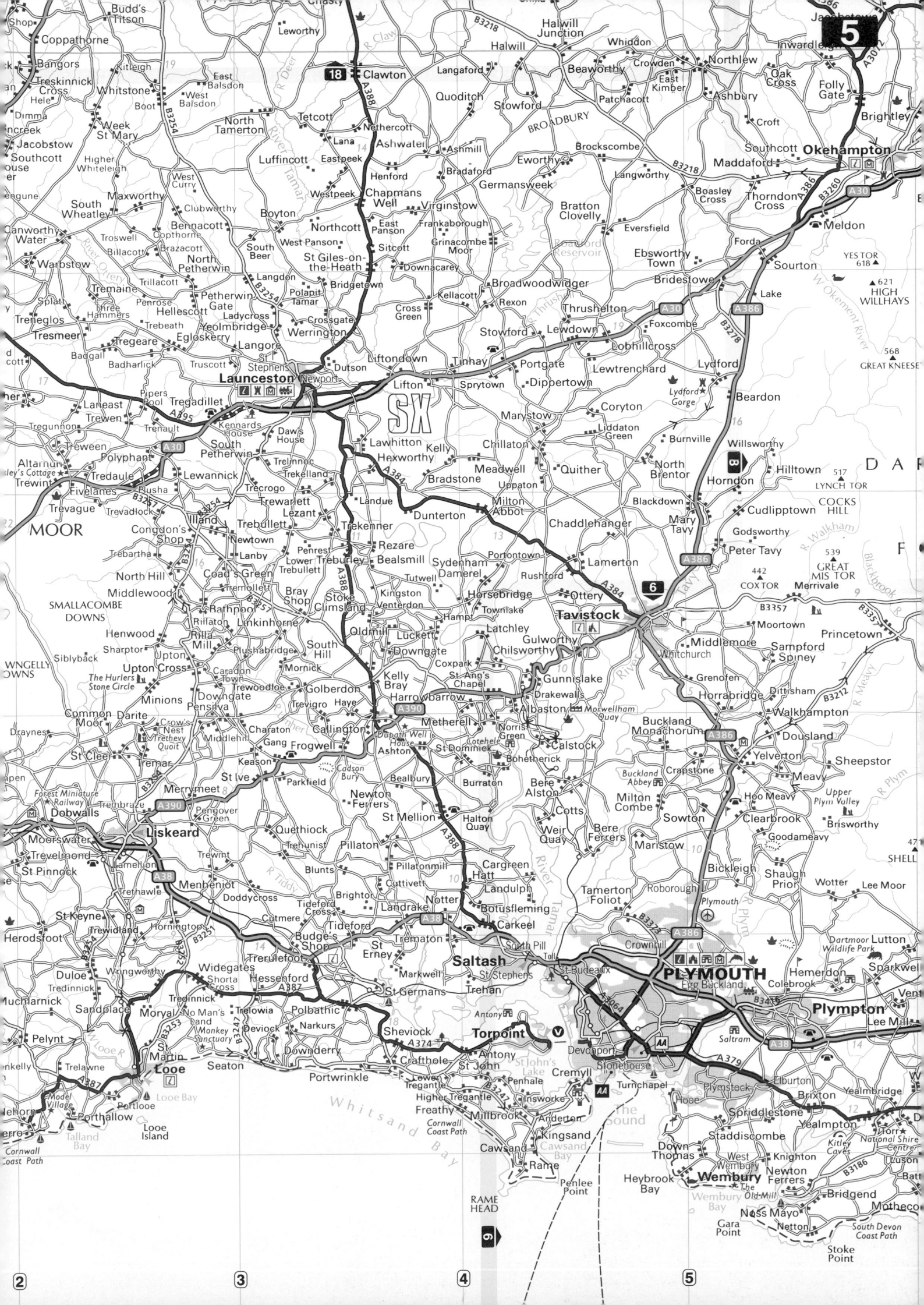

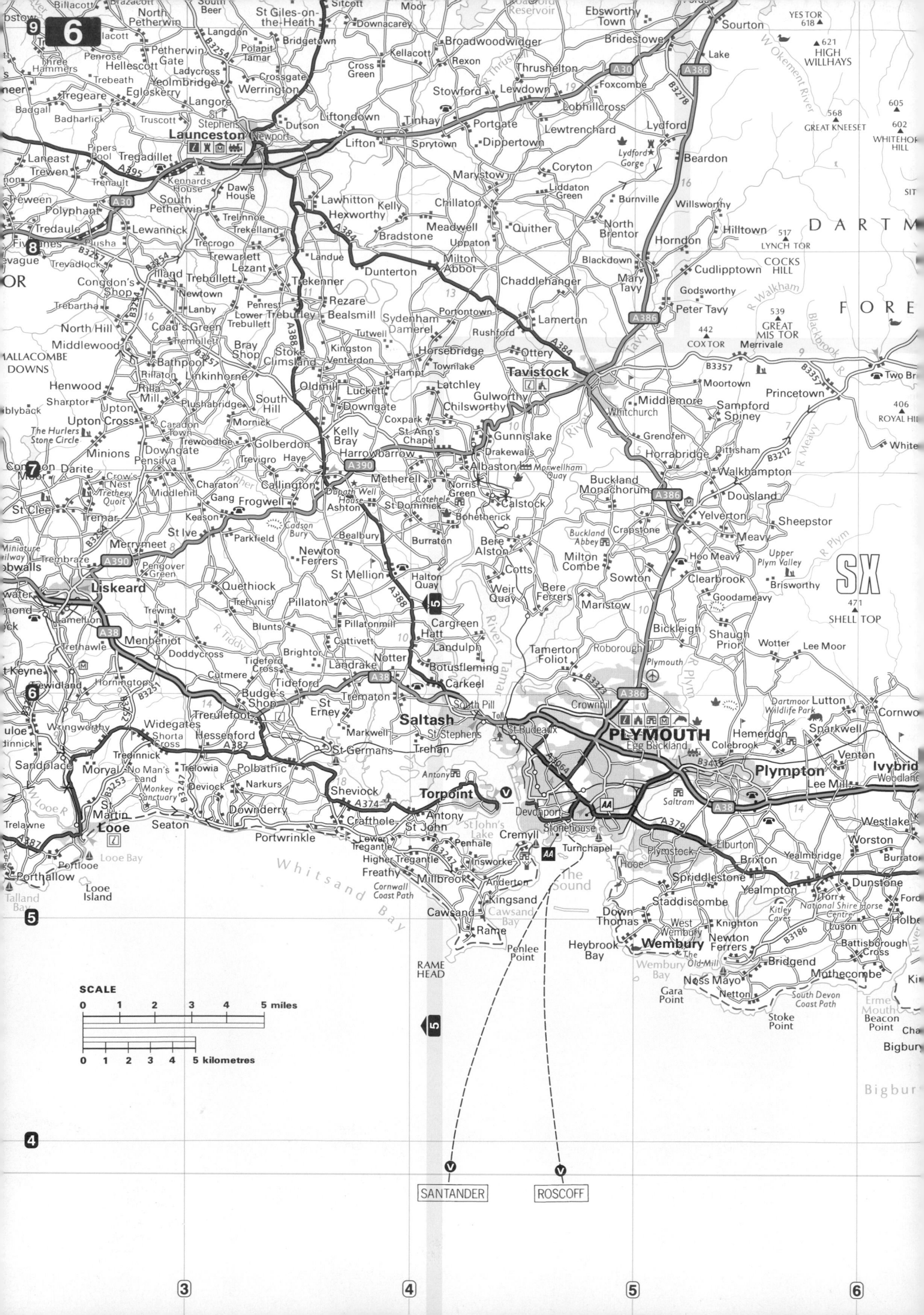

5

4

3

2

1

0

**LUNDY
ISLAND**

North West
Point

142

*Marisco*

Surf Point

**SCALE**

| 0 | 1 | 2 | 3 | 4 | 5 miles |

| 0 | 1 | 2 | 3 | 4 | 5 kilometres |

B A R N S T A P L E

O R

B I D E F O R D   B A Y

Bull Point
Rockham
Bay
Morte Point
Mortehoe
Woolacombe
Morte Bay
Pickwell
Baggy Point
Putsborough
Croyde Bay
Croyde Bay
Georgel
Croyde
Darracott
Knov
Saunton
Lobb
Braunton
Wraf

Appledore
Westward Ho!
Northam
We
Eastleig
Pil
Bideford
Landcros

HARTLAND
POINT
Shipload
Bay
Damehole
Point
Titchberry
Somerset and
North Devon
Coast Path
Brownsham
Clovelly
Court
Clovelly
Buck's
Mills
Hartland
Velly
Sierra
Abbotsham
Fairy
Cross
Ford
Yeo
Vale
Hartland
Quay
Stoke
B3248
Dyke
Horns
Cross
Woodtown
Spekes Mill
Mouth
Milford
Philham
A39
Buck's
Cross
Cranford
Goldworthy
Parkham
Littleham
Saltrens
Elmscott
Woolfardisworthy
Cabbacott
Buckland
Brewer
Monkleig
Hardisworthy
Parkham
Ash
Melbury
Frithelstock
South
Hole
Frithelstock
Stone
Taddiport
Welcombe
Ashmansworthy
Thornehillhead
Southcott
Mead
Darracott
Meddon
West
Putford
East Putford
Langtree
Lan
We
Woolley
East
Youlstone
Dinworthy
Colscott
Gooseham
Easteott
16
Morwenstow
Higher Sharpnose
Point
Shop
West
Youlstone
Bradworthy
Haytown
Bulkworthy
Stibb
Cross
Berry
Cross
Lower Sharpnose
Point
Upper Tamar
Reservoir
Kimworthy
Alfardisworthy
Abbots
Bickington
Newton
St Petrock
Steeple
Point
Kilkhampton
Darracott
Sutcombemill
Sutcombe
Venngreen
Sandy
Mouth
Thurdon
Soldon
Cross
Soldon
Milton Damerel
Stibb
A39
B3254
Dunsdon
Thornbury
Shebbear
Buckland
Filleigh
Northcott
Mouth
Poughill
Ebbersham
Venn
Holsworthy
Beacon
Brendon
Little
Lashbrook
Bradford
Priestacott
Dipper mill
Maer
Bush
Grimscott
Lana
Cookbury
Hole
Bude
Flexbury
Stratton
Launcells
Kingford
Chilsworthy
Cookbury
Wick
Holemoor
Lashbrook
Black
Torring
Bude
Bay
Bude
Launcells
Cross
Pancrasweek
Holsworthy
Anvil
Corner
13
Lynstone
A3072
Red
Cross
Buttsbear
Cross
Derril
Whimble
Brandis
Corner
A3072
Odham
Upton
Derriton
Chasty
Hollacombe
Chilla
Helebridge
Marhamchurch
Bridgerule
Pyworthy
Chasty
B3218
Widemouth
Bay
Budd's
Titson
Leworthy
Halwill
Junction
Box's Shop
Coppathorne
Halwill
Whiddon
Millook
Dizzard Point
Poundstock
Kitleigh
19
Langaford
Beaworthy
Dizzard
Bangors
Treskinnick
Cross
East
Balsdon
Clawton
Quoditch
Cro
St Gennys
Penlean
Tregole
imma
Whitstone
Boot
West
Balsdon
Tetcott
Stowford
Patchacon
ackington Haven
Coxford
Trenreek
Week
St Mary
th
Tamerton
Nethercott
BROADBURY
Cambeak
Rosecare
Jacobstow
Lana
Ashwater

4

1          2          3          4          5

SS

EXMOOR

FOREST

Foreland Point

Lynmouth Bay

Countisbury Cove

Hurtstone Point

Porlock Bay

Woody Bay

Lynton

Countisbury

Bossington

Lynbridge

Lynmouth

Brendon

Culbone

West Porlock

Porlock Weir

Elwill Bay

Martinhoe

West Lyn

Wilsham

Malmsmead

Porlock

Trentishoe

Dean

Barbrook

Rockford

Oare

Horner

Woody Bay

Kemacott

West Ilkerton

East Ilkerton

Cheriton

Tippacott

Lucott

Luccombe

Water Mouth

Combe Martin Bay

Heale

Killington

Woolhanger

Furzehill

Dry Hill

Dunkery Hill

Hele Bay

Watermouth

Haggington Hill

Combe Martin

Parracombe

Churchtown

HOAROAK HILL 474

River Exe

Edgcott

Exford

Luckwell Bridge

Hele

Chambercombe Manor

Sterridge

Berrynarbor

Dean

Swincombe

Challacombe

Simonsbath

Newland

Blackland

Withypool

Great Nurco

Two Pots

Ruggaton

Patchole

Arlington Beccott

Stowford

Barton Town

B3358

B3223

River Barle

410

Winsford

Mullacott Cross

West Down

Berry Down Cross

Kentisbury

Leworthy

Kinsford Water

Knaplock

Liscombe

Bittadon

East Down

Kentisbury Ford

Knightacott

Fullaford

SPAN HEAD 493

WORTH HILL

Tarr Steps

Tarr

Halsinger

Churchill

Arlington

Exmoor Bird Gardens

Loxhore

Lower Loxhore

Whitefield

North Radworthy

Twitchen

Hawkridge

Milltown

Higher Muddiford

Muddiford

Upcott

Loxhore Cott

Bratton Fleming

Benton

Lydcott

Brayford

Bentwichen

North Heasley

South Radworthy

Marwood

Guineaford

Shirwell

High Bray

North Heanton Punchardon

Kingsheanton

Shirwell Cross

Stoke Rivers

Charles

Heasley Mill

Northmoor

Ashford

Northleigh

Goodleigh

Whitsford

Molland

Slade

West Anstey

East Anstey

Dulverton

Bradiford Pilton

Willesleigh

Gunn

Stoodleigh

Upcott

Battleton

Barnstaple

Bradninch

Accott

West Buckland

Elwell

East Buckland

North Molton

Nightcott

Newport

Landkey Town

Landkey

Yarnacott

Bremridge

South Molton

Aller

Knowstone

Oakfordbridge

Lake

Bishop's Tawton

Swimbridge

Castle Hill

Bish Mill

Newtown

Ash Mill

Oldways End

Sowerhill

Oakford

Harracott

Herner

Traveller's Rest

Filleigh

Quince Honey Farm

Radley

Bishop's Nympton

East Knowstone

Westcott

Newton Tracey

Hiscott

Chapelton

Gobbaton

East Slowford

Clapworthy

George Nympton

Alswear

Mariansleigh

Yard

Rose Ash

Crooked Oak

A361

Chittlehampton

Umberleigh

Warkleigh

Satterleigh

Romansleigh

Meshaw

Creacombe

Rackenford

Atherington

Langridge Ford

Chittlehamholt

King's Nympton

Queen Dart

Loxbeare

High Bickington

Cadbury Barton

Week

Huntshaw Cross

Roborough

Burrington

Witheridge

Edgeworthy

Templeton

Withleigh

Great Torrington

St Giles in the Wood

Kingscott

Elstone

Colleton Mills

Chulmleigh

Worlington

Nomansland

Rosemoor

Beaford

Ashreigney

Cheldon

Drayford

Washford Pyne

Cruwys Morchard

Little Potheridge

Riddlecombe

Bridge Reeve

Chawleigh

Pennymoor

Great Potheridge

Dolton

Chittlehampton

Ashley

Eggesford

Filleigh

Hele Lane

Littleborough

Puddington

Way Village

Well Town

Huish

Hollocombe

Wembworthy

Nymet Rowland

Eastington

Black Dog

Poughill

Upham

Petrockstowe

Iddesleigh

Winkleigh

Moor End

Lapford

Woolfardisworthy

Cadeleigh

Ash

Meeth

Brushford Barton

Coldridge

Morchard Bishop

Kennerleigh

Stockleigh English

Uppincott

Monkokehampton

Barwick

Ingleigh Green

Broadwood Kelly

West Leigh

East Leigh

Nymet Tracey

Weeke

East Village

Cheriton Fitzpaine

Splatt

Bondleigh

Lowton

Zeal Monachorum

Loosebeare

Weeke

Newbuildings

Upton Hellions

Chilton

Hatherleigh

Honeychurch

North Tawton

Barons Wood

Down St Mary

Copplestone

Sandford

Lower Creedy

Stockleigh Pomeroy

Jacobstowe

Exbourne

Sampford Courtenay

Sutton

Clannaborough

Woolsgrove

West Sandford

Creedy Park

Little Silver

West Raddon

Inwardleigh

Trecott

Broadnymett

Bow

Coleford

Knowle

Penstone

Golebrooke

Efford

Northlew

Oak Cross

Folly Gate

Rowden

Itton

Spestos

Hillerton

Yeoford

Crediton

Neopardy

Fordton

Wyke

Shobrooke

Shute

Pennicott

Brightley

Taw Green

Corscombe

Spreyton

Woodland Head

Highfield

River Troney

Uton

Hookway

Smallbrook

Newton St Cyres

Netta

Bram

Sweetham

Venny Tedburn

Ashbury

SX

Croft

SW

41

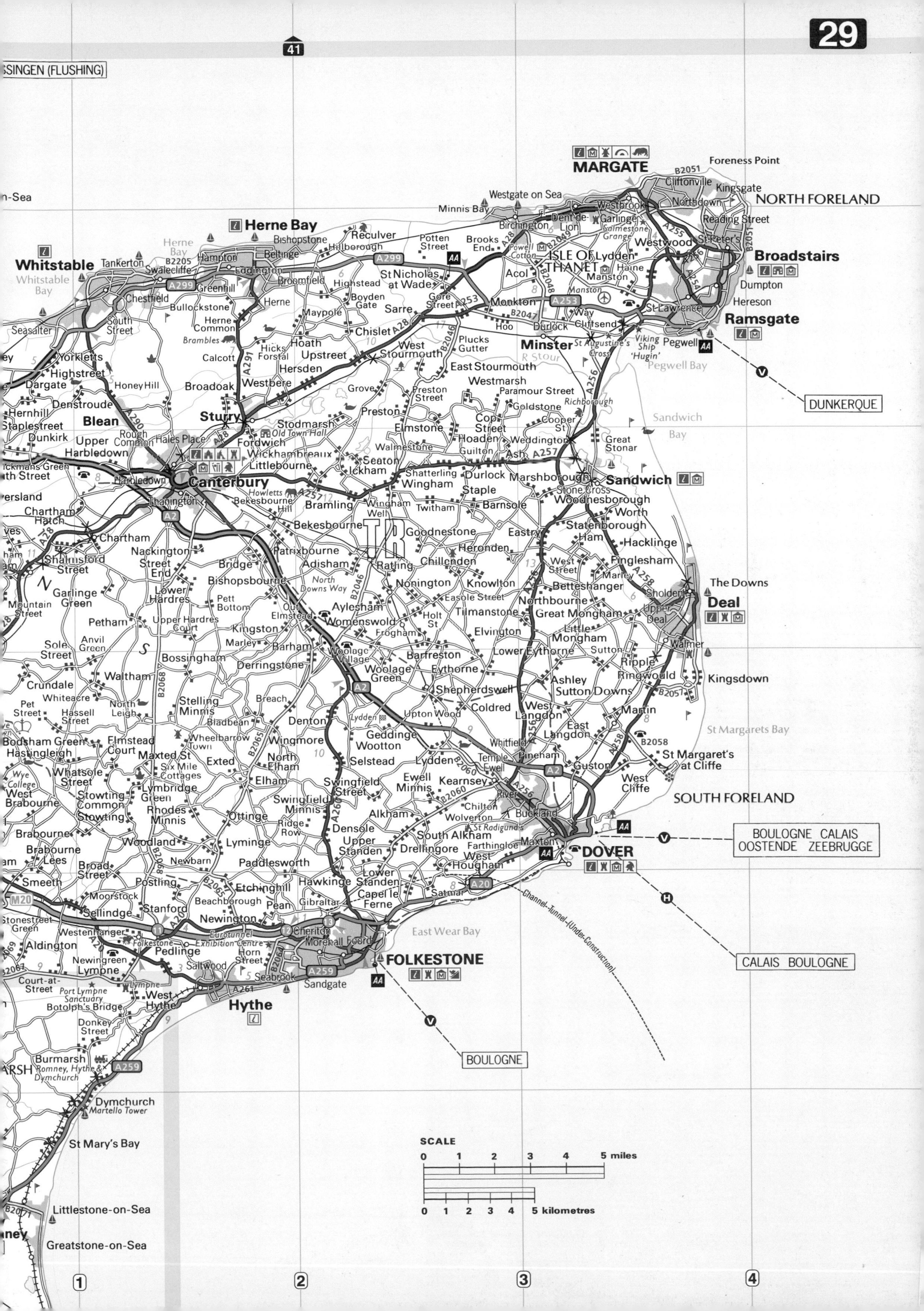

SSINGEN (FLUSHING)

**MARGATE**
Foreness Point
Cliftonville  Kingsgate
Westgate on Sea  Westbrook  Northdown  **NORTH FORELAND**
Minnis Bay  Dent-de-Lion  Garlinge  Reading Street
Birchington  St Peter's
**Herne Bay**  Reculver  Brooks End  Powell  Westwood  **Broadstairs**
Bishopstone  Hillborough  Potten Street  Cotton  ISLE OF  Lydden  Dumpton
Beltinge  Street  THANET  Haine  Hereson
**Whitstable**  Tankerton  Swalecliffe  Hampton  Eddington  Broomfield  Acol  Manston  St Lawrence  **Ramsgate**
Whitstable Bay  Greenhill  St Nicholas at Wade  Monkton  Way  Cliffsend
Chestfield  Herne  Boyden Gate  Sarre  Hoo  Durlock  **Minster**
Seasalter  Bullockstone  Maypole  Gore Street  Chislet  Pluck's Gutter  Viking Ship 'Hugin'  Pegwell  **DUNKERQUE**
South Street  Herne Common  Hoath  Upstreet  R Stour  St Augustine's Cross  Pegwell Bay
Yorkletts  Brambles  Hicks Forstal  Hersden  West Stourmouth  East Stourmouth  Westmarsh  Richborough  Sandwich Bay
Highstreet  Calcott  Broadoak  Westbere  Grove  Preston Street  Paramour Street  Goldstone
Dargate  Honey Hill  Sturry  Preston  Cooper St  Great Stonar
Denstroude  Stodmarsh  Elmstone  Hoaden  Weddington  Woodnesborough  **Sandwich**
Hernhill  Staplestreet  Rough Common  Old Town Hall  Walmestone  Guilton  Ash  Stone Cross  Worth
**Blean**  Upper Harbledown  Hales Place  Fordwich  Wickhambreaux  Seaton  Ickham  Shatterling  Durlock  Marshborough  Statenborough
Dunkirk  Harbledown  Littlebourne  Wingham  Staple  Barnsole  Ham  Hacklinge
Rickmans Green  **Canterbury**  Bekesbourne  Bramling  Twitham  Goodnestone  Eastry  Marley  Finglesham
Thanington  Hill  Bekesbourne  Wingham Well  Heronden  West Street  Betteshanger  Sholden  The Downs
Chartham Hatch  Patrixbourne  Ratling  Chillenden  Knowlton  Northbourne  Great Mongham  Upper Deal  **Deal**
Shalmsford Street  Chartham  Adisham  Nonington  Easole Street  Tilmanstone  Little Mongham  Walmer
Nackington  Bridge  Bishopsbourne  Frogham  Holt St  Elvington  Sutton  Ripple
Street End  Pett Bottom  Out Elmstead  Aylesham  Eythorne  Lower Eythorne  Ashley  Ringwould
Garlinge Green  Lower Hardres  Womenswold  Barfreston  Sutton Downs  Kingsdown
Mountain Street  Upper Hardres Court  Kingston  Marley  Woolage Village  Shepherdswell  West Langdon  Martin
Petham  Barham  Woolage Green  Coldred  East Langdon  B2058  St Margarets Bay
Sole Street  Bossingham  Derringstone  Upton Wood  Whitfield  St Margaret's at Cliffe
Anvil Green  Waltham  Breach  Denton  Lydden  Temple Ewell  Pineham  West Cliffe
Crundale  Whiteacre  Stelling Minnis  Bladbean  Geddinge  Wootton  Guston  **SOUTH FORELAND**
Pet Street  North Leigh  Wheelbarrow Town  Selstead  Ewell Minnis  River  Buckland
Hassell Street  Elmsted Court  Wingmore  North Elham  Lydden  Kearsney  Maxton
Bodsham Green  Six Mile Cottages  Exted  Swingfield Street  Chilton  Wolverton  St Radigund's  **DOVER**
Hastingleigh  Maxted St  Elham  Swingfield Minnis  Alkham  South Alkham  Farthingloe  BOULOGNE CALAIS OOSTENDE ZEEBRUGGE
Wye College  Whatsole Street  Lymbridge Green  Ridge Row  Densole  Drellingore  West Houghton
West Brabourne  Stowting Common  Rhodes Minnis  Ottinge  Upper Standen  Maxton
Brabourne  Stowting  Woodland  Lyminge  Lower Standen  CALAIS BOULOGNE
Brabourne Lees  Broad Street  Newbarn  Paddlesworth  Hawkinge  Capel le Ferne  Satmar  Channel Tunnel (Under Construction)
Smeeth  Postling  Etchinghill  Gibraltar  East Wear Bay
Moorstock  Beachborough  Pean  Morehall  Foord
Sellindge  Stanford  Newington  Cheriton  **FOLKESTONE**
Stonestreet Green  Aldington  Westenhanger  Eurotunnel Exhibition Centre  Horn Street
Newingreen  Folkestone  Pedlinge  Saltwood  Seabrook  Sandgate
Lympne  Court-at-Street  West Hythe  Port Lympne Sanctuary  **Hythe**  BOULOGNE
Botolph's Bridge  Wympne
Donkey Street  Lympne
Burmarsh  Romney, Hythe & Dymchurch
MARSH
Dymchurch  Martello Tower
St Mary's Bay

SCALE
0  1  2  3  4  5 miles
0  1  2  3  4  5 kilometres

Littlestone-on-Sea
Greatstone-on-Sea

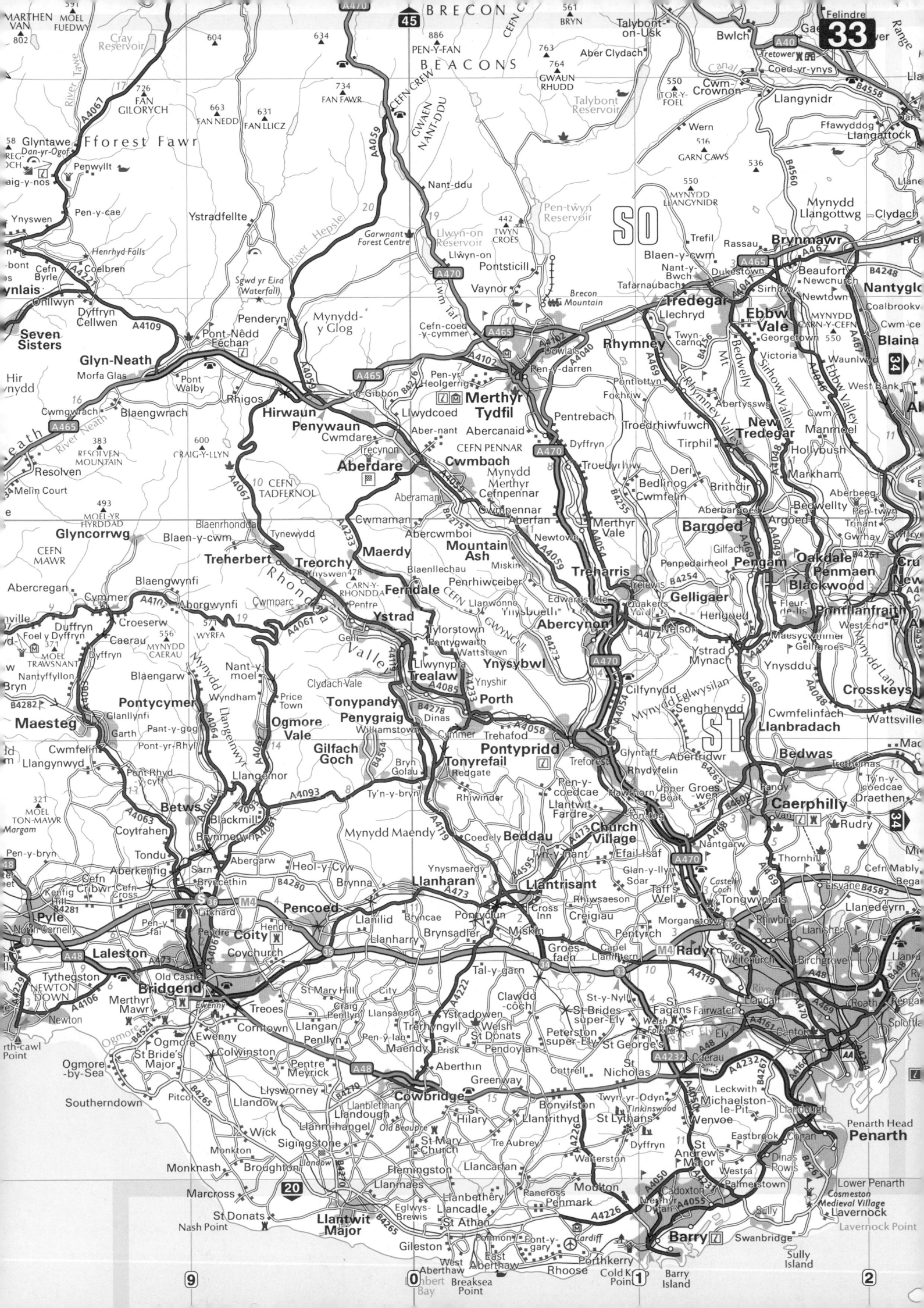

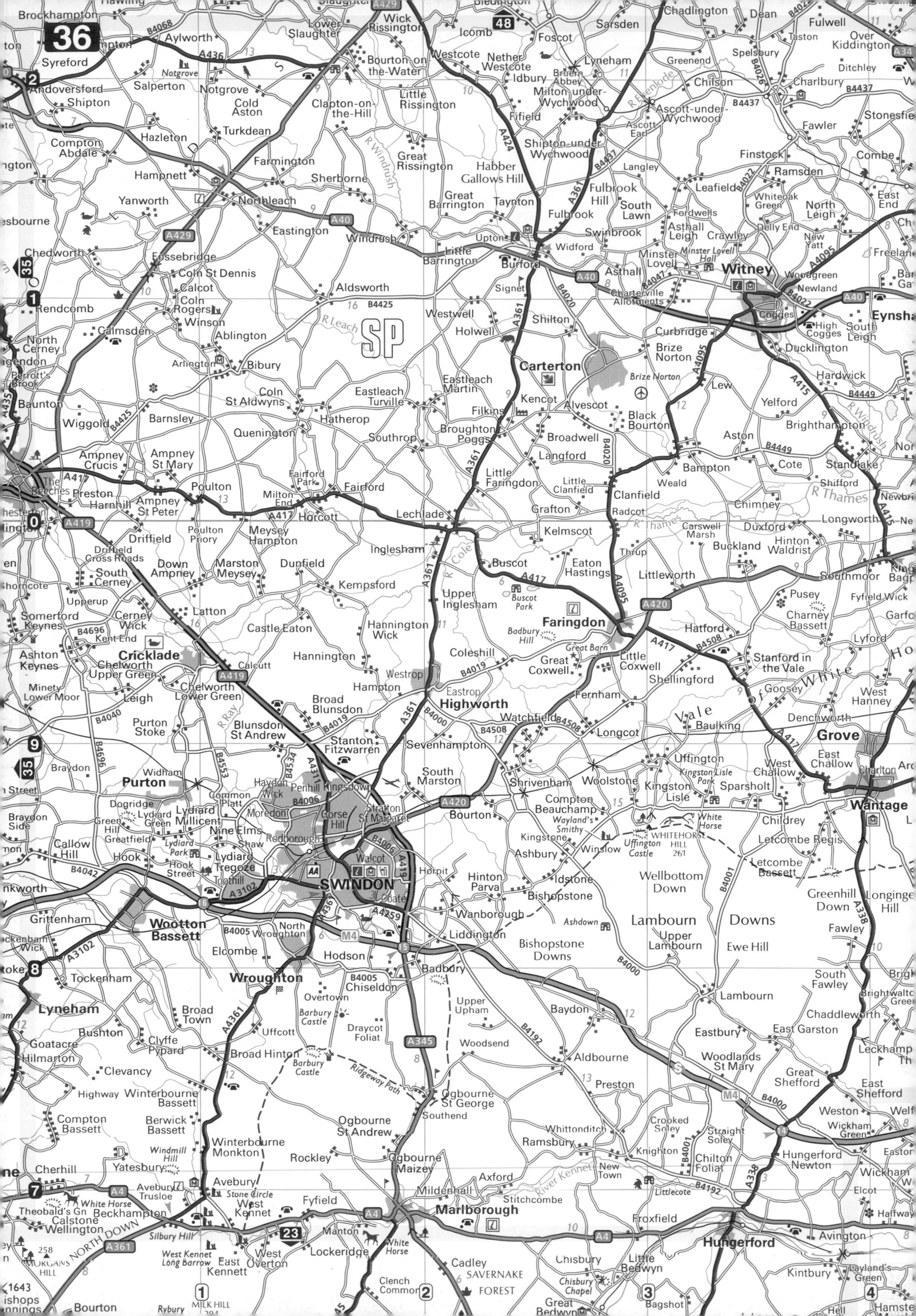

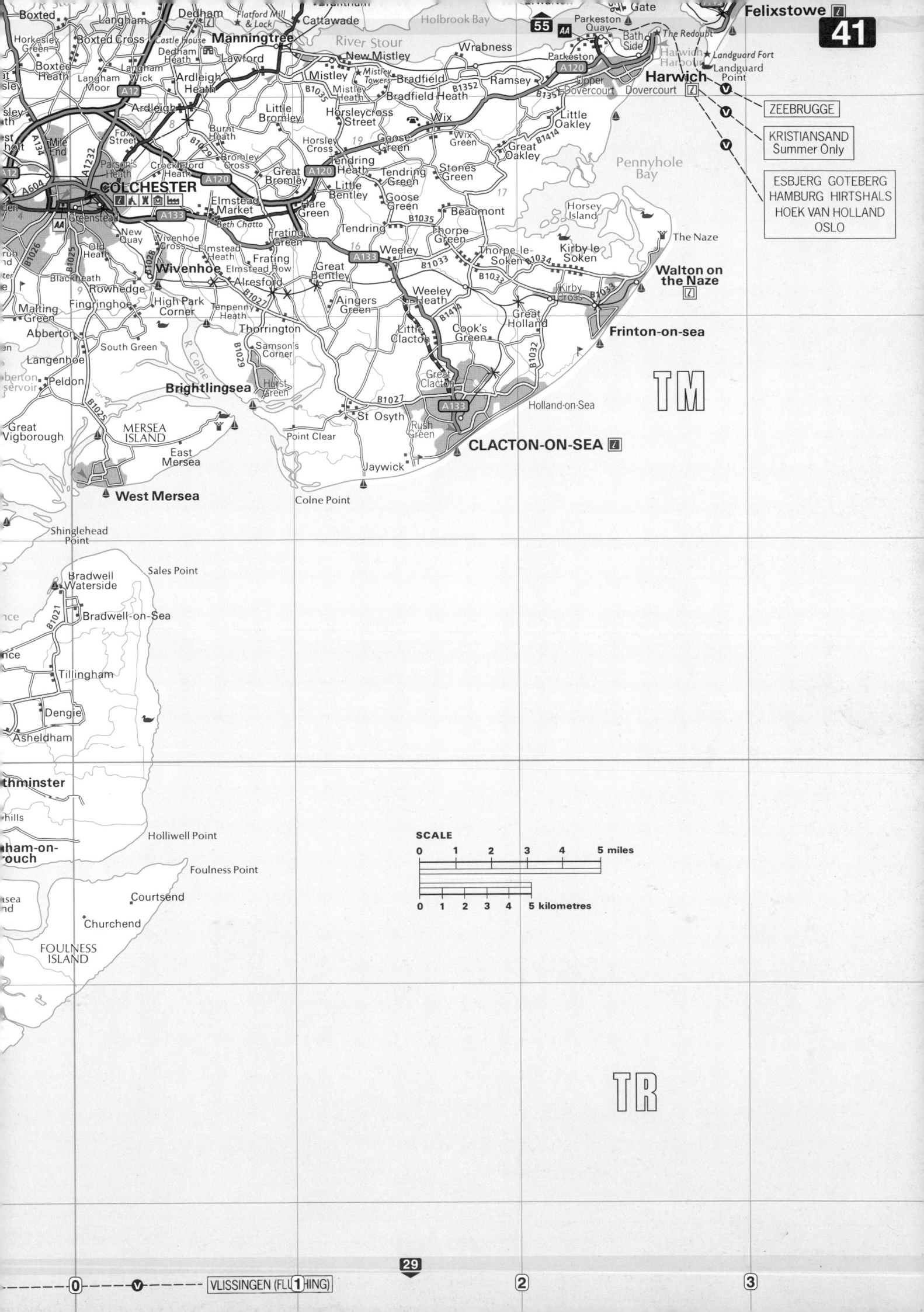

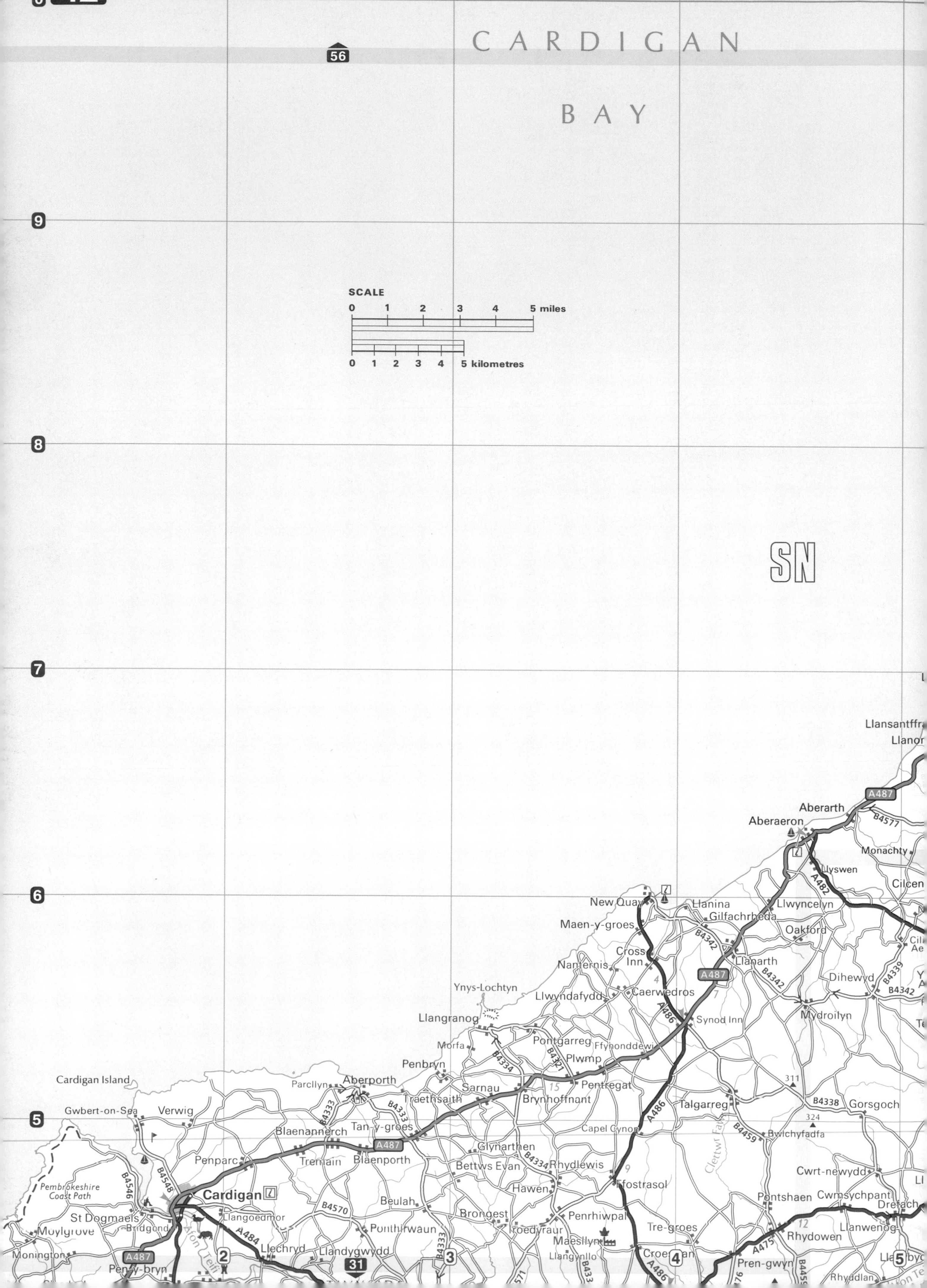

56

# CARDIGAN

# BAY

9

8

SN

7

Llansantffr
Llanor

A487

Aberarth
Aberaeron
B4577

Monachty

Llyswen

Cilcen

6 New Quay Llanina Llwyncelyn
Gilfachrheda
Maen-y-groes B4342 Oakford
Cross Cil
Nanternis Inn Llanarth Ae
4 Caerwedros A487 B4342
Ynys-Lochtyn A486 Llanarth Dihewyd B4339 Y
Llwyndafydd 7 Mydroilyn B4342
Llangranog Synod Inn Te

Morfa Pontgarreg Ffynonddewi
Penbryn B4321 Plwmp 311
B4334
Cardigan Island Aberporth Sarnau Pentregat B4338 Gorsgoch
Parcllyn Traethsaith Brynhoffnant Talgarreg
Gwbert-on-Sea Verwig B4333 A486 B4459 Bwlchyfadfa 324
5 B4333 Capel Cynon
Blaenannerch Tan-y-groes 9
Penparc Glynarthen Cwrt-newydd
Trewain Blaenporth Bettws Evan Rhydlewis Pontshaen Cwmsychpant
Pembrokeshire B4546 B4570 B4334 Ffostrasol Dref ach
Coast Path Cardigan Beulah Hawen Penrhiwpal A475 Llanwenog
Moylgrove Llangoedmor Brongest Tre-groes Rhydowen 12 5
Bridgend Ponthirwaun Troedyraur Penrhiwpal Lle by
Monington Llechryd B4333 Maesllyn A486 Pren-gwyn
A487 A484 Llandygwydd Croes an Rhyddlan
Pen-y-bryn 2 31 3 Llangynllo 4

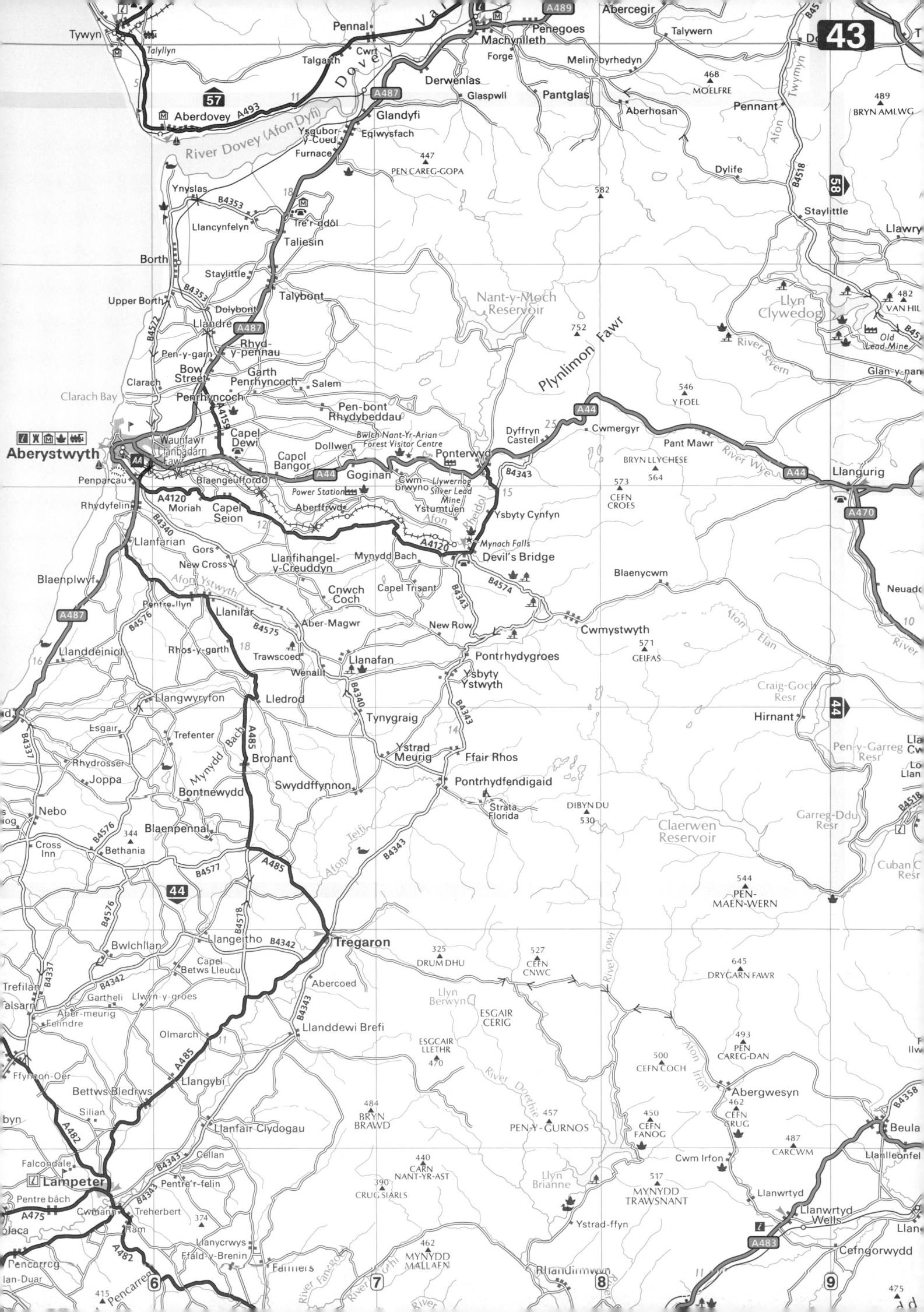

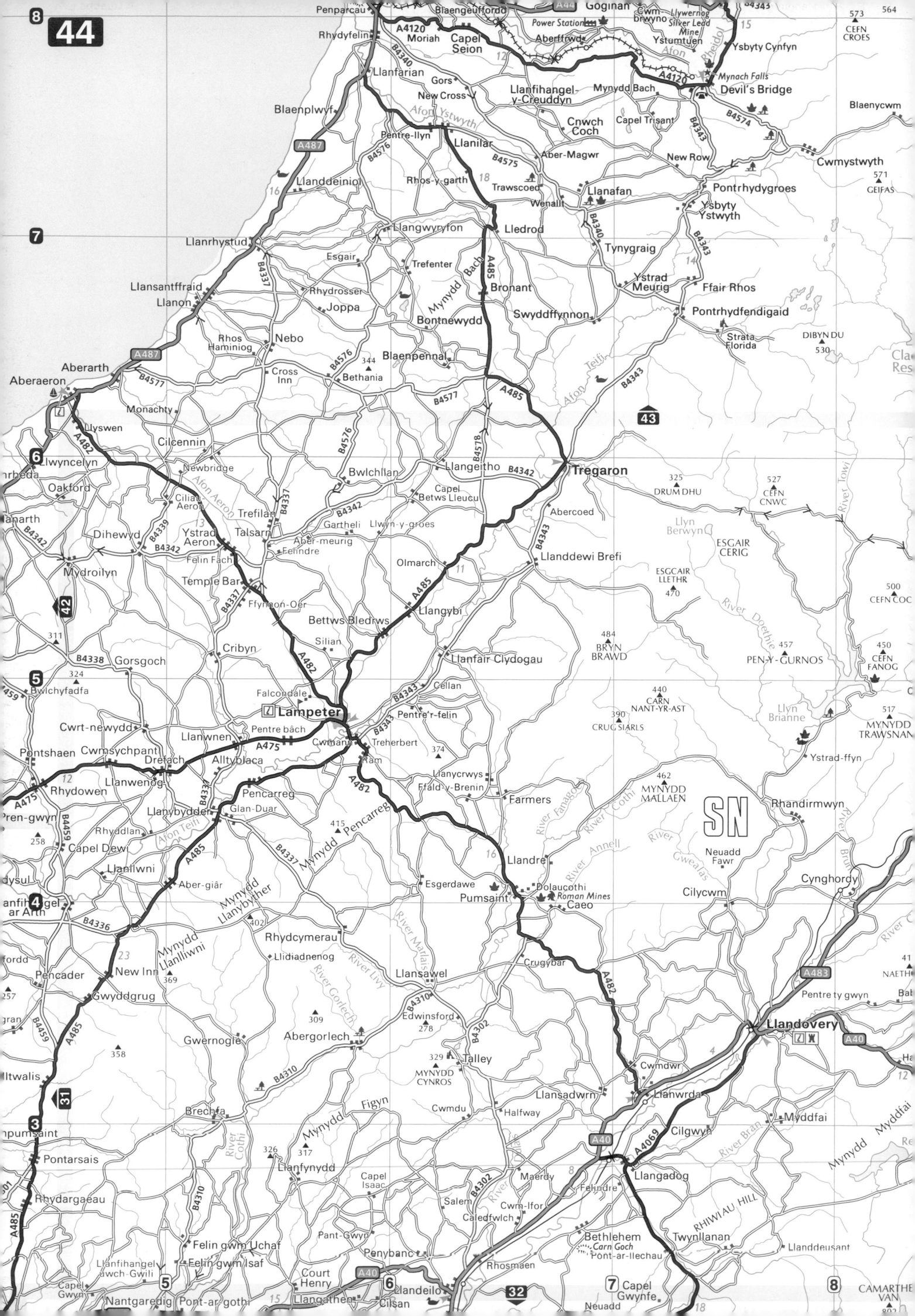

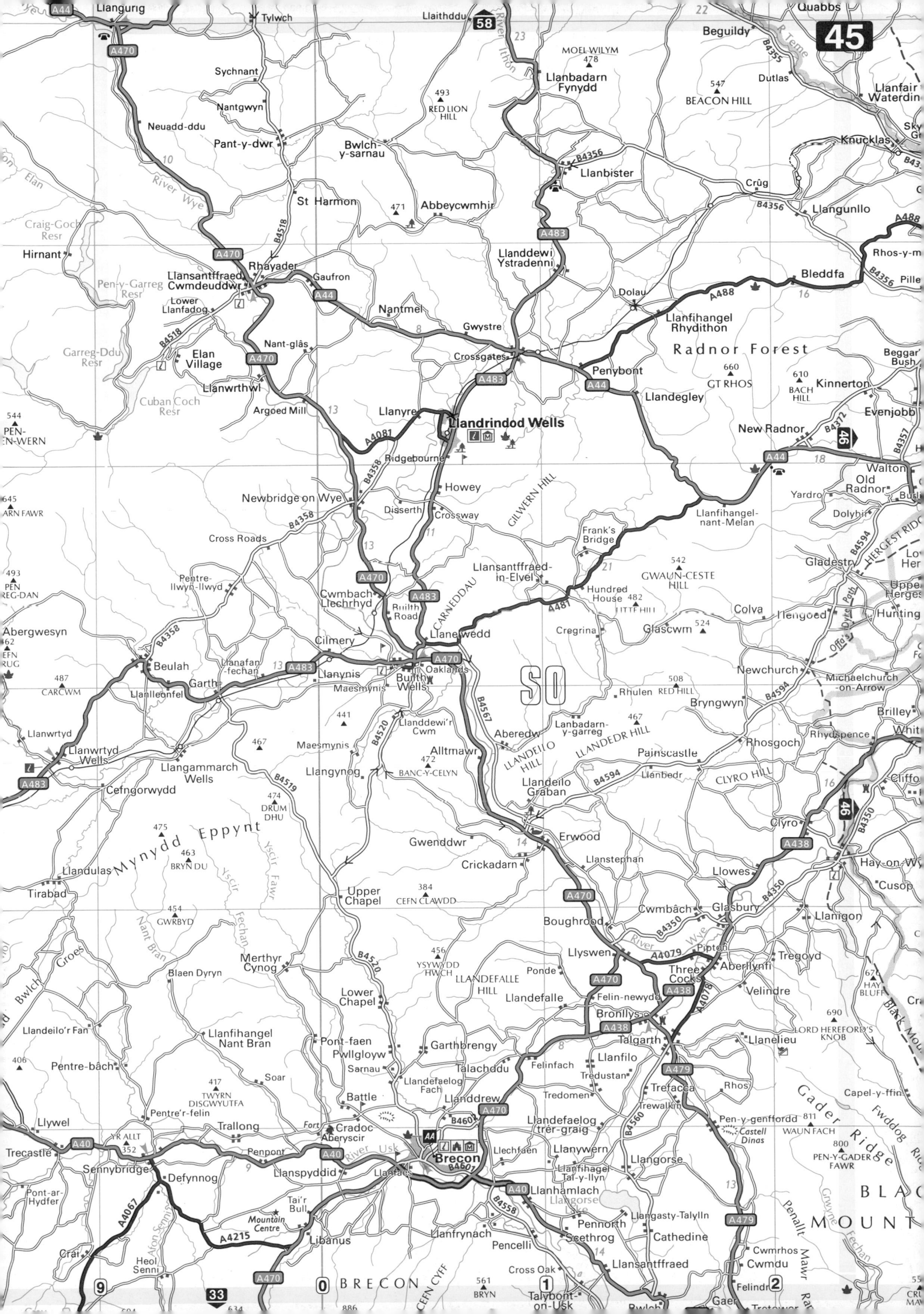

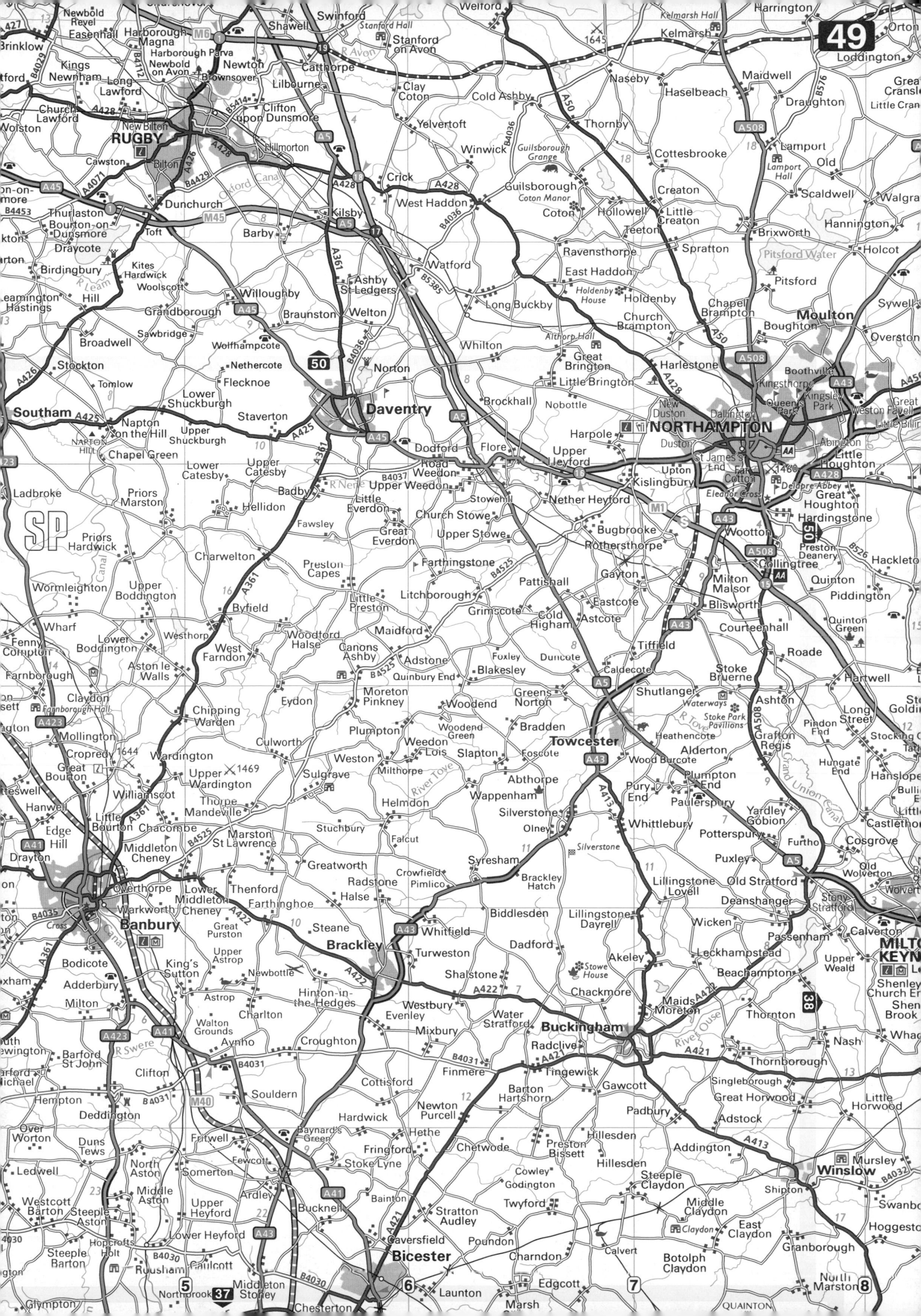

5

68

4

3

2

1

0

Aberdesach
Clynnog-fawr
Gyrn-goch
Old Welsh
Country Life
Llanllyfni
Nebo
Nasareth
Pant-gla
A487
Bryn
Capeluchaf
Upper
Clynnog
19
A499
522
Y GYRN-DDU
Trevor
Llanaelhaearn
Tre'r Ceiri
Glan-Dwyfach
Trwyn y
Grolech
Llithfaen
Pistyll
B4417
20
21
St Cybi's Well
Rhoslan
PENINSULA
Carreg Ddu
Porth
Nefyn
Llwyndyrys
Pencaenewydd
Llangybi
Morfa Nefyn
Porth Dinllaen
Groesffordd
Nefyn
Fron
B4354
Rhos
fawr
Llanarmon
Chwilog
B4354
Llanystumdwy
Aton Dwyf
Edern
Bodfuan
Penarth Fawr
Rhos-y-llan
Porth Ysgaden
LLEYN
Llandudwen
A497
Llannor
Efailnewydd
Denio
Abererch
13
C
Tudweiliog
Dinas
371
Garn
Rhyd-
y-clafdy
Pen-ychain
Porth Colman
Carn Fadrun
14
B4417
Bryn
mawr
Llaniestyn
Penrhos
Pwllheli
i
Llangwnnadl
Pen-y-graig
Meyllteyrn
B4415
Botwnnog
Llanbedrog
Porthor
B4413
Sarn
17
Mynytho
B4413
Trwyn Llanbedrog
Bryncroes
Nanhoron
Rhydlios
Rhoshirwaun
Llandegwning
St Tudwal's
Road
Anelog
B4413
Penycaerau
Plas-Yn-Rhiw
Llangian
A499
Abersoch
St Tudwal's
Island East
Uwchmynydd
Y Rhiw
Llanfaelrhys
Llanengan
Sarn-bâch
Marchros
Aberdaron
Porth Neigwl
Bwlchtocyn
St Tudwal's
Island West
Bardsey Sound
Aberdaron Bay
Porth
Ysgo
Porth
Ceiriad
St Mary's
BARDSEY
ISLAND

SCALE
0  1  2  3  4  5 miles

0  1  2  3  4  5 kilometres

42

C A R D I G A N

B A Y

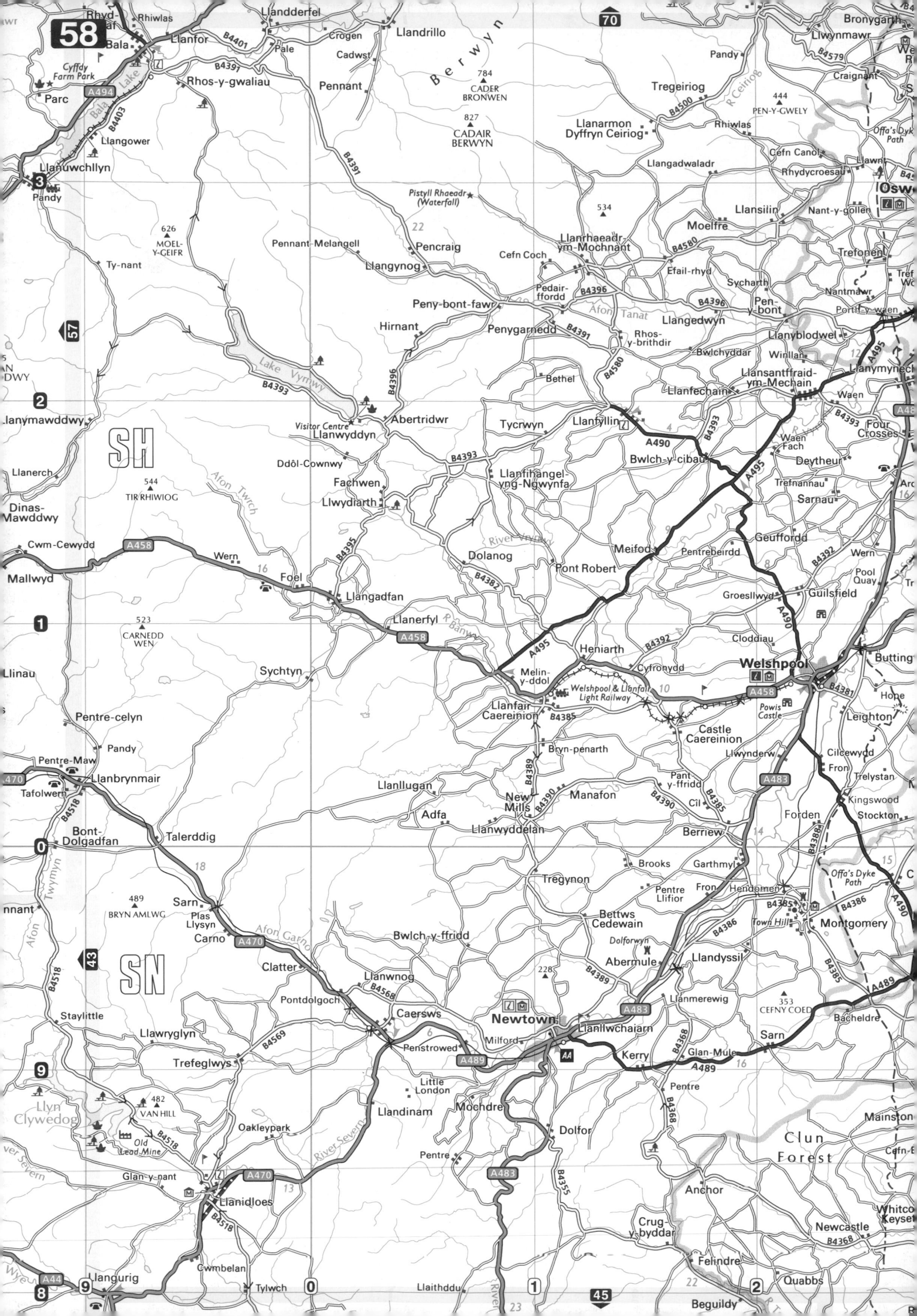

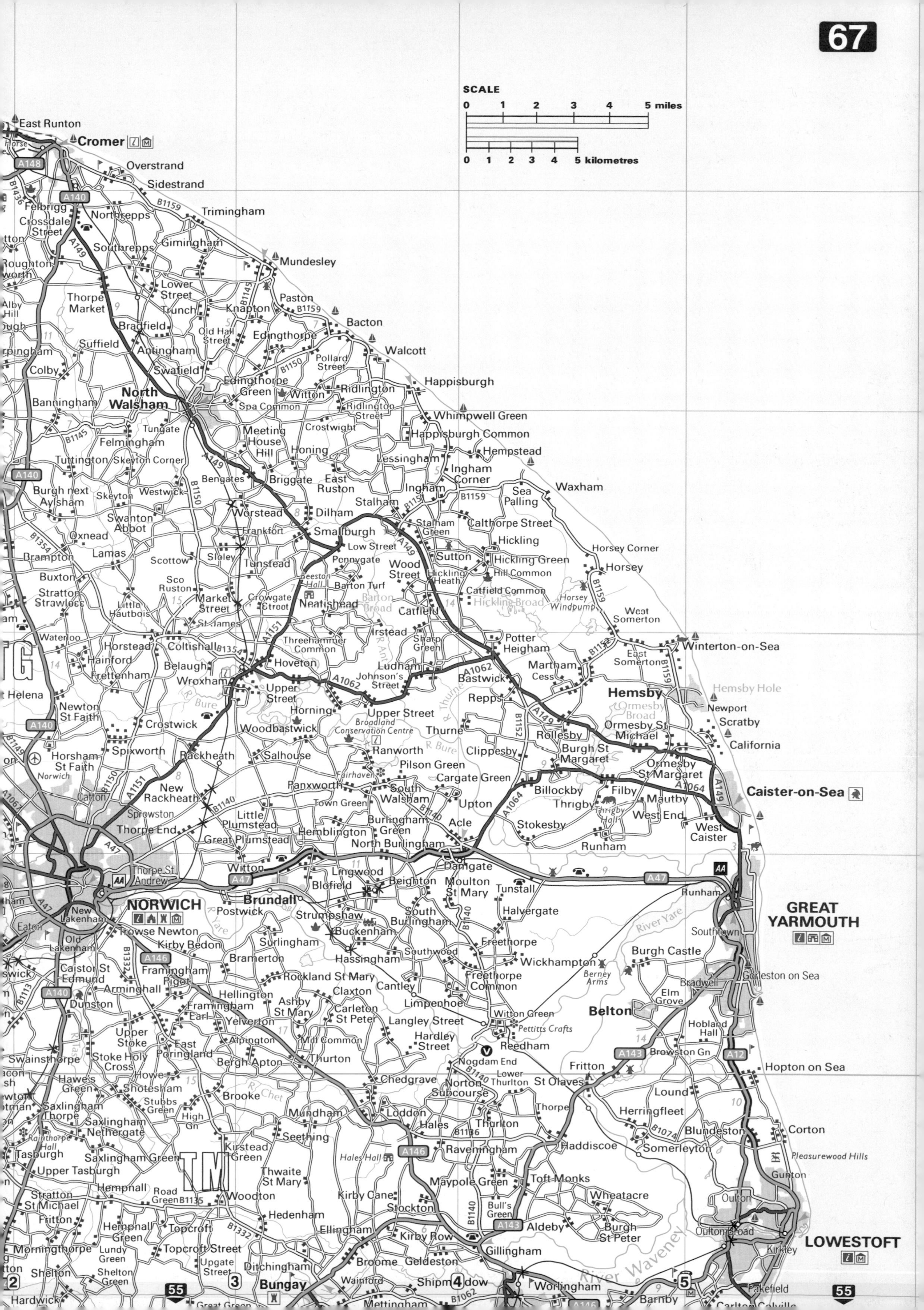

SCALE

0 1 2 3 4 5 miles

0 1 2 3 4 5 kilometres

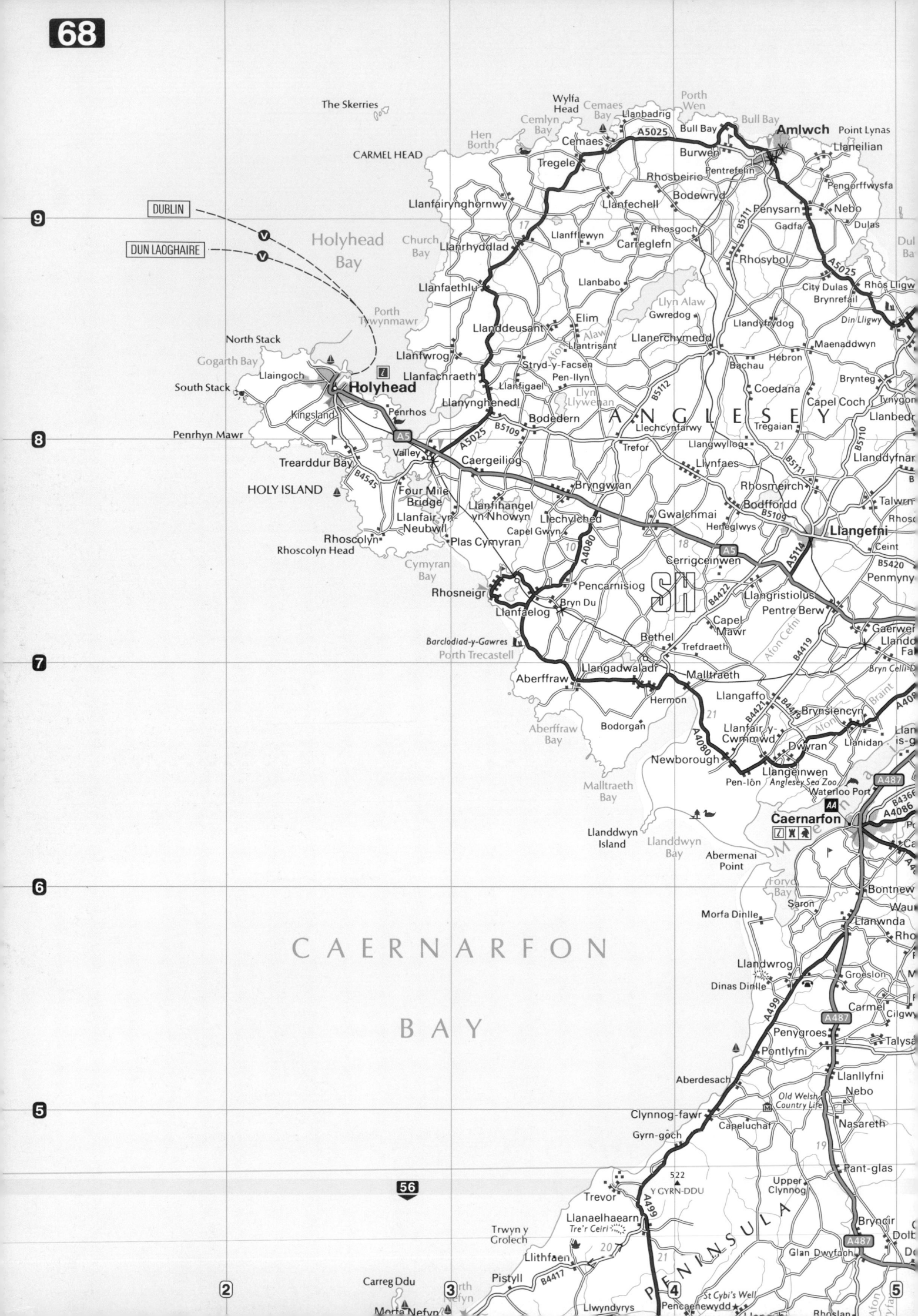

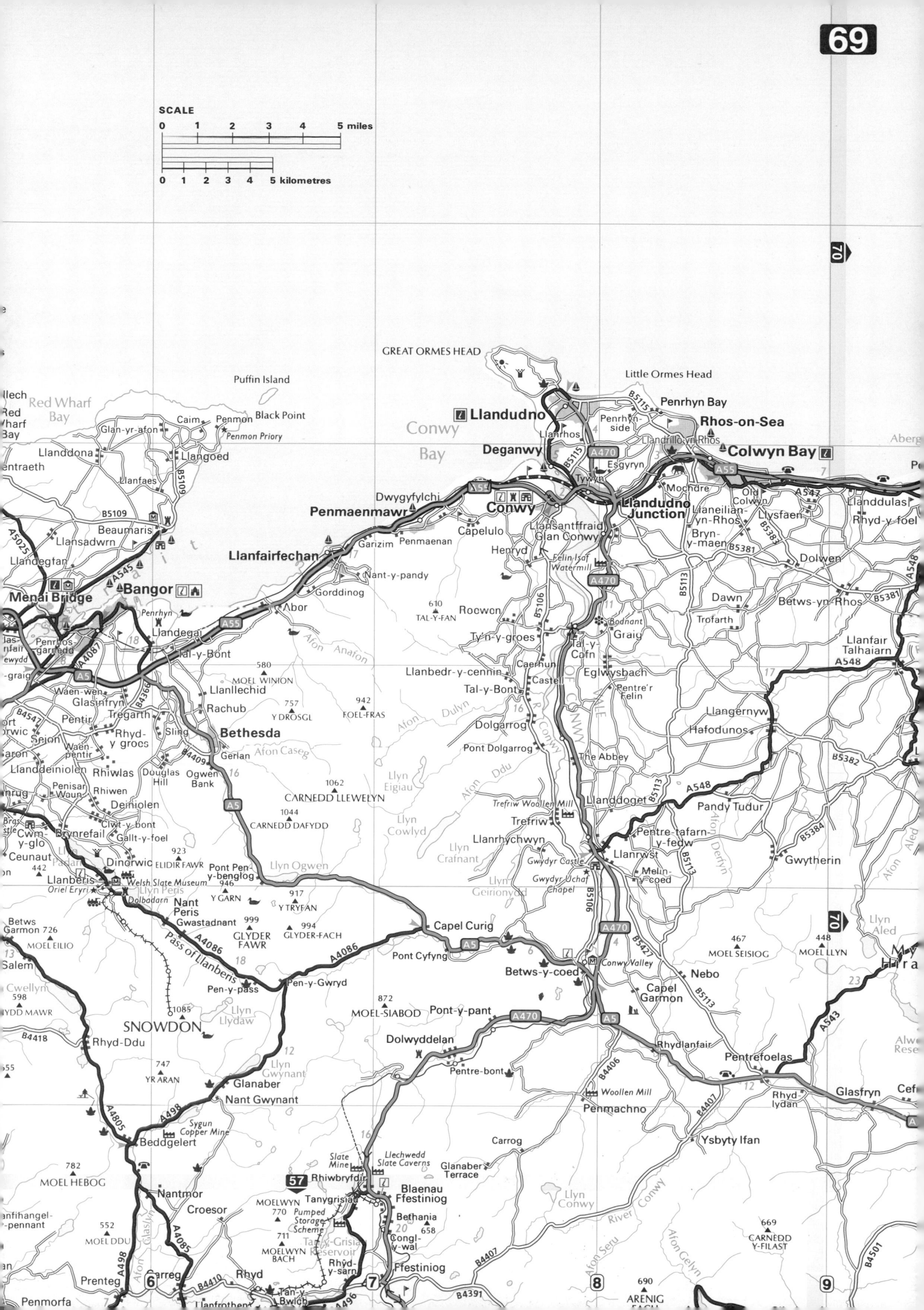

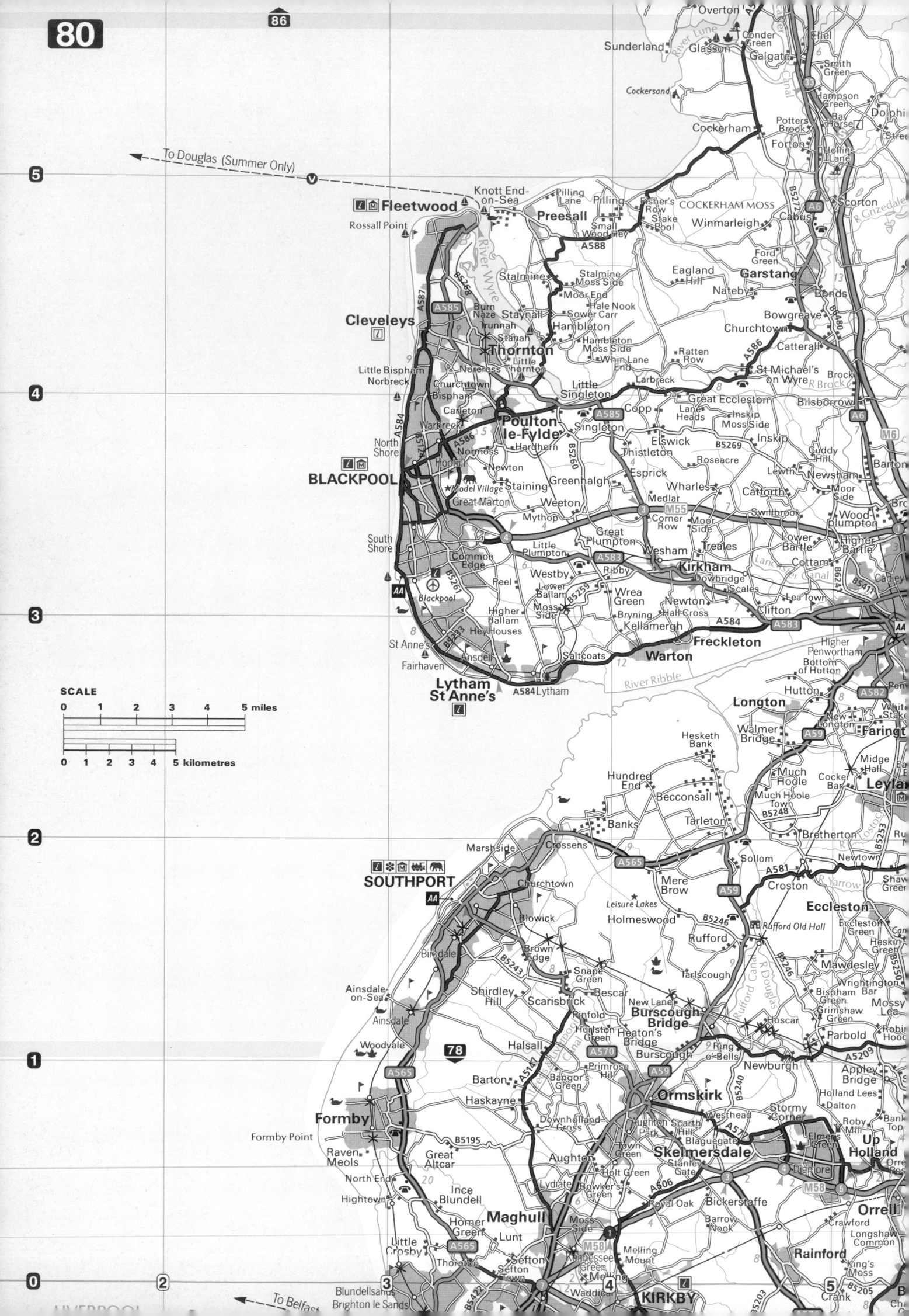

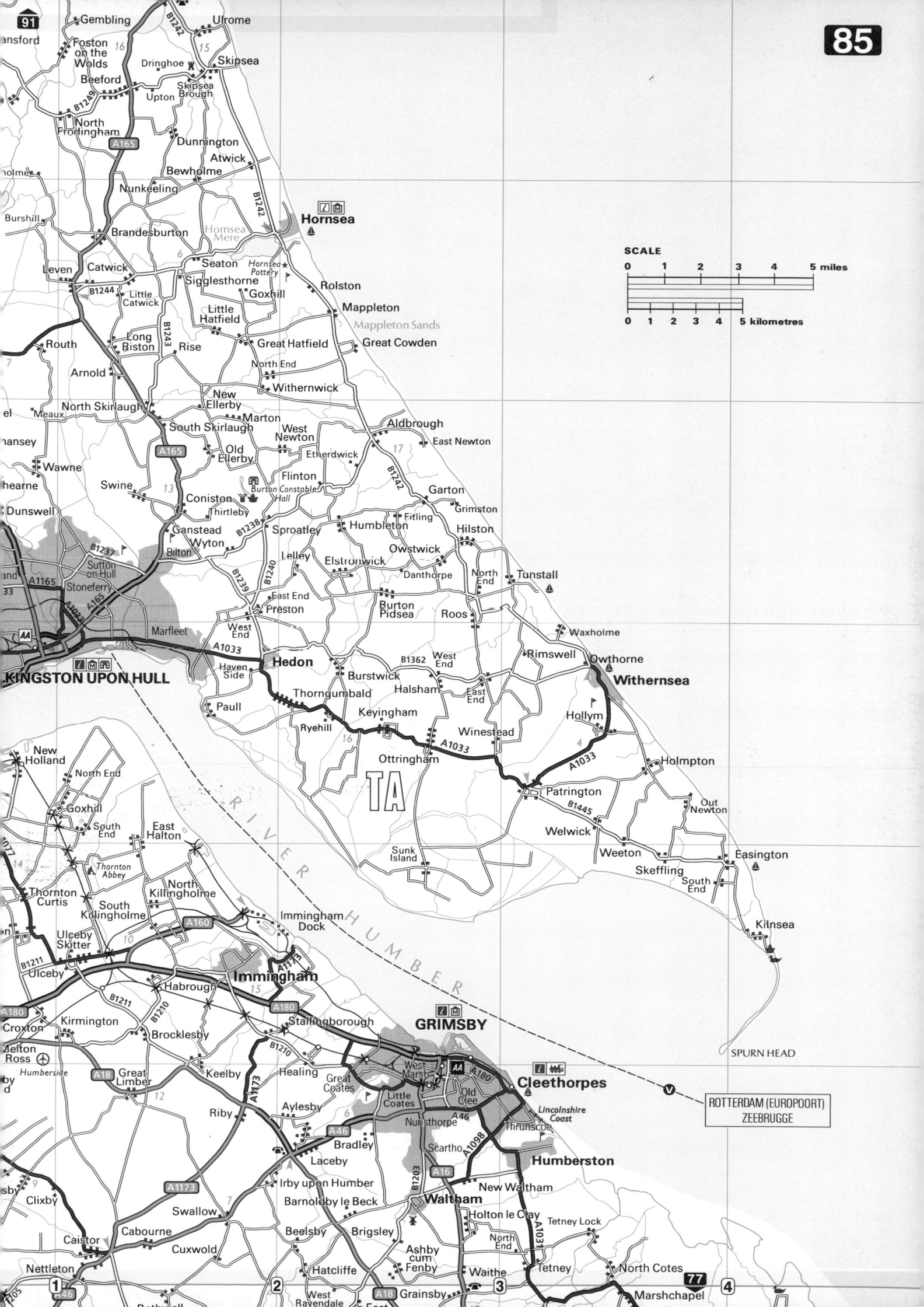

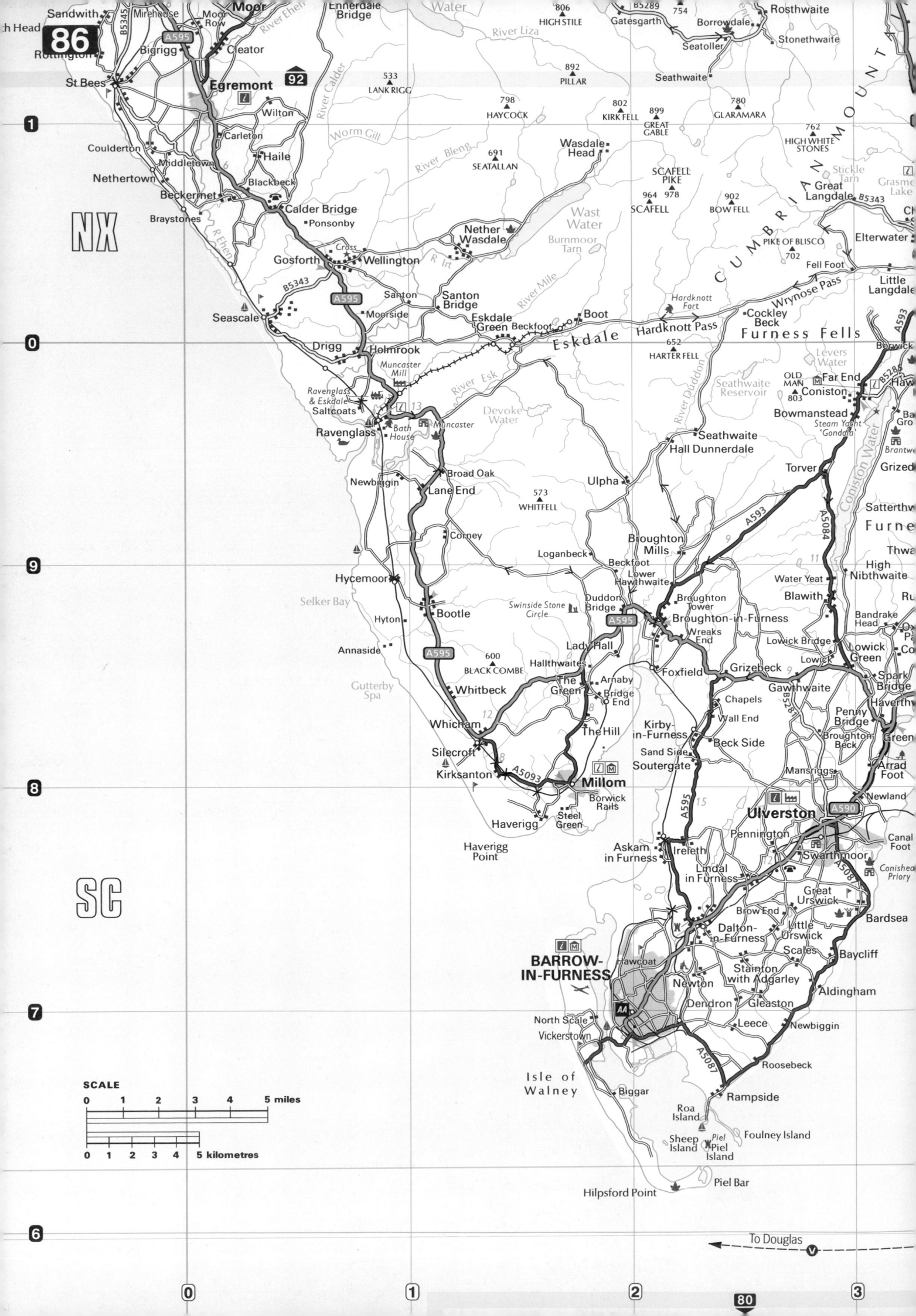

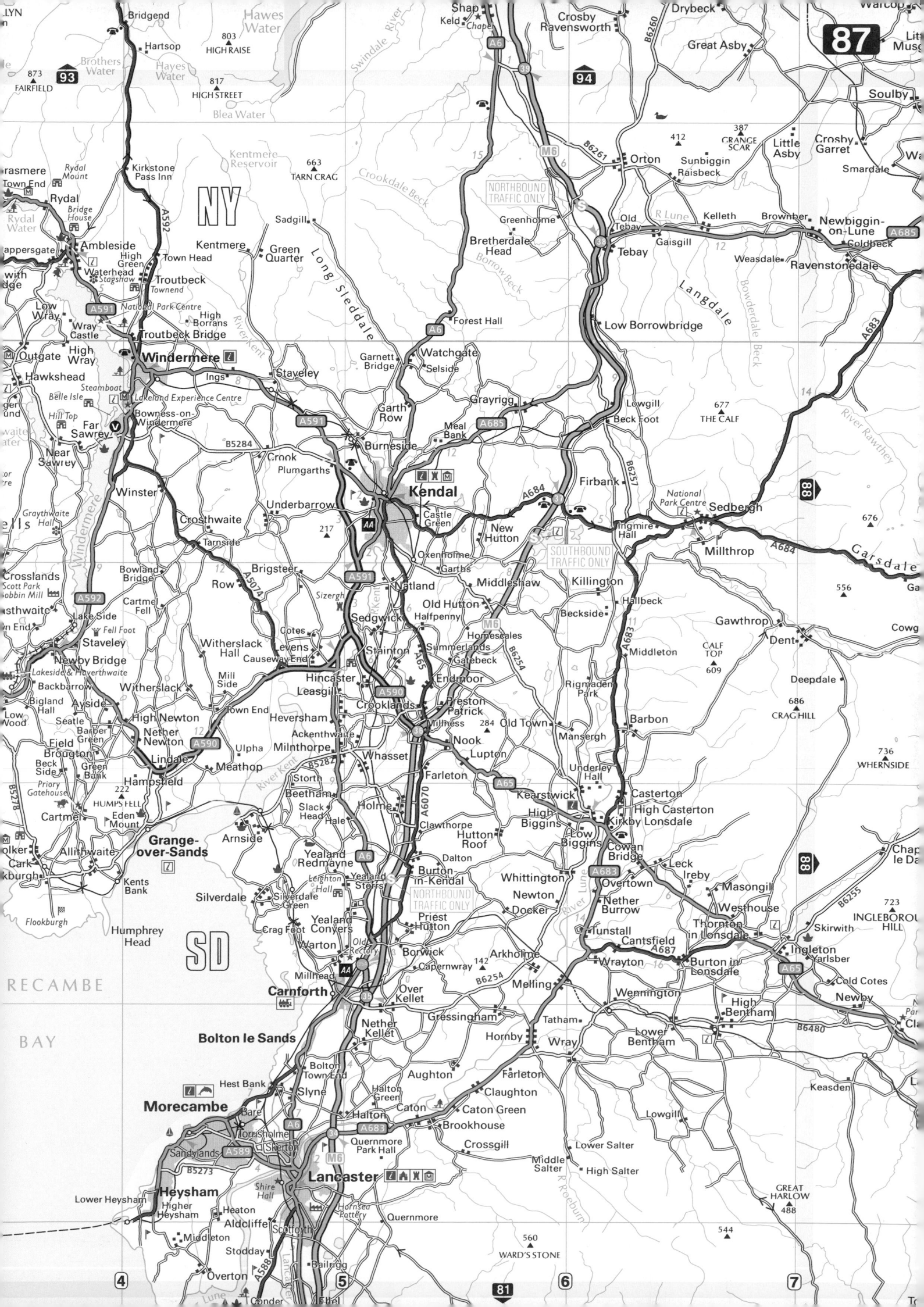

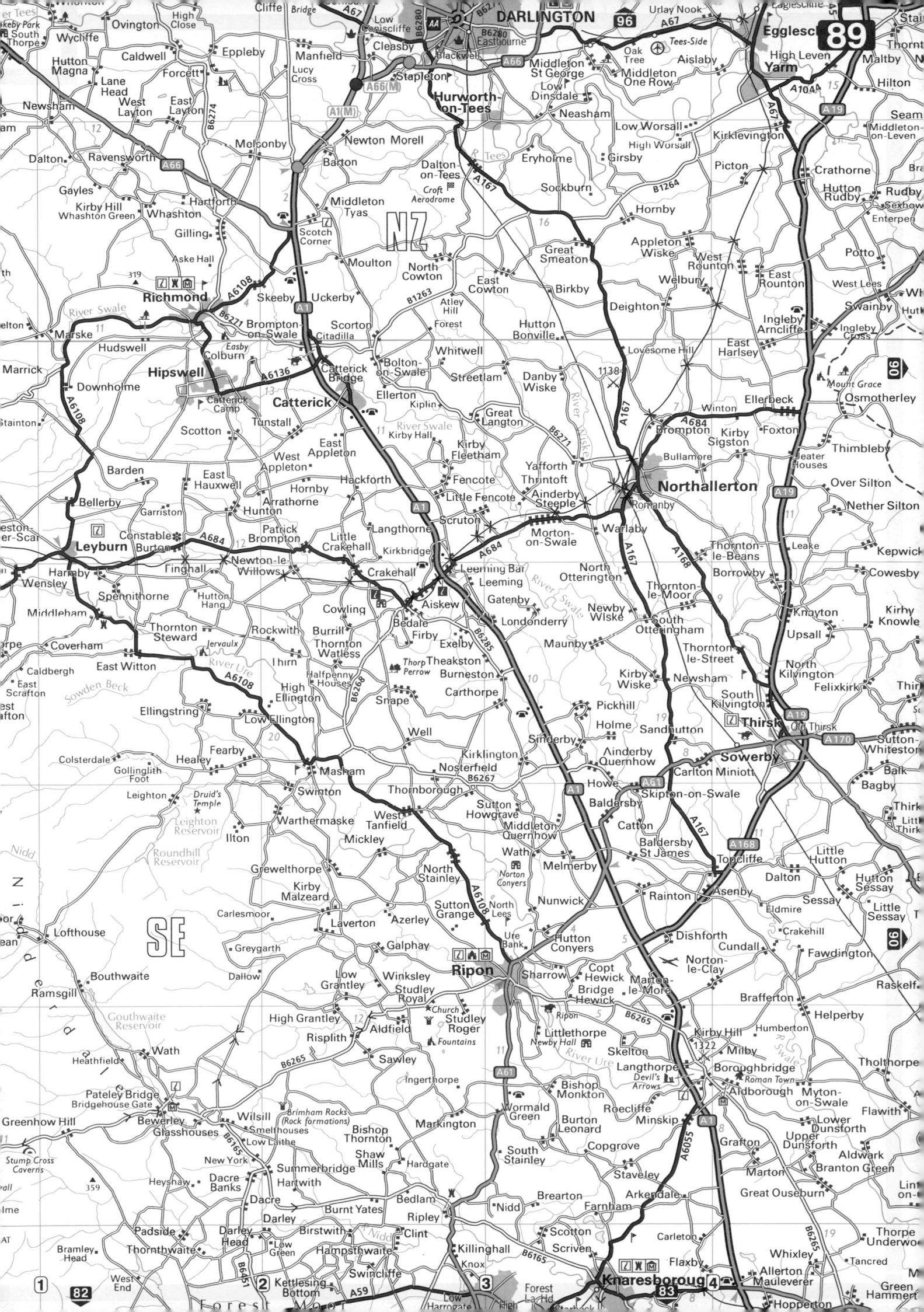

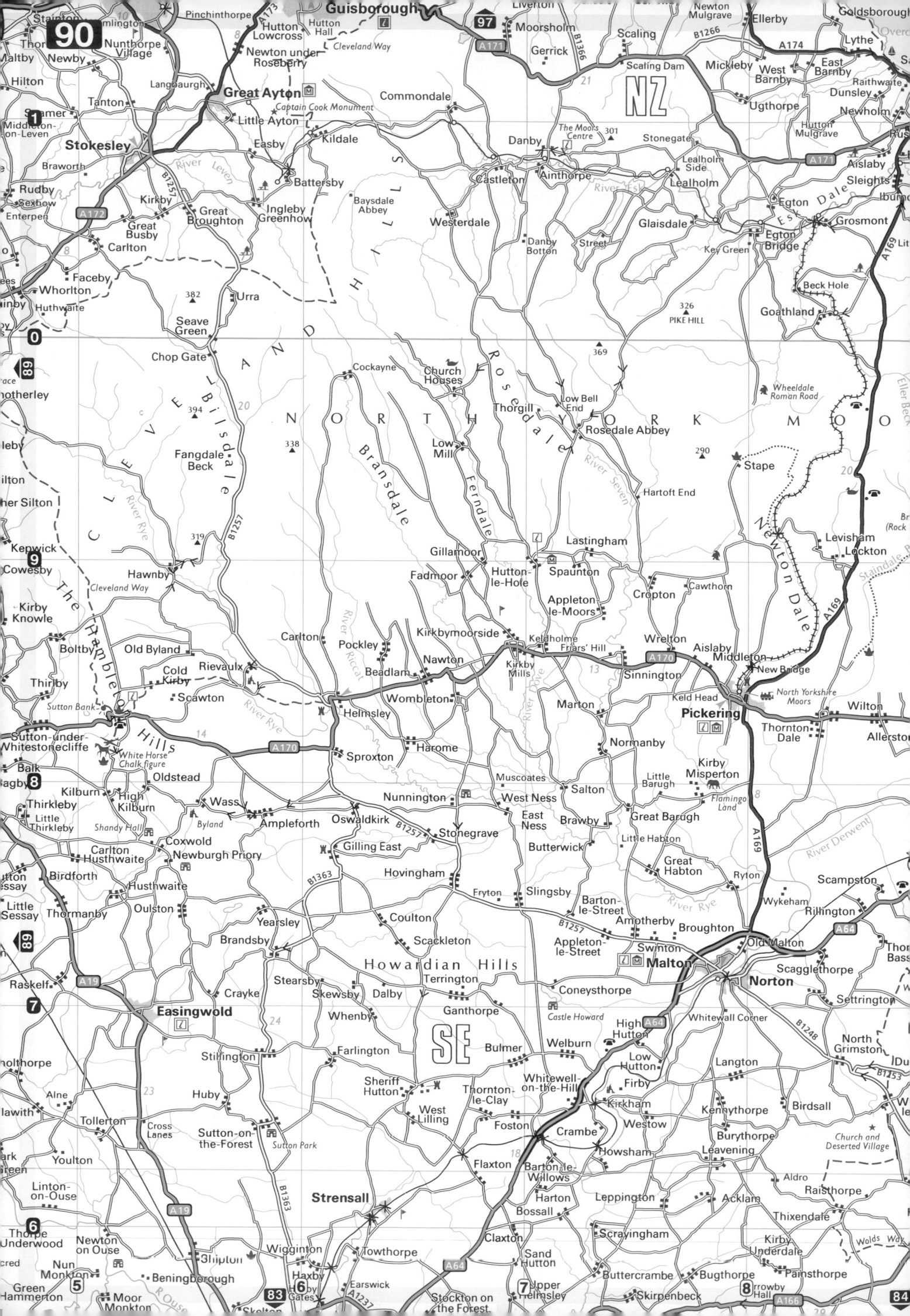

Wyke
**Whitby** 🛈⛺🏛
Saltwick Bay
Stainsacre
Sneaton  High Hawsker
ebarnby  Low Hawsker
Sneatonthorpe  Raw  Ness Point or
North Cheek
Robin Hood's Bay
Fylingthorpe
Robin Hood's
Bay
Old Peak or
South Cheek
Ravenscar

20
A171
Staintondale
Hayburn Wyke
Cloughton
Newlands
Harwood Dale
Cloughton Wyke
R. Derwent
Silpho  Cloughton
Broxa  Burniston  Cromer Point
Bickley  Cleveland Way
Langdale  Suffield  Scalby
End  Hackness  Newby
Wrench Green  Everley
**Scarborough** 🛈🍴🏛🐘⛱
Falsgrave
River Derwent  Sea Cut  Oliver's Mount
Bee Dale
West  East  A170  AA  A165
Sawdon  Ayton  Ayton  Osgodby
Hutton  Cayton Bay
Ebberston  Buscel  Irton  High Killerby  The Wyke
Ruston  Seamer  B1267
A170  17  Wykeham  Cayton  Lebberston
Brompton  Filey Brigg
Snainton  Gristhorpe
Yedingham  A64  Folkton  **Filey** 🛈
The  Willerby  R. Hertford  Muston
Staxton  A1039  West  Filey Bay
Sherburn  Flixton  7  Flotmanby
16  A64  Ganton  Hunmanby
East Heslerton  Potter  A165
West  Brompton  Reighton
Heslerton  B1249  Fordon  Speeton
ringham  B1229
Foxholes  Wold  Thornwick Bay
Newton  Burton  Buckton
Butterwick  Fleming  Bempton
Weaverthorpe  Grindale  11  Selwicks Bay
Thwing  FLAMBOROUGH
Helperthorpe  Octon  HEAD
West  East Lutton  Flamborough
Lutton  B1253  Boynton  Sewerby
Kirby  Langtoft  Rudston  BRIDLINGTON
Grindalythe  Monolith  Bessingby
Low  Cottam  **Bridlington** 🛈🏛
Mowthorpe  Sledmere  Carnaby  Hilderthorpe
Towthorpe  Kilham  Haisthorpe  Carnaby  BAY
B1251  B1252  Burton  Thornholme  A165
Ruston Parva  Agnes  Norman
B1249  12  Manor House  Fraisthorpe
Garton on-  Harpham
A166  the-Wolds  Lowthorpe  Gransmoor
thorpe  Wetwang  A166  Nafferton  Great  Barmston
Elmswell  **Great**  Little  Kelk  Lisset
**Driffield**  Kelk
B1248  Little  Gembling  85  B1242  Ulrome
9  Driffield  1  B1249  Wansford  2

SCALE
0  1  2  3  4  5 miles
0  1  2  3  4  5 kilometres

TA

0

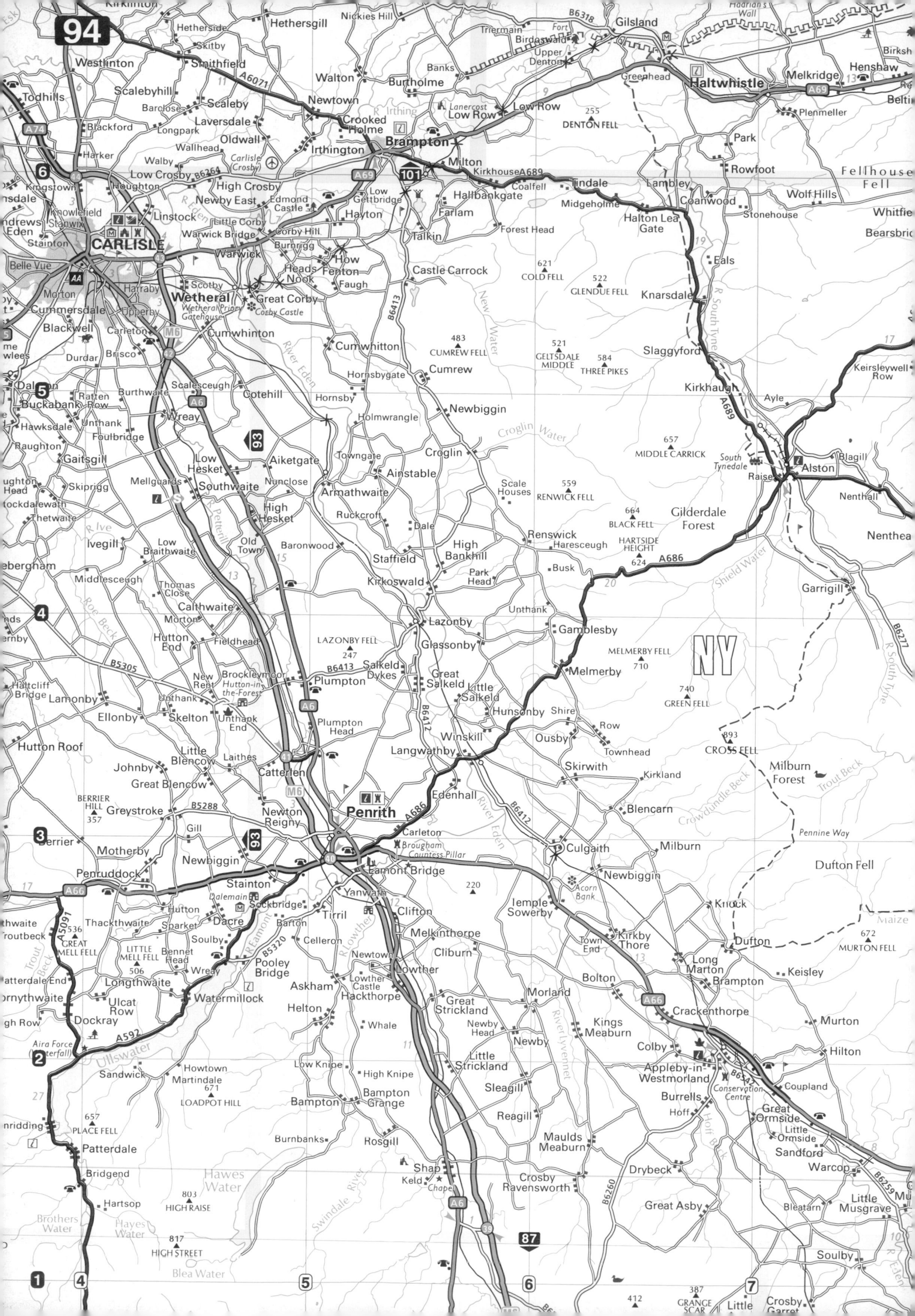

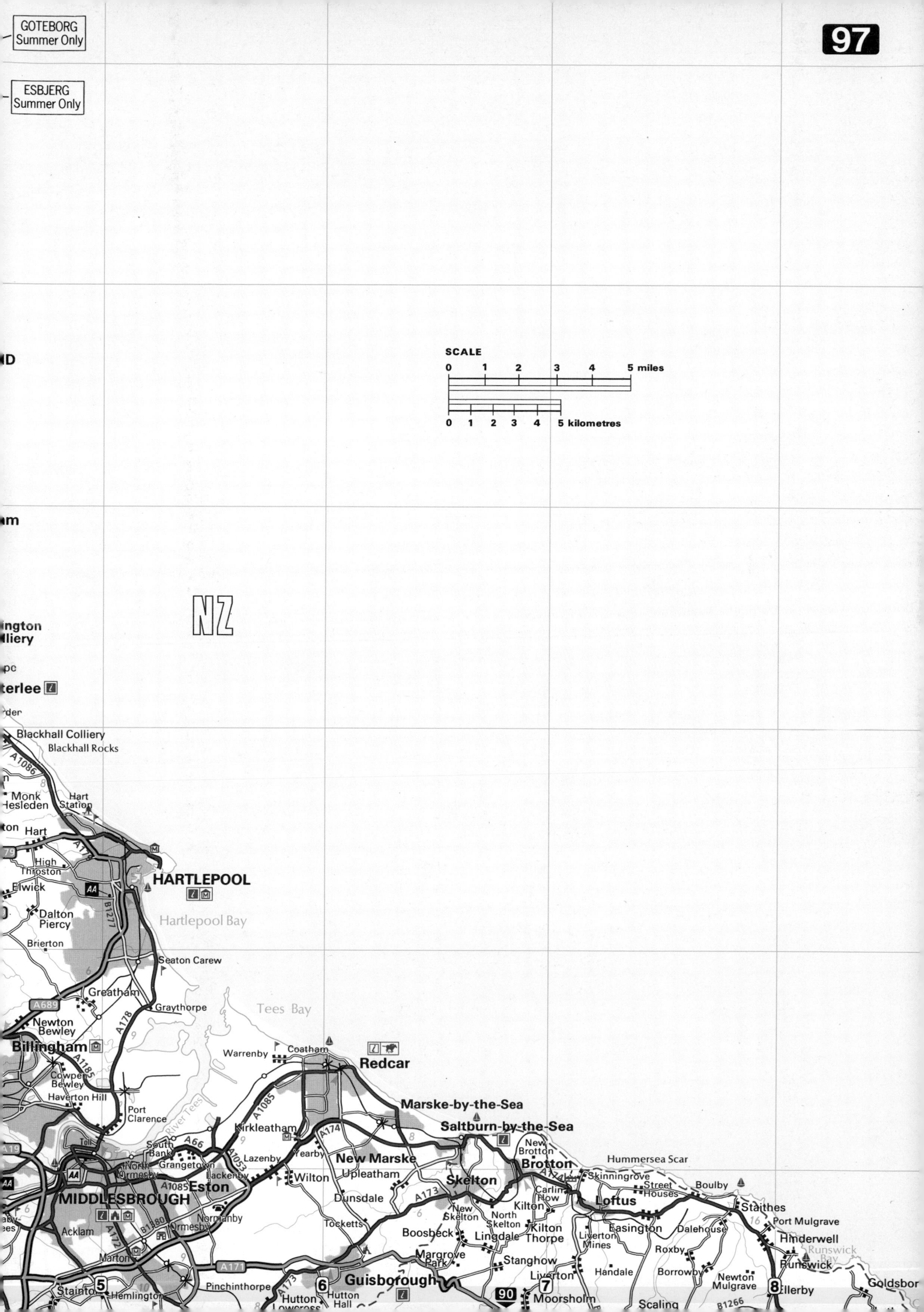

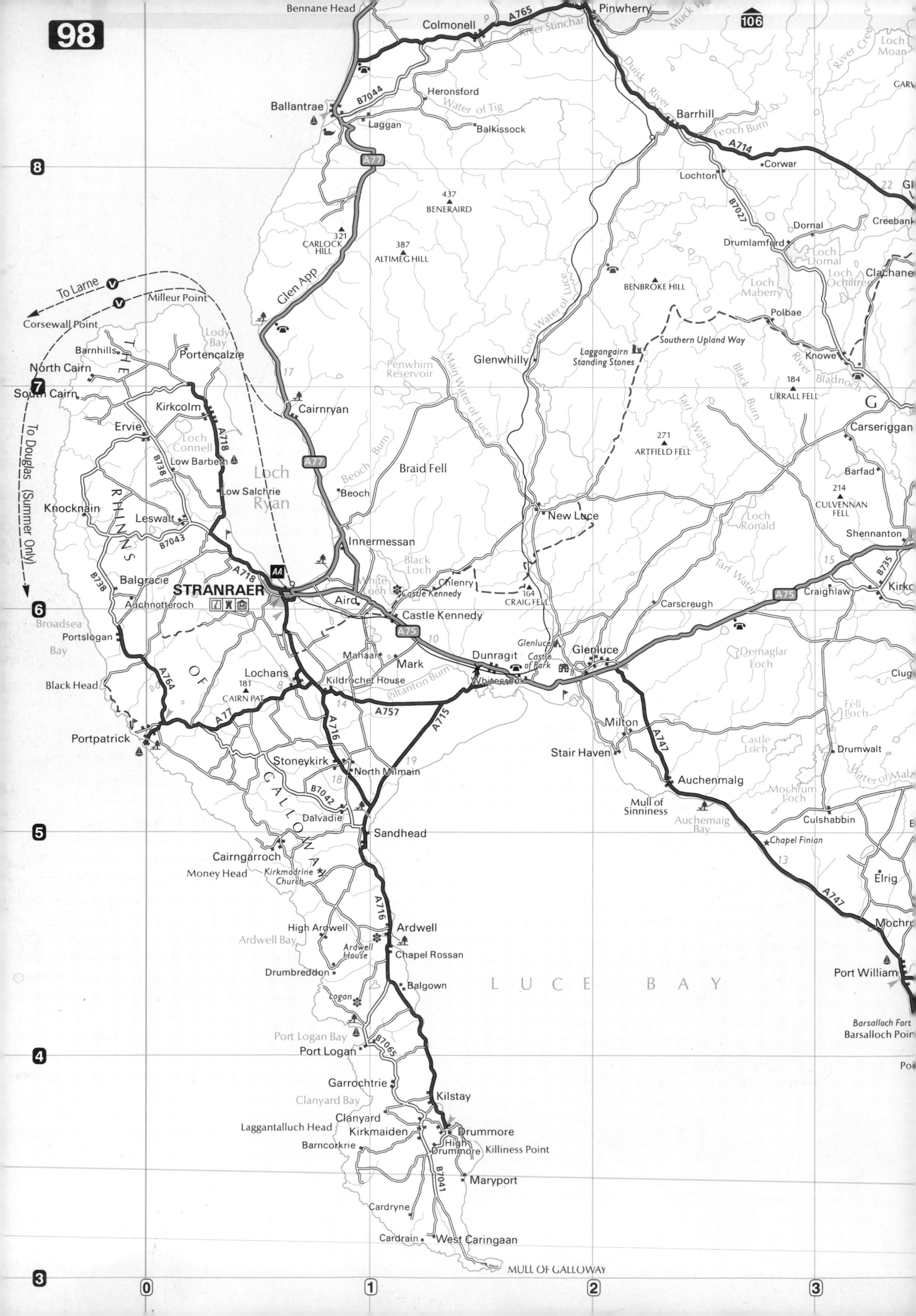

KIRRIEREOCH HILL

CORSERINE

107

WETHER HILL

842 MERRICK

Loch Enoch

813

716 MILFIRE

Loch Dungeon

13

A702

Loch Howie

Loch Urr

Loch Neidricken

Knocksheen

A713

Blawquhairn

Milnmark

Bogue

12

B7000

Glen Trool Lodge

Loch Trool

Garroch

St John's Town of Dalry

Glenlee

Drumwhirn

Loch Dee

BENNAN

380

Bruce's Stone

Deer Museum

New Galloway

A762

Balmaclellan

Troquhain

A712

Crogo

716 LAMACHAN HILL

675 LARG HILL

MILLFORE

Clatteringshaws Loch

A712

19

ROUND FELL 402

Black Water of Dee

CAIRN EDWARD 325

A713

Ironmacannie

Larglear Hill 281

Corsock

B794

440 GARLICK HILL

Wild Goat Park

Craigdews

Craigdews

L L O W A Y

Loch Grannoch

FELL OF FLEET 471

A762

Drumrash

Airds of Kells

Parton

Drumrash

13

Knockvennie Smithy

Kirk Du

100

R Cree

Penkill Burn

Minnigaff

Palnure Brook

CAIRNSMORE OF FLEET 710

Loch Fleet

AUCHENCLOY HILL 208

Mossdale

Loch Ken

Loch Roan

Walbutt

Challoch

Greebridge

NX

Loch Skerrow

Slogarie

Loch Skerrow

Woodhall Loch

Crossmichael

Crofts

Clarebrand

Newton Stewart

A75

A714

Palnure

WHITE TOP OF CULREACH 335

Laurieston

B795

19

Townhead of Greenlaw

A713

Baltersan

A75

Big Water of Fleet

Loch Whinyeon

Kirkconnell

Longwood

Threave

Causeway End

7

Gem Rock

Upper Ruscoe

BENGRAY 367

Bridge of Dee

Ringford

A75

A711

Threave Rhonehouse or Kelton H

Torhouse

B733

Kirkland

Creetown

Glen

Loch Whinyeon

A762

10

River Dee

Slagnaw

Airieland

Craigl

Wigtown

18

Kirkmabreck

CAIRNHARROW 455

Cairn Holy Chambered Cairns

Anwoth

Gatehouse of Fleet

B727

Littleton

15

Tongland

B727

381 BENGA

Malzie

Kirwaugh

Bladnoch

Carsluith

Cardoness

B727

Girthon

A75

Twynholm

Compstonend

Power Station and Dam

Little Sypland

THE CHERS

Braehead

Kirkinner

Ravenshall Point

Mossyard

Lennox Plunton

A755

8

Kirkchrist

Whinnie Liggate

Culnaightri

Au

A714

Whauphill

Orchardton Bay

Fleet Bay

Margrie

Gledpark

Kirkcudbright

Cairnfield

Little Airies

B7004

Culscadden

Islands of Fleet

Knockbrex

Borgue

Ingleston

Mutehill

Dundrennan

12

Sorbie

Millisle

B7052

Kirkandrews

Balmangan

A711

oddan

Drummoddie

Pouton

Garlieston

Wigtown Bay

Barness

Ross

Balmae

Netherlaw

92

Broughton Mains

B7063

Cruggleton Bay

Ringdoo Point

Little Ross

Abbey Head

Wren's Egg' anding Stones

B7021 Priory

B7004

Cults

onreith

Appleby

Excavations

Low Skeog

Rispain Camp

Whithorn

M

alcraig

A747

A746

Portyerrock

10

Craiglemine

A750

Glasserton

A747

St Ninian's Cave

Kidsdale

St Ninian's Chapel

Isle of Whithorn

Cutcloy

BURROW HEAD

SCALE

0 1 2 3 4 5 miles

0 1 2 3 4 5 kilometres

4    5    6    7

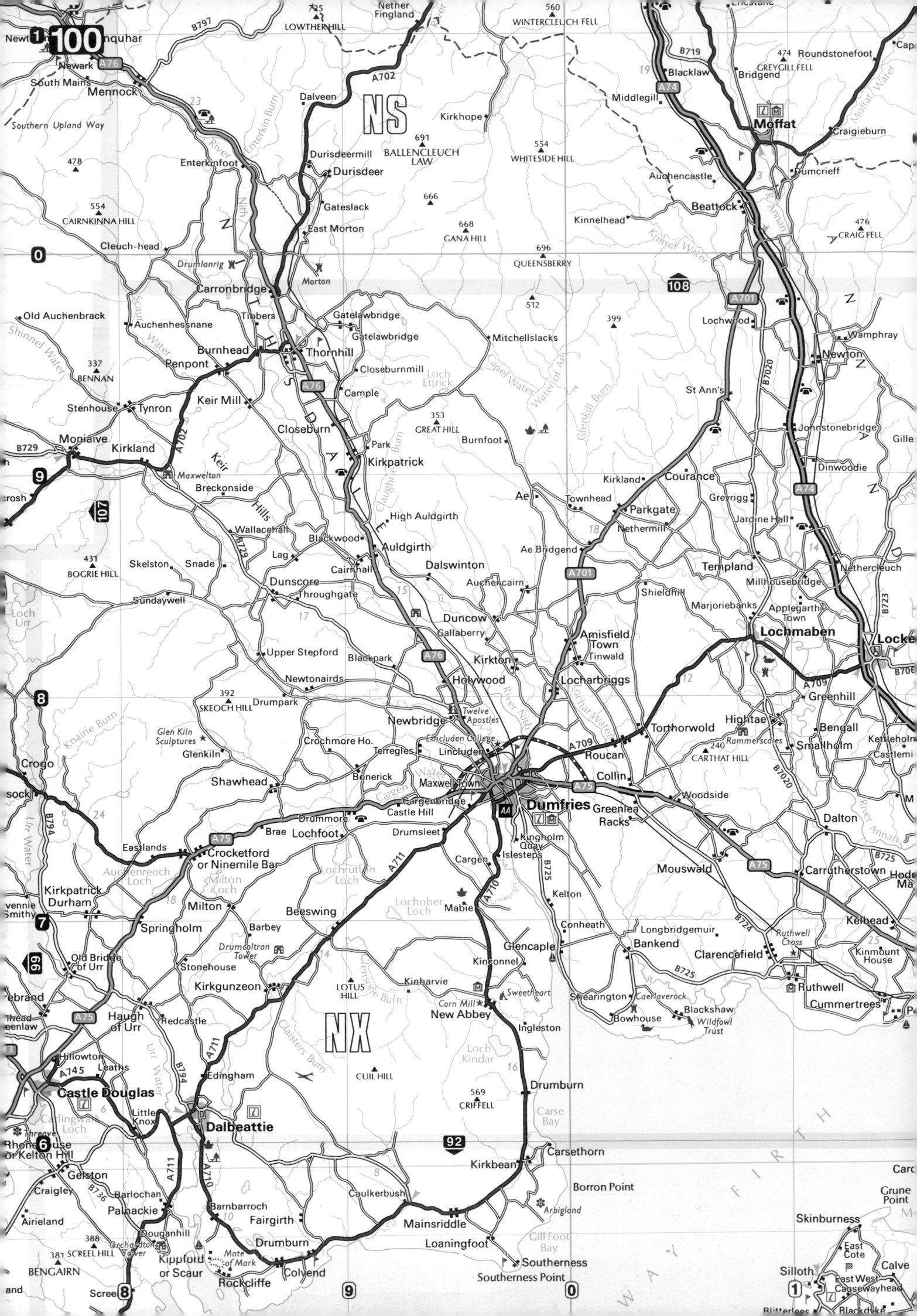

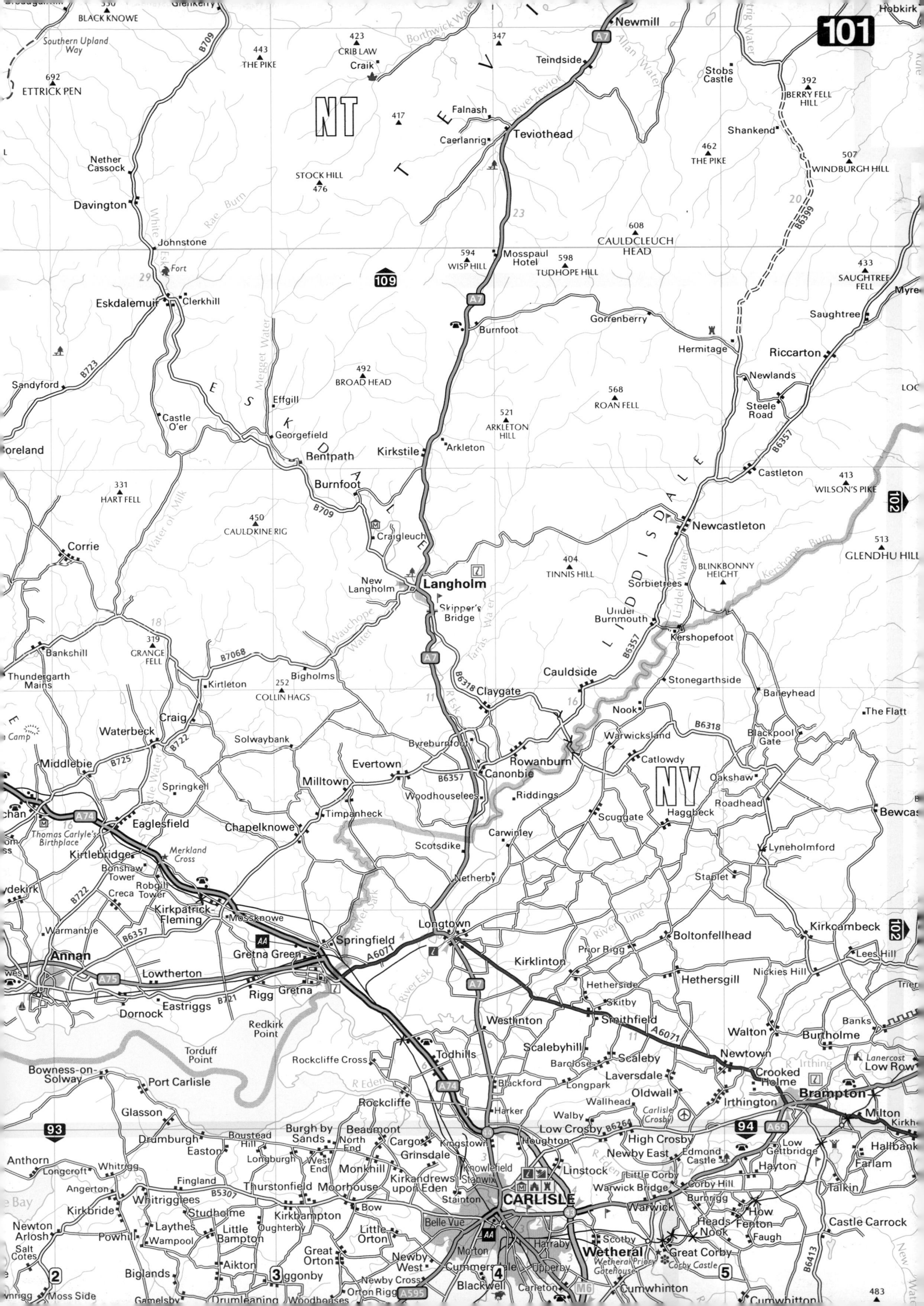

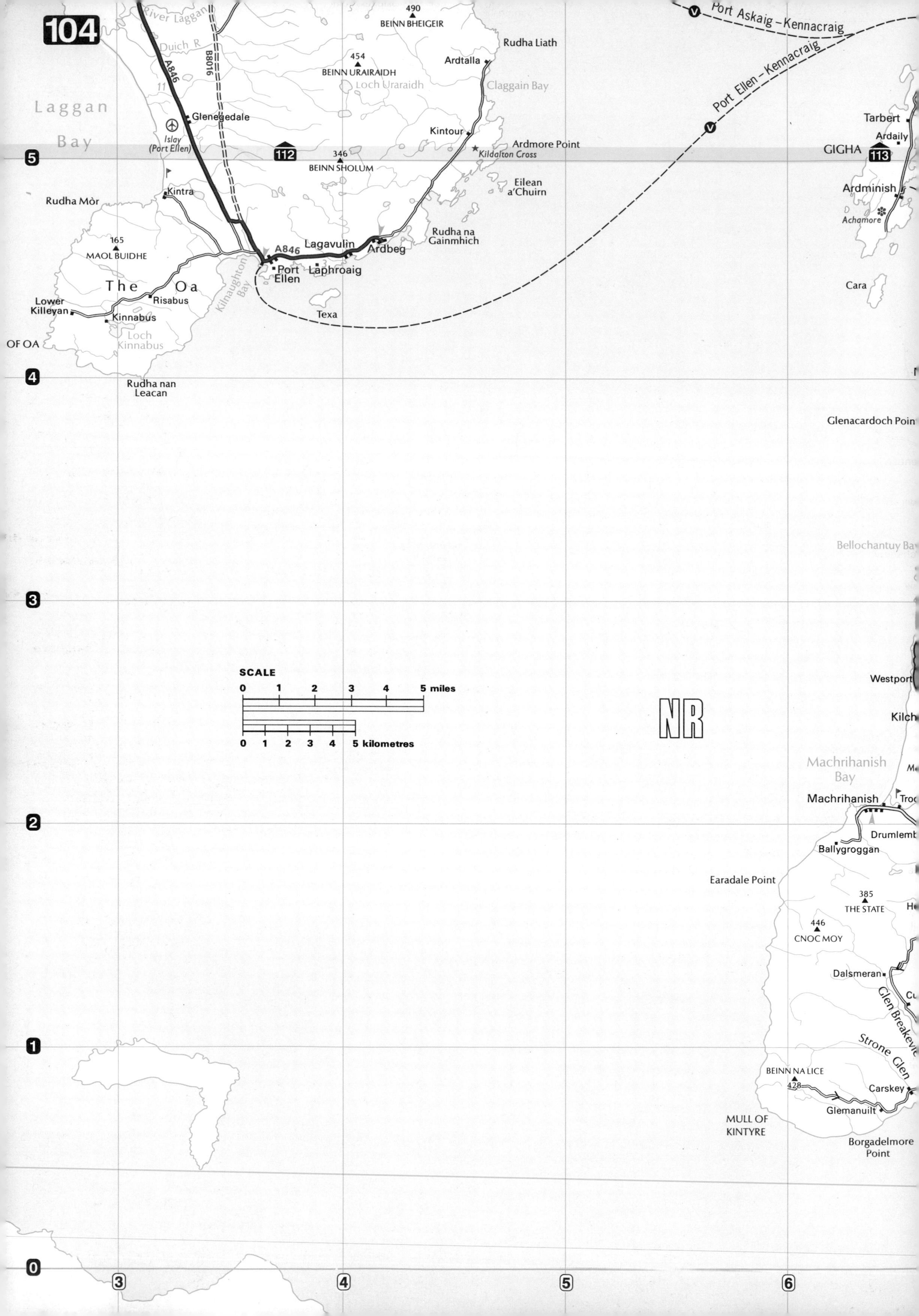

River Laggan

Duich R

490
BEINN BHEIGEIR

Rudha Liath

A846

B8016

454
BEINN URAIRAIDH

Ardtalla

Loch Uraraidh

Claggain Bay

**Laggan**

Glenegedale

Kintour

Tarbert

Ardaily

Islay
(Port Ellen)

Ardmore Point

GIGHA

**5**

**Bay**

**112**

346
BEINN SHOLUM

Kildalton Cross

Ardminish

**113**

Rudha Mòr

Kintra

Eilean
a'Chuirn

Achamore

165
MAOL BUIDHE

Rudha na
Gainmhich

A846

Lagavulin

Ardbeg

**The    Oa**

Risabus

Port
Ellen

Laphroaig

Cara

Lower
Killeyan

Kinnabus

Texa

OF OA

Loch
Kinnabus

**4**

Rudha nan
Leacan

Glenacardoch Poin

Bellochantuy Ba

**3**

**SCALE**

| 0 | 1 | 2 | 3 | 4 | 5 miles |

| 0 | 1 | 2 | 3 | 4 | 5 kilometres |

**NR**

Westport

Kilch

Machrihanish
Bay

Machrihanish

Troo

**2**

Drumlemb

Ballygroggan

Earadale Point

385
THE STATE

He

446
CNOC MOY

Dalsmeran

Cu

Glen Breakevi

**1**

Strone Glen

BEINN NA LICE
428

Carskey

MULL OF
KINTYRE

Glemanuilt

Borgadelmore
Point

**0**

**3**        **4**        **5**        **6**

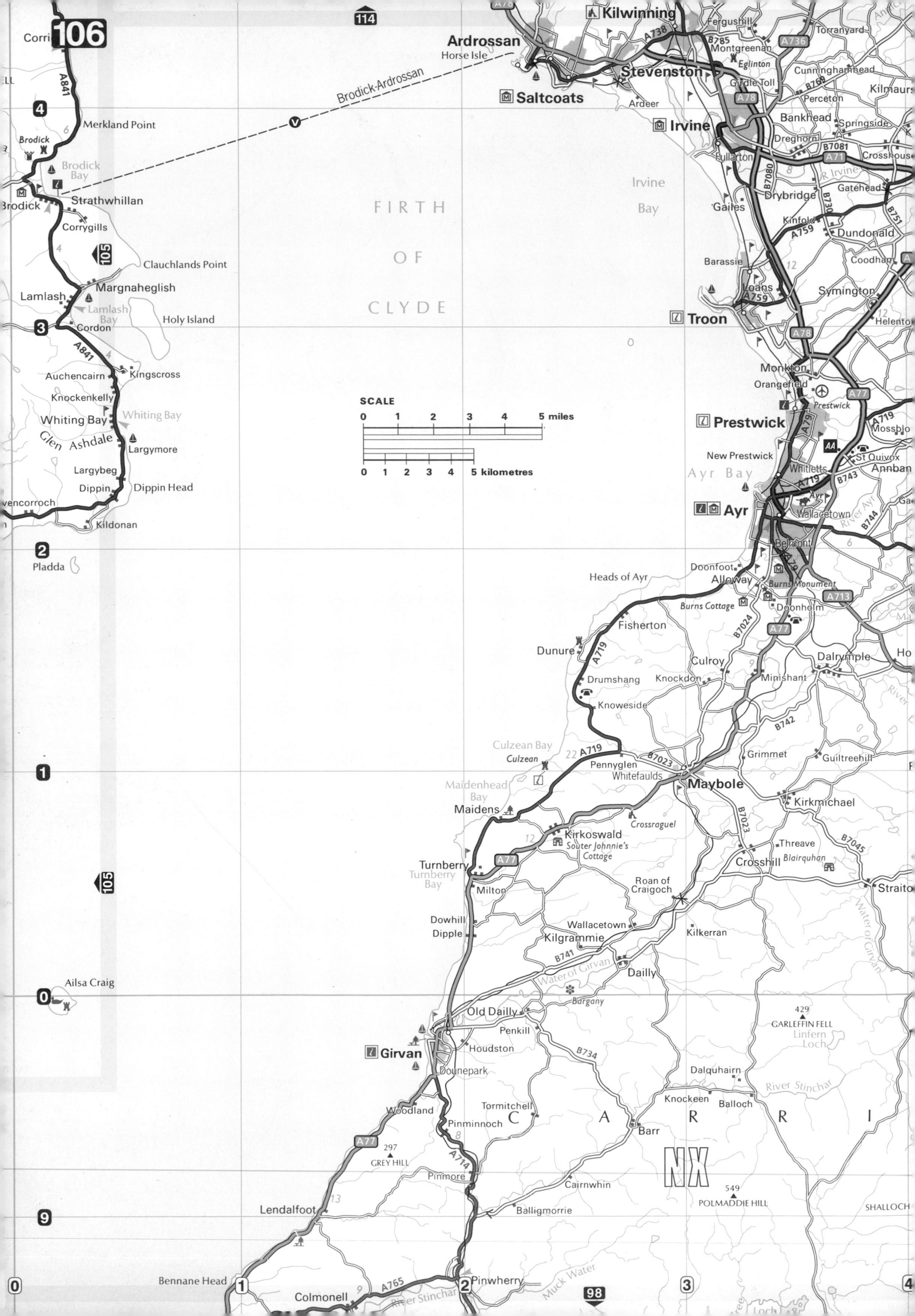

Corri

A841

4

6

*Brodick*

Merkland Point

Brodick Bay

Brodick

Strathwhillan

Corrygills

105

4

Clauchlands Point

Lamlash

3

Margnaheglish

Lamlash Bay

Holy Island

A841

Gordon

4

Auchencairn

Kingscross

Knockenkelly

Whiting Bay

Whiting Bay

*Glen Ashdale*

Largymore

Largybeg

Dippin

Dippin Head

vencorroch

Kildonan

2

Pladda

1

105

0

Ailsa Craig

9

0

Bennane Head

1

Colmonell

FIRTH OF CLYDE

114

Kilwinning

Ardrossan

Horse Isle

Brodick-Ardrossan

V

Saltcoats

A738

A785

B785

Fergushill

Montgreenan

Eglinton

Torranyard

A736

Cunninghamhead

B769

Kilmaurs

Girdle Toll

A78

Perceton

Bankhead

Springside

Irvine

Ardeer

Fullarton

Dreghorn

A71

Crosshouse

B7081

A78

B7080

8

Drybridge

Gatehead

B751

Irvine Bay

'Gailes

B759

Kinfold

Dundonald

12

Loans

A759

Coodham

Barassie

A78

Symington

Helento

Troon

12

Monkton

Orangefield

Prestwick

A77

A719

Mossblo

Prestwick

AA

St Quivox

Annban

New Prestwick

Whitletts

B743

Ayr Bay

Ayr

Wallacetown

River Ayr

A744

Ga

A713

Belmont

6

A77

Doonfoot

Alloway

Burns Monument

Heads of Ayr

Burns Cottage

Doonholm

Fisherton

B7024

Culroy

Dalrymple

Dunure

A719

Knockdon

Minishant

Ho

Drumshang

Knoweside

B742

River

Culzean Bay

*Culzean*

22 A719

Pennyglen

B7023

Grimmet

Guiltreehill

Maidenhead Bay

Whitefaulds

Maybole

Kirkmichael

Maidens

Crossraguel

B7023

Turnberry

12

Kirkoswald

*Souter Johnnie's Cottage*

Crosshill

Blairquhan

Straito

Turnberry Bay

A77

Roan of Craigoch

Milton

Dowhill

Wallacetown

Kilkerran

Dipple

Kilgrammie

B741

Water of Girvan

Dailly

Bargany

429

Old Dailly

GARLEFFIN FELL

Linfern Loch

Penkill

Girvan

Houdston

Dalquhairn

Dounepark

B734

Knockeen

Balloch

River Stinchar

Woodland

Tormitchell

C       A       R       R       I

Pinminnoch

Barr

8

NX

A77

297

GREY HILL

A714

Cairnwhin

549

POLMADDIE HILL

SHALLOCH

Pinmore

13

Lendalfoot

Balligmorrie

A765

Pinwherry

River Stinchar

Muck Water

98

3

SCALE

0    1    2    3    4    5 miles

0  1  2  3  4  5 kilometres

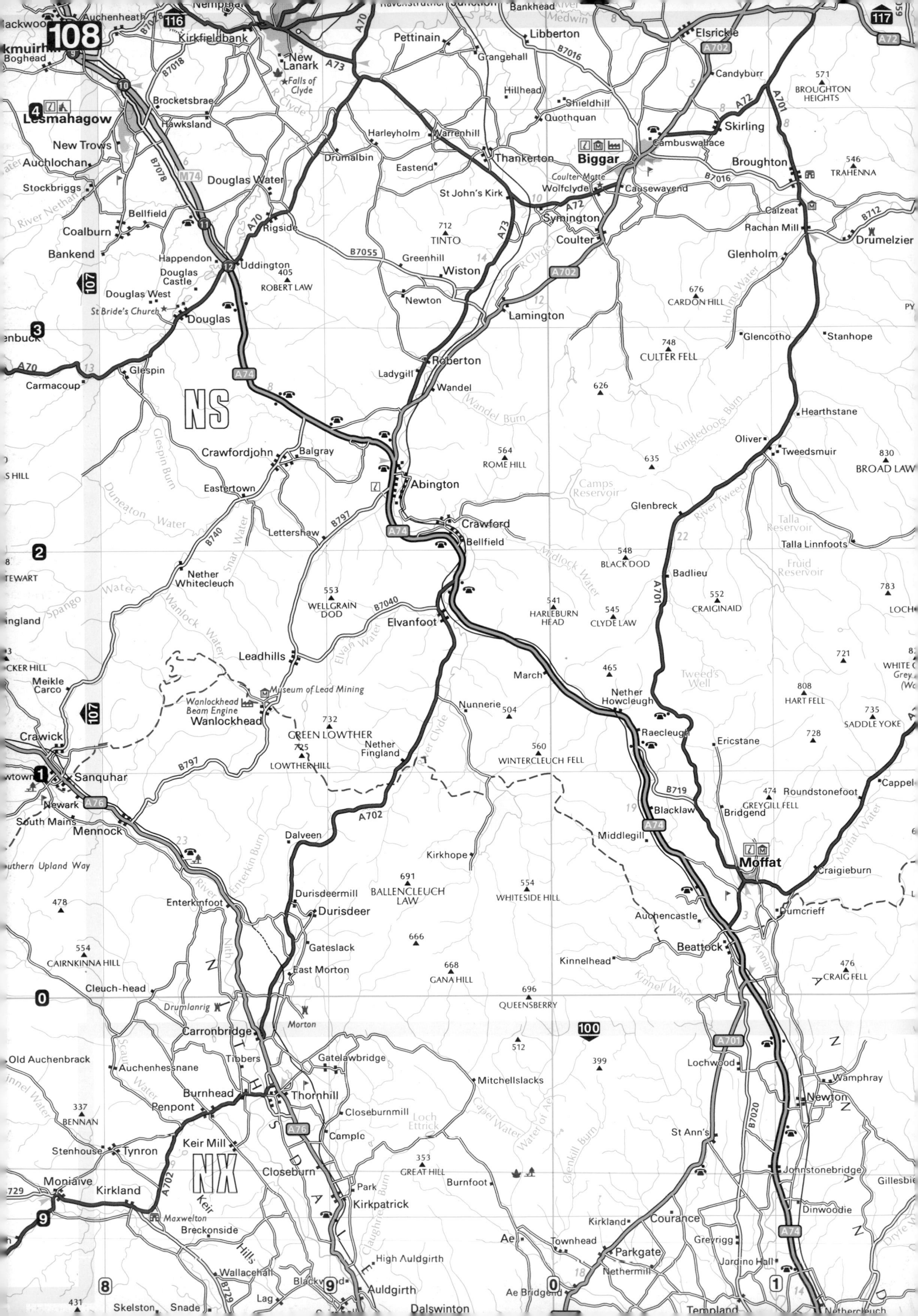

SCALE

0  1  2  3  4  5 miles

0  1  2  3  4  5 kilometres

Berwick-upon-Tweed

Barracks
Town Ramparts
Tweedmouth
Spittal
Ord
Huds Head

Unthank
Scremerston
Cheswick
West Allerdean
Ancroft
Gŏswick
Haggerston
Berrington
Beal
Bowsden
Kyloe
Lowick
East Kyloe
Fenwick
Buckton
Smeafield
Holburn
Detchant
Middleton
St Cuthbert's Cave
North Hazelrigg
Belford
Easington
Outchester
Spindlestone
Bellshill
Warenton
Adderstone
Warenford

HOLY ISLAND

CAUSEWAY
FLOODED
AT HIGH TIDE

Holy
Island
Lindisfarne
Lindisfarne
Priory
Castle Point
Fenham
Guile Point

Elwick
Ross
Low Middleton
Budle
Bay
Waren
Mill
Budle
Glororum
Burton
Bradford
Elford

Bamburgh

FARNE
ISLANDS
Staple
Sound
Inner
Sound

Seahouses
North
Sunderland
Beadnell

Nesbit
Doddington
West
Horton
East
Horton
South
Hazelrigg
Lucker
Newham
Swinhoe
Beadnell Bay

the Lady
erford Hall
B6353
B6525
nton
own

embleton
Woolcr
West
Weetwood
Chatton
Earle
Haugh Head
Newtown
Liburn
Tower
North
Middleton
South
Middleton
Chillingham
Hepbu
Ros Castle
CATERAN HILL
267

NU

Warenford
Newstead
Ellingham
North
Charlton
Doxford
Falloden

Chathill
Preston
Brunton
Christon
Bank

Tughall
High Newton
by-the-Sea
Embleton
Dunstan
Steads
Dunstanburgh
Embleton
Bay

Ilderton
Roseden
Roddham
New
Bewick
Old Bewick
Ditchburn
Harehope
Eglingham

South
Charlton
Rock
Dunstan
Craster
Rennington
Stamford
Howick
Hall

567
NMOOR HILL
Brandon
Ingram
Fawdon
Branton
Powburn
Glanton
Glanton Pike
Beanley
Titlington
East
Bolton
Shipley
Broxfield
Littlehoughton
Cullernose Point
Howick
Longhoughton

Prendwick
Great
Ryle
Shawdon
Hill
Bolton
Abberwick
Broome Park
Denwick
Boulmer

334
COCHRANE
PIKE

Alnham
Whittingham
Little Ryle
Thrunton
Lemmington
Hall
Alnwick
Hawkhill
Lesbury
Seaton Point
Bilton
Alnmouth

Elilaw
Scrainwood
Yetlington
Callaly
Edlingham
Bilton
Banks
High
Buston
Alnmouth
Bay

Netherton
Burradon
High
Trewhitt
Cartington
Lorbotle
260
GRANTLEES
HILL
Newton-
on-the-Moor
Swarland
Estate
Shilbottle
Low Buston
Birling
Warkworth
Hermitage

Sharperton
Snitter
Warton
Flotterton
Rothbury
Cragside
Thropton
Great
Tosson
Newtown
Whitton
Bickerton
Swindon
Caistron

Longframlington
North End
Pauperhaugh
Brinkburn
Swarland
Guyzance
Gloster
Hill
Amble
Coquet Island

Togston
Hauxley
Acklington
Radcliffe
East
Thirston
Felton
South
Broomhill
Broomhill
East
Chevington
Red Row
Chevington
Drift

Forest

TOSSON HILL

Eshott

West

Druridge

Middleton Hall
North
Charlton

A1
A697
A1068
B6341
B6344
B6346
B6347
B6348
B6349
B1340
B1341
B1342
B1339
B1330
B6345

River Till
River Breamish
River Aln
R Coquet

103
0
1
2
3

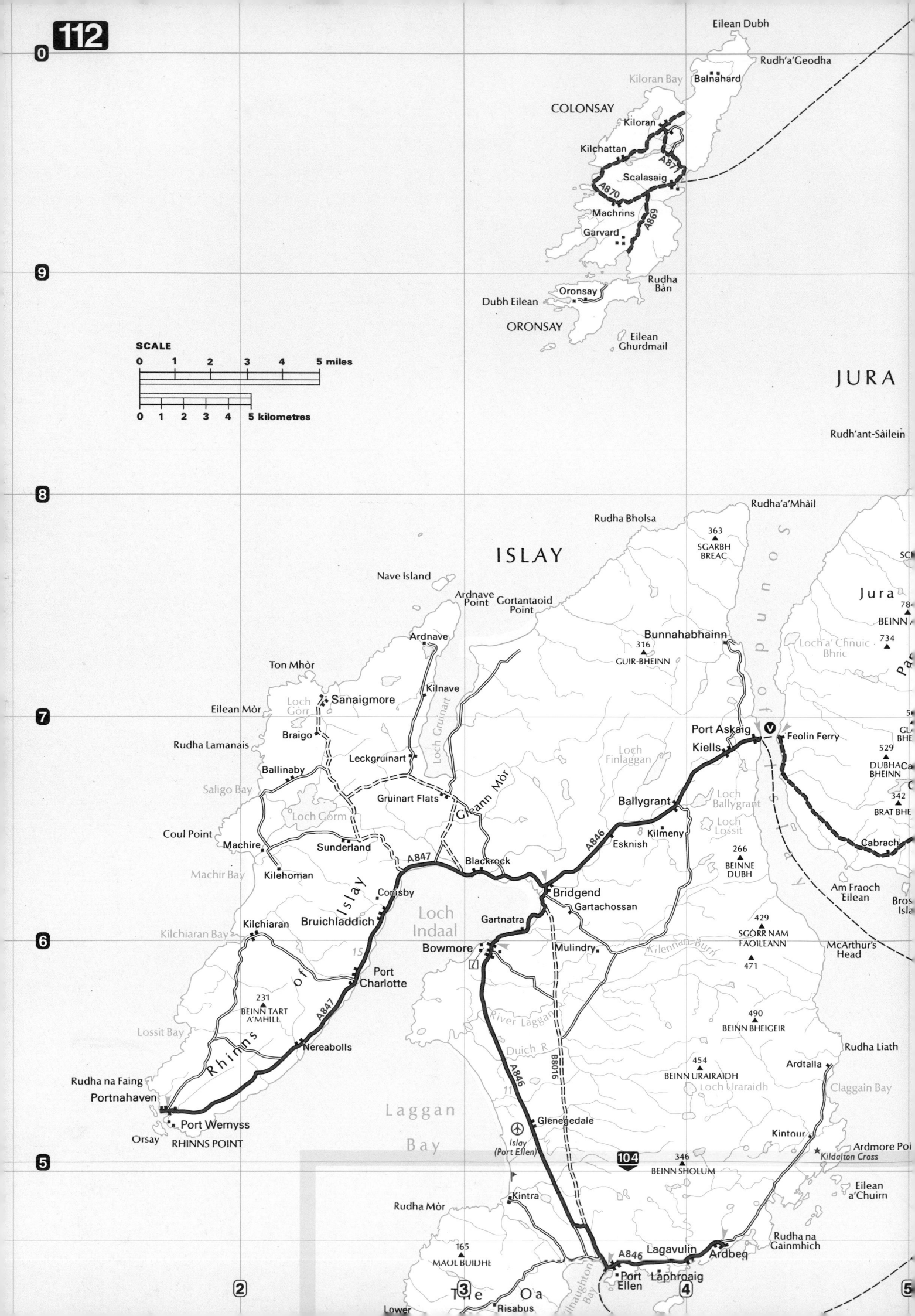

**SCALE**

0  1  2  3  4  5 miles

0  1  2  3  4  5 kilometres

**COLONSAY**

Eilean Dubh
Rudh'a'Geodha
Kiloran Bay
Balnahard
Kiloran
Kilchattan
A871
Scalasaig
A870
Machrins
A869
Garvard

**ORONSAY**

Oronsay
Rudha Bàn
Dubh Eilean
Eilean Ghurdmail

**JURA**

Rudh'ant-Sàilein

Rudha'a'Mhàil

**ISLAY**

Rudha Bholsa
SGARBH BREAC  363
Nave Island
Ardnave Point
Gortantaoid Point
Bunnahabhainn
GUIR-BHEINN  316

Ton Mhòr
Ardnave
Kilnave
Loch Gorr
Sanaigmore
Eilean Mòr
Braigo
Loch Gruinart
Port Askaig
Kiells
Feolin Ferry

Rudha Lamanais
Leckgruinart
Ballinaby
Loch Finlaggan
Ballygrant
Loch Ballygrant
Loch Lossit
529
DUBHA Ca BHEINN

Saligo Bay
Gleann Mòr
Gruinart Flats
Kilmeny  8
Esknish
342
BRAT BHE

Loch Gorm
Machire
Sunderland
A847
Blackrock
266
BEINNE DUBH
Cabrach

Coul Point
Machir Bay
Kilchoman
Comisby
Bridgend
Gartachossan
Am Fraoch Eilean
Bros Isla

Kilchiaran
Bruichladdich
Loch Indaal
Gartnatra
429
SGÒRR NAM FAOILEANN
McArthur's Head

Kilchiaran Bay
Bowmore
Mulindry
Kilennan Burn
471

15
Port Charlotte
490
BEINN BHEIGEIR

BEINN TART A'MHILL  231
A847
River Laggan
Rudha Liath

Lossit Bay
Nereabolls
Duich R
B8016
454
BEINN URAIRAIDH
Ardtalla

Rhinns of Islay
A846
Loch Uraraidh
Claggain Bay

Rudha na Faing
Portnahaven
11
Kintour
Ardmore Poi

Laggan Bay
Glenegedale
Kildalton Cross

Port Wemyss
Islay (Port Ellen)
104
346
BEINN SHOLUM
Orsay
RHINNS POINT

Rudha Mòr
Kintra
Eilean a'Chuirn

165
MAOL BUIDHE
Rudha na Gainmhich

A846
Lagavulin
Ardbeg
Port Ellen
Laphroaig

The Oa

Lower
Risabus

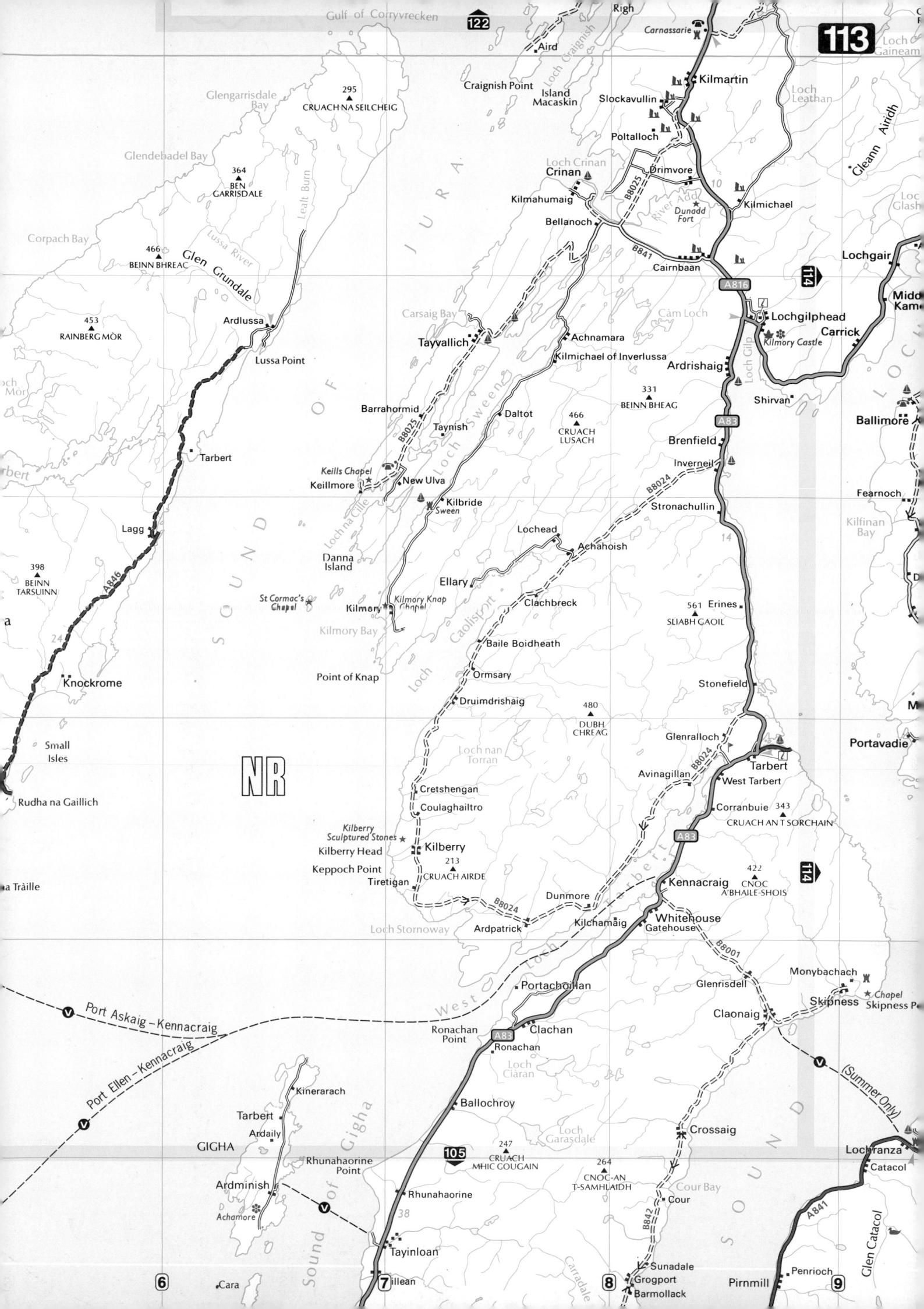

Gulf of Corryvrecken

122

Right
Carnassarie
Aird
Craignish Point
Island Macaskin
Kilmartin
Slockavullin
Poltalloch
Loch Craignish
Loch Gaineam
Loch Leathan

295
CRUACH NA SEILCHEIG
Glengarrisdale Bay

Glendebadel Bay

364
BEN GARRISDALE

Corpach Bay

466
BEINN BHREAC
Glen Grundale

453
RAINBERG MÒR
Ardlussa

Lussa Point

Tarbert

398
BEINN TARSUINN

Lagg

Knockrome

Small Isles

Rudha na Gaillich

NR

Carsaig Bay
Tayvallich

Barrahormid
Taynish
Daltot

Keills Chapel
Keillmore
New Ulva

Kilbride
Sween

Danna Island

St Cormac's Chapel

Kilmory
Kilmory Knap Chapel

Kilmory Bay

Point of Knap

Loch Sween

Loch na Cille

Achnamara
Kilmichael of Inverlussa

466
CRUACH LUSACH

Lochead
Achahoish

Ellary
Clachbreck

Baile Boidheath

Ormsary

Druimdrishaig

Cretshengan

Coulaghailtro

Kilberry Sculptured Stones
Kilberry Head
Keppoch Point
Tiretigan
Kilberry

213
CRUACH AIRDE

Loch nan Torran

480
DUBH CHREAG

B8024

Crinan
Loch Crinan
Kilmahumaig
Bellanoch

River Add
Dunadd Fort

Drimvore
Kilmichael

10

Cairnbaan
A816

331
BEINN BHEAG

Lochgilphead
Kilmory Castle
Carrick

Ardrishaig
Shirvan

Brenfield

Inverneil

Stronachullin

B8024

14

561
SLIABH GAOIL
Erines

Stonefield

Glenralloch

Avinagillan

Tarbert
West Tarbert

Corranbuie

343
CRUACH AN T SORCHAIN

A83

422
CNOC A'BHAILE-SHOIS

Kennacraig

Dunmore

Ardpatrick

Kilchamaig
Gatehouse

Whitehouse

B8001

Loch Stornoway

Lochgair
Midd Kam

Càm Loch

Ballimore

Fearnoch

Kilfinan Bay

Portavadie

114

Loch Gilp

Monybachach
Chapel
Skipness
Skipness P

Glenrisdell

Claonaig

West Loch

Portachoillan

Ronachan Point

Port Askaig – Kennacraig
Port Ellen – Kennacraig

Kinerarach

Tarbert
Ardaily
GIGHA

Rhunahaorine Point

Ardminish
Achamore

Cara

Clachan
Ronachan

A83

Ballochroy

105

247
CRUACH MHIC GOUGAIN

Loch Ciaran

Loch Garasdale

264
CNOC-AN T-SAMHLAIDH

Rhunahaorine

illean
Tayinloan

Crossaig

Cour Bay
Cour

B842

Sunadale
Grogport
Barmollack

(Summer Only)

Lochranza
Catacol

A841

Glen Catacol

Pirnrioch

Penrioch

6        7        8        9

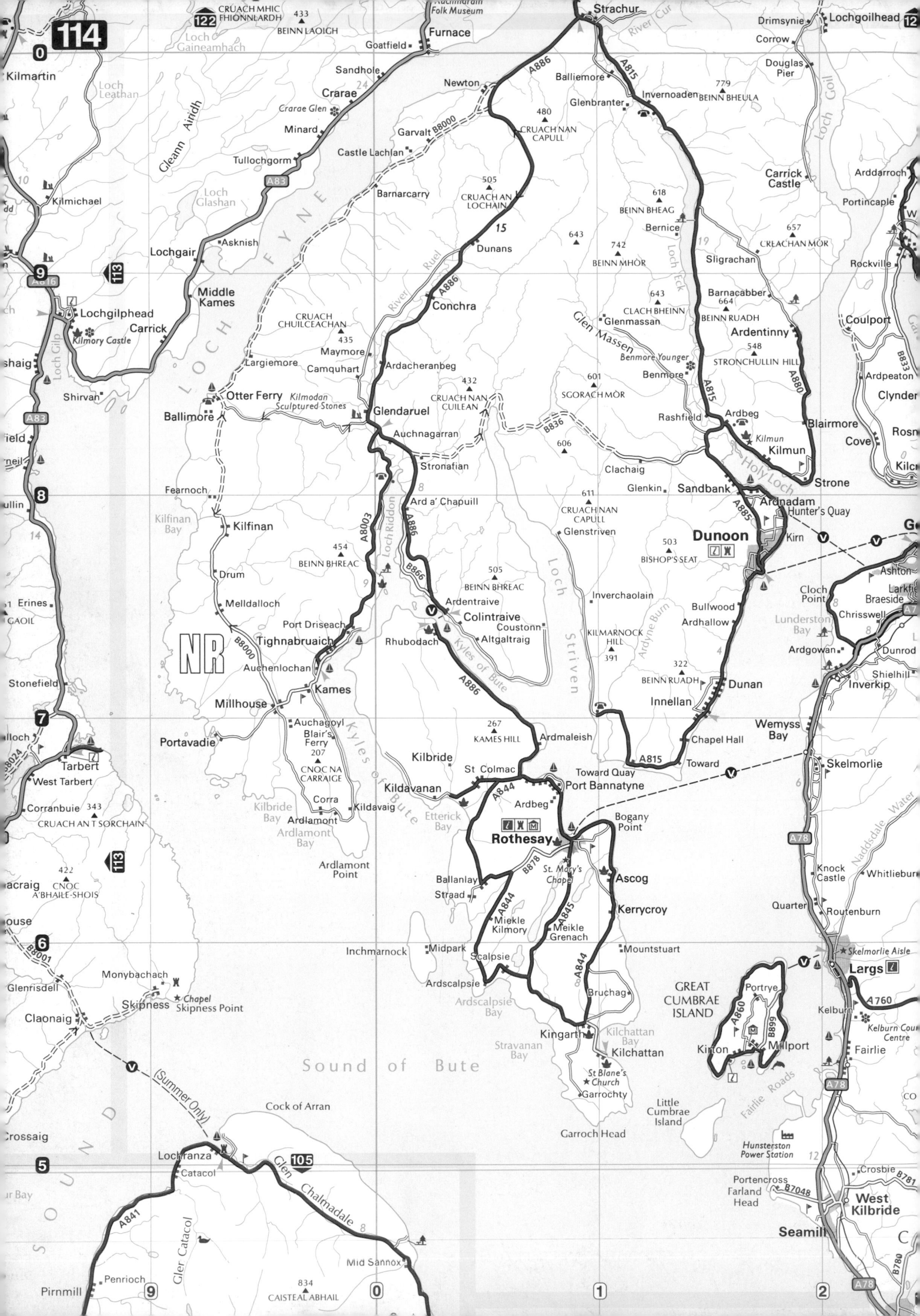

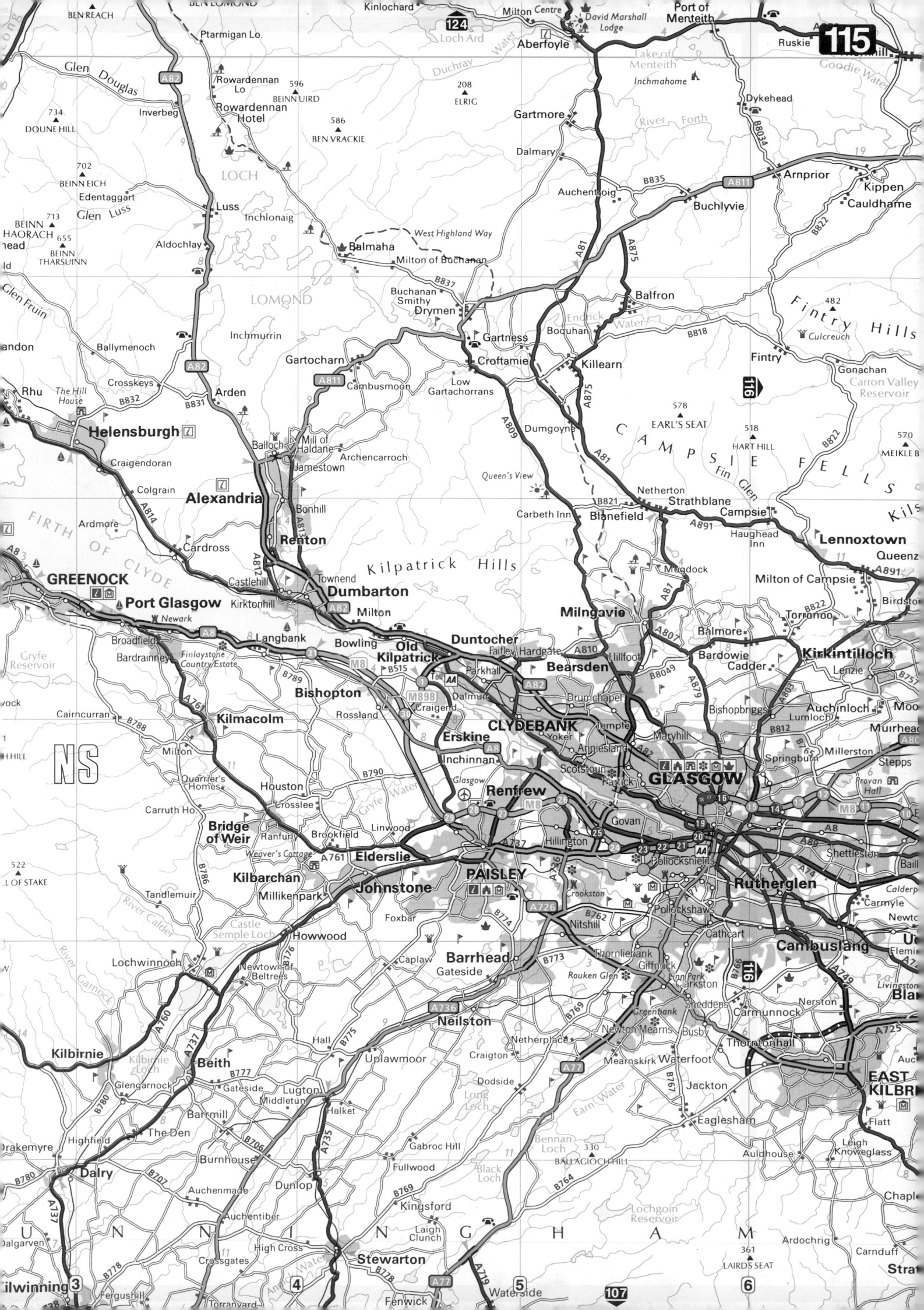

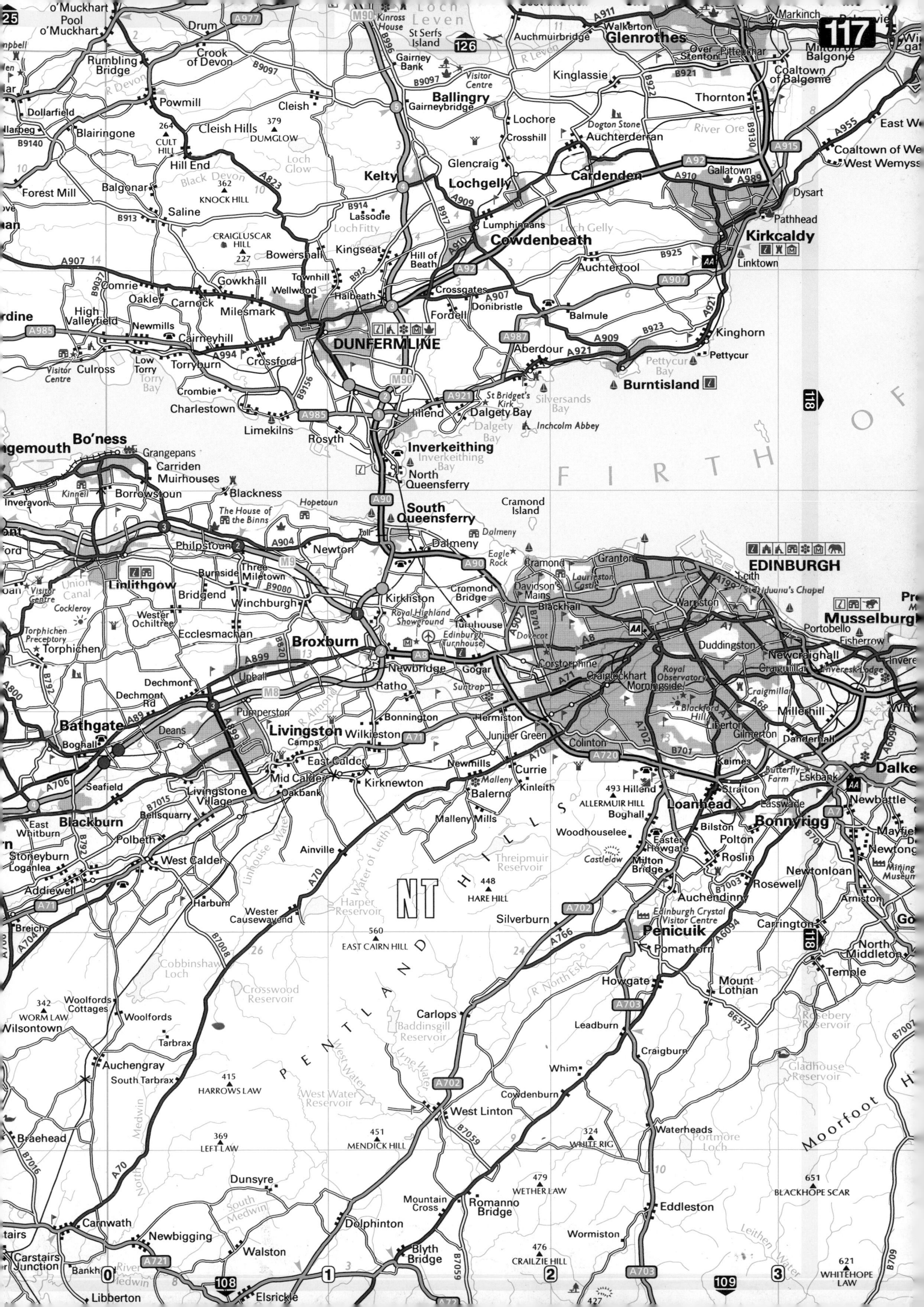

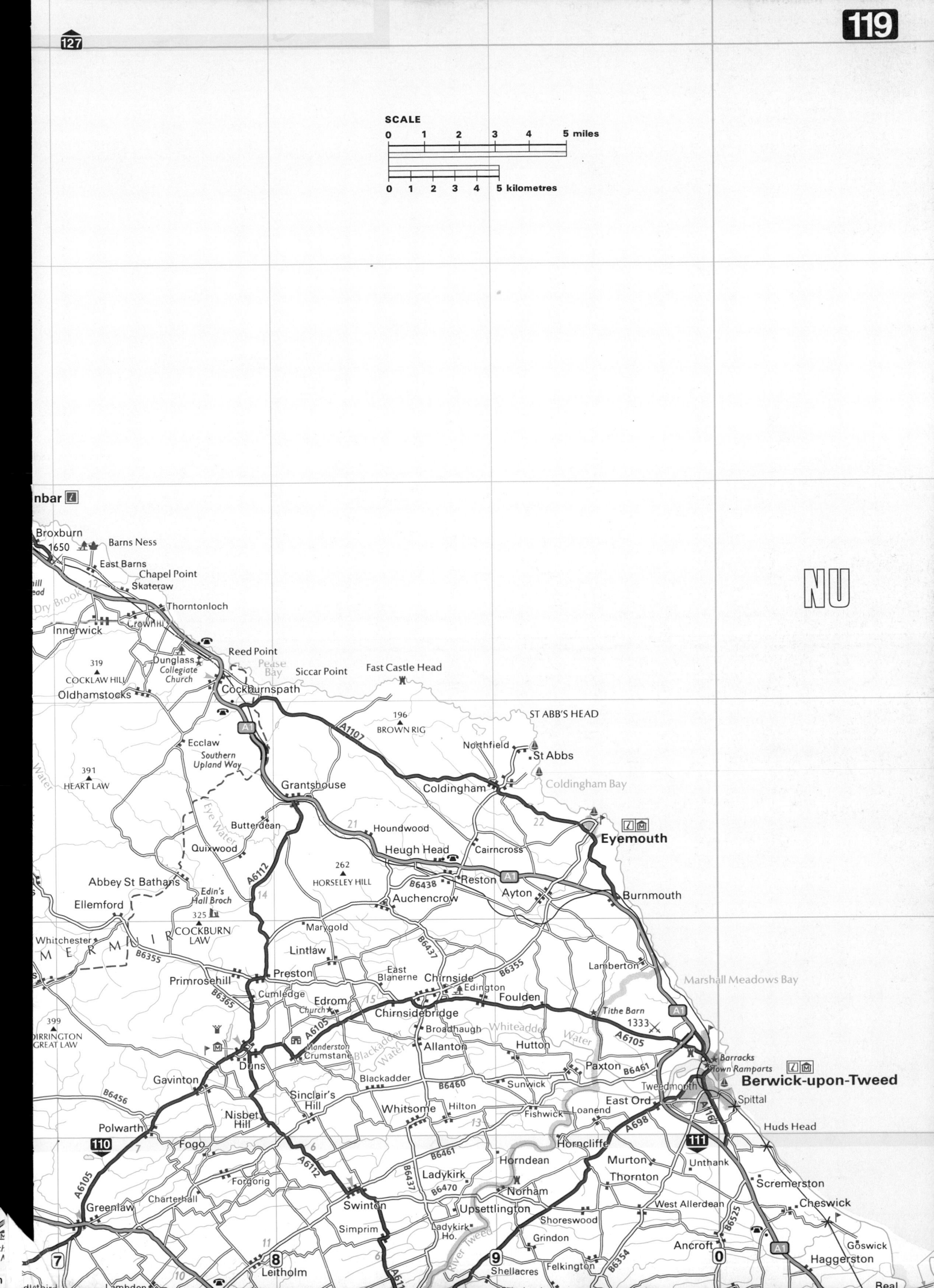

SCALE

0   1   2   3   4   5 miles

0  1  2  3  4  5 kilometres

NU

nbar

Broxburn
1650
Barns Ness
East Barns
Chapel Point
Skateraw
Thorntonloch
Dry Brook
hill
ead
Innerwick
Crown Hill
Reed Point
Dunglass
*Collegiate
Church*
Pease Bay
Siccar Point
Fast Castle Head
319
COCKLAW HILL
Oldhamstocks
Cockburnspath
ST ABB'S HEAD
Ecclaw
*Southern Upland Way*
391
HEART LAW
A1
A1107
196
BROWN RIG
Northfield
St Abbs
Grantshouse
Coldingham
Coldingham Bay
Water
Eye Water
Butterdean
Quixwood
21
Houndwood
22
Eyemouth
Heugh Head
Cairncross
Abbey St Bathans
*Edin's Hall Broch*
A6112
262
HORSELEY HILL
B6438
Reston
A1
Ayton
Burnmouth
Ellemford
14
325
Auchencrow
MERMIR
Whitchester
COCKBURN LAW
Marygold
Lintlaw
B6437
Lamberton
Marshall Meadows Bay
B6355
Preston
East Blanerne
Chirnside
B6355
Primrosehill
B6365
Cumledge
Edrom
*Church*
15
Edington
Foulden
Tithe Barn
1333
A1
399
IRRINGTON
GREAT LAW
Chirnsidebridge
Broadhaugh
Whiteadder
Water
A6105
Barracks
Manderston
Crumstane
Blackadder
Water
Allanton
Hutton
A6105
Town Ramparts
Berwick-upon-Tweed
Duns
Gavinton
Blackadder
B6460
Sunwick
Paxton
B6461
Tweedmouth
Spittal
B6456
Sinclair's
Hill
Whitsome
Hilton
Fishwick
East Ord
Huds Head
Nisbet
Hill
13
Loanend
Polwarth
110
Fogo
6
B6461
Horncliffe
Murton
111
Unthank
A698
A6112
Horndean
Thornton
Scremerston
A6105
Charterhall
Ladykirk
B6437
B6470
Norham
West Allerdean
B6525
Cheswick
Greenlaw
Forgorig
Swinton
Upsettlington
Shoreswood
Ancroft
A1
Göswick
7
8
Simprim
Ladykirk
Ho.
9
Grindon
0
Haggerston
11
10
6
River Tweed
Felkington
B6354
Furn
Leitholm
Shellacres
Beal

128

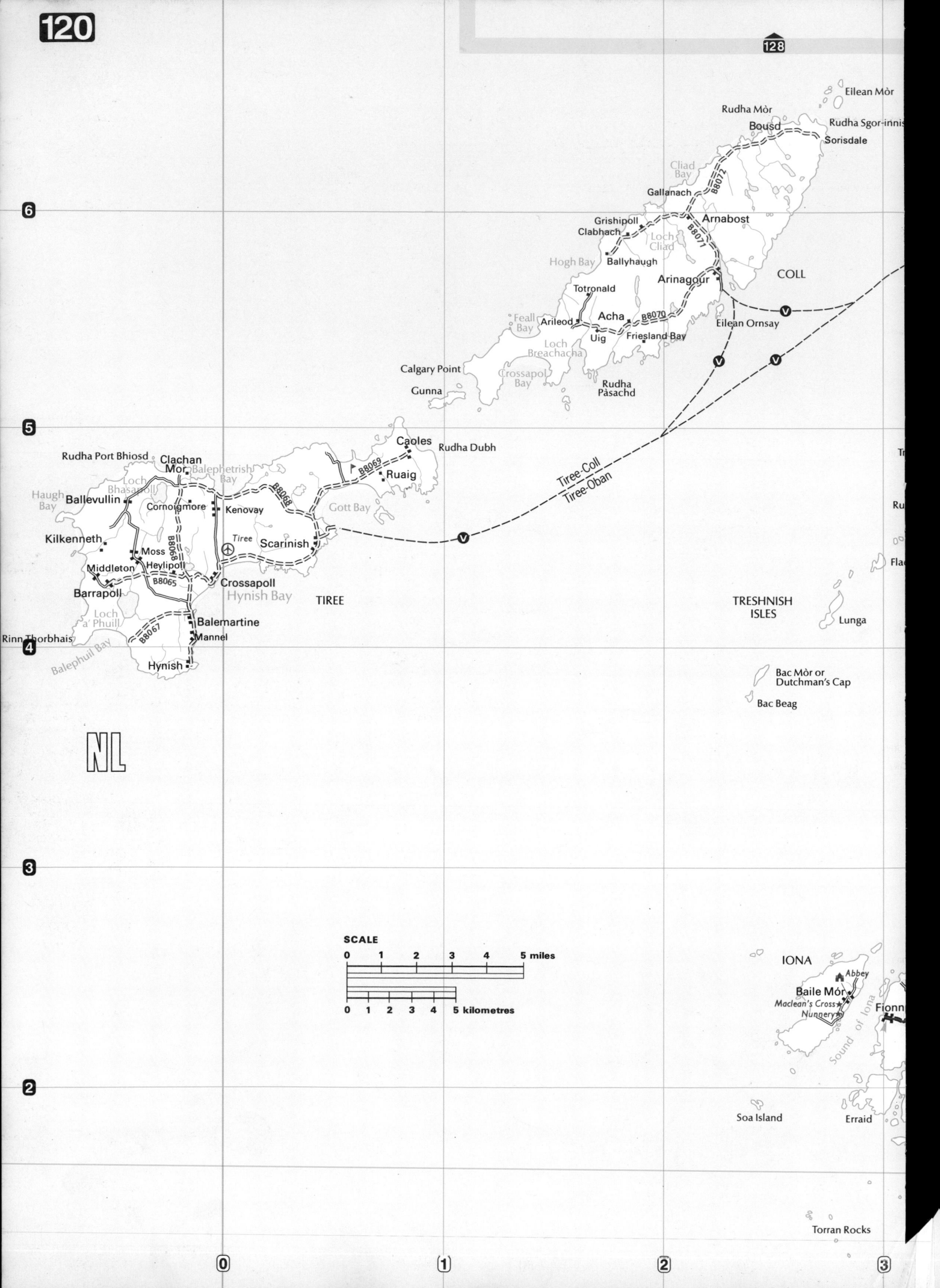

Eilean Mòr
Rudha Mòr
Rudha Sgor-innis
Bousd
Sorisdale
Cliad Bay
Gallanach
B8072
Grishipoll
Clabhach
Arnabost
Loch Cliad
B8071
COLL
Hogh Bay
Ballyhaugh
Arinagour
Totronald
Feall Bay
Arileod
Acha
B8070
Eilean Ornsay
Uig
Friesland Bay
Loch Breachacha
Calgary Point
Crossapol Bay
Rudha Pàsachd
Gunna

Caoles
Rudha Dubh
Rudha Port Bhiosd
Clachan Mor
Balephetrish Bay
B8069
Ruaig
Tiree-Coll
Tiree-Oban
Loch Bhasapoll
B8068
Haugh Bay
Ballevullin
Cornaigmore
Kenovay
Gott Bay
Kilkenneth
Tiree
Scarinish
B8068
Moss
Heylipoll
Middleton
B8065
Crossapoll
Barrapoll
Hynish Bay
TIREE
TRESHNISH ISLES
Lunga
Loch a' Phuill
Balemartine
B8067
Rinn Thorbhais
Mannel
Bac Mòr or Dutchman's Cap
Balephuil Bay
Hynish
Bac Beag

NL

SCALE
0  1  2  3  4  5 miles

0  1  2  3  4  5 kilometres

IONA
Abbey
Baile Mòr
Maclean's Cross
Nunnery
Fionn

Soa Island
Erraid

Torran Rocks

0        1        2        3

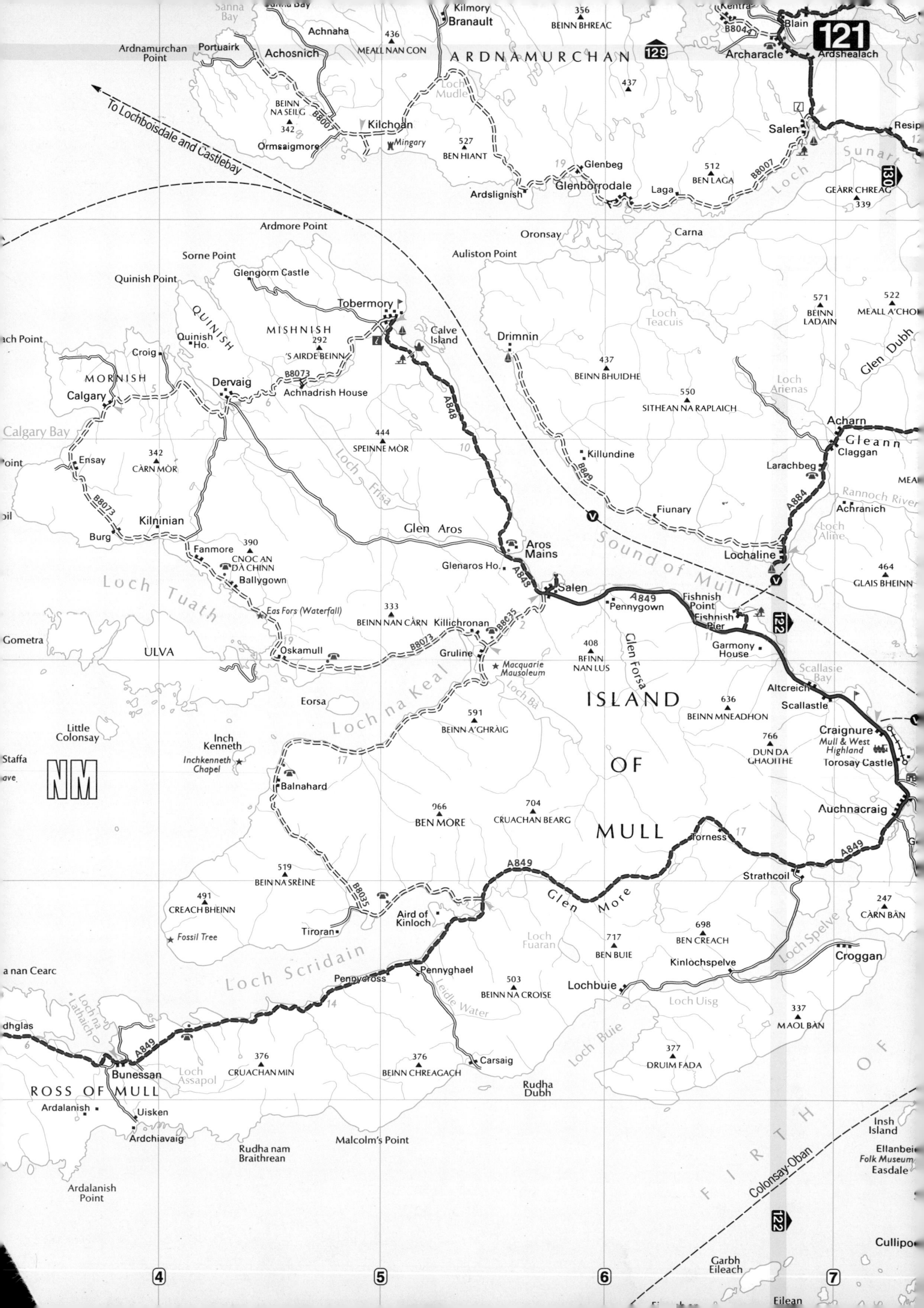

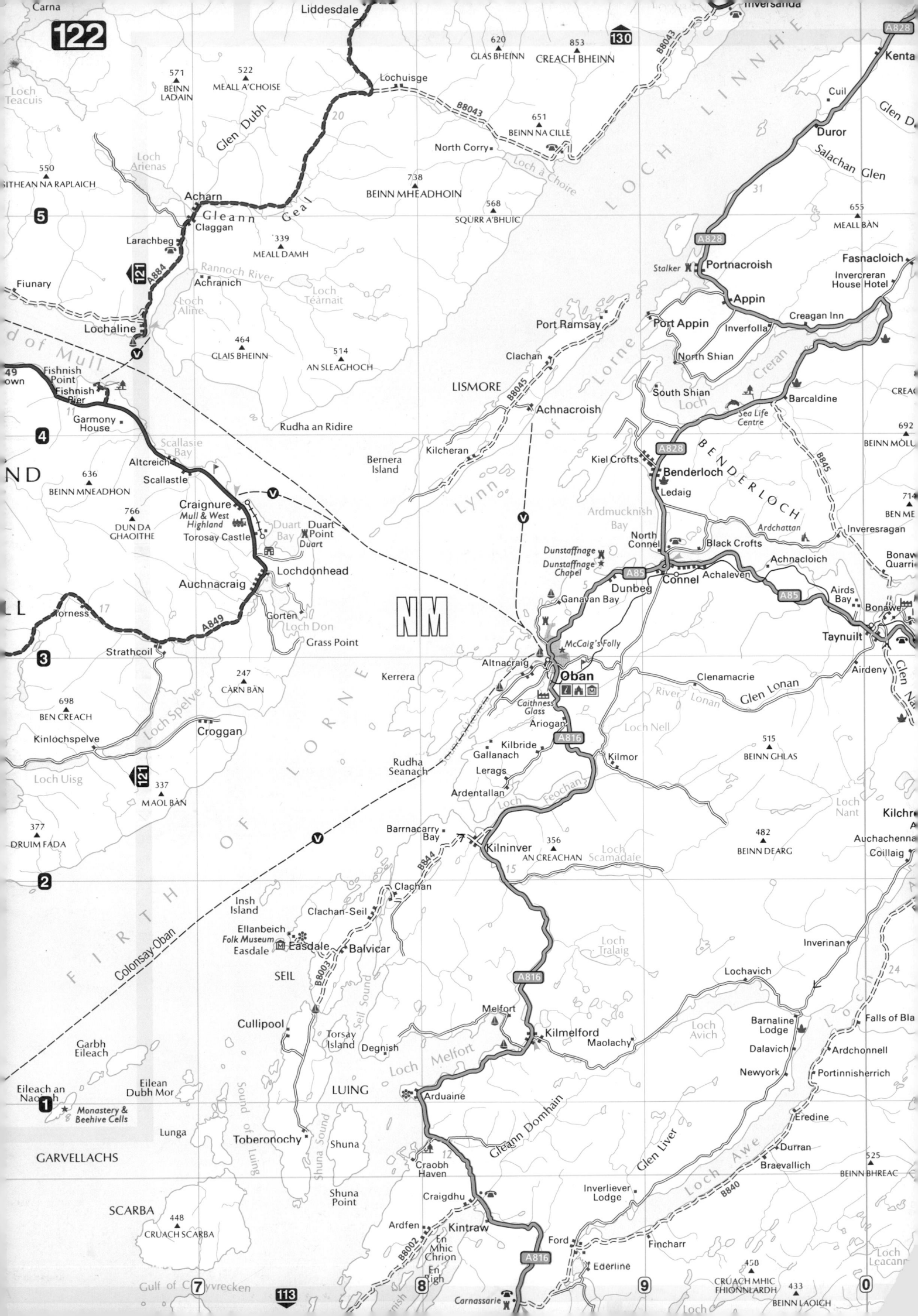

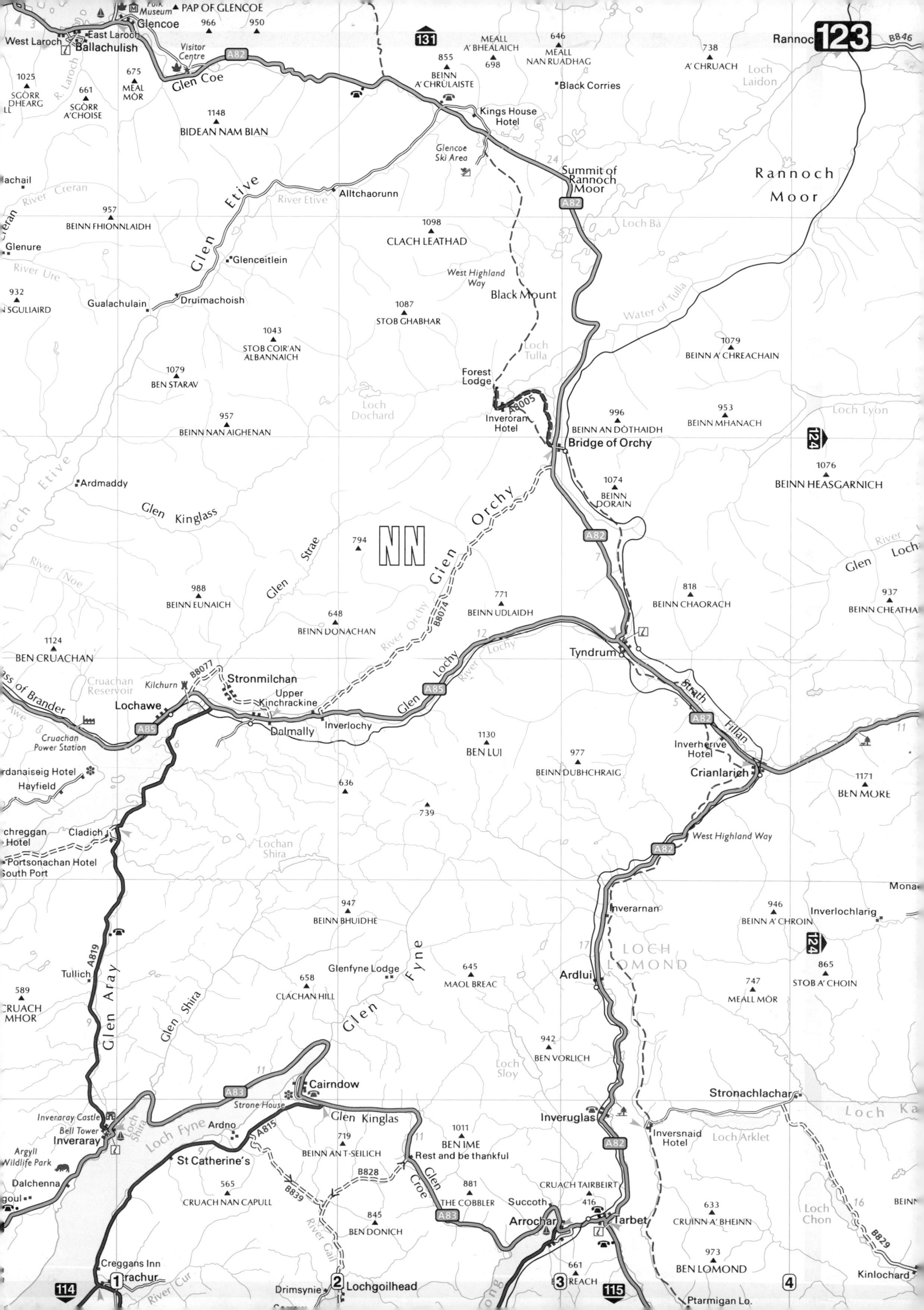

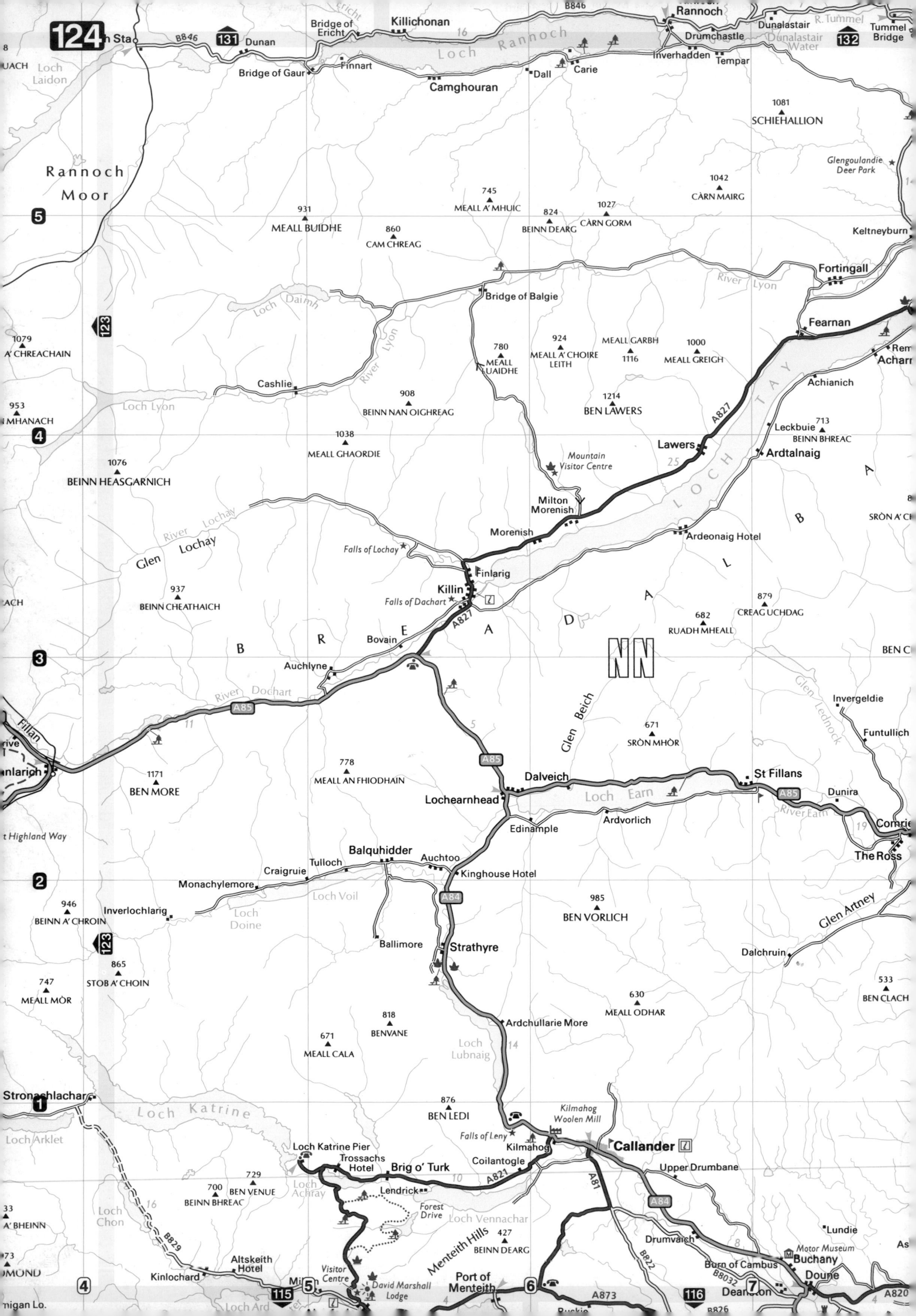

SCALE

0   1   2   3   4   5 miles

0  1  2  3  4  5 kilometres

LUNAN BAY

ST ANDREWS BAY

FIFE NESS

BUDDON NESS

Scurdie Ness
Ferryden
Kirkton of Craig
Fishtown of Usan
Boddin
Boddin Point
Braehead
Lunan
Red Head

Castle
Maryton
Carcary
Westerton
Bolshan
WUDDY LAW  132
Glasterlaw
Kinnell
Boysack
Inverkeilor
Cauldcots
B965
Letham Grange
Marywell
Auchmithie
St Vigeans
Carlingheugh Bay
The Deil's Head
**Arbroath**

Farnell
A934
A933
Priockheim
Leysmill
Chapelton
Colliston
Arbirlot
Bonnington

Finavon
Crosston
Aberlemno
Pitkennedy
Melgund Castle
Kemp's Castle
Turin
Carse Gray
Lunanhead
Clochtow
Restenneth Priory
Reswallie
B9113
Balgavies
Guthrie
Pitmuies
**Forfar**
Burnside
Dunnichen
Letham
Balmuir
Idvies
Kingsmuir
Bowriefauld
Craichie

Battledykes
Oathlaw
B9134
A94
shoe
134

Inverarity
Whigstreet
Redford
B9127
Kirkbuddo
Hatton
Hayhillock
Carmyllie
B978
B961
B9127
Elliot Water

Petterden
odhills
CARROT HILL  259
Affleck
Kirkton of Monikie
Craigton
Monikie
Muirdrum
Salmond's Muir
East Haven
Panbride
Carnoustie
Greystone

ewbigging
Bucklerheads
Wellbank
Newbigging
Upper Victoria
rnside of untrune
Kellas
Templehall
Barry
uglas Angus
Murroes
B961
Baldovie
A92
Monifieth
Buddon
Barnhill
Broughty Ferry
**DUNDEE**

Tayport
Scotscraig
**Newport on-Tay**
B945
Carrick
A919
Leuchars
Earlshall
Balmullo
Guardbridge
River Eden
Kincaple
A91
**St Andrews**
Brownhills
Boarhills
Stravithie
Kingsbarns
B9131
athkinness
Botanic Gardens
Denhead
B939
lebocraigs
cottie
A915
Baldinnie
B940
Radernie
Peat Inn
Kingsmuir
B940
Dunino
Balcomie Links
**Crail**
Largoward
Lathones
Lochty
Carnbee
B9171
A917
Kellie
Easter Pitkierie
Arncroach
Wester Pitkierie
Kilrenny
Anstruther Easter
Colinsburgh
B941
B9131
Fisheries Museum
**Anstruther**
Drumeldrie
B942
Abercrombie
Kilconquhar
Pittenweem
A917
St Monans
Elie
Earlsferry
A917
118
119
Isle of May

5          6          7          8

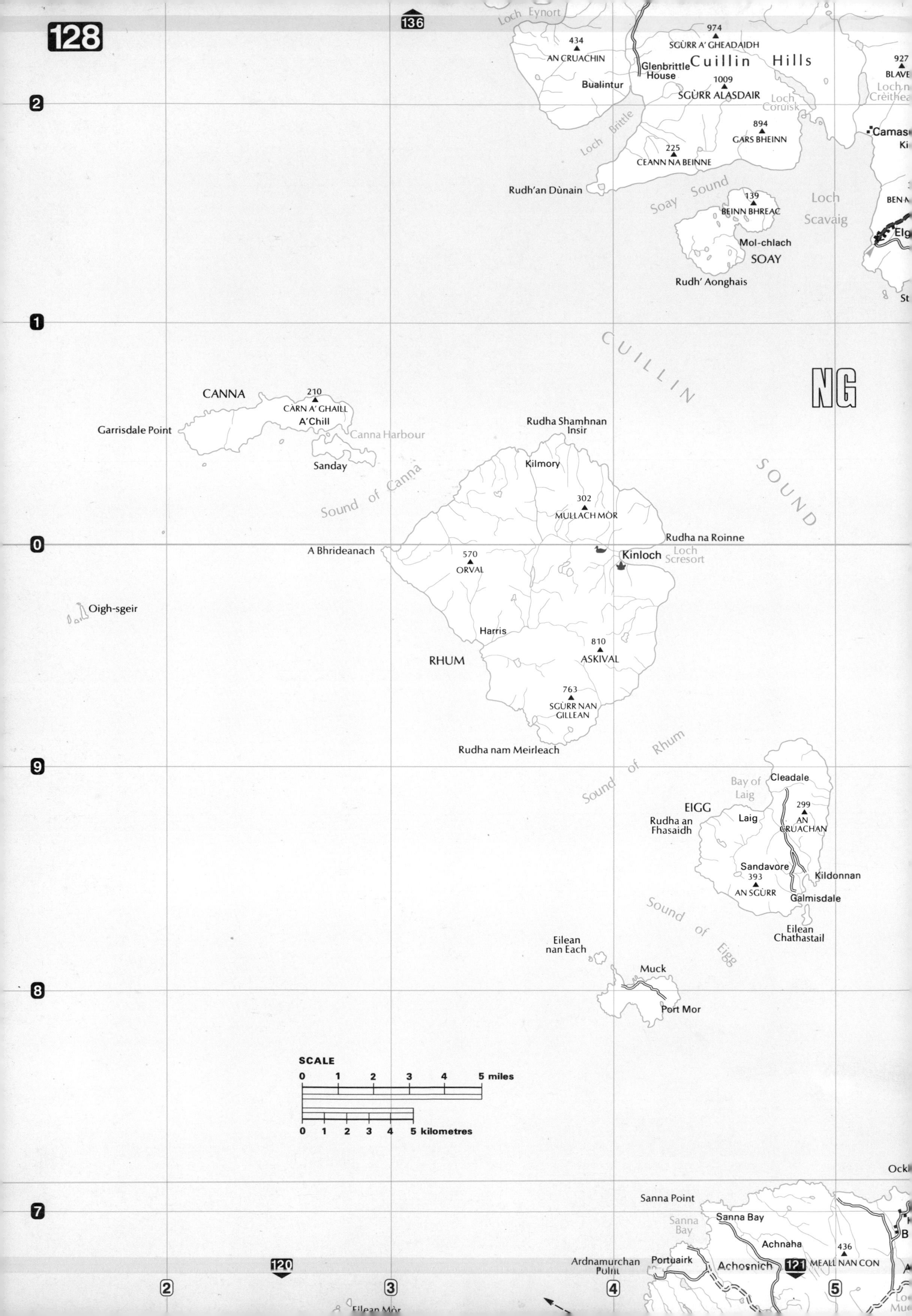

**136**

Loch Eynort

974
SGÙRR A' GHEADAIDH
434
AN CRUACHIN
Glenbrittle      Cuillin Hills
House
Bualintur                     927
1009              BLAVE
SGÙRR ALASDAIR        Loch
Loch
Coruisk        Crèithea

894
GARS BHEINN                Camas
Ki
225
CEANN NA BEINNE

Rudh'an Dùnain                    Loch
Soay   Sound        Scavaig
139
BEINN BHREAC            BEN
Mol-chlach                Elg

SOAY                  St

Rudh' Aonghais

**2**

**1**

**NG**

CANNA
210
CÀRN A' GHAILL
A'Chill
Garrisdale Point        Canna Harbour
C
U
I
L
Rudha Shamhnan        L
Insir        I
N

Sanday        Kilmory        S
O
Sound of Canna        U
N
302        D
MULLACH MÒR

**0**
A Bhrideanach        Rudha na Roinne
570
ORVAL        Kinloch   Loch
Scresort

Oigh-sgeir

Harris
810
ASKIVAL
RHUM

763
SGÙRR NAN
GILLEAN

Rudha nam Meirleach        Sound of Rhum

**9**
Cleadale
Bay of
Laig
EIGG        299
Rudha an        AN
Fhasaidh        Laig        CRUACHAN

Sandavore        Kildonnan
393
AN SGÙRR        Galmisdale

Eilean
Chathastail
Eilean
nan Each        Sound of Eigg
Muck

**8**
Port Mor

**SCALE**

0    1    2    3    4    5 miles

0   1   2   3   4   5 kilometres

**7**
Sanna Point
Sanna        Sanna Bay
Bay
Achnaha        B
436
Ardnamurchan        Portuairk        MEALL NAN CON
Point        Achosnich   **121**
Ock

Eilean Mòr

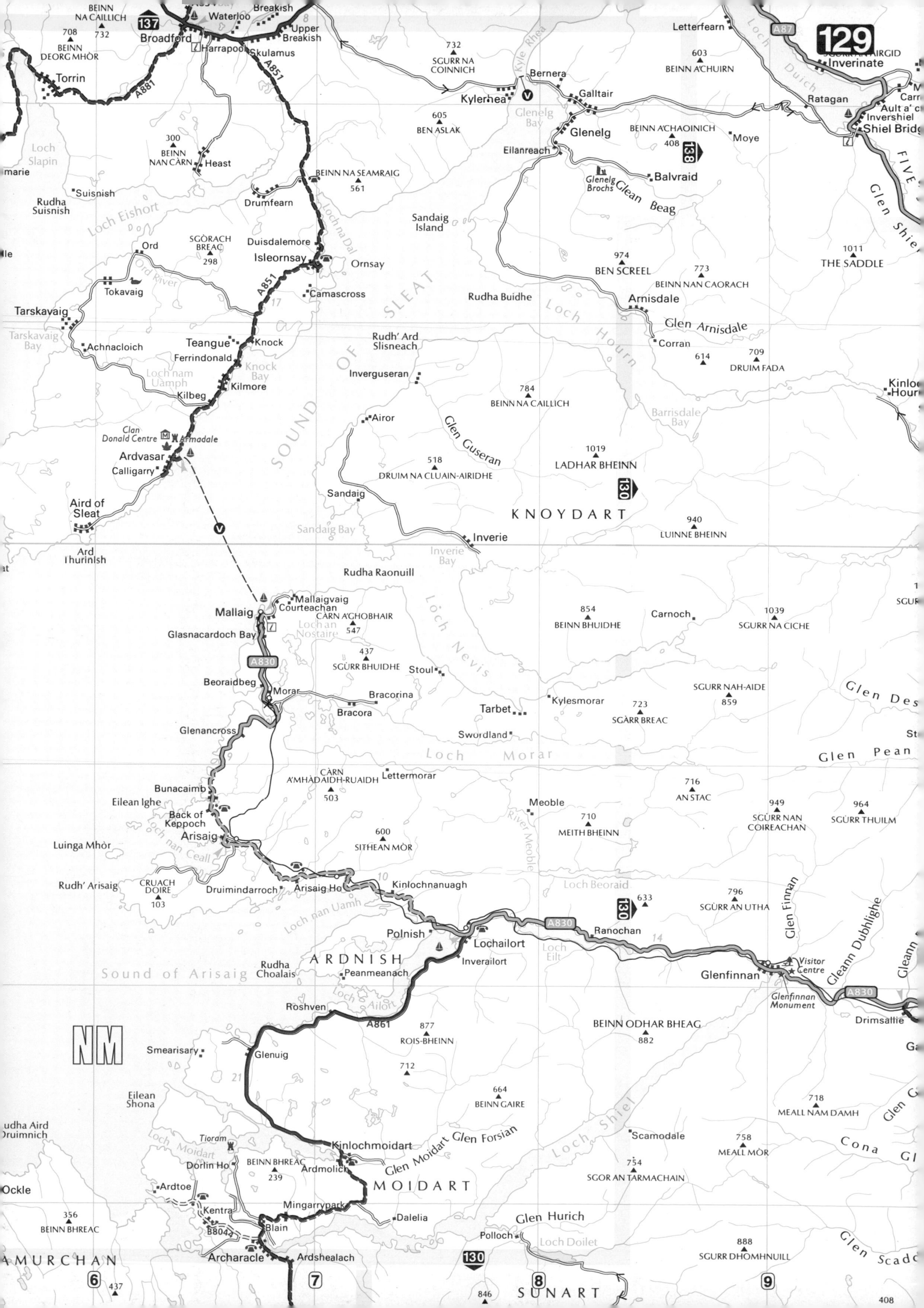

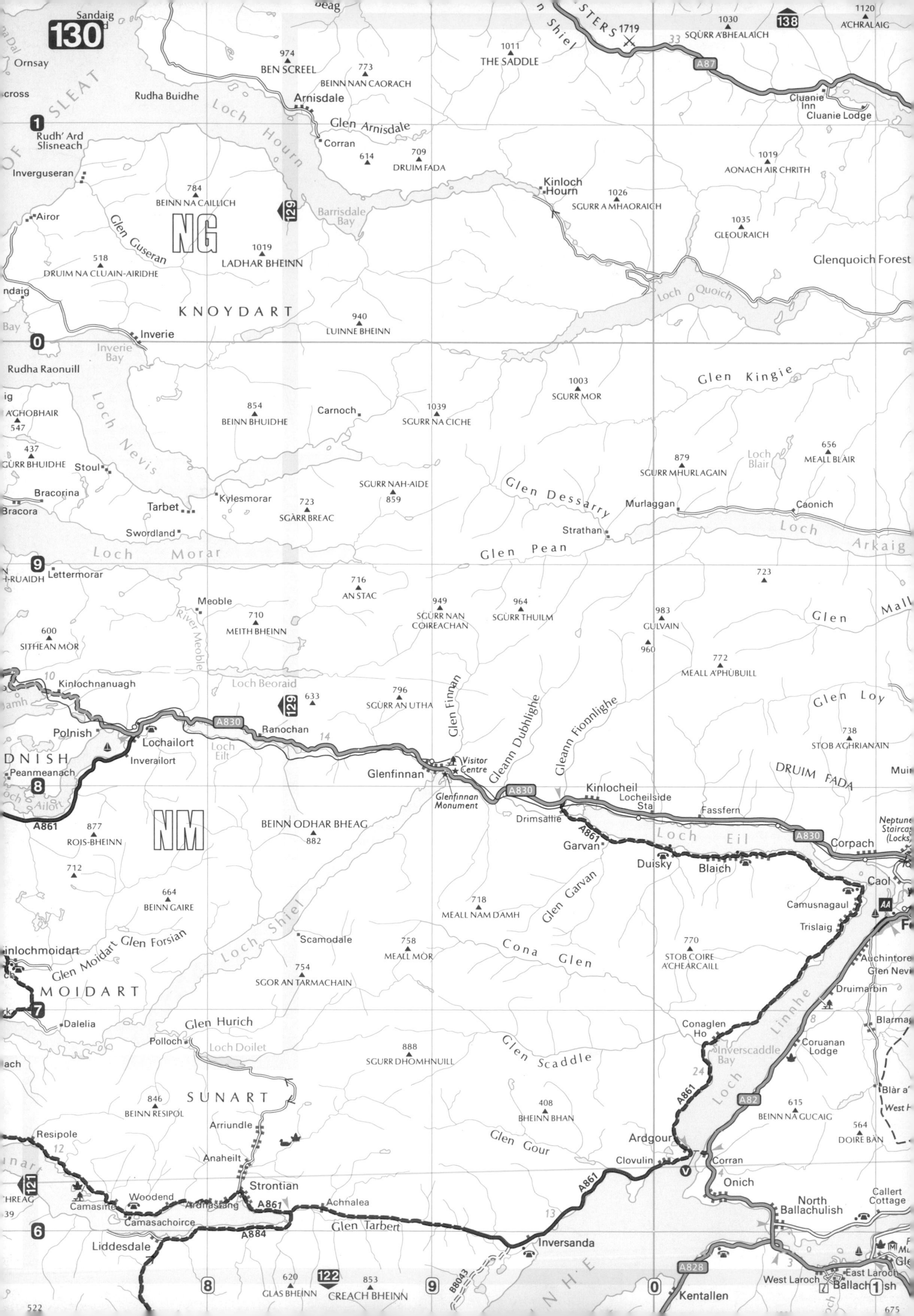

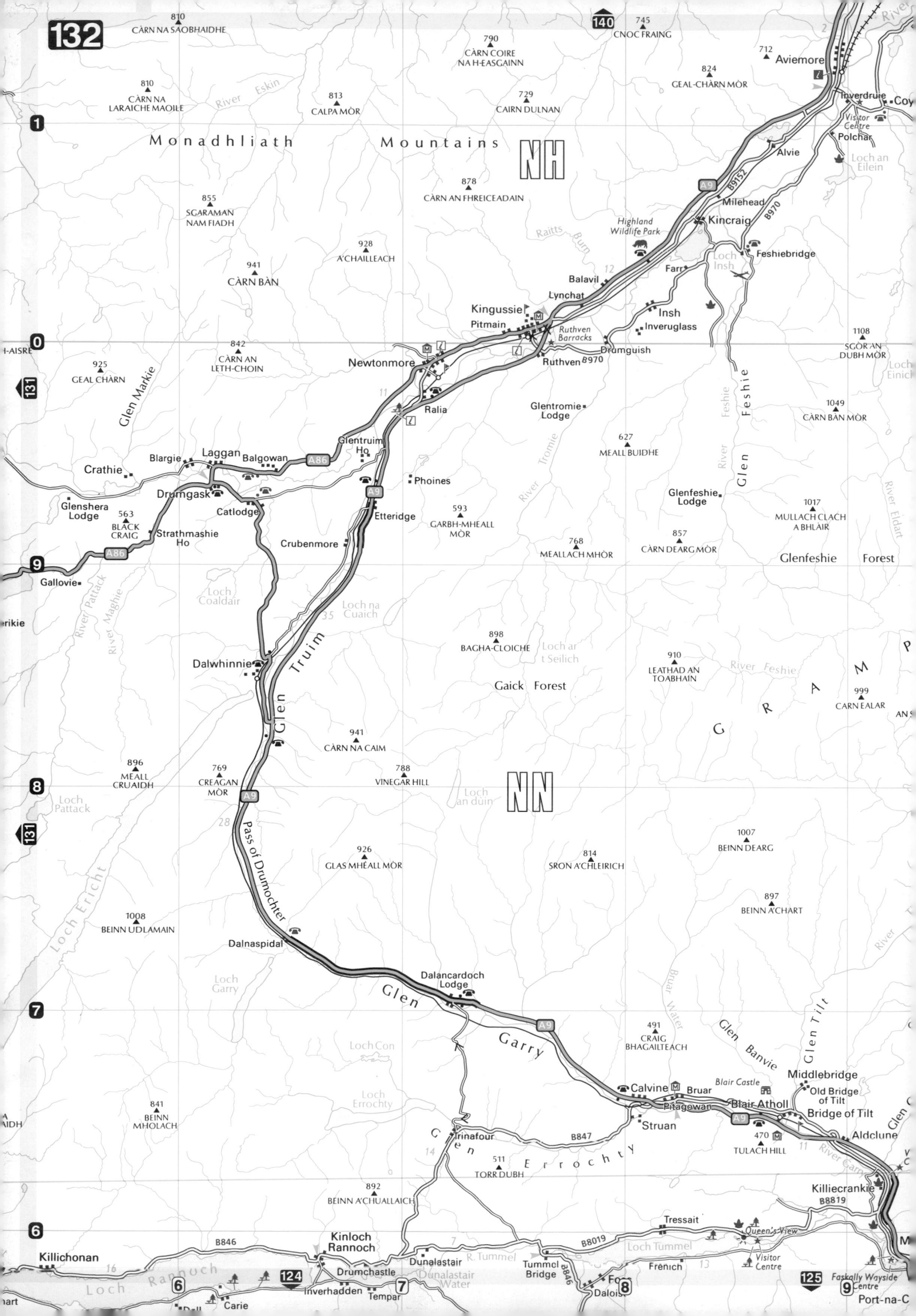

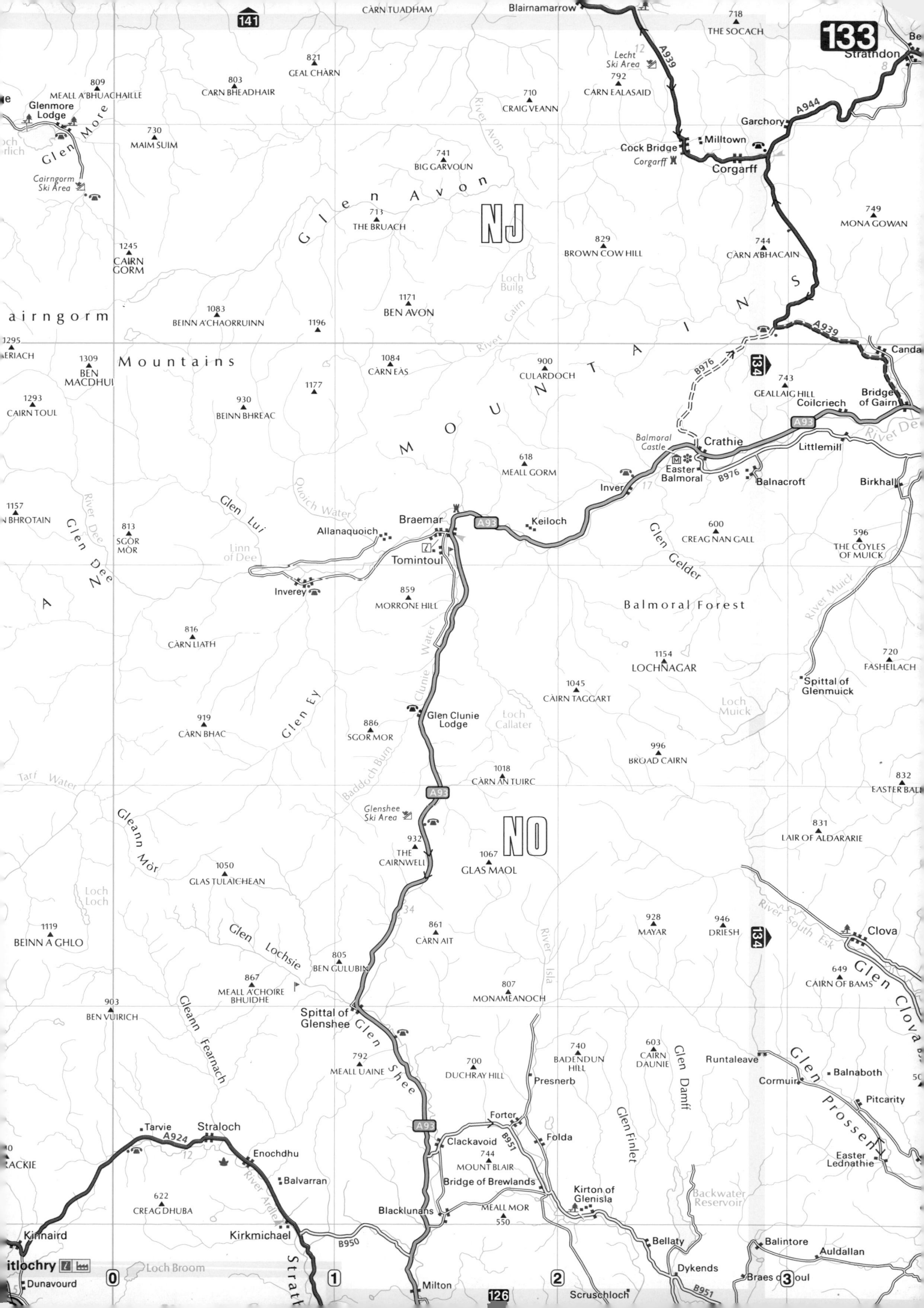

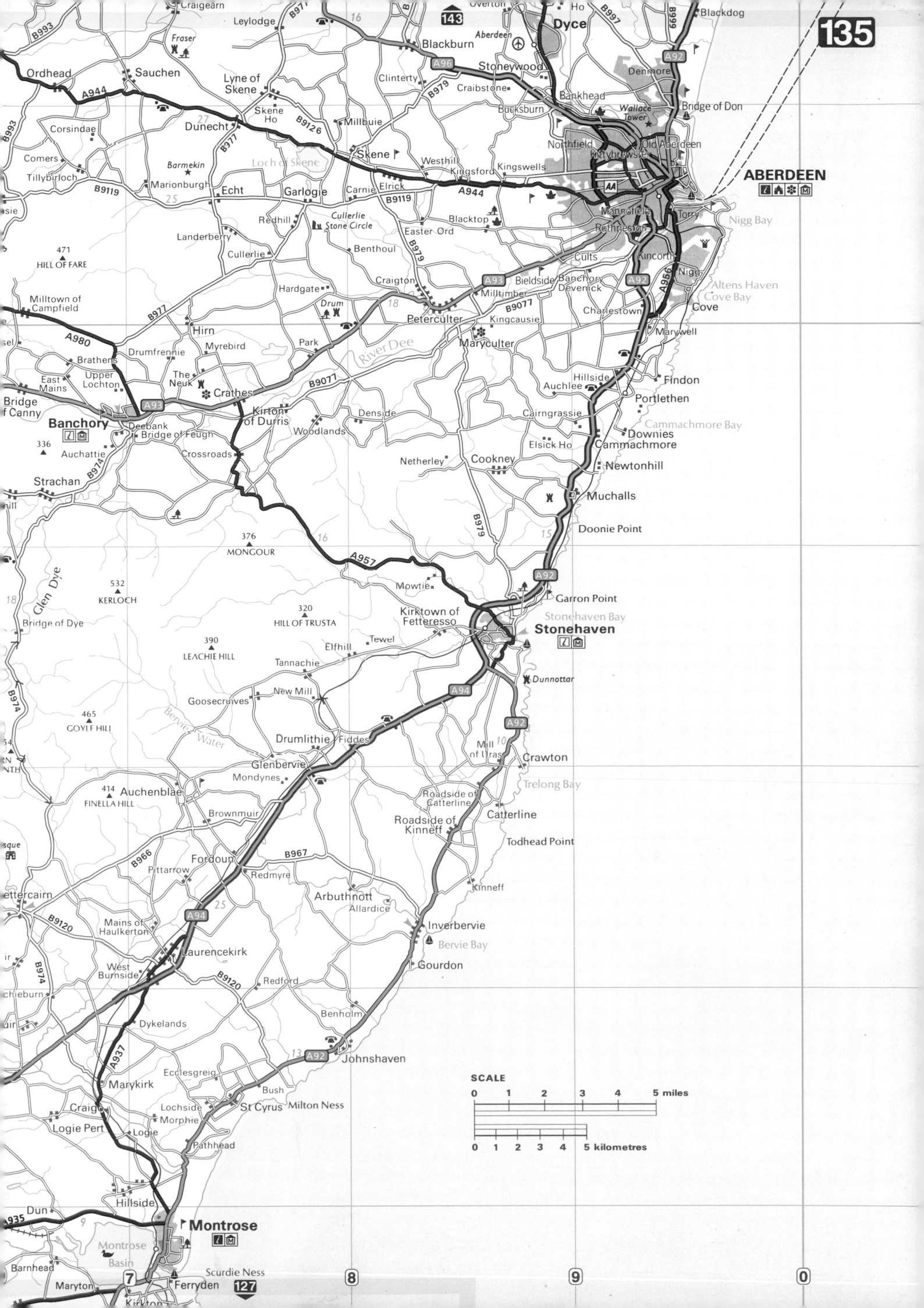

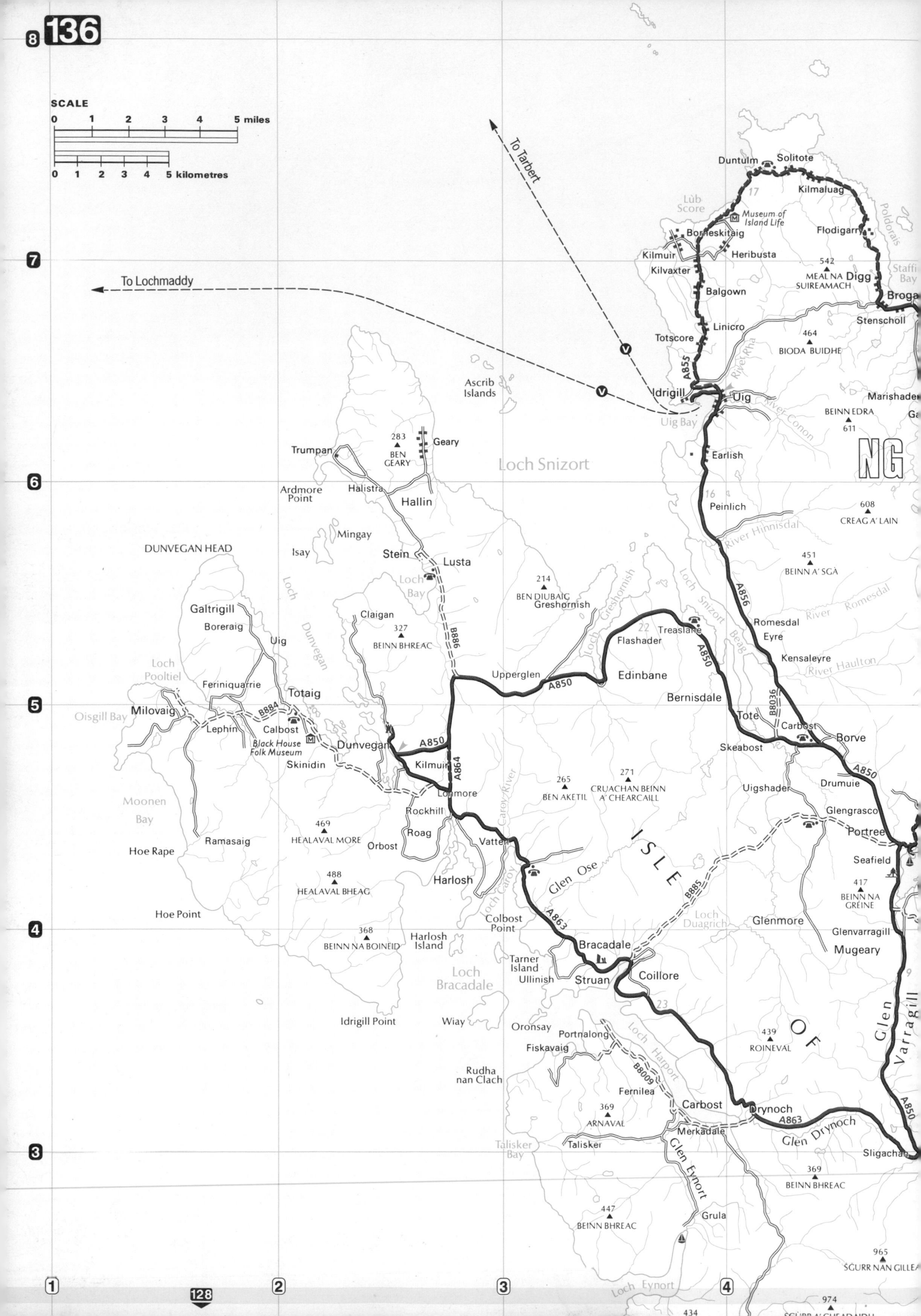

SCALE

0 1 2 3 4 5 miles

0 1 2 3 4 5 kilometres

To Tarbert

To Lochmaddy

Duntulm  Solitote
Kilmaluag
Lùb
Score  17
Museum of
Island Life  Flodigarry
Borneskitaig
Kilmuir  Heribusta
Kilvaxter  542
Balgown  MEAL NA  Digg  Staffin
SUIREAMACH  Bay
Linicro  Stenscholl  Broga
Totscore  464
BIODA BUIDHE

Ascrib
Islands  Idrigill  Uig
Marishader
BEINN EDRA  Ga
611
283  Geary  Earlish
Trumpan  BEN  Loch Snizort
GEARY  16  NG
Ardmore  Halistra  Peinlich  608
Point  Hallin  CREAG A' LAIN
Mingay
Isay  Stein  Lusta  451
DUNVEGAN HEAD  Loch  BEINN A' SGA
Bay  214
BEN DIUBAIG  River Hinnisdal
Galtrigill  Greshornish
Boreraig  Claigan  22 Treaslane  Romesdal
Uig  327  Flashader  Eyre  River
BEINN BHREAC  Upperglen  A850  Edinbane  Kensaleyre
Loch  Feriniquarrie  A850  Romesdal
Pooltiel  Totaig  Bernisdale  River Haulton
Milovaig  Calbost  Skeabost  Tote  Carbost
Oisgill Bay  Lephin  Black House  Dunvegan  Borve
Folk Museum  Uigshader  A850
Skinidin  Kilmuir  265  271  Drumuie
Loch  Lonmore  BEN AKETIL  CRUACHAN BEINN  Glengrasco
A' CHEARCAILL
Moonen  Rockhill  Portree
Bay  Roag  469  Vatten  ISLE  Seafield
HEALAVAL MORE  417
Ramasaig  Orbost  BEINN NA
Hoe Rape  GREINE
488  Glen Ose  Glenmore
HEALAVAL BHEAG  Harlosh  Glenvarragill
Hoe Point  Colbost  Mugeary
368  Point  Bracadale
Harlosh  A863
BEINN NA BOINEID  Island  Tarner  Coillore
Loch  Island  Struan
Bracadale  Ullinish
Idrigill Point  Wiay  Oronsay  23  O F
Portnalong  ROINEVAL
Fiskavaig  439
Rudha  B8009
nan Clach  Fernilea  Carbost  Drynoch  Glen Drynoch
369  Merkadale  A863  Sligachan
Talisker  ARNAVAL  Talisker
Bay  Talisker  369
BEINN BHREAC
447
BEINN BHREAC  Grula
965
SGURR NAN GILLE
974
434

North Erradale
B8021
Big Sand
Longa Island
Strath
Smithstown
Gairloch
Loch
Gairloch
Auchtercairn
Heritage Museum
A832
Poolewe
Londubh
MEALL NA

Port
Henderson
Eilean
Horrisdale
Charlestown
MEALL AN DOIRFIN
421

B8056
Badachro
Opinan
South Erradale

Loch
Mare
20

Red Point

Kilt Rock Waterfall
Ellishader
Valtos
Rudha nam
Brathairean
Tote

Loch a'Bhràige

619
BEINN BHREAC

Loch
Torridon
Craig
River

Rudha na Fearn
Fearnmore
Fearnbeg
Arinacrinachd
Cuaig
Kenmore

ISLAND
OF
RONA

Loch
Diabaig
Lower Diabaig
Alligin Shuas
Inveralligin
Torridon Ho
102
LIATHA

985
BEINN ALLIGIN

Loch
Leathan

Eilean
Tigh

Kalnalkill

492
AN GARBH-MHEALL

Ardheslaig
Loch
Shieldaig
Shieldaig
Island
Shieldaig
Torr
Annat

SOUND OF RAASAY

Eilean
Fladday

Lonbain

493
CRÒIC-BHEINN

Glenshieldaig
Forest

Loch
Damh

902
BEINN DAMH
MAO

Umachan

Torran
Arnish

Manish Point
Loch
Arnish

Loch
Lundie

ISLAND
OF
RAASAY

Brochel

River Applecross

Loch
Coultrie
730
SGURR A GHARAIDH

12
g

895
BEINN BHAN

DÜN
CAAN
444

Applecross
Bay

Applecross
Milton
Camusteel
Camusterrach

SGÙRR
A'CHAORACHAIN
774

INNER SOUND

Rudha
na' Leac

412
ANAVAIG

Camastianavaig

Oskaig

Clachan

310
BEINN NA LEAC

Inverarish

Tianavaig
Bay
Ollach

Upper
Ollach
B883
tailor

The
Braes

chorran

Sconser

773
LAMAIG

Eilean
Meadhonach

Eilean
Mòr

CROWLIN
ISLANDS

Culduie

Bealach-Na-Ba

Toscaig

River Toscaig

Kishorn
Island

Ardaneaskan

Kirkton

Ardarroch
Achintraid

Lochcarron
Slumbay

BAD A CHREAMHA
394

Strome

Ardnarff

Loch Carron

Achmore

Plockton

Stromeferry

BEINN RAIMH
447

Sallachy

Eyre Point

Suisnish
Point

Caolas Mòr

SCALPAY

67
Longay

Port-an-Eorna
Duirinish

Drumbuie
Erbusaig

Badicaul
Balmacara

Lochalsh House
& Garden
Auchtertyre

Conchra
Nostie

Bundal

YE

564
GLAS BHEINN
MHÒR

Duan
Luib

Caolas Scalpay

27
Pabay

Kyle of Lochalsh

Kyleakin

Kirkton

A87

Ardelve
Dornie

Carndu

Eilean Donan

Keppoch
A87

396
MULLACH NA
CARN

Loch Ainort
17

A850

A850

Loch Alsh

Letterfearn

BEINN
NA
LLICH
708
732

6

Corry
A854
Waterloo

Broadford

Broadford
Bay
Lower
Breakish

Upper
Breakish

7

8

9
A87

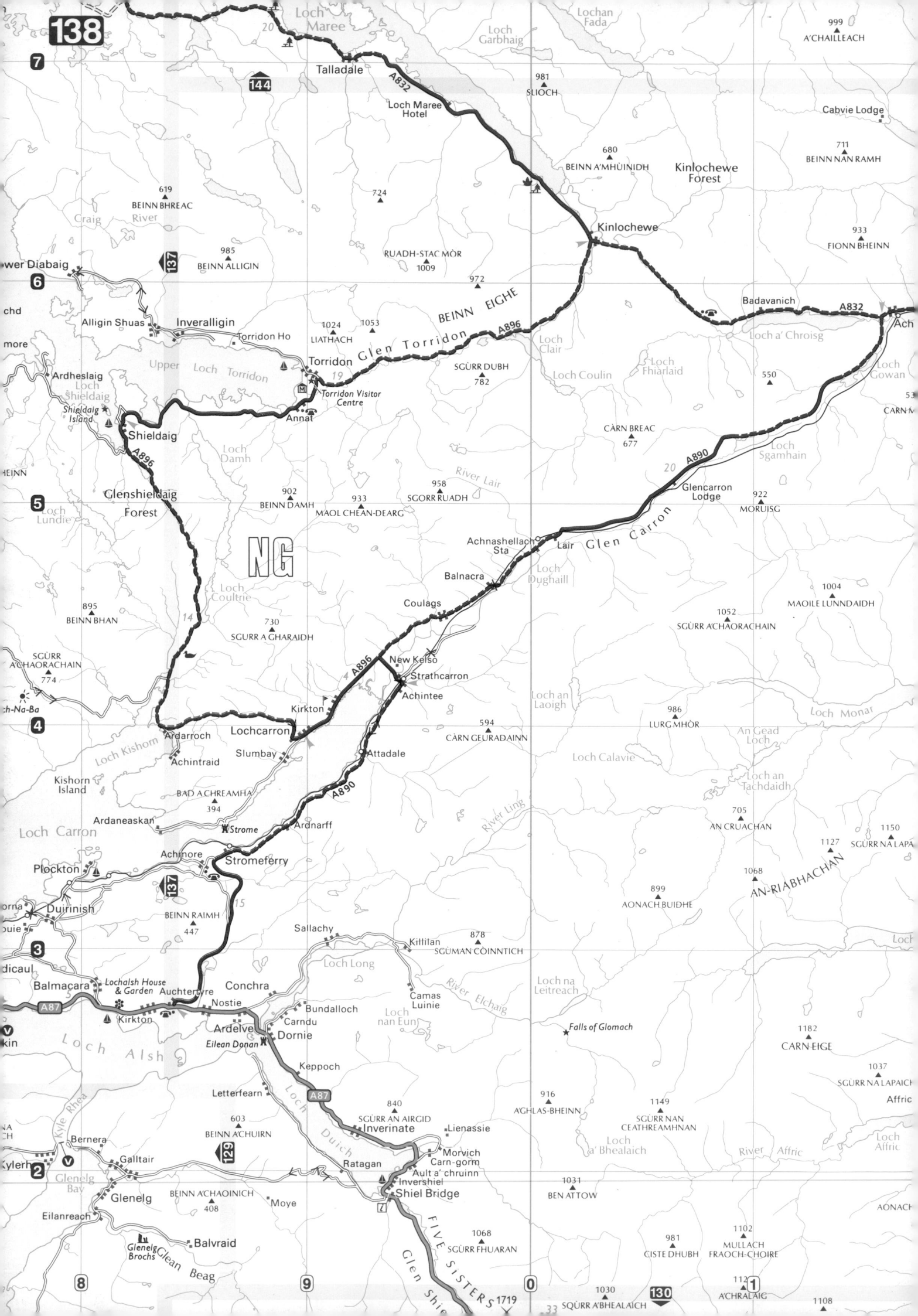

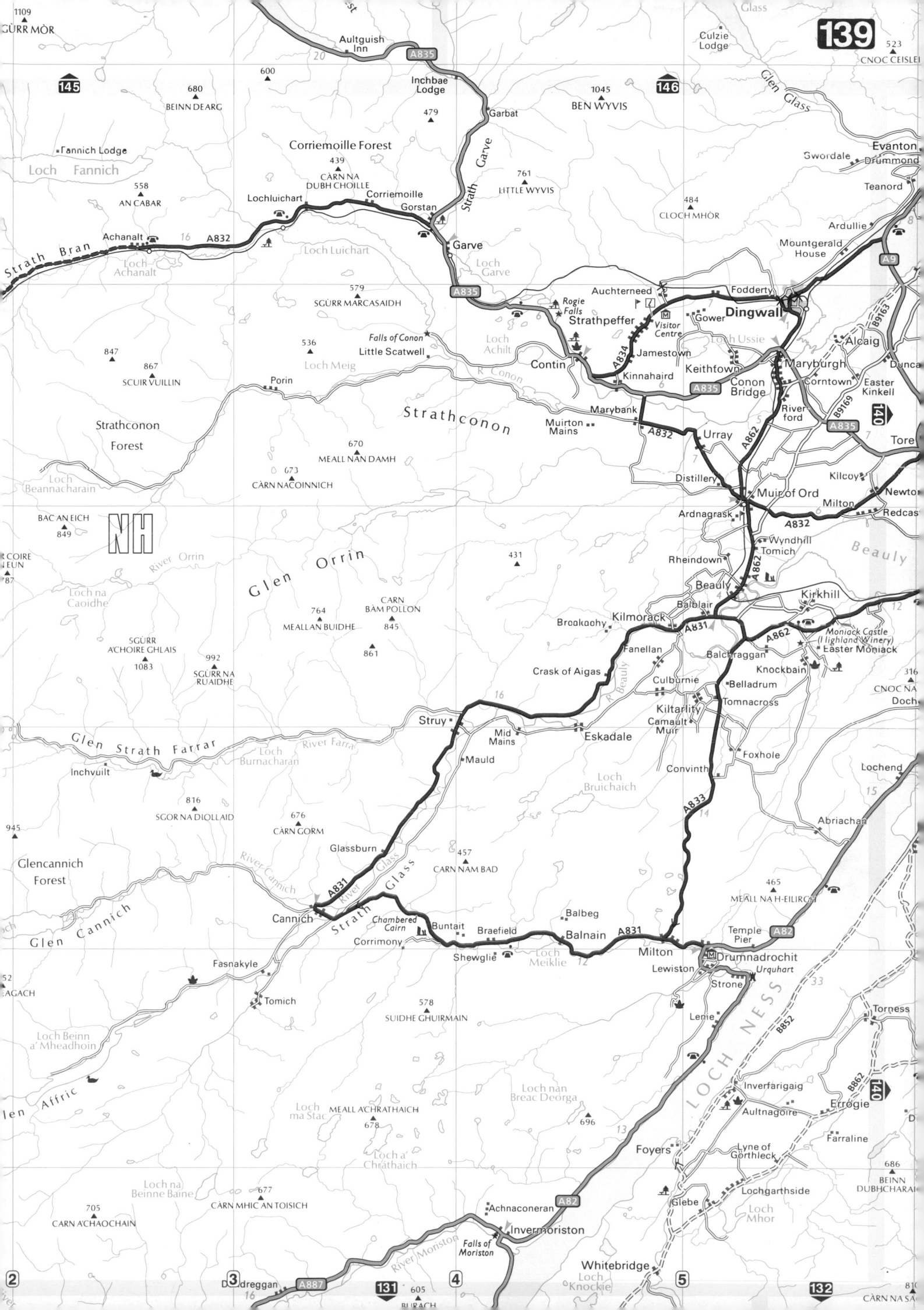

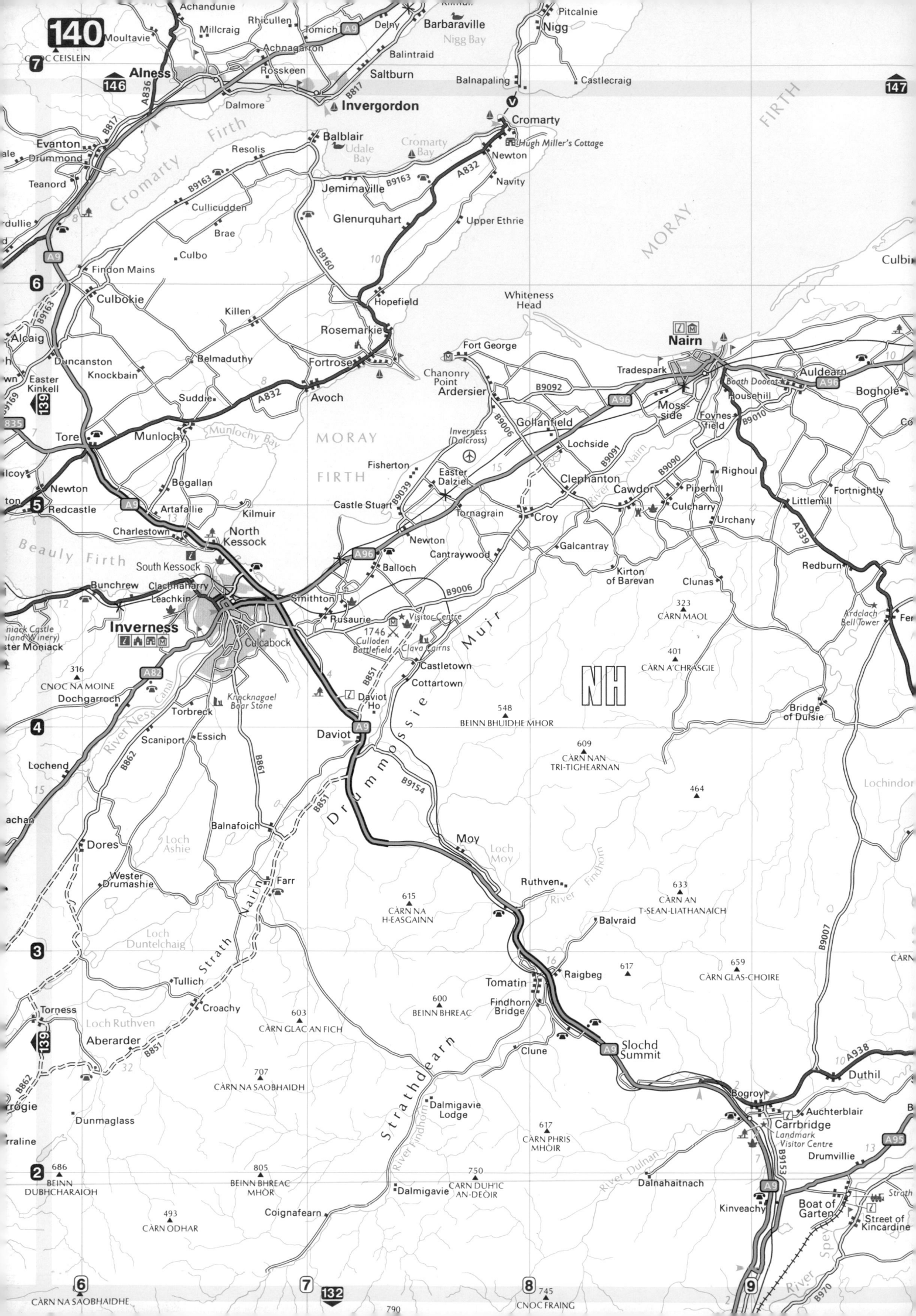

Troup Head
Cullykhan Bay
Roseherty
Sandhaven
Kinnairds Head
**Fraserburgh**
Pittulie
Pittulie
Peathill
Craigiefold
Percyhorner
Pilblae
Kirktown
Fraserburgh Bay
Cairnbulg
e Bay
Crovie
21
Pennan
Coburby
Mid Ardlaw
Inverallochy
Protstonhill
New Aberdour
Boyndlie
B9031
B9032
Memsie
St Combs
10
A92
B9033
A98
Rathen
Netherbrae
221
BRACKLAMORE HILL
Newburgh
Lonmay
Crofts of Savoch
12
A981
12
A952
Crimonmogate
Loch of Strathbeg
Old Rattray
Rattray Head
234
WAUGHTON HILL
Crimond
New Pitsligo
B9030
Strichen
Blackhill
18
B9027
New Byth
B9030
New Leeds
Longhill
St Fergus
Bonnykelly
5
A950
B9093
Denhead
Leys
Backfolds
Oldwhat
Garmond
Balthangie
A981
Fetterangus
Rora
inestown
13
Fedderate
B9106
6
Deer Abbey
Dunshillock
Mintlaw
River Ugie
A92
B9170
Maud
Old Deer
Visitor Centre
Longside
Inverugie
Buchanhaven
**Peterhead**
New Deer
Blackhill of Clackriach
B9029
A948
Drymuir
Bulwark
Stuartfield
Inverquhomery
A950
Hillhead of Cocklaw
Peterhead Bay
Maryhill
Slacks of Cairnbanno
Nethermuir
Millbreck
Nether Kinmundy
Burnhaven
Millbrex
Kirkton
B9170
Knaven
B9030
Kinnadie
Clola
Little Dens
Boddam
Buchan Ness
Cottown
Auchnagatt
12
Blackhill
Stirling
Cairnorrie
Kinknockie
Lendrum Terrace
henty
B9005
Brownhill
Inkhorn
Blackhill
Coldwells
NK
Coldwells
A952
Bullers of Buchan
dhead
Haddo
Methlick
Muirtack
Hatton
Auchiries
North Haven
To Stromness
14
A92
17
Cruden Bay
To Lerwick
R Ythan
B9005
Arthrath
Bogbrae
Port Errol
Barthol Chapel
Haddo
Birness
Chapel Hill
Bay of Cruden
Earlsford
A948
The Skares
Wedderlairs
Auchedly
Artrochie
A975
Medieval Tomb
Ythsie
Kinharrachie
Auchmacoy
Tulloch
Tarves
Kirktown of Slains
Craigdam
Esslemont
**Ellon**
Kirkton of Logie Buchan
Collieston
Tolquhon
B999
10
Idrum
A920
Pitmedden
B9000
V V
Kirktown of Bourtie
Carnbrogie
Udny Green
Housieside
32
urie
Whiterashes
Woodland
Pettymuk
Cultercullen
Newburgh
A947
Nether Crimond
Tillygreig
B999
B9000
Foveran
A92
Straloch
Reisque
Delfrigs
Kinmuck
New Machar
Causeyend
17
l Church
B979
Whitecairns
Balmedie
B977
Kinmundy
Belhelvie
Hatton of Fintray
Dyce Symbol Stones
B977
B997
Potterton
B999
8
6
135
Overton
Parkhill
Blackdog
0
1
9
**Dyce**

SCALE
0 1 2 3 4 5 miles
0 1 2 3 4 5 kilometres

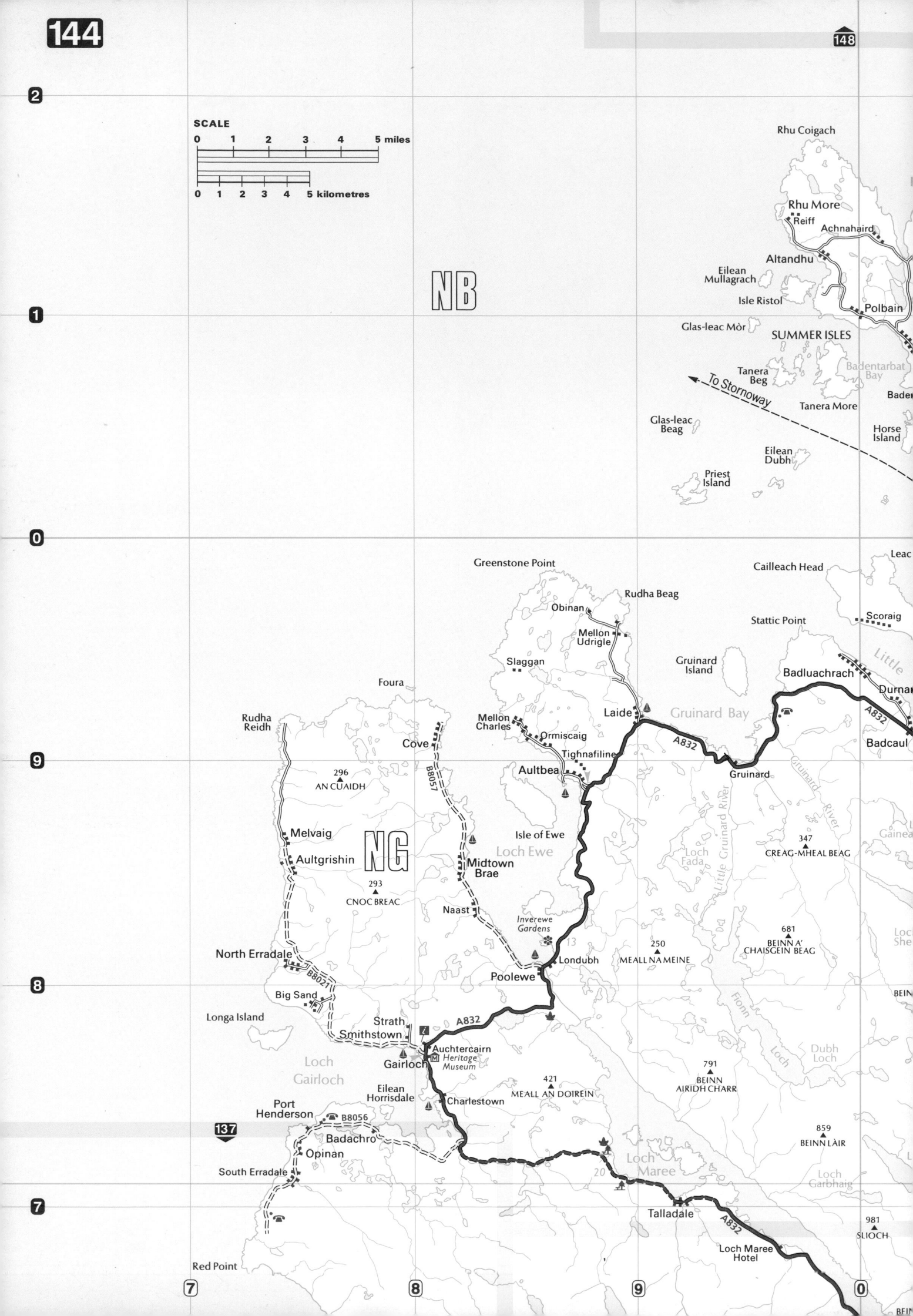

SCALE

0   1   2   3   4   5 miles

0   1   2   3   4   5 kilometres

NB

Rhu Coigach

Rhu More
Reiff
Achnahaird

Altandhu

Eilean
Mullagrach

Isle Ristol

Polbain

Glas-leac Mòr

SUMMER ISLES

Baden tarbat
Bay

To Stornoway

Tanera
Beg

Bade

Glas-leac
Beag

Tanera More

Eilean
Dubh

Horse
Island

Priest
Island

Leac

Greenstone Point

Cailleach Head

Rudha Beag

Obinan

Stattic Point

Scoraig

Mellon
Udrigle

Gruinard
Island

Badluachrach

Little

Slaggan

Durna

A832

Foura

Mellon
Charles

Laide

Gruinard Bay

Badcaul

Rudha
Reidh

Cove

Ormiscaig

Tighnafiline

A832

Gruinard

296
AN CUAIDH

B8057

Aultbea

347
CREAG-MHEAL BEAG

Gainea

Melvaig

Isle of Ewe

Loch Ewe

NG

Loch
Fada

Little Gruinard River

Gruinard River

Aultgrishin

293
CNOC BREAC

Midtown
Brae

250
MEALL NA MEINE

681
BEINN A'
CHAISGEIN BEAG

Loch
She

Naast

Inverewe
Gardens

13

North Erradale

B8021

Londubh

Fionn

Dubh
Loch

Big Sand

Poolewe

A832

Longa Island

Strath
Smithstown

Gairloch

Auchtercairn
Heritage
Museum

421
MEALL AN DOIREIN

791
BEINN
AIRIDH CHARR

Loch

Loch
Gairloch

Eilean
Horrisdale

Charlestown

859
BEINN LÀIR

Port
Henderson

B8056

137

Badachro

Loch
Maree

Loch
Garbhaig

Opinan

South Erradale

20

7

Talladale

A832

981
SLIOCH

Red Point

Loch Maree
Hotel

BEIN

148

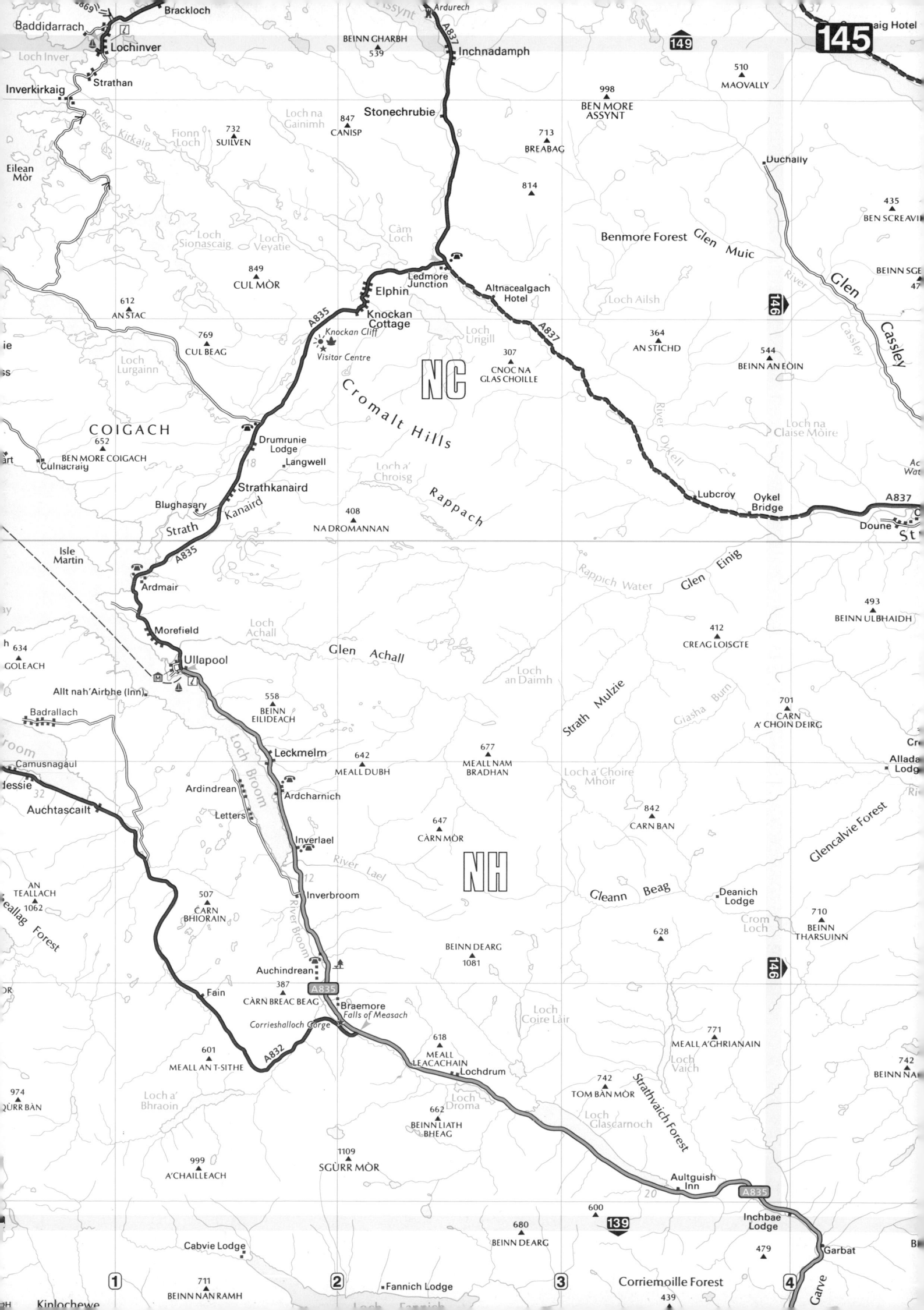

149
146

Bracloch
Baddidarrach
Lochinver
Loch Inver
Strathan
Inverkirkaig
Eilean Mòr

Ardurech
A837
BEINN GHARBH 539
Inchnadamph

510 MAOVALLY
998 BEN MORE ASSYNT
713 BREABAG
814
Duchally
435 BEN SCREAVI
BEINN SGE 47

Stonechrubie

Loch na Gainimh
847 CANISP
732 SUILVEN
Fionn Loch

Loch Sionascaig
Loch Veyatie
849 CUL MÒR
612 AN STAC

Càm Loch

Ledmore Junction
Elphin
Knockan Cottage
Knockan Cliff
Visitor Centre

Altnacealgach Hotel
A837

Benmore Forest
Glen Muic
River
Glen
Cassley
Loch Ailsh
364 AN STICHD
544 BEINN AN EÒIN

Loch na Claise Mòire

NC

769 CUL BEAG
Loch Lurgainn

Cromalt Hills

Loch Urigill
307 CNOC NA GLAS CHOILLE

COIGACH
652 BEN MORE COIGACH
Culnacraig

Drumrunie Lodge
Langwell
Strathkanaird
Blughasary
Kanaird
Strath
A835

Rappach
408 NA DROMANNAN

River Oykell
Lubcroy
Oykel Bridge
A837
Doune
St

Isle Martin
A835
Ardmair

Rappich Water
Glen Einig
493 BEINN ULBHAIDH

h 634 GOLEACH
Morefield
Loch Achall
Glen Achall
412 CREAG LOISGTE

Ullapool
Loch an Daimh
701 CARN A' CHOIN DEIRG

Allt nah'Airbhe (Inn)
Badrallach
558 BEINN EILIDEACH

Strath Mulzie
Giasha Burn
Cre
Allada Lodge

Leckmelm
642 MEALL DUBH
677 MEALL NAM BRADHAN
Loch a' Choire Mhòir
842 CARN BAN

Camusnagaul
essie 32
Auchtascailt

Ardindrean
Letters
Ardcharnich
Inverlael
River Lael
647 CÀRN MÒR

NH

Gleann Beag
Deanich Lodge
710 BEINN THARSUINN

AN TEALLACH 1062
eallag Forest

507 CARN BHIORAIN
Inverbroom

Glencalvie Forest

Loch Broom

BEINN DEARG 1081
628

Crom Loch

146

Fain
387 CÀRN BREAC BEAG
Auchindrean
A835
Braemore
Falls of Measach
Corrieshalloch Gorge
A832

771 MEALL A' GHRIANAIN
Loch Vaich

601 MEALL AN T-SITHE

618 MEALL LEACACHAIN
Lochdrum
742 TOM BÀN MÒR

Strathvaich Forest

742 BEINN NA

974 GÙRR BÀN
Loch a' Bhraoin

Loch Droma
662 BEINN LIATH BHEAG

Loch Glascarnoch

999 A'CHAILLEACH
1109 SGÙRR MÒR

Aultguish Inn
A835
20

600
139
Inchbae Lodge

OR
1
Cabvie Lodge
711 BEINN NAN RAMH
Kinlochewe

2
Fannich Lodge

680 BEINN DEARG
Corriemoille Forest
439

3

479
Garbat
Bi

4
Garve

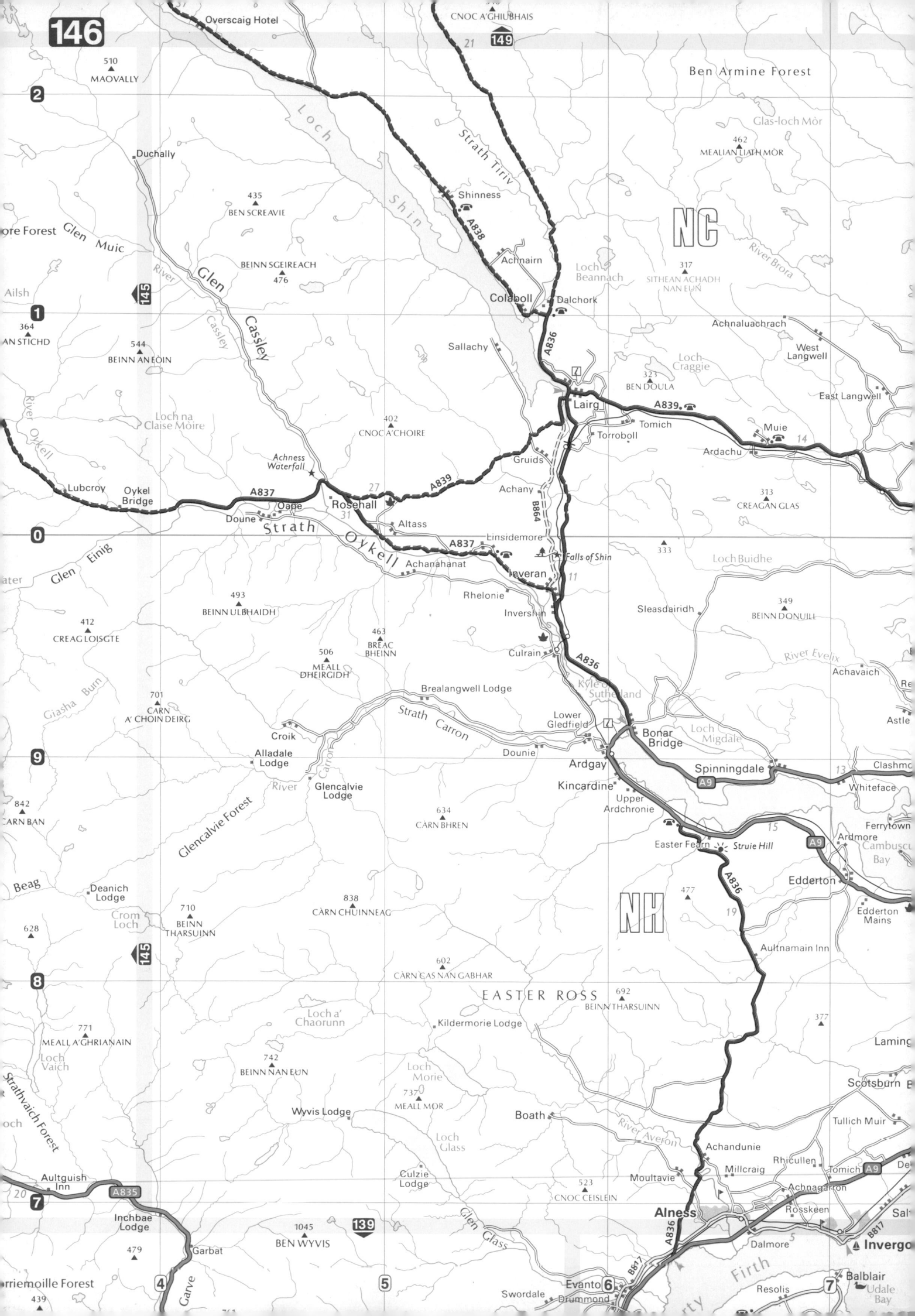

Overscaig Hotel

CNOC A'CHIUBHAIS

21  149

Ben Armine Forest

510
MAOVALLY

2

Duchally

Loch Shin

Strath Tirry

Glas-loch Mòr

NC

462
MEALLAN LIATH MÒR

River Brora

435
BEN SCREAVIE

Shinness

ore Forest

Glen Muic

Glen Cassley

River Cassley

BEINN SGEIREACH
476

A838

Achnairn

Loch
Beannach

SITHEAN ACHADH
NAN EUN

Achnaluachrach

317

West
Langwell

Ailsh

145

Colaboll

Dalchork

Loch
Craggie

East Langwell

River

364
AN STICHD

1

544
BEINN AN EOIN

Loch na
Claise Mòire

Sallachy

A836

323
BEN DOULA

Lairg

A839

Muie

Ardachu

14

River Oykell

402
CNOC A'CHOIRE

Achness
Waterfall

A839

Gruids

Tomich
Torroboll

313
CREAGAN GLAS

0

Lubcroy

Oykel
Bridge

A837

27

Rosehall

Achany

B864

Glen Einig

Oape

Doune

31

Altass

Linsidemore

Falls of Shin

333

Loch Buidhe

Strath Oykell

A837

349
BEINN DONUILL

ater

Glen

493
BEINN ULBHAIDH

Achanahanat

Inveran

11

Rhelonie

Sleasdairidh

412
CREAG LOISGTE

463
BREAC
BHEINN

Invershin

River Evelix

Achavaich

506
MEALL
DHEIRGIDH

Culrain

A836

Re

Giasha Burn

701
CARN
A' CHOIN DEIRG

Brealangwell Lodge

Kyle of
Sutherland

Astle

9

Croik

Strath Carron

Lower
Gledfield

Bonar
Bridge

Loch
Migdale

842
ARN BAN

Alladale
Lodge

River Carron

Dounie

Ardgay

Spinningdale

13

Clashm

Glencalvie Forest

Glencalvie
Lodge

Kincardine

A9

Whiteface

628

Beag

Deanich
Lodge

634
CÀRN BHREN

Upper
Ardchronie

15

A9

Ferrytown
Ardmore
Cambusc
Bay

Crom
Loch

710
BEINN
THARSUINN

838
CÀRN CHUINNEAG

477

A836

Easter Fearn

Struie Hill

Edderton

145

NH

19

Edderton
Mains

8

771
MEALL A'GHRIANAIN

602
CÀRN CAS NAN GABHAR

E A S T E R   R O S S

692
BEINN THARSUINN

Aultnamain Inn

377

Loch
Vaich

Loch a'
Chaorunn

Kildermorie Lodge

742
BEINN NAN EUN

Laming

Loch
Morie

737
MEALL MÒR

Scotsburn

Wyvis Lodge

0

Boath

River Averon

Tullich Muir

Strathvaich Forest

Culzie
Lodge

Achandunie

Rhicullen

Tomich

A9

Millcraig

och

Aultguish
Inn

20

A835

7

Inchbae
Lodge

Glen Glass

523
CNOC CEISLEIN

Moultavie

Alness

A836

Achnagarron

Rosskeen

B817

Sal

479

1045
BEN WYVIS

139

Garbat

riemoille Forest

4

Garve

5

Swordale

Evanto

6

Dalmore

5

Inverg

Firth

7

Balblair

439

761

Drummond

ty Firth

Resolis

Udale
Bay

CNOC NA
BREUN-CHOILLE

388
CREAG NAM FIADH

Cairns, Stone Rows
& Stone Circle

CREAG SCALABSDALE

Langwell
Ho.

150

151

Kildonan
Lodge

Kildonan    416
BEINN DUBHAIN

401
CNOC NA MAOILE

337
CNOC NA
H-INNSE MOIRE

Strath of Kildonan

17

Kilphedir

404

A9

A9

421
CNOC NAN
CRUBAG MOR

624
BEINN DHORAIN

River Helmsdale

Torrish

A897

Marrel

Ord of Caithness

Navidale

591
BEINN NA MEILICH

West
Helmsdale

East Helmsdale

Helmsdale

Black Water

Balnacoil Lodge

539
COL-BHEINN

Gartymore

Portgower

ND

Strath Brora

Lothmore

West Garty

River Brora

Ireavoch Lodge

Lothbeg

ochan

Gordonbush

Loch
Brora

Lothbeg

520
BEN HORN

Kintradwell    A9

ockarthur

Loch
Horn

Clynelish

Achrimsdale

Dalchalm

378
CAGAR FEOSAIG

Doll

Brora

Golspie Burn

Backies

Uppat
House

446
BEINN LUNDIE

Rhives

Cairn Liath

Dunrobin Castle

A9

Golspie

The Mound

Loch
Fleet

Littleferry

Skelbo

Skelbo Street

Fourpenny

7

17

B9168

Embo

Embo Street

Pitgrudy

A949

Camore

Dornoch

Tarbat Ness

NJ

Wilkhaven

Brucefield

Innis Mhor

Dornoch Firth

Portmahomack

Bindal

hill

Rockfield

Inver

Arboll

B9165

Toulvaddie

Lochslin

A9

Loch
Eye

Rhynie

B9165

Fearn

Balmuchy

11

Newfield

Hill-of-Fearn

Hilton of Cadboll Chapel

Tullich

B9166

Hilton of
Cadboll

ain

Arabella

B9175

Balintore

Ankerville

Shandwick

Shandwick Bay

Milton

Wester Rarichie

Kilmuir

Pitcalnie

aaraville

Nigg

Nigg Bay

SCALE

0    1    2    3    4    5 miles

0  1  2  3  4  5 kilometres

Balnapaling

140

Castlecraig

141

Burghead

St Hopeman
Aethans

Burghead Well

FIRTH

Cummingston

Cromarty

Miller's Cottage

9

0

Burghead
Bay

Roseisle

College of F

Newton

22

8

1

B901

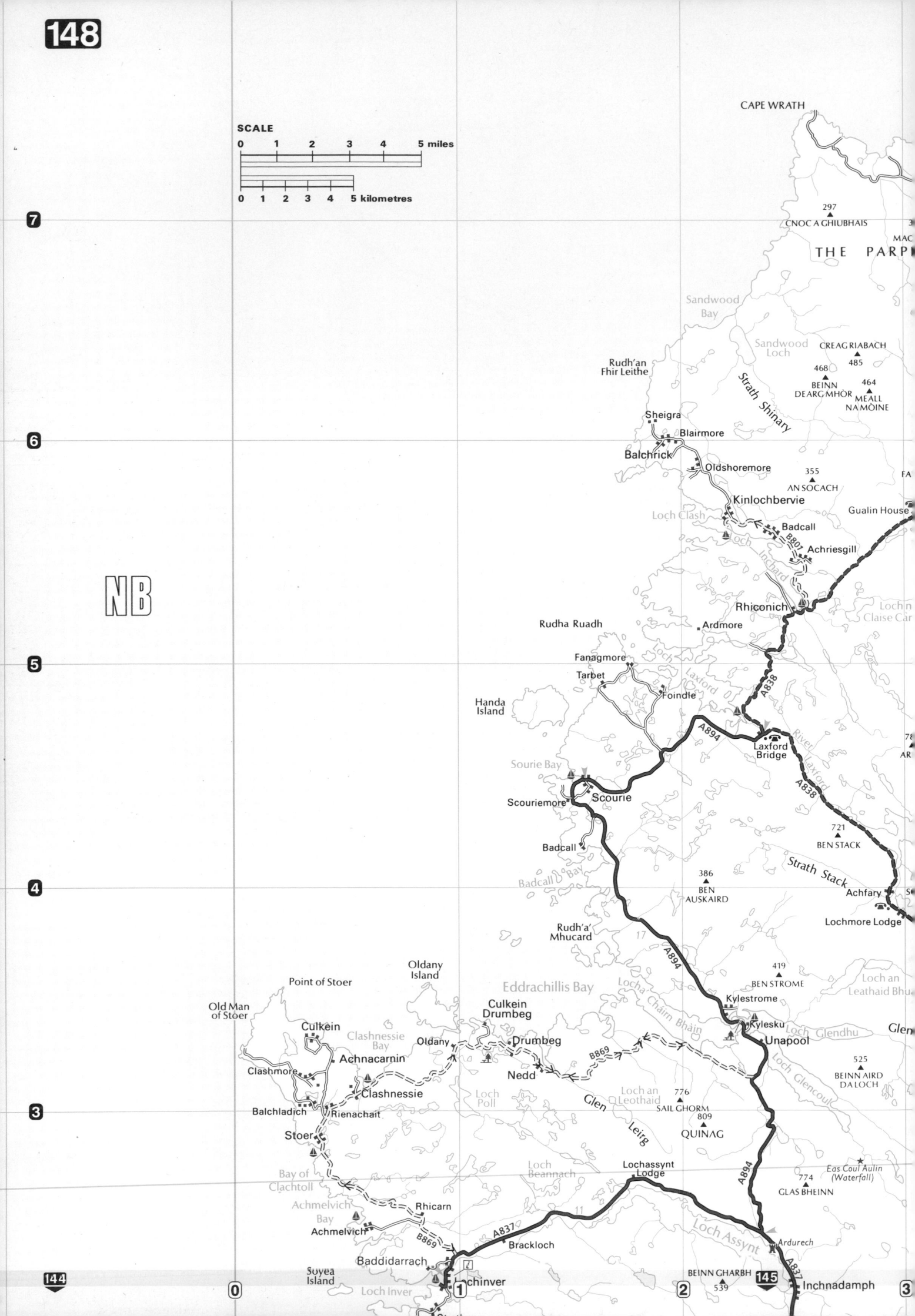

**SCALE**

0   1   2   3   4   5 miles

0   1   2   3   4   5 kilometres

NB

CAPE WRATH

THE PARP

MAC

297
CNOC A GHIUBHAIS

*Sandwood Bay*

*Sandwood Loch*

CREAG RIABACH

468   485

BEINN
DEARG MHÒR
464
MEALL
NA MÒINE

Rudh'an
Fhir Leithe

*Strath Shinary*

Sheigra
Blairmore
Balchrick
Oldshoremore

355
AN SOCACH

FA

Kinlochbervie
*Loch Clash*
Badcall
B807
Achriesgill

Gualin House

*Loch Inchard*

Rhiconich

*Loch na Claise Car*

Rudha Ruadh
Ardmore

Fanagmore
Tarbet
Foindle

*Laxford*

A838

Handa
Island

A894
Laxford
Bridge

*River Laxford*

78

AR

*Sourie Bay*
Scouriemore   Scourie

7

BEN STACK
721

Badcall

*Badcall Bay*

386
BEN
AUSKAIRD

A894
17

Strath Stack
Achfary

Lochmore Lodge

S

Rudh'a'
Mhucard

419
BEN STROME

*Loch an
Leathaid Bhu*

Point of Stoer
Old Man
of Stoer
Culkein
Clashmore
Achnacarnin
Clashnessie
Balchladich   Rienachait
Stoer

Oldany
Island

*Clashnessie
Bay*

Oldany

Culkein
Drumbeg
Drumbeg

Nedd

*Eddrachillis Bay*

*Locha Chàirn Bhàin*

B869

Kylestrome

Kylesku
Unapool

*Loch Glendhu*   Glen

525
BEINN AIRD
DA LOCH

*Loch
Poll*

*Glen Leirg*

*Loch an
Leothaid*
776
SAIL GHORM
809
QUINAG

*Loch Glencoul*

774
GLAS BHEINN

Eas Coul Aulin
(Waterfall)

A894

*Bay of
Clachtoll*

*Achmelvich
Bay*
Achmelvich   Rhicarn
B869

*Loch
Beannach*
11

Lochassynt
Lodge

A837

Brackloch

*Loch Assynt*
Ardurech

A837

Baddidarrach

*Suyea
Island*

Achinver

*Loch Inver*

BEINN GHARBH
539

Inchnadamph

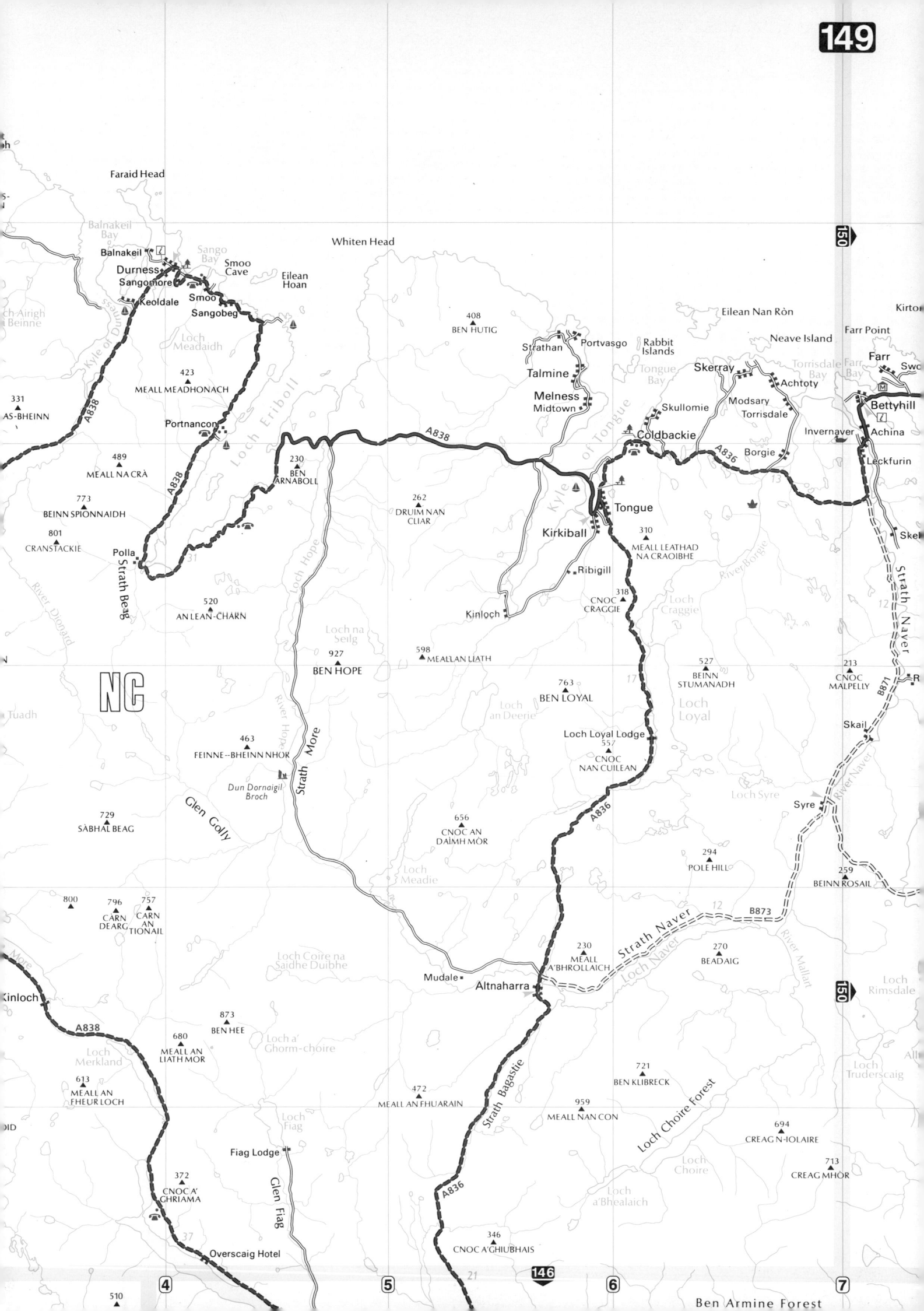

Faraid Head

Balnakeil
Bay

Whiten Head

Balnakeil
Durness
Sangomore
Keoldale    Smoo Cave
Sango Bay
Smoo
Sangobeg

Eilean
Hoan

Loch
Meadaidh

Loch Eriboll

408
BEN HUTIG

Eilean Nan Ròn

Strathan    Portvasgo
Rabbit
Islands

Neave Island

Farr Point

Farr
Swo

331
AS-BHEINN

423
MEALL MEADHONACH

Portnancon

A838

A838

A838    A838

Talmine

Melness
Midtown

Skerray

Skullomie

Achtoty

Modsary
Torrisdale

Torrisdale
Bay

Farr
Bay

M

Bettyhill

489
MEALL NA CRÀ

230
BEN
ARNABOLL

262
DRUIM NAN
CLIAR

A838

Coldbackie

Invernaver
Borgie

Achina

Leckfurin

773
BEINN SPIONNAIDH

Tongue

310
MEALL LEATHAD
NA CRAOIBHE

A836

13

River Borgie

Skel

801
CRANSTACKIE

Polla

Strath Beag

Kirkiball

Ribigill

Kinloch

318
CNOC
CRAGGIE

Loch
Craggie

River Diongrd

31

520
AN LEAN-CHARN

Loch na
Seilg

598
MEALLAN LIATH

527
BEINN
STUMANADH

Loch
Loyal

213
CNOC
MALPELLY

B871

12

Strath Naver

NC

927
BEN HOPE

763
BEN LOYAL

Loch
an Deirie

17

R

Tuadh

Loch Hope

463
FEINNE-BHEINN NHOR

Strath More

River Hope

Loch Loyal Lodge

557
CNOC
NAN CUILEAN

Loch Syre

Skail

Syre

River Naver

729
SÀBHAL BEAG

Dun Dornaigil
Broch

Glen Golly

656
CNOC AN
DAIMH MÒR

A836

Loch
Meadie

294
POLE HILL

259
BEINN ROSAIL

800
796
CARN
DEARG
757
CARN
AN
TIONAIL

Loch Coire na
Saidhe Duibhe

230
MEALL
A'BHROLLAICH

Strath Naver

12    B873

River Mallart

Kinloch

A838

Mudale

Altnaharra

270
BEADAIG

150

Loch
Rimsdale

613
MEALL AN
FHEUR LOCH

873
BEN HEE

680
MEALL AN
LIATH MOR

Loch a'
Ghorm-choire

Strath Bagastie

721
BEN KLIBRECK

Loch Choire Forest

Loch
Truderscaig

OID

472
MEALL AN FHUARAIN

Loch
Fiag

959
MEALL NAN CON

694
CREAG N-IOLAIRE

Fiag Lodge

A836

Loch
Choire

713
CREAG MHÒR

372
CNOC A'
GHRIAMA

Glen Fiag

37

Overscaig Hotel

346
CNOC A'GHIUBHAIS

Loch
a'Bhealaich

21

510

4            5            146    6            7

Ben Armine Forest

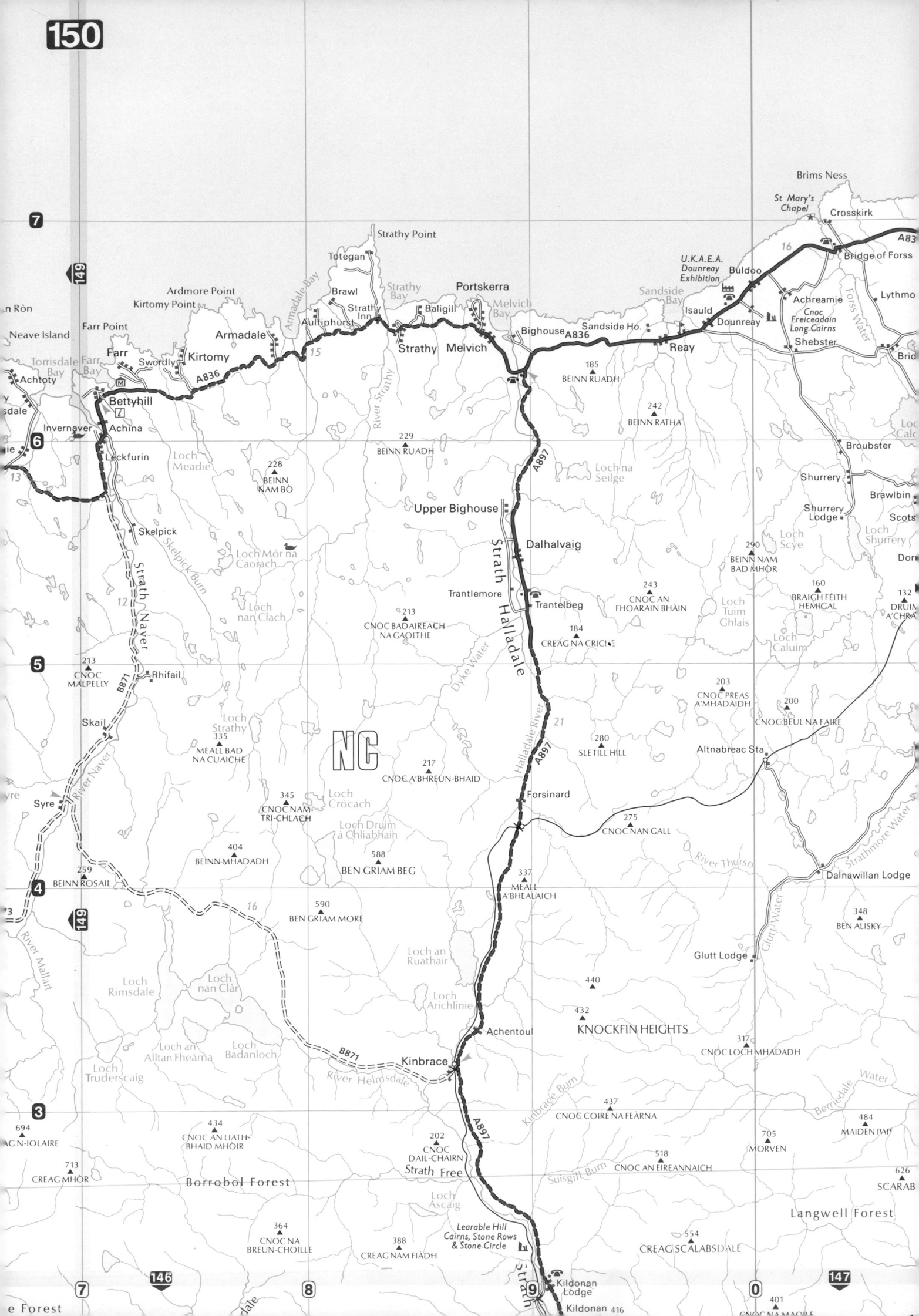

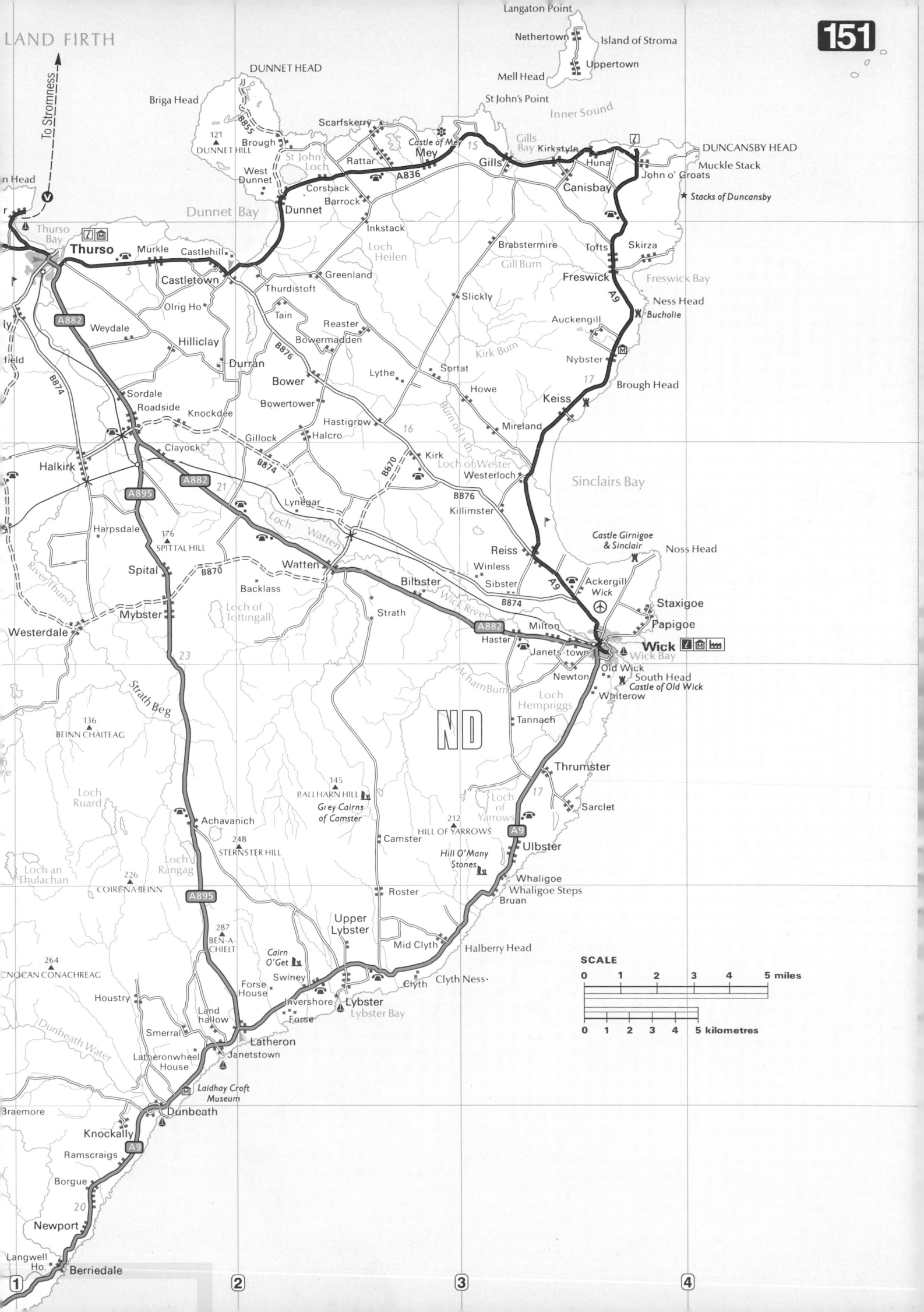

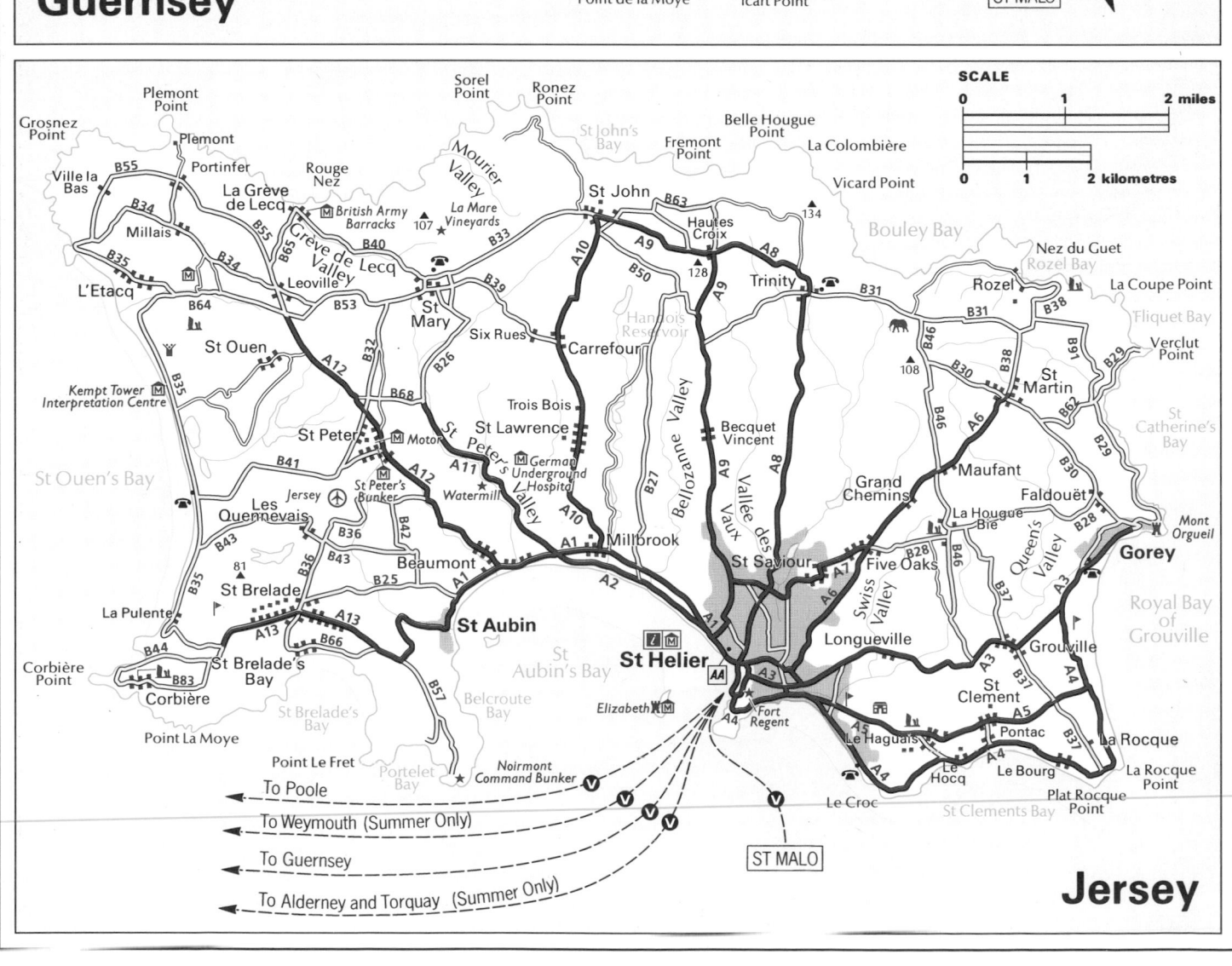

## The Channel Islands

St Anne ○
ALDERNEY

HERM
St Peter ○
Port
SARK
GUERNSEY

JERSEY

○ St Helier

0   5   10 mls

0   10   20 kms

FRANCE

SCALE

0        1        2 miles

0     1        2 kilometres

### Guernsey

To Alderney and Torquay (Summer Only)

L'Ancresse Bay
Le Fort Marchant
L'Ancresse
La Fontenelle
Dehus Dolmen
Clos du Valle
Vale
La Grève
Grande Havre
Bordeaux
La Passee
Islet Village
St Sampson

To Weymouth (Summer Only)
To Poole
To Portsmouth (Summer Only)

Grandes Rocques
Pleinheaume
Saline Bay
Capelles
Les Quartiers
Belle Grève Bay
St Peter Port

Cobo Bay
Fort Hommet
Cobo
Le Villocq
La Rousaillerie
Le Villocq
Butterfly Farm

Vazon Bay
Castel
Havelet Bay

Lihou Island
Richmond Fort
Perelle Bay
Perelle
Mont Saint
Kings Mills
Les Terres Point

CHERBOURG (Tues & Sat) Summer Only

L'Erée
Les Lohiers
St Andrew
Four Cabots

Roquaine Bay
La Houguette
St Saviour
Le Gron
German Underground Hospital
St Martin
Les Hubits
La Bellieuse

Fort Grey Maritime Museum
Les Arquêts
Villiaze
Mouilpied
Putron Village

Les Sages
St Peter's
Guernsey ✈ Le Bourg
La Villette

Pleinmont Point
Les Murchez
Les Nicolles
La Fosse

Torteval
Forest
German Occupation Museum
Jerbourg

Le Bigard
Les Villets
Petit Bot Bay
Moulin Huet Bay
St Martins Point

To Jersey

ST MALO

Point de la Moye
Icart Point

### Jersey

SCALE
0        1        2 miles
0     1        2 kilometres

Grosnez Point
Plemont Point
Plemont
Sorel Point
Ronez Point
Belle Hougue Point
St John's Bay
Fremont Point
La Colombière
Vicard Point
Bouley Bay

Ville la Bas
B55
Portinfer
Rouge Nez
Mourier Valley
St John
B63
Hautes Croix
134
Nez du Guet
Rozel Bay

La Grève de Lecq
B34
British Army Barracks
La Mare Vineyards
107
A10
A9
128
A8
Rozel
La Coupe Point

Millais
B35
B34
Crève de Lecq Valley
B40
B33
B50
Trinity
B31
Fliquet Bay
Verclut Point

L'Etacq
B64
Leoville
B65
St Mary
B39
Six Rues
Carrefour
Hambis Reservoir
A9
108
B46
B30
B38
St Martin
B91
B29

St Ouen
A12
B32
B53
B68
B26
Trois Bois
St Lawrence
German Underground Hospital
B27
Bellozanne Valley
Becquet Vincent
A8
B46
A6
B62
St Catherine's Bay

Kempt Tower Interpretation Centre
B35
St Peter
Motor
St Peter's Valley
Vallée des Vaux
Grand Chemins
Maufant
B30
B28
Faldouët

St Ouen's Bay
B41
St Peter's Bunker
Watermill
A11
A10
La Hougue Bie
Mont Orgueil

Jersey ✈
Les Quennevais
B43
B36
B42
A1
Millbrook
St Saviour
Five Oaks
B46
Queen's Valley
A3
Gorey

81
B36
B25
Beaumont
A2
A1
Swiss Valley
Longueville
Grouville
A4
Royal Bay of Grouville

St Brelade
B43
A13
La Pulente
B35
La Hougue Bie
A3
St Clement
A5

La Pulente
A13
B66
St Aubin
St Aubin's Bay
St Helier
A3
Le Haguais
Pontac
La Rocque

Corbière Point
B44
St Brelade's Bay
B83
Corbière
B57
Belcroute Bay
Elizabeth
A3
Le Bourg
La Rocque Point

Point La Moye
St Brelade's Bay
Fort Regent
Le Hocq
Le Croc
Plat Rocque Point

Point Le Fret
Portelet Bay
Noirmont Command Bunker
St Clements Bay

To Poole
To Weymouth (Summer Only)
To Guernsey
To Alderney and Torquay (Summer Only)

ST MALO

# Isle of Man

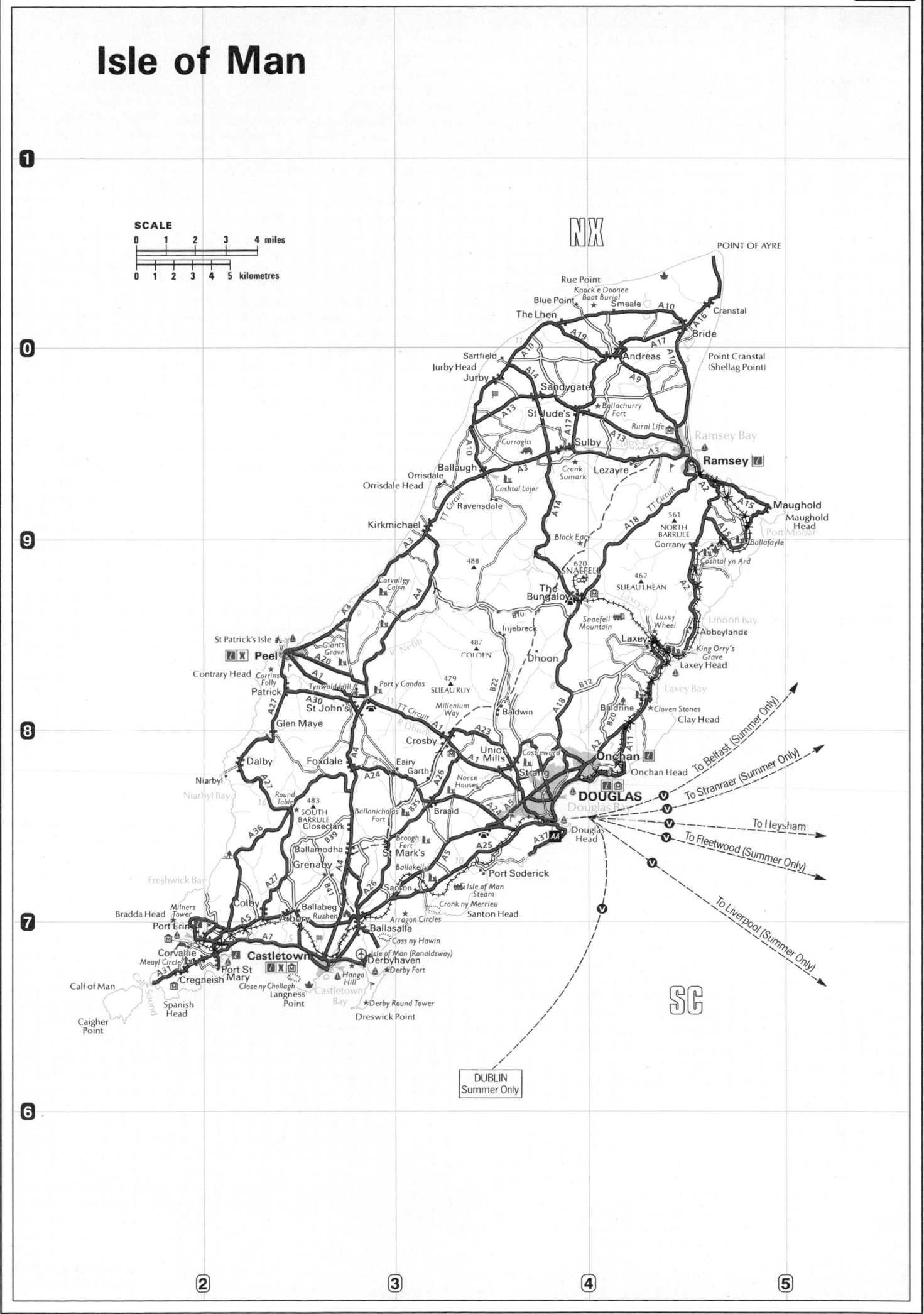

SCALE

0 1 2 3 4 miles

0 1 2 3 4 5 kilometres

NX

POINT OF AYRE

Rue Point
Knock e Doonee
Boat Burial
Blue Point
The Lhen
Smeale
A10
Cranstal
A16
Bride

Sartfield
Jurby Head
Jurby
A10
A19
Andreas
A10
A17
Point Cranstal
(Shellag Point)
A14
Sandygate
A9
St Jude's
Ballachurry Fort
Rural Life
Curraghs
A13
Sulby
A13
Ramsey Bay
Ballaugh
A3
Sulby R.
A3
Ramsey
Orrisdale
A3
Cronk Sumark
Lezayre
Maughold
Orrisdale Head
Cashtal Lajer
A14
TT Circuit
A18
561
NORTH BARRULE
A2
A15
Maughold Head
Port Mooar
Ravensdale
Block Eary
Corrany
Cashtal yn Ard
Ballafayle
Kirkmichael
A3
488
620
SNAEFELL
462
SLIEAU LHEAN
A2
Corvalley Cairn
A4
B10
The Bungalow
Dhoon Bay
St Patrick's Isle
Giants Grave
A20
A9
Injebreck
Snaefell Mountain
Luxey Wheel
Abboylands
Peel
487
COLDEN
B22
Luxey R.
Laxey
King Orry's Grave
Contrary Head
Corrins Folly
A1
Port y Candas
479
SLIEAU RUY
Dhoon
Laxey Head
Patrick
Tynwald Hill
11
B12
Baldrine
Laxey Bay
A30
St John's
TT Circuit
Millenium Way
Baldwin
A18
Cloven Stones
Clay Head
Glen Maye
A1
A23
B20
Crosby
A11
To Belfast (Summer Only)
Dalby
Foxdale
A4
Eairy Garth
Union Mills
Castleward
Onchan
Onchan Head
To Stranraer (Summer Only)
Niarbyl
A27
A24
A26
Norse Houses
Strang
DOUGLAS
Niarbyl Bay
Round Table
16
483
SOUTH BARRULE
Ballanicholas Fort
B35
Braaid
A5
Douglas Bay
To Heysham
Closeclark
B39
A24
A25
A37
Douglas Head
To Fleetwood (Summer Only)
Brough Fort
A26
A5
Ballamodha
St Mark's
AA
Grenaby
B41
A4
Ballakelly
10
Port Soderick
To Liverpool (Summer Only)
Santon
Isle of Man Steam
Freshwick Bay
Colby
A5
Cronk ny Merriu
Arragon Circles
Santon Head
Milners Tower
Ballabeg
Rushen
Ballasalla
Cass ny Hawin
Bradda Head
Arbory
Isle of Man (Ronaldsway)
Port Erin
A7
A7
V
Corvalie
Castletown
Derbyhaven
Meayl Circle
A31
Port St Mary
Hango Hill
Derby Fort
SC
Calf of Man
Cregneish
Close ny Chollagh
Langness Point
Castletown Bay
Derby Round Tower
Spanish Head
Dreswick Point
Caigher Point

DUBLIN
Summer Only

# Outer Hebrides

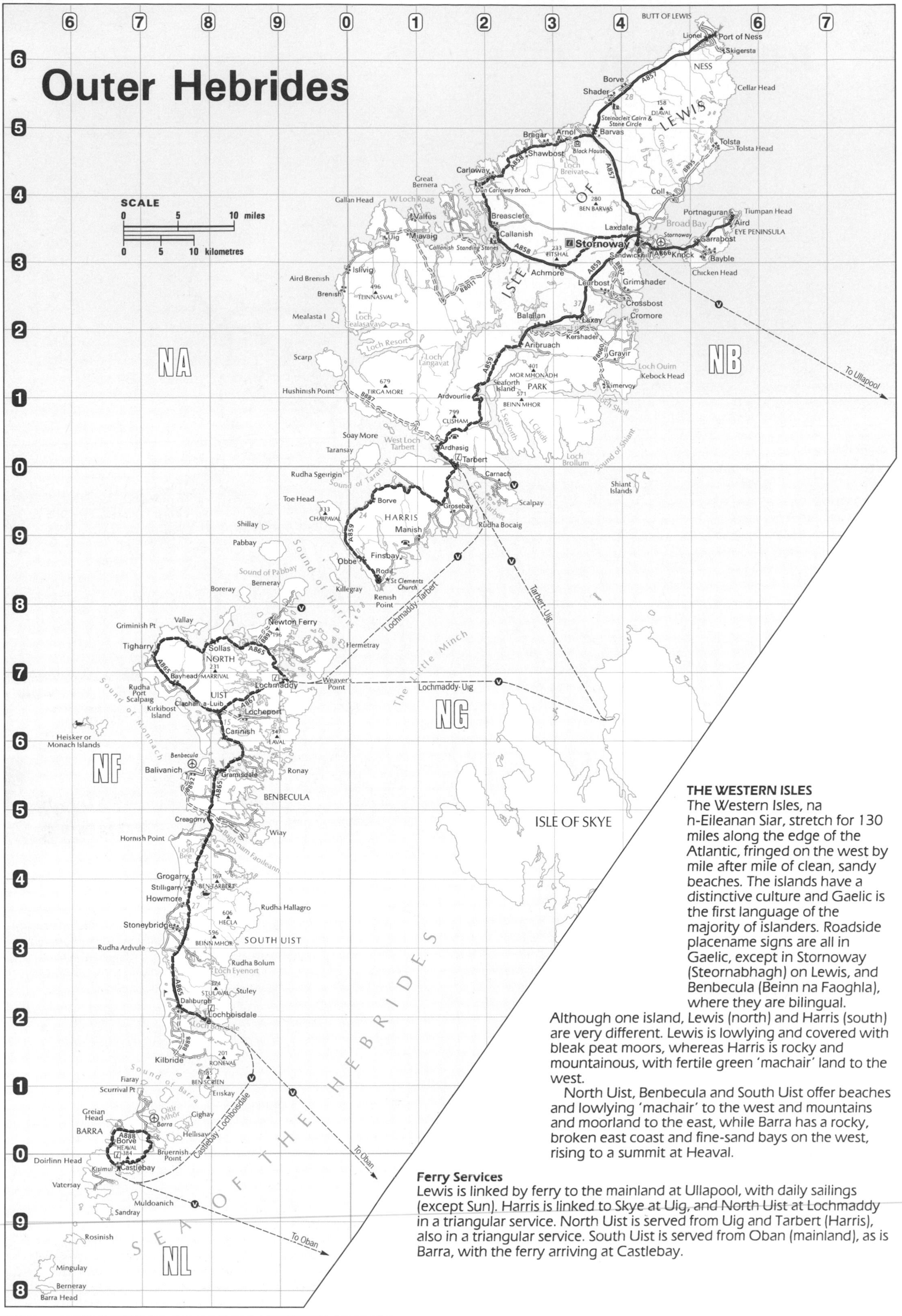

SCALE
0 5 10 miles
0 5 10 kilometres
BUTT OF LEWIS
Lionel
Port of Ness
Skigersta
NESS
Borve
Shader
Cellar Head
Steinacleit Cairn & Stone Circle
DIAVAL
LEWIS
Barvas
Arnol
Bragar
Black House
Shawbost
Tolsta
Tolsta Head
Loch Breivat
Carloway
Great Bernera
Dun Carloway Broch
280 BEN BARVAS
Coll
Gallan Head
W Loch Roag
Valtos
Breasclete
ISLE OF
Portnaguran
Tiumpan Head
Aird
EYE PENINSULA
Broad Bay
Laxdale
Uig
Miavaig
Callanish
Callanish Standing Stones
Stornoway
Garrabost
Sandwickhill
Knock
Bayble
233 EITSHAL
Achmore
Chicken Head
Islivig
Aird Brenish
Brenish
496 TEINNASVAL
Leurbost
Grimshader
Crossbost
Cromore
Mealasta I
Loch Tealasavay
Balallan
Laxay
Kershader
Loch Resort
Aribruach
Gravir
Scarp
NA
Loch Langavat
401 MOR MHONADH
Seaforth Island
PARK
Loch Ouirn
Kebock Head
NB
Hushinish Point
679 TIRGA MORE
Ardvourlie
Kimervay
571 BEINN MHOR
799 CLISHAM
Loch Seaforth
Loch Claidh
Loch Shell
To Ullapool
Soay More
Taransay
West Loch Tarbert
Ardhasig
Tarbert
Loch Brollum
Sound of Shiant
Rudha Sgeirigin
Sound of Taransay
Carnach
Shiant Islands
Toe Head
333 CHAIPAVAL
Borve
HARRIS
Grosebay
Scalpay
Shillay
Manish
Rudha Bocaig
Pabbay
Finsbay
Obbe
Rodil
St Clements Church
Sound of Pabbay
Sound of Harris
Berneray
Boreray
Killegray
Renish Point
Lochmaddy-Tarbert
Tarbert-Uig
Griminish Pt
Vallay
Newton Ferry
Tigharry
Sollas
NORTH
Hermetray
231 MARRIVAL
Bayhead
UIST
Lochmaddy
Weaver's Point
Lochmaddy-Uig
The Little Minch
Rudha Port Scalpaig
Clachan-a-Luib
Kirkibost Island
Locheport
Sound of Monach
Carinish
347 EAVAL
NG
Heisker or Monach Islands
Benbecula
Balivanich
Gramisdale
Ronay
NF
BENBECULA
ISLE OF SKYE
Creagorry
Wiay
Hornish Point
Bagh-nam Faoileann
Loch Bee
Grogarry
167 BEN TARBERT
Stilligarry
Howmore
Rudha Hallagro
606 HECLA
Stoneybridge
596 BEINN MHOR
SOUTH UIST
Rudha Ardvule
Rudha Bolum
Loch Eyenort
STULAVAL
Stuley
Dalburgh
Lochboisdale
Loch Boisdale
201 RONEVAL
Kilbride
Sound of Barra
185 BEN SCRIEN
Fiaray
Scurrival Pt
Eriskay
Greian Head
Oitir Mhòr
Barra
Cighay
BARRA
Hellisay
Borve
HEAVAL 384
Bruernish Point
Castlebay-Lochboisdale
To Oban
Doirlinn Head
Kisimul
Castlebay
Vatersay
Muldoanich
Sandray
SEA OF THE HEBRIDES
To Oban
Rosinish
NL
Mingulay
Berneray
Barra Head


**THE WESTERN ISLES**

The Western Isles, na h-Eileanan Siar, stretch for 130 miles along the edge of the Atlantic, fringed on the west by mile after mile of clean, sandy beaches. The islands have a distinctive culture and Gaelic is the first language of the majority of islanders. Roadside placename signs are all in Gaelic, except in Stornoway (Steornabhagh) on Lewis, and Benbecula (Beinn na Faoghla), where they are bilingual.

Although one island, Lewis (north) and Harris (south) are very different. Lewis is lowlying and covered with bleak peat moors, whereas Harris is rocky and mountainous, with fertile green 'machair' land to the west.

North Uist, Benbecula and South Uist offer beaches and lowlying 'machair' to the west and mountains and moorland to the east, while Barra has a rocky, broken east coast and fine-sand bays on the west, rising to a summit at Heaval.

**Ferry Services**

Lewis is linked by ferry to the mainland at Ullapool, with daily sailings (except Sun). Harris is linked to Skye at Uig, and North Uist at Lochmaddy in a triangular service. North Uist is served from Uig and Tarbert (Harris), also in a triangular service. South Uist is served from Oban (mainland), as is Barra, with the ferry arriving at Castlebay.

# Scottish Islands

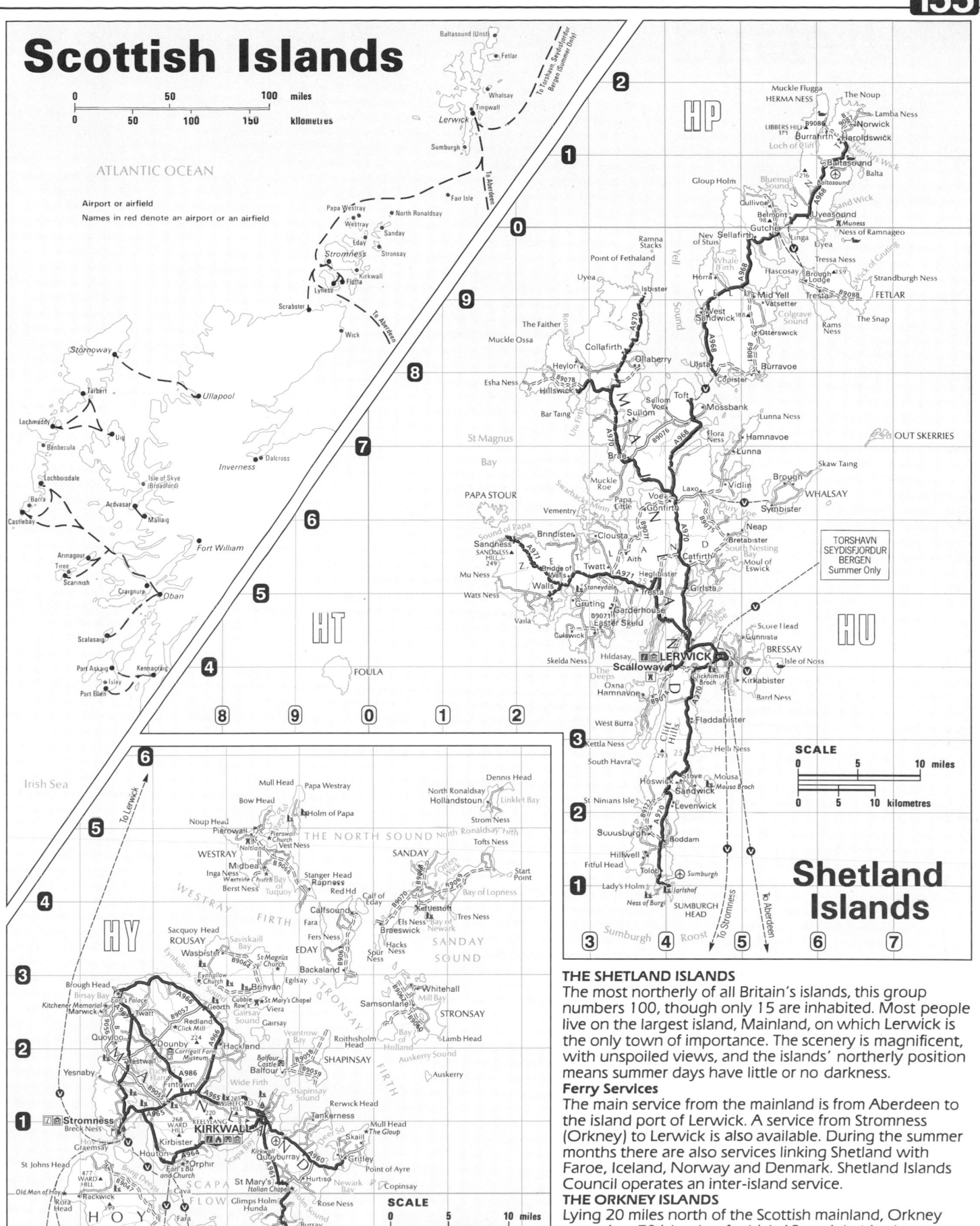

## Shetland Islands

## Orkney Islands

### THE SHETLAND ISLANDS
The most northerly of all Britain's islands, this group numbers 100, though only 15 are inhabited. Most people live on the largest island, Mainland, on which Lerwick is the only town of importance. The scenery is magnificent, with unspoiled views, and the islands' northerly position means summer days have little or no darkness.

### Ferry Services
The main service from the mainland is from Aberdeen to the island port of Lerwick. A service from Stromness (Orkney) to Lerwick is also available. During the summer months there are also services linking Shetland with Faroe, Iceland, Norway and Denmark. Shetland Islands Council operates an inter-island service.

### THE ORKNEY ISLANDS
Lying 20 miles north of the Scottish mainland, Orkney comprises 70 islands, of which 18 are inhabited, Mainland being the largest. Apart from Hoy, Orkney is generally green and flat, with few trees. The islands abound with prehistoric antiquities and rare bird life. The climate is one of even temperatures and 'twilight' summer nights but with violent winds at times.

### Ferry Services
The main service is from Scrabster on Caithness coast to the island port of Stromness. A service from Aberdeen to Stromness provides a link to Shetland at Lerwick. Inter-island services are also operated (advance reservations necessary).

# Ireland

**LEGEND**

| | |
|---|---|
| M1 | Motorway |
| N17 | National Primary Route |
| N54 | National Secondary Route |
| R182 | Regional Road |
| A4 | Primary Route |
| A21 | A Road |
| B75 | B Road |

Republic of Ireland

Northern Ireland

Distance in miles between symbols

International Boundary

Frontier Posts

Scale: 16 miles to 1 inch (approx)

0    10    20    30    miles

0   10   20   30   40   kilometres

G

F

E

D

1

2

Aran Island

Gweebarr

Rossan Point
Malin More
Glencolumbkille Folk Museum
Glencolumbkille (Gleann Cholm Cille)
1972 Carrick (An Charra)
SLIEVE LEAGUE
Kilcar (Cill Charthaigh)
R263
Killyb

St John's Point

Donegal

Inishmurray
R279
Grange
Lissadell House 1722 BENBU
Rosses Point
N15
Sligo Bay R29
Strandhill R292
SI
Dro
Ballys

Erris Head
Broad Haven
Downpatrick Head
Ballycastle
R314
Easky
Dromore West
Enniscrone
N59 32
N59
Colooney

Belmullet (Béal an Mhuirhead)
Bunnahowen
Carrowmore Lough
R315
R314
Killala
Killala Bay
N59
OX MTS
R29

Inishkea
R313
Bangor Erris
N59
Crossmolina
Ballina
Bunnyconnellan
R310
N57
R294
N17
Ballymo

Duvillaun More
Blacksod Bay
Lough
2369
2646 NEPHIN
R312
Connaught Regional Airport
Tobercurry
R296
R293
Ballymo

2204
SLIEVE MORE
Keel
R317
R315
Foxford
N58
N57
Charlestown
Carracastle
R294
R294

Achill Head
Achill Island
R319
Lough Feeagh
R312
Lough Conn
Curry
N5

Clare
Clew Bay
Newport
R311
Turlough
N5
Swinford
R320
Kilkelly R322
R325
Ballaghaderre
N5

Westport
N60
Castlebar
N60
R324
Kiltimagh
N17
R293
R325
Frenchpark

Inishturk
Caher
R335
Louisburgh
CROAGH PATRICK 2510
Westport Zoo
R330
Ballyhean
Balla
Knock
R323
Ballyhaunis
R29
Loughglinn
Castlerea

Inishbofin
Inishark
2239
Claremorris
R331
Partry
N60
Ballindine
R327
R360
R364
Ballinlough
R36
Bally

Cruagh
Letterfrack
2395
Clifden
N59
R344
R376
Leenene
Neale
Kilmaine
Dunmore
Glenamaddy
R362
Creggs
Ros

Ballyconneely
R341
R342
R340
Roundstone
Clonbur (An Fhairche)
Cornamona
R347
Shrule
Tuam
N17
R333
R322
R364
Bally

Slyne Head
Glinsk Glinsce
R340
Oughterard
Headford
N84
N83
Mount Bellew
Caltra

Croagnakeela
Kilkieran (Cill Ciaráin)
R336
N59
Oranmore
N63
Monivea
R339
R356
Ahascragh

Gorumna Island
Galway
N17
N64
Athenry
R348
R359
Kilco

Rock
Inishmore
Spiddal (An Spideal)
Clarinbridge
Kilcolgan
N18
R347
Craughwell
Loughrea
N6
N65

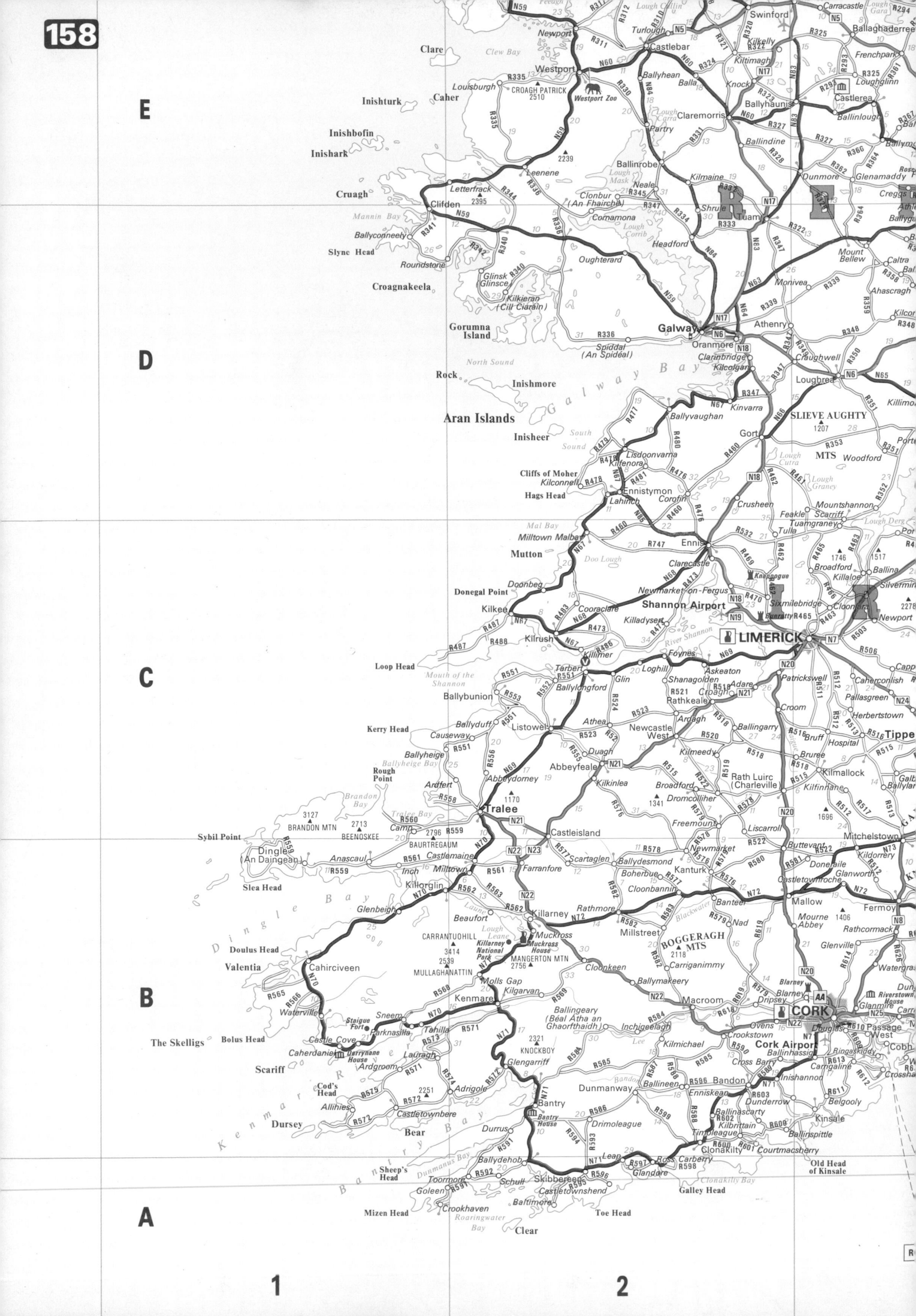

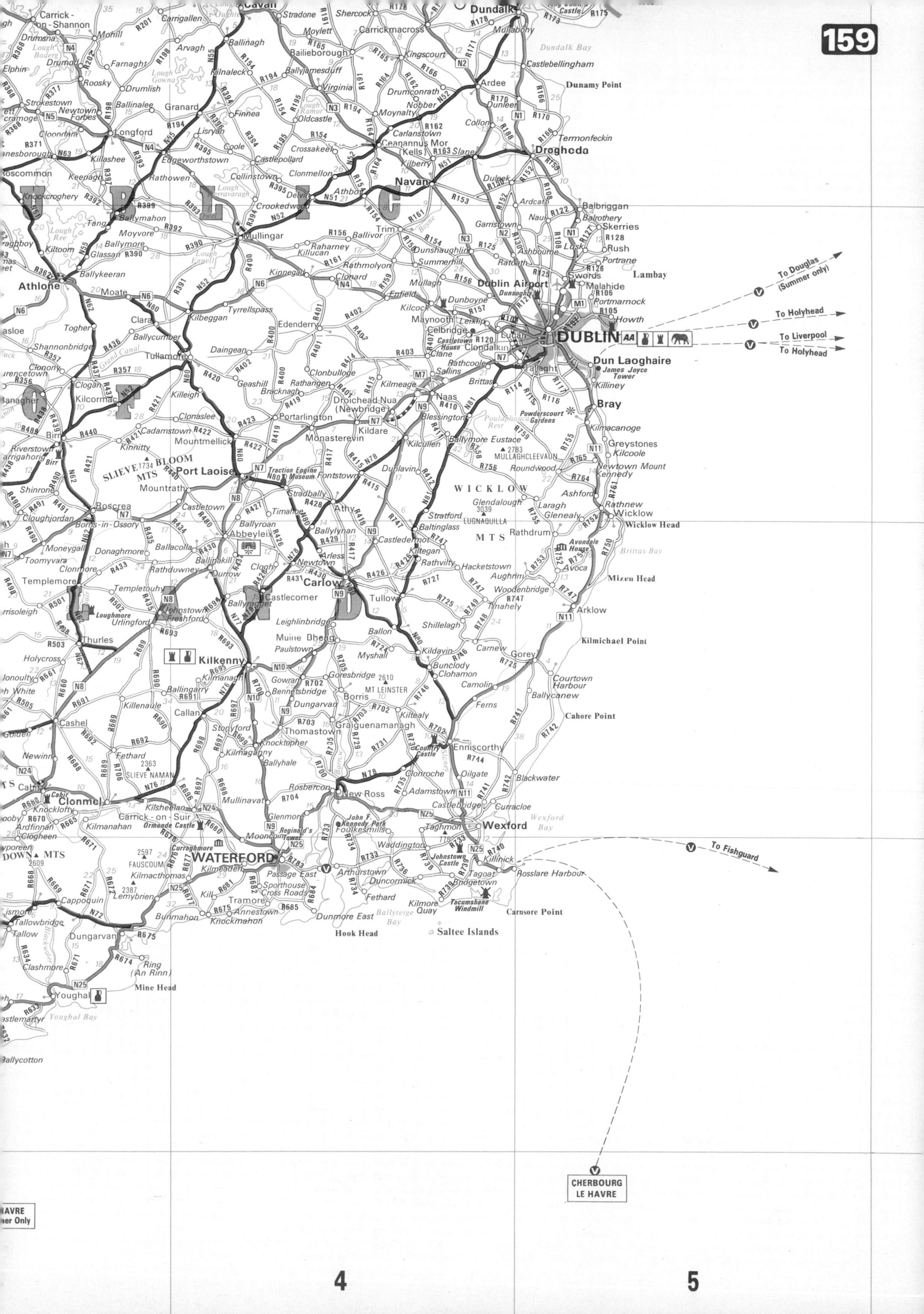

# INDEX To Ireland

The map for Ireland employs an arbitrary system of grid reference. Each entry is identified by the page number, and is followed by a letter on the left-hand side of the map and by a number at the top or the bottom. The entry can be located in the square where the lettered and numbered sections converge, e.g., Londonderry is to be found in the square marked by the dissecting blue lines of G4.

# London

# Inner London

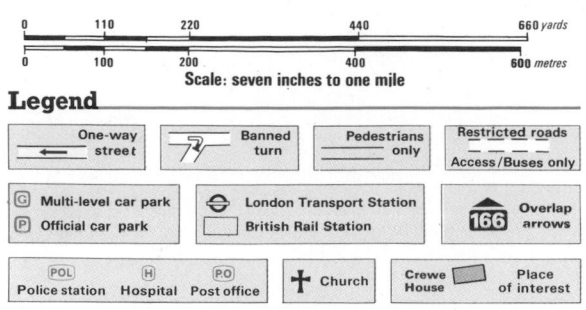

Scale: seven inches to one mile

**Legend**

| | | | |
|---|---|---|---|
| One-way street | Banned turn | Pedestrians only | Restricted roads Access/Buses only |
| Ⓖ Multi-level car park | Ⓟ Official car park | London Transport Station / British Rail Station | Overlap arrows |
| POL Police station | H Hospital P.O Post office | ✝ Church | Crewe House / Place of interest |

The one–way streets and banned turns shown on this map are in operation at time of going to press. Some of these are experimental and liable to change. Only the more important banned turns are shown, some of which operate between 7am and 7pm only, and these are sign–posted accordingly. No waiting or unilateral waiting restrictions apply to many streets. All such restrictions are indicated by official signs.

**Key to Map Pages**

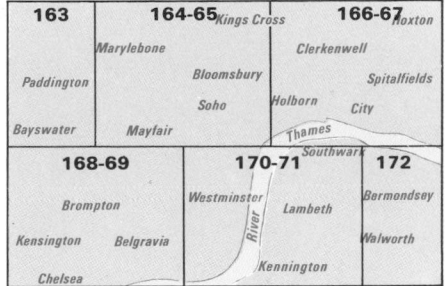

# Theatreland

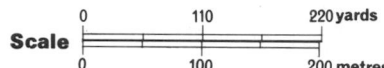

*(map of Theatreland showing Soho, Covent Garden, Strand, Charing Cross and Trafalgar Square areas, with labelled streets and theatres including Oxford Street, Charing Cross Road, Shaftesbury Avenue, Drury Lane, Kingsway, The Strand, Pall Mall, Whitehall, Haymarket, Regent Street, and landmarks such as the National Gallery, National Portrait Gallery, Nelson's Column, Charing Cross Station, Royal Opera House, Covent Garden, Somerset House and the River Thames)*

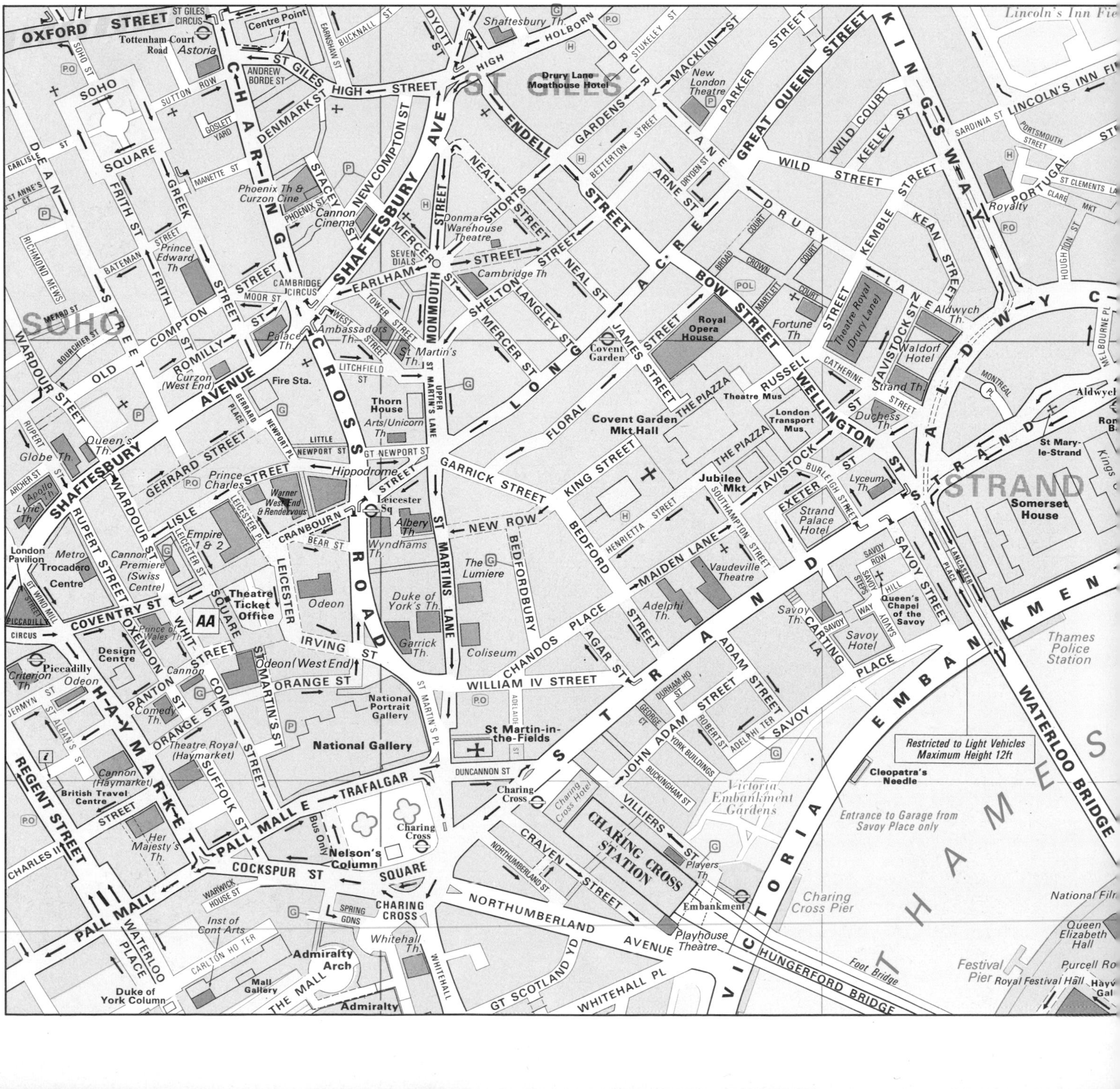

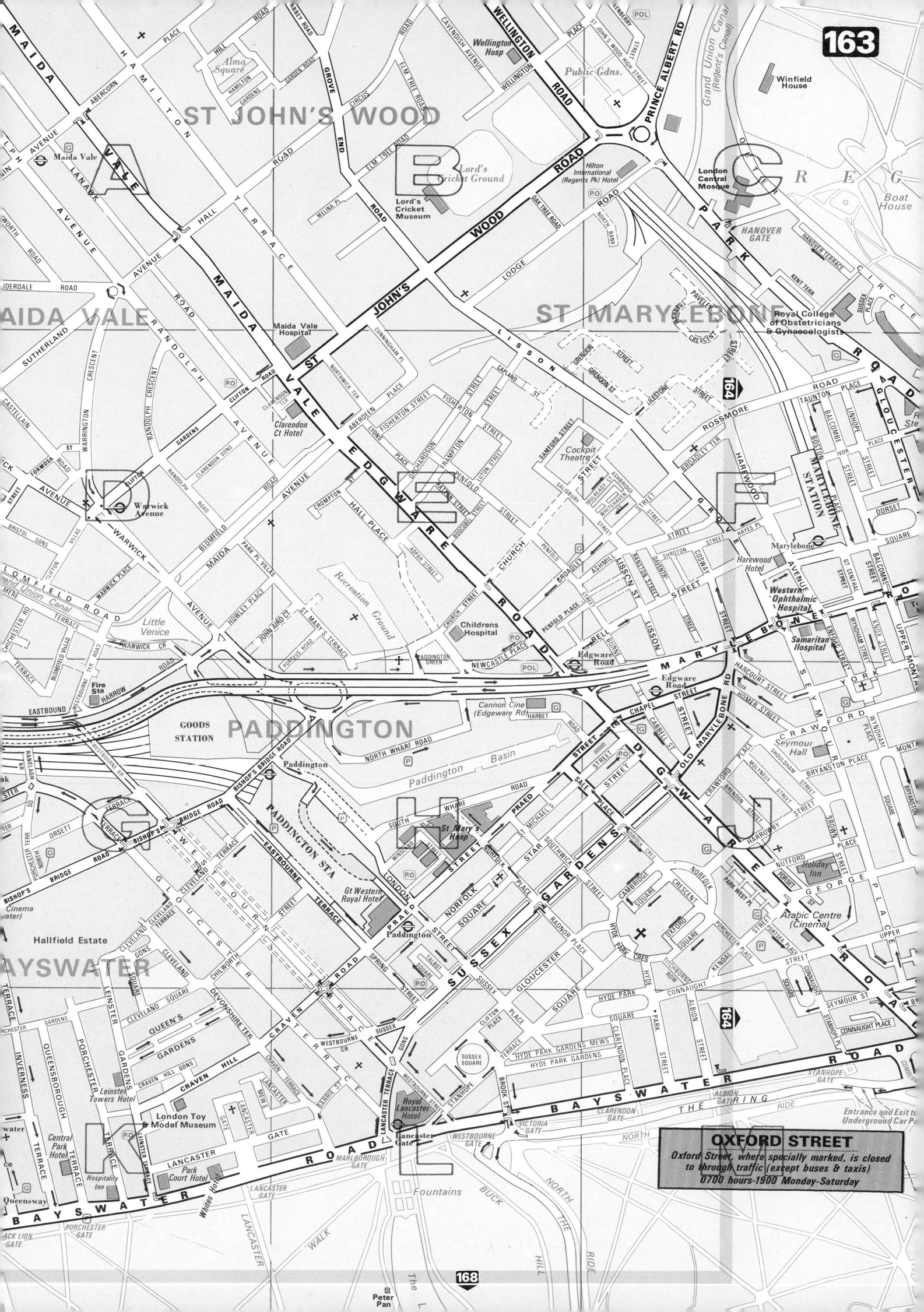

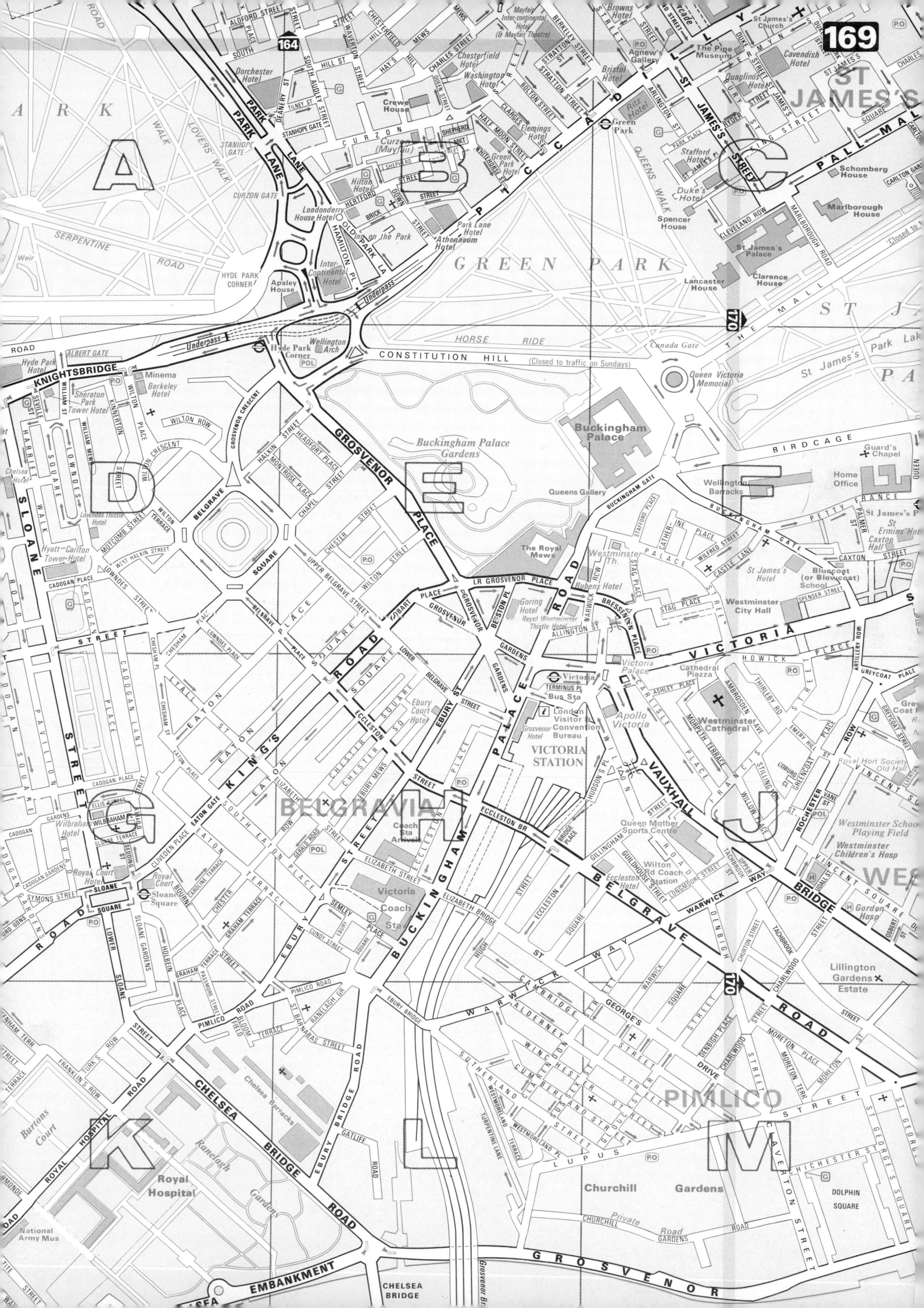

# INDEX To Inner London Maps

This map employs an arbitrary system of grid reference. Pages are identified by numbers and divided into twelve squares. Each square contains a black letter; all references give the page number first, followed by the letter of the square in which a particular street can be found. Reference for Exhibition Road is *168E*, meaning that the relevant map is on page *168* and that the street appears in the square designated E.

175

# Key to Town Plans

# Airports and Seaports

Most people who leave Britain by air or sea use the airports and seaports detailed in these pages. The maps indicate the approach roads into each complex with information on parking and telephone numbers through which details on costs and other travel information can be obtained. The hotels listed are AA-appointed, and the garages have been selected because they provide adequate long term parking facilities.

## HEATHROW AIRPORT Tel: 01-759 4321 (Airport Information)

Heathrow, one of the world's busiest international airports, lies sixteen miles west of London. The airport is situated on the Piccadilly Underground line at Heathrow Central station. It is also served by local bus and long distance coach services. For short-term parking, multi-storey car parks are sited at each of the passenger terminals Tel: 01-745 7160 (terminals 1, 2, 3) & 01-759 4931 (terminal 4). Charges for the long-term car parks on the northern perimeter road are designed to encourage their use for a stay in excess of four hours. A free coach takes passengers to and from the terminals. Commercial garages offering long-term parking facilities within easy reach of the airport include: Airways Garage Ltd. Tel: 01-759 9661/4; Quo-Vadis Airport Parking Tel: 01-759 2778; Cranford Parking Tel: 01-759 9661; Flyaway Car Storage Tel: 01-759 1567 or 2020; Kenning Car Hire Tel: 01-759 9701; and National Car Parks Tel: 01-759 9878. Car Hire: Avis Rent-A-Car Tel: 01-897 9321; Budget Rent-A-Car Tel: 01-759 2216; Godfrey Davis Europcar Tel: 01-897 0811/5; Guy Salmon Tel: 01-897 0541; Hertz Rent-A-Car Tel: 01-897 3347; and Kenning Car Hire Tel: 01-759 9701. The 4-star hotels in the area are The Excelsior Tel: 01-759 6611; the Heathrow Penta Tel: 01-897 6363; the Holiday Inn Tel: (0895) 445555 and the Sheraton-Heathrow Tel: 01-759 2424. The 3-star hotels are the Berkeley Arms Tel: 01-897 2121; the Ariel Tel: 01-759 2552; the Post House Tel: 01-759 2323; and the Skyway Tel: 01-759 6311.

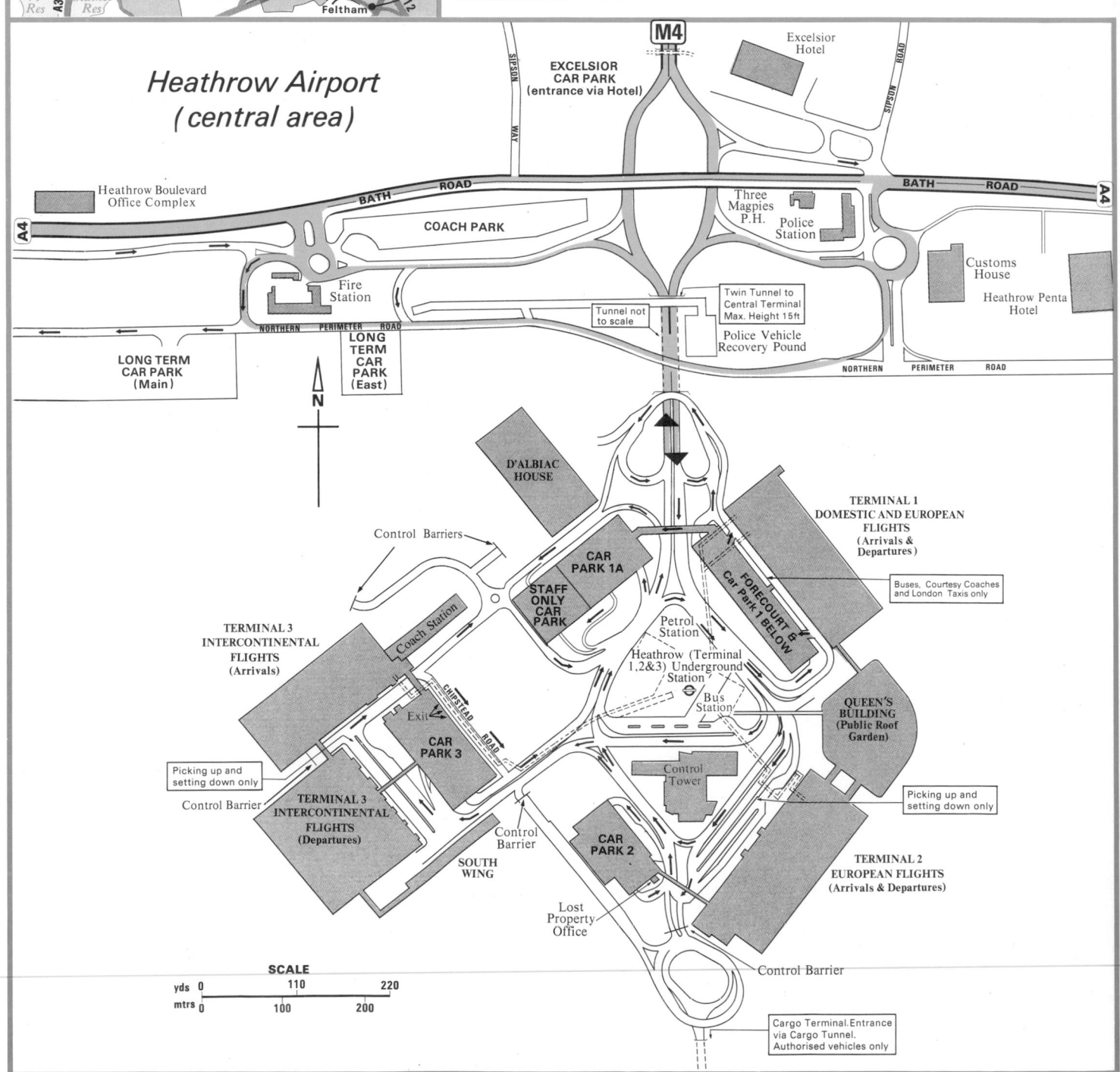

*Heathrow Airport (central area)*

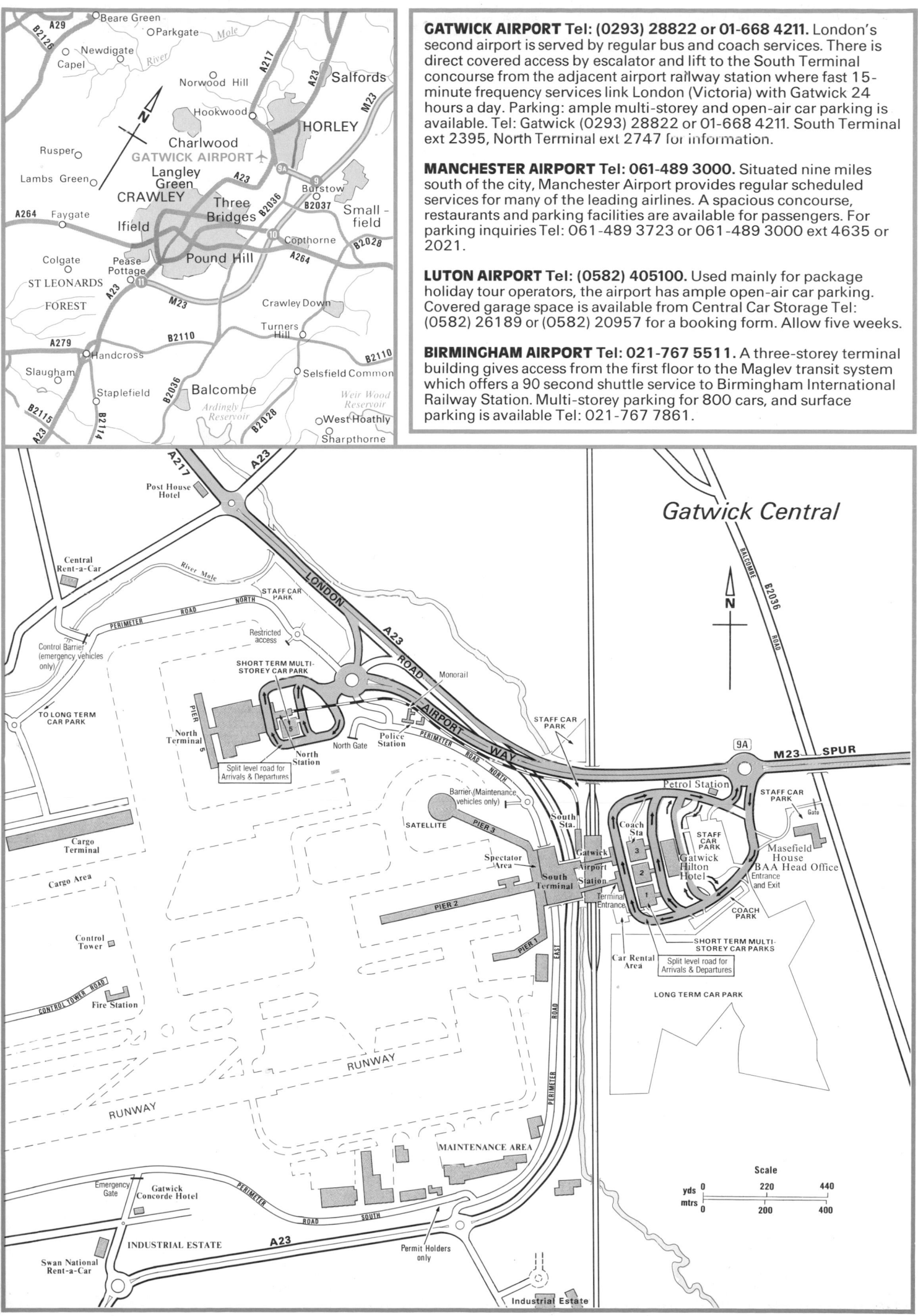

**GATWICK AIRPORT Tel: (0293) 28822 or 01-668 4211.** London's second airport is served by regular bus and coach services. There is direct covered access by escalator and lift to the South Terminal concourse from the adjacent airport railway station where fast 15-minute frequency services link London (Victoria) with Gatwick 24 hours a day. Parking: ample multi-storey and open-air car parking is available. Tel: Gatwick (0293) 28822 or 01-668 4211. South Terminal ext 2395, North Terminal ext 2747 for information.

**MANCHESTER AIRPORT Tel: 061-489 3000.** Situated nine miles south of the city, Manchester Airport provides regular scheduled services for many of the leading airlines. A spacious concourse, restaurants and parking facilities are available for passengers. For parking inquiries Tel: 061-489 3723 or 061-489 3000 ext 4635 or 2021.

**LUTON AIRPORT Tel: (0582) 405100.** Used mainly for package holiday tour operators, the airport has ample open-air car parking. Covered garage space is available from Central Car Storage Tel: (0582) 26189 or (0582) 20957 for a booking form. Allow five weeks.

**BIRMINGHAM AIRPORT Tel: 021-767 5511.** A three-storey terminal building gives access from the first floor to the Maglev transit system which offers a 90 second shuttle service to Birmingham International Railway Station. Multi-storey parking for 800 cars, and surface parking is available Tel: 021-767 7861.

*Gatwick Central*

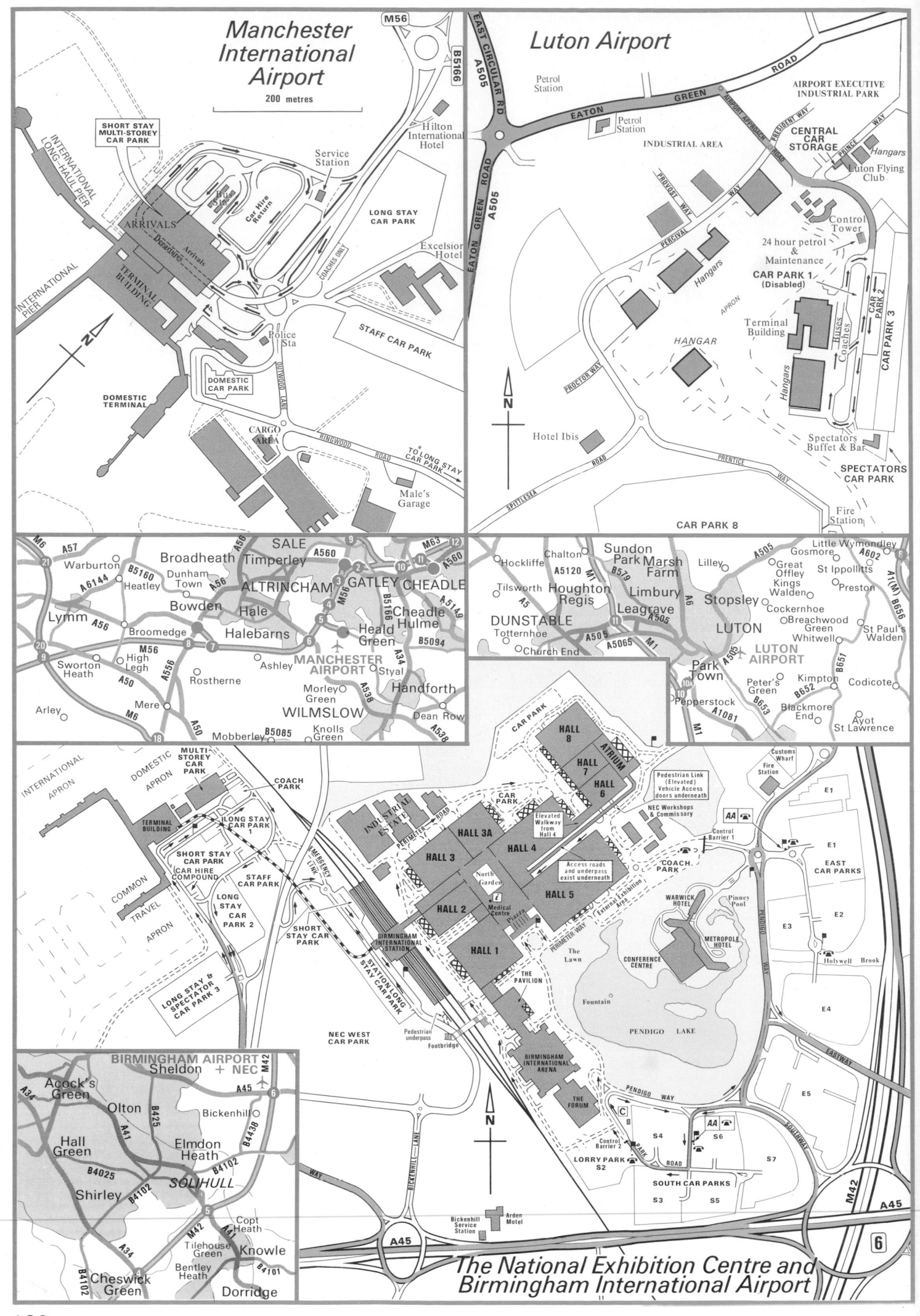

# Manchester International Airport

200 metres

SHORT STAY MULTI-STOREY CAR PARK

INTERNATIONAL LONG-HAUL PIER

Hilton International Hotel

Service Station

Bus Sta

Car Hire Return

ARRIVALS

Departures

Arrivals

COACHES ONLY

LONG STAY CAR PARK

Excelsior Hotel

INTERNATIONAL PIER

TERMINAL BUILDING

N

STAFF CAR PARK

Police Sta

DOMESTIC CAR PARK

DUNWOOD LANE

DOMESTIC TERMINAL

CARGO AREA

RINGWOOD ROAD

TO LONG STAY CAR PARK

Male's Garage

## Luton Airport

EAST CIRCULAR RD

A505

EATON GREEN ROAD

B5166

AIRPORT APPROACH

PRESIDENT WAY

Petrol Station

AIRPORT EXECUTIVE INDUSTRIAL PARK

EATON GREEN ROAD

Petrol Station

INDUSTRIAL AREA

PRINCE WAY

CENTRAL CAR STORAGE

Hangars

Luton Flying Club

PROVOST WAY

PERCIVAL WAY

Hangars

Control Tower

24 hour petrol & Maintenance

CAR PARK 1 (Disabled)

CAR PARK 2

CAR PARK 3

APRON

PROCTOR WAY

HANGAR

Terminal Building

Buses Coaches

N

Hotel Ibis

Hangars

Spectators Buffet & Bar

SPITTLESEA ROAD

PRENTICE WAY

SPECTATORS CAR PARK

CAR PARK 8

Fire Station

## (Manchester area map)

M6 A57
21 Warburton B5160
A6144 Heatley A56
Lymm A56 Bowden
Broomedge
20 M56
9 Sworton Heath A50
High Legh A556
Arley Mere
M6 Rostherne
18 A50 Mobberley B5085
Knolls Green

SALE 9
Broadheath Timperley A560
Dunham Town A56
ALTRINCHAM GATLEY CHEADLE M63 12
Hale M56 B5166 B5149
Halebarns A34
8 7 Heald Green B5094
Ashley MANCHESTER AIRPORT Styal
Morley Green
WILMSLOW A538 Handforth
Dean Row A538

## (Luton area map)

Hockliffe Chalton
A5120 Sundon Park Marsh Farm
Tilsworth Houghton Regis B579 Limbury
DUNSTABLE Leagrave
Totternhoe A505
Church End A5065 M1 11
10A
10 Pepperstock
A1081 M1

Little Wymondley A602 6
Gosmore St Ippollitts
Lilley Great Offley A1(M) B656
Kings Walden Preston
Stopsley Cockernhoe
Breachwood Green St Paul's Walden
Whitwell
LUTON B651
LUTON AIRPORT
Park Town A505 B652 Codicote
Peter's Green Kimpton B653
Blackmore End
Ayot St Lawrence

## The National Exhibition Centre and Birmingham International Airport

INTERNATIONAL APRON

DOMESTIC APRON

MULTI-STOREY CAR PARK

COACH PARK

TERMINAL BUILDING

LONG STAY CAR PARK 1

SHORT STAY CAR PARK

CAR HIRE COMPOUND

COMMON TRAVEL APRON

LONG STAY CAR PARK 2

STAFF CAR PARK

SHORT STAY CAR PARK

LONG STAY & SPECTATOR CAR PARK 3

EMERGENCY LINK

PERIMETER ROAD

INDUSTRIAL ESTATE

CAR PARK

HALL 8

HALL 7

HALL 6

ATRIUM

HALL 3A

HALL 3

HALL 4

HALL 2

North Garden

HALL 5

i

Medical Centre

Piazza

HALL 1

Elevated Walkway from Hall 4

Access roads and underpass exist underneath

Pedestrian Link (Elevated) Vehicle Access doors underneath

NEC Workshops & Commissary

AA

Control Barrier 1

COACH PARK

WARWICK HOTEL

Pinney's Pool

METROPOLE HOTEL

Customs Wharf

Fire Station

E1

E1

EAST CAR PARKS

E3

E2

PENDIGO WAY

Holywell Brook

E4

BIRMINGHAM INTERNATIONAL STATION

STATION LONG STAY CAR PARK

NEC WEST CAR PARK

THE PAVILION

External Exhibition Area

CONFERENCE CENTRE

The Lawn

Fountain

PENDIGO LAKE

E5

Pedestrian underpass Footbridge

BIRMINGHAM INTERNATIONAL ARENA

N

THE FORUM

PENDIGO WAY

C

Control Barrier 2

LORRY PARK S2

AA

S4

S6

S7

EASTWAY

M42

BICKENHILL LANE

A45

Bickenhill Service Station

Arden Motel

SOUTH CAR PARKS

S3

S5

A45

6

### (Birmingham inset map)

BIRMINGHAM AIRPORT + NEC
Sheldon M42
Acock's Green A34
Olton B425 Bickenhill A45 6
Hall Green A41 B443B
Shirley B4025 Elmdon Heath B4102
SOLIHULL
B4102 Copt Heath
M42 Tilehouse Green
Cheswick A34 Bentley Green B4101 Knowle
B4102 Green Heath Dorridge

180

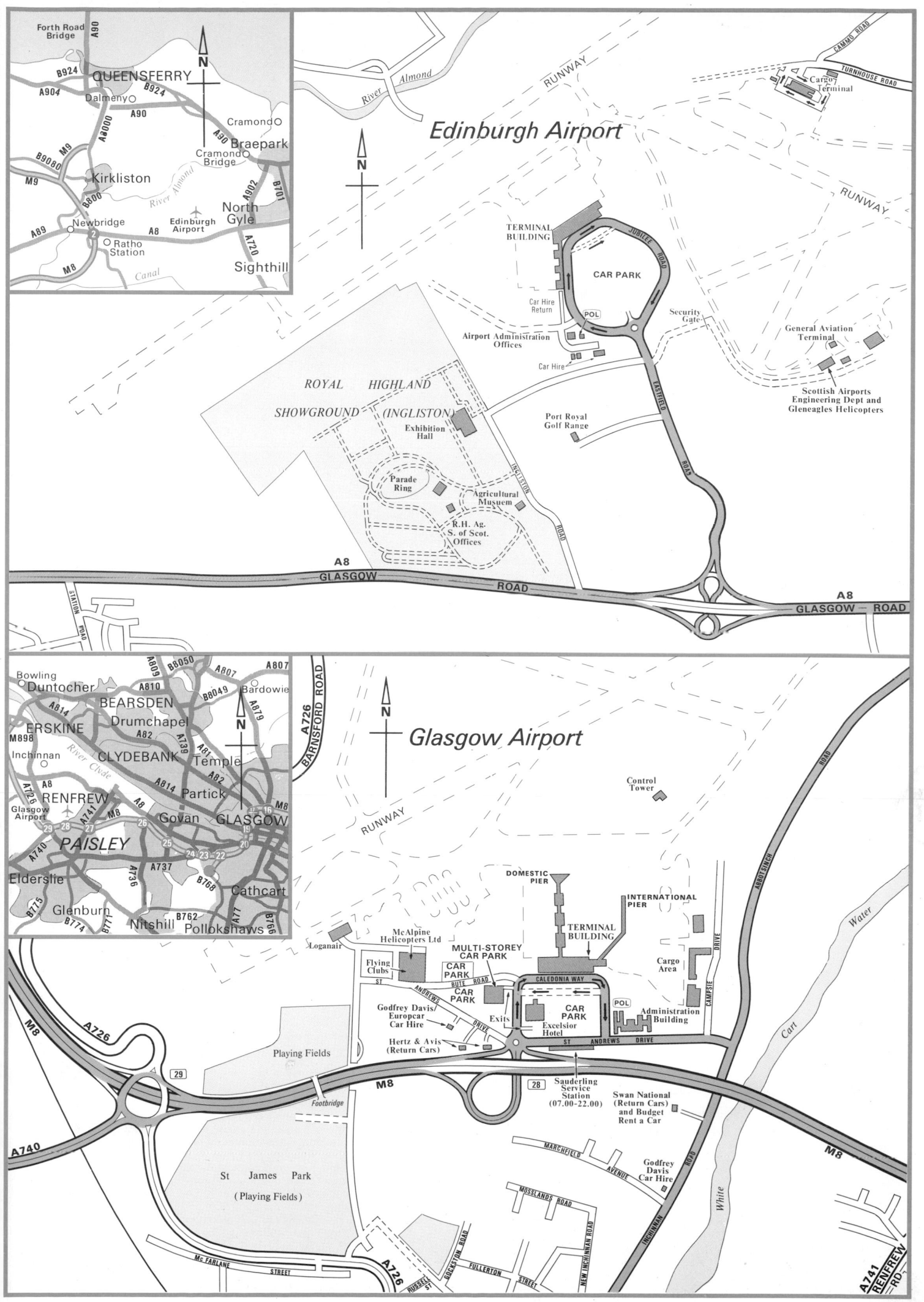

## Edinburgh Airport

Forth Road Bridge
QUEENSFERRY
B924
A904
Dalmeny
A90
A9000
B924
A90
Cramond
CramondO
Braepark
Cramond Bridge
B9080
M9
Kirkliston
B800
River Almond
A902
B701
North Gyle
M9
A89
Newbridge
2
A8
Edinburgh Airport
A720
Ratho Station
Sighthill
M8
Canal

River Almond
River Almond
RUNWAY
RUNWAY
CAMMO ROAD
TURNHOUSE ROAD
Cargo Terminal

N

TERMINAL BUILDING
JUBILEE ROAD
CAR PARK
Car Hire Return
POL
Security Gate
General Aviation Terminal
Airport Administration Offices
Car Hire
EASTFIELD
Scottish Airports Engineering Dept and Gleneagles Helicopters

ROYAL    HIGHLAND
SHOWGROUND    (INGLISTON)
Exhibition Hall
Port Royal Golf Range

INGLISTON ROAD

Parade Ring
Agricultural Musuem
R.H. Ag. S. of Scot. Offices

A8
GLASGOW    ROAD
A8
GLASGOW — ROAD

## Glasgow Airport

Bowling
Duntocher
B8050
A809
B8049
A807
A807
BEARSDEN
A810
Bardowie
A819
Drumchapel
ERSKINE
A814
A82
A81
N
M898
CLYDEBANK
Temple
Inchinnan
River Clyde
A814
A82
A82
M8
RENFREW
A8
Partick
A8
A726
A741
M8
Govan
GLASGOW
Glasgow Airport
29
28
27
26
25
19
A740
PAISLEY
24 23 22
20
Elderslie
A736
A737
B768
Cathcart
B775
B774
B771
A77
B762
B766
Glenburn
Nitshill
Pollokshaws

A726
BARNSFORD ROAD

N

RUNWAY
Control Tower
ABBOTSINCH ROAD
White Cart Water

DOMESTIC PIER
INTERNATIONAL PIER
Loganair
McAlpine Helicopters Ltd
MULTI-STOREY CAR PARK
TERMINAL BUILDING
Cargo Area
CAMPSIE DRIVE
Flying Clubs
ST ANDREWS DRIVE
CAR PARK
BUTE ROAD
CALEDONIA WAY
CAR PARK
CAR PARK
POL
Administration Building
Godfrey Davis/ Europcar Car Hire
Exits
Excelsior Hotel
M8
A726
Hertz & Avis (Return Cars)
ST    ANDREWS    DRIVE
29
Playing Fields
Footbridge
M8
28
Sauderling Service Station (07.00-22.00)
Swan National (Return Cars) and Budget Rent a Car
MARCHFIELD AVENUE
Godfrey Davis Car Hire
A740
St    James    Park
( Playing Fields )
MOSSLANDS ROAD
NEW INCHINNAN ROAD
White Cart
M8
McFarlane Street
A726
RUSSELL ST
BUCKSTON ROAD
FULLERTON STREET
INCHINNAN ROAD
A741
RENFREW RD

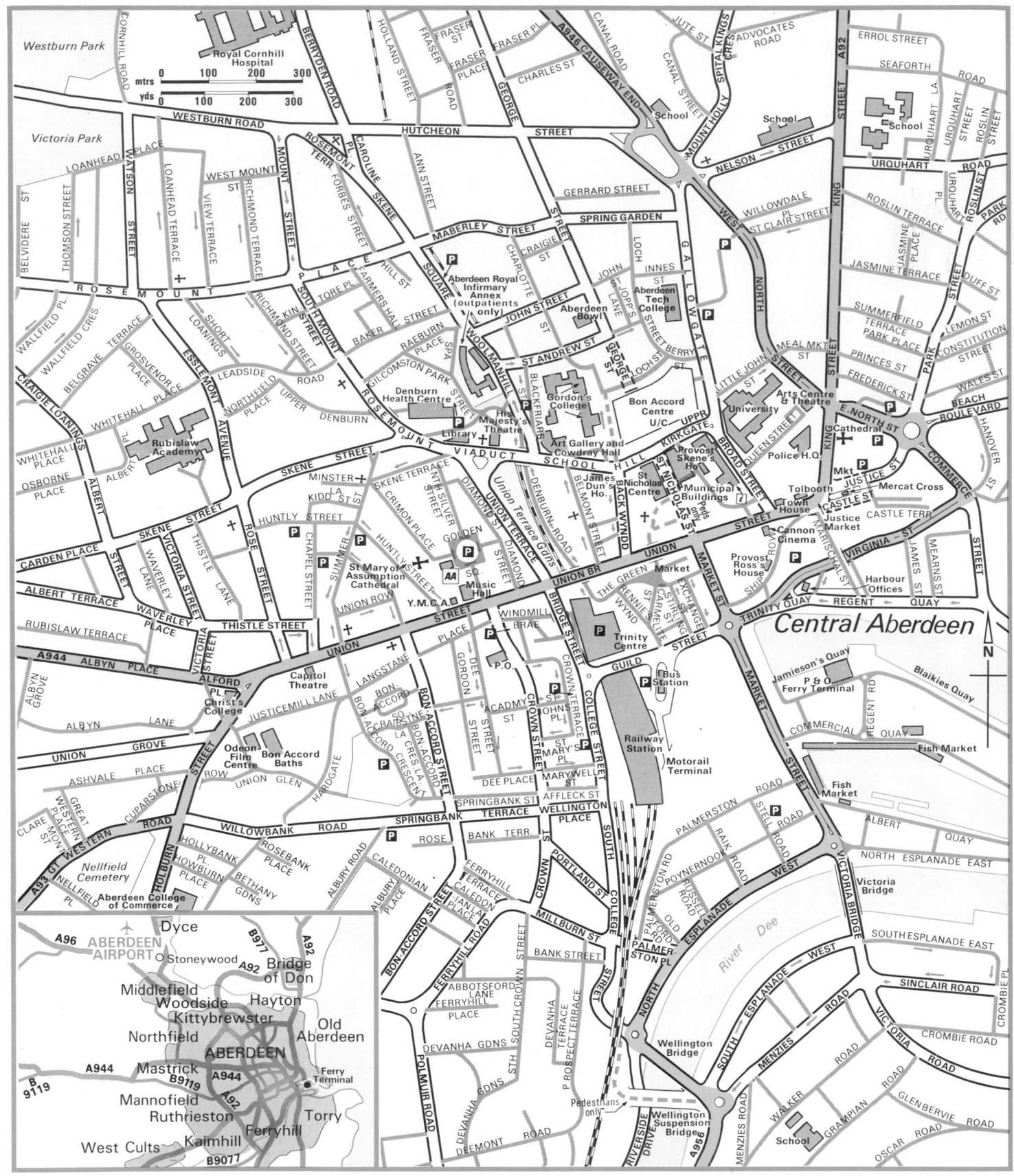

Central Aberdeen

**EDINBURGH AIRPORT Tel: 031-333 1000**
A regular coach service operates between Edinburgh (Waverley Bridge) and the airport seven miles away. The service also links with Glasgow and Glasgow Airport. The airport has parking for 1,400 vehicles, all open air, Tel: 031-344 3197. The information desk is located on the main concourse. Tel: 031-333 1000 or 031-344 3136. There are several top class hotels within easy reach of the airport, and car hire facilities are provided by Avis Tel: 031-333 1866, Europcar Tel: 031-333 2588, Hertz Tel: 031-333 1019 and Swan National Tel: 031-333 1922.

**GLASGOW AIRPORT Tel: 041-887 1111**
Situated eight miles west of Glasgow, the airport is linked with Central Glasgow and Edinburgh by regular coach services. Nearly 2,000 parking spaces are available, some under cover. Tel: 041-889 2751. The information desk is located on the first floor Tel: 041-887 1111 ext 4552. There is one 4-star hotel within easy reach of the airport, as well as four 3-star and one 2-star hotel. Car hire is available, from among others, Avis Tel: 041-887 2261, Hertz Tel: 041-887 2451, Europcar Tel: 041-887 0414 and Swan National Tel: 041-887 7915.

**ABERDEEN AIRPORT AND HELIPORT Tel: (0224) 722331**
Situated seven miles north-west of Aberdeen, the airport has its main access from the A96 which also serves for the West Heliport. Coach services operate between Aberdeen City Centre and the Main Terminal/West Heliport. Bus services from Aberdeen pass the entrance to East heliport. There is open air parking for 900 vehicles. Tel: (0224) 722331, extension 5142. At the Heliport there is open air parking for 300 vehicles. The information desk is in the check-in area. Tel: (0224) 722331 extension 5312. There are three 4-star hotels in the airport area and car hire is available through Avis. Tel: (0224) 722282, Europcar Tel: (0224) 723404, Hertz Tel: (0224) 722373, Budget Rent-a-Car Tel: (0224) 725067.

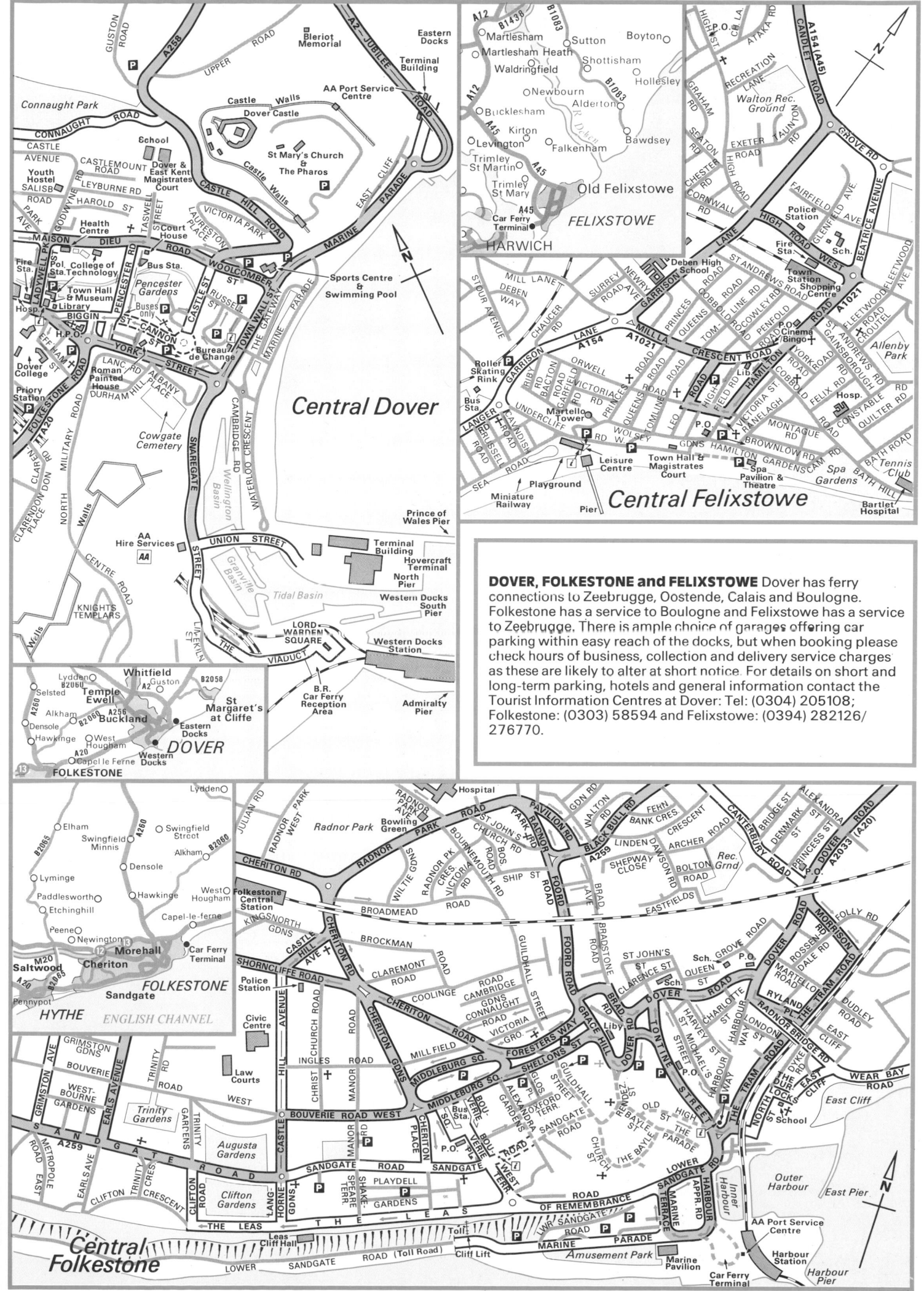

**Central Dover**

**Central Felixstowe**

**Central Folkestone**

**DOVER, FOLKESTONE and FELIXSTOWE** Dover has ferry connections to Zeebrugge, Oostende, Calais and Boulogne. Folkestone has a service to Boulogne and Felixstowe has a service to Zeebrugge. There is ample choice of garages offering car parking within easy reach of the docks, but when booking please check hours of business, collection and delivery service charges as these are likely to alter at short notice. For details on short and long-term parking, hotels and general information contact the Tourist Information Centres at Dover: Tel: (0304) 205108; Folkestone: (0303) 58594 and Felixstowe: (0394) 282126/ 276770.

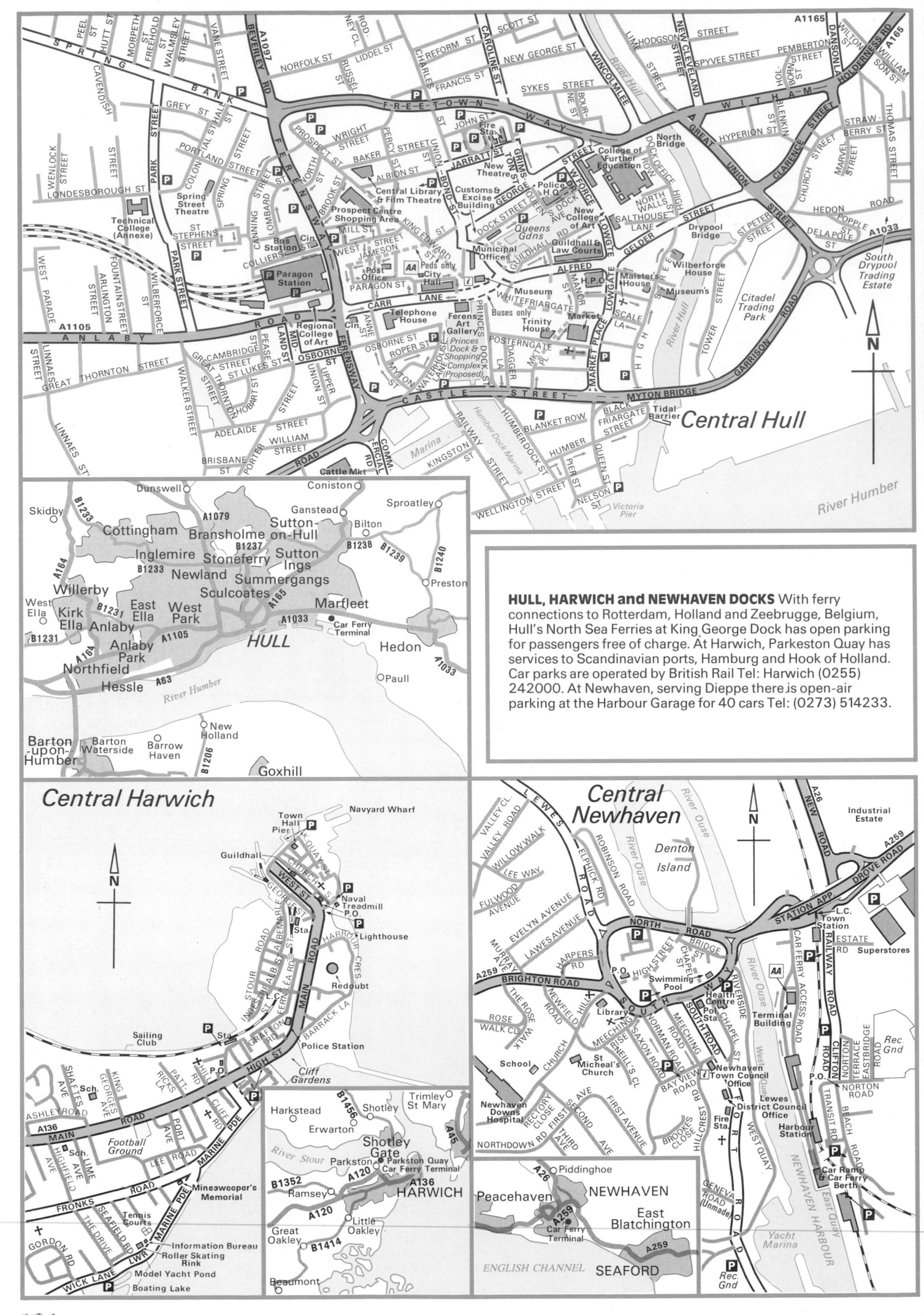

**Central Hull**

**HULL, HARWICH and NEWHAVEN DOCKS** With ferry connections to Rotterdam, Holland and Zeebrugge, Belgium, Hull's North Sea Ferries at King George Dock has open parking for passengers free of charge. At Harwich, Parkeston Quay has services to Scandinavian ports, Hamburg and Hook of Holland. Car parks are operated by British Rail Tel: Harwich (0255) 242000. At Newhaven, serving Dieppe there is open-air parking at the Harbour Garage for 40 cars Tel: (0273) 514233.

**Central Harwich**

**Central Newhaven**

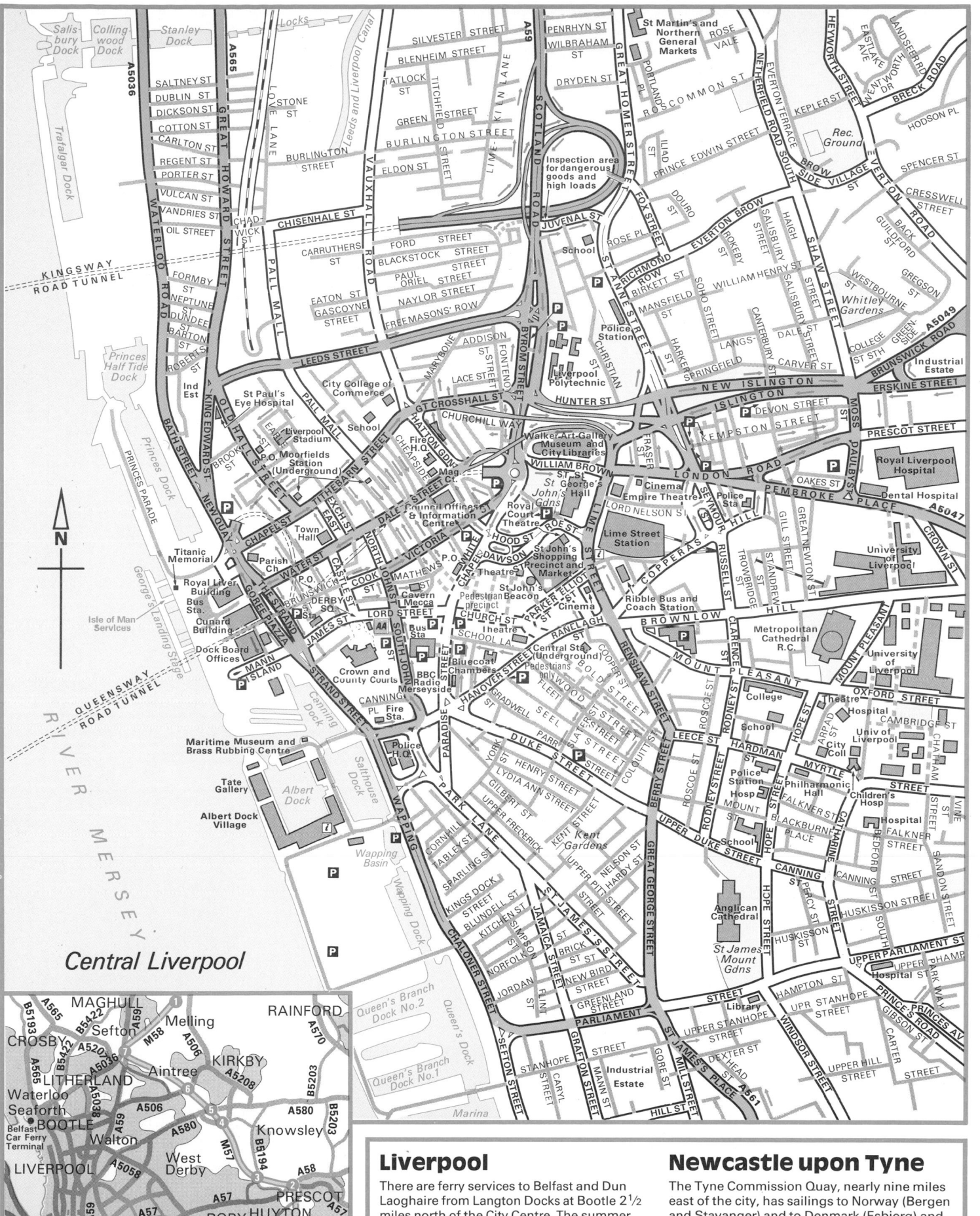

## Central Liverpool

## Liverpool

There are ferry services to Belfast and Dun Laoghaire from Langton Docks at Bootle 2½ miles north of the City Centre. The summer service to the Isle of Man leaves from Pier Head in Liverpool. Free open air parking for 70 cars is available close to Langton Dock for travellers to Ireland. For travellers to the Isle of Man numerous public car parks and a garage are available in the city centre close to Pier Head, contact Mersey Docks & Harbour Co for details, Tel: 051-200 2020. There are two 4-star, two 3-star and two 2-star hotels in Liverpool.

## Newcastle upon Tyne

The Tyne Commission Quay, nearly nine miles east of the city, has sailings to Norway (Bergen and Stavanger) and to Denmark (Esbjerg) and to Sweden (Göteborg). Garage accommodation is normally available near the quay, but covered parking is scarce, particularly during the summer. Advance booking is necessary. Send applications to E J Turnbull & Son Ltd, Albion Road, North Shields, Tel: 091-257 1201 who have a collection and delivery service. Accommodation is available in 3-star hotels at Tynemouth or Wallsend. Other hotels are in Whitley Bay.

# Central Newcastle Upon Tyne

# Weymouth

Weymouth, which handles sailings to Cherbourg and the Channel Islands, provides garage facilities at Channel Ferry Car Parks, Tel: (0305) 783408. Open parking available for 600 cars. Collection and delivery service from the ferry terminal is free. Caravan Transit Service Tel: (0305) 783408 provides parking for caravanners arriving in Weymouth a day prior to shipping and on their return. Weymouth has seven 2-star hotels and one 1-star.

# Central Weymouth

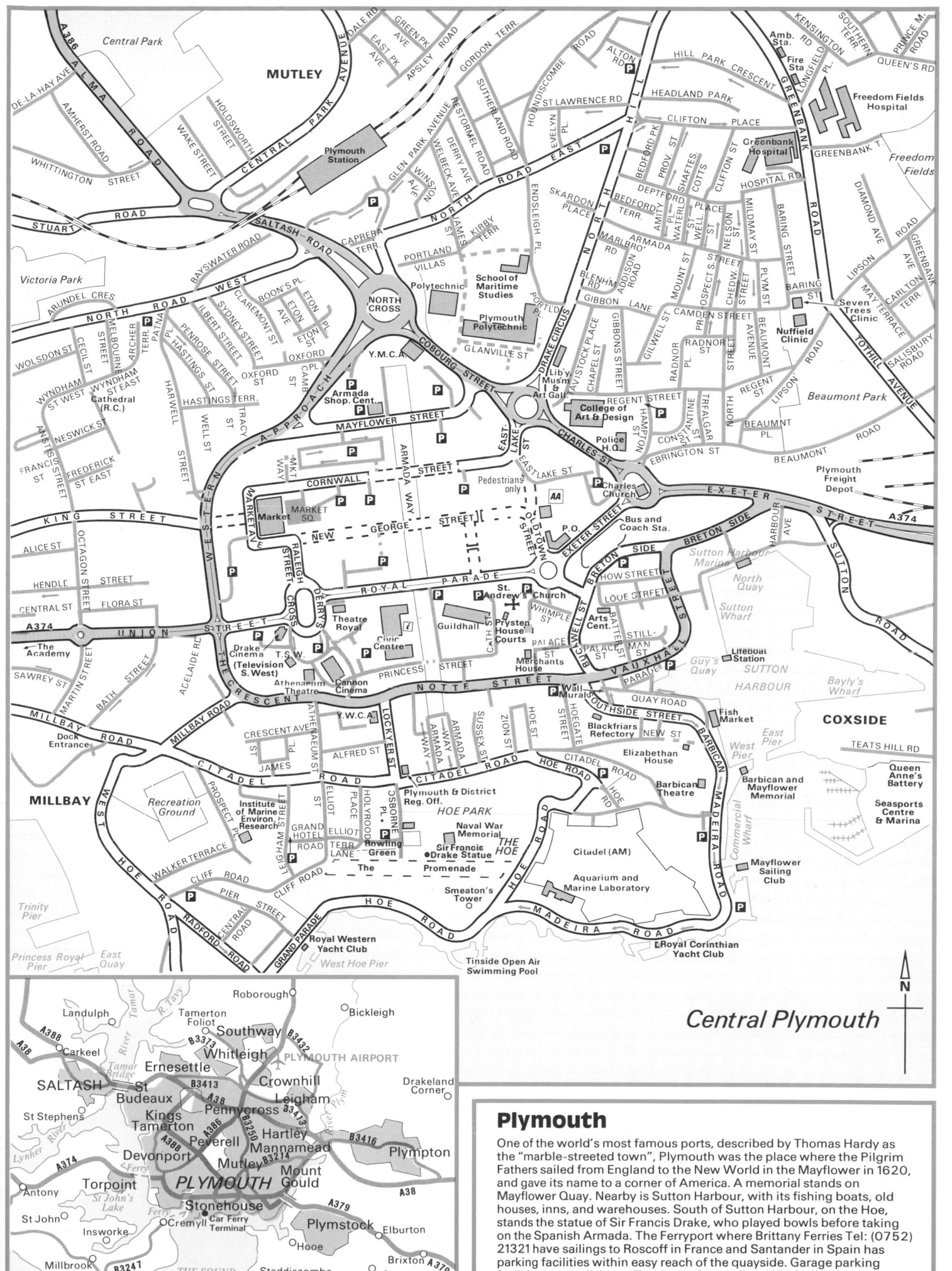

## Central Plymouth

N

## Plymouth

One of the world's most famous ports, described by Thomas Hardy as the "marble-streeted town", Plymouth was the place where the Pilgrim Fathers sailed from England to the New World in the Mayflower in 1620, and gave its name to a corner of America. A memorial stands on Mayflower Quay. Nearby is Sutton Harbour, with its fishing boats, old houses, inns, and warehouses. South of Sutton Harbour, on the Hoe, stands the statue of Sir Francis Drake, who played bowls before taking on the Spanish Armada. The Ferryport where Brittany Ferries Tel: (0752) 21321 have sailings to Roscoff in France and Santander in Spain has parking facilities within easy reach of the quayside. Garage parking facilities are available at Turnbull's Garage Tel: (0752) 667111, covered parking for six cars is one mile from the quay. There is also a collection and delivery service. Two 4-star, four 3-star, three 2-star and three 1-star hotels are near the Ferryport.

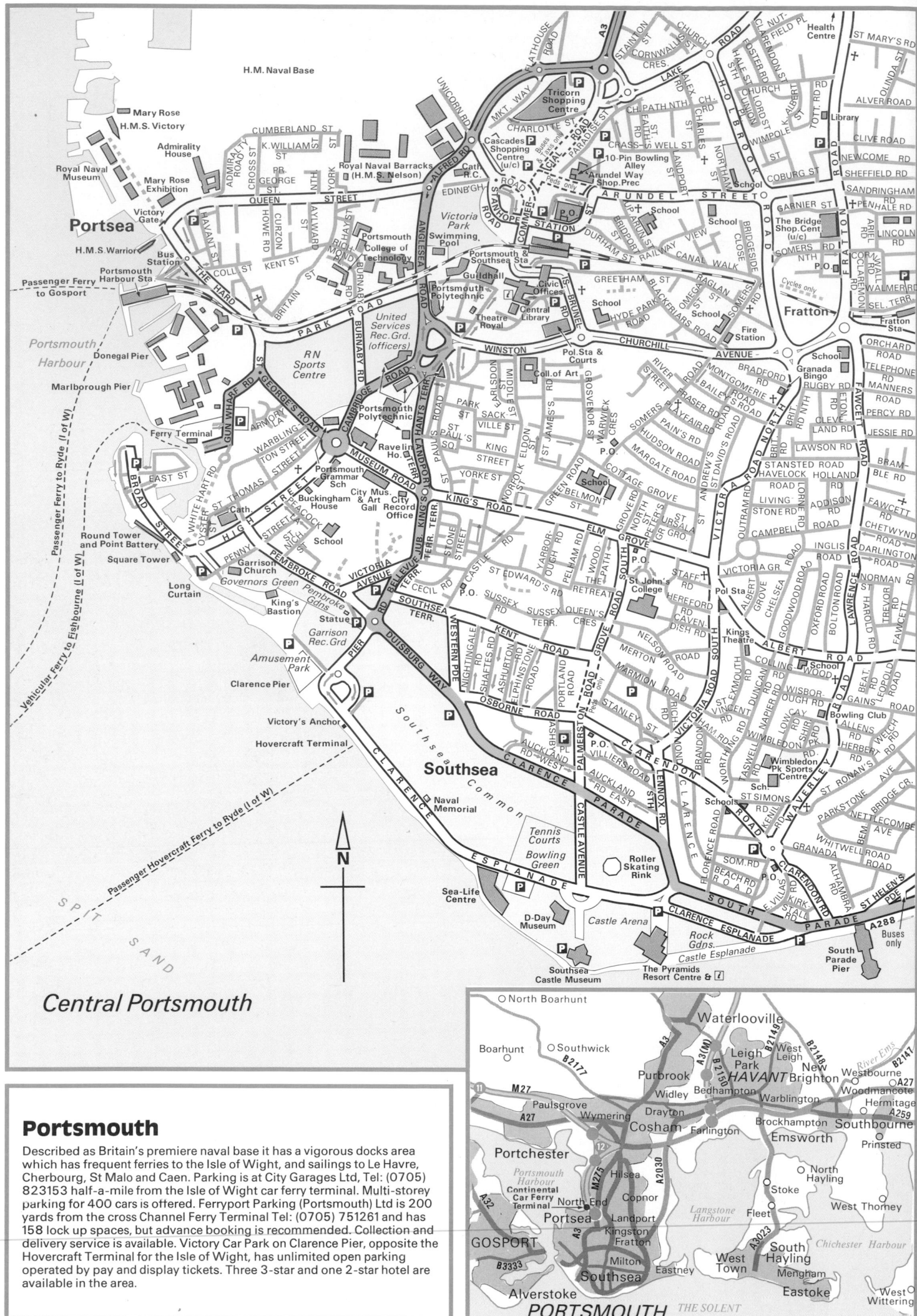

**Central Portsmouth**

# Portsmouth

Described as Britain's premiere naval base it has a vigorous docks area which has frequent ferries to the Isle of Wight, and sailings to Le Havre, Cherbourg, St Malo and Caen. Parking is at City Garages Ltd, Tel: (0705) 823153 half-a-mile from the Isle of Wight car ferry terminal. Multi-storey parking for 400 cars is offered. Ferryport Parking (Portsmouth) Ltd is 200 yards from the cross Channel Ferry Terminal Tel: (0705) 751261 and has 158 lock up spaces, but advance booking is recommended. Collection and delivery service is available. Victory Car Park on Clarence Pier, opposite the Hovercraft Terminal for the Isle of Wight, has unlimited open parking operated by pay and display tickets. Three 3-star and one 2-star hotel are available in the area.

188

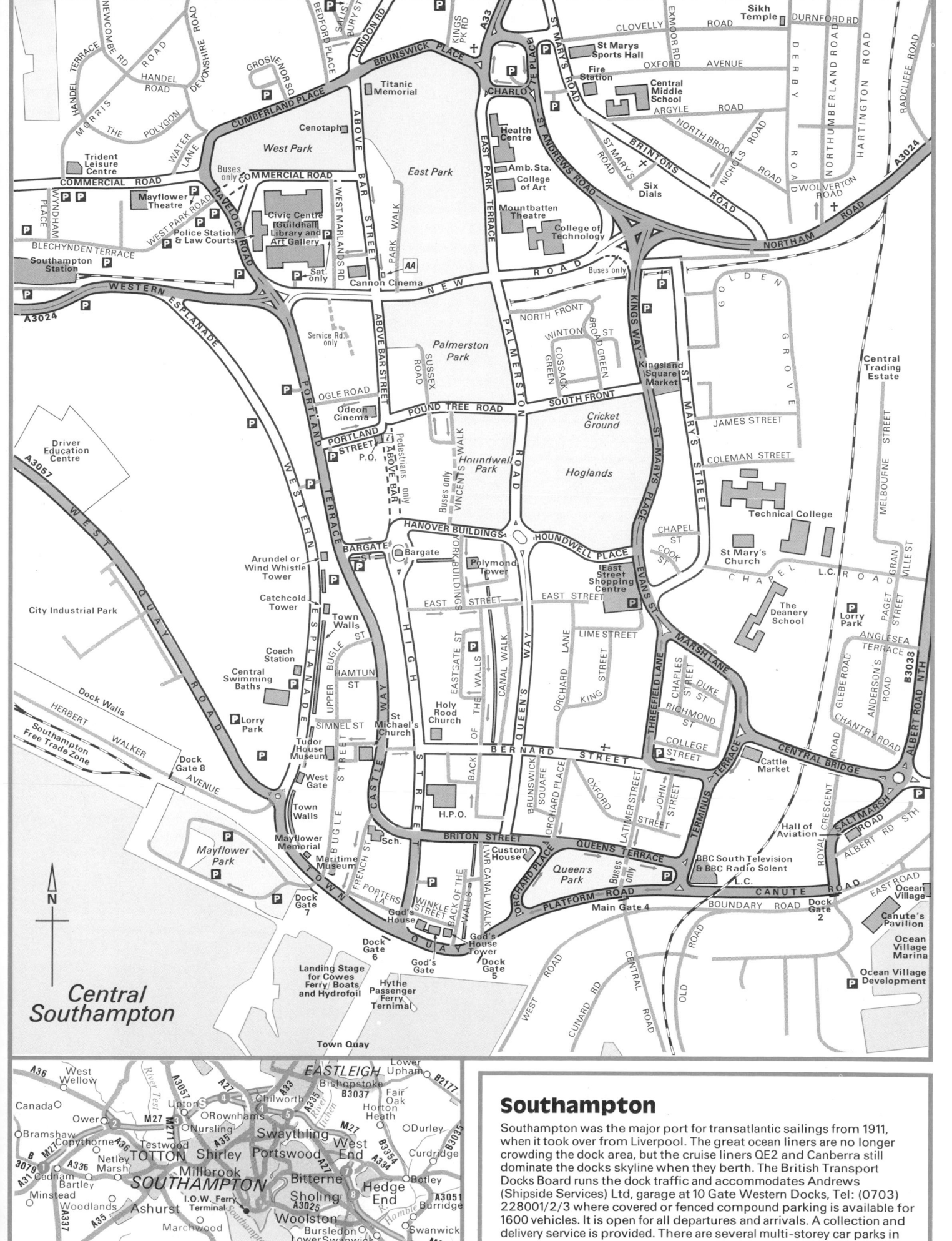

# Central Southampton

N

## Southampton

Southampton was the major port for transatlantic sailings from 1911, when it took over from Liverpool. The great ocean liners are no longer crowding the dock area, but the cruise liners QE2 and Canberra still dominate the docks skyline when they berth. The British Transport Docks Board runs the dock traffic and accommodates Andrews (Shipside Services) Ltd, garage at 10 Gate Western Docks, Tel: (0703) 228001/2/3 where covered or fenced compound parking is available for 1600 vehicles. It is open for all departures and arrivals. A collection and delivery service is provided. There are several multi-storey car parks in the city centre area. There are a number of AA-appointed hotels within a mile or so of the dock area, and these include four 3-star and one 2-star hotel.

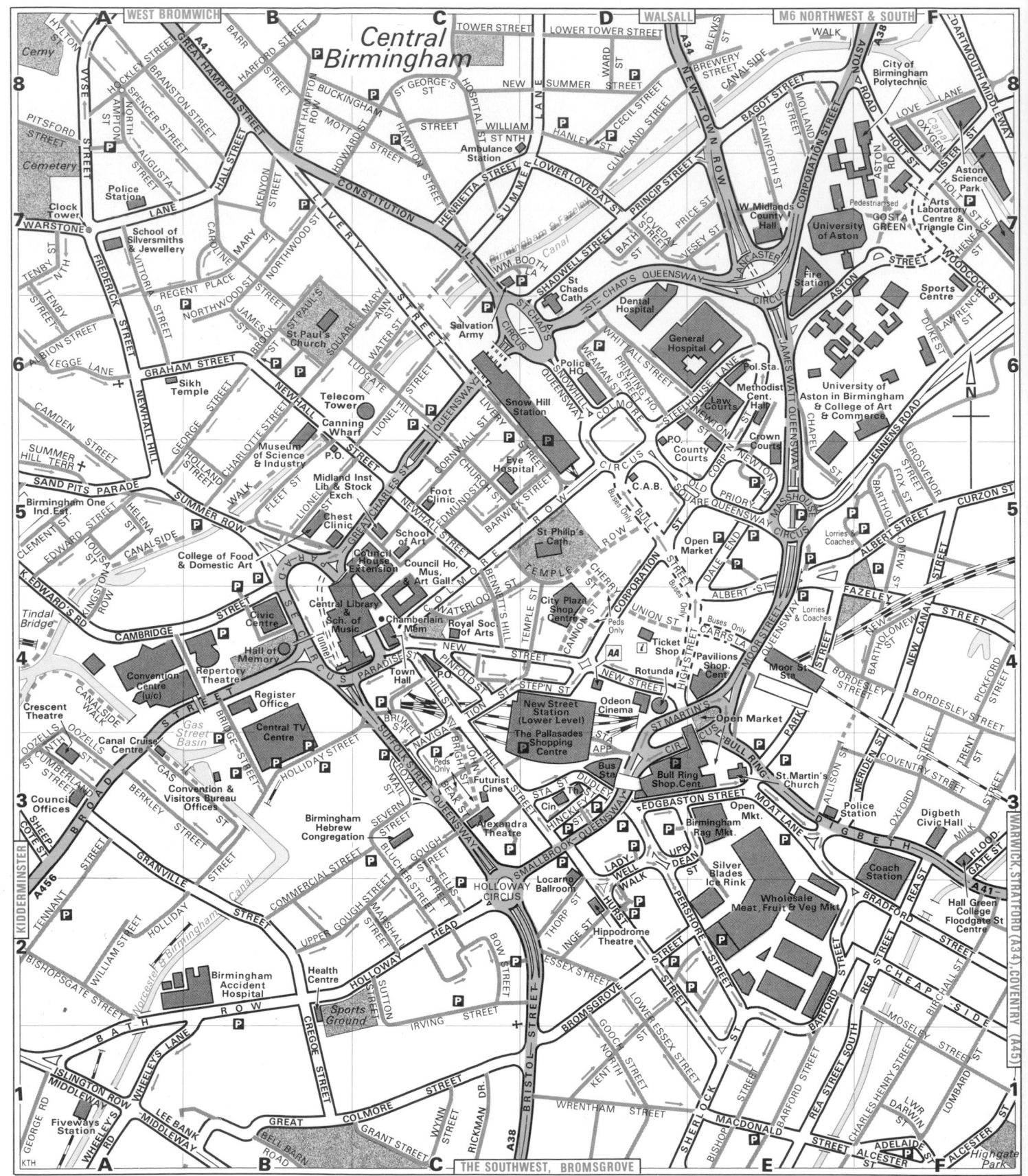

# Birmingham

It is very difficult to visualise Birmingham as it was before it began the growth which eventually made it the second-largest city in England. When the Romans were in Britain it was little more than a staging post on Icknield Street. Throughout medieval times it was a sleepy agricultural centre in the middle of a heavily-forested region. Timbered houses clustered together round a green that was eventually to be called the Bull Ring. But by the 16th century, although still a tiny and unimportant village by today's standards, it had begun to gain a reputation as a manufacturing centre. Tens of thousands of sword blades were made here during the Civil War. Throughout the 18th century more and more land was built on. In 1770 the Birmingham Canal was completed, making trade very much easier and increasing the town's development dramatically. All of that pales into near insignificance compared with what happened in the 19th century. Birmingham was not represented in Parliament until 1832 and had no town council until 1838. Yet by 1889 it had already been made a city, and after only another 20 years it had become the second largest city in England. Many of Birmingham's most imposing public buildings date from the 19th century, when the city was growing so rapidly. Surprisingly, the city has more miles of waterway than Venice.

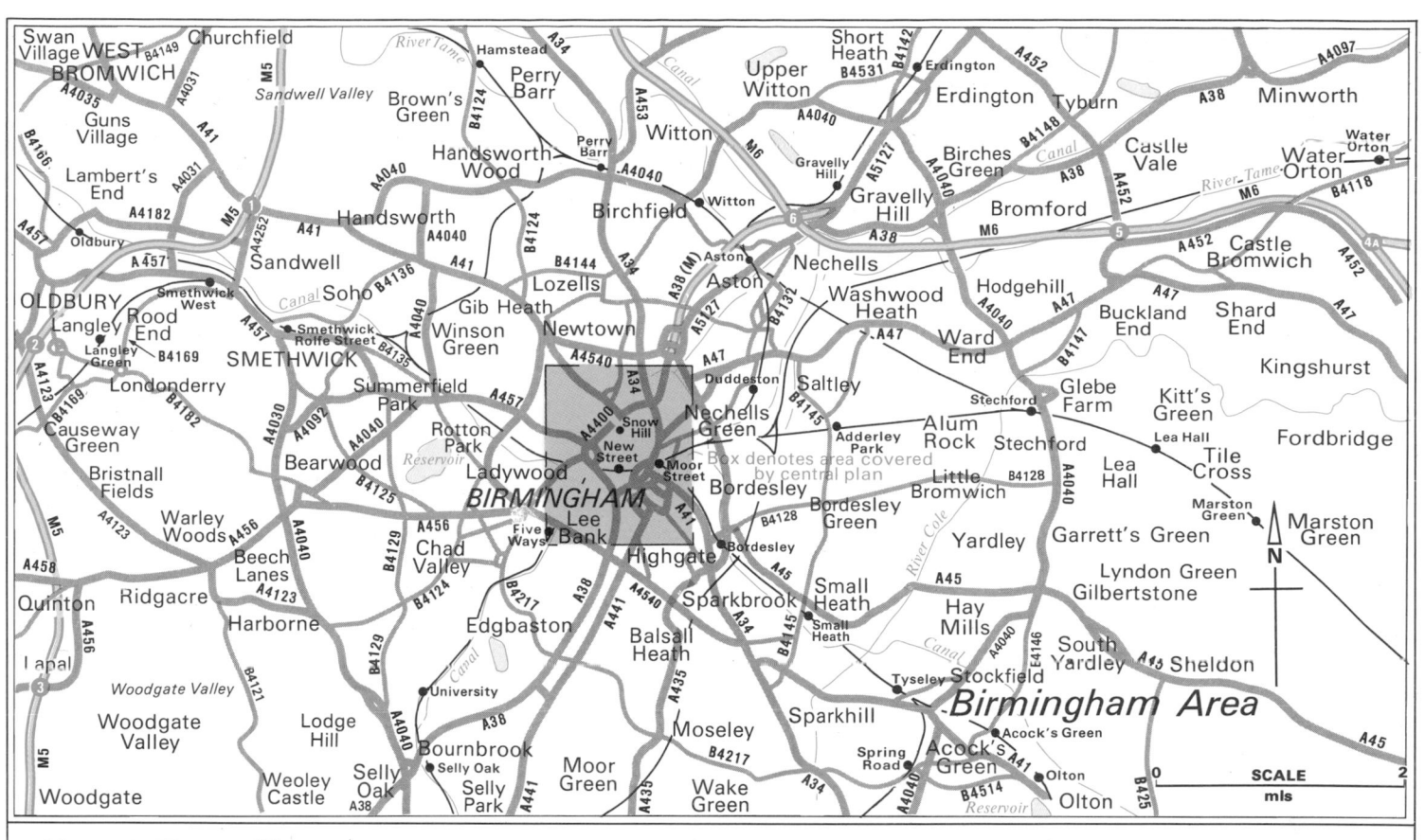

## Key to Town Plan and Area Plan

### Town Plan

| | |
|---|---|
| AA Recommended roads | |
| Restricted roads | |
| Other roads | |
| Buildings of interest | Station |
| One Way Streets | |
| Car Parks | P |
| Parks and open spaces | |
| Churches | + |

### Area Plan

| | |
|---|---|
| A roads | |
| B roads | |
| Locations | Meer End O |
| Urban area | |

## Street Index with Grid Reference

### Birmingham

| | |
|---|---|
| Adelaide Street | F1 |
| Albert Street | E4-E5-F5 |
| Albion Street | A6 |
| Alcester Street | F1 |
| Allison Street | E3 |
| Aston Road | F8-E8-F8-F7 |
| Aston Street | E6-E7-F7 |
| Augusta Street | A7-A8 |
| Bagot Street | E8 |
| Barford Street | E1-E2-F2 |
| Barr Street | B8 |
| Bartholomew Street | F4-F5 |
| Barwick Street | C5-D5 |
| Bath Row | A1-A2-B2 |
| Bath Street | D7 |
| Beak Street | C3 |
| Bell Barn Road | B1 |
| Bennett's Hill | C4-C5 |
| Berkley Street | A3-B3 |
| Birchall Street | F1-F2 |
| Bishop Street | E1 |
| Bishopsgate Street | A2 |
| Blews Street | E8 |
| Blucher Street | C2-C3 |
| Bordesley Street | E4-F4-F3 |
| Bow Street | C2 |
| Bradford Street | E3-E2-F2 |
| Branston Street | A8-B8-B7 |
| Brewery Street | E8 |
| Bridge Street | B3-B4 |
| Bristol Street | C1-D1-D2-C2 |
| Broad Street | A2-A3-A4-B4 |
| Bromsgrove Street | D1-D2-E2 |
| Brook Street | B6 |
| Brunel Street | C3-C4 |
| Buckingham Street | B8-C8 |
| Bull Ring | E3 |
| Bull Street | D5-E5-E4 |
| Cambridge Street | A4-B4-B5 |
| Camden Street | A5-A6 |
| Cannon Street | D4 |
| Caroline Street | B6-B7 |
| Carrs Lane | E4 |
| Cecil Street | D8 |
| Chapel Street | E5-E6 |
| Charles Henry Street | F1 |
| Charlotte Street | B5-B6 |
| Cheapside | F1 F2 |
| Cherry Street | D4-D5 |
| Church Street | C6-C5-D5 |
| Clement Street | A5 |
| Cleveland Street | D7-D8-E8 |
| Colmore Circus | D5-D6 |
| Colmore Row | C4-C5-D5 |
| Commercial Street | B2-B3-C3 |
| Constitution Hill | B7-C7 |
| Cornwall Street | C5-C6 |
| Corporation Street | D4-D5-E5-E6-E7-E8-F8 |
| Coventry Street | E3-F3 |
| Cregoe Street | B1-B2 |
| Cumberland Street | A3 |
| Curzon Street | F5 |
| Dale End | E4-E5 |
| Dartmouth Middleway | F7-F8 |
| Digbeth | E3-F3 |
| Dudley Street | D3 |
| Duke Street | F6 |
| Edgbaston Street | D3-E3 |
| Edmund Street | C5-D5 |
| Edward Street | A5 |
| Ellis Street | C2-C3 |
| Essex Street | D2 |
| Fazeley Street | E5-E4-F4 |
| Fleet Street | B5 |
| Floodgate Street | F3 |
| Fox Street | F5 |
| Frederick Street | A6-A7 |
| Gas Street | A3-B3 |
| George Road | A1 |
| George Street | A5-B5-B6 |
| Gooch Street North | D1-D2 |
| Gosta Green | F7 |
| Gough Street | C3 |
| Graham Street | A6-B6 |
| Grant Street | C1 |
| Granville Street | A3-A2-B2 |
| Great Charles St Queensway | B5-C5-C6 |
| Great Colmore Street | B1-C1-D1 |
| Great Hampton Row | B8 |
| Great Hampton Street | A8-B8 |
| Grosvenor Street | F5-F6 |
| Hall Street | B7-B8 |
| Hampton Street | C7-C8 |
| Harford Street | B8 |
| Hanley Street | D7-D8 |
| Helena Street | A5 |
| Heneage Street | F7 |
| Henrietta Street | C7-D7 |
| High Street | D4-E4 |
| Hill Street | C4-C3-D3 |
| Hinckley Street | D3 |
| Hockley Street | A8-B8 |
| Holland Street | B5 |
| Holliday Street | A2-B2-B3-C3-C4 |
| Holloway Circus | C2-C3-D3-D2 |
| Holloway Head | B2-C2 |
| Holt Street | F7-F8 |
| Hospital Street | C7-C8 |
| Howard Street | B7-C7-C8 |
| Hurst Street | D3-D2-E2-E1 |
| Hylton Street | A8 |
| Inge Street | D2 |
| Irving Street | C2-D2 |
| Islington Row Middleway | A1 |
| James Street | B6 |
| James Watt Queensway | E5-E6 |
| Jennens Road | E5-F5-F6 |
| John Bright Street | C3-C4 |
| Kent Street | D1-D2 |
| Kenyon Street | B7 |
| King Edward's Road | A4-A5 |
| Kingston Row | A4 |
| Ladywell Walk | D2-D3 |
| Lancaster Circus | E6-E7 |
| Lawrence Street | F6-F7 |
| Lee Bank Middleway | A1-B1 |
| Legge Lane | A6 |
| Lionel Street | B5-C5-C6 |
| Lister Street | F7-F8 |
| Livery Street | B7-C7-C6-D6-D5 |
| Lombard Street | F1-F2 |
| Louisa Street | A5 |
| Love Lane | F8 |
| Loveday Street | D7 |
| Lower Darwin Street | F1 |
| Lower Essex Street | D2-D1-E1 |
| Lower Loveday Street | D7 |
| Lower Tower Street | D8 |
| Ludgate Hill | B6-C6 |
| Macdonald Street | E1-F1 |
| Marshall Street | C2 |
| Mary Street | B7 |
| Mary Ann Street | C6-C7 |
| Masshouse Circus | E5 |
| Meriden Street | E3-F3 |
| Milk Street | F3 |
| Moat Lane | E3 |
| Molland Street | E8 |
| Moor Street Queensway | E4-E5 |
| Moseley Street | E2-F2-F1 |
| Mott Street | B8-C8-C7 |
| Navigation Street | C3-C4 |
| New Street | C4-D4 |
| New Bartholomew Street | F4 |
| New Canal Street | F4-F5 |
| Newhall Hill | A5-A6 |
| Newhall Street | B6-B5-C5 |
| New Summer Street | C8-D8 |
| Newton Street | E5 |
| New Town Row | D8-E8-E7 |
| Northampton Street | A8 |
| Northwood Street | B6-B7 |
| Old Square | D5-E5 |
| Oozells Street | A3-A4 |
| Oozells Street North | A3-A4 |
| Oxford Street | F3-F4 |
| Oxygen Street | F7-F8 |
| Paradise Circus | B4-B5 |
| Paradise Street | C4 |
| Park Street | E3-E4 |
| Pershore Street | D3-D2-E2 |
| Pickford Street | F4 |
| Pinfold Street | C4 |
| Pitsford Street | A8 |
| Price Street | D7-E7 |
| Princip Street | D7-E7-E8 |
| Printing House Street | D6 |
| Priory Queensway | E5 |
| Rea Street | E2-F2-F3 |
| Rea Street South | E1-F1-F2 |
| Regent Place | A7-B7 |
| Rickman Drive | C1 |
| Royal Mail Street | C3 |
| St Chad's Circus | C7-C6-D6 |
| St Chad's Queensway | D6-D7-E7 |
| St George's Street | C8 |
| St Martin's Circus | D3-D4-E4-E3 |
| St Paul's Square | B7-B6-C6 |
| Sand Pits Parade | A5 |
| Severn Street | C3 |
| Shadwell Street | D6-D7 |
| Sheepcote Street | A3 |
| Sherlock Street | D1-E1-E2 |
| Smallbrook Queensway | C3-D3 |
| Snow Hill Queensway | D6 |
| Spencer Street | A8-A7-B7 |
| Staniforth Street | E7-E8 |
| Station Approach | D3 |
| Station Street | D3 |
| Steelhouse Lane | D6-E6 |
| Stephenson Street | C4-D4 |
| Suffolk Street Queensway | B4-C4-C3 |
| Summer Hill Terrace | A5 |
| Summer Row | A5-B5 |
| Summer Lane | C7-D7-D8 |
| Sutton Street | C2 |
| Temple Row | C5-D5 |
| Temple Street | D4-D5 |
| Tenby Street | A6-A7 |
| Tenby Street North | A7 |
| Tennant Street | A2-A3 |
| Thorp Street | D2-D3 |
| Tower Street | C8-D8 |
| Trent Street | F3-F4 |
| Union Street | D4 |
| Upper Dean Street | D3-E3 |
| Upper Gough Street | B2-C2-C3 |
| Vesey Street | D7-E7 |
| Vittoria Street | A6-A7 |
| Vyse Street | A7-A8 |
| Ward Street | D8 |
| Warstone Lane | A7-B7 |
| Water Street | C6 |
| Waterloo Street | C4-C5-D5 |
| Weaman Street | D6 |
| Wheeley's Lane | A1-B1-B2 |
| Wheeley's Road | A1 |
| Whittall Street | D6-E6 |
| William Booth Lane | C7-D7 |
| William Street | A2 |
| William Street North | C8-D8 |
| Woodcock Street | F6-F7 |
| Wrentham Street | D1-E1 |
| Wynn Street | C1 |

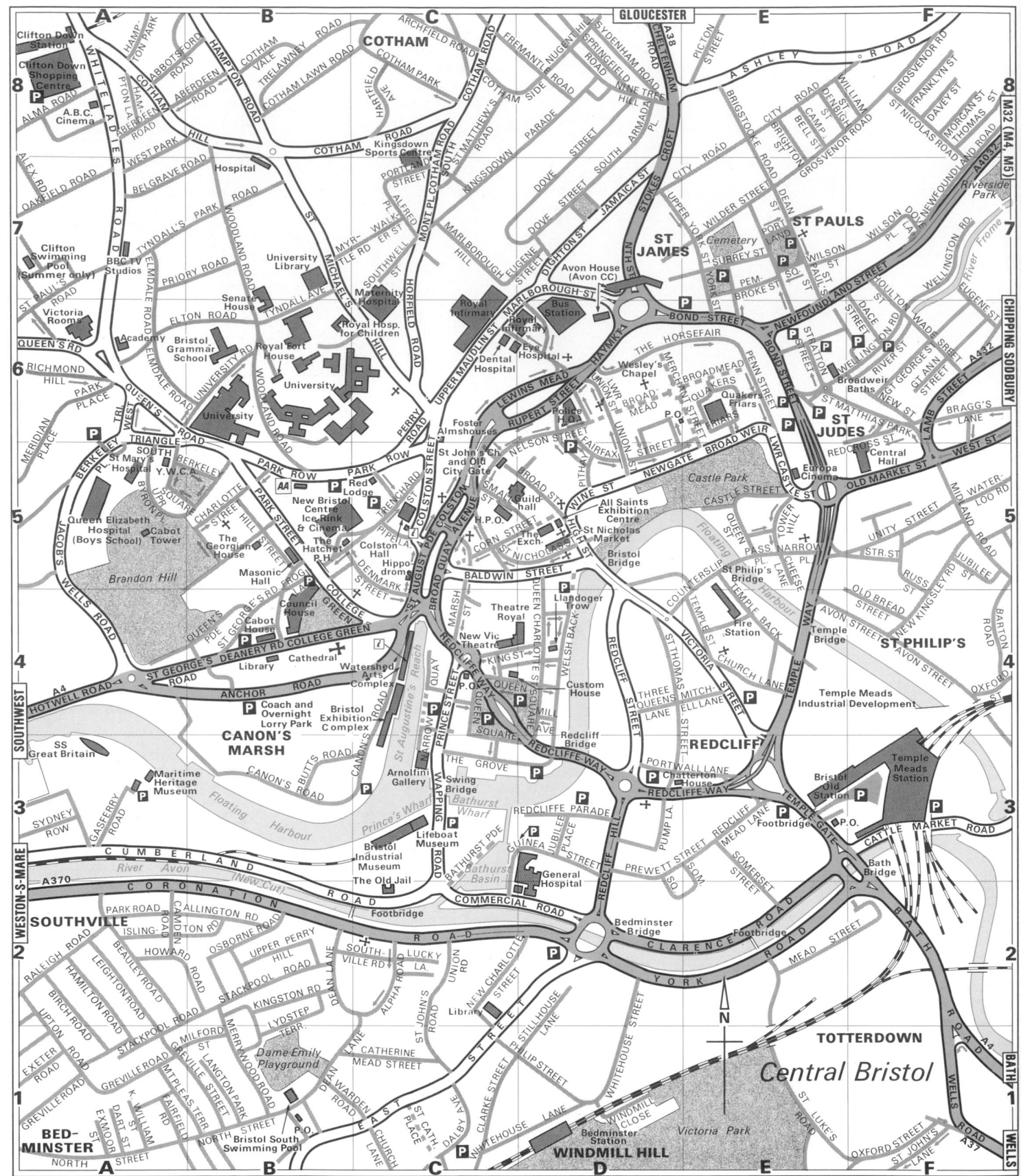

*Central Bristol*

# Bristol

One of Britain's most historic seaports, Bristol retains many of its visible links with the past, despite terrible damage inflicted during bombing raids in World War II. Most imposing is the cathedral, founded as an abbey church in 1140. Perhaps even more famous than the cathedral is the Church of St Mary Redcliffe. Ranking among the finest churches in the country, it owes much of its splendour to 14th- and 15th-century merchants who bestowed huge sums of money on it.

The merchant families brought wealth to the whole of Bristol, and their trading links with the world are continued in today's modern aerospace and technological industries. Much of the best of Bristol can be seen in the area of the Floating Harbour – an arm of the Avon. Several of the old warehouses have been converted into museums, galleries and exhibition centres. Among them are genuinely picturesque old pubs, the best-known of which is the Llandoger Trow. It is a timbered 17th-century house, the finest of its kind in Bristol. Further up the same street – King Street – is the Theatre Royal, built in 1766 and the oldest theatre in the country. In Corn Street, the heart of the business area, is a magnificent 18th-century corn exchange. In front of it are the four pillars known as the 'nails', on which merchants used to make cash transactions, hence 'to pay on the nail'.

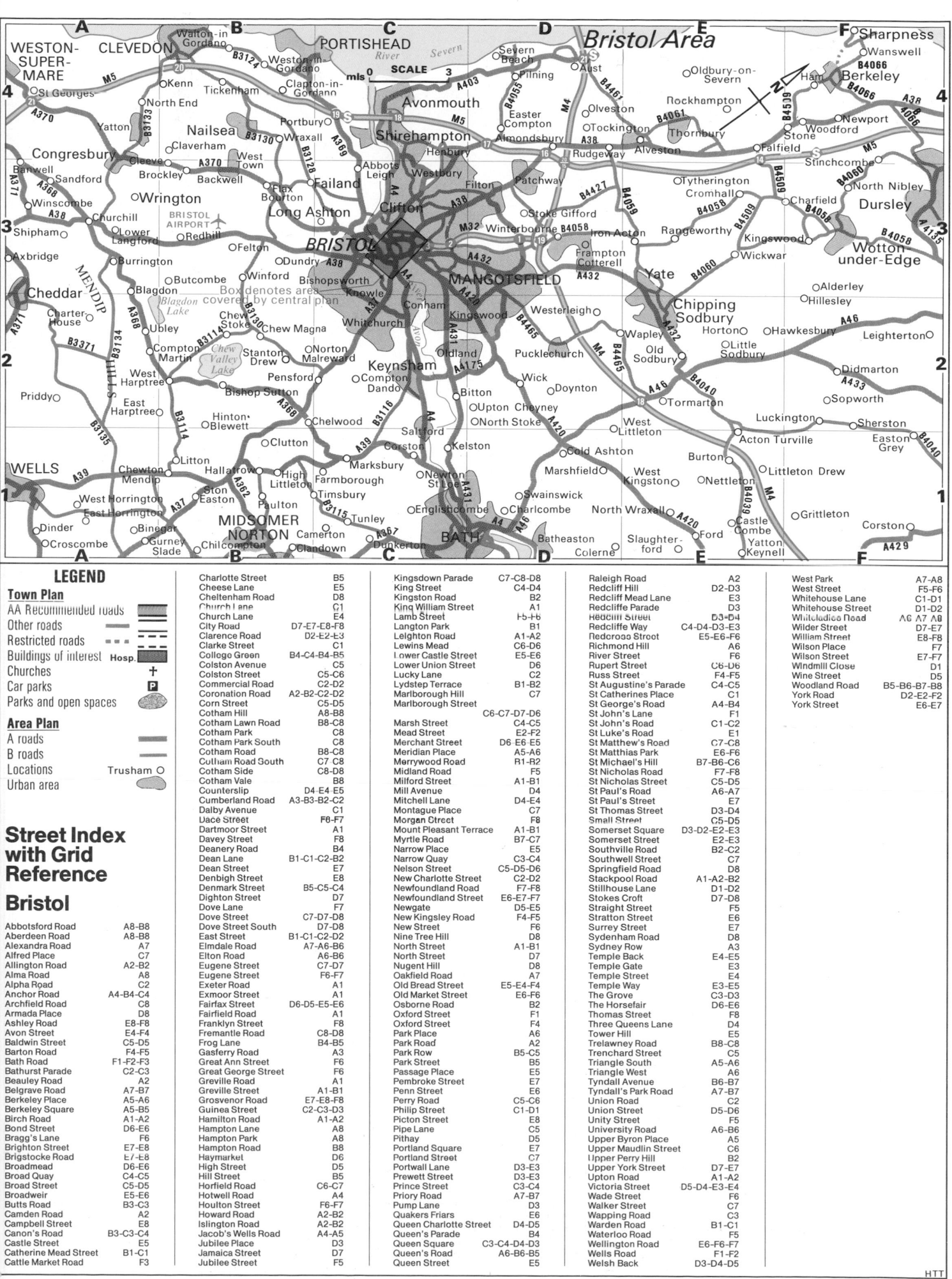

## LEGEND

**Town Plan**
- AA Recommended roads
- Other roads
- Restricted roads
- Buildings of interest  **Hosp.**
- Churches †
- Car parks P
- Parks and open spaces

**Area Plan**
- A roads
- B roads
- Locations  Trusham ○
- Urban area

# Street Index with Grid Reference

## Bristol

|  |  |
|---|---|
| Abbotsford Road | A8-B8 |
| Aberdeen Road | A8-B8 |
| Alexandra Road | A7 |
| Alfred Place | C7 |
| Allington Road | A2-B2 |
| Alma Road | A8 |
| Alpha Road | C2 |
| Anchor Road | A4-B4-C4 |
| Archfield Road | C8 |
| Armada Place | D8 |
| Ashley Road | E8-F8 |
| Avon Street | E4-F4 |
| Baldwin Street | C5-D5 |
| Barton Road | F4-F5 |
| Bath Road | F1-F2-F3 |
| Bathurst Parade | C2-C3 |
| Beauley Road | A2 |
| Belgrave Road | A7-B7 |
| Berkeley Place | A5-A6 |
| Berkeley Square | A5-B5 |
| Birch Road | A1-A2 |
| Bond Street | D6-E6 |
| Bragg's Lane | F6 |
| Brighton Street | E7-E8 |
| Brigstocke Road | E7-E8 |
| Broadmead | D6-E6 |
| Broad Quay | C4-C5 |
| Broad Street | C5-D5 |
| Broadweir | E5-E6 |
| Butts Road | B3-C3 |
| Camden Road | A2 |
| Campbell Street | E8 |
| Canon's Road | B3-C3-C4 |
| Castle Street | E5 |
| Catherine Mead Street | B1-C1 |
| Cattle Market Road | F3 |
| Charlotte Street | B5 |
| Cheese Lane | E5 |
| Cheltenham Road | D8 |
| Church Lane | C1 |
| Church Lane | E4 |
| City Road | D7-E7-E8-F8 |
| Clarence Road | D2-E2-E3 |
| Clarke Street | C1 |
| College Green | B4-C4-B4-B5 |
| Colston Avenue | C5 |
| Colston Street | C5-C6 |
| Commercial Road | C2-D2 |
| Coronation Road | A2-B2-C2-D2 |
| Corn Street | C5-D5 |
| Cotham Hill | A8-B8 |
| Cotham Lawn Road | B8-C8 |
| Cotham Park | C8 |
| Cotham Park South | C8 |
| Cotham Road | B8-C8 |
| Cotham Road South | C7-C8 |
| Cotham Side | C8-D8 |
| Cotham Vale | B8 |
| Counterslip | D4-E4-E5 |
| Cumberland Road | A3-B3-B2-C2 |
| Dalby Avenue | C1 |
| Dace Street | F6-F7 |
| Dartmoor Street | A1 |
| Davey Street | F8 |
| Deanery Road | B4 |
| Dean Lane | B1-C1-C2-B2 |
| Dean Street | E7 |
| Denbigh Street | E8 |
| Denmark Street | B5-C5-C4 |
| Dighton Street | D7 |
| Dove Lane | F7 |
| Dove Street | C7-D7-D8 |
| Dove Street South | D7-D8 |
| East Street | B1-C1-C2-D2 |
| Elmdale Road | A7-A6-B6 |
| Elton Road | A6-B6 |
| Eugene Street | C7-D7 |
| Eugene Street | F6-F7 |
| Exeter Road | A1 |
| Exmoor Street | A1 |
| Fairfax Street | D6-D5-E5-E6 |
| Fairfield Road | A1 |
| Franklyn Street | F8 |
| Fremantle Road | C8-D8 |
| Frog Lane | B4-B5 |
| Gasferry Road | A3 |
| Great Ann Street | F6 |
| Great George Street | F6 |
| Greville Road | A1 |
| Greville Road | A1-B1 |
| Grosvenor Road | E7-E8-F8 |
| Guinea Street | C2-C3-D3 |
| Hamilton Road | A1-A2 |
| Hampton Lane | A8 |
| Hampton Park | A8 |
| Hampton Road | B8 |
| Haymarket | D6 |
| High Street | D5 |
| Hill Street | B5 |
| Horfield Road | C6-C7 |
| Hotwell Road | A4 |
| Houlton Street | F6-F7 |
| Howard Road | A2-B2 |
| Islington Road | A2-B2 |
| Jacob's Wells Road | A4-A5 |
| Jubilee Place | D3 |
| Jamaica Street | D7 |
| Jubilee Street | F5 |
| Kingsdown Parade | C7-C8-D8 |
| King Street | C4-D4 |
| Kingston Road | B2 |
| King William Street | A1 |
| Lamb Street | F5-F6 |
| Langton Park | B1 |
| Leighton Road | A1-A2 |
| Lewins Mead | C6-D6 |
| Lower Castle Street | E5-E6 |
| Lower Union Street | D6 |
| Lucky Lane | C2 |
| Lydstep Terrace | B1-B2 |
| Marlborough Hill | C7 |
| Marlborough Street | C6-C7-D7-D6 |
| Marsh Street | C4-C5 |
| Mead Street | E2-F2 |
| Merchant Street | D6-E6-E5 |
| Meridian Place | A5-A6 |
| Merrywood Road | B1-B2 |
| Midland Road | F5 |
| Milford Street | A1-B1 |
| Mill Avenue | D4 |
| Mitchell Lane | D4-E4 |
| Montague Place | C7 |
| Morgan Street | F8 |
| Mount Pleasant Terrace | A1-B1 |
| Myrtle Road | B7-C7 |
| Narrow Place | E5 |
| Narrow Quay | C3-C4 |
| Nelson Street | C5-D5-D6 |
| New Charlotte Street | C2-D2 |
| Newfoundland Road | F7-F8 |
| Newfoundland Street | E6-E7-F7 |
| Newgate | D5-E5 |
| New Kingsley Road | F4-F5 |
| New Street | F6 |
| Nine Tree Hill | D8 |
| North Street | A1-B1 |
| North Street | D7 |
| Nugent Hill | D8 |
| Oakfield Road | A7 |
| Old Bread Street | E5-E4-F4 |
| Old Market Street | E6-F6 |
| Osborne Road | B2 |
| Oxford Street | F1 |
| Oxford Street | F4 |
| Park Place | A6 |
| Park Road | A2 |
| Park Row | B5-C5 |
| Park Street | B5 |
| Passage Place | E5 |
| Pembroke Street | E7 |
| Penn Street | E6 |
| Perry Road | C5-C6 |
| Philip Street | C1-D1 |
| Picton Street | E8 |
| Pipe Lane | C5 |
| Pithay | D5 |
| Portland Square | E7 |
| Portland Street | C7 |
| Portwall Lane | D3-E3 |
| Prewett Street | D3-E3 |
| Prince Street | C3-C4 |
| Priory Road | A7-B7 |
| Pump Lane | D3 |
| Quakers Friars | E6 |
| Queen Charlotte Street | D4-D5 |
| Queen's Parade | B4 |
| Queen Square | C3-C4-D4-D3 |
| Queen's Road | A6-B6-B5 |
| Queen Street | E5 |
| Raleigh Road | A2 |
| Redcliff Hill | D2-D3 |
| Redcliff Mead Lane | E3 |
| Redcliffe Parade | D3 |
| Redcliff Street | D3-D4 |
| Redcliffe Way | C4-D4-D3-E3 |
| Redcross Street | E5-E6-F6 |
| Richmond Hill | A6 |
| River Street | F6 |
| Rupert Street | C6-D6 |
| Russ Street | F4-F5 |
| St Augustine's Parade | C4-C5 |
| St Catherines Place | C1 |
| St George's Road | A4-B4 |
| St John's Lane | F1 |
| St John's Road | C1-C2 |
| St Luke's Road | E1 |
| St Matthew's Road | C7-C8 |
| St Matthias Park | E6-F6 |
| St Michael's Hill | B7-B6-C6 |
| St Nicholas Road | F7-F8 |
| St Nicholas Street | C5-D5 |
| St Paul's Road | A6-A7 |
| St Paul's Street | E7 |
| St Thomas Street | D3-D4 |
| Small Street | C5-D5 |
| Somerset Square | D3-D2-E2-E3 |
| Somerset Street | E2-E3 |
| Southville Road | B2-C2 |
| Southwell Street | C7 |
| Springfield Road | D8 |
| Stackpool Road | A1-A2-B2 |
| Stillhouse Lane | D1-D2 |
| Stokes Croft | D7-D8 |
| Straight Street | F5 |
| Stratton Street | E6 |
| Surrey Street | E7 |
| Sydenham Road | D8 |
| Sydney Row | A3 |
| Temple Back | E4-E5 |
| Temple Gate | E3 |
| Temple Street | E4 |
| Temple Way | E3-E5 |
| The Grove | C3-D3 |
| The Horsefair | D6-E6 |
| Thomas Street | F8 |
| Three Queens Lane | D4 |
| Tower Hill | E5 |
| Trelawney Road | B8-C8 |
| Trenchard Street | C5 |
| Triangle South | A5-A6 |
| Triangle West | A6 |
| Tyndall Avenue | B6-B7 |
| Tyndall's Park Road | A7-B7 |
| Union Road | C2 |
| Union Street | D5-D6 |
| Unity Street | F5 |
| University Road | A6-B6 |
| Upper Byron Place | A5 |
| Upper Maudlin Street | C6 |
| Upper Perry Hill | B2 |
| Upper York Street | D7-E7 |
| Upton Road | A1-A2 |
| Victoria Road | D5-D4-E3-E4 |
| Wade Street | F6 |
| Walker Street | C7 |
| Wapping Road | C3 |
| Warden Road | B1-C1 |
| Waterloo Road | E6 |
| Wellington Road | E6-F6-F7 |
| Wells Road | F1-F2 |
| Welsh Back | D3-D4-D5 |
| West Park | A7-A8 |
| West Street | F5-F6 |
| Whitehouse Lane | C1-D1 |
| Whitehouse Street | D1-D2 |
| Whiteladies Road | A6-A7-A8 |
| Wilder Street | D7-E7 |
| William Street | E8-F8 |
| Wilson Place | F7 |
| Wilson Street | E7-F7 |
| Windmill Close | D1 |
| Wine Street | D5 |
| Woodland Road | B5-B6-B7-B8 |
| York Road | D2-E2-F2 |
| York Street | E6-E7 |

HTT

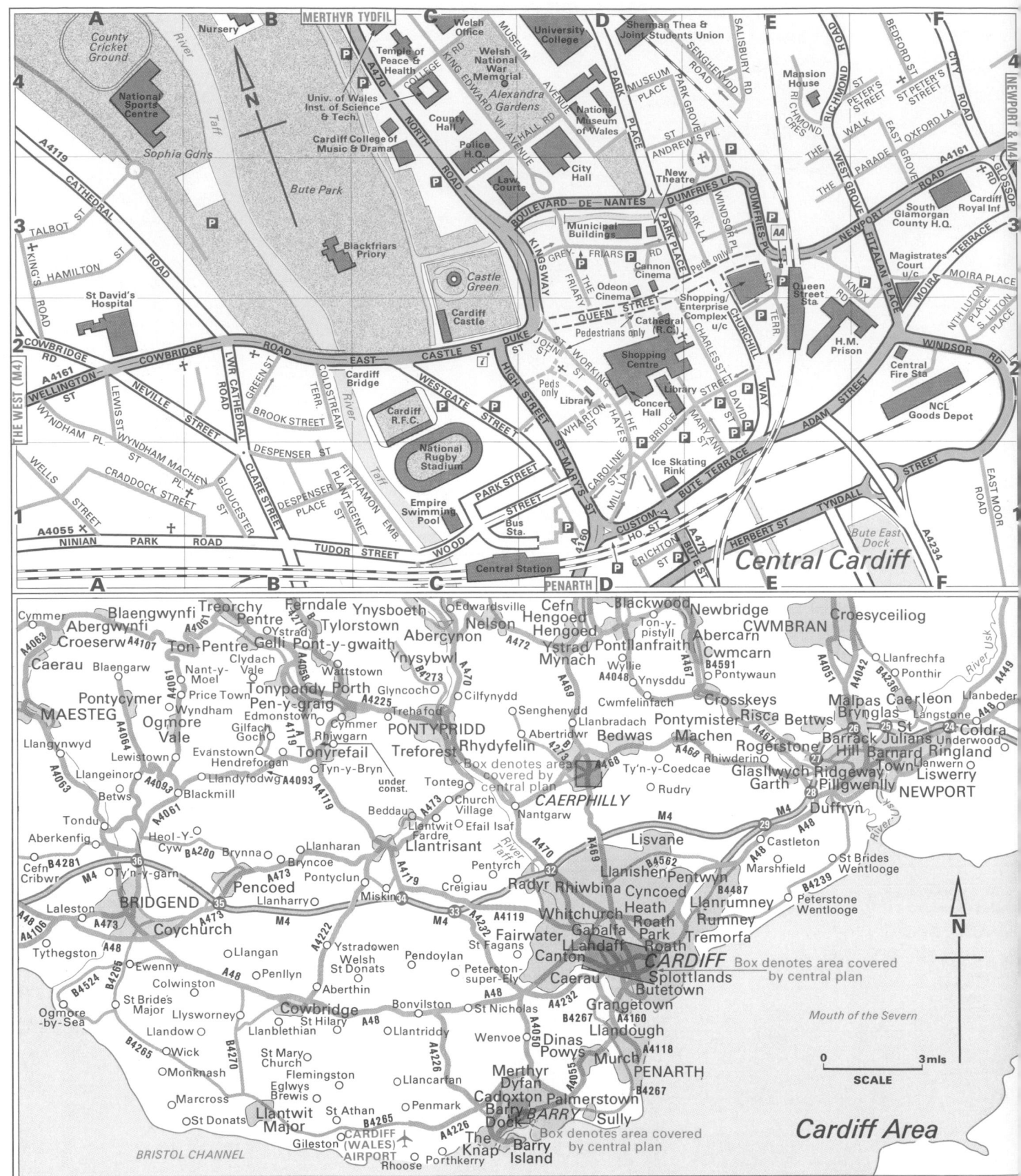

**Central Cardiff**

**Cardiff Area**

# Cardiff

Strategically important to both the Romans and the Normans, Cardiff slipped from prominence in medieval times and remained a quiet market town in a remote area until it was transformed – almost overnight – by the effects of the Industrial Revolution. The valleys of South Wales were a principal source of iron and coal – raw materials which helped to change the shape and course of the 19th-century world. Cardiff became a teeming export centre; by the end of the 19th century it was the largest coal-exporting city in the world.

Close to the castle – an exciting place with features from Roman times to the 19th century – is the city's civic centre – a fine concourse of buildings dating largely from the early part of the 20th century. Among them is the National Museum of Wales – a superb collection of art and antiquities from Wales and around the world.

**Barry** has sandy beaches, landscaped gardens and parks, entertainment arcades and funfairs. Like Cardiff it grew as a result of the demand for coal and steel, but now its dock complex is involved in the petrochemical and oil industries.

**Caerphilly** is famous for two things – a castle and cheese. The cheese is no longer made here, but the 13th-century castle, slighted by Cromwell, still looms above its moat. No castle in Britain – except Windsor – is larger.

194

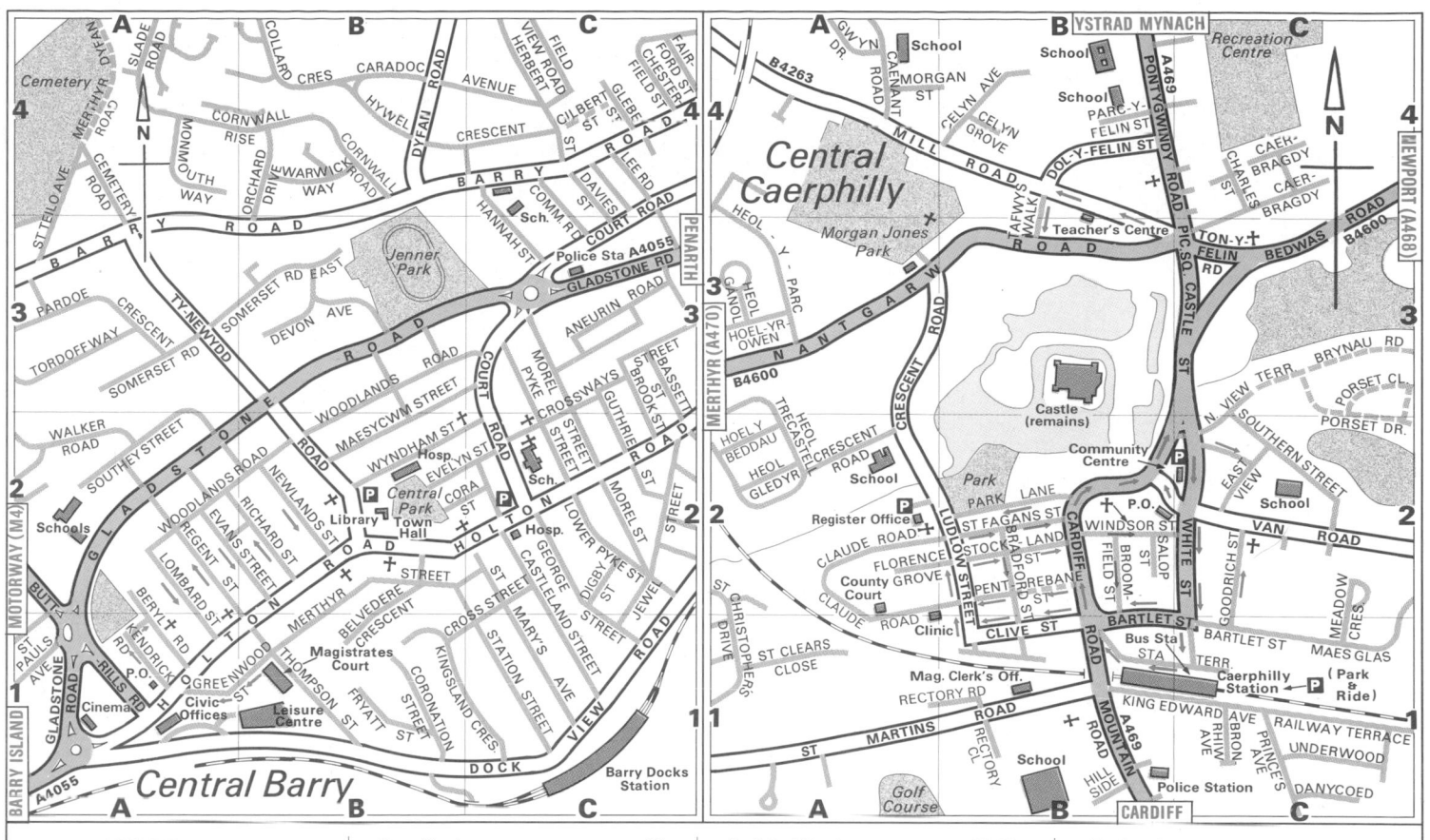

## LEGEND

**Town Plan**
AA recommended route
Restricted roads
Other roads
Buildings of interest    Cinema
Car parks    P
Parks and open spaces
One way streets
**Area Plan**
A roads
B roads
Locations    Glyncoch ◯
Urban area

## Street Index with Grid Reference

### Cardiff

| | |
|---|---|
| Adam Street | E1-E2-F2 |
| Bedford Street | F4 |
| Boulevard de Nantes | C3-D3 |
| Bridge Street | D1-D2-E2 |
| Brook Street | B2 |
| Bute Street | D1-E1 |
| Bute Terrace | D1-E1 |
| Caroline Street | D1 |
| Castle Street | C2 |
| Cathedral Street | A4-A3-B3-B2-A2 |
| Charles Street | D2-E2 |
| Churchill Way | E2-E3 |
| City Hall Road | C3-C4-D4 |
| City Road | F4 |
| Clare Street | B1 |
| Coldstream Terrace | B2 |
| College Road | C4 |
| Cowbridge Road | A2 |
| Cowbridge Road East | A2-B2-C2 |
| Craddock Street | A1-B1 |
| Crichton Street | D1 |
| Customhouse Street | D1 |
| David Street | E2 |
| Despenser Place | B1 |
| Despenser Street | B1 |
| Duke Street | C2-D2 |
| Dumfries Lane | D3-E3 |
| Dumfries Place | E3 |
| East Grove | F4-F3 |
| East Moor Road | F1 |
| Fitzalan Place | F3-F2 |
| Fitzhamon Embankment | B1-C1 |
| Glossop Road | F3 |
| Gloucester Street | B1 |
| Green Street | B2 |
| Greyfriars Road | D3 |
| Hamilton Street | A3 |
| Herbert Street | E1 |
| High Street | C2-D2 |
| King Edward VII Avenue | C4-D4-D3-C3 |
| King's Road | A2-A3 |
| Kingsway | C3-D3-D2 |
| Knox Road | E3-F3-F2 |
| Lewis Street | A2 |
| Lower Cathedral Road | B1-B2 |
| Machen Place | A1-B1 |
| Mary Ann Street | E1-E2 |
| Mill Lane | D1 |
| Moira Place | F3 |
| Moira Terrace | F2-F3 |
| Museum Avenue | C4-D4 |
| Museum Place | D4 |
| Neville Street | A2-B2-B1 |
| Newport Road | E3-F3-F4 |
| Ninian Park Road | A1-B1 |
| North Luton Place | F2-F3 |
| North Road | B4-C4-C3 |
| Oxford Lane | F4 |
| Park Grove | D4-E4 |
| Park Lane | D3-E3 |
| Park Place | D4-D3-E3 |
| Park Street | C1-D1 |
| Plantagenet Street | B1-C1 |
| Queen Street | D2-D3 |
| Richmond Crescent | E4 |
| Richmond Road | E4 |
| St Andrew's Place | D4-E4 |
| St John Street | D2 |
| St Mary's Street | D1-D2 |
| St Peter's Street | E4-F4 |
| Salisbury Road | E4 |
| Senghenydd Road | D4-E4 |
| South Luton Place | F2-F3 |
| Station Terrace | E2-E3 |
| The Friary | D2-D3 |
| The Hayes | D1-D2 |
| The Parade | E3-F3-F4 |
| The Walk | E3-E4-F4 |
| Talbot Street | A3 |
| Tudor Street | B1-C1 |
| Tyndall Street | E1-F1 |
| Wellington Street | A2 |
| Wells Street | A1 |
| Westgate Street | C2-D2-D1 |
| West Grove | E4-E3-F3 |
| Wharton Street | D2 |
| Windsor Place | E3 |
| Windsor Road | F2 |
| Wood Street | C1-D1 |
| Working Street | D2 |
| Wyndham Place | A2 |
| Wyndham Street | A1-A2 |

### Barry

| | |
|---|---|
| Aneurin Road | C3 |
| Barry Road | A3-A4-B3-B4-C4 |
| Bassett Street | C2-C3 |
| Belvedere Crescent | B1-B2 |
| Beryl Road | A1-A2 |
| Brook Street | C2-C3 |
| Buttrills Road | A1-A2 |
| Caradoc Avenue | B4-C4 |
| Castleland Street | C1-C2 |
| Cemetery Road | A3-A4 |
| Chesterfield Street | C4 |
| Collard Crescent | B4 |
| Commercial Road | C3-C4 |
| Cora Street | B2-C2 |
| Cornwall Rise | A3-A4 |
| Cornwall Road | B4 |
| Coronation Street | B1 |
| Cross Street | B1-C1-C2 |
| Crossways Street | C2-C3 |
| Court Road | C2-C3-C4 |
| Davies Street | C3-C4 |
| Devon Avenue | B3 |
| Digby Street | C2 |
| Dock View Road | B1-C1-C2 |
| Dyfan Road | B4 |
| Evans Street | A2-B2 |
| Evelyn Street | B2-C2 |
| Fairford Street | C4 |
| Field View Road | C4 |
| Fryatt Street | B1 |
| George Street | C1-C2 |
| Gilbert Street | C4 |
| Gladstone Road | A1-A2-B2-B3-C3 |
| Glebe Street | C4 |
| Greenwood Street | A1-B1 |
| Guthrie Street | C3-C2 |
| Hannah Street | C4-C3 |
| Herbert Street | C4 |
| Holton Road | A1-B1-B2-C2 |
| Hywel Crescent | B4-C4 |
| Jewel Street | C1-C2 |
| Kendrick Road | A1 |
| Kingsland Crescent | B1-C1 |
| Lee Road | C4 |
| Lombard Street | A1-A2 |
| Lower Pyke Street | C2 |
| Maesycwm Street | B2-B3-C3 |
| Merthyr Dyfan Road | A4 |
| Merthyr Street | B1-B2-C2 |
| Monmouth Way | A4 |
| Morel Street | C2-C3 |
| Newlands Street | B2 |
| Orchard Drive | B3-B4 |
| Pardoe Crescent | A3 |
| Pyke Street | C3-C2 |
| Regent Street | A2-B2 |
| Richard Street | A2-B2 |
| St Mary's Avenue | C1-C2 |
| St Pauls Avenue | A1 |
| St Teilo Avenue | A3-A4 |
| Slade Road | A4 |
| Somerset Road | A3 |
| Somerset Road East | A3-B3 |
| Southey Street | A2-A3 |
| Station Street | C1 |
| Thompson Street | B1 |
| Tordoff Way | A3 |
| Ty-Newydd Road | A3-B3-B2 |
| Walker Road | A2 |
| Warwick Way | B4 |
| Woodlands Road | A2-B2-B3-C3 |
| Wyndham Street | B2-C2 |

### Caerphilly

| | |
|---|---|
| Bartlet Street | B2-B1-C1 |
| Bedwas Road | C3-C4 |
| Bradford Street | D1-D2 |
| Broomfield Street | B2 |
| Bronrhiw Avenue | C1 |
| Brynau Road | C3 |
| Caenant Road | A4 |
| Caer Bragdy | C4 |
| Cardiff Road | B1-B2 |
| Castle Street | C3 |
| Celyn Avenue | B4 |
| Celyn Grove | B4 |
| Charles Street | C4 |
| Claude Road | A1-A2-B2 |
| Clive Street | B1-B2 |
| Crescent Rod | A2-A3-B3 |
| Danycoed | C1 |
| Davies Street | B4 |
| Dol-y-Felen Street | B4 |
| East View | C2 |
| Florence Grove | A2-B2 |
| Goodrich Street | C1-C2 |
| Gwyn Drive | A4 |
| Heol Ganol | A3 |
| Heol Gledyr | A2 |
| Heol Trecastell | A2-A3 |
| Hillside | B1 |
| Heol y Beddau | A2 |
| Heol-yr-Owen | A3 |
| King Edward Avenue | B1-C1 |
| Ludlow Street | A2-B2-B1 |
| Maes Glas | C1 |
| Meadow Crescent | C1-C2 |
| Mill Road | A4-B4-B3 |
| Morgan Street | A4-B4 |
| Mountain Road | B1 |
| Nantgarw Road | A3-B3 |
| North View Terrace | C2-C3 |
| Parc-y-Felin Street | B4 |
| Park Lane | B2 |
| Pentrebone Street | B2 |
| Piccadilly Square | B1 |
| Pontygwindy Road | B4-C4 |
| Porset Close | C3 |
| Porset Drive | C2-C3 |
| Prince's Avenue | C1 |
| Railway Terrace | C1 |
| Rectory Road | A1-B1 |
| Rectory Close | B1 |
| St Christopher's Drive | A1-A2 |
| St Clears Close | A1 |
| St Fagans Street | B2 |
| St Martins Road | A1-B1 |
| Salop Street | B2 |
| Southern Street | C2-C3 |
| Station Terrace | B1-C1 |
| Stockland Street | B2 |
| Tafwy Walk | B3-B4 |
| Ton-y-Felin Road | C3 |
| Underwood | C1 |
| Van Road | C2 |
| White Street | C2 |
| Windsor Street | B2 |

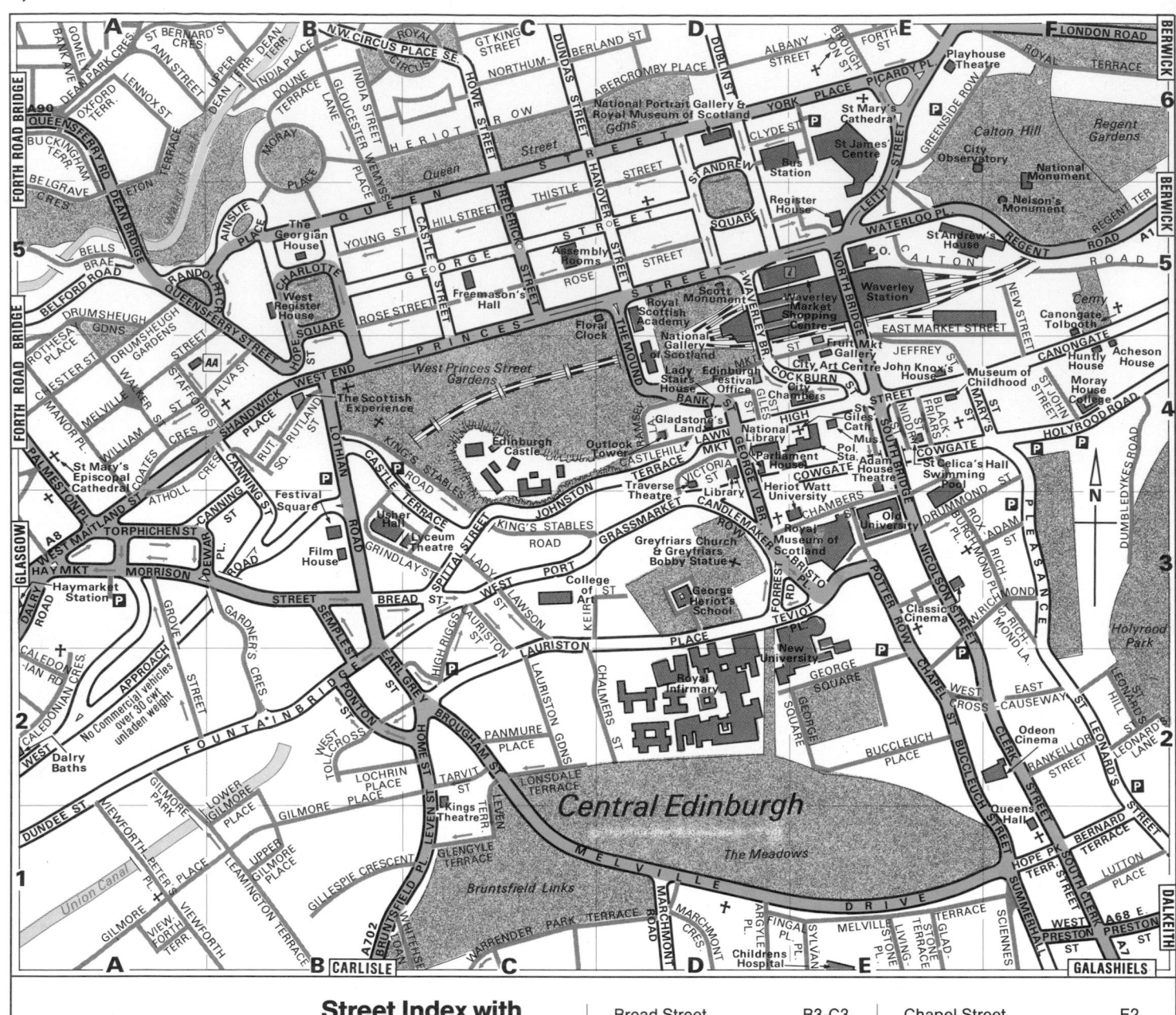

## Key to Town Plan and Area Plan

### Town Plan

| | |
|---|---|
| A A Recommended roads | ▬▬ |
| Other roads | ▬▬ |
| Restricted roads | ‑ ‑ ‑ |
| Buildings of intrest | Gallery ▬ |
| Car Parks | P |
| Parks and open spaces | ▒ |
| A A Service Centre | AA |
| Churches | + |

### Area Plan

| | |
|---|---|
| A roads | ▬▬ |
| B roads | ▬▬ |
| Locations | Newcraighall O |
| Urban area | ▒ |

## Street Index with Grid Reference

### Edinburgh

| | | | | | |
|---|---|---|---|---|---|
| Abercromby Place | C6-D6 | Bread Street | B3-C3 | Chapel Street | E2 |
| Adam Street | F3 | Bristo Place | D3-E3 | Chester Street | A4 |
| Ainslie Place | B5 | Brougham Street | C2 | Clerk Street | F1-F2 |
| Albany Street | D6-E6 | Broughton Street | E6 | Clyde Street | D6-E6 |
| Alva Street | A4-B4 | Bruntsfield Place | B1-C1 | Coates Crescent | A4-B4 |
| Ann Street | A6 | Buccleuch Place | E2 | Cockburn Street | D4-E4 |
| Argyle Place | D1 | Buccleauch Street | E2-F2-F1 | Comely Bank Avenue | A6 |
| Athol Crescent | A3-A4-B4 | Buckingham Terrace | A5-A6 | Cowgate | D4-E4-F4 |
| Bank Street | D4 | Caledonian Crescent | A2 | Dalry Road | A3 |
| Belford Road | A5 | Caledonian Road | A2 | Dean Bridge | A5 |
| Belgrave Crescent | A5 | Calton Road | E5-F5 | Dean Park Crescent | A6 |
| Bells Brae | A5 | Candlemaker Row | D3 | Dean Terrace | B6 |
| Bernard Terrace | F1 | Canning Street | A3-B3-B4 | Dewar Place | A3-B3 |
| Blackfriars Street | E4 | Canongate | E4-F4-F5 | Doune Terrace | B6 |
| | | Castle Hill | D4 | Drummond Street | E3-F3-F4 |
| | | Castle Street | C5 | Drumsheugh Gardens | A4-A5 |
| | | Castle Terrace | B4-B3-C3 | Dublin Street | D6 |
| | | Chalmers Street | C2-D2 | Dumbiedykes Road | F3-F4 |
| | | Chambers Street | D3-E3 | Dundas Street | C6 |
| | | Charlotte Square | B4-B5 | Dundee Street | A1-A2 |

# Edinburgh

Scotland's ancient capital, dubbed the "Athens of the North", is one of the most splendid cities in the whole of Europe. Its buildings, its history and its cultural life give it an international importance which is celebrated every year in its world-famous festival. The whole city is overshadowed by the craggy castle which seems to grow out of the rock itself. There has been a fortress here since the 7th century and most of the great figures of Scottish history have been associated with it. The old town grew up around the base of Castle Rock within the boundaries of the defensive King's Wall and, unable to spread outwards, grew upwards in a maze of tenements. However, during the 18th century new prosperity from the shipping trade resulted in the building of the New Town and the regular, spacious layout of the Georgian development makes a striking contrast with the old hotch-potch of streets. Princes Street is the main east-west thoroughfare with excellent shops on one side and Princes Street Gardens with their famous floral clock on the south side.

As befits such a splendid capital city there are numerous museums and art galleries packed with priceless treasures. Among these are the famous picture gallery in 16th-century Holyroodhouse, the present Royal Palace, and the fascinating and unusual Museum of Childhood.

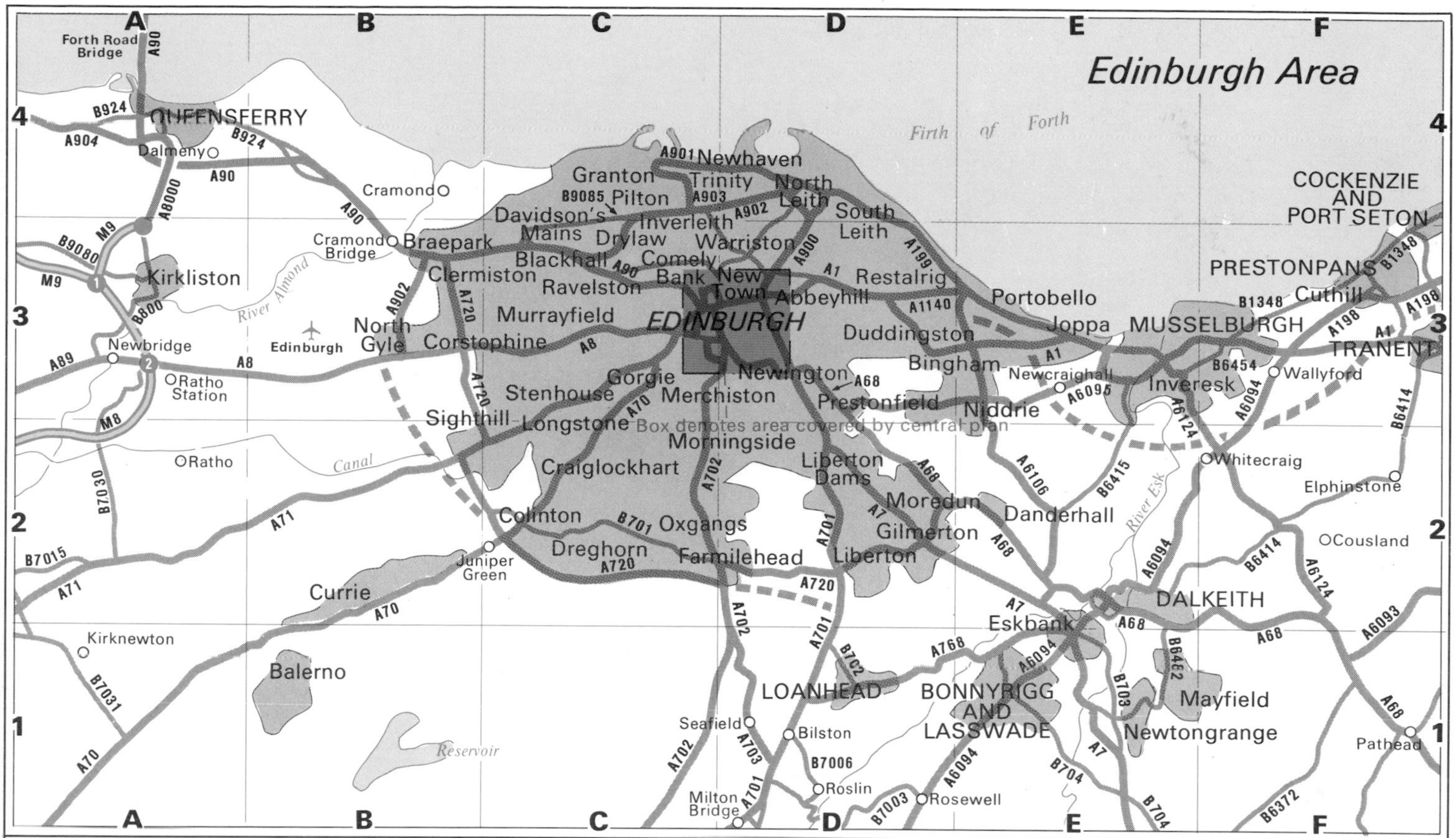

# Edinburgh Area

**EDINBURGH**
Holyrood Palace orginated as a guest house for the Abbey of Holyrood in the 16th century, but most of the present building was built for Charles II. Mary Queen of Scots was one of its most famous inhabitants.

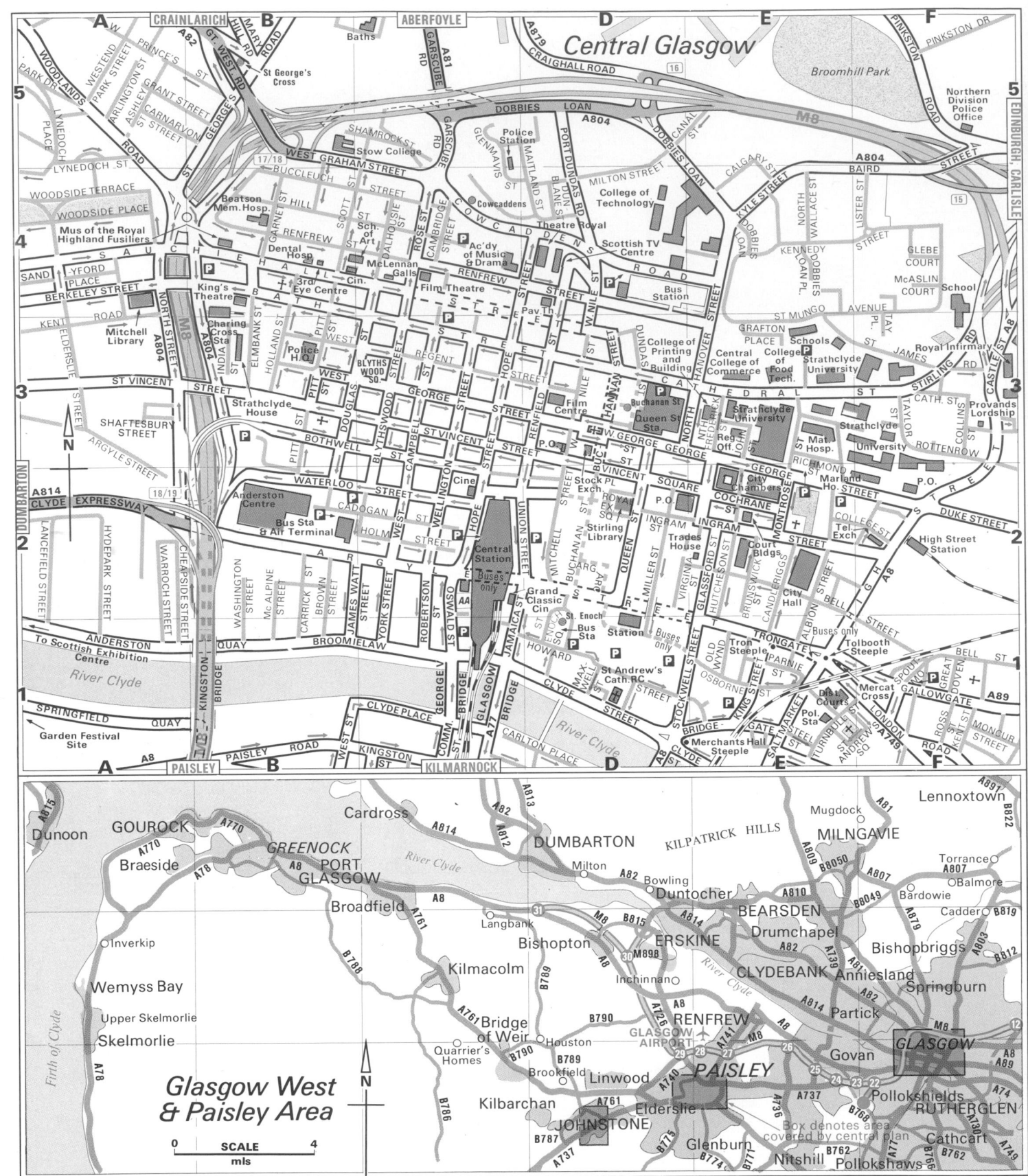

# Glasgow

Although much of Glasgow is distinctly Victorian in character, its roots go back very many centuries. Best link with the past is the cathedral; founded in the 6th century, it has features from many succeeding centuries, including an exceptional 13th-century crypt. Nearby is Provand's Lordship, the city's oldest house. It dates from 1471 and is now a museum. Two much larger museums are to be found a little out of the centre – the Art Gallery and Museum contains one of the finest collections of paintings in Britain, while the Hunterian Museum, attached to the University, covers geology, archaeology, ethnography and more general subjects. On Glasgow Green is People's Palace – a museum of city life. Most imposing of the Victorian buildings are the City Chambers and City Hall which was built in 1841 as a concert hall but now houses the Scottish National Orchestra.

*Paisley* is famous for the lovely fabric pattern to which it gives its name. It was taken from fabrics brought from the Near East in the early 19th century, and its manufacture, along with the production of thread, is still important. Coats Observatory is one of the best-equipped in the country.

*Johnstone* grew rapidly as a planned industrial town in the 19th century, but suffered from the effects of the Industrial Revolution. Today, engineering is the main industry.

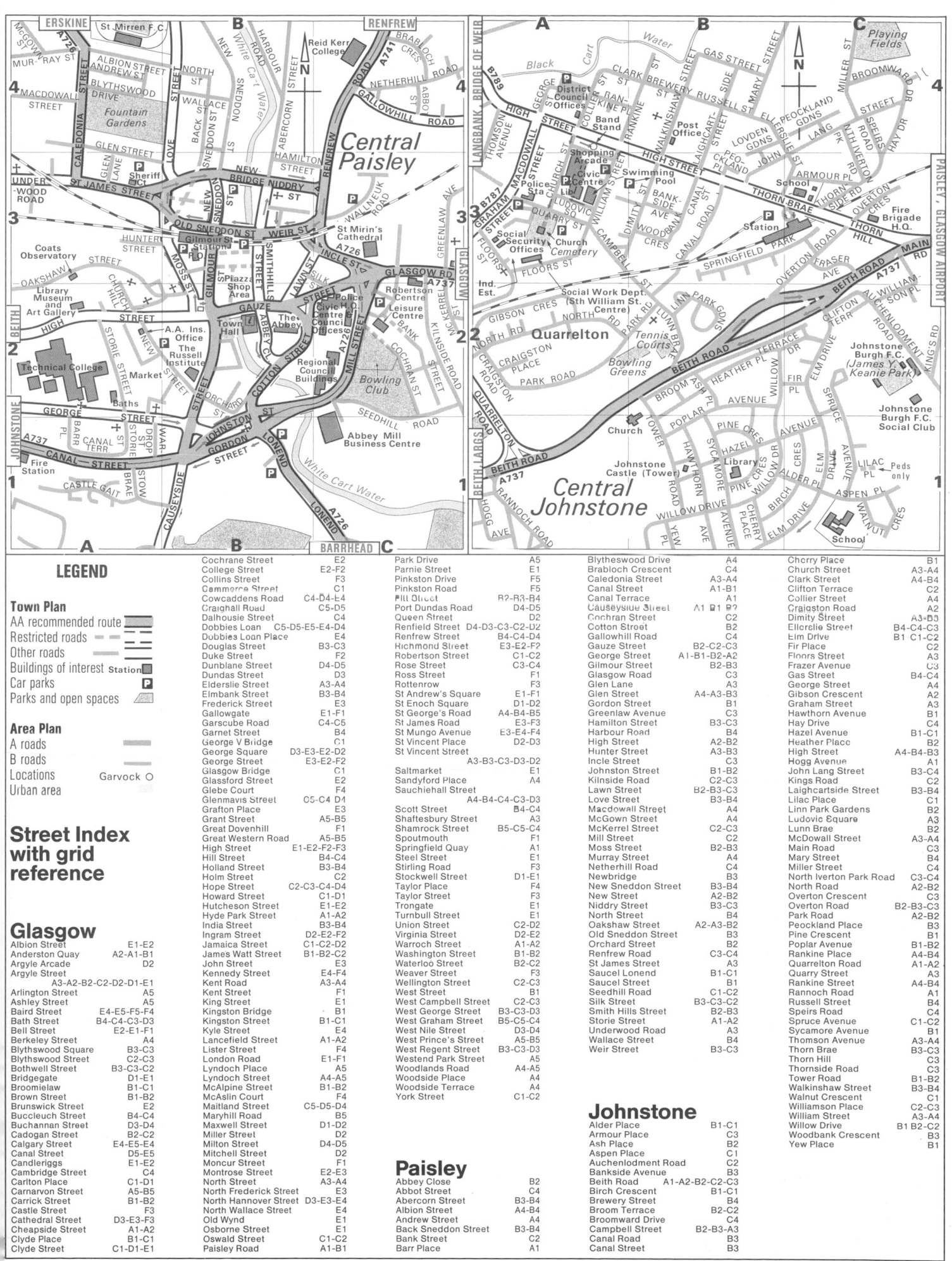

## LEGEND

**Town Plan**

- AA recommended route
- Restricted roads
- Other roads
- Buildings of interest  Station
- Car parks  P
- Parks and open spaces

**Area Plan**

- A roads
- B roads
- Locations  Garvock O
- Urban area

## Street Index with grid reference

### Glasgow

| | |
|---|---|
| Albion Street | E1-E2 |
| Anderston Quay | A2-A1-B1 |
| Argyle Arcade | D2 |
| Argyle Street | A3-A2-B2-C2-D2-D1-E1 |
| Arlington Street | A5 |
| Ashley Street | A5 |
| Baird Street | E4-E5-F5-F4 |
| Bath Street | B4-C4-C3-D3 |
| Bell Street | E2-E1-F1 |
| Berkeley Street | A4 |
| Blythswood Square | B3-C3 |
| Blythswood Street | C2-C3 |
| Bothwell Street | B3-C3-C2 |
| Bridgegate | D1-E1 |
| Broomielaw | B1-C1 |
| Brown Street | B1-B2 |
| Brunswick Street | E2 |
| Buccleuch Street | B4-C4 |
| Buchannan Street | D3-D4 |
| Cadogan Street | B2-C2 |
| Calgary Street | E4-E5-E4 |
| Canal Street | D5-E5 |
| Candleriggs | E1-E2 |
| Cambridge Street | C4 |
| Carlton Place | C1-D1 |
| Carnarvon Street | A5-B5 |
| Carrick Street | B1-B2 |
| Castle Street | F3 |
| Cathedral Street | D3-E3-F3 |
| Cheapside Street | A1-A2 |
| Clyde Place | B1-C1 |
| Clyde Street | C1-D1-E1 |
| Cochrane Street | E2 |
| College Street | E2-F2-F2 |
| Collins Street | F3 |
| Commerce Street | C1 |
| Cowcaddens Road | C4-D4-E4 |
| Craighall Road | C5-D5 |
| Dalhousie Street | C4 |
| Dobbies Loan | C5-D5-E5-E4-D4 |
| Dobbies Loan Place | E4 |
| Douglas Street | B3-C3 |
| Duke Street | F2 |
| Dunblane Street | D4-D5 |
| Dundas Street | D3 |
| Elderslie Street | A3-A4 |
| Elmbank Street | B3-B4 |
| Frederick Street | E3 |
| Gallowgate | E1-F1 |
| Garscube Road | C4-C5 |
| Garnet Street | B4 |
| George V Bridge | C1 |
| George Square | D3-E3-E2-D2 |
| George Street | E3-E2-F2 |
| Glasgow Bridge | C1 |
| Glassford Street | E2 |
| Glebe Court | F4 |
| Glenmavis Street | C5-C4-D4 |
| Grafton Place | E3 |
| Grant Street | A5-B5 |
| Great Dovenhill | F1 |
| Great Western Road | A5-B5 |
| High Street | E1-E2-F2-F3 |
| Hill Street | B4-C4 |
| Holland Street | B3-B4 |
| Holm Street | C2 |
| Hope Street | C2-C3-C4-D4 |
| Howard Street | C1-D1 |
| Hutcheson Street | E1-E2 |
| Hyde Park Street | A1-A2 |
| India Street | B3-B4 |
| Ingram Street | D2-E2-F2 |
| Jamaica Street | C1-C2-D2 |
| James Watt Street | B1-B2-C2 |
| John Street | E3 |
| Kennedy Street | E4-F4 |
| Kent Road | A3-A4 |
| Kent Street | F1 |
| King Street | E1 |
| Kingston Bridge | B1 |
| Kingston Street | B1-C1 |
| Kyle Street | E4 |
| Lancefield Street | A1-A2 |
| Lister Street | F4 |
| London Road | E1-F1 |
| Lyndoch Place | A5 |
| Lyndoch Street | A4-A5 |
| McAlpine Street | B1-B2 |
| McAslin Court | F4 |
| Maitland Street | C5-D5-D4 |
| Maryhill Road | B5 |
| Maxwell Street | D1-D2 |
| Miller Street | D2 |
| Milton Street | D4-D5 |
| Mitchell Street | D2 |
| Moncur Street | F1 |
| Montrose Street | E2-E3 |
| North Street | A3-A4 |
| North Frederick Street | E3 |
| North Hannover Street | D3-E3-E4 |
| North Wallace Street | E4 |
| Old Wynd | E1 |
| Osborne Street | E1 |
| Oswald Street | C1-C2 |
| Paisley Road | A1-B1 |
| Park Drive | A5 |
| Parnie Street | E1 |
| Pinkston Drive | F5 |
| Pinkston Road | F5 |
| Pitt Street | B2-B3-B4 |
| Port Dundas Road | D4-D5 |
| Queen Street | D2 |
| Renfield Street | D4-D3-C3-C2-D2 |
| Renfrew Street | B4-C4-D4 |
| Richmond Street | E3-E2-F2 |
| Robertson Street | C1-C2 |
| Rose Street | C3-C4 |
| Ross Street | F1 |
| Rottenrow | F3 |
| St Andrew's Square | E1-F1 |
| St Enoch Square | D1-D2 |
| St George's Road | A4-B4-B5 |
| St James Road | E3-F3 |
| St Mungo Avenue | E3-E4-F4 |
| St Vincent Place | D2-D3 |
| St Vincent Street | A3-B3-C3-D3-D2 |
| Saltmarket | E1 |
| Sandyford Place | A4 |
| Sauchiehall Street | A4-B4-C4-C3-D3 |
| Scott Street | B4-C4 |
| Shaftesbury Street | A3 |
| Shamrock Street | B5-C5-C4 |
| Spoutmouth | F1 |
| Springfield Quay | A1 |
| Steel Street | E1 |
| Stirling Road | F3 |
| Stockwell Street | D1-E1 |
| Taylor Place | F4 |
| Taylor Street | F3 |
| Trongate | E1 |
| Turnbull Street | E1 |
| Union Street | C2-D2 |
| Virginia Street | D2-E2 |
| Warroch Street | A1-A2 |
| Washington Street | B1-B2 |
| Waterloo Street | B2-C2 |
| Weaver Street | F3 |
| Wellington Street | C2-C3 |
| West Street | B1 |
| West Campbell Street | C2-C3 |
| West George Street | B3-C3-D3 |
| West Graham Street | B5-C5-C4 |
| West Nile Street | D3-D4 |
| West Prince's Street | A5-B5 |
| West Regent Street | B3-C3-D3 |
| Westend Park Street | A5 |
| Woodlands Road | A4-A5 |
| Woodside Place | A4 |
| Woodside Terrace | A4 |
| York Street | C1-C2 |

### Paisley

| | |
|---|---|
| Abbey Close | B2 |
| Abbot Street | C4 |
| Abercorn Street | B3-B4 |
| Albion Street | A4-B4 |
| Andrew Street | A4 |
| Back Sneddon Street | B3-B4 |
| Bank Street | C2 |
| Barr Place | A1 |
| Blytheswood Drive | A4 |
| Brabloch Crescent | C4 |
| Caledonia Street | A3-A4 |
| Canal Street | A1-B1 |
| Canal Terrace | A1 |
| Causeyside Street | A1-B1-B2 |
| Cochran Street | C2 |
| Cotton Street | B2 |
| County Place | B3 |
| Gauze Street | B2-C2-C3 |
| George Street | A1-B1-B2-A2 |
| Gilmour Street | B2-B3 |
| Glasgow Road | C3 |
| Glen Lane | A3 |
| Glen Street | A4-A3-B3 |
| Gordon Street | B1 |
| Greenlaw Avenue | C3 |
| Hamilton Street | B3-C3 |
| Harbour Road | B4 |
| High Street | A2-B2 |
| Hunter Street | A3-B3 |
| Incle Street | C3 |
| Johnston Street | B1-B2 |
| Kilnside Road | C2-C3 |
| Lawn Street | B2-B3-C3 |
| Love Street | B3-B4 |
| Macdowall Street | A4 |
| McGown Street | A4 |
| McKerrel Street | C2-C3 |
| Mill Street | C2 |
| Moss Street | B2-B3 |
| Murray Street | A4 |
| Netherhill Road | C4 |
| Newbridge | B3 |
| New Sneddon Street | B3-B4 |
| New Street | A2-B2 |
| Niddry Street | B3-C3 |
| North Street | B4 |
| Oakshaw Street | A2-A3-B2 |
| Old Sneddon Street | B3 |
| Orchard Street | B2 |
| Renfrew Road | C3-C4 |
| St James Street | A3 |
| Saucel Lonend | B1-C1 |
| Saucel Street | B1 |
| Seedhill Road | C1-C2 |
| Silk Street | B3-C3-C2 |
| Smith Hills Street | B2-B3 |
| Storie Street | A1-A2 |
| Underwood Road | A3 |
| Wallace Street | B4 |
| Weir Street | B3-C3 |

### Johnstone

| | |
|---|---|
| Alder Place | B1-C1 |
| Armour Place | C3 |
| Ash Place | B2 |
| Aspen Place | C1 |
| Auchenlodment Road | C2 |
| Bankside Avenue | B3 |
| Beith Road | A1-A2-B2-C2-C3 |
| Birch Crescent | B1-C1 |
| Brewery Street | B4 |
| Broom Terrace | B2-C2 |
| Broomward Drive | C4 |
| Campbell Street | B2-B3-A3 |
| Canal Road | B3 |
| Canal Street | B3 |
| Cherry Place | B1 |
| Church Street | A3-A4 |
| Clark Street | A4-B4 |
| Clifton Terrace | C2 |
| Collier Street | A4 |
| Craigston Road | A2 |
| Dimity Street | A3-B3 |
| Ellerslie Street | B4-C4-C3 |
| Elm Drive | B1 C1-C2 |
| Fir Place | C2 |
| Floors Street | A3 |
| Frazer Avenue | C3 |
| Gas Street | B4-C4 |
| George Street | A4 |
| Gibson Crescent | A2 |
| Graham Street | A3 |
| Hawthorn Avenue | B1 |
| Hay Drive | C4 |
| Hazel Avenue | B1-C1 |
| Heather Place | B2 |
| High Street | A4-B4-B3 |
| Hogg Avenue | A1 |
| John Lang Street | B3-C4 |
| Kings Road | C2 |
| Laighcartside Street | B3-B4 |
| Lilac Place | C1 |
| Linn Park Gardens | B2 |
| Ludovic Square | A3 |
| Lunn Brae | B2 |
| McDowall Street | A3-A4 |
| Main Road | C3 |
| Mary Street | B4 |
| Miller Street | C3 |
| North Iverton Park Road | C3-C4 |
| North Road | A2-B2 |
| Overton Crescent | C3 |
| Overton Road | B2-B3-C3 |
| Park Road | A2-B2 |
| Peockland Place | B3 |
| Pine Crescent | B1 |
| Poplar Avenue | B1-B2 |
| Rankine Place | A4-B4 |
| Quarrelton Road | A1-A2 |
| Quarry Street | A3 |
| Rankine Street | A4-B4 |
| Rannoch Road | A1 |
| Russell Street | B4 |
| Speirs Road | C4 |
| Spruce Avenue | C1-C2 |
| Sycamore Avenue | B1 |
| Thomson Avenue | A3-A4 |
| Thorn Brae | B3-C3 |
| Thorn Hill | C3 |
| Thornside Road | C3 |
| Tower Road | B1-B2 |
| Walkinshaw Street | B3-B4 |
| Walnut Crescent | C1 |
| Williamson Place | C2-C3 |
| William Street | C3 |
| Willow Drive | B1 B2-C2 |
| Woodbank Crescent | B3 |
| Yew Place | B1 |

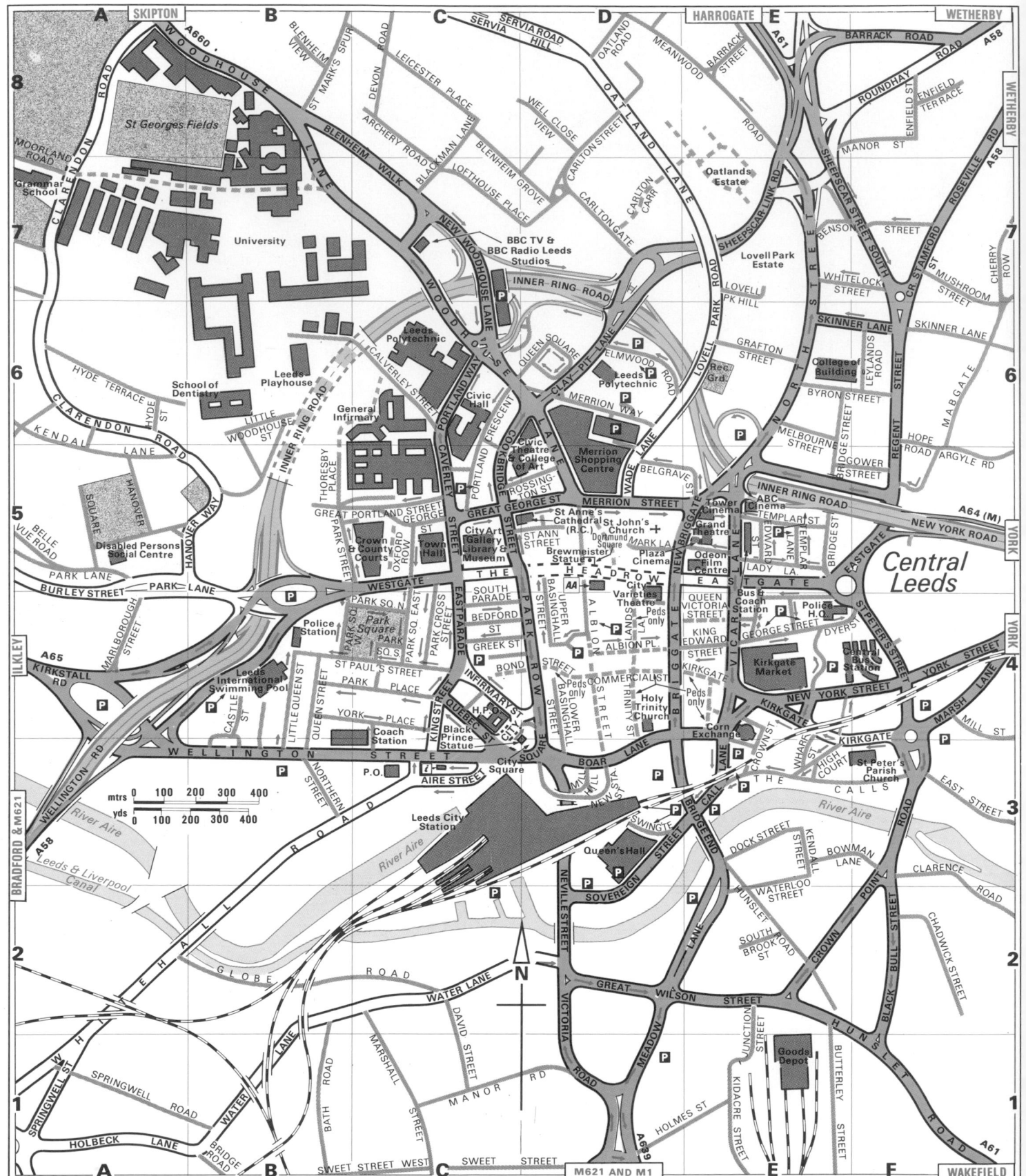

# Leeds

In the centre of Leeds is its town hall – a monumental piece of architecture with a 225ft clock-tower. It was opened by Queen Victoria in 1858, and has been a kind of mascot for the city ever since. It exudes civic pride; such buildings could only have been created in the heyday of Victorian prosperity and confidence. Leeds' staple industry has always been the wool trade, but it

only became a boom town towards the end of the 18th century, when textile mills were introduced. Today, the wool trade and ready-made clothing (Mr Hepworth and Mr Burton began their work here) are still important, though industries like paper, leather, furniture and electrical equipment are prominent.

Across Calverley Street from the town hall is the City Art Gallery, Library and Museum. Its collections include sculpture by Henry Moore, who

was a student at Leeds School of Art. Nearby is the Headrow, Leeds' foremost shopping thoroughfare. On it is the City Varieties Theatre, venue for many years of the famous television programme 'The Good Old Days'. Off the Headrow are several shopping arcades, of which Leeds has many handsome examples. Leeds has a good number of interesting churches; perhaps the finest is St John's, unusual in that it dates from 1634, a time when few churches were built.

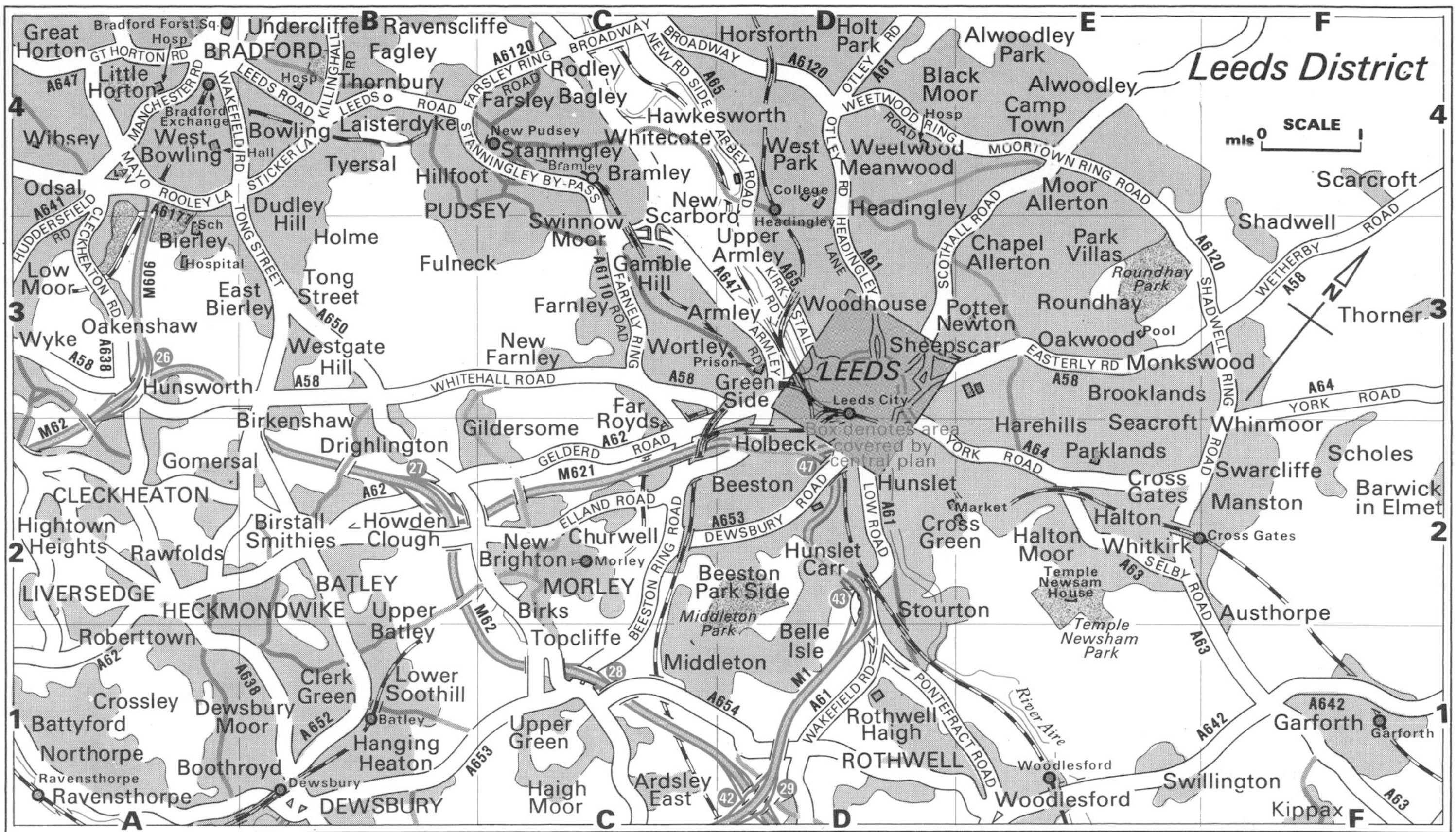

# Leeds District

SCALE
mls 0 ___ 1

Box denotes area covered by central plan

*Map labels include:* Great Horton, Bradford Forst Sq. Hosp, Undercliffe, Ravenscliffe, Fagley, BRADFORD, Thornbury, Little Horton, GT HORTON RD, Bradford Exchange, Bowling, Laisterdyke, Farsley, Rodley, Thornbury, Horsforth, Holt Park, Alwoodley Park, Black Moor, Alwoodley, Camp Town, Scarcroft, Shadwell, Thorner, Wibsey, West Bowling, Tyersal, Hillfoot, Stanningley, New Pudsey, Hawkesworth, Whitecote, West Park, Weetwood, Weelwood, Meanwood, Headingley, Chapel Allerton, Park Villas, Roundhay Park, Roundhay, Monkswood, Odsal, Bierley, Dudley Hill, Holme, PUDSEY, Swinnow Moor, Bramley, New Scarboro, Upper Armley, College, Headingley, Woodhouse, Potter Newton, Sheepscar, Oakwood, Brooklands, Low Moor, East Bierley, Tong Street, Fulneck, Gamble Hill, Farnley, Armley, Wortley, Prison, Green Side, LEEDS, Leeds City, Harehills, Seacroft, Whinmoor, Scholes, Swarcliffe, Barwick in Elmet, Wyke, Oakenshaw, Westgate Hill, New Farnley, Far Royds, Holbeck, Beeston, Hunslet, Cross Green, Cross Gates, Manston, Hunsworth, Birkenshaw, Drighlington, Gildersome, Churwell, Beeston Park Side, Middleton Park, Hunslet Carr, Halton Moor, Halton, Whitkirk, Cross Gates, Temple Newsam House, Austhorpe, CLECKHEATON, Gomersal, Birstall, Howden Clough, Smithies, New Brighton, Morley, Belle Isle, Temple Newsham Park, River Aire, Hightown Heights, Rawfolds, BATLEY, Birks, Topcliffe, Middleton, Stourton, LIVERSEDGE, HECKMONDWIKE, Upper Batley, Lower Soothill, Robertown, Clerk Green, Dewsbury Moor, Batley, Upper Green, Haigh Moor, Ardsley East, Rothwell Haigh, ROTHWELL, Woodlesford, Swillington, Garforth, Crossley, Battyford, Northorpe, Hanging Heaton, Boothroyd, Ravensthorpe, DEWSBURY, Kippax

---

## LEGEND

### Town Plan
| | |
|---|---|
| AA Recommended roads | ▬▬▬ |
| Other roads | ═══ |
| Restricted roads | - - - |
| Buildings of interset | Museum ▪ |
| AA Centre | AA |
| Parks and open spaces | ▪ |
| Car Parks | P |
| Churches | † |
| One way streets | ← |

### District Plan
| | |
|---|---|
| A roads | ▬▬ |
| B roads | ─── |
| Stations | Kirkgate ○ |
| Urban area | ▪ |
| Buildings of interest | Hospital ▪ |

## Street Index with Grid Reference

### Leeds

| | |
|---|---|
| Aire Street | C3 |
| Albion Place | D4 |
| Albion Street | D3-D4-D5 |
| Archery Road | C7-C8 |
| Argyle Road | F5 |
| Barrack Road | E8-F8 |
| Barrack Street | E8 |
| Bath Road | B1-B2 |
| Bedford Street | C4 |
| Belgrave Street | D5-E5 |
| Belle Vue Road | A5 |
| Benson Street | E7-F7 |
| Black Bull Street | F1-F2-F3 |
| Blackman Lane | C7-C8 |
| Blenheim Grove | C8-C7-D7 |
| Blenheim View | B8 |
| Blenheim Walk | B8-C8-C7 |
| Boar Lane | D3-D4 |
| Bond Street | C4-D4 |
| Bowman Lane | E3-F3 |
| Bridge End | D3-E3 |
| Bridge Road | B1 |
| Bridge Street | E5-E6 |
| Briggate | D3-D4-D5 |
| Burley Street | A4-A5 |
| Butterley Street | E1-E2 |
| Byron Street | E6-F6 |
| Call Lane | E3 |
| Calverley Street | C5-C6 |
| Carlton Carr | D7 |
| Carlton Gate | D7 |
| Carlton Street | D7-D8 |
| Castle Street | B3-B4 |
| Chadwick Street | F2 |
| Chapletown Road | E8 |
| Cherry Row | F7 |
| City Square | C3-C4-D4-D3 |
| Clarence Road | F2-F3 |
| Clarendon Road | A8-A7-A6-A5-B5 |
| Clay Pit Lane | D6 |
| Commercial Street | D4 |
| Cookbridge Street | C5-C6-D6 |
| Cross Stamford Street | F6-F7 |
| Crown Street | E3-E4 |
| Crown Point Road | E2-F2-F3 |
| David Street | C1-C2 |
| Devon Road | C8 |
| Dock Street | E3 |
| Dyer Street | E4-F4 |
| East Parade | C4-C5 |
| East Street | F3 |
| Eastgate | E5-F5 |
| Edward Street | E5 |
| Elmwood Road | D6 |
| Enfield Street | F8 |
| Enfield Terrace | F8 |
| George Street | C5 |
| George Street | E4 |
| Globe Road | A2-B2-C2 |
| Gower Street | E5-F5 |
| Grafton Street | E6 |
| Great George Street | C5-D5 |
| Great Portland Street | B5-C5 |
| Great Wilson Street | D2-E2 |
| Greek Street | C4-D4 |
| Hanover Square | A5 |
| Hanover Way | A5-B5 |
| High Court | E3 |
| Holbeck Lane | A1-B1 |
| Holmes Street | D1-E1 |
| Hope Road | F5-F6 |
| Hunslett Road | E3-E2-E1-F1-F2 |
| Hyde Street | A6 |
| Hyde Terrace | A6 |
| Infirmary Street | C4-D4 |
| Inner Ring Road | B5-B6-C6-C7-D7-D6-E6-E5-F5 |
| Junction Street | E1-E2 |
| Kendal Lane | A5-A6 |
| Kendal Street | E3 |
| Kidacre Street | E1 |
| King Street | C3-C4 |
| King Edward Street | D4-E4 |
| Kirkgate | E4-E3-F3-F4 |
| Kirkstall Road | A4 |
| Lady Lane | E5 |
| Lands Lane | D4-D5 |
| Leicester Place | C8 |
| Leylands Road | F6 |
| Lisbon Street | B3-B4 |
| Little Queen Street | B3-B4 |
| Little Woodhouse Street | B6 |
| Lofthouse Place | C7-D7 |
| Lovell Park Hill | E7 |
| Lovell Park Road | D6-E6-E7 |
| Lower Basinghall Street | D3-D4 |
| Mabgate | F6 |
| Manor Road | C1-D1 |
| Manor Street | E8-F8 |
| Mark Lane | D5 |
| Marlborough Street | A4 |
| Marsh Lane | F4 |
| Marshall Street | C1-C2 |
| Meadow Lane | D1-D2-E2-E3 |
| Meanwood Road | D8-E8 |
| Melbourne Street | E6 |
| Merrion Street | D5-E5 |
| Merrion Way | D6 |
| Mill Hill | D3 |
| Mill Street | F4 |
| Moorland Road | A7-A8 |
| Mushroom Street | F6-F7 |
| Neville Street | D2-D3 |
| New Briggate | D5-E5 |
| New Station Street | D3 |
| New Woodhouse Lane | C6-C7 |
| New York Road | F5 |
| New York Street | E4-F4 |
| North Street | E5-E6-E7 |
| Northern Street | B3 |
| Oatland Lane | D8-D7-E7 |
| Oatland Road | D8 |
| Oxford Row | C5 |
| Park Cross Street | C4-C5 |
| Park Lane | A5-B5-B4 |
| Park Place | B4-C4 |
| Park Row | C4-C5-D5-D4 |
| Park Square East | C4 |
| Park Square North | B4-C4 |
| Park Square South | C4 |
| Park Square West | B4 |
| Park Street | B5-C5 |
| Portland Crescent | C5-C6 |
| Portland Way | C6 |
| Quebec Street | C3-C4 |
| Queen Street | B3-R4 |
| Queen Square | C6-D6 |
| Queen Victoria Street | D4-E4 |
| Regent Street | F5-F6 |
| Roseville Road | F7-F8 |
| Rossington Street | C5-D5 |
| Roundhay Road | E8-F8 |
| St Ann Street | C5-D5 |
| St Mark's Spur | B8-C8 |
| St Paul's Street | B4-C4 |
| St Peter's Street | E4-F4 |
| Servia Hill | C8-D8 |
| Servia Road | C8-D8 |
| Sheepscar Link Road | E7-E8 |
| Sheepscar Street North | E8 |
| Sheepscar Street South | E8-E7-F7 |
| Skinner Lane | E6-F6 |
| South Brook Street | F2 |
| South Parade | C4 |
| Sovereign Street | D2-D3-E3 |
| Springwell Road | A1-B1 |
| Springwell Street | A1 |
| Sweet Street | C1-D1 |
| Sweet Street West | B1-C1 |
| Swinegate | D3 |
| The Calls | E3-F3 |
| The Headrow | C5-D5 |
| Templar Lane | E5 |
| Templar Street | E5 |
| Thoresby Place | B5-B6 |
| Trinity Street | D4 |
| Upper Basinghall Street | D4-D5 |
| Vicar Lane | E4-E5 |
| Victoria Road | D1-D2 |
| Wade Lane | D5-D6 |
| Water Lane | B1-B2-C2-D2 |
| Waterloo Street | E2-E3 |
| Well Close View | D8 |
| Wellington Road | A3 |
| Wellington Street | A3-B3-C3 |
| Westgate | B4-B5-C5-C4 |
| Wharf Street | E3-E4 |
| Whitehall Road | A1-A2-B2-B3-C3 |
| Whitelock Street | E7-F7 |
| Woodhouse Lane | A8-B8-B7-C7-C6-D6-D5 |
| York Place | B4-C4 |
| York Street | F4 |

LEEDS
Offices now occupy the handsome twin-towered Civic Hall which stands in Calverley Street in front of the new buildings of Leeds Polytechnic. This area of the city – the commercial centre – has been extensively redeveloped

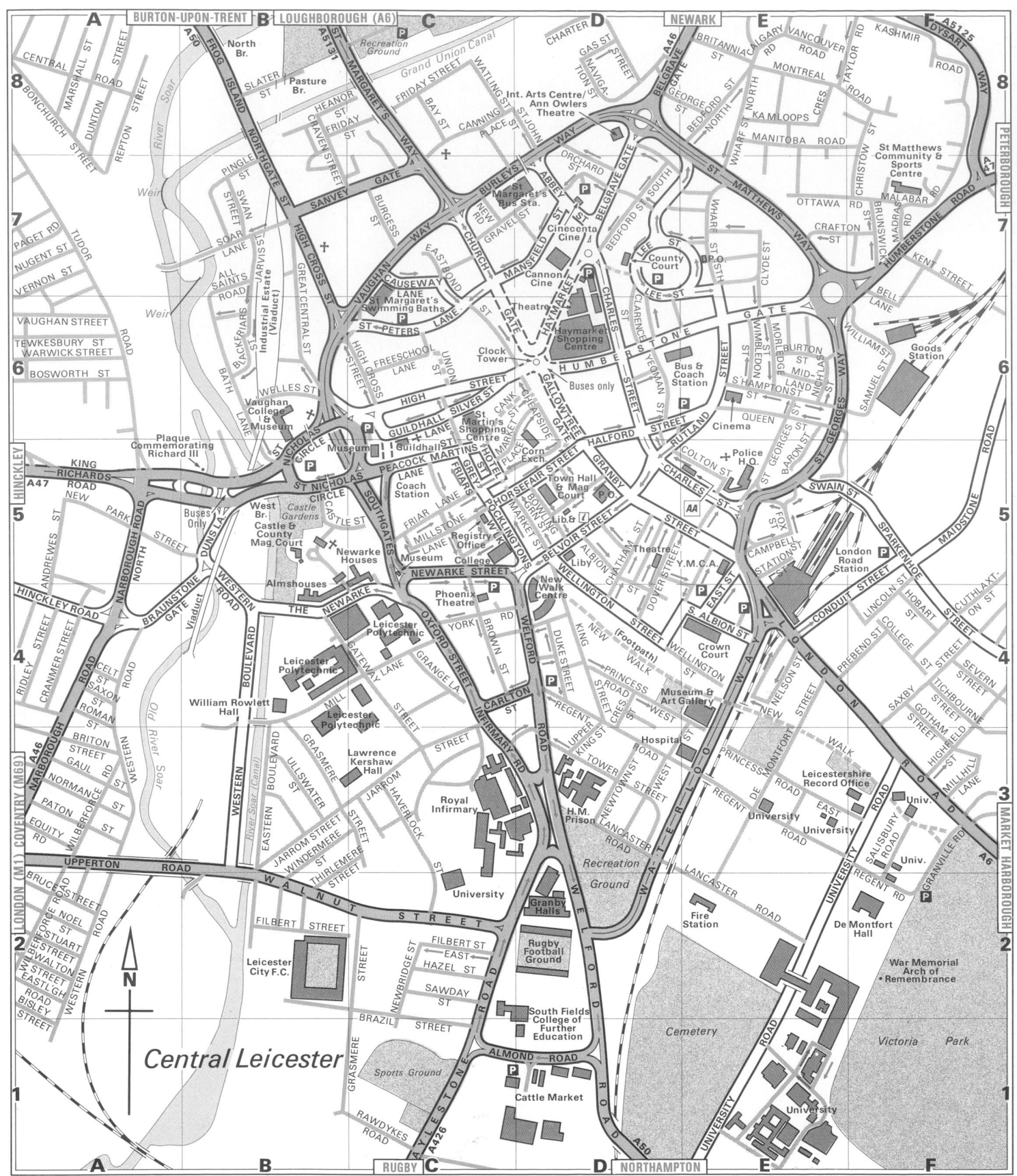

Central Leicester

# Leicester

A regional capital in Roman times, Leicester has retained many buildings from its eventful and distinguished past. Today the city is a thriving modern place, a centre for industry and commerce, serving much of the Midlands. Among the most outstanding monuments from the past is the Jewry Wall, a great bastion of Roman masonry. Close by are remains of the Roman baths and

several other contemporary buildings. Attached is a museum covering all periods from prehistoric times to 1500. Numerous other museums include the Wygston's House Museum of Costume, with displays covering the period 1769 to 1924; Newarke House, with collections showing changing social conditions in Leicester through four hundred years; and Leicestershire Museum and Art Gallery, with collections of drawings, paintings, ceramics, geology and natural history.

The medieval Guildhall has many features of interest, including a great hall, library and police cells. Leicester's castle, although remodelled in the 17th century, retains a 12th-century great hall. The Church of St Mary de Castro, across the road from the castle, has features going back at least as far as Norman times; while St Nicholas's Church is even older, with Roman and Saxon foundations. St Martin's Cathedral dates mainly from the 13th to 15th centuries and has a notable Bishop's throne.

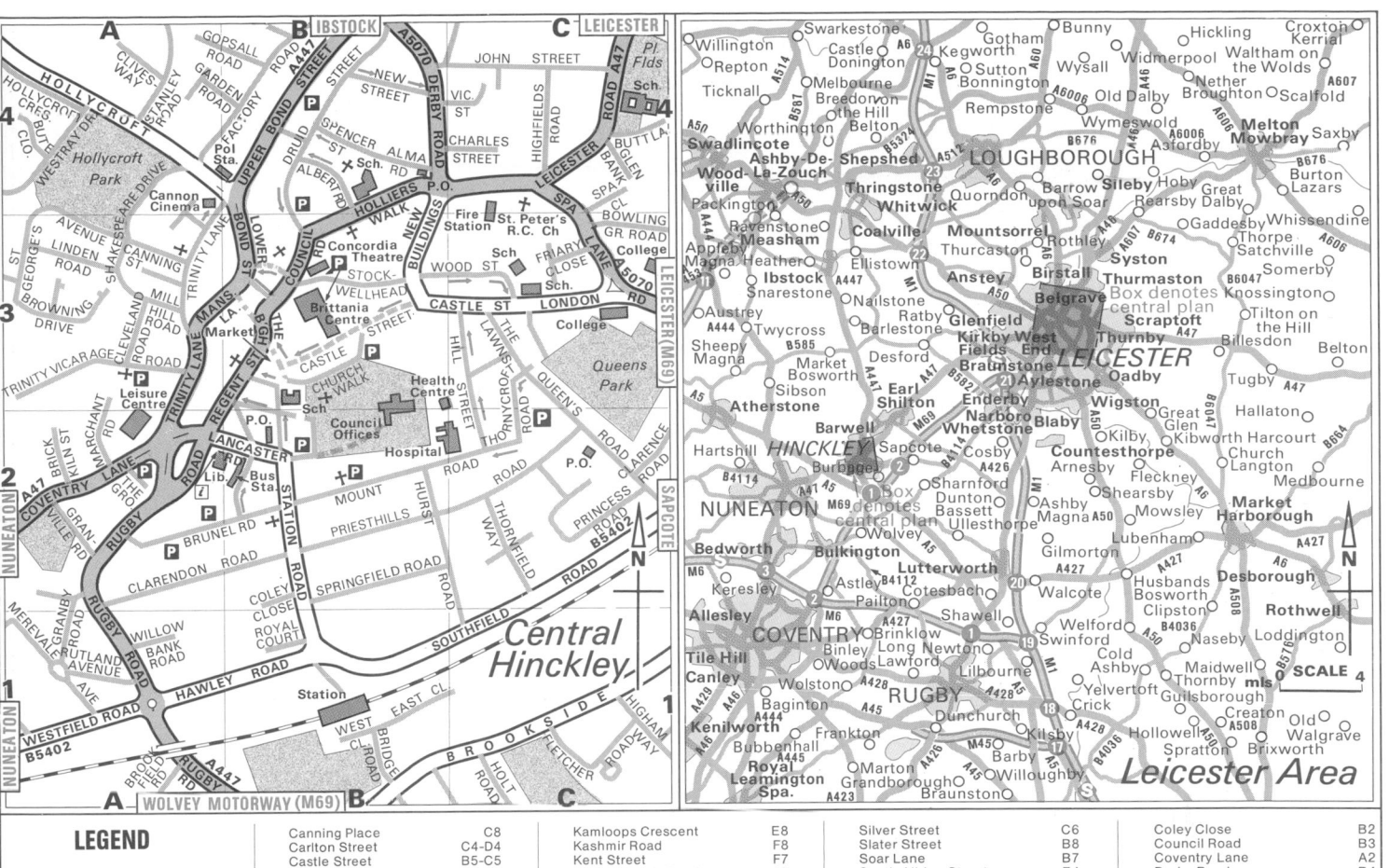

**Central Hinckley**

**Leicester Area**

---

LLTT

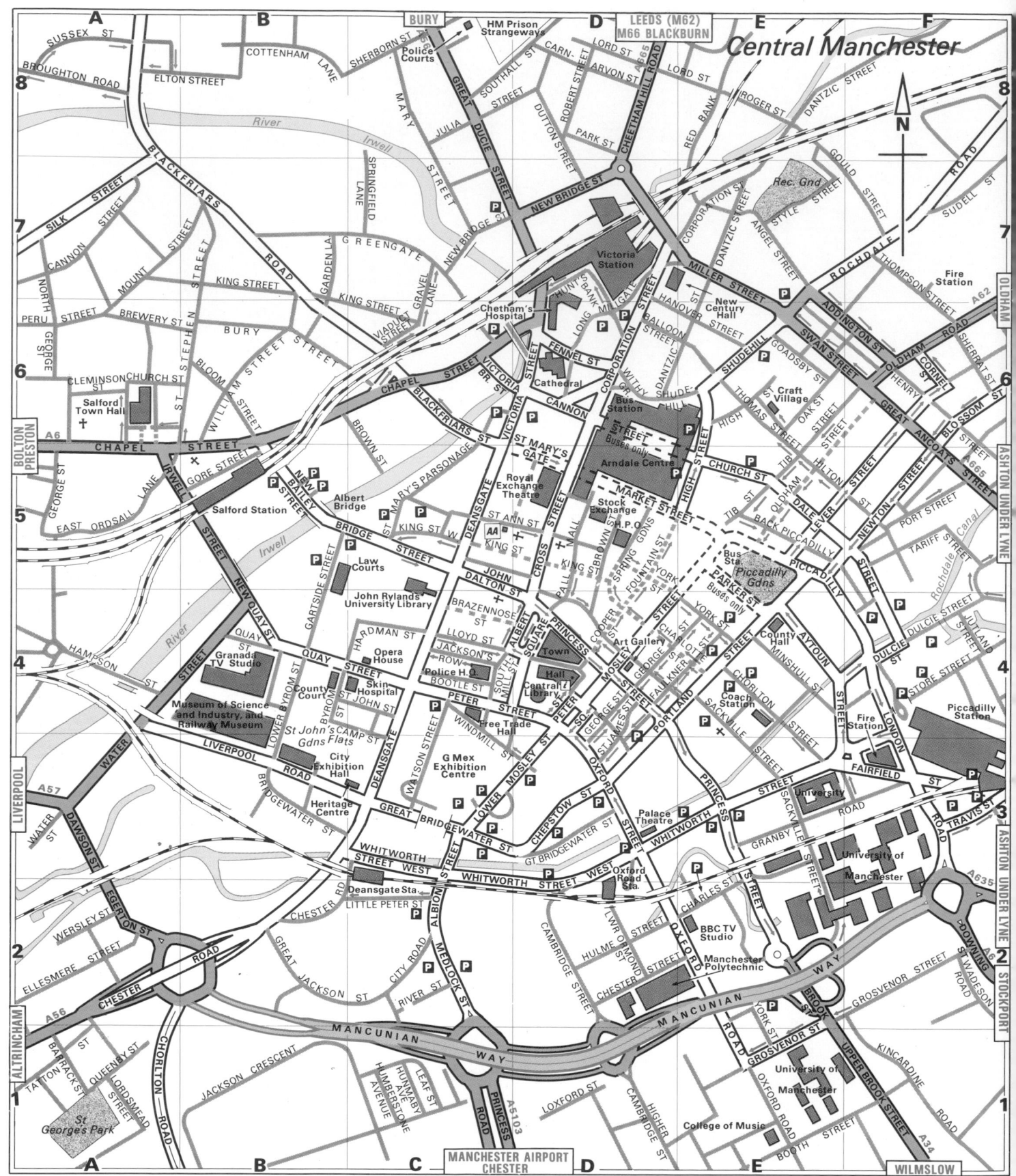

# Manchester

The gigantic conurbation called Greater Manchester covers a staggering 60 square miles, reinforcing Manchester's claim to be Britain's second city. Commerce and industry are vital aspects of the city's character, but it is also an important cultural centre – the Halle Orchestra has its home at the Free Trade Hall (a venue for many concerts besides classical music), there are several theatres, a library (the John Rylands) which houses one of the most important collections of books in the world, and a number of museums and galleries, including the Whitworth Gallery with its lovely watercolours.

Like many great cities it suffered badly during the bombing raids of World War II, but some older buildings remain, including the town hall, a huge building designed in Gothic style by Alfred Waterhouse and opened in 1877. Manchester Cathedral dates mainly from the 15th century and is noted for its fine tower and outstanding carved woodwork. Nearby is Chetham's Hospital, also 15th-century and now housing a music school. Much new development has taken place, and more is planned. Shopping precincts cater for the vast population, and huge hotels have provided services up to international standards. On the edge of the city is the Belle Vue centre, a large entertainments complex including concert and exhibition facilities, and a speedway stadium.

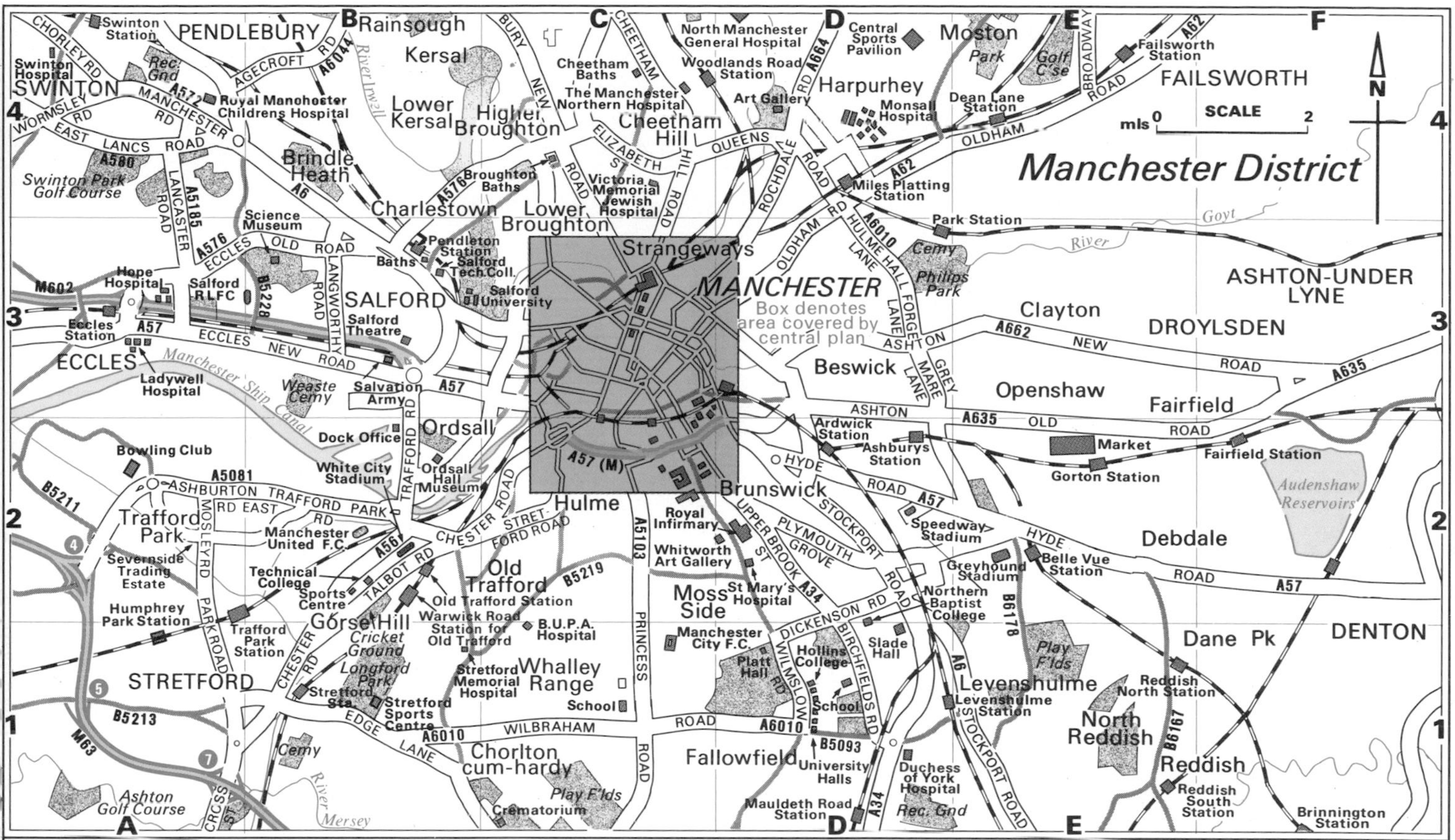

# Key to Town Plan and Area Plan

## Town Plan

| | |
|---|---|
| AA Recommended roads | |
| Other roads | |
| Restricted roads | |
| Buildings of interest | Baths |
| Car parks | P |
| Parks and open spaces | |
| Churches | † |
| AA Centre | AA |
| One Way Streets | ← |

## District Plan

| | |
|---|---|
| A roads | |
| B roads | |

## STREET INDEX
### -with grid reference

### Manchester

|  |  |
|---|---|
| Addington Street | E7-E6-F6 |
| Albert Square | C4-D4 |
| Albion Street | C2-C3 |
| Angel Street | E7 |
| Aytoun Street | E4-F4-F3-E3 |
| Back Piccadilly | E5-F5-F4 |
| Balloon Street | D6-E6 |
| Barrack Street | A1 |
| Blackfriars Road | A8-A7-B7-B6-C6 |
| Blackfriars Street | C5-C6 |
| Bloom Street | B6 |
| Blossom Street | F6 |
| Booth Street | E1-F1 |
| Bootle Street | C4 |
| Brazennose Street | C4-D4 |
| Brewery Street | A6-B6 |
| Bridge Street | B5-C5 |
| Bridgewater Street | B3 |
| Brook Street | E2 |
| Broughton Road | A8 |
| Brown Street | B6-C6-C5 |
| Brown Street | D4-D5 |
| Bury Street | B6-C6 |
| Byrom Street | B4 |
| Cambridge Street | D2 |
| Camp Street | B4-C4-C3 |
| Cannon Street | A7 |
| Cannon Street | D6-D5-E5 |
| Carnarvon Street | D8 |
| Chapel Street | A6-A5-B5-B6-C6-D6 |
| Charles Street | E2 |
| Charlotte Street | D4-E4 |
| Cheetham Hill Road | D7-D8 |
| Chepstow Street | D3 |
| Chester Road | A1-A2-B2-C2-C3 |
| Chester Street | D2-E2 |
| Chorlton Road | B2-A2-A1-B1 |
| Chorlton Street | E3-E4 |
| Church Street | A6-B6 |
| Church Street | E5 |
| Cleminson Street | A6 |
| City Road | C2 |
| Cooper Street | D4 |
| Cornel Street | F6 |
| Corporation Street | D6-D7-E7 |
| Cottenham Lane | B8 |
| Cross Street | D4-D5-D6 |
| Dale Street | E5-F5-F4 |
| Dantzic Street | D6-E6-E7-E8-F8 |
| Dawson Street | A3 |
| Deansgate | C3-C4-C5 |
| Downing Street | F2 |
| Dulcie Street | F4 |
| Dutton Street | D7-D8 |
| East Ordsall Lane | A5 |
| Egerton Street | A2 |
| Ellesmere Street | A2 |
| Elton Street | A8-B8 |
| Fairfield Street | F3 |
| Faulkner Street | D4-E4 |
| Fennel Street | D6 |
| Fountain Street | D4-D5 |
| Garden Lane | B6-B7 |
| Gartside Street | B4-B5 |
| George Street | A5 |
| George Street | D3-D4-E4 |
| Goadsby Street | E6 |
| Gore Street | B5 |
| Gould Street | E8-E7-F7 |
| Granby Road | E3-F3 |
| Gravel Lane | C6-C7 |
| Great Ancoats Street | F5-F6 |
| Great Bridgewater Street | C3-D3 |
| Great Ducie Street | C8-C7-D7 |
| Great Jackson Street | B2-C2 |
| Greengate | B7-C7 |
| Grosvenor Street | E1-E2-F2 |
| Hampson Street | A4 |
| Hanover Street | D7-D6-E6 |
| Hardman Street | C4 |
| Henry Street | F5-F6 |
| High Street | E5-E6 |
| Higher Cambridge Street | D1 |
| Hilton Street | E5-F5 |
| Hulme Street | D2 |
| Humberstone Avenue | C1 |
| Hunmaby Avenue | C1 |
| Hunt's Bank | D6-D7 |
| Irwell Street | A5-B5 |
| Jackson Crescent | B1-C1 |
| Jackson's Row | C4 |
| John Dalton Street | C5-C4-D4-D5 |
| Julia Street | C8-D8 |
| Jutland Street | F4 |
| Kincardine Road | F1-F2 |
| King Street | A7-B7-B6-C6 |
| King Street | C5-D5 |
| King St West | C5 |
| Leaf Street | C1 |
| Lever Street | E5-F5-F6 |
| Little Peter Street | B2-C2 |
| Liverpool Road | A4-A3-B4-B3-C3 |
| Lloyd Street | C4 |
| London Road | F3-F4 |
| Long Millgate | D6-D7 |
| Lord Street | D8-E8 |
| Lordsmead Street | A1 |
| Lower Byrom Street | B3-B4 |
| Lower Mosley Street | C3-D3-D4 |
| Lower Ormond Street | D2 |
| Loxford Street | D1 |
| Mancunian Way | B2-B1-C2-C1-D1-D2-E2-F2 |
| Market Street | D5-E5 |
| Mary Street | C7-C8 |
| Medlock Street | C2 |
| Miller Street | D7-E7-E6 |
| Minshull Street | E4 |
| Mosley Street | D4-D5-E4-E5 |
| Mount Street | A6-A7-B7 |
| Newton Street | F5 |
| New Bailey Street | B5 |
| New Bridge Street | C7-D7 |
| North George Street | A6-A7 |
| New Quay Street | B4-B5 |
| Oak Street | E6 |
| Oldham Road | F6-F7 |
| Oldham Street | E5-E6-F6 |
| Oxford Road | D2-E2-E1 |
| Oxford Street | D4-D3-D2 |
| Pall Mall | D4-D5 |
| Park Street | D8 |
| Parker Street | E4-E5 |
| Peru Street | A6 |
| Peter Street | C4-D4 |
| Piccadilly | E5-E4-F4 |
| Port Street | F5 |
| Portland Street | D3-D4-E4-E5 |
| Princess Road | C1-D1 |
| Princess Street | D4-E4-D3-E3-E2 |
| Quay Street | B4-C4 |
| Queenby Street | A1 |
| Red Bank | E7-E8 |
| River Street | C2 |
| Robert Street | D8 |
| Rochdale Road | E7-F7-F8 |
| Roger Street | E8 |
| St Ann Street | C5-D5 |
| St Mary's Gate | C5-C6-D5-D6 |
| St Mary's Parsonage | C5-C6 |
| St James Street | D3-D4 |
| St John Street | B4-C4 |
| St Peter Square | D4 |
| St Stephen Street | A6-B6-B7 |
| Sackville Street | E2-E3-E4 |
| Sherrat Street | F6 |
| Sherborn Street | B8-C8 |
| Shudehill | D6-E6 |
| Silk Street | A7 |
| Southall Street | C8-D8 |
| Southmill Street | C4 |
| Spring Gardens | D4-D5 |
| Springfield Lane | C7-C8 |
| Store Street | F4 |
| Style Street | E7-E8 |
| Sudell Street | F7-F8 |
| Sussex Street | A8 |
| Swan Street | E6-F6 |
| Tatton Street | A1 |
| Tariff Street | F5 |
| Thomas Street | E5-E6 |
| Thompson Street | F6-F7 |
| Tib Street | E5-E6-F6 |
| Travis Street | F3 |
| Upper Brook Street | E2-E1-F1 |
| Viaduct Street | C6 |
| Victoria Bridge Street | C6-D6 |
| Victoria Street | C6-D6 |
| Wadeson Road | F2 |
| Water Street | A3-A4-B4 |
| Watson Street | C3-C4 |
| Wersley Street | A2 |
| Whitworth Street | D3-E3 |
| Whitworth Street West | B3-C3-C2-D2-D3 |
| William Street | B6 |
| Windmill Street | C4-C3-D3 |
| Withy Green | D6 |
| York Street | D5-D4-E4 |

## MANCHESTER

The Barton Swing Bridge carries the Bridgewater Canal over the Manchester Ship Canal, which links Manchester with the sea nearly 40 miles away. Completed in 1894, the canal is navigable by vessels up to 15,000 tons.

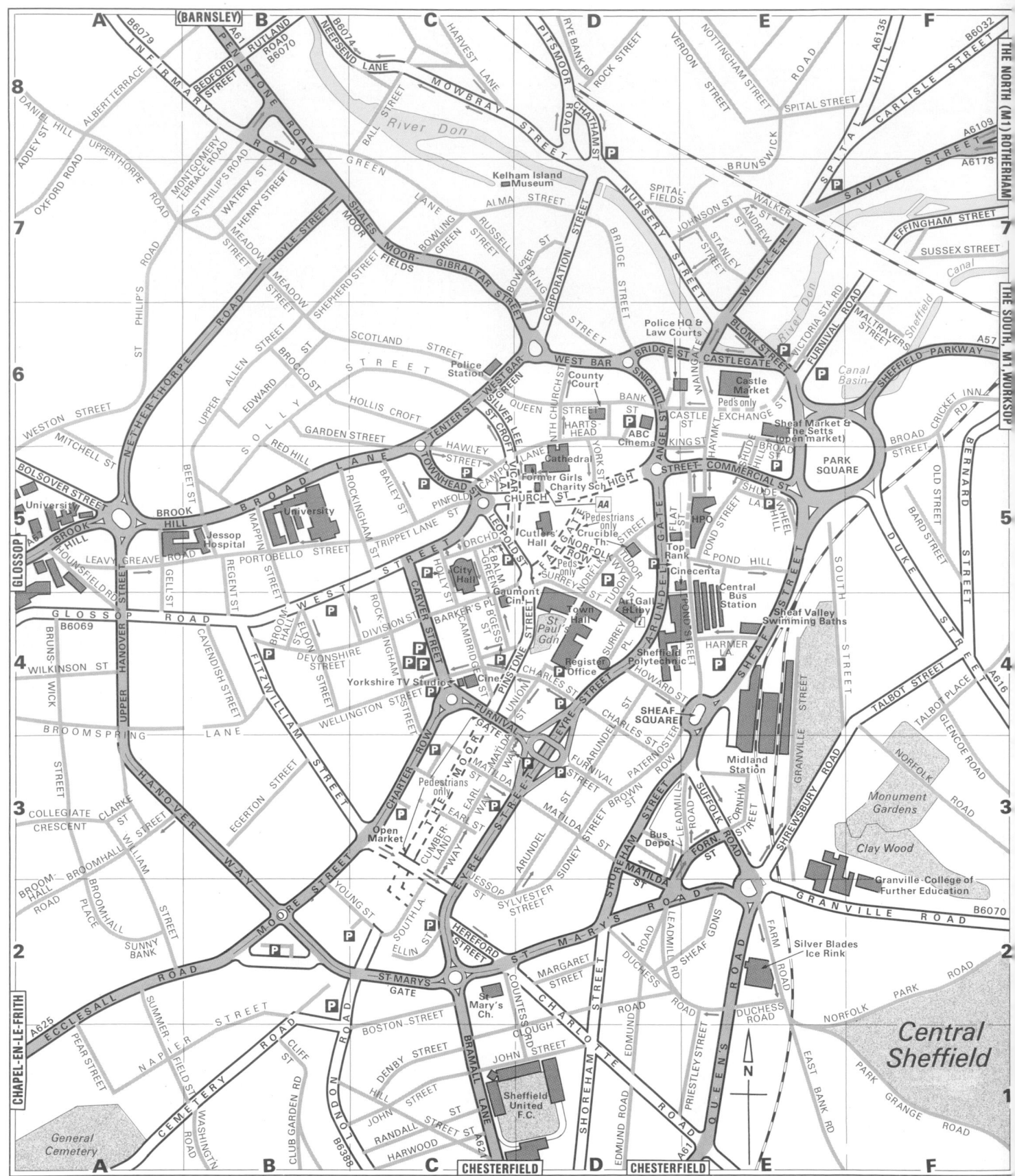

# Sheffield

Cutlery – which has made the name of Sheffield famous throughout the world – has been manufactured here since at least as early as the time of Chaucer. The god of blacksmiths, Vulcan, is the symbol of the city's industry, and he crowns the town hall, which was opened in 1897 by Queen Victoria. At the centre of the industry, however, is Cutlers' Hall, the headquarters of the Company of Cutlers. This society was founded in 1624 and has the right to grant trade marks to articles of a sufficiently high standard. In the hall is the company's collection of silver, with examples of craftsmanship dating back every year to 1773. A really large collection of cutlery is kept in the city museum. Steel production, a vital component of the industry, was greatly improved when the crucible process was invented here in 1740. At Abbeydale Industrial Hamlet, 3½ miles south-west of the city centre, is a complete restored site open as a museum and showing 18th-century methods of steel production. Sheffield's centre, transformed since World War II, is one of the finest and most modern in Europe. There are no soot-grimed industrial eyesores here, for the city has stringent pollution controls and its buildings are carefully planned and set within excellent landscaping projects. Many parks are set in and around the city, and the Pennines are within easy reach.

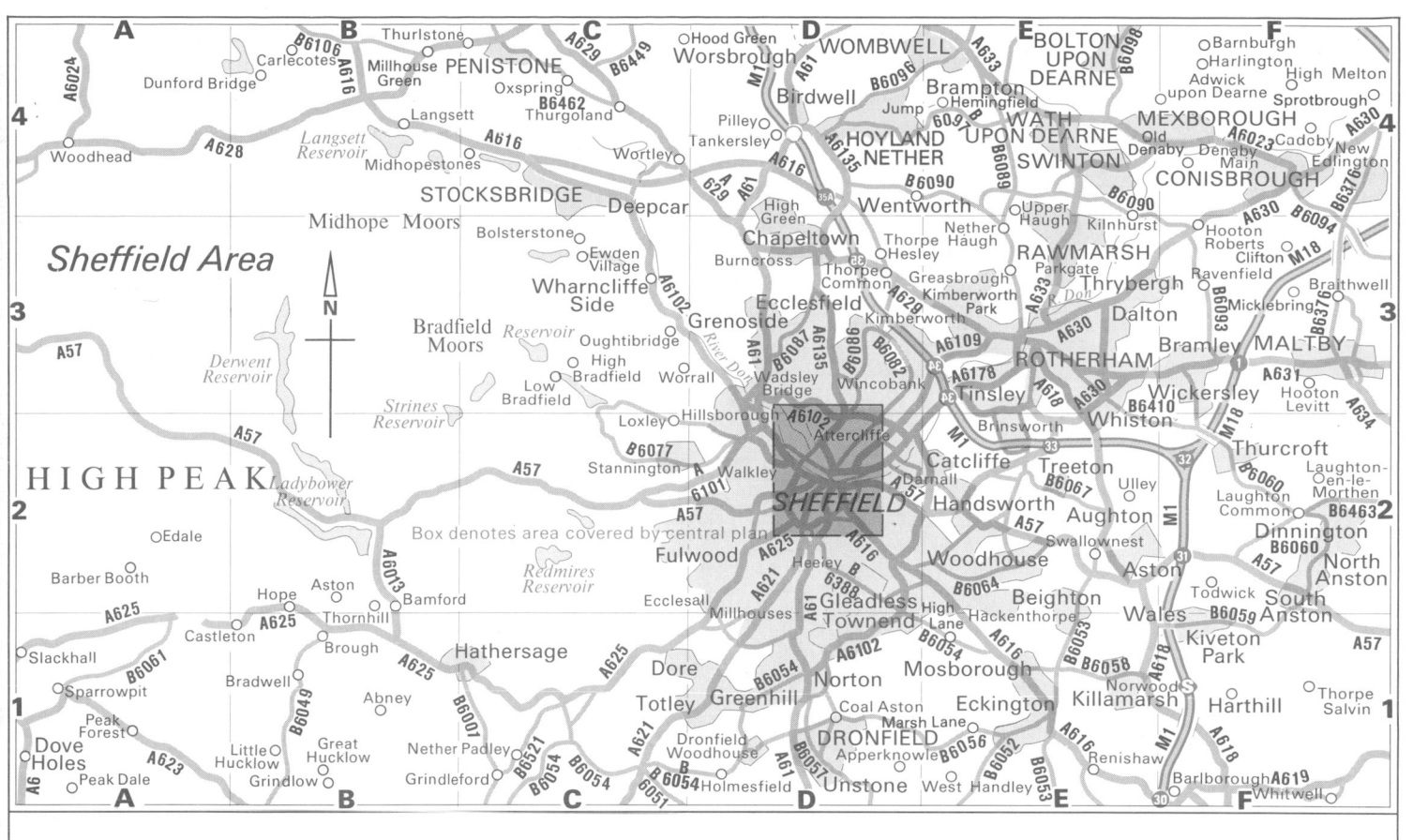

## LEGEND

### Town Plan
AA Recommended roads
Other roads
Restricted roads
Buildings of interest
AA Centre
Car Parks
Parks and open spaces

### Area Plan
A roads
B roads
Locations    Oakworth ○
Urban area

## Street Index with grid reference

### Sheffield

| | |
|---|---|
| Addey Street | A7-A8 |
| Albert Terrace | A8 |
| Alma Street | C7 D7 |
| Andrew Street | E7 |
| Angel Street | D5-D6 |
| Arundel Gate | D4-D5 |
| Arundel Street | C2-D2-D3-D4 |
| Bailey Street | C5 |
| Ball Street | C8 |
| Balm Green | C4-C5 |
| Bank Street | D6 |
| Bard Street | F5 |
| Barker's Pool | C4-C5-D5 |
| Bedford Street | B8 |
| Beet Street | B5 |
| Bernard Street | F4-F5-F6 |
| Blonk Street | E6 |
| Bolsover Street | A5 |
| Boston Street | C1-C2 |
| Bower Street | C7-D7 |
| Bowling Green | C7 |
| Bramall Lane | C1-C2 |
| Bridge Street | D7-D6-E6 |
| Broad Lane | B5-C5-C6 |
| Broad Street | F6-F5-F6 |
| Brocco Street | B6 |
| Brook Hill | A5-B5 |
| Broomhall Place | A2 |
| Broomhall Road | A2 |
| Broomhall Street | A2-A3-B4 |
| Broomspring Lane | A4-B4 |
| Brown Street | D3 |

| | |
|---|---|
| Brunswick Street | A3-A4 |
| Brunswick Road | E7-E8 |
| Burgess Street | C4 |
| Cambridge Street | C4 |
| Campo Lane | C5-D5-D6 |
| Carlisle Street | F8 |
| Carver Street | C4-C5 |
| Castle Street | D6-E6 |
| Castlegate | D6 |
| Cavendish Street | B4 |
| Cemetery Road | A1-B1-B2 |
| Charles Street | D3-D4 |
| Charlotte Road | C2-D2-D1-E1 |
| Charter Row | C3-C4 |
| Chatham Street | D7-D8 |
| Church Street | C5-D5 |
| Clarke Street | A3 |
| Cliff Street | B1 |
| Clough Road | C1-D1-D2 |
| Club Garden Road | B1 |
| Collegiate Crescent | A3 |
| Commercial Street | E5 |
| Corporation Street | D6-D7 |
| Countess Road | C2-D2-D1 |
| Cricket Inn Road | F6 |
| Cumberland Way | C3 |
| Daniel Hill | A8 |
| Denby Street | C1 |
| Devonshire Street | B4-C4 |
| Division Street | C4 |
| Duchess Road | D2-E2 |
| Duke Street | F4-F5 |
| Earl Street | C3 |
| Earl Way | C3 |
| East Bank Road | E1-E2 |
| Ecclesall Road | A1-A2-B2 |
| Edmund Road | D1-D2 |
| Edward Street | B6 |
| Effingham Street | F7 |
| Egerton Street | B3 |
| Eldon Street | B4 |
| Ellin Street | C2 |
| Eyre Street | C2-C3-D3-D4 |
| Exchange Street | D6 |
| Fargate | D5 |
| Farm Road | E2 |
| Fitzwilliam Street | B4-B3-C3 |
| Flat Street | E5 |
| Fornham Street | E3 |
| Furnival Gate | C3-C4-D3-D4 |
| Furnival Road | E6-F6-F7 |
| Furnival Street | D3 |
| Garden Street | B6-C6-C5 |
| Gell Street | A4-A5 |
| Gibralter Street | C7-C6-D6 |
| Glencoe Road | F3-F4 |
| Glossop Road | A4-B4 |
| Granville Road | E2-F2 |
| Granville Street | E3-E4 |
| Green Lane | B8-C8-C7 |
| Hanover Way | A3-B3-B2 |
| Harmer Lane | E4 |
| Hartshead | D6 |
| Harwood Street | C1 |
| Harvest Lane | C8 |

| | |
|---|---|
| Hawley Street | C5 |
| Haymarket | E5-E6 |
| Henry Street | B7 |
| Hereford Street | C2 |
| High Street | D5-E5 |
| Hill Street | B1-C1 |
| Hollis Croft | D6-C6 |
| Holly Street | C4-C5 |
| Hounsfield Road | A4-A5 |
| Howard Street | D4-E4 |
| Hoyle Street | B7 |
| Infirmary Road | A8-B8 B7 |
| Jessop Street | C2 |
| John Street | C1-D1 |
| Johnson Street | D7-E7 |
| King Street | D5-E5-E6 |
| Leadmill Road | D2-D3-E3 |
| Leavy Greave Road | A5-B5 |
| Lee Croft | C5-C6 |
| Leopold Street | C5-D5 |
| London Road | C1-B1-B2-C2 |
| Maltravers Street | F6 |
| Mappin Street | B4-B5 |
| Margaret Street | D2 |
| Matilda Street | C3-D3-D2 |
| Matilda Way | C3 |
| Meadow Street | B6-B7 |
| Mitchell Street | A5-A6 |
| Montgomery Terrace Road | A7-B7-B8 |
| Moorfields | C7 |
| Moore Street | B2-B3-C3 |
| Mowbray Street | C8-D8-D7 |
| Napier Street | A1-B1-B2 |
| Neepsend Lane | B8-C8 |
| Netherthorpe Road | A5-A6-B6-B7 |
| Norfolk Park Road | E1-E2-F2 |
| Norfolk Road | F3-F4 |
| Norfolk Row | D5 |
| Norfolk Street | D4-D5 |
| North Church Street | D6 |
| Nottingham Street | E8 |
| Nursery Street | D7-E7-E6 |
| Old Street | F5-F6 |
| Orchard Lane | C5 |
| Oxford Road | A7-A8 |
| Park Grange Road | E1-F1 |
| Park Square | E5-E6-F6-F5 |
| Paternoster Row | D3-D4-E4 |
| Pear Street | A1 |
| Penistone Road | B7-B8 |
| Pinfold Street | C5 |
| Pinstone Street | C4-D4-D5 |
| Pitsmoor Road | D8 |
| Pond Hill | E5 |
| Pond Street | E4-E5 |
| Portobello Street | B5-C5 |
| Priestley Street | D1-E1-E2 |
| Queen Street | C6-D6 |
| Queen's Road | E1-E2 |
| Randall Street | C1 |
| Red Hill | B5-B6 |
| Regent Street | B4-B5 |
| Rock Street | D8 |
| Rockingham Street | B5-C5-C4 |
| Russell Street | C7 |

| | |
|---|---|
| Rutland Road | B8 |
| Rye Bank Road | D8 |
| St Mary's Gate | C2 |
| St Mary's Road | C2-D2-E2 |
| St Philip's Road | A6-A7-B7-B8 |
| Savile Street | E7-F7-F8 |
| Scotland Street | B6-C6 |
| Shales Moor | B7-C7 |
| Sheaf Gardens | D2-E2 |
| Sheaf Street | E4-E5 |
| Sheffield Parkway | F6 |
| Shepherd Street | B6-B7-C7 |
| Shoreham Street | D1-D2-D3-E3 |
| Shrewsbury Road | E3-E4-F3-F4 |
| Shude Lane | E5 |
| Shude Hill | E5-E6 |
| Sidney Street | D3 |
| Silver Street | C6 |
| Snig Hill | D6 |
| Solly Street | B5-B6-C6 |
| South Lane | C2 |
| South Street | E4-E5 |
| Spital Hill | E7-E8-F8 |
| Spital Street | E8-F8 |
| Spitalfields | D7-E7 |
| Spring Street | D6-D7 |
| Stanley Street | E7 |
| Suffolk Road | E3 |
| Summerfield Street | A2-A1-B1 |
| Sunny Bank | A2 |
| Surrey Place | D4 |
| Surrey Street | D4-D5 |
| Sussex Street | F7 |
| Sylvester Street | C2-D2 |
| Talbot Place | F4 |
| Talbot Street | F4 |
| Tenter Street | C6 |
| The Moor | C3-C4 |
| Townhead Street | C5 |
| Trippet Lane | C5 |
| Tudor Street | D4-D5 |
| Tudor Way | D5 |
| Union Street | C4-D4 |
| Upper Allen Street | B6 |
| Upper Hanover Street | A3-A4-A5 |
| Upperthorpe Road | A7-A8 |
| Verdon Street | D8-E8 |
| Vicar Lane | C5-D5 |
| Victoria Station Road | E6-E7-F7 |
| Waingate | E6 |
| Walker Street | E7 |
| Washington Road | B1 |
| Watery Street | B7-B8 |
| Wellington Street | B4-C4 |
| West Bar | D6 |
| West Bar Green | C6-D6 |
| West Street | B4-B5-C5 |
| Weston Street | A5-A6 |
| Wheel Hill | E5 |
| Wicker | E6-E7 |
| Wilkinson Street | A4 |
| William Street | A2-A3 |
| York Street | D5-D6 |
| Young Street | B2-C2 |

# INDEX TO ATLAS

**This index contains over 32,000 entries.**
**All towns and large villages are included, as are locally important settlements.**

To locate a place in the atlas, first look up the name of the town or village required in the index. Turn to the page number indicated in *italic* type, and find the location using the last four numbers. Taking Hythe *Kent* ........................... **29** TR1634 as our example, take the first **bold** figure of the reference, 1, which refers to the number along the bottom of the page. The second figure, 6, tells you the distance to move in tenths to the right of this numbered line. A vertical line through this point is the first half of the reference. The third, **bold** figure, 3, refers to the number on the lefthand side of the page. Finally, the fourth figure, 4, indicates the distance to move in tenths above this numbered line. A horizontal line drawn through this point to intersect with the first line gives the precise location of the place in question. (For an explanation of the double letters, ie TR, in the reference, see the national grid page.)

Street plans of towns included within the index on the pages shown:

A'Chill Amber Row


A'Chill *Highld* 128 NG2705
Ab Kettleby *Leics* 63 SK7223
Ab Lench *H & W* 47 SP0152
Abbas Combe *Somset* 22 ST7022
Abberley *H & W* 47 SO7568
Abberley Common *H & W* 47 SO7467
Abberton *Essex* 41 TM0019
Abberton *H & W* 47 SO9953
Abberwick *Nthumb* 111 NU1313
Abbess Roding *Essex* 40 TL5711
Abbey *Devon* 9 ST1410
Abbey Cowpe *Cumb* 92 NY1550
Abbey Dore *H & W* 46 SO3830
Abbey Gate *Devon* 10 SY2996
Abbey Green *Staffs* 72 SJ9757
Abbey Hill *Somset* 9 ST1717
Abbey St. Bathans *Border* 119 NT7661
Abbey Town *Cumb* 93 NY1750
Abbey Village *Lancs* 81 SD6422
Abbey Wood *Gt Lon* 27 TQ4779
Abbeycwmhir *Powys* 45 SO0571
Abbeydale *S York* 74 SK3282
Abbeylands *IOM* 153 SC4585
Abbeystead *Lancs* 81 SD5654
Abbot's Chair *Derbys* 74 SK0290
Abbot's Salford *Warwks* 48 SP0650
Abbotrule *Border* 110 NT6113
Abbots Bickington *Devon* 18 SS3813
Abbots Bromley *Staffs* 73 SK0824
Abbots Deuglie *Tays* 126 NO1111
Abbots Langley *Herts* 26 TL0902
Abbots Leigh *Avon* 34 ST5474
Abbots Morton *H & W* 48 SP0255
Abbots Ripton *Cambs* 52 TL2377
Abbots Worthy *Hants* 24 SU4932
Abbotsford *Border* 109 NT5034
Abbotsham *Devon* 18 SS4226
Abbotskerswell *Devon* 7 SX8569
Abbotsleigh *Devon* 7 SX8048
Abbotsley *Cambs* 52 TL2256
Abbotstone *Hants* 24 SU5634
Abbotswood *Hants* 23 SU3623
Abbott Street *Dorset* 11 ST9800
Abbotts Ann *Hants* 23 SU3243
Abbottsbury *Dorset* 10 SY5785
Abcott *Shrops* 46 SO3978
Abdon *Shrops* 59 SO5786
Abenhall *Gloucs* 35 SO6717
Aber *Gwynd* 69 SH6572
Aber Clydach *Powys* 33 SO1021
Aber-arad *Dyfed* 31 SN3140
Aber-banc *Dyfed* 31 SN3541
Aber-giar *Dyfed* 44 SN5040
Aber-Magwr *Dyfed* 43 SN6673
Aber-meurig *Dyfed* 44 SN5656
Aber-nant *M Glam* 33 SO0103
Aberaeron *Dyfed* 42 SN4562
Aberaman *M Glam* 33 SO0101
Aberangell *Powys* 57 SH8410
Aberarder *Highld* 140 NH6235
Aberargie *Tays* 126 NO1615
Aberarth *Dyfed* 42 SN4763
Aberavon *W Glam* 32 SS7589
Aberbargoed *M Glam* 33 SO1500
Aberbargoed *M Glam* 33 ST1699
Aberbeeg *Gwent* 33 SO2102
Abercairny *Tays* 108 NS9122
Abercanaid *M Glam* 33 SO0503
Abercarn *Gwent* 33 ST2195
Abercastle *Dyfed* 30 SM8533
Abercegir *Powys* 57 SH8001
Aberchader Lodge *Highld* 131 NH3403
Aberchirder *Gramp* 142 NJ6252
Abercraf *Powys* 33 SN8213
Abercregan *W Glam* 33 SS8496
Abercrombie *Fife* 127 NO5102
Abercwmboi *M Glam* 33 ST0299
Abercych *Dyfed* 31 SN2441
Abercynon *M Glam* 33 ST0794
Aberdalgie *Tays* 125 NO0720
Aberdare *Powys* 35 SO0002
Aberdaron *Gwynd* 56 SH1726
Aberdeen *Gramp* 135 NJ9306
Aberdesach *Gwynd* 68 SH4251
Aberdour *Fife* 117 NT1985
Aberdovey *Gwynd* 43 SN6196
Aberdulais *W Glam* 32 SS7799
Aberedw *Powys* 45 SO0847
Abereiddy *Dyfed* 30 SM7931
Abererch *Gwynd* 56 SH3936
Aberfan *M Glam* 33 SO0700
Aberfeldy *Tays* 125 NN8549
Aberffraw *Gwynd* 68 SH3560
Aberffrwd *Dyfed* 43 SN6879
Aberford *W York* 83 SE4336
Aberfoyle *Cent* 115 NN5200
Abergarw *M Glam* 33 SS9184
Abergarwed *W Glam* 33 SN8102
Abergavenny *Gwent* 34 SO2914
Abergele *Clwyd* 70 SH9477
Abergorlech *Dyfed* 44 SN5833
Abergwesyn *Powys* 45 SN8552
Abergwili *Dyfed* 31 SN4320
Abergwydel *Powys* 57 SH7902
Abergwynfi *W Glam* 33 SS8995
Abergynolwyn *Gwynd* 57 SH6707
Aberhosan *Powys* 43 SN8197
Aberkenfig *M Glam* 33 SS8984
Aberlady *Loth* 118 NT4679
Aberlemno *Tays* 127 NO5255
Aberllefenni *Gwynd* 57 SH7609
Aberllynfi *Powys* 45 SO1737
Aberlour *Gramp* 141 NJ2642
Abermorddu *Clwyd* 71 SJ3056
Abermule *Powys* 58 SO1594
Abernant *Dyfed* 31 SN3423
Abernethy *Tays* 126 NO1916
Abernyte *Tays* 126 NO2531
Aberporth *Dyfed* 42 SN2651
Abersoch *Gwynd* 56 SH3128
Abersychan *Gwent* 34 SO2604
Aberthin *S Glam* 33 ST0075
Abertillery *Gwent* 33 SO2104
Abertridwr *M Glam* 33 ST1289
Abertridwr *Powys* 58 SJ0319
Abertysswg *M Glam* 33 SO1305
Aberuthven *Tays* 125 NN9815
Aberyscir *Powys* 45 SN9929
Aberystwyth *Dyfed* 43 SN5881
Abingdon *Oxon* 37 SU4997
Abinger *Surrey* 14 TQ1145
Abinger Hammer *Surrey* 14 TQ0947
Abington *Nhants* 50 SP7860
Abington *Strath* 108 NS9323
Abington Pigotts *Cambs* 39 TL3044
Ablington *Gloucs* 36 SP1007
Ablington *Wilts* 23 SU1645
Abney *Derbys* 74 SK1980
Above Church *Staffs* 73 SK0150
Aboyne *Gramp* 134 NO5298
Abram *Gt Man* 78 SD6001
Abriachan *Highld* 139 NH5535
Abridge *Essex* 27 TQ4696
Abson *Avon* 35 ST7074
Abthorpe *Nhants* 49 SP6446
Aby *Lincs* 77 TF4078
Acaster Malbis *N York* 83 SE5845
Acaster Selby *N York* 83 SE5741
Accott *Devon* 19 SS6432
Accrington *Lancs* 81 SD7628
Accurach *Strath* 123 NN1120
Acha *Strath* 120 NM1854
Achalader *Tays* 126 NO1245
Achaleven *Strath* 122 NM9233
Achanalt *Highld* 139 NH2561
Achanamara *Strath* 113 NR7887
Achandunie *Highld* 146 NH6472
Achanoish *Strath* 113 NR7877
Achany *Highld* 146 NC5602
Acharn *Tays* 124 NN7543
Achavanich *Highld* 151 ND1842
Achduart *Highld* 145 NC0403
Achentoul *Highld* 150 NC8733
Achfary *Highld* 148 NC2939
Achianich *Tays* 124 NN7242
Achiltibuie *Highld* 144 NC0208
Achina *Highld* 150 NC7060
Achintee *Highld* 138 NG9441
Achintoan *Strath* 105 NR7516
Achintraid *Highld* 138 NG8438
Achlain *Highld* 131 NH3712
Achlyness *Highld* 148 NC2452
Achmelvich *Highld* 148 NC0524
Achmore *Cent* 124 NN5832
Achmore *Highld* 138 NG8533
Achmore *W Isls* 154 NB3029
Achnacarnin *Highld* 148 NC0332
Achnacarry *Highld* 131 NN1787
Achnacloich *Highld* 129 NG5908
Achnacloich *Strath* 122 NM9534
Achnaconeran *Highld* 139 NH4118
Achnacroish *Strath* 122 NM8541
Achnadrish House *Strath* 121 NM4652
Achnafauld *Tays* 125 NN8736
Achnagarron *Highld* 146 NH6870
Achnaha *Highld* 128 NM4668
Achnahaird *Highld* 144 NC0110
Achnahanat *Highld* 146 NH5198
Achnairn *Highld* 146 NC5512
Achnalea *Highld* 130 NM8561
Achnaluachrach *Highld* 146 NC6709
Achnasheen *Highld* 138 NH1658
Achnashellach Station *Highld* 138 NH0047
Achnastank *Gramp* 141 NJ2733
Achosnich *Highld* 121 NM4467
Achranich *Highld* 122 NM7047
Achreamie *Highld* 150 ND0166
Achriabhach *Highld* 131 NN1468
Achriesgill *Highld* 148 NC2554
Achtoty *Highld* 149 NC6762
Achurch *Nhants* 51 TL0282
Achvaich *Highld* 146 NH7194
Ackenthwaite *Cumb* 87 SD5082
Ackergill *Highld* 151 ND3553
Acklam *Cleve* 97 NZ4817
Acklam *N York* 90 SE7861
Ackleton *Shrops* 60 SO7798
Acklington *Nthumb* 103 NU2302
Ackton *W York* 83 SE4121
Ackworth Moor Top *W York* 83 SE4316
Acle *Norfk* 67 TG4010
Acock's Green *W Mids* 61 SP1283
Acol *Kent* 29 TR3067
Acomb *N York* 83 SE5751
Acomb *Nthumb* 102 NY9366
Acombe *Somset* 9 ST1913
Aconbury *H & W* 46 SO5133
Acre *Lancs* 81 SD7924
Acrefair *Clwyd* 70 SJ2843
Acresford *Derbys* 61 SK2913
Acton *Ches* 71 SJ6352
Acton *Dorset* 11 SY9878
Acton *Gt Lon* 26 TQ2080
Acton *H & W* 47 SO8467
Acton *Shrops* 59 SO3185
Acton *Staffs* 72 SJ8241
Acton *Suffk* 54 TL8945
Acton Beauchamp *H & W* 47 SO6750
Acton Bridge *Ches* 71 SJ6075
Acton Burnell *Shrops* 59 SJ5302
Acton Green *H & W* 47 SO6950
Acton Park *Clwyd* 71 SJ3451
Acton Pigott *Shrops* 59 SJ5402
Acton Round *Shrops* 59 SO6395
Acton Scott *Shrops* 59 SO4589
Acton Trussell *Staffs* 72 SJ9317
Acton Turville *Avon* 35 ST8080
Adbaston *Staffs* 72 SJ7628
Adber *Dorset* 21 ST5920
Adbolton *Notts* 62 SK5938
Adderbury *Oxon* 49 SP4735
Adderley *Shrops* 72 SJ6640
Adderstone *Nthumb* 111 NU1330
Addiewell *Loth* 117 NS9962
Addingham *W York* 82 SE0749
Addington *Bucks* 49 SP7428
Addington *Gt Lon* 27 TQ3763
Addington *Kent* 28 TQ6559
Addiscombe *Gt Lon* 27 TQ3366
Addlestone *Surrey* 26 TQ0565
Addlestonemore *Surrey* 26 TQ0565
Addlethorpe *Lincs* 77 TF5469
Adeney *Shrops* 72 SJ7018
Adeyfield *Herts* 38 TL0708
Adfa *Powys* 58 SJ0601
Adforton *H & W* 46 SO4071
Adisham *Kent* 29 TR2253
Adlestrop *Gloucs* 48 SP2426
Adlingfleet *Humb* 84 SE8421
Adlington *Ches* 79 SJ9180
Adlington *Lancs* 81 SD6013
Admaston *Shrops* 59 SJ6313
Admaston *Staffs* 73 SK0423
Admington *Warwks* 48 SP2045
Adsborough *Somset* 20 ST2729
Adscombe *Somset* 20 ST1838
Adstock *Bucks* 49 SP7330
Adstone *Nhants* 49 SP5951
Adswood *Gt Man* 79 SJ8888
Adversane *W Susx* 14 TQ0723
Adwalton *W York* 82 SE2228
Adwell *Oxon* 37 SU6999
Adwick le Street *S York* 83 SE5308
Adwick upon Dearne *S York* 83 SE4601
AE Bridgend *D & G* 100 NY0186
Ae *D & G* 100 NX9889
Affeton Barton *Devon* 19 SS7513
Affetside *Gt Man* 81 SD7513
Affleck *Gramp* 142 NJ5540
Affleck *Gramp* 142 NJ5540
Affpuddle *Dorset* 11 SY8093
Affric Lodge *Highld* 138 NH1823
Afon-wen *Clwyd* 70 SJ1371
Afton *Devon* 7 SX8462
Afton *IOW* 12 SZ3486
Afton Bridgend *Strath* 107 NS6213
Agglethorpe *N York* 89 SE0886
Aigburth *Mersyd* 78 SJ3886
Aike *Humb* 84 TA0445
Aiketgate *Cumb* 94 NY4846
Aikhead *Cumb* 93 NY2349
Aikton *Cumb* 93 NY2753
Ailby *Lincs* 77 TF4476
Ailey *H & W* 46 SO3348
Ailsworth *Cambs* 64 TL1198
Ainderby *N York* 89 SE3480
Ainderby Quernhow *N York* 89 SE3480
Ainderby Steeple *N York* 89 SE3392
Aingers Green *Essex* 41 TM1120
Ainsdale *Mersyd* 80 SD3112
Ainsdale-on-Sea *Mersyd* 80 SD3012
Ainstable *Cumb* 94 NY5246
Ainsworth *Gt Man* 79 SD7610
Ainthorpe *N York* 90 NZ7007
Aintree *Mersyd* 78 SJ3898
Aird *D & G* 98 NX0960
Aird *W Isls* 154 NB5635
Aird *Strath* 113 NM7600
Aird of Kinloch *Strath* 121 NM5228
Aird of Sleat *Highld* 129 NG5900
Airdeny *Strath* 122 NM9929
Airdrie *Strath* 116 NS7665
Airdriehill *Strath* 116 NS7867
Airds Bay *Strath* 122 NM9932
Airds of Kells *D & G* 99 NX6770
Airieland *D & G* 99 NX7556
Airmyn *Humb* 84 SE7224
Airntully *Tays* 125 NO0935
Airor *Highld* 129 NG7205
Airth *Cent* 116 NS8987
Airton *N York* 88 SD9059
Aisby *Lincs* 76 SK8792
Aisby *Lincs* 64 TF0138
Aisgill *Cumb* 88 SD7797
Aish *Devon* 7 SX6960
Aish *Devon* 7 SX8458
Aiskew *N York* 89 SE2788
Aislaby *Cleve* 89 NZ4012
Aislaby *N York* 90 NZ8508
Aislaby *N York* 90 SE7785
Aisthorpe *Lincs* 76 SK9480
Aisthorpe *Lincs* 76 SK9480
Aith *Shet* 155 HU3455
Akeld *Nthumb* 111 NT9529
Akeley *Bucks* 49 SP7037
Akenham *Suffk* 54 TM1449
Albaston *Devon* 6 SX4270
Alberbury *Shrops* 59 SJ3614
Albert Street *Clwyd* 70 SJ2660
Albourne *W Susx* 15 TQ2616
Albourne Green *W Susx* 15 TQ2616
Albrighton *Shrops* 59 SJ4918
Albrighton *Shrops* 60 SJ8104
Alburgh *Norfk* 55 TM2687
Albury *Herts* 39 TL4324
Albury *Oxon* 37 SP6505
Albury *Surrey* 14 TQ0547
Albury End *Herts* 39 TL4223
Albury Heath *Surrey* 14 TQ0646
Alby Hill *Norfk* 67 TG1934
Alcaig *Highld* 139 NH5657
Alcaston *Shrops* 59 SO4687
Alcester *Warwks* 48 SP0857
Alcester Lane End *W Mids* 61 SP0780
Alciston *E Susx* 16 TQ5005
Alcombe *Wilts* 35 ST8069
Alconbury *Cambs* 52 TL1876
Alconbury Weston *Cambs* 52 TL1777
Aldborough *N York* 89 SE4066
Aldborough *Norfk* 66 TG1834
Aldbourne *Wilts* 36 SU2675
Aldbrough *Humb* 85 TA2438
Aldbury *Herts* 38 SP9612
Aldcliffe *Cumb* 87 SD4660
Aldclune *Tays* 132 NN8964
Aldeburgh *Suffk* 55 TM4656
Aldeby *Norfk* 67 TM4593
Aldenham *Herts* 26 TQ1498
Alder Moor *Staffs* 73 SK2227
Alderbury *Wilts* 23 SU1827
Aldercar *Derbys* 62 SK4447
Alderford *Norfk* 66 TG1218
Alderholt *Dorset* 12 SU1212
Alderley *Gloucs* 35 ST7690
Alderley Edge *Ches* 79 SJ8478
Aldermans Green *W Mids* 61 SP3583
Aldermaston *Berks* 24 SU5965
Alderminster *Warwks* 48 SP2248
Aldershot *Hants* 25 SU8650
Alderton *Gloucs* 47 SP0033
Alderton *Nhants* 49 SP7346
Alderton *Shrops* 59 SJ4924
Alderton *Suffk* 55 TM3441
Alderton *Wilts* 35 ST8482
Alderwasley *Derbys* 74 SK3153
Aldfield *N York* 89 SE2669
Aldford *Ches* 71 SJ4159
Aldgate *Leics* 63 SK9804
Aldham *Essex* 40 TL9126
Aldham *Suffk* 54 TM0545
Aldingbourne *W Susx* 14 SU9205
Aldingham *Cumb* 86 SD2870
Aldington *H & W* 48 SP0644
Aldington *Kent* 29 TR0736
Aldington Corner *Kent* 28 TR0536
Aldivalloch *Gramp* 141 NJ3536
Aldochlay *Strath* 115 NS3591
Aldon *Shrops* 46 SO4379
Aldoth *Cumb* 92 NY1448
Aldreth *Cambs* 53 TL4473
Aldridge *W Mids* 61 SK0500
Aldringham *Suffk* 55 TM4461
Aldro *N York* 90 SE8162
Aldsworth *Gloucs* 36 SP1510
Aldsworth *W Susx* 14 SU7608
Aldunie *Gramp* 141 NJ3626
Aldwark *Derbys* 74 SK2257
Aldwark *N York* 89 SE4663
Aldwick *W Susx* 14 SZ9199
Aldwincle *Nhants* 51 TL0081
Aldworth *Berks* 37 SU5579
Alexandria *Strath* 115 NS3980
Aley *Somset* 20 ST1837
Alfardisworthy *Devon* 18 SS2911
Alfington *Devon* 9 SY1197
Alfold *Surrey* 14 TQ0334
Alfold Bars *W Susx* 14 TQ0333
Alford *Gramp* 142 NJ5715
Alford *Lincs* 77 TF4575
Alford *Somset* 21 ST6032
Alford Crossways *Surrey* 14 TQ0435
Alfreton *Derbys* 74 SK4155
Alfrick *H & W* 47 SO7453
Alfrick Pound *H & W* 47 SO7352
Alfriston *E Susx* 16 TQ5103
Algarkirk *Lincs* 64 TF2935
Alhampton *Somset* 21 ST6234
Alkborough *Humb* 84 SE8821
Alkerton *Gloucs* 35 SO7705
Alkerton *Oxon* 48 SP3743
Alkham *Kent* 29 TR2542
Alkington *Shrops* 71 SJ5339
Alkmonton *Derbys* 73 SK1838
All Cannings *Wilts* 36 SU0771
All Saints South Elmham *Suffk* 55 TM3482
All Stretton *Shrops* 59 SO4695
Alladale Lodge *Highld* 146 NH4489
Allaleigh *Devon* 7 SX8053
Allanaquoich *Gramp* 133 NO1291
Allanbank *Strath* 116 NS8458
Allanton *Border* 119 NT8654
Allanton *Strath* 116 NS7454
Allanton *Strath* 116 NS8457
Allardice *Gramp* 135 NO8173
Allardice *Gramp* 135 NO8173
Allaston *Gloucs* 35 SO6304
Allbrook *Hants* 13 SU4521
Allen's Green *Herts* 39 TL4516
Allendale Town *Nthumb* 95 NY8455
Allenheads *Nthumb* 95 NY8645
Allensford *Dur* 95 NZ0749
Allensmore *H & W* 46 SO4635
Allenton *Derbys* 62 SK3732
Aller *Devon* 19 SS7625
Aller *Somset* 21 ST4029
Allerby *Cumb* 92 NY0839
Allercombe *Devon* 9 SY0494
Allerford *Somset* 20 SS9047
Allerston *N York* 90 SE8782
Allerthorpe *Humb* 84 SE7847
Allerton *Mersyd* 78 SJ3987
Allerton *W York* 82 SE1234
Allerton Bywater *W York* 83 SE4127
Allerton Mauleverer *N York* 89 SE4458
Allesley *W Mids* 61 SP2980
Allestree *Derbys* 62 SK3439
Allet Common *Cnwll* 3 SW7948
Allexton *Leics* 51 SK8100
Allgreave *Ches* 72 SJ9767
Allhallows *Kent* 28 TQ8377
Allhallows-on-Sea *Kent* 40 TQ8478
Alligin Shuas *Highld* 137 NG8358
Allimore Green *Staffs* 72 SJ8519
Allington *Dorset* 10 SY4693
Allington *Kent* 28 TQ7557
Allington *Lincs* 63 SK8540
Allington *Wilts* 35 ST8975
Allington *Wilts* 23 SU0663
Allington *Wilts* 23 SU2039
Allithwaite *Cumb* 87 SD3876
Allen End *Warwks* 61 SP1696
Alloa *Cent* 116 NS8893
Allonby *Cumb* 92 NY0843
Alloway *Strath* 106 NS3318
Allowenshay *Somset* 10 ST3913
Allscott *Shrops* 60 SO7396
Allscott *Shrops* 59 SJ6113
Allt Na h'Airbhe Inn *Highld* 145 NH1193
Alltami *Clwyd* 70 SJ2665
Alltchaorunn *Highld* 123 NN1951
Alltmawr *Powys* 45 SO0746
Alltwalis *Dyfed* 31 SN4431
Alltwen *W Glam* 32 SN7303
Alltyblaca *Dyfed* 44 SN5245
Allweston *Dorset* 11 ST6614
Allwood Green *Suffk* 54 TM0472
Almeley *H & W* 46 SO3351
Almeley Wooton *H & W* 46 SO3352
Almer *Dorset* 11 SY9098
Almholme *S York* 83 SE5008
Almington *Staffs* 72 SJ7034
Alminstone Cross *Devon* 18 SS3420
Almodington *W Susx* 14 SZ8297
Almondbank *Tays* 125 NO0625
Almondbury *W York* 82 SE1615
Almondsbury *Avon* 34 ST6083
Alne *N York* 90 SE4965
Alnesbourn Priory *Suffk* 55 TM1940
Alness *Highld* 146 NH6599
Alnham *Nthumb* 111 NT9810
Alnmouth *Nthumb* 111 NU2410
Alnwick *Nthumb* 111 NU1813
Alperton *Gt Lon* 26 TQ1884
Alphamstone *Essex* 54 TL8835
Alpheton *Suffk* 54 TL8850
Alphington *Devon* 9 SX9090
Alpington *Norfk* 67 TG2901
Alport *Derbys* 74 SK2264
Alpraham *Ches* 71 SJ5859
Alresford *Essex* 41 TM0721
Alrewas *Staffs* 73 SK1715
Alsager *Ches* 72 SJ7955
Alsagers Bank *Staffs* 72 SJ8048
Alshot *Somset* 20 ST1936
Alsop en le Dale *Derbys* 73 SK1655
Alston *Devon* 10 ST3002
Alston Sutton *Somset* 21 ST4151
Alstone *Gloucs* 47 SO9832
Alstone *Somset* 21 ST3147
Alstone Green *Staffs* 72 SJ8618
Alstonefield *Staffs* 73 SK1355
Alswear *Devon* 19 SS7222
Alt *Gt Man* 79 SD9403
Altandhu *Highld* 144 NB9812
Altarnun *Cnwll* 5 SX2281
Altass *Highld* 146 NC5000
Altcreich *Strath* 122 NM6939
Altgaltraig *Strath* 114 NS0473
Altham *Lancs* 81 SD7733
Althorne *Essex* 40 TQ9199
Althorpe *Humb* 84 SE8309
Altnabreac Station *Highld* 150 ND0045
Altnacealgach Hotel *Highld* 145 NC2810
Altnacraig *Strath* 122 NM8429
Altnaharra *Highld* 149 NC5635
Altofts *W York* 83 SE3723
Alton *Derbys* 74 SK3664
Alton *Hants* 24 SU7139
Alton *Staffs* 73 SK0742
Alton *Wilts* 23 SU1546
Alton Barnes *Wilts* 23 SU1062
Alton Pancras *Dorset* 11 ST6902
Alton Priors *Wilts* 23 SU1062
Altrincham *Gt Man* 79 SJ7687
Alva *Cent* 116 NS8897
Alvanley *Ches* 71 SJ4974
Alvaston *Derbys* 62 SK3833
Alvechurch *H & W* 61 SP0372
Alvecote *Warwks* 61 SK2404
Alvediston *Wilts* 22 ST9723
Alveley *Shrops* 60 SO7684
Alverdiscott *Devon* 19 SS5225
Alverstoke *Hants* 13 SZ6098
Alverstone *IOW* 13 SZ5785
Alverthorpe *W York* 82 SE3121
Alverton *Notts* 63 SK7942
Alves *Gramp* 141 NJ1362
Alvescot *Oxon* 36 SP2704
Alveston *Avon* 35 ST6388
Alveston *Warwks* 48 SP2256
Alvie *Highld* 132 NH8609
Alvingham *Lincs* 77 TF3691
Alvington *Gloucs* 34 SO6000
Alwalton *Cambs* 64 TL1396
Alwinton *Nthumb* 110 NT9106
Alwoodley *W York* 82 SE2840
Alwoodley Gates *W York* 82 SE3140
Alyth *Tays* 126 NO2448
Amber Hill *Lincs* 76 TF2346
Amber Row *Derbys* 74 SK3856

Ambergate
Astonlane


Ambergate *Derbys* 74 SK3451
Amberley *Gloucs* 35 SO8401
Amberley *W Susx* 14 TQ0313
Ambirstone *E Susx* 16 TQ5911
Amble *Nthumb* 103 NU2604
Amblecote *W Mids* 60 SO8985
Ambler Thorn *W York* 82 SE0929
Ambleside *Cumb* 87 NY3704
Ambleston *Dyfed* 30 SN0026
Ambrosden *Oxon* 37 SP6019
Amcotts *Humb* 84 SE8514
America *Cambs* 53 TL4378
Amersham *Bucks* 26 SU9597
Amersham-on-the-Hill *Bucks* 26 SU9798
Amerton *Staffs* 73 SJ9927
Amesbury *Wilts* 23 SU1541
Amhuinnsuidhe *W Isls* 154 NB0408
Amington *Staffs* 61 SK2304
Amisfield Town *D & G* 100 NY0082
Amlwch *Gwynd* 68 SH4492
Ammanford *Dyfed* 32 SN6212
Amotherby *N York* 90 SE7473
Ampfield *Hants* 13 SU4023
Ampleforth *N York* 90 SE5878
Ampney Crucis *Gloucs* 36 SP0602
Ampney St. Mary *Gloucs* 36 SP0802
Ampney St. Peter *Gloucs* 36 SP0801
Amport *Hants* 23 SU3044
Ampthill *Beds* 38 TL0337
Ampton *Suffk* 54 TL8671
Amroth *Dyfed* 31 SN1608
Amwell *Herts* 39 TL1613
Anaheilt *Highld* 130 NM8162
Ancaster *Lincs* 63 SK9843
Anchor *Shrops* 58 SO1784
Ancroft *Nthumb* 111 NU0045
Ancrum *Border* 110 NT6224
Ancton *W Susx* 14 SU9800
Anderby *Lincs* 77 TF5275
Andersea *Somset* 21 ST3333
Andersfield *Somset* 20 ST2733
Anderson *Dorset* 11 SY8797
Anderton *Ches* 79 SJ6475
Anderton *M Glam* 6 SX4351
Andover *Hants* 23 SU3645
Andoversford *Gloucs* 35 SP0219
Andreas *IOM* 153 SC4199
Anelog *Gwynd* 56 SH1527
Anerley *Gt Lon* 27 TQ3369
Anfield *Mersyd* 78 SJ3692
Angarrack *Cnwll* 2 SW5838
Angarrick *Cnwll* 3 SW7937
Angelbank *Shrops* 46 SO5776
Angersleigh *Somset* 20 ST1918
Angerton *Cumb* 93 NY2257
Angle *Dyfed* 30 SM8603
Angmering *W Susx* 14 TQ0604
Angram *N York* 88 SD8899
Angram *N York* 83 SE5248
Angrouse *Cnwll* 2 SW6619
Anick *Nthumb* 102 NY9465
Ankerville *Highld* 147 NH8174
Ankle Hill *Leics* 63 SK7518
Anlaby *Humb* 84 TA0352
Anlaby *Humb* 84 TA0328
Anmer *Norfk* 65 TF7429
Anmore *Hants* 13 SU6711
Anna Valley *Hants* 23 SU3443
Annan *D & G* 101 NY1966
Annaside *Cumb* 86 SD0986
Annat *Highld* 138 NG8954
Annat *Strath* 122 NN0322
Annathill *Strath* 116 NS7270
Annbank *Strath* 106 NS4023
Annelsey Woodhouse *Notts* 75 SK4953
Annesley *Notts* 75 SK5153
Annfield Plain *Dur* 96 NZ1751
Anniesland *Strath* 115 NS5368
Annitsford *T & W* 103 NZ2674
Annscroft *Shrops* 59 SJ4508
Ansdell *Lancs* 80 SD3428
Ansford *Somset* 21 ST6432
Ansley *Warwks* 61 SP3091
Anslow *Staffs* 73 SK1924
Anslow Gate *Staffs* 73 SK2125
Anslow Lees *Staffs* 73 SK2024
Ansteadbrook *Surrey* 14 SU9332
Anstey *Hants* 24 SU7240
Anstey *Herts* 39 TL4033
Anstey *Leics* 62 SK5408
Anston *S York* 75 SK5184
Anstruther *Fife* 127 NO5703
Anstruther Easter *Fife* 127 NO5704
Ansty *W Susx* 15 TQ2923
Ansty *Warwks* 61 SP4083
Ansty *Wilts* 22 ST9526
Ansty Cross *Dorset* 11 ST7603
Anthill Common *Hants* 13 SU6412
Anthony's *Surrey* 26 TQ0161
Anthorn *Cumb* 93 NY1958
Antingham *Norfk* 67 TG2533
Antony *Cnwll* 5 SX3954
Antony *M Glam* 5 SX4054
Antrobus *Ches* 79 SJ6480
Antron *Cnwll* 2 SW6327
Anvil Corner *Devon* 18 SS3704
Anvil Green *Kent* 29 TR1049
Anwick *Lincs* 76 TF1150
Anwoth *D & G* 99 NX5856
Aperfield *Gt Lon* 27 TQ4158
Apes Dale *H & W* 60 SO9973
Apethorpe *Nhants* 51 TL0295
Apeton *Staffs* 72 SJ8518
Apley *Lincs* 76 TF1075
Apley Park *Shrops* 60 SO7199
Apperknowle *Derbys* 74 SK3878
Apperley *Gloucs* 47 SO8628
Apperley Bridge *W York* 82 SE1838
Apperley Dene *Nthumb* 95 NZ0558
Appersett *N York* 88 SD8590
Appin *Strath* 122 NM9346
Appleby *D & G* 99 NX4140
Appleby *Humb* 84 SE9414
Appleby Magna *Leics* 61 SK3109
Appleby Parva *Leics* 61 SK3008
Appleby Street *Herts* 39 TL3304
Appleby-in-Westmorland *Cumb* 94 NY6820
Applecross *Highld* 137 NG7144
Appledore *Devon* 18 SS4630
Appledore *Devon* 9 ST0614
Appledore *Kent* 17 TQ9529
Appledore Heath *Kent* 17 TQ9530
Appleford *Oxon* 37 SU5293
Applegarth Town *D & G* 100 NY1084
Applehaugh *S York* 83 SE3512
Appleshaw *Hants* 23 SU3048
Applethwaite *Cumb* 93 NY2625
Appleton *Ches* 78 SJ5186
Appleton *Oxon* 37 SP4401
Appleton Roebuck *N York* 83 SE5542
Appleton Thorn *Ches* 79 SJ6483
Appleton Wiske *N York* 89 NZ3904
Appleton-le-Moors *N York* 90 SE7387
Appleton-le-Street *N York* 90 SE7373
Appletreehall *Border* 109 NT5117
Appletreewick *N York* 88 SE0560
Appley *Somset* 20 ST0721
Appley Bridge *Lancs* 78 SD5209
Apse Heath *IOW* 13 SZ5683
Apsley End *Beds* 38 TL1232
Apsley Heath *Warwks* 61 SP0970
Apuldram *W Susx* 14 SU8403
Arabella *Highld* 147 NH7975
Arbeadie *Gramp* 135 NO6996
Arbirlot *Tays* 127 NO6040
Arboll *Highld* 147 NH8782
Arborfield *Berks* 24 SU7567
Arborfield Cross *Berks* 24 SU7666
Arbory *IOM* 153 SC2470
Arbourthorpe *S York* 74 SK3685
Arbroath *Tays* 127 NO6441
Arbuthnott *Gramp* 135 NO8074
Arcadia *Kent* 28 TQ8736
Archaracle *Highld* 121 NM6767
Archddu *Dyfed* 32 SN4401
Archdeacon Newton *Dur* 96 NZ2517
Archlestown *Gramp* 141 NJ2344
Arclid Green *Ches* 72 SJ7962
Ard a'Chapuill *Strath* 114 NS0179
Ardacheranbeg *Strath* 114 NS0085
Ardachu *Highld* 146 NC6603
Ardaily *Strath* 104 NR6450
Ardalanish *Strath* 121 NM3619
Ardanaiseig *Strath* 123 NN0824
Ardaneaskan *Highld* 137 NG8335
Ardarroch *Highld* 137 NG8339
Ardarroch *Strath* 114 NS2394
Ardbeg *Strath* 104 NR4146
Ardbeg *Strath* 114 NS0766
Ardbeg *Strath* 114 NS1583
Ardcharnich *Highld* 145 NH1788
Ardchiavaig *Strath* 121 NM3818
Ardchonnel *Strath* 122 NM9812
Ardchullarie More *Cent* 124 NN5813
Ardchyle *Cent* 124 NN5229
Arddleen *Powys* 58 SJ2616
Ardechive *Highld* 131 NN1490
Ardeer *Strath* 106 NS2740
Ardeley *Herts* 39 TL3027
Ardelve *Highld* 138 NG8727
Arden *Strath* 115 NS3684
Ardens Grafton *Warwks* 48 SP1154
Ardentinny *Strath* 114 NS1887
Ardeonaig *Cent* 124 NN6635
Ardersier *Highld* 140 NH7854
Ardessie *Highld* 145 NH0689
Ardfern *Strath* 122 NM8004
Ardgartan *Strath* 123 NN2703
Ardgay *Highld* 146 NH5990
Ardgour *Highld* 130 NN0163
Ardgowan *Strath* 114 NS2073
Ardhallow *Strath* 114 NS1574
Ardhasig *W Isls* 154 NB1303
Ardheslaig *Highld* 137 NG7855
Ardindrean *Highld* 145 NH1588
Ardingly *W Susx* 15 TQ3429
Ardington *Oxon* 36 SU4388
Ardington Wick *Oxon* 36 SU4389
Ardivachar *W Isls* 154 NF7445
Ardlamont House *Strath* 114 NR9865
Ardleigh *Essex* 41 TM0529
Ardleigh Heath *Essex* 41 TM0430
Ardler *Tays* 126 NO2642
Ardley *Oxon* 49 SP5427
Ardley End *Essex* 39 TL5214
Ardlui *Strath* 123 NN3115
Ardlussa *Strath* 113 NR6487
Ardmaddy *Strath* 123 NN0837
Ardmair *Highld* 145 NH1198
Ardmaleish *Strath* 114 NS0768
Ardmay *Strath* 123 NN2802
Ardminish *Strath* 104 NR6448
Ardmolich *Highld* 129 NM7171
Ardmore *Highld* 146 NH7086
Ardmore *Highld* 148 NC2151
Ardmore *Strath* 115 NS3178
Ardnadam *Strath* 114 NS1780
Ardnagrask *Highld* 139 NH5249
Ardnarff *Highld* 138 NG8935
Ardnastang *Highld* 130 NM8061
Ardnave *Strath* 112 NR2873
Ardno *Strath* 123 NN1508
Ardochrig *Strath* 116 NS6346
Ardochy House *Highld* 131 NH3002
Ardpatrick *Strath* 113 NR7660
Ardpeaton *Strath* 114 NS2185
Ardrishaig *Strath* 113 NR8585
Ardroil *W Isls* 154 NB0432
Ardrossan *Strath* 106 NS2342
Ardscalpsie *Strath* 114 NS0558
Ardshealach *Highld* 121 NM6867
Ardsley *S York* 83 SE3805
Ardsley East *W York* 82 SE3024
Ardslignish *Highld* 121 NM5661
Ardtalnaig *Tays* 124 NN7039
Ardtoe *Highld* 129 NM6270
Ardullie *Highld* 139 NH5862
Ardvaine *Strath* 122 NM7910
Ardvasar *Highld* 129 NG6303
Ardverikie *Highld* 131 NN5087
Ardvorlich *Tays* 124 NN6322
Ardvourlie *W Isls* 154 NB1911
Ardwell *D & G* 98 NX1045
Ardwick *Gt Man* 79 SJ8597
Areley Kings *H & W* 60 SO7970
Arford *Hants* 14 SU8236
Argoed *Gwent* 33 SO1700
Argoed *Shrops* 59 SJ3221
Argoed Mill *Powys* 45 SN9962
Argos Hill *E Susx* 16 TQ5628
Aribrauch *W Isls* 154 NB2518
Aridhglas *Strath* 120 NM3123
Arileod *Strath* 120 NM1655
Arinacrinachd *Highld* 137 NG7458
Arinagour *Strath* 120 NM2257
Ariogan *Strath* 122 NM8627
Arisaig *Highld* 129 NM6686
Arisaig House *Highld* 129 NM6984
Arivruach *W Isls* 154 NB2417
Arkendale *N York* 89 SE3861
Arkesden *Essex* 39 TL4834
Arkholme *Lancs* 87 SD5871
Arkleby *Cumb* 92 NY1439
Arkleton *D & G* 101 NY3791
Arkley *Gt Lon* 26 TQ2295
Arksey *S York* 83 SE5807
Arkwright Town *Derbys* 74 SK4270
Arle *Gloucs* 47 SO9223
Arlecdon *Cumb* 92 NY0419
Arlescote *Warwks* 48 SP3848
Arleston *Shrops* 60 SJ6610
Arley *Ches* 79 SJ6780
Arley *Warwks* 61 SP2890
Arlingham *Gloucs* 35 SO7010
Arlington *Devon* 19 SS6140
Arlington *E Susx* 16 TQ5407
Arlington *Gloucs* 36 SP1006
Arlington Beccott *Devon* 19 SS6240
Armadale *Highld* 150 NC7864
Armadale *Loth* 116 NS9368
Armadale Castle *Highld* 129 NG6304
Armaside *Cumb* 92 NY1527
Armathwaite *Cumb* 94 NY5046
Arminghall *Norfk* 67 TG2504
Armitage *Staffs* 73 SK0816
Armitage Bridge *W York* 82 SE1313
Armley *W York* 82 SE2733
Armshead *Staffs* 72 SJ9348
Armston *Nhants* 51 TL0686
Armthorpe *S York* 83 SE6205
Arnabost *Strath* 120 NM2159
Arnaby *Cumb* 86 SD1884
Arnburn *Strath* 115 NS3588
Arncliffe *N York* 88 SD9371
Arncliffe Cote *N York* 88 SD9470
Arncroach *Fife* 127 NO5105
Arndilly House *Gramp* 141 NJ2847
Arne *Dorset* 11 SY9788
Arnesby *Leics* 50 SP6192
Arnfield *Derbys* 79 SK0198
Arngask *Tays* 126 NO1411
Arnicle *Strath* 105 NR7138
Arnisdale *Highld* 130 NG8410
Arnish *Highld* 137 NG5948
Arniston *Loth* 118 NT3362
Arnol *W Isls* 154 NB3148
Arnold *Humb* 85 TA1241
Arnold *Notts* 62 SK5845
Arnprior *Cent* 116 NS6194
Arnside *Cumb* 87 SD4578
Aros Mains *Strath* 121 NM5645
Arotalla *Strath* 112 NR3654
Arowry *Clwyd* 71 SJ4639
Arrad Foot *Cumb* 86 SD3080
Arram *Humb* 84 TA0344
Arrathorne *N York* 89 SE2093
Arreton *IOW* 13 SZ5386
Arrington *Cambs* 52 TL3250
Arriundle *Highld* 130 NM8264
Arrochar *Strath* 123 NN3004
Arrow *Warwks* 48 SP0856
Arrowfield Top *H & W* 61 SP0374
Arscott *Shrops* 59 SJ4308
Artafallie *Highld* 140 NH6349
Arthington *W York* 82 SE2644
Arthingworth *Nhants* 50 SP7581
Arthog *Gwynd* 57 SH6414
Arthrath *Gramp* 143 NJ9636
Arthursdale *W York* 83 SE3737
Artrochie *Gramp* 143 NK0032
Arundel *W Susx* 14 TQ0107
Asby *Cumb* 92 NY0620
Ascog *Strath* 114 NS1062
Ascot *Berks* 25 SU9268
Ascott *Warwks* 48 SP3234
Ascott Earl *Oxon* 36 SP3018
Ascott-under-Whychwood *Oxon* 36 SP3018
Asenby *N York* 89 SE3975
Asfordby *Leics* 63 SK7018
Asfordby Hill *Leics* 63 SK7219
Asgarby *Lincs* 64 TF1145
Asgarby *Lincs* 77 TF3366
Ash *Devon* 19 SS5208
Ash *Devon* 7 SX8350
Ash *Dorset* 11 ST8610
Ash *Kent* 29 TR2858
Ash *Kent* 27 TQ6064
Ash *Somset* 20 ST2822
Ash *Somset* 21 ST4720
Ash *Surrey* 25 SU8950
Ash Bullayne *Devon* 8 SS7704
Ash Green *Surrey* 25 SU9049
Ash Green *Warwks* 61 SP3385
Ash Magna *Shrops* 71 SJ5739
Ash Mill *Devon* 19 SS7823
Ash Parva *Shrops* 71 SJ5739
Ash Priors *Somset* 20 ST1529
Ash Street *Suffk* 54 TM0146
Ash Thomas *Devon* 9 ST0010
Ash Vale *Surrey* 25 SU8952
Ashampstead *Berks* 37 SU5676
Ashampstead Green *Berks* 37 SU5677
Ashbocking *Suffk* 54 TM1754
Ashbocking Green *Suffk* 54 TM1854
Ashbourne *Derbys* 73 SK1846
Ashbourne Green *Derbys* 73 SK1947
Ashbrittle *Somset* 20 ST0521
Ashburnham Place *E Susx* 16 TQ6814
Ashburton *Devon* 7 SX7569
Ashbury *Devon* 5 SX5097
Ashbury *Oxon* 36 SU2685
Ashby *Humb* 84 SE9008
Ashby by Partney *Lincs* 77 TF4266
Ashby cum Fenby *Humb* 77 TA2500
Ashby de la Launde *Lincs* 76 TF0555
Ashby Folville *Leics* 63 SK7012
Ashby Magna *Leics* 50 SP5690
Ashby Parva *Leics* 50 SP5288
Ashby Puerorum *Lincs* 77 TF3271
Ashby St. Ledgers *Nhants* 50 SP5768
Ashby St. Mary *Norfk* 67 TG3202
Ashby-de-la-Zouch *Leics* 62 SK3516
Ashchurch *Gloucs* 47 SO9233
Ashcombe *Avon* 21 ST3361
Ashcombe *Devon* 9 SX9179
Ashcott *Somset* 21 ST4336
Ashcott Corner *Somset* 21 ST4539
Ashculme *Devon* 9 ST1415
Ashdon *Essex* 53 TL5842
Ashe *Hants* 24 SU5350
Asheldham *Essex* 41 TL9701
Ashen *Essex* 53 TL7442
Ashendon *Bucks* 37 SP7014
Asheridge *Bucks* 38 SP9304
Ashfield *Cent* 124 NN7803
Ashfield *Hants* 12 SU3619
Ashfield *Suffk* 55 TM2162
Ashfield Green *Suffk* 53 TL7656
Ashfield Green *Suffk* 55 TM2673
Ashfields *Shrops* 72 SJ7026
Ashfold Crossways *W Susx* 15 TQ2328
Ashford *Derbys* 74 SK1969
Ashford *Devon* 19 SS5335
Ashford *Devon* 7 SX6848
Ashford *Kent* 28 TR0142
Ashford *Surrey* 26 TQ0771
Ashford Bowdler *Shrops* 46 SO5170
Ashford Carbonel *Shrops* 46 SO5270
Ashford Hill *Hants* 24 SU5562
Ashgill *Strath* 116 NS7850
Ashill *Devon* 9 ST0811
Ashill *Norfk* 66 TF8804
Ashill *Somset* 10 ST3217
Ashingdon *Essex* 40 TQ8693
Ashington *Nthumb* 103 NZ2787
Ashington *Somset* 21 ST5621
Ashington *W Susx* 15 TQ1315
Ashkirk *Border* 109 NT4722
Ashlett *Hants* 13 SU4603
Ashleworth *Gloucs* 47 SO8125
Ashleworth Quay *Gloucs* 47 SO8125
Ashley *Cambs* 53 TL6961
Ashley *Ches* 79 SJ7784
Ashley *Devon* 19 SS6411
Ashley *Gloucs* 35 ST9394
Ashley *Hants* 12 SZ2595
Ashley *Hants* 23 SU3831
Ashley *Kent* 29 TR3048
Ashley *Nhants* 50 SP7990
Ashley *Staffs* 72 SJ7536
Ashley *Wilts* 22 ST8168
Ashley Green *Bucks* 38 SP9705
Ashley Moor *H & W* 46 SO4767
Ashmansworth *Hants* 24 SU4157
Ashmansworthy *Devon* 18 SS3317
Ashmead Green *Gloucs* 35 ST7699
Ashmill *Devon* 5 SX3995
Ashmore *Dorset* 11 ST9117
Ashmore Green *Berks* 24 SU5069
Ashorne *Warwks* 48 SP3057
Ashover *Derbys* 74 SK3463
Ashover Hay *Derbys* 74 SK3460
Ashow *Warwks* 61 SP3170
Ashperton *H & W* 47 SO6441
Ashprington *Devon* 7 SX8157
Ashreigney *Devon* 19 SS6213
Ashridge Park *Herts* 38 SP9912
Ashtead *Surrey* 26 TQ1858
Ashton *Cambs* 64 TF1005
Ashton *Ches* 71 SJ5069
Ashton *Cnwll* 2 SW6028
Ashton *Devon* 8 SX8584
Ashton *H & W* 46 SO5164
Ashton *Hants* 13 SU5519
Ashton *M Glam* 5 SX3868
Ashton *Nhants* 49 SP7649
Ashton *Nhants* 51 TL0588
Ashton *Somset* 21 ST4149
Ashton Common *Wilts* 22 ST8958
Ashton Hill *Wilts* 22 ST9057
Ashton Keynes *Wilts* 36 SU0494
Ashton under Hill *H & W* 47 SO9938
Ashton upon Mersey *Gt Man* 79 SJ7892
Ashton Watering *Avon* 34 ST5370
Ashton-under-Lyne *Gt Man* 79 SJ9399
Ashurst *Hants* 12 SU3310
Ashurst *Kent* 16 TQ5138
Ashurst *W Susx* 15 TQ1716
Ashurstwood *W Susx* 15 TQ4136
Ashwater *Devon* 5 SX3895
Ashwell *Herts* 39 TL2639
Ashwell *Leics* 63 SK8613
Ashwell End *Herts* 39 TL2540
Ashwellthorpe *Norfk* 66 TM1497
Ashwick *Somset* 21 ST6447
Ashwicken *Norfk* 65 TF7018
Ashwood *Staffs* 60 SO8688
Askam in Furness *Cumb* 86 SD2177
Aske Hall *N York* 89 NZ1703
Askern *S York* 83 SE5613
Askerswell *Dorset* 10 SY5292
Askett *Bucks* 38 SP8105
Askham *Cumb* 94 NY5123
Askham *Notts* 75 SK7374
Askham Bryan *N York* 83 SE5548
Askham Richard *N York* 83 SE5347
Asknish *Strath* 114 NR9391
Askrigg *N York* 88 SD9490
Askwith *N York* 82 SE1648
Aslackby *Lincs* 64 TF0830
Aslacton *Norfk* 66 TM1591
Aslockton *Notts* 63 SK7440
Asney *Somset* 21 ST4637
Aspall *Suffk* 54 TM1664
Aspatria *Cumb* 92 NY1442
Aspenden *Herts* 39 TL3528
Asperton *Lincs* 64 TF2637
Aspley *Staffs* 72 SJ8133
Aspley Guise *Beds* 38 SP9335
Aspley Heath *Beds* 38 SP9334
Aspull *Gt Man* 78 SD6108
Aspull Common *Gt Man* 79 SJ6498
Asselby *Humb* 84 SE7127
Asserby *Lincs* 77 TF4977
Asserby Turn *Lincs* 77 TF4777
Assington *Suffk* 54 TL9338
Assington Green *Suffk* 53 TL7751
Astbury *Ches* 72 SJ8461
Astcote *Nhants* 49 SP6753
Asterby *Lincs* 77 TF2678
Asterley *Shrops* 59 SJ3707
Asterton *Shrops* 59 SO3991
Asterton *Shrops* 59 SO3991
Asthall *Oxon* 36 SP2811
Asthall Leigh *Oxon* 36 SP3013
Astle *Highld* 146 NH7391
Astley *Gt Man* 79 SD7000
Astley *H & W* 47 SO7867
Astley *Shrops* 59 SJ5319
Astley *W York* 83 SE3828
Astley *Warwks* 61 SP3189
Astley Abbots *Shrops* 60 SO7196
Astley Bridge *Gt Man* 81 SD7111
Astley Cross *H & W* 47 SO8069
Astley Green *Gt Man* 79 SJ7099
Astley Town *H & W* 47 SO7968
Aston *Berks* 37 SU7884
Aston *Ches* 71 SJ5578
Aston *Ches* 71 SJ6146
Aston *Clwyd* 71 SJ3067
Aston *Derbys* 74 SK1883
Aston *H & W* 46 SO4662
Aston *H & W* 46 SO4671
Aston *Herts* 39 TL2722
Aston *Oxon* 36 SP3403
Aston *S York* 75 SK4685
Aston *Shrops* 60 SO8093
Aston *Shrops* 59 SJ5328
Aston *Shrops* 59 SJ6109
Aston *Staffs* 72 SJ8923
Aston *Staffs* 72 SJ7541
Aston *Staffs* 72 SJ9131
Aston *W Mids* 61 SP0888
Aston Abbotts *Bucks* 38 SP8419
Aston Botterell *Shrops* 59 SO6284
Aston Cantlow *Warwks* 48 SP1360
Aston Clinton *Bucks* 38 SP8812
Aston Crews *H & W* 47 SO6723
Aston Cross *Gloucs* 47 SO9433
Aston End *Herts* 39 TL2724
Aston Eyre *Shrops* 59 SO6594
Aston Fields *H & W* 47 SO9669
Aston Flamville *Leics* 50 SP4692
Aston Heath *Ches* 71 SJ5679
Aston Ingham *H & W* 47 SO6823
Aston juxta Mondrum *Ches* 72 SJ6457
Aston le Walls *Nhants* 49 SP4950
Aston Magna *Gloucs* 48 SP1935
Aston on Clun *Shrops* 59 SO3982
Aston Pigott *Shrops* 59 SJ3306
Aston Rogers *Shrops* 59 SJ3406
Aston Rowant *Oxon* 37 SU7299
Aston Sandford *Bucks* 37 SP7507
Aston Somerville *H & W* 48 SP0438
Aston Subedge *Gloucs* 48 SP1341
Aston Tirrold *Oxon* 37 SU5586
Aston Upthorpe *Oxon* 37 SU5586
Aston-in-Makerfield *Gt Man* 78 SJ5799
Aston-on-Trent *Derbys* 62 SK4129
Astonlane *Shrops* 59 SO6494

Astrop

Barford

Astrop *Nhants* 49 SP5036
Astrope *Herts* 38 SP8914
Astwick *Beds* 39 TL2138
Astwith *Derbys* 75 SK4364
Astwood *Bucks* 38 SP9547
Astwood *H & W* 47 SO9365
Astwood Bank *H & W* 48 SP0462
Aswarby *Lincs* 64 TF0639
Aswardby *Lincs* 77 TF3770
Atch Lench *H & W* 48 SP0350
Atcham *Shrops* 59 SJ5409
Athelhampton *Dorset* 11 SY7694
Athelington *Suffk* 55 TM2171
Athelney *Somset* 21 ST3428
Athelstaneford *Loth* 118 NT5377
Atherfield Green *IOW* 13 SZ4679
Atherington *Devon* 19 SS5923
Atherington *W Susx* 14 TQ0000
Atherstone *Somset* 10 ST3816
Atherstone *Warwks* 61 SP3097
Atherstone on Stour *Warwks* 48 SP2050
Atherton *Gt Man* 79 SD6703
Atley Hill *N York* 89 NZ2802
Atlow *Derbys* 73 SK2348
Attadale *Highld* 138 NG9238
Attenborough *Notts* 62 SK5134
Atterby *Lincs* 76 SK9893
Attercliffe *S York* 74 SK3788
Atterley *Shrops* 59 SO6397
Atterton *Leics* 61 SP3598
Attleborough *Norfk* 66 TM0495
Attleborough *Warwks* 61 SP3790
Attlebridge *Norfk* 66 TG1317
Attleton Green *Suffk* 53 TL7454
Attonburn *Border* 110 NT8122
Atwick *Humb* 85 TA1850
Atworth *Wilts* 22 ST8565
Auberrow *H & W* 46 SO4947
Aubourn *Lincs* 76 SK9262
Auchachenna *Strath* 122 NN0221
Auchagallon *Strath* 105 NR8934
Auchagoyl *Strath* 114 NR9669
Auchedly *Gramp* 143 NJ8932
Auchenblae *Gramp* 135 NO7278
Auchenbowie *Cent* 116 NS7988
Auchencairn *D & G* 92 NX7951
Auchencairn *D & G* 100 NX9885
Auchencarroch *Strath* 115 NS4182
Auchencastle *D & G* 108 NT0603
Auchencrow *Border* 119 NT8560
Auchendinny *Loth* 117 NT2561
Auchengray *Strath* 117 NS9954
Auchenhalrig *Gramp* 141 NJ3761
Auchenheath *Strath* 108 NS8043
Auchenhessnane *D & G* 100 NX8096
Auchenlochan *Strath* 114 NR9772
Auchenmade *Strath* 115 NS3548
Auchenmalg *D & G* 98 NX2352
Auchentibber *Strath* 116 NS6755
Auchentiber *Strath* 115 NS3647
Auchentroig *Cent* 115 NS5493
Auchindrain *Strath* 122 NN0303
Auchindrean *Highld* 145 NH1080
Auchininna *Gramp* 142 NJ6566
Auchinleck *Strath* 107 NS5521
Auchinloch *Strath* 116 NS6570
Auchinstarry *Strath* 116 NS7176
Auchintore *Highld* 130 NN0972
Auchiries *Gramp* 143 NK0737
Auchlee *Gramp* 135 NO8996
Auchlee *Gramp* 135 NO8996
Auchleven *Gramp* 142 NJ6224
Auchlochan *Strath* 107 NS7937
Auchlossan *Gramp* 134 NJ5701
Auchlyne *Cent* 124 NN5129
Auchmacoy *Gramp* 143 NJ9931
Auchmillan *Strath* 107 NS5129
Auchmithie *Tays* 127 NO6743
Auchmuirbridge *Fife* 126 NO2101
Auchnacraig *Strath* 122 NM7233
Auchnacree *Tays* 134 NO4663
Auchnagarran *Strath* 114 NS0082
Auchnagatt *Gramp* 143 NJ9241
Auchnangoul *Strath* 123 NN0605
Auchronie *Tays* 134 NO4480
Auchtascailt *Highld* 145 NH0987
Auchterarder *Tays* 125 NN9412
Auchteraw *Highld* 131 NH3507
Auchterblair *Highld* 140 NH9222
Auchtercairn *Highld* 144 NG8077
Auchterhouse *Tays* 126 NO3337
Auchterless *Gramp* 142 NJ7141
Auchtermuchty *Fife* 126 NO2311
Auchterneed *Highld* 139 NH4859
Auchtertool *Fife* 117 NT2190
Auchtertyre *Highld* 137 NG8327
Auchtoo *Cent* 124 NN5520
Auckengill *Highld* 151 ND3664
Auckley *S York* 83 SE6501
Audenshaw *Gt Man* 79 SJ9197
Audlem *Ches* 72 SJ6543
Audley *Staffs* 72 SJ7950
Audley End *Essex* 54 TL8037
Audley End *Essex* 39 TL5237
Audley End *Suffk* 54 TL8553
Audmore *Staffs* 72 SJ8321
Aughertree *Cumb* 93 NY2538
Aughton *Humb* 84 SE7038
Aughton *Lancs* 87 SD5467
Aughton *Lancs* 80 SD3950
Aughton *Lancs* 78 SD3905
Aughton *S York* 75 SK4586
Aughton *Wilts* 23 SU2356
Aughton Park *Lancs* 78 SD4006
Auldallan *Tays* 134 NO3158
Auldearn *Highld* 140 NH9155
Aulden *H & W* 46 SO4654
Auldgirth *D & G* 100 NX9186
Auldhame *Loth* 118 NT5984
Auldhouse *Strath* 116 NS6250
Ault Hucknall *Derbys* 75 SK4665
Ault-a-Chruinn *Highld* 138 NG9420
Aultbea *Highld* 144 NG8789
Aultgrishan *Highld* 144 NG7485
Aultguish Inn *Highld* 145 NH3570
Aultiphurst *Highld* 150 NC8065
Aultmore *Gramp* 142 NJ4053
Aultnagoire *Highld* 139 NH5423
Aultnamain Inn *Highld* 146 NH6681
Aunby *Lincs* 64 TF0214
Aunk *Devon* 9 ST0400
Aunsby *Lincs* 64 TF0438
Aust *Avon* 34 ST5789
Austendike *Lincs* 64 TF2821
Austerfield *Notts* 75 SK6594
Austerlands *Gt Man* 79 SD9505
Austhorpe *W York* 83 SE3634
Austonley *W York* 82 SE1207
Austrey *Warwks* 61 SK2906
Austwick *N York* 88 SD7668
Authorpe *Lincs* 77 TF3980
Authorpe Row *Lincs* 77 TF5373
Avebury *Wilts* 36 SU1069
Avebury Trusloe *Wilts* 36 SU0969
Aveley *Essex* 27 TQ5680
Avening *Gloucs* 35 ST8897
Averham *Notts* 75 SK7654
Aveton Gifford *Devon* 7 SX6947
Aviemore *Highld* 132 NH8913
Avinagillan *Strath* 113 NR8367
Avington *Berks* 23 SU3767
Avoch *Highld* 140 NH6955
Avon *Dorset* 12 SZ1498
Avon Dassett *Warwks* 49 SP4150
Avonbridge *Cent* 116 NS9172
Avonmouth *Avon* 34 ST5178
Avonwick *Devon* 7 SX7158
Awkley *Avon* 34 ST5885
Awliscombe *Devon* 9 ST1301
Awre *Gloucs* 35 SO7008
Awsworth *Notts* 62 SK4844
Axborough *H & W* 60 SO8579
Axbridge *Somset* 21 ST4354
Axford *Hants* 24 SU6043
Axford *Wilts* 36 SU2370
Axminster *Devon* 10 SY2998
Axmouth *Devon* 10 SY2591
Axton *Clwyd* 70 SJ1080
Aycliffe *Dur* 96 NZ2822
Aylburton *Gloucs* 34 SO6101
Ayle *Cumb* 94 NY7149
Aylesbeare *Devon* 9 SY0391
Aylesbury *Bucks* 38 SP8214
Aylesby *Humb* 85 TA2007
Aylesford *Kent* 28 TQ7359
Aylesham *Kent* 29 TR2352
Aylestone *Leics* 50 SK5700
Aylestone Park *Leics* 62 SK5801
Aylmerton *Norfk* 66 TG1839
Aylsham *Norfk* 67 TG1926
Aylton *H & W* 47 SO6537
Aylworth *Gloucs* 36 SP1021
Aymestrey *H & W* 46 SO4265
Aynho *Nhants* 49 SP5133
Ayot Green *Herts* 39 TL2214
Ayot St. Lawrence *Herts* 39 TL1916
Ayot St. Peter *Herts* 39 TL2115
Ayr *Strath* 106 NS3321
Aysgarth *N York* 88 SE0088
Ayshford *Devon* 9 ST0415
Ayside *Cumb* 87 SD3983
Ayston *Leics* 63 SK8601
Aythorpe Roding *Essex* 40 TL5815
Ayton *Border* 119 NT9261
Azerley *N York* 89 SE2574

# B

Babbacombe *Devon* 7 SX9265
Babbington *Notts* 62 SK4943
Babbinswood *Shrops* 59 SJ3330
Babbs Green *Herts* 39 TL3916
Babcary *Somset* 21 ST5628
Babel *Dyfed* 44 SN8235
Babel Green *Suffk* 53 TL7348
Babell *Clwyd* 70 SJ1573
Babeny *Devon* 7 SX6774
Babington *Somset* 22 ST7051
Bablock Hythe *Oxon* 36 SP4304
Babraham *Cambs* 53 TL5150
Babworth *Notts* 75 SK6880
Bachau *Gwynd* 68 SH4383
Bache *Shrops* 59 SO4782
Bacheldre *Powys* 58 SO2492
Bachelor Bump *E Susx* 17 TQ8312
Back o' th' Brook *Staffs* 73 SK0751
Back of Keppoch *Highld* 129 NM6587
Back Street *Suffk* 53 TL7458
Backaland *Ork* 155 HY5630
Backbarrow *Cumb* 87 SD3584
Backe *Dyfed* 31 SN2615
Backfolds *Gramp* 143 NK0252
Backford *Ches* 71 SJ4071
Backford Cross *Ches* 71 SJ3873
Backhill of Trustach *Gramp* 134 NO6397
Backies *Highld* 147 NC8302
Backlass *Highld* 151 ND2053
Backwell *Avon* 21 ST4968
Backworth *T & W* 103 NZ3072
Bacon End *Essex* 40 TL6018
Bacon's End *W Mids* 61 SP1887
Baconsthorpe *Norfk* 66 TG1237
Bacton *H & W* 46 SO3732
Bacton *Norfk* 67 TG3433
Bacton *Suffk* 54 TM0567
Bacton Green *Suffk* 54 TM0365
Bacup *Lancs* 81 SD8623
Badachro *Highld* 137 NG7873
Badavanich *Highld* 138 NH1058
Badbury *Wilts* 36 SU1980
Badby *Nhants* 49 SP5559
Badcall *Highld* 148 NC1541
Badcall *Highld* 148 NC2455
Badcaul *Highld* 144 NH0291
Baddeley Edge *Staffs* 72 SJ9150
Baddeley Green *Staffs* 72 SJ9151
Baddesley Clinton *Warwks* 61 SP2071
Baddesley Ensor *Warwks* 61 SP2798
Baddidarach *Highld* 145 NC0822
Badenscallie *Highld* 144 NC0306
Badenscoth *Gramp* 142 NJ7038
Badenyon *Gramp* 141 NJ3319
Badgall *Cnwll* 5 SX2386
Badgeney *Cambs* 65 TL4397
Badger *Shrops* 60 SO7699
Badger's Cross *Cnwll* 2 SW4833
Badgers Mount *Kent* 27 TQ4962
Badgeworth *Gloucs* 35 SO9019
Badgworth *Somset* 21 ST3952
Badharlick *Cnwll* 5 SX2686
Badicaul *Highld* 137 NG7528
Badingham *Suffk* 55 TM3068
Badlesmere *Kent* 28 TR0153
Badlieu *Border* 108 NT0518
Badluachrach *Highld* 144 NG9994
Badninish *Highld* 147 NH7594
Badrallach *Highld* 145 NH0691
Badsey *H & W* 48 SP0743
Badshot Lea *Surrey* 25 SU8648
Badsworth *W York* 83 SE4614
Badwell Ash *Suffk* 54 TL9969
Badwell Green *Suffk* 54 TM0169
Bag Enderby *Lincs* 77 TF3573
Bagber *Dorset* 11 ST7513
Bagby *N York* 89 SE4680
Bage The *H & W* 46 SO3243
Bagendon *Gloucs* 35 SP0006
Bagginswood *Shrops* 60 SO6881
Baggrow *Cumb* 93 NY1742
Bagham *Kent* 29 TR0753
Bagillt *Clwyd* 70 SJ2175
Baginton *Warwks* 61 SP3474
Baglan *W Glam* 32 SS7492
Bagley *Shrops* 59 SJ4027
Bagley *Somset* 21 ST4745
Bagley *W York* 82 SE2235
Bagmore *Hants* 24 SU6645
Bagnall *Staffs* 72 SJ9250
Bagnor *Berks* 24 SU4569
Bagot *Shrops* 46 SO5973
Bagshot *Surrey* 25 SU9063
Bagshot *Wilts* 23 SU3165
Bagstone *Avon* 35 ST6987
Bagthorpe *Notts* 75 SK4751
Bagworth *Leics* 62 SK4408
Bagwy Llydiart *H & W* 46 SO4426
Baildon *W York* 82 SE1539
Baildon Green *W York* 82 SE1439
Baile Boidheath *Strath* 113 NR7473
Baile Mor *Strath* 120 NM2824
Bailey Green *Hants* 13 SU6627
Baileyhead *Cumb* 101 NY5181
Bailiff Bridge *W York* 82 SE1425
Baillieston *Strath* 116 NS6763
Bailrigg *Lancs* 87 SD4858
Bainahaitnach *Highld* 140 NH8519
Bainbridge *N York* 88 SD9390
Bainshole *Gramp* 142 NJ6035
Bainton *Cambs* 64 TF0906
Bainton *Humb* 84 SE9652
Bainton *Oxon* 49 SP5827
Baintown *Fife* 126 NO3503
Bairnkine *Border* 110 NT6515
Baker Street *Essex* 40 TQ6381
Baker's End *Herts* 39 TL3917
Bakewell *Derbys* 74 SK2168
Bala *Gwynd* 58 SH9236
Balallan *W Isls* 154 NB2720
Balavil *Highld* 132 NH7902
Balbeg *Highld* 139 NH4431
Balbeggie *Tays* 126 NO1629
Balblair *Highld* 139 NH5145
Balblair *Highld* 140 NH7066
Balby *S York* 75 SE5600
Balcary *D & G* 92 NX8149
Balchladich *Highld* 148 NC0330
Balchraggan *Highld* 139 NH5343
Balchrick *Highld* 148 NC1959
Balcombe *W Susx* 15 TQ3130
Balcombe Lane *W Susx* 15 TQ3132
Balcomie Links *Fife* 127 NO6209
Balcurvie *Fife* 126 NO3401
Baldersby *N York* 89 SE3578
Baldersby St. James *N York* 89 SE3676
Balderstone *Gt Man* 81 SD9011
Balderstone *Lancs* 81 SD6332
Balderton *Leics* 75 SK8151
Baldhu *Cnwll* 3 SW7743
Baldinnie *Fife* 127 NO4211
Baldinnies *Tays* 125 NO0217
Baldock *Herts* 39 TL2434
Baldovie *Tays* 127 NO4533
Baldrine *IOM* 153 SC4281
Baldslow *E Susx* 17 TQ8013
Baldwin *IOM* 153 SC3581
Baldwin's Gate *Staffs* 72 SJ7940
Baldwinholme *Cumb* 93 NY3352
Bale *Norfk* 66 TG0136
Baledgarno *Tays* 126 NO2730
Balemartine *Strath* 120 NL9841
Balerno *Loth* 117 NT1666
Balfarg *Fife* 126 NO2803
Balfield *Tays* 134 NO5468
Balfour *Ork* 155 HY4716
Balfron *Cent* 115 NS5488
Balgarva *W Isls* 154 NF7647
Balgaveny *Gramp* 142 NJ6540
Balgavies *Tays* 127 NO5451
Balgedie *Tays* 126 NO1604
Balgonar *Fife* 117 NT0293
Balgowan *Highld* 132 NN6494
Balgown *D & G* 98 NX1142
Balgown *Highld* 136 NG3868
Balgracie *D & G* 98 NW9761
Balgray *Tays* 126 NO4038
Balhalgardy *Gramp* 142 NJ7623
Balham *Gt Lon* 27 TQ2873
Balhary *Tays* 126 NO2646
Balholmie *Tays* 126 NO1436
Baligill *Highld* 150 NC8565
Balintore *Highld* 147 NH8675
Balintore *Tays* 133 NO2859
Balintraid *Highld* 146 NH7370
Balivanich *W Isls* 154 NF7755
Balk *N York* 89 SE4781
Balkeerie *Tays* 126 NO3344
Balkholme *Humb* 84 SE7828
Balkissock *Strath* 98 NX1482
Ball *Shrops* 59 SJ3026
Ball Green *Staffs* 72 SJ8952
Ball Haye Green *Staffs* 72 SJ9857
Ball Hill *Hants* 24 SU4263
Ball's Green *Gloucs* 35 ST8699
Ballabeg *IOM* 153 SC2470
Ballacannell *IOM* 153 SC4382
Ballacarnane Beg *IOM* 153 SC3088
Ballachgair *Strath* 105 NR7727
Ballajora *IOM* 153 SC4790
Ballamodha *IOM* 153 SC2773
Ballantrae *Strath* 98 NX0882
Ballards Gore *Essex* 40 TQ9092
Ballards Green *Warwks* 61 SP2791
Ballasalla *IOM* 153 SC2870
Ballasalla *IOM* 153 SC3497
Ballater *Gramp* 134 NO3795
Ballaugh *IOM* 153 SC3493
Ballchraggan *Highld* 147 NH7675
Ballechin *Tays* 125 NN9353
Ballencrieff *Loth* 118 NT4878
Ballevullin *Strath* 120 NL9546
Ballidon *Derbys* 73 SK2054
Balliekine *Strath* 105 NR8739
Balliemore *Strath* 114 NS1099
Ballig *IOM* 153 SC2882
Balligmorrie *Strath* 106 NX2290
Ballimore *Cent* 124 NN5317
Ballimore *Strath* 114 NR9283
Ballinaby *Strath* 112 NR2267
Ballindalloch *Gramp* 141 NJ1636
Ballindean *Tays* 126 NO2529
Ballingdon *Essex* 54 TL8840
Ballinger Common *Bucks* 38 SP9103
Ballingham *H & W* 46 SO5731
Ballingry *Fife* 117 NT1797
Ballinluig *Tays* 125 NN9752
Ballinshoe *Tays* 126 NO4153
Ballintuim *Tays* 126 NO1055
Balloch *Highld* 140 NH7246
Balloch *Strath* 106 NX3295
Balloch *Tays* 125 NN8419
Ballochroy *Strath* 113 NR7352
Ballogie *Gramp* 134 NO5795
Ballogie *Gramp* 134 NO5795
Balls Cross *W Susx* 14 SU9826
Balls Green *E Susx* 16 TQ4936
Ballygown *Strath* 121 NM4343
Ballygrant *Strath* 112 NR3966
Ballygroggan *Strath* 104 NR6219
Ballyhaugh *Strath* 120 NM1758
Ballymenoch *Strath* 115 NS3086
Ballymichael *Strath* 105 NR9231
Balmacara *Highld* 137 NG8028
Balmaclellan *D & G* 99 NX6579
Balmacneil *Tays* 125 NN9750
Balmae *D & G* 99 NX6845
Balmaha *Cent* 115 NS4290
Balmalcolm *Fife* 126 NO3208
Balmangan *D & G* 99 NX6445
Balmedie *Gramp* 143 NJ9618
Balmer Heath *Shrops* 59 SJ4434
Balmerino *Fife* 126 NO3524
Balmerlawn *Hants* 12 SU3003
Balmore *Strath* 115 NS5973
Balmuchy *Highld* 147 NH8678
Balmuir *Tays* 127 NO5648
Balmule *Fife* 117 NT2088
Balmullo *Fife* 127 NO4320
Balnaboth *Tays* 134 NO3166
Balnacoil Lodge *Highld* 147 NC8011
Balnacra *Highld* 138 NG9746
Balnacroft *Gramp* 133 NO2894
Balnafoich *Highld* 140 NH6835
Balnaguard *Tays* 125 NN9451
Balnahard *Strath* 112 NR4199
Balnahard *Strath* 121 NM4534
Balnain *Highld* 139 NH4430
Balnakeil *Highld* 149 NC3968
Balnapaling *Highld* 147 NH7969
Balquharn *Tays* 125 NO0235
Balquhidder *Cent* 124 NN5320
Balruddery House *Tays* 126 NO3132
Balsall *W Mids* 61 SP2376
Balsall Common *W Mids* 61 SP2477
Balsall Heath *W Mids* 61 SP0784
Balsall Street *W Mids* 61 SP2276
Balscote *Oxon* 48 SP3941
Balsham *Cambs* 53 TL5850
Baltasound *Shet* 155 HP6208
Balterley *Staffs* 72 SJ7550
Balterley Green *Staffs* 72 SJ7650
Baltersan *D & G* 99 NX4261
Balthangie *Gramp* 143 NJ8351
Baltonsborough *Somset* 21 ST5434
Balvarran *Tays* 130 NN0761
Balvicar *Strath* 122 NM7616
Balvraid *Highld* 140 NH8231
Balvraid *Highld* 129 NG8416
Balwest *Cnwll* 2 SW5930
Balwin's Hill *Surrey* 15 TQ3839
Bamber Bridge *Lancs* 81 SD5625
Bamber's Green *Essex* 40 TL5722
Bamburgh *Nthumb* 111 NU1735
Bamff *Tays* 126 NO2251
Bamford *Derbys* 74 SK2083
Bamford *Gt Man* 81 SD8612
Bampton *Cumb* 94 NY5118
Bampton *Devon* 20 SS9522
Bampton *Oxon* 36 SP3103
Bampton Grange *Cumb* 94 NY5218
Banavie *Highld* 130 NN1177
Banbury *Oxon* 49 SP4540
Banc-y-ffordd *Dyfed* 31 SN4037
Bancffosfelem *Dyfed* 32 SN4811
Banchory *Gramp* 135 NO6995
Banchory-Devenick *Gramp* 135 NJ9101
Bancycapel *Dyfed* 31 SN4315
Bancyfelin *Dyfed* 31 SN3218
Bandirran *Tays* 126 NO2030
Bandrake Head *Cumb* 101 NY3187
Banff *Gramp* 142 NJ6864
Bangor *Gwynd* 69 SH5872
Bangor *Gwynd* 69 SH5872
Bangor's Green *Lancs* 78 SD3709
Bangor-is-y-coed *Clwyd* 71 SJ3945
Bangors *Cnwll* 18 SX2099
Bangrove *Suffk* 54 TL9463
Banham *Norfk* 54 TM0688
Bank *Hants* 12 SU2807
Bank *Hants* 12 SU2807
Bank Ground *Cumb* 101 NY3196
Bank Newton *N York* 81 SD9053
Bank Street *H & W* 47 SO6362
Bank Top *Lancs* 78 SD5207
Bank Top *W York* 82 SE1024
Bankend *D & G* 100 NY0268
Bankend *Strath* 108 NS8033
Bankfoot *Tays* 125 NO0635
Bankglen *Strath* 107 NS5912
Bankhead *Gramp* 135 NJ8910
Bankhead *Strath* 106 NS3739
Banknock *Cent* 116 NS7779
Banks *Cumb* 101 NY5664
Banks *Lancs* 80 SD3820
Banks Green *H & W* 47 SO9967
Bankshill *D & G* 101 NY1982
Banningham *Norfk* 67 TG2129
Bannister Green *Essex* 40 TL6921
Bannockburn *Cent* 116 NS8190
Banstead *Surrey* 27 TQ2559
Bantham *Devon* 7 SX6643
Banton *Strath* 116 NS7480
Banwell *Avon* 21 ST3959
Bapchild *Kent* 28 TQ9263
Bapton *Wilts* 22 ST9938
Bar Hill *Cambs* 52 TL3863
Barassie *Strath* 106 NS3232
Barbaraville *Highld* 146 NH7472
Barber Booth *Derbys* 74 SK1184
Barber Green *Cumb* 101 NY3982
Barbey *D & G* 100 NX8569
Barbieston *Strath* 107 NS4317
Barbon *Cumb* 87 SD6282
Barbreck House *Strath* 122 NM8206
Barbridge *Ches* 71 SJ6156
Barbrook *Devon* 19 SS7147
Barby *Nhants* 50 SP5470
Barcaldine *Strath* 122 NM9641
Barcheston *Warwks* 48 SP2639
Barclose *Cumb* 101 NY4462
Barcombe *E Susx* 16 TQ4214
Barcombe Cross *E Susx* 16 TQ4216
Barcroft *W York* 82 SE0437
Barden *N York* 89 SE1493
Barden Park *Kent* 16 TQ5746
Bardfield End Green *Essex* 40 TL6231
Bardfield Saling *Essex* 40 TL6826
Bardney *Lincs* 76 TF1169
Bardon *Leics* 62 SK4412
Bardon Mill *Nthumb* 102 NY7764
Bardowie *Strath* 115 NS5873
Bardown *E Susx* 16 TQ6629
Bardrainney *Strath* 115 NS3372
Bardsea *Cumb* 86 SD2974
Bardsey *W York* 83 SE3643
Bardsley *Gt Man* 79 SD9201
Bardwell *Suffk* 54 TL9473
Bare *Lancs* 87 SD4464
Bareppa *Cnwll* 3 SW7729
Barewood *H & W* 46 SO3856
Barfad *D & G* 98 NX3266
Barford *Norfk* 66 TG1107
Barford *Warwks* 48 SP2760

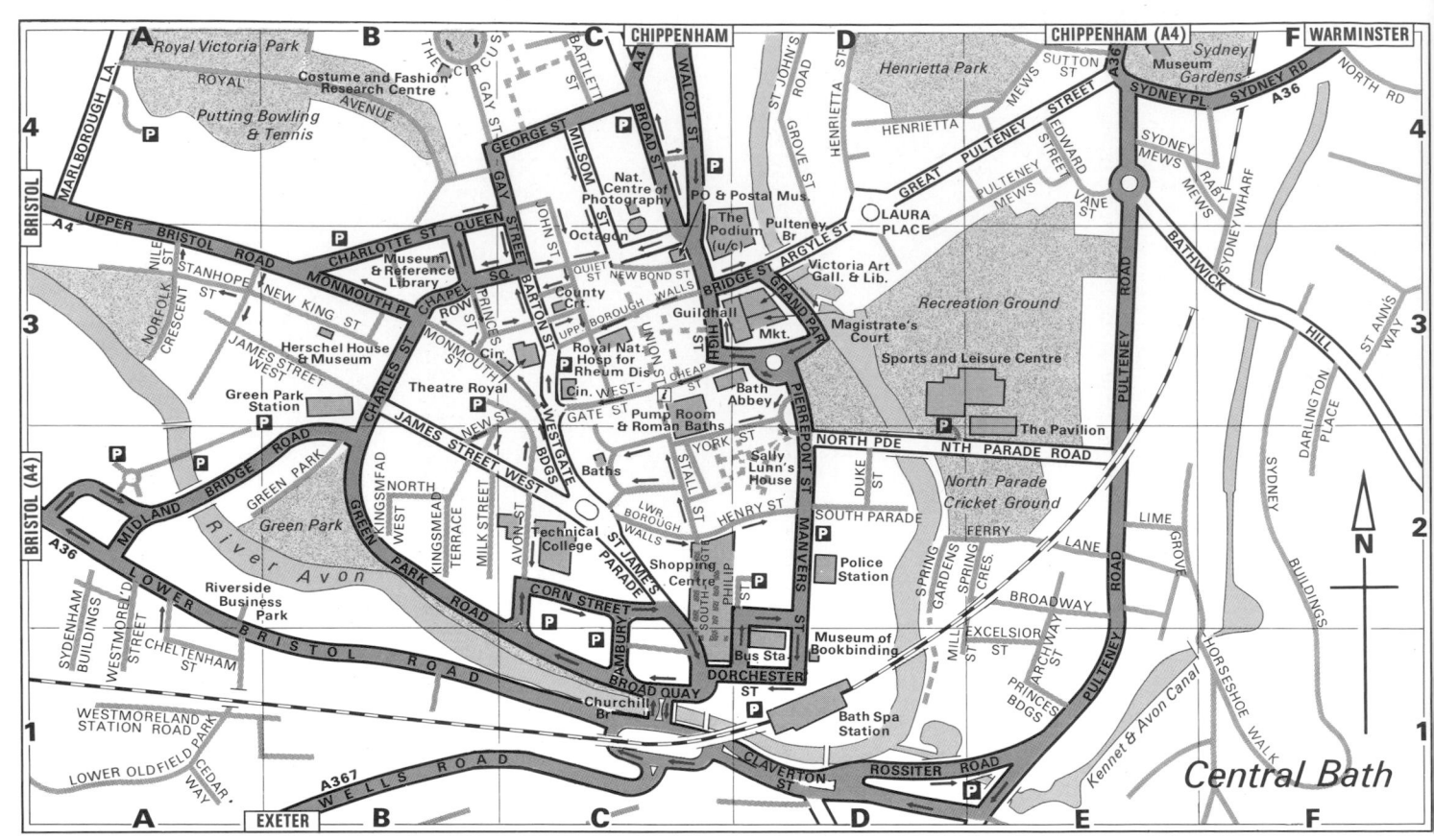

Central Bath

| Place | Page | Grid Ref |
|---|---|---|
| Baythorne End *Essex* | 53 | TL7242 |
| Bayton *H & W* | 60 | SO6973 |
| Bayton Common *H & W* | 60 | SO7172 |
| Bayworth *Oxon* | 37 | SP4901 |
| Beach *Avon* | 35 | ST7070 |
| Beachampton *Bucks* | 45 | SP7736 |
| Beachamwell *Norfk* | 65 | TF7505 |
| Beachborough *Kent* | 29 | TR1638 |
| Beachley *Gloucs* | 34 | ST5491 |
| Beacon *Devon* | 9 | ST1705 |
| Beacon End *Essex* | 40 | TL9524 |
| Beacon Hill *E Susx* | 16 | TQ5030 |
| Beacon Hill *Kent* | 17 | TQ8232 |
| Beacon Hill *Notts* | 75 | SK8153 |
| Beacon Hill *Surrey* | 14 | SU8736 |
| Beacon's Bottom *Bucks* | 37 | SU7895 |
| Beaconsfield *Bucks* | 26 | SU9490 |
| Beacontree *Gt Lon* | 27 | TQ4786 |
| Beadlam *N York* | 90 | SE6584 |
| Beadlow *Beds* | 38 | TL1038 |
| Beadnell *Nthumb* | 111 | NU2229 |
| Beaford *Devon* | 19 | SS5515 |
| Beal *N York* | 83 | SE5325 |
| Beal *Nthumb* | 111 | NU0642 |
| Bealbury *M Glam* | 5 | SX3766 |
| Bealsmill *Cnwll* | 5 | SX3677 |
| Beam Hill *Staffs* | 73 | SK2326 |
| Beamhurst *Staffs* | 73 | SK0536 |
| Beaminster *Dorset* | 10 | ST4801 |
| Beamish *Dur* | 96 | NZ2253 |
| Beamsley *N York* | 82 | SE0752 |
| Bean *Kent* | 27 | TQ5872 |
| Beanacre *Wilts* | 22 | ST9066 |
| Beanley *Nthumb* | 111 | NU0818 |
| Beara Charter Barton *Devon* | 19 | SS5238 |
| Beardon *Devon* | 5 | SX5184 |
| Beardwood *Lancs* | 81 | SD6629 |
| Beare *Devon* | 9 | SS9800 |
| Beare Green *Surrey* | 15 | TQ1742 |
| Bearley *Warwks* | 48 | SP1860 |
| Bearley Cross *Warwks* | 48 | SP1761 |
| Bearpark *Dur* | 96 | NZ2343 |
| Bearsbridge *Nthumb* | 94 | NY7857 |
| Bearsden *Strath* | 115 | NS5372 |
| Bearstead *Kent* | 28 | TQ8055 |
| Bearstone *Shrops* | 72 | SJ7239 |
| Bearwood *W Mids* | 60 | SP0286 |
| Beatley Heath *Herts* | 27 | TQ2599 |
| Beattock *D & G* | 108 | NT0702 |
| Beauchamp Roding *Essex* | 40 | TL5809 |
| Beauchief *S York* | 74 | SK3381 |
| Beaudesert *Warwks* | 48 | SP1565 |
| Beaufort *Gwent* | 33 | SO1611 |
| Beaulieu *Hants* | 12 | SU3802 |
| Beauly *Highld* | 139 | NH5246 |
| Beaumaris *Gwynd* | 69 | SH6076 |
| Beaumont *Cumb* | 93 | NY3459 |
| Beaumont *Essex* | 41 | TM1625 |
| Beaumont *Jersey* | 152 | JS0000 |
| Beaumont Hill *Dur* | 96 | NZ2918 |
| Beausale *Warwks* | 61 | SP2470 |
| Beauworth *Hants* | 25 | SU7960 |
| Beauworth *Hants* | 13 | SU5726 |
| Beaver *Kent* | 28 | TR0040 |
| Beaver Green *Kent* | 28 | TR0041 |
| Beaworthy *Devon* | 18 | SX4699 |
| Beazley End *Essex* | 40 | TL7429 |
| Bebington *Mersyd* | 70 | SJ3382 |
| Bebside *Nthumb* | 103 | NZ2781 |
| Beccles *Suffk* | 55 | TM4290 |
| Becconsall *Lancs* | 80 | SD4523 |
| Beck Foot *Cumb* | 87 | SD6196 |
| Beck Hole *N York* | 90 | NZ8102 |
| Beck Row *Suffk* | 53 | TL6977 |
| Beck Side *Cumb* | 86 | SD2382 |
| Beckbury *Shrops* | 60 | SJ7601 |
| Beckenham *Gt Lon* | 27 | TQ3769 |
| Beckering *Lincs* | 76 | TF1180 |
| Beckermet *Cumb* | 86 | NY0206 |
| Beckett End *Norfk* | 65 | TL7798 |
| Beckfoot *Cumb* | 86 | SD1989 |
| Beckfoot *Cumb* | 92 | NY0949 |
| Beckfoot *Cumb* | 86 | NY1600 |
| Beckford *H & W* | 47 | SO9735 |
| Beckhampton *Wilts* | 23 | SU0868 |
| Beckingham *Lincs* | 76 | SK8753 |
| Beckingham *Notts* | 75 | SK7889 |
| Beckington *Somset* | 22 | ST7951 |
| Beckjay *Shrops* | 46 | SO3977 |
| Beckley *E Susx* | 17 | TQ8523 |
| Beckley *Hants* | 12 | SZ2297 |
| Beckley *Oxon* | 37 | SP5611 |
| Becks *W York* | 82 | SE0345 |
| Beckside *Cumb* | 87 | SD6187 |
| Beckton *Gt Lon* | 27 | TQ4381 |
| Beckwithshaw *N York* | 82 | SE2653 |
| Becquet Vincent *Jersey* | 152 | JS0000 |
| Bedale *N York* | 89 | SE2687 |
| Bedburn *Dur* | 95 | NZ0931 |
| Bedchester *Dorset* | 11 | ST8517 |
| Beddau *M Glam* | 33 | ST0585 |
| Beddgelert *Gwynd* | 69 | SH5848 |
| Beddingham *E Susx* | 16 | TQ4407 |
| Beddington *Gt Lon* | 27 | TQ3065 |
| Beddington Corner *Gt Lon* | 27 | TQ2866 |
| Bedfield *Suffk* | 55 | TM2266 |
| Bedfield Little Green *Suffk* | 55 | TM2365 |
| Bedford *Beds* | 38 | TL0449 |
| Bedgebury Cross *Kent* | 17 | TQ7134 |
| Bedham *W Susx* | 14 | TQ0122 |
| Bedhampton *Hants* | 13 | SU6906 |
| Bedingfield *Suffk* | 54 | TM1768 |
| Bedingfield Green *Suffk* | 54 | TM1866 |
| Bedingfield Street *Suffk* | 54 | TM1767 |
| Bedlam *N York* | 89 | SE2661 |
| Bedlam Lane *Kent* | 28 | TQ8845 |
| Bedlington *T & W* | 103 | NZ2581 |
| Bedlinog *M Glam* | 33 | SO0901 |
| Bedminster *Avon* | 34 | ST5771 |
| Bedminster Down *Avon* | 34 | ST5770 |
| Bedmond *Herts* | 38 | TL0903 |
| Bednall *Staffs* | 72 | SJ9517 |
| Bedrule *Border* | 110 | NT6017 |
| Bedstone *Shrops* | 46 | SO3776 |
| Bedwas *M Glam* | 33 | ST1789 |
| Bedwellty *Gwent* | 33 | SO1600 |
| Bedworth *Warwks* | 61 | SP3687 |
| Bedworth Woodlands *Warwks* | 61 | SP3487 |
| Beeby *Leics* | 63 | SK6608 |
| Beech *Hants* | 24 | SU6938 |
| Beech *Staffs* | 72 | SJ8538 |
| Beech Hill *Berks* | 24 | SU6964 |
| Beechingstoke *Wilts* | 23 | SU0859 |
| Beedon *Berks* | 37 | SU4877 |
| Beedon Hill *Berks* | 37 | SU4877 |
| Beeford *Humb* | 85 | TA1253 |
| Beeley *Derbys* | 74 | SK2667 |
| Beelsby *Humb* | 85 | TA2001 |
| Beenham *Berks* | 24 | SU5868 |
| Beer *Devon* | 9 | SY2289 |
| Beer *Somset* | 21 | ST4031 |
| Beer Hackett *Dorset* | 10 | ST5911 |
| Beercrocombe *Somset* | 21 | ST3220 |
| Beesands *Devon* | 7 | SX8140 |
| Beesby *Lincs* | 77 | TF4680 |
| Beeson *Devon* | 7 | SX8140 |
| Beeston *Beds* | 52 | TL1648 |
| Beeston *Ches* | 71 | SJ5458 |
| Beeston *Norfk* | 66 | TF9015 |
| Beeston *Notts* | 62 | SK5336 |
| Beeston *W York* | 82 | SE2930 |
| Beeston Regis *Norfk* | 66 | TG1742 |
| Beeswing *D & G* | 100 | NX8969 |
| Beetham *Cumb* | 87 | SD4979 |
| Beetham *Somset* | 10 | ST2712 |
| Beetley *Norfk* | 66 | TF9718 |
| Began *S Glam* | 34 | ST2283 |
| Begbroke *Oxon* | 37 | SP4613 |
| Begdale *Cambs* | 65 | TF4506 |
| Begelly *Dyfed* | 31 | SN1107 |
| Beggar's Bush *Powys* | 46 | SO2664 |
| Beggarinton Hill *W York* | 82 | SE2824 |
| Beguildy *Powys* | 45 | SO1979 |
| Beighton *Norfk* | 67 | TG3808 |
| Beighton *S York* | 75 | SK4483 |
| Beighton Hill *Derbys* | 73 | SK2951 |
| Bein Inn *Tays* | 126 | NO1613 |
| Beith *Strath* | 115 | NS3553 |
| Bekesbourne *Kent* | 29 | TR1955 |
| Bekesbourne Hill *Kent* | 29 | TR1856 |
| Belaugh *Norfk* | 67 | TG2818 |
| Belbroughton *H & W* | 60 | SO9277 |
| Belchalwell *Dorset* | 11 | ST7909 |
| Belchalwell Street *Dorset* | 11 | ST7908 |
| Belchamp Otten *Essex* | 54 | TL8041 |
| Belchamp St. Paul *Essex* | 53 | TL7942 |
| Belchamp Walter *Essex* | 54 | TL8240 |
| Belchford *Lincs* | 77 | TF2975 |
| Belford *Nthumb* | 111 | NU1034 |
| Belgrave *Leics* | 62 | SK5906 |
| Belhelvie *Gramp* | 143 | NJ9417 |
| Belhinnie *Gramp* | 142 | NJ4627 |
| Bell Bar *Herts* | 39 | TL2505 |
| Bell Busk *N York* | 81 | SD9056 |
| Bell End *H & W* | 60 | SO9477 |
| Bell Heath *H & W* | 60 | SO9577 |
| Bell Hill *Hants* | 13 | SU7424 |
| Bell o' th'Hill *Ches* | 71 | SJ5245 |
| Bellabeg *Gramp* | 134 | NJ3513 |
| Belladrum *Highld* | 139 | NH5142 |
| Bellanoch *Strath* | 113 | NR7992 |
| Bellasize *Humb* | 84 | SE8227 |
| Bellaty *Tays* | 133 | NO2359 |
| Belle Vue *Cumb* | 93 | NY3756 |
| Belle Vue *Cumb* | 92 | NY1232 |
| Belle Vue *W York* | 83 | SE3419 |
| Belleau *Lincs* | 77 | TF4078 |
| Bellerby *N York* | 89 | SE1192 |
| Bellever *Devon* | 8 | SX6577 |
| Bellfield *Strath* | 108 | NS8234 |
| Bellfield *Strath* | 108 | NS9620 |
| Bellimoor *H & W* | 46 | SO3840 |
| Bellingdon *Bucks* | 38 | SP9405 |
| Bellingham *Nthumb* | 102 | NY8383 |
| Belloch *Strath* | 104 | NR3738 |
| Bellochantuy *Strath* | 104 | NR6632 |
| Bells Cross *Suffk* | 54 | TM1552 |
| Bells Yew Green *E Susx* | 16 | TQ6035 |
| Bellshill *Nthumb* | 111 | NU1230 |
| Bellside *Strath* | 116 | NS8058 |
| Bellsmyre *Strath* | 115 | NS4076 |
| Bellsquarry *Loth* | 117 | NT0465 |
| Belluton *Avon* | 21 | ST6164 |
| Belmaduthy *Highld* | 140 | NH6456 |
| Belmesthorpe *Leics* | 64 | TF0410 |
| Belmont *Gt Lon* | 27 | TQ2562 |
| Belmont *Lancs* | 81 | SD6715 |
| Belmont *Shet* | 155 | HP5600 |
| Belmont *Strath* | 106 | NS3520 |
| Belnacraig *Gramp* | 141 | NJ3716 |
| Belowda *Cnwll* | 4 | SW9661 |
| Belper *Derbys* | 62 | SK3447 |
| Belper Lane End *Derbys* | 74 | SK3349 |
| Belph *Notts* | 90 | SK5475 |
| Belsay *Nthumb* | 103 | NZ0978 |
| Belsay Castle *Nthumb* | 103 | NZ0878 |
| Belses *Border* | 110 | NT5725 |
| Belsford *Devon* | 7 | SX7659 |
| Belsize *Herts* | 26 | TL0301 |
| Belstead *Suffk* | 54 | TM1241 |
| Belstone *Devon* | 8 | SX6193 |
| Belstone Corner *Devon* | 8 | SX6298 |
| Belthorn *Lancs* | 81 | SD7124 |
| Beltinge *Kent* | 29 | TR1967 |
| Beltingham *Nthumb* | 102 | NY7863 |
| Beltoft *Humb* | 84 | SE8006 |
| Belton *Humb* | 84 | SE7806 |
| Belton *Leics* | 62 | SK4420 |
| Belton *Lincs* | 63 | SK8101 |
| Belton *Lincs* | 63 | SK9339 |
| Belton *Norfk* | 67 | TG4802 |
| Beltring *Kent* | 28 | TQ6747 |
| Belvedere *Gt Lon* | 27 | TQ4978 |
| Belvoir *Leics* | 63 | SK8133 |
| Bembridge *IOW* | 13 | SZ6488 |
| Bemersley Green *Staffs* | 72 | SJ8854 |
| Bemersyde *Border* | 110 | NT5933 |
| Bemerton *Wilts* | 23 | SU1230 |
| Bempton *Humb* | 91 | TA1972 |
| Ben Rhydding *W York* | 82 | SE1448 |
| Benacre *Suffk* | 55 | TM5184 |
| Benbuie *D & G* | 107 | NX7196 |
| Benderloch *Strath* | 122 | NM9038 |
| Benenden *Kent* | 17 | TQ8033 |
| Benfield *D & G* | 99 | NX3764 |
| Benfieldside *Dur* | 95 | NZ0952 |
| Bengall *D & G* | 100 | NY1178 |
| Bengates *Norfk* | 67 | TG3027 |
| Bengeworth *H & W* | 48 | SP0443 |
| Benhall Green *Suffk* | 55 | TM3961 |
| Benhall Street *Suffk* | 55 | TM3561 |
| Benholm *Gramp* | 135 | NO8069 |
| Beningbrough *N York* | 90 | SE5257 |
| Benington *Herts* | 39 | TL2923 |
| Benington *Lincs* | 77 | TF3946 |
| Benllech *Gwynd* | 68 | SH5182 |
| Benmore *Cent* | 124 | NN4125 |
| Benmore *Strath* | 114 | NS1385 |
| Bennacott *Cnwll* | 5 | SX2992 |
| Bennan *Strath* | 105 | NR9921 |
| Bennet Head *Cumb* | 93 | NY4423 |
| Bennetland *Humb* | 84 | SE8228 |
| Bennett End *Bucks* | 37 | SU7897 |
| Bennington Sea End *Lincs* | 65 | TF4145 |
| Benniworth *Lincs* | 76 | TF2081 |
| Benny *Cnwll* | 4 | SX1192 |
| Benover *Kent* | 28 | TQ7048 |
| Benson *Oxon* | 37 | SU6291 |
| Benthall Green *Essex* | 39 | TL5025 |
| Benthall *Shrops* | 60 | SJ6602 |
| Benthall *Gloucs* | 35 | SO9116 |
| Benthoul *Gramp* | 135 | NJ8003 |
| Bentlawnt *Shrops* | 59 | SJ3301 |
| Bentley *Hants* | 25 | SU7844 |
| Bentley *Humb* | 84 | TA0135 |
| Bentley *S York* | 83 | SE5605 |
| Bentley *Suffk* | 55 | TM1238 |
| Bentley *Warwks* | 61 | SP2895 |
| Bentley Heath *W Mids* | 61 | SP1676 |
| Bentley Rise *S York* | 83 | SE5605 |
| Benton *Devon* | 19 | SS6536 |
| Benton Polliwilline *Strath* | 105 | NR7310 |
| Bentpath *D & G* | 101 | NY3190 |
| Bentwichen *Devon* | 19 | SS7334 |
| Bentworth *Hants* | 24 | SU6640 |
| Benvie *Tays* | 126 | NO3231 |
| Benville *Dorset* | 10 | ST5403 |
| Benwick *Cambs* | 52 | TL3490 |
| Beoch *D & G* | 98 | NX0865 |
| Beoley *H & W* | 48 | SP0669 |
| Beoraidbeg *Highld* | 129 | NM6793 |
| Bepton *W Susx* | 14 | SU8618 |
| Berden *Essex* | 39 | TL4629 |
| Bere Alston *Devon* | 6 | SX4466 |
| Bere Ferrers *Devon* | 6 | SX4563 |
| Bere Regis *Dorset* | 11 | SY8494 |
| Berea *Dyfed* | 30 | SM7930 |
| Berepper *Cnwll* | 2 | SW6522 |
| Bergh Apton *Norfk* | 67 | TG3000 |
| Berhill *Somset* | 21 | ST4455 |
| Berinsfield *Oxon* | 37 | SU5696 |
| Berkeley *Gloucs* | 35 | ST6899 |
| Berkeley Heath *Gloucs* | 35 | ST6999 |
| Berkeley Road *Gloucs* | 35 | ST7299 |
| Berkhamsted *Herts* | 38 | SP9907 |
| Berkley *Somset* | 22 | ST8049 |
| Berkswell *W Mids* | 61 | SP2479 |
| Bermondsey *Gt Lon* | 27 | TQ3479 |
| Bernera *Highld* | 129 | NG8021 |
| Bernice *Strath* | 114 | NS1391 |
| Bernisdale *Highld* | 136 | NG4050 |
| Berrick Prior *Oxon* | 37 | SU6294 |
| Berrick Salome *Oxon* | 37 | SU6293 |
| Berriedale *Highld* | 147 | ND1222 |
| Berrier *Cumb* | 93 | NY3929 |
| Berrier *Cumb* | 93 | NY3929 |
| Berriew *Powys* | 58 | SJ1801 |
| Berrington *H & W* | 46 | SO5767 |
| Berrington *Nthumb* | 111 | NU0043 |
| Berrington *Shrops* | 59 | SJ5207 |
| Berrington Green *H & W* | 46 | SO5866 |
| Berrow *Somset* | 20 | ST2952 |
| Berry Brow *W York* | 82 | SE1514 |
| Berry Cross *Devon* | 18 | SS4714 |
| Berry Down Cross *Devon* | 19 | SS5573 |
| Berry Head *Devon* | 7 | SX9456 |
| Berry Hill *Dyfed* | 30 | SN0640 |
| Berry Hill *Gloucs* | 34 | SO5712 |
| Berry Pomeroy *Devon* | 7 | SX8261 |
| Berry's Green *Gt Lon* | 27 | TQ4356 |
| Berryhillock *Gramp* | 142 | NJ5054 |
| Berryhillock *Gramp* | 142 | NJ5060 |
| Berryhillock *Gramp* | 142 | NJ5054 |
| Berrynarbor *Devon* | 19 | SS5546 |
| Bersham *Clwyd* | 71 | SJ3048 |
| Berthengam *Temp* | 70 | SJ1179 |
| Berwick *E Susx* | 16 | TQ5105 |
| Berwick Bassett *Wilts* | 36 | SU0973 |
| Berwick Hill *Nthumb* | 103 | NZ1775 |
| Berwick St. James *Wilts* | 23 | SU0739 |
| Berwick St. John *Wilts* | 22 | ST9421 |
| Berwick St. Leonard *Wilts* | 22 | ST9233 |
| Berwick-upon-Tweed *Nthumb* | 119 | NT9953 |
| Bescaby *Leics* | 63 | SK8126 |
| Bescar *Cumb* | 80 | SD3913 |
| Besford *H & W* | 47 | SO9145 |
| Besford *Shrops* | 59 | SJ5525 |
| Besom Hill *Gt Man* | 79 | SD9508 |
| Bessacarr *S York* | 83 | SE6101 |
| Bessels Leigh *Oxon* | 37 | SP4501 |
| Bessingby *Humb* | 91 | TA1565 |
| Bessingham *Norfk* | 66 | TG1536 |
| Bestbeech Hill *E Susx* | 16 | TQ6131 |
| Besthorpe *Norfk* | 66 | TM0595 |
| Besthorpe *Notts* | 75 | SK8264 |
| Beswick *Humb* | 84 | TA0148 |
| Betchcott *Shrops* | 59 | SO4399 |
| Betchworth *Surrey* | 26 | TQ2150 |
| Bethania *Dyfed* | 43 | SN5763 |
| Bethania *Gwynd* | 57 | SH7044 |
| Bethel *Gwynd* | 70 | SH9839 |
| Bethel *Gwynd* | 68 | SH3970 |
| Bethel *Gwynd* | 68 | SH5265 |
| Bethel *Powys* | 58 | SJ1021 |
| Bethersden *Kent* | 28 | TQ9240 |
| Bethesda *Dyfed* | 31 | SN0918 |
| Bethesda *Gwynd* | 69 | SH6266 |
| Bethlehem *Dyfed* | 44 | SN6825 |
| Bethnal Green *Gt Lon* | 27 | TQ3482 |
| Betley *Staffs* | 72 | SJ7548 |
| Betsham *Kent* | 27 | TQ6071 |
| Betteshanger *Kent* | 29 | TR3152 |
| Bettiscombe *Dorset* | 10 | SY3999 |
| Bettisfield *Clwyd* | 59 | SJ4635 |
| Betton *Shrops* | 72 | SJ6937 |
| Betton Strange *Shrops* | 59 | SJ5109 |
| Bettws *Gwent* | 34 | ST2990 |
| Bettws Bledrws *Dyfed* | 44 | SN5952 |
| Bettws Cedewain *Powys* | 58 | SO1296 |
| Bettws Evan *Dyfed* | 42 | SN3047 |
| Bettws Gwerfil Goch *Clwyd* | 70 | SJ0346 |
| Bettws Malpas *Gwent* | 34 | ST3090 |
| Bettws-yn-Rhos *Clwyd* | 69 | SH9073 |
| Beulah *Dyfed* | 42 | SN2846 |
| Beulah *Powys* | 45 | SN9251 |
| Bevendean *E Susx* | 15 | TQ3406 |
| Bevercotes *Notts* | 75 | SK6972 |
| Beverley *Humb* | 84 | TA0339 |
| Beverston *Gloucs* | 35 | ST8693 |
| Bewaldeth *Cumb* | 93 | NY2034 |
| Bewcastle *Cumb* | 101 | NY5674 |
| Bewdley *H & W* | 60 | SO7875 |
| Bewerley *N York* | 89 | SE1564 |
| Bewholme *Humb* | 85 | TA1649 |
| Bewlbridge *Kent* | 16 | TQ6834 |
| Bewlie *Border* | 109 | NT5626 |
| Bexhill *E Susx* | 17 | TQ7407 |
| Bexley *Gt Lon* | 27 | TQ4973 |
| Bexley Heath *Gt Lon* | 27 | TQ4875 |
| Bexleyhill *W Susx* | 14 | SU9125 |
| Bexwell *Norfk* | 65 | TF6303 |
| Beyton *Suffk* | 54 | TL9363 |
| Beyton Green *Suffk* | 54 | TL9363 |
| Bibstone *Avon* | 35 | ST6991 |
| Bibury *Gloucs* | 36 | SP1106 |
| Bicester *Oxon* | 37 | SP5822 |
| Bickenhill *W Mids* | 61 | SP1882 |
| Bicker *Lincs* | 64 | TF2237 |
| Bicker Bar *Lincs* | 64 | TF2438 |
| Bicker Gauntlet *Lincs* | 64 | TF2139 |
| Bickershaw *Gt Man* | 79 | SD6701 |
| Bickerstaffe *Lancs* | 78 | SD4404 |
| Bickerton *Ches* | 71 | SJ5052 |
| Bickerton *Devon* | 7 | SX8139 |
| Bickerton *N York* | 83 | SE4450 |
| Bickerton *Nthumb* | 103 | NT9900 |
| Bickford *Staffs* | 60 | SJ8814 |
| Bickington *Devon* | 19 | SS5332 |
| Bickington *Devon* | 7 | SX7972 |
| Bickleigh *Devon* | 9 | SS9407 |
| Bickleigh *Devon* | 6 | SX5262 |
| Bickleton *Devon* | 19 | SS5031 |
| Bickley *Ches* | 71 | SJ5448 |
| Bickley *Gt Lon* | 27 | TQ4268 |
| Bickley *N York* | 91 | SE9191 |
| Bickley Moss *Ches* | 71 | SJ5449 |
| Bicknacre *Essex* | 40 | TL7802 |
| Bicknoller *Somset* | 20 | ST1039 |
| Bicknor *Kent* | 28 | TQ8658 |
| Bickton *H & W* | 47 | SO6573 |
| Bickton *Hants* | 12 | SU1412 |
| Bicton *H & W* | 46 | SO4566 |
| Bicton *Shrops* | 59 | SJ4415 |
| Bicton *Shrops* | 59 | SO2983 |
| Bidborough *Kent* | 16 | TQ5643 |
| Bidden *Hants* | 24 | SU7049 |
| Biddenden *Kent* | 28 | TQ8538 |
| Biddenden Green *Kent* | 28 | TQ8842 |
| Biddenham *Beds* | 38 | TL0250 |
| Biddestone *Wilts* | 35 | ST8673 |
| Biddisham *Somset* | 21 | ST3853 |
| Biddlesden *Bucks* | 49 | SP6340 |
| Biddlestone *Nthumb* | 111 | NT9508 |
| Biddulph *Staffs* | 72 | SJ8857 |
| Biddulph Moor *Staffs* | 72 | SJ9058 |
| Bideford *Devon* | 18 | SS4426 |
| Bidford-on-Avon *Warwks* | 48 | SP1052 |
| Bidston *Mersyd* | 78 | SJ2890 |
| Bielby *Humb* | 84 | SE7843 |
| Bieldside *Gramp* | 135 | NJ8702 |
| Bierley *IOW* | 13 | SZ5178 |
| Bierton *Bucks* | 38 | SP8315 |
| Big Balcraig *D & G* | 99 | NX3843 |
| Big Corlae *D & G* | 107 | NX6697 |
| Big Sand *Highld* | 144 | NG7579 |
| Bigbury *Devon* | 7 | SX6646 |
| Bigbury-on-Sea *Devon* | 7 | SX6544 |
| Bigby *Lincs* | 84 | TA0507 |
| Biggar *Cumb* | 86 | SD1966 |
| Biggar *Strath* | 108 | NT0437 |
| Biggin *Derbys* | 74 | SK1559 |
| Biggin *Derbys* | 73 | SK2549 |
| Biggin *N York* | 83 | SE5434 |
| Biggin Hill *Gt Lon* | 27 | TQ4159 |
| Biggleswade *Beds* | 39 | TL1944 |
| Bigholms *D & G* | 101 | NY3181 |
| Bighouse *Highld* | 150 | NC8964 |
| Bighton *Hants* | 24 | SU6134 |
| Biglands *Cumb* | 93 | NY2553 |
| Bignor *W Susx* | 14 | SU9814 |
| Bigrigg *Cumb* | 92 | NY0013 |
| Bilborough *Notts* | 62 | SK5241 |
| Bilbrook *Somset* | 20 | ST0341 |
| Bilbrook *Staffs* | 60 | SJ8703 |
| Bilbrough *N York* | 83 | SE5246 |
| Bilbster *Highld* | 151 | ND2853 |
| Bildershaw *Dur* | 96 | NZ2024 |
| Bildeston *Suffk* | 54 | TL9949 |
| Bildeston *Suffk* | 54 | TL9949 |
| Bill Street *Kent* | 28 | TQ7073 |
| Billacott *Cnwll* | 5 | SX2691 |
| Billericay *Essex* | 40 | TQ6794 |
| Billesdon *Leics* | 63 | SK7202 |
| Billesley *Warwks* | 48 | SP1456 |
| Billingborough *Lincs* | 64 | TF1134 |
| Billinge *Mersyd* | 78 | SD5200 |
| Billingford *Norfk* | 66 | TG0120 |
| Billingford *Norfk* | 54 | TM1678 |
| Billingham *Cleve* | 97 | NZ4624 |
| Billinghay *Lincs* | 76 | TF1554 |
| Billingley *S York* | 83 | SE4304 |
| Billingshurst *W Susx* | 14 | TQ0825 |
| Billingsley *Shrops* | 60 | SO7085 |
| Billington *Beds* | 38 | SP9422 |
| Billington *Lancs* | 81 | SD7235 |
| Billington *Staffs* | 72 | SJ8820 |
| Billockby *Norfk* | 67 | TG4313 |
| Billy Row *Dur* | 96 | NZ1637 |
| Bilsborrow *Lancs* | 80 | SD5139 |
| Bilsby *Lincs* | 77 | TF4776 |
| Bilsham *W Susx* | 14 | SU9702 |
| Bilsington *Kent* | 17 | TR0434 |
| Bilsthorpe *Notts* | 75 | SK6460 |
| Bilsthorpe Manor *Notts* | 75 | SK6560 |
| Bilston *Loth* | 117 | NT2664 |
| Bilston *W Mids* | 60 | SO9596 |
| Bilstone *Leics* | 62 | SK3605 |
| Bilting *Kent* | 28 | TR0549 |
| Bilton *Humb* | 85 | TA1532 |
| Bilton *N York* | 83 | SE4749 |
| Bilton *N York* | 83 | SE4749 |
| Bilton *Nthumb* | 111 | NU2211 |
| Bilton *Warwks* | 50 | SP4073 |
| Bilton Banks *Nthumb* | 111 | NU2010 |
| Binbrook *Lincs* | 76 | TF2093 |
| Binchester Blocks *Dur* | 96 | NZ2231 |
| Bincombe *Dorset* | 11 | SY6884 |
| Bindal *Highld* | 147 | NH9284 |
| Binegar *Somset* | 21 | ST6149 |
| Bines Green *W Susx* | 15 | TQ1817 |
| Binfield *Berks* | 25 | SU8471 |
| Binfield Heath *Oxon* | 37 | SU7477 |
| Bingfield *Nthumb* | 102 | NY9772 |
| Bingham *Notts* | 63 | SK7039 |
| Bingham's Melcombe *Dorset* | 11 | ST7701 |
| Bingley *W York* | 82 | SE1039 |
| Bings *Shrops* | 59 | SJ5318 |
| Binham *Norfk* | 66 | TF9839 |
| Binley *Hants* | 24 | SU4153 |
| Binley *W Mids* | 61 | SP3778 |
| Binnegar *Dorset* | 11 | SY8887 |
| Binniehill *Cent* | 116 | NS8572 |
| Binns Farm *Gramp* | 141 | NJ3164 |
| Binscombe *Surrey* | 25 | SU9746 |
| Binsey *Oxon* | 37 | SP4907 |
| Binstead *Hants* | 25 | SU7741 |
| Binstead *IOW* | 13 | SZ5792 |
| Binsted *W Susx* | 14 | SU9806 |
| Binton *Warwks* | 48 | SP1454 |
| Bintree *Norfk* | 66 | TG0123 |
| Binweston *Shrops* | 59 | SJ3004 |
| Birch *Essex* | 40 | TL9420 |
| Birch *Gt Man* | 79 | SD8507 |
| Birch Close *Dorset* | 11 | ST8803 |
| Birch Cross *Staffs* | 73 | SK1230 |
| Birch Green *Essex* | 40 | TL9418 |
| Birch Green *Herts* | 39 | TL2911 |
| Birch Heath *Ches* | 71 | SJ5461 |
| Birch Hill *Ches* | 71 | SJ5473 |
| Birch Vale *Derbys* | 74 | SK0286 |
| Bircham Newton *Norfk* | 65 | TF7734 |
| Bircham Tofts *Norfk* | 65 | TF7732 |
| Birchanger *Essex* | 39 | TL5122 |
| Birchencliffe *W York* | 82 | SE1218 |
| Bircher *H & W* | 46 | SO4765 |
| Bircher *H & W* | 46 | SO4765 |
| Birchfield *W Mids* | 61 | SP0690 |
| Birchgrove *E Susx* | 15 | TQ4029 |
| Birchgrove *S Glam* | 33 | ST1679 |
| Birchgrove *W Glam* | 32 | SS7098 |

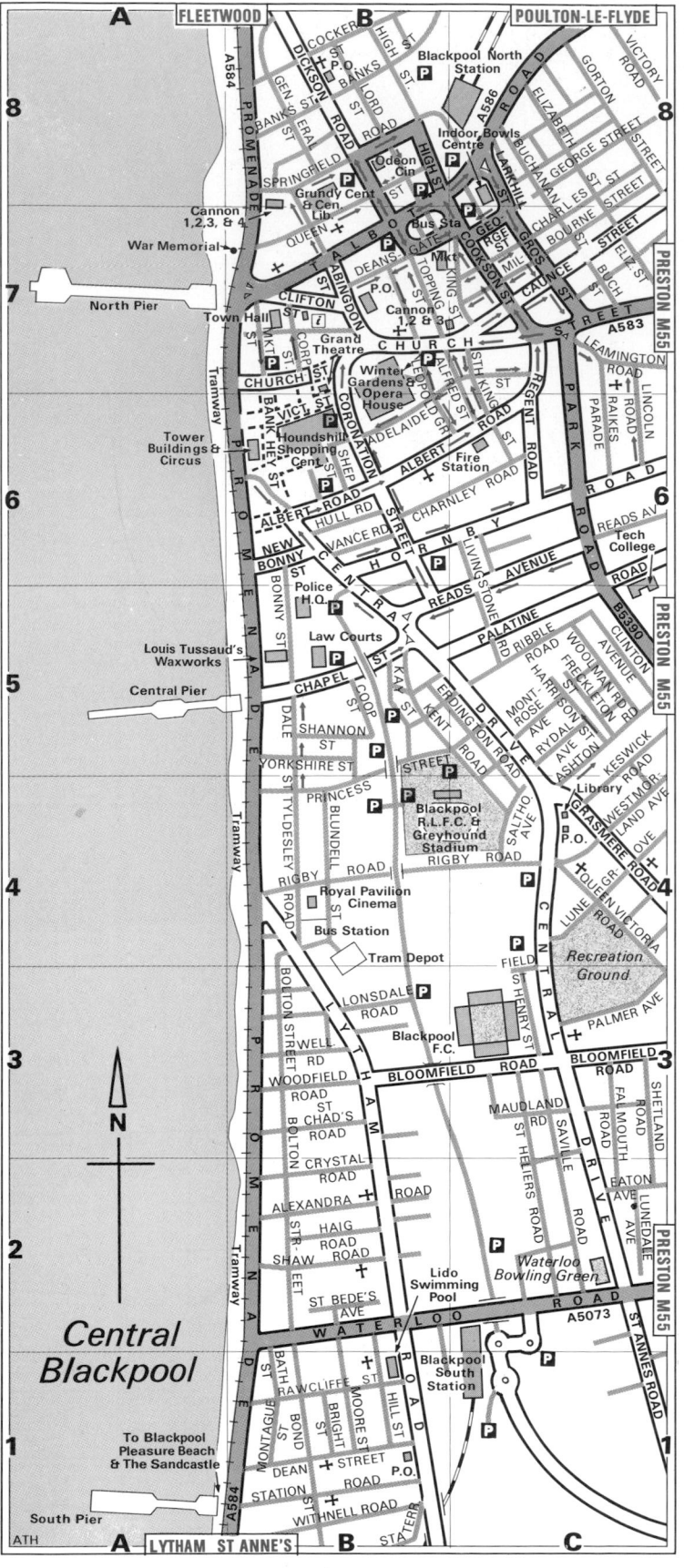

*Central Blackpool*

To Blackpool Pleasure Beach & The Sandcastle

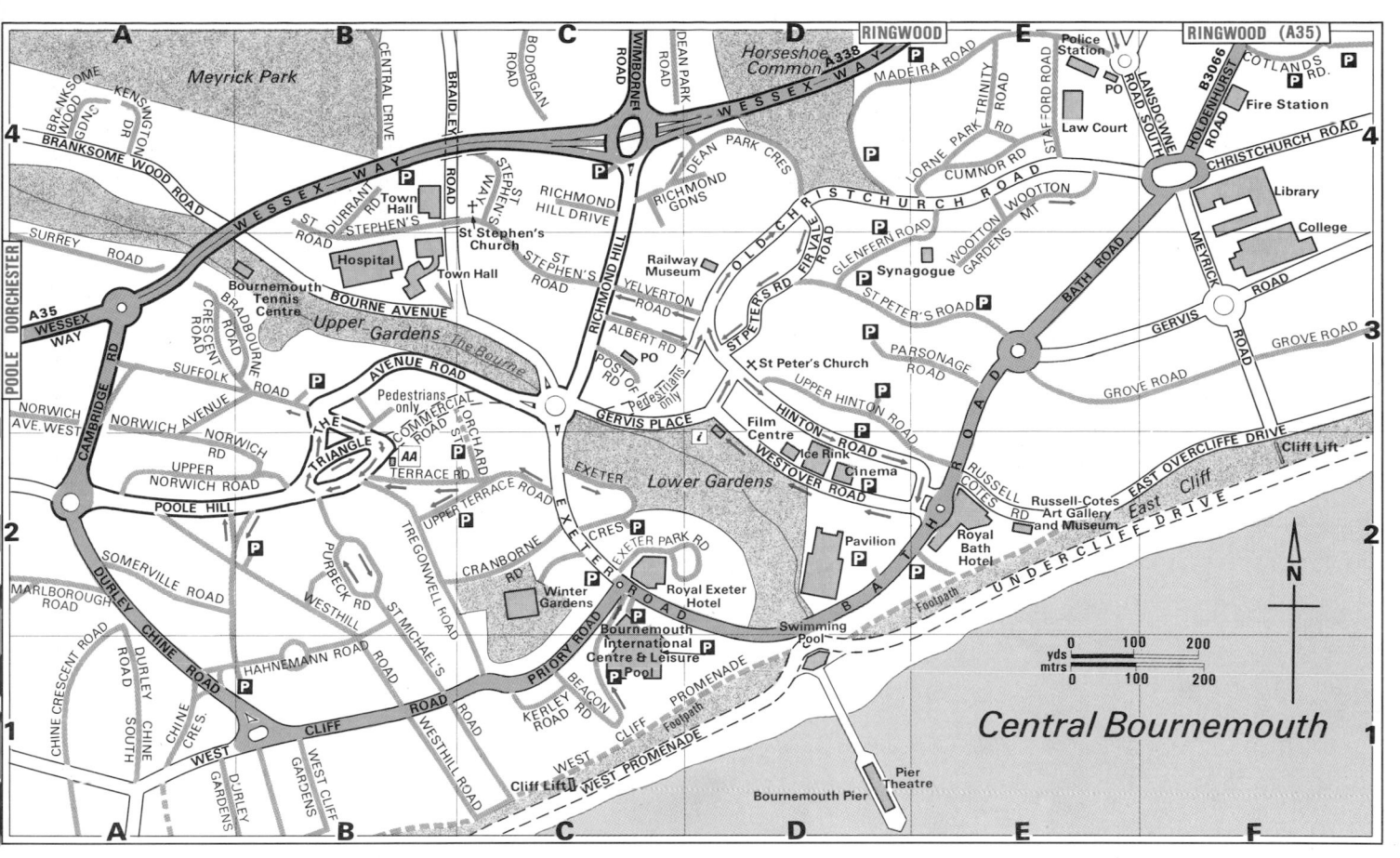

Central Bournemouth

| | | | |
|---|---|---|---|
| Blankney *Lincs* | 76 | TF0660 |
| Blantyre *Strath* | 116 | NS6857 |
| Blar a' Chaorainn *Highld* | 130 | NN1066 |
| Blargie *Highld* | 132 | NN6094 |
| Blarmachfoldach *Highld* | 130 | NN0969 |
| Blashford *Hants* | 12 | SU1406 |
| Blaston *Leics* | 51 | SP8095 |
| Blatherwycke *Nhants* | 51 | SP9795 |
| Blawith *Cumb* | 86 | SD2888 |
| Blawquhairn *D & G* | 99 | NX6282 |
| Blaxhall *Suffk* | 55 | TM3657 |
| Blaxton *S York* | 75 | SE6600 |
| Blaydon *T & W* | 103 | NZ1863 |
| Bleadney *Somset* | 21 | ST4845 |
| Bleadon *Somset* | 21 | ST3456 |
| Bleak Street *Somset* | 22 | ST7631 |
| Blean *Kent* | 29 | TR1260 |
| Bleasby *Lincs* | 75 | SK7149 |
| Bleasby *Lincs* | 76 | TF1384 |
| Bleasdale *Lancs* | 81 | SD5745 |
| Bleatarn *Cumb* | 94 | NY7313 |
| Bleathwood *H & W* | 46 | SO5570 |
| Blebocraigs *Fife* | 127 | NO4215 |
| Bleddfa *Powys* | 45 | SO2168 |
| Bledington *Gloucs* | 36 | SP2422 |
| Bledlow *Bucks* | 37 | SP7702 |
| Bledlow Ridge *Bucks* | 37 | SU7997 |
| Blegbie *Loth* | 118 | NT4861 |
| Blencarn *Cumb* | 94 | NY6331 |
| Blencogo *Cumb* | 93 | NY1947 |
| Blendworth *Hants* | 13 | SU7113 |
| Blennerhasset *Cumb* | 93 | NY1741 |
| Bletchingdon *Oxon* | 37 | SP5017 |
| Bletchingley *Surrey* | 27 | TQ3250 |
| Bletchley *Bucks* | 38 | SP8633 |
| Bletchley *Shrops* | 59 | SJ6233 |
| Bletherston *Dyfed* | 31 | SN0721 |
| Bletsoe *Beds* | 51 | TL0258 |
| Blewbury *Oxon* | 37 | SU5385 |
| Blickling *Norfk* | 66 | TG1728 |
| Blidworth *Notts* | 75 | SK5956 |
| Blidworth Bottoms *Notts* | 75 | SK5954 |
| Blindburn *Nthumb* | 110 | NT8210 |
| Blindley Heath *Surrey* | 15 | TQ3645 |
| Blisland *Cnwll* | 4 | SX0973 |
| Bliss Gate *H & W* | 60 | SO7472 |
| Blissford *Hants* | 12 | SU1713 |
| Blisworth *Nhants* | 49 | SP7253 |
| Blithbury *Staffs* | 73 | SK0819 |
| Blo Norton *Norfk* | 54 | TM0179 |
| Blockley *Gloucs* | 48 | SP1634 |
| Blofield *Norfk* | 67 | TG3309 |
| Bloomfield *Border* | 110 | NT5824 |
| Blore *Staffs* | 72 | SJ7234 |
| Blore *Staffs* | 73 | SK1349 |
| Blounts Green *Staffs* | 73 | SK0832 |
| Blowick *Mersyd* | 80 | SD3516 |
| Bloxham *Oxon* | 49 | SP4235 |
| Bloxwich *W Mids* | 60 | SJ9902 |
| Bloxworth *Dorset* | 11 | SY8894 |
| Blubberhouses *N York* | 82 | SE1655 |
| Blue Anchor *Cnwll* | 4 | SW9158 |
| Blue Anchor *Somset* | 20 | ST0243 |
| Blue Bell Hill *Kent* | 28 | TQ7462 |
| Blue Point *IOM* | 153 | NX3902 |
| Blughasary *Highld* | 145 | NC1301 |
| Blundellsands *Mersyd* | 78 | SJ3099 |
| Blundeston *Suffk* | 67 | TM5197 |
| Blunham *Beds* | 52 | TL1551 |
| Blunsdon St. Andrew *Wilts* | 36 | SU1389 |
| Bluntington *H & W* | 60 | SO8974 |
| Bluntisham *Cambs* | 52 | TL3674 |
| Blunts *Cnwll* | 5 | SX3462 |
| Blunts Green *Warwks* | 48 | SP1468 |
| Blurton *Staffs* | 72 | SJ8942 |
| Blyborough *Lincs* | 76 | SK9394 |
| Blyford *Suffk* | 55 | TM4276 |
| Blymhill *Staffs* | 60 | SJ8112 |
| Blymhill Lawn *Staffs* | 60 | SJ8211 |
| Blyth *Notts* | 75 | SK6287 |
| Blyth *Nthumb* | 103 | NZ3181 |
| Blyth Bridge *Border* | 117 | NT1345 |
| Blythburgh *Suffk* | 55 | TM4575 |
| Blythe *Border* | 110 | NT5849 |
| Blythe Bridge *Staffs* | 72 | SJ9541 |
| Blythe Bridge *Staffs* | 72 | SJ9541 |
| Blythe End *Warwks* | 61 | SP2190 |
| Blyton *Lincs* | 76 | SK8594 |
| Bo'Ness *Cent* | 117 | NT0081 |
| Boar's Head *Gt Man* | 78 | SD5708 |
| Boarhills *Fife* | 127 | NO5614 |
| Boarhunt *Hants* | 13 | SU6008 |
| Boarley *Kent* | 28 | TQ7659 |
| Boars Hill *Oxon* | 37 | SP4902 |
| Boarsgreave *Lancs* | 81 | SD8420 |
| Boarshead *E Susx* | 16 | TQ5332 |
| Boarstall *Bucks* | 37 | SP6214 |
| Boasley Cross *Devon* | 5 | SX5093 |
| Boat of Garten *Highld* | 140 | NH9319 |
| Boath *Highld* | 146 | NH5774 |
| Bobbing *Kent* | 28 | TQ8865 |
| Bobbington *Staffs* | 60 | SO8190 |
| Bobbingworth *Essex* | 39 | TL5305 |
| Bocaddon *Cnwll* | 4 | SX1858 |
| Bochym *Cnwll* | 2 | SW6820 |
| Bocking *Essex* | 40 | TL7624 |
| Bocking Churchstreet *Essex* | 40 | TL7626 |
| Bockleton *H & W* | 46 | SO5961 |
| Boconnoc *Cnwll* | 4 | SX1460 |
| Boddam *Gramp* | 143 | NK1342 |
| Boddam *Shet* | 155 | HU3915 |
| Boddin *Tays* | 127 | NO7153 |
| Boddington *Gloucs* | 47 | SO8925 |
| Bodedern *Gwynd* | 68 | SH3380 |
| Bodelwyddan *Clwyd* | 70 | SJ0075 |
| Bodelwyddan *Clwyd* | 70 | SJ0075 |
| Bodenham *H & W* | 46 | SO5351 |
| Bodenham *Wilts* | 23 | SU1626 |
| Bodenham Moor *H & W* | 46 | SO5450 |
| Bodewryd *Gwynd* | 68 | SH3990 |
| Bodfari *Clwyd* | 70 | SJ0970 |
| Bodffordd *Gwynd* | 68 | SH4276 |
| Bodfuan *Gwynd* | 56 | SH3237 |
| Bodham Street *Norfk* | 66 | TG1240 |
| Bodiam *E Susx* | 17 | TQ7825 |
| Bodicote *Oxon* | 49 | SP4538 |
| Bodieve *Cnwll* | 4 | SW9973 |
| Bodinnick *Cnwll* | 3 | SX1352 |
| Bodior *Gwynd* | 68 | SH2876 |
| Bodle Street Green *E Susx* | 16 | TQ6514 |
| Bodmin *Cnwll* | 4 | SX0767 |
| Bodney *Norfk* | 66 | TL8398 |
| Bodorgan *Gwynd* | 68 | SH3867 |
| Bodrean *Cnwll* | 3 | SW8448 |
| Bodsham Green *Kent* | 29 | TR1045 |
| Bodwen *Cnwll* | 4 | SX0360 |
| Bodymoor Heath *Warwks* | 61 | SP1996 |
| Bogallan *Highld* | 140 | NH6530 |
| Bogbrae *Gramp* | 143 | NK0335 |
| Boghall *Loth* | 117 | NS9968 |
| Boghall *Loth* | 117 | NT2465 |
| Boghead *Strath* | 107 | NS7742 |
| Boghead Farm *Gramp* | 141 | NJ3559 |
| Boghole *Highld* | 140 | NH9655 |
| Bogmoor *Gramp* | 141 | NJ3563 |
| Bogmuir *Gramp* | 135 | NO6571 |
| Bogmuir *Gramp* | 135 | NO6571 |
| Bogniebrae *Gramp* | 142 | NJ5945 |
| Bognor Regis *W Susx* | 14 | SZ9399 |
| Bogroy *Highld* | 140 | NH9023 |
| Bogue *D & G* | 99 | NX6481 |
| Bohetherick *Devon* | 5 | SX4167 |
| Bohortha *Cnwll* | 3 | SW8632 |
| Bohuntine *Highld* | 131 | NN2883 |
| Bojewyan *Cnwll* | 2 | SW3934 |
| Bokiddick *Cnwll* | 4 | SX0562 |
| Bolam *Dur* | 96 | NZ1922 |
| Bolam *Nthumb* | 103 | NZ1082 |
| Bolberry *Devon* | 7 | SX6939 |
| Bold Heath *Mersyd* | 78 | SJ5389 |
| Boldmere *W Mids* | 61 | SP1194 |
| Boldon *T & W* | 96 | NZ3461 |
| Boldon Colliery *T & W* | 96 | NZ3462 |
| Boldre *Hants* | 12 | SZ3198 |
| Boldron *Dur* | 95 | NZ0314 |
| Bole *Notts* | 75 | SK7987 |
| Bole Hill *Derbys* | 74 | SK3374 |
| Bolehill *Derbys* | 73 | SK2956 |
| Bolenowe *Cnwll* | 2 | SW6738 |
| Bolfracks *Tays* | 125 | NN8248 |
| Bolham *Devon* | 9 | SS9514 |
| Bolham Water *Devon* | 9 | ST1612 |
| Bolingey *Cnwll* | 3 | SW7653 |
| Bollington *Ches* | 79 | SJ7286 |
| Bollington *Ches* | 79 | SJ9377 |
| Bollington Cross *Ches* | 79 | SJ9277 |
| Bolney *W Susx* | 15 | TQ2622 |
| Bolnhurst *Beds* | 51 | TL0859 |
| Bolshan *Tays* | 127 | NO6252 |
| Bolsover *Derbys* | 75 | SK4470 |
| Bolster Moor *W York* | 82 | SE0815 |
| Bolsterstone *S York* | 74 | SK2696 |
| Bolstone *H & W* | 46 | SO5532 |
| Bolt Head *Devon* | 7 | SX7236 |
| Bolt Tail *Devon* | 7 | SX6639 |
| Boltby *N York* | 90 | SE4886 |
| Bolter End *Bucks* | 37 | SU7992 |
| Boltinstone *Gramp* | 134 | NJ4110 |
| Bolton *Cumb* | 94 | NY6323 |
| Bolton *Gt Man* | 79 | SD7109 |
| Bolton *Humb* | 84 | SE7752 |
| Bolton *Loth* | 118 | NT5070 |
| Bolton *Nthumb* | 111 | NU1013 |
| Bolton Abbey *N York* | 82 | SE0754 |
| Bolton Bridge *N York* | 82 | SE0653 |
| Bolton by Bowland *Lancs* | 81 | SD7849 |
| Bolton Hall *N York* | 88 | SE0789 |
| Bolton le Sands *Lancs* | 87 | SD4867 |
| Bolton New Houses *Cumb* | 93 | NY2444 |
| Bolton Percy *N York* | 83 | SE5341 |
| Bolton Town End *Lancs* | 87 | SD4667 |
| Bolton Upon Dearne *S York* | 83 | SE4502 |
| Bolton-on-Swale *N York* | 89 | SE2599 |
| Boltonfellend *Cumb* | 101 | NY4768 |
| Boltongate *Cumb* | 93 | NY2240 |
| Bolventor *Cnwll* | 4 | SX1876 |
| Bomere Heath *Shrops* | 59 | SJ4719 |
| Bon-y-Maen *W Glam* | 32 | SS6895 |
| Bonar Bridge *Highld* | 146 | NH6191 |
| Bonawe *Strath* | 122 | NN0141 |
| Bonawe Quarries *Strath* | 122 | NN0033 |
| Bonby *Humb* | 84 | TA0015 |
| Boncath *Dyfed* | 31 | SN2038 |
| Bonchester Bridge *Border* | 110 | NT5812 |
| Bonchurch *IOW* | 13 | SZ5778 |
| Bond's Green *H & W* | 46 | SO3554 |
| Bondleigh *Devon* | 8 | SS6504 |
| Bonds *Lancs* | 80 | SD4945 |
| Bone *Cnwll* | 2 | SW4632 |
| Bonehill *Staffs* | 61 | SK1902 |
| Bonerick *D & G* | 100 | NX9076 |
| Boney Hay *Staffs* | 61 | SK0510 |
| Bonhill *Strath* | 115 | NS3979 |
| Boningale *Shrops* | 60 | SJ8202 |
| Bonjedward *Border* | 110 | NT6522 |
| Bonnington *Kent* | 17 | TR0535 |
| Bonnington *Loth* | 117 | NT1269 |
| Bonnington *Tays* | 127 | NO5740 |
| Bonnybridge *Cent* | 116 | NS8280 |
| Bonnykelly *Gramp* | 143 | NJ8663 |
| Bonnyrigg *Loth* | 117 | NT3065 |
| Bonnyton *Tays* | 126 | NO3338 |
| Bonsall *Derbys* | 74 | SK2758 |
| Bont *Gwent* | 34 | SO3819 |
| Bont-Dolgadfan *Powys* | 57 | SH8800 |
| Bontddu *Gwynd* | 57 | SH6719 |
| Bonthorpe *Lincs* | 77 | TF4872 |
| Bontnewydd *Dyfed* | 43 | SN6165 |
| Bontnewydd *Gwynd* | 68 | SH4859 |
| Bontuchel *Clwyd* | 70 | SJ0857 |
| Bonvilston *S Glam* | 33 | ST0673 |
| Bonwm *Clwyd* | 70 | SJ1042 |
| Boode *Devon* | 19 | SS5038 |
| Booham *Devon* | 7 | SX8892 |
| Boohay *Devon* | 7 | SX8551 |
| Booker *Bucks* | 37 | SU8391 |
| Booley *Shrops* | 59 | SJ5725 |
| Boon Hill *Staffs* | 72 | SJ8050 |
| Boorley Green *Hants* | 13 | SU5014 |
| Boosbeck *Cleve* | 97 | NZ6616 |
| Boose's Green *Essex* | 40 | TL8531 |
| Boot *Cnwll* | 5 | SX2697 |
| Boot *Cumb* | 86 | NY1701 |
| Boot Street *Suffk* | 55 | TM2248 |
| Booth *Humb* | 84 | SE7326 |
| Booth *W York* | 82 | SE0427 |
| Booth Green *Ches* | 79 | SJ9281 |
| Booth Town *W York* | 82 | SE0926 |
| Boothby Graffoe *Lincs* | 76 | SK9859 |
| Boothby Pagnell *Lincs* | 63 | SK9730 |
| Boothstown *Gt Man* | 79 | SD7201 |
| Boothville *Nhants* | 50 | SP7864 |
| Bootle *Cumb* | 86 | SD1088 |
| Bootle *Mersyd* | 78 | SJ3495 |
| Bootle Station *Cumb* | 86 | SD0989 |
| Boots Green *Ches* | 79 | SJ7572 |
| Booze *N York* | 88 | NZ0102 |
| Boquhan *Cent* | 115 | NS5387 |
| Boraston *Shrops* | 46 | SO6169 |
| Bordeaux *Guern* | 46 | GN0000 |
| Bordeaux *Jersey* | 152 | JS0000 |
| Borden *Kent* | 28 | TQ8862 |
| Borden *W Susx* | 14 | SU8324 |
| Border *Cumb* | 92 | NY1654 |
| Bordley *N York* | 88 | SD9465 |
| Bordon *Hants* | 14 | SU7935 |
| Bordon Camp *Hants* | 14 | SU7936 |
| Boreham *Essex* | 40 | TL7610 |
| Boreham *Wilts* | 22 | ST8944 |
| Boreham Street *E Susx* | 16 | TQ6611 |
| Borehamwood *Herts* | 26 | TQ1996 |
| Boreland *D & G* | 101 | NY1790 |
| Boreraig *Highld* | 136 | NG1853 |
| Boreston *Devon* | 7 | SX7753 |
| Boreton *Ches* | 59 | SJ5106 |
| Borgie *Highld* | 149 | NC6759 |
| Borgue *D & G* | 99 | NX6248 |
| Borgue *Highld* | 151 | ND1326 |
| Borley *Essex* | 54 | TL8442 |
| Borley Green *Essex* | 54 | TL8543 |
| Borley Green *Suffk* | 54 | TL9960 |
| Borneskitaig *Highld* | 136 | NG3771 |
| Borness *D & G* | 99 | NX6145 |
| Borough Green *Kent* | 27 | TQ6057 |
| Boroughbridge *N York* | 89 | SE3966 |
| Borras Head *Clwyd* | 71 | SJ3653 |
| Borrowash *Derbys* | 62 | SK4134 |

Borrowby Bridge Hewick


| | | |
|---|---|---|
| Borrowby *N York* | 97 | NZ7715 |
| Borrowby *N York* | 89 | SE4289 |
| Borrowdale *Cumb* | 93 | NY2514 |
| Borrowdale Hotel *Cumb* | 93 | NY2618 |
| Borrowstoun *Cent* | 117 | NS9980 |
| Borstal *Kent* | 28 | TQ7366 |
| Borth *Dyfed* | 43 | SN6090 |
| Borth-y-Gest *Gwynd* | 57 | SH5637 |
| Borthwick *Loth* | 118 | NT3659 |
| Borthwickbrae *Border* | 109 | NT4113 |
| Borthwickshiels *Border* | 109 | NT4315 |
| Borve *W Isls* | 154 | NB4157 |
| Borve *Highld* | 136 | NG4448 |
| Borve *W Isls* | 154 | NF6501 |
| Borve *W Isls* | 154 | NF9181 |
| Borwick *Lancs* | 87 | SD5273 |
| Borwick Lodge *Cumb* | 109 | NY3499 |
| Borwick Rails *Cumb* | 86 | SD1879 |
| Bosavern *Cnwll* | 2 | SW3730 |
| Bosbury *H & W* | 47 | SO6943 |
| Boscarne *Cnwll* | 4 | SX0367 |
| Boscastle *Cnwll* | 4 | SX0990 |
| Boscombe *Dorset* | 12 | SZ1191 |
| Boscombe *Wilts* | 23 | SU2038 |
| Boscoppa *Cnwll* | 3 | SX0353 |
| Bosham *W Susx* | 14 | SU8004 |
| Bosham Hoe *W Susx* | 14 | SU8102 |
| Bosherton *Dyfed* | 30 | SR9694 |
| Boskednan *Cnwll* | 2 | SW4434 |
| Boskennal *Cnwll* | 2 | SW4323 |
| Bosley *Ches* | 72 | SJ9165 |
| Bosoughan *Cnwll* | 4 | SW8760 |
| Bossall *N York* | 90 | SE7160 |
| Bossiney *Cnwll* | 4 | SX0688 |
| Bossingham *Kent* | 29 | TR1549 |
| Bossington *Somset* | 19 | SS8947 |
| Bostock Green *Ches* | 79 | SJ6769 |
| Boston *Lincs* | 64 | TF3243 |
| Boston Spa *W York* | 83 | SE4245 |
| Boswarthan *Cnwll* | 2 | SW4433 |
| Boswinger *Cnwll* | 3 | SW9941 |
| Botallack *Cnwll* | 2 | SW3632 |
| Botany Bay *Gt Lon* | 27 | TQ2999 |
| Botcheston *Leics* | 62 | SK4804 |
| Botesdale *Suffk* | 54 | TM0576 |
| Bothal *Nthumb* | 103 | NZ2386 |
| Bothampstead *Berks* | 37 | SU5076 |
| Bothamsall *Notts* | 75 | SK6773 |
| Bothel *Cumb* | 93 | NY1838 |
| Bothenhampton *Dorset* | 10 | SY4791 |
| Bothwell *Strath* | 116 | NS7058 |
| Botley *Bucks* | 26 | SP9802 |
| Botley *Hants* | 13 | SU5113 |
| Botley *Oxon* | 37 | SP4806 |
| Botolph Claydon *Bucks* | 49 | SP7324 |
| Botolph's Bridge *Kent* | 17 | TR1233 |
| Botolphs *W Susx* | 15 | TQ1909 |
| Bottesford *Humb* | 84 | SE8907 |
| Bottesford *Leics* | 63 | SK8038 |
| Bottisham *Cambs* | 53 | TL5460 |
| Bottom of Hutton *Lancs* | 80 | SD4827 |
| Bottomcraig *Fife* | 126 | NO3724 |
| Bottoms *Cnwll* | 2 | SW3824 |
| Bottoms *W York* | 81 | SD9321 |
| Botton o' the' Moor *Gt Man* | 81 | SD6511 |
| Botts Green *Warwks* | 61 | SP2492 |
| Botusfleming *Cnwll* | 5 | SX4060 |
| Botwnnog *Gwynd* | 56 | SH2631 |
| Bough Beech *Kent* | 16 | TQ4847 |
| Boughrood *Powys* | 45 | SO1239 |
| Boughspring *Gloucs* | 34 | ST5597 |
| Boughton *Cambs* | 52 | TL1965 |
| Boughton *Nhants* | 50 | SP7565 |
| Boughton *Norfk* | 65 | TF7002 |
| Boughton *Notts* | 75 | SK6768 |
| Boughton Aluph *Kent* | 28 | TR0348 |
| Boughton End *Beds* | 38 | SP9838 |
| Boughton Green *Kent* | 28 | TQ7651 |
| Boughton Lees *Kent* | 28 | TR0246 |
| Boughton Malherbe *Kent* | 28 | TQ8849 |
| Boughton Monchelsea *Kent* | 28 | TQ7749 |
| Boughton Street *Kent* | 28 | TR0559 |
| Boulby *Cleve* | 97 | NZ7618 |
| Boulder Clough *W York* | 82 | SE0324 |
| Bouldnor *IOW* | 12 | SZ3789 |
| Bouldon *Shrops* | 59 | SO5485 |
| Bouley Bay *Jersey* | 152 | JS0000 |
| Boulge *Suffk* | 55 | TM2552 |
| Boulmer *Nthumb* | 111 | NU2614 |
| Boulston *Dyfed* | 30 | SM9712 |
| Boultham *Lincs* | 76 | SK9775 |
| Boultham *Lincs* | 76 | SK9568 |
| Boulton Low Houses *Cumb* | 93 | NY2344 |
| Bourn *Cambs* | 52 | TL3256 |
| Bourne *Devon* | 19 | SS6514 |
| Bourne *Lincs* | 64 | TF0920 |
| Bourne End *Beds* | 51 | TL0260 |
| Bourne End *Beds* | 38 | SP9644 |
| Bourne End *Bucks* | 26 | SU8987 |
| Bourne End *Herts* | 38 | TL0206 |
| Bournebridge *Essex* | 27 | TQ5094 |
| Bournebrook *W Mids* | 60 | SP0482 |
| Bournemouth *Dorset* | 12 | SZ0991 |
| Bournes Green *Essex* | 40 | TQ9186 |
| Bournes Green *Gloucs* | 35 | SO9104 |
| Bournheath *H & W* | 60 | SO9474 |
| Bournmoor *T & W* | 96 | NZ3150 |
| Bournstream *Gloucs* | 35 | ST7594 |
| Bournville *W Mids* | 61 | SP0481 |
| Bourton *Avon* | 21 | ST3864 |
| Bourton *Dorset* | 22 | ST7630 |
| Bourton *Oxon* | 36 | SU2386 |
| Bourton *Shrops* | 59 | SO5996 |
| Bourton *Wilts* | 23 | SU0464 |
| Bourton on Dunsmore *Warwks* | 50 | SP4370 |
| Bourton-on-the- Hill *Gloucs* | 48 | SP1732 |
| Bourton-on-the-Water *Gloucs* | 36 | SP1620 |
| Bousd *Strath* | 120 | NM2563 |
| Boustead Hill *Cumb* | 93 | NY2959 |
| Bouth *Cumb* | 86 | SD3385 |
| Bouthwaite *N York* | 89 | SE1171 |
| Bovain *Cent* | 124 | NN5430 |
| Boveney *Berks* | 26 | SU9377 |
| Boveridge *Dorset* | 12 | SU0615 |
| Bovey Tracey *Devon* | 8 | SX8178 |
| Bovingdon *Herts* | 38 | TL0103 |
| Bovingdon Green *Bucks* | 37 | SU8386 |
| Bovinger *Essex* | 39 | TL5215 |
| Bovington Camp *Dorset* | 11 | SY8389 |
| Bow *Cumb* | 93 | NY3356 |
| Bow *Devon* | 8 | SS7201 |
| Bow *Devon* | 7 | SX8156 |
| Bow *Ork* | 155 | ND3693 |
| Bow Brickhill *Bucks* | 38 | SP9034 |
| Bow End *Cumb* | 101 | NY2674 |
| Bow Fife *Fife* | 126 | NO3212 |
| Bow Street *Dyfed* | 43 | SN6285 |
| Bow Street *Norfk* | 66 | TM0198 |
| Bowbank *Dur* | 95 | NY9423 |
| Bowbridge *Gloucs* | 35 | SO8605 |
| Bowburn *Dur* | 96 | NZ3038 |
| Bowcombe *IOW* | 13 | SZ4786 |
| Bowd *Devon* | 9 | SY1190 |
| Bowden *Border* | 109 | NT5530 |
| Bowden *Devon* | 7 | SX8448 |
| Bowden Hill *Wilts* | 22 | ST9367 |
| Bowdon *Gt Man* | 79 | SJ7686 |
| Bower *Highld* | 151 | ND2362 |
| Bower Ashton *Avon* | 34 | ST5671 |
| Bower Hinton *Somset* | 10 | ST4517 |
| Bower House Tye *Suffk* | 54 | TL9941 |
| Bower's Row *W York* | 83 | SE4027 |
| Bowerchalke *Wilts* | 22 | SU0122 |
| Bowerhill *Wilts* | 22 | ST9162 |
| Bowermadden *Highld* | 151 | ND2464 |
| Bowers *Staffs* | 72 | SJ8135 |
| Bowers Gifford *Essex* | 40 | TQ7588 |
| Bowershall *Fife* | 117 | NT0991 |
| Bowertower *Highld* | 151 | ND2361 |
| Bowes *Dur* | 95 | NY9913 |
| Bowgreave *Lancs* | 80 | SD4943 |
| Bowhill *Border* | 109 | NT4227 |
| Bowithick *Cnwll* | 4 | SX1882 |
| Bowker's Green *Lancs* | 78 | SD4004 |
| Bowland *Border* | 109 | NT4540 |
| Bowland Bridge *Cumb* | 87 | SD4189 |
| Bowlee *Gt Man* | 79 | SD8406 |
| Bowley *H & W* | 46 | SO5452 |
| Bowley Town *H & W* | 46 | SO5352 |
| Bowlhead Green *Surrey* | 25 | SU9138 |
| Bowling *Strath* | 115 | NS4373 |
| Bowling *W York* | 82 | SE1731 |
| Bowling Bank *Clwyd* | 71 | SJ3949 |
| Bowling Green *H & W* | 47 | SO8151 |
| Bowmanstead *Cumb* | 86 | SD3096 |
| Bowmore *Strath* | 112 | NR3159 |
| Bowness-on-Solway *Cumb* | 101 | NY2262 |
| Bowness-on-Windermere *Cumb* | 87 | SD4097 |
| Bowscale *Cumb* | 93 | NY3532 |
| Bowsden *Nthumb* | 111 | NT9941 |
| Bowthorpe *Norfk* | 66 | TG1709 |
| Box *Gloucs* | 35 | SO8600 |
| Box *Wilts* | 22 | ST8268 |
| Box End *Beds* | 38 | TL0049 |
| Box Hill *Surrey* | 26 | TQ2051 |
| Box's Shop *Cnwll* | 18 | SS2101 |
| Boxbush *Gloucs* | 35 | SO6720 |
| Boxbush *Gloucs* | 35 | SO7412 |
| Boxford *Berks* | 24 | SU4271 |
| Boxford *Suffk* | 54 | TL9640 |
| Boxgrove *W Susx* | 14 | SU9007 |
| Boxholme *Lincs* | 76 | TF0653 |
| Boxley *Kent* | 28 | TQ7758 |
| Boxmoor *Herts* | 38 | TL0406 |
| Boxted *Essex* | 41 | TL9933 |
| Boxted *Suffk* | 54 | TL8251 |
| Boxted Cross *Essex* | 41 | TM0032 |
| Boxted Heath *Essex* | 41 | TM0031 |
| Boxwell *Gloucs* | 35 | ST8192 |
| Boxworth *Cambs* | 52 | TL3464 |
| Boxworth End *Cambs* | 52 | TL3667 |
| Boyden End *Suffk* | 53 | TL7355 |
| Boyden Gate *Kent* | 29 | TR2265 |
| Boylestone *Derbys* | 73 | SK1835 |
| Boyndie *Gramp* | 142 | NJ6463 |
| Boyndlie *Gramp* | 143 | NJ9162 |
| Boynton *Humb* | 91 | TA1368 |
| Boys Hill *Dorset* | 11 | ST6709 |
| Boysack *Tays* | 127 | NO6249 |
| Boythorpe *Derbys* | 74 | SK3869 |
| Boyton *Cnwll* | 5 | SX3192 |
| Boyton *Suffk* | 55 | TM3747 |
| Boyton *Wilts* | 22 | ST9539 |
| Boyton Cross *Essex* | 40 | TL6409 |
| Boyton End *Suffk* | 53 | TL7244 |
| Bozeat *Nhants* | 51 | SP9058 |
| Braaid *IOM* | 153 | SC3176 |
| Brabling Green *Suffk* | 55 | TM2964 |
| Brabourne *Kent* | 29 | TR1041 |
| Brabourne Lees *Kent* | 29 | TR0840 |
| Brabstermire *Highld* | 151 | ND3169 |
| Bracadale *Highld* | 136 | NG3538 |
| Braceborough *Lincs* | 64 | TF0713 |
| Bracebridge Heath *Lincs* | 76 | SK9867 |
| Bracebridge Low Fields *Lincs* | 76 | SK9666 |
| Braceby *Lincs* | 64 | TF0135 |
| Bracewell *Lancs* | 81 | SD8648 |
| Brackenfield *Derbys* | 74 | SK3759 |
| Brackenhurst *Strath* | 116 | NS7468 |
| Brackenthwaite *Cumb* | 93 | NY2946 |
| Brackenthwaite *Cumb* | 92 | NY1522 |
| Brackenthwaite *N York* | 82 | SE2851 |
| Bracklesham *W Susx* | 14 | SZ8096 |
| Brackletter *Highld* | 131 | NN1882 |
| Brackley *Nhants* | 49 | SP5837 |
| Brackley Hatch *Nhants* | 49 | SP6441 |
| Brackloch *Highld* | 148 | NC1224 |
| Bracknell *Berks* | 25 | SU8769 |
| Braco *Tays* | 125 | NN8309 |
| Bracobrae *Gramp* | 142 | NJ5053 |
| Bracon *Humb* | 84 | SE7807 |
| Bracon Ash *Norfk* | 66 | TM1899 |
| Bracora *Highld* | 129 | NM7192 |
| Bracorina *Highld* | 129 | NM7292 |
| Bradaford *Devon* | 5 | SX3994 |
| Bradbourne *Derbys* | 73 | SK2052 |
| Bradbury *Dur* | 96 | NZ3128 |
| Bradda *IOM* | 153 | SC1970 |
| Bradden *Nhants* | 49 | SP6448 |
| Braddock *Cnwll* | 4 | SX1662 |
| Bradeley *Staffs* | 72 | SJ8851 |
| Bradenham *Bucks* | 37 | SU8297 |
| Bradenstoke *Wilts* | 35 | SU0079 |
| Bradfield *Berks* | 24 | SU6072 |
| Bradfield *Devon* | 9 | ST0509 |
| Bradfield *Essex* | 41 | TM1430 |
| Bradfield *Norfk* | 67 | TG2633 |
| Bradfield *S York* | 74 | SK2692 |
| Bradfield Combust *Suffk* | 54 | TL8957 |
| Bradfield Green *Ches* | 72 | SJ6859 |
| Bradfield Heath *Essex* | 41 | TM1430 |
| Bradfield St. Clare *Suffk* | 54 | TL9158 |
| Bradfield St. George *Suffk* | 54 | TL9060 |
| Bradford *Cnwll* | 4 | SX1175 |
| Bradford *Devon* | 18 | SS4207 |
| Bradford *Nthumb* | 103 | NZ0679 |
| Bradford *Nthumb* | 111 | NU1532 |
| Bradford *W York* | 82 | SE1633 |
| Bradford Abbas *Dorset* | 10 | ST5814 |
| Bradford Leigh *Wilts* | 22 | ST8362 |
| Bradford on Avon *Wilts* | 22 | ST8260 |
| Bradford Peverell *Dorset* | 11 | SY6593 |
| Bradford-on-Tone *Somset* | 20 | ST1722 |
| Brading *IOW* | 13 | SZ6087 |
| Bradley *Ches* | 71 | SJ5377 |
| Bradley *Clwyd* | 71 | SJ3253 |
| Bradley *Derbys* | 73 | SK2246 |
| Bradley *H & W* | 47 | SO9860 |
| Bradley *Hants* | 24 | SU6341 |
| Bradley *Humb* | 85 | TA2406 |
| Bradley *N York* | 88 | SE0380 |
| Bradley *Staffs* | 72 | SJ8717 |
| Bradley *W Mids* | 60 | SO9595 |
| Bradley *W York* | 82 | SE1720 |
| Bradley Green *Ches* | 71 | SJ5046 |
| Bradley Green *H & W* | 47 | SO9862 |
| Bradley Green *Somset* | 20 | ST2538 |
| Bradley Green *Warwks* | 61 | SK2800 |
| Bradley in the Moors *Staffs* | 73 | SK0541 |
| Bradley Stoke *Avon* | 34 | ST6081 |
| Bradmore *Notts* | 62 | SK5831 |
| Bradney *Somset* | 21 | ST3338 |
| Bradninch *Devon* | 9 | SS9903 |
| Bradninch *Devon* | 19 | SS6133 |
| Bradnop *Staffs* | 73 | SK0155 |
| Bradnor Green *H & W* | 46 | SO2957 |
| Bradpole *Dorset* | 10 | SY4794 |
| Bradshaw *Gt Man* | 81 | SD7312 |
| Bradshaw *W York* | 82 | SE0514 |
| Bradshaw *W York* | 82 | SE0729 |
| Bradstone *Devon* | 5 | SX3880 |
| Bradwall Green *Ches* | 72 | SJ7663 |
| Bradwell *Bucks* | 38 | SP8340 |
| Bradwell *Derbys* | 74 | SK1781 |
| Bradwell *Devon* | 19 | SS5042 |
| Bradwell *Essex* | 40 | TL8222 |
| Bradwell *Norfk* | 67 | TG5003 |
| Bradwell Waterside *Essex* | 41 | TL9907 |
| Bradwell-on-Sea *Essex* | 41 | TM0007 |
| Bradworthy *Devon* | 18 | SS3213 |
| Brae *D & G* | 100 | NX8674 |
| Brae *D & G* | 100 | NX8674 |
| Brae *Highld* | 140 | NH6662 |
| Brae *Shet* | 155 | HU3568 |
| Brae Roy Lodge *Highld* | 131 | NN3391 |
| Braeface *Cent* | 116 | NS7880 |
| Braefield *Highld* | 139 | NH4130 |
| Braegrum *Tays* | 125 | NO0025 |
| Braehead *D & G* | 99 | NX4252 |
| Braehead *D & G* | 99 | NX4252 |
| Braehead *Strath* | 117 | NS9550 |
| Braehead *Tays* | 127 | NO6952 |
| Braehour *Highld* | 151 | ND0953 |
| Braelangwell Lodge *Highld* | 146 | NH5192 |
| Braemar *Gramp* | 133 | NO1591 |
| Braemore *Highld* | 150 | ND0829 |
| Braemore *Highld* | 145 | NH2078 |
| Braes of Coul *Tays* | 133 | NO2857 |
| Braes of Enzie *Gramp* | 142 | NJ3957 |
| Braes The *Highld* | 137 | NG5234 |
| Braeside *Strath* | 114 | NS2375 |
| Braeswick *Ork* | 155 | HY6037 |
| Braevallich *Strath* | 122 | NM9507 |
| Brafferton *Dur* | 96 | NZ2921 |
| Brafferton *N York* | 89 | SE4370 |
| Brafield-on-the-Green *Nhants* | 51 | SP8258 |
| Bragar *W Isls* | 154 | NB2847 |
| Bragbury End *Herts* | 39 | TL2621 |
| Brahen Hill *W York* | 83 | SE4317 |
| Braidwood *Strath* | 116 | NS8448 |
| Braigo *Strath* | 112 | NR2369 |
| Brailsford *Derbys* | 73 | SK2541 |
| Brailsford Green *Derbys* | 73 | SK2541 |
| Brain's Green *Gloucs* | 35 | SO6608 |
| Braintree *Essex* | 40 | TL7523 |
| Braiseworth *Suffk* | 54 | TM1372 |
| Braishfield *Hants* | 23 | SU3725 |
| Braithwaite *Cumb* | 93 | NY2323 |
| Braithwaite *W York* | 82 | SE0341 |
| Braithwell *S York* | 75 | SK5394 |
| Bramber *W Susx* | 15 | TQ1811 |
| Brambridge *Hants* | 13 | SU4721 |
| Bramcote *Notts* | 62 | SK5037 |
| Bramcote *Warwks* | 61 | SP4088 |
| Bramdean *Hants* | 24 | SU6128 |
| Bramerton *Norfk* | 67 | TG2904 |
| Bramfield *Herts* | 39 | TL2915 |
| Bramfield *Suffk* | 55 | TM4074 |
| Bramford *Suffk* | 54 | TM1246 |
| Bramhall *Gt Man* | 79 | SJ8984 |
| Bramham *W York* | 83 | SE4242 |
| Bramhope *W York* | 82 | SE2443 |
| Bramley *Derbys* | 74 | SK3979 |
| Bramley *Derbys* | 74 | SK3979 |
| Bramley *Hants* | 24 | SU6559 |
| Bramley *S York* | 75 | SK4892 |
| Bramley *Surrey* | 25 | TQ0044 |
| Bramley *W York* | 82 | SE2435 |
| Bramley Corner *Hants* | 24 | SU6359 |
| Bramley Green *Hants* | 24 | SU6658 |
| Bramleyhead *N York* | 83 | SE5218 |
| Bramling *Kent* | 29 | TR2256 |
| Brampford Speke *Devon* | 9 | SX9298 |
| Brampton *Cambs* | 52 | TL2170 |
| Brampton *Cumb* | 101 | NY5361 |
| Brampton *Cumb* | 94 | NY6723 |
| Brampton *Lincs* | 76 | SK8479 |
| Brampton *Norfk* | 67 | TG2223 |
| Brampton *S York* | 83 | SE4101 |
| Brampton *Suffk* | 55 | TM4381 |
| Brampton Abbotts *H & W* | 46 | SO6026 |
| Brampton Ash *Nhants* | 50 | SP7987 |
| Brampton Bryan *H & W* | 46 | SO3672 |
| Brampton-en-le-Morthen *S York* | 75 | SK4888 |
| Bramshall *Staffs* | 73 | SK0633 |
| Bramshaw *Hants* | 12 | SU2715 |
| Bramshill *Hants* | 24 | SU7461 |
| Bramshott *Hants* | 14 | SU8432 |
| Bramwell *Somset* | 21 | ST4229 |
| Bran End *Essex* | 40 | TL6525 |
| Branault *Highld* | 128 | NM5269 |
| Brancaster *Norfk* | 65 | TF7743 |
| Brancaster Staithe *Norfk* | 66 | TF7944 |
| Brancepeth *Dur* | 96 | NZ2237 |
| Branch End *Nthumb* | 103 | NZ0662 |
| Branchill *Gramp* | 141 | NJ0852 |
| Brand End *Lincs* | 64 | TF3844 |
| Brand Green *Gloucs* | 47 | SO7328 |
| Branderburgh *Gramp* | 141 | NJ2371 |
| Brandesburton *Humb* | 85 | TA1147 |
| Brandeston *Suffk* | 55 | TM2460 |
| Brandis Corner *Devon* | 18 | SS4104 |
| Brandiston *Norfk* | 66 | TG1421 |
| Brandon *Dur* | 96 | NZ2439 |
| Brandon *Lincs* | 76 | SK9048 |
| Brandon *Nthumb* | 111 | NU0417 |
| Brandon *Suffk* | 53 | TL7886 |
| Brandon *Warwks* | 50 | SP4176 |
| Brandon Bank *Cambs* | 53 | TL6289 |
| Brandon Creek *Norfk* | 65 | TL6091 |
| Brandon Parva *Norfk* | 66 | TG0708 |
| Brandsby *N York* | 90 | SE5872 |
| Brandy Wharf *Lincs* | 76 | TF0196 |
| Brane *Cnwll* | 2 | SW4028 |
| Branksome *Dorset* | 12 | SZ0393 |
| Branksome Park *Dorset* | 12 | SZ0590 |
| Bransbury *Hants* | 24 | SU4242 |
| Bransby *Lincs* | 76 | SK8979 |
| Branscombe *Devon* | 9 | SY1988 |
| Bransford *H & W* | 47 | SO7952 |
| Bransgore *Hants* | 12 | SZ1897 |
| Bransley *Shrops* | 47 | SO6575 |
| Branson's Cross *H & W* | 61 | SP0970 |
| Branston *Leics* | 63 | SK8129 |
| Branston *Lincs* | 76 | TF0166 |
| Branston *Staffs* | 73 | SK2221 |
| Branston Booths *Lincs* | 76 | TF0669 |
| Branstone *IOW* | 13 | SZ5583 |
| Brant Broughton *Lincs* | 76 | SK9154 |
| Brantham *Suffk* | 54 | TM1134 |
| Branthwaite *Cumb* | 92 | NY0525 |
| Branthwaite *Cumb* | 93 | NY2937 |
| Brantingham *Humb* | 84 | SE9429 |
| Branton *Nthumb* | 111 | NU0416 |
| Branton *S York* | 83 | SE6401 |
| Branton Green *N York* | 89 | SE4462 |
| Branxton *Nthumb* | 110 | NT8937 |
| Brassey Green *Ches* | 71 | SJ5260 |
| Brassington *Derbys* | 73 | SK2354 |
| Brasted *Kent* | 27 | TQ4855 |
| Brasted Chart *Gt Lon* | 27 | TQ4653 |
| Brathens *Gramp* | 135 | NO6798 |
| Bratoft *Lincs* | 77 | TF4764 |
| Brattleby *Lincs* | 76 | SK9481 |
| Bratton *Shrops* | 59 | SJ6314 |
| Bratton *Somset* | 20 | SS9546 |
| Bratton *Wilts* | 22 | ST9152 |
| Bratton Clovelly *Devon* | 5 | SX4691 |
| Bratton Fleming *Devon* | 19 | SS6437 |
| Bratton Seymour *Somset* | 22 | ST6729 |
| Braughing *Herts* | 39 | TL3925 |
| Braughing Friars *Herts* | 39 | TL4124 |
| Braunston *Leics* | 63 | SK8306 |
| Braunston *Nhants* | 50 | SP5466 |
| Braunstone *Leics* | 62 | SK5502 |
| Braunton *Devon* | 18 | SS4836 |
| Brawby *N York* | 90 | SE7378 |
| Brawdy *Dyfed* | 30 | SM8524 |
| Brawl *Highld* | 150 | NC8166 |
| Brawlbin *Highld* | 150 | ND0757 |
| Braworth *N York* | 90 | NZ5007 |
| Bray *Berks* | 26 | SU9079 |
| Bray Shop *Cnwll* | 5 | SX3374 |
| Bray's Hill *E Susx* | 16 | TQ6714 |
| Braybrooke *Nhants* | 50 | SP7684 |
| Braydon *Wilts* | 36 | SU0588 |
| Braydon Brook *Wilts* | 35 | ST9891 |
| Braydon Side *Wilts* | 35 | SU0185 |
| Brayford *Devon* | 19 | SS6934 |
| Braystones *Cumb* | 86 | NY0106 |
| Braythorn *N York* | 82 | SE2449 |
| Brayton *N York* | 83 | SE6030 |
| Braywick *Berks* | 26 | SU8979 |
| Braywoodside *Berks* | 26 | SU8775 |
| Brazacott *Cnwll* | 5 | SX2691 |
| Breach *Kent* | 28 | TQ8465 |
| Breach *Kent* | 29 | TR1947 |
| Breachwood Green *Herts* | 39 | TL1522 |
| Breaclete *W Isls* | 154 | NB1537 |
| Breaden Heath *Shrops* | 59 | SJ4436 |
| Breadsall *Derbys* | 62 | SK3639 |
| Breadstone *Gloucs* | 35 | SO7000 |
| Breadward *H & W* | 46 | SO2854 |
| Breage *Cnwll* | 2 | SW6128 |
| Breakachy *Highld* | 139 | NH4644 |
| Bream *Gloucs* | 34 | SO6005 |
| Bream's Meend *Gloucs* | 34 | SO5905 |
| Breamore *Hants* | 12 | SU1517 |
| Brean *Somset* | 20 | ST2955 |
| Brearley *W York* | 82 | SE0226 |
| Brearton *N York* | 89 | SE3260 |
| Breasclete *W Isls* | 154 | NB2135 |
| Breaston *Derbys* | 62 | SK4633 |
| Brechfa *Dyfed* | 44 | SN5230 |
| Brechin *Tays* | 134 | NO6060 |
| Breckles *Norfk* | 66 | TL9594 |
| Breckonside *D & G* | 100 | NX8489 |
| Breckrey *Highld* | 137 | NG5061 |
| Brecon *Powys* | 45 | SO0428 |
| Bredbury *Gt Man* | 79 | SJ9291 |
| Brede *E Susx* | 17 | TQ8218 |
| Bredenbury *H & W* | 46 | SO6056 |
| Bredfield *Suffk* | 55 | TM2753 |
| Bredgar *Kent* | 28 | TQ8860 |
| Bredhurst *Kent* | 28 | TQ7962 |
| Bredon *H & W* | 47 | SO9236 |
| Bredon's Hardwick *H & W* | 47 | SO9135 |
| Bredon's Norton *H & W* | 47 | SO9339 |
| Bredwardine *H & W* | 46 | SO3344 |
| Breedon on the Hill *Leics* | 62 | SK4022 |
| Breich *Loth* | 117 | NS9560 |
| Breightmet *Gt Man* | 79 | SD7409 |
| Breighton *Humb* | 84 | SE7033 |
| Breinton *H & W* | 46 | SO4739 |
| Bremhill *Wilts* | 35 | ST9873 |
| Bremley *Devon* | 19 | SS8128 |
| Bremridge *Devon* | 19 | SS6929 |
| Brenchley *Kent* | 28 | TQ6741 |
| Brendon *Devon* | 18 | SS3607 |
| Brendon *Devon* | 19 | SS7648 |
| Brenfield *Strath* | 113 | NR8482 |
| Brenish *W Isls* | 154 | NA9926 |
| Brenkley *T & W* | 103 | NZ2175 |
| Brent Eleigh *Suffk* | 54 | TL9448 |
| Brent Knoll *Somset* | 21 | ST3350 |
| Brent Knoll *Somset* | 21 | ST3350 |
| Brent Mill *Devon* | 7 | SX7059 |
| Brent Pelham *Herts* | 39 | TL4330 |
| Brentford *Gt Lon* | 26 | TQ1777 |
| Brentingby *Leics* | 63 | SK7818 |
| Brentwood *Essex* | 27 | TQ5993 |
| Brenzett *Kent* | 17 | TR0027 |
| Brenzett Green *Kent* | 17 | TR0028 |
| Brereton *Staffs* | 73 | SK0516 |
| Brereton Cross *Staffs* | 73 | SK0615 |
| Brereton Green *Ches* | 72 | SJ7764 |
| Brereton Heath *Ches* | 72 | SJ8065 |
| Brereton Hill *Staffs* | 73 | SK0615 |
| Bressingham *Norfk* | 54 | TM0780 |
| Bressingham Common *Norfk* | 54 | TM0982 |
| Bretabister *Shet* | 155 | HU4857 |
| Bretby *Derbys* | 73 | SK2923 |
| Bretford *Warwks* | 50 | SP4377 |
| Bretforton *H & W* | 48 | SP0944 |
| Bretherton *Lancs* | 80 | SD4720 |
| Brettenham *Norfk* | 54 | TL9383 |
| Brettenham *Suffk* | 54 | TL9654 |
| Bretton *Clwyd* | 71 | SJ3564 |
| Bretton *Derbys* | 74 | SK2078 |
| Brewer Street *Surrey* | 27 | TQ3251 |
| Brewers End *Essex* | 39 | TL5521 |
| Brewhouse *D & G* | 100 | NY0165 |
| Brewood *Staffs* | 60 | SJ8808 |
| Brgoed *M Glam* | 33 | ST1599 |
| Briantspuddle *Dorset* | 11 | SY8193 |
| Brick End *Essex* | 40 | TL5725 |
| Brick Houses *S York* | 74 | SK3081 |
| Bricket Wood *Herts* | 26 | TL1302 |
| Brickkiln Green *Essex* | 40 | TL7331 |
| Bricklehampton *H & W* | 47 | SO9842 |
| Bride *IOM* | 153 | NX4501 |
| Bridekirk *Cumb* | 92 | NY1133 |
| Bridell *Dyfed* | 31 | SN1742 |
| Bridestowe *Devon* | 5 | SX5189 |
| Brideswell *Gramp* | 142 | NJ5739 |
| Bridford *Devon* | 8 | SX8186 |
| Bridge *Cnwll* | 2 | SW6744 |
| Bridge *Kent* | 29 | TR1854 |
| Bridge End *Beds* | 38 | TL0050 |
| Bridge End *Cumb* | 93 | NY3748 |
| Bridge End *Cumb* | 86 | SD1884 |
| Bridge End *Devon* | 7 | SX7046 |
| Bridge End *Dur* | 95 | NZ0236 |
| Bridge End *Essex* | 40 | TL6731 |
| Bridge End *Lincs* | 64 | TF1436 |
| Bridge End *Nthumb* | 102 | NY8965 |
| Bridge End *Surrey* | 26 | TQ0757 |
| Bridge Fields *Leics* | 62 | SK4927 |
| Bridge Green *Essex* | 39 | TL4636 |
| Bridge Hewick *N York* | 89 | SE3370 |

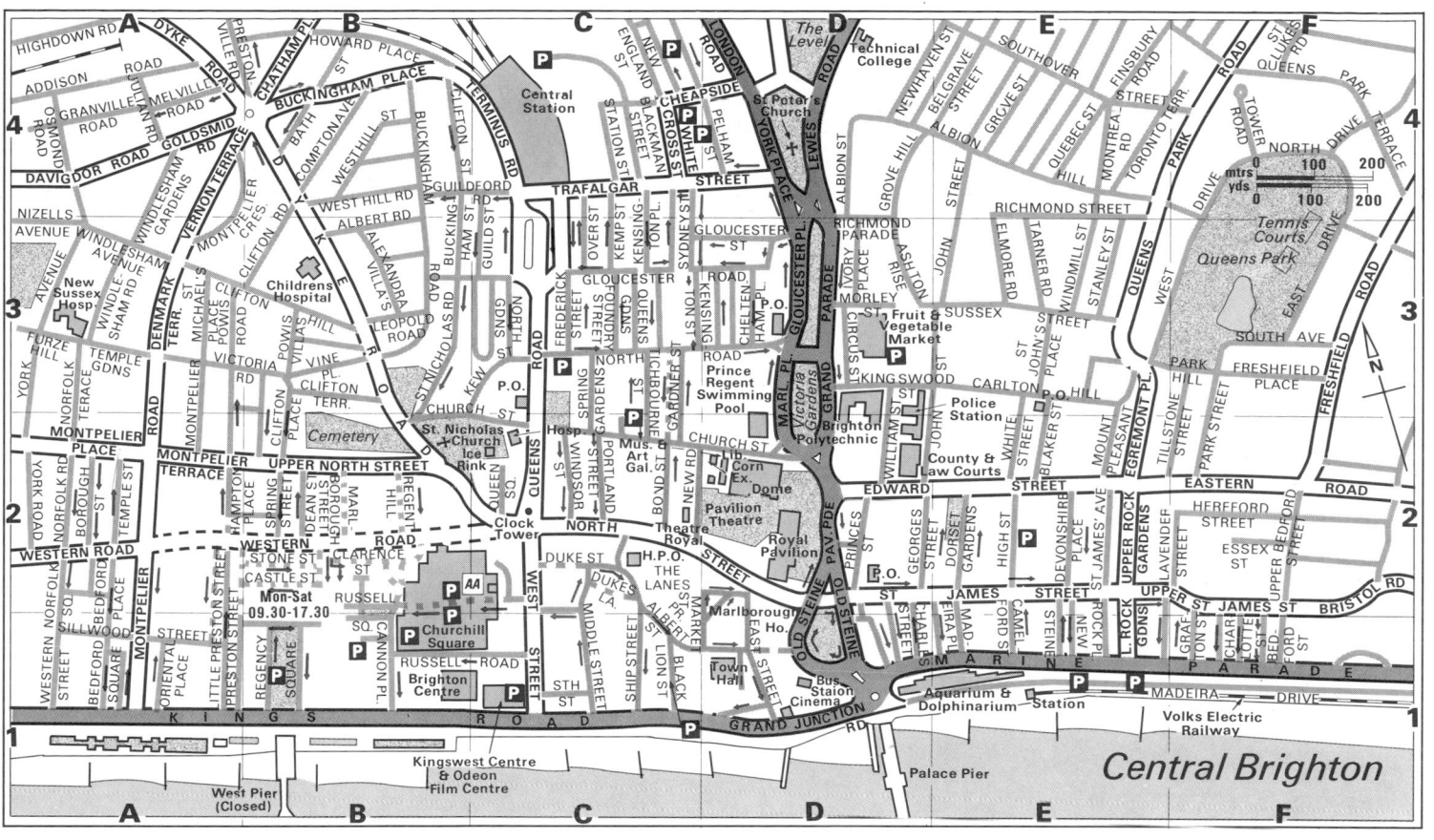

Central Brighton

Burton Carmyllie


Burton *Somset* 20 ST1944
Burton *Somset* 10 ST5313
Burton *Wilts* 22 ST8232
Burton *Wilts* 35 ST8179
Burton Agnes *Humb* 91 TA1063
Burton Bradstock *Dorset* 10 SY4889
Burton Coggles *Lincs* 63 SK9725
Burton Dassett *Warwks* 48 SP3051
Burton End *Essex* 39 TL5323
Burton End *Suffk* 53 TL6645
Burton Fleming *Humb* 91 TA0872
Burton Green *Clwyd* 71 SJ3458
Burton Green *Warwks* 61 SP2675
Burton Hastings *Warwks* 50 SP4190
Burton in Lonsdale *N York* 87 SD6572
Burton Joyce *Notts* 63 SK6443
Burton Latimer *Nhants* 51 SP9074
Burton Lazars *Leics* 63 SK7716
Burton Leonard *N York* 89 SE3263
Burton Overy *Leics* 50 SP6798
Burton on the Wolds *Leics* 62 SK5921
Burton Pedwardine *Lincs* 64 TF1142
Burton Pidsea *Humb* 85 TA2431
Burton Salmon *N York* 83 SE4827
Burton upon Stather *Humb* 84 SE8617
Burton upon Trent *Staffs* 73 SK2423
Burton's Green *Essex* 40 TL8327
Burton-in-Lonsdale *N York* 87 SD6572
Burtonwood *Ches* 78 SJ5692
Burwardsley *Ches* 71 SJ5156
Burwarton *Shrops* 59 SO6185
Burwash *E Susx* 16 TQ6724
Burwash Common *E Susx* 16 TQ6423
Burwash Weald *E Susx* 16 TQ6523
Burwell *Cambs* 53 TL5866
Burwell *Lincs* 77 TF3579
Burwen *Gwynd* 68 SH4293
Burwick *Ork* 155 ND4384
Bury *Cambs* 52 TL2883
Bury *Gt Man* 81 SD8111
Bury *Somset* 20 SS9427
Bury *W Susx* 14 TQ0113
Bury End *Beds* 38 TL1235
Bury End *Bucks* 26 SU9597
Bury Green *Herts* 39 TL4521
Bury Hill *Hants* 23 SU3443
Bury St. Edmunds *Suffk* 54 TL8564
Burythorpe *N York* 90 SE7964
Busby *Strath* 115 NS5756
Buscot *Wilts* 36 SU2298
Bush *Cnwll* 18 SS2307
Bush *Gramp* 135 NO7565
Bush *Gramp* 135 NO7565
Bush Bank *H & W* 46 SO4551
Bush Green *Norfk* 55 TM2187
Bush Green *Suffk* 54 TL9157
Bush Hill Park *Gt Lon* 27 TQ3395
Bushbury *W Mids* 60 SJ9202
Bushby *Leics* 63 SK6504
Bushey *Herts* 26 TQ1395
Bushey Heath *Herts* 26 TQ1494
Bushley *H & W* 47 SO8734
Bushley Green *H & W* 47 SO8634
Bushmead *Beds* 52 TL1160
Bushton *Wilts* 36 SU0677
Busk *Cumb* 94 NY6042
Buslingthorpe *Lincs* 76 TF0885
Bussage *Gloucs* 35 SO8803
Bussex *Somset* 21 ST3435
Butcher Hill *W York* 81 SD9322
Butcher's Cross *E Susx* 16 TQ5525
Butcher's Pasture *Essex* 40 TL6024
Butchers Row *W Susx* 15 TQ1720
Butcombe *Avon* 21 ST5162
Butleigh *Somset* 21 ST5233
Butleigh Wootton *Somset* 21 ST5034
Butler's Cross *Bucks* 38 SP8407
Butler's Hill *Notts* 75 SK5448
Butlers Green *Staffs* 72 SJ8150
Butlers Marston *Warwks* 48 SP3150
Butley *Suffk* 55 TM3751
Butley Corner *Suffk* 55 TM3849
Butt Green *Ches* 72 SJ6751
Butt Lane *Staffs* 72 SJ8254
Butt's Green *Essex* 40 TL7603
Buttercrambe *N York* 90 SE7358
Butterdean *Border* 119 NT7964
Butterhill Bank *Staffs* 72 SJ9330
Butterknowle *Dur* 95 NZ1025
Butterleigh *Devon* 9 SS9708
Butterley *Derbys* 74 SK4051
Buttermere *Cumb* 93 NY1726
Buttermere *Wilts* 23 SU3361
Buttermere *Wilts* 23 SU3361
Buttershaw *W York* 82 SE1329
Butterstone *Tays* 125 NO0645
Butterton *Staffs* 72 SJ8242
Butterton *Staffs* 73 SK0756
Butterwick *Dur* 96 NZ3829
Butterwick *Lincs* 64 TF3844
Butterwick *N York* 90 SE7377
Butterwick *N York* 91 SE9871
Buttington *Powys* 58 SJ2508
Buttonbridge *Shrops* 60 SO7379
Buttonoak *Shrops* 60 SO7578
Buttsash *Hants* 13 SU4205
Buttsbear Cross *Cnwll* 18 SS2604
Buxhall *Suffk* 54 TM0057
Buxted *E Susx* 16 TQ4923
Buxton *Derbys* 74 SK0673
Buxton *Norfk* 67 TG2322
Buxton Heath *Norfk* 66 TG1821
Bwchall Fen Street *Suffk* 54 TM0059
Bwlch *Powys* 33 SO1522
Bwlch-y-cibau *Powys* 58 SJ1717
Bwlch-y-ffridd *Powys* 58 SO0795
Bwlch-y-groes *Dyfed* 31 SN2436
Bwlch-y-sarnau *Powys* 45 SO0374
Bwlchgwyn *Clwyd* 70 SJ2653
Bwlchllan *Dyfed* 44 SN5758
Bwlchnewydd *Dyfed* 31 SN3624
Bwlchtocyn *Gwynd* 56 SH3125
Bwlchyddar *Clwyd* 58 SJ1722
Bwlchyfadfa *Dyfed* 42 SN4349
Bwlchymyrdd *W Glam* 32 SS5798
Byermoor *T & W* 96 NZ1857
Byers Garth *Dur* 96 NZ3141
Byers Green *Dur* 96 NZ2233
Byfield *Nhants* 49 SP5153
Byfield *Nhants* 49 SP5153
Byfleet *Surrey* 26 TQ0661
Byford *H & W* 46 SO3942
Byker *T & W* 103 NZ2764
Bylchau *Clwyd* 70 SH9762
Byley *Ches* 79 SJ7269
Bynea *Dyfed* 32 SS5499
Byre Burnfoot *D & G* 101 NY3877
Byrewalls *Border* 110 NT6643
Byrness *Nthumb* 102 NT7602
Bystock *Devon* 9 SY0283
Bythorn *Cambs* 51 TL0575
Byton *H & W* 46 SO3764
Bywell *Nthumb* 103 NZ0461
Byworth *W Susx* 14 SU9820

# C

Cabourne *Lincs* 85 TA1401
Cabrach *Gramp* 141 NJ3826
Cabrach *Strath* 112 NR4964
Cabus *Lancs* 80 SD4948
Cabvie Lodge *Highld* 138 NH1567
Cackle Green *E Susx* 16 TQ6919
Cackle Street *E Susx* 16 TQ4526
Cackle Street *E Susx* 17 TQ8219
Cacrabank *Border* 109 NT3017
Cadbury *Devon* 9 SS9105
Cadbury Barton *Devon* 19 SS6917
Cadder *Strath* 116 NS6172
Caddington *Beds* 38 TL0619
Caddonfoot *Border* 109 NT4535
Cade Street *E Susx* 16 TQ6021
Cadeby *Leics* 62 SK4202
Cadeby *S York* 75 SE5100
Cadeleigh *Devon* 9 SS9107
Cadgwith *Cnwll* 3 SW7214
Cadham *Fife* 126 NO2802
Cadishead *Gt Man* 79 SJ7191
Cadle *W Glam* 32 SS6296
Cadley *Wilts* 23 SU2454
Cadley *Wilts* 23 SU2066
Cadmore End *Bucks* 37 SU7892
Cadnam *Hants* 12 SU2913
Cadney *Humb* 84 TA0103
Cadole *Clwyd* 70 SJ2062
Cadoxton *S Glam* 20 ST1269
Cadoxton Juxta-Neath *W Glam* 32 SS7598
Cadsden *Bucks* 38 SP8204
Cadwst *Clwyd* 58 SJ0235
Cae'r bryn *Dyfed* 32 SN5913
Cae'r-bont *Powys* 32 SN8011
Caeathro *Gwynd* 68 SH5061
Caehopkin *Powys* 33 SN8212
Caenby *Lincs* 76 TF0089
Caenby Corner *Lincs* 76 SK9689
Caeo *Dyfed* 44 SN6739
Caer Farchell *Dyfed* 30 SM7927
Caerau *M Glam* 33 SS8694
Caerau *S Glam* 33 ST1375
Caerdeon *Gwynd* 57 SH6518
Caergeiliog *Gwynd* 68 SH3178
Caergwrle *Clwyd* 71 SJ3057
Caerhun *Gwynd* 69 SH7770
Caerlanrig *Border* 109 NT3904
Caerleon *Gwent* 34 ST3491
Caernarfon *Gwynd* 68 SH4862
Caerphilly *M Glam* 33 ST1587
Caersws *Powys* 58 SO0392
Caerwedros *Dyfed* 42 SN3755
Caerwent *Gwent* 34 ST4790
Caerwys *Clwyd* 70 SJ1272
Caerynwch *Gwynd* 57 SH7617
Caggle Street *Gwent* 34 SO3717
Caim *Gwynd* 69 SH6280
Cairnbaan *Strath* 113 NR8390
Cairnbrogie *Gramp* 143 NJ8527
Cairnbulg *Gramp* 143 NK0365
Cairncross *Border* 119 NT8963
Cairncurran *Strath* 115 NS3170
Cairndow *Strath* 123 NN1810
Cairneyhill *Fife* 117 NT0486
Cairnfield *D & G* 99 NX3848
Cairnfield House *Gramp* 142 NJ4162
Cairngarroch *D & G* 98 NX0649
Cairngrassie *Gramp* 135 NO9095
Cairngrassie *Gramp* 135 NO9095
Cairnie *Gramp* 142 NJ4844
Cairnorrie *Gramp* 143 NJ8641
Cairnryan *D & G* 98 NX0668
Cairnty Auchroisk *Gramp* 141 NJ3351
Cairnwhin *Strath* 106 NX2491
Caister-on-Sea *Norfk* 67 TG5212
Caistor *Lincs* 85 TA1101
Caistor St. Edmund *Norfk* 67 TG2303
Caistron *Nthumb* 103 NT9901
Cake Street *Norfk* 54 TM0790
Cakebole *H & W* 60 SO8772
Calais Street *Suffk* 54 TL9740
Calbost *Highld* 136 NG2148
Calbourne *IOW* 13 SZ4286
Calceby *Lincs* 77 TF3877
Calcot *Berks* 24 SU6671
Calcot *Clwyd* 70 SJ1775
Calcot *Gloucs* 36 SP0910
Calcot Row *Berks* 24 SU6771
Calcots *Gramp* 141 NJ2563
Calcott *Kent* 29 TR1762
Calcott *Shrops* 59 SJ4414
Calcutt *Wilts* 36 SU1193
Caldbeck *Cumb* 93 NY3240
Caldbergh *N York* 89 SE0985
Caldecote *Cambs* 52 TL1488
Caldecote *Cambs* 52 TL3456
Caldecote *Herts* 39 TL2338
Caldecote *Nhants* 49 SP6851
Caldecote Highfields *Cambs* 52 TL3559
Caldecott *Leics* 51 SP8693
Caldecott *Nhants* 51 SP9868
Caldecott *Oxon* 37 SU4996
Calder Bridge *Cumb* 86 NY0306
Calder Grove *W York* 82 SE3016
Calder Vale *Lancs* 80 SD5345
Calderbank *Strath* 116 NS7663
Calderbrook *Gt Man* 82 SD9418
Caldercote *Bucks* 38 SP8935
Caldercruix *Strath* 116 NS8167
Caldermill *Strath* 107 NS6642
Caldermore *Gt Man* 81 SD9316
Caldicot *Gwent* 34 ST4888
Caldwell *N York* 89 NZ1613
Caldy *Mersyd* 78 SJ2285
Calendra *Cnwll* 3 SW9240
Calenick *Cnwll* 3 SW8243
Calford Green *Suffk* 53 TL7045
Calfsound *Ork* 155 HY5738
Calgary *Strath* 121 NM3751
Califer *Gramp* 141 NJ0857
California *Cent* 116 NS9076
California *Derbys* 62 SK3335
California *Norfk* 67 TG5114
California *Suffk* 54 TM0641
California Cross *Devon* 7 SX7053
Calke *Derbys* 62 SK3722
Callaly *Nthumb* 111 NU0509
Callander *Cent* 124 NN6208
Callanish *W Isls* 154 NB2133
Callaughton *Shrops* 59 SO6197
Callert Cottage *Highld* 130 NN1060
Callestick *Cnwll* 3 SW7750
Calligarry *Highld* 129 NG6203
Callington *Cnwll* 5 SX3669
Callingwood *Staffs* 73 SK1823
Callow *H & W* 46 SO4934
Callow End *H & W* 47 SO8349
Callow Hill *H & W* 47 SP0164
Callow Hill *H & W* 60 SO7573
Callow Hill *Wilts* 36 SU0385
Callows Grave *H & W* 46 SO5966
Calmore *Hants* 12 SU3314
Calmsden *Gloucs* 36 SP0508
Calne *Wilts* 35 ST9971
Calow *Derbys* 74 SK4071
Calshot *Hants* 13 SU4701
Calstock *Cnwll* 6 SX4368
Calstone Wellington *Wilts* 23 SU0268
Calthorpe *Norfk* 66 TG1831
Calthorpe Street *Norfk* 67 TG4025
Calthwaite *Cumb* 93 NY4640
Calton *N York* 88 SD9259
Calton *N York* 88 SD9059
Calton *Staffs* 73 SK1050
Calton Green *Staffs* 73 SK1050
Calveley *Ches* 71 SJ5958
Calver *Derbys* 74 SK2474
Calver Hill *H & W* 46 SO3748
Calver Sough *Derbys* 74 SK2374
Calverhall *Shrops* 59 SJ6037
Calverleigh *Devon* 9 SS9214
Calverley *W York* 82 SE2036
Calvert *Bucks* 49 SP6824
Calverton *Bucks* 38 SP7938
Calverton *Notts* 75 SK6149
Calvine *Tays* 132 NN8065
Calvo *Cumb* 92 NY1453
Calzeat *Border* 108 NT1135
Cam *Gloucs* 35 ST7599
Camas - luinie *Highld* 138 NG9428
Camasachoirce *Highld* 130 NM7660
Camascross *Highld* 129 NG6911
Camasine *Highld* 130 NM7561
Camastianavaig *Highld* 137 NG5039
Camasunary *Highld* 128 NG5118
Camault Muir *Highld* 139 NH5040
Camber *E Susx* 17 TQ9618
Camberley *Surrey* 25 SU8860
Camberwell *Gt Lon* 27 TQ3276
Camblesforth *N York* 83 SE6425
Cambo *Nthumb* 103 NZ0285
Cambois *Nthumb* 103 NZ3083
Camborne *Cnwll* 2 SW6440
Cambridge *Cambs* 53 TL4558
Cambridge *Gloucs* 35 SO7403
Cambrose *Cnwll* 2 SW6845
Cambus *Cent* 116 NS8593
Cambus O' May *Gramp* 134 NO4198
Cambusavie Platform *Highld* 147 NH7696
Cambusbarron *Cent* 116 NS7792
Cambuskenneth *Cent* 116 NS8094
Cambuskenneth *Cent* 116 NS8094
Cambusmoon *Strath* 115 NS4285
Cambuswallace *Strath* 108 NT0438
Camden Town *Gt Lon* 27 TQ2784
Cameley *Avon* 21 ST6157
Camelford *Cnwll* 4 SX1083
Camelon *Cent* 116 NS8680
Camelot *Lancs* 80 SD5315
Camer's Green *H & W* 47 SO7735
Camerory *Highld* 141 NJ0131
Camerton *Avon* 22 ST6857
Camerton *Cumb* 92 NY0431
Camghouran *Tays* 124 NN5556
Cammachmore *Gramp* 135 NO9195
Cammeringham *Lincs* 76 SK9482
Camore *Highld* 147 NH7889
Camp The *Gloucs* 35 SO9109
Campbeltown *Strath* 105 NR7120
Camperdown *T & W* 103 NZ2772
Cample *D & G* 100 NX8993
Campmuir *Tays* 126 NO2137
Camps *Loth* 117 NT0968
Camps End *Cambs* 53 TL6142
Campsall *S York* 83 SE5313
Campsea Ashe *Suffk* 55 TM3356
Campsie *Strath* 116 NS6179
Campton *Beds* 38 TL1238
Campton *Beds* 38 TL1238
Camptown *Border* 110 NT6813
Camquhart *Strath* 114 NR9985
Camrose *Dyfed* 30 SM9220
Camserney *Tays* 125 NN8149
Camster *Highld* 151 ND2642
Camusnagaul *Highld* 145 NH0589
Camusnagaul *Highld* 130 NN0874
Camusteel *Highld* 137 NG7042
Camusterrach *Highld* 137 NG7141
Canada *Hants* 12 SU2818
Canal Foot *Cumb* 86 SD3177
Canaston Bridge *Dyfed* 30 SN0615
Candacraig *Gramp* 134 NO3499
Candle Street *Suffk* 54 TM0374
Candlesby *Lincs* 77 TF4567
Candover Green *Shrops* 59 SJ5005
Candyburn *Strath* 108 NT0741
Cane End *Oxon* 37 SU6779
Canewdon *Essex* 40 TQ9094
Canfield End *Essex* 40 TL5821
Canford Bottom *Dorset* 12 SU0300
Canford Cliffs *Dorset* 12 SZ0689
Canford Magna *Dorset* 12 SZ0398
Canhams Green *Suffk* 54 TM0565
Canisbay *Highld* 151 ND3472
Canklow *S York* 74 SK4291
Canley *W Mids* 61 SP3077
Cann *Dorset* 22 ST8723
Cannich *Highld* 139 NH3331
Cannington *Somset* 20 ST2539
Cannock *Staffs* 60 SJ9810
Cannock Wood *Staffs* 61 SK0412
Cannon Bridge *H & W* 46 SO4340
Canon Frome *H & W* 47 SO6543
Canon Pyon *H & W* 46 SO4548
Canonbie *D & G* 101 NY3976
Canons Ashby *Nhants* 49 SP5750
Canonstown *Cnwll* 2 SW5335
Canterbury *Kent* 29 TR1457
Cantley *Norfk* 67 TG3804
Cantley *S York* 83 SE6202
Cantlop *Shrops* 59 SJ5205
Canton *S Glam* 33 ST1676
Cantraywood *Highld* 140 NH7847
Cantsfield *Lancs* 87 SD6172
Canvey Island *Essex* 40 TQ7983
Canwick *Lincs* 76 SK9869
Canworthy Water *Cnwll* 5 SX2291
Caol *Highld* 130 NN1075
Caoles *Strath* 120 NM0848
Caonich *Highld* 130 NN0692
Capel *Kent* 16 TQ6344
Capel *Surrey* 15 TQ1740
Capel Bangor *Dyfed* 43 SN6580
Capel Betws Lleucu *Dyfed* 44 SN6058
Capel Coch *Gwynd* 68 SH4582
Capel Curig *Gwynd* 69 SH7258
Capel Cynon *Dyfed* 42 SN3849
Capel Dewi *Dyfed* 31 SN4542
Capel Dewi *Dyfed* 32 SN4720
Capel Garmon *Gwynd* 69 SH8155
Capel Green *Suffk* 55 TM3749
Capel Gwyn *Dyfed* 32 SN4622
Capel Gwyn *Gwynd* 68 SH3575
Capel Gwynfe *Dyfed* 32 SN7222
Capel Hendre *Dyfed* 32 SN5911
Capel Isaac *Dyfed* 44 SN5926
Capel Iwan *Dyfed* 31 SN2836
Capel Llanilltern *M Glam* 33 ST0979
Capel le Ferne *Kent* 29 TR2439
Capel Mawr *Gwynd* 68 SH4171
Capel Seion *Dyfed* 43 SN6379
Capel St. Andrews *Suffk* 55 TM3748
Capel St. Mary *Suffk* 54 TM0838
Capel Trisant *Dyfed* 43 SN7175
Capel-Dewi *Dyfed* 43 SN6282
Capel-y-ffin *Powys* 46 SO2531
Capel-y-graig *Gwynd* 69 SH5469
Capelles *Guern* 152 GN0000
Capelulo *Gwynd* 69 SH7476
Capelulo *Gwynd* 69 SH7476
Capenhurst *Ches* 71 SJ3673
Capernwray *Lancs* 87 SD5372
Capheaton *Nthumb* 103 NZ0380
Caplaw *Strath* 115 NS4458
Capon's Green *Suffk* 55 TM2867
Cappelgill *D & G* 108 NT1409
Cappercleuch *Border* 109 NT2423
Capstone *Kent* 28 TQ7865
Capton *Devon* 7 SX8353
Capton *Somset* 20 ST0739
Caputh *Tays* 125 NO0840
Car Colston *Notts* 63 SK7242
Caradon Town *Cnwll* 5 SX2971
Carbeth Inn *Cent* 115 NS5279
Carbis *Cnwll* 4 SW9959
Carbis Bay *Cnwll* 2 SW5238
Carbost *Highld* 136 NG3732
Carbost *Highld* 136 NG4248
Carbrook *S York* 74 SK3889
Carbrooke *Norfk* 66 TF9502
Carburton *Notts* 75 SK6173
Carcary *Tays* 127 NO6455
Carclaze *Cnwll* 3 SX0254
Carclew *Cnwll* 3 SW7838
Carcroft *S York* 83 SE5409
Cardenden *Fife* 117 NT2195
Cardeston *Shrops* 59 SJ3912
Cardewlees *Cumb* 93 NY3551
Cardiff *S Glam* 33 ST1876
Cardigan *Dyfed* 42 SN1846
Cardinal's Green *Cambs* 53 TL6147
Cardington *Beds* 38 TL0847
Cardington *Shrops* 59 SO5095
Cardinham *Cnwll* 4 SX1268
Cardow *Gramp* 141 NJ1943
Cardrain *D & G* 98 NX1231
Cardrona *Border* 109 NT3038
Cardross *Strath* 115 NS3477
Cardryne *D & G* 98 NX1132
Cardurnock *Cumb* 93 NY1758
Careby *Lincs* 64 TF0216
Careston *Tays* 134 NO5260
Carew *Dyfed* 30 SN0404
Carew Cheriton *Dyfed* 30 SN0402
Carew Newton *Dyfed* 30 SN0404
Carey *H & W* 46 SO5730
Carfin *Strath* 116 NS7759
Carfraemill *Border* 118 NT5053
Cargate Green *Norfk* 67 TG3913
Cargen *D & G* 100 NX9672
Cargenbridge *D & G* 100 NX9275
Cargill *Tays* 126 NO1536
Cargo *Cumb* 93 NY3659
Cargreen *Cnwll* 6 SX4262
Cargurrel *Cnwll* 3 SW8837
Carham *Nthumb* 110 NT7938
Carhampton *Somset* 20 ST0042
Carharrack *Cnwll* 3 SW7341
Carie *Tays* 124 NN6257
Carie *Tays* 124 NN6437
Carinish *W Isls* 154 NF8159
Carisbrooke *IOW* 13 SZ4888
Cark *Cumb* 87 SD3676
Carkeel *Cnwll* 5 SX4060
Carland Cross *Cnwll* 3 SW8454
Carlbury *Dur* 96 NZ2116
Carlby *Lincs* 64 TF0514
Carlcroft *Nthumb* 110 NT8311
Carlecotes *S York* 82 SE1703
Carleen *Cnwll* 2 SW6130
Carlesmoor *N York* 89 SE2073
Carleton *Cumb* 94 NY5330
Carleton *Cumb* 93 NY4253
Carleton *Lancs* 80 SD3339
Carleton *N York* 89 SE3959
Carleton *N York* 82 SD9749
Carleton *W York* 83 SE4620
Carleton Forehoe *Norfk* 66 TG0905
Carleton Rode *Norfk* 66 TM1193
Carleton St. Peter *Norfk* 67 TG3402
Carlidnack *Cnwll* 3 SW7729
Carlin How *Cleve* 97 NZ7018
Carlincraig *Gramp* 142 NJ6743
Carlincraig *Gramp* 142 NJ6743
Carlingcott *Avon* 22 ST6958
Carlisle *Cumb* 93 NY3955
Carloggas *Cnwll* 4 SW8765
Carlops *Border* 117 NT1656
Carloway *W Isls* 154 NB2042
Carlton *Beds* 51 SP9555
Carlton *Cambs* 53 TL6452
Carlton *Cleve* 96 NZ3921
Carlton *Cumb* 86 NY0109
Carlton *Leics* 62 SK3905
Carlton *N York* 83 SE6423
Carlton *N York* 90 NZ5004
Carlton *N York* 88 SE0684
Carlton *N York* 90 SE6086
Carlton *N York* 83 SE6423
Carlton *Notts* 62 SK6041
Carlton *S York* 83 SE3610
Carlton *Suffk* 55 TM3864
Carlton *W York* 83 SE3327
Carlton Colville *Suffk* 55 TM5190
Carlton Curlieu *Leics* 50 SP6997
Carlton Green *Cambs* 53 TL6451
Carlton Husthwaite *N York* 90 SE4976
Carlton in Lindrick *Notts* 75 SK5984
Carlton Miniott *N York* 89 SE3980
Carlton Scroop *Lincs* 63 SK9445
Carlton-le-Moorland *Lincs* 76 SK9058
Carlton-on-Trent *Notts* 75 SK7963
Carluddon *Cnwll* 3 SX0255
Carluke *Strath* 116 NS8450
Carmacoup *Strath* 107 NS7927
Carmarthen *Dyfed* 31 SN4020
Carmel *Clwyd* 70 SJ1676
Carmel *Dyfed* 32 SN5816
Carmel *Gwynd* 68 SH3882
Carmel *Gwynd* 68 SH4954
Carminowe *Cnwll* 2 SW6624
Carmunnock *Strath* 115 NS5957
Carmyle *Strath* 116 NS6462
Carmyllie *Tays* 127 NO5542

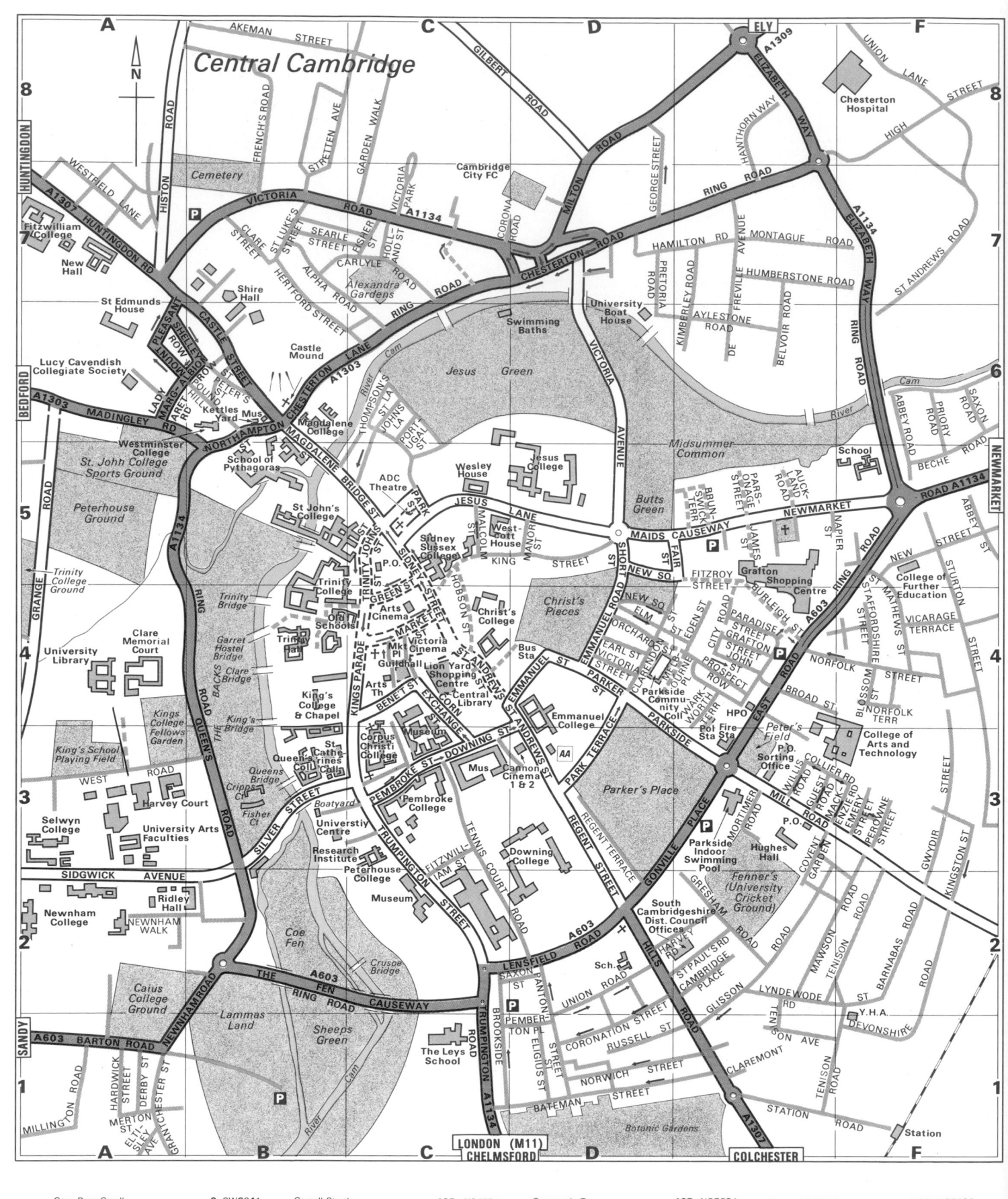

Central Cambridge

Clunie Corriegour


Clunie *Tays* **126** NO1043
Clunton *Shrops* **59** SO3381
Clutton *Avon* **21** ST6159
Clutton *Ches* **71** SJ4654
Clutton Hill *Avon* **21** ST6359
Clwt-y-bont *Gwynd* **69** SH5763
Clydach *Gwent* **34** SO2213
Clydach *W Glam* **32** SN6801
Clydach Vale *M Glam* **33** SS9792
Clydebank *Strath* **115** NS5069
Clydey *Dyfed* **31** SN2535
Clyffe Pypard *Wilts* **36** SU0776
Clynder *Strath* **114** NS2484
Clynderwen *Dyfed* **31** SN1219
Clyne *W Glam* **32** SN8000
Clynelish *Highld* **147** NC8905
Clynnog-fawr *Gwynd* **68** SH4149
Clyro *Powys* **45** SO2143
Clyst Honiton *Devon* **9** SX9893
Clyst Hydon *Devon* **9** ST0301
Clyst St. George *Devon* **9** SX9888
Clyst St. Lawrence *Devon* **9** ST0200
Clyst St. Mary *Devon* **9** SX9790
Clyth *Highld* **151** ND2836
Cnwch Coch *Dyfed* **43** SN6775
Coad's Green *Cnwll* **5** SX2976
Coal Aston *Derbys* **74** SK3679
Coal Pool *W Mids* **60** SK0100
Coal Street *Suffk* **55** TM2371
Coalbrookdale *Shrops* **60** SJ6603
Coalbrookvale *Gwent* **33** SO1909
Coalburn *Strath* **108** NS8134
Coalburns *T & W* **96** NZ1261
Coalcleugh *Nthumb* **95** NY8045
Coaley *Gloucs* **35** SO7701
Coalfel *Cumb* **94** NY5959
Coalhill *Essex* **40** TQ7598
Coalmoor *Shrops* **60** SJ6607
Coalpit Heath *Avon* **35** ST6781
Coalport *Shrops* **60** SJ6902
Coalsnaughton *Cent* **116** NS9295
Coaltown of Balgonie *Fife* **117** NT3099
Coaltown of Wemyss *Fife* **118** NT3295
Coalville *Leics* **62** SK4214
Coanwood *Nthumb* **94** NY6759
Coat *Somset* **21** ST4520
Coatbridge *Strath* **116** NS7365
Coatdyke *Strath* **116** NS7465
Coate *Wilts* **23** SU0461
Coate *Wilts* **36** SU1783
Coates *Cambs* **64** TL3097
Coates *Gloucs* **35** SO9700
Coates *Lincs* **75** SK8181
Coates *Lincs* **76** SK9083
Coates *W Susx* **14** SU9917
Coatham *Cleve* **97** NZ5925
Coatham Mundeville *Dur* **96** NZ2820
Cobbaton *Devon* **19** SS6126
Coberley *Gloucs* **35** SO9616
Cobhall Common *H & W* **46** SO4535
Cobham *Kent* **28** TQ6768
Cobham *Surrey* **26** TQ1060
Coblers Green *Essex* **40** TL6819
Cobley *Dorset* **12** SU0220
Cobnash *H & W* **46** SO4560
Cobo *Guern* **152** GN0000
Cobridge *Staffs* **72** SJ8748
Coburby *Gramp* **143** NJ9164
Cock Alley *Derbys* **74** SK4170
Cock Bank *Clwyd* **71** SJ3545
Cock Bridge *Gramp* **133** NJ2508
Cock Clarks *Essex* **40** TL8103
Cock End *Suffk* **53** TL7253
Cock Green *Essex* **40** TL6920
Cock Marling *E Susx* **17** TQ8719
Cock Street *Kent* **28** TQ7850
Cockayne *N York* **90** SE6298
Cockayne Hatley *Beds* **52** TL2549
Cockburnspath *Border* **119** NT7770
Cockenzie and Port Seton *Loth* **118** NT4075
Cocker Bar *Lancs* **80** SD5022
Cocker Brook *Lancs* **81** SD7425
Cockerdale *W York* **82** SE2329
Cockerham *Lancs* **80** SD4651
Cockermouth *Cumb* **92** NY1230
Cockernhoe Green *Herts* **38** TL1223
Cockett *W Glam* **32** SS6394
Cockfield *Dur* **96** NZ1224
Cockfield *Suffk* **54** TL9054
Cockfosters *Gt Lon* **27** TQ2796
Cocking *W Susx* **14** SU8717
Cocking Causeway *W Susx* **14** SU8819
Cockington *Devon* **7** SX8964
Cocklake *Somset* **21** ST4349
Cockley Beck *Cumb* **86** NY2501
Cockley Cley *Norfk* **66** TF7904
Cockpole Green *Berks* **37** SU7981
Cocks *Cnwll* **3** SW7652
Cockshutford *Shrops* **59** SO5885
Cockshutt *Shrops* **59** SJ4328
Cockthorpe *Norfk* **66** TF9842
Cockwells *Cnwll* **2** SW5234
Cockwood *Devon* **9** SX9780
Cockwood *Somset* **20** ST2223
Cockyard *Derbys* **74** SK0480
Cockyard *H & W* **46** SO4133
Coddenham *Suffk* **54** TM1354
Coddington *Ches* **71** SJ4555
Coddington *H & W* **47** SO7142
Coddington *Notts* **76** SK8354
Codford St. Mary *Wilts* **22** ST9739
Codford St. Peter *Wilts* **22** ST9640
Codicote *Herts* **39** TL2118
Codmore Hill *W Susx* **14** TQ0520
Codnor *Derbys* **74** SK4149
Codrington *Avon* **35** ST7278
Codsall *Staffs* **60** SJ8603
Codsall Wood *Staffs* **60** SJ8405
Coed Morgan *Gwent* **34** SO3511
Coed Talon *Clwyd* **70** SJ2658
Coed Ystumgwern *Gwynd* **57** SH5824
Coed-y-caerau *Gwent* **34** ST3891
Coed-y-paen *Gwent* **34** ST3398
Coed-yr-ynys *Powys* **33** SO1520
Coedana *Gwynd* **68** SH4381
Coedely *M Glam* **33** ST0285
Coedkernew *Gwent* **34** ST2783
Coedpoeth *Clwyd* **71** SJ2850
Coedway *Powys* **59** SJ3315
Coelbren *Powys* **33** SN8511
Coffinswell *Devon* **7** SX8868
Coffle End *Beds* **51** TL0059
Cofnpennar *Gwent* **34** SO3006
Cofton Hackett *H & W* **60** SP0075
Cogan *S Glam* **33** ST1772
Cogenhoe *Nhants* **51** SP8260
Cogges *Oxon* **36** SP3609
Coggeshall *Essex* **40** TL8522
Coggin's Mill *E Susx* **16** TQ5927
Coignafearn *Highld* **140** NH7017
Coilacriech *Gramp* **134** NO3296
Coilantogle *Cent* **124** NN5907
Coillaig *Strath* **122** NN0120
Coillore *Highld* **136** NG3538
Coiltry *Highld* **131** NH3506
Coity *M Glam* **33** SS9281
Colaboll *Highld* **146** NC5610
Colan *Cnwll* **4** SW8661
Colaton Raleigh *Devon* **9** SY0787
Colbone *Somset* **19** SS8448
Colburn *N York* **89** SE1999
Colbury *Hants* **12** SU3410
Colby *Cumb* **94** NY6620
Colby *IOM* **153** SC2370
Colby *Norfk* **67** TG2231
Colchester *Essex* **41** TL9925
Cold Ash *Berks* **24** SU5169
Cold Ashby *Nhants* **50** SP6576
Cold Ashton *Avon* **35** ST7472
Cold Aston *Gloucs* **36** SP1219
Cold Blow *Dyfed* **31** SN1212
Cold Brayfield *Bucks* **38** SP9252
Cold Cotes *N York* **88** SD7171
Cold Green *H & W* **47** SO6842
Cold Hanworth *Lincs* **76** TF0383
Cold Harbour *Herts* **38** TL1415
Cold Harbour *Oxon* **37** SU6379
Cold Harbour *Wilts* **22** ST8646
Cold Hatton *Shrops* **59** SJ6121
Cold Hatton Heath *Shrops* **59** SJ6321
Cold Hesledon *Dur* **96** NZ4146
Cold Hiendly *W York* **83** SE3714
Cold Higham *Nhants* **49** SP6653
Cold Kirby *N York* **90** SE5384
Cold Newton *Leics* **63** SK7106
Cold Northcott *Cnwll* **5** SX2086
Cold Norton *Essex* **40** TL8500
Cold Overton *Leics* **63** SK8110
Cold Weston *Shrops* **59** SO5583
Coldbackie *Highld* **149** NC6160
Coldbeck *Cumb* **88** NY7104
Coldblow *Gt Lon* **27** TQ5073
Coldean *E Susx* **15** TQ3308
Coldeast *Devon* **7** SX8274
Colden *W York* **82** SD9628
Colden Common *Hants* **13** SU4822
Coldfair Green *Suffk* **55** TM4361
Coldham *Cambs* **65** TF4302
Coldharbour *Cnwll* **3** SW7548
Coldharbour *Devon* **9** ST0612
Coldharbour *Gloucs* **34** SO5503
Coldharbour *Surrey* **26** TQ0360
Coldharbour *Surrey* **15** TQ1443
Coldingham *Border* **119** NT9065
Coldmeece *Staffs* **72** SJ8532
Coldred *Kent* **29** TR2747
Coldridge *Devon* **8** SS6907
Coldstone *Kent* **27** TQ2961
Coldstream *Border* **110** NT8439
Coldwaltham *W Susx* **14** TQ0216
Coldwell *H & W* **46** SO4235
Coldwells *Gramp* **143** NJ9538
Coldwells *Gramp* **143** NK1039
Cole *Somset* **22** ST6633
Cole End *Warwks* **61** SP1989
Cole Green *Herts* **39** TL4330
Cole Green *Herts* **39** TL2911
Cole Henley *Hants* **24** SU4751
Cole's Cross *Devon* **7** SX7747
Colebatch *Shrops* **59** SO3187
Colebrook *Devon* **6** SX5457
Colebrook *Devon* **9** ST0006
Colebrooke *Devon* **8** SX7799
Coleby *Humb* **84** SE8919
Coleby *Lincs* **76** SK9760
Coleford *Devon* **8** SS7701
Coleford *Gloucs* **34** SO5710
Coleford *Somset* **22** ST6848
Coleford Water *Somset* **20** ST1234
Colegate End *Norfk* **55** TM1988
Colehill *Dorset* **12** SU0300
Coleman Green *Herts* **39** TL1812
Coleman's Hatch *E Susx* **16** TQ4533
Colemere *Shrops* **59** SJ4232
Colemore *Hants* **24** SU7030
Colemore Green *Shrops* **60** SO7097
Colenden *Tays* **126** NO1029
Coleorton *Leics* **62** SK3917
Colerne *Wilts* **35** ST8171
Coles Cross *Dorset* **10** ST3902
Coles Green *Suffk* **54** TM1041
Colesbourne *Gloucs* **35** SP0013
Colesden *Beds* **52** TL1255
Coleshill *Bucks* **26** SU9495
Coleshill *Oxon* **36** SU2393
Coleshill *Warwks* **61** SP2089
Colestocks *Devon* **9** ST0900
Coleton *Devon* **7** SX9051
Coley *Avon* **21** ST5855
Colgate *W Susx* **15** TQ2332
Colgrain *Strath* **115** NS3280
Colinsburgh *Fife* **127** NO4703
Colinton *Loth* **117** NT2268
Colintraive *Strath* **114** NS0374
Colkirk *Norfk* **66** TF9126
Coll *W Isls* **154** NB4539
Collace *Tays* **126** NO2032
Collafirth *Shet* **155** HU3482
Collation *Devon* **7** SX7338
Collaton *Devon* **7** SX7952
Collaton St. Mary *Devon* **7** SX8660
College Green *Somset* **21** ST5736
College of Roseisle *Gramp* **141** NJ1466
College Town *Berks* **25** SU8560
Collessie *Fife* **126** NO2813
Colleton Mills *Devon* **19** SS6615
Collier Row *Gt Lon* **27** TQ4991
Collier Street *Kent* **28** TQ7145
Collier's End *Herts* **39** TL3720
Collier's Green *Kent* **17** TQ7822
Colliers Green *Kent* **28** TQ7439
Colliery Row *T & W* **96** NZ3349
Collieston *Gramp* **143** NK0328
Collin *D & G* **100** NY0276
Collingbourne Ducis *Wilts* **23** SU2453
Collingbourne Kingston *Wilts* **23** SU2355
Collingham *Notts* **75** SK8261
Collingham *W York* **83** SE3845
Collington *H & W* **47** SO6460
Collingtree *Nhants* **49** SP7555
Collins Green *Ches* **78** SJ5694
Colliston *Tays* **127** NO6045
Colliton *Devon* **9** ST0804
Collyweston *Nhants* **63** SK9902
Colmonell *Strath* **98** NX1485
Colmworth *Beds* **51** TL1058
Coln Rogers *Gloucs* **36** SP0809
Coln St. Aldwyns *Gloucs* **36** SP1405
Coln St. Dennis *Gloucs* **36** SP0811
Colnbrook *Gt Lon* **26** TQ0277
Colne *Cambs* **52** TL3776
Colne *Lancs* **81** SD8940
Colne Bridge *W York* **82** SE1720
Colne Edge *Lancs* **81** SD8841
Colne Engaine *Essex* **40** TL8530
Colney *Norfk* **66** TG1807
Colney Heath *Herts* **39** TL2005
Colney Street *Herts* **26** TL1502
Colpy *Gramp* **142** NJ6432
Colquhar *Border* **109** NT3341
Colquite *Cnwll* **4** SX0570
Colscott *Devon* **18** SS3614
Colsterdale *N York* **89** SE1381
Colsterworth *Lincs* **63** SK9324
Colston Bassett *Notts* **63** SK7033
Colt Hill *Hants* **24** SU7451
Colt's Hill *Kent* **16** TQ6443
Coltfield *Gramp* **141** NJ1163
Coltishall *Norfk* **67** TG2619
Colton *Cumb* **86** SD3186
Colton *N York* **83** SE5444
Colton *Norfk* **66** TG1009
Colton *Staffs* **73** SK0520
Colton *W York* **83** SE3732
Columbjohn *Devon* **9** SX9699
Colva *Powys* **45** SO1952
Colvend *D & G* **92** NX8654
Colwall Green *H & W* **47** SO7441
Colwall Stone *H & W* **47** SO7542
Colwell *Nthumb* **102** NY9575
Colwich *Staffs* **73** SK0121
Colwick *Notts* **62** SK6140
Colwinston *S Glam* **33** SS9375
Colworth *W Susx* **14** SU9102
Colwyn Bay *Clwyd* **69** SH8479
Colyford *Devon* **9** SY2492
Colyton *Devon* **9** SY2493
Combe *Berks* **23** SU3760
Combe *Devon* **7** SX9173
Combe *Devon* **7** SX8448
Combe *Devon* **7** SX7138
Combe *H & W* **46** SO3463
Combe *Oxon* **36** SP4116
Combe Almer *Dorset* **11** SY9497
Combe Common *Surrey* **14** SU9436
Combe Fishacre *Devon* **7** SX8465
Combe Florey *Somset* **20** ST1531
Combe Hay *Avon* **22** ST7359
Combe Martin *Devon* **19** SS5846
Combe Moor *H & W* **46** SO3663
Combe Raleigh *Devon* **9** ST1502
Combe St. Nicholas *Somset* **10** ST3011
Combebow *Devon* **5** SX4888
Combeinteignhead *Devon* **7** SX9071
Comberbach *Ches* **79** SJ6477
Comberford *Staffs* **61** SK1907
Comberton *Cambs* **52** TL3856
Comberton *H & W* **46** SO4968
Combridge *Staffs* **73** SK0937
Combrook *Warwks* **48** SP3051
Combs *Derbys* **74** SK0478
Combs *Suffk* **54** TM0456
Combs Ford *Suffk* **54** TM0557
Combwich *Somset* **20** ST2542
Comedivock *Cumb* **93** NY3449
Comers *Gramp* **135** NJ6707
Comhampton *H & W* **47** SO8366
Commercial *Dyfed* **31** SN1416
Commercial End *Cambs* **53** TL5563
Commins Coch *Powys* **57** SH8403
Common Edge *Lancs* **80** SD3232
Common End *Cumb* **92** NY0022
Common Moor *Cnwll* **5** SX2469
Common Platt *Wilts* **36** SU1186
Common Side *Derbys* **74** SK3375
Common The *Wilts* **23** SU2432
Commondale *N York* **90** NZ6610
Commonside *Ches* **71** SJ5573
Commonside *Derbys* **73** SK2441
Commonwood *Clwyd* **71** SJ3753
Commonwood *Shrops* **59** SJ4828
Compass *Somset* **20** ST2934
Compstall *Gt Man* **79** SJ9690
Compstonend *D & G* **99** NX6652
Compton *Berks* **37** SU5280
Compton *Devon* **7** SX8664
Compton *Hants* **23** SU3529
Compton *Hants* **13** SU4625
Compton *Staffs* **60** SO8285
Compton *Surrey* **25** SU9547
Compton *W Susx* **14** SU7714
Compton *Wilts* **23** SU1352
Compton Abbas *Dorset* **22** ST8718
Compton Abdale *Gloucs* **36** SP0516
Compton Bassett *Wilts* **36** SU0372
Compton Beauchamp *Oxon* **36** SU2886
Compton Bishop *Somset* **21** ST3955
Compton Chamberlayne *Wilts* **23** SU0229
Compton Dando *Avon* **21** ST6464
Compton Dundon *Somset* **21** ST4933
Compton Durville *Somset* **10** ST4117
Compton Greenfield *Avon* **34** ST5682
Compton Martin *Avon* **21** ST5456
Compton Pauncefoot *Somset* **21** ST6425
Compton Valence *Dorset* **10** SY5993
Compton Verney *Warwks* **48** SP3152
Comrie *Fife* **117** NT0289
Comrie *Tays* **124** NN7722
Conaglen House *Highld* **130** NN0268
Conchra *Highld* **138** NG8828
Conchra *Strath* **114** NS0288
Concraigie *Tays* **126** NO1044
Conderton *H & W* **47** SO9637
Condicote *Gloucs* **48** SP1528
Condorrat *Strath* **116** NS7373
Condover *Shrops* **59** SJ4906
Coney Hill *Gloucs* **35** SO8516
Coney Weston *Suffk* **54** TL9578
Coneyhurst Common *W Susx* **14** TQ1024
Coneysthorpe *N York* **90** SE7171
Conford *Hants* **14** SU8233
Congdon's Shop *Cnwll* **5** SX2778
Congerstone *Leics* **62** SK3605
Congham *Norfk* **65** TF7123
Conghurst *Kent* **17** TQ7628
Congl-y-wal *Gwynd* **57** SH7044
Congleton *Ches* **72** SJ8563
Congresbury *Avon* **21** ST4363
Congreve *Staffs* **60** SJ8914
Conicavel *Gramp* **140** NH9853
Conichan *Tays* **125** NN8432
Coningsby *Lincs* **76** TF2258
Conington *Cambs* **52** TL1885
Conington *Cambs* **52** TL3266
Conisbrough *S York* **75** SK5098
Conisby *Strath* **112** NR2661
Conisholme *Lincs* **77** TF3995
Coniston *Cumb* **86** SD3097
Coniston *Humb* **85** TA1535
Coniston Cold *N York* **81** SD9054
Conistone *N York* **88** SD9867
Connah's Quay *Clwyd* **71** SJ2969
Connel *Strath* **122** NM9133
Connel Park *Strath* **107** NS6012
Connor Downs *Cnwll* **2** SW5939
Conon Bridge *Highld* **139** NH5455
Cononley *N York* **82** SD9847
Consall *Staffs* **72** SJ9748
Consett *Dur* **95** NZ1150
Constable Burton *N York* **89** SE1690
Constable Lee *Lancs* **81** SD8123
Constantine *Cnwll* **3** SW7329
Contin *Highld* **139** NH4556
Convinth *Highld* **139** NH5138
Conwy *Gwynd* **69** SH7777
Conyer *Kent* **28** TQ9664
Conyer's Green *Suffk* **54** TL8867
Cooden *E Susx* **17** TQ7107
Coodham *Strath* **106** NS3932
Cooil *IOM* **153** SC3475
Cook's Green *Essex* **41** TM1819
Cookbury *Devon* **18** SS4005
Cookbury Wick *Devon* **18** SS3805
Cookham *Berks* **26** SU8985
Cookham Dean *Berks* **26** SU8685
Cookham Rise *Berks* **26** SU8885
Cookhill *Warwks* **48** SP0558
Cookley *H & W* **60** SO8480
Cookley *Suffk* **55** TM3475
Cookley Green *Oxon* **37** SU6990
Cookney *Gramp* **135** NO8693
Cooks Green *Suffk* **54** TL9853
Cooksbridge *E Susx* **15** TQ4013
Cooksey Green *H & W* **47** SO9069
Cookshill *Staffs* **72** SJ9443
Cooksland *Cnwll* **4** SX0867
Cooksmill Green *Essex* **40** TL6306
Cookson Green *Ches* **71** SJ5774
Cookson's Green *Dur* **96** NZ2933
Coolham *W Susx* **14** TQ1222
Cooling *Kent* **28** TQ7575
Cooling Street *Kent* **28** TQ7474
Coombe *Cnwll* **2** SW6242
Coombe *Cnwll* **3** SW8340
Coombe *Cnwll* **3** SW9551
Coombe *Devon* **20** SS9725
Coombe *Devon* **7** SX8384
Coombe *Devon* **9** SY1092
Coombe *Gloucs* **35** ST7693
Coombe *Hants* **13** SU6620
Coombe *Wilts* **23** SU1550
Coombe Bissett *Wilts* **23** SU1026
Coombe Cellars *Devon* **7** SX9072
Coombe Cross *Hants* **13** SU6621
Coombe End *Somset* **20** ST0329
Coombe Hill *Gloucs* **47** SO8827
Coombe Keynes *Dorset* **11** SY8484
Coombe Pafford *Devon* **7** SX9267
Coombe Street *Somset* **22** ST7531
Coombes *W Susx* **15** TQ1908
Coombeswood *W Mids* **60** SO9685
Cooper Street *Kent* **29** TR3060
Cooper Turning *Gt Man* **79** SD6308
Cooper's Corner *Kent* **16** TQ4849
Cooperhill *Gramp* **141** NH9953
Coopers Green *E Susx* **16** TQ4723
Coopersale Common *Essex* **27** TL4702
Coopersale Street *Essex* **27** TL4701
Cootham *W Susx* **14** TQ0714
Cop Street *Kent* **27** TQ2960
Copdock *Suffk* **54** TM1242
Copetown *W York* **83** SE3923
Copford Green *Essex* **40** TL9222
Copgrove *N York* **89** SE3463
Copister *Shet* **155** HU4878
Cople *Beds* **38** TL1048
Copley *Dur* **95** NZ0825
Copley *Gt Man* **79** SJ9798
Copley *W York* **82** SE0822
Coplow Dale *Derbys* **74** SK1679
Copmanthorpe *N York* **83** SE5646
Copmere End *Staffs* **72** SJ8029
Copp *Lancs* **80** SD4239
Coppathorne *Cnwll* **18** SS2000
Coppenhall *Staffs* **72** SJ9019
Coppenhall Moss *Ches* **72** SJ7058
Copperhouse *Cnwll* **2** SW5738
Coppers Green *Herts* **39** TL1909
Coppicegate *Shrops* **60** SO7380
Coppingford *Cambs* **52** TL1680
Coppins Corner *Kent* **28** TQ9448
Copplestone *Devon* **8** SS7702
Coppull *Lancs* **81** SD5614
Coppull Moor *Lancs* **81** SD5512
Copsale *W Susx* **15** TQ1724
Copster Green *Lancs* **81** SD6733
Copston Magna *Warwks* **50** SP4588
Copt Heath *W Mids* **61** SP1778
Copt Hewick *N York* **89** SE3471
Copthall Green *Essex* **27** TL4200
Copthorne *Cnwll* **5** SX2692
Copthorne *W Susx* **15** TQ3139
Copy's Green *Norfk* **66** TF9439
Copythorne *Hants* **12** SU3014
Coram Street *Suffk* **54** TM0042
Corbets Tay *Gt Lon* **27** TQ5685
Corbiere *Jersey* **152** JS0000
Corbridge *Nthumb* **103** NY9964
Corby *Nhants* **51** SP8988
Corby Glen *Lincs* **63** SK9925
Corby Hill *Cumb* **94** NY4857
Cordon *Strath* **105** NS0230
Cordwell Unthank *Derbys* **74** SK2076
Coreley *Shrops* **47** SO6273
Cores End *Bucks* **26** SU9087
Corfe *Somset* **20** ST2319
Corfe Castle *Dorset* **11** SY9681
Corfe Mullen *Dorset* **11** SY9798
Corfton *Shrops* **59** SO4985
Corgarff *Gramp* **133** NJ2708
Corhampton *Hants* **13** SU6120
Corks Pond *Kent* **28** TQ6540
Corley *Warwks* **61** SP3085
Corley Ash *Warwks* **61** SP2986
Corley Moor *Warwks* **61** SP2885
Cormuir *Tays* **134** NO3066
Cornabus *Strath* **104** NR3346
Cornard Tye *Suffk* **54** TL9041
Corndon *Devon* **8** SX6885
Cornelly *M Glam* **33** SS8281
Corner Row *Lancs* **80** SD4134
Corney *Cumb* **86** SD1191
Cornforth *Dur* **96** NZ3134
Cornheath *D & G* **100** NX9969
Cornhill *Gramp* **142** NJ5858
Cornhill-on-Tweed *Nthumb* **110** NT8639
Cornholme *W York* **81** SD9126
Cornish Hall End *Essex* **53** TL6836
Cornoigmore *Strath* **120** NL9846
Cornriggs *Dur* **95** NY8441
Cornsay *Dur* **96** NZ1443
Cornsay Colliery *Dur* **96** NZ1643
Corntown *Highld* **139** NH5556
Corntown *M Glam* **33** SS9177
Cornwell *Oxon* **48** SP2727
Cornwood *Devon* **6** SX6059
Cornworthy *Devon* **7** SX8255
Corpach *Highld* **130** NN0976
Corpusty *Norfk* **66** TG1130
Corra *Strath* **114** NR9765
Corrachree *Gramp* **134** NJ4604
Corran *Cnwll* **3** SW9946
Corran *Highld* **130** NG8509
Corran *Highld* **130** NN0263
Corranbuie *Strath* **113** NR8465
Corrany *IOM* **153** SC4589
Corrie *D & G* **101** NY2086
Corrie *Strath* **105** NS0242
Corriecravie *Strath* **105** NR9223
Corriegour *Highld* **131** NN2692

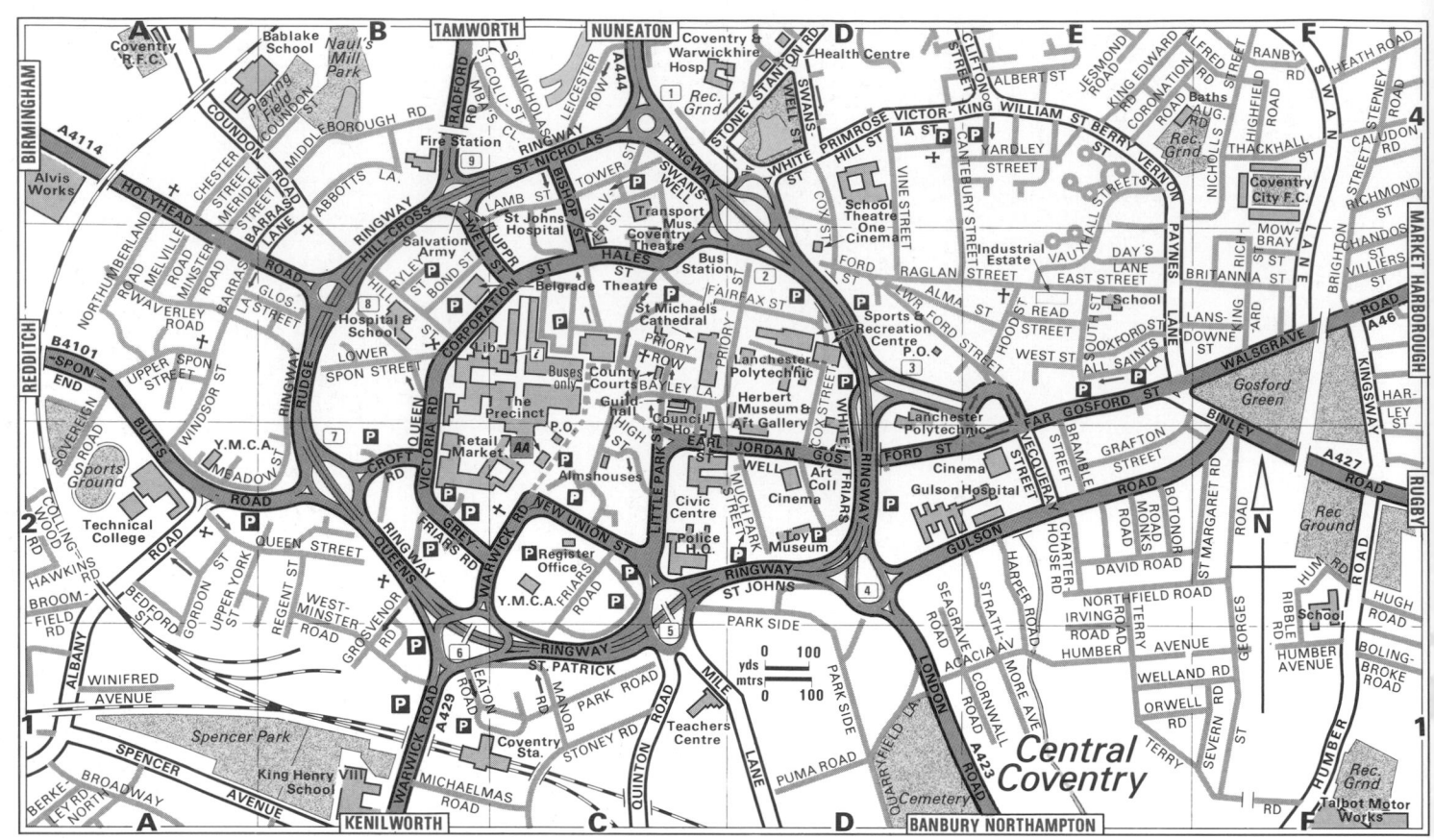

Central Coventry

| | | |
|---|---|---|
| Corriemoille *Highld* | 139 | NH3663 |
| Corrimony *Highld* | 139 | NH3730 |
| Corringham *Essex* | 40 | TQ7083 |
| Corringham *Lincs* | 76 | SK8691 |
| Corris *Gwynd* | 57 | SH7507 |
| Corris Uchaf *Gwynd* | 57 | SH7408 |
| Corrow *Strath* | 114 | NN1800 |
| Corry *Highld* | 137 | NG6424 |
| Corrygills *Strath* | 105 | NS0335 |
| Cors-y-Gedol *Gwynd* | 57 | SH6022 |
| Corsback *Highld* | 151 | ND2372 |
| Corscombe *Devon* | 8 | SX6296 |
| Corscombe *Dorset* | 10 | ST5105 |
| Corse *Gloucs* | 47 | SO7926 |
| Corse *Gramp* | 142 | NJ6040 |
| Corse Lawn *Gloucs* | 47 | SO8330 |
| Corsham *Wilts* | 35 | ST8670 |
| Corsindae *Gramp* | 135 | NJ6808 |
| Corsley *Wilts* | 22 | ST8246 |
| Corsley Heath *Wilts* | 22 | ST8245 |
| Corsock *D & G* | 99 | NX7675 |
| Corston *Avon* | 22 | ST6965 |
| Corston *Wilts* | 35 | ST9283 |
| Corstorphine *Loth* | 117 | NT1972 |
| Cortachy *Tays* | 134 | NO3959 |
| Corton *Suffk* | 67 | TM5497 |
| Corton *Wilts* | 22 | ST9340 |
| Corton Denham *Somset* | 21 | ST6322 |
| Coruanan Lodge *Highld* | 130 | NN0668 |
| Corvallie *IOM* | 153 | SC1968 |
| Corwar *Strath* | 98 | NX2780 |
| Corwen *Clwyd* | 70 | SJ0743 |
| Coryates *Dorset* | 10 | SY6285 |
| Coryton *Devon* | 5 | SX4583 |
| Coryton *Essex* | 40 | TQ7482 |
| Cosby *Leics* | 50 | SP5495 |
| Coseley *W Mids* | 60 | SO9494 |
| Cosford *Shrops* | 60 | SJ8005 |
| Cosgrove *Nhants* | 38 | SP7942 |
| Cosham *Hants* | 13 | SU6505 |
| Cosheston *Dyfed* | 30 | SN0003 |
| Coshieville *Tays* | 124 | NN7749 |
| Cossall *Notts* | 62 | SK4842 |
| Cossall Marsh *Notts* | 62 | SK4842 |
| Cossington *Leics* | 62 | SK6013 |
| Cossington *Somset* | 21 | ST3540 |
| Costallack *Cnwll* | 2 | SW4525 |
| Costessey *Norfk* | 66 | TG1712 |
| Costock *Notts* | 62 | SK5726 |
| Coston *Leics* | 63 | SK8422 |
| Coston *Norfk* | 66 | TG0606 |
| Cote *Oxon* | 36 | SP3502 |
| Cote *Somset* | 21 | ST3544 |
| Cotebrook *Ches* | 71 | SJ5765 |
| Cotehill *Cumb* | 93 | NY4650 |
| Cotes *Cumb* | 87 | SD4886 |
| Cotes *Leics* | 62 | SK5520 |
| Cotes *Staffs* | 72 | SJ8434 |
| Cotes Heath *Staffs* | 72 | SJ8334 |
| Cotesbach *Leics* | 50 | SP5382 |
| Cotgrave *Notts* | 63 | SK6435 |
| Cotham *Notts* | 63 | SK7947 |
| Cothelstone *Somset* | 20 | ST1831 |
| Cotherstone *Dur* | 95 | NZ0119 |
| Cothill *Oxon* | 37 | SU4699 |
| Cotleigh *Devon* | 9 | ST2002 |
| Cotmanhay *Derbys* | 62 | SK4643 |
| Coton *Cambs* | 52 | TL4058 |
| Coton *Nhants* | 50 | SP6771 |
| Coton *Shrops* | 59 | SJ5334 |
| Coton *Staffs* | 61 | SK1805 |
| Coton *Staffs* | 72 | SJ8120 |
| Coton *Staffs* | 72 | SJ9832 |
| Coton Clanford *Staffs* | 72 | SJ8723 |
| Coton Hayes *Staffs* | 72 | SJ9832 |
| Coton Hill *Shrops* | 59 | SJ4913 |
| Coton in the Clay *Staffs* | 73 | SK1629 |
| Coton in the Elms *Derbys* | 73 | SK2415 |
| Coton Park *Derbys* | 73 | SK2717 |
| Cott *Devon* | 7 | SX7861 |
| Cottage End *Hants* | 24 | SU4143 |
| Cottam *Humb* | 91 | SE9964 |
| Cottam *Lancs* | 80 | SD5032 |
| Cottam *Notts* | 75 | SK8179 |
| Cottartown *Highld* | 140 | NH7442 |
| Cottenham *Cambs* | 53 | TL4467 |
| Cotterdale *N York* | 88 | SD8393 |
| Cottered *Herts* | 39 | TL3129 |
| Cotteridge *W Mids* | 61 | SP0480 |
| Cotterstock *Nhants* | 51 | TL0490 |
| Cottesbrooke *Nhants* | 50 | SP7173 |
| Cottesmore *Leics* | 63 | SK9013 |
| Cottingham *Humb* | 84 | TA0532 |
| Cottingham *Nhants* | 51 | SP8490 |
| Cottingley *W York* | 82 | SE1139 |
| Cottisford *Oxon* | 49 | SP5831 |
| Cottivett *M Glam* | 5 | SX3662 |
| Cotton *Suffk* | 54 | TM0767 |
| Cotton End *Beds* | 38 | TL0845 |
| Cotton Tree *Lancs* | 81 | SD9040 |
| Cottown *Gramp* | 142 | NJ5026 |
| Cottown *Gramp* | 142 | NJ7715 |
| Cottown *Gramp* | 143 | NJ8140 |
| Cottrell *S Glam* | 33 | ST0774 |
| Cotts *Devon* | 6 | SX4365 |
| Cotwall *Shrops* | 59 | SJ6017 |
| Cotwalton *Staffs* | 72 | SJ9234 |
| Couch's Mill *Cnwll* | 4 | SX1459 |
| Coughton *H & W* | 34 | SO5921 |
| Coughton *Warwks* | 48 | SP0860 |
| Coulaghailtro *Strath* | 113 | NR7165 |
| Coulags *Highld* | 138 | NG9645 |
| Coulderton *Cumb* | 86 | NX9809 |
| Coull *Gramp* | 134 | NJ5102 |
| Coulport *Strath* | 114 | NS2191 |
| Coulsdon *Gt Lon* | 27 | TQ2959 |
| Coulston *Strath* | 108 | NT0234 |
| Coultershaw Bridge *W Susx* | 14 | SU9719 |
| Coultings *Somset* | 20 | ST2241 |
| Coulton *N York* | 90 | SE6373 |
| Coultra *Fife* | 126 | NO3523 |
| Cound *Shrops* | 59 | SJ5505 |
| Coundlane *Shrops* | 59 | SJ5705 |
| Coundon *Dur* | 96 | NZ2429 |
| Coundon Grange *Dur* | 96 | NZ2328 |
| Countersett *N York* | 88 | SD9187 |
| Countess *Wilts* | 23 | SU1542 |
| Countess Cross *Essex* | 40 | TL8631 |
| Countess Wear *Devon* | 9 | SX9489 |
| Countesthorpe *Leics* | 50 | SP5895 |
| Countisbury *Devon* | 19 | SS7449 |
| Coup Green *Lancs* | 81 | SD5927 |
| Coupar Angus *Tays* | 126 | NO2239 |
| Coupland *Cumb* | 94 | NY7018 |
| Coupland *Nthumb* | 110 | NT9331 |
| Cour *Strath* | 105 | NR8248 |
| Courance *D & G* | 100 | NY0590 |
| Court Henry *Dyfed* | 32 | SN5522 |
| Court-at-Street *Kent* | 17 | TR0935 |
| Courteachan *Highld* | 129 | NM4897 |
| Courteenhall *Nhants* | 49 | SP7653 |
| Courtsend *Essex* | 41 | TR0293 |
| Courtway *Somset* | 20 | ST2033 |
| Cousland *Loth* | 118 | NT3768 |
| Cousley Wood *E Susx* | 16 | TQ6433 |
| Coustoun *Strath* | 114 | NS0774 |
| Cove *Devon* | 20 | SS9519 |
| Cove *Hants* | 25 | SU8555 |
| Cove *Highld* | 144 | NG8090 |
| Cove *Strath* | 114 | NS2282 |
| Cove Bay *Gramp* | 135 | NJ9501 |
| Cove Bottom *Suffk* | 55 | TM4980 |
| Covehithe *Suffk* | 55 | TM5282 |
| Coven *Staffs* | 60 | SJ9006 |
| Coven Lawn *Staffs* | 60 | SJ9005 |
| Coveney *Cambs* | 53 | TL4882 |
| Covenham St. Bartholomew *Lincs* | 77 | TF3395 |
| Covenham St. Mary *Lincs* | 77 | TF3394 |
| Coventry *W Mids* | 61 | SP3379 |
| Coverack *Cnwll* | 3 | SW7818 |
| Coverack Bridges *Cnwll* | 2 | SW6630 |
| Coverham *N York* | 89 | SE1086 |
| Covington *Cambs* | 51 | TL0570 |
| Cow Green *Suffk* | 54 | TM0565 |
| Cow Honeybourne *H & W* | 48 | SP1143 |
| Cowan Bridge *Lancs* | 87 | SD6376 |
| Cowbeech *E Susx* | 16 | TQ6114 |
| Cowbit *Lincs* | 64 | TF2518 |
| Cowbridge *S Glam* | 33 | SS9974 |
| Cowdale *Derbys* | 74 | SK0872 |
| Cowden *Kent* | 16 | TQ4640 |
| Cowden Pound *Kent* | 16 | TQ4642 |
| Cowden Station *Kent* | 16 | TQ4741 |
| Cowdenbeath *Fife* | 117 | NT1691 |
| Cowdenburn *Border* | 117 | NT2052 |
| Cowers Lane *Derbys* | 73 | SK3046 |
| Cowes *IOW* | 13 | SZ4995 |
| Cowesby *N York* | 89 | SE4689 |
| Cowesfield Green *Wilts* | 23 | SU2623 |
| Cowfold *W Susx* | 15 | TQ2122 |
| Cowgill *Cumb* | 88 | SD7586 |
| Cowhill *Avon* | 34 | ST6191 |
| Cowie *Cent* | 116 | NS8389 |
| Cowley *Derbys* | 74 | SK3377 |
| Cowley *Devon* | 9 | SX9095 |
| Cowley *Gloucs* | 35 | SO9614 |
| Cowley *Gt Lon* | 26 | TQ0582 |
| Cowley *Oxon* | 37 | SP5404 |
| Cowley *Oxon* | 49 | SP6628 |
| Cowling *Lancs* | 81 | SD5917 |
| Cowling *N York* | 89 | SE2387 |
| Cowling *N York* | 82 | SD9643 |
| Cowlinge *Suffk* | 53 | TL7154 |
| Cowmess *W York* | 82 | SE1815 |
| Cowpe *Lancs* | 81 | SD8320 |
| Cowpen *Nthumb* | 103 | NZ2981 |
| Cowpen Bewley *Cleve* | 97 | NZ4824 |
| Cowplain *Hants* | 13 | SU6911 |
| Cowshill *Dur* | 95 | NY8540 |
| Cowslip Green *Avon* | 21 | ST4862 |
| Cowthorpe *N York* | 83 | SE4252 |
| Cowton *Somset* | 20 | ST1919 |
| Cox Common *Suffk* | 55 | TM4082 |
| Coxall *Shrops* | 46 | SO3774 |
| Coxbank *Ches* | 72 | SJ6541 |
| Coxbench *Derbys* | 62 | SK3743 |
| Coxbridge *Somset* | 21 | ST5436 |
| Coxford *Cnwll* | 4 | SX1696 |
| Coxford *Norfk* | 66 | TF8529 |
| Coxgreen *Staffs* | 60 | SO8086 |
| Coxheath *Kent* | 28 | TQ7451 |
| Coxhoe *Dur* | 96 | NZ3235 |
| Coxley *Somset* | 21 | ST5343 |
| Coxley *W York* | 82 | SE2717 |
| Coxley Wick *Somset* | 21 | ST5244 |
| Coxpark *M Glam* | 5 | SX4072 |
| Coxtie Green *Essex* | 27 | TQ5696 |
| Coxwold *N York* | 90 | SE5377 |
| Coychurch *M Glam* | 33 | SS9379 |
| Coylton *Strath* | 107 | NS4219 |
| Coylumbridge *Highld* | 132 | NH9110 |
| Coytrahen *M Glam* | 33 | SS8985 |
| Crab Orchard *Dorset* | 12 | SU0806 |
| Crabadon *Devon* | 7 | SX7655 |
| Crabbs Cross *H & W* | 48 | SP0465 |
| Crabtree *W Susx* | 15 | TQ2225 |
| Crabtree Green *Clwyd* | 71 | SJ3344 |
| Crackenthorpe *Cumb* | 94 | NY6622 |
| Crackington Haven *Cnwll* | 4 | SX1496 |
| Crackley *Staffs* | 72 | SJ8350 |
| Crackley *Warwks* | 61 | SP2973 |
| Cracklybank *Shrops* | 60 | SJ7611 |
| Crackpot *N York* | 88 | SD9696 |
| Cracoe *N York* | 88 | SD9760 |
| Craddock *Devon* | 9 | ST0812 |
| Craddock *Devon* | 9 | ST0812 |
| Cradle End *Herts* | 39 | TL4621 |
| Cradley *H & W* | 47 | SO7347 |
| Cradley *W Mids* | 60 | SO9484 |
| Cradoc *Powys* | 45 | SO0130 |
| Crafthole *Cnwll* | 5 | SX3654 |
| Crafton *Bucks* | 38 | SP8819 |
| Crag Foot *Lancs* | 87 | SD4873 |
| Cragabus *Strath* | 104 | NR3245 |
| Cragg *W York* | 82 | SE0023 |
| Cragg Hill *W York* | 82 | SE2437 |
| Craggan *Highld* | 141 | NJ0226 |
| Craghead *Dur* | 96 | NZ2150 |
| Crai *Powys* | 45 | SN8924 |
| Craibstone *Gramp* | 142 | NJ4959 |
| Craibstone *Gramp* | 135 | NJ8710 |
| Craichie *Tays* | 127 | NO5047 |
| Craig *D & G* | 101 | NY2678 |
| Craig Llangiwg *W Glam* | 32 | SN7304 |
| Craig Penllyn *S Glam* | 33 | SS9777 |
| Craig's End *Essex* | 53 | TL7137 |
| Craig-y-Duke *W Glam* | 32 | SN7102 |
| Craig-y-nos *Powys* | 33 | SN8415 |
| Craigburn *Border* | 117 | NT2354 |
| Craigcefnparc *W Glam* | 32 | SN6702 |
| Craigdam *Gramp* | 143 | NJ8430 |
| Craigdarroch *D & G* | 107 | NX7391 |
| Craigdarroch *Strath* | 107 | NS6306 |
| Craigdews *D & G* | 99 | NX5072 |
| Craigdhu *Strath* | 122 | NM8205 |
| Craigearn *Gramp* | 142 | NJ7214 |
| Craigellachie *Gramp* | 141 | NJ2844 |
| Craigend *Strath* | 115 | NS4670 |
| Craigend *Tays* | 126 | NO1120 |
| Craigendoran *Strath* | 115 | NS3181 |
| Craigengillan *Strath* | 115 | NS4702 |
| Craigenhouses *Strath* | 113 | NR5267 |
| Craighat *Cent* | 115 | NS4984 |
| Craighlaw *D & G* | 98 | NX3061 |
| Craigleuch *D & G* | 101 | NY3487 |
| Craigie *Strath* | 107 | NS4232 |
| Craigie *Tays* | 126 | NO1143 |
| Craigieburn *D & G* | 108 | NT1105 |
| Craigiefold *Gramp* | 143 | NJ9265 |
| Craiglemine *D & G* | 99 | NX4039 |
| Craigley *D & G* | 99 | NX7658 |
| Craiglockhart *Fife* | 117 | NT2271 |
| Craiglug *Gramp* | 141 | NJ3354 |
| Craigmillar *Loth* | 117 | NT3071 |
| Craignant *Shrops* | 58 | SJ2535 |
| Craigneston *D & G* | 107 | NX7588 |
| Craigneuk *Strath* | 116 | NS7656 |
| Craignure *Strath* | 122 | NM7236 |
| Craigo *Tays* | 135 | NO6864 |
| Craigrothie *Fife* | 126 | NO3810 |
| Craigruie *Cent* | 124 | NN5021 |
| Craigs *Strath* | 105 | NR6923 |
| Craigton *Gramp* | 135 | NJ8301 |
| Craigton *Strath* | 115 | NS4954 |
| Craigton *Tays* | 126 | NO3250 |
| Craigton *Tays* | 127 | NU5138 |
| Craik *Border* | 109 | NT3408 |
| Crail *Fife* | 127 | NO6107 |
| Crailing *Border* | 110 | NT6824 |
| Crailinghall *Border* | 110 | NT6922 |
| Crakehall *N York* | 89 | SE2489 |
| Crakehill *N York* | 89 | SE4273 |
| Crakemarsh *Staffs* | 73 | SK0936 |

224

Crambe Cwmfelin Boeth


Crambe *N York* 90 SE7364
Cramlington *Nthumb* 103 NZ2676
Cramond *Loth* 117 NT1976
Cramond Bridge *Loth* 117 NT1775
Cranage *Ches* 79 SJ7568
Cranberry *Staffs* 72 SJ8235
Cranborne *Dorset* 12 SU0513
Cranbrook *Devon* 8 SX7488
Cranbrook *Kent* 28 TQ7730
Cranbrook Common *Kent* 28 TQ7838
Crane Moor *S York* 82 SE3001
Crane's Corner *Norfk* 66 TF9113
Cranfield *Beds* 38 SP9542
Cranford *Devon* 18 SS3421
Cranford *Gt Lon* 26 TQ1077
Cranford St. Andrew *Nhants* 51 SP9277
Cranford St. John *Nhants* 51 SP9276
Cranham *Gloucs* 35 SO8913
Cranham *Gt Lon* 27 TQ5786
Cranhill *Warwks* 48 SP1253
Crank *Mersyd* 78 SJ5099
Cranleigh *Surrey* 14 TQ0639
Cranmer Green *Suffk* 54 TM0271
Cranmore *IOW* 13 SZ3990
Cranmore *Somset* 22 ST6843
Cranoe *Leics* 50 SP7695
Cransford *Suffk* 55 TM3164
Cranshaws *Border* 118 NT6861
Cranstal *IOM* 153 NX4602
Cranswick *Humb* 84 TA0252
Crantock *Cnwll* 4 SW7960
Cranwell *Lincs* 76 TF0349
Cranwich *Norfk* 65 TL7795
Cranworth *Norfk* 66 TF9804
Crapstone *Devon* 6 SX5067
Crarae *Strath* 114 NR9897
Crask of Aigas *Highld* 139 NH4642
Craster *Nthumb* 111 NU2520
Craswall *H & W* 46 SO2735
Crateford *Staffs* 60 SJ9009
Cratfield *Suffk* 55 TM3175
Crathes *Gramp* 135 NO7596
Crathie *Gramp* 133 NO2695
Crathie *Highld* 132 NN5794
Crathorne *N York* 89 NZ4407
Craven Arms *Shrops* 59 SO4382
Crawcrook *T & W* 103 NZ1363
Crawford *Lancs* 78 SD5003
Crawford *Strath* 108 NS9520
Crawfordjohn *Strath* 108 NS8824
Crawick *D & G* 107 NS7811
Crawley *Hants* 24 SU4234
Crawley *Oxon* 36 SP3412
Crawley *W Susx* 15 TQ2636
Crawley Down *W Susx* 15 TQ3437
Crawleyside *Dur* 95 NY9840
Crawshawbooth *Lancs* 81 SD8125
Crawton *Gramp* 135 NO8779
Cray *N York* 88 SD9479
Cray's Pond *Oxon* 37 SU6380
Crayford *Gt Lon* 27 TQ5175
Crayke *N York* 90 SE5670
Craymere Beck *Norfk* 66 TG0631
Crays Hill *Essex* 40 TQ7192
Craythorne *Staffs* 73 SK2426
Craze Lowman *Devon* 9 SS9814
Creacombe *Devon* 19 SS8119
Creagan Inn *Strath* 122 NM9744
Creagorry *W Isls* 154 NF7948
Creaguaineach Lodge *Highld* 131 NN3068
Creamore Bank *Shrops* 59 SJ5130
Creaton *Nhants* 50 SP7071
Creca *D & G* 101 NY2270
Credenhill *H & W* 46 SO4543
Crediton *Devon* 8 SS8300
Creebank *D & G* 98 NX3477
Creech Heathfield *Somset* 20 ST2827
Creech St. Michael *Somset* 20 ST2725
Creed *Cnwll* 3 SW9347
Creedy Park *Devon* 8 SS8302
Creekmouth *Gt Lon* 27 TQ4581
Creeting St. Mary *Suffk* 54 TM0956
Creeton *Lincs* 64 TF0120
Creetown *D & G* 99 NX4758
Creggans Hotel *Strath* 123 NN0902
Cregneish *IOM* 153 SC1967
Cregrina *Powys* 45 SO1252
Creich *Fife* 126 NO3221
Creigiau *M Glam* 33 ST0781
Crelly *Cnwll* 2 SW6732
Cremyll *Cnwll* 6 SX4553
Cressage *Shrops* 59 SJ5904
Cressbrook *Derbys* 74 SK1673
Cresselly *Dyfed* 30 SN0606
Cressex *Bucks* 37 SU8392
Cressing *Essex* 40 TL7920
Cresswell *Dyfed* 30 SN0506
Cresswell *Nthumb* 103 NZ2993
Cresswell *Staffs* 72 SJ9739
Creswell *Derbys* 75 SK5274
Creswell Green *Staffs* 61 SK0710
Cretingham *Suffk* 55 TM2260
Cretshengan *Strath* 113 NR7166
Crew Green *Powys* 59 SJ3215
Crewe *Ches* 71 SJ4253
Crewe *Ches* 72 SJ7055
Crewe Green *Ches* 72 SJ7255
Crewkerne *Somset* 10 ST4409
Crews Hill *H & W* 35 SO6722
Crews Hill Station *Herts* 27 TL3100
Crewton *Derbys* 62 SK3733
Crianlarich *Strath* 123 NN3825
Cribb's Causeway *Avon* 34 ST5780
Cribyn *Dyfed* 44 SN5251
Criccieth *Gwynd* 56 SH4938
Crich *Derbys* 74 SK3554
Crich Carr *Derbys* 74 SK3354
Crich Common *Derbys* 74 SK3553
Crichton *Loth* 118 NT3862
Crick *Gwent* 34 ST4890
Crick *Nhants* 50 SP5972
Crickadarn *Powys* 45 SO0942
Cricket St. Thomas *Somset* 10 ST3708
Crickheath *Shrops* 59 SJ2923
Crickhowell *Powys* 33 SO2118
Cricklade *Wilts* 36 SU0993
Cricklewood *Gt Lon* 26 TQ2385
Cridling Stubbs *N York* 83 SE5221
Crieff *Tays* 125 NN8621
Criggan *Cnwll* 4 SX0160
Criggion *Powys* 59 SJ2915
Crigglestone *W York* 82 SE3116
Crimble *Gt Man* 81 SD8611
Crimesthorpe *S York* 74 SK3690
Crimond *Gramp* 143 NK0556
Crimonmogate *Gramp* 143 NK0358
Crimplesham *Norfk* 65 TF6503
Crimscote *Warwks* 48 SP2347
Crinan *Strath* 113 NR7894
Crindledyke *Strath* 116 NS8356
Cringleford *Norfk* 67 TG1905
Cringles *N York* 82 SE0448
Crinow *Dyfed* 31 SN1214
Cripp's Corner *E Susx* 17 TQ7721
Cripplesease *Cnwll* 2 SW5036
Cripplestyle *Dorset* 12 SU0912
Crizeley *H & W* 46 SO4432
Croachy *Highld* 140 NH6527
Croanford *Cnwll* 4 SX0371
Croasdale *Cumb* 92 NY0917
Crochmare House *D & G* 100 NX8977
Crock Street *Somset* 10 ST3213
Crockenhill *Kent* 27 TQ5067
Crocker End *Oxon* 37 SU7086
Crocker's Ash *H & W* 34 SO5316
Crockerhill *W Susx* 14 SU9207
Crockernwell *Devon* 8 SX7592
Crockerton *Wilts* 22 ST8642
Crockey Hill *N York* 83 SE6246
Crockham Hill *Kent* 27 TQ4450
Crockhurst Street *Kent* 16 TQ6235
Crockleford Heath *Essex* 41 TM0426
Croes-lan *Dyfed* 42 SN3844
Croes-y-mwyalch *Gwent* 34 ST3092
Croes-y-pant *Gwent* 34 SO3104
Croeserw *W Glam* 33 SS8795
Croesgoch *Dyfed* 30 SM8330
Croesor *Gwynd* 57 SH6344
Croesyceiliog *Dyfed* 31 SN4016
Croesyceiliog *Gwent* 34 ST3096
Croesywaun *Gwynd* 68 SH5159
Croft *Ches* 79 SJ6393
Croft *Devon* 5 SX5296
Croft *Leics* 50 SP5195
Croft *Lincs* 77 TF5162
Croft Michael *Cnwll* 2 SW6637
Croftamie *Cent* 115 NS4786
Crofton *Cumb* 93 NY3050
Crofton *Devon* 9 SX9680
Crofton *W York* 83 SE3717
Crofton *Wilts* 23 SU2562
Crofts *Gramp* 141 NJ2850
Crofts of Dipple *Gramp* 141 NJ3258
Crofts of Savoch *Gramp* 143 NK0460
Crofty *W Glam* 32 SS5295
Crogen *Gwynd* 58 SJ0036
Croggan *Strath* 122 NM7027
Croglin *Cumb* 94 NY5747
Crogo *D & G* 99 NX7576
Croick *Highld* 146 NH4591
Croig *Strath* 121 NM3953
Cromarty *Highld* 140 NH7867
Crombie *Fife* 117 NT0584
Cromdale *Highld* 141 NJ0728
Cromer *Herts* 52 TL2980
Cromer *Herts* 39 TL2928
Cromer *Norfk* 67 TG2242
Cromford *Derbys* 73 SK2956
Cromhall *Avon* 35 ST6990
Cromhall Common *Avon* 35 ST6989
Cromore *W Isls* 154 NB4021
Crompton Fold *Gt Man* 79 SD9409
Cromwell *Notts* 75 SK7761
Cronberry *Strath* 107 NS6022
Crondall *Hants* 25 SU7948
Cronk The *IOM* 153 SC3495
Cronk-y-Voddy *IOM* 153 SC3086
Cronton *Mersyd* 78 SJ4988
Crook *Cumb* 87 SD4695
Crook *Dur* 96 NZ1635
Crook of Devon *Tays* 117 NO0300
Crookdake *Cumb* 93 NY1943
Crooke *Gt Man* 78 SD5507
Crooked End *Gloucs* 35 SO6217
Crooked Holme *Cumb* 101 NY5162
Crooked Soley *Wilts* 34 ST3172
Crookedholm *Strath* 107 NS4537
Crookes *S York* 74 SK3288
Crookhall *Dur* 95 NZ1150
Crookham *Berks* 24 SU5364
Crookham *Nthumb* 110 NT9138
Crookham Village *Hants* 25 SU7952
Crooklands *Cumb* 87 SD5383
Cropper *Derbys* 73 SK2335
Cropredy *Oxon* 49 SP4646
Cropston *Leics* 62 SK5511
Cropthorne *H & W* 47 SO9944
Cropton *N York* 90 SE7589
Cropwell Bishop *Notts* 63 SK6835
Cropwell Butler *Notts* 63 SK6837
Crosbie *Strath* 114 NS2149
Crosby *Cumb* 92 NY0738
Crosby *Humb* 84 SE8912
Crosby *IOM* 153 SC3279
Crosby *Mersyd* 78 SJ3198
Crosby Garrett *Cumb* 88 NY7309
Crosby Ravensworth *Cumb* 94 NY6214
Crosby Villa *Cumb* 92 NY0939
Croscombe *Somset* 21 ST5844
Crosemere *Shrops* 59 SJ4329
Cross *Somset* 21 ST4154
Cross Ash *Gwent* 34 SO4019
Cross Bush *W Susx* 14 TQ0306
Cross Coombe *Cnwll* 3 SW7351
Cross End *Beds* 51 TL0658
Cross End *Essex* 54 TL8634
Cross Flatts *W York* 82 SE1040
Cross Gates *W York* 83 SE3534
Cross Green *Devon* 5 SX3888
Cross Green *Devon* 5 SX3888
Cross Green *Staffs* 60 SJ9105
Cross Green *Suffk* 54 TL8353
Cross Green *Suffk* 54 TL8955
Cross Green *Suffk* 54 TL9953
Cross Hands *Dyfed* 31 SN0712
Cross Hands *Dyfed* 32 SN5612
Cross Hill *Derbys* 74 SK4148
Cross Hills *N York* 82 SE0145
Cross Houses *Shrops* 60 SO6991
Cross Houses *Shrops* 59 SJ5307
Cross Inn *Dyfed* 42 SN3957
Cross Inn *Dyfed* 43 SN5463
Cross Inn *Dyfed* 44 SN7725
Cross Inn *M Glam* 33 ST0583
Cross in Hand *E Susx* 16 TQ5521
Cross Keys *Wilts* 35 ST8771
Cross Lane *IOW* 13 SZ5090
Cross Lane Head *Shrops* 60 SO7095
Cross Lanes *Clwyd* 71 SJ3746
Cross Lanes *Cnwll* 2 SW6921
Cross Lanes *Cnwll* 3 SW7642
Cross Lanes *N York* 90 SE5264
Cross Oak *Powys* 45 SO1023
Cross o' th' hands *Derbys* 73 SK2846
Cross of Jackston *Gramp* 142 NJ7432
Cross Roads *Devon* 5 SX4586
Cross Roads *Powys* 45 SN9756
Cross Street *Suffk* 54 TM1876
Cross Town *Ches* 79 SJ7578
Cross Ways *Dorset* 11 SY7688
Cross-at-Hand *Kent* 28 TQ7846
Crossaig *Strath* 113 NR8351
Crossapoll *Strath* 120 NL9943
Crossbost *Highld* 999 NB3924
Crosscanonby *Cumb* 92 NY0739
Crossdale Street *Norfk* 67 TG2239
Crossens *Mersyd* 80 SD3720
Crossford *Fife* 117 NT0786
Crossford *Strath* 116 NS8246
Crossgate *Lincs* 64 TF2426
Crossgate *M Glam* 5 SX3488
Crossgate *Staffs* 72 SJ9437
Crossgatehall *Loth* 118 NT3669
Crossgates *Fife* 117 NT1488
Crossgates *Powys* 45 SO0865
Crossgates *Strath* 115 NS3744
Crossgill *Lancs* 87 SD5563
Crosshands *Dyfed* 31 SN1923
Crosshands *Strath* 107 NS4830
Crosshill *Fife* 117 NT1796
Crosshill *Strath* 106 NS3206
Crosshouse *Strath* 106 NS3938
Crosskeys *Gwent* 34 ST2292
Crosskeys *Strath* 115 NS3385
Crosskirk *Highld* 150 ND0369
Crossland Edge *W York* 82 SE1212
Crossland Hill *W York* 82 SE1114
Crosslands *Cumb* 101 NY3489
Crosslanes *Shrops* 59 SJ3218
Crosslee *Border* 109 NT3018
Crosslee *Strath* 115 NS4066
Crossley *W York* 82 SE2021
Crossmichael *D & G* 99 NX7367
Crosspost *W Susx* 15 TQ2522
Crossroads *Gramp* 134 NJ5607
Crossroads *Gramp* 135 NO7594
Crossroads *Gramp* 134 NJ5607
Crosston *Tays* 127 NO5256
Crossway *Dyfed* 31 SN1542
Crossway *Gwent* 34 SO4419
Crossway *Powys* 45 SO0558
Crossway Green *Gwent* 34 ST5294
Crossway Green *H & W* 47 SO8368
Crosswell *Dyfed* 31 SN1236
Crosthwaite *Cumb* 87 SD4391
Croston *Lancs* 80 SD4918
Crostwick *Norfk* 67 TG2515
Crostwight *Norfk* 67 TG3429
Crouch *Kent* 28 TR0458
Crouch End *Gt Lon* 27 TQ3088
Crouch Hill *Dorset* 11 ST7010
Croucheston *Wilts* 23 SU0625
Crough House Green *Kent* 16 TQ4346
Croughton *Nhants* 49 SP5433
Crovie *Gramp* 143 NJ8065
Crow *Hants* 12 SU1603
Crow Edge *S York* 82 SE1804
Crow End *Cambs* 52 TL3257
Crow Hill *H & W* 47 SO6326
Crow Street *Essex* 27 TQ5796
Crow's Green *Essex* 40 TL6926
Crow's Nest *Cnwll* 5 SX2669
Crowan *Cnwll* 2 SW6434
Crowborough *E Susx* 16 TQ5131
Crowborough Town *E Susx* 16 TQ5031
Crowcombe *Somset* 20 ST1336
Crowden *Derbys* 74 SK0699
Crowden *Devon* 18 SX4999
Crowdhill *Hants* 13 SU4920
Crowdicote *Derbys* 74 SK1065
Crowdleham *Kent* 27 TQ5658
Crowell *Oxon* 37 SU7499
Crowfield *Nhants* 49 SP6141
Crowfield *Suffk* 54 TM1557
Crowfield Green *Suffk* 54 TM1458
Crowgate Street *Norfk* 67 TG3121
Crowhill *Loth* 119 NT7374
Crowhole *Derbys* 74 SK3375
Crowhurst *E Susx* 17 TQ7512
Crowhurst *Surrey* 15 TQ3847
Crowhurst Lane End *Surrey* 15 TQ3847
Crowland *Lincs* 64 TF2410
Crowland *Suffk* 54 TM0170
Crowlas *Cnwll* 2 SW5133
Crowle *H & W* 47 SO9256
Crowle *Humb* 84 SE7712
Crowle Green *H & W* 47 SO9256
Crowmarsh Gifford *Oxon* 37 SU6189
Crown Corner *Suffk* 55 TM2570
Crownhill *Devon* 6 SX4857
Crownpits *Surrey* 25 SU9743
Crownthorpe *Norfk* 66 TG0803
Crowntown *Cnwll* 2 SW6331
Crows-an-Wra *Cnwll* 2 SW3927
Crowshill *Norfk* 66 TF9406
Crowsnest *Shrops* 59 SJ3701
Crowthorne *Berks* 25 SU8464
Crowton *Ches* 71 SJ5774
Croxall *Staffs* 61 SK1913
Croxby *Lincs* 76 TF1898
Croxdale *Dur* 96 NZ2636
Croxden *Staffs* 73 SK0639
Croxley Green *Herts* 26 TQ0795
Croxton *Cambs* 52 TL2460
Croxton *Humb* 85 TA0912
Croxton *Norfk* 66 TF9831
Croxton *Norfk* 54 TL8786
Croxton *Staffs* 72 SJ7832
Croxton Green *Ches* 71 SJ5552
Croxton Kerrial *Leics* 63 SK8329
Croxtonbank *Staffs* 72 SJ7832
Croy *Highld* 140 NH7949
Croy *Strath* 116 NS7275
Croyde *Devon* 18 SS4439
Croyde Bay *Devon* 18 SS4339
Croydon *Cambs* 52 TL3149
Croydon *Gt Lon* 27 TQ3265
Crubenmore *Highld* 132 NN6790
Cruckmeole *Shrops* 59 SJ4309
Cruckton *Shrops* 59 SJ4310
Cruden Bay *Gramp* 143 NK0836
Crudgington *Shrops* 59 SJ6318
Crudwell *Wilts* 35 ST9592
Crug *Powys* 45 SO1972
Crug-y-byddar *Powys* 58 SO1682
Crugmeer *Cnwll* 4 SW9076
Crugybar *Dyfed* 44 SN6537
Crulivig *W Isls* 154 NB1733
Crumlin *Gwent* 33 ST2198
Crumplehorn *Cnwll* 5 SX2051
Crumpsall *Gt Man* 79 SD8402
Crumstane *Border* 119 NT8053
Crundale *Dyfed* 30 SM9718
Crundale *Kent* 29 TR0749
Crunwear *Dyfed* 31 SN1810
Cruwys Morchard *Devon* 19 SS8712
Crux Easton *Hants* 24 SU4256
Cruxton *Dorset* 10 SY6096
Crwbin *Dyfed* 32 SN4713
Cryers Hill *Bucks* 26 SU8797
Crymmych *Dyfed* 31 SN1833
Crynant *W Glam* 32 SN7904
Crystal Palace *Gt Lon* 27 TQ3371
Cuaig *Highld* 137 NG7057
Cubbington *Warwks* 48 SP3468
Cubert *Cnwll* 4 SW7857
Cubley *S York* 82 SE2401
Cublington *Bucks* 38 SP8422
Cublington *H & W* 46 SO3938
Cuckfield *W Susx* 15 TQ3025
Cucklington *Somset* 22 ST7527
Cuckney *Notts* 75 SK5671
Cuckold's Green *Kent* 28 TQ8276
Cuckoo Bridge *Lincs* 64 TF2020
Cuckoo's Corner *Hants* 24 SU7441
Cuckoo's Nest *Ches* 71 SJ3860
Cuddesdon *Oxon* 37 SP5903
Cuddington *Bucks* 37 SP7311
Cuddington *Ches* 71 SJ5971
Cuddington Heath *Ches* 71 SJ4747
Cuddy Hill *Lancs* 80 SD4937
Cudham *Gt Lon* 27 TQ4459
Cudliptown *Devon* 5 SX5279
Cudworth *S York* 83 SE3808
Cudworth *Somset* 10 ST3810
Cudworth Common *S York* 83 SE4007
Cuerden Green *Lancs* 80 SD5425
Cuerdley Cross *Ches* 78 SJ5487
Cufaude *Hants* 24 SU6557
Cuffley *Herts* 39 TL3003
Culbo *Highld* 140 NH6461
Culbokie *Highld* 140 NH6059
Culburnie *Highld* 139 NH4941
Culcabock *Highld* 140 NH6844
Culcharry *Highld* 140 NH8650
Culcheth *Ches* 79 SJ6694
Culdrain *Gramp* 142 NJ5134
Culduie *Highld* 137 NG7140
Culford *Suffk* 54 TL8370
Culgaith *Cumb* 94 NY6029
Culham *Oxon* 37 SU5095
Culinlongart *Strath* 104 NR6511
Culkein *Highld* 148 NC0333
Culkein Drumbeg *Highld* 148 NC1133
Culkerton *Gloucs* 35 ST9395
Cullen *Gramp* 142 NJ5167
Cullercoats *T & W* 103 NZ3671
Cullerlie *Gramp* 135 NJ7603
Cullicudden *Highld* 140 NH6463
Cullingworth *W York* 82 SE0636
Cullipool *Strath* 122 NM7313
Cullivoe *Shet* 155 HP5402
Cullompton *Devon* 9 ST0207
Culm Davy *Devon* 9 ST1215
Culmalzie *D & G* 99 NX3752
Culmington *Shrops* 59 SO4982
Culmstock *Devon* 9 ST1013
Culnacraig *Highld* 145 NC0603
Culnaightrie *D & G* 92 NX7750
Culnaknock *Highld* 137 NG5263
Culpho *Suffk* 55 TM2149
Culrain *Highld* 146 NH5794
Culross *Fife* 117 NS9886
Culroy *Strath* 106 NS3114
Culscadden *D & G* 99 NX4748
Culshabbin *D & G* 98 NX3050
Culswick *Shet* 155 HU2745
Cultercullen *Gramp* 143 NJ9223
Cults *D & G* 99 NX4643
Cults *Gramp* 135 NJ8903
Culverlane *Devon* 7 SX7460
Culverstone Green *Kent* 27 TQ6362
Culverthorpe *Lincs* 64 TF0240
Culworth *Nhants* 49 SP5446
Culzie Lodge *Highld* 146 NH5171
Cum brwyno *Dyfed* 43 SN7180
Cumbernauld *Strath* 116 NS7674
Cumberworth *Lincs* 77 TF5073
Cumergyr *Dyfed* 43 SN7982
Cuminestown *Gramp* 143 NJ8050
Cummersdale *Cumb* 93 NY3953
Cummertrees *D & G* 100 NY1366
Cummingston *Gramp* 141 NJ1368
Cumnor *Oxon* 37 SP4504
Cumrew *Cumb* 94 NY5450
Cumwhinton *Cumb* 93 NY4552
Cumwhitton *Cumb* 94 NY5052
Cundall *N York* 89 SE4272
Cunninghamhead *Strath* 106 NS3741
Cupar *Fife* 126 NO3714
Cupar Muir *Fife* 126 NO3613
Cupernham *Hants* 23 SU3622
Curbar *Derbys* 74 SK2574
Curbridge *Hants* 13 SU5211
Curbridge *Oxon* 36 SP3208
Curdridge *Hants* 13 SU5313
Curdworth *Warwks* 61 SP1892
Curland *Somset* 10 ST2716
Currarie *Strath* 106 NX1691
Curridge *Berks* 24 SU4972
Currie *Loth* 117 NT1867
Curry Mallet *Somset* 21 ST3221
Curry Rivel *Somset* 21 ST3824
Curt *Gwynd* 57 SN6899
Curteis Corner *Kent* 28 TQ8539
Curtisden Green *Kent* 28 TQ7440
Curtisknowle *Devon* 7 SX7353
Cury *Cnwll* 2 SW6721
Cusgarne *Cnwll* 3 SW7540
Cushuish *Somset* 20 ST1930
Cusop *H & W* 46 SO2441
Cutcloy *D & G* 99 NX4534
Cutcombe *Somset* 20 SS9239
Cutgate *Gt Man* 81 SD8614
Cuthill *Highld* 147 NH7587
Cutiau *Gwynd* 57 SH6317
Cutler's Green *Essex* 40 TL5930
Cutmadoc *Cnwll* 4 SX0963
Cutmere *M Glam* 5 SX3260
Cutnall Green *H & W* 47 SO8868
Cutsdean *Gloucs* 48 SP0831
Cutthorpe *Derbys* 74 SK3473
Cuxham *Oxon* 37 SU6695
Cuxton *Kent* 28 TQ7066
Cuxton *Kent* 28 TQ7066
Cuxwold *Lincs* 85 TA1701
Cwm *Clwyd* 70 SJ0677
Cwm *Gwent* 33 SO1805
Cwm *W Glam* 32 SS6895
Cwm Capel *Dyfed* 32 SN4502
Cwm Irfon *Powys* 45 SN8549
Cwm Morgan *Dyfed* 31 SN2935
Cwm-bach *Dyfed* 32 SN4801
Cwm-Cewydd *Gwynd* 57 SH8713
Cwm-Crownon *Powy's* 33 SO1419
Cwm-celyn *Gwent* 33 SO2008
Cwm-Llinau *Powys* 57 SH8408
Cwm-y-glo *Gwynd* 69 SH5562
Cwmafan *W Glam* 32 SS7791
Cwmaman *M Glam* 33 ST0099
Cwmann *Dyfed* 44 SN5847
Cwmavon *Gwent* 34 SO2706
Cwmbach *Dyfed* 31 SN2526
Cwmbach *M Glam* 33 SO0201
Cwmbach *Powys* 45 SO1639
Cwmbach Llechrhyd *Powys* 45 SO0254
Cwmbelan *Powys* 58 SN9481
Cwmbran *Gwent* 34 ST2994
Cwmcarn *Gwent* 34 ST2293
Cwmcarvan *Gwent* 34 SO4707
Cwmcoy *Dyfed* 31 SN2942
Cwmdare *M Glam* 33 SN9803
Cwmdu *Dyfed* 44 SN6330
Cwmdu *Powys* 45 SO1823
Cwmdu *W Glam* 32 SS6494
Cwmduad *Dyfed* 31 SN3731
Cwmdwr *Dyfed* 44 SN7132
Cwmfelin *M Glam* 33 SO0901
Cwmfelin *M Glam* 33 SS8689
Cwmfelin Boeth *Dyfed* 31 SN1919

Cwmfelin Mynach

Doley

Cwmfelin Mynach *Dyfed* 31 SN2324
Cwmfelinfach *Gwent* 33 ST1891
Cwmffrwd *Dyfed* 31 SN4217
Cwmgiedd *Powys* 32 SN7911
Cwmgorse *W Glam* 32 SN7010
Cwmgwili *Dyfed* 32 SN5710
Cwmgwrach *W Glam* 33 SN8604
Cwmhiraeth *Dyfed* 31 SN3438
Cwmisfael *Dyfed* 32 SN4915
Cwmllynfell *Dyfed* 32 SN7412
Cwmparc *M Glam* 33 SS9495
Cwmpengraig *Dyfed* 31 SN3436
Cwmpennar *M Glam* 33 SO0400
Cwmrhos *Powys* 31 SN1824
Cwmrhydyceirw *W Glam* 32 SS6699
Cwmsychpant *Dyfed* 44 SN4746
Cwmtillery *Gwent* 33 SO2105
Cwmyoy *Gwent* 46 SO2923
Cwmystwyth *Dyfed* 43 SN7874
Cwn-y-glo *Dyfed* 32 SN5513
Cwrt-newydd *Dyfed* 44 SN4847
Cwrt-y-gollen *Powys* 34 SO2317
Cyffylliog *Clwyd* 70 SJ0557
Cyfronydd *Powys* 58 SJ1408
Cylibebyll *W Glam* 32 SN7404
Cymmer *M Glam* 33 ST0290
Cymmer *W Glam* 33 SS8696
Cynghardy *Dyfed* 44 SN8040
Cynheidre *Dyfed* 32 SN4907
Cynonville *W Glam* 33 SS8395
Cynwyd *Clwyd* 70 SJ0541
Cynwyl Elfed *Dyfed* 31 SN3727

# D

Daccombe *Devon* 7 SX9068
Dacre *Cumb* 93 NY4526
Dacre *N York* 89 SE1960
Dacre Banks *N York* 89 SE1962
Daddry Shield *Dur* 95 NY8937
Dadford *Bucks* 49 SP6638
Dadlington *Leics* 61 SP4098
Dafen *Dyfed* 32 SN5201
Daffy Green *Norfk* 66 TF9609
Dagenham *Gt Lon* 27 TQ5084
Daglingworth *Gloucs* 35 SO9905
Dagnall *Bucks* 38 SP9916
Dagworth *Suffk* 54 TM0361
Dailly *Strath* 106 NS2701
Dainton *Devon* 7 SX8466
Dairsie *Fife* 126 NO4117
Daisy Hill *Gt Man* 79 SD6504
Daisy Hill *W York* 82 SE2728
Dalavich *Strath* 122 NM9612
Dalbeattie *D & G* 100 NX8361
Dalbeg *W Isls* 154 NB2345
Dalblair *Strath* 107 NS6419
Dalbog *Tays* 134 NO5871
Dalbury *Derbys* 73 SK2634
Dalby *IOM* 153 SC2178
Dalby *Lincs* 77 TF4169
Dalby *N York* 90 SE6370
Dalcapon *Tays* 125 NN9754
Dalchalm *Highld* 147 NC9105
Dalchenna *Strath* 123 NN0706
Dalchork *Highld* 146 NC5710
Dalchreichart *Highld* 131 NH2912
Dalchriun *Tays* 124 NN7116
Dalcrue *Tays* 125 NO0417
Dalderby *Lincs* 77 TF2465
Dalditch *Devon* 4 SX0483
Dale *Cumb* 94 NY5443
Dale *Derbys* 62 SK4338
Dale *Dyfed* 30 SM8005
Dale End *Derbys* 74 SK2161
Dale End *N York* 82 SD9646
DaleHead *Cumb* 93 NY4316
Dale Hill *E Susx* 16 TQ7030
Dalebottom *Cumb* 93 NY2921
Dalehouse *N York* 97 NZ7717
Dalelia *Highld* 129 NM7369
Dalgarven *Strath* 115 NS2846
Dalgety Bay *Fife* 117 NT1683
Dalgig *Strath* 107 NS5513
Dalginross *Tays* 124 NN7721
Dalguise *Tays* 125 NN9947
Dalhalvaig *Highld* 150 NC8954
Dalham *Suffk* 53 TL7261
Daliburgh *W Isls* 154 NF7421
Dalkeith *Loth* 118 NT3367
Dall *Tays* 124 NN5956
Dallas *Gramp* 141 NJ1252
Dalleagles *Strath* 107 NS5610
Dallinghoo *Suffk* 55 TM2655
Dallington *E Susx* 16 TQ6519
Dallow *N York* 89 SE1971
Dalmally *Strath* 123 NN1527
Dalmarnock *Tays* 117 NS9945
Dalmary *Cent* 115 NS5195
Dalmellington *Strath* 107 NS4706
Dalmeny *Loth* 117 NT1477
Dalmigavie *Highld* 140 NH7319
Dalmigavie Lodge *Highld* 140 NH7523
Dalmore *Highld* 140 NH6668
Dalnacardoch Lodge *Tays* 132 NN7270
Dalnaspidal *Tays* 132 NN6473
Dalnawillan Lodge *Highld* 150 ND0240
Daloist *Tays* 124 NN7857
Dalqueich *Tays* 125 NO0704
Dalquhairn *Strath* 106 NX3296
Dalreavoch Lodge *Highld* 147 NC7508
Dalry *Strath* 115 NS2949
Dalrymple *Strath* 106 NS3514
Dalserf *Strath* 116 NS7950
Dalsmeran *Strath* 104 NR6413
Dalston *Cumb* 93 NY3650
Dalston *Gt Lon* 27 TQ3384
Dalswinton *D & G* 100 NX9385
Dalton *Cumb* 87 SD5476
Dalton *D & G* 100 NY1173
Dalton *Lancs* 78 SD4908
Dalton *N York* 89 NZ1108
Dalton *N York* 89 SE4376
Dalton *Nthumb* 103 NZ1172
Dalton *S York* 75 SK4594
Dalton in Furness *Cumb* 86 SD2273
Dalton Magna *S York* 75 SK4693
Dalton Parva *S York* 75 SK4593
Dalton Piercy *Cleve* 97 NZ4631
Dalton-le-Dale *Dur* 96 NZ4047
Dalton-on-Tees *N York* 89 NZ2907
Daltot *Strath* 113 NR7583
Dalvadie *D & G* 98 NX0851
Dalveich *Cent* 124 NN6124
Dalwhinnie *Highld* 132 NN6385
Dalwood *Devon* 9 ST2400
Dam Green *Norfk* 54 TM0485
Damask Green *Herts* 39 TL2529
Damerham *Hants* 12 SU1015
Damgate *Norfk* 67 TG4009
Dan's Castle *Dur* 95 NZ1149
Dan-y-Parc *Powys* 34 SO2217
Danaway *Kent* 28 TQ8663
Danbury *Essex* 40 TL7805
Danby *N York* 90 NZ7008
Danby Bottom *N York* 90 NZ6904
Danby Wiske *N York* 89 SE3398
Dandaleith *Gramp* 141 NJ2845
Danderhall *Loth* 117 NT3069
Dane End *Herts* 39 TL3321
Dane Hills *Leics* 62 SK5605
Dane Street *Kent* 28 TR0552
Danebridge *Ches* 72 SJ9665
Danegate *E Susx* 16 TQ5634
Danehill *E Susx* 15 TQ4027
Danemoor Green *Norfk* 66 TG0505
Danesford *Shrops* 60 SO7391
Danesmoor *Derbys* 74 SK4263
Daniel's Water *Kent* 28 TQ9541
Danshillack *Gramp* 142 NJ7157
Danskine *Loth* 118 NT5667
Danthorpe *Humb* 85 TA2732
Danzey Green *Warwks* 48 SP1269
Dapple Heath *Staffs* 73 SK0425
Darass Hall *T & W* 103 NZ1570
Darby Green *Hants* 25 SU8360
Darcy Lever *Gt Man* 79 SD7308
Daren-felen *Gwent* 34 SO2212
Darenth *Kent* 27 TQ5571
Daresbury *Ches* 78 SJ5882
Darfield *S York* 83 SE4104
Dargate *Kent* 29 TR0761
Darite *Cnwll* 5 SX2569
Darland *Clwyd* 71 SJ3757
Darland *Kent* 28 TQ7964
Darlaston *Staffs* 72 SJ8835
Darlaston *W Mids* 60 SO9796
Darlaston Green *W Mids* 60 SO9797
Darley *N York* 89 SE2059
Darley Abbey *Derbys* 62 SK3538
Darley Bridge *Derbys* 74 SK2661
Darley Dale *Derbys* 74 SK2663
Darley Green *Warwks* 61 SP1874
Darley Head *N York* 89 SE1959
Darleyhall *Herts* 38 TL1422
Darlingscott *Warwks* 48 SP2342
Darlington *Dur* 89 NZ2914
Darliston *Shrops* 59 SJ5833
Darlton *Notts* 75 SK7773
Darnford *Staffs* 61 SK1308
Darowen *Powys* 57 SH8301
Darra *Gramp* 142 NJ7447
Darracott *Devon* 18 SS2317
Darracott *Devon* 18 SS4739
Darrington *W York* 83 SE4919
Darsham *Suffk* 55 TM4170
Dartford *Kent* 27 TQ5474
Dartington *Devon* 7 SX7862
Dartmeet *Devon* 7 SX6773
Dartmouth *Devon* 7 SX8751
Darton *S York* 82 SE3110
Darvel *Strath* 107 NS5637
Darwell Hole *E Susx* 16 TQ6919
Darwen *Lancs* 81 SD6922
Datchet *Berks* 26 SU9877
Datchworth *Herts* 39 TL2619
Datchworth Green *Herts* 39 TL2618
Daubhill *Gt Man* 79 SD7007
Dauntsey *Wilts* 35 ST9782
Dauntsey Green *Wilts* 35 ST9982
Dava *Highld* 141 NJ0138
Davenham *Ches* 79 SJ6571
Davenport *Gt Man* 79 SJ9088
Davenport Green *Ches* 79 SJ8379
Davenport Green *Gt Man* 79 SJ8086
Daventry *Nhants* 49 SP5762
David Street *Kent* 27 TQ6466
Davidson's Mains *Loth* 117 NT2175
Davidstow *Cnwll* 4 SX1587
Davington *D & G* 109 NT2302
Davington Hill *Kent* 28 TR0161
Daviot *Gramp* 142 NJ7528
Daviot *Highld* 140 NH7239
Daviot House *Highld* 140 NH7240
Davis Street *Berks* 25 SU7872
Davis's Town *E Susx* 16 TQ5217
Davoch of Grange *Gramp* 142 NJ4851
Daw End *W Mids* 61 SK0300
Daw's House *Cnwll* 5 SX3182
Dawesgreen *Surrey* 15 TQ2147
Dawley *Shrops* 60 SJ6807
Dawlish *Devon* 9 SX9676
Dawlish Warren *Devon* 9 SX9778
Dawn *Clwyd* 69 SH8672
Daws Green *Somset* 20 ST2021
Daws Heath *Essex* 40 TQ8188
Dawsmere *Lincs* 65 TF4430
Day Green *Ches* 72 SJ7757
Daybrook *Notts* 62 SK5745
Dayhills *Staffs* 72 SJ9532
Dayhouse Bank *H & W* 60 SO9678
Daylesford *Gloucs* 48 SP2425
Ddol *Clwyd* 70 SJ1471
Ddol-Cownwy *Powys* 58 SJ0117
Deal *Kent* 29 TR3752
Dean *Cumb* 92 NY0725
Dean *Devon* 19 SS6245
Dean *Devon* 19 SS7048
Dean *Devon* 7 SX7364
Dean *Dorset* 11 ST9715
Dean *Hants* 24 SU4431
Dean *Hants* 13 SU5619
Dean *Lancs* 81 SD8526
Dean *Oxon* 36 SP3422
Dean *Somset* 22 ST6743
Dean Bottom *Kent* 27 TQ5868
Dean Court *Oxon* 37 SP4705
Dean Cross *Devon* 19 SS5042
Dean End *Dorset* 11 ST9617
Dean Head *S York* 74 SE2500
Dean Prior *Devon* 7 SX7363
Dean Row *Ches* 79 SJ8781
Dean Street *Kent* 28 TQ7451
Deanburnhaugh *Border* 109 NT3912
Deancombe *Devon* 7 SX7264
Deane *Gt Man* 79 SD6907
Deane *Hants* 24 SU5450
Deanhead *W York* 82 SE0415
Deanich Lodge *Highld* 145 NH3683
Deanland *Dorset* 22 ST9918
Deanlane End *W Susx* 13 SU7412
Deanraw *Nthumb* 102 NY8162
Deanscale *Cumb* 92 NY0926
Deanshanger *Nhants* 49 SP7639
Deanshaugh *Gramp* 141 NJ3550
Deanston *Cent* 116 NN7101
Dearnley *Gt Man* 81 SD9215
Debach *Suffk* 55 TM2454
Debden *Essex* 39 TL5533
Debden Cross *Essex* 40 TL5731
Debden Green *Essex* 40 TL5732
Debden Green *Essex* 27 TQ4398
Debenham *Suffk* 54 TM1763
Deblin's Green *H & W* 47 SO8149
Dechmont *Loth* 117 NT0470
Dechmont Road *Loth* 117 NT0269
Deddington *Oxon* 49 SP4631
Dedham *Essex* 41 TM0533
Dedham Heath *Essex* 41 TM0531
Dedworth *Berks* 26 SU9476
Deebank *Gramp* 135 NO6994
Deebank *Gramp* 135 NO6994
Deene *Nhants* 51 SP9492
Deenethorpe *Nhants* 51 SP9591
Deepcar *S York* 74 SK2897
Deepcut *Surrey* 25 SU9057
Deepdale *Cumb* 88 SD7284
Deepdale *N York* 88 SD8989
Deeping Gate *Lincs* 64 TF1509
Deeping St. James *Lincs* 64 TF1609
Deeping St. Nicholas *Lincs* 64 TF2115
Deerhurst *Gloucs* 47 SO8729
Deerhurst Walton *Gloucs* 47 SO8828
Deerton Street *Kent* 28 TQ9762
Defford *H & W* 47 SO9143
Defynnog *Powys* 45 SN9227
Deganwy *Gwynd* 69 SH7779
Degnish *Strath* 122 NM7812
Deighton *N York* 89 NZ3801
Deighton *N York* 83 SE6244
Deighton *W York* 82 SE1519
Deiniolen *Gwynd* 69 SH5863
Delabole *Cnwll* 4 SX0683
Delamere *Ches* 71 SJ5668
Delfrigs *Gramp* 143 NJ9620
Dell Quay *W Susx* 14 SU8302
Delley *Devon* 19 SS5424
Delliefure *Highld* 141 NJ0731
Delly End *Oxon* 36 SP3513
Delmonden Green *Kent* 17 TQ7330
Delnashaugh Hotel *Gramp* 141 NJ1835
Delnato *Gramp* 141 NJ1517
Delny *Highld* 146 NH7372
Delph *Gt Man* 82 SD9807
Delves *Dur* 95 NZ1149
Delvine *Tays* 126 NO1240
Dembleby *Lincs* 64 TF0437
Demelza *Cnwll* 4 SW9763
Denaby *S York* 75 SK4899
Denaby Main *S York* 75 SK4999
Denbies *Surrey* 26 TQ1450
Denbigh *Clwyd* 70 SJ0566
Denbrae *Fife* 126 NO3818
Denbury *Devon* 7 SX8268
Denby *Derbys* 62 SK3946
Denby Bottles *Derbys* 62 SK3846
Denby Dale *W York* 82 SE2208
Denchworth *Oxon* 36 SU3891
Dendron *Cumb* 86 SD2470
Denel End *Beds* 38 TL0335
Denfield *Strath* 108 NS9517
Denford *Nhants* 51 SP9976
Dengie *Essex* 41 TL9802
Denham *Bucks* 26 TQ0487
Denham *Suffk* 53 TL7561
Denham *Suffk* 55 TM1974
Denham End *Suffk* 53 TL7663
Denham Green *Bucks* 26 TQ0388
Denham Green *Suffk* 55 TM1974
Denhead *Fife* 127 NO4613
Denhead *Gramp* 143 NJ9952
Denhead of Gray *Tays* 126 NO3531
Denholm *Border* 110 NT5718
Denholme *W York* 82 SE0734
Denholme Clough *W York* 82 SE0732
Denio *Gwynd* 56 SH3635
Denmead *Hants* 13 SU6512
Denmore *Gramp* 135 NJ9411
Denne Park *W Susx* 15 TQ1628
Dennington *Suffk* 55 TM2867
Dennis Park *W Mids* 60 SO9585
Denny *Cent* 116 NS8082
Dennyloanhead *Cent* 116 NS8180
Denshaw *Gt Man* 82 SD9710
Denside *Gramp* 135 NO8095
Densole *Kent* 29 TR2141
Denston *Suffk* 53 TL7652
Denstone *Staffs* 73 SK0940
Denstroude *Kent* 29 TR1061
Dent *Cumb* 87 SD7087
Dent-de-Lion *Kent* 29 TR3269
Denton *Cambs* 52 TL1487
Denton *Dur* 96 NZ2118
Denton *E Susx* 16 TQ4502
Denton *Gt Man* 79 SJ9295
Denton *Kent* 28 TQ6673
Denton *Kent* 29 TR2147
Denton *Lincs* 63 SK8632
Denton *N York* 82 SE1448
Denton *Nhants* 51 SP8358
Denton *Norfk* 55 TM2888
Denton *Oxon* 37 SP5902
Denver *Norfk* 65 TF6101
Denwick *Nthumb* 111 NU2014
Deopham *Norfk* 66 TG0500
Deopham Green *Norfk* 66 TM0499
Depden *Suffk* 53 TL7857
Depden Green *Suffk* 53 TL7756
Deptford *Gt Lon* 27 TQ3777
Deptford *Wilts* 22 SU0038
Derby *Derbys* 62 SK3536
Derbyhaven *IOM* 153 SC2867
Derculich *Tays* 125 NN8852
Deri *M Glam* 33 SO1201
Derril *Devon* 18 SS3003
Derringstone *Kent* 29 TR2049
Derrington *Staffs* 72 SJ8922
Derriton *Devon* 18 SS3303
Derry Hill *Wilts* 35 ST9670
Derrythorpe *Humb* 84 SE8208
Dersingham *Norfk* 65 TF6830
Dervaig *Strath* 121 NM4352
Derwen *Clwyd* 70 SJ0750
Derwenlas *Powys* 57 SN7298
Desborough *Nhants* 51 SP8083
Desford *Leics* 62 SK4703
Deskford *Gramp* 142 NJ5061
Deskford *Gramp* 142 NJ5061
Detchant *Nthumb* 111 NU0836
Detling *Kent* 28 TQ7958
Deuxhill *Shrops* 60 SO6987
Devauden *Gwent* 34 ST4898
Devil's Bridge *Dyfed* 43 SN7477
Deviock *M Glam* 5 SX3155
Devitts Green *Warwks* 61 SP2790
Devizes *Wilts* 22 SU0061
Devonport *Devon* 6 SX4554
Devonside *Cent* 116 NS9296
Devoran *Cnwll* 3 SW7939
Dewarton *Loth* 118 NT3763
Dewlish *Dorset* 11 SY7798
Dewsbury *W York* 82 SE2422
Dewsbury Moor *W York* 82 SE2321
Deytheur *Powys* 58 SJ2417
Dhoon *IOM* 153 SC3784
Dhoor *IOM* 153 SC4396
Dhowin *IOM* 153 NX4101
Dial *Avon* 21 ST5367
Dial Green *W Susx* 14 SU9227
Dial Post *W Susx* 15 TQ1519
Dibberford *Dorset* 10 ST4504
Dibden *Hants* 13 SU4108
Dibden Purlieu *Hants* 13 SU4106
Dickens Heath *W Mids* 61 SP1076
Dickleburgh *Norfk* 54 TM1682
Didbrook *Gloucs* 48 SP0531
Didcot *Oxon* 37 SU5190
Diddington *Cambs* 52 TL1965
Diddlebury *Shrops* 59 SO5085
Didley *H & W* 46 SO4532
Didling *W Susx* 14 SU8318
Didmarton *Gloucs* 35 ST8287
Didsbury *Gt Man* 79 SJ8392
Didworthy *Devon* 7 SX6862
Digby *Lincs* 76 TF0854
Digg *Highld* 136 NG4669
Diggle *Gt Man* 82 SE0008
Digmore *Lancs* 78 SD4805
Digswell *Herts* 39 TL2415
Digswell Water *Herts* 39 TL2414
Dihewyd *Dyfed* 44 SN4855
Dilham *Norfk* 67 TG3325
Dilhorne *Staffs* 72 SJ9743
Dillington *Cambs* 52 TL1365
Dilston *Nthumb* 102 NY9763
Dilton *Wilts* 22 ST8548
Dilton Marsh *Wilts* 22 ST8449
Dilwyn *H & W* 46 SO4154
Dimma *Cnwll* 5 SX1997
Dimple *Gt Man* 81 SD7015
Dinas *Cnwll* 4 SW9174
Dinas *Dyfed* 31 SN2730
Dinas *Dyfed* 30 SN0139
Dinas *Gwynd* 56 SH2736
Dinas *M Glam* 33 ST0091
Dinas Dinlle *Gwynd* 68 SH4356
Dinas Powis *S Glam* 33 ST1571
Dinas-Mawddwy *Gwynd* 57 SH8615
Dinder *Somset* 21 ST5744
Dinedor *H & W* 46 SO5336
Dingestow *Gwent* 34 SO4510
Dinghurst *Avon* 21 ST4459
Dingle *Mersyd* 78 SJ3687
Dingleden *Kent* 17 TQ8131
Dingley *Nhants* 50 SP7787
Dingwall *Highld* 139 NH5458
Dinham *Gwent* 34 ST4792
Dinmael *Clwyd* 70 SJ0044
Dinnet *Gramp* 134 NO4598
Dinnington *S York* 75 SK5386
Dinnington *Somset* 10 ST4012
Dinnington *T & W* 103 NZ2073
Dinorwic *Gwynd* 69 SH5961
Dinton *Bucks* 37 SP7611
Dinton *Wilts* 22 SU0131
Dinwoodie *D & G* 100 NY1090
Dinworthy *Devon* 18 SS3015
Dipford *Somset* 20 ST2022
Dipley *Hants* 24 SU7457
Dippen *Strath* 105 NR7937
Dippenhall *Surrey* 25 SU8146
Dippermill *Devon* 18 SS4406
Dippertown *Devon* 5 SX4385
Dippin *Strath* 105 NS0422
Dipple *Gramp* 141 NJ3258
Dipple *Strath* 106 NS2002
Diptford *Devon* 7 SX7256
Dipton *Dur* 96 NZ1554
Diptonmill *Nthumb* 102 NY9361
Dirleton *Loth* 118 NT5184
Dirt Pot *Nthumb* 95 NY8546
Discoed *Powys* 46 SO2764
Diseworth *Leics* 62 SK4524
Dishforth *N York* 89 SE3873
Disley *Ches* 79 SJ9784
Diss *Norfk* 54 TM1180
Disserth *Powys* 45 SO0358
Distington *Cumb* 92 NY0023
Ditchampton *Wilts* 23 SU0831
Ditchburn *Nthumb* 111 NU1320
Ditcheat *Somset* 21 ST6236
Ditchingham *Norfk* 67 TM3391
Ditchley *Oxon* 36 SP3820
Ditchling *E Susx* 15 TQ3215
Ditherington *Shrops* 59 SJ5014
Ditteridge *Wilts* 35 ST8169
Dittisham *Devon* 6 SX5370
Dittisham *Devon* 7 SX8654
Ditton *Ches* 78 SJ4986
Ditton *Kent* 28 TQ7158
Ditton Green *Cambs* 53 TL6558
Ditton Priors *Shrops* 59 SO6089
Dixton *Gloucs* 47 SO9830
Dixton *Gwent* 34 SO5113
Dizzard *Cnwll* 4 SX1698
Dobcross *Gt Man* 82 SD9906
Dobroyd Castle *W York* 81 SD9323
Dobwalls *Cnwll* 5 SX2165
Doccombe *Devon* 8 SX7786
Dochgarroch *Highld* 140 NH6241
Docker *Lancs* 87 SD5774
Docking *Norfk* 65 TF7636
Docklow *H & W* 46 SO5557
Dockray *Cumb* 93 NY2649
Dockray *Cumb* 93 NY3921
Dod's Leigh *Staffs* 73 SK0134
Dodbrooke *Devon* 7 SX7444
Dodd's Green *Ches* 71 SJ6043
Doddinghurst *Essex* 27 TQ5999
Doddington *Cambs* 52 TL4090
Doddington *Kent* 28 TQ9357
Doddington *Lincs* 76 SK9070
Doddington *Nthumb* 111 NT9932
Doddington *Shrops* 46 SO6176
Doddiscombsleigh *Devon* 8 SX8586
Doddshill *Norfk* 65 TF6930
Doddy Cross *M Glam* 5 SX3062
Dodford *H & W* 60 SO9373
Dodford *Nhants* 49 SP6160
Dodington *Avon* 35 ST7580
Dodington *Somset* 20 ST1740
Dodleston *Ches* 71 SJ3661
Dodscott *Devon* 19 SS5419
Dodside *Strath* 115 NS5053
Dodworth *S York* 82 SE3105
Dodworth Bottom *S York* 83 SE3205
Dodworth Green *S York* 82 SE3103
Doe Bank *W Mids* 61 SP1197
Doe Lea *Derbys* 75 SK4566
Dog Village *Devon* 9 SX9896
Dogdyke *Lincs* 76 TF2055
Dogley Lane *W York* 82 SE1914
Dogmersfield *Hants* 25 SU7852
Dogridge *Wilts* 36 SU0787
Dogsthorpe *Cambs* 64 TF1901
Dol-for *Powys* 57 SH8106
Dol-gran *Dyfed* 31 SN4334
Dolanog *Powys* 58 SJ0612
Dolau *Powys* 45 SO1367
Dolbenmaen *Gwynd* 56 SH5043
Dolcombe *Devon* 8 SX7786
Doley *Shrops* 72 SJ7429

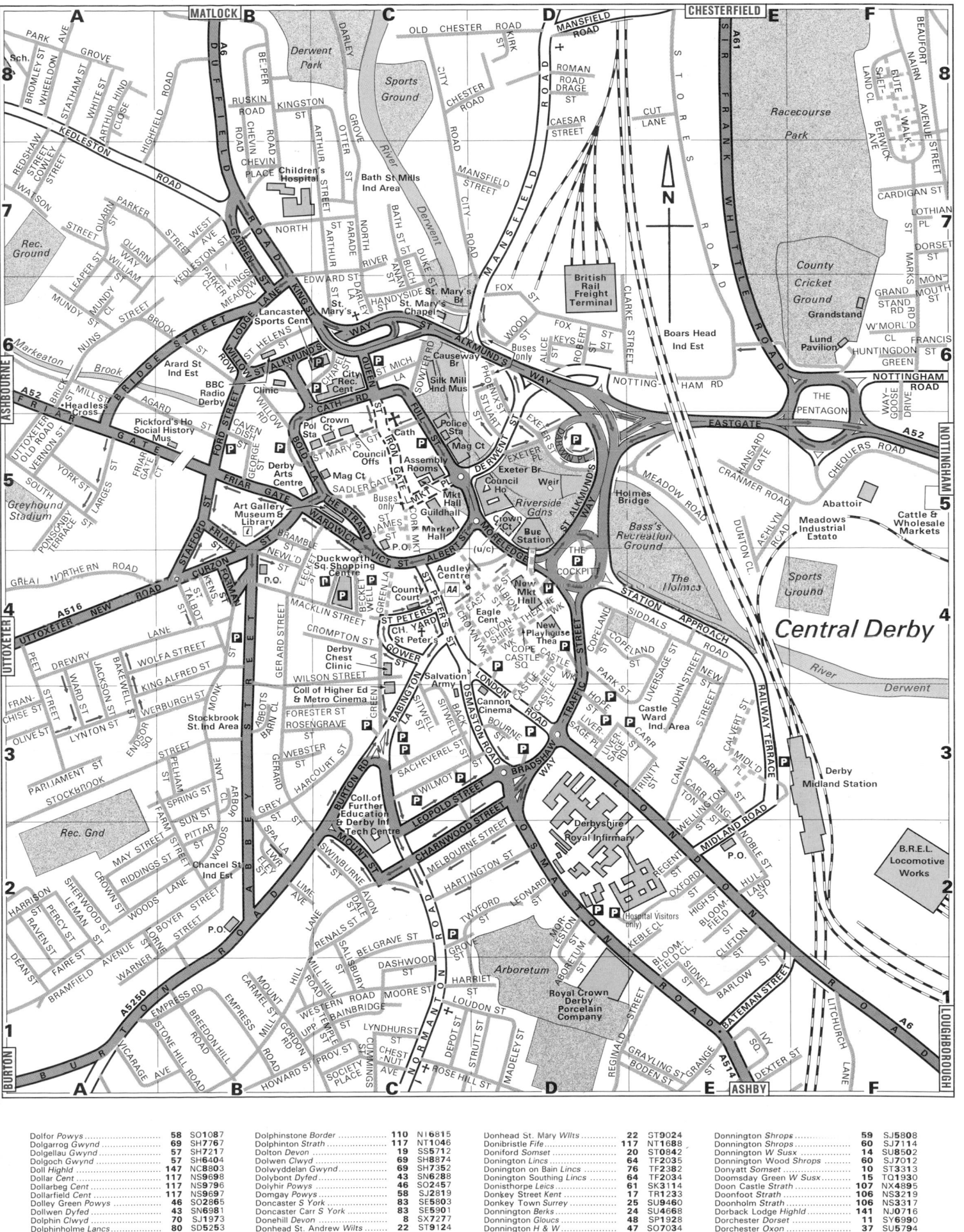

**Central Derby**

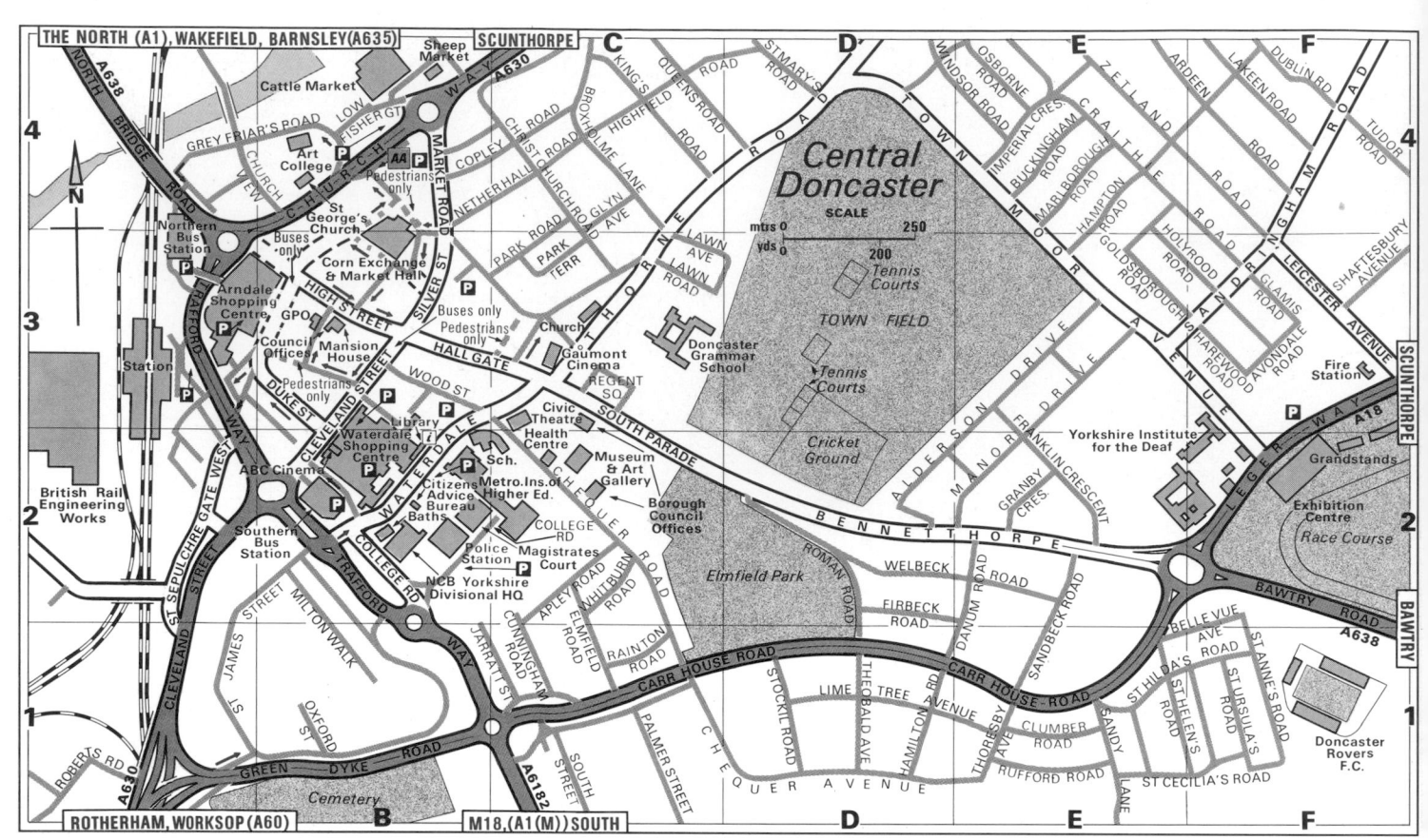

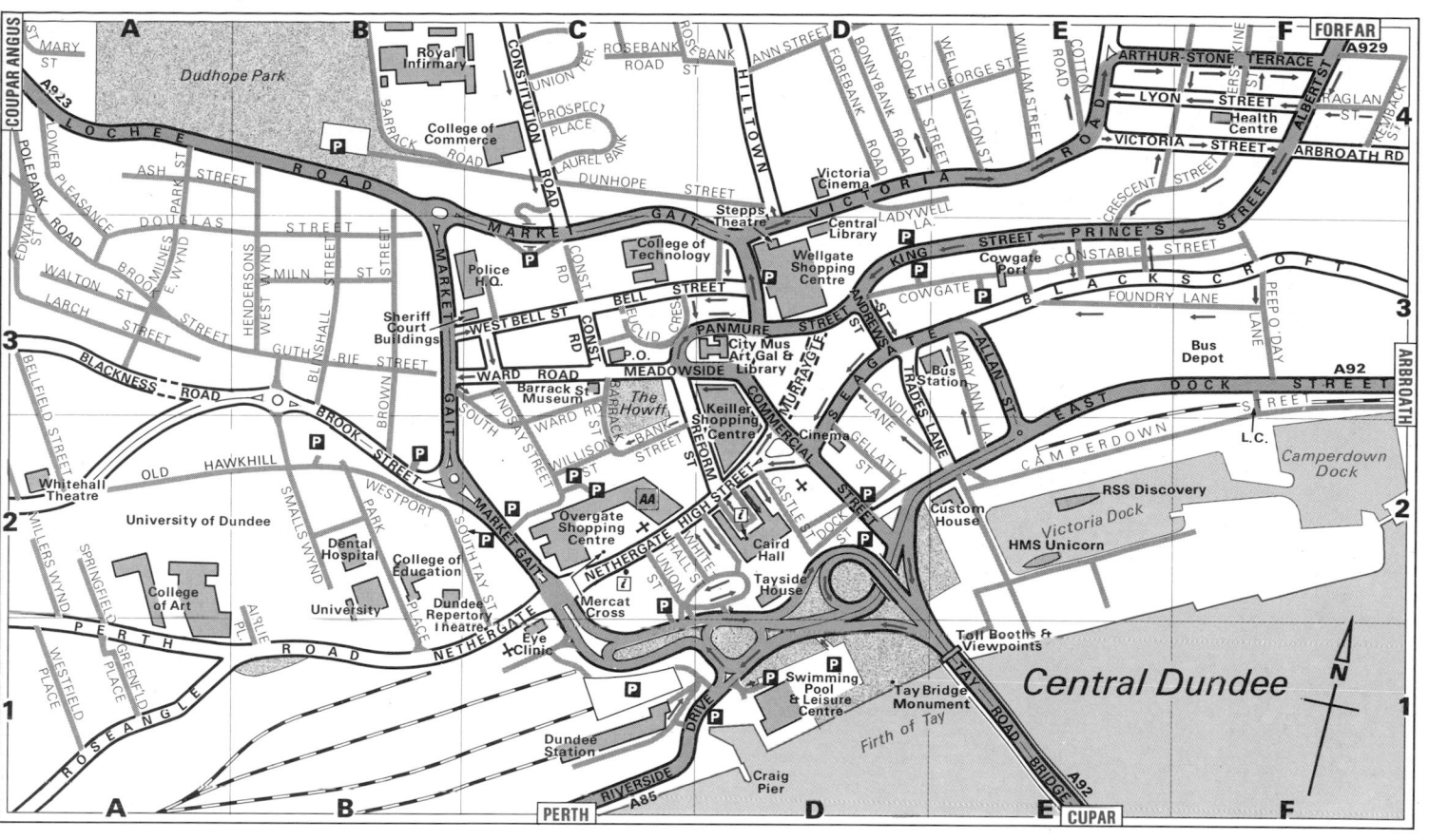

Central Dundee

## E

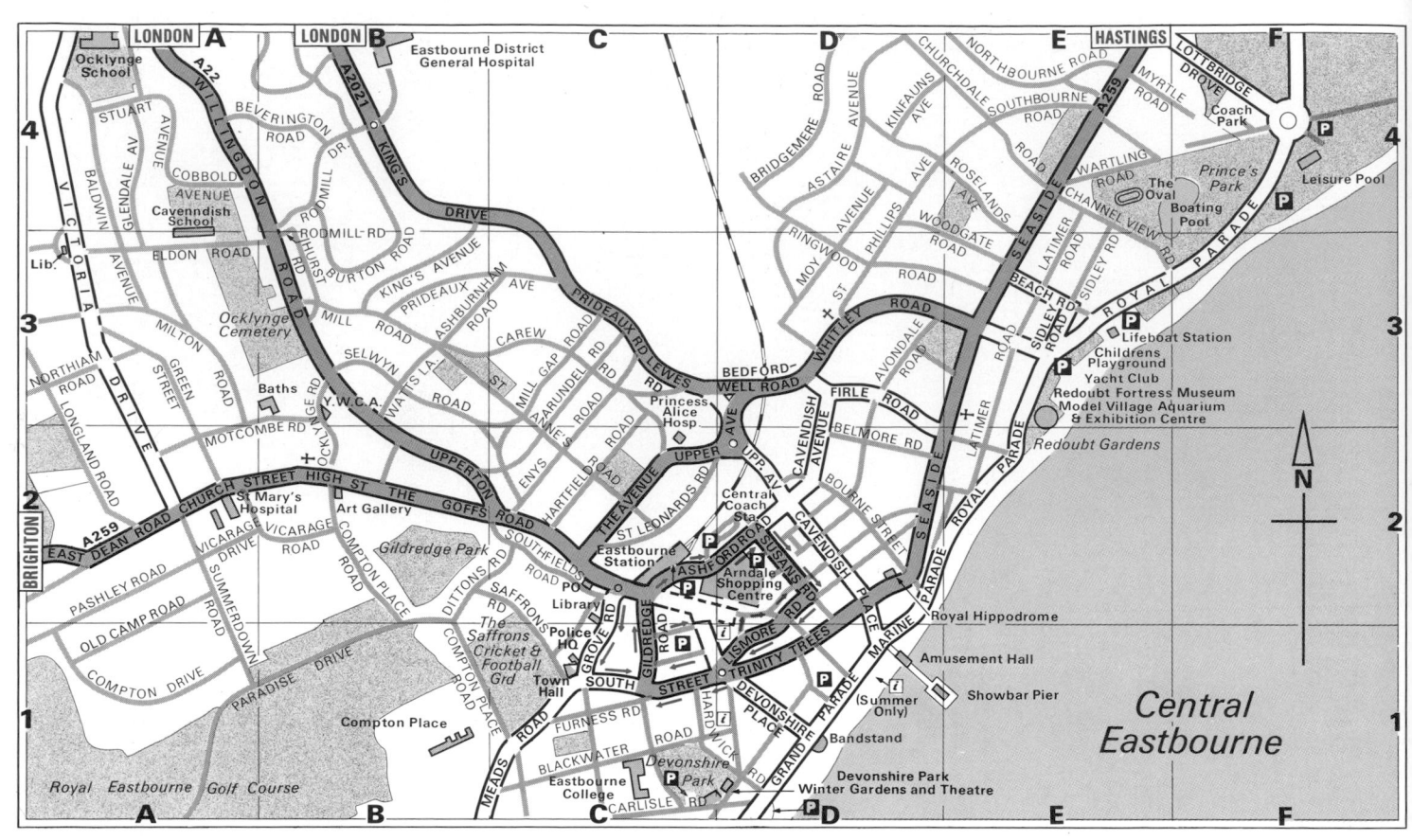

Central Eastbourne

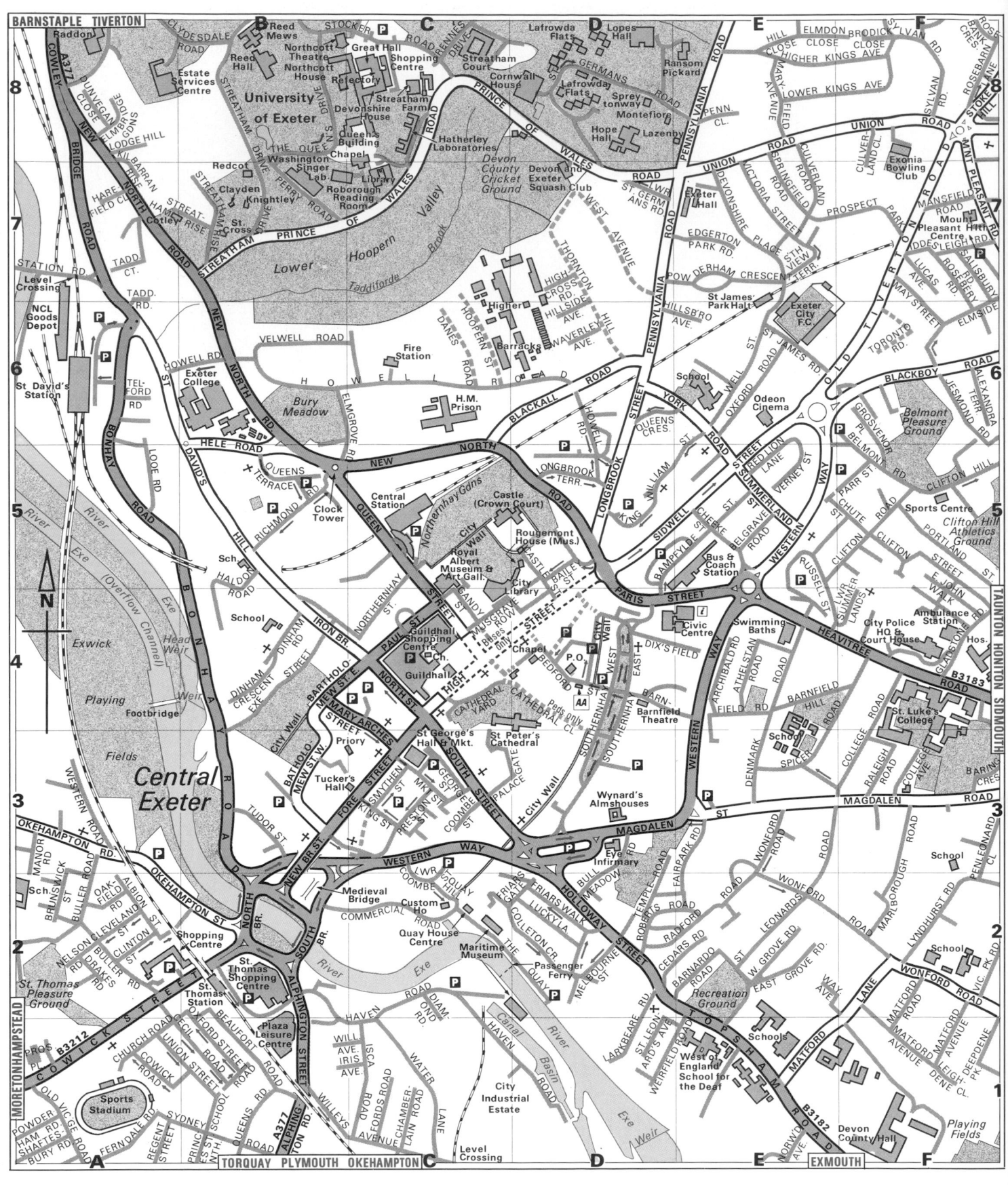

Faccombe Ford

# F

Faccombe *Hants* 23 SU3958
Faceby *N York* 90 NZ4902
Fachwen *Powys* 58 SJ0316
Facit *Lancs* 81 SD8819
Fackley *Notts* 75 SK4761
Faddiley *Ches* 71 SJ5852
Fadmoor *N York* 90 SE6789
Failand *Avon* 34 ST5171
Failford *Strath* 107 NS4626
Failsworth *Gt Man* 79 SD8901
Fain *Highld* 145 NH1379
Fair Oak *Hants* 13 SU4918
Fair Oak Green *Hants* 24 SU6660
Fairbourne *Gwynd* 57 SH6113
Fairburn *N York* 83 SE4727
Fairfield *Derbys* 74 SK0674
Fairfield *H & W* 60 SO9475
Fairfield *Kent* 17 TQ9626
Fairford *Gloucs* 36 SP1501
Fairford Park *Gloucs* 36 SP1501
Fairgirth *D & G* 92 NX8756
Fairhaven *Lancs* 80 SD3228
Fairlie *Strath* 114 NS2154
Fairlight *E Susx* 17 TQ8511
Fairmile *Devon* 9 SY0997
Fairmile *Surrey* 26 TQ1161
Fairnilee *Border* 109 NT4532
Fairoak *Staffs* 72 SJ7632
Fairseat *Kent* 27 TQ6261
Fairstead *Essex* 40 TL7616
Fairwarp *E Susx* 16 TQ4626
Fairwater *S Glam* 33 ST1477
Fairy Cross *Devon* 18 SS4024
Fakenham *Norfk* 66 TF9229
Fakenham Magna *Suffk* 54 TL9076
Fala *Loth* 118 NT4461
Fala Dam *Loth* 118 NT4361
Falcondale *Dyfed* 44 SN5649
Falcut *Nhants* 49 SP5942
Faldingworth *Lincs* 76 TF0684
Faldouet *Jersey* 152 JS0000
Falfield *Gloucs* 35 ST6893
Falkenham *Suffk* 55 TM2939
Falkirk *Cent* 116 NS8880
Falkland *Fife* 126 NO2507
Fallgate *Derbys* 74 SK3561
Fallin *Cent* 116 NS8391
Falloden *Nthumb* 111 NU1922
Fallowfield *Gt Man* 79 SJ8594
Fallowfield *Nthumb* 102 NY9268
Falls of Blarghour *Strath* 122 NM9913
Falmer *E Susx* 15 TQ3509
Falmouth *Cnwll* 3 SW8032
Falnash *Border* 109 NT3906
Falsgrave *N York* 91 TA0287
Falstone *Nthumb* 102 NY7287
Fambridge Station *Essex* 40 TQ8698
Fanagmore *Highld* 148 NC1750
Fancott *Beds* 38 TL0127
Fanellan *Highld* 139 NH4842
Fangdale Beck *N York* 90 SE5694
Fangfoss *Humb* 84 SE7653
Fanmore *Strath* 121 NM4144
Fannich Lodge *Highld* 139 NH2266
Fans *Border* 110 NT6140
Far Bletchley *Bucks* 38 SP8533
Far Cotton *Nhants* 49 SP7459
Far End *Cumb* 101 NY3098
Far Forest *H & W* 60 SO7274
Far Green *Gloucs* 35 SO7700
Far Moor *Gt Man* 78 SD5204
Far Oakridge *Gloucs* 35 SO9203
Far Sawrey *Cumb* 87 SD3795
Far Thorpe *Lincs* 77 TF2673
Farcet *Cambs* 64 TL2094
Farden *Shrops* 46 SO5775
Fareham *Hants* 13 SU5806
Farewell *Staffs* 61 SK0811
Farforth *Lincs* 77 TF3178
Faringdon *Oxon* 36 SU2895
Farington *Lancs* 80 SD5325
Farkhill *Tays* 125 NO0435
Farlam *Cumb* 94 NY5558
Farleigh *Avon* 21 ST4969
Farleigh *Devon* 7 SX7553
Farleigh *Surrey* 27 TQ3760
Farleigh Hungerford *Somset* 22 ST7957
Farleigh Wallop *Hants* 24 SU6246
Farlesthorpe *Lincs* 77 TF4774
Farleton *Cumb* 87 SD5380
Farleton *Lancs* 87 SD5767
Farley *Derbys* 74 SK2962
Farley *Staffs* 73 SK0644
Farley *Wilts* 23 SU2229
Farley Green *Suffk* 53 TL7353
Farley Green *Surrey* 14 TQ0545
Farley Hill *Berks* 24 SU7564
Farleys End *Gloucs* 35 SO7615
Farlington *N York* 90 SE6167
Farlow *Shrops* 59 SO6380
Farm Town *Leics* 62 SK3916
Farmborough *Avon* 21 ST6560
Farmbridge End *Essex* 40 TL6211
Farmcote *Gloucs* 48 SP0629
Farmcote *Shrops* 60 SO7892
Farmers *Dyfed* 44 SN6444
Farmington *Gloucs* 36 SP1315
Farmoor *Oxon* 37 SP4506
Farms Common *Cnwll* 2 SW6734
Farmtown *Gramp* 142 NJ5051
Farnachty *Gramp* 142 NJ4261
Farnah Green *Derbys* 62 SK3347
Farnborough *Berks* 36 SU4381
Farnborough *Gt Lon* 27 TQ4564
Farnborough *Hants* 25 SU8753
Farnborough *Warwks* 49 SP4349
Farnborough *Warwks* 49 SP4349
Farnborough Park *Hants* 25 SU8755
Farnborough Street *Hants* 25 SU8556
Farncombe *Surrey* 25 SU9745
Farndish *Beds* 51 SP9263
Farndon *Ches* 71 SJ4154
Farndon *Notts* 75 SK7651
Farnell *Tays* 127 NO6255
Farnham *Dorset* 11 ST9514
Farnham *Essex* 39 TL4724
Farnham *N York* 89 SE3460
Farnham *Suffk* 55 TM3660
Farnham *Surrey* 25 SU8446
Farnham Common *Bucks* 26 SU9585
Farnham Green *Essex* 39 TL4625
Farnham Royal *Bucks* 26 SU9583
Farningham *Kent* 27 TQ5467
Farnley *N York* 82 SE2147
Farnley *W York* 82 SE2533
Farnley Tyas *W York* 82 SE1612
Farnsfield *Notts* 75 SK6456
Farnworth *Ches* 78 SJ5187
Farnworth *Gt Man* 79 SD7306
Farnworth *Gt Man* 79 SD7306
Farr *Highld* 150 NC7163
Farr *Highld* 140 NH6833
Farr *Highld* 132 NH8203
Farraline *Highld* 139 NH5621
Farringdon *Devon* 9 SY0191
Farrington Gurney *Avon* 21 ST6255
Farsley *W York* 82 SE2135
Farther Howegreen *Essex* 40 TL8401
Farthing Green *Kent* 28 TQ8146
Farthing Street *Gt Lon* 27 TQ4262
Farthinghoe *Nhants* 49 SP5339
Farthingloe *Kent* 29 TR2940
Farthingstone *Nhants* 49 SP6154
Fartown *W York* 82 SE1518
Fartown *W York* 82 SE2232
Farway *Devon* 9 SY1895
Fasnacloich *Strath* 122 NN0247
Fasnakyle *Highld* 139 NH3128
Fasque *Gramp* 135 NO6575
Fassfern *Highld* 130 NN0278
Fatfield *T & W* 96 NZ2954
Faugh *Cumb* 94 NY5154
Fauld *Staffs* 73 SK1728
Faulkbourne *Essex* 40 TL7917
Faulkland *Somset* 22 ST7354
Fauls *Shrops* 59 SJ5932
Faversham *Kent* 28 TR0161
Fawdington *N York* 89 SE4372
Fawdon *Nthumb* 111 NU0315
Fawfieldhead *Staffs* 74 SK0763
Fawkham Green *Kent* 27 TQ5865
Fawler *Oxon* 36 SP3717
Fawley *Berks* 36 SU3981
Fawley *Bucks* 37 SU7586
Fawley *Hants* 13 SU4503
Fawley Chapel *H & W* 46 SO5829
Fawnog *Clwyd* 70 SJ2466
Fawsley *Nhants* 49 SP5656
Faxfleet *Humb* 84 SE8624
Faygate *W Susx* 15 TQ2134
Fazakerley *Mersyd* 78 SJ3797
Fazeley *Staffs* 61 SK2001
Fearby *N York* 89 SE1981
Fearn *Highld* 147 NH8378
Fearnan *Tays* 124 NN7244
Fearnbeg *Highld* 137 NG7359
Fearnhead *Ches* 79 SJ6390
Fearnmore *Highld* 137 NG7260
Fearnoch *Strath* 114 NR9279
Featherstone *Staffs* 60 SJ9305
Featherstone *W York* 83 SE4221
Feckenham *H & W* 47 SP0162
Fedderate *Gramp* 143 NJ8949
Feering *Essex* 40 TL8720
Feetham *N York* 88 SD9898
Feindside *Border* 109 NT4408
Feizor *N York* 88 SD7867
Felbridge *Surrey* 15 TQ3739
Felbrigg *Norfk* 67 TG2039
Felcourt *Surrey* 15 TQ3841
Felday *Surrey* 14 TQ1144
Felden *Herts* 38 TL0404
Felin Fach *Dyfed* 44 SN5255
Felin Gwm Uchaf *Dyfed* 31 SN4034
Felin-gwm Uchaf *Dyfed* 44 SN5024
Felin-newydd *Powys* 45 SO1135
Felindre *Dyfed* 32 SN5521
Felindre *Dyfed* 44 SN5555
Felindre *Dyfed* 44 SN7027
Felindre *Powys* 31 SN1723
Felindre *Powys* 58 SO1681
Felinfach *Powys* 45 SO0933
Felinfoel *Dyfed* 32 SN5202
Felingem Isaf *Dyfed* 44 SN5023
Felixkirk *N York* 89 SE4684
Felixstowe *Suffk* 55 TM3035
Felixstoweferry *Suffk* 55 TM3237
Felkington *Nthumb* 110 NT9444
Felkirk *W York* 83 SE3812
Fell Foot *Cumb* 86 NY2903
Fell Lane *W York* 82 SE0440
Fell Side *Cumb* 93 NY3037
Felling *T & W* 96 NZ2761
Felmersham *Beds* 51 SP9957
Felmingham *Norfk* 67 TG2529
Felpham *W Susx* 14 SZ9599
Felsham *Suffk* 54 TL9457
Felsted *Essex* 40 TL6720
Feltham *Gt Lon* 26 TQ1073
Felthamhill *Gt Lon* 26 TQ0971
Felthorpe *Norfk* 66 TG1618
Felton *Avon* 21 ST5265
Felton *H & W* 46 SO5748
Felton *Nthumb* 103 NU1800
Felton Butler *Shrops* 59 SJ3917
Feltwell *Norfk* 53 TL7190
Fen Ditton *Cambs* 53 TL4860
Fen Drayton *Cambs* 52 TL3368
Fen End *Lincs* 64 TF2420
Fen End *W Mids* 61 SP2274
Fen Street *Norfk* 66 TL9895
Fen Street *Suffk* 54 TM1862
Fenay Bridge *W York* 82 SE1815
Fence *Lancs* 81 SD8237
Fence *S York* 75 SK4485
Fencehouses *T & W* 96 NZ3249
Fencote *N York* 89 SE2893
Fencott *Oxon* 37 SP5716
Fendike Corner *Lincs* 77 TF4560
Fenham *Nthumb* 103 NU0800
Fenham *T & W* 103 NZ2264
Feniscliffe *Lancs* 81 SD6526
Feniscowles *Lancs* 81 SD6425
Feniton *Devon* 9 SY1199
Fenn Green *Shrops* 60 SO7783
Fenn Street *Kent* 28 TQ7975
Fenny Bentley *Derbys* 73 SK1750
Fenny Bridges *Devon* 9 SY1198
Fenny Compton *Warwks* 49 SP4151
Fenny Drayton *Leics* 61 SP3597
Fenny Stratford *Bucks* 38 SP8834
Fenrother *Nthumb* 103 NZ1792
Fenstanton *Cambs* 52 TL3168
Fenstead End *Suffk* 54 TL8050
Fenton *Cambs* 52 TL3279
Fenton *Lincs* 76 SK8476
Fenton *Lincs* 76 SK8751
Fenton *Notts* 75 SK7984
Fenton *Staffs* 72 SJ8944
Fenton Town *Nthumb* 111 NT9734
Fenwick *Nthumb* 111 NU0640
Fenwick *Nthumb* 103 NZ0572
Fenwick *S York* 83 SE5916
Fenwick *Strath* 107 NS4643
Feochaig *Strath* 105 NR7613
Feock *Cnwll* 3 SW8238
Feolin Ferry *Strath* 112 NR4469
Feriniquarrie *Highld* 136 NG1750
Fern *Tays* 134 NO4861
Ferndale *M Glam* 33 SS9996
Ferndown *Dorset* 12 SU0700
Ferness *Highld* 140 NH9645
Fernham *Oxon* 36 SU2991
Fernhill Heath *H & W* 47 SO8659
Fernhurst *W Susx* 14 SU8928
Fernie *Fife* 126 NO3115
Ferniegair *Strath* 116 NS7354
Fernilea *Highld* 136 NG3732
Fernilee *Derbys* 79 SK0178
Ferny Common *H & W* 46 SO3651
Ferriby Sluice *Humb* 84 SE9720
Ferrindonald *Highld* 129 NG6608
Ferring *W Susx* 14 TQ0902
Ferry Point *Highld* 146 NH7385
Ferrybridge *W York* 83 SE4824
Ferryden *Tays* 127 NO7156
Ferryhill *Dur* 96 NZ2932
Ferryside *Dyfed* 31 SN3610
Ferrytown *Highld* 146 NH7387
Fersfield *Norfk* 54 TM0683
Fersit *Highld* 131 NN3577
Fetcham *Surrey* 26 TQ1455
Fetterangus *Gramp* 143 NJ9850
Fettercairn *Gramp* 135 NO6573
Feus *Tays* 126 NO3533
Fewcott *Oxon* 49 SP5328
Fewston *N York* 82 SE1954
Ffair Rhos *Dyfed* 43 SN7368
Ffairfach *Dyfed* 32 SN6220
Ffawyddog *Powys* 33 SO2018
Ffestiniog *Gwynd* 57 SH7042
Ffordd-Las *Clwyd* 70 SJ1264
Fforest *Dyfed* 32 SN5804
Fforest *Gwent* 34 SO2820
Fforest Fach *W Glam* 32 SS6295
Fforest Goch *W Glam* 32 SN7401
Ffostrasol *Dyfed* 42 SN3747
Ffridd Uchaf *Gwynd* 69 SH5751
Ffrith *Clwyd* 70 SJ2855
Ffrwdgrech *Powys* 45 SO0227
Ffynnon-Oer *Dyfed* 44 SN5353
Ffynnongroew *Clwyd* 70 SJ1381
Ffynonddewi *Dyfed* 42 SN3853
Fiag Lodge *Highld* 149 NC4528
Fickleshole *Surrey* 27 TQ3860
Fiddes *Gramp* 135 NO8080
Fiddington *Gloucs* 47 SO9231
Fiddington *Somset* 20 ST2140
Fiddleford *Dorset* 11 ST8013
Fiddlers Green *Cnwll* 3 SW8254
Fiddlers Hamlet *Essex* 27 TL4701
Field *Staffs* 73 SK0233
Field Broughton *Cumb* 87 SD3881
Field Dalling *Norfk* 66 TG0039
Field Head *Leics* 62 SK4909
Fieldhead *Cumb* 93 NY4539
Fife Keith *Gramp* 142 NJ4250
Fifehead Magdalen *Dorset* 22 ST7721
Fifehead Neville *Dorset* 11 ST7610
Fifehead St. Quinton *Dorset* 11 ST7710
Fifield *Berks* 26 SU9076
Fifield *Oxon* 36 SP2318
Fifield *Wilts* 23 SU1450
Figheldean *Wilts* 23 SU1547
Filands *Wilts* 35 ST9388
Filby *Norfk* 67 TG4613
Filey *N York* 91 TA1180
Filgrave *Bucks* 38 SP8648
Filkins *Oxon* 36 SP2304
Filleigh *Devon* 19 SS6628
Filleigh *Devon* 19 SS7410
Fillingham *Lincs* 76 SK9485
Fillongley *Warwks* 61 SP2887
Filmore Hill *Hants* 13 SU6627
Filton *Avon* 34 ST6079
Fimber *Humb* 91 SE8960
Finavon *Tays* 127 NO4956
Fincham *Norfk* 65 TF6806
Finchampstead *Berks* 25 SU7963
Fincharn *Strath* 122 NM9003
Finchdean *Hants* 13 SU7312
Finchingfield *Essex* 40 TL6832
Finchley *Gt Lon* 27 TQ2690
Find O' Gask *Tays* 125 NO0019
Findern *Derbys* 73 SK3030
Findhorn *Gramp* 141 NJ0463
Findhorn Bridge *Highld* 140 NH8027
Findochty *Gramp* 142 NJ4667
Findon *Gramp* 135 NO9397
Findon *W Susx* 14 TQ1208
Findon Mains *Highld* 140 NH6060
Findrack House *Gramp* 134 NJ6004
Finedon *Nhants* 51 SP9172
Fingal Street *Suffk* 55 TM2270
Fingask *Gramp* 142 NJ7827
Fingask *Tays* 126 NO1619
Fingest *Bucks* 37 SU7791
Finghall *N York* 89 SE1789
Fingland *Cumb* 93 NY2557
Fingland *D & G* 107 NS7517
Finglesham *Kent* 29 TR3353
Fingringhoe *Essex* 41 TM0320
Finkle Green *Essex* 53 TL7040
Finkle Street *S York* 74 SK3099
Finlarig *Cent* 124 NN5733
Finmere *Oxon* 49 SP6333
Finnart *Tays* 124 NN5157
Finningham *Suffk* 54 TM0669
Finningley *Notts* 75 SK6699
Finsbay *W Isls* 154 NG0786
Finstall *H & W* 60 SO9870
Finsthwaite *Cumb* 87 SD3687
Finstock *Oxon* 36 SP3616
Finstown *Ork* 155 HY3514
Fintry *Cent* 116 NS6186
Fintry *Gramp* 142 NJ7554
Finzean *Gramp* 134 NO5993
Finzean *Gramp* 134 NO5993
Fionnphort *Strath* 120 NM3023
Fir Tree *Dur* 96 NZ1434
Firbank *Cumb* 87 SD6293
Firbeck *S York* 75 SK5688
Firby *N York* 90 SE7466
Firby *N York* 89 SE2686
Firgrove *Gt Man* 81 SD9113
Firsby *Lincs* 77 TF4562
Fishbourne *IOW* 13 SZ5592
Fishbourne *W Susx* 14 SU8304
Fishburn *Dur* 96 NZ3632
Fishcross *Cent* 116 NS8995
Fisher *W Susx* 14 SU8700
Fisher's Pond *Hants* 13 SU4820
Fisher's Row *Lancs* 80 SD4148
Fisherford *Gramp* 142 NJ6735
Fisherrow *Loth* 118 NT3472
Fisherstreet *W Susx* 14 SU9531
Fisherton *Highld* 140 NH7451
Fisherton *Strath* 106 NS2717
Fisherton de la Mere *Wilts* 22 ST9938
Fishery Estate *Berks* 26 SU8980
Fishguard *Dyfed* 30 SM9637
Fishinghurst *Kent* 28 TQ7537
Fishlake *S York* 83 SE6513
Fishleigh *Devon* 8 SS5405
Fishmere End *Lincs* 64 TF2837
Fishnish Pier *Strath* 121 NM6542
Fishpond Bottom *Dorset* 10 SY3698
Fishponds *Avon* 35 ST6375
Fishpool *Gt Man* 79 SD8009
Fishtoft *Lincs* 64 TF3642
Fishtoft Drove *Lincs* 77 TF3148
Fishtown of Usan *Tays* 127 NO7254
Fishwick *Border* 119 NT9151
Fishwick *Lancs* 81 SD5529
Fiskavaig *Highld* 136 NG3334
Fiskerton *Lincs* 76 TF0472
Fiskerton *Notts* 75 SK7351
Fitling *Humb* 85 TA2534
Fittleton *Wilts* 23 SU1449
Fittleworth *W Susx* 14 TQ0119
Fitton End *Cambs* 65 TF4313
Fitz *Shrops* 59 SJ4418
Fitzhead *Somset* 20 ST1228
Fitzroy *Somset* 20 ST1927
Fitzwilliam *W York* 83 SE4115
Fiunary *Highld* 121 NM6246
Five Acres *Gloucs* 34 SO5712
Five Ash Down *E Susx* 16 TQ4724
Five Ashes *E Susx* 16 TQ5525
Five Bells *Somset* 20 ST0642
Five Bridges *H & W* 47 SO6446
Five Lanes *Gwent* 34 ST4490
Five Oak Green *Kent* 16 TQ6445
Five Oaks *Jersey* 152 JS0000
Five Oaks *W Susx* 14 TQ0928
Five Roads *Dyfed* 32 SN4905
Five Wents *Kent* 28 TQ8050
Fivecrosses *Ches* 71 SJ5376
Fivehead *Somset* 21 ST3522
Fivelanes *Cnwll* 5 SX2280
Fiveways *Warwks* 61 SP2370
Flack's Green *Essex* 40 TL7614
Flackwell Heath *Bucks* 26 SU8990
Fladbury *H & W* 47 SO9946
Fladdabister *Shet* 155 HU4332
Flagg *Derbys* 74 SK1368
Flamborough *Humb* 91 TA2270
Flamstead *Herts* 38 TL0714
Flansham *W Susx* 14 SU9601
Flanshow *W York* 82 SE3020
Flappit Spring *W York* 82 SE0536
Flasby *N York* 82 SD9456
Flash *Staffs* 74 SK0267
Flashader *Highld* 136 NG3453
Flatt *Strath* 116 NS6551
Flatt The *Cumb* 101 NY5678
Flaunden *Herts* 26 TL0100
Flawborough *Notts* 63 SK7842
Flawith *N York* 90 SE4865
Flax Bourton *Avon* 21 ST5069
Flaxby *N York* 89 SE3957
Flaxley *Gloucs* 35 SO6815
Flaxmere *Ches* 71 SJ5672
Flaxpool *Somset* 20 ST1435
Flaxton *N York* 90 SE6762
Fleckney *Leics* 50 SP6493
Flecknoe *Warwks* 49 SP5163
Fledborough *Notts* 75 SK8072
Fleet *Dorset* 10 SY6380
Fleet *Hants* 13 SU7201
Fleet *Hants* 25 SU8053
Fleet *Lincs* 65 TF3923
Fleet Hargate *Lincs* 65 TF3924
Fleetend *Hants* 13 SU5006
Fleetwood *Lancs* 80 SD3348
Flemingston *S Glam* 33 ST0170
Flemington *Strath* 116 NS6559
Flempton *Suffk* 54 TL8169
Fletcher Green *Kent* 16 TQ5349
Fletchersbridge *Cnwll* 4 SX1065
Fletchertown *Cumb* 93 NY2042
Fletching *E Susx* 16 TQ4223
Fleur-de-lis *M Glam* 58 SO1596
Flexbury *Cnwll* 18 SS2107
Flexford *Surrey* 25 SU9350
Flimby *Cumb* 92 NY0233
Flimwell *E Susx* 17 TQ7131
Flint *Clwyd* 70 SJ2472
Flint Mountain *Clwyd* 70 SJ2470
Flint's Green *W Mids* 61 SP2680
Flintham *Notts* 63 SK7445
Flinton *Humb* 85 TA2136
Flitcham *Norfk* 65 TF7326
Flitton *Beds* 38 TL0535
Flitwick *Beds* 38 TL0334
Flixborough *Humb* 84 SE8715
Flixborough Stather *Humb* 84 SE8614
Flixton *Gt Man* 79 SJ7494
Flixton *N York* 91 TA0479
Flixton *Suffk* 55 TM3186
Flockton *W York* 82 SE2314
Flockton Green *W York* 82 SE2614
Flodda *W Isls* 154 NF8455
Flodden *Nthumb* 110 NT9235
Flodigarry *Highld* 136 NG4671
Flookburgh *Cumb* 87 SD3675
Flordon *Norfk* 66 TM1897
Flore *Nhants* 49 SP6460
Flotterton *Nthumb* 103 NT9902
Flowers Green *E Susx* 16 TQ6311
Flowton *Suffk* 54 TM0847
Flushdyke *W York* 82 SE2821
Flushing *Cnwll* 3 SW8034
Fluxton *Devon* 9 SY0892
Flyford Flavell *H & W* 47 SO9854
Fobbing *Essex* 40 TQ7184
Fochabers *Gramp* 141 NJ3458
Fochriw *M Glam* 33 SO1005
Fockerby *Humb* 84 SE8519
Fodderty *Highld* 139 NH5159
Foddington *Somset* 21 ST5829
Foel *Powys* 58 SH9911
Foel y Dyffryn *M Glam* 33 SS8594
Foelgastell *Dyfed* 32 SN5415
Foffarty *Tays* 126 NO4145
Foggathorpe *Humb* 84 SE7537
Fogo *Border* 110 NT7749
Fogwatt *Gramp* 141 NJ2356
Foindle *Highld* 148 NC1948
Folda *Tays* 133 NO1963
Fole *Staffs* 73 SK0437
Foleshill *W Mids* 61 SP3582
Foliejon Park *Berks* 25 SU8974
Folke *Dorset* 11 ST6513
Folkestone *Kent* 29 TR2336
Folkingham *Lincs* 64 TF0733
Folkington *E Susx* 16 TQ5603
Folksworth *Cambs* 52 TL1489
Folkton *N York* 91 TA0579
Folla Rule *Gramp* 142 NJ7332
Follifoot *N York* 83 SE3452
Folly Gate *Devon* 8 SX5797
Folly Hill *Surrey* 25 SU8348
Fonmon *S Glam* 20 ST0467
Font-y-gary *S Glam* 20 ST0566
Fonthill Bishop *Wilts* 22 ST9332
Fonthill Gifford *Wilts* 22 ST9231
Fontmell Magna *Dorset* 11 ST8616
Fontmell Parva *Dorset* 11 ST8214
Fontwell *W Susx* 14 SU9507
Foolow *Derbys* 74 SK1976
Foord *Kent* 29 TR2236
Footbridge *Cumb* 93 NY4148
Foots Cray *Gt Lon* 27 TQ4770
Forbestown *Gramp* 134 NJ3613
Forcett *N York* 89 NZ1712
Ford *Bucks* 37 SP7709

Ford Garton End


Ford Derbys 74 SK4080
Ford Devon 6 SX6150
Ford Devon 7 SX7945
Ford Devon 18 SS4024
Ford Gloucs 48 SP0829
Ford Nthumb 110 NT9437
Ford Shrops 59 SJ4113
Ford Somset 20 ST0928
Ford Somset 21 ST5853
Ford Staffs 73 SK0653
Ford Strath 122 NM8603
Ford W Susx 14 TQ0003
Ford Wilts 35 ST8475
Ford Barton Devon 20 SS9118
Ford End Essex 40 TL6716
Ford Green Lancs 80 SD4746
Ford Heath Shrops 59 SJ4011
Ford Street Somset 20 ST1518
Ford's Green Suffk 54 TM0666
Forda Devon 8 SX5391
Fordcombe Kent 16 TQ5240
Fordell Fife 117 NT1588
Forden Powys 58 SJ2201
Forder Devon 8 SX6789
Forder Green Devon 7 SX7867
Fordham Cambs 53 TL6370
Fordham Essex 41 TL9328
Fordham Norfk 65 TL6199
Fordham Heath Essex 40 TL9426
Fordingbridge Hants 12 SU1413
Fordon Humb 91 TA0475
Fordoun Gramp 135 NO7475
Fordstreet Essex 40 TL9226
Fordton Devon 8 SX8298
Fordwells Oxon 36 SP3014
Fordwich Kent 29 TR1859
Fordyce Gramp 142 NJ5563
Forebridge Staffs 72 SJ9222
Foremark Derbys 62 SK3326
Forest Dur 95 NY8629
Forest Guern 152 GN0000
Forest N York 89 NZ2700
Forest Becks Lancs 81 SD7851
Forest Gate Gt Lon 27 TQ4085
Forest Green Surrey 14 TQ1241
Forest Hall Cumb 87 NY5401
Forest Head Cumb 94 NY5857
Forest Hill Gt Lon 27 TQ3671
Forest Hill Oxon 37 SP5807
Forest Lane Head N York 83 SE3356
Forest Lodge Strath 123 NN2642
Forest Mill Cent 117 NS9694
Forest Moor N York 82 SE2256
Forest Row E Susx 16 TQ4234
Forest Side IOW 13 SZ4889
Forest Town Notts 75 SK5662
Forestburn Gate Nthumb 103 NZ0696
Forestfield Strath 116 NS8566
Forestside W Susx 13 SU7512
Forfar Tays 127 NO4550
Forgandenny Tays 125 NO0818
Forge Powys 57 SN7699
Forge Side Gwent 34 SO2408
Forge-Hammer Gwent 34 ST2895
Forgie Gramp 141 NJ3854
Forgieside Gramp 142 NJ4053
Forgorig Border 110 NT7748
Forhill H & W 61 SP0575
Formby Mersyd 78 SD3007
Forncett End Norfk 66 TM1494
Forncett St. Mary Norfk 66 TM1694
Forncett St. Peter Norfk 66 TM1693
Forneth Tays 126 NO1044
Fornham All Saints Suffk 54 TL8367
Fornham St. Martin Suffk 54 TL8567
Fornside Cumb 93 NY3230
Forres Gramp 141 NJ0358
Forsbrook Staffs 72 SJ9641
Forse Highld 151 ND2234
Forse House Highld 151 ND2135
Forshaw Heath Warwks 61 SP0873
Forsinard Highld 150 NC8943
Forstal The Kent 28 TQ8946
Forston Dorset 11 SY6695
Fort Augustus Highld 131 NH3709
Fort George Highld 140 NH7656
Fort Hommet Guern 152 GN0000
Fort le Marchant Guern 152 GN0000
Fort William Highld 130 NN1074
Forter Tays 133 NO1864
Fortescue Devon 9 SY1388
Forteviot Tays 125 NO0517
Forth Strath 116 NS9453
Forthampton Gloucs 47 SO8532
Fortingall Tays 124 NN7447
Fortnighty Highld 140 NH9350
Forton Hants 24 SU4243
Forton Lancs 80 SD4851
Forton Shrops 59 SJ4216
Forton Somset 10 ST3306
Forton Staffs 72 SJ7521
Fortrose Highld 140 NH7256
Fortuneswell Dorset 11 SY6873
Forty Green Bucks 26 SU9291
Forty Hill Gt Lon 27 TQ3398
Forward Green Suffk 54 TM1060
Fosbury Wilts 23 SU3157
Foscot Oxon 36 SP2421
Foscote Nhants 49 SP6546
Fosdyke Lincs 64 TF3133
Fosdyke Bridge Lincs 64 TF3132
Foss Tays 132 NN7958
Foss-y-ffin Dyfed 42 SN4460
Fossebridge Gloucs 36 SP0811
Foster Street Essex 39 TL4709
Foster Street Essex 39 TL4909
Fosterhouses S York 83 SE6514
Foston Derbys 73 SK1831
Foston Leics 50 SP6094
Foston Lincs 63 SK8542
Foston N York 90 SE6965
Foston on the Wolds Humb 85 TA1055
Fotherby Lincs 77 TF3191
Fothergill Cumb 92 NY0234
Fotheringhay Nhants 51 TL0593
Fotrie Gramp 142 NJ6645
Foul End Warwks 61 SP2494
Foul Mile E Susx 16 TQ6115
Foulby W York 83 SE3917
Foulden Border 119 NT9256
Foulden Norfk 65 TL7699
Foulridge Lancs 81 SD8942
Foulsham Norfk 66 TG0325
Fountainhall Border 118 NT4349
Four Ashes Staffs 60 SO8087
Four Ashes Staffs 60 SJ9108
Four Ashes Suffk 54 TM0070
Four Ashes W Mids 61 SP1575
Four Cabots Guern 61 GN0000
Four Crosses Powys 58 SJ2618
Four Crosses Staffs 60 SJ9509
Four Cabots Guern 152 GN0000
Four Elms Kent 16 TQ4648
Four Foot Somset 21 ST5733
Four Forks Somset 20 ST2336
Four Gates Gt Man 79 SD6507
Four Gotes Cambs 65 TF4516
Four Lane End S York 82 SE2702
Four Lane Ends Ches 71 SJ5661
Four Lanes Cnwll 2 SW6838
Four Marks Hants 24 SU6634
Four Mile Bridge Gwynd 68 SH2778
Four Oaks E Susx 17 TQ8524
Four Oaks Gloucs 47 SO6928
Four Oaks W Mids 61 SP1098
Four Oaks W Mids 61 SP2480
Four Points Berks 37 SU5579
Four Roads Dyfed 32 SN4409
Four Shire Stone Warwks 48 SP2332
Four Throws Kent 17 TQ7729
Four Wents Kent 27 TQ6251
Fourlanes End Ches 72 SJ8059
Fourpenny Highld 147 NH8094
Fourstones Nthumb 102 NY8867
Fovant Wilts 22 SU0028
Foveran Gramp 143 NJ9824
Fowey Cnwll 3 SX1251
Fowley Common Ches 79 SJ6796
Fowlhall Kent 28 TQ6946
Fowlis Tays 126 NO3233
Fowlis Wester Tays 125 NN9324
Fowlmere Cambs 53 TL4245
Fownhope H & W 46 SO5834
Fox Corner Surrey 25 SU9655
Fox Hatch Essex 27 TQ5798
Fox House Inn S York 74 SK2680
Fox Street Essex 41 TM0227
Foxbar Strath 115 NS4561
Foxcombe Devon 5 SX4887
Foxcote Gloucs 35 SP0118
Foxcote Somset 22 ST7155
Foxcotte Hants 23 SU3447
Foxdale IOM 153 SC2778
Foxearth Essex 54 TL8344
Foxendown Kent 28 TQ6666
Foxfield Cumb 86 SD2085
Foxham Wilts 35 ST9777
Foxhills Hants 12 SU3411
Foxhole Cnwll 3 SW9654
Foxhole Highld 139 NH5239
Foxhole W Glam 32 SS6694
Foxholes N York 91 TA0173
Foxhunt Green E Susx 17 TQ5417
Foxley Nhants 49 SP6451
Foxley Norfk 66 TG0321
Foxley Wilts 35 ST8985
Foxley Green Wilts 35 ST8985
Foxlydiate H & W 47 SP0167
Foxt Staffs 73 SK0348
Foxton Cambs 52 TL4148
Foxton Dur 96 NZ3624
Foxton Leics 50 SP7089
Foxton N York 89 SE4295
Foxup N York 88 SD8676
Foxwist Green Ches 71 SJ6268
Foxwood Shrops 47 SO6276
Foy H & W 46 SO5928
Foyers Highld 139 NH4921
Foynesfield Highld 140 NH8855
Fraddam Cnwll 2 SW5834
Fraddon Cnwll 4 SW9158
Fradley Staffs 61 SK1513
Fradswell Staffs 73 SJ9931
Fraisthorpe Humb 91 TA1561
Framfield E Susx 16 TQ4920
Framingham Earl Norfk 67 TG2702
Framingham Pigot Norfk 67 TG2703
Framlingham Suffk 55 TM2863
Frampton Dorset 10 SY6294
Frampton Lincs 64 TF3239
Frampton Cotterell Avon 35 ST6682
Frampton Mansell Gloucs 35 SO9202
Frampton on Severn Gloucs 35 SO7407
Frampton West End Lincs 64 TF2941
Framsden Suffk 55 TM1959
Framwellgate Moor Dur 96 NZ2644
Frances Green Lancs 81 SD6236
Franche H & W 60 SO8178
Frandley Ches 71 SJ6379
Frank's Bridge Powys 45 SO1156
Frankaborough Devon 5 SX3992
Frankby Mersyd 78 SJ2486
Frankfort Norfk 67 TG3024
Franklands Gate H & W 46 SO5346
Frankley H & W 60 SO9980
Frankton Warwks 50 SP4270
Frant E Susx 16 TQ5835
Fraserburgh Gramp 143 NJ9966
Frating Essex 41 TM0822
Frating Green Essex 41 TM0923
Fratton Hants 13 SU6500
Freathy Cnwll 5 SX3952
Freckenham Suffk 53 TL6672
Freckleton Lancs 80 SD4329
Freebirch Derbys 74 SK3173
Freeby Leics 63 SK8020
Freefolk Hants 24 SU4848
Freehay Staffs 73 SK0241
Freeland Oxon 36 SP4112
Freethorpe Norfk 67 TG4005
Freethorpe Common Norfk 67 TG4004
Freiston Lincs 64 TF3743
Fremington Devon 19 SS5132
French Street Kent 27 TQ4652
Frenchay Avon 35 ST6377
Frenchbeer Devon 8 SX6785
Frenich Tays 132 NN8258
Frensham Surrey 25 SU8441
Freshfield Mersyd 78 SD2908
Freshiebridge Highld 132 NH8504
Freshwater IOW 12 SZ3487
Freshwater Bay IOW 12 SZ3485
Fressingfield Suffk 55 TM2677
Freston Suffk 54 TM1739
Freswick Highld 151 ND3667
Fretherne Gloucs 35 SO7210
Frettenham Norfk 67 TG2417
Freuchie Fife 126 NO2806
Freystrop Dyfed 30 SM9511
Friar Waddon Dorset 11 SY6485
Friar's Gate E Susx 16 TQ4933
Friars' Hill N York 90 SE7385
Friday Bridge Cambs 65 TF4605
Friday Street E Susx 16 TQ6203
Friday Street Suffk 55 TM3760
Friday Street Suffk 55 TM2459
Friday Street Suffk 55 TM3352
Friday Street Surrey 14 TQ1245
Fridaythorpe Humb 90 SE8759
Fridaythorpe Humb 90 SE8759
Friden Derbys 74 SK1660
Friendly W York 82 SE0524
Friern Barnet Gt Lon 27 TQ2892
Friesland Bay Strath 120 NM1954
Friesthorpe Lincs 76 TF0683
Frieston Lincs 63 SK9347
Frieth Bucks 37 SU7990
Friezeland Notts 75 SK4750
Frilford Oxon 37 SU4497
Frilsham Berks 24 SU5473
Frimley Surrey 25 SU8758
Frindsbury Kent 28 TQ7369
Fring Norfk 65 TF7334
Fringford Oxon 49 SP6029
Frinsted Kent 28 TQ8957
Frinton-on-Sea Essex 41 TM2320
Friockheim Tays 127 NO5949
Friog Gwynd 57 SH6111
Frisby on the Wreake Leics 63 SK6917
Friskney Lincs 77 TF4655
Friskney Eaudike Lincs 77 TF4755
Friston E Susx 16 TV5598
Friston Suffk 55 TM4160
Fritchley Derbys 74 SK3553
Frith Bank Lincs 77 TF3147
Frith Common H & W 47 SO6969
Fritham Hants 12 SU2413
Frithelstock Devon 18 SS4619
Frithelstock Stone Devon 18 SS4518
Frithend Hants 25 SU8039
Frithsden Herts 38 TL0009
Frithville Lincs 77 TF3150
Frittenden Kent 28 TQ8140
Frittiscombe Devon 7 SX8043
Fritton Norfk 67 TG4700
Fritton Norfk 67 TM2293
Fritwell Oxon 49 SP5229
Frizinghall W York 82 SE1436
Frizington Cumb 92 NY0316
Frocester Gloucs 35 SO7803
Frodesley Shrops 59 SJ5101
Frodsham Ches 71 SJ5177
Frog End Cambs 53 TL5358
Frog End Cambs 52 TL3946
Frog Pool H & W 47 SO8065
Frogbury Devon 8 SS6806
Frogden Border 110 NT7628
Froggatt Derbys 74 SK2476
Froghall Staffs 73 SK0247
Frogham Hants 12 SU1612
Frogham Kent 29 TR2550
Frogmore Devon 7 SX7742
Frognall Lincs 64 TF1610
Frogwell Cnwll 5 SX3468
Frolesworth Leics 50 SP5090
Frome Somset 22 ST7747
Frome St. Quintin Dorset 10 ST5902
Frome Whitfield Dorset 11 SY6991
Fromes Hill H & W 47 SO6846
Fron Gwynd 56 SH3539
Fron Gwynd 68 SH5055
Fron Powys 58 SO1797
Fron Powys 58 SJ2303
Fron Cysyllte Clwyd 70 SJ2740
Fron Isaf Clwyd 70 SJ2740
Fron-goch Gwynd 70 SH9039
Frostenden Suffk 55 TM4881
Frosterley Dur 95 NZ0237
Froxfield Beds 38 SP9733
Froxfield Wilts 23 SU2968
Froxfield Green Hants 13 SU7025
Fryern Hill Hants 13 SU4321
Fryerning Essex 40 TL6300
Fryton N York 90 SE6874
Fulbeck Lincs 76 SK9449
Fulbourn Cambs 53 TL5256
Fulbrook Oxon 36 SP2513
Fulflood Hants 24 SU4730
Fulford N York 83 SE6149
Fulford Somset 20 ST2129
Fulford Staffs 72 SJ9537
Fulham Gt Lon 27 TQ2576
Fulking W Susx 15 TQ2411
Full Sutton Humb 84 SE7455
Fullabrook Devon 19 SS5240
Fullaford Devon 19 SS6838
Fullarton Strath 106 NS3238
Fuller Street Essex 40 TL7416
Fuller Street Kent 27 TQ5656
Fuller's End Essex 39 TL5325
Fuller's Moor Ches 71 SJ4954
Fullerton Hants 23 SU3739
Fulletby Lincs 77 TF2973
Fullready Warwks 48 SP2846
Fullwood Strath 115 NS4450
Fulmer Bucks 26 SU9985
Fulmodeston Norfk 66 TF9931
Fulneck W York 82 SE2232
Fulnetby Lincs 76 TF0979
Fulstone W York 82 SE1709
Fulstow Lincs 77 TF3246
Fulwell Oxon 48 SP3723
Fulwell T & W 96 NZ3959
Fulwood Lancs 80 SD5431
Fulwood Notts 75 SK4757
Fulwood S York 74 SK3085
Fulwood Somset 20 ST2120
Fundenhall Norfk 66 TM1596
Funtington W Susx 14 SU8008
Funtley Hants 13 SU5608
Funtullich Guern 124 NN7526
Furley Devon 10 ST2704
Furnace Dyfed 32 SN5001
Furnace Dyfed 43 SN6895
Furnace Strath 114 NN0200
Furnace End Warwks 61 SP2491
Furnace Vale Derbys 79 SK0083
Furner's Green E Susx 15 TQ4126
Furneux Pelham Herts 39 TL4327
Furnther Quarter Kent 28 TQ8939
Furtho Nhants 49 SP7743
Furze Platt Berks 26 SU8782
Furzehill Devon 19 SS7245
Furzehill Dorset 11 SU0002
Furzehills Lincs 77 TF2572
Furzeley Corner Hants 13 SU6510
Furzley Hants 12 SU2816
Furzley Hants 12 SU2816
Fyfett Somset 9 ST2314
Fyfield Essex 40 TL5707
Fyfield Hants 23 SU2946
Fyfield Hants 23 SU2946
Fyfield Oxon 36 SU4298
Fyfield Wilts 23 SU1760
Fyfield Wilts 23 SU1468
Fyfield Bavant Wilts 22 SU0125
Fyfield Wick Oxon 36 SU4196
Fylingthorpe N York 91 NZ9404
Fyning W Susx 14 SU8124
Fyvie Gramp 142 NJ7637


# G


Gabroc Hill Strath 115 NS4551
Gaddesby Leics 63 SK6813
Gaddesden Row Herts 38 TL0512
Gadfa Gwynd 68 SH4589
Gadlas Shrops 59 SJ3737
Gadoirth Strath 106 NS4022
Gaer Powys 33 SO1721
Gaer-llwyd Gwent 34 ST4496
Gaerwen Gwynd 68 SH4871
Gagingwell Oxon 48 SP4025
Gailes Strath 106 NS3235
Gailey Staffs 60 SJ9110
Gainford Dur 96 NZ1716
Gainsborough Lincs 75 SK8189
Gainsford End Essex 53 TL7335
Gairloch Highld 144 NG8076
Gairlochy Highld 131 NN1784
Gairney Bank Tays 117 NT1299
Gairneybridge Tays 117 NT1397
Gaisby W York 82 SE1536
Gaisland Cent 115 NS5390
Gaitsgill Cumb 93 NY3847
Galashiels Border 109 NT4936
Galby Leics 50 SK6900
Galcantray Highld 140 NH8147
Galgate Lancs 80 SD4855
Galhampton Somset 21 ST6329
Gallaberry D & G 100 NX9682
Gallanach Strath 120 NM2160
Gallanach Strath 122 NM8326
Gallantry Bank Ches 71 SJ5153
Gallatown Fife 117 NT2994
Galley Common Warwks 61 SP3192
Galleywood Essex 40 TL7003
Gallovie Highld 132 NN5589
Gallowfauld Tays 127 NO4342
Gallowhill Tays 126 NO1635
Gallows Green Essex 54 TL9246
Gallows Green H & W 47 SO9363
Gallows Green Staffs 73 SK0741
Gallowstree Common Oxon 37 SU6980
Gallt-y-foel Gwynd 69 SH5862
Galltair Highld 129 NG8120
Gally Hill Hants 25 SU8051
Gallypot Street E Susx 16 TQ4635
Galmisdale Highld 128 NM4784
Galmpton Devon 7 SX6940
Galmpton Devon 7 SX8856
Galphay N York 89 SE2572
Galsgill Cumb 87 NY6305
Galston Strath 107 NS5036
Galtbrook Notts 62 SK4845
Galton Dorset 11 SY7785
Galtrigill Highld 136 NG1854
Gamballs Green Staffs 74 SK0367
Gambles Green Essex 40 TL7615
Gamblesby Cumb 94 NY6039
Gambling Humb 91 TA1057
Gamelsby Cumb 93 NY2552
Gamesley Gt Man 79 SK0194
Gamlingay Cambs 52 TL2452
Gamlingay Cinques Cambs 52 TL2352
Gamlingay Great Heath Beds 52 TL2151
Gammersgill N York 88 SE0582
Gamrie Gramp 143 NJ7962
Gamston Notts 75 SK7076
Ganarew H & W 34 SO5216
Ganavan Bay Strath 122 NM8632
Gang Cnwll 5 SX3068
Ganllwyd Gwynd 57 SH7224
Gannachy Tays 134 NO5970
Ganstead Humb 85 TA1434
Ganthorpe N York 90 SE6870
Ganton N York 91 SE9877
Ganwick Corner Herts 27 TQ2599
Gappah Devon 9 SX8677
Garbat Highld 139 NH4168
Garbity Gramp 141 NJ3052
Garboldisham Norfk 54 TM0081
Garchory Gramp 134 NJ2909
Garden City Clwyd 71 SJ3269
Garden Village Derbys 74 SK2698
Gardeners Green Berks 25 SU8266
Gardenstown Gramp 143 NJ7964
Garderhouse Shet 155 HU3347
Gardham Humb 84 SE9542
Gare Hill Somset 22 ST7840
Garelochhead Strath 114 NS2491
Garenin W Isls 154 NB1944
Garford Oxon 36 SU4296
Garforth W York 83 SE4033
Garforth Bridge W York 83 SE3932
Gargrave N York 81 SD9354
Gargunnock Cent 116 NS7094
Garizim Gwynd 69 SH6975
Garlandhayes Devon 9 ST1716
Garlic Street Norfk 55 TM2183
Garlieston D & G 99 NX4746
Garlinge Kent 29 TR3369
Garlinge Green Kent 29 TR1152
Garlogie Gramp 135 NJ7805
Garmond Gramp 143 NJ8052
Garmondsway Dur 96 NZ3434
Garmony House Strath 121 NM6640
Garmouth Gramp 141 NJ3364
Garmston Shrops 59 SJ6006
Garn Gwynd 56 SH2734
Garn-Dolbenmaen Gwynd 56 SH4944
Garnant Dyfed 32 SN6813
Garnett Bridge Cumb 87 SD5298
Garnkirk Strath 116 NS6768
Garnlydan Gwent 33 SO1612
Garnoch Highld 130 NM8696
Garnswllt W Glam 32 SN6209
Garrabost W Isls 154 NB5133
Garrallan Strath 107 NS5418
Garraron Strath 122 NM8008
Garras Cnwll 2 SW7023
Garreg Gwynd 57 SH6141
Garrigill Cumb 94 NY7441
Garriston N York 89 SE1592
Garroch D & G 99 NX5981
Garrochtrie D & G 98 NX1038
Garrochty Strath 114 NS0953
Garros Highld 136 NG4963
Garsdale Cumb 88 SD7489
Garsdale Head Cumb 88 SD7892
Garsdon Wilts 35 ST9687
Garshall Green Staffs 72 SJ9634
Garsington Oxon 37 SP5802
Garstang Lancs 80 SD4945
Garston Herts 26 TL1100
Garston Mersyd 78 SJ4084
Gartachossan Strath 112 NR3461
Gartcosh Strath 116 NS6968
Garth Clwyd 70 SJ2542
Garth Gwent 34 ST3492
Garth IOM 153 SC3177
Garth M Glam 33 SS8690
Garth Powys 45 SN9549
Garth Powys 46 SO2772
Garth Penrhyncoch Dyfed 43 SN6484
Garth Row Cumb 87 SD5297
Garthbrengy Powys 45 SO0433
Gartheli Dyfed 44 SN5856
Garthmyl Powys 68 SO1999
Garthorpe Humb 84 SE8419
Garthorpe Leics 63 SK8320
Garths Cumb 87 SD5489
Gartly Gramp 142 NJ5232
Gartmore Cent 115 NS5297
Gartnatra Strath 112 NR3260
Gartness Cent 115 NS5086
Gartness Strath 116 NS7864
Gartocharn Strath 115 NS4286
Garton Humb 85 TA2635
Garton End Cambs 64 TF1909

Garton-on-the-Wolds Graims

Garton-on-the-Wolds Humb 91 SE9759
Gartsherrie Strath 116 NS7265
Gartymore Highld 147 ND0114
Garvald Loth 118 NT5870
Garvalt Strath 114 NS0296
Garvan Highld 130 NM9777
Garvard Strath 112 NR3691
Garve Highld 139 NH3961
Garvestone Norfk 66 TG0207
Garvock Strath 114 NS2570
Garway H & W 34 SO4522
Garway Common H & W 34 SO4622
Garway Hill H & W 46 SO4425
Garynahine W Isls 154 NB2331
Gasper Wilts 22 ST7533
Gass Strath 106 NS4105
Gastard Wilts 22 ST8868
Gasthorpe Norfk 54 TL9781
Gaston Green Essex 39 TL4917
Gatcombe IOW 13 SZ4885
Gate Burton Lincs 76 SK8382
Gate Helmsley N York 83 SE6855
Gatebeck Cumb 87 SD5485
Gateford Notts 75 SK5781
Gateforth N York 83 SE5628
Gatehead Strath 106 NS3936
Gatehouse Nthumb 102 NY7989
Gatehouse Strath 113 NR8160
Gatehouse of Fleet D & G 99 NX5956
Gatelawbridge D & G 100 NX9096
Gateley Norfk 66 TF9624
Gatenby N York 89 SE3287
Gates Heath Ches 71 SJ4760
Gatesgarth Cumb 93 NY1925
Gatesgarth Cumb 93 NY1915
Gateshaw Border 110 NT7722
Gateshead T & W 96 NZ2562
Gateside Fife 126 NO1809
Gateside Strath 115 NS4858
Gateside Strath 115 NS3653
Gateside Tays 127 NO4344
Gateslack D & G 108 NS8902
Gathurst Gt Man 78 SD5507
Gatley Gt Man 79 SJ8488
Gatton Surrey 27 TQ2752
Gattonside Border 109 NT5435
Gauldry Fife 126 NO3723
Gauldswell Tays 126 NO2151
Gaulkthorn Lancs 81 SD7526
Gaultree Norfk 65 TF4907
Gaunt's Common Dorset 12 SU0205
Gaunt's End Essex 39 TL5525
Gaunton's Bank Ches 71 SJ5647
Gautby Lincs 76 TF1772
Gavinton Border 119 NT7652
Gawber S York 83 SE3207
Gawcott Bucks 49 SP6831
Gawsworth Ches 79 SJ8969
Gawthorpe W York 82 SE2721
Gawthrop Cumb 87 SD6987
Gawthwaite Cumb 86 SD2784
Gay Bowers Essex 40 TL7904
Gay Street W Susx 14 TQ0820
Gaydon Warwks 48 SP3654
Gayhurst Bucks 38 SP8446
Gayle N York 88 SD8688
Gayles N York 89 NZ1207
Gayton Mersyd 78 SJ2780
Gayton Nhants 49 SP7054
Gayton Norfk 65 TF7219
Gayton Staffs 72 SJ9828
Gayton le Marsh Lincs 77 TF4284
Gayton Thorpe Norfk 65 TF7418
Gaywood Norfk 65 TF6320
Gazeley Suffk 53 TL7264
Gear Cnwll 3 SW7224
Geary Highld 136 NG2661
Gedding Suffk 54 TL9458
Geddinge Kent 29 TR2346
Geddington Nhants 51 SP8983
Gedintailor Highld 137 NG5235
Gedling Notts 62 SK6142
Gedney Lincs 65 TF4024
Gedney Broadgate Lincs 65 TF4022
Gedney Drove End Lincs 65 TF4629
Gedney Dyke Lincs 65 TF4126
Gedney Hill Lincs 64 TF3311
Gee Cross Gt Man 79 SJ9593
Geldeston Norfk 67 TM3991
Gelli Gwent 34 ST2793
Gelli M Glam 33 SS9794
Gelli Gynan Clwyd 70 SJ1854
Gellideg M Glam 33 SO0207
Gellifor Clwyd 70 SJ1262
Gelligaer M Glam 33 ST1397
Gelligroes Gwent 33 ST1794
Gelligron W Glam 32 SN7104
Gellilydan Gwynd 57 SH6839
Gellinudd W Glam 32 SN7304
Gellinudd W Glam 32 SN7303
Gelly Dyfed 31 SN0819
Gellyburn Tays 125 NO0939
Gellywen Dyfed 31 SN2723
Gelston D & G 92 NX7758
Gelston Lincs 63 SK9145
Gentleshaw Staffs 61 SK0511
George Green Bucks 26 TQ0081
George Nympton Devon 19 SS7023
Georgefield D & G 101 NY3091
Georgeham Devon 18 SS4639
Georgetown Gwent 33 SO1508
Georgia Cnwll 2 SW4836
Georth Ork 155 HY3626
Gerlan Gwynd 69 SH6366
Germansweek Devon 5 SX4394
Germoe Cnwll 2 SW5829
Gerrans Cnwll 3 SW8735
Gerrards Cross Bucks 26 TQ0088
Gerrick Cleve 90 NZ7012
Geshader W Isls 154 NB1131
Gestingthorpe Essex 54 TL8138
Geuffordd Powys 58 SJ2114
Geufron Powys 45 SN9968
Gib Hill Ches 79 SJ6478
Gibraltar Lincs 77 TF5558
Gibralter Kent 29 TR2038
Gibsmere Notts 75 SK7248
Giddeahall Wilts 35 ST8674
Giddy Green Dorset 11 SY8286
Gidea Park Gt Lon 27 TQ5290
Gidleigh Devon 8 SX6788
Gidleigh Devon 8 SX6788
Giffnock Strath 115 NS5658
Gifford Loth 118 NT5368
Giffordtown Fife 126 NO2811
Giggleswick N York 88 SD8163
Gilberdyke Humb 84 SE8329
Gilbert Street Hants 24 SU6532
Gilbert's Cross Staffs 60 SO8186
Gilbert's End H & W 47 SO8242
Gilchriston Loth 118 NT4865
Gilcrux Cumb 92 NY1138
Gildersome W York 82 SE2429
Gildingwells S York 75 SK5585
Gilesgate Moor Dur 96 NZ2943
Gileston S Glam 20 ST0167
Gilfach M Glam 33 ST1598
Gilfach M Glam 33 ST1598
Gilfach Goch M Glam 33 SS9890
Gilfachrheda Dyfed 42 SN4159
Gilgarran Cumb 92 NY0323
Gill Cumb 93 NY4429
Gill's Green Kent 17 TQ7532
Gillamore N York 90 SE6890
Gillesbie D & G 100 NY1691
Gilling N York 89 NZ1805
Gilling East N York 90 SE6176
Gillingham Dorset 22 ST8026
Gillingham Kent 28 TQ7768
Gillingham Norfk 67 TM4191
Gillock Highld 151 ND2159
Gillow Heath Staffs 72 SJ8858
Gills Highld 151 ND3272
Gilmanscleuch Border 109 NT3321
Gilmerton Loth 117 NT2968
Gilmerton Tays 125 NN8823
Gilmonby Dur 95 NY9912
Gilmorton Leics 50 SP5787
Gilsland Nthumb 102 NY6366
Gilson Warwks 61 SP1890
Gilstead W York 82 SE1131
Gilston Herts 39 TL4413
Gilwern Gwent 34 SO2414
Gimingham Norfk 67 TG2836
Ginclough Ches 79 SJ9576
Ginger Green E Susx 16 TQ6212
Gipping Suffk 54 TM0763
Gipsey Bridge Lincs 77 TF2849
Girdle Toll Strath 106 NS3440
Girlington W York 82 SE1334
Girlsta Shet 155 HU4250
Girsby Cleve 89 NZ3508
Girtford Beds 52 TL1649
Girthon D & G 99 NX6053
Girton Cambs 53 TL4262
Girton Notts 75 SK8266
Girvan Strath 106 NX1897
Gisburn Lancs 81 SD8248
Gisleham Suffk 55 TM5188
Gislingham Suffk 54 TM0771
Gissing Norfk 54 TM1485
Gittisham Devon 9 SY1398
Gladestry Powys 45 SO2355
Gladsmuir Loth 118 NT4573
Glais W Glam 32 SN7000
Glaisdale N York 90 NZ7705
Glamis Tays 126 NO3846
Glan-Duar Dyfed 44 SN5243
Glan-Mule Powys 58 SO1690
Glan-rhyd W Glam 32 SN7809
Glan-y-don Clwyd 70 SJ1679
Glan-y-llyn M Glam 33 ST1184
Glan-y-nant Powys 58 SN9384
Glan-yr-afon Gwynd 69 SH6080
Glan-yr-afon Gwynd 70 SH9140
Glan-yr-afon Gwynd 70 SJ0142
Glanaber Gwynd 69 SH6350
Glanaber Terrace Gwynd 69 SH7547
Glanafon Dyfed 30 SM9517
Glanaman Dyfed 32 SN6713
Glandford Norfk 66 TG0441
Glandwr Dyfed 31 SN1928
Glandyfi Dyfed 43 SN6996
Glangrwyne Powys 34 SO2416
Glanllynfi M Glam 33 SS8690
Glanrhyd Dyfed 31 SN1442
Glanton Nthumb 111 NU0714
Glanton Pike Nthumb 111 NU0514
Glanvilles Wootton Dorset 11 ST6708
Glapthorn Nhants 51 TL0290
Glapwell Derbys 75 SK4766
Glasbury Powys 45 SO1739
Glascoed Clwyd 70 SH9973
Glascoed Gwent 34 SO3201
Glascote Staffs 61 SK2203
Glascwm Powys 45 SO1552
Glasfryn Clwyd 70 SH9250
Glasgow Strath 115 NS5865
Glasinfryn Gwynd 69 SH5868
Glaslaw Gramp 135 NO8585
Glasnacardoch Bay Highld 129 NM6795
Glasnakille Highld 128 NG5313
Glaspwll Powys 43 SN7397
Glass Houghton W York 83 SE4324
Glassburn Highld 139 NH3634
Glassel Gramp 135 NO6599
Glassel Gramp 135 NO6599
Glassenbury Kent 28 TQ7536
Glasserton D & G 99 NX4237
Glassford Strath 116 NS7247
Glasshouse Gloucs 35 SO7021
Glasshouse Hill Gloucs 35 SO7020
Glasshouses N York 89 SE1764
Glasson Cumb 101 NY2560
Glasson Lancs 80 SD4456
Glassonby Cumb 94 NY5738
Glasterlaw Tays 127 NO5951
Glaston Leics 51 SK8900
Glastonbury Somset 21 ST4938
Glatton Cambs 52 TL1586
Glazebury Ches 79 SJ6797
Glazeley Shrops 60 SO7088
Gleadless Townend Derbys 74 SK3883
Gleadsmoss Ches 79 SJ8168
Gleaston Cumb 86 SD2570
Gledhow W York 82 SE3137
Gleding Notts 62 SK5132
Gledpark D & G 99 NX6250
Gledrid Shrops 59 SJ2936
Glehearn Tays 126 NO1016
Glemanault Strath 104 NR6407
Glemsford Suffk 54 TL8348
Glen D & G 99 NX5457
Glen Auldyn IOM 153 SC4393
Glen Clunie Lodge Gramp 133 NO1383
Glen Nevis House Highld 130 NN1272
Glen of Foudland Gramp 142 NJ6035
Glen of Foudland Gramp 142 NJ6035
Glen Parva Leics 50 SP5798
Glen Trool Lodge D & G 99 NX4080
Glen Village Cent 116 NS8878
Glen Vine IOM 153 SC3378
Glenancross Highld 129 NM6691
Glenaros House Strath 121 NM5544
Glenbarr Strath 105 NR6736
Glenbeg Highld 121 NM5862
Glenbervie Gramp 135 NO7680
Glenboig Strath 116 NS7269
Glenborrodale Highld 121 NM6061
Glenbranter Strath 114 NS1197
Glenbreck Border 108 NT0521
Glenbrittle House Highld 128 NG4121
Glenbuck Strath 107 NS7429
Glencally Tays 134 NO3562
Glencalvie Lodge Highld 146 NH4689
Glencaple D & G 100 NX9968
Glencarron Lodge Highld 138 NH0650
Glencarse Tays 126 NO1922
Glenceitlein Highld 123 NN1548
Glencoe Highld 130 NN1058
Glencothe Border 108 NT0829
Glencraig Fife 117 NT1894
Glencrosh D & G 107 NX7689
Glendaruel Strath 114 NR9983
Glendevon Tays 125 NN9904
Glendoe Lodge Highld 131 NH4009
Glendoik Tays 126 NO2022
Glenduckie Fife 126 NO2818
Gleneagles Tays 125 NN9209
Glenegedale Strath 112 NR3351
Glenelg Highld 129 NG8119
Glenerney Gramp 141 NJ0146
Glenfarg Tays 126 NO1310
Glenfeshie Lodge Highld 132 NN8493
Glenfield Leics 62 SK5306
Glenfinnan Highld 130 NM8980
Glenfinntaig Lodge Highld 131 NN2286
Glenfoot Tays 126 NO1815
Glenfyne Lodge Strath 123 NN2215
Glengarnock Strath 115 NS3252
Glengolly Highld 151 ND1065
Glengorm Castle Strath 121 NM4357
Glengrasco Highld 136 NG4444
Glenholm Border 108 NT1033
Glenhoul D & G 107 NX6187
Glenkerry Border 109 NT2711
Glenkiln D & G 100 NX8477
Glenkin Strath 114 NS1280
Glenkindie Gramp 142 NJ4314
Glenlee D & G 99 NX6080
Glenlochar D & G 99 NX7364
Glenloig Strath 105 NR9435
Glenluce D & G 98 NX1957
Glenmallan Strath 114 NS2595
Glenmark Tays 134 NO4283
Glenmassan Strath 114 NS1087
Glenmavis Strath 116 NS7467
Glenmaye IOM 153 SC2380
Glenmore Highld 136 NG4340
Glenmore Strath 122 NM8412
Glenmore Lodge Highld 133 NH9709
Glenmuirshaw Strath 107 NS6920
Glenquiech Tays 134 NO4266
Glenralloch Strath 113 NR8569
Glenridding Cumb 93 NY3817
Glenrisdell Strath 113 NR8658
Glenrothes Fife 117 NO2700
Glenshero Lodge Highld 132 NN5593
Glenstriven Strath 114 NS0878
Glentham Lincs 76 TF0090
Glentromie Lodge Highld 132 NN7897
Glentrool Village D & G 98 NX3578
Glentruim House Highld 132 NN6894
Glentworth Lincs 76 SK9488
Glenuig Highld 129 NM6676
Glenure Strath 123 NN0448
Glenurquhart Highld 140 NH7462
Glenvarragill Highld 136 NG4739
Glenwhilly D & G 98 NX1771
Glespin Strath 108 NS8128
Glewstone H & W 34 SO5521
Glinton Cambs 64 TF1505
Glooston Leics 50 SP7595
Glororum Nthumb 111 NU1633
Glossop Derbys 74 SK0493
Gloster Hill Nthumb 103 NU2504
Gloucester Gloucs 35 SO8318
Glover's Hill Staffs 73 SK0416
Glusburn N York 82 SE0044
Glutt Lodge Highld 150 ND0036
Gluvian Cnwll 4 SW9164
Glympton Oxon 36 SP4221
Glyn Ceiriog Clwyd 70 SJ2038
Glyn-Neath W Glam 33 SN8806
Glynarthen Dyfed 42 SN3140
Glyncoch M Glam 33 ST0792
Glyncorrwg W Glam 33 SS8799
Glynde E Susx 16 TQ4509
Glyndebourne E Susx 16 TQ4510
Glyndyfrdwy Clwyd 70 SJ1442
Glynn Cnwll 4 SX1165
Glynogwr M Glam 33 SS9585
Glyntaff M Glam 33 ST0889
Glyntawe Powys 33 SN8416
Glynteg Dyfed 31 SN3638
Gnosall Staffs 72 SJ8220
Gnosall Heath Staffs 72 SJ8220
Goadby Leics 50 SP7598
Goadby Marwood Leics 63 SK7826
Goat Lees Kent 28 TR0145
Goatacre Wilts 35 SU0176
Goatfield Strath 114 NN0100
Goatham Green E Susx 17 TQ8120
Goathill Dorset 11 ST6717
Goathland N York 90 NZ8301
Goathurst Somset 20 ST2534
Goathurst Common Kent 27 TQ4952
Gobowen Shrops 59 SJ3033
Godalming Surrey 25 SU9743
Godameavy Devon 6 SX5364
Goddard's Corner Suffk 55 TM2868
Goddard's Green Kent 17 TQ8134
Godford Cross Devon 9 ST1302
Godington Bucks 49 SP6427
Godley Gt Man 79 SJ9595
Godmanchester Cambs 52 TL2470
Godmanstone Dorset 11 SY6697
Godmersham Kent 28 TR0550
Godney Somset 21 ST4842
Godolphin Cross Cnwll 2 SW6031
Godre'r-graig W Glam 32 SN7506
Godshill Hants 12 SU1714
Godshill IOW 13 SZ5281
Godstone Staffs 73 SK0134
Godstone Surrey 27 TQ3551
Godstone Station Surrey 15 TQ3648
Godsworthy Devon 5 SX5277
Godwinscroft Hants 12 SZ1896
Goetre Gwent 34 SO3206
Goff's Oak Herts 39 TL3203
Gogar Loth 117 NT1672
Goginan Dyfed 43 SN6981
Golan Gwynd 57 SH5242
Golant Cnwll 3 SX1254
Golberdon Cnwll 5 SX3271
Golborne Gt Man 78 SJ6097
Golcar W York 82 SE0915
Gold Hill Cambs 65 TL5392
Gold Hill Dorset 11 ST8213
Goldcliff Gwent 34 ST3683
Golden Cross E Susx 16 TQ5312
Golden Green Kent 16 TQ6348
Golden Grove Dyfed 32 SN5919
Golden Hill Dyfed 30 SM9802
Golden Pot Hants 24 SU7043
Golden Valley Derbys 74 SK4251
Goldenhill Staffs 72 SJ8553
Golders Green Gt Lon 26 TQ2487
Goldfinch Bottom Berks 24 SU5063
Goldhanger Essex 40 TL9009
Golding Shrops 59 SJ5403
Goldington Beds 38 TL0750
Golds Green W Mids 60 SO9893
Goldsborough N York 90 NZ8314
Goldsborough N York 83 SE3856
Goldsithney Cnwll 2 SW5430
Goldstone Shrops 72 SJ7028
Goldsworth Surrey 25 SU9958
Goldthorpe S York 83 SE4604
Goldworthy Devon 18 SS3923
Golford Kent 28 TQ7936
Golford Green Kent 28 TQ7936
Gollanfield Highld 140 NH8053
Gollinglith Foot N York 89 SE1480
Golly Clwyd 71 SJ3358
Golsoncott Somset 20 ST0338
Golspie Highld 132 NH8300
Gomeldon Wilts 23 SU1936
Gomersal W York 82 SE2026
Gomshall Surrey 14 TQ0847
Gonachan Cent 116 NS6386
Gonalston Notts 63 SK6747
Gonerby Hill Foot Lincs 63 SK9037
Gonfirth Shet 155 HU3761
Good Easter Essex 40 TL6212
Gooderstone Norfk 65 TF7602
Goodleigh Devon 19 SS6034
Goodmanham Humb 84 SE8842
Goodnestone Kent 28 TR0461
Goodnestone Kent 29 TR2554
Goodrich H & W 34 SO5719
Goodrich Cross H & W 34 SO5619
Goodrington Devon 7 SX8958
Goodshaw Lancs 81 SD8125
Goodshaw Fold Lancs 81 SD8026
Goodstone Devon 7 SX7871
Goodwick Dyfed 30 SM9438
Goodworth Clatford Hants 23 SU3642
Goodyers End Warwks 61 SP3385
Goole Humb 84 SE7423
Goolefields Humb 84 SE7520
Goonbell Cnwll 3 SW7249
Goonhavern Cnwll 3 SW7853
Goonvrea Cnwll 2 SW7149
Goose Green Avon 35 ST6774
Goose Green Essex 41 TM1425
Goose Green Essex 41 TM1425
Goose Green Gt Man 78 SD5603
Goose Green Kent 28 TQ8437
Goose Green Kent 27 TQ6451
Goose Green W Susx 14 TQ1118
Goose Pool H & W 46 SO4636
Goosecruives Gramp 135 NO7583
Goosecruives Gramp 135 NO7583
Gooseford Devon 8 SX6892
Gooseham Cnwll 18 SS2316
Goosehill Green H & W 47 SO9361
Goosemoor Somset 20 SS9635
Goosetrey Ches 79 SJ7770
Goosey Oxon 36 SU3591
Goosnargh Lancs 81 SD5536
Gorddinog Gwynd 69 SH6773
Gordon Border 110 NT6443
Gordon Arms Hotel Border 109 NT3125
Gordonbush Highld 147 NC8409
Gordonstown Gramp 142 NJ5656
Gordonstown Gramp 142 NJ7138
Gore Powys 46 SO2658
Gore Pit Essex 40 TL8719
Gore Street Kent 27 TQ2765
Gorebridge Loth 118 NT3461
Gorefield Cambs 65 TF4112
Gores Wilts 23 SU1158
Gorey Jersey 152 JS0000
Goring Oxon 37 SU6080
Goring Heath Oxon 37 SU6579
Goring-by-Sea W Susx 14 TQ1102
Gorleston on Sea Norfk 67 TG5204
Gorrachie Gramp 142 NJ7358
Gorran Churchtown Cnwll 3 SW9942
Gorran Haven Cnwll 3 SX0141
Gorran High Lanes Cnwll 3 SW9843
Gorrenberry Border 109 NY4699
Gorrowby Hall Humb 90 SE7957
Gors Dyfed 43 SN6277
Gorse Hill Wilts 36 SU1586
Gorsedd Clwyd 70 SJ1576
Gorseinon W Glam 32 SS5998
Gorseybank Derbys 73 SK2953
Gorsgoch Dyfed 44 SN4850
Gorslas Dyfed 32 SN5713
Gorsley Gloucs 47 SO6925
Gorsley Common Gloucs 47 SO6225
Gorsley Green Ches 79 SJ8469
Gorst Hill H & W 60 SO7473
Gorstage Ches 71 SJ6172
Gorstan Highld 139 NH3863
Gorstello Ches 71 SJ3562
Gorsty Common H & W 46 SO4437
Gorsty Hill Staffs 73 SK1029
Gorten Strath 122 NM7432
Gorton Gt Man 79 SJ8896
Gosbeck Suffk 54 TM1555
Gosberton Lincs 64 TF2331
Gosberton Clough Lincs 64 TF1929
Gosfield Essex 40 TL7829
Gosford Devon 4 SX1197
Gosforth Cumb 86 NY0603
Gosforth T & W 103 NZ2467
Gosland Green Ches 71 SJ5758
Gosling Street Somset 21 ST5633
Gosmore Herts 39 TL1827
Gospel End Staffs 60 SO8993
Gospel Green W Susx 14 SU9331
Gosport Hants 13 SZ6199
Gossard Green Beds 38 SP9643
Goswick Nthumb 111 NU0645
Gotham Notts 62 SK5330
Gotherington Gloucs 47 SO9629
Gotton Somset 20 ST2428
Goudhurst Kent 28 TQ7237
Goulceby Lincs 77 TF2579
Gourdas Gramp 142 NJ7741
Gourdie Tays 126 NO3532
Gourdon Gramp 135 NO8271
Gourock Strath 114 NS2477
Govan Strath 115 NS5465
Goveton Devon 7 SX7546
Govilon Gwent 34 SO2614
Gowdall Humb 83 SE6122
Gower Highld 139 NH5058
Gowerton W Glam 32 SS5896
Gowkhall Fife 117 NT0589
Gowthorpe Humb 84 SE7654
Goxhill Humb 85 TA1021
Goxhill Humb 85 TA1844
Graby Lincs 64 TF0929
Grade Cnwll 2 SW7114
Gradeley Green Ches 71 SJ5851
Graffham W Susx 14 SU9217
Grafham Cambs 52 TL1669
Grafham Surrey 14 TQ0241
Grafton H & W 46 SO5761
Grafton H & W 46 SO4936
Grafton H & W 47 SO9837
Grafton H & W 46 SO5761
Grafton N York 89 SE4163
Grafton Oxon 36 SP2600
Grafton Shrops 59 SJ4319
Grafton Flyford H & W 47 SO9656
Grafton Regis Nhants 49 SP7546
Grafton Underwood Nhants 51 SP9280
Grafty Green Kent 28 TQ8748
Graianrhyd Clwyd 70 SJ2156
Graig Clwyd 70 SJ0872
Graig Gwynd 69 SH8071
Graig-fechan Clwyd 70 SJ1454
Grains Kent 28 TQ8876

Graims Bar
Gussage St Michael

Grains Bar *Gt Man* 79 SD9608
Grains o'the Beck Bridge *Dur* 95 NY8621
Grainsby *Lincs* 77 TF2799
Grainthorpe *Lincs* 77 TF3896
Gramisdale *W Isls* 154 NF8155
Grampound *Cnwll* 3 SW9348
Grampound Road *Cnwll* 3 SW9150
Gramsdale *W Isls* 154 NF8255
Granborough *Bucks* 49 SP7625
Granby *Notts* 63 SK7536
Grand Chemins *Jersey* 152 JS0000
Grandborough *Warwks* 50 SP4967
Grandes Rocques *Guern* 152 GN0000
Grandtully *Tays* 125 NN9153
Grange *Cumb* 93 NY2517
Grange *Kent* 28 TQ7968
Grange *Mersyd* 78 SJ2286
Grange *Tays* 126 NO2625
Grange Crossroads *Gramp* 142 NJ4754
Grange Gate *Dorset* 11 SY9182
Grange Hall *Gramp* 141 NJ0660
Grange Hill *Gt Lon* 27 TQ4492
Grange Lindores *Fife* 126 NO2516
Grange Moor *W York* 82 SE2216
Grange Villa *Dur* 96 NZ2352
Grange-over-Sands *Cumb* 87 SD4077
Grangehall *Strath* 108 NS9642
Grangemill *Derbys* 74 SK2457
Grangemouth *Cent* 116 NS9282
Grangepans *Cent* 117 NT0181
Grangetown *Cleve* 97 NZ5420
Gransmoor *Humb* 91 TA1259
Gransmore Green *Essex* 40 TL6922
Granston *Dyfed* 30 SM8934
Grantchester *Cambs* 53 TL4355
Grantham *Lincs* 63 SK9135
Granton *Fife* 117 NT2277
Grantown-on-Spey *Highld* 141 NJ0328
Grantsfield *H & W* 46 SO5360
Grantshouse *Border* 119 NT8165
Grappenhall *Ches* 79 SJ6486
Grasby *Lincs* 85 TA0804
Grasmere *Cumb* 86 NY3307
Grass Green *Essex* 53 TL7338
Grasscroft *Gt Man* 82 SD9704
Grassendale *Mersyd* 78 SJ3985
Grassgartin *Cumb* 93 NY3444
Grassington *N York* 88 SE0063
Grassmoor *Derbys* 74 SK4067
Grassthorpe *Notts* 75 SK7967
Grateley *Hants* 23 SU2742
Gratwich *Staffs* 73 SK0231
Graveley *Cambs* 52 TL2564
Graveley *Herts* 39 TL2327
Gravelly Hill *W Mids* 61 SP1090
Gravelsbank *Shrops* 59 SJ3600
Graveney *Kent* 28 TR0562
Gravesend *Kent* 27 TQ6474
Gravir *W Isls* 154 NB3715
Grayingham *Lincs* 76 SK9396
Grayrigg *Cumb* 87 SD5796
Grays *Essex* 27 TQ6177
Grayshott *Hants* 14 SU8735
Grayswood *Surrey* 14 SU9134
Graythorpe *Cleve* 97 NZ5227
Grazeley *Berks* 24 SU6966
Grazies Hill *Oxon* 37 SU7980
Greasbrough *S York* 74 SK4195
Greasby *Mersyd* 78 SJ2587
Greasley *Notts* 62 SK4947
Great Abington *Cambs* 53 TL5348
Great Addington *Nhants* 51 SP9675
Great Alne *Warwks* 48 SP1259
Great Altcar *Lancs* 78 SD3306
Great Amwell *Herts* 39 TL3712
Great Asby *Cumb* 94 NY6713
Great Ashfield *Suffk* 54 TL9967
Great Ayton *N York* 90 NZ5510
Great Baddow *Essex* 40 TL7305
Great Badminton *Avon* 35 ST8082
Great Bardfield *Essex* 40 TL6730
Great Barford *Beds* 52 TL1352
Great Barr *W Mids* 61 SP0495
Great Barrington *Gloucs* 36 SP2013
Great Barrow *Ches* 71 SJ4768
Great Barton *Suffk* 54 TL8967
Great Barugh *N York* 90 SE7478
Great Bavington *Nthumb* 102 NY9880
Great Bealings *Suffk* 55 TM2349
Great Bedwyn *Wilts* 23 SU2764
Great Bentley *Essex* 41 TM1021
Great Billing *Nhants* 51 SP8162
Great Bircham *Norfk* 65 TF7732
Great Blakenham *Suffk* 54 TM1150
Great Bolas *Shrops* 72 SJ6421
Great Bookham *Surrey* 26 TQ1354
Great Bosullow *Cnwll* 2 SW4133
Great Bourton *Oxon* 49 SP4545
Great Bowden *Leics* 50 SP7488
Great Bradley *Suffk* 53 TL6753
Great Braxted *Essex* 40 TL8614
Great Bricett *Suffk* 54 TM0350
Great Brickhill *Bucks* 38 SP9030
Great Bridge *W Mids* 60 SO9792
Great Bridgeford *Staffs* 72 SJ8827
Great Brington *Nhants* 50 SP6665
Great Bromley *Essex* 41 TM0826
Great Broughton *Cumb* 92 NY0731
Great Broughton *N York* 90 NZ5405
Great Budworth *Ches* 79 SJ6677
Great Burdon *Dur* 96 NZ3116
Great Burstead *Essex* 40 TQ6892
Great Busby *N York* 90 NZ5205
Great Canfield *Essex* 40 TL5918
Great Carlton *Lincs* 77 TF4085
Great Casterton *Leics* 63 TF0009
Great Chart *Kent* 28 TQ9741
Great Chatfield *Wilts* 22 ST8663
Great Chatwell *Staffs* 60 SJ7914
Great Chell *Staffs* 72 SJ8752
Great Chesterford *Essex* 39 TL5042
Great Cheverell *Wilts* 22 ST9858
Great Chishill *Cambs* 39 TL4238
Great Clacton *Essex* 41 TM1716
Great Cliffe *W York* 82 SE3015
Great Clifton *Cumb* 92 NY0429
Great Coates *Humb* 85 TA2309
Great Comberton *H & W* 47 SO9542
Great Comp *Kent* 27 TQ6356
Great Corby *Cumb* 93 NY4754
Great Cornard *Suffk* 54 TL8840
Great Cowden *Humb* 85 TA2342
Great Coxwell *Oxon* 36 SU2693
Great Cransley *Nhants* 51 SP8376
Great Cressingham *Norfk* 66 TF8501
Great Crosthwaite *Cumb* 93 NY2624
Great Cubley *Derbys* 73 SK1638
Great Dalby *Leics* 63 SK7414
Great Doddington *Nhants* 51 SP8864
Great Doward *H & W* 34 SO5416
Great Driffield *Humb* 91 TA0257
Great Dunham *Norfk* 66 TF8714
Great Dunmow *Essex* 40 TL6222
Great Durnford *Wilts* 23 SU1338
Great Easton *Essex* 40 TL6025
Great Easton *Leics* 51 SP8493
Great Eccleston *Lancs* 80 SD4240
Great Ellingham *Norfk* 66 TM0196
Great Elm *Somset* 22 ST7449
Great Englebourne *Devon* 7 SX7756
Great Everdon *Nhants* 49 SP5957
Great Eversden *Cambs* 52 TL3653
Great Finborough *Suffk* 54 TM0158
Great Fransham *Norfk* 66 TF8913
Great Gaddesden *Herts* 38 TL0211
Great Gidding *Cambs* 52 TL1183
Great Givendale *Humb* 84 SE8153
Great Glemham *Suffk* 55 TM3361
Great Glen *Leics* 50 SP6597
Great Gonerby *Lincs* 63 SK8938
Great Gransden *Cambs* 52 TL2655
Great Green *Cambs* 39 TL2844
Great Green *Norfk* 55 TM2889
Great Green *Suffk* 54 TL9365
Great Green *Suffk* 54 TL9156
Great Habton *N York* 90 SE7576
Great Hale *Lincs* 64 TF1442
Great Hallingbury *Essex* 39 TL5119
Great Hanwood *Shrops* 59 SJ4409
Great Harrowden *Nhants* 51 SP8770
Great Harwood *Lancs* 81 SD7332
Great Haseley *Oxon* 37 SP6401
Great Hatfield *Humb* 85 TA1842
Great Haywood *Staffs* 73 SJ9922
Great Heck *N York* 83 SE5921
Great Henny *Essex* 54 TL8637
Great Hinton *Wilts* 22 ST9058
Great Hockham *Norfk* 66 TL9592
Great Holland *Essex* 41 TM2019
Great Horkesley *Essex* 41 TL9731
Great Hormead *Herts* 39 TL4030
Great Horton *W York* 82 SE1411
Great Horwood *Bucks* 49 SP7731
Great Houghton *Nhants* 50 SP7958
Great Houghton *S York* 83 SE4206
Great Hucklow *Derbys* 74 SK1777
Great Kelk *Humb* 91 TA1058
Great Kimble *Bucks* 38 SP8206
Great Kingshill *Bucks* 26 SU8797
Great Langdale *Cumb* 86 NY2906
Great Langton *N York* 89 SE2996
Great Leighs *Essex* 40 TL7217
Great Limber *Lincs* 85 TA1308
Great Linford *Bucks* 38 SP8542
Great Livermere *Suffk* 54 TL8871
Great Longstone *Derbys* 74 SK1971
Great Lumley *T & W* 96 NZ2949
Great Lyth *Shrops* 59 SJ4507
Great Malvern *H & W* 47 SO7845
Great Maplestead *Essex* 54 TL8134
Great Marton *Lancs* 80 SD3235
Great Massingham *Norfk* 66 TF7923
Great Melton *Norfk* 66 TG1206
Great Meols *Mersyd* 78 SJ2390
Great Milton *Oxon* 37 SP6202
Great Missenden *Bucks* 26 SP8901
Great Mitton *Lancs* 81 SD7138
Great Mongeham *Kent* 29 TR3551
Great Moulton *Norfk* 54 TM1690
Great Munden *Herts* 39 TL3524
Great Ness *Shrops* 59 SJ3919
Great Nurcott *Somset* 20 SS9036
Great Oak *Gwent* 34 SO3809
Great Oakley *Essex* 41 TM1927
Great Oakley *Nhants* 51 SP8686
Great Offley *Herts* 38 TL1427
Great Ormside *Cumb* 94 NY7017
Great Orton *Cumb* 93 NY3254
Great Ouseburn *N York* 89 SE4461
Great Oxendon *Nhants* 50 SP7383
Great Oxney Green *Essex* 40 TL6606
Great Pattenden *Kent* 28 TQ7345
Great Paxton *Cambs* 52 TL2063
Great Plumpton *Lancs* 80 SD3833
Great Plumstead *Norfk* 67 TG3010
Great Ponton *Lincs* 63 SK9230
Great Potheridge *Devon* 19 SS5114
Great Preston *W York* 83 SE4029
Great Purston *Nhants* 49 SP5139
Great Raveley *Cambs* 52 TL2581
Great Rissington *Gloucs* 36 SP1917
Great Rollright *Oxon* 48 SP3231
Great Rudbaxton *Dyfed* 30 SM9620
Great Ryburgh *Norfk* 66 TF9527
Great Ryle *Nthumb* 111 NU0212
Great Ryton *Shrops* 59 SJ4803
Great Saling *Essex* 40 TL7026
Great Salkeld *Cumb* 94 NY5436
Great Sampford *Essex* 53 TL6435
Great Sankey *Ches* 78 SJ5688
Great Saredon *Staffs* 60 SJ9508
Great Saughall *Ches* 71 SJ3669
Great Saxham *Suffk* 53 TL7862
Great Shefford *Berks* 36 SU3875
Great Shelford *Cambs* 53 TL4652
Great Smeaton *N York* 89 NZ3404
Great Snoring *Norfk* 66 TF9434
Great Somerford *Wilts* 35 ST9682
Great Soudley *Shrops* 72 SJ7229
Great Stainton *Dur* 96 NZ3322
Great Stambridge *Essex* 40 TQ8992
Great Staughton *Cambs* 52 TL1264
Great Steeping *Lincs* 77 TF4364
Great Stoke *Avon* 35 ST6280
Great Stonar *Kent* 29 TR3359
Great Strickland *Cumb* 94 NY5522
Great Stukeley *Cambs* 52 TL2274
Great Sturton *Lincs* 76 TF2176
Great Sutton *Ches* 71 SJ3775
Great Sutton *Shrops* 59 SO5183
Great Swinburne *Nthumb* 102 NY9375
Great Tew *Oxon* 48 SP3929
Great Tey *Essex* 40 TL8925
Great Torrington *Devon* 18 SS4919
Great Tosson *Nthumb* 103 NU0200
Great Totham *Essex* 40 TL8611
Great Totham *Essex* 40 TL8713
Great Tows *Lincs* 76 TF2290
Great Urswick *Cumb* 86 SD2674
Great Wakering *Essex* 40 TQ9487
Great Waldingfield *Suffk* 54 TL9144
Great Walsingham *Norfk* 66 TF9437
Great Waltham *Essex* 40 TL6913
Great Warley *Essex* 27 TQ5890
Great Washbourne *Gloucs* 47 SO9834
Great Weeke *Devon* 8 SX7187
Great Weldon *Nhants* 51 SP9289
Great Welnetham *Suffk* 54 TL8859
Great Wenham *Suffk* 54 TM0738
Great Whittington *Nthumb* 103 NZ0070
Great Wigborough *Essex* 41 TL9615
Great Wilbraham *Cambs* 53 TL5557
Great Wishford *Wilts* 23 SU0835
Great Witchingham *Norfk* 66 TG1020
Great Witcombe *Gloucs* 35 SO9114
Great Witley *H & W* 47 SO7566
Great Wolford *Warwks* 48 SP2534
Great Wratting *Essex* 53 TL6848
Great Wymondley *Herts* 39 TL2128
Great Wyrley *Staffs* 60 SJ9907
Great Wytheford *Shrops* 59 SJ5719
Great Yarmouth *Norfk* 67 TG5207
Great Yeldham *Essex* 53 TL7638
Greatfield *Wilts* 36 SU0785
Greatford *Lincs* 64 TF0811
Greatgate *Staffs* 73 SK0540
Greatham *Cleve* 97 NZ4927
Greatham *Hants* 14 SU7730
Greatham *W Susx* 14 TQ0415
Greatstone-on-Sea *Kent* 17 TR0822
Greatworth *Nhants* 49 SP5542
Grebby *Lincs* 77 TF4368
Green Bank *Cumb* 101 NY3780
Green Cross *Surrey* 14 SU8634
Green Down *Somset* 21 ST5753
Green End *Beds* 51 TL1063
Green End *Beds* 51 TL0864
Green End *Beds* 38 TL0147
Green End *Beds* 52 TL1252
Green End *Cambs* 53 TL4668
Green End *Cambs* 53 TL4861
Green End *Cambs* 52 TL2274
Green End *Cambs* 52 TL3856
Green End *Herts* 39 TL3333
Green End *Herts* 39 TL3122
Green End *Herts* 39 TL2630
Green End *Warwks* 61 SP2686
Green Hammerton *N York* 83 SE4656
Green Head *Cumb* 93 NY3649
Green Heath *Staffs* 60 SJ9913
Green Hill *Nthumb* 95 NY8647
Green Hill *Wilts* 36 SU0686
Green Hills *Cambs* 53 TL6072
Green Lane *Devon* 8 SX7877
Green Lane *H & W* 48 SP0665
Green Moor *S York* 74 SK2899
Green Oak *Humb* 84 SE8127
Green Ore *Somset* 21 ST5749
Green Quarter *Cumb* 87 NY4603
Green Street *E Susx* 17 TQ7611
Green Street *Gloucs* 35 SO8915
Green Street *H & W* 47 SO8749
Green Street *Herts* 39 TL4521
Green Street *Herts* 26 TQ1998
Green Street *W Susx* 15 TQ1522
Green Street Green *Gt Lon* 27 TQ4563
Green Street Green *Kent* 27 TQ5870
Green The *Cumb* 86 SD1784
Green Tye *Herts* 39 TL4418
Greenburn *Loth* 116 NS9360
Greencroft *Norfk* 66 TG0243
Greencroft Hall *Dur* 96 NZ1549
Greenend *Oxon* 36 SP3221
Greenfield *Beds* 38 TL0534
Greenfield *Clwyd* 70 SJ1977
Greenfield *Gt Man* 82 SD9904
Greenfield *Highld* 131 NH2000
Greenfield *Oxon* 37 SU7191
Greenfield *Strath* 114 NS2490
Greenford *Gt Lon* 26 TQ1482
Greengairs *Strath* 116 NS7870
Greengates *W York* 82 SE1937
Greenhalgh *Lancs* 80 SD4035
Greenham *Berks* 24 SU4865
Greenham *Somset* 20 ST0719
Greenhaugh *Nthumb* 102 NY7987
Greenhead *Nthumb* 102 NY6565
Greenhey *Gt Man* 79 SD7104
Greenhill *Cent* 116 NS8279
Greenhill *D & G* 100 NY1079
Greenhill *H & W* 47 SO7248
Greenhill *Kent* 29 TR1666
Greenhill *S York* 74 SK3481
Greenhill *Strath* 108 NS9333
Greenhillocks *Derbys* 74 SK4049
Greenhithe *Kent* 27 TQ5875
Greenholm *Strath* 107 NS5437
Greenholme *Cumb* 87 NY5905
Greenhouse *Border* 109 NT5624
Greenhow Hill *N York* 89 SE1164
Greenland *Highld* 151 ND2367
Greenland *S York* 74 SK3988
Greenlands *Bucks* 37 SU7785
Greenlaw *Border* 110 NT7146
Greenlea *D & G* 100 NY0375
Greenloaning *Tays* 125 NN8307
Greenmoor Hill *Oxon* 37 SU6481
Greenmount *Gt Man* 81 SD7714
Greenock *Strath* 115 NS2776
Greenodd *Cumb* 86 SD3182
Greens Norton *Nhants* 49 SP6649
Greensgate *Norfk* 66 TG1015
Greenside *T & W* 96 NZ1362
Greenside *W York* 82 SE1616
Greenstead *Essex* 41 TM0125
Greenstead Green *Essex* 40 TL8227
Greensted *Essex* 39 TL5303
Greenstreet Green *Suffk* 54 TM0450
Greenway *Gloucs* 47 SO7032
Greenway *H & W* 60 SO7470
Greenway *S Glam* 33 ST0574
Greenway *Somset* 21 ST3124
Greenwich *Gt Lon* 27 TQ3877
Greet *Gloucs* 48 SP0230
Greete *Shrops* 46 SO5771
Greetham *Leics* 63 SK9214
Greetham *Lincs* 77 TF3070
Greetland *W York* 82 SE0821
Gregson Lane *Lancs* 81 SD5926
Greinton *Somset* 21 ST4136
Grenaby *IOM* 153 SC2672
Grendon *Nhants* 51 SP8760
Grendon *Warwks* 61 SP2799
Grendon Green *H & W* 46 SO5957
Grendon Underwood *Bucks* 37 SP6820
Grenofen *Devon* 6 SX5671
Grenofen *Devon* 6 SX4971
Grenoside *S York* 74 SK3394
Gresford *Clwyd* 71 SJ3454
Gresham *Norfk* 66 TG1638
Greshornish *Highld* 136 NG3454
Gressenhall *Norfk* 66 TF9615
Gressenhall Green *Norfk* 66 TF9616
Gressingham *Lancs* 87 SD5769
Grestey Green *Ches* 72 SJ7054
Greta Bridge *Dur* 95 NZ0813
Gretna *D & G* 101 NY3167
Gretna Green *D & G* 101 NY3268
Gretton *Gloucs* 47 SP0030
Gretton *Nhants* 51 SP8994
Gretton *Shrops* 59 SO5195
Grewelthorpe *N York* 89 SE2376
Grey Friars *Suffk* 55 TM4770
Grey Green *Humb* 84 SE7807
Grey's Green *Oxon* 37 SU7183
Greygarth *N York* 89 SE1872
Greylake *Somset* 21 ST3833
Greyrigg *D & G* 100 NY0889
Greyson Green *Cumb* 92 NX9925
Greysouthen *Cumb* 92 NY0729
Greysouthern *Cumb* 92 NY0629
Greystoke *Cumb* 93 NY4330
Greystone *Tays* 127 NO5343
Greywell *Hants* 24 SU7151
Gribb *Dorset* 10 ST3703
Gribthorpe *Humb* 84 SE7635
Griff *Warwks* 61 SP3689
Griffithstown *Gwent* 34 ST2999
Griffydam *Leics* 62 SK4118
Grigghall *Cumb* 87 SD4691
Griggs Green *Hants* 14 SU8231
Grimeford Village *Lancs* 81 SD6112
Grimethorpe *S York* 83 SE4109
Grimley *H & W* 47 SO8360
Grimmet *Strath* 106 NS3210
Grimoldby *Lincs* 77 TF3988
Grimpo *Shrops* 59 SJ3526
Grimsargh *Lancs* 81 SD5834
Grimsby *Humb* 85 TA2710
Grimscote *Nhants* 49 SP6553
Grimscott *Cnwll* 18 SS2607
Grimshader *W Isls* 154 NB4026
Grimshaw *Lancs* 81 SD7024
Grimshaw Green *Lancs* 80 SD4912
Grimsthorpe *Lincs* 64 TF0422
Grimston *Humb* 85 TA2735
Grimston *Leics* 63 SK6821
Grimston *Norfk* 65 TF7222
Grimston Hill *Notts* 75 SK6865
Grimstone *Dorset* 10 SY6393
Grimstone End *Suffk* 54 TL9368
Grinacombe Moor *Devon* 5 SX4191
Grindale *Humb* 91 TA1271
Grindle *Shrops* 60 SJ7503
Grindleford *Derbys* 74 SK2477
Grindleton *Lancs* 81 SD7545
Grindley Brook *Shrops* 71 SJ5242
Grindlow *Derbys* 74 SK1878
Grindon *Cleve* 96 NZ3925
Grindon *Nthumb* 110 NT9144
Grindon *Staffs* 73 SK0854
Grindonrigg *Nthumb* 110 NT9243
Gringley on the Hill *Notts* 75 SK7390
Grinsdale *Cumb* 93 NY3758
Grinshill *Shrops* 59 SJ5223
Grinton *N York* 88 SE0498
Grishipoll *Strath* 120 NM1959
Grisling Common *E Susx* 16 TQ4422
Gristhorpe *N York* 91 TA0881
Griston *Norfk* 66 TL9499
Gritley *Ork* 155 HY5604
Grittenham *Wilts* 36 SU0382
Grittleton *Wilts* 35 ST8580
Grizebeck *Cumb* 86 SD2384
Grizedale *Cumb* 86 SD3394
Groby *Leics* 62 SK5207
Groes *Clwyd* 70 SJ0064
Groes *W Glam* 32 SS7986
Groes-faen *M Glam* 33 ST0680
Groes-Wen *M Glam* 33 ST1286
Groesffordd *Gwynd* 56 SH2739
Groesffordd Marli *Clwyd* 70 SJ0073
Groeslon *Gwynd* 68 SH4755
Groeslon *Gwynd* 68 SH5260
Grogport *Strath* 105 NR8044
Gromford *Suffk* 55 TM3858
Gronant *Clwyd* 70 SJ0883
Groom's Hill *H & W* 47 SP0154
Groombridge *E Susx* 16 TQ5337
Grosebay *W Isls* 154 NG1592
Grosmont *Gwent* 46 SO4024
Grosmont *N York* 90 NZ8305
Grossington *Gloucs* 35 SO7302
Groton *Suffk* 54 TL9641
Grotton *Gt Man* 79 SD9604
Grouville *Jersey* 152 JS0000
Grove *Bucks* 38 SP9122
Grove *Dorset* 11 SY6972
Grove *Dyfed* 30 SM9900
Grove *Kent* 29 TR2362
Grove *Notts* 75 SK7379
Grove *Oxon* 36 SU4090
Grove Green *Kent* 28 TQ7856
Grove Park *Gt Lon* 27 TQ4072
Grove Vale *W Mids* 61 SP0394
Grovenhurst *Kent* 28 TQ7140
Grovesend *Avon* 35 ST6489
Grovesend *W Glam* 32 SN5900
Grubb Street *Kent* 27 TQ5869
Gruesllwyd *Powys* 58 SJ2111
Gruids *Highld* 146 NC5603
Gruinard *Highld* 144 NG9489
Gruinart Flats *Strath* 112 NR2866
Grula *Highld* 136 NG3826
Gruline *Strath* 121 NM5440
Grumbla *Cnwll* 2 SW4029
Grundisburgh *Suffk* 55 TM2251
Gruting *Shet* 155 HU2849
Gualachulain *Highld* 123 NN1145
Gualin House *Highld* 148 NC3056
Guanockgate *Lincs* 64 TF3710
Guardbridge *Fife* 127 NO4518
Guarlford *H & W* 47 SO8145
Guay *Tays* 125 NO0049
Guestling Green *E Susx* 17 TQ8513
Guestling Thorn *E Susx* 17 TQ8516
Guestwick *Norfk* 66 TG0627
Guide *Lancs* 81 SD7025
Guide Bridge *Gt Man* 70 SH9297
Guide Post *T & W* 103 NZ2585
Guilden Down *Shrops* 59 SO3083
Guilden Morden *Cambs* 39 TL2744
Guilden Sutton *Ches* 71 SJ4468
Guildford *Surrey* 25 SU9949
Guildstead *Kent* 28 TQ8262
Guildtown *Tays* 126 NO1331
Guilreehill *Strath* 106 NS3610
Guilsborough *Nhants* 50 SP6772
Guilsfield *Powys* 58 SJ2211
Guilton *Kent* 29 TR2858
Guineaford *Devon* 19 SS5537
Guisborough *Cleve* 97 NZ6115
Guiseley *W York* 82 SE1942
Guist *Norfk* 66 TF9925
Guiting Power *Gloucs* 48 SP0924
Gullane *Loth* 118 NT4882
Gulling Green *Suffk* 54 TL8356
Gulval *Cnwll* 2 SW4831
Gulworthy *Devon* 6 SX4572
Gumfreston *Dyfed* 31 SN1101
Gumley *Leics* 50 SP6890
Gummow's Shop *Cnwll* 4 SW8657
Gun Green *Kent* 17 TQ7731
Gun Hill *E Susx* 16 TQ5614
Gun Hill *Warwks* 61 SP2889
Gunby *Humb* 84 SE7135
Gunby *Lincs* 63 SK9121
Gunby *Lincs* 77 TF4667
Gundleton *Hants* 24 SU6133
Gunn *Devon* 19 SS6333
Gunnerside *N York* 88 SD9598
Gunnerton *Nthumb* 102 NY9074
Gunness *Humb* 84 SE8411
Gunnislake *Devon* 6 SX4371
Gunnista *Shet* 155 HU5043
Gunthorpe *Cambs* 64 TF1803
Gunthorpe *Norfk* 66 TG0134
Gunthorpe *Notts* 63 SK6844
Gunton *Suffk* 67 TM5395
Gunville *IOW* 13 SZ4889
Gupworthy *Somset* 20 SS9735
Gurnard *IOW* 13 SZ4795
Gurnett *Ches* 79 SJ9271
Gurney Slade *Somset* 21 ST6249
Gurnos *W Glam* 32 SN7709
Gushmere *Kent* 28 TR0457
Gussage All Saints *Dorset* 11 SU0010
Gussage St. Michael *Dorset* 11 ST9811

Guston Harwich


Guston *Kent* 29 TR3244
Gutcher *Shet* 155 HU5499
Guthrie *Tays* 127 NO5650
Guy's Marsh *Dorset* 22 ST8420
Guyhirn *Cambs* 65 TF4003
Guyhirn Gull *Cambs* 65 TF3903
Guyzance *Nthumb* 103 NU2104
Gwaenysgor *Clwyd* 70 SJ0780
Gwalchmai *Gwynd* 68 SH3876
Gwastadnant *Gwynd* 69 SH6157
Gwaun-Cae-Gurwen *W Glam* 32 SN7011
Gwbert-on-Sea *Dyfed* 42 SN1649
Gwealavellan *Cnwll* 2 SW5942
Gwealeath *Cnwll* 2 SW6922
Gweek *Cnwll* 2 SW7026
Gwehelog *Gwent* 34 SO3804
Gwenddwr *Powys* 45 SO0643
Gwendreath *Cnwll* 3 SW7216
Gwennap *Cnwll* 3 SW7340
Gwenter *Cnwll* 3 SW7417
Gwern-y-Steeple *S Glam* 33 ST0775
Gwernaffield *Clwyd* 70 SJ2065
Gwernesney *Gwent* 34 SO4101
Gwernogle *Dyfed* 44 SN5334
Gwernymynydd *Clwyd* 70 SJ2162
Gwersyllt *Clwyd* 71 SJ3153
Gwespyr *Clwyd* 70 SJ1183
Gwindra *Cnwll* 3 SW9552
Gwinear *Cnwll* 2 SW5937
Gwithian *Cnwll* 2 SW5841
Gwredog *Gwynd* 68 SH4086
Gwrhay *Gwent* 33 ST1899
Gwyddelwern *Clwyd* 70 SJ0746
Gwyddgrug *Dyfed* 44 SN4635
Gwynfryn *Clwyd* 70 SJ2552
Gwystre *Powys* 45 SO0665
Gwytherin *Clwyd* 69 SH8761
Gyfelia *Clwyd* 71 SJ3245
Gyrn-goch *Gwynd* 68 SH4048


# H


Habberley *H & W* 60 SO8176
Habberley *Shrops* 59 SJ3903
Habergham *Lancs* 81 SD8033
Habertoft *Lincs* 77 TF5069
Habin *W Susx* 14 SU8022
Habrough *Humb* 85 TA1413
Haccombe *Devon* 7 SX8970
Hacconby *Lincs* 64 TF1025
Haceby *Lincs* 64 TF0236
Hacheston *Suffk* 55 TM3059
Hack Green *Ches* 72 SJ6448
Hackenthorpe *S York* 74 SK4183
Hackford *Norfk* 66 TG0502
Hackforth *N York* 89 SE2493
Hackland *Ork* 155 HY3920
Hackleton *Nhants* 51 SP8055
Hacklinge *Kent* 29 TR3454
Hackman's Gate *H & W* 60 SO8978
Hackness *N York* 91 SE9790
Hackness *Somset* 21 ST3345
Hackney *Gt Lon* 27 TQ3484
Hackthorn *Lincs* 76 SK9982
Hackthorpe *Cumb* 94 NY5323
Hacton *Gt Lon* 27 TQ5585
Hadden *Border* 110 NT7836
Haddenham *Bucks* 37 SP7308
Haddenham *Cambs* 53 TL4675
Haddington *Lincs* 76 SK9163
Haddington *Loth* 118 NT5173
Haddiscoe *Norfk* 67 TM4497
Haddo *Gramp* 143 NJ8337
Haddon *Cambs* 64 TL1392
Hade Edge *W York* 82 SE1404
Hademore *Staffs* 61 SK1708
Hadfield *Derbys* 74 SK0296
Hadham Cross *Herts* 39 TL4218
Hadham Ford *Herts* 39 TL4321
Hadleigh *Essex* 40 TQ8187
Hadleigh *Suffk* 54 TM0242
Hadleigh Heath *Suffk* 54 TL9941
Hadley *H & W* 47 SO8664
Hadley *Shrops* 60 SJ6712
Hadley End *Staffs* 73 SK1320
Hadley Wood *Gt Lon* 27 TQ2698
Hadlow *Kent* 27 TQ6350
Hadlow Down *E Susx* 16 TQ5324
Hadnall *Shrops* 59 SJ5220
Hadstock *Essex* 53 TL5644
Hadzor *H & W* 47 SO9162
Haffenden Quarter *Kent* 28 TQ8840
Hafod-y-bwch *Clwyd* 71 SJ3147
Hafod-y-coed *Gwent* 34 SO2200
Hafodunos *Clwyd* 69 SH8667
Hafodyrynys *Gwent* 34 ST2299
Hafodyrynys *Gwent* 34 ST2499
Haggate *Lancs* 81 SD8735
Haggbeck *Cumb* 101 NY4774
Haggerston *Nthumb* 111 NU0443
Haggington Hill *Devon* 19 SS5547
Haggs *Cent* 116 NS7979
Hagley *H & W* 46 SO5641
Hagley *H & W* 60 SO9181
Hagnaby *Lincs* 77 TF3462
Hagworthingham *Lincs* 77 TF3469
Haigh *Gt Man* 78 SD6009
Haighton Green *Lancs* 81 SD5634
Hail Weston *Cambs* 52 TL1662
Haile *Cumb* 86 NY0308
Hailes *Gloucs* 48 SP0430
Hailey *Herts* 39 TL3710
Hailey *Oxon* 37 SU6485
Hailsham *E Susx* 16 TQ5909
Hainault *Gt Lon* 27 TQ4591
Haine *Kent* 29 TR3566
Hainford *Norfk* 67 TG2318
Hainton *Lincs* 76 TF1784
Hainworth *W York* 82 SE0639
Haisthorpe *Humb* 91 TA1264
Hakin *Dyfed* 30 SM8905
Halam *Notts* 75 SK6754
Halbeath *Fife* 117 NT1289
Halberton *Devon* 9 ST0012
Halcro *Highld* 151 ND2360
Hale *Ches* 78 SJ4782
Hale *Cumb* 87 SD5078
Hale *Gt Man* 79 SJ7786
Hale *Hants* 12 SU1919
Hale *Somset* 22 ST7527
Hale *Surrey* 25 SU8448
Hale Bank *Ches* 78 SJ4884
Hale Green *E Susx* 16 TQ5514
Hale Nook *Lancs* 80 SD3944
Hale Street *Kent* 28 TQ6749
Halebarns *Gt Man* 79 SJ7985
Hales *Norfk* 67 TM3897
Hales *Staffs* 72 SJ7134
Hales Green *Derbys* 73 SK1841
Hales Place *Kent* 29 TR1459
Halesgate *Lincs* 64 TF3226
Halesowen *W Mids* 60 SO9683
Halesworth *Suffk* 55 TM3877
Halewood *Mersyd* 78 SJ4585
Halewood Green *Mersyd* 78 SJ4486
Half Penny *Cumb* 87 SD5387
Halford *Shrops* 59 SO4383
Halford *Warwks* 48 SP2545
Halford Blackpool *Devon* 7 SX8175
Halfpenny Green *Staffs* 60 SO8291
Halfpenny Houses *N York* 89 SE2284
Halfway *Berks* 24 SU4068
Halfway *Dyfed* 44 SN6430
Halfway *Powys* 44 SN8332
Halfway *S York* 75 SK4381
Halfway Bridge *W Susx* 14 SU9322
Halfway House *Shrops* 59 SJ3411
Halfway Houses *Kent* 28 TQ9372
Halifax *W York* 82 SE0925
Halistra *Highld* 136 NG2459
Halket *Strath* 115 NS4252
Halkirk *Highld* 151 ND1359
Halkyn *Clwyd* 70 SJ2171
Hall *Strath* 115 NS4154
Hall Cliffe *W York* 82 SE2918
Hall cross *Lancs* 80 SD4230
Hall Dunnerdale *Cumb* 86 SD2195
Hall End *Beds* 38 TL0737
Hall End *Beds* 38 TL0045
Hall End *W Mids* 60 SP0092
Hall Green *Ches* 72 SJ8356
Hall Green *W Mids* 61 SP1181
Hall's Green *Essex* 39 TL4108
Hall's Green *Herts* 39 TL2728
Hallam Fields *Derbys* 62 SK4739
Halland *E Susx* 16 TQ4916
Hallaton *Leics* 50 SP7896
Hallatrow *Avon* 21 ST6356
Hallbankgate *Cumb* 94 NY5859
Hallbeck *Cumb* 87 SD6288
Hallen *Avon* 34 ST5480
Hallfield Gate *Derbys* 74 SK3958
Hallgarth *Dur* 96 NZ3343
Hallin *Highld* 136 NG2558
Halling *Kent* 28 TQ7063
Hallington *Lincs* 77 TF3085
Hallington *Nthumb* 102 NY9875
Hallins *Derbys* 74 SK3371
Halliwell *Gt Man* 79 SD6910
Halloughton *Notts* 75 SK6951
Hallow *H & W* 47 SO8258
Hallow Heath *H & W* 47 SO8259
Hallrule *Border* 110 NT5914
Hallsands *Devon* 7 SX8138
Hallthwaites *Cumb* 86 SD1785
Halltoft End *Lincs* 64 TF3645
Hallworthy *Cnwll* 4 SX1887
Hallyne *Border* 109 NT1940
Halmer End *Staffs* 72 SJ7949
Halmond's Frome *H & W* 47 SO6647
Halmore *Gloucs* 35 SO6902
Halnaker *W Susx* 14 SU9008
Halsall *Lancs* 78 SD3710
Halse *Nhants* 49 SP5640
Halse *Somset* 20 ST1428
Halsetown *Cnwll* 2 SW5038
Halsham *Humb* 85 TA2627
Halsinger *Devon* 19 SS5138
Halstead *Essex* 40 TL8130
Halstead *Kent* 27 TQ4961
Halstead *Leics* 63 SK7505
Halstock *Dorset* 10 ST5308
Halsway *Somset* 20 ST1338
Haltham *Lincs* 77 TF2463
Halton *Bucks* 38 SP8710
Halton *Ches* 78 SJ5481
Halton *Clwyd* 71 SJ3039
Halton *Lancs* 87 SD5064
Halton *Nthumb* 103 NY9967
Halton *W York* 83 SE3533
Halton East *N York* 82 SE0454
Halton Fenside *Lincs* 77 TF4263
Halton Gill *N York* 88 SD8876
Halton Green *Lancs* 87 SD5165
Halton Holegate *Lincs* 77 TF4165
Halton Lea Gate *Nthumb* 94 NY6458
Halton Quay *M Glam* 5 SX4165
Halton Shields *Nthumb* 103 NZ0168
Halton West *N York* 81 SD8454
Haltwhistle *Nthumb* 102 NY7064
Halvergate *Norfk* 67 TG4207
Halwell *Devon* 7 SX7753
Halwill *Devon* 5 SX4392
Halwill *Devon* 18 SX4299
Halwill Junction *Devon* 18 SS4400
Ham *Devon* 9 ST2301
Ham *Gloucs* 35 ST6898
Ham *Gloucs* 35 SO9721
Ham *Gt Lon* 26 TQ1772
Ham *Kent* 29 TR3354
Ham *Somset* 20 ST2825
Ham *Somset* 22 ST6748
Ham *Wilts* 23 SU3262
Ham Common *Dorset* 22 ST8125
Ham Green *Avon* 34 ST5375
Ham Green *H & W* 47 SO7444
Ham Green *H & W* 47 SP0164
Ham Green *Kent* 17 TQ8926
Ham Green *Kent* 28 TQ8468
Ham Hill *Kent* 28 TQ6960
Ham Street *Somset* 21 ST5534
Hamble *Hants* 13 SU4806
Hambleden *Bucks* 37 SU7886
Hambledon *Hants* 13 SU6415
Hambledon *Surrey* 25 SU9638
Hambleton *Lancs* 80 SD3742
Hambleton *N York* 83 SE5430
Hambleton Moss Side *Lancs* 80 SD3842
Hambridge *Somset* 21 ST5936
Hambridge *Somset* 21 ST3921
Hambrook *Avon* 35 ST6378
Hambrook *W Susx* 14 SU7806
Hamels *Herts* 39 TL3724
Hameringham *Lincs* 77 TF3067
Hamerton *Cambs* 52 TL1379
Hamilton *Strath* 116 NS7255
Hamlet *Dorset* 10 ST5908
Hamlins *E Susx* 16 TQ5909
Hammerpot *W Susx* 14 TQ0705
Hammersmith *Gt Lon* 26 TQ2378
Hammerwich *Staffs* 61 SK0607
Hammerwood *E Susx* 16 TQ4339
Hammond Street *Herts* 39 TL3304
Hammoon *Dorset* 11 ST8114
Hamnavoe *Shet* 155 HU3735
Hamnavoe *Shet* 155 HU4971
Hampden Park *E Susx* 16 TQ6002
Hampden Row *Bucks* 26 SP8501
Hamperden End *Essex* 40 TL5730
Hampnett *Gloucs* 36 SP0915
Hampole *S York* 83 SE5010
Hampreston *Dorset* 12 SZ0598
Hampsfield *Cumb* 87 SD4080
Hampson Green *Lancs* 80 SD4954
Hampstead *Gt Lon* 27 TQ2685
Hampstead Norrey's *Berks* 37 SU5276
Hampsthwaite *N York* 89 SE2558
Hampt *M Glam* 5 SX3974
Hampton *Devon* 5 SX2696
Hampton *Gt Lon* 26 TQ1369
Hampton *H & W* 48 SP0243
Hampton *Kent* 29 TR1568
Hampton *Shrops* 60 SO7486
Hampton *Wilts* 36 SU1892
Hampton Bishop *H & W* 46 SO5537
Hampton Green *Ches* 71 SJ5140
Hampton Green *Ches* 71 SJ5149
Hampton Heath *Ches* 71 SJ4949
Hampton in Arden *W Mids* 61 SP2081
Hampton Loade *Shrops* 60 SO7486
Hampton Lovett *H & W* 47 SO8865
Hampton Lucy *Warwks* 48 SP2557
Hampton on the Hill *Warwks* 48 SP2564
Hampton Poyle *Oxon* 37 SP5015
Hampton Wick *Gt Lon* 26 TQ1769
Hamptworth *Wilts* 12 SU2419
Hamrow *Norfk* 66 TF9124
Hamsey *E Susx* 15 TQ4012
Hamsey Green *Gt Lon* 27 TQ3760
Hamstall Ridware *Staffs* 73 SK1019
Hamstead *IOW* 13 SZ4091
Hamstead *W Mids* 61 SP0592
Hamstead Marshall *Berks* 24 SU4165
Hamsterley *Dur* 95 NZ1131
Hamsterley *Dur* 95 NZ1156
Hamstreet *Kent* 17 TR0034
Hamwood *Avon* 21 ST3756
Hanbury *H & W* 47 SO9664
Hanbury *Staffs* 73 SK1727
Hanby *Lincs* 64 TF0231
Hanchet End *Suffk* 53 TL6446
Hanchurch *Staffs* 72 SJ8441
Hand and Pen *Devon* 9 SY0495
Hand Green *Ches* 71 SJ5460
Handale *Cleve* 97 NZ7215
Handbridge *Ches* 71 SJ4065
Handcross *W Susx* 15 TQ2629
Handforth *Ches* 79 SJ8583
Handley *Ches* 71 SJ4657
Handley *Derbys* 74 SK3761
Handley Green *Essex* 40 TL6601
Handsacre *Staffs* 73 SK0916
Handsworth *S York* 74 SK4186
Handsworth *W Mids* 61 SP0589
Handy Cross *Bucks* 26 SU8490
Hanford *Dorset* 11 ST8410
Hanford *Staffs* 72 SJ8642
Hanging Langford *Wilts* 23 SU0237
Hangleton *E Susx* 15 TQ2607
Hangleton *W Susx* 14 TQ0803
Hanham *Avon* 35 ST6372
Hankelow *Ches* 72 SJ6745
Hankerton *Wilts* 35 ST9690
Hankham *E Susx* 16 TQ6105
Hanley *Staffs* 72 SJ8847
Hanley Castle *H & W* 47 SO8342
Hanley Child *H & W* 47 SO6565
Hanley Swan *H & W* 47 SO8143
Hanley William *H & W* 47 SO6766
Hanlith *N York* 88 SD8960
Hanmer *Clwyd* 71 SJ4540
Hannaford *Devon* 19 SS6029
Hannah *Lincs* 77 TF4979
Hannington *Hants* 24 SU5455
Hannington *Nhants* 51 SP8170
Hannington *Wilts* 36 SU1793
Hannington Wick *Wilts* 36 SU1795
Hanscombe End *Beds* 38 TL1133
Hanslope *Bucks* 38 SP8046
Hanthorpe *Lincs* 64 TF0823
Hanwell *Gt Lon* 26 TQ1579
Hanwell *Oxon* 49 SP4343
Hanworth *Gt Lon* 26 TQ1271
Hanworth *Norfk* 67 TG1935
Happendon *Strath* 108 NS8533
Happisburgh *Norfk* 67 TG3831
Happisburgh Common *Norfk* 67 TG3729
Hapsford *Ches* 71 SJ4774
Hapton *Lancs* 81 SD7931
Hapton *Norfk* 66 TM1796
Harberton *Devon* 7 SX7758
Harbertonford *Devon* 7 SX7856
Harbledown *Kent* 29 TR1357
Harborne *W Mids* 60 SP0284
Harborough Magna *Warwks* 50 SP4778
Harborough Parva *Warwks* 50 SP4778
Harbottle *Nthumb* 102 NT9304
Harbours Hill *H & W* 47 SO9566
Harbridge *Hants* 12 SU1409
Harbridge Green *Hants* 12 SU1411
Harburn *Loth* 117 NT0462
Harbury *Warwks* 48 SP3760
Harby *Leics* 63 SK7431
Harby *Notts* 76 SK8770
Harcombe *Devon* 9 SX8881
Harcombe *Devon* 9 SY1590
Harcombe Bottom *Devon* 10 SY3395
Harden *W Mids* 60 SK0101
Harden *W York* 82 SE0838
Hardenhuish *Wilts* 35 ST9074
Hardgate *Gramp* 135 NJ7901
Hardgate *N York* 89 SE2662
Hardgate *Strath* 115 NS5073
Hardham *W Susx* 14 TQ0317
Hardhorn *Lancs* 80 SD3537
Hardingham *Norfk* 66 TG0403
Hardings Wood *Staffs* 72 SJ8254
Hardingstone *Nhants* 49 SP7657
Hardington *Somset* 22 ST7452
Hardington Mandeville *Somset* 10 ST5111
Hardington Marsh *Somset* 10 ST5009
Hardington Moor *Somset* 10 ST5212
Hardley *Hants* 13 SU4205
Hardley Street *Norfk* 67 TG3801
Hardmead *Bucks* 38 SP9347
Hardraw *N York* 88 SD8691
Hardsough *Lancs* 81 SD7920
Hardstoft *Derbys* 75 SK4463
Hardway *Hants* 13 SU6101
Hardway *Somset* 22 ST7134
Hardwick *Bucks* 38 SP8019
Hardwick *Cambs* 52 TL3758
Hardwick *Lincs* 76 SK8675
Hardwick *Nhants* 51 SP8469
Hardwick *Norfk* 55 TM2290
Hardwick *Oxon* 36 SP3706
Hardwick *Oxon* 49 SP5729
Hardwick *S York* 75 SK4885
Hardwick *W Mids* 61 SP0798
Hardwick Green *H & W* 47 SO8133
Hardwicke *Gloucs* 35 SO7912
Hardwicke *Gloucs* 47 SO9027
Hardy's Green *Essex* 40 TL9320
Hare Croft *W York* 82 SE0835
Hare Green *Essex* 41 TM1025
Hare Hatch *Berks* 37 SU8077
Hare Street *Essex* 27 TL5300
Hare Street *Essex* 39 TL4209
Hare Street *Herts* 39 TL3929
Harebeating *E Susx* 16 TQ5910
Hareby *Lincs* 77 TF3365
Harefield *Gt Lon* 26 TQ0590
Harehill *Derbys* 73 SK1735
Harehills *W York* 82 SE3135
Harehope *Nthumb* 111 NU0920
Harelaw *Border* 109 NT5323
Harelaw *Dur* 96 NZ1552
Hareplain *Kent* 28 TQ8140
Haresceugh *Cumb* 94 NY6043
Harescombe *Gloucs* 35 SO8310
Haresfield *Gloucs* 35 SO8110
Harestock *Hants* 24 SU4631
Harewood *W York* 83 SE3245
Harewood End *H & W* 46 SO5227
Harford *Devon* 6 SX6359
Hargate *Norfk* 66 TM1291
Hargatewell *Derbys* 74 SK1274
Hargrave *Ches* 71 SJ4862
Hargrave *Nhants* 51 TL0370
Hargrave *Suffk* 53 TL7760
Hargrave Green *Suffk* 53 TL7759
Harker *Cumb* 101 NY3960
Harkstead *Suffk* 54 TM1834
Harlaston *Staffs* 61 SK2110
Harlaxton *Lincs* 63 SK8832
Harle Syke *Lancs* 81 SD8635
Harlech *Gwynd* 57 SH5831
Harlescott *Shrops* 59 SJ5115
Harlesden *Gt Lon* 26 TQ2383
Harlesthorpe *Derbys* 75 SK4976
Harleston *Devon* 7 SX7945
Harleston *Norfk* 55 TM2483
Harleston *Suffk* 54 TM0160
Harlestone *Nhants* 49 SP7064
Harley *S York* 74 SK3698
Harley *Shrops* 59 SJ5901
Harleyholm *Strath* 108 NS9238
Harlington *Beds* 38 TL0330
Harlington *Gt Lon* 26 TQ0877
Harlington *S York* 83 SE4802
Harlosh *Highld* 136 NG2841
Harlow *Herts* 39 TL4711
Harlow Hill *Nthumb* 103 NZ0768
Harlthorpe *Humb* 84 SE7337
Harlton *Cambs* 52 TL3852
Harlyn Bay *Cnwll* 4 SW8775
Harman's Cross *Dorset* 11 SY9880
Harmby *N York* 89 SE1289
Harmer Green *Herts* 39 TL2515
Harmer Hill *Shrops* 59 SJ4822
Harmondsworth *Gt Lon* 26 TQ0577
Harmston *Lincs* 76 SK9762
Harnage *Shrops* 59 SJ5604
Harnham *Nthumb* 103 NZ0781
Harnhill *Gloucs* 36 SP0600
Harold Hill *Gt Lon* 27 TQ5392
Harold Wood *Gt Lon* 27 TQ5590
Haroldston West *Dyfed* 30 SM8615
Haroldswick *Shet* 155 HP6312
Harome *N York* 90 SE6481
Harpenden *Herts* 38 TL1314
Harpford *Devon* 9 SY0890
Harpham *Humb* 91 TA0961
Harpley *H & W* 47 SO6861
Harpley *Norfk* 65 TF7825
Harpole *Nhants* 49 SP6961
Harpsdale *Highld* 151 ND1355
Harpsden *Oxon* 37 SU7680
Harpswell *Lincs* 76 SK9389
Harpur Hill *Derbys* 74 SK0671
Harpurhey *Gt Man* 79 SD8501
Harraby *Cumb* 93 NY4154
Harracott *Devon* 19 SS5627
Harrapool *Highld* 129 NG6522
Harrietfield *Tays* 125 NN9829
Harrietsham *Kent* 28 TQ8652
Harringay *Gt Lon* 27 TQ3188
Harrington *Cumb* 92 NX9926
Harrington *H & W* 60 SO8774
Harrington *Lincs* 77 TF3671
Harrington *Nhants* 50 SP7780
Harringworth *Nhants* 51 SP9197
Harris *Highld* 134 NO3396
Harriseahead *Staffs* 72 SJ8656
Harriston *Cumb* 92 NY1641
Harrogate *N York* 82 SE3055
Harrold *Beds* 51 SP9456
Harrop Dale *Gt Man* 82 SE0008
Harrow *Gt Lon* 26 TQ1588
Harrow Green *Suffk* 54 TL8654
Harrow on the Hill *Gt Lon* 26 TQ1587
Harrow Weald *Gt Lon* 26 TQ1591
Harrowbarrow *Cnwll* 5 SX3969
Harrowden *Beds* 38 TL0646
Harrowgate Village *Dur* 96 NZ2917
Harsgeir *W Isls* 154 NB1040
Harston *Cambs* 53 TL4250
Harston *Leics* 63 SK8331
Harswell *Humb* 84 SE8240
Hart *Cleve* 97 NZ4734
Hart Station *Cleve* 97 NZ4836
Hartburn *Nthumb* 103 NZ0886
Hartest *Suffk* 54 TL8352
Hartfield *E Susx* 16 TQ4735
Hartford *Cambs* 52 TL2572
Hartford *Ches* 71 SJ6372
Hartford *Somset* 20 SS9629
Hartford End *Essex* 40 TL6817
Hartfordbridge *Hants* 25 SU7757
Hartforth *N York* 89 NZ1606
Harthill *Ches* 71 SJ4955
Harthill *Loth* 116 NS9064
Harthill *S York* 75 SK4980
Hartington *Derbys* 74 SK1260
Hartland *Devon* 18 SS2624
Hartland Quay *Devon* 18 SS2224
Hartlebury *H & W* 60 SO8471
Hartlepool *Cleve* 97 NZ5032
Hartley *Cumb* 88 NY7808
Hartley *Kent* 27 TQ6166
Hartley *Kent* 17 TQ7634
Hartley *Nthumb* 103 NZ3475
Hartley Green *Kent* 27 TQ6066
Hartley Green *Staffs* 72 SJ9729
Hartley Wespall *Hants* 24 SU6958
Hartley Wintney *Hants* 24 SU7656
Hartlip *Kent* 28 TQ8364
Hartoft End *N York* 90 SE7592
Harton *N York* 90 SE7061
Harton *Shrops* 59 SO4888
Harton *T & W* 103 NZ3765
Hartpury *Gloucs* 47 SO7924
Hartshead *W York* 82 SE1822
Hartshead Moor Side *W York* 82 SE1625
Hartshill *Staffs* 72 SJ8645
Hartshill *Warwks* 61 SP3294
Hartshorne *Derbys* 62 SK3221
Hartside *Nthumb* 111 NT9716
Hartsop *Cumb* 93 NY4013
Hartswell *Somset* 20 ST0826
Hartwell *Nhants* 38 SP7850
Hartwith *N York* 89 SE2161
Hartwood *Strath* 116 NS8459
Hartwood *Strath* 116 NS8459
Hartwood Myres *Border* 109 NT4324
Harvel *Kent* 28 TQ6563
Harvington *H & W* 48 SP0548
Harwell *Notts* 75 SK6891
Harwell *Oxon* 37 SU4989
Harwich *Essex* 41 TM2531

Harwood Heylor


Harwood *Gt Man* **79** SD7410
Harwood *Nthumb* **103** NZ0189
Harwood *Nthumb* **95** NY8133
Harwood Dale *N York* **91** SE9695
Harwood Lee *Gt Man* **81** SD7412
Harworth *Notts* **75** SK6291
Hasbury *W Mids* **60** SO9583
Hascombe *Surrey* **25** TQ0039
Haselbeach *Nhants* **50** SP7177
Haselbury Plucknett *Somset* **10** ST4711
Haseley *Warwks* **48** SP2367
Haseley Green *Warwks* **48** SP2369
Haseley Knob *Warwks* **61** SP2371
Haselor *Warwks* **48** SP1257
Hasfield *Gloucs* **47** SO8227
Hasguard *Dyfed* **30** SM8509
Haskayne *Lancs* **78** SD3508
Hasketon *Suffk* **55** TM2450
Hasland *Derbys* **74** SK3969
Hasland Green *Derbys* **74** SK3978
Haslemere *Surrey* **14** SU9032
Haslingden *Lancs* **81** SD7823
Haslingfield *Cambs* **52** TL4052
Haslington *Ches* **72** SJ7355
Haslington Grane *Lancs* **81** SD7523
Hassall *Ches* **72** SJ7657
Hassall Green *Ches* **72** SJ7858
Hassell Street *Kent* **29** TR0946
Hassendean *Border* **109** NT5420
Hassingham *Norfk* **67** TG3705
Hassness *Cumb* **93** NY1816
Hassness *Cumb* **93** NY1826
Hassocks *W Susx* **15** TQ3015
Hassop *Derbys* **74** SK2272
Haste Hill *Surrey* **14** SU9032
Haster *Highld* **151** ND3251
Hasthorpe *Lincs* **77** TF4869
Hastigrow *Highld* **151** ND2660
Hastingleigh *Kent* **29** TR0945
Hastings *E Susx* **17** TQ8209
Hastings *Somset* **10** ST3816
Hastings *Somset* **10** ST3316
Hastingwood *Essex* **39** TL4807
Hastoe *Herts* **38** SP9209
Haswell *Dur* **96** NZ3743
Haswell Plough *Dur* **96** NZ3741
Hatch *Beds* **52** TL1547
Hatch Beauchamp *Somset* **20** ST3020
Hatch End *Beds* **51** TL0760
Hatch End *Herts* **26** TQ1391
Hatchet Gate *Hants* **12** SU3701
Hatching Green *Herts* **38** TL1313
Hatchmere *Ches* **71** SJ5571
Hatcliffe *Humb* **76** TA2100
Hatfield *H & W* **46** SO5959
Hatfield *H & W* **47** SO8750
Hatfield *Herts* **39** TL2308
Hatfield *S York* **83** SE6509
Hatfield Broad Oak *Essex* **39** TL5416
Hatfield Heath *Essex* **39** TL5215
Hatfield Peverel *Essex* **40** TL7911
Hatfield Woodhouse *S York* **83** SE6708
Hatford *Oxon* **36** SU3394
Hatford *Oxon* **36** SU3394
Hatherden *Hants* **23** SU3450
Hatherleigh *Devon* **8** SS5404
Hathern *Leics* **62** SK5022
Hatherop *Gloucs* **36** SP1505
Hathersage *Derbys* **74** SK2381
Hathersage Books *Derbys* **74** SK2480
Hatherton *Ches* **72** SJ6847
Hatherton *Staffs* **60** SJ9510
Hatley St. George *Cambs* **52** TL2751
Hatt *Cnwll* **5** SX3961
Hattingley *Hants* **24** SU6437
Hatton *Ches* **78** SJ5982
Hatton *Derbys* **73** SK2130
Hatton *Gramp* **143** NK0537
Hatton *Gt Lon* **26** TQ0975
Hatton *Lincs* **76** TF1776
Hatton *Shrops* **59** SO4690
Hatton *Tays* **127** NO4642
Hatton *Warwks* **48** SP2367
Hatton Heath *Ches* **71** SJ4561
Hatton of Fintray *Gramp* **143** NJ8316
Haugh *Lincs* **77** TF4175
Haugh *Strath* **107** NS4925
Haugh *W York* **81** SD9311
Haugh Head *Nthumb* **111** NU0026
Haugh of Glass *Gramp* **142** NJ4239
Haugh of Urr *D & G* **100** NX8066
Haugham *Lincs* **77** TF3381
Haughhead Inn *Strath* **116** NS6178
Haughley *Suffk* **54** TM0262
Haughley Green *Suffk* **54** TM0364
Haughton *Notts* **75** SK6772
Haughton *Powys* **59** SJ3018
Haughton *Shrops* **59** SJ3726
Haughton *Shrops* **59** SJ5516
Haughton *Shrops* **60** SJ7408
Haughton *Shrops* **60** SO6896
Haughton *Staffs* **72** SJ8620
Haughton Green *Gt Man* **79** SJ9393
Haughton le Skerne *Dur* **96** NZ3116
Haughton Moss *Ches* **71** SJ5756
Haultwick *Herts* **39** TL3323
Haunton *Staffs* **61** SK2310
Hautes Croix *Jersey* **152** JS0000
Hauxley *Nthumb* **103** NU2703
Hauxton *Cambs* **53** TL4352
Havannah *Ches* **72** SJ8764
Havant *Hants* **13** SU7106
Haven *H & W* **46** SO4054
Haven Bank *Lincs* **76** TF2352
Haven Side *Humb* **85** TA1827
Havenhouse Station *Lincs* **77** TF5259
Havenstreet *IOW* **13** SZ5690
Havercroft *W York* **83** SE3813
Haverfordwest *Dyfed* **30** SM9515
Haverhill *Suffk* **53** TL6745
Haverigg *Cumb* **86** SD1578
Havering-atte-Bower *Essex* **27** TQ5193
Haversham *Bucks* **38** SP8242
Haverthwaite *Cumb* **87** SD3483
Haverton Hill *Cleve* **97** NZ4822
Havyat *Avon* **21** ST4761
Havyatt *Somset* **21** ST5338
Hawarden *Clwyd* **71** SJ3165
Hawbridge *H & W* **47** SO9049
Hawbush Green *Essex* **40** TL7820
Hawcoat *Cumb* **101** NY2271
Hawdsdale *Cumb* **93** NY3648
Hawe's Green *Norfk* **67** TM2499
Hawen *Dyfed* **42** SN3447
Hawes *N York* **88** SD8789
Hawford *H & W* **47** SO8460
Hawick *Border* **109** NT5014
Hawk Green *Gt Man* **79** SJ9687
Hawkchurch *Devon* **10** ST3400
Hawkedon *Suffk* **53** TL7953
Hawkenbury *Kent* **28** TQ8045
Hawkeridge *Wilts* **22** ST8653
Hawkerland *Devon* **9** SY0589
Hawkes End *W Mids* **61** SP2983
Hawkesbury *Avon* **35** ST7686
Hawkesbury *Warwks* **61** SP3784
Hawkesbury Upton *Avon* **35** ST7786
Hawkhill *Nthumb* **111** NU2212
Hawkhurst *Kent* **17** TQ7530
Hawkhurst Common *E Susx* **16** TQ5317
Hawkinge *Kent* **29** TR2139
Hawkley *Hants* **24** SU7429
Hawkridge *Devon* **19** SS8630
Hawkshaw *Gt Man* **81** SD7615
Hawkshead *Cumb* **87** SD3598
Hawkshead Hill *Cumb* **101** NY3398
Hawksland *Strath* **108** NS8439
Hawkspur Green *Essex* **40** TL6532
Hawkstone *Shrops* **59** SJ5830
Hawkswick *N York* **88** SD9570
Hawksworth *Notts* **63** SK7543
Hawksworth *W York* **82** SE1641
Hawkwell *Essex* **40** TQ8591
Hawley *Hants* **25** SU8558
Hawley *Kent* **27** TQ5571
Hawling *Gloucs* **48** SP0623
Hawnby *N York* **90** SE5489
Haworth *W York* **82** SE0337
Hawstead *Suffk* **54** TL8559
Hawstead Green *Suffk* **54** TL8658
Hawthorn *Dur* **96** NZ4145
Hawthorn *Hants* **24** SU6733
Hawthorn *M Glam* **33** ST0987
Hawthorn Hill *Berks* **25** SU8873
Hawthorn Hill *Lincs* **76** TF2155
Hawthorpe *Lincs* **64** TF0427
Hawton *Notts* **75** SK7851
Haxby *N York* **90** SE6058
Haxby Gates *N York* **83** SE6056
Haxey *Humb* **75** SK7699
Haxey Turbary *Humb* **84** SE7501
Haxted *Surrey* **16** TQ4245
Haxton *Wilts* **23** SU1549
Hay *Cnwll* **3** SW8651
Hay *Cnwll* **3** SW9243
Hay *Cnwll* **4** SW9770
Hay *Cnwll* **3** SW9552
Hay Green *Norfk* **65** TF5418
Hay Street *Herts* **39** TL3926
Hay-on-Wye *Powys* **45** SO2342
Haydock *Mersyd* **78** SJ5697
Haydon *Dorset* **11** ST6615
Haydon *Somset* **20** ST2523
Haydon Bridge *Nthumb* **102** NY8464
Haydon Wick *Wilts* **36** SU1387
Haye *Cnwll* **5** SX3570
Hayes *Gt Lon* **26** TQ0980
Hayes *Gt Lon* **27** TQ4066
Hayes End *Gt Lon* **26** TQ0882
Hayfield *Derbys* **74** SK0386
Hayfield *Strath* **123** NN0723
Haygate *Shrops* **59** SJ6410
Hayhillock *Tays* **127** NO5242
Hayle *Cnwll* **2** SW5537
Hayley Green *W Mids* **60** SO9482
Haymoor Green *Ches* **72** SJ6850
Hayne *Devon* **8** SX7685
Hayne *Devon* **9** SS9515
Haynes *Beds* **38** TL0740
Haynes West End *Beds* **38** TL0640
Hayscastle *Dyfed* **30** SM8925
Hayscastle Cross *Dyfed* **30** SM9125
Haysden *Kent* **16** TQ5645
Hayton *Cumb* **94** NY5057
Hayton *Humb* **84** SE8145
Hayton *Notts* **75** SK7284
Hayton's Bent *Shrops* **59** SO5280
Haytor Vale *Devon* **8** SX7677
Haytown *Devon* **18** SS3814
Haywards Heath *W Susx* **15** TQ3324
Haywood *H & W* **46** SO4834
Haywood *S York* **83** SE5812
Haywood Oaks *Notts* **75** SK6055
Hazards Green *E Susx* **16** TQ6812
Hazel Grove *Gt Man* **79** SJ9287
Hazel Street *Kent* **28** TQ6939
Hazel Stub *Suffk* **53** TL6544
Hazelbank *Strath* **116** NS8345
Hazelbury Bryan *Dorset* **11** ST7408
Hazeleigh *Essex* **40** TL8203
Hazeley *Hants* **24** SU7459
Hazelhurst *Gt Man* **79** SD9600
Hazelrigg *T & W* **103** NZ2472
Hazelslade *Staffs* **60** SK0212
Hazelton Walls *Fife* **126** NO3322
Hazelwood *Derbys* **62** SK3245
Hazlemere *Bucks* **26** SU8895
Hazles *Staffs* **73** SK0047
Hazleton *Gloucs* **36** SP0718
Heacham *Norfk* **65** TF6737
Head of Muir *Cent* **116** NS8080
Headbourne Worthy *Hants* **24** SU4831
Headbrook *H & W* **46** SO2956
Headcorn *Kent* **28** TQ8344
Headingley *W York* **82** SE2836
Headington *Oxon* **37** SP5307
Headlam *Dur* **96** NZ1818
Headless Cross *H & W* **48** SP0365
Headlesscross *Strath* **116** NS9158
Headley *Hants* **24** SU5162
Headley *Hants* **14** SU8236
Headley *Surrey* **26** TQ2054
Headley Down *Hants* **14** SU8436
Headley Heath *H & W* **61** SP0676
Headon *Notts* **75** SK7476
Heads *Strath* **116** NS7147
Heads Nook *Cumb* **94** NY5054
Heads Nook *Cumb* **94** NY4955
Heage *Derbys* **74** SK3650
Healaugh *N York* **88** SE0198
Healaugh *N York* **83** SE4947
Heald Green *Gt Man* **79** SJ8486
Heale *Devon* **19** SS6446
Heale *Somset* **21** ST3825
Heale *Somset* **20** ST2420
Healey *Lancs* **81** SD8817
Healey *N York* **89** SE1780
Healey *Nthumb* **95** NZ0158
Healey *W York* **82** SE2719
Healeyfield *Dur* **95** NZ0648
Healing *Humb* **85** TA2110
Heamoor *Cnwll* **2** SW4631
Heanor *Derbys* **62** SK4346
Heanton Punchardon *Devon* **19** SS5035
Heapey *Lancs* **81** SD5920
Heapham *Lincs* **76** SK8788
Hearn *Hants* **14** SU8337
Hearthstane *Border* **108** NT1126
Hearts Delight *Kent* **17** TQ8820
Heasley Mill *Devon* **19** SS7332
Heast *Highld* **129** NG6417
Heath *Derbys* **75** SK4467
Heath *W York* **83** SE3520
Heath and Reach *Beds* **38** SP9228
Heath Common *W Susx* **14** TQ1014
Heath End *Bucks* **26** SU8798
Heath End *Hants* **24** SU4162
Heath End *Hants* **24** SU5762
Heath End *Leics* **62** SK3621
Heath End *Surrey* **25** SU8449
Heath End *Warwks* **48** SP2360
Heath Green *H & W* **61** SP0771
Heath Hayes *Staffs* **60** SK0110
Heath Hill *Shrops* **60** SJ7614
Heath House *Somset* **21** ST4146
Heath Town *W Mids* **60** SO9399
Heathbrook *Shrops* **59** SJ6228
Heathcote *Derbys* **74** SK1460
Heathcote *Shrops* **72** SJ6528
Heathencote *Nhants* **49** SP7047
Heather *Leics* **62** SK3910
Heathfield *Devon* **8** SX8376
Heathfield *E Susx* **16** TQ5821
Heathfield *N York* **89** SE1367
Heathfield *Somset* **20** ST1626
Heathton *Shrops* **60** SO8192
Heatley *Gt Man* **79** SJ7088
Heatley *Staffs* **73** SK0626
Heaton *Gt Man* **79** SD6909
Heaton *Lancs* **87** SD4460
Heaton *Staffs* **72** SJ9562
Heaton *T & W* **103** NZ2666
Heaton *W York* **82** SE1335
Heaton Chapel *Gt Man* **79** SJ8991
Heaton Mersey *Gt Man* **79** SJ8690
Heaton Norris *Gt Man* **79** SJ8891
Heaton's Bridge *Lancs* **78** SD3905
Heaton's Bridge *Lancs* **80** SD4011
Heaverham *Kent* **27** TQ5758
Heaviley *Gt Man* **79** SJ9088
Heavitree *Devon* **9** SX9392
Hebburn *T & W* **103** NZ3263
Hebden *N York* **88** SE0263
Hebden Bridge *W York* **82** SD9927
Hebden Green *Ches* **71** SJ6365
Hebing End *Herts* **39** TL3122
Hebron *Dyfed* **31** SN1827
Hebron *Nthumb* **103** NZ1989
Heckfield *Hants* **24** SU7260
Heckfield Green *Suffk* **54** TM1875
Heckfordbridge *Essex* **40** TL9421
Heckington *Lincs* **64** TF1444
Heckmondwike *W York* **82** SE2123
Heddington *Wilts* **22** ST9966
Heddon-on-the-Wall *Nthumb* **103** NZ1366
Hedenham *Norfk* **67** TM3193
Hedge End *Hants* **13** SU4912
Hedgerley *Bucks* **26** SU9687
Hedgerley Green *Bucks* **26** SU9787
Hedging *Somset* **20** ST3029
Hedley on the Hill *Nthumb* **95** NZ0759
Hednesford *Staffs* **60** SK0012
Hedon *Humb* **85** TA1928
Hedsor *Bucks* **26** SU9086
Hegdon Hill *H & W* **46** SO5853
Heglibister *Shet* **155** HU3851
Heighington *Dur* **96** NZ2422
Heighington *Lincs* **76** TF0269
Heightington *H & W* **60** SO7671
Heiton *Border* **110** NT7130
Hele *Cnwll* **5** SX2197
Hele *Devon* **19** SS5347
Hele *Devon* **9** SS9902
Hele *Devon* **7** SX7470
Hele *Somset* **20** ST1824
Hele Lane *Devon* **19** SS7910
Helebridge *Cnwll* **18** SS2103
Helensburgh *Strath* **115** NS2982
Helenton *Strath* **106** NS3820
Helford *Cnwll* **3** SW7526
Helford Passage *Cnwll* **3** SW7627
Helhoughton *Norfk* **66** TF8626
Helions Bumpstead *Essex* **53** TL6541
Hell Corner *Berks* **23** SU3864
Helland *Cnwll* **4** SX0771
Hellandbridge *Cnwll* **4** SX0671
Hellescott *Cnwll* **5** SX2888
Hellesdon *Norfk* **67** TG2010
Hellesvear *Cnwll* **2** SW5040
Hellidon *Nhants* **49** SP5158
Hellifield *N York* **81** SD8556
Hellingly *E Susx* **16** TQ5812
Hellington *Norfk* **67** TG3103
Helmdon *Nhants* **49** SP5943
Helme *W York* **82** SE0912
Helmingham *Suffk* **55** TM1957
Helmington Row *Dur* **96** NZ1835
Helmsdale *Highld* **147** ND0315
Helmshore *Lancs* **81** SD7821
Helmsley *N York* **90** SE6183
Helperby *N York* **89** SE4369
Helperthorpe *N York* **91** SE9570
Helpringham *Lincs* **64** TF1340
Helpston *Cambs* **64** TF1205
Helsby *Ches* **71** SJ4975
Helsey *Lincs* **77** TF5172
Helston *Cnwll* **2** SW6527
Helstone *Cnwll* **4** SX0881
Helton *Cumb* **94** NY5021
Helwith *N York* **88** NZ0702
Helwith Bridge *N York* **88** SD8169
Hemblington *Norfk* **67** TG3411
Hemel Hempstead *Herts* **38** TL0507
Hemerdon *Devon* **6** SX5657
Hemerdon *Devon* **6** SX5657
Hemingbrough *N York* **83** SE6730
Hemingby *Lincs* **76** TF2375
Hemingfield *S York* **83** SE3801
Hemingford Abbots *Cambs* **52** TL2871
Hemingford Grey *Cambs* **52** TL2970
Hemingstone *Suffk* **54** TM1454
Hemington *Nhants* **51** TL0985
Hemington *Somset* **22** ST7253
Hemley *Suffk* **55** TM2842
Hemlington *Cleve* **90** NZ5014
Hemp Green *Suffk* **55** TM3769
Hempholme *Humb* **85** TA0850
Hempnall *Norfk* **67** TM2494
Hempnall Green *Norfk* **67** TM2493
Hempriggs *Gramp* **141** NJ1064
Hempstead *Essex* **53** TL6338
Hempstead *Kent* **28** TQ7964
Hempstead *Norfk* **66** TG1037
Hempstead *Norfk* **67** TG4028
Hempsted Rea *Gloucs* **35** SO8116
Hempton *Norfk* **66** TF9129
Hempton *Oxon* **49** SP4431
Hemsby *Norfk* **67** TG4917
Hemswell *Lincs* **76** SK9290
Hemsworth *W York* **83** SE4213
Hemyock *Devon* **9** ST1313
Henbury *Avon* **34** ST5678
Henbury *Ches* **79** SJ8873
Hendersyde Park *Border* **110** NT7435
Hendham *Devon* **7** SX7450
Hendomen *Powys* **58** SO2198
Hendon *Gt Lon* **26** TQ2389
Hendon *T & W* **96** NZ4055
Hendra *Cnwll* **3** SW7237
Hendra *Cnwll* **4** SX0275
Hendre *M Glam* **33** SS9381
Hendy *Dyfed* **32** SN5803
Heneglwys *Gwynd* **68** SH4276
Henfield *W Susx* **15** TQ2116
Henford *Devon* **5** SX3794
Henghurst *Kent* **28** TQ9536
Hengoed *M Glam* **33** ST1595
Hengoed *Powys* **45** SO2253
Hengoed *Shrops* **58** SJ2833
Hengrave *Suffk* **54** TL8269
Henham *Essex* **39** TL5428
Henhurst *Kent* **28** TQ6669
Heniarth *Powys* **58** SJ1208
Henlade *Somset* **20** ST2624
Henley *Dorset* **11** ST6904
Henley *Gloucs* **35** SO9016
Henley *Shrops* **59** SO4588
Henley *Shrops* **46** SO5476
Henley *Somset* **21** ST4232
Henley *Suffk* **54** TM1551
Henley *W Susx* **14** SU8925
Henley Green *W Mids* **61** SP3681
Henley on Thames *Oxon* **37** SU7682
Henley Park *Surrey* **25** SU9352
Henley Street *Kent* **28** TQ6667
Henley's Down *E Susx* **17** TQ7312
Henley-in-Arden *Warwks* **48** SP1566
Henllan *Clwyd* **70** SJ0268
Henllan *Dyfed* **31** SN3540
Henllan Amgoed *Dyfed* **31** SN1820
Henllys *Gwent* **34** ST2691
Henlow *Beds* **39** TL1738
Hennock *Devon* **8** SX8381
Henny Street *Essex* **54** TL8738
Henry's Moat (Castell Hen *Dyfed* **30** SN0427
Henryd *Gwynd* **69** SH7774
Henryd *Gwynd* **69** SH7674
Hensall *N York* **83** SE5923
Henshaw *Nthumb* **102** NY7664
Hensingham *Cumb* **92** NX9816
Henstead *Suffk* **55** TM4986
Hensting *Hants* **13** SU4922
Henstride Ash *Somset* **22** ST7220
Henstridge *Somset* **22** ST7219
Henstridge Marsh *Somset* **22** ST7420
Henton *Oxon* **37** SP7602
Henton *Somset* **21** ST4845
Henwick *H & W* **47** SO8354
Henwood *Cnwll* **5** SX2673
Heol Senni *Powys* **45** SN9223
Heol-las *W Glam* **32** SS6998
Heol-y-Cyw *M Glam* **33** SS9484
Hepburn *Nthumb* **111** NU0624
Hepscott *Nthumb* **103** NZ2284
Heptonstall *W York* **82** SD9828
Hepworth *Suffk* **54** TL9874
Hepworth *W York* **82** SE1606
Herbrandston *Dyfed* **30** SM8707
Hereford *H & W* **46** SO5039
Hereson *Kent* **29** TR3865
Hergest *H & W* **46** SO2655
Heribusta *Highld* **136** NG3970
Heriot *Loth* **118** NT3952
Hermiston *Loth* **117** NT1870
Hermit Hill *S York* **74** SE3200
Hermitage *Berks* **24** SU5072
Hermitage *Border* **101** NY5095
Hermitage *Dorset* **10** ST6306
Hermitage *Hants* **13** SU7505
Hermon *Dyfed* **31** SN2032
Hermon *Gwynd* **68** SH3868
Herne *Kent* **29** TR1865
Herne Bay *Kent* **29** TR1768
Herne Common *Kent* **29** TR1764
Herne Pound *Kent* **28** TQ6554
Herner *Devon* **19** SS5926
Hernhill *Kent* **29** TR0660
Herodsfoot *Cnwll* **5** SX2160
Heronden *Kent* **29** TR2954
Herongate *Essex* **40** TQ6391
Heronsford *Strath* **98** NX1283
Heronsgate *Herts* **26** TQ0294
Herriard *Hants* **24** SU6645
Herring's Green *Beds* **38** TL0844
Herringfleet *Suffk* **67** TM4797
Herringswell *Suffk* **53** TL7270
Herringthorpe *S York* **75** SK4492
Herrington *T & W* **96** NZ3443
Hersden *Kent* **29** TR2062
Hersham *Cnwll* **18** SS2507
Hersham *Surrey* **26** TQ1164
Herstmonceux *E Susx* **16** TQ6410
Herston *Dorset* **12** SZ0278
Herston *Ork* **155** ND4291
Herston *Ork* **155** ND4291
Hertford *Herts* **39** TL3212
Hertford Heath *Herts* **39** TL3510
Hertingfordbury *Herts* **39** TL3011
Hesket Newmarket *Cumb* **93** NY3438
Hesketh Bank *Lancs* **80** SD4423
Hesketh Lane *Lancs* **81** SD6141
Heskin Green *Lancs* **80** SD5315
Hesleden *Dur* **96** NZ4438
Hesleden *N York* **88** SD8874
Hesleyside *Nthumb* **102** NY8183
Heslington *N York* **83** SE6250
Hessay *N York* **83** SE5253
Hessenford *Cnwll* **5** SX3057
Hessett *Suffk* **54** TL9361
Hessle *Humb* **84** TA0226
Hessle *W York* **83** SE4217
Hest Bank *Lancs* **87** SD4666
Hestley Green *Suffk* **54** TM1567
Heston *Gt Lon* **26** TQ1277
Hestwall *Ork* **155** HY2616
Heswall *Mersyd* **78** SJ2781
Hethe *Oxon* **49** SP5929
Hethersett *Norfk* **66** TG1505
Hethersgill *Cumb* **101** NY4767
Hetherside *Cumb* **101** NY4366
Hetherson Green *Ches* **71** SJ5249
Hethpool *Nthumb* **110** NT8928
Hett *Dur* **96** NZ2836
Hetton *N York* **88** SD9658
Hetton Steads *Nthumb* **111** NU0335
Hetton-le-Hole *T & W* **96** NZ3548
Heugh *Nthumb* **103** NZ0873
Heugh Head *Border* **119** NT8762
Heugh-Head *Gramp* **134** NJ3811
Heveningham *Suffk* **55** TM3372
Hever *Kent* **16** TQ4745
Heversham *Cumb* **87** SD4983
Hevingham *Norfk* **67** TG2021
Hewas Water *Cnwll* **3** SW9649
Hewelsfield *Gloucs* **34** SO5602
Hewenden *W York* **82** SE0736
Hewish *Avon* **21** ST4064
Hewish *Somset* **10** ST4108
Hewood *Dorset* **10** ST3502
Hexham *Nthumb* **102** NY9464
Hextable *Kent* **27** TQ5170
Hexthorpe *S York* **83** SE5602
Hexton *Herts* **38** TL1030
Hexworthy *Devon* **7** SX6572
Hexworthy *M Glam* **5** SX3681
Hey *Lancs* **81** SD8843
Hey Houses *Lancs* **80** SD3429
Heybridge *Essex* **40** TL8508
Heybridge *Essex* **40** TQ6398
Heybridge Basin *Essex* **40** TL8707
Heybrook Bay *Devon* **6** SX4949
Heydon *Cambs* **39** TL4340
Heydon *Norfk* **66** TG1127
Heydour *Lincs* **63** TF0039
Heyhead *Gt Man* **79** SJ8285
Heylipoll *Strath* **120** NL9743
Heylor *Shet* **155** HU2980

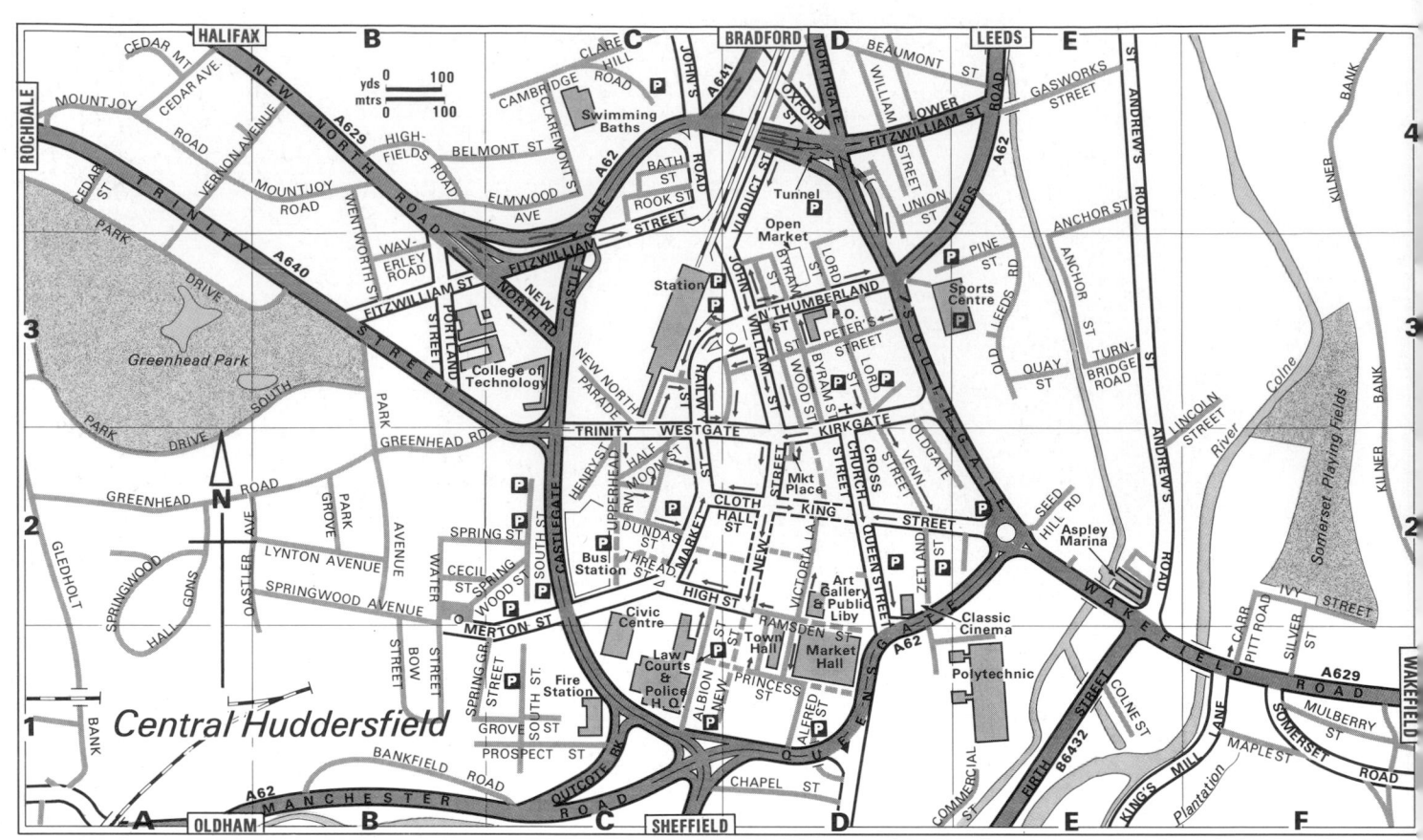

Central Huddersfield

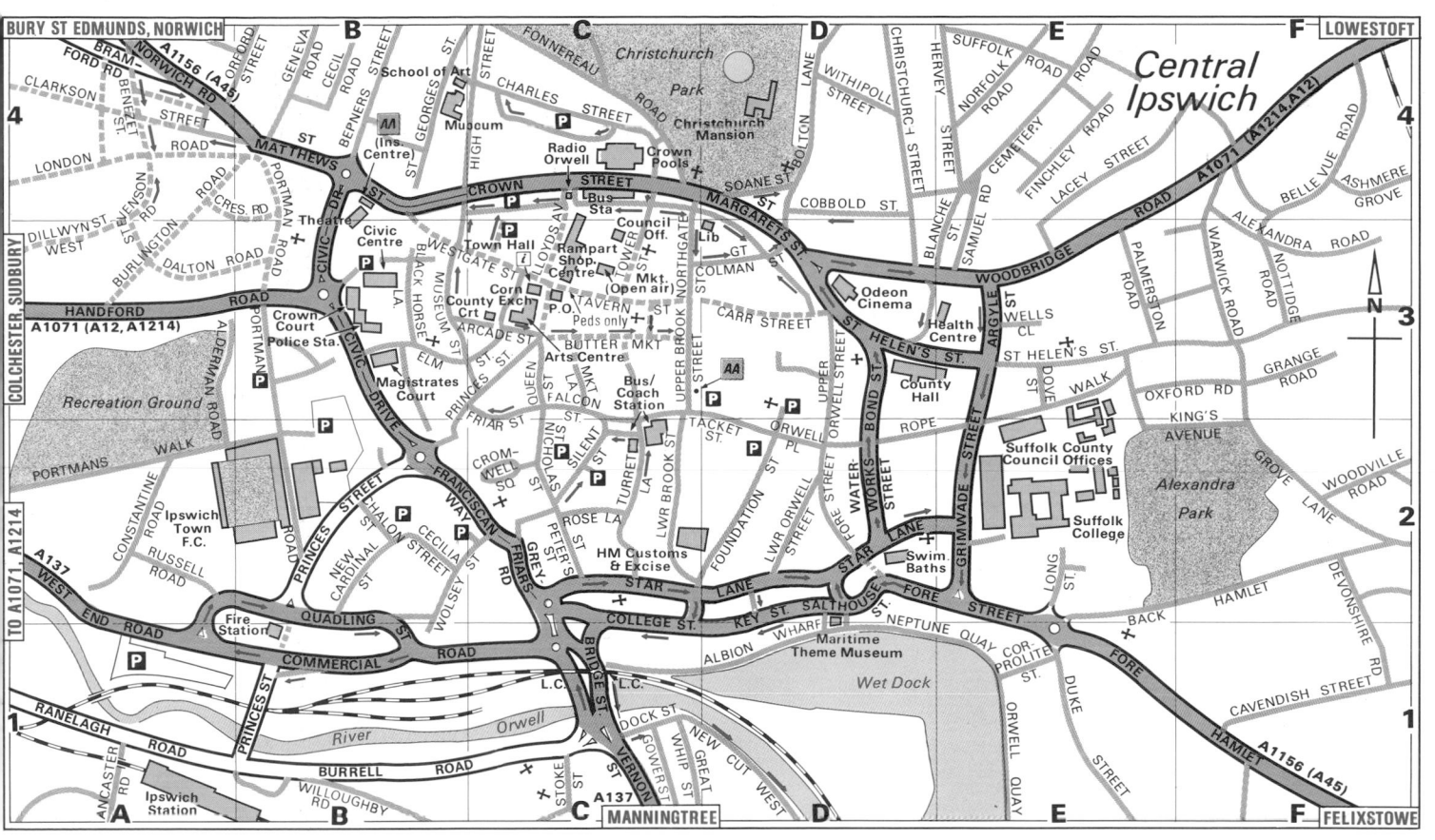

Ilchester Kilbride


Ilchester *Somset* 21 ST5222
Ilderton *Nthumb* 111 NU0121
Ilford *Gt Lon* 27 TQ4486
Ilford *Somset* 10 ST3617
Ilfracombe *Devon* 19 SS5147
Ilkeston *Derbys* 62 SK4642
Ilketshall St. Andrew *Suffk* 55 TM3887
Ilketshall St. Margaret *Suffk* 55 TM3485
Ilkley *W York* 82 SE1147
Illand *Cnwll* 5 SX2978
Illey *W Mids* 60 SO9881
Illidge Green *Ches* 72 SJ7963
Illingworth *W York* 82 SE0728
Illogan *Cnwll* 2 SW6743
Illston on the Hill *Leics* 50 SP7099
Ilmer *Bucks* 37 SP7605
Ilmington *Warwks* 48 SP2143
Ilminster *Somset* 10 ST3614
Ilsington *Dorset* 11 SY7592
Ilsington *Devon* 8 SX7876
Ilston *W Glam* 32 SS5590
Ilton *N York* 89 SE1878
Ilton *Somset* 10 ST3517
Imachar *Strath* 105 NR8640
Immingham *Humb* 85 TA1714
Immingham Dock *Humb* 85 TA1916
Impington *Cambs* 53 TL4463
Ince *Ches* 71 SJ4576
Ince Blundell *Mersyd* 78 SD3203
Ince-in-Makerfield *Gt Man* 78 SD5904
Inchbae Lodge *Highld* 146 NH4069
Inchbare *Tays* 134 NO6065
Inchberry *Gramp* 141 NJ3055
Inchinnan *Strath* 115 NS4868
Inchlaggan *Highld* 131 NH1801
Inchmagranachan *Tays* 125 NO0044
Inchmichael *Tays* 126 NO2425
Inchnacardoch *Highld* 131 NH3810
Inchnadamph *Highld* 145 NC2522
Inchture *Tays* 126 NO2728
Inchvuilt *Highld* 139 NH2438
Inchyra *Tays* 126 NO1820
Indian Queens *Cnwll* 4 SW9159
Ingate Place *Suffk* 55 TM4288
Ingatestone *Essex* 40 TQ6499
Ingbirchworth *S York* 82 SE2205
Ingerthorpe *N York* 89 SE2866
Ingestre *Staffs* 72 SJ9724
Ingham *Lincs* 76 SK9483
Ingham *Norfk* 67 TG3926
Ingham *Suffk* 54 TL8570
Ingham Corner *Norfk* 67 TG3927
Ingleborough *Norfk* 65 TF4715
Ingleby *Derbys* 62 SK3426
Ingleby Arncliffe *N York* 89 NZ4400
Ingleby Cross *N York* 89 NZ4500
Ingleby Greenhow *N York* 90 NZ5806
Ingleigh Green *Devon* 8 SS6007
Inglesbatch *Avon* 22 ST7061
Inglesham *Wilts* 36 SU2098
Ingleston *D & G* 100 NX9765
Ingleston *D & G* 99 NX6048
Ingleton *Dur* 96 NZ1720
Ingleton *N York* 87 SD6972
Inglewhite *Lancs* 80 SD5440
Ingliston *Tays* 127 NO4248
Ingmire Hall *Cumb* 87 SD6391
Ingoe *Nthumb* 103 NZ0374
Ingoldisthorpe *Norfk* 65 TF6832
Ingoldmells *Lincs* 77 TF5668
Ingoldsby *Lincs* 64 TF0130
Ingon *Warwks* 48 SP2158
Ingram *Nthumb* 111 NU0116
Ingrave *Essex* 40 TQ6291
Ingrow *W York* 82 SE0539
Ings *Cumb* 87 SD4498
Ingst *Avon* 34 ST5887
Ingst *Avon* 34 ST5887
Ingthorpe *Leics* 63 SK9908
Ingworth *Norfk* 67 TG1929
Injebreck *IOM* 153 SC3585
Inkberrow *H & W* 47 SP0157
Inkerman *Dur* 95 NZ1140
Inkhorn *Gramp* 143 NJ9239
Inkpen *Berks* 23 SU3664
Inkstack *Highld* 151 ND2570
Inmarsh *Wilts* 22 ST9460
Innellan *Strath* 114 NS1470
Innerleithen *Border* 109 NT3336
Innerleven *Fife* 118 NO3700
Innermessan *D & G* 98 NX0863
Innerwick *Loth* 119 NT7273
Innesmill *Gramp* 141 NJ2863
Insch *Gramp* 142 NJ6328
Insh *Highld* 132 NH8101
Inskip *Lancs* 80 SD4637
Inskip Moss Side *Lancs* 80 SD4539
Instow *Devon* 18 SS4730
Insworke *Cnwll* 6 SX4252
Intake *S York* 74 SK3884
Intake *S York* 74 SK3884
Inver *Gramp* 133 NO2393
Inver *Highld* 147 NH8682
Inver *Tays* 125 NO0142
Inver-Boyndie *Gramp* 142 NJ6664
Inver-Boyndie *Gramp* 135 NJ6607
Inverailort *Highld* 129 NM7681
Inveralligin *Highld* 138 NG8457
Inverallochy *Gramp* 143 NK0464
Inveran *Highld* 146 NH5797
Inveraray *Strath* 123 NN0908
Inverarish *Highld* 137 NG5535
Inverarity *Tays* 127 NO4544
Inverarnan *Cent* 123 NN3218
Inveravon *Cent* 117 NS9579
Inverawe *Strath* 122 NN0231
Inverbervie *Gramp* 135 NO8372
Inverbroom *Highld* 145 NH1883
Inverchaolain *Strath* 114 NS0975
Invercreran House Hotel *Strath* 122 NN0147
Inverdruie *Highld* 132 NH8910
Inveresk *Loth* 118 NT3571
Inveresragan *Strath* 122 NM9935
Inverey *Gramp* 133 NO0889
Inverfarigaig *Highld* 139 NH5223
Inverfolla *Strath* 122 NM9544
Invergarry *Highld* 131 NH3101
Invergeldie *Tays* 124 NN7327
Invergloy *Highld* 131 NN2288
Invergordon *Highld* 140 NH7068
Invergowrie *Tays* 126 NO3430
Inverguseran *Highld* 129 NG7407
Inverhadden *Tays* 124 NN6757
Inverherive *Cent* 123 NN3626
Inverie *Highld* 129 NG7600
Inverinan *Strath* 122 NM9917
Inverinate *Highld* 138 NG9221
Inverkeilor *Tays* 127 NO6649
Inverkeithing *Fife* 117 NT1383
Inverkeithny *Gramp* 142 NJ6246
Inverkip *Strath* 114 NS2071
Inverkirkaig *Highld* 145 NC0819
Inverlael *Highld* 145 NH1886
Inverlair *Highld* 131 NN3379
Inverliever Lodge *Strath* 122 NM8905
Inverlochlarig *Cent* 124 NN4318
Inverlochy *Strath* 123 NN1927
Invermarkie *Gramp* 142 NJ4239
Invermoriston *Highld* 139 NH4217
Invernaver *Highld* 150 NC7060
Inverneg *Strath* 115 NS3497
Inverneil *Strath* 113 NR8481
Inverness *Highld* 140 NH6645
Invernoaden *Strath* 114 NS1297
Inveroran Hotel *Strath* 123 NN2741
Inverquharity *Tays* 134 NO4057
Inverquhomery *Gramp* 143 NK0246
Inverroy *Highld* 131 NN2581
Inversanda *Highld* 130 NM9459
Invershiel *Highld* 138 NG9319
Invershin *Highld* 146 NH5796
Invershore *Highld* 151 ND2435
Inversnaid *Cent* 123 NN3408
Inverugie *Gramp* 143 NK0947
Inveruglas *Strath* 123 NN3109
Inveruglass *Highld* 132 NH8000
Inverurie *Gramp* 142 NJ7721
Inwardleigh *Devon* 8 SX5699
Inworth *Essex* 40 TL8718
Iping *W Susx* 14 SU8522
Ipplepen *Devon* 7 SX8366
Ipsden *Oxon* 37 SU6285
Ipstones *Staffs* 73 SK0249
Ipswich *Suffk* 54 TM1644
Irby *Mersyd* 78 SJ2584
Irby in the Marsh *Lincs* 77 TF4763
Irby upon Humber *Humb* 85 TA1904
Irchester *Nhants* 51 SP9265
Ireby *Cumb* 93 NY2338
Ireby *Lancs* 87 SD6575
Ireland *Beds* 38 TL1341
Irelands Cross *Shrops* 72 SJ7341
Ireleth *Cumb* 86 SD2277
Ireshopeburn *Dur* 95 NY8638
Ireton Wood *Derbys* 73 SK2847
Irlam *Gt Man* 79 SJ7294
Irnham *Lincs* 64 TF0226
Iron Acton *Avon* 35 ST6783
Iron Bridge *Cambs* 65 TL4897
Iron Cross *Warwks* 48 SP0552
Ironmacannie *D & G* 99 NX6675
Irons Bottom *Surrey* 15 TQ2546
Ironville *Derbys* 75 SK4351
Irstead *Norfk* 67 TG3620
Irthington *Cumb* 101 NY4961
Irthlingborough *Nhants* 51 SP9470
Irton *N York* 91 TA0184
Irvine *Strath* 106 NS3239
Isauld *Highld* 150 NC9865
Isbister *Shet* 155 HU3790
Isfield *E Susx* 16 TQ4417
Isham *Nhants* 51 SP8873
Isington *Hants* 25 SU7742
Islandpool *H & W* 60 SO8680
Isle Abbotts *Somset* 21 ST3520
Isle Brewers *Somset* 21 ST3621
Isle of Whithorn *D & G* 99 NX4736
Isleham *Cambs* 53 TL6474
Isleornsay *Highld* 129 NG6912
Islet Village *Guern* 152 GN0000
Isley Walton *Leics* 62 SK4225
Islington *Gt Lon* 27 TQ3184
Islip *Nhants* 51 SP9879
Islip *Oxon* 37 SP5214
Islivig *W Isls* 154 NA9927
Isombridge *Shrops* 59 SJ6113
Istead Rise *Kent* 27 TQ6369
Itchen Abbas *Hants* 24 SU5332
Itchen Stoke *Hants* 24 SU5532
Itchingfield *W Susx* 15 TQ1328
Itchington *Avon* 35 ST6587
Itteringham *Norfk* 66 TG1430
Itton *Devon* 8 SX6898
Itton *Gwent* 34 ST4995
Itton Common *Gwent* 34 ST4895
Ivegill *Cumb* 93 NY4143
Ivelet *N York* 88 SD9398
Iver *Bucks* 26 TQ0381
Iver Heath *Bucks* 26 TQ0283
Iveston *Dur* 96 NZ1350
Ivinghoe *Bucks* 38 SP9416
Ivinghoe Aston *Bucks* 38 SP9517
Ivington *H & W* 46 SO4756
Ivington Green *H & W* 46 SO4656
Ivy Cross *Dorset* 22 ST8623
Ivy Hatch *Kent* 27 TQ5854
Ivy Todd *Norfk* 66 TF8909
Ivybridge *Devon* 6 SX6356
Ivychurch *Kent* 17 TR0227
Iwade *Kent* 28 TQ8967
Iwerne Courney *Dorset* 11 ST8512
Iwerne Minster *Dorset* 11 ST8614
Ixworth *Suffk* 54 TL9370
Ixworth Thorpe *Suffk* 54 TL9173

# J

Jack Green *Lancs* 81 SD5926
Jack Hill *N York* 82 SE1951
Jack-in-the-Green *Devon* 9 SY0195
Jacksdale *Notts* 75 SK4451
Jackson Bridge *W York* 82 SE1606
Jackton *Strath* 115 NS5952
Jacobs Well *Surrey* 25 SU9952
Jacobstow *Cnwll* 5 SX1995
Jacobstowe *Devon* 8 SS5801
Jameston *Dyfed* 30 SS0599
Jamestown *Highld* 139 NH4756
Jamestown *Strath* 115 NS3981
Janets-town *Highld* 151 ND3551
Janetstown *Highld* 151 ND1932
Jardine Hall *D & G* 100 NY1088
Jarrow *T & W* 103 NZ3065
Jarvis Brook *E Susx* 16 TQ5329
Jasper's Green *Essex* 40 TL7226
Jawcraig *Cent* 116 NS8475
Jaywick *Essex* 41 TM1513
Jealott's Hill *Berks* 25 SU8673
Jeater Houses *N York* 89 SE4394
Jedburgh *Border* 110 NT6420
Jeffreyston *Dyfed* 31 SN0806
Jemimaville *Highld* 140 NH7165
Jenkins Green *E Susx* 16 TQ6205
Jerbourg *Guern* 152 GN0000
Jerusalem *Lincs* 76 SK9170
Jesmond *T & W* 103 NZ2566
Jevington *E Susx* 16 TQ5601
Jingle Street *Gwent* 34 SO4710
Jockey End *Herts* 38 TL0413
Jodrell Bank *Ches* 79 SJ7970
John O'Groats *Highld* 151 ND3872
John's Cross *E Susx* 17 TQ7421
Johnby *Cumb* 93 NY4333
Johnshaven *Gramp* 135 NO7967
Johnson's Street *Norfk* 67 TG3717
Johnston *Dyfed* 31 SN3919
Johnston *Dyfed* 30 SM9310
Johnstone *D & G* 108 NT1400
Johnstone *Strath* 115 NS4263
Johnstonebridge *D & G* 100 NY1092
Johnstown *Clwyd* 71 SJ3046
Joppa *Dyfed* 43 SN5666
Joppa *Strath* 106 NS4119
Jordans *Bucks* 26 SU9791
Jordanston *Dyfed* 30 SM9232
Jordanthorpe *S York* 74 SK3581
Jubilee Corner *Kent* 28 TQ8447
Jump *S York* 83 SE3701
Jumper's Town *E Susx* 16 TQ4632
Juniper Green *Loth* 117 NT1968
Jurby *IOM* 153 SC3598

# K

Kaber *Cumb* 88 NY7911
Kaimes *Loth* 117 NT2768
Kalnakill *Highld* 137 NG6955
Kames *Strath* 122 NM8211
Kames *Strath* 114 NR9771
Kames *Strath* 107 NS6926
Kea *Cnwll* 3 SW8142
Keadby *Humb* 84 SE8311
Keal Cotes *Lincs* 77 TF3661
Kearby Town End *N York* 83 SE3446
Kearnsey *Kent* 29 TR2844
Kearsley *Gt Man* 79 SD7504
Kearstwick *Cumb* 87 SD6079
Kearton *N York* 88 SD9998
Keasden *N York* 88 SD7266
Keason *M Glam* 5 SX3168
Keaton *Devon* 7 SX6454
Keckwick *Ches* 78 SJ5783
Keddington *Lincs* 77 TF3488
Keddington Corner *Lincs* 77 TF3589
Kedington *Suffk* 53 TL7046
Kedleston *Derbys* 73 SK3041
Keelby *Lincs* 85 TA1610
Keele *Staffs* 72 SJ8045
Keele University *Staffs* 72 SJ8145
Keeley Green *Beds* 38 TL0046
Keelham *W York* 82 SE0732
Keeston *Dyfed* 30 SM9019
Keevil *Wilts* 22 ST9157
Kegworth *Leics* 62 SK4826
Kehelland *Cnwll* 2 SW6241
Keig *Gramp* 142 NJ6119
Keighley *W York* 82 SE0641
Keilarsbrae *Cent* 116 NS8993
Keilarsbrae *Cent* 116 NS8993
Keillmore *Strath* 113 NR6880
Keillour *Tays* 125 NN9725
Keiloch *Gramp* 133 NO1891
Keils *Strath* 113 NR5268
Keinton Mandeville *Somset* 21 ST5430
Keir Mill *D & G* 100 NX8593
Keirsleywell Row *Nthumb* 94 NY7751
Keisby *Lincs* 64 TF0328
Keisley *Cumb* 94 NY7124
Keiss *Highld* 151 ND3461
Keith *Gramp* 142 NJ4250
Keithick *Tays* 126 NO2038
Keithock *Tays* 134 NO6063
Keithtown *Gramp* 139 NH5256
Kelbrook *Lancs* 81 SD9044
Kelburn *Strath* 114 NS2156
Kelby *Lincs* 63 TF0041
Keld *Cumb* 94 NY5514
Keld *Cumb* 94 NY5514
Keld *N York* 88 NY8901
Keld Head *N York* 90 SE7884
Keldholme *N York* 90 SE7086
Kelfield *Humb* 84 SE8201
Kelfield *N York* 83 SE5938
Kelham *Notts* 75 SK7755
Kelhead *D & G* 100 NY1469
Kellacott *Devon* 5 SX4089
Kellamergh *Lancs* 80 SD4029
Kellas *Gramp* 141 NJ1654
Kellas *Tays* 127 NO4535
Kellaton *Devon* 7 SX8039
Kelleth *Cumb* 87 NY6605
Kelling *Norfk* 66 TG0942
Kellington *N York* 83 SE5524
Kelloe *Dur* 96 NZ3436
Kells *Cumb* 92 NX9616
Kelly *Devon* 5 SX3981
Kelly Bray *Cnwll* 5 SX3571
Kelmarsh *Nhants* 50 SP7379
Kelmscot *Oxon* 36 SU2499
Kelsale *Suffk* 55 TM3865
Kelsall *Ches* 71 SJ5268
Kelshall *Herts* 39 TL3236
Kelsick *Cumb* 93 NY1950
Kelso *Border* 110 NT7234
Kelstedge *Derbys* 74 SK3363
Kelstern *Lincs* 77 TF2489
Kelsterton *Clwyd* 70 SJ2770
Kelston *Avon* 22 ST7067
Keltneyburn *Tays* 124 NN7749
Kelton *D & G* 100 NX9970
Kelty *Fife* 117 NT1494
Kelvedon *Essex* 40 TL8619
Kelvedon Hatch *Essex* 27 TQ5698
Kelynack *Cnwll* 2 SW3729
Kemacott *Devon* 19 SS6647
Kemback *Fife* 126 NO4115
Kemberton *Shrops* 60 SJ7204
Kemble *Wilts* 35 ST9897
Kemble Wick *Gloucs* 35 ST9895
Kemerton *H & W* 47 SO9437
Kemnay *Gramp* 142 NJ7316
Kemneys Commander *Gwent* 34 SO3404
Kemp Town *E Susx* 15 TQ3303
Kempe's Corner *Kent* 28 TR0346
Kempley *Gloucs* 47 SO6729
Kempley Green *Gloucs* 47 SO6728
Kemps Green *Warwks* 61 SP1470
Kempsey *H & W* 47 SO8549
Kempsford *Gloucs* 36 SU1597
Kempshott *Hants* 24 SU6050
Kempston *Beds* 38 TL0347
Kempston Hardwick *Beds* 38 TL0344
Kempton *Shrops* 59 SO3682
Kemsing *Kent* 27 TQ5558
Kemsley *Kent* 28 TQ9166
Kemsley Street *Kent* 28 TQ8062
Kenardington *Kent* 17 TQ9732
Kenchester *H & W* 46 SO4342
Kencot *Oxon* 36 SP2504
Kendal *Cumb* 87 SD5192
Kenderchurch *H & W* 46 SO4028
Kendleshire *Avon* 35 ST6679
Kenfig *M Glam* 32 SS8081
Kenfig Hill *M Glam* 33 SS8382
Kenilworth *Warwks* 61 SP2971
Kenley *Gt Lon* 27 TQ3260
Kenley *Shrops* 59 SJ5600
Kenmore *Highld* 137 NG7557
Kenmore *Tays* 124 NN7745
Kenn *Avon* 21 ST4269
Kenn *Devon* 9 SX9285
Kennacraig *Strath* 113 NR8262
Kennards House *Cnwll* 5 SX2883
Kenneggy *Cnwll* 2 SW5629
Kennerleigh *Devon* 8 SS8107
Kennessee Green *Mersyd* 78 SD3801
Kennet *Cent* 116 NS9291
Kennethmont *Gramp* 142 NJ5428
Kennett *Cambs* 53 TL7068
Kennford *Devon* 9 SX9186
Kenninghall *Norfk* 54 TM0386
Kennington *Kent* 28 TR0245
Kennington *Oxon* 37 SP5101
Kennoway *Fife* 126 NO3502
Kenny *Somset* 10 ST3118
Kennyhill *Suffk* 53 TL6680
Kennythorpe *N York* 90 SE7865
Kenovay *Strath* 120 NL9946
Kensaleyre *Highld* 136 NG4251
Kensham Green *Kent* 17 TQ8229
Kensington *Gt Lon* 27 TQ2579
Kensworth *Beds* 38 TL0319
Kensworth Common *Beds* 38 TL0318
Kent End *Wilts* 36 SU0594
Kent Green *Ches* 72 SJ8458
Kent Street *E Susx* 17 TQ7816
Kent's Green *Gloucs* 47 SO7423
Kent's Oak *Hants* 23 SU3224
Kentallen *Highld* 122 NN0057
Kentchurch *H & W* 46 SO4125
Kentford *Suffk* 53 TL7066
Kentisbeare *Devon* 9 ST0608
Kentisbury *Devon* 19 SS6244
Kentisbury Ford *Devon* 19 SS6242
Kentish Town *Gt Lon* 27 TQ2984
Kentmere *Cumb* 87 NY4504
Kenton *Devon* 9 SX9583
Kenton *Gt Lon* 26 TQ1788
Kenton *Suffk* 55 TM1965
Kenton *T & W* 103 NZ2267
Kenton Bank Foot *Nthumb* 103 NZ2069
Kentra *Highld* 129 NM6569
Kents Bank *Cumb* 87 SD3976
Kenwick *Shrops* 59 SJ4230
Kenwyn *Cnwll* 3 SW8145
Kenyon *Gt Man* 79 SJ6395
Keoldale *Highld* 149 NC3866
Keppoch *Highld* 138 NG8924
Keprigan *Strath* 105 NR6810
Kepwick *N York* 89 SE4690
Keresley *W Mids* 61 SP3282
Keresley Green *Warwks* 61 SP3184
Kergilliak *Cnwll* 3 SW7833
Kernborough *Devon* 7 SX7940
Kerne Bridge *H & W* 34 SO5818
Kerridge *Ches* 79 SJ9377
Kerridge-end *Ches* 79 SJ9475
Kerris *Cnwll* 2 SW4427
Kerry *Powys* 58 SO1490
Kerry's Gate *H & W* 46 SO3933
Kerrycroy *Strath* 114 NS1061
Kersall *Notts* 75 SK7162
Kersbrook *Devon* 9 SY0683
Kerscott *Devon* 19 SS6329
Kersey *Suffk* 54 TM0044
Kersey Tye *Suffk* 54 TL9843
Kersey Upland *Suffk* 54 TL9942
Kershader *W Isls* 154 NB3419
Kershopefoot *D & G* 101 NY4782
Kersoe *H & W* 47 SO9939
Kerswell *Devon* 9 ST0806
Kerswell Green *H & W* 47 SO8646
Kerthen Wood *Cnwll* 2 SW5833
Kesgrave *Suffk* 55 TM2245
Kessingland *Suffk* 55 TM5286
Kessingland Beach *Suffk* 55 TM5385
Kestle *Cnwll* 3 SW9845
Kestle Mill *Cnwll* 4 SW8459
Keston *Gt Lon* 27 TQ4164
Keswick *Cumb* 93 NY2623
Keswick *Norfk* 67 TG2004
Ketsby *Lincs* 77 TF3676
Kettering *Nhants* 51 SP8678
Ketteringham *Norfk* 66 TG1603
Kettins *Tays* 126 NO2339
Kettle Green *Herts* 39 TL4118
Kettlebaston *Suffk* 54 TL9650
Kettlebridge *Fife* 126 NO3007
Kettlebrook *Staffs* 61 SK2103
Kettleburgh *Suffk* 55 TM2660
Kettleshulme *Ches* 79 SJ9879
Kettlesing *N York* 82 SE2155
Kettlesing Bottom *N York* 89 SE2257
Kettletoft *Ork* 155 HY6538
Kettlestone *Norfk* 66 TF9631
Kettlethorpe *Lincs* 76 SK8475
Kettlewell *N York* 88 SD9772
Ketton *Leics* 63 SK9804
Kew *Gt Lon* 26 TQ1877
Kexbrough *S York* 82 SE2909
Kexby *Lincs* 76 SK8785
Kexby *N York* 84 SE7050
Key Green *Ches* 72 SJ8963
Key Green *N York* 90 NZ8004
Key Street *Kent* 28 TQ8864
Key's Toft *Lincs* 77 TF4858
Keyham *Leics* 63 SK6706
Keyhaven *Hants* 12 SZ3091
Keyingham *Humb* 85 TA2425
Keymer *W Susx* 15 TQ3115
Keynsham *Avon* 21 ST6568
Keysoe *Beds* 51 TL0762
Keysoe Row *Beds* 51 TL0861
Keyston *Cambs* 51 TL0475
Keyworth *Notts* 62 SK6130
Kibbear *Somset* 20 ST2122
Kibblesworth *T & W* 96 NZ2456
Kibworth Beauchamp *Leics* 50 SP6893
Kibworth Harcourt *Leics* 50 SP6894
Kidbrooke *Gt Lon* 27 TQ4076
Kidburngill *Cumb* 92 NY0621
Kidd's Moor *Norfk* 66 TG1103
Kiddemore Green *Staffs* 60 SJ8509
Kidderminster *H & W* 60 SO8376
Kiddington *Oxon* 49 SP4123
Kidlington *Oxon* 37 SP4913
Kidmore End *Oxon* 37 SU6979
Kidsdale *D & G* 99 NX4336
Kidsgrove *Staffs* 72 SJ8354
Kidstones *N York* 88 SD9581
Kidwelly *Dyfed* 31 SN4006
Kiel Crofts *Strath* 122 NM9039
Kielder *Nthumb* 102 NY6293
Kiells *Strath* 112 NR4168
Kilbagie *Cent* 116 NS9290
Kilbeg *Highld* 129 NG6506
Kilberry *Strath* 113 NR7164
Kilbirnie *Strath* 115 NS3154
Kilbride *Highld* 129 NG5820
Kilbride *Strath* 122 NM8525
Kilbride *Strath* 113 NR7279
Kilbride *Strath* 114 NS0367

Kneesworth

Lee


| | | |
|---|---|---|
| Kneesworth *Cambs* | **39** | TL3444 |
| Kneeton *Notts* | **63** | SK7146 |
| Knelston *W Glam* | **32** | SS4689 |
| Knenhall *Staffs* | **72** | SJ9237 |
| Knettishall *Suffk* | **54** | TL9780 |
| Knightacott *Devon* | **19** | SS6539 |
| Knightcote *Warwks* | **48** | SP3954 |
| Knightley *Staffs* | **72** | SJ8125 |
| Knightley Dale *Staffs* | **72** | SJ8123 |
| Knighton *Devon* | **6** | SX5249 |
| Knighton *Dorset* | **10** | ST6111 |
| Knighton *Dorset* | **12** | SZ0497 |
| Knighton *Leics* | **62** | SK6001 |
| Knighton *Powys* | **46** | SO2872 |
| Knighton *Somset* | **20** | ST1944 |
| Knighton *Staffs* | **72** | SJ7240 |
| Knighton *Staffs* | **72** | SJ7427 |
| Knighton *Wilts* | **36** | SU2971 |
| Knighton on Teme *H & W* | **47** | SO6369 |
| Knightsmill *Cnwll* | **4** | SX0780 |
| Knightwick *H & W* | **47** | SO7355 |
| Knill *H & W* | **46** | SO2960 |
| Knipton *Leics* | **63** | SK8231 |
| Knitsley *Dur* | **95** | NZ1048 |
| Kniveton *Derbys* | **73** | SK2050 |
| Knock *Cumb* | **94** | NY6727 |
| Knock *Gramp* | **142** | NJ5452 |
| Knock *W Isls* | **154** | NB4931 |
| Knock *Highld* | **129** | NG6709 |
| Knock Castle *Strath* | **114** | NS1963 |
| Knockally *Highld* | **151** | ND1429 |
| Knockan *Highld* | **145** | NC2110 |
| Knockandhu *Gramp* | **141** | NJ2023 |
| Knockando *Gramp* | **141** | NJ1941 |
| Knockarthur *Highld* | **147** | NC7506 |
| Knockbain *Highld* | **140** | NH6256 |
| Knockbain *Highld* | **139** | NH5543 |
| Knockbrex *D & G* | **99** | NX5849 |
| Knockdee *Highld* | **151** | ND1760 |
| Knockdolian *Strath* | **98** | NX1285 |
| Knockdown *Wilts* | **35** | ST8388 |
| Knockeen *Strath* | **106** | NX3195 |
| Knockenkelly *Strath* | **105** | NS0427 |
| Knockentiber *Strath* | **106** | NS4039 |
| Knockespoch House *Gramp* | **142** | NJ5423 |
| Knockespoch House *Gramp* | **142** | NJ5423 |
| Knockhall *Kent* | **27** | TQ5974 |
| Knockholt *Kent* | **27** | TQ4658 |
| Knockholt Pound *Kent* | **27** | TQ4859 |
| Knockin *Shrops* | **59** | SJ3322 |
| Knockinlaw *Strath* | **107** | NS4239 |
| Knockmill *Kent* | **27** | TQ5761 |
| Knocknaha *Strath* | **105** | NR6818 |
| Knocknain *D & G* | **98** | NW9765 |
| Knockrome *Strath* | **113** | NR5571 |
| Knocksharry *IOM* | **153** | SC2785 |
| Knocksheen *D & G* | **99** | NX5882 |
| Knockvennie Smithy *D & G* | **99** | NX7571 |
| Knodishall *Suffk* | **55** | TM4262 |
| Knole *Somset* | **21** | ST4825 |
| Knole Park *Avon* | **34** | ST5983 |
| Knolls Green *Ches* | **79** | SJ8079 |
| Knolton *Clwyd* | **71** | SJ3739 |
| Knook *Wilts* | **22** | ST9341 |
| Knossington *Leics* | **63** | SK8008 |
| Knott End-on-Sea *Lancs* | **80** | SD3548 |
| Knotting *Beds* | **51** | TL0063 |
| Knotting Green *Beds* | **51** | TL0062 |
| Knottingley *W York* | **83** | SE5023 |
| Knotty Green *Bucks* | **26** | SU9392 |
| Knowbury *Shrops* | **46** | SO5875 |
| Knowe *D & G* | **98** | NX3171 |
| Knowehead *D & G* | **107** | NX6090 |
| Knowesgate *Nthumb* | **102** | NY9885 |
| Knoweside *Strath* | **106** | NS2513 |
| Knowl Green *Essex* | **53** | TL7841 |
| Knowl Hill *Berks* | **37** | SU8279 |
| Knowle *Avon* | **34** | ST6070 |
| Knowle *Devon* | **18** | SS4938 |
| Knowle *Devon* | **8** | SS7801 |
| Knowle *Devon* | **9** | SY0482 |
| Knowle *Devon* | **9** | ST0006 |
| Knowle *Devon* | **9** | ST0006 |
| Knowle *Shrops* | **46** | SO5974 |
| Knowle *Somset* | **20** | SS9643 |
| Knowle *W Mids* | **61** | SP1876 |
| Knowle Cross *Devon* | **9** | SY0397 |
| Knowle Green *Lancs* | **81** | SD6338 |
| Knowle Hill *Surrey* | **25** | SU9966 |
| Knowle St. Giles *Somset* | **10** | ST3411 |
| Knowlton *Dorset* | **12** | SU0209 |
| Knowlton *Kent* | **29** | TR2853 |
| Knowsley *Mersyd* | **78** | SJ4395 |
| Knowstone *Devon* | **19** | SS8323 |
| Knox *N York* | **89** | SE2958 |
| Knox Bridge *Kent* | **28** | TQ7840 |
| Knox Bridge *Kent* | **28** | TQ7840 |
| Knucklas *Powys* | **46** | SO2574 |
| Knuston *Nhants* | **51** | SP9266 |
| Knutsford *Ches* | **79** | SJ7578 |
| Knutton *Staffs* | **72** | SJ8347 |
| Knypersley *Staffs* | **72** | SJ8856 |
| Krumlin *W York* | **82** | SE0518 |
| Kuggar *Cnwll* | **3** | SW7216 |
| Kyle of Lochalsh *Highld* | **137** | NG7627 |
| Kyleakin *Highld* | **137** | NG7526 |
| Kylerhea *Highld* | **129** | NG7820 |
| Kylesku *Highld* | **148** | NC2233 |
| Kylesmorar *Highld* | **129** | NM8093 |
| Kylestrome *Highld* | **148** | NC2234 |
| Kyloe *Nthumb* | **111** | NU0540 |
| Kymin *Gwent* | **34** | SO5212 |
| Kynaston *H & W* | **47** | SO6435 |
| Kynaston *Shrops* | **59** | SJ3520 |
| Kynnersley *Shrops* | **72** | SJ6716 |
| Kyre Green *H & W* | **46** | SO6162 |
| Kyre Park *H & W* | **47** | SO6264 |
| Kyrewood *H & W* | **46** | SO5967 |
| Kyrle *Somset* | **20** | ST0522 |


# L


| | | |
|---|---|---|
| L'Ancresse *Guern* | **152** | GN0000 |
| L'Eree *Guern* | **152** | GN0000 |
| L'Etacq *Jersey* | **152** | JS0000 |
| La Beilleuse *Guern* | **152** | GN0000 |
| La Fontenelle *Guern* | **152** | GN0000 |
| La Fosse *Guern* | **152** | GN0000 |
| La Greve *Guern* | **152** | GN0000 |
| La Greve de Lecq *Jersey* | **152** | JS0000 |
| La Hougette *Guern* | **152** | GN0000 |
| La Hougue Bie *Jersey* | **152** | JS0000 |
| La Houguette *Guern* | **152** | GN0000 |
| La Passee *Guern* | **152** | GN0000 |
| La Pulente *Jersey* | **152** | JS0000 |
| La Rocque *Jersey* | **152** | JS0000 |
| La Rousaillerie *Guern* | **152** | GN0000 |
| La Villette *Guern* | **152** | GN0000 |
| La Villocq *Guern* | **152** | GN0000 |
| Labbacott *Devon* | **18** | SS4220 |
| Laceby *Humb* | **85** | TA2106 |
| Lacey Green *Bucks* | **37** | SP8200 |
| Lach Dennis *Ches* | **79** | SJ7071 |
| Lackenby *Cleve* | **97** | NZ5619 |
| Lackford *Suffk* | **53** | TL7970 |
| Lackford Green *Suffk* | **53** | TL7971 |
| Lacock *Wilts* | **22** | ST9168 |
| Ladbroke *Warwks* | **49** | SP4158 |
| Ladderedge *Staffs* | **72** | SJ9654 |
| Laddingford *Kent* | **28** | TQ6948 |
| Lade Bank *Lincs* | **77** | TF3954 |
| Ladock *Cnwll* | **3** | SW8950 |
| Lady Hall *Cumb* | **86** | SD1986 |
| Lady's Green *Suffk* | **53** | TL7559 |
| Ladybank *Fife* | **126** | NO3009 |
| Ladycross *Cnwll* | **5** | SX3288 |
| Ladygill *Strath* | **108** | NS9428 |
| Ladykirk *Border* | **110** | NT8847 |
| Ladykirk Ho *Border* | **110** | NT8845 |
| Ladywood *H & W* | **47** | SO8761 |
| Ladywood *W Mids* | **61** | SP0586 |
| Lag *D & G* | **100** | NX8786 |
| Laga *Highld* | **121** | NM6360 |
| Lagavulin *Strath* | **104** | NR4045 |
| Lagg *Strath* | **113** | NR5978 |
| Lagg *Strath* | **105** | NR9521 |
| Laggan *Highld* | **131** | NN2997 |
| Laggan *Highld* | **132** | NN6194 |
| Laggan *Strath* | **98** | NX1082 |
| Laide *Highld* | **144** | NG8992 |
| Laig *Highld* | **128** | NM4687 |
| Laigh Church *Strath* | **115** | NS4647 |
| Laigh Fenwick *Strath* | **107** | NS4542 |
| Laigh Glenmuir *Strath* | **107** | NS6120 |
| Laighstonehall *Strath* | **116** | NS7054 |
| Laindon *Essex* | **40** | TQ6789 |
| Lair *Highld* | **138** | NH0148 |
| Lairg *Highld* | **146** | NC5806 |
| Laisterdyke *W York* | **82** | SE1832 |
| Laithes *Cumb* | **93** | NY4633 |
| Lake *Devon* | **8** | SX5388 |
| Lake *Devon* | **19** | SS5531 |
| Lake *Devon* | **18** | SS4402 |
| Lake *IOW* | **13** | SZ5983 |
| Lake *Wilts* | **23** | SU1239 |
| Lake Side *Cumb* | **87** | SD3787 |
| Lakenheath *Suffk* | **53** | TL7182 |
| Laker's Green *Surrey* | **14** | TQ0335 |
| Lakesend *Norfk* | **65** | TL5196 |
| Lakley Lanes *Bucks* | **38** | SP8250 |
| Laleham *Surrey* | **26** | TQ0568 |
| Laleston *M Glam* | **33** | SS8779 |
| Lamanva *Cnwll* | **3** | SW7631 |
| Lamarsh *Essex* | **54** | TL8835 |
| Lamas *Norfk* | **67** | TG2423 |
| Lamb Roe *Lancs* | **81** | SD7337 |
| Lambden *Border* | **110** | NT7443 |
| Lamberhurst *Kent* | **16** | TQ6735 |
| Lamberhurst Down *Kent* | **16** | TQ6735 |
| Lamberton *Border* | **119** | NT9658 |
| Lambfair Green *Suffk* | **53** | TL7154 |
| Lambfell Moar *IOM* | **153** | SC2984 |
| Lambley *Notts* | **63** | SK6345 |
| Lambley *Nthumb* | **94** | NY6659 |
| Lambourn *Berks* | **36** | SU3278 |
| Lambourne End *Essex* | **27** | TQ4794 |
| Lambs Green *W Susx* | **15** | TQ2136 |
| Lambston *Dyfed* | **30** | SM9016 |
| Lamellion *Cnwll* | **5** | SX2463 |
| Lamerton *Devon* | **5** | SX4476 |
| Lamesley *T & W* | **96** | NZ2557 |
| Lamington *Highld* | **146** | NH7477 |
| Lamington *Strath* | **108** | NS9731 |
| Lamlash *Strath* | **105** | NS0231 |
| Lamonby *Cumb* | **93** | NY4136 |
| Lamorick *Cnwll* | **4** | SX0364 |
| Lamorna *Cnwll* | **2** | SW4424 |
| Lamorran *Cnwll* | **3** | SW8741 |
| Lampen *Cnwll* | **4** | SX1867 |
| Lampeter *Dyfed* | **44** | SN5748 |
| Lampeter-Velfrey *Dyfed* | **31** | SN1514 |
| Lamphey *Dyfed* | **30** | SN0100 |
| Lamplugh *Cumb* | **92** | NY0820 |
| Lamport *Nhants* | **50** | SP7574 |
| Lamyatt *Somset* | **21** | ST6535 |
| Lana *Devon* | **18** | SS3007 |
| Lana *Devon* | **5** | SX3496 |
| Lanark *Strath* | **108** | NS8843 |
| Lanarth *Cnwll* | **3** | SW7621 |
| Lanby *Cnwll* | **5** | SX2977 |
| Lancaster *Lancs* | **87** | SD4761 |
| Lancaut *Gloucs* | **34** | ST5396 |
| Lanchester *Dur* | **96** | NZ1647 |
| Lancing *W Susx* | **15** | TQ1804 |
| Land-hallow *Highld* | **151** | ND1833 |
| Landbeach *Cambs* | **53** | TL4765 |
| Landcross *Devon* | **18** | SS4523 |
| Landerberry *Gramp* | **135** | NJ7404 |
| Landewednack *Cnwll* | **2** | SW7012 |
| Landford *Wilts* | **12** | SU2519 |
| Landford *Wilts* | **12** | SU2519 |
| Landford Manor *Wilts* | **12** | SU2620 |
| Landimore *W Glam* | **32** | SS4693 |
| Landkey Town *Devon* | **19** | SS5930 |
| Landore *W Glam* | **32** | SS6695 |
| Landrake *Cnwll* | **5** | SX3760 |
| Lands End *Cnwll* | **2** | SW3425 |
| Landscove *Devon* | **7** | SX7766 |
| Landshipping *Dyfed* | **30** | SN0211 |
| Landue *M Glam* | **5** | SX3579 |
| Landulph *Cnwll* | **6** | SX4262 |
| Landwade *Cambs* | **53** | TL6268 |
| Landywood *Staffs* | **60** | SJ9806 |
| Lane *Cnwll* | **4** | SW8260 |
| Lane Bottom *Lancs* | **81** | SD8735 |
| Lane End *Bucks* | **37** | SU8091 |
| Lane End *Ches* | **79** | SJ6990 |
| Lane End *Cnwll* | **4** | SX0369 |
| Lane End *Cumb* | **86** | SD1093 |
| Lane End *Hants* | **13** | SU5525 |
| Lane End *Kent* | **27** | TQ5671 |
| Lane End *Lancs* | **81** | SD8747 |
| Lane End *Wilts* | **22** | ST8145 |
| Lane Ends *Derbys* | **73** | SK2334 |
| Lane Ends *Dur* | **96** | NZ1933 |
| Lane Ends *Lancs* | **81** | SD7930 |
| Lane Ends *N York* | **82** | SD9743 |
| Lane Green *Staffs* | **60** | SJ8802 |
| Lane Head *Dur* | **89** | NZ1211 |
| Lane Head *Gt Man* | **79** | SJ6296 |
| Lane Head *W Mids* | **60** | SO9799 |
| Lane Heads *Lancs* | **80** | SD4339 |
| Lane Side *Lancs* | **81** | SD7922 |
| Laneast *Cnwll* | **5** | SX2283 |
| Laneham *Notts* | **75** | SK8076 |
| Lanehead *Dur* | **95** | NY8441 |
| Lanehead *Nthumb* | **102** | NY7865 |
| Lanes *Cnwll* | **3** | SW9040 |
| Laneshaw Bridge *Lancs* | **81** | SD9240 |
| Langaford *Devon* | **18** | SX4199 |
| Langaller *Somset* | **20** | ST2626 |
| Langar *Notts* | **63** | SK7234 |
| Langbank *Strath* | **115** | NS3873 |
| Langbar *N York* | **82** | SE0951 |
| Langbaurgh *N York* | **90** | NZ5611 |
| Langcliffe *N York* | **88** | SD8264 |
| Langdale End *N York* | **91** | SE9391 |
| Langdon *M Glam* | **5** | SX3089 |
| Langdon Beck *Dur* | **95** | NY8531 |
| Langdown *Hants* | **13** | SU4206 |
| Langdyke *Fife* | **126** | NO3304 |
| Langenhoe *Essex* | **41** | TM0018 |
| Langford *Avon* | **21** | ST4561 |
| Langford *Beds* | **39** | TL1841 |
| Langford *Devon* | **9** | ST0203 |
| Langford *Essex* | **40** | TL8309 |
| Langford *Notts* | **75** | SK8258 |
| Langford *Oxon* | **36** | SP2402 |
| Langford Budville *Somset* | **20** | ST1122 |
| Langford End *Beds* | **52** | TL1653 |
| Langford Green *Devon* | **9** | ST0302 |
| Langham *Dorset* | **22** | ST7725 |
| Langham *Essex* | **41** | TM0333 |
| Langham *Leics* | **63** | SK8411 |
| Langham *Norfk* | **66** | TG0041 |
| Langham *Suffk* | **54** | TL9770 |
| Langham Moor *Essex* | **41** | TM0131 |
| Langham Wick *Essex* | **41** | TM0231 |
| Langho *Lancs* | **81** | SD7034 |
| Langholm *D & G* | **101** | NY3684 |
| Langley *Berks* | **26** | TQ0178 |
| Langley *Ches* | **79** | SJ9471 |
| Langley *Derbys* | **62** | SK4446 |
| Langley *Essex* | **39** | TL4334 |
| Langley *Gloucs* | **47** | SP0128 |
| Langley *Gt Man* | **79** | SD8506 |
| Langley *Hants* | **13** | SU4401 |
| Langley *Herts* | **39** | TL2122 |
| Langley *Nthumb* | **102** | NY8361 |
| Langley *Oxon* | **36** | SP2915 |
| Langley *Somset* | **20** | ST0828 |
| Langley *W Susx* | **14** | SU8029 |
| Langley *Warwks* | **48** | SP1965 |
| Langley Burrell *Wilts* | **35** | ST9375 |
| Langley Castle *Nthumb* | **102** | NY8362 |
| Langley Common *Derbys* | **73** | SK2938 |
| Langley Green *Derbys* | **73** | SK2738 |
| Langley Green *Essex* | **40** | TL8822 |
| Langley Green *Warwks* | **48** | SP1962 |
| Langley Marsh *Somset* | **20** | ST0729 |
| Langley Mill *Derbys* | **62** | SK4447 |
| Langley Moor *Dur* | **96** | NZ2440 |
| Langley Park *Dur* | **96** | NZ2144 |
| Langley Street *Norfk* | **67** | TG3601 |
| Langleybury *Herts* | **26** | TL0700 |
| Langney *E Susx* | **16** | TQ6302 |
| Langold *Notts* | **75** | SK5886 |
| Langore *Cnwll* | **5** | SX2986 |
| Langport *Somset* | **21** | ST4226 |
| Langrick *Lincs* | **77** | TF2648 |
| Langridge *Avon* | **35** | ST7469 |
| Langridge Ford *Devon* | **19** | SS5722 |
| Langrigg *Cumb* | **92** | NY1645 |
| Langrish *Hants* | **13** | SU7023 |
| Langsett *S York* | **74** | SE2100 |
| Langshaw *Border* | **109** | NT5139 |
| Langside *Tays* | **125** | NN7913 |
| Langstone *Gwent* | **34** | ST3789 |
| Langstone *Hants* | **13** | SU7105 |
| Langthorne *N York* | **89** | SE2491 |
| Langthorpe *N York* | **89** | SE3867 |
| Langthwaite *N York* | **88** | NZ0001 |
| Langtoft *Humb* | **91** | TA0166 |
| Langtoft *Lincs* | **64** | TF1212 |
| Langton *Dur* | **96** | NZ1719 |
| Langton *Lincs* | **76** | TF2368 |
| Langton *Lincs* | **77** | TF3970 |
| Langton *N York* | **90** | SE7967 |
| Langton by Wragby *Lincs* | **76** | TF1476 |
| Langton Green *Kent* | **16** | TQ5439 |
| Langton Green *Kent* | **16** | TQ5439 |
| Langton Green *Suffk* | **54** | TM1474 |
| Langton Herring *Dorset* | **10** | SY6182 |
| Langton Matravers *Dorset* | **11** | SY9978 |
| Langtree *Devon* | **18** | SS4515 |
| Langtree Week *Devon* | **18** | SS4705 |
| Langwathby *Cumb* | **94** | NY5733 |
| Langwell *Highld* | **145** | NC1703 |
| Langwell House *Highld* | **147** | ND1122 |
| Langwith *Derbys* | **75** | SK5370 |
| Langworth *Lincs* | **76** | TF0676 |
| Langworthy *Devon* | **5** | SX4895 |
| Lanieth *Cnwll* | **3** | SW9752 |
| Lanivet *Cnwll* | **4** | SX0364 |
| Lank *Cnwll* | **4** | SX0975 |
| Lanlivery *Cnwll* | **4** | SX0759 |
| Lanner *Cnwll* | **2** | SW7139 |
| Lanoy *Cnwll* | **5** | SX2977 |
| Lanreath *Cnwll* | **4** | SX1857 |
| Lansallos *Cnwll* | **4** | SX1751 |
| Lansdown *Avon* | **22** | ST7268 |
| Lanteglos *Cnwll* | **4** | SX0882 |
| Lanteglos Highway *Cnwll* | **3** | SX1453 |
| Lantilio-Crossenny *Gwent* | **34** | SO3914 |
| Lanton *Border* | **110** | NT6122 |
| Lanton *Nthumb* | **110** | NT9231 |
| Lapford *Devon* | **19** | SS7308 |
| Laphroaig *Strath* | **104** | NR3845 |
| Lapley *Staffs* | **60** | SJ8713 |
| Lapworth *Warwks* | **61** | SP1671 |
| Larachbeg *Highld* | **122** | NM6948 |
| Larbert *Cent* | **116** | NS8582 |
| Larbreck *Lancs* | **80** | SD4040 |
| Largie *Gramp* | **142** | NJ6131 |
| Largiemore *Strath* | **114** | NR9486 |
| Largoward *Fife* | **127** | NO4607 |
| Largs *Strath* | **114** | NS2059 |
| Largybeg *Strath* | **105** | NS0423 |
| Largymore *Strath* | **105** | NS0424 |
| Larkfield *Kent* | **28** | TQ7058 |
| Larkfield *Strath* | **114** | NS2376 |
| Larkhall *Strath* | **116** | NS7651 |
| Larkhill *Wilts* | **23** | SU1243 |
| Larling *Norfk* | **54** | TL9889 |
| Larrick *Cnwll* | **5** | SX3078 |
| Larriston *Border* | **101** | NY5494 |
| Lartington *Dur* | **95** | NZ0117 |
| Lasborough *Gloucs* | **35** | ST8294 |
| Lasham *Hants* | **24** | SU6742 |
| Lashbrook *Devon* | **18** | SS4305 |
| Lashenden *Kent* | **28** | TQ8440 |
| Lask Edge *Staffs* | **72** | SJ9156 |
| Lassodie *Fife* | **117** | NT1292 |
| Lasswade *Loth* | **117** | NT3065 |
| Lastingham *N York* | **90** | SE7290 |
| Latcham *Somset* | **21** | ST4447 |
| Latchford *Herts* | **39** | TL3920 |
| Latchford *Oxon* | **37** | SP6501 |
| Latchingdon and Snoreham *Essex* | **40** | TL8800 |
| Latchley *Cnwll* | **5** | SX4173 |
| Latebrook *Staffs* | **72** | SJ8453 |
| Lately Common *Gt Man* | **79** | SJ6797 |
| Lathbury *Bucks* | **38** | SP8744 |
| Latheron *Highld* | **151** | ND2033 |
| Latheronwheel House *Highld* | **151** | ND1832 |
| Lathones *Fife* | **127** | NO4708 |
| Latimer *Bucks* | **26** | TQ0199 |
| Lator *Devon* | **7** | SX7872 |
| Latteridge *Avon* | **35** | ST6684 |
| Lattiford *Somset* | **22** | ST6926 |
| Latton *Wilts* | **36** | SU0995 |
| Lauder *Border* | **118** | NT5347 |
| Laugharne *Dyfed* | **31** | SN3011 |
| Laughterton *Lincs* | **76** | SK8375 |
| Laughton *E Susx* | **16** | TQ4913 |
| Laughton *Leics* | **50** | SP6688 |
| Laughton *Lincs* | **64** | TF0731 |
| Laughton *Lincs* | **76** | SK8497 |
| Laughton-en-le-Morthen *S York* | **75** | SK5188 |
| Launcells *Cnwll* | **18** | SS2405 |
| Launcells Cross *Cnwll* | **18** | SS2505 |
| Launceston *Cnwll* | **5** | SX3384 |
| Launton *Oxon* | **37** | SP6022 |
| Laurencekirk *Gramp* | **135** | NO7171 |
| Laurieston *Cent* | **116** | NS9179 |
| Laurieston *D & G* | **99** | NX6864 |
| Lavendon *Bucks* | **51** | SP9153 |
| Lavenham *Suffk* | **54** | TL9149 |
| Lavernock *S Glam* | **20** | ST1868 |
| Laversdale *Cumb* | **101** | NY4762 |
| Laverstock *Wilts* | **23** | SU1530 |
| Laverstoke *Hants* | **24** | SU4948 |
| Laverton *Gloucs* | **48** | SP0735 |
| Laverton *N York* | **89** | SE2273 |
| Laverton *Somset* | **22** | ST7753 |
| Lavister *Clwyd* | **71** | SJ3758 |
| Law *Strath* | **116** | NS8152 |
| Law Hill *Strath* | **116** | NS8251 |
| Lawers *Tays* | **124** | NN6739 |
| Lawers *Tays* | **125** | NN7923 |
| Lawford *Essex* | **41** | TM0831 |
| Lawford *Somset* | **20** | ST1437 |
| Lawgrove *Tays* | **125** | NO0926 |
| Lawhitton *Cnwll* | **5** | SX3582 |
| Lawkland *N York* | **88** | SD7766 |
| Lawkland Green *N York* | **88** | SD7865 |
| Lawley *Shrops* | **60** | SJ6608 |
| Lawnhead *Staffs* | **72** | SJ8224 |
| Lawrence End *Herts* | **38** | TL1419 |
| Lawrenny *Dyfed* | **30** | SN0107 |
| Lawshall *Suffk* | **54** | TL8654 |
| Lawshall Green *Suffk* | **54** | TL8853 |
| Lawton *H & W* | **46** | SO4459 |
| Laxay *W Isls* | **154** | NB3321 |
| Laxdale *W Isls* | **154** | NB4234 |
| Laxey *IOM* | **153** | SC4384 |
| Laxfield *Suffk* | **55** | TM2972 |
| Laxford Bridge *Highld* | **148** | NC2346 |
| Laxo *Shet* | **155** | HU4463 |
| Laxton *Humb* | **84** | SE7825 |
| Laxton *Nhants* | **51** | SP9596 |
| Laxton *Notts* | **75** | SK7266 |
| Laycock *W York* | **82** | SE0341 |
| Layer Breton *Essex* | **40** | TL9418 |
| Layer Marney *Essex* | **40** | TL9217 |
| Layer-de-la-Haye *Essex* | **41** | TL9620 |
| Layham *Suffk* | **54** | TM0340 |
| Layland's Green *Berks* | **23** | SU3866 |
| Laymore *Dorset* | **10** | ST3804 |
| Laysters Pole *H & W* | **46** | SO5563 |
| Layter's Green *Bucks* | **26** | SU9890 |
| Laytham *Humb* | **84** | SE7439 |
| Laythes *Cumb* | **93** | NY2455 |
| Lazenby *Cleve* | **97** | NZ5719 |
| Lazonby *Cumb* | **94** | NY5449 |
| Le Bigard *Guern* | **152** | GN0000 |
| Le Bourg *Guern* | **152** | GN0000 |
| Le Bourg *Jersey* | **152** | JS0000 |
| Le Bron *Guern* | **152** | GN0000 |
| Le Haquais *Jersey* | **152** | JS0000 |
| Le Hocq *Jersey* | **152** | JS0000 |
| Le Villocq *Guern* | **152** | GN0000 |
| Le Villocq *Guern* | **152** | GN0000 |
| Lea *Derbys* | **74** | SK3257 |
| Lea *H & W* | **35** | SO6521 |
| Lea *Lincs* | **75** | SK8286 |
| Lea *Shrops* | **59** | SJ4108 |
| Lea *Shrops* | **59** | SO3589 |
| Lea *Wilts* | **35** | ST9586 |
| Lea Bridge *Derbys* | **74** | SK3156 |
| Lea Heath *Staffs* | **73** | SK0225 |
| Lea Marston *Warwks* | **61** | SP2093 |
| Lea Town *Lancs* | **80** | SD4730 |
| Lea Yeat *Cumb* | **88** | SD7586 |
| Leachkin *Highld* | **140** | NH6445 |
| Leadburn *Loth* | **117** | NT2355 |
| Leaden Roding *Essex* | **40** | TL5913 |
| Leadenham *Lincs* | **76** | SK9452 |
| Leadgate *Cumb* | **94** | NY7043 |
| Leadgate *Dur* | **96** | NZ1251 |
| Leadgate *Nthumb* | **95** | NZ1159 |
| Leadhills *Strath* | **108** | NS8815 |
| Leadingcross Green *Kent* | **28** | TQ8951 |
| Leadmill *Derbys* | **74** | SK2380 |
| Leafield *Oxon* | **36** | SP3115 |
| Leagrave *Beds* | **38** | TL0523 |
| Leahead *Ches* | **72** | SJ6964 |
| Leaholm Side *N York* | **90** | NZ7607 |
| Leake *N York* | **89** | SE4390 |
| Leake Common Side *Lincs* | **77** | TF3952 |
| Lealholm *N York* | **90** | NZ7607 |
| Lealt *Highld* | **137** | NG5060 |
| Leam *Derbys* | **74** | SK2379 |
| Leamington Hastings *Warwks* | **50** | SP4467 |
| Leamonsley *Staffs* | **61** | SK1009 |
| Leap Cross *E Susx* | **16** | TQ5810 |
| Leargybreck *Strath* | **113** | NR5371 |
| Leasgill *Cumb* | **87** | SD4984 |
| Leasingham *Lincs* | **76** | TF0548 |
| Leasingthorne *Dur* | **96** | NZ2530 |
| Leatherhead *Surrey* | **26** | TQ1656 |
| Leathley *N York* | **82** | SE2346 |
| Leaths *D & G* | **100** | NX7863 |
| Leaton *Shrops* | **59** | SJ6111 |
| Leaton *Shrops* | **59** | SJ4618 |
| Leaveland *Kent* | **28** | TR0053 |
| Leavenheath *Suffk* | **54** | TL9537 |
| Leavening *N York* | **90** | SE7863 |
| Leaves Green *Gt Lon* | **27** | TQ4161 |
| Lebberston *N York* | **91** | TA0782 |
| Lechampstead Thicket *Berks* | **36** | SU4276 |
| Lechlade *Wilts* | **36** | SU2199 |
| Leck *Lancs* | **87** | SD6476 |
| Leckbuie *Tays* | **124** | NN7040 |
| Leckford *Hants* | **23** | SU3737 |
| Leckfurin *Highld* | **150** | NC7059 |
| Leckgruinart *Strath* | **112** | NR2768 |
| Leckhampstead *Berks* | **36** | SU4375 |
| Leckhampstead *Bucks* | **49** | SP7237 |
| Leckhampton *Gloucs* | **35** | SO9419 |
| Leckhamstead *Bucks* | **49** | SP7237 |
| Leckmelm *Highld* | **145** | NH1790 |
| Leckwith *S Glam* | **33** | ST1574 |
| Leconfield *Humb* | **84** | TA0143 |
| Ledaig *Strath* | **122** | NM9037 |
| Ledburn *Bucks* | **38** | SP9021 |
| Ledbury *H & W* | **47** | SO7037 |
| Ledgemoor *H & W* | **46** | SO4150 |
| Ledicot *H & W* | **46** | SO4162 |
| Ledmore Junction *Highld* | **145** | NC2412 |
| Ledsham *Ches* | **71** | SJ3574 |
| Ledsham *W York* | **83** | SE4529 |
| Ledston *W York* | **83** | SE4328 |
| Ledstone *Devon* | **7** | SX7446 |
| Ledwell *Oxon* | **49** | SP4128 |
| Lee *Devon* | **18** | SS4846 |
| Lee *Gt Lon* | **27** | TQ3875 |
| Lee *Hants* | **12** | SU3617 |
| Lee *Shrops* | **59** | SJ4032 |

Lee Little Singleton


Lee Strath 121 NM4022
Lee Brockhurst Shrops 59 SJ5427
Lee Chapel Essex 40 TQ6987
Lee Clump Bucks 38 SP9004
Lee Common Bucks 38 SP9303
Lee Green Ches 72 SJ6562
Lee Mill Devon 6 SX5855
Lee Moor Devon 6 SX5762
Lee Street Surrey 15 TQ2743
Lee-on-the-Solent Hants 13 SU5600
Leebotwood Shrops 59 SO4798
Leece Cumb 86 SD2469
Leedon Beds 38 SP9325
Leeds Kent 28 TQ8253
Leeds W York 82 SE3034
Leeds Beck Lincs 76 TF2065
Leedstown Cnwll 2 SW6034
Leek Staffs 72 SJ9856
Leek Wootton Warwks 48 SP2968
Leeming N York 89 SE2989
Leeming W York 82 SE0434
Leeming Bar N York 89 SE2889
Lees Derbys 73 SK2637
Lees Gt Man 79 SD9504
Lees Gt Man 79 SD9504
Lees W York 82 SE0437
Lees Green Derbys 73 SK2637
Lees Hill Cumb 101 NY5568
Leesthorpe Leics 63 SK7813
Leetown Tays 126 NO2121
Leftwich Ches 79 SJ6672
Legbourne Lincs 77 TF3684
Legburthwaite Cumb 93 NY3219
Legerwood Border 110 NT5843
Legsby Lincs 76 TF1385
Leicester Leics 62 SK5804
Leicester Forest East Leics 62 SK5303
Leigh Devon 9 SS9115
Leigh Dorset 10 ST6108
Leigh Gloucs 47 SO8626
Leigh H & W 47 SO7853
Leigh Kent 16 TQ5446
Leigh Mersyd 79 SJ6599
Leigh Shrops 59 SJ3303
Leigh Surrey 15 TQ2246
Leigh Wilts 36 SU0692
Leigh Beck Essex 40 TQ8183
Leigh Delamere Wilts 35 ST8879
Leigh Green Kent 17 TQ9033
Leigh Knoweglass Strath 116 NS6350
Leigh Sinton H & W 47 SO7750
Leigh upon Mendip Somset 22 ST6847
Leigh Woods Avon 34 ST5572
Leigh-on-Sea Essex 40 TQ8286
Leighland Chapel Somset 20 ST0336
Leighterton Gloucs 35 ST8290
Leighton N York 89 SE1679
Leighton Powys 58 SJ2406
Leighton Shrops 59 SJ6105
Leighton Somset 22 ST7043
Leighton Bromswold Cambs 52 TL1175
Leighton Buzzard Beds 38 SP9225
Leinthall Earls H & W 46 SO4467
Leinthall Starkes H & W 46 SO4369
Leintwardine H & W 46 SO4074
Leire Leics 50 SP5290
Leiston Suffk 55 TM4462
Leitfie Tays 126 NO2545
Leith Loth 117 NT2676
Leitholm Border 110 NT7944
Lelant Cnwll 2 SW5437
Lelley Humb 85 TA2032
Lem Hill H & W 60 SO7275
Lemmington Hall Nthumb 111 NU1211
Lempitlaw Border 110 NT7832
Lemreway W Isls 154 NB3711
Lemsford Herts 39 TL2212
Lenchwick H & W 48 SP0347
Lendalfoot Strath 106 NX1390
Lendrick Cent 124 NN5506
Lendrum Terrace Gramp 143 NK1141
Lenham Kent 28 TQ8952
Lenham Heath Kent 28 TQ9249
Lenie Highld 139 NH5126
Lennel Border 110 NT8540
Lennox Plunton D & G 99 NX6051
Lennoxlove Loth 118 NT5172
Lennoxtown Strath 116 NS6277
Lent Bucks 26 SU9381
Lenton Lincs 64 TF0230
Lenton Notts 62 SK5539
Lenwade Norfk 66 TG0918
Lenzie Strath 116 NS6572
Leochel-Cushnie Gramp 134 NJ5210
Leominster H & W 46 SO4958
Leonard Stanley Gloucs 35 SO8003
Leorin Strath 104 NR3548
Leoville Jersey 152 JS0000
Lepe Hants 13 SZ4598
Lephin Highld 136 NG1749
Lephinchapel Strath 114 NR9690
Lephinmore Strath 114 NR9892
Leppington N York 90 SE7661
Lepton W York 82 SE2015
Lerags Strath 122 NM8324
Lerryn Cnwll 4 SX1457
Lerwick Shet 155 HU4741
Les Arquets Guern 152 GN0000
Les Hubits Guern 152 GN0000
Les Lohiers Guern 152 GN0000
Les Murchez Guern 152 GN0000
Les Nicolles Guern 152 GN0000
Les Quartiers Guern 152 GN0000
Les Quennevais Jersey 152 JS0000
Les Sages Guern 152 GN0000
Les Villets Guern 152 GN0000
Lesbury Nthumb 111 NU2312
Leslie Fife 126 NO2501
Leslie Gramp 142 NJ5924
Lesmahagow Strath 108 NS8139
Lesnewth Cnwll 4 SX1390
Lessingham Norfk 67 TG3928
Lessonhall Cumb 93 NY2249
Lessonhall Cumb 93 NY2249
Lestowder Cnwll 3 SW7924
Leswalt D & G 98 NX0164
Letchmore Heath Herts 26 TQ1597
Letchworth Herts 39 TL2232
Letcombe Bassett Oxon 36 SU3785
Letcombe Regis Oxon 36 SU3786
Letham Border 110 NT6708
Letham Fife 126 NO3014
Letham Tays 127 NO5348
Letham Grange Tays 127 NO6345
Lethenty Gramp 142 NJ5820
Lethenty Gramp 143 NJ8140
Lethenty Gramp 142 NJ5820
Letheringham Suffk 55 TM2757
Letheringsett Norfk 66 TG0639
Lett's Green Kent 27 TQ4558
Lettaford Devon 8 SX7084
Letterfearn Highld 138 NG8823
Letterfinley Lodge Hotel Highld 131 NN2591
Lettermorar Highld 129 NM7389
Letters Highld 145 NH1687
Lettershaw Strath 108 NS8920
Letterston Dyfed 30 SM9429
Lettoch Highld 141 NJ0219
Lettoch Highld 141 NJ0932
Letton H & W 46 SO3346
Letton H & W 46 SO3770
Letty Green Herts 39 TL2810
Letwell S York 75 SK5587
Leuchars Fife 127 NO4521
Leurbost W Isls 154 NB3725
Levalsa Moor Cnwll 3 SX0049
Levedale Staffs 72 SJ9016
Level's Green Essex 39 TL4724
Leven Fife 118 NO3800
Leven Humb 85 TA1045
Levencorroch Strath 105 NS0021
Levens Cumb 87 SD4886
Levens Green Herts 39 TL3522
Levenshulme Gt Man 79 SJ8794
Levenwick Shet 155 HU4021
Leverburgh W Isls 154 NG0186
Leverington Cambs 65 TF4411
Leverstock Green Herts 38 TL0806
Leverton Lincs 77 TF3947
Levington Suffk 55 TM2339
Levisham N York 90 SE8390
Lew Oxon 36 SP3206
Lew Middleton Nthumb 111 NU1036
Lewannick Cnwll 5 SX2780
Lewdown Devon 5 SX4486
Lewes E Susx 15 TQ4110
Leweston Dorset 10 ST6312
Leweston Dyfed 30 SM9422
Lewis Wych H & W 46 SO3357
Lewisham Gt Lon 27 TQ3774
Lewiston Highld 139 NH5129
Lewknor Oxon 37 SU7197
Leworthy Devon 19 SS6738
Leworthy Devon 18 SS3201
Lewson Street Kent 28 TQ9661
Lewth Lancs 80 SD4836
Lewtrenchard Devon 5 SX4686
Lexden Essex 41 TL9625
Lexworthy Somset 20 ST2535
Ley Cnwll 4 SX1766
Leybourne Kent 28 TQ6858
Leyburn N York 89 SE1190
Leycett Staffs 72 SJ7946
Leygreen Herts 39 TL1624
Leyland Lancs 80 SD5422
Leyland Green Mersyd 78 SD5500
Leylodge Gramp 135 NJ7613
Leys Gramp 143 NK0052
Leys Tays 126 NO2537
Leys of Cossans Tays 126 NO3849
Leysdown-on-Sea Kent 28 TR0370
Leysmill Tays 127 NO6047
Leyton Gt Lon 27 TQ3886
Leytonstone Gt Lon 27 TQ3987
Lezant Cnwll 5 SX3379
Lezayre IOM 153 SC4294
Lezerea Cnwll 2 SW6833
Lhanbryde Gramp 141 NJ2761
Lhen The IOM 153 NX3801
Little Cheverell Wilts 22 ST9853
Libanus Powys 45 SN9925
Libberton Strath 108 NS9943
Liberton Loth 117 NT2769
Lichfield Staffs 61 SK1109
Lickey H & W 60 SO9975
Lickey End H & W 60 SO9772
Lickey Rock H & W 60 SO9774
Lickfold W Susx 14 SU9226
Liddaton Green Devon 5 SX4582
Liddesdale Highld 130 NM7759
Liddington Wilts 36 SU2081
Lidgate Suffk 53 TL7258
Lidget S York 75 SE6500
Lidgett Notts 75 SK6365
Lidham Hill E Susx 17 TQ8316
Lidlington Beds 38 SP9839
Lidsing Kent 28 TQ7862
Lienassie Highld 138 NG9621
Liff Tays 126 NO3332
Lifford W Mids 61 SP0580
Lifton Devon 5 SX3885
Liftondown Devon 5 SX3685
Lighthazles W York 82 SE0220
Lighthorne Warwks 48 SP3355
Lightwater Surrey 25 SU9362
Lightwood Staffs 72 SJ9241
Lightwood Green Ches 63 SK6342
Lightwood Green Clwyd 71 SJ3840
Lilbourne Nhants 50 SP5677
Lilburn Tower Nthumb 111 NU0224
Lilleshall Shrops 72 SJ7315
Lilley Berks 37 SU4479
Lilley Herts 38 TL1226
Lilliesleaf Border 109 NT5325
Lillingstone Dayrell Bucks 49 SP7039
Lillingstone Lovell Bucks 49 SP7140
Lillington Dorset 10 ST6212
Lilstock Somset 20 ST1644
Lilyhurst Shrops 60 SJ7413
Limbrick Lancs 81 SD6016
Limbury Beds 38 TL0724
Lime Street H & W 47 SO8130
Limebrook H & W 46 SO3766
Limefield Gt Man 81 SD8013
Limekilnburn Strath 116 NS7050
Limekilns Fife 117 NT0883
Limerigg Cent 116 NS8570
Limerstone IOW 13 SZ4482
Limestone Brae Nthumb 95 NY7949
Limington Somset 21 ST5422
Limmerhaugh Strath 107 NS6127
Limpenhoe Norfk 67 TG3903
Limpley Stoke Wilts 22 ST7760
Limpsfield Surrey 27 TQ4053
Linby Notts 75 SK5351
Linchmere W Susx 14 SU8731
Lincoln Lincs 76 SK9771
Lincomb H & W 47 SO8269
Lincombe Devon 7 SX7340
Lincombe Devon 7 SX7458
Lindal in Furness Cumb 86 SD2475
Lindale Cumb 87 SD4180
Lindean Border 109 NT4931
Lindfield W Susx 15 TQ3425
Lindfold Hants 14 SU8036
Lindford Magna Lincs 76 TF1988
Lindley W York 82 SE1218
Lindley Green N York 82 SE2248
Lindores Fife 126 NO2617
Lindow End Ches 79 SJ8178
Lindridge H & W 47 SO6769
Lindsell Essex 40 TL6427
Lindsey Suffk 54 TL9745
Lindsey Tye Suffk 54 TL9845
Liney Somset 21 ST3535
Linford Essex 40 TQ6779
Linford Hants 12 SU1707
Ling Bob W York 82 SE0935
Lingague IOM 153 SC2172
Lingdale Cleve 97 NZ6716
Lingen H & W 46 SO3667
Lingfield Surrey 15 TQ3843
Lingfield Common Surrey 15 TQ3844
Lingley Green Ches 78 SJ5589
Lingwood Norfk 67 TG3608
Liniclett W Isls 154 NF7949
Linicro Highld 136 NG3967
Linkend H & W 47 SO8231
Linkenholt Hants 23 SU3658
Linkhill Kent 17 TQ8128
Linkinhorne Cnwll 5 SX3173
Linktown Fife 117 NT2890
Linkwood Gramp 141 NJ2361
Linley Shrops 59 SO3592
Linley Green H & W 47 SO6953
Linleygreen Shrops 60 SO6898
Linlithgow Loth 117 NS9977
Linnels Bridge Nthumb 102 NY9562
Linshiels Nthumb 110 NT8906
Linsidemore Highld 146 NH5499
Linslade Beds 38 SP9125
Linstead Parva Suffk 55 TM3377
Linstock Cumb 93 NY4258
Linthurst H & W 60 SO9972
Linthwaite W York 82 SE1014
Linthwaite W York 82 SE0913
Lintlaw Border 119 NT8258
Lintmill Gramp 142 NJ5165
Linton Border 110 NT7726
Linton Cambs 53 TL5646
Linton Derbys 73 SK2716
Linton Gloucs 35 SO7918
Linton H & W 47 SO6625
Linton Kent 28 TQ7550
Linton N York 88 SD9962
Linton W York 83 SE3846
Linton Heath Derbys 73 SK2816
Linton Hill Gloucs 47 SO6624
Linton-on-Ouse N York 90 SE4860
Linwood Hants 12 SU1809
Linwood Lincs 76 TF1186
Linwood Strath 115 NS4464
Lionel W Isls 154 NB5263
Lions Green E Susx 16 TQ5518
Liphook Hants 14 SU8431
Lipley Shrops 72 SJ7330
Liscard Mersyd 78 SJ2991
Liscombe Devon 19 SS8732
Liskeard Cnwll 5 SX2564
Liss Hants 14 SU7727
Liss Forest Hants 14 SU7829
Lissett Humb 91 TA1458
Lissington Lincs 76 TF1083
Liston Essex 54 TL8544
Lisvane S Glam 33 ST1983
Liswerry Gwent 34 ST3487
Litcham Norfk 66 TF8817
Litchard M Glam 33 SS9182
Litchborough Nhants 49 SP6354
Litchfield Hants 24 SU4653
Litherland Mersyd 78 SJ3397
Litlington Cambs 39 TL3142
Litlington E Susx 16 TQ5201
Little Abington Cambs 53 TL5349
Little Addington Nhants 51 SP9673
Little Airies D & G 99 NX4248
Little Almshoe Herts 39 TL2025
Little Alne Warwks 48 SP1461
Little Amwell Herts 39 TL3511
Little Asby Cumb 87 NY6909
Little Aston Staffs 61 SK0900
Little Atherfield IOW 13 SZ4680
Little Ayton N York 90 NZ5610
Little Baddow Essex 40 TL7708
Little Badminton Avon 35 ST8084
Little Bampton Cumb 93 NY2755
Little Bardfield Essex 40 TL6531
Little Barford Beds 52 TL1756
Little Barningham Norfk 66 TG1333
Little Barrington Gloucs 36 SP2012
Little Barrow Ches 71 SJ4770
Little Barugh N York 90 SE7579
Little Bavington Nthumb 102 NY9878
Little Bayton Warwks 61 SP3585
Little Bealings Suffk 55 TM2348
Little Bedwyn Wilts 23 SU2966
Little Bentley Essex 41 TM1125
Little Berkhamsted Herts 39 TL2907
Little Billing Nhants 51 SP8061
Little Billington Beds 38 SP9322
Little Birch H & W 46 SO5130
Little Bispham Lancs 80 SD3141
Little Blakenham Suffk 54 TM1049
Little Blencow Cumb 93 NY4532
Little Bloxwich W Mids 60 SK0003
Little Bognor W Susx 14 TQ0020
Little Bolehill Derbys 73 SK2954
Little Bookham Surrey 26 TQ1254
Little Bourton Oxon 49 SP4543
Little Bowden Leics 50 SP7487
Little Bradley Suffk 53 TL6852
Little Brampton H & W 46 SO3061
Little Brampton Shrops 59 SO3681
Little Braxted Essex 40 TL8314
Little Brechin Tays 134 NO5862
Little Brickhill Bucks 38 SP9032
Little Bridgeford Staffs 72 SJ8727
Little Brington Nhants 49 SP6663
Little Bromley Essex 41 TM0928
Little Budworth Ches 71 SJ6065
Little Burstead Essex 40 TQ6692
Little Bytham Lincs 64 TF0118
Little Carlton Lincs 77 TF3985
Little Carlton Notts 75 SK7757
Little Casterton Leics 64 TF0109
Little Catwick Humb 85 TA1444
Little Catworth Cambs 51 TL1072
Little Cawthorpe Lincs 77 TF3583
Little Chalfont Bucks 26 SU9997
Little Charlinch Somset 20 ST2437
Little Chart Kent 28 TQ9446
Little Chatfield Wilts 22 ST8563
Little Chesterford Essex 39 TL5141
Little Cheveney Kent 28 TQ7243
Little Chishill Cambs 39 TL4237
Little Clacton Essex 41 TM1618
Little Clanfield Oxon 36 SP2701
Little Clifton Cumb 92 NY0528
Little Coates Humb 85 TA2408
Little Comberton H & W 47 SO9643
Little Common E Susx 17 TQ7108
Little Comp Kent 27 TQ6357
Little Compton Warwks 48 SP2530
Little Corby Cumb 93 NY4757
Little Cornard Suffk 54 TL9039
Little Cowarne H & W 46 SO6051
Little Coxwell Oxon 36 SU2893
Little Crakehall N York 89 SE2490
Little Cransley Nhants 51 SP8376
Little Creaton Nhants 50 SP7171
Little Cressingham Norfk 66 TF8700
Little Crosby Mersyd 78 SD3201
Little Crosthwaite Cumb 93 NY2336
Little Cubley Derbys 73 SK1537
Little Dalby Leics 63 SK7714
Little Dens Gramp 143 NK0643
Little Dewchurch H & W 46 SO5231
Little Ditton Cambs 53 TL6658
Little Doward H & W 34 SO5416
Little Driffield Humb 91 TA0058
Little Dunham Norfk 66 TF8612
Little Dunkeld Tays 125 NO0342
Little Dunmow Essex 40 TL6521
Little Durnford Wilts 23 SU1234
Little Easton Essex 40 TL6023
Little Eaton Derbys 62 SK3641
Little Ellingham Norfk 66 TM0099
Little Elm Somset 22 ST7246
Little Everdon Nhants 49 SP5957
Little Eversden Cambs 52 TL3753
Little Faringdon S York 36 SP2201
Little Fencote N York 89 SE2793
Little Fenton N York 83 SE5135
Little Fransham Norfk 66 TF9011
Little Gaddesden Herts 38 SP9913
Little Garway H & W 46 SO4424
Little Gidding Cambs 52 TL1282
Little Glemham Suffk 55 TM3458
Little Gorsley H & W 47 SO6824
Little Gransden Cambs 52 TL2755
Little Green Notts 63 SK7243
Little Green Somset 22 ST7248
Little Grimsby Lincs 77 TF3291
Little Grindley Notts 75 SK7380
Little Habton N York 90 SE7477
Little Hadham Herts 39 TL4322
Little Hale Lincs 64 TF1441
Little Hallam Derbys 62 SK4640
Little Hallingbury Essex 39 TL5017
Little Hanford Dorset 11 ST8311
Little Harrowden Nhants 51 SP8771
Little Hartlip Kent 28 TQ8464
Little Haseley Oxon 37 SP6400
Little Hatfield Humb 85 TA1743
Little Hautbois Norfk 67 TG2521
Little Haven Dyfed 30 SM8513
Little Hay Staffs 61 SK1202
Little Haywood Staffs 73 SK0021
Little Heath Berks 24 SU6537
Little Heath Staffs 72 SJ9017
Little Heath W Mids 61 SP3482
Little Hereford H & W 46 SO5568
Little Hermitage Kent 28 TQ7170
Little Horkesley Essex 41 TL9632
Little Hormead Herts 39 TL4028
Little Horsted E Susx 16 TQ4718
Little Horton W York 82 SE1531
Little Horton Wilts 23 SU0462
Little Horwood Bucks 38 SP7930
Little Houghton Nhants 51 SP8059
Little Houghton S York 83 SE4205
Little Hucklow Derbys 74 SK1678
Little Hulton Gt Man 79 SD7203
Little Hungerford Berks 24 SU5173
Little Hutton N York 89 SE4576
Little Ingestre Staffs 73 SJ9924
Little Irchester Nhants 51 SP9066
Little Keak Humb 91 TA0959
Little Keyford Somset 22 ST7746
Little Kimble Bucks 38 SP8207
Little Kineton Warwks 48 SP3350
Little Kingshill Bucks 26 SU8899
Little Knox D & G 100 NX8060
Little Langdale Cumb 86 NY3103
Little Langford Wilts 23 SU0436
Little Lashbrook Devon 18 SS4007
Little Laver Essex 39 TL5409
Little Leigh Ches 71 SJ6175
Little Leighs Essex 40 TL7117
Little Lever Gt Man 79 SD7507
Little Linford Bucks 38 SP8434
Little Linton Cambs 53 TL5547
Little Load Somset 21 ST4624
Little London Cambs 65 TL4196
Little London E Susx 16 TQ5720
Little London Essex 39 TL4729
Little London Essex 53 TL6835
Little London Gloucs 35 SO7018
Little London Hants 23 SU3749
Little London Hants 24 SU6259
Little London Lincs 65 TF4323
Little London Lincs 77 TF3375
Little London Lincs 64 TF2321
Little London Norfk 65 TF5620
Little London Oxon 37 SP6412
Little London Powys 58 SO0489
Little London W York 82 SE2039
Little Longstone Derbys 74 SK1871
Little Madeley Staffs 72 SJ7745
Little Malvern H & W 47 SO7740
Little Mancot Clwyd 71 SJ3266
Little Maplestead Essex 54 TL8234
Little Marcle H & W 47 SO6736
Little Marlow Bucks 26 SU8787
Little Massingham Norfk 66 TF7924
Little Melton Norfk 66 TG1607
Little Mill Gwent 34 SO3203
Little Milton Oxon 37 SP6100
Little Missenden Bucks 26 SU9298
Little Mongham Kent 29 TR3351
Little Moor Somset 21 ST3232
Little Musgrave Cumb 94 NY7613
Little Ness Shrops 59 SJ4019
Little Neston Ches 71 SJ3076
Little Newcastle Dyfed 30 SM9829
Little Newsham Dur 96 NZ1217
Little Norton Somset 10 ST4815
Little Norton Staffs 60 SK0208
Little Oakley Essex 41 TM2129
Little Oakley Nhants 51 SP8985
Little Odell Beds 51 SP9557
Little Offley Herts 38 TL1228
Little Onn Staffs 72 SJ8315
Little Ormside Cumb 94 NY7016
Little Orton Cumb 93 NY3555
Little Oxendon Nhants 50 SP7184
Little Packington Warwks 61 SP2184
Little Pattenden Kent 28 TQ7445
Little Paxton Cambs 52 TL1862
Little Petherick Cnwll 4 SW9172
Little Plumpton Lancs 80 SD3832
Little Plumstead Norfk 67 TG3112
Little Ponton Lincs 63 SK9232
Little Posbrook Hants 13 SU5304
Little Potheridge Devon 19 SS5214
Little Preston Nhants 49 SP5854
Little Preston W York 83 SE3830
Little Raveley Cambs 52 TL2579
Little Reedness Humb 84 SE8022
Little Ribston N York 83 SE3853
Little Rissington Gloucs 36 SP1819
Little Rollright Oxon 48 SP2930
Little Rowsley Derbys 74 SK2566
Little Ryburgh Norfk 66 TF9628
Little Ryle Nthumb 111 NU0111
Little Ryton Shrops 59 SJ4803
Little Salkeld Cumb 94 NY5636
Little Sampford Essex 40 TL6533
Little Sandhurst Berks 25 SU8262
Little Saredon Staffs 60 SJ9407
Little Saughall Ches 71 SJ3769
Little Saxham Suffk 54 TL8063
Little Scatwell Highld 139 NH3856
Little Sessay N York 89 SE4674
Little Shelford Cambs 53 TL4551
Little Silver Devon 9 SS8601
Little Silver Devon 9 SS9109
Little Singleton Lancs 80 SD3739

Little Skipwith
Locheilside Station


| | | |
|---|---|---|
| Little Skipwith *N York* | **83** | SE**6538** |
| Little Smeaton *N York* | **83** | SE**5217** |
| Little Snoring *Norfk* | **66** | TF**9532** |
| Little Sodbury *Avon* | **35** | ST**7583** |
| Little Sodbury End *Avon* | **35** | ST**7483** |
| Little Somborne *Hants* | **23** | SU**3832** |
| Little Somerford *Wilts* | **35** | ST**9684** |
| Little Soudley *Shrops* | **72** | SJ**7128** |
| Little Stainforth *N York* | **88** | SD**8166** |
| Little Stainton *Dur* | **96** | NZ**3420** |
| Little Stanney *Ches* | **71** | SJ**4174** |
| Little Staughton *Beds* | **51** | TL**1062** |
| Little Steeping *Lincs* | **77** | TF**4362** |
| Little Stoke *Staffs* | **72** | SJ**9132** |
| Little Stonham *Suffk* | **54** | TM**1160** |
| Little Stretton *Leics* | **50** | SK**6600** |
| Little Stretton *Shrops* | **59** | SO**4492** |
| Little Strickland *Cumb* | **94** | NY**5619** |
| Little Stukeley *Cambs* | **52** | TL**2175** |
| Little Sugnall *Staffs* | **72** | SJ**8031** |
| Little Sutton *Ches* | **71** | SJ**3776** |
| Little Sutton *Shrops* | **59** | SO**5182** |
| Little Sypland *D & G* | **99** | NX**7253** |
| Little Tew *Oxon* | **48** | SP**3828** |
| Little Tey *Essex* | **40** | TL**8923** |
| Little Thetford *Cambs* | **53** | TL**5376** |
| Little Thirkleby *N York* | **89** | SE**4778** |
| Little Thornage *Norfk* | **66** | TG**0538** |
| Little Thornton *Lancs* | **80** | SD**3541** |
| Little Thorpe *Dur* | **96** | NZ**4242** |
| Little Thurlow *Suffk* | **53** | TL**6751** |
| Little Thurlow Green *Suffk* | **53** | TL**6851** |
| Little Thurrock *Essex* | **27** | TQ**6277** |
| Little Torrington *Devon* | **18** | SS**4916** |
| Little Totham *Essex* | **40** | TL**8912** |
| Little Town *Ches* | **79** | SJ**6494** |
| Little Town *Cumb* | **93** | NY**2319** |
| Little Town *Lancs* | **81** | SD**6635** |
| Little Twycross *Leics* | **62** | SK**3405** |
| Little Urswick *Cumb* | **101** | NY**2673** |
| Little Wakering *Essex* | **40** | TQ**9388** |
| Little Walden *Essex* | **39** | TL**5541** |
| Little Waldingfield *Suffk* | **54** | TL**9245** |
| Little Walsingham *Norfk* | **66** | TF**9336** |
| Little Waltham *Essex* | **40** | TL**7013** |
| Little Warley *Essex* | **40** | TQ**6090** |
| Little Washbourne *Gloucs* | **47** | SO**9833** |
| Little Weighton *Humb* | **84** | SE**9833** |
| Little Weldon *Nhants* | **51** | SP**9289** |
| Little Welnetham *Suffk* | **54** | TL**8960** |
| Little Welton *Lincs* | **77** | TF**3087** |
| Little Wenham *Suffk* | **54** | TM**0839** |
| Little Wenlock *Shrops* | **59** | SJ**6407** |
| Little Weston *Somset* | **21** | ST**6125** |
| Little Whitefield *IOW* | **13** | SZ**5989** |
| Little Whittington *Nthumb* | **102** | NY**9869** |
| Little Wilbraham *Cambs* | **53** | TL**5458** |
| Little Witcombe *Gloucs* | **35** | SO**9115** |
| Little Witley *H & W* | **47** | SO**7864** |
| Little Wittenham *Oxon* | **37** | SU**5693** |
| Little Wolford *Warwks* | **48** | SP**2635** |
| Little Woodcote *Surrey* | **27** | TQ**2861** |
| Little Wratting *Suffk* | **53** | TL**6847** |
| Little Wymington *Beds* | **51** | SP**9565** |
| Little Wymondley *Herts* | **39** | TL**2127** |
| Little Wyrley *Staffs* | **60** | SK**0105** |
| Little Yeldham *Essex* | **53** | TL**7839** |
| Littlebarn *Devon* | **18** | SS**4323** |
| Littlebeck *N York* | **90** | NZ**8704** |
| Littleborough *Devon* | **19** | SS**8210** |
| Littleborough *Gt Man* | **81** | SD**9316** |
| Littleborough *Notts* | **75** | SK**8282** |
| Littlebourne *Kent* | **29** | TR**2057** |
| Littlebredy *Dorset* | **10** | SY**5888** |
| Littlebury *Essex* | **39** | TL**5139** |
| Littlebury Green *Essex* | **39** | TL**4938** |
| Littlecott *Wilts* | **23** | SU**1451** |
| Littledean *Gloucs* | **35** | SO**6713** |
| Littledown *Hants* | **23** | SU**3558** |
| Littleferry *Highld* | **147** | NH**8095** |
| Littleham *Devon* | **18** | SS**4323** |
| Littleham *Devon* | **9** | SY**0281** |
| Littlehampton *W Susx* | **14** | TQ**0202** |
| Littleharle Tower *Nthumb* | **103** | NZ**0183** |
| Littlehempston *Devon* | **7** | SX**8162** |
| Littlehoughton *Nthumb* | **111** | NU**2216** |
| Littlemill *Gramp* | **134** | NO**3295** |
| Littlemill *Highld* | **140** | NH**9150** |
| Littlemill *Strath* | **107** | NS**4515** |
| Littlemoor *Derbys* | **74** | SK**3663** |
| Littlemore *Oxon* | **37** | SP**5302** |
| Littleover *Derbys* | **62** | SK**3234** |
| Littleport *Cambs* | **53** | TL**5686** |
| Littleport Bridge *Cambs* | **53** | TL**5787** |
| Littler *Ches* | **71** | SJ**6366** |
| Littlestone-on-Sea *Kent* | **17** | TR**0824** |
| Littlethorpe *Leics* | **50** | SP**5496** |
| Littlethorpe *N York* | **89** | SE**3268** |
| Littleton *Avon* | **21** | ST**5564** |
| Littleton *Ches* | **71** | SJ**4466** |
| Littleton *D & G* | **99** | NX**6355** |
| Littleton *Dorset* | **11** | ST**8904** |
| Littleton *Hants* | **24** | SU**4532** |
| Littleton *Somset* | **21** | ST**4830** |
| Littleton *Surrey* | **25** | SU**9847** |
| Littleton *Surrey* | **26** | TQ**0668** |
| Littleton Drew *Wilts* | **35** | ST**8380** |
| Littleton Pannell *Wilts* | **22** | ST**9954** |
| Littleton-on-Severn *Avon* | **34** | ST**5990** |
| Littletown *Dur* | **96** | NZ**3343** |
| Littletown *IOW* | **13** | SZ**5390** |
| Littlewick Green *Berks* | **37** | SU**8379** |
| Littlewindsor *Dorset* | **10** | ST**4303** |
| Littlewood *Staffs* | **60** | SJ**9807** |
| Littleworth *Bucks* | **38** | SP**8823** |
| Littleworth *H & W* | **47** | SO**9962** |
| Littleworth *H & W* | **47** | SO**8850** |
| Littleworth *Oxon* | **36** | SU**3197** |
| Littleworth *Staffs* | **72** | SJ**9323** |
| Littleworth *Staffs* | **60** | SK**0112** |
| Littleworth *W Susx* | **15** | TQ**1920** |
| Littleworth Common *Bucks* | **26** | SU**9386** |
| Littleworth End *Cambs* | **52** | TL**2266** |
| Littley Green *Essex* | **40** | TL**6917** |
| Litton *Derbys* | **74** | SK**1675** |
| Litton *N York* | **88** | SD**9074** |
| Litton *Somset* | **21** | ST**5954** |
| Litton Cheney *Dorset* | **10** | SY**5490** |
| Liverpool *Mersyd* | **78** | SJ**3490** |
| Liverton *Cleve* | **97** | NZ**7115** |
| Liverton *Devon* | **7** | SX**8075** |
| Liverton Mines *Cleve* | **97** | NZ**7117** |
| Liverton Street *Kent* | **28** | TQ**8749** |
| Livesey Street *Kent* | **28** | TQ**7054** |
| Livingston *Loth* | **117** | NT**0668** |
| Livingston Village *Loth* | **117** | NT**0366** |
| Lixton *Devon* | **7** | SX**6950** |
| Llxwm *Clwyd* | **70** | SJ**1771** |
| Lizard *Cnwll* | **2** | SW**7012** |
| Llaingoch *Gwynd* | **68** | SH**2282** |
| Llaithddu *Powys* | **58** | SO**0680** |
| Llan-y-pwll *Clwyd* | **71** | SJ**3752** |
| Llanaber *Gwynd* | **57** | SH**6018** |
| Llanaelhaearn *Gwynd* | **56** | SH**3844** |
| Llanafan *Dyfed* | **43** | SN**6872** |
| Llanafan-fechan *Powys* | **45** | SN**9750** |
| Llanallgo *Gwynd* | **68** | SH**5085** |
| Llanarmon *Gwynd* | **56** | SH**4239** |
| Llanarmon Dyffryn Ceiriog *Clwyd* | **58** | SJ**1532** |
| Llanarmon-yn-lal *Clwyd* | **70** | SJ**1956** |
| Llanarth *Dyfed* | **42** | SN**4257** |
| Llanarth *Gwent* | **34** | SO**3710** |
| Llanarthney *Dyfed* | **32** | SN**5320** |
| Llanasa *Clwyd* | **70** | SJ**1081** |
| Llanbabo *Gwynd* | **68** | SH**3786** |
| Llanbadarn Fawr *Dyfed* | **43** | SN**6080** |
| Llanbadarn Fynydd *Powys* | **45** | SO**0977** |
| Llanbadarn-y-garreg *Powys* | **45** | SO**1148** |
| Llanbadoc *Gwent* | **34** | ST**3799** |
| Llanbadrig *Gwynd* | **68** | SH**3794** |
| Llanbeder *Gwent* | **34** | ST**3890** |
| Llanbedr *Gwynd* | **57** | SH**5826** |
| Llanbedr *Powys* | **45** | SO**1446** |
| Llanbedr *Powys* | **34** | SO**2320** |
| Llanbedr-Dyffryn-Clwyd *Clwyd* | **70** | SJ**1459** |
| Llanbedr-y-cennin *Gwynd* | **69** | SH**7669** |
| Llanbedrgoch *Gwynd* | **68** | SH**5180** |
| Llanbedrog *Gwynd* | **56** | SH**3231** |
| Llanberis *Gwynd* | **69** | SH**5760** |
| Llanbethery *S Glam* | **20** | ST**0369** |
| Llanbister *Powys* | **45** | SO**1073** |
| Llanblethian *S Glam* | **33** | SS**9873** |
| Llanboidy *Dyfed* | **31** | SN**2123** |
| Llanbradach *M Glam* | **33** | ST**1490** |
| Llanbrynmair *Powys* | **57** | SH**8902** |
| Llancadle *S Glam* | **20** | ST**2368** |
| Llancarfan *S Glam* | **33** | ST**0570** |
| Llancayo *Gwent* | **34** | SO**3603** |
| Llancillo *H & W* | **46** | SO**3625** |
| Llancloudy *H & W* | **34** | SO**4920** |
| Llancynfelyn *Dyfed* | **43** | SN**6492** |
| Llandaff *S Glam* | **33** | ST**1578** |
| Llandanwg *Gwynd* | **57** | SH**5728** |
| Llandawke *Dyfed* | **31** | SN**2811** |
| Llanddaniel Fab *Gwynd* | **68** | SH**4970** |
| Llanddarog *Dyfed* | **32** | SN**5016** |
| Llanddeiniol *Dyfed* | **43** | SN**5572** |
| Llanddeiniolen *Gwynd* | **69** | SH**5465** |
| Llandderfel *Gwynd* | **58** | SH**9837** |
| Llanddeusant *Dyfed* | **44** | SN**7724** |
| Llanddeusant *Gwynd* | **68** | SH**3485** |
| Llanddewi *W Glam* | **32** | SS**4685** |
| Llanddewi *W Glam* | **32** | SS**4689** |
| Llanddewi Brefi *Dyfed* | **44** | SN**6655** |
| Llanddewi Rhydderch *Gwent* | **34** | SO**3513** |
| Llanddewi Velfrey *Dyfed* | **31** | SN**1416** |
| Llanddewi Ystradenni *Powys* | **45** | SO**1068** |
| Llanddewi'r Cwm *Powys* | **45** | SO**0348** |
| Llanddoget *Gwynd* | **69** | SH**8063** |
| Llanddona *Gwynd* | **69** | SH**5779** |
| Llanddowror *Dyfed* | **31** | SN**2514** |
| Llanddrew *Powys* | **45** | SO**0530** |
| Llanddulas *Clwyd* | **69** | SH**9078** |
| Llanddyfnan *Gwynd* | **68** | SH**5078** |
| Llandecwyn *Gwynd* | **57** | SH**6337** |
| Llandefaelog Fach *Powy's* | **45** | SO**0332** |
| Llandefaelogtrer-graig *Powys* | **45** | SO**1229** |
| Llandefalle *Powys* | **45** | SO**1035** |
| Llandegai *Gwynd* | **69** | SH**5971** |
| Llandegfan *Gwynd* | **69** | SH**5674** |
| Llandegla *Clwyd* | **70** | SJ**1952** |
| Llandegley *Powys* | **45** | SO**1463** |
| Llandegveth *Gwent* | **34** | ST**3395** |
| Llandegwning *Gwynd* | **56** | SH**2630** |
| Llandeilo *Dyfed* | **32** | SN**6322** |
| Llandeilo Graban *Powys* | **45** | SO**0944** |
| Llandeilo'r Fan *Powys* | **45** | SN**8934** |
| Llandeloy *Dyfed* | **30** | SM**8526** |
| Llandenny *Gwent* | **34** | SO**4104** |
| Llandenny Walks *Gwent* | **34** | SO**4003** |
| Llandevaud *Gwent* | **34** | ST**4090** |
| Llandevenny *Gwent* | **34** | ST**4186** |
| Llandinabo *H & W* | **46** | SO**5128** |
| Llandinam *Powys* | **58** | SO**0288** |
| Llandissilio *Dyfed* | **31** | SN**1221** |
| Llandogo *Gwent* | **34** | SO**5203** |
| Llandough *S Glam* | **33** | SS**9972** |
| Llandough *S Glam* | **33** | ST**1673** |
| Llandovery *Dyfed* | **44** | SN**7634** |
| Llandow *S Glam* | **33** | SS**9473** |
| Llandre *Dyfed* | **43** | SN**6286** |
| Llandre *Dyfed* | **44** | SN**6741** |
| Llandre Isaf *Dyfed* | **31** | SN**1328** |
| Llandrillo *Clwyd* | **58** | SJ**0337** |
| Llandrillo-yn-Rhos *Clwyd* | **69** | SH**8380** |
| Llandrindod Wells *Powys* | **45** | SO**0561** |
| Llandrinio *Powys* | **58** | SJ**2817** |
| Llandudno *Gwynd* | **69** | SH**7882** |
| Llandudno Junction *Gwynd* | **69** | SH**7977** |
| Llandudwen *Gwynd* | **56** | SH**2736** |
| Llandulas *Powys* | **45** | SN**8841** |
| Llandwrog *Gwynd* | **68** | SH**4556** |
| Llandybie *Dyfed* | **32** | SN**6215** |
| Llandyfaelog *Dyfed* | **31** | SN**4111** |
| Llandyfan *Dyfed* | **32** | SN**6417** |
| Llandyfriog *Dyfed* | **31** | SN**3341** |
| Llandyfrydog *Gwynd* | **68** | SH**4485** |
| Llandygwydd *Dyfed* | **31** | SN**2443** |
| Llandyrnog *Clwyd* | **70** | SJ**1065** |
| Llandyssil *Powys* | **58** | SO**1995** |
| Llandysul *Dyfed* | **31** | SN**4140** |
| Llanedeyrn *S Glam* | **34** | ST**2282** |
| Llanedi *Dyfed* | **32** | SN**5806** |
| Llanegryn *Gwynd* | **57** | SH**6005** |
| Llanegryn *Gwynd* | **57** | SH**5905** |
| Llanegwad *Dyfed* | **32** | SN**5121** |
| Llaneilian *Gwynd* | **68** | SH**4692** |
| Llanelian-yn-Rhos *Clwyd* | **69** | SH**8676** |
| Llanelidan *Clwyd* | **70** | SJ**1150** |
| Llanelieu *Powys* | **45** | SO**1834** |
| Llanellen *Gwent* | **34** | SO**3010** |
| Llanelli *Dyfed* | **32** | SN**5000** |
| Llanelltyd *Gwynd* | **57** | SH**7119** |
| Llanelly *Gwent* | **34** | SO**2314** |
| Llanelwedd *Powys* | **45** | SO**0451** |
| Llanenddwyn *Gwynd* | **57** | SH**5823** |
| Llanengan *Gwynd* | **56** | SH**2926** |
| Llanerch *Gwynd* | **57** | SH**8816** |
| Llanerch *Powys* | **59** | SO**3094** |
| Llanerchymedd *Gwynd* | **68** | SH**4184** |
| Llanerfyl *Powys* | **58** | SJ**0309** |
| Llanfachraeth *Gwynd* | **68** | SH**3182** |
| Llanfachreth *Gwynd* | **57** | SH**7522** |
| Llanfaelog *Gwynd* | **68** | SH**3373** |
| Llanfaelrhys *Gwynd* | **56** | SH**2227** |
| Llanfaenor *Gwent* | **34** | SO**4217** |
| Llanfaes *Gwynd* | **69** | SH**6077** |
| Llanfaes *Powys* | **45** | SO**0328** |
| Llanfaethlu *Gwynd* | **68** | SH**3186** |
| Llanfair *Gwynd* | **57** | SH**5729** |
| Llanfair *H & W* | **46** | SO**2444** |
| Llanfair Caereinion *Powys* | **58** | SJ**1006** |
| Llanfair Clydogau *Dyfed* | **44** | SN**6251** |
| Llanfair Dyffryn Clwyd *Clwyd* | **70** | SJ**1355** |
| Llanfair Kilgeddin *Gwent* | **34** | SO**3407** |
| Llanfair P G *Gwynd* | **69** | SH**5371** |
| Llanfair Talhaiarn *Clwyd* | **70** | SH**9269** |
| Llanfair Waterdine *Shrops* | **45** | SO**2376** |
| Llanfair-is-gaer *Gwynd* | **68** | SH**5267** |
| Llanfair-Nant-Gwyn *Dyfed* | **31** | SN**1637** |
| Llanfair-y-Cwmmwd *Gwynd* | **68** | SH**4466** |
| Llanfair-yn-Neubwll *Gwynd* | **68** | SH**3077** |
| Llanfairfechan *Gwynd* | **69** | SH**6874** |
| Llanfairynghornwy *Gwynd* | **68** | SH**3290** |
| Llanfallteg *Dyfed* | **31** | SN**1520** |
| Llanfallteg West *Dyfed* | **31** | SN**1419** |
| Llanfaredd *M Glam* | **45** | SO**0651** |
| Llanfarian *Dyfed* | **43** | SN**5977** |
| Llanfechain *Powys* | **58** | SJ**1820** |
| Llanfechelli *Gwynd* | **68** | SH**3691** |
| Llanfendigaid *Gwynd* | **57** | SH**5605** |
| Llanferres *Clwyd* | **70** | SJ**1960** |
| Llanfflewyn *Gwynd* | **68** | SH**3689** |
| Llanfihagel Tal-y-llyn *Powys* | **45** | SO**1128** |
| Llanfihangel ar-Arth *Dyfed* | **31** | SN**4539** |
| Llanfihangel Glyn Myfyr *Clwyd* | **70** | SH**9849** |
| Llanfihangel Nant Bran *Powys* | **45** | SN**9434** |
| Llanfihangel Rhydithon *Powys* | **45** | SO**1566** |
| Llanfihangel Rogiet *Gwent* | **34** | ST**4487** |
| Llanfihangel yn Nhowyn *Gwynd* | **68** | SH**3277** |
| Llanfihangel-nant-Melan *Powys* | **45** | SO**1858** |
| Llanfihangel-uwch-Gwili *Dyfed* | **44** | SN**4923** |
| Llanfihangel-y-Creuddyn *Dyfed* | **43** | SN**6675** |
| Llanfihangel-y-pennant *Gwynd* | **57** | SH**5245** |
| Llanfihangel-y-pennant *Gwynd* | **57** | SH**6708** |
| Llanfihangel-y-traethau *Gwynd* | **57** | SH**5935** |
| Llanfihangel-yng-Ngwynfa *Powys* | **58** | SJ**0816** |
| Llanfilo *Powys* | **45** | SO**1132** |
| Llanfoist *Gwent* | **34** | SO**2813** |
| Llanfor *Gwynd* | **58** | SH**9336** |
| Llanfrechfa *Gwent* | **34** | ST**3293** |
| Llanfrothen *Gwynd* | **57** | SH**6241** |
| Llanfrynach *Powys* | **45** | SO**0725** |
| Llanfwrog *Clwyd* | **70** | SJ**1157** |
| Llanfwrog *Gwynd* | **68** | SH**3083** |
| Llanfyllin *Powys* | **58** | SJ**1419** |
| Llanfynydd *Clwyd* | **70** | SJ**2756** |
| Llanfynydd *Dyfed* | **44** | SN**5527** |
| Llanfyrnach *Dyfed* | **31** | SN**2231** |
| Llangadfan *Powys* | **58** | SJ**0111** |
| Llangadog *Dyfed* | **31** | SN**4207** |
| Llangadog *Dyfed* | **44** | SN**7028** |
| Llangadwaladr *Clwyd* | **58** | SJ**1830** |
| Llangadwaladr *Gwynd* | **68** | SH**3869** |
| Llangaffo *Gwynd* | **68** | SH**4468** |
| Llangain *Dyfed* | **31** | SN**3815** |
| Llangammarch Wells *Powys* | **45** | SN**9347** |
| Llangan *S Glam* | **33** | SS**9577** |
| Llangarron *H & W* | **34** | SO**5220** |
| Llangasty-Talylln *Powys* | **45** | SO**1326** |
| Llangathen *Dyfed* | **32** | SN**5822** |
| Llangattock *Powys* | **33** | SO**2117** |
| Llangattock Lingoed *Gwent* | **34** | SO**3620** |
| Llangattock-Vibon-Avel *Gwent* | **34** | SO**4515** |
| Llangedwyn *Clwyd* | **58** | SJ**1824** |
| Llangefni *Gwynd* | **68** | SH**4675** |
| Llangeinor *M Glam* | **33** | SS**9187** |
| Llangeinwen *Gwynd* | **68** | SH**4465** |
| Llangeitho *Dyfed* | **44** | SN**6259** |
| Llangeler *Dyfed* | **31** | SN**3739** |
| Llangelynin *Gwynd* | **57** | SH**5707** |
| Llangendeirne *Dyfed* | **32** | SN**4514** |
| Llangennech *Dyfed* | **32** | SN**5601** |
| Llangennith *W Glam* | **31** | SS**4291** |
| Llangenny *Powys* | **34** | SO**2418** |
| Llangernyw *Clwyd* | **69** | SH**8767** |
| Llangian *Gwynd* | **56** | SH**2928** |
| Llangiwg *W Glam* | **32** | SN**7205** |
| Llangloffan *Dyfed* | **30** | SM**9032** |
| Llanglydwen *Dyfed* | **31** | SN**1827** |
| Llangoed *Gwynd* | **69** | SH**6079** |
| Llangoedmor *Dyfed* | **42** | SN**1945** |
| Llangollen *Clwyd* | **70** | SJ**2141** |
| Llangolman *Dyfed* | **31** | SN**1127** |
| Llangorse *Powys* | **45** | SO**1327** |
| Llangovan *Gwent* | **34** | SO**4505** |
| Llangower *Gwynd* | **58** | SH**9032** |
| Llangranog *Dyfed* | **42** | SN**3154** |
| Llangristiolus *Gwynd* | **68** | SH**4373** |
| Llangrove *H & W* | **34** | SO**5219** |
| Llangua *Gwent* | **46** | SO**3925** |
| Llangunllo *Powys* | **45** | SO**2171** |
| Llangunnor *Dyfed* | **31** | SN**4320** |
| Llangurig *Powys* | **43** | SN**9080** |
| Llangwm *Clwyd* | **70** | SH**9644** |
| Llangwm *Dyfed* | **30** | SM**9909** |
| Llangwm *Gwent* | **34** | ST**4299** |
| Llangwm-isaf *Gwent* | **34** | SO**4300** |
| Llangwyfan *Clwyd* | **70** | SJ**1266** |
| Llangwyllog *Gwynd* | **68** | SH**4379** |
| Llangwyryfon *Dyfed* | **43** | SN**5970** |
| Llangybi *Dyfed* | **44** | SN**6053** |
| Llangybi *Gwent* | **34** | ST**3797** |
| Llangybi *Gwynd* | **56** | SH**4240** |
| Llangyfelach *W Glam* | **32** | SS**6498** |
| Llangynhafal *Clwyd* | **70** | SJ**1263** |
| Llangynidr *Powys* | **33** | SO**1519** |
| Llangynin *Dyfed* | **31** | SN**2519** |
| Llangynllo *Dyfed* | **42** | SN**3544** |
| Llangynog *Dyfed* | **31** | SN**3314** |
| Llangynog *Powys* | **58** | SJ**0526** |
| Llangynog *Powys* | **45** | SO**0145** |
| Llangynwyd *M Glam* | **33** | SS**8588** |
| Llangynwyd *M Glam* | **33** | SS**8988** |
| Llanhamlach *Powys* | **45** | SO**0926** |
| Llanharan *M Glam* | **33** | ST**0083** |
| Llanharry *M Glam* | **33** | ST**0080** |
| Llanhennock *Gwent* | **34** | ST**3592** |
| Llanhilleth *Gwent* | **33** | SO**2100** |
| Llanidan *Gwynd* | **68** | SH**4966** |
| Llanidloes *Powys* | **58** | SN**9584** |
| Llaniestyn *Gwynd* | **56** | SH**2633** |
| Llanigon *Powys* | **45** | SO**2139** |
| Llanilar *Dyfed* | **43** | SN**6275** |
| Llanilid *M Glam* | **33** | SS**9781** |
| Llanina *Dyfed* | **42** | SN**4059** |
| Llanishen *Gwent* | **34** | SO**4703** |
| Llanishen *S Glam* | **33** | ST**1781** |
| Llanllechid *Gwynd* | **69** | SH**6268** |
| Llanlleonfel *Powys* | **45** | SN**9350** |
| Llanllowell *Gwent* | **34** | ST**3998** |
| Llanllugan *Powys* | **58** | SJ**0502** |
| Llanllwch *Dyfed* | **31** | SN**3818** |
| Llanllwchaiarn *Powys* | **58** | SO**1292** |
| Llanllwni *Dyfed* | **44** | SN**4741** |
| Llanllyfni *Gwynd* | **68** | SH**4651** |
| Llanmadoc *W Glam* | **32** | SS**4493** |
| Llanmaes *S Glam* | **20** | SS**9869** |
| Llanmartin *Gwent* | **34** | ST**3989** |
| Llanmerewig *Powys* | **58** | SO**1593** |
| Llanmerewig *Powys* | **58** | SO**1593** |
| Llanmihangel *S Glam* | **33** | SS**9872** |
| Llanmiloe *Dyfed* | **31** | SN**2508** |
| Llanmorlais *W Glam* | **32** | SS**5294** |
| Llannefydd *Clwyd* | **70** | SH**9870** |
| Llannon *Dyfed* | **32** | SN**5308** |
| Llannor *Gwynd* | **56** | SH**3537** |
| Llanon *Dyfed* | **42** | SN**5166** |
| Llanover *Gwent* | **34** | SO**3109** |
| Llanpumsaint *Dyfed* | **31** | SN**4229** |
| Llanrhaeadr *Clwyd* | **70** | SJ**0763** |
| Llanrhaeadr-ym-Mochnant *Clwyd* | **58** | SJ**1226** |
| Llanrhidian *W Glam* | **32** | SS**4992** |
| Llanrhos *Gwynd* | **69** | SH**7880** |
| Llanrhychwyn *Gwynd* | **69** | SH**7761** |
| Llanrhyddlad *Gwynd* | **68** | SH**3389** |
| Llanrhystud *Dyfed* | **43** | SN**5369** |
| Llanrian *Dyfed* | **30** | SM**8131** |
| Llanrothal *H & W* | **34** | SO**4718** |
| Llanrug *Gwynd* | **69** | SH**5363** |
| Llanrumney *S Glam* | **34** | ST**2280** |
| Llanrwst *Gwynd* | **69** | SH**7961** |
| Llansadurnen *Dyfed* | **31** | SN**2810** |
| Llansadwrn *Dyfed* | **44** | SN**6931** |
| Llansadwrn *Gwynd* | **69** | SH**5575** |
| Llansaint *Dyfed* | **31** | SN**3808** |
| Llansamlet *W Glam* | **32** | SS**6897** |
| Llansannan *Clwyd* | **70** | SH**9365** |
| Llansannor *S Glam* | **33** | SS**9977** |
| Llansantffraed *Powys* | **45** | SO**1223** |
| Llansantffraed-Cwmdeuddwr *Powys* | **45** | SN**9667** |
| Llansantffraed-in-Elvel *Powys* | **45** | SO**0954** |
| Llansantffraid *Dyfed* | **42** | SN**5167** |
| Llansantffraid Glan Conwy *Gwynd* | **69** | SH**8075** |
| Llansantffraid-ym-Mechain *Powys* | **58** | SJ**2220** |
| Llansawel *Dyfed* | **44** | SN**6136** |
| Llansilin *Clwyd* | **58** | SJ**2128** |
| Llansoy *Gwent* | **34** | SO**4402** |
| Llanspyddid *Powys* | **45** | SO**0128** |
| Llanstadwell *Dyfed* | **30** | SM**9505** |
| Llanstephan *Dyfed* | **31** | SN**3511** |
| Llanstephan *Powys* | **45** | SO**1141** |
| Llantarnam *Gwent* | **34** | ST**3093** |
| Llanteg *Dyfed* | **31** | SN**1810** |
| Llanthewy Skirrid *Gwent* | **34** | SO**3416** |
| Llanthony *Gwent* | **46** | SO**2827** |
| Llantilio Pertholey *Gwent* | **34** | SO**3116** |
| Llantrisant *Gwent* | **34** | ST**3997** |
| Llantrisant *Gwynd* | **68** | SH**3683** |
| Llantrisant *M Glam* | **33** | ST**0483** |
| Llantrithyd *S Glam* | **33** | ST**0472** |
| Llantwit Fardre *M Glam* | **33** | ST**0886** |
| Llantwit Major *S Glam* | **20** | SS**9668** |
| Llantysilio *Clwyd* | **70** | SJ**1943** |
| Llanuwchllyn *Gwynd* | **57** | SH**8730** |
| Llanvaches *Gwent* | **34** | ST**4391** |
| Llanvair Discoed *Gwent* | **34** | ST**4492** |
| Llanvapley *Gwent* | **34** | SO**3614** |
| Llanvetherine *Gwent* | **34** | SO**3617** |
| Llanveynoe *H & W* | **46** | SO**3031** |
| Llanvihangel Crucorney *Gwent* | **34** | SO**3220** |
| Llanvihangel Gobion *Gwent* | **34** | SO**3409** |
| Llanvihangel-Ystern-Llewe *Gwent* | **34** | SO**4313** |
| Llanwarne *H & W* | **46** | SO**5027** |
| Llanwddyn *Powys* | **58** | SJ**0219** |
| Llanwenarth *Gwent* | **34** | SO**2714** |
| Llanwenog *Dyfed* | **44** | SN**4945** |
| Llanwern *Gwent* | **34** | ST**3688** |
| Llanwinio *Dyfed* | **31** | SN**2626** |
| Llanwnda *Dyfed* | **30** | SM**9339** |
| Llanwnda *Gwynd* | **68** | SH**4758** |
| Llanwnen *Dyfed* | **44** | SN**5347** |
| Llanwnog *Powys* | **58** | SO**0293** |
| Llanwonno *M Glam* | **33** | ST**0395** |
| Llanwrda *Dyfed* | **44** | SN**7131** |
| Llanwrin *Powys* | **57** | SH**7803** |
| Llanwrthwl *Powys* | **45** | SN**9763** |
| Llanwrtyd *Powys* | **45** | SN**8647** |
| Llanwrtyd Wells *Powys* | **45** | SN**8846** |
| Llanwyddelan *Powys* | **58** | SJ**0801** |
| Llanyblodwel *Shrops* | **58** | SJ**2423** |
| Llanybri *Dyfed* | **31** | SN**3312** |
| Llanybydder *Dyfed* | **44** | SN**5244** |
| Llanycefn *Dyfed* | **31** | SN**0923** |
| Llanychaer Bridge *Dyfed* | **30** | SM**9835** |
| Llanycrwys *Dyfed* | **44** | SN**6445** |
| Llanymawddwy *Gwynd* | **58** | SH**9019** |
| Llanymynech *Shrops* | **58** | SJ**2620** |
| Llanynghenedl *Gwynd* | **68** | SH**3181** |
| Llanynis *Powys* | **45** | SN**9950** |
| Llanynys *Clwyd* | **70** | SJ**1062** |
| Llanyre *Powys* | **45** | SO**0462** |
| Llanystumdwy *Gwynd* | **56** | SH**4738** |
| Llanywern *Powys* | **45** | SO**1028** |
| Llawhaden *Dyfed* | **31** | SN**0717** |
| Llawnt *Shrops* | **58** | SJ**2430** |
| Llawryglyn *Powys* | **58** | SN**9291** |
| Llay *Clwyd* | **71** | SJ**3355** |
| Llechcynfarwy *Gwynd* | **68** | SH**3881** |
| Llechfaen *Powys* | **45** | SO**0828** |
| Llechryd *Dyfed* | **31** | SN**2243** |
| Llechryd *M Glam* | **33** | SO**1009** |
| Lledrod *Dyfed* | **43** | SN**6470** |
| Llidiadnenog *Dyfed* | **44** | SN**5437** |
| Llidiardau *Gwynd* | **57** | SH**8738** |
| Llidiart-y-parc *Clwyd* | **70** | SJ**1243** |
| Llithfaen *Gwynd* | **56** | SH**3542** |
| Llong *Clwyd* | **70** | SJ**2662** |
| Llowes *Powys* | **45** | SO**1941** |
| Llwydcoed *M Glam* | **33** | SN**9904** |
| Llwydiarth *Powys* | **58** | SJ**0315** |
| Llwyn-drain *Dyfed* | **31** | SN**2634** |
| Llwyn-du *Gwent* | **34** | SO**2816** |
| Llwyn-on *M Glam* | **33** | SO**0111** |
| Llwyn-y-brain *Dyfed* | **31** | SN**1914** |
| Llwyn-y-Groes *Dyfed* | **44** | SN**5956** |
| Llwyncelyn *Dyfed* | **42** | SN**4459** |
| Llwyndafydd *Dyfed* | **42** | SN**3755** |
| Llwynderw *Powys* | **58** | SJ**2004** |
| Llwyndyrys *Gwynd* | **56** | SH**3740** |
| Llwyngwril *Gwynd* | **57** | SH**5909** |
| Llwynhendy *Dyfed* | **32** | SS**5399** |
| Llwynmawr *Clwyd* | **58** | SJ**2237** |
| Llwynypia *M Glam* | **33** | SS**9993** |
| Llyn-y-pandy *Clwyd* | **70** | SJ**2065** |
| Llynclys *Shrops* | **58** | SJ**2823** |
| Llynfaes *Gwynd* | **68** | SH**4178** |
| Llys-y-fran *Dyfed* | **30** | SN**0424** |
| Llysfaen *Clwyd* | **69** | SH**8977** |
| Llysfaen *Clwyd* | **69** | SH**8977** |
| Llyswen *Dyfed* | **42** | SN**4561** |
| Llyswen *Powys* | **45** | SO**1337** |
| Llysworney *S Glam* | **33** | SS**9674** |
| Llywel *Powys* | **45** | SN**8730** |
| Load Brook *S York* | **74** | SK**2788** |
| Loan *Cent* | **117** | NS**9675** |
| Loanend *Nthumb* | **119** | NT**9450** |
| Loanhead *Loth* | **117** | NT**2865** |
| Loaningfoot *D & G* | **92** | NX**9656** |
| Loans *Strath* | **106** | NS**3431** |
| Lobb *Devon* | **18** | SS**4637** |
| Lobhillcross *Devon* | **5** | SX**4686** |
| Loceport *W Isls* | **154** | NF**8563** |
| Loch Katrine Pier *Cent* | **124** | NN**4907** |
| Loch Loyal Lodge *Highld* | **149** | NC**6146** |
| Loch Maree Hotel *Highld* | **138** | NG**9668** |
| Loch Skipport *W Isls* | **154** | NF**8238** |
| Lochailort *Highld* | **129** | NM**7682** |
| Lochans *D & G* | **98** | NX**0656** |
| Lochassynt Lodge *Highld* | **148** | NC**1727** |
| Lochavich *Strath* | **122** | NM**9415** |
| Lochawe *Strath* | **123** | NN**1227** |
| Lochboisdale *W Isls* | **154** | NF**7820** |
| Lochbuie *Strath* | **121** | NM**6125** |
| Lochcarron *Highld* | **138** | NG**8939** |
| Lochdochart House *Cent* | **124** | NN**4327** |
| Lochdrum *Highld* | **145** | NH**2585** |
| Lochead *Strath* | **113** | NR**7778** |
| Lochearnhead *Cent* | **124** | NN**5823** |
| Lochee *Tays* | **126** | NO**3731** |
| Locheilside Station *Highld* | **130** | NM**9978** |

Ludborough Mashbury


Ludborough *Lincs* 77 TF2995
Ludbrook *Devon* 7 SX6654
Ludchurch *Dyfed* 31 SN1411
Luddenden *W York* 82 SE0426
Luddenden Foot *W York* 82 SE0325
Luddenham Court *Kent* 28 TQ9962
Luddesdown *Kent* 28 TQ6766
Luddington *Humb* 84 SE8216
Luddington *Warwks* 48 SP1652
Luddington in the Brook *Nhants* 51 TL1083
Ludford *Lincs* 76 TF1989
Ludford *Shrops* 46 SO5174
Ludgershall *Bucks* 37 SP6517
Ludgershall *Wilts* 23 SU2650
Ludgershall *Wilts* 23 SU2650
Ludgvan *Cnwll* 2 SW5033
Ludham *Norfk* 67 TG3818
Ludlow *Shrops* 46 SO5175
Ludney *Somset* 10 ST3812
Ludwell *Wilts* 22 ST9122
Ludworth *Dur* 96 NZ3641
Luffenhall *Herts* 39 TL2928
Luffincott *Devon* 5 SX3394
Lufflands *Devon* 18 SS3209
Luffness *Loth* 118 NT4780
Lugar *Strath* 107 NS5821
Lugg Green *H & W* 46 SO4462
Luggate Burn *Loth* 118 NT6074
Luggiebank *Strath* 116 NS7672
Lugsdale *Ches* 78 SJ5285
Lugton *Strath* 115 NS4152
Lugwardine *H & W* 46 SO5540
Luib *Highld* 137 NG5627
Lulham *H & W* 46 SO4141
Lullington *Derbys* 61 SK2513
Lullington *E Susx* 16 TQ5202
Lullington *Somset* 22 ST7851
Lulsgate Bottom *Avon* 21 ST5165
Lulsley *H & W* 47 SO7455
Lulworth Camp *Dorset* 11 SY8381
Lumb *Lancs* 81 SD8324
Lumb *W York* 82 SE0321
Lumbutts *W York* 82 SD9528
Lumby *N York* 83 SE4830
Lumloch *Strath* 116 NS6370
Lumphanan *Gramp* 134 NJ5804
Lumphinnans *Fife* 117 NT1692
Lumsden *Gramp* 142 NJ4722
Lunan *Tays* 127 NO6851
Lunanhead *Tays* 127 NO4752
Luncarty *Tays* 125 NO0929
Lund *Humb* 84 SE9647
Lund *N York* 83 SE6532
Lundie *Cent* 124 NN7304
Lundie *Tays* 126 NO2836
Lundin Links *Fife* 126 NO4002
Lundy Green *Norfk* 67 TM2392
Lunna *Shet* 155 HU4869
Lunsford *Kent* 28 TQ6959
Lunsford's Cross *E Susx* 17 TQ7210
Lunt *Mersyd* 78 SD3402
Luntley *H & W* 46 SO3955
Luppitt *Devon* 9 ST1606
Lupridge *Devon* 7 SX7153
Lupset *W York* 82 SE3119
Lupton *Cumb* 87 SD5581
Lurgashall *W Susx* 14 SU9327
Lurley *Devon* 9 SS9214
Lusby *Lincs* 77 TF3367
Luscombe *Devon* 7 SX7957
Luskentyre *W Isls* 154 NG0699
Luson *Devon* 6 SX6050
Luss *Strath* 115 NS3692
Lusta *Highld* 136 NG2756
Lustleigh *Devon* 8 SX7881
Luston *H & W* 46 SO4863
Luthermuir *Gramp* 135 NO6568
Luthrie *Fife* 126 NO3319
Lutley *W Mids* 60 SO9483
Luton *Beds* 38 TL0921
Luton *Devon* 9 ST0802
Luton *Devon* 9 SX9076
Luton *Kent* 28 TQ7766
Lutterworth *Leics* 50 SP5484
Lutton *Devon* 6 SX5959
Lutton *Dorset* 11 SY8980
Lutton *Lincs* 65 TF4325
Lutton *Nhants* 52 TL1187
Lutworthy *Devon* 19 SS7615
Luxborough *Somset* 20 SS9738
Luxulyan *Cnwll* 4 SX0458
Luzley *Gt Man* 79 SD9601
Lybster *Highld* 151 ND2435
Lydbury North *Shrops* 59 SO3486
Lydcott *Devon* 19 SS6936
Lydd *Kent* 17 TR0420
Lydden *Kent* 29 TR3567
Lydden *Kent* 29 TR2645
Lyddington *Leics* 51 SP8797
Lyde Green *Hants* 24 SU7057
Lydeard St. Lawrence *Somset* 20 ST1232
Lydford *Devon* 5 SX5084
Lydford on Fosse *Somset* 21 ST5630
Lydgate *Derbys* 74 SK3177
Lydgate *Gt Man* 82 SD9526
Lydgate *W York* 81 SD9225
Lydham *Shrops* 59 SO3391
Lydiard Green *Wilts* 36 SU0885
Lydiard Millicent *Wilts* 36 SU0986
Lydiard Tregoze *Wilts* 36 SU1085
Lydiate *Mersyd* 78 SD3604
Lydiate Ash *H & W* 60 SO9775
Lydlinch *Dorset* 11 ST7413
Lydney *Gloucs* 35 SO6303
Lydstep *Dyfed* 31 SS0898
Lye *W Mids* 60 SO9284
Lye Cross *Avon* 21 ST4962
Lye Green *Bucks* 38 SP9703
Lye Green *E Susx* 16 TQ5034
Lye Green *Warwks* 48 SP1965
Lye Head *H & W* 60 SO7573
Lye's Green *Wilts* 22 ST8246
Lyford *Oxon* 36 SU3994
Lymbridge Green *Kent* 29 TR1244
Lyme *Border* 109 NT2041
Lyme Regis *Dorset* 10 SY3492
Lyminge *Kent* 29 TR1641
Lymington *Hants* 12 SZ3295
Lyminster *W Susx* 14 TQ0204
Lymm *Ches* 79 SJ6887
Lympne *Kent* 17 TR1135
Lympsham *Somset* 21 ST3454
Lympstone *Devon* 9 SX9984
Lynbridge *Devon* 19 SS7248
Lynch *Somset* 20 SS9047
Lynch Green *Norfk* 66 TG1505
Lynchat *Highld* 132 NH7801
Lyndhurst *Hants* 12 SU2907
Lyndon *Leics* 63 SK9004
Lyndon Green *W Mids* 61 SP1485
Lyne *Surrey* 26 TQ0166
Lyne Down *H & W* 47 SO6530
Lyne Hill *Staffs* 60 SJ9212
Lyne of Gorthleck *Highld* 139 NH5420
Lyne of Skene *Gramp* 135 NJ7610
Lyneal *Shrops* 59 SJ4433
Lynegar *Highld* 151 ND2256
Lyneham *Devon* 8 SX8579
Lyneham *Oxon* 36 SP2720
Lyneham *Wilts* 35 SU0278
Lyneholmford *Cumb* 101 NY5172
Lynemouth *Nthumb* 103 NZ2991
Lyness *Ork* 155 ND3094
Lyng *Norfk* 66 TG0717
Lyng *Somset* 21 ST3328
Lynhales *H & W* 46 SO3255
Lynmouth *Devon* 19 SS7249
Lynn *Shrops* 72 SJ7815
Lynn of Shenval *Gramp* 141 NJ2129
Lynsted *Kent* 28 TQ9460
Lynstone *Cnwll* 18 SS2005
Lynton *Devon* 19 SS7149
Lyon's Gate *Dorset* 11 ST6605
Lyonshall *H & W* 46 SO3355
Lytchett Matravers *Dorset* 11 SY9495
Lytchett Minster *Dorset* 11 SY9593
Lytham *Lancs* 80 SD3627
Lytham St. Anne's *Lancs* 80 SD3427
Lythbank *Shrops* 59 SJ4607
Lythe *Highld* 151 ND2762
Lythe *N York* 90 NZ8413
Lythmore *Highld* 150 ND0566


# M


Maaruig *W Isls* 154 NB1906
Mabe Burnthouse *Cnwll* 3 SW7634
Mabie *D & G* 100 NX9570
Mablethorpe *Lincs* 77 TF5085
Macclesfield *Ches* 79 SJ9173
Macclesfield Forest *Ches* 79 SJ9772
Macduff *Gramp* 142 NJ7064
Macharioch *Strath* 105 NR7309
Machen *M Glam* 33 ST2189
Machire *Strath* 112 NR2064
Machrie Farm *Strath* 105 NR9033
Machrihanish *Strath* 104 NR6320
Machrins *Strath* 112 NR3693
Machynlleth *Powys* 57 SH7400
Machynys *Dyfed* 32 SS5198
Mackworth *Derbys* 62 SK3137
Macmerry *Loth* 118 NT4372
Maddaford *Devon* 8 SX5495
Madderty *Tays* 125 NN9522
Maddington *Wilts* 23 SU0643
Maddiston *Cent* 116 NS9476
Madehurst *W Susx* 14 SU9810
Madeley *Shrops* 60 SJ6904
Madeley *Staffs* 72 SJ7744
Madeley Heath *Staffs* 72 SJ7845
Madford *Devon* 9 ST1411
Madingley *Cambs* 52 TL3960
Madley *H & W* 46 SO4238
Madresfield *H & W* 47 SO8047
Madron *Cnwll* 2 SW4532
Maen-y-groes *Dyfed* 42 SN3858
Maenaddwyn *Gwynd* 68 SH4684
Maenclochog *Dyfed* 31 SN0827
Maendy *S Glam* 33 ST0076
Maenporth *Cnwll* 3 SW7829
Maentwrog *Gwynd* 57 SH6640
Maer *Cnwll* 18 SS2008
Maer *Staffs* 72 SJ7938
Maerdy *Clwyd* 70 SJ0144
Maerdy *M Glam* 33 SS9798
Maes-glas *Gwent* 34 ST2986
Maes-y-cwmmer *M Glam* 33 ST1794
Maesbrook *Shrops* 59 SJ3021
Maesbury *Shrops* 59 SJ3026
Maesbury Marsh *Shrops* 59 SJ3125
Maesgwynne *Dyfed* 31 SN2024
Maeshafn *Clwyd* 70 SJ2061
Maesllyn *Dyfed* 42 SN3644
Maesmynis *Powys* 45 SO0350
Maesmynis *Powys* 45 SO0147
Maesteg *M Glam* 33 SS8590
Maesybont *Dyfed* 32 SN5616
Maesycwmmer *M Glam* 33 ST1594
Magdalen Laver *Essex* 39 TL5108
Maggieknockater *Gramp* 141 NJ3145
Maggots End *Essex* 39 TL4727
Magham Down *E Susx* 16 TQ6011
Maghull *Mersyd* 78 SD3703
Magor *Gwent* 34 ST4287
Mahaar *D & G* 98 NX1058
Maiden Bradley *Wilts* 22 ST7938
Maiden Head *Avon* 21 ST5666
Maiden Law *Dur* 96 NZ1749
Maiden Newton *Dorset* 10 SY5997
Maiden Rushdett *Gt Lon* 26 TQ1761
Maiden Wells *Dyfed* 30 SR9799
Maidencombe *Devon* 7 SX9268
Maidenhayne *Devon* 10 SY2795
Maidenhead *Berks* 26 SU8980
Maidens *Strath* 106 NS2107
Maidens Green *Berks* 25 SU8972
Maidenwell *Lincs* 77 TF3179
Maidford *Nhants* 49 SP6052
Maids Moreton *Bucks* 49 SP7035
Maidstone *Kent* 28 TQ7555
Maidwell *Nhants* 50 SP7476
Maindee *Gwent* 34 ST3288
Mains of Allardice *Gramp* 135 NO8375
Mains of Bainakettle *Gramp* 134 NO6274
Mains of Bainakettle *Gramp* 134 NO6274
Mains of Balhall *Tays* 134 NO5163
Mains of Cairnbarrow *Gramp* 142 NJ4640
Mains of Dalvey *Highld* 141 NJ1031
Mains of Dillavaird *Gramp* 135 NO7482
Mains of Haulkerton *Gramp* 135 NO7172
Mains of Haulkerton *Gramp* 135 NO7172
Mains of Throsk *Cent* 116 NS8690
Mainsforth *Dur* 96 NZ3131
Mainsriddle *D & G* 92 NX9557
Mainstone *Shrops* 58 SO2787
Maisemore *Gloucs* 35 SO8121
Major's Green *H & W* 61 SP1077
Makeney *Derbys* 62 SK3544
Malborough *Devon* 7 SX7039
Malcoff *Derbys* 74 SK0782
Malden *Surrey* 26 TQ2175
Malden *Surrey* 26 TQ2166
Maldon *Essex* 40 TL8507
Malham *N York* 88 SD9062
Mallaig *Highld* 129 NM6796
Mallaigvaig *Highld* 129 NM6897
Malleny Mills *Loth* 117 NT1665
Mallows Green *Essex* 39 TL4726
Malltraeth *Gwynd* 68 SH4069
Mallwyd *Gwynd* 57 SH8612
Malmesbury *Wilts* 35 ST9387
Malmsmead *Somset* 19 SS7947
Malpas *Ches* 71 SJ4847
Malpas *Cnwll* 3 SW8442
Malpas *Gwent* 34 ST3090
Malshanger House *Hants* 24 SU5652
Maltby *Cleve* 89 NZ4613
Maltby *Lincs* 77 TF3083
Maltby *S York* 75 SK5392
Maltby le Marsh *Lincs* 77 TF4681
Malting Green *Essex* 41 TL9720
Maltman's Hill *Kent* 28 TQ9043
Malton *N York* 90 SE7871
Malvern Link *H & W* 47 SO7847
Malvern Wells *H & W* 47 SO7741
Malzie *D & G* 99 NX3754
Mamble *H & W* 60 SO6971
Mamhilad *Gwent* 34 SO3003
Manaccan *Cnwll* 3 SW7625
Manafon *Powys* 58 SJ1102
Manaton *Devon* 8 SX7581
Manby *Lincs* 77 TF3986
Mancetter *Warwks* 61 SP3296
Manchester *Gt Man* 79 SJ8497
Mancot *Clwyd* 71 SJ3267
Mandally *Highld* 131 NH2900
Manea *Cambs* 53 TL4789
Maneight *Strath* 107 NS5409
Maney *W Mids* 61 SP1295
Manfield *N York* 89 NZ2213
Mangersta *W Isls* 154 NB0131
Mangerton *Dorset* 10 SY4995
Mangotsfield *Avon* 35 ST6676
Mangrove End *Herts* 38 TL1223
Manhay *Cnwll* 2 SW6930
Manish *W Isls* 154 NA9513
Manish *W Isls* 154 NG1089
Mankinholes *W York* 82 SD9623
Mankinholes *W York* 82 SD9623
Manley *Ches* 71 SJ5071
Manmoel *Gwent* 33 SO1803
Manning's Heath *W Susx* 15 TQ2028
Manningford Bohune *Wilts* 23 SU1357
Manningford Bruce *Wilts* 23 SU1359
Manningham *W York* 82 SE1435
Mannington *Dorset* 12 SU0605
Manningtree *Essex* 41 TM1032
Mannofield *Gramp* 135 NJ9204
Manor Park *Gt Lon* 27 TQ4286
Manorbier *Dyfed* 30 SS0697
Manorbier Newton *Dyfed* 30 SN0400
Manorhill *Border* 110 NT6632
Manorowen *Dyfed* 30 SM9336
Mansell Gamage *H & W* 46 SO3944
Mansell Lacy *H & W* 46 SO4245
Mansergh *Cumb* 87 SD6082
Mansfield *Notts* 75 SK5361
Mansfield *Strath* 107 NS6214
Mansfield Woodhouse *Notts* 75 SK5363
Mansriggs *Cumb* 86 SD2880
Manston *Dorset* 11 ST8115
Manston *Kent* 29 TR3466
Manston *W York* 83 SE3634
Manswood *Dorset* 11 ST9708
Manthorpe *Lincs* 63 SK9237
Manthorpe *Lincs* 64 TF0715
Manton *Humb* 84 SE9302
Manton *Leics* 63 SK8704
Manton *Notts* 75 SK6078
Manton *Wilts* 23 SU1768
Manuden *Essex* 39 TL4926
Manwood End *Essex* 39 TL5412
Maolachy *Strath* 122 NM8912
Maperton *Somset* 22 ST6726
Maple Cross *Herts* 26 TQ0392
Maplebeck *Notts* 75 SK7160
Mapledurham *Oxon* 37 SU6776
Mapledurwell *Hants* 24 SU6851
Maplehurst *W Susx* 15 TQ1824
Maplescombe *Kent* 27 TQ5664
Mapleton *Derbys* 73 SK1648
Mapleton *Kent* 16 TQ4649
Mapperley *Derbys* 62 SK4343
Mapperley Park *Notts* 62 SK5742
Mapperton *Dorset* 10 SY5099
Mappleborough Green *Warwks* 48 SP0866
Mappleton *Humb* 85 TA2243
Mappowder *Dorset* 11 ST7105
Marazanvose *Cnwll* 3 SW8050
Marazion *Cnwll* 2 SW5130
Marbury *Ches* 71 SJ5645
March *Cambs* 65 TL4297
March *Strath* 108 NS9914
Marcham *Oxon* 37 SU4596
Marchamley *Shrops* 59 SJ5929
Marchamley Wood *Shrops* 59 SJ5831
Marchington *Staffs* 73 SK1330
Marchington Woodlands *Staffs* 73 SK1128
Marchros *Gwynd* 56 SH3126
Marchwiel *Clwyd* 71 SJ3547
Marchwood *Hants* 12 SU3810
Marcross *S Glam* 20 SS9269
Marden *H & W* 46 SO5146
Marden *Kent* 28 TQ7444
Marden *Wilts* 23 SU0857
Marden Ash *Essex* 27 TL5502
Marden Beech *Kent* 28 TQ7343
Marden Thorn *Kent* 28 TQ7643
Mardens Hill *E Susx* 16 TQ5032
Mardleybury *Herts* 39 TL2618
Mardy *Gwent* 34 SO3015
Mare Green *Somset* 21 ST3326
Marefield *Leics* 63 SK7407
Mareham le Fen *Lincs* 77 TF2761
Mareham on the Hill *Lincs* 77 TF2867
Marehay *Derbys* 74 SK3948
Marehill *W Susx* 14 TQ0618
Maresfield *E Susx* 16 TQ4624
Marfleet *Humb* 85 TA1329
Marford *Clwyd* 59 SJ3635
Margam *W Glam* 32 SS7887
Margaret Marsh *Dorset* 22 ST8218
Margaretting *Essex* 40 TL6701
Margaretting Tye *Essex* 40 TL6801
Margate *Kent* 29 TR3571
Margnaheglish *Strath* 105 NS0332
Margrie *D & G* 99 NX5950
Margrove Park *Cleve* 97 NZ6515
Marham *Norfk* 65 TF7110
Marhamchurch *Cnwll* 18 SS2203
Marholm *Cambs* 64 TF1402
Marian-glas *Gwynd* 68 SH5084
Mariansleigh *Devon* 19 SS7422
Marine Town *Kent* 28 TQ9274
Marionburgh *Gramp* 135 NJ7006
Marishader *Highld* 136 NG4963
Maristow *Devon* 6 SX4764
Marjoriebanks *D & G* 100 NY0883
Mark *D & G* 98 NX1158
Mark *Somset* 21 ST3747
Mark Causeway *Somset* 21 ST3547
Mark Cross *E Susx* 16 TQ5010
Mark Cross *E Susx* 16 TQ5831
Mark's Corner *IOW* 13 SZ4792
Markbeech *Kent* 16 TQ4742
Markby *Lincs* 77 TF4878
Markeaton *Derbys* 62 SK3337
Market Bosworth *Leics* 62 SK4003
Market Deeping *Lincs* 64 TF1310
Market Drayton *Shrops* 72 SJ6734
Market Harborough *Leics* 50 SP7387
Market Lavington *Wilts* 22 SU0154
Market Overton *Leics* 63 SK8816
Market Rasen *Lincs* 76 TF1089
Market Stainton *Lincs* 76 TF2279
Market Street *Norfk* 67 TG2921
Market Weighton *Humb* 84 SE8741
Market Weston *Suffk* 54 TL9877
Markfield *Leics* 62 SK4810
Markham *Gwent* 33 SO1601
Markham Moor *Notts* 75 SK7274
Markinch *Fife* 126 NO2901
Markington *N York* 89 SE2864
Marks Tey *Essex* 40 TL9023
Marksbury *Avon* 22 ST6662
Markshall *Essex* 40 TL8425
Markwell *Cnwll* 5 SX3658
Markyate *Herts* 38 TL0616
Marl Bank *H & W* 47 SO7840
Marlborough *Wilts* 36 SU1869
Marlbrook *H & W* 46 SO5054
Marlbrook *H & W* 60 SO9774
Marlcliff *Warwks* 48 SP0950
Marldon *Devon* 7 SX8663
Marle Green *E Susx* 16 TQ5816
Marlesford *Suffk* 55 TM3258
Marley *Kent* 29 TR1750
Marley *Kent* 29 TR3352
Marley Green *Ches* 71 SJ5745
Marlingford *Norfk* 66 TG1309
Marloes *Dyfed* 30 SM7908
Marlow *Bucks* 26 SU8486
Marlow *H & W* 46 SO4076
Marlpit Hill *Kent* 16 TQ4447
Marlpits *E Susx* 16 TQ4528
Marlpits *E Susx* 16 TQ7013
Marlpool *Derbys* 62 SK4345
Marnhull *Dorset* 22 ST7718
Marnoch *Gramp* 142 NJ5950
Marple *Gt Man* 79 SJ9588
Marple Bridge *Gt Man* 79 SJ9789
Marr *S York* 83 SE5105
Marrel *Highld* 147 ND0117
Marrick *N York* 88 SE0798
Marros *Dyfed* 31 SN2009
Marsden *T & W* 103 NZ4064
Marsden *W York* 82 SE0411
Marsden Height *Lancs* 81 SD8636
Marsett *N York* 88 SD9085
Marsh *Bucks* 38 SP8109
Marsh *Somset* 10 ST2510
Marsh *W York* 82 SE0236
Marsh Baldon *Oxon* 37 SU5699
Marsh Gibbon *Bucks* 37 SP6422
Marsh Green *Devon* 9 SY0493
Marsh Green *Kent* 16 TQ4344
Marsh Green *Shrops* 59 SJ6014
Marsh Green *Staffs* 72 SJ8859
Marsh Lane *Derbys* 74 SK4079
Marsh Lane *Gloucs* 34 SO5807
Marsh Street *Somset* 20 SS9944
Marsh The *Powys* 59 SO3197
Marshall's Heath *Herts* 39 TL1614
Marshalswick *Herts* 39 TL1608
Marsham *Norfk* 67 TG1924
Marshborough *Kent* 29 TR2958
Marshbrook *Shrops* 59 SO4489
Marshchapel *Lincs* 77 TF3599
Marshfield *Avon* 35 ST7773
Marshfield *Gwent* 34 ST2582
Marshgate *Cnwll* 4 SX1592
Marshland Green *Gt Man* 79 SJ6899
Marshland St. James *Norfk* 65 TF5209
Marshside *Mersyd* 80 SD3619
Marshwood *Dorset* 10 SY3899
Marske *N York* 89 NZ1000
Marske-by-the-Sea *Cleve* 97 NZ6322
Marston *Ches* 79 SJ6775
Marston *H & W* 46 SO3557
Marston *Lincs* 63 SK8943
Marston *Oxon* 37 SP5208
Marston *Staffs* 60 SJ8314
Marston *Staffs* 72 SJ9227
Marston *Warwks* 61 SP2195
Marston *Wilts* 22 ST9656
Marston Green *W Mids* 61 SP1785
Marston Jabbet *Warwks* 61 SP3788
Marston Magna *Somset* 21 ST5922
Marston Meysey *Wilts* 36 SU1297
Marston Montgomery *Derbys* 73 SK1338
Marston Moretaine *Beds* 38 SP9941
Marston on Dove *Derbys* 73 SK2329
Marston St. Lawrence *Nhants* 49 SP5342
Marston Stannet *H & W* 46 SO5655
Marston Trussell *Nhants* 50 SP6985
Marstow *H & W* 34 SO5518
Marsworth *Bucks* 38 SP9214
Marten *Wilts* 23 SU2860
Marthall *Ches* 79 SJ8075
Martham *Norfk* 67 TG4518
Martin *Hants* 12 SU0719
Martin *Kent* 29 TR3347
Martin *Lincs* 76 TF2366
Martin *Lincs* 76 TF1259
Martin Dales *Lincs* 76 TF1762
Martin Drove End *Hants* 12 SU0420
Martin Hussingtree *H & W* 47 SO8860
Martindale *Cumb* 93 NY4319
Martinhoe *Devon* 19 SS6648
Martinscroft *Ches* 79 SJ6589
Martinstown *Dorset* 11 SY6488
Martlesham *Suffk* 55 TM2547
Martletwy *Dyfed* 30 SN0310
Martock *Somset* 21 ST4619
Marton *Ches* 71 SJ6267
Marton *Ches* 79 SJ8568
Marton *Cleve* 97 NZ5115
Marton *Humb* 85 TA1839
Marton *Lincs* 76 SK8381
Marton *N York* 89 SE4162
Marton *N York* 90 SE7383
Marton *Shrops* 58 SJ2802
Marton *Warwks* 48 SP4069
Marton-le-Moor *N York* 89 SE3670
Martyr Worthy *Hants* 24 SU5132
Martyr's Green *Surrey* 26 TQ0857
Marwick *Ork* 155 HY2324
Marwood *Devon* 19 SS5437
Mary Tavy *Devon* 5 SX5079
Marybank *Highld* 139 NH4853
Maryburgh *Highld* 139 NH5456
Maryculter *Gramp* 135 NO8599
Maryculter *Gramp* 135 NO8599
Maryfield *Cnwll* 6 SX4256
Maryhill *Gramp* 143 NJ8245
Maryhill *Strath* 115 NS5669
Marykirk *Gramp* 135 NO6865
Maryland *Gwent* 34 SO5105
Marylebone *Gt Man* 78 SD5807
Marypark *Gramp* 141 NJ1938
Maryport *Cumb* 92 NY0336
Maryport *D & G* 98 NX1434
Marystow *Devon* 5 SX4383
Maryton *Tays* 127 NO6856
Marywell *Gramp* 135 NO9399
Marywell *Gramp* 135 NO9399
Marywell *Tays* 134 NO5896
Marywell *Tays* 127 NO6544
Masham *N York* 89 SE2280
Mashbury *Essex* 40 TL6511

Mason Milton


Mason T & W 103 NZ2073
Masongill N York 87 SD6675
Mastin Moor Derbys 75 SK4575
Matching Essex 39 TL5212
Matching Green Essex 39 TL5311
Matching Tye Essex 39 TL5111
Matfen Nthumb 103 NZ0371
Matfield Kent 28 TQ6541
Mathern Gwent 34 ST5291
Mathon H & W 47 SO7345
Mathry Dyfed 30 SM8832
Matlaske Norfk 66 TG1534
Matlock Derbys 74 SK3060
Matlock Bank Derbys 74 SK3060
Matlock Bath Derbys 74 SK2958
Matlock Dale Derbys 74 SK2959
Matson Gloucs 35 SO8515
Matterdale End Cumb 93 NY3933
Mattersey Notts 75 SK6889
Mattersey Thorpe Notts 75 SK6889
Mattingley Hants 24 SU7357
Mattishall Norfk 66 TG0511
Mattishall Burgh Norfk 66 TG0512
Mauchline Strath 107 NS4927
Maud Gramp 143 NJ9247
Maufant Jersey 152 JS0000
Maugersbury Gloucs 48 SP1925
Maughold IOM 153 SC4991
Mauld Highld 139 NH4038
Maulden Beds 38 TL0538
Maulds Meaburn Cumb 94 NY6216
Maunby N York 89 SE3486
Maund Bryan H & W 46 SO5650
Maundown Somset 20 ST0528
Mautby Norfk 67 TG4812
Mavesyn Ridware Staffs 73 SK0816
Mavis Enderby Lincs 77 TF3666
Maw Green Ches 72 SJ7157
Maw Green W Mids 60 SP0196
Mawbray Cumb 92 NY0846
Mawdesley Lancs 80 SD4914
Mawdlam M Glam 32 SS8081
Mawgan Cnwll 2 SW7025
Mawgan Cross Cnwll 2 SW7024
Mawgan Porth Cnwll 4 SW8467
Mawla Cnwll 2 SW7045
Mawnan Cnwll 3 SW7827
Mawnan Smith Cnwll 3 SW7728
Mawthorpe Lincs 77 TF4672
Maxey Cambs 64 TF1208
Maxstoke Warwks 61 SP2386
Maxted Street Kent 29 TR1244
Maxton Border 110 NT6130
Maxton Kent 29 TR3041
Maxwellheugh Border 110 NT7333
Maxwelltown D & G 100 NX9676
Maxworthy Cnwll 5 SX2593
May Bank Staffs 72 SJ8547
May's Green Oxon 37 SU7580
May's Green Surrey 26 TQ0957
Mayals W Glam 32 SS6090
Maybole Strath 106 NS2909
Maybury Surrey 26 TQ0158
Mayes Green Surrey 14 TQ1239
Mayfield E Susx 16 TQ5827
Mayfield Loth 118 NT3565
Mayfield Staffs 73 SK1545
Mayford Surrey 25 SU9956
Mayland Essex 40 TL9201
Maymore Strath 114 NR9986
Maynard's Green E Susx 16 TQ5818
Maypole Gwent 34 SO4716
Maypole Kent 29 TR2064
Maypole W Mids 61 SP0878
Maypole Green Norfk 67 TM4195
Maypole Green Suffk 54 TL9159
Maypole Green Suffk 55 TM2767
Mead Devon 18 SS2217
Meadgate Avon 22 ST6758
Meadle Bucks 38 SP8006
Meadowtown Shrops 59 SJ3101
Meadwell Devon 5 SX4081
Meal Bank Cumb 87 SD5495
Mealrigg Cumb 92 NY1345
Mealsgate Cumb 93 NY2142
Mearnskirk Strath 115 NS5455
Meanwood W York 82 SE2837
Mearbeck N York 88 SD8160
Meare Somset 21 ST4541
Meare Green Somset 20 ST2922
Mears Ashby Nhants 51 SP8366
Measham Leics 62 SK3312
Meathop Cumb 87 SD4380
Meaux Humb 85 TA0839
Meavy Devon 6 SX5467
Med Avon 22 ST7358
Medbourne Leics 51 SP8093
Meddon Devon 18 SS2717
Meden Vale Notts 75 SK5870
Medlam Lincs 77 TF3156
Medlar Lancs 80 SD4135
Medmenham Berks 37 SU8084
Medomsley Dur 96 NZ1254
Medstead Hants 24 SU6537
Meer Common H & W 46 SO3652
Meer End W Mids 61 SP2474
Meerbrook Staffs 72 SJ9860
Meesden Herts 39 TL4322
Meeson Shrops 72 SJ6420
Meeth Devon 19 SS5408
Meeting Green Suffk 53 TL7455
Meeting House Hill Norfk 67 TG3028
Meidrim Dyfed 31 SN2820
Meifod Powys 58 SJ1513
Meigle Tays 126 NO2944
Meikle Carco D & G 107 NS7813
Meikle Earnock Strath 116 NS7053
Meikle Grenach Strath 114 NS0760
Meikle Kilmory Strath 114 NS0561
Meikle Obney Tays 125 NO0337
Meikle Wartle Gramp 142 NJ7231
Meikleour Tays 126 NO1539
Meinciau Dyfed 32 SN4610
Meir Staffs 72 SJ9342
Meirheath Staffs 72 SJ9240
Melbourn Cambs 39 TL3844
Melbourne Derbys 62 SK3825
Melbourne Humb 84 SE7543
Melbury Devon 18 SS3719
Melbury Abbas Dorset 22 ST8820
Melbury Bubb Dorset 10 ST5906
Melbury Osmond Dorset 10 ST5707
Melbury Sampford Dorset 10 ST5705
Melchbourne Beds 51 TL0365
Melcombe Bingham Dorset 11 ST7602
Meldon Devon 8 SX5692
Meldon Nthumb 103 NZ1183
Meldreth Cambs 52 TL3746
Meldrum Cent 116 NS7199
Meledon Cnwll 3 SW9254
Melfort Strath 122 NM8313
Melgund Castle Tays 127 NO5455
Meliden Clwyd 70 SJ0580
Melin Court W Glam 33 SN8201
Melin-byrhedyn Powys 57 SN8198
Melin-y-coed Gwynd 69 SH8160
Melin-y-ddol Powys 58 SJ0807
Melin-y-wig Clwyd 70 SJ0448
Melinau Dyfed 31 SN1613
Melkinthorpe Cumb 94 NY5525
Melkridge Nthumb 102 NY7363
Melksham Wilts 22 ST9063
Mell Green Berks 37 SU4577
Mellangoose Cnwll 2 SW6826
Melldalloch Strath 114 NR9375
Mellguards Cumb 93 NY4446
Melling Lancs 87 SD5970
Melling Mersyd 78 SD3800
Melling Mount Mersyd 78 SD4001
Mellis Suffk 54 TM0974
Mellon Charles Highld 144 NG8491
Mellon Udrigle Highld 144 NG8895
Mellor Gt Man 79 SJ9888
Mellor Lancs 81 SD6530
Mellor Brook Lancs 81 SD6431
Mells Somset 22 ST7249
Mells Suffk 55 TM4076
Melmerby Cumb 94 NY6137
Melmerby N York 88 SE0785
Melmerby N York 89 SE3376
Melness Highld 149 NC5861
Melon Green Suffk 54 TL8456
Melplash Dorset 10 SY4797
Melrose Border 109 NT5434
Melsetter Ork 155 ND2689
Melsonby N York 89 NZ1908
Meltham W York 82 SE0910
Meltham W York 82 SE1010
Meltham Mills W York 82 SE1010
Melton Humb 84 SE9726
Melton Suffk 55 TM2850
Melton Constable Norfk 66 TG0433
Melton Mowbray Leics 63 SK7518
Melton Ross Humb 84 TA0610
Meltonby Humb 84 SE7952
Melvaig Highld 144 NG7486
Melverley Shrops 59 SJ3316
Melverley Green Shrops 59 SJ3317
Melvich Highld 150 NC8764
Membury Devon 10 ST2703
Memsie Gramp 143 NJ9762
Menabilly Cnwll 3 SX0951
Menagissey Cnwll 2 SW7146
Menai Bridge Gwynd 69 SH5571
Mendham Suffk 55 TM2783
Mendlesham Suffk 54 TM1065
Mendlesham Green Suffk 54 TM0963
Menethorpe N York 90 SE7667
Menheniot Cnwll 5 SX2862
Menithwood H & W 47 SO7069
Mennock D & G 108 NS8008
Menston W York 82 SE1743
Menstrie Cent 116 NS8596
Menthorpe N York 83 SE6934
Mentmore Bucks 38 SP9019
Meoble Highld 129 NM7987
Meole Brace Shrops 59 SJ4810
Meonstoke Hants 13 SU6119
Meopham Kent 27 TQ6466
Meopham Green Kent 27 TQ6465
Meopham Station Kent 27 TQ6467
Mepal Cambs 53 TL4481
Meppershall Beds 38 TL1336
Mere Ches 79 SJ7281
Mere Wilts 22 ST8132
Mere Brow Lancs 80 SD4218
Mere Green H & W 47 SO9562
Mere Green W Mids 61 SP1298
Mere Heath Ches 79 SJ6670
Mereclough Lancs 81 SD8730
Meresborough Kent 28 TQ8264
Mereworth Kent 28 TQ6553
Meriden W Mids 61 SP2482
Merkadale Highld 136 NG3931
Merlin's Bridge Dyfed 30 SM9414
Merrifield Devon 7 SX8147
Merrington Shrops 59 SJ4720
Merriott Somset 10 ST4412
Merrivale Devon 6 SX5475
Merrow Surrey 26 TQ0250
Merry Field Hill Dorset 12 SU0201
Merry Hill Herts 26 TQ1394
Merry Hill W Mids 60 SO9386
Merry Lees Leics 62 SK4705
Merryhill W Mids 60 SO8897
Merrymeet Cnwll 5 SX2766
Mersham Kent 28 TR0540
Merstham Surrey 27 TQ2953
Merston W Susx 14 SU8903
Merstone IOW 13 SZ5285
Merther Cnwll 3 SW8644
Merthyr Dyfed 31 SN3520
Merthyr Cynog Powys 45 SN9837
Merthyr Dyfan S Glam 20 ST1169
Merthyr Mawr M Glam 33 SS8877
Merthyr Tydfil M Glam 33 SO0506
Merthyr Vale M Glam 33 ST0799
Merthyr Vale M Glam 33 ST0899
Merton Devon 19 SS5212
Merton Gt Lon 27 TQ2570
Merton Norfk 66 TL9098
Merton Oxon 37 SP5717
Mervinslaw Border 110 NT6713
Meshaw Devon 19 SS7519
Messing Essex 40 TL8919
Messingham Humb 84 SE8904
Metcombe Devon 9 SY0791
Metfield Suffk 55 TM2980
Metherell Cnwll 5 SX4069
Metherin Cnwll 4 SX1174
Metheringham Lincs 76 TF0661
Methil Fife 118 NT3799
Methleigh Cnwll 2 SW6226
Methley W York 83 SE3826
Methley Junction W York 83 SE3926
Methlick Gramp 143 NJ8537
Methven Tays 125 NO0226
Methwold Norfk 65 TL7394
Methwold Hythe Norfk 65 TL7195
Mettingham Suffk 55 TM3690
Metton Norfk 67 TG1937
Mevagissey Cnwll 3 SX0144
Mexborough S York 75 SE4700
Mey Highld 151 ND2872
Meyllteyrn Gwynd 56 SH2332
Meyllteyrn Gwynd 56 SH2333
Meysey Hampton Gloucs 36 SU1199
Miavaig W Isls 154 NB0834
Michaelchurch H & W 46 SO5125
Michaelchurch Escley H & W 46 SO3134
Michaelchurch-on-Arrow Powys 46 SO2450
Michaelston-le-Pit S Glam 33 ST1573
Michaelstone-y-Fedw Gwent 34 ST2484
Michaelstow Cnwll 4 SX0878
Michelcombe Devon 7 SX6968
Micheldever Hants 24 SU5139
Micheldever Station Hants 24 SU5143
Michelmersh Hants 23 SU3426
Mickfield Suffk 54 TM1361
Mickle Trafford Ches 71 SJ4469
Micklebring S York 75 SK5194
Mickleby N York 90 NZ8012
Micklefield W York 83 SE4432
Micklefield Green Herts 26 TQ0498
Mickleham Surrey 26 TQ1753
Mickleover Derbys 73 SK3034
Micklethwaite Cumb 93 NY2850
Micklethwaite W York 82 SE1041
Mickleton Dur 95 NY9623
Mickleton Gloucs 48 SP1643
Mickleton W York 83 SE4027
Mickley Derbys 74 SK3379
Mickley N York 89 SE2576
Mickley Green Suffk 54 TL8457
Mickley Square Nthumb 103 NZ0762
Mid Ardlaw Gramp 143 NJ9464
Mid Beltie Gramp 134 NJ6200
Mid Bockhampton Hants 12 SZ1796
Mid Calder Loth 117 NT0767
Mid Clyth Highld 151 ND2937
Mid Lavant W Susx 14 SU8508
Mid Mains Highld 139 NH4239
Mid Sannox Strath 105 NS0145
Mid Thorpe Lincs 77 TF2572
Mid Yell Shet 155 HU5191
Midbea Ork 155 HY4444
Middle Assendon Oxon 37 SU7385
Middle Aston Oxon 49 SP4726
Middle Chinnock Somset 10 ST4713
Middle Claydon Bucks 49 SP7225
Middle Duntisbourne Gloucs 35 SO9806
Middle Handley Derbys 74 SK4077
Middle Harling Norfk 54 TL9885
Middle Kames Strath 114 NR9189
Middle Littleton H & W 48 SP0847
Middle Madeley Staffs 72 SJ7745
Middle Maes-coed H & W 46 SO3333
Middle Mayfield Staffs 73 SK1444
Middle Mill Dyfed 30 SM8026
Middle Quarter Kent 28 TQ8937
Middle Rasen Lincs 76 TF0889
Middle Rocombe Devon 7 SX9069
Middle Salter Lancs 87 SD6063
Middle Stoford Somset 20 ST1821
Middle Stoke Kent 28 TQ8275
Middle Stoughton Somset 21 ST4248
Middle Street Essex 39 TL4005
Middle Street Gloucs 35 SO7803
Middle Taphouse Cnwll 4 SX1763
Middle Town IOS 2 SV8808
Middle Tysoe Warwks 48 SP3344
Middle Wallop Hants 23 SU2938
Middle Winterslow Wilts 23 SU2432
Middle Woodford Wilts 23 SU1136
Middle Yard Gloucs 35 SO8103
Middlebie D & G 101 NY2176
Middlecliffe S York 83 SE4204
Middlecott Devon 8 SX7186
Middlegill D & G 108 NT0407
Middleham N York 89 SE1287
Middlehill Cnwll 5 SX2869
Middlehill Wilts 35 ST8169
Middlehope Shrops 59 SO4988
Middlemarsh Dorset 11 ST6707
Middlemore Devon 6 SX5073
Middlesbrough Cleve 97 NZ4920
Middlesceugh Cumb 93 NY3942
Middleshaw Cumb 87 SD5589
Middleshaw D & G 100 NY1475
Middlesmoor N York 88 SE0973
Middlestone Dur 96 NZ2531
Middlestone Moor Dur 96 NZ2432
Middlestown W York 82 SE2617
Middlethird Border 110 NT6743
Middleton Cumb 87 SD6285
Middleton Derbys 74 SK1963
Middleton Derbys 73 SK2756
Middleton Essex 54 TL8739
Middleton Gt Man 79 SD8705
Middleton H & W 46 SO5469
Middleton Hants 24 SU4244
Middleton Lancs 87 SD4258
Middleton Loth 118 NT3758
Middleton N York 90 SE7885
Middleton Nhants 51 SP8489
Middleton Norfk 65 TF6616
Middleton Nthumb 111 NU0024
Middleton Nthumb 111 NU1035
Middleton Nthumb 103 NZ0584
Middleton Shrops 59 SJ3129
Middleton Shrops 46 SO5477
Middleton Strath 120 NL9443
Middleton Strath 115 NS3952
Middleton Suffk 55 TM4267
Middleton Tays 126 NO1206
Middleton W Glam 31 SS4287
Middleton W York 82 SE1249
Middleton W York 83 SE3027
Middleton Warwks 61 SP1798
Middleton Cheney Nhants 49 SP4941
Middleton Green Staffs 73 SJ9935
Middleton Hall Nthumb 111 NT9825
Middleton Moor Suffk 55 TM4167
Middleton one Tow Dur 89 NZ3512
Middleton Priors Shrops 59 SO6290
Middleton Quernhow N York 89 SE3378
Middleton Scriven Shrops 60 SO6887
Middleton St. George Dur 89 NZ3412
Middleton Stoney Oxon 49 SP5323
Middleton Tyas N York 89 NZ2205
Middleton-in-Teesdale Dur 95 NY9425
Middleton-on-Leven N York 89 NZ4609
Middleton-on-Sea W Susx 14 SU9800
Middleton-on-the-Hill H & W 46 SO5364
Middleton-on-the-Wolds Humb 84 SE9449
Middletown Avon 34 ST4571
Middletown Cumb 86 NX9908
Middletown Powys 59 SJ3012
Middlewich Ches 72 SJ7066
Middlewood Cnwll 5 SX2775
Middlewood H & W 46 SO2844
Middlewood Green Suffk 54 TM0961
Middleyard Strath 107 NS5132
Middlezoy Somset 21 ST3733
Middridge Dur 96 NZ2526
Midford Avon 22 ST7660
Midge Hall Lancs 80 SD5123
Midgeholme Cumb 94 NY6359
Midgham Berks 24 SU5567
Midgley W York 82 SE2714
Midgley W York 82 SE0226
Midhopestones S York 74 SK2399
Midhurst W Susx 14 SU8821
Midlem Border 109 NT5227
Midney Somset 21 ST4927
Midpark Strath 114 NS0259
Midsomer Norton Avon 22 ST6654
Midtown Highld 144 NG8285
Midtown Highld 149 NC5861
Midville Lincs 77 TF3756
Midway Ches 79 SJ9282
Migvie Gramp 134 NJ4306
Milarrochy Cent 115 NS4092
Milborne Port Somset 22 ST6718
Milborne St. Andrew Dorset 11 SY8097
Milborne Wick Somset 22 ST6620
Milbourne Nthumb 103 NZ1175
Milbourne Wilts 35 ST9587
Milburn Cumb 94 NY6529
Milbury Heath Avon 35 ST6790
Milby N York 89 SE4067
Milcombe Oxon 49 SP4134
Milden Suffk 54 TL9546
Mildenhall Suffk 53 TL7174
Mildenhall Wilts 36 SU2069
Mile Elm Wilts 35 ST9969
Mile End Essex 41 TL9927
Mile End Gloucs 34 SO5811
Mile End Suffk 55 TM3489
Mile Head Lancs 87 SD4970
Mile Oak E Susx 15 TQ2407
Mile Oak Kent 28 TQ6743
Mile Oak Staffs 61 SK1802
Mile Town Kent 28 TQ9274
Milebrook Powys 46 SO3172
Milebush Kent 28 TQ7545
Mileham Norfk 66 TF9119
Milehead Highld 132 NH8406
Miles Hope H & W 46 SO5764
Miles Platting Gt Man 79 SJ8599
Milesmark Fife 117 NT0688
Milfield Nthumb 110 NT9333
Milford Derbys 62 SK3545
Milford Devon 18 SS2322
Milford Powys 58 SO0991
Milford Staffs 72 SJ9721
Milford Surrey 25 SU9442
Milford Haven Dyfed 30 SM9006
Milford on Sea Hants 12 SZ2891
Milkwall Gloucs 34 SO5809
Mill Bank W York 82 SE0321
Mill Brow Gt Man 79 SJ9889
Mill Common Norfk 67 TG3301
Mill Common Suffk 55 TM4082
Mill Cross Devon 7 SX7361
Mill End Bucks 37 SU7885
Mill End Cambs 52 TL3180
Mill End Herts 39 TL3332
Mill Green Cambs 53 TL6245
Mill Green Essex 40 TL6301
Mill Green Herts 39 TL2410
Mill Green Lincs 64 TF2223
Mill Green Norfk 54 TM1384
Mill Green Staffs 73 SK0821
Mill Green Suffk 54 TM1360
Mill Green Suffk 55 TM3161
Mill Green Suffk 54 TL9957
Mill Green Suffk 54 TL9542
Mill Green W Mids 61 SK0701
Mill Hill E Susx 16 TQ6104
Mill Hill Gt Lon 26 TQ2292
Mill Meece Staffs 72 SJ8333
Mill of Cammie Gramp 135 NO6993
Mill of Drummond Tays 125 NN8315
Mill of Grange Gramp 141 NJ0460
Mill of Haldane Strath 115 NS4083
Mill of Uras Gramp 135 NO8680
Mill of Uras Gramp 135 NO8680
Mill Side Cumb 87 SD4484
Mill Street Kent 28 TQ6957
Mill Street Norfk 66 TG0118
Mill Street Norfk 66 TG0517
Mill Street Suffk 54 TM0672
Millais Jersey 152 JS0000
Milland W Susx 14 SU8328
Milland Marsh W Susx 14 SU8326
Millbeck Cumb 93 NY2526
Millbreck Gramp 143 NK0044
Millbrex Gramp 143 NJ8144
Millbridge Surrey 25 SU8442
Millbrook Beds 38 TL0138
Millbrook Cnwll 6 SX4252
Millbrook Gt Man 79 SJ9799
Millbrook Hants 12 SU3813
Millbrook Jersey 152 JS0000
Millbuie Gramp 135 NJ7909
Millburn Strath 107 NS4429
Millcombe Devon 7 SX8050
Millcorner E Susx 17 TQ8223
Millcraig Highld 146 NH6571
Milldale Staffs 73 SK1354
Millend Gloucs 34 SO5608
Millend Gloucs 35 ST7496
Miller's Dale Derbys 74 SK1373
Miller's Green Essex 40 TL5808
Millerhill Loth 118 NT3269
Millers Green Derbys 73 SK2752
Millerston Strath 116 NS6467
Millgate Lancs 81 SD8819
Millgreen Shrops 72 SJ6828
Millhalf H & W 46 SO2847
Millhayes Devon 9 ST2303
Millheugh Strath 116 NS7450
Millholme Cumb 87 SD5690
Millhouse Cumb 93 NY3637
Millhouse S York 74 SK3484
Millhouse Strath 114 NR9570
Millhouse Green S York 82 SE2203
Millhousebridge D & G 100 NY1085
Millhouses S York 74 SK3484
Millhouses S York 83 SE4204
Millikenpark Strath 115 NS4162
Millin Cross Dyfed 30 SM9914
Millington Humb 84 SE8351
Millisle D & G 99 NX4547
Millness Cumb 87 SD5383
Millom Cumb 86 SD1780
Millook Cnwll 18 SX1899
Millpool Cnwll 2 SW5730
Millpool Cnwll 4 SX1170
Millport Strath 114 NS1655
Millthrop Cumb 87 SD6691
Milltimber Gramp 135 NJ8501
Milltown D & G 101 NY3375
Milltown Derbys 74 SK3561
Milltown Devon 19 SS5539
Milltown Gramp 133 NJ2609
Milltown Gramp 142 NJ4716
Milltown of Campfield Gramp 135 NJ6500
Milltown of Edinvillie Gramp 141 NJ2639
Milltown of Learney Gramp 134 NJ6303
Milnathort Tays 126 NO1204
Milngavie Strath 115 NS5574
Milnmark D & G 99 NX6582
Milnrow Gt Man 81 SD9212
Milnthorpe Cumb 87 SD4981
Milnthorpe W York 83 SE3317
Milovaig Highld 136 NG1550
Milson Shrops 47 SO6472
Milsted Kent 28 TQ9058
Milston Wilts 23 SU1645
Milthorpe Lincs 64 TF1030
Milthorpe Nhants 49 SP5946
Milton Avon 21 ST3462
Milton Cambs 53 TL4762
Milton Cent 115 NN5001
Milton Cent 115 NS4490
Milton Cumb 101 NY5560
Milton D & G 98 NX2154
Milton D & G 100 NX8470
Milton Derbys 62 SK3126
Milton Dyfed 30 SN0303
Milton Gramp 142 NJ5163
Milton Gwent 34 ST3688
Milton Highld 151 ND3451
Milton Highld 139 NH5030
Milton Highld 137 NG7134
Milton Highld 139 NH4930

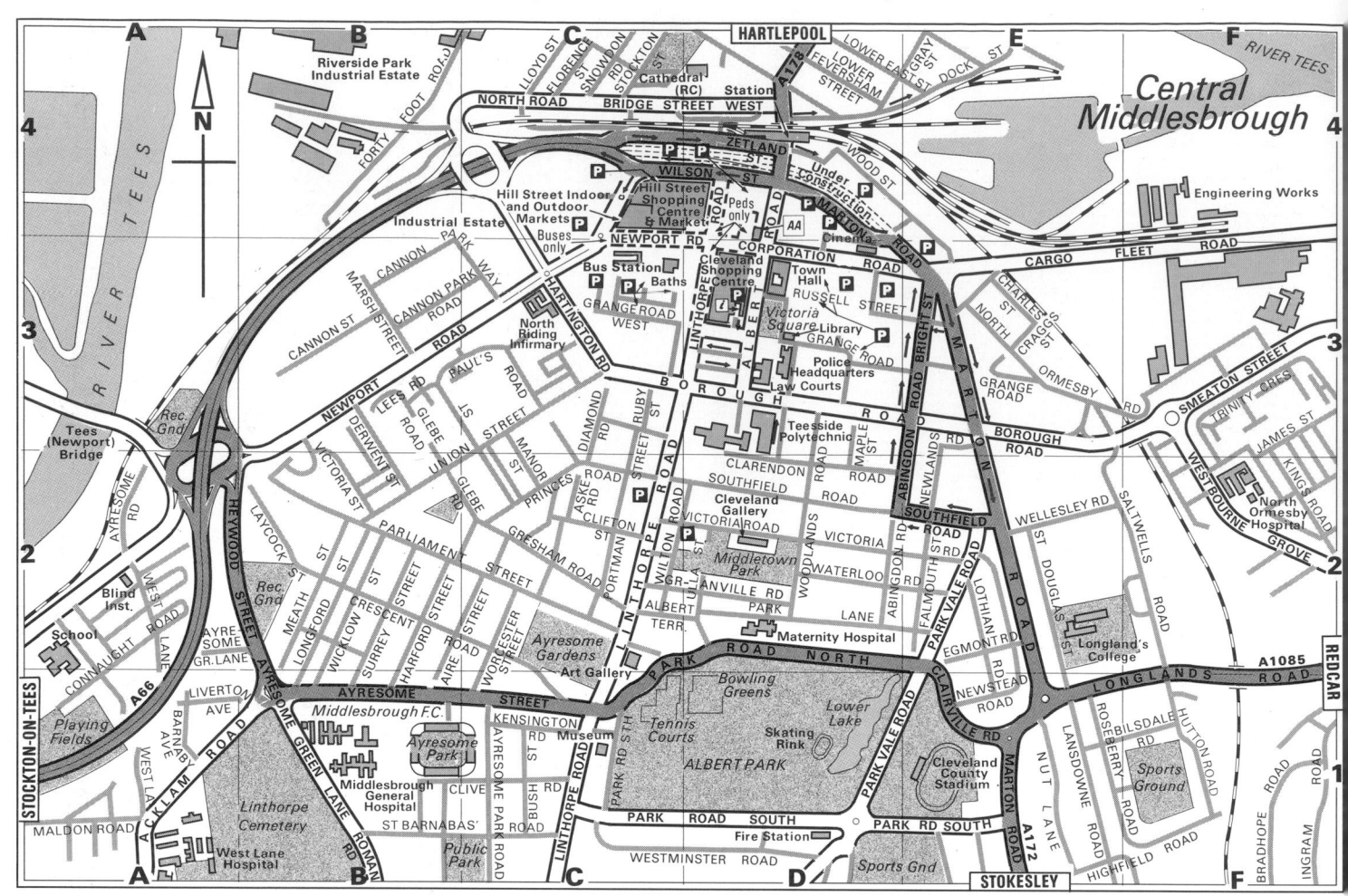

Moresby
New Broughton

Moresby *Cumb* 92 NX9821
Moresby Parks *Cumb* 92 NY0019
Morestead *Hants* 13 SU5025
Moreton *Dorset* 11 SY8089
Moreton *Essex* 39 TL5307
Moreton *H & W* 46 SO5164
Moreton *Mersyd* 78 SJ2690
Moreton *Oxon* 37 SP6904
Moreton *Staffs* 73 SK1429
Moreton *Staffs* 72 SJ7817
Moreton Corbet *Shrops* 59 SJ5523
Moreton Jeffries *H & W* 46 SO6048
Moreton Mill *Shrops* 59 SJ5823
Moreton Morrell *Warwks* 48 SP3155
Moreton on Lugg *H & W* 46 SO5045
Moreton Paddox *Warwks* 48 SP3054
Moreton Pinkney *Nhants* 49 SP5749
Moreton Say *Shrops* 59 SJ6234
Moreton Valence *Gloucs* 35 SO7809
Moreton-in-Marsh *Gloucs* 48 SP2032
Moretonhampstead *Devon* 8 SX7586
Morfa *Dyfed* 42 SN3053
Morfa Bychan *Gwynd* 57 SH5437
Morfa Glas *W Glam* 33 SN8706
Morfa Nefyn *Gwynd* 56 SH2840
Morgan's Vale *Wilts* 12 SU1921
Morganstown *S Glam* 33 ST1281
Morham *Loth* 118 NT5571
Moriah *Dyfed* 43 SN6279
Morland *Cumb* 94 NY6022
Morley *Ches* 79 SJ8282
Morley *Derbys* 62 SK3941
Morley *Dur* 96 NZ1227
Morley *W York* 82 SE2627
Morley Green *Ches* 79 SJ8281
Morley St. Botolph *Norfk* 66 TM0799
Mornick *Cnwll* 5 SX3172
Morningside *Loth* 117 NT2470
Morningside *Strath* 116 NS8355
Morningthorpe *Norfk* 67 TM2192
Morpeth *Nthumb* 103 NZ2085
Morphie *Gramp* 135 NO7164
Morrey *Staffs* 73 SK1218
Morridge Side *Staffs* 73 SK0254
Morridge Top *Staffs* 74 SK0365
Morriston *W Glam* 32 SS6697
Morston *Norfk* 66 TG0043
Mortehoe *Devon* 18 SS4545
Morthen *S York* 75 SK4789
Mortimer *Berks* 24 SU6564
Mortimer Common *Berks* 24 SU6565
Mortimer West End *Hants* 24 SU6363
Mortimer's Cross *H & W* 46 SO4263
Mortlake *Gt Lon* 26 TQ2075
Morton *Cumb* 93 NY4539
Morton *Cumb* 93 NY3855
Morton *Derbys* 74 SK4060
Morton *IOW* 13 SZ6086
Morton *Lincs* 75 SK8091
Morton *Lincs* 64 TF0923
Morton *Norfk* 66 TG1217
Morton *Notts* 75 SK7252
Morton *Shrops* 59 SJ2924
Morton Bagot *Warwks* 48 SP1164
Morton Hall *Lincs* 76 SK8863
Morton Tinmouth *Dur* 96 NZ1821
Morton-on-Swale *N York* 89 SE3292
Morvah *Cnwll* 2 SW4035
Morval *Cnwll* 5 SX2656
Morvich *Highld* 138 NC6311
Morville *Shrops* 60 SO6794
Morville Heath *Shrops* 60 SO6893
Morwenstow *Cnwll* 18 SS2015
Mosborough *S York* 74 SK4281
Moscow *Strath* 107 NS4840
Mose *Shrops* 60 SO7590
Mosedale *Cumb* 93 NY3532
Moseley *H & W* 47 SO8159
Moseley *W Mids* 60 SO9398
Moseley *W Mids* 61 SP0783
Moses Gate *Gt Man* 79 SD7306
Moss *Clwyd* 71 SJ3053
Moss *S York* 83 SE5914
Moss *Strath* 120 NL9644
Moss Bank *Mersyd* 78 SJ5198
Moss End *Ches* 79 SJ6778
Moss Nook *Gt Man* 79 SJ8385
Moss Side *Cumb* 93 NY1952
Moss Side *Lancs* 80 SD3730
Moss Side *Mersyd* 78 SD3802
Moss-Side *Highld* 140 NH8554
Mossat *Gramp* 142 NJ4719
Mossbank *Shet* 155 HU4575
Mossbay *Cumb* 92 NX9927
Mossblown *Strath* 106 NS3925
Mossbrow *Gt Man* 79 SJ7189
Mossburnford *Border* 110 NT6616
Mossdale *D & G* 99 NX6570
Mossdale *Strath* 107 NS4904
Mossend *Strath* 116 NS7360
Mosser Mains *Cumb* 92 NY1125
Mossgiel *Strath* 107 NS4828
Mossknowe *D & G* 101 NY2769
Mossley *Ches* 72 SJ8861
Mossley *Gt Man* 82 SD9702
Mossley *Staffs* 73 SK0417
Mosspaul Hotel *Border* 109 NY4099
Mosstodloch *Gramp* 141 NJ3259
Mossy Lea *Lancs* 80 SD5312
Mossyard *D & G* 99 NX5551
Mosterton *Dorset* 10 ST4505
Moston *Gt Man* 79 SD8701
Moston *Shrops* 59 SJ5626
Moston Green *Ches* 72 SJ7261
Mostyn *Clwyd* 70 SJ1580
Motcombe *Dorset* 22 ST8425
Motherby *Cumb* 93 NY4228
Mothercombe *Devon* 6 SX6147
Motherwell *Strath* 116 NS7457
Motspur Park *Gt Lon* 26 TQ2267
Mottingham *Gt Lon* 27 TQ4272
Mottisfont *Hants* 23 SU3226
Mottistone *IOW* 13 SZ4083
Mottram in Longdendale *Gt Man* 79 SJ9995
Mottram in Longdendale *Gt Man* 79 SJ9995
Mouilpied *Guern* 152 GN0000
Mouldsworth *Ches* 71 SJ5071
Moulin *Tays* 132 NN9459
Moulsecoomb *E Susx* 15 TQ3307
Moulsford *Oxon* 37 SU5984
Moulsoe *Bucks* 38 SP9041
Moultavie *Highld* 146 NH6371
Moulton *Ches* 79 SJ6569
Moulton *Lincs* 64 TF3023
Moulton *N York* 89 NZ2303
Moulton *Nhants* 50 SP7866
Moulton *S Glam* 33 ST0770
Moulton *Suffk* 53 TL6964
Moulton Chapel *Lincs* 64 TF2918
Moulton Seas End *Lincs* 64 TF3227
Moulton St. Mary *Norfk* 67 TG3907
Mount *Cnwll* 4 SX1468
Mount *Cnwll* 3 SW7856
Mount *W York* 82 SE0918
Mount Ambrose *Cnwll* 2 SW7143
Mount Bures *Essex* 40 TL9032
Mount Hawke *Cnwll* 2 SW7147
Mount Hermon *Cnwll* 2 SW6915
Mount Lothian *Loth* 117 NT2757
Mount Pleasant *Ches* 72 SJ8456
Mount Pleasant *Derbys* 74 SK3448
Mount Pleasant *Dur* 96 NZ2634
Mount Pleasant *E Susx* 16 TQ4216
Mount Pleasant *H & W* 47 SP0064
Mount Pleasant *Norfk* 66 TL9994
Mount Pleasant *Suffk* 53 TL7347
Mount Sorrel *Wilts* 23 SU0324
Mount Tabor *W York* 82 SE0527
Mountain *W York* 82 SE0931
Mountain Ash *M Glam* 33 ST0499
Mountain Cross *Border* 117 NT1547
Mountain Street *Kent* 29 TR0652
Mountblairy *Gramp* 142 NJ6954
Mountblairy *Gramp* 142 NJ6954
Mountfield *E Susx* 17 TQ7320
Mountgerald House *Highld* 139 NH5661
Mountjoy *Cnwll* 4 SW8760
Mountjoy *Cnwll* 4 SW8760
Mountnessing *Essex* 40 TQ6297
Mounton *Gwent* 34 ST5193
Mountsorrel *Leics* 62 SK5814
Mountstuart *Strath* 114 NS1159
Mousehill *Surrey* 25 SU9441
Mousehole *Cnwll* 2 SW4626
Mouswald *D & G* 100 NY0672
Mow Cop *Ches* 72 SJ8557
Mowacre Hill *Leics* 62 SK5707
Mowhaugh *Border* 110 NT8120
Mowmacre Hill *Leics* 62 SK5807
Mowsley *Leics* 50 SP6489
Mowtie *Gramp* 135 NO8388
Moy *Highld* 140 NH7634
Moy *Highld* 131 NN4282
Moye *Highld* 138 NG8818
Moyles Court *Hants* 12 SU1607
Moylgrove *Dyfed* 42 SN1144
Muasdale *Strath* 105 NR6840
Much Birch *H & W* 46 SO5030
Much Cowarne *H & W* 46 SO6147
Much Dewchurch *H & W* 46 SO4831
Much Hadham *Herts* 39 TL4219
Much Hoole *Lancs* 80 SD4723
Much Hoole Town *Lancs* 80 SD4722
Much Marcle *H & W* 47 SO6533
Much Wenlock *Shrops* 59 SO6299
Muchalls *Gramp* 135 NO9092
Muchelney *Somset* 21 ST4224
Muchelney Ham *Somset* 21 ST4323
Muchlarnick *Cnwll* 5 SX2156
Mucking *Essex* 40 TQ6881
Muckingford *Essex* 40 TQ6779
Muckleford *Dorset* 10 SY6393
Mucklestone *Staffs* 72 SJ7237
Muckton *Lincs* 77 TF3781
Mucomir *Highld* 131 NN1884
Mud Row *Kent* 28 TR0072
Mudale *Highld* 149 NC5335
Muddiford *Devon* 19 SS5638
Muddlebridge *Devon* 19 SS5132
Muddles Green *E Susx* 16 TQ5413
Mudeford *Dorset* 12 SZ1892
Mudford *Somset* 21 ST5719
Mudford Sock *Somset* 21 ST5519
Mudgley *Somset* 21 ST4445
Mugdock *Cent* 115 NS5577
Mugeary *Highld* 136 NG4438
Mugginton *Derbys* 73 SK2842
Muggintonlane End *Derbys* 73 SK2844
Muggleswick *Dur* 95 NZ0449
Muie *Highld* 146 NC6704
Muir of Fowlis *Gramp* 134 NJ5612
Muir of Miltonduff *Gramp* 141 NJ1859
Muir of Ord *Highld* 139 NH5250
Muir of Thorn *Tays* 125 NO0637
Muirden *Gramp* 142 NJ7054
Muirdrum *Tays* 127 NO5637
Muiresk *Gramp* 142 NJ6948
Muirhead *Fife* 126 NO2805
Muirhead *Strath* 116 NS6869
Muirhead *Tays* 126 NO3434
Muirhouselaw *Border* 110 NT6328
Muirhouses *Cent* 117 NT0180
Muirkirk *Strath* 107 NS6927
Muirmill *Cent* 116 NS7283
Muirshearlich *Highld* 131 NN1380
Muirtack *Gramp* 143 NJ9937
Muirton Mains *Highld* 139 NH3553
Muirton of Ardblair *Tays* 126 NO1643
Muirtown *Tays* 125 NN9211
Muker *N York* 88 SD9098
Mulbarton *Norfk* 67 TG1901
Mulben *Gramp* 141 NJ3550
Mulfra *Cnwll* 2 SW4534
Mulindry *Strath* 112 NR3659
Mullacott Cross *Devon* 19 SS5144
Mullion *Cnwll* 2 SW6719
Mumby *Lincs* 77 TF5174
Muncher's Green *Herts* 39 TL3126
Munderfield Row *H & W* 47 SO6451
Munderfield Stocks *H & W* 47 SO6550
Mundesley *Norfk* 67 TG3136
Mundford *Norfk* 66 TL8093
Mundham *Norfk* 67 TM3397
Mundon Hill *Essex* 40 TL8602
Munerigie *Highld* 131 NH2602
Mungrisdale *Cumb* 93 NY3630
Munlochy *Highld* 140 NH6453
Munnoch *Strath* 114 NS2548
Munsley *H & W* 47 SO6641
Munslow *Shrops* 59 SO5287
Munslow Aston *Shrops* 59 SO5186
Murchington *Devon* 8 SX6888
Murcot *H & W* 48 SP0640
Murcott *Oxon* 37 SP5815
Murcott *Wilts* 35 ST9591
Murkle *Highld* 151 ND1668
Murlaggan *Highld* 130 NN0192
Murrell Green *Hants* 24 SU7455
Murroes *Tays* 127 NO4635
Murrow *Cambs* 64 TF3707
Mursley *Bucks* 38 SP8128
Murthill *Tays* 134 NO4657
Murthly *Tays* 126 NO1038
Murton *Cumb* 94 NY7221
Murton *Dur* 96 NZ3947
Murton *N York* 83 SE6452
Murton *N York* 83 SE6452
Murton *Nthumb* 111 NT9748
Murton *T & W* 103 NZ3270
Musbury *Devon* 10 SY2794
Muscoates *N York* 90 SE6879
Musselburgh *Loth* 118 NT3472
Muston *Leics* 63 SK8237
Muston *N York* 91 TA0979
Mustow Green *H & W* 60 SO8774
Muswell Hill *Gt Lon* 27 TQ2889
Mutehill *D & G* 99 NX6848
Mutford *Suffk* 55 TM4888
Muthill *Tays* 125 NN8616
Mutterton *Devon* 9 ST0305
Muxton *Shrops* 60 SJ7114
Mybster *Highld* 151 ND1652
Myddfai *Dyfed* 44 SN7730
Myddle *Shrops* 59 SJ4623
Mydroilyn *Dyfed* 42 SN4555
Mylor *Cnwll* 3 SW8135
Mylor Bridge *Cnwll* 3 SW8036
Mynachlog-ddu *Dyfed* 31 SN1430
Myndd-llan *Clwyd* 70 SJ1572
Myndtown *Shrops* 59 SO3999
Mynydd Buch *Dyfed* 43 SN7276
Mynydd Isa *Clwyd* 70 SJ2363
Mynydd-bach *Gwent* 34 ST4894
Mynydd-bach *W Glam* 32 SS6597
Mynyddgarreg *Dyfed* 31 SN4208
Mynytho *Gwynd* 56 SH3031
Myrebird *Gramp* 135 NO7398
Myredykes *Border* 102 NY5998
Mytchett *Surrey* 25 SU8855
Mytholm *W York* 82 SD9827
Mytholmroyd *W York* 82 SE0126
Mythop *Lancs* 80 SD3634
Myton-on-Swale *N York* 89 SE4466

# N

Naast *Highld* 144 NG8283
Nab's Head *Lancs* 81 SD6229
Naburn *N York* 83 SE5945
Nackholt *Kent* 28 TR0543
Nackington *Kent* 29 TR1554
Nacton *Suffk* 55 TM2240
Nafferton *Humb* 91 TA0559
Nag's Head *Gloucs* 35 ST8898
Nailbridge *Gloucs* 35 SO6416
Nailsbourne *Somset* 20 ST2128
Nailsea *Avon* 34 ST4770
Nailstone *Leics* 62 SK4107
Nailsworth *Gloucs* 35 ST8499
Nairn *Highld* 140 NH8756
Nalderswood *Surrey* 15 TQ2345
Nancegollan *Cnwll* 2 SW6332
Nancledra *Cnwll* 2 SW4936
Nanhoron *Gwynd* 56 SH2731
Nannerch *Clwyd* 70 SJ1669
Nanpantan *Leics* 62 SK5017
Nanpean *Cnwll* 3 SW9656
Nanquidno *Cnwll* 2 SW3629
Nanstallon *Cnwll* 4 SX0367
Nant Gwynant *Gwynd* 69 SH6350
Nant Peris *Gwynd* 69 SH6058
Nant-ddu *Powys* 33 SO0015
Nant-glas *Powys* 45 SN9965
Nant-y-Bwch *Gwent* 33 SO1210
Nant-y-caws *Dyfed* 32 SN4518
Nant-y-derry *Gwent* 34 SO3306
Nant-y-gollen *Shrops* 58 SJ2429
Nant-y-moel *M Glam* 33 SS9392
Nant-y-pandy *Gwynd* 69 SH6974
Nanternis *Dyfed* 42 SN3756
Nantgaredig *Dyfed* 32 SN4921
Nantgarw *M Glam* 33 ST1285
Nantglyn *Clwyd* 70 SJ0061
Nantgwyn *Powys* 45 SN9776
Nantlle *Gwynd* 68 SH5053
Nantmawr *Shrops* 58 SJ2524
Nantmel *Powys* 45 SO0366
Nantmor *Gwynd* 57 SH6046
Nantwich *Ches* 72 SJ6552
Nantyffyllon *M Glam* 33 SS8592
Nantyglo *Gwent* 33 SO1910
Naphill *Bucks* 26 SU8496
Napleton *H & W* 47 SO8648
Nappa *N York* 81 SD8553
Napton on the Hill *Warwks* 49 SP4661
Narberth *Dyfed* 31 SN1114
Narborough *Leics* 50 SP5497
Narborough *Norfk* 65 TF7412
Narkurs *M Glam* 5 SX3255
Nasareth *Gwynd* 68 SH4749
Naseby *Nhants* 50 SP6978
Nash *Bucks* 38 SP7833
Nash *Gt Lon* 27 TQ4063
Nash *Gwent* 34 ST3483
Nash *H & W* 46 SO3062
Nash *Shrops* 46 SO6071
Nash End *H & W* 60 SO7781
Nash Lee *Bucks* 38 SP8408
Nash Street *Kent* 27 TQ6469
Nash's Green *Hants* 24 SU6745
Nassington *Nhants* 51 TL0696
Nasty *Herts* 39 TL3524
Nateby *Cumb* 88 NY7706
Nateby *Lancs* 80 SD4644
Natland *Cumb* 87 SD5289
Naughton *Suffk* 54 TM0249
Naunton *Gloucs* 48 SP1123
Naunton *H & W* 47 SO8739
Naunton *H & W* 47 SO8645
Naunton Beauchamp *H & W* 47 SO9652
Navenby *Lincs* 76 SK9857
Navestock *Essex* 27 TQ5397
Navestock Side *Essex* 27 TQ5697
Navidale *Highld* 147 ND0316
Navity *Highld* 140 NH7864
Nawton *N York* 90 SE6584
Nayland *Suffk* 54 TL9734
Nazeing *Essex* 39 TL4106
Nazeing Gate *Essex* 39 TL4105
Neacroft *Hants* 12 SZ1897
Neal's Green *Warwks* 61 SP3384
Nealhouse *Cumb* 93 NY3351
Neap *Shet* 155 HU5058
Near Cotton *Staffs* 73 SK0646
Near Sawry *Cumb* 87 SD3795
Nearsden *Gt Lon* 26 TQ2185
Neasham *Dur* 89 NZ3210
Neath *W Glam* 32 SS7597
Neatham *Hants* 24 SU7440
Neatishead *Norfk* 67 TG3421
Nebo *Dyfed* 43 SN5464
Nebo *Gwynd* 68 SH4750
Nebo *Gwynd* 69 SH8356
Necton *Norfk* 66 TF8709
Nedd *Highld* 148 NC1331
Nedging *Suffk* 54 TM0048
Nedging Tye *Suffk* 54 TM0250
Needham *Norfk* 55 TM2281
Needham Market *Suffk* 54 TM0855
Needham Street *Suffk* 53 TL7265
Needingworth *Cambs* 52 TL3472
Neen Savage *Shrops* 60 SO6777
Neen Sollars *Shrops* 47 SO6572
Neenton *Shrops* 59 SO6388
Nefyn *Gwynd* 56 SH3040
Neilston *Strath* 115 NS4857
Nelson *Lancs* 81 SD8638
Nelson *M Glam* 33 ST1195
Nemphlar *Strath* 116 NS8544
Nempnett Thrubwell *Avon* 21 ST5260
Nenthall *Cumb* 94 NY7545
Nenthead *Cumb* 94 NY7743
Nenthorn *Border* 110 NT6837
Neopardy *Devon* 8 SX7998
Nep Town *W Susx* 15 TQ2115
Nercwys *Clwyd* 70 SJ2360
Nereabolls *Strath* 112 NR2255
Nerston *Strath* 116 NS6457
Nesbit *Nthumb* 111 NT9833
Nesfield *N York* 82 SE0949
Ness *Ches* 71 SJ3076
Nesscliffe *Shrops* 59 SJ3819
Neston *Ches* 71 SJ2977
Neston *Wilts* 22 ST8667
Netchwood *Shrops* 59 SO6291
Nether Alderley *Ches* 79 SJ8476
Nether Blainslie *Border* 109 NT5443
Nether Broughton *Notts* 63 SK6925
Nether Burrow *Lancs* 87 SD6174
Nether Cassock *D & G* 109 NT2303
Nether Cerne *Dorset* 11 SY6698
Nether Compton *Dorset* 10 ST5917
Nether Crimond *Gramp* 143 NJ8222
Nether Dallachy *Gramp* 141 NJ3664
Nether Exe *Devon* 9 SS9300
Nether Fingland *Strath* 108 NS9310
Nether Handley *Derbys* 74 SK4176
Nether Handwick *Tays* 126 NO3641
Nether Haugh *S York* 74 SK4196
Nether Headon *Notts* 75 SK7477
Nether Heage *Derbys* 74 SK3650
Nether Heyford *Nhants* 49 SP6658
Nether Howecleuch *Strath* 108 NT0312
Nether Kellet *Lancs* 87 SD5067
Nether Kinmundy *Gramp* 143 NK0543
Nether Moor *Derbys* 74 SK3866
Nether Newton *Cumb* 87 SD4082
Nether Padley *Derbys* 74 SK2478
Nether Poppleton *N York* 83 SE5654
Nether Row *Cumb* 93 NY3238
Nether Silton *N York* 89 SE4592
Nether Skyborry *Shrops* 46 SO2773
Nether Stowey *Somset* 20 ST1939
Nether Street *Essex* 40 TL5812
Nether Wallop *Hants* 23 SU3036
Nether Wasdale *Cumb* 86 NY1204
Nether Wasdale *Cumb* 86 NY1204
Nether Wellwood *Strath* 107 NS6526
Nether Welton *Cumb* 93 NY3545
Nether Westcote *Oxon* 36 SP2220
Nether Whitacre *Warwks* 61 SP2392
Nether Whitecleuch *Strath* 108 NS8319
Netheravon *Wilts* 23 SU1448
Netherbrae *Gramp* 143 NJ7959
Netherburn *Strath* 116 NS7947
Netherbury *Dorset* 10 SY4799
Netherby *Cumb* 101 NY3971
Netherby *N York* 83 SE3346
Nethercleuch *D & G* 100 NY1186
Nethercote *Warwks* 49 SP5164
Nethercott *Devon* 18 SS4839
Nethercott *Devon* 5 SX3596
Netherend *Gloucs* 34 SO5900
Netherfield *E Susx* 16 TQ7019
Netherfield *Leics* 62 SK5816
Netherfield *Notts* 62 SK6140
Netherfield Road *E Susx* 17 TQ7417
Nethergate *Norfk* 66 TG0529
Nethergate *Notts* 75 SK7599
Netherhampton *Wilts* 23 SU1029
Netherhay *Dorset* 10 ST4105
Netherland Green *Staffs* 73 SK1030
Netherlaw *D & G* 99 NX7445
Netherley *Gramp* 135 NO8493
Nethermill *D & G* 100 NY0487
Nethermuir *Gramp* 143 NJ9144
Netheroyd Hill *W York* 82 SE1419
Netherplace *Strath* 115 NS5255
Netherseal *Derbys* 61 SK2813
Netherstreet *Wilts* 22 ST9764
Netherthong *W York* 82 SE1309
Netherthorpe *Derbys* 75 SK4574
Netherton *Cent* 115 NS5579
Netherton *Devon* 7 SX8971
Netherton *H & W* 46 SO5126
Netherton *H & W* 47 SO9941
Netherton *Hants* 23 SU3757
Netherton *Nthumb* 103 NZ2382
Netherton *Nthumb* 111 NT9807
Netherton *Oxon* 34 ST4199
Netherton *Shrops* 60 SO7382
Netherton *Strath* 116 NS7854
Netherton *Tays* 126 NO1452
Netherton *Tays* 134 NO5457
Netherton *W Mids* 60 SO9488
Netherton *W York* 82 SE2716
Netherton *W York* 82 SE1313
Nethertown *Cumb* 86 NX9807
Nethertown *Highld* 151 ND3578
Nethertown *Lancs* 81 SD7236
Nethertown *Staffs* 73 SK1017
Netherwitton *Nthumb* 103 NZ0990
Nethy Bridge *Highld* 141 NJ0020
Netley *Hants* 13 SU4508
Netley Marsh *Hants* 12 SU3313
Nettacott *Devon* 9 SX9099
Nettlebed *Oxon* 37 SU6986
Nettlebridge *Somset* 21 ST6448
Nettlecombe *Dorset* 10 SY5195
Nettlecombe *IOW* 13 SZ5278
Nettleden *Herts* 38 TL0110
Nettleham *Lincs* 76 TF0075
Nettlestead *Kent* 28 TQ6852
Nettlestead Green *Kent* 28 TQ6850
Nettlestone *IOW* 13 SZ6290
Nettlesworth *Dur* 96 NZ2547
Nettleton *Lincs* 76 TA1100
Nettleton *Wilts* 35 ST8178
Nettleton Shrub *Wilts* 35 ST8277
Netton *Devon* 6 SX5546
Netton *Wilts* 23 SU1236
Neuadd *Dyfed* 32 SN7021
Neuadd Fawr *Dyfed* 44 SN7541
Neuadd-ddu *Powys* 45 SN9275
Nevendon *Essex* 40 TQ7390
Nevern *Dyfed* 31 SN0840
Nevill Holt *Leics* 51 SP8193
New Abbey *D & G* 100 NX9666
New Aberdour *Gramp* 143 NJ8863
New Addington *Gt Lon* 27 TQ3763
New Alresford *Hants* 24 SU5832
New Alyth *Tays* 126 NO2447
New Arram *Humb* 84 TA0344
New Ash Green *Kent* 27 TQ6064
New Balderton *Notts* 75 SK8152
New Barn *Kent* 27 TQ6168
New Barnet *Gt Lon* 27 TQ2695
New Barton *Nhants* 51 SP8564
New Bewick *Nthumb* 111 NU0620
New Bilton *Warwks* 50 SP4975
New Bolingbroke *Lincs* 77 TF3057
New Bradwell *Bucks* 38 SP8341
New Brampton *Derbys* 74 SK3671
New Brancepeth *Dur* 96 NZ2241
New Bridge *N York* 90 SE8085
New Brighton *Clwyd* 70 SJ2565
New Brighton *Mersyd* 78 SJ3193
New Brinsley *Notts* 75 SK4650
New Brotton *Cleve* 97 NZ6820
New Broughton *Clwyd* 71 SJ3151

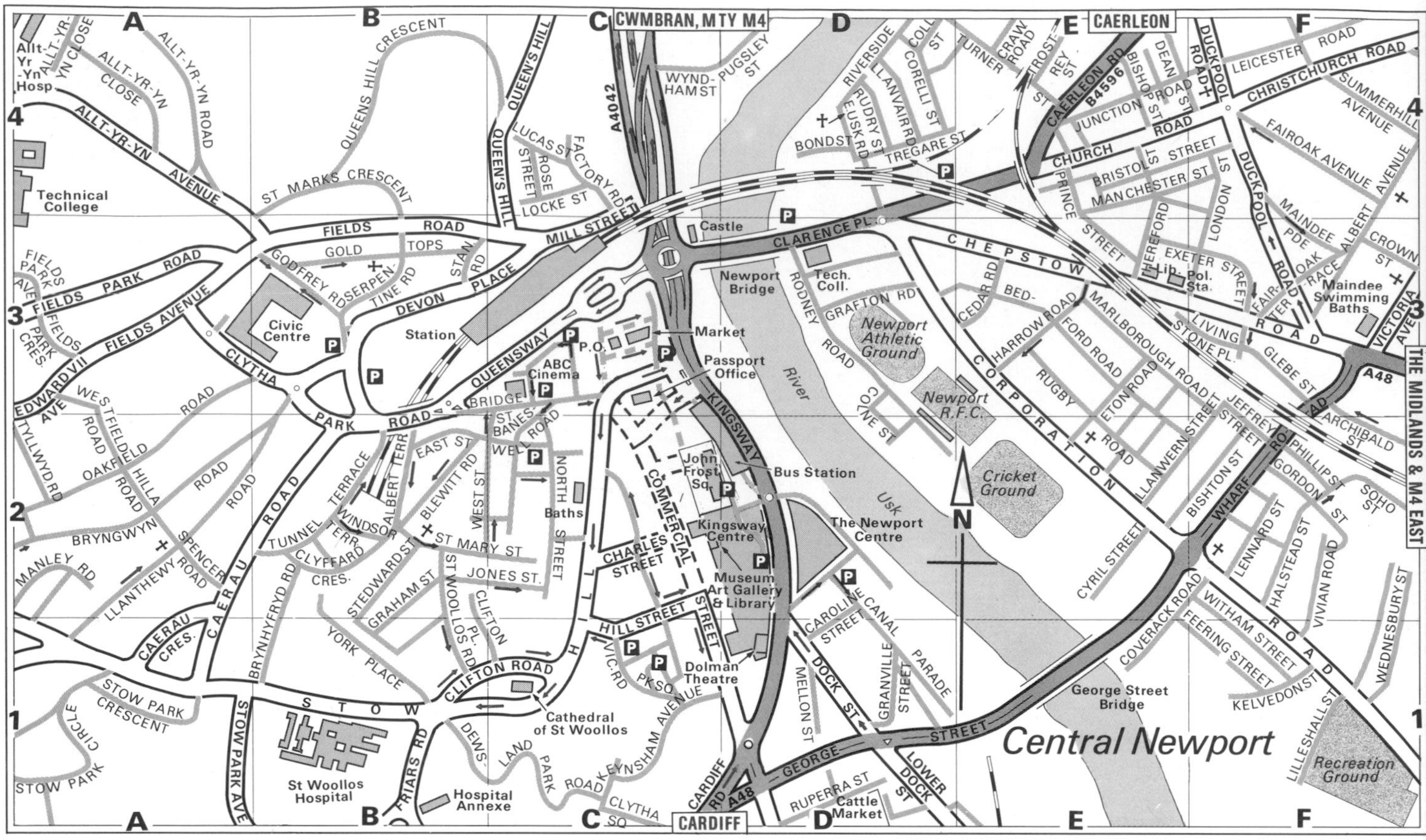

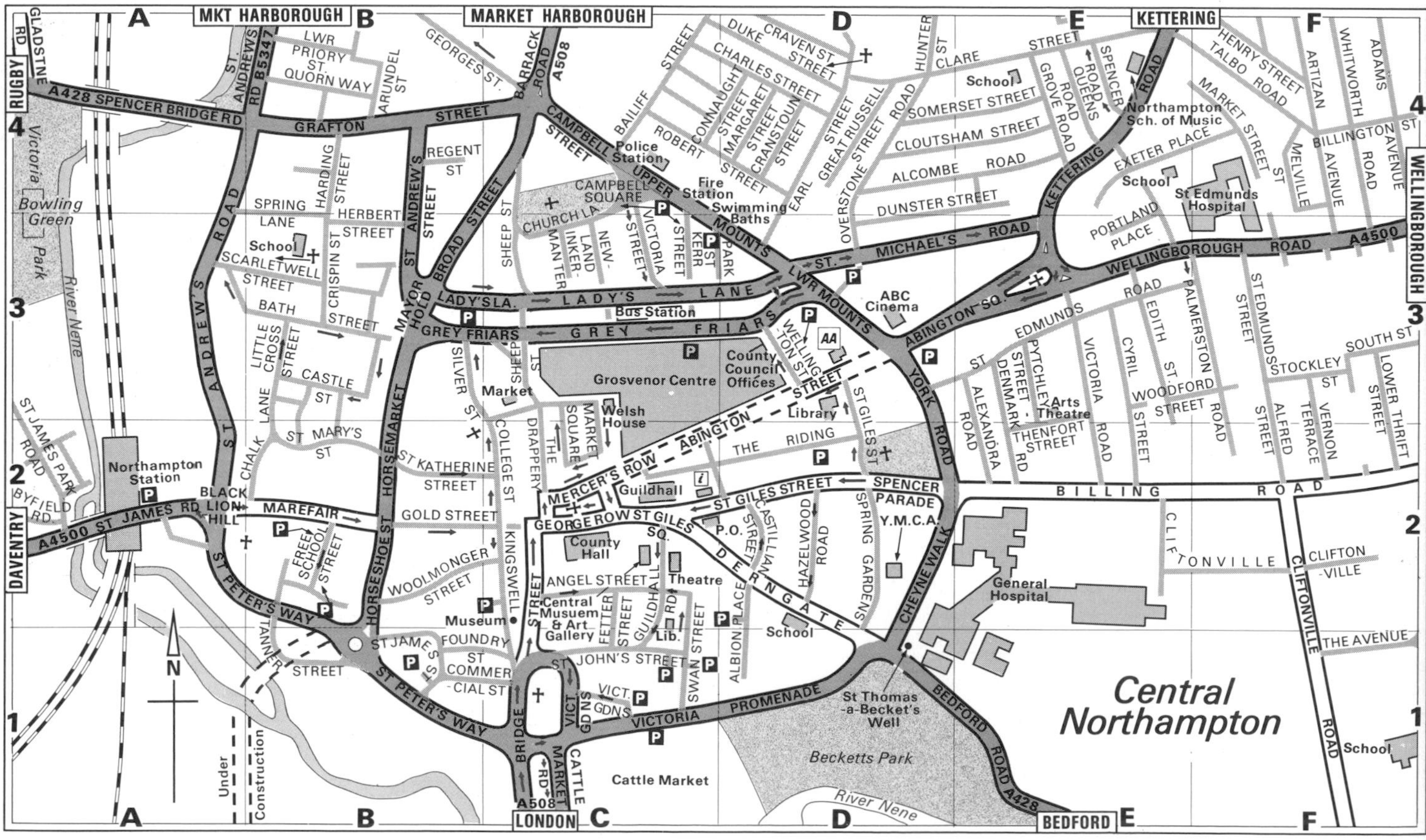

## Central Newport

## Central Northampton

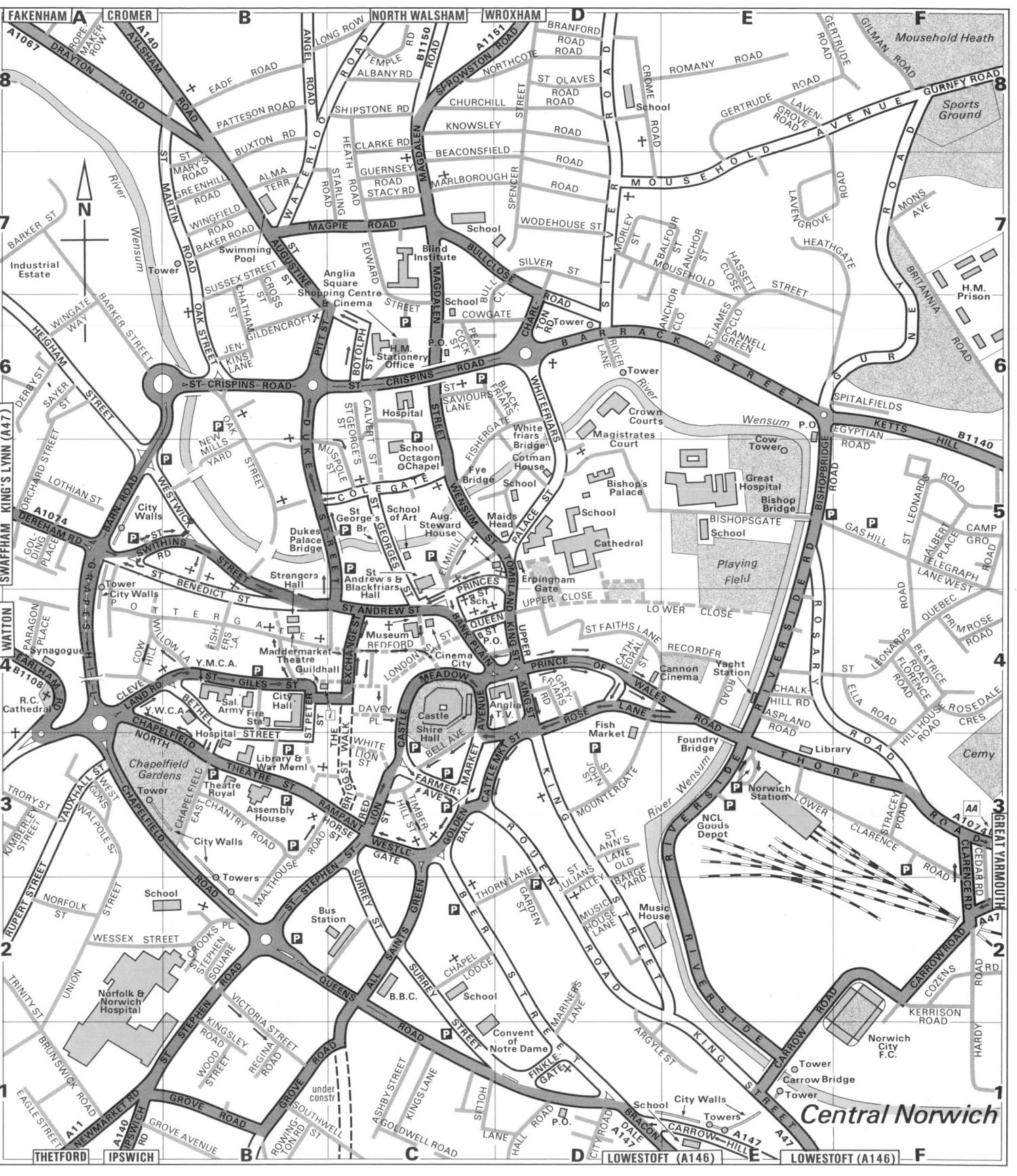

Central Norwich

New Swannington North Otterington


New Swannington *Leics* 62 SK4215
New Thundersley *Essex* 40 TQ7789
New Town *Dorset* 22 ST8318
New Town *Dorset* 11 ST9907
New Town *Dorset* 11 ST9515
New Town *Dorset* 22 ST9918
New Town *E Susx* 16 TQ4720
New Town *Loth* 118 NT4470
New Town *Nhants* 51 SP9677
New Town *Wilts* 36 SU2871
New Tredegar *M Glam* 33 SO1403
New Trows *Strath* 108 NS8038
New Tupton *Derbys* 74 SK3966
New Ulva *Strath* 113 NR7080
New Village *Humb* 84 SE8530
New Walsoken *Cambs* 65 TF4609
New Waltham *Humb* 85 TA2804
New Whittington *Derbys* 74 SK4075
New Wimpole *Cambs* 52 TL3449
New Winton *Loth* 118 NT4271
New Yatt *Oxon* 36 SP3713
New York *Lincs* 77 TF2455
New York *N York* 89 SE1962
New York *T & W* 103 NZ3270
New Zealand *Derbys* 62 SK3336
Newall *W York* 82 SE1946
Newark *Cambs* 64 TF2100
Newark *D & G* 107 NS7809
Newark-on-Trent *Notts* 75 SK7953
Newarthill *Strath* 116 NS7859
Newbarn *Kent* 29 TR1540
Newbattle *Loth* 118 NT3365
Newbie *D & G* 101 NY1764
Newbiggin *Cumb* 86 SD0993
Newbiggin *Cumb* 93 NY4729
Newbiggin *Cumb* 94 NY5549
Newbiggin *Cumb* 94 NY6228
Newbiggin *Cumb* 86 SD2669
Newbiggin *Dur* 96 NZ1447
Newbiggin *Dur* 95 NY9127
Newbiggin *N York* 88 SD9591
Newbiggin *N York* 88 SE0085
Newbiggin *Nthumb* 102 NY9461
Newbiggin-by-the-Sea *Nthumb* 103 NZ3087
Newbiggin-on-Lune *Cumb* 87 NY7005
Newbigging *Strath* 117 NT0145
Newbigging *Tays* 126 NO2842
Newbigging *Tays* 127 NO4237
Newbold *Derbys* 74 SK3773
Newbold *Leics* 62 SK4019
Newbold on Avon *Warwks* 50 SP4977
Newbold on Stour *Warwks* 48 SP2446
Newbold Pacey *Warwks* 48 SP2957
Newbold Revel *Warwks* 50 SP4580
Newbold Verdon *Leics* 62 SK4403
Newborough *Cambs* 64 TF2006
Newborough *Gwynd* 68 SH4265
Newborough *Staffs* 73 SK1325
Newbottle *Nhants* 49 SP5236
Newbottle *T & W* 96 NZ3351
Newbourn *Suffk* 55 TM2743
Newbridge *Clwyd* 70 SJ2841
Newbridge *Cnwll* 3 SW7944
Newbridge *Cnwll* 2 SW4231
Newbridge *D & G* 100 NX9579
Newbridge *Dyfed* 30 SM9431
Newbridge *Dyfed* 44 SN5059
Newbridge *Gwent* 33 ST2097
Newbridge *Hants* 12 SU2915
Newbridge *IOW* 13 SZ4187
Newbridge *Loth* 117 NT1272
Newbridge *Oxon* 36 SP4001
Newbridge Green *H & W* 47 SO8439
Newbridge on Wye *Powys* 45 SO0158
Newbridge-on-Usk *Gwent* 34 ST3894
Newbrough *Nthumb* 102 NY8767
Newbuildings *Devon* 8 SS7903
Newburgh *Fife* 126 NO2318
Newburgh *Gramp* 143 NJ9659
Newburgh *Gramp* 143 NJ9925
Newburgh *Lancs* 78 SD4810
Newburgh Priory *N York* 90 SE5476
Newburn *T & W* 103 NZ1665
Newbury *Berks* 24 SU4666
Newbury *Somset* 22 ST6950
Newbury *Wilts* 22 ST8241
Newby *Cumb* 94 NY5921
Newby *Lancs* 81 SD8146
Newby *N York* 91 TA0190
Newby *N York* 90 NZ5012
Newby *N York* 88 SD7269
Newby Bridge *Cumb* 87 SD3686
Newby Cross *Cumb* 93 NY3653
Newby East *Cumb* 93 NY4758
Newby Head *Cumb* 94 NY5821
Newby West *Cumb* 93 NY3654
Newby Wiske *N York* 89 SE3687
Newcastle *Gwent* 34 SO4417
Newcastle *Shrops* 58 SO2482
Newcastle Emlyn *Dyfed* 31 SN3040
Newcastle upon Tyne *T & W* 103 NZ2464
Newcastle-under-Lyme *Staffs* 72 SJ8445
Newcastleton *D & G* 101 NY4887
Newchapel *Dyfed* 31 SN2239
Newchapel *Staffs* 72 SJ8654
Newchapel *Surrey* 15 TQ3642
Newchurch *Gwent* 33 SO1710
Newchurch *Gwent* 34 ST4597
Newchurch *H & W* 46 SO3550
Newchurch *IOW* 13 SZ5685
Newchurch *Kent* 17 TR0531
Newchurch *Powys* 45 SO2150
Newchurch *Staffs* 73 SK1423
Newchurch in Pendle *Lancs* 81 SD8239
Newcott *Devon* 9 ST2309
Newcraighall *Loth* 117 NT2973
Newdigate *Surrey* 15 TQ1942
Newell Green *Berks* 25 SU8771
Newenden *Kent* 17 TQ8327
Newent *Gloucs* 47 SO7226
Newfield *Dur* 96 NZ2452
Newfield *Dur* 96 NZ2033
Newfield *Highld* 147 NH7877
Newfound *Hants* 24 SU5851
Newgale *Dyfed* 30 SM8422
Newgate *Cambs* 52 TL3990
Newgate *Norfk* 66 TG0443
Newgate Street *Herts* 39 TL3005
Newhall *Ches* 71 SJ6145
Newhall *Derbys* 73 SK2821
Newham *Gt Lon* 27 TQ4081
Newham *Nthumb* 111 NU1728
Newhaven *E Susx* 16 TQ4401
Newhaven Hotel *Derbys* 74 SK1660
Newholm *N York* 90 NZ8610
Newhouse *Strath* 116 NS7961
Newick *E Susx* 15 TQ4121
Newingreen *Kent* 29 TR1236
Newington *Kent* 28 TQ8564
Newington *Kent* 29 TR1837
Newington *Oxon* 37 SU6096
Newington *Shrops* 59 SO4283
Newington Bagpath *Gloucs* 35 ST8194
Newland *Cumb* 101 NY2979
Newland *Gloucs* 34 SO5409
Newland *H & W* 47 SO7948
Newland *Humb* 84 SE8029
Newland *Humb* 84 TA0631
Newland *N York* 83 SE6824
Newland *Oxon* 36 SP3610
Newland *Somset* 19 SS8338
Newlandrig *Loth* 118 NT3762
Newlands *Border* 101 NY5194
Newlands *Cumb* 93 NY3439
Newlands *Nthumb* 95 NZ0855
Newlands of Dundurlas *Gramp* 141 NJ2950
Newlyn *Cnwll* 2 SW4628
Newlyn East *Cnwll* 3 SW8256
Newmains *Strath* 116 NS8256
Newman's End *Essex* 39 TL5112
Newman's Green *Suffk* 54 TL8843
Newmarket *Cumb* 93 NY3338
Newmarket *Suffk* 53 TL6463
Newmill *Border* 109 NT4510
Newmill *Gramp* 142 NJ4352
Newmill of Inshewan *Tays* 134 NO4260
Newmillerdam *W York* 83 SE3215
Newmills *Fife* 117 NT0186
Newmills *Gwent* 34 SO5107
Newmills *Loth* 117 NT1667
Newmiln *Tays* 126 NO1230
Newmilns *Strath* 107 NS5337
Newnes *Shrops* 59 SJ3834
Newney Green *Essex* 40 TL6507
Newnham *Gloucs* 35 SO6911
Newnham *H & W* 47 SO6469
Newnham *Hants* 24 SU7054
Newnham *Herts* 39 TL2437
Newnham *Kent* 28 TQ9557
Newnham Paddox *Warwks* 50 SP4783
Newport *Devon* 19 SS5631
Newport *Dorset* 11 SY8895
Newport *Dyfed* 30 SN0539
Newport *Essex* 39 TL5234
Newport *Gloucs* 35 ST7097
Newport *Gwent* 34 ST3188
Newport *Highld* 151 ND1324
Newport *Humb* 84 SE8530
Newport *IOW* 13 SZ4989
Newport *Norfk* 67 TG5016
Newport *Shrops* 72 SJ7419
Newport Bagnell *Bucks* 38 SP8743
Newport-on-Tay *Fife* 127 NO4228
Newpound Common *W Susx* 14 TQ0627
Newquay *Cnwll* 4 SW8161
Newsam Green *W York* 83 SE3630
Newsbank *Ches* 72 SJ8366
Newseat *Gramp* 142 NJ7033
Newsham *Lancs* 80 SD5136
Newsham *N York* 89 SE3884
Newsham *N York* 89 NZ1010
Newsham *Nthumb* 103 NZ3080
Newsholme *Humb* 84 SE7129
Newsholme *Lancs* 81 SD8451
Newstead *Border* 109 NT5634
Newstead *Notts* 75 SK5152
Newstead *Nthumb* 111 NU1527
Newstead *W York* 83 SE4014
Newtack *Gramp* 142 NJ4446
Newthorpe *N York* 83 SE4632
Newtimber Place *W Susx* 15 TQ2613
Newton *Beds* 39 TL2344
Newton *Border* 110 NT6020
Newton *Cambs* 65 TF4314
Newton *Cambs* 53 TL4349
Newton *Ches* 71 SJ4167
Newton *Ches* 71 SJ5059
Newton *Cumb* 86 SD2271
Newton *D & G* 100 NY1194
Newton *Derbys* 75 SK4459
Newton *Gramp* 141 NJ3362
Newton *Gramp* 141 NJ1663
Newton *H & W* 46 SO3769
Newton *H & W* 46 SO3432
Newton *H & W* 46 SO5153
Newton *Highld* 151 ND3449
Newton *Highld* 139 NH5850
Newton *Highld* 140 NH7448
Newton *Highld* 140 NH7866
Newton *Lancs* 80 SD3436
Newton *Lancs* 80 SD4430
Newton *Lancs* 87 SD5974
Newton *Lancs* 81 SD6950
Newton *Lincs* 64 TF0436
Newton *Loth* 117 NT0977
Newton *M Glam* 33 SS8377
Newton *N York* 90 SE8872
Newton *Nhants* 51 SP8883
Newton *Norfk* 66 TF8315
Newton *Notts* 63 SK6841
Newton *Nthumb* 110 NT9407
Newton *Nthumb* 103 NZ0364
Newton *S Glam* 34 ST2378
Newton *Shrops* 59 SJ4234
Newton *Staffs* 73 SK0325
Newton *Strath* 114 NS0498
Newton *Strath* 116 NS6560
Newton *Strath* 108 NS9331
Newton *Suffk* 54 TL9240
Newton *W Glam* 32 SS6088
Newton *W Isls* 154 NF8877
Newton *W Mids* 61 SP0393
Newton *W York* 83 SE4427
Newton *Warwks* 50 SP5378
Newton *Wilts* 23 SU2322
Newton Abbot *Devon* 7 SX8671
Newton Arlosh *Cumb* 93 NY2055
Newton Aycliffe *Dur* 96 NZ2724
Newton Bewley *Cleve* 97 NZ4626
Newton Blossomville *Bucks* 38 SP9251
Newton Bromswold *Beds* 51 SP9966
Newton Burgoland *Leics* 62 SK3709
Newton by Toft *Lincs* 76 TF0487
Newton Ferrers *Devon* 6 SX5447
Newton Ferrers *M Glam* 5 SX3466
Newton Flotman *Norfk* 67 TM2198
Newton Green *Gwent* 34 ST5191
Newton Harcourt *Leics* 50 SP6497
Newton Heath *Gt Man* 79 SD8700
Newton Hill *Gramp* 135 NO9193
Newton Hill *W York* 83 SE3222
Newton Kyme *N York* 83 SE4644
Newton Longville *Bucks* 38 SP8431
Newton Mearns *Strath* 115 NS5355
Newton Morrel *N York* 89 NZ2309
Newton Mountain *Dyfed* 30 SM9807
Newton Mulgrave *N York* 97 NZ7815
Newton of Balcanquhal *Tays* 126 NO1610
Newton on Ouse *N York* 90 SE5159
Newton on Trent *Lincs* 76 SK8374
Newton on the Hill *Shrops* 59 SJ4823
Newton Poppleford *Devon* 9 SY0889
Newton Purcell *Oxon* 49 SP6230
Newton Regis *Warwks* 61 SK2707
Newton Reigny *Cumb* 93 NY4731
Newton Solney *Derbys* 73 SK2825
Newton St. Cyres *Devon* 9 SX8797
Newton St. Faith *Norfk* 67 TG2217
Newton St. Loe *Avon* 22 ST7064
Newton St. Petrock *Devon* 18 SS4112
Newton Stacey *Hants* 24 SU4140
Newton Stewart *D & G* 99 NX4165
Newton Toney *Wilts* 23 SU2140
Newton Tracey *Devon* 19 SS5226
Newton Underwood *Nthumb* 103 NZ1486
Newton under Roseberry *Cleve* 90 NZ5613
Newton upon Derwent *Humb* 84 SE7149
Newton Valence *Hants* 24 SU7232
Newton-le-Willows *Mersyd* 78 SJ5995
Newton-le-Willows *N York* 89 SE2189
Newton-on-the-Moor *Nthumb* 111 NU1705
Newtonairds *D & G* 100 NX8880
Newtongarry Croft *Gramp* 142 NJ5735
Newtongrange *Loth* 118 NT3364
Newtonloan *Loth* 118 NT3362
Newtonmill *Tays* 134 NO6064
Newtonmore *Highld* 132 NN7198
Newtown *Beds* 52 TL1945
Newtown *Ches* 71 SJ5374
Newtown *Ches* 72 SJ9060
Newtown *Ches* 71 SJ6247
Newtown *Cnwll* 2 SW5729
Newtown *Cnwll* 3 SX1052
Newtown *Cnwll* 5 SX2978
Newtown *Cnwll* 3 SW7423
Newtown *Cumb* 92 NY0948
Newtown *Cumb* 101 NY5262
Newtown *D & G* 107 NS7710
Newtown *Derbys* 79 SJ9984
Newtown *Devon* 18 SX0699
Newtown *Devon* 19 SS7625
Newtown *Dorset* 10 ST4701
Newtown *Dorset* 12 SZ0393
Newtown *Gloucs* 35 SO6702
Newtown *Gt Man* 78 SD5605
Newtown *Gwent* 33 SO1710
Newtown *H & W* 60 SO9478
Newtown *H & W* 46 SO4757
Newtown *H & W* 46 SO5333
Newtown *H & W* 46 SO6145
Newtown *H & W* 47 SO8655
Newtown *H & W* 47 SO7037
Newtown *Hants* 12 SU2710
Newtown *Hants* 24 SU4763
Newtown *Hants* 13 SU6113
Newtown *Hants* 12 SU2710
Newtown *Highld* 131 NH3504
Newtown *IOM* 153 SC3273
Newtown *IOW* 13 SZ4290
Newtown *Lancs* 80 SD5118
Newtown *M Glam* 33 ST0598
Newtown *Nthumb* 111 NT9631
Newtown *Nthumb* 103 NU0300
Newtown *Powys* 58 SO1091
Newtown *Shrops* 59 SJ4222
Newtown *Shrops* 59 SJ4831
Newtown *Somset* 10 ST2712
Newtown *Staffs* 60 SJ9904
Newtown *Wilts* 22 ST9128
Newtown *Wilts* 23 SU2963
Newtown Linford *Leics* 62 SK5110
Newtown of Beltrees *Strath* 115 NS3758
Newtown St. Boswells *Border* 110 NT5732
Newtown Unthank *Leics* 62 SK4904
Newtyle *Tays* 126 NO2941
Newyears Green *Gt Lon* 26 TQ0788
Newyork *Strath* 122 NM9611
Nextend *H & W* 46 SO3357
Neyland *Dyfed* 30 SM9605
Niarbyl *IOM* 153 SC2177
Nibley *Avon* 35 ST6982
Nibley *Gloucs* 35 SO6606
Nibley Green *Gloucs* 35 ST7296
Nicholashayne *Devon* 9 ST1016
Nicholaston *W Glam* 32 SS5288
Nickies Hill *Cumb* 101 NY5467
Nidd *N York* 89 SE3060
Nigg *Gramp* 135 NJ9402
Nigg *Highld* 147 NH8071
Nightcott *Devon* 19 SS8925
Nine Ashes *Essex* 27 TL5902
Nine Elms *Wilts* 36 SU1085
Nine Wells *Dyfed* 30 SM7824
Ninebanks *Nthumb* 94 NY7853
Ninemile Bar or Crocketfo *D & G* 100 NX8373
Nineveh *H & W* 47 SO6265
Ninfield *E Susx* 16 TQ7012
Ningwood *IOW* 13 SZ3989
Nisbet *Border* 110 NT6725
Nisbet Hill *Border* 119 NT7850
Niton *IOW* 13 SZ5076
Nitshill *Strath* 115 NS5260
No Man's Heath *Ches* 71 SJ5148
No Man's Heath *Warwks* 61 SK2909
No Man's Land *Cnwll* 4 SW9470
No Man's Land *Cnwll* 5 SX2756
Noah's Ark *Kent* 27 TQ5557
Noak Green *Essex* 40 TQ6990
Noak Hill *Essex* 27 TQ5494
Noblethorpe *W York* 82 SE2805
Nobold *Shrops* 59 SJ4609
Nobottle *Nhants* 49 SP6763
Nocton *Lincs* 76 TF0564
Nogdam End *Norfk* 67 TG3900
Noke *Oxon* 37 SP5413
Nolton *Dyfed* 30 SM8718
Nolton Haven *Dyfed* 30 SM8618
Nomansland *Devon* 19 SS8313
Nomansland *Wilts* 12 SU2517
Noneley *Shrops* 59 SJ4728
Nonington *Kent* 29 TR2552
Nook *Cumb* 87 SD5482
Nook *Cumb* 101 NY4679
Norbiton Common *Gt Lon* 26 TQ2167
Norbreck *Lancs* 80 SD3140
Norbridge *H & W* 47 SO7144
Norbury *Ches* 71 SJ5547
Norbury *Derbys* 73 SK1241
Norbury *Gt Lon* 27 TQ3069
Norbury *Shrops* 59 SO3693
Norbury *Staffs* 72 SJ7823
Norbury Common *Ches* 71 SJ5548
Norbury Junction *Staffs* 72 SJ7923
Norby *N York* 89 SE4381
Norchard *H & W* 47 SO8568
Norcott Brook *Ches* 78 SJ6180
Norcross *Lancs* 80 SD3341
Nordam *Humb* 84 SE8932
Nordelph *Norfk* 65 TF5501
Norden *Gt Man* 81 SD8614
Nordley *Shrops* 60 SO6997
Norham *Nthumb* 110 NT9047
Norland Town *W York* 82 SE0622
Norley *Ches* 71 SJ5772
Norley *Devon* 18 SS4900
Norleywood *Hants* 12 SZ3597
Norlington *E Susx* 16 TQ4413
Norman Cross *Cambs* 64 TL1691
Norman's Bay *E Susx* 16 TQ6805
Norman's Green *Devon* 9 ST0503
Normanby *Cleve* 97 NZ5518
Normanby *Humb* 84 SE8716
Normanby *Lincs* 76 TF0088
Normanby *N York* 90 SE7381
Normanby le Wold *Lincs* 76 TF1295
Normandy *Surrey* 25 SU9251
Normansland *Wilts* 12 SU2517
Normanton *Derbys* 62 SK3433
Normanton *Leics* 63 SK8140
Normanton *Lincs* 63 SK9446
Normanton *Notts* 75 SK7054
Normanton *W York* 83 SE3822
Normanton *Wilts* 23 SU1340
Normanton le Heath *Leics* 62 SK3712
Normanton on Soar *Notts* 62 SK5123
Normanton on Trent *Notts* 75 SK7868
Normanton on the Wolds *Notts* 62 SK6232
Normoss *Lancs* 80 SD3437
Normoss *Lancs* 80 SD3437
Norney *Surrey* 25 SU9444
Norrington Common *Wilts* 22 ST8864
Norris Green *Cnwll* 5 SX4169
Norristhorpe *W York* 82 SE2123
North Anston *S York* 75 SK5184
North Aston *Oxon* 49 SP4728
North Baddesley *Hants* 13 SU3920
North Ballchulish *Highld* 130 NN0560
North Barrow *Somset* 21 ST6029
North Barsham *Norfk* 66 TF9135
North Benfleet *Essex* 40 TQ7690
North Bersted *W Susx* 14 SU9200
North Berwick *Loth* 118 NT5485
North Biddick *T & W* 97 NZ5153
North Bitchburn *Dur* 96 NZ1733
North Boarhunt *Hants* 13 SU6010
North Bockhampton *Hants* 12 SZ1797
North Bovey *Devon* 8 SX7483
North Bradley *Wilts* 22 ST8554
North Brentor *Devon* 5 SX4881
North Brewham *Somset* 22 ST7236
North Bridge *Surrey* 14 SU9636
North Brook End *Cambs* 39 TL2844
North Buckland *Devon* 18 SS4840
North Burlingham *Norfk* 67 TG3610
North Cadbury *Somset* 21 ST6327
North Cairn *D & G* 98 NW9770
North Carlton *Lincs* 76 SK9477
North Carlton *Notts* 75 SK5885
North Cave *Humb* 84 SE8832
North Cerney *Gloucs* 35 SP0208
North Charford *Hants* 12 SU1919
North Charlton *Nthumb* 111 NU1622
North Cheam *Gt Lon* 26 TQ2365
North Cheriton *Somset* 22 ST6825
North Chideock *Dorset* 10 SY4294
North Cliffe *Humb* 84 SE8737
North Clifton *Notts* 75 SK8272
North Close *Dur* 96 NZ2532
North Cockerington *Lincs* 77 TF3790
North Collingham *Notts* 76 SK8362
North Common *E Susx* 15 TQ3921
North Connel *Strath* 122 NM9135
North Cornelly *M Glam* 33 SS8281
North Corner *Cnwll* 3 SW7818
North Corry *Highld* 122 NM8353
North Cotes *Lincs* 77 TA3400
North Cottingham *Notts* 75 SK8061
North Country *Cnwll* 2 SW6943
North Cove *Suffk* 55 TM4689
North Cowton *N York* 89 NZ2803
North Crawley *Bucks* 38 SP9244
North Cray *Gt Lon* 27 TQ4872
North Creake *Norfk* 66 TF8538
North Curry *Somset* 21 ST3125
North Dalton *Humb* 84 SE9352
North Deighton *N York* 83 SE3851
North Duffield *N York* 83 SE6837
North Elham *Kent* 29 TR1844
North Elkington *Lincs* 77 TF2890
North Elmham *Norfk* 66 TF9820
North Elmsall *W York* 83 SE4712
North End *Avon* 21 ST4267
North End *Dorset* 22 ST8427
North End *Essex* 40 TL6619
North End *Hants* 12 SU1016
North End *Hants* 24 SU5829
North End *Hants* 13 SU6502
North End *Humb* 85 TA1941
North End *Humb* 85 TA2931
North End *Humb* 85 TA3007
North End *Humb* 85 TA1022
North End *Leics* 62 SK5715
North End *Lincs* 76 TF0499
North End *Lincs* 64 TF2341
North End *Lincs* 77 TF4289
North End *Mersyd* 78 SD3004
North End *Nhants* 51 SP9668
North End *Norfk* 66 TL9992
North End *Nthumb* 108 NT1301
North End *W Susx* 14 SU9804
North End *W Susx* 14 TQ1209
North Erradale *Highld* 144 NG7481
North Evington *Leics* 62 SK6204
North Fambridge *Essex* 40 TQ8597
North Feorline *Strath* 105 NR9129
North Ferriby *Humb* 84 SE9826
North Frodingham *Humb* 85 TA1053
North Gorley *Hants* 12 SU1611
North Green *Norfk* 55 TM2288
North Green *Suffk* 55 TM3162
North Green *Suffk* 55 TM3966
North Grimston *N York* 90 SE8467
North Halling *Kent* 28 TQ7065
North Hayling *Hants* 13 SU7303
North Hazelrigg *Nthumb* 111 NU0533
North Heasley *Devon* 19 SS7333
North Heath *W Susx* 14 TQ0621
North Hele *Somset* 20 ST0323
North Hill *Cnwll* 5 SX2776
North Hillingdon *Gt Lon* 26 TQ0784
North Hinksey *Oxon* 37 SP4805
North Huish *Devon* 7 SX7156
North Hykeham *Lincs* 76 SK9466
North Kelsey *Humb* 84 TA0401
North Kessock *Highld* 140 NH6548
North Killingholme *Humb* 85 TA1417
North Kilvington *N York* 89 SE4284
North Kilworth *Leics* 50 SP6183
North Kingston *Hants* 12 SU1603
North Kyme *Lincs* 76 TF1552
North Lee *Bucks* 38 SP8308
North Lees *N York* 89 SE3073
North Leigh *Kent* 29 TR1447
North Leigh *Oxon* 36 SP3813
North Leverton with Habbl *Notts* 75 SK7882
North Littleton *H & W* 48 SP0847
North Lopham *Norfk* 54 TM0383
North Luffenham *Leics* 63 SK9303
North Marden *W Susx* 14 SU8016
North Marston *Bucks* 37 SP7722
North Middleton *Loth* 118 NT3559
North Middleton *Nthumb* 111 NT9924
North Milmain *D & G* 98 NX0952
North Molton *Devon* 19 SS7329
North Moreton *Oxon* 37 SU5689
North Mundham *W Susx* 14 SU8702
North Muskham *Notts* 75 SK7958
North Newbald *Humb* 84 SE9136
North Newington *Oxon* 49 SP4139
North Newnton *Wilts* 23 SU1257
North Newton *Gwent* 20 ST2931
North Newton *Somset* 20 ST3031
North Nibley *Gloucs* 35 ST7395
North Oakley *Hants* 24 SU5354
North Ockendon *Gt Lon* 27 TQ5985
North Ormsby *Lincs* 77 TF2893
North Otterington *N York* 89 SE3689

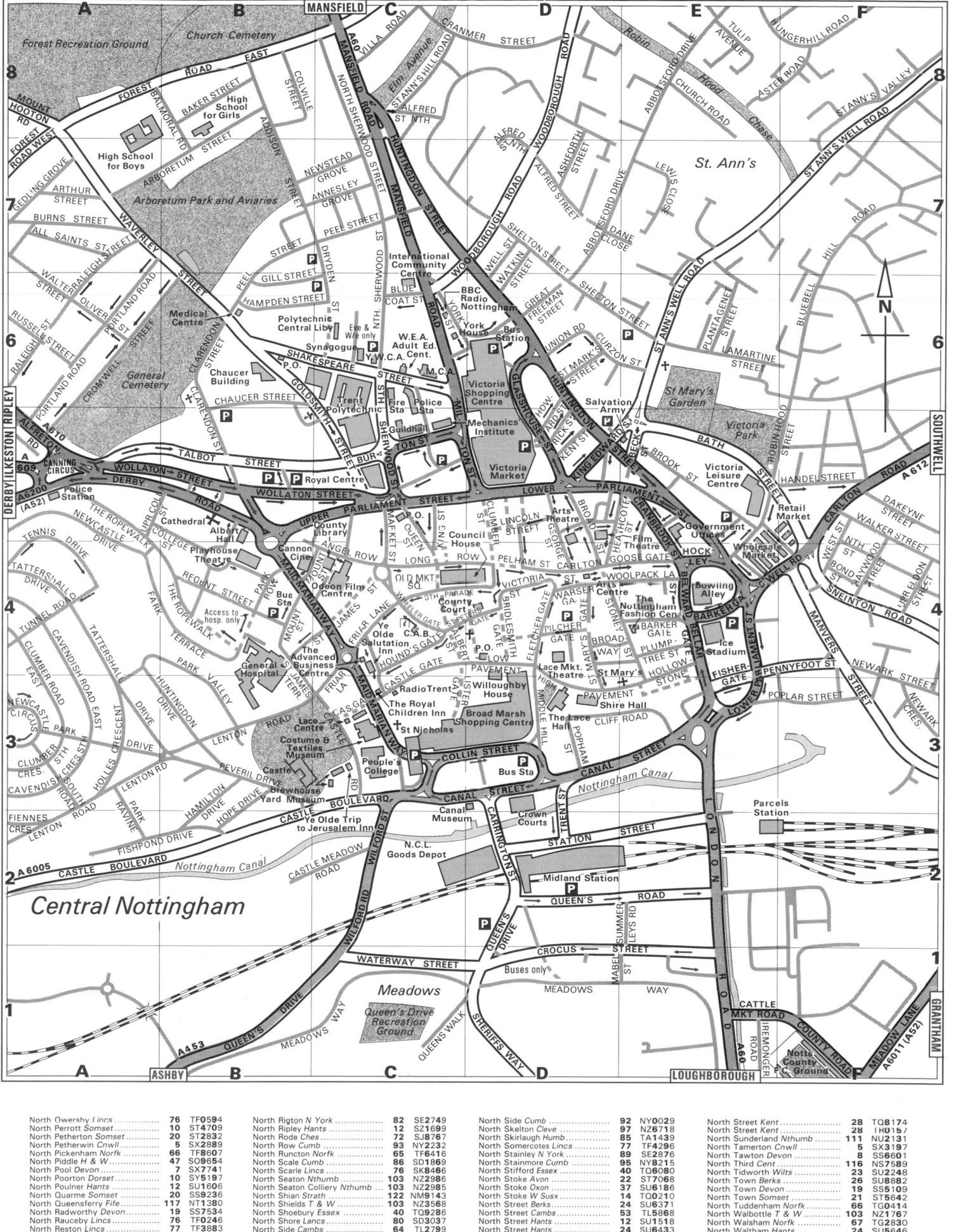

*Central Nottingham*

North Warnborough

Otterham Quay

North Warnborough Hants 24 SU7351
North Weald Basset Essex 39 TL4904
North Weston Avon 34 ST4674
North Wheatley Notts 75 SK7685
North Whilborough Devon 7 SX8766
North Wick Avon 21 ST5865
North Widcombe Somset 21 ST5758
North Willingham Lincs 76 TF1688
North Wingfield Derbys 74 SK4064
North Witham Lincs 63 SK9221
North Wootton Dorset 11 ST6614
North Wootton Norfk 65 TF6424
North Wootton Somset 21 ST5641
North Wraxall Wilts 35 ST8175
North Wroughton Wilts 36 SU1481
Northacre Norfk 66 TL9598
Northall Bucks 38 SP9520
Northall Green Norfk 66 TF9915
Northallerton N York 89 SE3793
Northam Devon 18 SS4429
Northam Hants 13 SU4312
Northampton H & W 47 SO8365
Northampton Nhants 49 SP7560
Northaw Herts 27 TL2702
Northay Somset 10 ST2811
Northborough Cambs 64 TF1507
Northbourne Kent 29 TR3352
Northbridge Street E Susx 17 TQ7423
Northbrook Hants 24 SU5139
Northbrook Oxon 37 SP4922
Northchapel W Susx 14 SU9529
Northchurch Herts 38 SP9708
Northcott Devon 9 ST0912
Northcott Devon 9 ST1109
Northcott Devon 5 SX3392
Northcourt Oxon 37 SU5098
Northdown Kent 29 TR3770
Northedge Derbys 74 SK3565
Northend Bucks 37 SU7392
Northend Warwks 48 SP3852
Northend Woods Bucks 26 SU9089
Northenden Gt Man 79 SJ8290
Northfield Gramp 135 NJ9008
Northfield Humb 84 TA0328
Northfield W Mids 60 SP0279
Northfields Lincs 64 TF0208
Northfleet Essex 27 TQ6274
Northiam E Susx 17 TQ8324
Northill Beds 52 TL1446
Northington Gloucs 35 SO7008
Northington Hants 24 SU5637
Northlands Lincs 77 TF3453
Northleach Gloucs 36 SP1114
Northleigh Devon 19 SS6034
Northleigh Devon 9 SY1995
Northlew Devon 19 SX5099
Northload Bridge Somset 21 ST4939
Northmoor Somset 20 SS9028
Northmoor Oxon 36 SP4202
Northmoor Green or Moorla Somset 21 ST3332
Northmuir Tays 126 NO3854
Northney Hants 13 SU7303
Northolt Gt Lon 26 TQ1384
Northop Clwyd 70 SJ2468
Northop Hall Clwyd 70 SJ2667
Northorpe Lincs 64 TF2036
Northorpe Lincs 76 SK8996
Northorpe Lincs 64 TF0917
Northorpe W York 82 SE2121
Northover Somset 21 ST4838
Northover Somset 21 ST5223
Northowram W York 82 SE1127
Northport Dorset 11 SY9288
Northrepps Norfk 67 TG2439
Northton W Isls 154 NF9889
Northway Somset 20 ST1329
Northway W Glam 32 SS5889
Northwich Ches 79 SJ6673
Northwick Avon 34 ST5686
Northwick H & W 47 SO8458
Northwick Somset 21 ST3548
Northwold Norfk 65 TL7597
Northwood Derbys 74 SK2664
Northwood Gt Lon 26 TQ0990
Northwood IOW 13 SZ4893
Northwood Shrops 59 SJ4633
Northwood Staffs 72 SJ8948
Northwood End Beds 38 TL0941
Northwood Green Gloucs 35 SO7216
Norton Avon 21 ST3463
Norton Ches 78 SJ5582
Norton Cleve 96 NZ4421
Norton Cnwll 4 SX0869
Norton E Susx 16 TQ4601
Norton Gloucs 47 SO8524
Norton Gwent 34 SO4420
Norton H & W 47 SO8751
Norton H & W 48 SP0448
Norton Herts 39 TL2334
Norton IOW 12 SZ3489
Norton N York 90 SE7971
Norton Nhants 49 SP5963
Norton Notts 75 SK5772
Norton Powys 46 SO3067
Norton S York 83 SE5415
Norton S York 74 SK3561
Norton S York 74 SK3581
Norton Shrops 59 SO4681
Norton Shrops 59 SJ5609
Norton Shrops 60 SJ7200
Norton Shrops 59 SO6482
Norton Shrops 59 SO4681
Norton Suffk 54 TL9565
Norton W Glam 32 SS6188
Norton W Susx 14 SU9306
Norton Wilts 35 ST8884
Norton Bavant Wilts 22 ST9043
Norton Bridge Staffs 72 SJ8730
Norton Brook Staffs 72 SJ9052
Norton Canes Staffs 60 SK0107
Norton Canon H & W 46 SO3847
Norton Corner Norfk 66 TG0928
Norton Disney Lincs 76 SK8859
Norton Ferris Wilts 22 ST7936
Norton Fitzwarren Somset 20 ST1925
Norton Green IOW 12 SZ3388
Norton Green Staffs 60 SK0107
Norton Hawkfield Avon 21 ST5964
Norton Heath Essex 40 TL6004
Norton in Hales Shrops 72 SJ7038
Norton in the Moors Staffs 72 SJ8951
Norton Lindsey Warwks 48 SP2263
Norton Little Green Suffk 54 TL9766
Norton Malreward Avon 21 ST6065
Norton Mandeville Essex 40 TL5804
Norton St. Philip Somset 22 ST7755
Norton Subcourse Norfk 67 TM4198
Norton sub Hamdon Somset 10 ST4615
Norton Wood H & W 46 SO3648
Norton-Juxta-Twycross Leics 61 SK3207
Norton-le-Clay N York 89 SE4071
Norwell Notts 75 SK7661
Norwell Woodhouse Notts 75 SK7362
Norwich Norfk 67 TG2308
Norwick Shet 155 HP6514
Norwood Cent 116 NS8793
Norwood Kent 17 TR0430
Norwood S York 75 SK4681
Norwood End Essex 40 TL5608
Norwood Green Gt Lon 26 TQ1378
Norwood Green W York 82 SE1427
Norwood Hill Surrey 15 TQ2443
Norwoodside Cambs 65 TL4197
Noseley Leics 50 SP7398
Noss Mayo Devon 6 SX5447
Nosterfield N York 89 SE2780
Nosterfield End Cambs 53 TL6344
Nostie Highld 138 NG8527
Notgrove Gloucs 36 SP1020
Nottage M Glam 33 SS8278
Notter M Glam 5 SX3961
Nottingham Notts 62 SK5739
Nottington Dorset 11 SY6582
Notton W York 83 SE3413
Notton Wilts 35 ST9169
Nottswood Hill Gloucs 35 SO7018
Nounsley Essex 40 TL7910
Noutard's Green H & W 47 SO8066
Nox Shrops 59 SJ4110
Nuffield Oxon 37 SU6687
Nun Monkton N York 90 SE5057
Nuncargate Notts 75 SK5054
Nunclose Cumb 94 NY4945
Nuneaton Warwks 61 SP3692
Nuneham Courtenay Oxon 37 SU5599
Nunhead Gt Lon 27 TQ3475
Nunkeeling Humb 85 TA1449
Nunnerie Strath 108 NS9612
Nunney Somset 22 ST7345
Nunney Catch Somset 22 ST7344
Nunnington H & W 46 SO5543
Nunnington N York 90 SE6679
Nunnykirk Nthumb 103 NZ0793
Nuns Moor T & W 103 NZ2266
Nunsthorpe Humb 85 TA2508
Nunthorpe N York 83 SE6050
Nunthorpe Village Cleve 90 NZ5313
Nunton W Isls 154 NF7653
Nunton Wilts 23 SU1525
Nunwick N York 89 SE3274
Nunwick Nthumb 102 NY8774
Nup End Bucks 38 SP8619
Nupdown Avon 35 ST6295
Nupend Gloucs 35 SO7806
Nuptow Berks 25 SU8873
Nursling Hants 12 SU3616
Nursted Hants 14 SU7621
Nursteed Wilts 23 SU0260
Nurton Staffs 60 SO8399
Nutbourne W Susx 14 SU7705
Nutbourne W Susx 14 TQ0718
Nutfield Surrey 27 TQ3050
Nuthall Notts 62 SK5144
Nuthampstead Herts 39 TL4034
Nuthurst W Susx 15 TQ1926
Nutley E Susx 16 TQ4427
Nutley Hants 24 SU6144
Nuttal Lane Gt Man 81 SD7915
Nutwell S York 83 SE6304
Nybster Highld 151 ND3663
Nyetimber W Susx 14 SZ8998
Nyewood W Susx 14 SU8021
Nymet Rowland Devon 19 SS7108
Nymet Tracey Devon 8 SS7200
Nympsfield Gloucs 35 SO8000
Nynehead Somset 20 ST1423
Nyton W Susx 14 SU9305

# O

Oad Street Kent 28 TQ8662
Oadby Leics 50 SK6200
Oak Cross Devon 8 SX5399
Oakall Green H & W 47 SO8161
Oakamoor Staffs 73 SK0544
Oakbank Loth 117 NT0766
Oakdale Gwent 33 ST1898
Oake Somset 20 ST1525
Oaken Staffs 60 SJ8502
Oakenclough Lancs 80 SD5447
Oakengates Shrops 60 SJ7010
Oakenholt Clwyd 70 SJ2571
Oakenshaw Dur 96 NZ1937
Oakenshaw W York 82 SE1728
Oaker Side Derbys 74 SK2761
Oakerthorpe Derbys 74 SK3854
Oakford Devon 20 SS9021
Oakford Dyfed 42 SN4558
Oakfordbridge Devon 20 SS9122
Oakgrove Ches 79 SJ9169
Oakham Leics 63 SK8608
Oakhanger Ches 72 SJ7654
Oakhanger Hants 14 SU7635
Oakhill Somset 21 ST6347
Oakhurst Kent 27 TQ5450
Oakington Cambs 52 TL4164
Oaklands Powys 45 SO0450
Oakle Street Gloucs 35 SO7517
Oakley Beds 51 TL0053
Oakley Bucks 37 SP6412
Oakley Dorset 11 SZ0198
Oakley Hants 24 SU5650
Oakley Oxon 37 SP7400
Oakley Suffk 54 TM1678
Oakley Green Berks 26 SU9276
Oakleypark Powys 58 SN9886
Oakridge Gloucs 35 SO9103
Oaks Dur 96 NZ1526
Oaks Lancs 81 SD6733
Oaks Shrops 59 SJ4204
Oaks Green Derbys 73 SK1533
Oaksey Wilts 35 ST9893
Oakshaw Cumb 101 NY5076
Oakshott Hants 13 SU7427
Oakthorpe Leics 61 SK3213
Oaktree Dur 89 NZ3613
Oakwood Border 109 NT4225
Oakwood Nthumb 102 NY9465
Oakwoodhill Surrey 15 TQ1337
Oakworth W York 82 SE0339
Oape Highld 146 NC4101
Oare Kent 28 TR0063
Oare Somset 19 SS8047
Oare Wilts 23 SU1563
Oasby Lincs 63 TF0039
Oath Somset 21 ST3827
Oathlaw Tays 127 NO4756
Oatlands Park Surrey 26 TQ0865
Oban Strath 122 NM8630
Obinan Highld 144 NG8796
Obney Tays 125 NO0237
Oborne Dorset 11 ST6518
Obthorpe Lincs 64 TF0915
Occlestone Green Ches 72 SJ6962
Occold Suffk 54 TM1570
Ochertyre Tays 125 NN8323
Ochiltree Strath 107 NS5121
Ockbrook Derbys 62 SK4235
Ocker Hill W Mids 60 SO9793
Ockeridge H & W 47 SO7762
Ockham Surrey 26 TQ0756
Ockle Highld 129 NM5570
Ockley Surrey 15 TQ1440
Ocle Pychard H & W 46 SO5946
Octon Humb 91 TA0369
Odcombe Somset 10 ST5015
Odd Down Avon 22 ST7462
Oddingley H & W 47 SO9159
Oddington Gloucs 48 SP2225
Oddington Oxon 37 SP5514
Odell Beds 51 SP9657
Odham Devon 18 SS4703
Odiham Hants 24 SU7451
Odsal W York 82 SE1529
Odsey Herts 39 TL2938
Odstock Wilts 23 SU1426
Odstone Leics 62 SK3907
Offchurch Warwks 48 SP3566
Offenham H & W 48 SP0546
Offerton T & W 96 NZ3455
Offham E Susx 15 TQ4012
Offham Kent 28 TQ6557
Offham W Susx 14 TQ0208
Offleymarsh Shrops 72 SJ7829
Offord Cluny Cambs 52 TL2267
Offord Darcy Cambs 52 TL2266
Offton Suffk 54 TM0649
Offwell Devon 9 SY1999
Ogbourne Maizey Wilts 36 SU1871
Ogbourne St. Andrew Wilts 36 SU1872
Ogbourne St. George Wilts 36 SU2074
Ogden W York 82 SE0730
Ogle Nthumb 103 NZ1378
Oglet Mersyd 78 SJ4481
Ogmore M Glam 33 SS8876
Ogmore Vale M Glam 33 SS9390
Ogmore-by-Sea M Glam 33 SS8675
Ogwen Bank Gwynd 69 SH6265
Okeford Fitzpaine Dorset 11 ST8010
Okehampton Devon 8 SX5895
Okehampton Camp Devon 8 SX5893
Olchard Devon 9 SX8776
Old Nhants 50 SP7873
Old Aberdeen Gramp 135 NJ9407
Old Alresford Hants 24 SU5834
Old Auchenbrack D & G 107 NX7597
Old Basford Notts 62 SK5543
Old Basing Hants 24 SU6652
Old Bewick Nthumb 111 NU0621
Old Bolingbroke Lincs 77 TF3564
Old Bracknell Berks 25 SU8668
Old Bramhope W York 82 SE2343
Old Brampton Derbys 74 SK3371
Old Bridge of Tilt Tays 132 NN8866
Old Bridge of Urr D & G 100 NX7767
Old Buckenham Norfk 66 TM0691
Old Burghclere Hants 24 SU4657
Old Byland N York 90 SE5485
Old Cassop Dur 96 NZ3339
Old Castle M Glam 33 SS9079
Old Church Stoke Powys 58 SO2894
Old Clee Humb 85 TA2808
Old Cleeve Somset 20 ST0342
Old Colwyn Clwyd 69 SH8678
Old Dailly Strath 106 NX2299
Old Dalby Leics 63 SK6723
Old Dam Derbys 74 SK1179
Old Deer Gramp 143 NJ9747
Old Ditch Somset 21 ST5049
Old Edington S York 75 SK5397
Old Eldon Dur 96 NZ2427
Old Ellerby Humb 85 TA1637
Old Felixstowe Suffk 55 TM3136
Old Fletton Cambs 64 TL1997
Old Forge H & W 34 SO5518
Old Furnace H & W 46 SO4923
Old Glossop Derbys 74 SK0494
Old Goole Humb 84 SE7422
Old Grimsby IOS 2 SV8915
Old Hall Green Herts 39 TL3622
Old Hall Street Norfk 67 TG3033
Old Harlow Essex 39 TL4711
Old Heath Essex 41 TM0122
Old Hunstanton Norfk 65 TF6842
Old Hutton Cumb 87 SD5688
Old Kea Cnwll 3 SW8441
Old Kilpatrick Strath 115 NS4673
Old Knebworth Herts 39 TL2320
Old Lakenham Norfk 67 TG2206
Old Langho Lancs 81 SD7035
Old Leake Lincs 77 TF4050
Old Malton N York 90 SE7972
Old Micklefield W York 83 SE4432
Old Milton Hants 12 SZ2494
Old Milverton Warwks 48 SP2967
Old Newton Suffk 54 TM0662
Old Quarrington Dur 96 NZ3237
Old Radford Notts 62 SK5540
Old Radnor Powys 46 SO2559
Old Ratray Gramp 143 NK0857
Old Rayne Gramp 142 NJ6728
Old Romney Kent 17 TR0325
Old Scone Tays 126 NO1226
Old Shoreham W Susx 15 TQ2006
Old Shoremore Highld 148 NC2059
Old Soar Kent 27 TQ6154
Old Sodbury Avon 35 ST7581
Old Somerby Lincs 63 SK9633
Old Stratford Nhants 49 SP7741
Old Sunnford W Mids 60 SO9083
Old Tebay Cumb 87 NY6105
Old Thirsk N York 89 SE4382
Old Town Cumb 93 NY4743
Old Town Cumb 87 SD5983
Old Town E Susx 16 TV5999
Old Town IOS 2 SV9110
Old Town Nthumb 102 NY8891
Old Town W York 82 SE0028
Old Trafford Gt Man 79 SJ8196
Old Tupton Derbys 74 SK3865
Old Warden Beds 38 TL1343
Old Weston Cambs 51 TL0977
Old Wick Highld 151 ND3649
Old Windsor Berks 25 SU9874
Old Wives Lees Kent 29 TR0754
Old Woking Surrey 26 TQ0156
Old Wolverton Bucks 38 SP8041
Oldany Highld 148 NC0932
Oldberrow Warwks 48 SP1266
Oldborough Devon 8 SS7706
Oldburry Kent 27 TQ5956
Oldbury Shrops 60 SO7192
Oldbury W Mids 60 SO9889
Oldbury Warwks 61 SP3194
Oldbury Naite Avon 35 ST6293
Oldbury on the Hill Gloucs 35 ST8287
Oldbury-on-Severn Avon 34 ST6092
Oldcastle Gwent 46 SO3224
Oldcastle Heath Ches 71 SJ4745
Oldcotes Notts 75 SK5888
Oldfield H & W 47 SO8465
Oldfield W York 82 SE0037
Oldford Somset 22 ST7849
Oldhall Green Suffk 54 TL8956
Oldham Gt Man 81 SD9215
Oldham Gt Man 79 SD9204
Oldhamstocks Loth 119 NT7470
Oldhurst Cambs 52 TL3077
Oldland Avon 35 ST6771
Oldley Shrops 46 SO3378
Oldmeldrum Gramp 143 NJ8027
Oldmill Cnwll 5 SX3774
Oldmixon Avon 21 ST3358
Oldridge Devon 8 SX8295
Oldstead N York 90 SE5279
Oldwall Cumb 101 NY4761
Oldwalls W Glam 32 SS4891
Oldways End Devon 19 SS8624
Oldwhat Gramp 143 NJ8661
Oldwoods Shrops 59 SJ4520
Olive Green Staffs 73 SK1118
Oliver Border 108 NT0924
Oliver's Battery Hants 13 SU4527
Ollaberry Shet 155 HU3680
Ollach Highld 137 NG5137
Ollerton Ches 79 SJ7776
Ollerton Notts 75 SK6567
Ollerton Shrops 72 SJ6425
Olmarch Dyfed 44 SN6255
Olmstead Green Cambs 53 TL6341
Olney Bucks 38 SP8851
Olney Nhants 49 SP6643
Olrig House Highld 151 ND1866
Olton W Mids 61 SP1382
Olveston Avon 34 ST6087
Ombersley H & W 47 SO8463
Ompton Notts 75 SK6865
Onchan IOM 153 SC4078
One House Suffk 54 TM0159
Onecote Staffs 73 SK0455
Onen Gwent 34 SO4314
Ongar Street H & W 46 SO3967
Onibury Shrops 46 SO4579
Onich Highld 130 NN0261
Onllwyn W Glam 33 SN8410
Onneley Staffs 72 SJ7543
Onslow Village Surrey 25 SU9849
Onston Ches 71 SJ5973
Openwoodgate Derbys 62 SK3647
Opinan Highld 137 NG7472
Orbliston Gramp 141 NJ3057
Orbost Highld 136 NG2543
Orby Lincs 77 TF4967
Orchard Portman Somset 20 ST2421
Orcheston Wilts 23 SU0545
Orcop H & W 46 SO4726
Orcop Hill H & W 46 SO4828
Ord Gramp 142 NJ6259
Ord Highld 129 NG6113
Ordhead Gramp 135 NJ6610
Ordie Gramp 134 NJ4501
Ordiequish Gramp 141 NJ3356
Ordley Nthumb 95 NY9559
Ordsall Notts 75 SK7079
Ore E Susx 17 TQ8311
Oreleton Common H & W 46 SO4768
Oreton Shrops 59 SO6581
Orford Ches 78 SJ6190
Orford Suffk 55 TM4250
Organford Dorset 11 SY9392
Orgreave Staffs 73 SK1415
Orlestone Kent 17 TR0034
Orleton H & W 46 SO4967
Orleton H & W 47 SO7067
Orlingbury Nhants 51 SP8572
Ormathwaite Cumb 93 NY2625
Ormesby Cleve 97 NZ5317
Ormesby St. Margaret Norfk 67 TG4914
Ormesby St. Michael Norfk 67 TG4814
Ormidale Strath 114 NS0081
Ormiscaig Highld 144 NG8590
Ormiston Loth 118 NT4269
Ormsaigmore Highld 121 NM4763
Ormsary Strath 113 NR7472
Ormskirk Lancs 78 SD4108
Ornsby Hill Dur 96 NZ1648
Oronsay Strath 112 NR3588
Orosay W Isls 154 NB3612
Orphir Ork 155 HY3405
Orpington Gt Lon 27 TQ4666
Orrell Gt Man 78 SD5303
Orrell Mersyd 78 SJ3496
Orrell Post Gt Man 78 SD5305
Orrisdale IOM 153 SC3293
Orrisdale Head IOM 153 SC3192
Orroland D & G 92 NX7746
Orsett Essex 40 TQ6482
Orslow Staffs 72 SJ8015
Orston Notts 63 SK7740
Orthwaite Cumb 93 NY2534
Orton Cumb 87 NY6208
Orton Nhants 51 SP8079
Orton Staffs 60 SO8795
Orton Longueville Cambs 64 TL1696
Orton Rigg Cumb 93 NY3352
Orton Waterville Cambs 64 TL1596
Orton-on-the-Hill Leics 61 SK3003
Orwell Cambs 52 TL3650
Osbaldeston Lancs 81 SD6431
Osbaldeston Green Lancs 81 SD6432
Osbaldwick N York 83 SE6251
Osbaston Leics 62 SK4204
Osbaston Shrops 59 SJ3222
Osborne IOW 13 SZ5194
Osbournby Lincs 64 TF0638
Oscroft Ches 71 SJ5067
Osgathorpe Leics 62 SK4219
Osgodby Lincs 76 TF0792
Osgodby N York 83 SE6433
Osgodby N York 91 TA0584
Oskaig Highld 137 NG5438
Oskamull Strath 121 NM4540
Osmaston Derbys 73 SK1943
Osmington Dorset 11 SY7282
Osmington Mills Dorset 11 SY7381
Osmondthorpe W York 83 SE3333
Osmotherley N York 89 SE4596
Osney Oxon 37 SP5006
Ospringe Kent 28 TR0060
Ossett W York 82 SE2720
Ossington Notts 75 SK7564
Ostend Essex 40 TQ9397
Oswaldkirk N York 90 SE6278
Oswaldtwistle Lancs 81 SD7327
Oswestry Shrops 58 SJ2829
Otford Kent 27 TQ5359
Otham Kent 28 TQ7954
Otham Hole Kent 28 TQ7952
Othery Somset 21 ST3831
Otley Suffk 55 TM2055
Otley W York 82 SE2045
Otley Green Suffk 55 TM2156
Otter Ferry Strath 114 NR9384
Otterbourne Hants 13 SU4523
Otterburn N York 88 SD8857
Otterburn Nthumb 102 NY8893
Otterham Cnwll 4 SX1690
Otterham Quay Kent 28 TQ8366

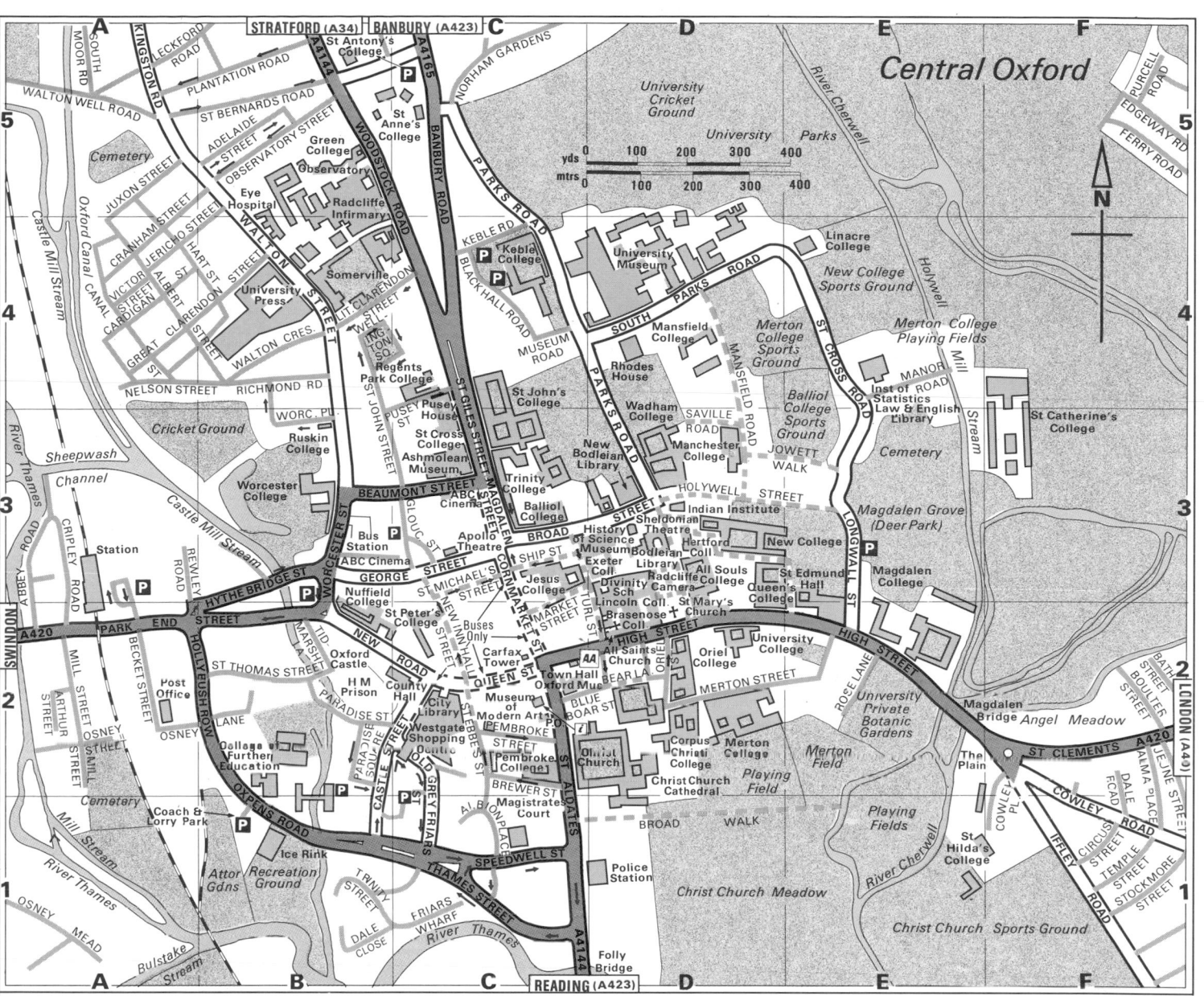

Central Oxford

Pottle Street

Redgrave

Pottle Street *Wilts* 22 ST8141
Potto *N York* 89 NZ4703
Potton *Beds* 52 TL2249
Poughill *Cnwll* 18 SS2207
Poughill *Devon* 19 SS8508
Poulner *Hants* 12 SU1606
Poulshot *Wilts* 22 ST9659
Poulston *Devon* 7 SX7754
Poulton *Gloucs* 36 SP0900
Poulton *Mersyd* 78 SJ3091
Poulton Priory *Gloucs* 36 SP0900
Poulton-le-Fylde *Lancs* 80 SD3439
Pound Bank *H & W* 60 SO7374
Pound Green *E Susx* 16 TQ5123
Pound Green *H & W* 60 SO7579
Pound Green *Hants* 24 SU5759
Pound Hill *W Susx* 15 TQ2937
Pound Street *Hants* 24 SU4561
Poundffald *W Glam* 32 SS5694
Poundgates *E Susx* 16 TQ4918
Poundon *Bucks* 49 SP6425
Poundsbridge *Kent* 16 TQ5341
Poundsgate *Devon* 7 SX7072
Poundstock *Cnwll* 18 SX2099
Pounsley *E Susx* 16 TQ5221
Pouton *D & G* 99 NX4645
Povey Cross *Surrey* 15 TQ2642
Pow Green *H & W* 47 SO7044
Powburn *Nthumb* 111 NU0616
Powderham *Devon* 9 SX9684
Powerstock *Dorset* 10 SY5196
Powfoot *D & G* 100 NY1465
Powhill *Cumb* 93 NY2355
Powick *H & W* 47 SO8351
Powler's Piece *Devon* 18 SS3618
Powmill *Tays* 117 NT0297
Poxwell *Dorset* 11 SY7484
Poyle *Gt Lon* 26 TQ0376
Poynings *W Susx* 15 TQ2612
Poynter's Lane End *Cnwll* 2 SW6743
Poyntington *Dorset* 21 ST6419
Poynton *Ches* 79 SJ9283
Poynton *Shrops* 59 SJ5717
Poynton Green *Shrops* 59 SJ5618
Poys Street *Suffk* 55 TM3570
Poyston Cross *Dyfed* 30 SM9819
Poystreet Green *Suffk* 54 TL9858
Praa Sands *Cnwll* 2 SW5828
Pratt's Bottom *Gt Lon* 27 TQ4762
Prawle Point *Devon* 7 SX7734
Praze-an-Beeble *Cnwll* 2 SW6336
Predannack Wollas *Cnwll* 2 SW6616
Prees *Shrops* 59 SJ5533
Prees Green *Shrops* 59 SJ5531
Prees Heath *Shrops* 71 SJ5538
Prees Higher Heath *Shrops* 59 SJ5636
Prees Lower Heath *Shrops* 59 SJ5732
Preesall *Lancs* 80 SD3647
Pren-gwyn *Dyfed* 42 SN4244
Prendwick *Nthumb* 111 NU0012
Prenteg *Gwynd* 57 SH5841
Prenton *Mersyd* 78 SJ3086
Prescot *Mersyd* 78 SJ4692
Prescott *Devon* 9 ST0814
Prescott *Shrops* 60 SO6681
Prescott *Shrops* 59 SJ4220
Presnerb *Tays* 133 NO1866
Pressen *Nthumb* 110 NT8335
Prestatyn *Clwyd* 70 SJ0682
Prestbury *Ches* 79 SJ9077
Prestbury *Gloucs* 47 SO9723
Presteigne *Powys* 46 SO3164
Prestleigh *Somset* 21 ST6340
Prestolee *Gt Man* 79 SD7505
Preston *Border* 119 NT7957
Preston *Devon* 7 SX8862
Preston *Devon* 7 SX7351
Preston *Devon* 7 SX8574
Preston *Dorset* 11 SY7083
Preston *E Susx* 15 TQ3106
Preston *Gloucs* 47 SO6734
Preston *Gloucs* 36 SP0400
Preston *Herts* 39 TL1824
Preston *Humb* 85 TA1830
Preston *Kent* 28 TR0260
Preston *Kent* 29 TR2561
Preston *Lancs* 80 SD5329
Preston *Leics* 63 SK8602
Preston *Loth* 118 NT5977
Preston *Nthumb* 111 NU1825
Preston *Shrops* 59 SJ5215
Preston *Somset* 20 ST1036
Preston *Suffk* 54 TL9450
Preston *Wilts* 36 SU2774
Preston Bagot *Warwks* 48 SP1766
Preston Bissett *Bucks* 49 SP6529
Preston Bowyer *Somset* 20 ST1326
Preston Brockhurst *Shrops* 59 SJ5324
Preston Brook *Ches* 78 SJ5680
Preston Candover *Hants* 24 SU6041
Preston Capes *Nhants* 49 SP5754
Preston Crowmarsh *Oxon* 37 SU6190
Preston Deanery *Nhants* 50 SP7855
Preston Green *Warwks* 48 SP1665
Preston Gubbals *Shrops* 59 SJ4919
Preston Montford *Shrops* 59 SJ4314
Preston on Stour *Warwks* 48 SP2049
Preston on the Hill *Ches* 78 SJ5780
Preston on Wye *H & W* 46 SO3842
Preston Patrick *Cumb* 87 SD5483
Preston Plucknett *Somset* 10 ST5515
Preston Streeet *Kent* 27 TQ2561
Preston upon the Weald Mo *Shrops* 72 SJ6815
Preston Wynne *H & W* 46 SO5546
Preston-under-Scar *N York* 88 SE0791
Prestonpans *Loth* 118 NT3874
Prestwich *Gt Man* 79 SD8104
Prestwick *Nthumb* 103 NZ1872
Prestwick *Strath* 106 NS3525
Prestwood *Bucks* 26 SP8700
Prestwood *Staffs* 60 SO8686
Price Town *M Glam* 33 SS9392
Prickwillow *Cambs* 53 TL5982
Priddy *Somset* 21 ST5250
Priest Hutton *Lancs* 87 SD5273
Priestacott *Devon* 18 SS4206
Priestcliffe *Derbys* 74 SK1471
Priestcliffe Ditch *Derbys* 74 SK1271
Priestend *Bucks* 37 SP6906
Priestly Green *W York* 82 SE1326
Priestweston *Shrops* 59 SO2997
Priestwood Green *Kent* 27 TQ6464
Primethorpe *Leics* 50 SP5293
Primrose Green *Norfk* 66 TG0616
Primrose Hill *Border* 119 NT7857
Primrose Hill *Cambs* 52 TL3889
Primrose Hill *Derbys* 75 SK4358
Primrose Hill *Lancs* 78 SD3809
Primrose Hill *W Mids* 60 SO9487
Primsidemill *Border* 110 NT8126
Princes Gate *Dyfed* 31 SN1312
Princes Risborough *Bucks* 38 SP8003
Princethorpe *Warwks* 61 SP4070
Princetown *Devon* 6 SX5873
Prinsted *W Susx* 14 SU7605
Prior-Rigg *Cumb* 101 NY4568
Priors Halton *Shrops* 46 SO4975
Priors Hardwick *Warwks* 49 SP4756
Priors Marston *Warwks* 49 SP4957
Priors Norton *Gloucs* 47 SO8624
Priory Wood *H & W* 46 SO2545
Prisk *S Glam* 33 ST0176
Priston *Avon* 22 ST6960
Pristow Green *Norfk* 54 TM1388
Prittlewell *Essex* 40 TQ8687
Privett *Hants* 13 SU6727
Prixton *Devon* 19 SS5436
Probus *Cnwll* 3 SW8947
Prospect *Cumb* 92 NY1041
Prospidnick *Cnwll* 2 SW6431
Protstonhill *Gramp* 143 NJ8163
Providence *Avon* 34 ST5370
Prowse *Devon* 8 SS8405
Prudhoe *Nthumb* 103 NZ0962
Prussia Cove *Cnwll* 2 SW5528
Ptarmigan Lodge *Cent* 115 NN3500
Publow *Avon* 21 ST6264
Puckeridge *Herts* 39 TL3823
Puckington *Somset* 10 ST3718
Pucklechurch *Avon* 35 ST6976
Puckrup *Gloucs* 47 SO8836
Puddinglake *Ches* 79 SJ7269
Puddington *Ches* 71 SJ3273
Puddington *Devon* 19 SS8310
Puddledock *Norfk* 66 TM0592
Puddletown *Dorset* 11 SY7594
Pudleston *H & W* 46 SO5659
Pudsey *W York* 82 SE2232
Pulborough *W Susx* 14 TQ0418
Puleston *Shrops* 72 SJ7322
Pulford *Ches* 71 SJ3759
Pulham *Dorset* 35 ST7080
Pulham *Dorset* 11 ST7008
Pulham Market *Norfk* 55 TM1986
Pulham St. Mary *Norfk* 55 TM2185
Pullens Green *Avon* 34 ST6192
Pulley *Shrops* 59 SJ4809
Pulloxhill *Beds* 38 TL0634
Pumpherston *Loth* 117 NT0669
Pumsaint *Dyfed* 44 SN6540
Puncheston *Dyfed* 30 SN0030
Puncknowle *Dorset* 10 SY5388
Punnett's Town *E Susx* 16 TQ6220
Purbrook *Hants* 13 SU6707
Purbrook Park *Hants* 13 SU6707
Purfleet *Essex* 27 TQ5578
Puriton *Somset* 21 ST3241
Purleigh *Essex* 40 TL8402
Purley *Berks* 37 SU6675
Purley *Gt Lon* 27 TQ3161
Purlogue *Shrops* 46 SO2877
Purlpit *Wilts* 22 ST8766
Purls Bridge *Cambs* 53 TL4787
Purse Caundle *Dorset* 11 ST6917
Purshall Green *H & W* 60 SO8971
Purslow *Shrops* 59 SO3681
Purslow *Shrops* 59 SO3681
Purston Jaglin *W York* 83 SE4319
Purtington *Somset* 10 ST3808
Purton *Gloucs* 35 SO6705
Purton *Gloucs* 35 SO6904
Purton *Wilts* 36 SU0887
Purton Stoke *Wilts* 36 SU0990
Pury End *Nhants* 49 SP7045
Pusey *Oxon* 36 SU3596
Putley *H & W* 47 SO6337
Putley Green *H & W* 47 SO6437
Putloe *Gloucs* 35 SO7809
Putney *Gt Lon* 26 TQ2374
Putron Village *Guern* 152 GN0000
Putsborough *Devon* 18 SS4540
Puttenham *Herts* 38 SP8814
Puttenham *Surrey* 25 SU9347
Puttock End *Essex* 54 TL8140
Puttock's End *Essex* 40 TL5619
Putton *Dorset* 11 SY6480
Puxley *Nhants* 49 SP7542
Puxton *Avon* 21 ST4063
Pwll *Dyfed* 32 SN4800
Pwll Trap *Dyfed* 31 SN2616
Pwll-du *Gwent* 34 SO2411
Pwll-y-glaw *W Glam* 32 SS7993
Pwllcrochan *Dyfed* 30 SM9202
Pwllglas *Clwyd* 70 SJ1154
Pwllgloyw *Powys* 45 SO0333
Pwllheli *Gwynd* 56 SH3734
Pwllmeyric *Gwent* 34 ST5192
Pye Bridge *Derbys* 75 SK4452
Pye Corner *Gwent* 34 ST3485
Pye Corner *Herts* 39 TL4412
Pye Green *Staffs* 60 SJ9814
Pyecombe *W Susx* 15 TQ2912
Pyle *M Glam* 33 SS8282
Pyleigh *Somset* 20 ST1331
Pylle *Somset* 21 ST6038
Pymore *Cambs* 53 TL4986
Pymore *Dorset* 10 SY4694
Pyrford *Surrey* 26 TQ0458
Pyrton *Oxon* 37 SU6896
Pytchley *Nhants* 51 SP8574
Pyworthy *Devon* 18 SS3002

# Q

Quabbs *Shrops* 58 SO2080
Quadring *Lincs* 64 TF2233
Quadring Eaudike *Lincs* 64 TF2433
Quainton *Bucks* 37 SP7420
Quaker's Yard *M Glam* 33 ST0996
Quaking Houses *Dur* 96 NZ1850
Quarley *Hants* 23 SU2743
Quarley *Hants* 23 SU2743
Quarndon *Derbys* 62 SK3340
Quarr Hill *IOW* 13 SZ5792
Quarrier's Homes *Strath* 115 NS3666
Quarrington *Lincs* 64 TF0544
Quarrington Hill *Dur* 96 NZ3337
Quarry Bank *W Mids* 60 SO9386
Quarrybank *Ches* 71 SJ5465
Quarrywood *Gramp* 141 NJ1764
Quarter *Strath* 116 NS7251
Quatford *Shrops* 60 SO7391
Quatt *Shrops* 60 SO7588
Quebec *Dur* 96 NZ1743
Quedgeley *Gloucs* 35 SO8113
Queen Adelaide *Cambs* 53 TL5681
Queen Camel *Somset* 21 ST5924
Queen Charlton *Avon* 21 ST6367
Queen Dart *Devon* 19 SS8316
Queen Oak *Dorset* 22 ST7840
Queen Street *Kent* 28 TQ6845
Queen Street *Wilts* 35 SU0287
Queen's Bower *IOW* 13 SZ5784
Queen's Head *Shrops* 59 SJ3327
Queen's Park *Beds* 38 TL0349
Queen's Park *Nhants* 49 SP7662
Queenborough *Kent* 28 TQ9172
Queenborough *Kent* 28 TQ9172
Queenhill *H & W* 47 SO8537
Queensbury *W York* 82 SE1030
Queensferry *Clwyd* 71 SJ3168
Queenzieburn *Strath* 116 NS6977
Quendon *Essex* 39 TL5130
Queniborough *Leics* 63 SK6412
Quenington *Gloucs* 36 SP1404
Quernhow *N York* 89 SE3480
Quernmore *Lancs* 87 SD5160
Quernmore Park Hall *Lancs* 87 SD5162
Queslett *W Mids* 61 SP0695
Quethiock *Cnwll* 5 SX3164
Quick's Green *Berks* 37 SU5876
Quidenham *Norfk* 54 TM0287
Quidhampton *Hants* 24 SU5150
Quidhampton *Wilts* 23 SU1030
Quina Brook *Shrops* 59 SJ5233
Quinberry End *Nhants* 49 SP6250
Quine's Hill *IOM* 153 SC3473
Quinish House *Strath* 121 NM4154
Quinton *Nhants* 49 SP7754
Quinton *W Mids* 60 SO9884
Quinton Green *Nhants* 38 SP7852
Quintrell Downs *Cnwll* 4 SW8460
Quither *Devon* 5 SX4481
Quixhall *Staffs* 73 SK1041
Quixwood *Border* 119 NT7863
Quoditch *Devon* 5 SX4097
Quorndon *Leics* 62 SK5616
Quothquan *Strath* 108 NS9939
Quoyburray *Ork* 155 HY5005
Quoyloo *Ork* 155 HY2421

# R

RAF College *Lincs* 76 TF0049
Rabbit's Cross *Kent* 28 TQ7848
Rableyheath *Herts* 39 TL2319
Raby *Cumb* 93 NY1951
Raby *Mersyd* 71 SJ3179
Rachan Mill *Border* 108 NT1134
Rachub *Gwynd* 69 SH6267
Rackenford *Devon* 19 SS8418
Rackham *W Susx* 14 TQ0513
Rackheath *Norfk* 67 TG2814
Racks *D & G* 100 NY0274
Rackwick *Ork* 155 ND2099
Radbourne *Derbys* 73 SK2836
Radcliffe *Gt Man* 79 SD7807
Radcliffe *Nthumb* 103 NU2602
Radcliffe on Trent *Notts* 63 SK6439
Radclive *Bucks* 49 SP6734
Radcot *Oxon* 36 SU2899
Raddington *Somset* 20 ST0225
Radernie *Fife* 127 NO4609
Radford Semele *Warwks* 48 SP3464
Radlet *Somset* 20 ST2038
Radlett *Herts* 26 TL1600
Radley *Devon* 19 SS7323
Radley *Oxon* 37 SU5399
Radley Green *Essex* 40 TL6205
Radmore Green *Ches* 71 SJ5955
Radnage *Bucks* 37 SU7897
Radstock *Avon* 22 ST6854
Radstone *Nhants* 49 SP5840
Radway *Warwks* 48 SP3648
Radway Green *Ches* 72 SJ7754
Radwell *Beds* 51 TL0057
Radwell *Herts* 39 TL2335
Radwinter *Essex* 53 TL6037
Radwinter End *Essex* 53 TL6139
Radyr *S Glam* 33 ST1380
Raecleugh *D & G* 108 NT0311
Rafford *Gramp* 141 NJ0656
Raftra *Cnwll* 2 SW3723
Ragdale *Leics* 63 SK6619
Ragdon *Shrops* 59 SO4591
Raginnis *Cnwll* 2 SW4625
Raglan *Gwent* 34 SO4107
Ragnall *Notts* 75 SK8073
Raigbeg *Highld* 140 NH8128
Rainbow Hill *H & W* 47 SO8656
Rainford *Gt Man* 78 SD4700
Rainham *Gt Lon* 27 TQ5282
Rainham *Kent* 28 TQ8165
Rainhill *Mersyd* 78 SJ4991
Rainhill Stoops *Mersyd* 78 SJ5090
Rainigadale *W Isls* 154 NB2201
Rainow *Ches* 79 SJ9475
Rainsough *Gt Man* 79 SD8002
Rainton *N York* 89 SE3775
Rainworth *Notts* 75 SK5958
Raisbeck *Cumb* 87 NY6407
Raise *Cumb* 94 NY7146
Raisthorpe *N York* 90 SE8561
Rait *Tays* 126 NO2226
Raithby *Lincs* 77 TF3084
Raithby *Lincs* 77 TF3767
Raithwaite *N York* 90 NZ8611
Rake *W Susx* 14 SU8027
Rakewood *Gt Man* 82 SD9414
Ralia *Highld* 132 NN7097
Raltcliff Bridge *Cumb* 93 NY3636
Ram *Dyfed* 44 SN5846
Ram Hill *Avon* 35 ST6779
Ram Lane *Kent* 28 TQ9646
Ramasaig *Highld* 136 NG1644
Rame *Cnwll* 6 SX4249
Rame *Cnwll* 3 SW7233
Rampisham *Dorset* 10 ST5502
Rampside *Cumb* 86 SD2366
Rampton *Cambs* 53 TL4268
Rampton *Notts* 75 SK8078
Ramridge End *Beds* 38 TL1022
Ramsbottom *Gt Man* 81 SD7916
Ramsbury *Wilts* 36 SU2771
Ramscraigs *Highld* 151 ND1427
Ramsdean *Hants* 13 SU7022
Ramsdell *Hants* 24 SU5957
Ramsden *H & W* 47 SO9246
Ramsden *Oxon* 36 SP3515
Ramsden Bellhouse *Essex* 40 TQ7194
Ramsden Heath *Essex* 40 TQ7095
Ramsey *Cambs* 52 TL2885
Ramsey *Essex* 41 TM2130
Ramsey *IOM* 153 SC4594
Ramsey Forty Foot *Cambs* 52 TL3087
Ramsey Heights *Cambs* 52 TL2484
Ramsey Island *Essex* 40 TL9506
Ramsey Mereside *Cambs* 52 TL2889
Ramsey St. Mary's *Cambs* 52 TL2588
Ramsgate *Kent* 29 TR3865
Ramsgill *N York* 89 SE1170
Ramshaw *Dur* 95 NY9547
Ramsholt *Suffk* 55 TM3141
Ramshope *Nthumb* 102 NT7304
Ramshorn *Staffs* 73 SK0845
Ramsley *Devon* 8 SX6493
Ramsnest Common *Surrey* 14 SU9533
Ranby *Lincs* 76 TF2278
Ranby *Notts* 75 SK6580
Rand *Lincs* 76 TF1078
Randwick *Gloucs* 35 SO8206
Ranfurly *Strath* 115 NS3864
Rangemore *Staffs* 73 SK1822
Rangeworthy *Avon* 35 ST6986
Rank's Green *Essex* 40 TL7518
Rankinston *Strath* 107 NS4513
Ranksborough *Leics* 63 SK8310
Rann *Lancs* 81 SD7124
Rannoch Station *Tays* 124 NN4257
Ranochan *Highld* 129 NM8282
Ranscombe *Somset* 20 SS9543
Ranskill *Notts* 75 SK6587
Ranton *Staffs* 72 SJ8524
Ranton Green *Staffs* 72 SJ8423
Ranworth *Norfk* 67 TG3514
Raploch *Cent* 116 NS7894
Rapness *Ork* 155 HY5041
Rapps *Somset* 10 ST3316
Rascarrel *D & G* 92 NX7948
Rashfield *Strath* 114 NS1483
Rashwood *H & W* 47 SO9165
Raskelf *N York* 90 SE4971
Rassau *Gwent* 33 SO1512
Ratagan *Highld* 138 NG9220
Ratby *Leics* 62 SK5105
Ratcliffe Culey *Leics* 61 SP3299
Ratcliffe on Soar *Notts* 62 SK4928
Ratcliffe on the Wreake *Leics* 63 SK6314
Ratfyn *Wilts* 23 SU1642
Rathen *Gramp* 143 NJ9960
Rathhead *Fife* 117 NT2992
Rathillet *Fife* 126 NO3620
Rathmell *N York* 88 SD8059
Ratho *Loth* 117 NT1370
Rathven *Gramp* 142 NJ4465
Ratlake *Hants* 13 SU4123
Ratley *Warwks* 48 SP3847
Ratling *Kent* 29 TR2453
Ratlinghope *Shrops* 59 SO4097
Rattan Row *Norfk* 65 TF5114
Rattar *Highld* 151 ND2673
Ratten Row *Cumb* 93 NY3949
Ratten Row *Cumb* 93 NY3140
Ratten Row *Lancs* 80 SD4241
Rattery *Devon* 7 SX7361
Rattlesden *Suffk* 54 TL9759
Ratton Village *E Susx* 16 TQ5901
Rattray *Tays* 126 NO1845
Raughton *Cumb* 93 NY3848
Raughton Head *Cumb* 93 NY3745
Raunds *Nhants* 51 SP9972
Raven Meols *Mersyd* 78 SD2905
Ravenfield *S York* 75 SK4895
Ravenglass *Cumb* 86 SD0896
Ravenhills Green *H & W* 47 SO7454
Raveningham *Norfk* 67 TM3996
Ravenscar *N York* 91 NZ9801
Ravenscliffe *Staffs* 72 SJ8452
Ravensdale *IOM* 153 SC3592
Ravensden *Beds* 51 TL0754
Ravenshead *Notts* 75 SK5654
Ravensmoor *Ches* 71 SJ6150
Ravensthorpe *Nhants* 50 SP6670
Ravensthorpe *W York* 82 SE2220
Ravenstone *Bucks* 38 SP8450
Ravenstone *Leics* 62 SK4013
Ravenstonedale *Cumb* 88 NY7203
Ravenstruther *Strath* 116 NS9245
Ravensworth *N York* 89 NZ1307
Raw *N York* 91 NZ9305
Rawcliffe *Humb* 83 SE6822
Rawcliffe *N York* 83 SE5854
Rawcliffe *N York* 83 SE5854
Rawcliffe Bridge *Humb* 83 SE6921
Rawdon *W York* 82 SE2139
Rawling Street *Kent* 28 TQ9059
Rawmarsh *S York* 75 SK4396
Rawnsley *Staffs* 60 SK0212
Rawreth *Essex* 40 TQ7893
Rawridge *Devon* 9 ST2006
Rawtenstall *Lancs* 81 SD8123
Raydon *Suffk* 54 TM0438
Raylees *Nthumb* 102 NY9291
Rayleigh *Essex* 40 TQ8090
Raymond's Hill *Devon* 10 SY3396
Rayne *Essex* 40 TL7222
Raynes Park *Gt Lon* 26 TQ2368
Reach *Cambs* 53 TL5666
Read *Lancs* 81 SD7734
Reading *Berks* 24 SU7173
Reading Street *Kent* 29 TR3868
Reading Street *Kent* 17 TQ9230
Reagill *Cumb* 94 NY6017
Rearquhar *Highld* 146 NH7492
Rearsby *Leics* 63 SK6514
Rease Heath *Shrops* 72 SJ6454
Reaster *Highld* 151 ND2565
Reay *Highld* 150 NC9664
Reculver *Kent* 29 TR2269
Red Ball *Devon* 9 ST0917
Red Bull *Ches* 72 SJ8255
Red Cross *Cambs* 53 TL4754
Red Cross *Cnwll* 18 SS2605
Red Dial *Cumb* 93 NY2546
Red Hill *Dorset* 12 SZ0995
Red Hill *Warwks* 48 SP1355
Red Lodge *Suffk* 53 TL6970
Red Lumb *Gt Man* 81 SD8415
Red Rock *Gt Man* 78 SD5809
Red Roses *Dyfed* 31 SN2012
Red Row *T & W* 103 NZ2599
Red Street *Staffs* 72 SJ8251
Red Wharf Bay *Gwynd* 68 SH5281
Redberth *Dyfed* 31 SN0804
Redbourn *Herts* 38 TL1012
Redbourne *Lincs* 76 SK9699
Redbrook *Clwyd* 71 SJ5040
Redbrook *Gloucs* 34 SO5309
Redbrook Street *Kent* 28 TQ9336
Redburn *Highld* 140 NH9447
Redburn *Nthumb* 102 NY7764
Redcar *Cleve* 97 NZ6024
Redcastle *D & G* 100 NX8165
Redcastle *Highld* 139 NH5849
Redcliff Bay *Avon* 34 ST4475
Redding *Cent* 116 NS9278
Reddingmuirhead *Cent* 116 NS9177
Reddish *Gt Man* 79 SJ8993
Redditch *H & W* 48 SP0467
Rede *Suffk* 54 TL8056
Redenhall *Norfk* 55 TM2684
Redenham *Hants* 23 SU3049
Redesmouth *Nthumb* 102 NY8681
Redford *Gramp* 135 NO7570
Redford *Gramp* 135 NO7570
Redford *Tays* 127 NO5644
Redford *W Susx* 14 SU8626
Redfordgreen *Border* 109 NT3616
Redgate *M Glam* 33 ST0188
Redgorton *Tays* 125 NO0828
Redgrave *Suffk* 54 TM0478

Redhill Roughton

Redhill Avon 21 ST4963
Redhill Gramp 135 NJ7704
Redhill Herts 39 TL3032
Redhill Surrey 27 TQ2850
Redisham Suffk 55 TM4084
Redland Avon 34 ST5775
Redland Ork 155 HY3724
Redlingfield Suffk 54 TM1870
Redlingfield Green Suffk 54 TM1871
Redlynch Somset 22 ST6933
Redlynch Wilts 12 SU2020
Redmain Cumb 92 NY1434
Redmarley H & W 47 SO7666
Redmarley D'Abitot Gloucs 47 SO7531
Redmarshall Cleve 96 NZ3821
Redmile Leics 63 SK7935
Redmire N York 88 SE0491
Redmyre Gramp 135 NO7575
Redmyre Gramp 135 NO7575
Rednal Shrops 59 SJ3628
Rednal W Mids 60 SP0076
Redpath Border 110 NT5835
Redruth Cnwll 2 SW6941
Redstocks Wilts 22 ST9362
Redstone Tays 126 NO1834
Redvales Gt Man 79 SD8008
Redwick Avon 34 ST5486
Redwick Gwent 34 ST4184
Redworth Dur 96 NZ2423
Reed Herts 39 TL3636
Reedham Norfk 67 TG4101
Reedness Humb 84 SE7923
Reeds Holme Lancs 81 SD8124
Reedy Devon 8 SX8189
Reef W Isls 154 NB1134
Reepham Lincs 76 TF0373
Reepham Norfk 66 TG1023
Reeth N York 88 SE0499
Reeves Green W Mids 61 SP2677
Regaby IOM 153 SC4397
Reiff Highld 144 NB9614
Reigate Surrey 27 TQ2550
Reighton N York 91 TA1375
Reinachait Highld 148 NC0430
Reisque Gramp 143 NJ8820
Reiss Highld 151 ND3354
Rejerrah Cnwll 3 SW8056
Releath Cnwll 2 SW6633
Relubbus Cnwll 2 SW5631
Relugas Gramp 141 NH9948
Remenham Berks 37 SU7783
Remenham Hill Berks 37 SU7882
Remony Tays 124 NN7643
Rempstone Notts 62 SK5724
Rendcomb Gloucs 35 SP0209
Rendham Suffk 55 TM3464
Renfrew Strath 115 NS4967
Renhold Beds 51 TL0953
Renishaw Derbys 75 SK4477
Rennington Nthumb 111 NU2118
Renton Strath 115 NS3878
Renwick Cumb 94 NY5943
Repps Norfk 67 TG4217
Repton Derbys 73 SK3026
Resaurie Highld 140 NH7045
Rescassa Cnwll 3 SW9842
Rescorla Cnwll 3 SW9848
Resipole Highld 121 NM7264
Reskadinnick Cnwll 2 SW6341
Resolis Highld 140 NH6765
Resolven W Glam 33 SN8302
Rest and be Thankful Strath 123 NN2307
Reston Border 119 NT8862
Restronguet Cnwll 3 SW8136
Reswallie Tays 127 NO5051
Reterth Cnwll 4 SW9463
Retew Cnwll 3 SW9256
Retford Notts 75 SK7081
Retire Cnwll 4 SX0064
Rettendon Essex 40 TQ7698
Retyn Cnwll 4 SW8858
Revesby Lincs 77 TF2961
Rew Devon 7 SX7570
Rew Street IOW 13 SZ4994
Rewe Devon 9 SX9499
Rexon Devon 5 SX4188
Rexon Cross Devon 5 SX4188
Reydon Suffk 55 TM4977
Reymerston Norfk 66 TG0206
Reynalton Dyfed 31 SN0908
Reynoldston W Glam 32 SS4890
Rezare Cnwll 5 SX3677
Rhadyr Gwent 34 SO3602
Rhandirmwyn Dyfed 44 SN7843
Rhayader Powys 45 SN9708
Rheindown Highld 139 NH5147
Rhelonie Highld 146 NH5597
Rhes-y-cae Clwyd 70 SJ1971
Rhewl Clwyd 70 SJ1160
Rhewl Clwyd 70 SJ1744
Rhewl Mostyn Clwyd 70 SJ1580
Rhewl-fawr Clwyd 70 SJ1580
Rhicarn Highld 148 NC0825
Rhiconich Highld 148 NC2552
Rhicullen Highld 146 NH6971
Rhifail Highld 150 NC7249
Rhigos M Glam 33 SN9205
Rhilochan Highld 146 NC7407
Rhireavach Highld 144 NH0295
Rhives Highld 147 NC8200
Rhiwbina S Glam 33 ST1682
Rhiwbryfdir Gwynd 57 SH6946
Rhiwderyn Gwent 34 ST2687
Rhiwen Gwynd 69 SH5763
Rhiwinder M Glam 33 ST0287
Rhiwlas Clwyd 58 SJ1932
Rhiwlas Gwynd 69 SH5765
Rhiwlas Gwynd 58 SH9237
Rhiwsaeson M Glam 33 ST0682
Rhode Somset 20 ST2734
Rhoden Green Kent 28 TQ6745
Rhodes Gt Man 79 SD8505
Rhodes Minnis Kent 29 TR1542
Rhodesia Notts 75 SK5680
Rhodiad-y-brenin Dyfed 30 SM7627
Rhonehouse or Kelton Hill D & G 99 NX7459
Rhoose S Glam 20 ST0666
Rhos Clwyd 70 SJ1261
Rhos Dyfed 31 SN3835
Rhos Powys 45 SO1731
Rhos W Glam 32 SN7403
Rhos Haminiog Dyfed 43 SN5364
Rhos Lligwy Gwynd 68 SH4986
Rhos y-brithdir Powys 58 SJ1323
Rhos-fawr Gwynd 56 SH3838
Rhos-hill Dyfed 31 SN1940
Rhos-on-Sea Clwyd 69 SH8480
Rhos-y-garth Dyfed 43 SN6373
Rhos-y-gwaliau Gwynd 58 SH9434
Rhos-y-llan Gwynd 56 SH2337
Rhos-y-meirch Powys 46 SO2769
Rhosaman Dyfed 32 SN7214
Rhoscefnhir Gwynd 68 SH5276
Rhoscolyn Gwynd 56 SH2735
Rhoscrowther Dyfed 30 SM9002
Rhosesmor Clwyd 70 SJ2168
Rhosgadfan Gwynd 68 SH5057
Rhosgoch Gwynd 68 SH4189
Rhosgoch Powys 45 SO1847
Rhoshirwaun Gwynd 56 SH1930
Rhoslan Gwynd 56 SH4841
Rhosllanerchrugog Clwyd 71 SJ2946
Rhosmaen Dyfed 44 SN6423
Rhosmeirch Gwynd 68 SH4677
Rhosneigr Gwynd 68 SH3172
Rhosnesni Clwyd 71 SJ3460
Rhosrobin Clwyd 71 SJ3452
Rhossili W Glam 31 SS4188
Rhostryfan Gwynd 68 SH4958
Rhostyllen Clwyd 71 SJ3148
Rhosybol Gwynd 68 SH4288
Rhosygadfa Shrops 59 SJ3234
Rhosymedre Clwyd 70 SJ2842
Rhu Strath 115 NS2783
Rhuallt Clwyd 70 SJ0774
Rhuban W Isls 154 NF7811
Rhubodach Strath 114 NS0273
Rhuddall Heath Ches 71 SJ5562
Rhuddlan Clwyd 70 SJ0277
Rhulen Powys 45 SO1349
Rhunahaorine Strath 105 NR7048
Rhyd Gwynd 57 SH6341
Rhyd-Ddu Gwynd 69 SH5652
Rhyd-lydan Clwyd 69 SH8950
Rhyd-uchaf Gwynd 58 SH9037
Rhyd-y pennau Dyfed 43 SN6386
Rhyd-y-clafdy Gwynd 56 SH3234
Rhyd-y-foel Clwyd 70 SH9176
Rhyd-y-groes Gwynd 69 SH5867
Rhyd-y-meirch Gwent 34 SO3107
Rhyd-y-sarn Gwynd 57 SH6842
Rhyd-yr-onnen Gwynd 57 SH6102
Rhydargaeau Dyfed 31 SN4326
Rhydcymerau Dyfed 44 SN5738
Rhydd H & W 47 SO8345
Rhydding W Glam 32 SS7499
Rhyddlan Dyfed 44 SN4943
Rhydgaled Clwyd 70 SH9964
Rhydlanfair Gwynd 69 SH8252
Rhydlewis Dyfed 42 SN3447
Rhydlios Gwynd 56 SH1830
Rhydowen Dyfed 42 SN4445
Rhydrosser Dyfed 43 SN5667
Rhydspence H & W 46 SO2447
Rhydtalog Clwyd 70 SJ2354
Rhydwyn Gwynd 68 SH3188
Rhydycroesau Shrops 58 SJ2430
Rhydyfelin Dyfed 43 SN5979
Rhydyfelin M Glam 33 ST0988
Rhydyfro W Glam 32 SN7105
Rhydymain Gwynd 57 SH7821
Rhydymwyn Clwyd 70 SJ2067
Rhyl Clwyd 70 SJ0181
Rhymney M Glam 33 SO1107
Rhynd Tays 126 NO1520
Rhynie Gramp 142 NJ4927
Rhynie Highld 147 NH8479
Ribbesford H & W 60 SO7874
Ribbleton Lancs 81 SD5631
Ribby Lancs 80 SD4031
Ribchester Lancs 81 SD6535
Riber Derbys 74 SK3059
Ribigill Highld 149 NC5854
Riby Lincs 85 TA1807
Riccall N York 83 SE6237
Riccarton Border 101 NY5495
Riccarton Strath 107 NS4236
Richards Castle H & W 46 SO4969
Richings Park Bucks 26 TQ0278
Richmond N York 89 NZ1701
Richmond S York 74 SK4085
Richmond Fort Guern 152 GN0000
Richmond upon Thames Gt Lon 26 TQ1874
Richs Halford Somset 20 ST1534
Rickerscote Staffs 72 SJ9220
Rickford Avon 21 ST4859
Rickham Devon 7 SX7437
Rickham Devon 7 SX7437
Rickinghall Inferior Suffk 54 TM0475
Rickinghall Superior Suffk 54 TM0375
Rickinghall Superior Suffk 54 TM0475
Rickling Essex 39 TL4931
Rickling Green Essex 39 TL5029
Rickmansworth Herts 26 TQ0694
Riddell Border 109 NT5124
Riddings Cumb 101 NY4075
Riddings Derbys 74 SK4252
Riddlecombe Devon 19 SS6013
Riddlesden W York 82 SE0742
Ridge Avon 21 ST5555
Ridge Dorset 11 SY9386
Ridge Herts 26 TL2100
Ridge Wilts 22 ST9531
Ridge Green Surrey 15 TQ3048
Ridge Lane Warwks 61 SP2994
Ridge Row Kent 29 TR2042
Ridgebourne Powys 45 SO0560
Ridgehill Avon 21 ST5362
Ridgeway Derbys 74 SK3551
Ridgeway Derbys 74 SK4081
Ridgeway H & W 48 SP0461
Ridgeway Cross H & W 47 SO7147
Ridgewell Essex 53 TL7340
Ridgewood E Susx 16 TQ4719
Ridgmont Beds 38 SP9736
Riding Mill Nthumb 103 NZ0161
Ridley Kent 27 TQ6164
Ridley Nthumb 102 NY7963
Ridley Green Ches 71 SJ5554
Ridlington Leics 63 SK8402
Ridlington Norfk 67 TG3431
Ridlington Street Norfk 67 TG3430
Ridsdale Nthumb 102 NY9084
Rievaulx N York 90 SE5785
Rigg D & G 101 NY2966
Riggend Strath 116 NS7670
Righoul Highld 140 NH8851
Rigmadon Park Cumb 87 SD6185
Rigsby Lincs 77 TF4375
Rigside Strath 108 NS8735
Riley Green Lancs 81 SD6225
Rileyhill Staffs 73 SK1115
Rilla Mill Cnwll 5 SX2973
Rillaton Cnwll 5 SX2973
Rillington N York 90 SE8574
Rimington Lancs 81 SD8045
Rimpton Somset 21 ST6021
Rimswell Humb 85 TA3028
Rinaston Dyfed 30 SM9826
Rindleford Shrops 60 SO7395
Ring O'Bells Lancs 78 SD4510
Ring's End Cambs 65 TF3902
Ringford D & G 99 NX6857
Ringinglow Derbys 74 SK2983
Ringland Norfk 66 TG1314
Ringles Cross E Susx 16 TQ4722
Ringlestone Kent 28 TQ8755
Ringley Gt Man 79 SD7605
Ringmer E Susx 16 TQ4412
Ringmore Devon 7 SX9272
Ringmore Devon 7 SX6545
Ringorm Gramp 141 NJ2644
Ringsfield Suffk 55 TM4088
Ringsfield Corner Suffk 55 TM4087
Ringshall Bucks 38 SP9814
Ringshall Suffk 54 TM0453
Ringshall Stocks Suffk 54 TM0551
Ringstead Nhants 51 SP9875
Ringstead Norfk 65 TF7040
Ringwood Hants 12 SU1405
Ringwould Kent 29 TR3548
Rinsey Cnwll 2 SW5927
Rinsey Croft Cnwll 2 SW6028
Ripe E Susx 16 TQ5110
Ripley Derbys 74 SK3950
Ripley Hants 12 SZ1698
Ripley N York 89 SE2860
Ripley Surrey 26 TQ0556
Riplingham Humb 84 SE9631
Riplington Hants 13 SU6623
Ripon N York 89 SE3171
Rippingale Lincs 64 TF0927
Ripple H & W 47 SO8737
Ripple Kent 29 TR3550
Ripponden W York 82 SE0319
Risabus Strath 104 NR3143
Risbury H & W 46 SO5454
Risby Humb 84 SE9114
Risby Suffk 53 TL7966
Risca Gwent 34 ST2391
Rise Humb 85 TA1542
Riseden E Susx 16 TQ6130
Risedown Kent 28 TQ7036
Risegate Lincs 64 TF2129
Riseholme Lincs 76 SK9670
Risehow Cumb 92 NY0335
Riseley Beds 51 TL0462
Riseley Berks 24 SU7263
Rishangles Suffk 54 TM1668
Rishton Lancs 81 SD7230
Rishworth W York 82 SE0318
Rising Bridge Lancs 81 SD7825
Risley Ches 79 SJ6592
Risley Derbys 62 SK4635
Risplith N York 89 SE2468
Rivar Wilts 23 SU3161
Rivenhall End Essex 40 TL8416
River Kent 29 TR2943
River W Susx 14 SU9322
River Bank Cambs 53 TL5368
Riverford Highld 139 NH5455
Riverhead Kent 27 TQ5156
Rivers Corner Dorset 11 ST7712
Rivington Lancs 81 SD6214
Roa Island Cumb 86 SD2364
Roachhill Devon 19 SS8422
Road Ashton Wilts 22 ST8856
Road Green Norfk 67 TM2694
Road Weedon Nhants 49 SP6359
Roade Nhants 49 SP7551
Roadhead Cumb 101 NY5175
Roadmeetings Strath 116 NS8649
Roadside Highld 151 ND1560
Roadside Strath 107 NS5717
Roadside of Catterline Gramp 135 NO8678
Roadside of Catterline Gramp 135 NO8678
Roadside of Kinneff Gramp 135 NO8477
Roadwater Somset 20 ST0238
Roag Highld 136 NG2744
Roan of Craigoch Strath 106 NS2904
Roast Green Essex 39 TL4632
Roath S Glam 33 ST1977
Roberton Border 109 NT4214
Roberton Strath 108 NS9428
Robertsbridge E Susx 17 TQ7423
Roberttown W York 82 SE1922
Robeston Wathen Dyfed 31 SN0815
Robgill Tower D & G 101 NY2471
Robin Hill Staffs 72 SJ9057
Robin Hood Lancs 80 SD5211
Robin Hood W York 83 SE3227
Robin Hood's Bay N York 91 NZ9505
Robinhood End Essex 53 TL7036
Roborough Devon 19 SS5717
Roby Mersyd 78 SJ4390
Roby Mill Lancs 78 SD5107
Rocester Staffs 73 SK1039
Roch Dyfed 30 SM8821
Roch Gate Dyfed 30 SM8720
Rochdale Gt Man 81 SD8913
Roche Cnwll 4 SW9860
Rochester Kent 28 TQ7468
Rochester Nthumb 102 NY8298
Rochford Essex 40 TQ8790
Rochford H & W 47 SO6368
Rochville Strath 114 NS2390
Rock Cnwll 4 SW9476
Rock H & W 60 SO7371
Rock Nthumb 111 NU2020
Rock W Glam 32 SS7893
Rock W Susx 14 TQ1214
Rock Ferry Mersyd 78 SJ3386
Rock Hill H & W 47 SO9569
Rockbeare Devon 9 SY0195
Rockbourne Hants 12 SU1118
Rockcliffe Cumb 101 NY3561
Rockcliffe D & G 92 NX8553
Rockcliffe Cross Cumb 101 NY3463
Rockesta Cnwll 2 SW3722
Rockfield Gwent 34 SO4814
Rockfield Highld 147 NH9283
Rockford Devon 19 SS7547
Rockford Hants 12 SU1608
Rockgreen Shrops 46 SO5275
Rockhampton Gloucs 35 ST6593
Rockhead Cnwll 4 SX0784
Rockhill Shrops 46 SO2879
Rockingham Nhants 51 SP8691
Rockland All Saints Norfk 66 TL9996
Rockland St. Mary Norfk 67 TG3104
Rockland St. Peter Norfk 66 TL9897
Rockley Notts 75 SK7174
Rockley Wilts 36 SU1571
Rockliffe Lancs 81 SD8722
Rockwell End Bucks 37 SU7988
Rockwell Green Somset 20 ST1320
Rodborough Gloucs 35 SO8304
Rodbourne Wilts 36 SU1485
Rodbourne Wilts 35 ST9383
Rodd H & W 46 SO3262
Roddam Nthumb 111 NU0220
Rodden Dorset 10 SY6184
Roddymoor Dur 96 NZ1536
Rode Somset 22 ST8053
Rode Heath Ches 72 SJ8767
Rode Heath Ches 72 SJ8057
Rodel W Isls 154 NG0483
Roden Shrops 59 SJ5716
Rodhuish Somset 20 ST0139
Rodington Shrops 59 SJ5814
Rodington Heath Shrops 59 SJ5814
Rodley Gloucs 35 SO7411
Rodley W York 82 SE2236
Rodmarton Gloucs 35 ST9497
Rodmell E Susx 15 TQ4106
Rodmersham Kent 28 TQ9261
Rodmersham Green Kent 28 TQ9161
Rodney Stoke Somset 21 ST4849
Rodono Border 109 NT2321
Rodsley Derbys 73 SK2040
Rodway Somset 20 ST2540
Roe Cross Gt Man 79 SJ9896
Roe Green Gt Man 79 SD7501
Roe Green Herts 39 TL2107
Roe Green Herts 39 TL3133
Roecliffe N York 89 SE3765
Roehampton Gt Lon 26 TQ2273
Roewen Gwynd 69 SH7672
Roffey W Susx 15 TQ1932
Rogart Highld 146 NC7304
Rogate W Susx 14 SU8023
Roger Ground Cumb 101 NY3597
Rogerstone Gwent 34 ST2788
Rogiet Gwent 34 ST4587
Roke Oxon 37 SU6293
Roker T & W 96 NZ4059
Rollesby Norfk 67 TG4415
Rolleston Leics 50 SK7300
Rolleston Notts 75 SK7452
Rolleston Staffs 73 SK2327
Rolston Humb 85 TA2145
Rolstone Avon 21 ST3862
Rolvenden Kent 17 TQ8431
Rolvenden Layne Kent 17 TQ8530
Romaldkirk Dur 95 NY9921
Romanby N York 89 SE3693
Romanno Bridge Border 117 NT1647
Romansleigh Devon 19 SS7220
Romden Castle Kent 28 TQ8941
Romesdal Highld 136 NG4033
Romford Dorset 12 SU0709
Romford Gt Lon 27 TQ5188
Romiley Gt Man 79 SJ9490
Romney Street Kent 27 TQ5461
Romsey Hants 12 SU3521
Romsley H & W 60 SO9679
Romsley Shrops 60 SO7883
Ronachan Strath 113 NR7454
Ronague IOM 153 SC2472
Rookhope Dur 95 NY9342
Rookley IOW 13 SZ5084
Rookley Green IOW 13 SZ5083
Rooks Bridge Somset 21 ST3752
Rooks Nest Somset 20 ST0339
Rookwith N York 89 SE2086
Roos Humb 85 TA2830
Roosebeck Cumb 101 NY2567
Roothams Green Beds 51 TL1057
Ropley Hants 24 SU6431
Ropley Dean Hants 24 SU6332
Ropley Soke Hants 24 SU6533
Ropsley Lincs 63 SK9934
Rora Gramp 143 NK0650
Rorrington Shrops 59 SJ3000
Rosarie Gramp 141 NJ3850
Roscroggan Cnwll 2 SW6542
Rose Cnwll 3 SW7754
Rose Ash Devon 19 SS7821
Rose Green Essex 40 TL9028
Rose Green Suffk 54 TL9337
Rose Green Suffk 54 TL9744
Rose Green W Susx 14 SZ9099
Rose Hill E Susx 16 TQ4516
Rose Hill Lancs 81 SD8231
Rose Lands E Susx 16 TQ6200
Roseacre Lancs 80 SD4336
Rosebank Strath 116 NS8049
Rosebush Dyfed 31 SN0729
Rosecare Cnwll 4 SX1695
Rosecliston Cnwll 4 SW8159
Rosedale Abbey N York 90 SE7296
Roseden Nthumb 111 NU0321
Rosehall Highld 146 NC4701
Rosehearty Gramp 143 NJ9367
Rosehill Shrops 59 SJ4717
Roseisle Gramp 141 NJ1466
Rosemarket Dyfed 30 SM9508
Rosemarkie Highld 140 NH7357
Rosemary Lane Devon 9 ST1514
Rosemount Tays 126 NO1843
Rosenannon Cnwll 4 SW9566
Rosenithon Cnwll 3 SW8021
Roser's Cross E Susx 16 TQ5420
Rosevean Cnwll 4 SX0258
Rosevine Cnwll 3 SW8736
Rosewarne Cnwll 2 SW6137
Rosewell Loth 117 NT2862
Roseworth Cleve 96 NZ4121
Roseworthy Cnwll 2 SW6139
Rosgill Cumb 94 NY5316
Roshven Highld 129 NM7078
Roskhill Highld 136 NG2745
Roskorwell Cnwll 3 SW7923
Roskrow Cnwll 3 SW7635
Rosley Cumb 93 NY3245
Roslin Loth 117 NT2763
Rosliston Derbys 73 SK2416
Rosneath Strath 114 NS2583
Ross D & G 99 NX6444
Ross Nthumb 111 NU1337
Ross Tays 124 NN7621
Ross-on-Wye H & W 46 SO6024
Rossett Clwyd 71 SJ3657
Rossett Green N York 82 SE2952
Rossie Orchill Tays 125 NO0912
Rossington Notts 75 SK6298
Rosskeen Highld 146 NH6869
Rossland Strath 115 NS4370
Roster Highld 151 ND2639
Rostherne Ches 79 SJ7483
Rosthwaite Cumb 93 NY2514
Roston Derbys 73 SK1241
Rosudgeon Cnwll 2 SW5529
Rosyth Loth 117 NT1182
Rothbury Nthumb 103 NU0501
Rotherby Leics 63 SK6716
Rotherfield E Susx 16 TQ5529
Rotherfield Greys Oxon 37 SU7282
Rotherfield Peppard Oxon 37 SU7082
Rotherham S York 75 SK4392
Rothersthorpe Nhants 49 SP7156
Rotherwick Hants 24 SU7156
Rothes Gramp 141 NJ2749
Rothesay Strath 114 NS0864
Rothiebrisbane Gramp 142 NJ7437
Rothiemay Gramp 142 NJ5448
Rothienorman Gramp 142 NJ7235
Rothley Leics 62 SK5812
Rothley Nthumb 103 NZ0488
Rothmaise Gramp 142 NJ6832
Rothwell Lincs 76 TF1499
Rothwell Nhants 51 SP8181
Rothwell W York 83 SE3428
Rothwell Haigh W York 83 SE3328
Rotsea Humb 84 TA0651
Rottal Tays 134 NO3769
Rottingdean E Susx 15 TQ3602
Rottington Cumb 92 NX9613
Roucan D & G 100 NY0277
Roud IOW 13 SZ5180
Rough Close Staffs 72 SJ9239
Rough Common Kent 29 TR1359
Rougham Norfk 66 TF8320
Rougham Green Suffk 54 TL9061
Roughlee Lancs 81 SD8440
Roughley W Mids 61 SP1399
Roughton Lincs 76 TF2364

Roughton Scholey Hill


Roughton *Norfk* 67 TG2237
Roughton *Shrops* 60 SO7594
Roughway *Kent* 27 TQ6153
Round Bush *Herts* 26 TQ1498
Round Green *Suffk* 53 TL7154
Round Street *Kent* 28 TQ6568
Roundbush *Essex* 40 TL8601
Roundbush Green *Essex* 40 TL5815
Roundham *Somset* 10 ST4209
Roundhay *W York* 83 SE3235
Rounds Green *W Mids* 60 SO9889
Roundstone Foot *D & G* 108 NT1308
Roundstreet Common *W Susx* 14 TQ0528
Roundway *Wilts* 22 SU0163
Roundyhill *Tays* 126 NO3750
Rous Lench *H & W* 47 SP0153
Rousdon *Devon* 10 SY2990
Rousham *Oxon* 49 SP4724
Rout's Green *Bucks* 37 SU7899
Routenbeck *Cumb* 93 NY1930
Routenburn *Strath* 114 NS1961
Routh *Humb* 85 TA0942
Row *Cnwll* 4 SX0976
Row *Cumb* 94 NY6235
Row *Cumb* 87 SD4589
Row Ash *Hants* 13 SU5413
Row Green *Essex* 40 TL7420
Rowanburn *D & G* 101 NY4177
Rowardennan *Cent* 115 NS3698
Rowarth *Derbys* 79 SK0189
Rowberrow *Somset* 21 ST4558
Rowborough *IOW* 13 SZ4685
Rowde *Wilts* 22 ST9762
Rowden *Devon* 8 SX6499
Rowfield *Derbys* 73 SK1949
Rowfoot *Nthumb* 102 NY6860
Rowford *Somset* 20 ST2327
Rowhedge *Essex* 41 TM0321
Rowhook *W Susx* 14 TQ1234
Rowington *Warwks* 48 SP2069
Rowland *Derbys* 74 SK2172
Rowland's Castle *Hants* 13 SU7310
Rowland's Gill *T & W* 96 NZ1658
Rowledge *Surrey* 25 SU8243
Rowley *Dur* 95 NZ0848
Rowley *Humb* 84 SE9732
Rowley *Shrops* 59 SJ3006
Rowley Green *W Mids* 61 SP3483
Rowley Hill *W York* 82 SE1915
Rowley Regis *W Mids* 60 SO9787
Rowlstone *H & W* 46 SO3727
Rowly *Surrey* 14 TQ0441
Rowner *Hants* 13 SU5801
Rowney Green *H & W* 61 SP0471
Rownhams *Hants* 12 SU3817
Rows of Trees *Ches* 79 SJ8379
Rowsham *Bucks* 38 SP8418
Rowsley *Derbys* 74 SK2566
Rowstock *Oxon* 37 SU4788
Rowston *Lincs* 76 TF0856
Rowthorne *Derbys* 75 SK4864
Rowton *Ches* 71 SJ4564
Rowton *Shrops* 59 SO4180
Rowton *Shrops* 59 SJ3612
Rowton *Shrops* 59 SJ6120
Rowtown *Surrey* 26 TQ0363
Roxburgh *Border* 110 NT6930
Roxby *Humb* 84 SE9217
Roxby *N York* 97 NZ7616
Roxton *Beds* 52 TL1554
Roxwell *Essex* 40 TL6408
Roy Bridge *Highld* 131 NN2681
Royal Leamington Spa *Warwks* 48 SP3265
Royal Oak *Dur* 96 NZ2023
Royal Oak *Lancs* 78 SD4103
Royal Tunbridge Wells *Kent* 16 TQ5839
Royal's Green *Ches* 71 SJ6242
Roydhouse *W York* 82 SE2112
Roydon *Essex* 39 TL4009
Roydon *Norfk* 65 TF7023
Roydon *Norfk* 54 TM0980
Roydon Hamlet *Essex* 39 TL4107
Royston *Herts* 39 TL3540
Royston *S York* 83 SE3611
Royton *Gt Man* 79 SD9107
Rozel *Jersey* 152 JS0000
Ruabon *Clwyd* 71 SJ3043
Ruaig *Strath* 120 NM0747
Ruan Lanihorne *Cnwll* 3 SW8942
Ruan Major *Cnwll* 2 SW7016
Ruan Minor *Cnwll* 3 SW7215
Ruardean *Gloucs* 34 SO6117
Ruardean Hill *Gloucs* 35 SO6317
Ruardean Woodside *Gloucs* 35 SO6215
Rubery *H & W* 60 SO9877
Ruckcroft *Cumb* 94 NY5344
Ruckhall Common *H & W* 46 SO4539
Ruckinge *Kent* 17 TR0233
Ruckland *Lincs* 77 TF3378
Ruckley *Shrops* 59 SJ5300
Rudby *N York* 89 NZ4706
Rudchester *Nthumb* 103 NZ1167
Ruddington *Notts* 62 SK5733
Ruddle *Gloucs* 35 SO6811
Ruddlemoor *Cnwll* 3 SX0054
Rudford *Gloucs* 35 SO7721
Rudge *Somset* 22 ST8252
Rudgeway *Avon* 35 ST6386
Rudgwick *W Susx* 14 TQ0833
Rudhall *H & W* 47 SO6225
Rudheath *Ches* 79 SJ7471
Rudley Green *Essex* 40 TL8303
Rudry *M Glam* 33 ST2086
Rudston *Humb* 91 TA0967
Rudway Barton *Devon* 9 SS9301
Rudyard *Staffs* 72 SJ9558
Ruecastle *Border* 110 NT6120
Rufford *Lancs* 80 SD4615
Rufforth *N York* 83 SE5251
Rug *Clwyd* 70 SJ0543
Rugby *Warwks* 50 SP5075
Rugeley *Staffs* 73 SK0418
Ruggaton *Devon* 19 SS5645
Ruishton *Somset* 20 ST2624
Ruislip *Gt Lon* 26 TQ0987
Ruletown Head *Border* 110 NT6113
Rumbach *Gramp* 141 NJ3852
Rumbling Bridge *Tays* 117 NT0199
Rumburgh *Suffk* 55 TM3481
Rumby Hill *Dur* 96 NZ1634
Rumford *Cent* 116 NS9377
Rumford *Cnwll* 4 SW8970
Rumney *S Glam* 33 ST2179
Rumwell *Somset* 20 ST1923
Runcorn *Ches* 78 SJ5182
Runcton *W Susx* 14 SU8802
Runcton Holme *Norfk* 65 TF6109
Runfold *Surrey* 25 SU8747
Runhall *Norfk* 66 TG0507
Runham *Norfk* 67 TG5108
Runham *Norfk* 67 TG4610
Running Waters *Dur* 96 NZ3340
Runnington *Somset* 20 ST1121
Runsell Green *Essex* 40 TL7905
Runshaw Moor *Lancs* 80 SD5319
Runswick *N York* 97 NZ8016
Runtaleave *Tays* 133 NO2867
Runwell *Essex* 40 TQ7594
Ruscombe *Berks* 37 SU8076
Rush Green *Ches* 79 SJ6987
Rush Green *Essex* 41 TM1615
Rush Green *Gt Lon* 27 TQ5187
Rush Green *Herts* 39 TL3325
Rush Green *Herts* 39 TL2123
Rushall *H & W* 47 SO6435
Rushall *Norfk* 55 TM1982
Rushall *W Mids* 60 SK0201
Rushall *Wilts* 23 SU1255
Rushbrooke *Suffk* 54 TL8961
Rushbury *Shrops* 59 SO5092
Rushden *Herts* 39 TL3031
Rushden *Nhants* 51 SP9566
Rushenden *Kent* 28 TQ9071
Rusher's Cross *E Susx* 16 TQ6028
Rushett Common *Surrey* 14 TQ0242
Rushford *Devon* 5 SX4476
Rushford *Norfk* 54 TL9281
Rushlake Green *E Susx* 16 TQ6218
Rushmere *Suffk* 55 TM4987
Rushmere St. Andrew *Suffk* 55 TM1946
Rushmoor *Surrey* 25 SU8740
Rushock *H & W* 46 SO3058
Rushock *H & W* 60 SO8871
Rusholme *Gt Man* 79 SJ8595
Rushton *Ches* 71 SJ5864
Rushton *Nhants* 51 SP8483
Rushton *Shrops* 59 SJ6008
Rushton Spencer *Staffs* 72 SJ9362
Rushwick *H & W* 47 SO8254
Rushyford *Dur* 96 NZ2828
Ruskie *Cent* 116 NN6200
Ruskington *Lincs* 76 TF0850
Rusland *Cumb* 87 SD3488
Rusper *W Susx* 15 TQ2037
Ruspidge *Gloucs* 35 SO6611
Russ Hill *Surrey* 15 TQ2340
Russel's Green *Suffk* 55 TM2572
Russell Green *Essex* 40 TL7413
Russell's Green *E Susx* 16 TQ7011
Russell's Water *Oxon* 37 SU7089
Rusthall *Kent* 16 TQ5639
Rusthall *Kent* 16 TQ5639
Rustington *W Susx* 14 TQ0502
Ruston *N York* 91 SE9583
Ruston Parva *Humb* 91 TA0661
Ruswarp *N York* 90 NZ8809
Ruthall *Shrops* 59 SO5990
Rutherford *Border* 110 NT6430
Rutherglen *Strath* 116 NS6162
Ruthernbridge *Cnwll* 4 SX0166
Ruthin *Clwyd* 70 SJ1258
Ruthrieston *Gramp* 135 NJ9204
Ruthven *Gramp* 142 NJ5046
Ruthven *Highld* 132 NN7699
Ruthven *Highld* 140 NH8132
Ruthven *Tays* 126 NO2848
Ruthven House *Tays* 126 NO3047
Ruthvoes *Cnwll* 4 SW9260
Ruthwaite *Cumb* 93 NY2336
Ruthwell *D & G* 100 NY1067
Ruxley Corner *Gt Lon* 27 TQ4770
Ruxton Green *H & W* 34 SO5419
Ruyton-XI-Towns *Shrops* 59 SJ3922
Ryal *Nthumb* 103 NZ0174
Ryall *Dorset* 10 SY4094
Ryall *H & W* 47 SO8640
Ryarsh *Kent* 28 TQ6660
Rycote *Oxon* 37 SP6705
Rydal *Cumb* 87 NY3606
Ryde *IOW* 13 SZ5992
Rye *E Susx* 17 TQ9220
Rye Cross *H & W* 47 SO7735
Rye Foreign *E Susx* 17 TQ8922
Rye Harbour *E Susx* 17 TQ9319
Rye Street *H & W* 47 SO7835
Ryebank *Shrops* 59 SJ5131
Ryeford *H & W* 35 SO6322
Ryeish Green *Nhants* 24 SU6267
Ryhall *Leics* 64 TF0310
Ryhill *W York* 83 SE3814
Ryhope *T & W* 96 NZ4152
Rylah *Derbys* 75 SK4667
Ryland *Lincs* 76 TF0179
Rylands *Notts* 62 SK5336
Rylstone *N York* 88 SD9658
Ryme Intrinseca *Dorset* 10 ST5810
Ryther *N York* 83 SE5539
Ryton *N York* 90 SE7975
Ryton *Shrops* 60 SJ7602
Ryton *T & W* 103 NZ1564
Ryton *Warwks* 61 SP3986
Ryton Woodside *T & W* 96 NZ1462
Ryton-on-Dunsmore *Warwks* 61 SP3874


# S


Sabden *Lancs* 81 SD7837
Sabine's Green *Essex* 27 TQ5496
Sacombe *Herts* 39 TL3319
Sacombe Green *Herts* 39 TL3419
Sacriston *T & W* 96 NZ2447
Sadberge *Dur* 96 NZ3416
Saddell *Strath* 105 NR7832
Saddington *Leics* 50 SP6591
Saddle Bow *Norfk* 65 TF6015
Saddlescombe *W Susx* 15 TQ2711
Sadgilk *Cumb* 87 NY4805
Saffron Walden *Essex* 39 TL5438
Sageston *Dyfed* 30 SN0503
Saham Hills *Norfk* 66 TF9003
Saham Toney *Norfk* 66 TF9001
Saighton *Ches* 71 SJ4462
Saint Hill *Devon* 9 ST0908
Saint Hill *W Susx* 15 TQ3835
Saintbury *Gloucs* 48 SP1139
Salachail *Strath* 123 NN0551
Salcombe *Devon* 7 SX7338
Salcombe Regis *Devon* 9 SY1588
Salcott *Essex* 40 TL9413
Sale *Gt Man* 79 SJ7991
Sale Green *H & W* 47 SO9358
Saleby *Lincs* 77 TF4578
Salehurst *E Susx* 17 TQ7424
Salem *Dyfed* 44 SN6236
Salem *Dyfed* 43 SN6684
Salem *Gwynd* 69 SH5456
Salen *Highld* 121 NM6864
Salen *Strath* 121 NM5743
Salesbury *Lancs* 81 SD6832
Salford *Beds* 38 SP9339
Salford *Gt Man* 79 SJ8198
Salford *Oxon* 48 SP2828
Salford Priors *Warwks* 48 SP0751
Salfords *Surrey* 15 TQ2846
Salhouse *Norfk* 67 TG3014
Saline *Fife* 117 NT0292
Salisbury *Wilts* 23 SU1429
Salkeld Dykes *Cumb* 94 NY5437
Sall *Norfk* 66 TG1025
Sallachy *Highld* 146 NC5408
Sallachy *Highld* 138 NG9130
Salmonby *Lincs* 77 TF3273
Salmond's Muir *Tays* 127 NO5838
Salperton *Gloucs* 36 SP0720
Salph End *Beds* 38 TL0852
Salsburgh *Strath* 116 NS8262
Salt *Staffs* 72 SJ9527
Salt Cotes *Cumb* 93 NY1853
Salta *Cumb* 92 NY0845
Saltaire *W York* 82 SE1337
Saltash *Cnwll* 6 SX4258
Saltburn *Highld* 146 NH7270
Saltburn-by-the-Sea *Cleve* 97 NZ6621
Saltby *Leics* 63 SK8526
Saltcoats *Cumb* 86 SD0797
Saltcoats *Lancs* 80 SD3728
Saltcoats *Strath* 106 NS2441
Saltdean *E Susx* 15 TQ3802
Salter *Lancs* 87 SD6063
Salterbeck *Cumb* 92 NX9926
Salterbeck *Cumb* 92 NX9926
Salterforth *IOM* 81 SD8845
Salterswall *Ches* 71 SJ6266
Salterton *Wilts* 23 SU1236
Salterton *Wilts* 23 SU1236
Saltfleet *Lincs* 77 TF4593
Saltfleetby All Saints *Lincs* 77 TF4590
Saltfleetby St. Clements *Lincs* 77 TF4591
Saltfleetby St. Peter *Lincs* 77 TF4489
Saltford *Avon* 22 ST6867
Salthouse *Norfk* 66 TG0743
Saltley *W Mids* 61 SP0987
Saltmarsh *Gwent* 34 ST3483
Saltmarshe *Humb* 84 SE7824
Saltney *Ches* 71 SJ3865
Salton *N York* 90 SE7179
Saltrens *Devon* 18 SS4521
Saltwick *Nthumb* 103 NZ1780
Saltwood *Kent* 29 TR1535
Salvington *W Susx* 15 TQ1305
Salwarpe *H & W* 47 SO8762
Salwayash *Dorset* 10 SY4596
Sambourne *Warwks* 48 SP0662
Sambrook *Shrops* 72 SJ7124
Samlesbury *Lancs* 81 SD5930
Samlesbury Bottoms *Lancs* 81 SD6229
Sampford Arundel *Somset* 20 ST1018
Sampford Brett *Somset* 20 ST0941
Sampford Courtnay *Devon* 8 SS6301
Sampford Moor *Somset* 20 ST1118
Sampford Peverell *Devon* 9 ST0214
Sampford Spiney *Devon* 6 SX5372
Samson's Corner *Essex* 41 TM0818
Samsonlane *Ork* 155 HY6525
Samuelston *Loth* 118 NT4870
Sanaigmore *Strath* 112 NR2370
Sancreed *Cnwll* 2 SW4129
Sancton *Humb* 84 SE8939
Sand *Somset* 21 ST4346
Sand Cross *E Susx* 16 TQ5820
Sand Hills *W York* 83 SE3739
Sand Hole *Humb* 84 SE8037
Sand Hutton *N York* 90 SE6958
Sand Side *Cumb* 86 SD2282
Sandaig *Highld* 129 NG7102
Sandal Magna *W York* 83 SE3417
Sandale *Cumb* 93 NY2440
Sandavore *Highld* 128 NM4785
Sandbach *Ches* 72 SJ7560
Sandbank *Strath* 114 NS1580
Sandbanks *Dorset* 12 SZ0487
Sandend *Gramp* 142 NJ5566
Sanderstead *Gt Lon* 27 TQ3461
Sandford *Avon* 21 ST4159
Sandford *Cumb* 94 NY7216
Sandford *Devon* 8 SS8202
Sandford *Dorset* 11 SY9289
Sandford *Hants* 12 SU1601
Sandford *IOW* 13 SZ5481
Sandford *Shrops* 59 SJ3423
Sandford *Shrops* 59 SJ5834
Sandford *Strath* 107 NS7143
Sandford Batch *Avon* 21 ST4158
Sandford Orcas *Dorset* 21 ST6220
Sandford St. Martin *Oxon* 49 SP4226
Sandford-on-Thames *Oxon* 37 SP5301
Sandgate *Kent* 29 TR2035
Sandhaven *Gramp* 143 NJ9667
Sandhead *D & G* 98 NX0949
Sandhill *S York* 75 SK4496
Sandhills *Dorset* 10 ST5800
Sandhills *Dorset* 11 ST6710
Sandhills *Oxon* 37 SP5507
Sandhills *Staffs* 61 SK0604
Sandhills *Surrey* 25 SU9438
Sandhoe *Nthumb* 102 NY9666
Sandhole *Strath* 114 NS0098
Sandholme *Humb* 84 SE8230
Sandholme *Lincs* 64 TF3337
Sandhurst *Berks* 25 SU8361
Sandhurst *Gloucs* 47 SO8223
Sandhurst *Kent* 17 TQ8028
Sandhurst Cross *Kent* 17 TQ7827
Sandhutton *N York* 89 SE3881
Sandiacre *Derbys* 62 SK4736
Sandilands *Lincs* 77 TF5280
Sandiway *Ches* 71 SJ6070
Sandleheath *Hants* 12 SU1214
Sandley *Dorset* 22 ST7724
Sandling *Kent* 28 TQ7557
Sandlow Green *Ches* 72 SJ7865
Sandness *Shet* 155 HU1957
Sandon *Essex* 40 TL7404
Sandon *Herts* 39 TL3234
Sandon *Staffs* 72 SJ9429
Sandon Bank *Staffs* 72 SJ9428
Sandown *IOW* 13 SZ5984
Sandplace *Cnwll* 5 SX2556
Sandridge *Herts* 39 TL1710
Sandridge *Wilts* 22 ST9465
Sandringham *Norfk* 65 TF6928
Sands *Bucks* 37 SU8393
Sandsend *N York* 90 NZ8612
Sandside House *Highld* 150 NC9565
Sandtoft *Humb* 84 SE7408
Sandwich *Kent* 29 TR3358
Sandwick *Cumb* 93 NY4219
Sandwick *Shet* 155 HU4323
Sandwith *Cumb* 92 NX9615
Sandwith Newtown *Cumb* 92 NX9614
Sandy *Beds* 52 TL1649
Sandy Bank *Lincs* 77 TF2654
Sandy Cross *H & W* 47 SO6757
Sandy Haven *Dyfed* 30 SM8507
Sandy Lane *Clwyd* 71 SJ4040
Sandy Lane *W York* 82 SE1136
Sandy Lane *Wilts* 22 ST9668
Sandy Park *Devon* 8 SX7189
Sandycroft *Clwyd* 71 SJ3366
Sandyford *D & G* 101 NY2093
Sandygate *Devon* 7 SX8674
Sandygate *IOM* 153 SC3797
Sandylands *Lancs* 87 SD4163
Sandylane *Staffs* 72 SJ7035
Sandylane *W Glam* 32 SS5589
Sandystones *Border* 110 NT5926
Sandyway *H & W* 46 SO4925
Sangobeg *Highld* 149 NC4266
Sangomore *Highld* 149 NC4067
Sankey Bridges *Ches* 78 SJ5887
Sankyn's Green *H & W* 47 SO7964
Sanna Bay *Highld* 128 NM4469
Santon *Cumb* 86 NY1001
Santon *IOM* 153 SC3171
Santon Bridge *Cumb* 86 NY1101
Santon Downham *Suffk* 54 TL8187
Sapcote *Leics* 50 SP4993
Sapey Common *H & W* 47 SO7064
Sapiston *Suffk* 54 TL9175
Sapley *Cambs* 52 TL2474
Sapperton *Derbys* 73 SK1834
Sapperton *Gloucs* 35 SO9403
Sapperton *Lincs* 64 TF0133
Saracen's Head *Lincs* 64 TF3427
Sarclet *Highld* 151 ND3443
Sarisbury *Hants* 13 SU5008
Sarn *Gwynd* 56 SH2432
Sarn *Gwynd* 56 SH2432
Sarn *M Glam* 33 SS9184
Sarn *Powys* 58 SN9597
Sarn *Powys* 58 SO2091
Sarn-bach *Gwynd* 56 SH3026
Sarn-wen *Powys* 58 SJ2718
Sarnau *Dyfed* 42 SN3151
Sarnau *Dyfed* 31 SN3318
Sarnau *Gwynd* 70 SH9739
Sarnau *Powys* 58 SJ2315
Sarnau *Powys* 45 SO0232
Sarnesfield *H & W* 46 SO3750
Saron *Dyfed* 31 SN3737
Saron *Dyfed* 32 SN6012
Saron *Gwynd* 69 SH5365
Sarratt *Herts* 26 TQ0499
Sarre *Kent* 29 TR2565
Sarsden *Oxon* 36 SP2822
Sarson *Hants* 23 SU3044
Sartfield *IOM* 153 SC3599
Satley *Dur* 95 NZ1143
Satmar *Kent* 29 TR2539
Satron *N York* 88 SD9397
Satterleigh *Devon* 19 SS6622
Satterthwaite *Cumb* 86 SD3392
Satwell *Oxon* 37 SU7083
Sauchen *Gramp* 135 NJ7011
Saucher *Tays* 126 NO1933
Sauchieburn *Gramp* 135 NO6669
Saughtree *Border* 101 NY5696
Saul *Gloucs* 35 SO7409
Saundby *Notts* 75 SK7888
Saundersfoot *Dyfed* 31 SN1304
Saunderton *Bucks* 37 SP7901
Saunton *Devon* 18 SS4637
Sausthorpe *Lincs* 77 TF3868
Saveock Water *Cnwll* 3 SW7645
Saverley Green *Staffs* 72 SJ9638
Savile Town *W York* 82 SE2420
Sawbridge *Warwks* 50 SP5065
Sawbridgeworth *Herts* 39 TL4814
Sawdon *N York* 91 SE9485
Sawley *Derbys* 62 SK4731
Sawley *Lancs* 81 SD7746
Sawley *N York* 89 SE2467
Sawry *Cumb* 87 SD3795
Sawston *Cambs* 53 TL4849
Sawtry *Cambs* 52 TL1683
Saxby *Leics* 63 SK8219
Saxby *Lincs* 76 TF0086
Saxby *W Susx* 14 SU9604
Saxby All Saints *Humb* 84 SE9816
Saxelbye *Leics* 63 SK7021
Saxham Street *Suffk* 54 TM0861
Saxilby *Lincs* 76 SK8875
Saxlingham *Norfk* 66 TG0239
Saxlingham Green *Norfk* 67 TM2496
Saxlingham Nethergate *Norfk* 67 TM2397
Saxlingham Thorpe *Norfk* 67 TM2198
Saxmundham *Suffk* 55 TM3863
Saxon Street *Cambs* 53 TL6579
Saxondale *Notts* 63 SK6839
Saxtead *Suffk* 55 TM2665
Saxtead Green *Suffk* 55 TM2564
Saxtead Little Green *Suffk* 55 TM2566
Saxthorpe *Norfk* 66 TG1130
Saxton *N York* 83 SE4736
Sayers Common *W Susx* 15 TQ2618
Scackleton *N York* 90 SE6472
Scaftworth *Notts* 75 SK6691
Scagglethorpe *N York* 90 SE8372
Scalasaig *Strath* 112 NR3994
Scalby *Humb* 84 SE8530
Scalby *N York* 91 TA0190
Scald End *Beds* 51 TL0457
Scaldwell *Nhants* 50 SP7672
Scale Houses *Cumb* 94 NY5845
Scaleby *Cumb* 101 NY4463
Scalebyhill *Cumb* 101 NY4363
Scales *Cumb* 93 NY3427
Scales *Cumb* 86 SD2772
Scales *Lancs* 80 SD4531
Scalesceugh *Cumb* 93 NY4450
Scalford *Leics* 63 SK7624
Scaling *N York* 90 NZ7413
Scaling Dam *N York* 90 NZ7412
Scalloway *Shet* 155 HU4039
Scalpay *W Isls* 154 NG2395
Scamblesby *Lincs* 77 TF2778
Scammonden *W York* 82 SE0515
Scamodale *Highld* 129 NM8373
Scampston *N York* 90 SE8575
Scampton *Lincs* 76 SK9479
Scancroft Hill *W York* 83 SE3741
Scaniport *Highld* 140 NH6239
Scapegoat Hill *W York* 82 SE0916
Scarborough *N York* 91 TA0388
Scarcewater *Cnwll* 3 SW9154
Scarcliffe *Derbys* 75 SK4968
Scarcroft *W York* 83 SE3540
Scarfskerry *Highld* 151 ND2674
Scargill *Dur* 88 NZ0510
Scarinish *Strath* 120 NM0444
Scarisbrick *Lancs* 80 SD3813
Scarness *Cumb* 93 NY2130
Scarning *Norfk* 66 TF9512
Scarrington *Notts* 63 SK7341
Scarth Hill *Lancs* 78 SD4206
Scarthingwell *N York* 83 SE4837
Scartho *Humb* 85 TA2606
Scawby *Humb* 84 SE9605
Scawsby *S York* 83 SE5305
Scawthorpe *S York* 83 SE5506
Scawton *N York* 90 SE5483
Scayne's Hill *W Susx* 15 TQ3623
Scethrog *Powys* 45 SO1025
Scholar Green *Staffs* 72 SJ8357
Scholes *Gt Man* 78 SD5905
Scholes *S York* 74 SK3896
Scholes *W York* 82 SE1507
Scholes *W York* 82 SE1726
Scholes *W York* 83 SE3736
Scholey Hill *W York* 83 SE3825

School Aycliffe Shrub End


School Aycliffe Dur 96 NZ2523
School Green Ches 72 SJ6464
School Green W York 82 SE1132
School House Dorset 10 ST3602
Schoolgreen Berks 24 SU6367
Scissett W York 82 SE2510
Scleddau Dyfed 30 SM9434
Sco Ruston Norfk 67 TG2822
Scofton Notts 75 SK6280
Scole Norfk 54 TM1579
Sconser Highld 137 NG5131
Scoonie Fife 126 NO3801
Scopwick Lincs 76 TF0757
Scoraig Highld 144 NH0096
Scorborough Humb 84 TA0145
Scorrier Cnwll 3 SW7244
Scorriton Devon 7 SX7068
Scorton Lancs 80 SD5048
Scorton N York 89 NZ2500
Scot Hay Staffs 72 SJ8047
Scot Lane End Gt Man 79 SD6209
Scot's Gap Nthumb 103 NZ0386
Scotby Cumb 93 NY4455
Scotch Corner N York 89 NZ2105
Scotforth Lancs 87 SD4859
Scothern Lincs 76 TF0377
Scotland Lincs 63 TF0030
Scotland W York 82 SE2340
Scotland Gate T & W 103 NZ2584
Scotlandwell Tays 126 NO1801
Scotsburn Highld 146 NH7275
Scotscalder Highld 151 ND0956
Scotscraig Fife 127 NO4428
Scotsdike Cumb 101 NY3872
Scotsmill Gramp 142 NJ5618
Scotsmill Gramp 142 NJ5618
Scotstoun Strath 115 NS5367
Scotswood T & W 103 NZ2064
Scotter Lincs 76 SE8800
Scotterthorpe Lincs 84 SE8701
Scottlethorpe Lincs 64 TF0520
Scotton Lincs 76 SK8899
Scotton N York 89 SE1895
Scotton N York 89 SE3259
Scottow Norfk 67 TG2823
Scoughall Loth 118 NT6183
Scoulton Norfk 66 TF9800
Scounslow Green Staffs 73 SK0929
Scourie Highld 148 NC1544
Scouriemore Highld 148 NC1443
Scousburgh Shet 155 HU3717
Scouthead Gt Man 79 SD9605
Scrabster Highld 151 ND1070
Scraesburgh Border 110 NT6718
Scrafield Lincs 77 TF3069
Scrainwood Nthumb 111 NT9808
Scrane End Lincs 64 TF3841
Scraptoft Leics 63 SK6405
Scratby Norfk 67 TG5115
Scrayingham N York 90 SE7360
Scrays E Susx 17 TQ7619
Scredington Lincs 64 TF0940
Screel D & G 92 NX7953
Scremby Lincs 77 TF4467
Scremerston Nthumb 111 NU0148
Screveton Notts 63 SK7343
Scrivelby Lincs 77 TF2766
Scriven N York 89 SE3458
Scrooby Notts 75 SK6590
Scropton Derbys 73 SK1930
Scrub Hill Lincs 76 TF2355
Scruschloch Tays 133 NO2357
Scruton N York 89 SE2992
Scuggate Cumb 101 NY4474
Sculthorpe Norfk 66 TF8931
Scunthorpe Humb 84 SE8910
Scurlage W Glam 32 SS4687
Sea Somset 10 ST3412
Sea Palling Norfk 67 TG4226
Seaborough Dorset 10 ST4205
Seabridge Staffs 72 SJ8343
Seabrook Kent 29 TR1835
Seaburn T & W 96 NZ4160
Seacombe Mersyd 78 SJ3290
Seacroft Lincs 77 TF5661
Seacroft W York 83 SE3536
Seafield Highld 136 NG4743
Seafield Loth 117 NT0066
Seaford E Susx 16 TV4899
Seaforth Mersyd 78 SJ3297
Seagrave Leics 62 SK6217
Seagry Heath Wilts 35 ST9581
Seaham Dur 96 NZ4149
Seahouses Nthumb 111 NU2232
Seal Kent 27 TQ5556
Seale Surrey 25 SU8947
Seamer N York 90 NZ4910
Seamer N York 91 TA0183
Seamill Strath 114 NS2047
Searby Lincs 84 TA0605
Seasalter Kent 29 TR0864
Seascale Cumb 86 NY0301
Seathwaite Cumb 93 NY2312
Seathwaite Cumb 86 SD2296
Seatoller Cumb 93 NY2414
Seaton Cnwll 5 SX3054
Seaton Cumb 92 NY0130
Seaton Devon 9 SY2490
Seaton Dur 96 NZ3949
Seaton Humb 85 TA1646
Seaton Kent 29 TR2258
Seaton Leics 51 SP9098
Seaton Nthumb 103 NZ3276
Seaton Burn T & W 103 NZ2373
Seaton Carew Cleve 97 NZ5229
Seaton Delaval Nthumb 103 NZ3075
Seaton Ross Humb 84 SE7740
Seaton Sluice Nthumb 103 NZ3376
Seatown Dorset 10 SY4191
Seave Green N York 90 NZ5600
Seaview IOW 13 SZ6291
Seaville Cumb 92 NY1553
Seavington St. Mary Somset 10 ST4014
Seavington St. Michael Somset 10 ST4015
Sebastopol Gwent 34 ST2998
Sebergham Cumb 93 NY3542
Seckington Warwks 61 SK2607
Sedbergh Cumb 87 SD6592
Sedbury Gloucs 34 ST5493
Sedbusk N York 88 SD8891
Sedgeberrow H & W 48 SP0238
Sedgebrook Lincs 63 SK8537
Sedgefield Dur 96 NZ3528
Sedgeford Norfk 65 TF7136
Sedgehill Wilts 22 ST8627
Sedgley W Mids 60 SO9193
Sedgley Park Gt Man 79 SD8202
Sedgwick Cumb 87 SD5186
Sedlescombe E Susx 17 TQ7818
Sedrup Bucks 38 SP7911
Seed Kent 28 TQ9456
Seend Wilts 22 ST9461
Seend Cleeve Wilts 22 ST9360
Seer Green Bucks 26 SU9691
Seething Norfk 67 TM3197
Sefton Mersyd 78 SD3501
Sefton Town Mersyd 78 SD3400
Seghill Nthumb 103 NZ2874
Seighford Staffs 72 SJ8725
Seilebost W Isls 154 NG0696
Seion Gwynd 69 SH5467
Seisdon Staffs 60 SO8495
Selattyn Shrops 58 SJ2633
Selborne Hants 24 SU7433
Selby N York 83 SE6132
Selham W Susx 14 SU9320
Selkirk Border 109 NT4728
Sellack H & W 46 SO5627
Sellafirth Shet 155 HU5297
Sellan Cnwll 2 SW4230
Sellick's Green Somset 20 ST2119
Sellindge Kent 29 TR0938
Selling Kent 28 TR0456
Sells Green Wilts 22 ST9462
Selly Oak W Mids 61 SP0482
Selmeston E Susx 16 TQ5007
Selsden Gt Lon 27 TQ3562
Selsey W Susx 14 SZ8593
Selsfield Common Gwynd 15 TQ3434
Selside Cumb 87 SD5298
Selside Gt Lon 27 TQ3267
Selside N York 88 SD7875
Selstead Kent 29 TR2144
Selston Notts 75 SK4653
Selworthy Somset 20 SS9146
Semer Suffk 54 TL9947
Semington Wilts 22 ST8960
Semley Wilts 22 ST8926
Send Surrey 26 TQ0255
Send Marsh Surrey 26 TQ0455
Senghenydd M Glam 33 ST1190
Sennen Cnwll 2 SW3525
Sennen Cove Cnwll 2 SW3526
Sennybridge Powys 45 SN9228
Serlby Notts 75 SK6389
Sessay N York 89 SE4575
Setchey Norfk 65 TF6313
Setley Hants 12 SU3000
Seton Mains Loth 118 NT4275
Setting Stones Nthumb 102 NY8468
Settle N York 88 SD8163
Settle N York 88 SD8163
Settrington N York 90 SE8370
Seven Ash Somset 20 ST1533
Seven Ash Somset 20 ST1533
Seven Kings Gt Lon 27 TQ4587
Seven Sisters W Glam 33 SN8208
Seven Springs Gloucs 35 SO9617
Seven Wells Gloucs 48 SP1134
Sevenhampton Gloucs 36 SP0321
Sevenhampton Wilts 36 SU2090
Sevenoaks Kent 27 TQ5255
Sevenoaks Weald Kent 27 TQ5250
Sever Star Green Essex 40 TL9326
Severn Beach Avon 34 ST5484
Severn Stoke H & W 47 SO8544
Sevicks End Beds 51 TL0954
Sevington Kent 28 TR0340
Sewards End Essex 53 TL5738
Sewardstonebury Gt Lon 27 TQ3995
Sewell Beds 38 SP9922
Sewerby Humb 91 TA2068
Seworgan Cnwll 2 SW7030
Sewstern Leics 63 SK8821
Sexhow N York 89 NZ4706
Sezincote Gloucs 48 SP1731
Shabbington Bucks 37 SP6606
Shacklecross Derbys 62 SK4234
Shackleford Surrey 25 SU9345
Shade W York 81 SD9323
Shader W Isls 154 NB3854
Shadforth Dur 96 NZ3441
Shadingfield Suffk 55 TM4384
Shadoxhurst Kent 28 TQ9737
Shadwell Norfk 54 TL9383
Shadwell W York 83 SE3439
Shaftenhoe End Herts 39 TL4037
Shaftesbury Dorset 22 ST8622
Shaftholme S York 83 SE5708
Shafton S York 83 SE3812
Shafton Two Gates S York 82 SE2910
Shalbourne Wilts 23 SU3163
Shalcombe IOW 13 SZ3985
Shalden Hants 24 SU6941
Shalden Green Hants 24 SU6943
Shaldon Devon 7 SX9372
Shalfleet IOW 13 SZ4189
Shalford Essex 40 TL7229
Shalford Surrey 25 TQ0047
Shalford Green Essex 40 TL7127
Shallowford Devon 19 SS7144
Shallowford Staffs 72 SJ8729
Shalmsford Street Kent 29 TR0954
Shalstone Bucks 49 SP6436
Shamley Green Surrey 14 TQ0343
Shandford Tays 134 NO4962
Shandon Strath 114 NS2586
Shandwick Highld 147 NH8575
Shangton Leics 50 SP7196
Shank End Border 109 NT5205
Shankhouse Nthumb 103 NZ2778
Shanklin IOW 13 SZ5881
Shap Cumb 94 NY5615
Shapwick Dorset 11 ST9301
Shapwick Somset 21 ST4137
Shard End W Mids 61 SP1588
Shardlow Derbys 62 SK4330
Shareshill Staffs 60 SJ9406
Sharkham Point Devon 7 SX9354
Sharlston W York 83 SE3818
Sharlston Common W York 83 SE3919
Sharman's Cross W Mids 61 SP1379
Sharnal Street Kent 28 TQ7974
Sharnbrook Beds 51 SP9959
Sharneyford Lancs 81 SD8824
Sharnford Leics 50 SP4891
Sharnhill Green Dorset 11 ST7105
Sharoe Green Lancs 80 SD5333
Sharow N York 89 SE3371
Sharp Green Norfk 67 TG3820
Sharpenhoe Beds 38 TL0630
Sharperton Nthumb 102 NT9503
Sharpness Gloucs 35 SO6702
Sharptor Cnwll 5 SX2573
Sharpway Gate H & W 47 SO9565
Sharrington Norfk 66 TG0337
Shatterford H & W 60 SO7981
Shatterling Kent 29 TR2658
Shaugh Prior Devon 6 SX5463
Shaughlaige-e-Caine IOM 153 SC3187
Shave Cross Dorset 10 SY4198
Shavington Ches 72 SJ6951
Shaw Berks 24 SU4768
Shaw Gt Man 79 SD9309
Shaw W York 82 SE0235
Shaw Wilts 22 ST8865
Shaw Wilts 36 SU1185
Shaw Common Gloucs 47 SO6927
Shaw Green Herts 39 TL2932
Shaw Green Lancs 80 SD5218
Shaw Green Lancs 80 SD5218
Shaw Green N York 82 SE2652
Shaw Hill Lancs 81 SD5721
Shaw Mills N York 89 SE2562
Shawbost W Isls 154 NB2646
Shawbury Shrops 59 SJ5521
Shawclough Gt Man 81 SD8914
Shawdon Hill Nthumb 111 NU0813
Shawell Leics 50 SP5480
Shawford Hants 13 SU4624
Shawforth Lancs 81 SD8920
Shawhead D & G 100 NX8676
Shawton Strath 116 NS6749
Shear Cross Wilts 22 ST8642
Shearington D & G 100 NY0266
Shearsby Leics 50 SP6291
Shebbear Devon 18 SS4309
Shebdon Staffs 72 SJ7625
Shebster Highld 150 ND0164
Shedfield Hants 13 SU5513
Sheen Derbys 74 SK1161
Sheep Hill Dur 96 NZ1757
Sheep-ridge W York 82 SE1519
Sheepbridge Derbys 74 SK3674
Sheepscar W York 82 SE3134
Sheepscombe Gloucs 35 SO8910
Sheepstor Devon 6 SX5667
Sheepwash Devon 18 SS4806
Sheepwash Nthumb 103 NZ2585
Sheepway Avon 34 ST4976
Sheepy Magna Leics 61 SK3201
Sheepy Parva Leics 62 SK3301
Sheering Essex 39 TL5014
Sheerness Kent 28 TQ9174
Sheerwater Surrey 26 TQ0461
Sheet Hants 13 SU7524
Sheffield Cnwll 2 SW4526
Sheffield S York 74 SK3587
Sheffield Bottom Berks 24 SU6469
Sheffield Green E Susx 15 TQ4125
Shefford Beds 38 TL1439
Shegra Highld 148 NC1860
Sheinton Shrops 59 SJ6104
Shelderton Shrops 46 SO4077
Sheldon Derbys 74 SK1768
Sheldon Devon 9 ST1208
Sheldon W Mids 61 SP1584
Sheldwich Kent 28 TR0156
Sheldwich Lees Kent 28 TR0156
Shelf W York 82 SE1228
Shelfanger Norfk 54 TM1083
Shelfield W Mids 61 SK0302
Shelfield Warwks 48 SP1263
Shelfield Green Warwks 48 SP1262
Shelford Notts 63 SK6642
Shelford Warwks 50 SP4289
Shellacres Border 110 NT8943
Shelley Essex 39 TL5505
Shelley Suffk 54 TM0338
Shelley W York 82 SE2011
Shelley Far Bank W York 82 SE2010
Shellingford Oxon 36 SU3193
Shellow Bowells Essex 40 TL6108
Shelsley Beauchamp H & W 47 SO7363
Shelsley Walsh H & W 47 SO7263
Shelston D & G 100 NX8285
Shelton Beds 51 TL0368
Shelton Norfk 67 TM2291
Shelton Notts 63 SK7844
Shelton Shrops 59 SJ4613
Shelton Green Norfk 55 TM2390
Shelton Lock Derbys 62 SK3731
Shelton Under Harley Staffs 72 SJ8139
Shelve Shrops 59 SO3399
Shelwick H & W 46 SO5242
Shenfield Essex 40 TQ6095
Shenington Oxon 48 SP3742
Shenley Herts 26 TL1800
Shenley Brook End Bucks 38 SP8335
Shenley Church End Bucks 38 SP8336
Shenleybury Herts 39 TL1803
Shenmore H & W 46 SO3937
Shennanton D & G 98 NX3463
Shenstone H & W 60 SO8673
Shenstone Staffs 61 SK1004
Shenstone Woodend Staffs 61 SK1101
Shenton Leics 61 SK3800
Shepeau Stow Lincs 64 TF3012
Sheperdswell Kent 29 TR2647
Shephall Herts 39 TL2623
Shepherd's Bush Gt Lon 26 TQ2379
Shepherds Cnwll 3 SW8154
Shepherds Green Oxon 37 SU7183
Shepherds Patch Gloucs 35 SO7304
Shepley W York 82 SE1909
Shepperdine Avon 35 ST6295
Shepperton Surrey 26 TQ0776
Shepperton Green Surrey 26 TQ0768
Shepreth Cambs 52 TL3947
Shepshed Leics 62 SK4719
Shepton Beauchamp Somset 10 ST4016
Shepton Mallet Somset 21 ST6143
Shepton Montague Somset 22 ST6731
Shepway Kent 28 TQ7753
Sheraton Dur 96 NZ4435
Sherborne Dorset 10 ST6316
Sherborne Gloucs 36 SP1714
Sherborne Somset 21 ST5855
Sherborne Causeway Dorset 22 ST8323
Sherborne St. John Hants 24 SU6255
Sherbourne Warwks 48 SP2661
Sherburn Dur 96 NZ3142
Sherburn N York 91 SE9577
Sherburn Hill Dur 96 NZ3342
Sherburn in Elmet N York 83 SE4933
Shere Surrey 14 TQ0747
Shereford Norfk 66 TF8829
Sherfield English Hants 23 SU2922
Sherfield English Hants 23 SU2922
Sherfield on Loddon Hants 24 SU6757
Sherfin Lancs 81 SD7925
Sherford Devon 7 SX7844
Sherford Dorset 11 SY9193
Sheriff Hutton N York 90 SE6566
Sheriffhales Shrops 60 SJ7512
Sheringham Norfk 66 TG1543
Sherington Bucks 38 SP8846
Shermanbury W Susx 15 TQ2019
Shernborne Norfk 65 TF7132
Sherril Devon 7 SX6774
Sherrington Wilts 22 ST9638
Sherston Wilts 35 ST8585
Sherwood Notts 62 SK5743
Sherwood Green Devon 19 SS5520
Shettleston Strath 116 NS6464
Shevington Gt Man 78 SD5408
Shevington Moor Gt Man 78 SD5410
Shevington Vale Gt Man 78 SD5309
Sheviock Cnwll 5 SX3655
Shewglie Highld 139 NH4129
Shibden Head W York 82 SE0929
Shide IOW 13 SZ4988
Shidlaw Nthumb 110 NT8038
Shiel Bridge Highld 138 NG9318
Shieldaig Highld 137 NG8153
Shieldhill Cent 116 NS8976
Shieldhill D & G 100 NY0385
Shieldhill Strath 108 NT0040
Shields Strath 116 NS7755
Shielhill Strath 114 NS2471
Shielhill Tays 134 NO4257
Shifford Oxon 36 SP3701
Shifnal Shrops 60 SJ7407
Shilbottle Nthumb 111 NU1908
Shildon Dur 96 NZ2326
Shillingford Devon 20 SS9723
Shillingford Oxon 37 SU5992
Shillingford Abbot Devon 9 SX9187
Shillingford St. George Devon 9 SX9087
Shillingstone Dorset 11 ST8211
Shillington Beds 38 TL1234
Shillmoor Nthumb 110 NT8807
Shiltenish W Isls 154 NB2819
Shilton Oxon 36 SP2608
Shilton Warwks 61 SP4084
Shilvinghampton Dorset 10 SY6284
Shimpling Norfk 54 TM1583
Shimpling Suffk 54 TL8651
Shimpling Street Suffk 54 TL8753
Shincliffe Dur 96 NZ2940
Shiney Row T & W 96 NZ3252
Shinfield Berks 24 SU7368
Shingay Cambs 52 TL3046
Shingle Street Suffk 55 TM3642
Shinnersbridge Devon 7 SX7863
Shinness Highld 146 NC5215
Shipbourne Kent 27 TQ5952
Shipbrookhill Ches 79 SJ6771
Shipdham Norfk 66 TF9607
Shipham Somset 21 ST4457
Shiphay Devon 7 SX8965
Shiplake Oxon 37 SU7678
Shiplake Row Oxon 37 SU7478
Shipley Nthumb 111 NU1416
Shipley Shrops 60 SO8096
Shipley W Susx 15 TQ1422
Shipley W York 82 SE1437
Shipley Bridge Surrey 15 TQ3040
Shipley Hatch Kent 28 TR0038
Shipmeadow Suffk 55 TM3890
Shippea Hill Halt Cambs 53 TL6484
Shippon Oxon 37 SU4898
Shipston on Stour Warwks 48 SP2540
Shipton Bucks 49 SP7727
Shipton Gloucs 36 SP0318
Shipton N York 90 SE5558
Shipton Shrops 59 SO5692
Shipton Bellinger Hants 23 SU2345
Shipton Gorge Dorset 10 SY4991
Shipton Green W Susx 14 SU8000
Shipton Moyne Gloucs 35 ST8989
Shipton-on-Cherwell Oxon 37 SP4617
Shipton-under-Wychwood Oxon 36 SP2717
Shiptonthorpe Humb 84 SE8543
Shirburn Oxon 37 SU6995
Shirdley Hill Lancs 80 SD3612
Shire Cumb 94 NY6135
Shire Oak W Mids 61 SK0504
Shirebrook Notts 75 SK5267
Shiregreen S York 74 SK3691
Shirehampton Avon 34 ST5377
Shiremoor T & W 103 NZ3171
Shirenewton Gwent 34 ST4793
Shireoaks Notts 75 SK5580
Shirkoak Kent 17 TQ9435
Shirl Heath H & W 46 SO4359
Shirland Derbys 74 SK3958
Shirlett Shrops 59 SO6597
Shirley Derbys 73 SK2141
Shirley Gt Lon 27 TQ3565
Shirley Hants 13 SU4013
Shirley W Mids 61 SP1278
Shirrell Heath Hants 13 SU5714
Shirven Strath 113 NR8784
Shirwell Devon 19 SS6037
Shirwell Cross Devon 19 SS5937
Shittlehope Dur 95 NZ0038
Shobdon H & W 46 SO4062
Shobley Hants 12 SU1806
Shobrooke Devon 9 SS8600
Shoby Leics 63 SK6820
Shocklach Green Ches 71 SJ4349
Shocklach Green Ches 71 SJ4349
Shoeburyness Essex 40 TQ9484
Sholden Kent 29 TR3552
Sholing Hants 13 SU4511
Shoose Cumb 92 NY0127
Shoot Hill Shrops 59 SJ4112
Shop Cnwll 18 SS2214
Shop Cnwll 4 SW8773
Shop Street Suffk 55 TM2268
Shopwyke W Susx 14 SU8805
Shore Gt Man 81 SD9217
Shoreditch Gt Lon 27 TQ3382
Shoreditch Somset 20 ST2422
Shoreham Kent 27 TQ5261
Shoreham-by-Sea W Susx 15 TQ2105
Shoreswood Nthumb 110 NT9446
Shorley Hants 13 SU5726
Shorncote Gloucs 35 SU0296
Shorne Kent 28 TQ6971
Shorne Ridgeway Kent 28 TQ6970
Short Heath W Mids 60 SJ9701
Short Heath W Mids 61 SP0992
Shorta Cross Cnwll 5 SX2857
Shortbridge E Susx 16 TQ4521
Shortfield Common Surrey 25 SU8442
Shortgate E Susx 16 TQ4915
Shortlanesend Cnwll 3 SW8047
Shorwell IOW 13 SZ4582
Shoscombe Avon 22 ST7156
Shotesham Norfk 67 TM2599
Shotgate Essex 40 TQ7593
Shotley Suffk 55 TM2335
Shotley Bridge Nthumb 95 NZ0853
Shotley Gate Suffk 41 TM2433
Shotley Street Suffk 55 TM2335
Shotleyfield Nthumb 95 NZ0653
Shottenden Kent 28 TR0454
Shottermill Surrey 14 SU8832
Shottery Warwks 48 SP1954
Shotteswell Warwks 49 SP4245
Shottisham Suffk 55 TM3244
Shottle Derbys 74 SK3149
Shottlegate Derbys 62 SK3147
Shotton Clwyd 71 SJ3168
Shotton Dur 96 NZ3625
Shotton Dur 96 NZ4139
Shotton Nthumb 103 NZ2277
Shotton Nthumb 110 NT8430
Shotwick Ches 71 SJ3472
Shougle Gramp 141 NJ2155
Shouldham Norfk 65 TF6709
Shouldham Thorpe Norfk 65 TF6607
Shoulton H & W 47 SO8158
Shover's Green E Susx 16 TQ6530
Shraleybrook Staffs 72 SJ7849
Shrawardine Shrops 59 SJ3915
Shrawley H & W 47 SO8065
Shreding Green Bucks 26 TQ0281
Shrewley Warwks 48 SP2167
Shrewsbury Shrops 59 SJ4912
Shrewton Wilts 23 SU0643
Shripney W Susx 14 SU9302
Shrivenham Oxon 36 SU2388
Shropham Norfk 66 TL9893
Shroton Dorset 11 ST8512
Shrub End Essex 41 TL9723

Shucknall
South Rauceby

Shucknall H & W 46 SO5842
Shudy Camps Cambs 53 TL6244
Shurdington Gloucs 35 SO9118
Shurlock Row Berks 25 SU8374
Shurnock H & W 48 SP0260
Shurrery Highld 150 ND0458
Shurrery Lodge Highld 150 ND0456
Shurton Somset 20 ST2044
Shustoke Warwks 61 SP2290
Shut End W Mids 60 SO9089
Shut Heath Staffs 72 SJ8621
Shute Devon 9 SS8900
Shute Devon 10 SY2597
Shutford Oxon 48 SP3840
Shuthonger Gloucs 47 SO8935
Shutlanger Nhants 49 SP7249
Shutt Green Staffs 60 SJ8709
Shutterton Devon 9 SX9678
Shuttington Warwks 61 SK2505
Shuttlewood Derbys 75 SK4672
Shuttlewood Common Derbys 75 SK4773
Shuttleworth Lancs 81 SD8017
Sibbertoft Nhants 50 SP6882
Sibdon Carwood Shrops 59 SO4081
Sibford Ferris Oxon 48 SP3537
Sibford Gower Oxon 48 SP3537
Sible Hedingham Essex 53 TL7734
Sibley's Green Essex 40 TL6128
Siblyback Cnwll 5 SX2372
Sibsey Lincs 77 TF3550
Sibsey Fenside Lincs 77 TF3452
Sibson Cambs 51 TL0997
Sibson Leics 61 SK3500
Sibster Highld 151 ND3253
Sibthorpe Notts 75 SK7272
Sibthorpe Notts 63 SK7645
Sibton Suffk 55 TM3669
Sicklesmere Suffk 54 TL8760
Sicklinghall N York 83 SE3648
Sid Devon 9 SY1388
Sid Cop S York 83 SE3809
Sidborough Devon 9 SS9014
Sidbrook Somset 20 ST2527
Sidbury Devon 9 SY1491
Sidbury Shrops 60 SO6885
Sidcot Somset 21 ST4257
Sidcup Gt Lon 27 TQ4672
Siddick Cumb 92 NY0131
Siddington Ches 79 SJ8470
Siddington Gloucs 36 SU0399
Sidemoor H & W 60 SO9571
Sidestrand Norfk 67 TG2539
Sidford Devon 9 SY1390
Sidinish W Isls 154 NF8763
Sidlesham W Susx 14 SZ8598
Sidlesham Common W Susx 14 SU8500
Sidley E Susx 17 TQ7409
Sidmouth Devon 9 SY1287
Siefton Shrops 59 SO4883
Sigford Devon 7 SX7773
Sigglesthorne Humb 85 TA1545
Sigingstone S Glam 33 SS9771
Signet Oxon 36 SP2410
Silchester Hants 24 SU6262
Sileby Leics 62 SK6015
Silecroft Cumb 86 SD1281
Silfield Norfk 66 TM1299
Silian Dyfed 44 SN5751
Silk Willoughby Lincs 64 TF0542
Silkstead Hants 13 SU4424
Silkstone S York 82 SE2905
Silkstone Common S York 82 SE2904
Silksworth T & W 96 NZ3752
Silloth Cumb 92 NY1153
Silpho N York 91 SE9692
Silsden W York 82 SE0446
Silsoe Beds 38 TL0835
Silton Dorset 22 ST7829
Silver End Beds 38 TL1042
Silver End Essex 40 TL8119
Silver Street H & W 61 SP0776
Silver Street Kent 28 TQ8761
Silver Street Somset 21 ST5433
Silverburn Loth 117 NT2060
Silverdale Lancs 87 SD4574
Silverdale Staffs 72 SJ8146
Silverdale Green Lancs 87 SD4674
Silverford Gramp 142 NJ7763
Silvergate Norfk 66 TG1727
Silverlace Green Suffk 55 TM3160
Silverley's Green Suffk 55 TM2976
Silverstone Nhants 49 SP6643
Silverton Devon 9 SS9503
Silverwell Cnwll 3 SW7448
Silvington Shrops 47 SO6279
Simmondley Derbys 74 SK0293
Simonburn Nthumb 102 NY8773
Simons Burrow Devon 9 ST1416
Simonsbath Somset 19 SS7739
Simonstone Lancs 81 SD7734
Simonstone N York 88 SD8791
Simpson Bucks 38 SP8835
Simpson Cross Dyfed 30 SM8919
Sinclair's Hill Border 119 NT8150
Sinclairston Strath 107 NS4716
Sincliffe N York 89 SE2458
Sinderby N York 89 SE3481
Sinderhope Nthumb 95 NY8451
Sinderland Green Gt Man 79 SJ7390
Sindlesham Berks 25 SU7769
Single Street Gt Lon 27 TQ4359
Singleborough Bucks 49 SP7631
Singleton Lancs 80 SD3838
Singleton W Susx 14 SU8713
Singlewell Kent 28 TQ6571
Sinkhurst Green Kent 28 TQ8142
Sinnahard Gramp 134 NJ4713
Sinnington N York 90 SE7485
Sinton H & W 47 SO8160
Sinton Green H & W 47 SO8160
Sipson Gt Lon 26 TQ0777
Sirhowy Gwent 33 SO1510
Sissinghurst Kent 28 TQ7937
Siston Avon 35 ST6875
Sitcott Devon 5 SX3691
Sithney Cnwll 2 SW6329
Sithney Common Cnwll 2 SW6428
Sithney Green Cnwll 2 SW6429
Sittingbourne Kent 28 TQ9063
Six Ashes Staffs 60 SO7988
Six Bells Gwent 34 SO2202
Six Mile Bottom Cambs 53 TL5756
Six Mile Cottages Kent 29 TR1344
Six Rues Jersey 152 JS0000
Sixhills Lincs 76 TF1787
Sixpenny Handley Dorset 11 ST9917
Sizewell Suffk 55 TM4762
Skail Highld 150 NC7146
Skaill Ork 155 HY5806
Skaith D & G 99 NX3766
Skares Strath 107 NS5217
Skateraw Loth 119 NT7375
Skeabost Highld 136 NG4148
Skeeby N York 89 NZ1902
Skeffington Leics 63 SK7402
Skeffling Humb 85 TA3719
Skegby Notts 75 SK7869
Skegby Notts 75 SK4961
Skegness Lincs 77 TF5663
Skelbo Highld 147 NH7895
Skelbo Street Highld 147 NH7994
Skelbrook S York 83 SE5112
Skeldyke Lincs 64 TF3337
Skellingthorpe Lincs 76 SK9272
Skellorm Green Ches 79 SJ9281
Skellow S York 83 SE5310
Skelmanthorpe W York 82 SE2210
Skelmersdale Lancs 78 SD4606
Skelmorlie Strath 114 NS1967
Skelpick Highld 150 NC7255
Skelton Cleve 97 NZ6619
Skelton Cumb 93 NY4335
Skelton Humb 84 SE7725
Skelton N York 89 NZ0900
Skelton N York 89 SE3668
Skelton N York 83 SE5656
Skelwith Bridge Cumb 87 NY3403
Skendleby Lincs 77 TF4369
Skene House Gramp 135 NJ7610
Skenfrith Gwent 34 SO4520
Skerne Humb 84 TA0455
Skerray Highld 149 NC6563
Skerton Lancs 87 SD4763
Sketchley Leics 50 SP4292
Sketty W Glam 32 SS6292
Skewen W Glam 32 SS7296
Skewsby N York 90 SE6270
Skeyton Norfk 67 TG2425
Skeyton Corner Norfk 67 TG2527
Skidbrooke Lincs 77 TF4393
Skidbrooke North End Lincs 77 TF4395
Skidby Humb 84 TA0133
Skigersta W Isls 154 NB5461
Skilgate Somset 20 SS9827
Skillington Lincs 63 SK8925
Skinburness Cumb 92 NY1356
Skinflats Cent 116 NS9082
Skinidin Highld 136 NG2247
Skinners Green Berks 24 SU4465
Skinningrove Cleve 97 NZ7119
Skipness Strath 114 NR9057
Skipper's Bridge Cumb 101 NY3783
Skiprigg Cumb 93 NY3845
Skipsea Humb 85 TA1654
Skipsea Brough Humb 85 TA1554
Skipton N York 82 SD9851
Skipton-on-Swale N York 89 SE3679
Skipwith N York 83 SE6638
Skirling Border 108 NT0739
Skirmett Bucks 37 SU7790
Skirpenbeck Humb 90 SE7457
Skirwith Cumb 94 NY6132
Skirwith N York 87 SD7073
Skirza Highld 151 ND3868
Skitby Cumb 101 NY4465
Skittle Green Bucks 37 SP7713
Skulamus Highld 129 NG6722
Skullomie Highld 149 NC6161
Skyborry Green Shrops 46 SO2674
Skye Green Essex 40 TL8722
Skye of Curr Highld 140 NH9824
Skyreholme N York 88 SE0660
Slabacombe Head Devon 7 SX9152
Slack Derbys 74 SK3362
Slack W York 82 SD9728
Slack Head Cumb 87 SD4978
Slack Side W York 82 SE1430
Slackadale Gramp 142 NJ7454
Slackcote Gt Man 82 SD9709
Slackhall Derbys 74 SK0781
Slackholme End Lincs 77 TF5370
Slacks of Cairnbanno Gramp 143 NJ8445
Slad Gloucs 35 SO8707
Slade Devon 19 SS5046
Slade Devon 9 ST1108
Slade Somset 19 SS8427
Slade End Oxon 37 SU5890
Slade Green Kent 27 TQ5276
Slade Heath Staffs 60 SJ9206
Slade Hooton S York 75 SK5288
Sladen Derbys 74 SK0772
Slades Green H & W 47 SO8134
Sladesbridge Cnwll 4 SX0171
Slaggan Highld 144 NG8494
Slaggyford Nthumb 94 NY6752
Slagnaw D & G 99 NX7458
Slaid Hill W York 83 SE3340
Slaidburn Lancs 81 SD7152
Slaithwaite W York 82 SE0813
Slaley Derbys 74 SK2757
Slaley Nthumb 95 NY9757
Slamannan Cent 116 NS8573
Slapton Bucks 38 SP9320
Slapton Devon 7 SX8244
Slapton Nhants 49 SP6446
Slattocks Gt Man 79 SD8808
Slaugham W Susx 15 TQ2528
Slaughterford Wilts 35 ST8473
Slawston Leics 50 SP7794
Sleaford Hants 25 SU8038
Sleaford Lincs 64 TF0645
Sleagill Cumb 94 NY5919
Sleap Shrops 59 SJ4826
Sleapford Shrops 59 SJ6315
Sleasdairidh Highld 146 NH6496
Sledmere Humb 91 SE9364
Sleight Dorset 11 SY9898
Sleightholme Dur 88 NY9510
Sleights N York 90 NZ8607
Slepe Dorset 11 SY9293
Slerra Devon 18 SS3124
Slickly Highld 151 ND2966
Sliddery Strath 105 NR9322
Sligachan Highld 136 NG4829
Sligrachan Strath 114 NS1791
Slimbridge Gloucs 35 SO7303
Slindon Staffs 72 SJ8232
Slindon W Susx 14 SU9608
Slinfold W Susx 14 TQ1131
Sling Gwynd 69 SH6066
Slingsby N York 90 SE6974
Slip End Beds 38 TL0818
Slip End Herts 39 TL2837
Slipton Nhants 51 SP9579
Slitting Mill Staffs 73 SK0217
Slockavullin Strath 113 NR8297
Slogarie D & G 99 NX6568
Sloley Norfk 67 TG2923
Sloncombe Devon 8 SX7386
Sloothby Lincs 77 TF4970
Slough Berks 26 SU9879
Slough Green Somset 20 ST2720
Slough Green W Susx 15 TQ2826
Slumbay Highld 138 NG8838
Slyfield Green Surrey 25 TQ0052
Slyne Lancs 87 SD4765
Smailholm Border 110 NT6436
Small Dole W Susx 15 TQ2112
Small Heath W Mids 61 SP1085
Small Hythe Kent 17 TQ8930
Small Wood Hey Lancs 80 SD3948
Smallbridge Gt Man 81 SD9115
Smallbrook Devon 9 SX8698
Smallbrook Gloucs 34 SO5900
Smallburgh Norfk 67 TG3324
Smalldale Derbys 74 SK1781
Smalldale Derbys 74 SK0977
Smalley Derbys 62 SK4044
Smalley Common Derbys 62 SK4142
Smalley Green Derbys 62 SK4043
Smallfield Surrey 15 TQ3143
Smallholm D & G 100 NY0977
Smallridge Devon 10 ST3001
Smallthorne Staffs 72 SJ8850
Smallwood Ches 72 SJ8060
Smallworth Norfk 54 TM0181
Smannell Hants 23 SU3849
Smardale Cumb 88 NY7308
Smarden Kent 28 TQ8742
Smarden Bell Kent 28 TQ8742
Smart's Hill Kent 16 TQ5242
Smeafield Nthumb 111 NU0937
Smeale IOM 153 NX4102
Smearisary Highld 129 NM6477
Smeatharpe Devon 9 ST1910
Smeeth Kent 29 TR0739
Smeeton Westerby Leics 50 SP6792
Smelthouses N York 89 SE1964
Smerclate W Isls 154 NF7415
Smerral Highld 151 ND1733
Smestow Staffs 60 SO8591
Smethwick W Mids 60 SP0288
Smethwick Green Ches 72 SJ8063
Smisby Derbys 62 SK3419
Smith End Green H & W 47 SO7752
Smith Green Lancs 80 SD4955
Smith's End Herts 39 TL4037
Smith's Green Essex 53 TL6640
Smith's Green Essex 40 TL5821
Smitheclose IOW 13 SZ5391
Smithfield Cumb 101 NY4465
Smithies S York 83 SE3508
Smithincott Devon 9 ST0611
Smithstown Highld 144 NG7977
Smithton Highld 140 NH7145
Smithy Green Ches 79 SJ7474
Smithy Green Gt Man 79 SJ8785
Smithy Houses Derbys 62 SK3847
Smockington Leics 50 SP4589
Smoo Highld 149 NC4167
Smythe's Green Essex 40 TL9218
Snade D & G 100 NX8486
Snaigow House Tays 125 NO0843
Snailbeach Shrops 59 SJ3702
Snailwell Cambs 53 TL6467
Snainton N York 91 SE9181
Snaith Humb 83 SE6422
Snake Inn Derbys 74 SK1190
Snape N York 89 SE2684
Snape Suffk 55 TM3959
Snape Green Mersyd 80 SD3814
Snape Street Suffk 55 TM3958
Snarestone Leics 62 SK3409
Snarford Lincs 76 TF0482
Snargate Kent 17 TQ9928
Snave Kent 17 TR0130
Sneachill H & W 47 SO9053
Snead Powys 59 SO3192
Sneath Common Norfk 54 TM1589
Sneaton N York 91 NZ8907
Sneatonthorpe N York 91 NZ9006
Snelland Lincs 76 TF0780
Snelston Derbys 73 SK1543
Snetterton Norfk 66 TL9991
Snettisham Norfk 65 TF6834
Snibston Leics 62 SK4113
Snig's End Gloucs 47 SO7828
Sniperhill Kent 28 TQ9163
Snitter Nthumb 103 NU0203
Snitterby Lincs 76 SK9894
Snitterfield Warwks 48 SP2159
Snitterton Derbys 74 SK2760
Snittlegarth Cumb 93 NY2138
Snitton Shrops 46 SO5575
Snoadhill Kent 28 TQ9342
Snodhill H & W 46 SO3240
Snodland Kent 28 TQ7061
Snoll Hatch Kent 28 TQ6637
Snow End Herts 39 TL4032
Snow Street Norfk 54 TM0981
Snowdon Hill S York 82 SE2600
Snowshill Gloucs 48 SP0933
Soake Hants 13 SU6611
Soar Gwynd 68 SH3872
Soar M Glam 33 ST0983
Soar Powys 45 SN9732
Soberton Hants 13 SU6116
Soberton Heath Hants 13 SU6014
Sockbridge Cumb 94 NY5127
Sockburn Nthumb 89 NZ3406
Sodylt Bank Shrops 71 SJ3440
Soham Cambs 53 TL5973
Soham Cotes Cambs 53 TL5774
Solbury Dyfed 30 SM8912
Soldon Devon 18 SS3210
Soldon Cross Devon 18 SS3210
Soldridge Hants 24 SU6535
Sole Street Kent 28 TQ6567
Sole Street Kent 29 TR0949
Solihull W Mids 61 SP1679
Solitote Highld 136 NG4274
Sollas W Isls 154 NF8074
Sollers Dilwyn H & W 46 SO4255
Sollers Hope H & W 46 SO6132
Sollom Lancs 80 SD4518
Solva Dyfed 30 SM8024
Solwaybank D & G 101 NY3077
Somerby Leics 63 SK7710
Somerby Lincs 84 TA0626
Somercotes Derbys 74 SK4253
Somerford Keynes Gloucs 35 SU0195
Somerley W Susx 14 SZ8198
Somerleyton Suffk 67 TM4897
Somersal Herbert Derbys 73 SK1335
Somersby Lincs 77 TF3472
Somersham Cambs 52 TL3678
Somersham Suffk 54 TM0848
Somerton Oxon 49 SP4928
Somerton Somset 21 ST4828
Somerton Suffk 54 TL8153
Somerwood Shrops 59 SJ5615
Sompting W Susx 15 TQ1605
Sonning Berks 37 SU7575
Sonning Common Oxon 37 SU7080
Sonning Eye Oxon 37 SU7576
Sontley Clwyd 71 SJ3347
Sopley Hants 12 SZ1596
Sopworth Wilts 35 ST8286
Sorbie D & G 99 NX4346
Sorbietrees Cumb 101 NY4884
Sordale Highld 151 ND1462
Sorisdale Strath 120 NM2763
Sorn Strath 107 NS5526
Sortat Highld 151 ND2863
Sosgill Cumb 92 NY1024
Sotby Lincs 76 TF2078
Sots Hole Lincs 76 TF1164
Sotterly Suffk 55 TM4585
Sotwell Oxon 37 SU5790
Soughton Clwyd 70 SJ2466
Soulbury Bucks 38 SP8826
Soulby Cumb 93 NY4625
Soulby Cumb 88 NY7410
Souldern Oxon 49 SP5231
Souldrop Beds 51 SP9861
Sound Muir Gramp 141 NJ3652
Soundwell Avon 35 ST6575
Sourton Devon 8 SX5390
Soutergate Cumb 86 SD2281
South Acre Norfk 66 TF8114
South Alkham Kent 29 TR2441
South Allington Devon 7 SX7938
South Alloa Cent 116 NS8791
South Ambersham W Susx 14 SU9120
South Anston S York 75 SK5183
South Ascot Berks 25 SU9268
South Ashford Kent 28 TR0041
South Baddesley Hants 12 SZ3596
South Bank Cleve 97 NZ5320
South Bank N York 83 SE5950
South Barrow Somset 21 ST6027
South Beddington Gt Lon 27 TQ2863
South Beer M Glam 5 SX3091
South Benfleet Essex 40 TQ7787
South Bersted W Susx 14 SU9300
South Bockhampton Dorset 12 SZ1796
South Bowood Dorset 10 SY4498
South Bramwith S York 83 SE6211
South Brent Devon 7 SX6960
South Brewham Somset 22 ST7236
South Broomhill Nthumb 103 NZ2499
South Burlingham Norfk 67 TG3807
South Cadbury Somset 21 ST6325
South Cairn D & G 98 NW9669
South Carlton Lincs 76 SK9476
South Carlton Notts 75 SK5883
South Carrine Strath 105 NR6709
South Cave Humb 84 SE9231
South Cerney Gloucs 36 SU0497
South Charlton Nthumb 111 NU1620
South Cheriton Somset 22 ST6924
South Church Dur 96 NZ2128
South Cleatlam Dur 96 NZ1217
South Cliffe Humb 84 SE8736
South Clifton Notts 75 SK8270
South Cockerington Lincs 76 TF1888
South Collingham Notts 75 SK8260
South Cornelly M Glam 33 SS8280
South Cottingham Notts 76 SK8362
South Cove Suffk 55 TM4981
South Creake Norfk 66 TF8536
South Crosland W York 82 SE1112
South Croxton Leics 63 SK6810
South Dalton Humb 84 SE9645
South Duffield N York 83 SE6733
South Elkington Lincs 77 TF2988
South Elmsall W York 83 SE4711
South End Berks 24 SU5970
South End Cumb 86 SD2063
South End H & W 47 SO7344
South End Hants 12 SU1015
South End Humb 85 TA3918
South End Norfk 54 TL9990
South Erradale Highld 137 NG7471
South Fambridge Essex 40 TQ8694
South Fawley Berks 36 SU3880
South Feorline Strath 105 NR9027
South Ferriby Humb 84 SE9820
South Field Humb 84 TA0225
South Godstone Surrey 15 TQ3546
South Gorley Hants 12 SU1610
South Gosforth T & W 103 NZ2467
South Green Essex 41 TM0319
South Green Essex 40 TQ6893
South Green Kent 28 TQ8560
South Green Norfk 66 TG0510
South Green Suffk 54 TM1775
South Hanningfield Essex 40 TQ7497
South Harting W Susx 14 SU7819
South Hayling Hants 13 SZ7299
South Hazelrigg Nthumb 111 NU0532
South Heath Bucks 26 SP9101
South Heighton E Susx 16 TQ4503
South Hetton Cleve 96 NZ3845
South Hiendley Strath 83 SE3912
South Hiendly W York 83 SE3912
South Hill Cnwll 5 SX3373
South Hill Somset 21 ST4727
South Hinksey Oxon 37 SP5003
South Hole Devon 18 SS2220
South Holmwood Surrey 15 TQ1745
South Hornchurch Gt Lon 27 TQ5283
South Huish Devon 7 SX6941
South Hykeham Lincs 76 SK9364
South Hylton T & W 96 NZ3556
South Kelsey Lincs 76 TF0398
South Kessock Highld 140 NH6547
South Killingholme Humb 85 TA1416
South Kilvington N York 89 SE4283
South Kilworth Nhants 50 SP6081
South Kirkby W York 83 SE4410
South Knighton Devon 7 SX8072
South Kyme Lincs 76 TF1749
South Lambeth Gt Lon 27 TQ3077
South Lawn Oxon 36 SP2814
South Leigh Oxon 36 SP3909
South Leverton Notts 75 SK7881
South Littleton H & W 48 SP0746
South Lochboisdale W Isls 154 NF7817
South Lopham Norfk 54 TM0481
South Luffenham Leics 63 SK9401
South Mains D & G 107 NS7808
South Malling E Susx 16 TQ4211
South Marston Wilts 36 SU1987
South Merstham Surrey 27 TQ2952
South Middleton Nthumb 111 NT9923
South Milford N York 83 SE4931
South Milton Devon 7 SX7042
South Mimms Herts 39 TL2210
South Molton Devon 19 SS7125
South Moor Dur 96 NZ1952
South Moreton Oxon 37 SU5688
South Mundham W Susx 14 SU8700
South Muskham Notts 75 SK7956
South Newbald Humb 84 SE9136
South Newington Oxon 48 SP4033
South Newton Wilts 23 SU0834
South Normanton Derbys 75 SK4456
South Norwood Gt Lon 27 TQ3368
South Nutfield Surrey 15 TQ3049
South Ockendon Essex 27 TQ5983
South Ormsby Lincs 77 TF3675
South Ossett W York 82 SE2819
South Otterington N York 89 SE3787
South Owersby Lincs 76 TF0693
South Park Surrey 15 TQ2548
South Perrott Dorset 10 ST4706
South Petherton Somset 10 ST4316
South Petherwin Cnwll 5 SX3181
South Pickenham Norfk 66 TF8504
South Pill M Glam 6 SX4259
South Pool Devon 7 SX7740
South Poorton Dorset 10 SY5197
South Port Strath 123 NN0420
South Quarme Somset 20 SS9236
South Queensferry Loth 117 NT1378
South Radworthy Devon 19 SS7432
South Rauceby Lincs 64 TF0245

South Raynham
Stanley

South Raynham *Norfk* 66 TF8723
South Reddish *Gt Man* 79 SJ8992
South Reston *Lincs* 77 TF4083
South Runcton *Norfk* 65 TF6308
South Scarle *Notts* 76 SK8463
South Shian *Strath* 122 NM9042
South Shields *T & W* 103 NZ3567
South Shore *Lancs* 80 SD3033
South Side *Humb* 85 TA1120
South Skirlaugh *Humb* 85 TA1438
South Somercotes *Lincs* 77 TF4193
South Stainley *N York* 89 SE3063
South Stifford *Essex* 27 TQ5977
South Stoke *Avon* 22 ST7461
South Stoke *Oxon* 37 SU5983
South Stoke *W Susx* 14 TQ0210
South Stour *Kent* 28 TR0338
South Street *E Susx* 15 TQ3918
South Street *Kent* 27 TQ6363
South Street *Kent* 29 TR1265
South Street *Kent* 28 TR0557
South Tarbrax *Strath* 117 NT0353
South Tawton *Devon* 8 SX6594
South Thoresby *Lincs* 77 TF4077
South Tidworth *Hants* 23 SU2347
South Town *Devon* 9 SX9683
South Town *Hants* 24 SU6536
South Walsham *Norfk* 67 TG3613
South Warnborough *Hants* 24 SU7247
South Weald *Essex* 27 TQ5793
South Weston *Oxon* 37 SU7098
South Wheatley *Cnwll* 5 SX2492
South Widcombe *Somset* 21 ST5756
South Wigston *Leics* 50 SP5897
South Willesborough *Kent* 28 TR0240
South Willingham *Lincs* 76 TF1983
South Wingate *Dur* 96 NZ4135
South Wingfield *Derbys* 74 SK3755
South Witham *Lincs* 63 SK9219
South Wonston *Hants* 24 SU4635
South Woodham Ferrers *Essex* 40 TQ8097
South Wootton *Norfk* 65 TF6422
South Wraxall *Wilts* 22 ST8364
South Yeo *Devon* 19 SS5100
South Zeal *Devon* 8 SX6493
Southall *Gt Lon* 26 TQ1279
Southam *Gloucs* 47 SO9725
Southam *Warwks* 49 SP4161
Southampton *Hants* 13 SU4211
Southborough *Gt Lon* 27 TQ4267
Southborough *Kent* 16 TQ5842
Southbourne *Dorset* 12 SZ1491
Southbourne *W Susx* 14 SU7605
Southbrook *Dorset* 11 SY8494
Southburgh *Norfk* 66 TG0004
Southburn *Humb* 84 SE9954
Southchurch *Essex* 40 TQ9086
Southcott *Cnwll* 5 SX1995
Southcott *Devon* 8 SX7580
Southcott *Devon* 18 SS4416
Southcott *Devon* 8 SX5495
Southcott *Wilts* 23 SU1659
Southcourt *Bucks* 38 SP8112
Southease *E Susx* 16 TQ4205
Southend *Strath* 105 NR6908
Southend *Wilts* 36 SU1973
Southend-on-Sea *Essex* 40 TQ8886
Southeranby *Cumb* 93 NY3739
Southerby *Cumb* 93 NY3639
Southernden *Kent* 28 TQ0045
Southerndown *M Glam* 33 SS8873
Southerness *D & G* 92 NX9754
Southerton *Devon* 4 SX0790
Southery *Norfk* 65 TL6294
Southfield *Cent* 116 NS8472
Southfleet *Kent* 27 TQ6171
Southford *IOW* 13 SZ5178
Southgate *Gt Lon* 27 TQ2994
Southgate *Norfk* 66 TF8635
Southgate *Norfk* 65 TF6833
Southgate *Norfk* 66 TG1324
Southgate *W Glam* 32 SS5587
Southill *Beds* 38 TL1442
Southington *Hants* 24 SU5049
Southleigh *Devon* 9 SY2093
Southminster *Essex* 40 TQ9599
Southmoor *Oxon* 36 SU3998
Southmuir *Tays* 126 NO3853
Southoe *Cambs* 52 TL1864
Southolt *Suffk* 55 TM1968
Southorpe *Cambs* 64 TF0803
Southover *Dorset* 10 SY6294
Southover *E Susx* 16 TQ6525
Southowram *W York* 82 SE1123
Southport *Mersyd* 80 SD3317
Southrepps *Norfk* 67 TG2536
Southrey *Lincs* 76 TF1366
Southrop *Gloucs* 36 SP1903
Southrope *Hants* 24 SU6744
Southsea *Clwyd* 71 SJ2951
Southsea *Hants* 13 SZ6498
Southside *Dur* 95 NZ1026
Southtown *Norfk* 67 TG5206
Southtown *Somset* 10 ST3216
Southwaite *Cumb* 93 NY4445
Southwark *Gt Lon* 27 TQ3279
Southwater *W Susx* 15 TQ1526
Southwater Street *W Susx* 15 TQ1527
Southway *Somset* 21 ST5142
Southwell *Dorset* 11 SY6870
Southwell *Notts* 75 SK7053
Southwick *Hants* 13 SU6208
Southwick *Nhants* 51 TL0192
Southwick *Somset* 21 ST3546
Southwick *T & W* 96 NZ3758
Southwick *W Susx* 15 TQ2405
Southwick *Wilts* 22 ST8354
Southwold *Suffk* 55 TM5076
Southwood *Norfk* 67 TG3905
Southwood *Somset* 21 ST5533
Soutra Mains *Loth* 118 NT4559
Sowe Common *W Mids* 61 SP3783
Sower Carr *Lancs* 80 SD3743
Sowerby *N York* 89 SE4281
Sowerby *W York* 82 SE0423
Sowerby Bridge *W York* 82 SE0523
Sowerby Row *Cumb* 93 NY3940
Sowerhill *Somset* 19 SS8924
Sowhill *Gwent* 34 SO2700
Sowley reen *Suffk* 53 TL7051
Sowood *W York* 82 SE0818
Sowton *Devon* 6 SX5065
Sowton *Devon* 9 SX9792
Soyland Town *W York* 82 SE0320
Spa Common *Norfk* 67 TG2930
Spain's End *Essex* 53 TL6637
Spalding *Lincs* 64 TF2422
Spaldington *Humb* 84 SE7533
Spaldwick *Cambs* 52 TL1372
Spalford *Notts* 76 SK8369
Spanish Green *Hants* 24 SU6959
Sparham *Norfk* 66 TG0719
Sparhamill *Norfk* 66 TG0819
Spark Bridge *Cumb* 86 SD3084
Sparket *Cumb* 93 NY4325
Sparkford *Somset* 21 ST6026
Sparkhill *W Mids* 61 SP1083
Sparkwell *Devon* 6 SX5757
Sparrow Green *Norfk* 66 TF9514
Sparrowpit *Derbys* 74 SK0880
Sparrows Green *E Susx* 16 TQ6332
Sparsholt *Hants* 24 SU4331
Sparsholt *Oxon* 36 SU3487
Spartylea *Cumb* 95 NY8548
Spath *Staffs* 73 SK0835
Spaunton *N York* 90 SE7289
Spaxton *Somset* 20 ST2236
Spean Bridge *Highld* 131 NN2281
Spear Hill *W Susx* 15 TQ1317
Spearywell *Hants* 23 SU3127
Speen *Berks* 24 SU4568
Speen *Bucks* 37 SU8399
Speeton *N York* 91 TA1574
Speke *Mersyd* 78 SJ4383
Speldhurst *Kent* 16 TQ5541
Spellbrook *Herts* 39 TL4817
Spelmonden *Kent* 28 TQ7037
Spelsbury *Oxon* 36 SP3421
Spen *W York* 82 SE1925
Spen Green *Ches* 72 SJ8260
Spencers Wood *Berks* 24 SU7167
Spennithorne *N York* 89 SE1489
Spennymoor *Dur* 96 NZ2533
Spernall *Warwks* 48 SP0862
Spestos *Devon* 8 SX7298
Spetchley *H & W* 47 SO8954
Spettisbury *Dorset* 11 ST9002
Spexhall *Suffk* 55 TM3780
Spey Bay *Gramp* 141 NJ3565
Speybridge *Highld* 141 NJ0326
Speyview *Gramp* 141 NJ2541
Spilsby *Lincs* 77 TF4065
Spindlestone *Nthumb* 111 NU1533
Spinkhill *Derbys* 75 SK4478
Spinningdale *Highld* 146 NH6789
Spirthill *Wilts* 35 ST9975
Spital *Berks* 26 SU9675
Spital *Mersyd* 78 SJ3482
Spital Hill *Notts* 75 SK6193
Spital in the Street *Lincs* 76 SK9690
Spithurst *E Susx* 16 TQ4217
Spittal *Dyfed* 30 SM9723
Spittal *Highld* 151 ND1654
Spittal *Loth* 118 NT4677
Spittal *Nthumb* 119 NU0051
Spittal of Glenmuick *Gramp* 134 NO3085
Spittal of Glenshee *Tays* 133 NO1069
Spittalfield *Tays* 126 NO1141
Spittalon Rule *Border* 110 NT5819
Spixworth *Norfk* 67 TG2415
Splatt *Cnwll* 4 SW9476
Splatt *Cnwll* 5 SX2288
Splatt *Devon* 8 SS6005
Splayne's Green *E Susx* 16 TQ4324
Splottlands *S Glam* 33 ST2077
Spodegreen *Ches* 79 SJ7385
Spofforth *N York* 83 SE3650
Spon Green *Clwyd* 71 SJ2963
Spondon *Derbys* 62 SK3935
Spooner Row *Norfk* 66 TM0997
Sporle *Norfk* 66 TF8411
Spott *Loth* 118 NT6775
Spottiswoode *Border* 110 NT6049
Spratton *Nhants* 50 SP7170
Spreakley *Surrey* 25 SU8441
Spreyton *Devon* 8 SX6997
Spriddlestone *Devon* 6 SX5351
Spridlington *Lincs* 76 TF0084
Spring Vale *S York* 82 SE2503
Springburn *Strath* 116 NS6068
Springfield *Essex* 40 TL7208
Springfield *Fife* 126 NO3411
Springhill *Staffs* 61 SK0706
Springhill *Staffs* 60 SJ9704
Springholm *D & G* 100 NX8070
Springkell *D & G* 101 NY2575
Springside *Strath* 106 NS3738
Springthorpe *Lincs* 76 SK8789
Springwell *T & W* 96 NZ2958
Sproatley *Humb* 85 TA1934
Sproston Green *Ches* 72 SJ7366
Sprotbrough *S York* 83 SE5301
Sproughton *Suffk* 54 TM1244
Sprouston *Border* 110 NT7535
Sprowston *Norfk* 67 TG2512
Sproxton *Leics* 63 SK8524
Sproxton *N York* 90 SE6181
Sprytown *Devon* 5 SX4185
Spunhill *Shrops* 59 SJ4133
Spurstow *Ches* 71 SJ5657
Spyway *Dorset* 10 SY5293
Squirrel's Heath *Gt Lon* 27 TQ5289
St Giles in the Wood *Devon* 19 SS5318
St-y-Nyll *S Glam* 33 ST0978
St. Abbs *Border* 119 NT9167
St. Aethans *Gramp* 141 NJ1168
St. Agnes *Cnwll* 3 SW7250
St. Agnes *Loth* 118 NT6763
St. Albans *Herts* 38 TL1407
St. Allen *Cnwll* 3 SW8250
St. Andrew *Guern* 152 GN0000
St. Andrew's Major *S Glam* 33 ST1371
St. Andrews *Fife* 127 NO5116
St. Andrews Well *Dorset* 10 SY4793
St. Ann's *D & G* 100 NY0793
St. Ann's Chapel *Devon* 5 SX4170
St. Ann's Chapel *Devon* 7 SX6647
St. Anne's *Lancs* 80 SD3228
St. Anthony *Cnwll* 3 SW7825
St. Anthony's Hill *E Susx* 16 TQ6201
St. Arvans *Gwent* 34 ST5196
St. Athan *S Glam* 20 ST0168
St. Aubin *Jersey* 152 JS0000
St. Austell *Cnwll* 3 SX0152
St. Bees *Cumb* 86 NX9611
St. Blazey *Cnwll* 3 SX0654
St. Blazey Gate *Cnwll* 3 SX0653
St. Boswells *Border* 110 NT5930
St. Brelade *Jersey* 152 JS0000
St. Brelades Bay *Jersey* 152 JS0000
St. Breock *Cnwll* 4 SW9771
St. Breward *Cnwll* 4 SX0977
St. Briavels *Gloucs* 34 SO5504
St. Bride's Major *M Glam* 33 SS8974
St. Brides *Dyfed* 30 SM8010
St. Brides Netherwent *Gwent* 34 ST4290
St. Brides super-Ely *S Glam* 33 ST0977
St. Brides Wentlooge *Gwent* 34 ST2982
St. Budeaux *Devon* 6 SX4558
St. Buryan *Cnwll* 2 SW4025
St. Cadoc *Cnwll* 4 SW8875
St. Catherine *Avon* 35 ST7770
St. Catherines *Strath* 123 NN1207
St. Chloe *Gloucs* 35 SO8401
St. Clears *Dyfed* 31 SN2716
St. Cleer *Cnwll* 5 SX2468
St. Clement *Cnwll* 3 SW8443
St. Clement *Jersey* 152 JS0000
St. Clether *Cnwll* 5 SX2084
St. Colmac *Strath* 114 NS0467
St. Columb Major *Cnwll* 4 SW9163
St. Columb Minor *Cnwll* 4 SW8362
St. Columb Road *Cnwll* 4 SW9159
St. Combs *Gramp* 143 NK0563
St. Cross South Elmham *Suffk* 55 TM2984
St. Cyrus *Gramp* 135 NO7464
St. David's *Tays* 125 NN9420
St. Davids *Dyfed* 30 SM7525
St. Day *Cnwll* 3 SW7242
St. Decumans *Somset* 20 ST0642
St. Dennis *Cnwll* 4 SW9557
St. Devereux *H & W* 46 SO4431
St. Dogmaels *Dyfed* 42 SN1646
St. Dogwells *Dyfed* 30 SM9728
St. Dominick *Cnwll* 5 SX3967
St. Donats *S Glam* 20 SS9368
St. Edith's Marsh *Wilts* 22 ST9764
St. Endellion *Cnwll* 4 SW9978
St. Enoder *Cnwll* 3 SW8956
St. Erme *Cnwll* 3 SW8449
St. Erney *Cnwll* 5 SX3659
St. Erth *Cnwll* 2 SW5535
St. Erth Praze *Cnwll* 2 SW5735
St. Ervan *Cnwll* 4 SW8970
St. Ewe *Cnwll* 3 SW9746
St. Fagans *S Glam* 33 ST1277
St. Fergus *Gramp* 143 NK0952
St. Fillans *Tays* 124 NN6924
St. Florence *Dyfed* 31 SN0801
St. Gennys *Cnwll* 4 SX1497
St. George *Clwyd* 70 SH9775
St. George's *S Glam* 33 ST1076
St. George's Hill *Surrey* 26 TQ0862
St. Georges *Avon* 21 ST3762
St. Germans *Cnwll* 5 SX3657
St. Giles-on-the-Heath *Devon* 31 SS3690
St. Gluvia's *Cnwll* 3 SW7834
St. Harmon *Powys* 45 SN9872
St. Helen Auckland *Dur* 96 NZ1826
St. Helena *Norfk* 67 TG1916
St. Helens *Cumb* 92 NY0132
St. Helens *E Susx* 17 TQ8212
St. Helens *IOW* 13 SZ6288
St. Helens *Mersyd* 78 SJ5195
St. Helier *Gt Lon* 27 TQ2667
St. Helier *Jersey* 152 JS0000
St. Hilary *Cnwll* 2 SW5531
St. Hilary *S Glam* 33 ST0173
St. Ibbs *Herts* 39 TL1926
St. Illtyd *Gwent* 33 SO2102
St. Ishmaels *Dyfed* 30 SM8307
St. Issey *Cnwll* 4 SW9271
St. Ive *Cnwll* 5 SX3167
St. Ives *Cambs* 52 TL3171
St. Ives *Cnwll* 2 SW5140
St. Ives *Dorset* 12 SU1203
St. Ives *W York* 82 SE0938
St. Jame's End *Nhants* 49 SP7460
St. James *Norfk* 67 TG2820
St. James South Elmham *Suffk* 55 TM3281
St. John *Cnwll* 5 SX4053
St. John *Jersey* 152 JS0000
St. John's *IOM* 153 SC2781
St. John's Chapel *Devon* 19 SS5329
St. John's Chapel *Dur* 95 NY8837
St. John's Fen End *Norfk* 65 TF5312
St. John's Highway *Norfk* 65 TF5214
St. John's Kirk *Strath* 108 NS9836
St. John's Town of Dalry *D & G* 99 NX6281
St. John's Wood *Gt Lon* 27 TQ2683
St. Johns *Dur* 95 NZ0733
St. Johns *H & W* 47 SO8453
St. Johns *Kent* 27 TQ5356
St. Johns *Surrey* 25 SU9858
St. Jude's *IOM* 153 SC3996
St. Just *Cnwll* 2 SW3631
St. Just *Cnwll* 3 SW8435
St. Just Lane *Cnwll* 3 SW8535
St. Katherines *Gramp* 142 NJ7834
St. Keverne *Cnwll* 3 SW7921
St. Kew *Cnwll* 4 SX0276
St. Kew Highway *Cnwll* 4 SX0375
St. Keyne *Cnwll* 5 SX2461
St. Laurence *Kent* 29 TR3665
St. Lawrence *Cnwll* 4 SX0466
St. Lawrence *Essex* 41 TL9604
St. Lawrence *IOW* 13 SZ5376
St. Lawrence *Jersey* 152 JS0000
St. Lenords *Bucks* 38 SP9007
St. Leonards *Dorset* 12 SU1002
St. Leonards *E Susx* 17 TQ8009
St. Leonards Street *Kent* 28 TQ6756
St. Levan *Cnwll* 2 SW3822
St. Lythans *S Glam* 33 ST1072
St. Mabyn *Cnwll* 4 SX0473
St. Margaret South Elmham *Suffk* 55 TM3184
St. Margaret's at Cliffe *Kent* 29 TR3544
St. Margarets *H & W* 46 SO3533
St. Margarets *Herts* 39 TL3811
St. Margarets Hope *Ork* 155 ND4493
St. Marks *IOM* 153 SC2974
St. Martin *Cnwll* 5 SX2655
St. Martin *Guern* 152 GN0000
St. Martin *Jersey* 152 JS0000
St. Martin's *Tays* 126 NO1530
St. Martin's Green *Cnwll* 3 SW7324
St. Martin's Moor *Shrops* 59 SJ3135
St. Martins *Shrops* 59 SJ3236
St. Mary *Jersey* 152 JS0000
St. Mary Bourne *Hants* 24 SU4250
St. Mary Church *S Glam* 33 ST0071
St. Mary Cray *Gt Lon* 27 TQ4767
St. Mary Hill *S Glam* 33 SS9678
St. Mary in the Marsh *Kent* 17 TR0628
St. Mary's *Ork* 155 HY4701
St. Mary's Bay *Kent* 17 TR0827
St. Mary's Grove *Avon* 21 ST4669
St. Mary's Hoo *Kent* 28 TQ8076
St. Marylebone *Gt Lon* 27 TQ2782
St. Marys Bay *Devon* 7 SX9355
St. Marys Church *Devon* 7 SX9166
St. Maughans *Gwent* 34 SO4617
St. Maughans Green *Gwent* 34 SO4717
St. Mawes *Cnwll* 3 SW8433
St. Mawgan *Cnwll* 4 SW8765
St. Mellion *Cnwll* 5 SX3865
St. Mellons *S Glam* 34 ST2281
St. Merryn *Cnwll* 4 SW8874
St. Mewan *Cnwll* 3 SW9951
St. Michael Caerhays *Cnwll* 3 SW9642
St. Michael Church *Somset* 21 ST3130
St. Michael Penkevil *Cnwll* 3 SW8542
St. Michael South Elmham *Suffk* 55 TM3483
St. Michael's on Wyre *Lancs* 80 SD4641
St. Michaels *H & W* 46 SO5865
St. Michaels *Kent* 17 TQ8835
St. Minver *Cnwll* 4 SW9677
St. Monans *Fife* 127 NO5201
St. Neot *Cnwll* 4 SX1867
St. Neots *Cambs* 52 TL1860
St. Nicholas *Dyfed* 30 SM9035
St. Nicholas *S Glam* 33 ST0974
St. Nicholas at Wade *Kent* 29 TR2666
St. Ninians *Cent* 116 NS7991
St. Olaves *Norfk* 67 TM4599
St. Osyth *Essex* 41 TM1215
St. Ouen *Jersey* 152 JS0000
St. Owens Cross *H & W* 46 SO5324
St. Paul's Walden *Herts* 39 TL1922
St. Pauls Cray *Gt Lon* 27 TQ4668
St. Peter *Jersey* 152 JS0000
St. Peter Port *Guern* 152 GN0000
St. Peter's *Guern* 152 GN0000
St. Peter's *Kent* 29 TR3768
St. Peter's Hill *Cambs* 52 TL2373
St. Petrox *Dyfed* 30 SR9797
St. Pinnock *Cnwll* 5 SX2063
St. Quivox *Strath* 106 NS3724
St. Ruan *Cnwll* 2 SW7115
St. Sampson *Guern* 152 GN0000
St. Saviour *Guern* 152 JS0000
St. Stephen *Cnwll* 3 SW9453
St. Stephen *Cnwll* 3 SW9453
St. Stephens *Cnwll* 5 SX3285
St. Stephens *Cnwll* 5 SX4158
St. Teath *Cnwll* 4 SX0680
St. Tudy *Cnwll* 4 SX0676
St. Twynnells *Dyfed* 30 SR9597
St. Veep *Cnwll* 3 SX1455
St. Vigeans *Tays* 127 NO6443
St. Wenn *Cnwll* 4 SW9664
St. Weonards *H & W* 46 SO4924
Stableford *Shrops* 60 SO7598
Stableford *Staffs* 72 SJ8138
Stacey Bank *Derbys* 74 SK2890
Stackhouse *N York* 88 SD8165
Stackpole *Dyfed* 30 SR9896
Stacksford *Norfk* 54 TM0590
Stacksteads *Lancs* 81 SD8521
Stadbury *Devon* 7 SX6845
Staddiscombe *Devon* 6 SX5151
Staddlethorpe *Humb* 84 SE8428
Stadhampton *Oxon* 37 SU6098
Staffield *Cumb* 94 NY5443
Staffin *Highld* 136 NG4967
Stafford *Staffs* 72 SJ9223
Stag Green *Cumb* 86 SD1679
Stag's Head *Devon* 19 SS6728
Stagsden *Beds* 38 SP9849
Stainburn *Cumb* 92 NY0229
Stainburn *N York* 82 SE2448
Stainby *Lincs* 63 SK9022
Staincross *S York* 83 SE3210
Staindrop *Dur* 96 NZ1220
Staines *Surrey* 26 TQ0371
Stainfield *Lincs* 64 TF0724
Stainfield *Lincs* 76 TF1172
Stainforth *N York* 88 SD8267
Stainforth *S York* 83 SE6411
Staining *Lancs* 80 SD3436
Stainland *W York* 82 SE0719
Stainsacre *N York* 91 NZ9108
Stainsby *Derbys* 75 SK4465
Stainton *Cleve* 89 NZ4714
Stainton *Cumb* 93 NY3857
Stainton *Cumb* 94 NY4828
Stainton *Cumb* 87 SD5285
Stainton *Dur* 95 NZ0718
Stainton *N York* 89 SE1096
Stainton *S York* 75 SK5593
Stainton by Langworth *Lincs* 76 TF0577
Stainton le Vale *Lincs* 76 TF1794
Stainton with Adgarley *Cumb* 86 SD2472
Staintondale *N York* 91 SE9898
Stair *Cumb* 93 NY2321
Stair *Strath* 107 NS4323
Stair Haven *D & G* 98 NX2153
Stairfoot *S York* 83 SE3705
Staithes *N York* 97 NZ7818
Stake Pool *Lancs* 80 SD4147
Stakeford *Nthumb* 103 NZ2785
Stakes *Hants* 13 SU6808
Stalbridge *Dorset* 11 ST7317
Stalbridge Weston *Dorset* 11 ST7216
Stalham *Norfk* 67 TG3725
Stalham Green *Norfk* 67 TG3824
Stalisfield Green *Kent* 28 TQ9552
Stallen *Dorset* 10 ST6016
Stalling Busk *N York* 88 SD9186
Stallingborough *Humb* 85 TA1911
Stallington *Staffs* 72 SJ9439
Stalmine *Lancs* 80 SD3745
Stalmine Moss Side *Lancs* 80 SD3845
Stalybridge *Gt Man* 79 SJ9698
Stambourne *Essex* 53 TL7238
Stambourne Green *Essex* 53 TL6938
Stamford *Lincs* 64 TF0307
Stamford *Nthumb* 111 NU2219
Stamford Bridge *Ches* 71 SJ4667
Stamford Bridge *Humb* 84 SE7155
Stamford Hill *Gt Lon* 27 TQ3387
Stamfordham *Nthumb* 103 NZ0772
Stamton Lees *Derbys* 74 SK2562
Stanah *Lancs* 80 SD3542
Stanborough *Herts* 39 TL2210
Stanbridge *Beds* 38 SP9624
Stanbridge *Dorset* 11 SU0003
Stanbury *W York* 82 SE0137
Stand *Gt Man* 79 SD7905
Stand *Strath* 116 NS7668
Standburn *Cent* 116 NS9274
Standeford *Staffs* 60 SJ9107
Standen *Kent* 28 TQ8540
Standen Street *Kent* 17 TQ8030
Standerwick *Somset* 22 ST8150
Standford *Hants* 14 SU8134
Standish *Gloucs* 35 SO8018
Standish *Gt Man* 78 SD5610
Standish Lower Ground *Gt Man* 78 SD5507
Standlake *Oxon* 36 SP3902
Standon *Hants* 13 SU4226
Standon *Herts* 39 TL3922
Standon *Staffs* 72 SJ8135
Standon Green End *Herts* 39 TL3620
Standwell Green *Suffk* 54 TM1370
Stane *Strath* 116 NS8859
Stanfield *Norfk* 66 TF9320
Stanford *Beds* 39 TL1640
Stanford *Kent* 29 TR1238
Stanford *Shrops* 59 SJ3313
Stanford Bishop *H & W* 47 SO6851
Stanford Bridge *H & W* 47 SO7165
Stanford Bridge *Shrops* 72 SJ7024
Stanford Dingley *Berks* 24 SU5771
Stanford in the Vale *Oxon* 36 SU3493
Stanford le Hope *Essex* 40 TQ6882
Stanford on Avon *Nhants* 50 SP5978
Stanford on Soar *Notts* 62 SK5422
Stanford on Teme *H & W* 47 SO7065
Stanford Rivers *Essex* 27 TL5301
Stanford's End *Kent* 16 TQ4444
Stanfree *Derbys* 75 SK4774
Stanghow *Cleve* 97 NZ6715
Stanground *Cambs* 64 TL2096
Stanhill *Lancs* 81 SD7227
Stanhoe *Norfk* 66 TF8036
Stanhope *Border* 108 NT1229
Stanhope *Dur* 95 NY9939
Stanhope Bretby *Derbys* 73 SK2921
Stanion *Nhants* 51 SP9186
Stanley *Derbys* 62 SK4140
Stanley *Dur* 96 NZ1953
Stanley *Notts* 75 SK4661
Stanley *Shrops* 60 SO7583
Stanley *Staffs* 72 SJ9352
Stanley *Tays* 126 NO1033
Stanley *W York* 83 SE3422

Stanley *W York* 83 SE3422
Stanley Common *Derbys* 62 SK4142
Stanley Crook *Dur* 96 NZ1638
Stanley Gate *Lancs* 78 SD4405
Stanley Moor *Staffs* 72 SJ9251
Stanley Pontlarge *Gloucs* 47 SO9930
Stanmer *E Susx* 15 TQ3309
Stanmore *Berks* 37 SU4778
Stanmore *Gt Lon* 26 TQ1692
Stanmore *Hants* 24 SU4628
Stannersburn *Nthumb* 102 NY7286
Stanningley *W York* 82 SE2234
Stannington *Nthumb* 103 NZ2179
Stannington *S York* 74 SK2988
Stansbatch *H & W* 46 SO3461
Stansfield *Suffk* 53 TL7852
Stanshope *Staffs* 73 SK1254
Stanstead *Suffk* 54 TL8449
Stanstead Abbots *Herts* 39 TL3811
Stanstead Street *Suffk* 54 TL8448
Stansted *Kent* 27 TQ6062
Stansted Mountfitchet *Essex* 39 TL5125
Stanton *Derbys* 73 SK2719
Stanton *Devon* 7 SX7050
Stanton *Gloucs* 48 SP0634
Stanton *Gwent* 34 SO3021
Stanton *Nthumb* 103 NZ1390
Stanton *Staffs* 73 SK1246
Stanton *Suffk* 54 TL9673
Stanton Butts *Cambs* 52 TL2372
Stanton by Bridge *Derbys* 62 SK3627
Stanton by Dale *Derbys* 62 SK4637
Stanton Drew *Avon* 21 ST5963
Stanton Fitzwarren *Wilts* 36 SU1790
Stanton Harcourt *Oxon* 36 SP4105
Stanton Hill *Notts* 75 SK4760
Stanton in Peak *Derbys* 74 SK2464
Stanton Lacy *Shrops* 46 SO4979
Stanton Long *Shrops* 59 SO5691
Stanton on the Wolds *Notts* 63 SK6330
Stanton Prior *Avon* 22 ST6762
Stanton St. Bernard *Wilts* 23 SU0962
Stanton St. John *Oxon* 37 SP5709
Stanton St. Quintin *Wilts* 35 ST9079
Stanton Street *Suffk* 54 TL9566
Stanton under Bardon *Leics* 62 SK4610
Stanton upon Hine Heath *Shrops* 59 SJ5624
Stanton Wick *Avon* 21 ST6162
Stantway *Gloucs* 35 SO7313
Stanwardine in the Field *Shrops* 59 SJ4124
Stanwardine in the Wood *Shrops* 59 SJ4227
Stanway *Essex* 40 TL9424
Stanway *Gloucs* 48 SP0632
Stanway Green *Essex* 41 TL9623
Stanway Green *Suffk* 55 TM2470
Stanwell *Surrey* 26 TQ0574
Stanwell Moor *Surrey* 26 TQ0474
Stanwick *Nhants* 51 SP9871
Stanwix *Cumb* 93 NY3957
Stape *N York* 90 SE7994
Stapehill *Dorset* 12 SU0500
Stapeley *Ches* 72 SJ6749
Stapenhill *Staffs* 73 SK2521
Staple *Kent* 29 TR2756
Staple *Somset* 20 ST1141
Staple Cross *Devon* 20 ST0320
Staple Cross *E Susx* 17 TQ7822
Staple Fitzpaine *Somset* 10 ST2618
Staple Hill *H & W* 60 SO9773
Staplefield *W Susx* 15 TQ2728
Stapleford *Cambs* 53 TL4751
Stapleford *Herts* 39 TL3117
Stapleford *Leics* 63 SK8018
Stapleford *Lincs* 76 SK8857
Stapleford *Notts* 62 SK4837
Stapleford *Wilts* 23 SU0637
Stapleford Abbotts *Essex* 27 TQ5194
Stapleford Tawney *Essex* 27 TQ5099
Staplegrove *Somset* 20 ST2126
Staplehay *Somset* 20 ST2121
Staplehurst *Kent* 28 TQ7843
Staplers *IOW* 13 SZ5189
Staplestreet *Kent* 29 TR0660
Stapleton *H & W* 46 SO3265
Stapleton *Leics* 50 SP4398
Stapleton *N York* 89 NZ2612
Stapleton *Shrops* 59 SJ4604
Stapleton *Somset* 21 ST4621
Stapley *Somset* 9 ST1813
Staploe *Beds* 52 TL1560
Staplow *H & W* 47 SO6941
Star *Dyfed* 31 SN2435
Star *Fife* 126 NO3103
Star *Somset* 21 ST4358
Star Hill *Gwent* 34 SO4702
Starbeck *N York* 83 SE3255
Starbotton *N York* 88 SD9574
Starcross *Devon* 9 SX9781
Stareton *Warwks* 61 SP3371
Starkholmes *Derbys* 74 SK3058
Starklin *H & W* 60 SO8574
Starling *Gt Man* 79 SD7710
Starlings Green *Essex* 39 TL4531
Starr's Green *E Susx* 17 TQ7615
Starston *Norfk* 55 TM2384
Start *Devon* 7 SX8144
Start Point *Devon* 7 SX8337
Startforth *Dur* 95 NZ0415
Startley *Wilts* 35 ST9482
Statenborough *Kent* 29 TR3155
Statham *Ches* 79 SJ6787
Stathe *Somset* 21 ST3728
Stathern *Leics* 63 SK7731
Station Town *Dur* 96 NZ4036
Staughton Green *Cambs* 52 TL1365
Staughton Highway *Cambs* 52 TL1364
Staunton *Gloucs* 34 SO5512
Staunton *Gloucs* 47 SO7929
Staunton Green *H & W* 46 SO3661
Staunton on Arrow *H & W* 46 SO3760
Staunton on Wye *H & W* 46 SO3644
Staveley *Cumb* 87 SD3786
Staveley *Cumb* 87 SD4698
Staveley *Derbys* 75 SK4374
Staveley *N York* 89 SE3662
Staverton *Devon* 7 SX7964
Staverton *Gloucs* 47 SO8923
Staverton *Nhants* 49 SP5461
Staverton *Wilts* 22 ST8560
Staverton Bridge *Gloucs* 35 SO8722
Stawell *Somset* 21 ST3638
Stawley *Somset* 20 ST0622
Staxigoe *Highld* 151 ND3852
Staxton *N York* 91 TA0179
Staylittle *Dyfed* 43 SN6489
Staylittle *Powys* 43 SN8892
Staynall *Lancs* 80 SD3643
Staythorpe *Notts* 75 SK7554
Stead *W York* 82 SE1446
Stean *N York* 89 SE0973
Steane *Nhants* 49 SP5538
Stearsby *N York* 90 SE6071
Steart *Somset* 20 ST2745
Stebbing *Essex* 40 TL6624
Stebbing Green *Essex* 40 TL6823
Stebbing Park *Essex* 40 TL6524
Stechford *W Mids* 61 SP1387
Stede Quarter *Kent* 28 TQ8737
Stedham *W Susx* 14 SU8622
Steel Cross *E Susx* 16 TQ5331
Steel Heath *Shrops* 59 SJ5436
Steele Road *Border* 101 NY5292
Steen's Bridge *H & W* 46 SO5357
Steep *Hants* 13 SU7425
Steep Lane *W York* 82 SE0223
Steephill *IOW* 13 SZ5477
Steeple *Dorset* 11 SY9080
Steeple *Essex* 40 TL9303
Steeple Ashton *Wilts* 22 ST9056
Steeple Aston *Oxon* 49 SP4725
Steeple Barton *Oxon* 49 SP4424
Steeple Bumpstead *Essex* 53 TL6841
Steeple Claydon *Bucks* 49 SP7026
Steeple Gidding *Cambs* 52 TL1381
Steeple Langford *Wilts* 23 SU0337
Steeple Morden *Cambs* 39 TL2842
Steeton *W York* 82 SE0344
Stein *Highld* 136 NG2656
Stella *T & W* 103 NZ1763
Stelling Minnis *Kent* 29 TR1447
Stembridge *Somset* 21 ST4220
Stenalees *Cnwll* 4 SX0157
Stenhouse *D & G* 107 NX7993
Stenhousemuir *Cent* 116 NS8682
Stenigot *Lincs* 77 TF2481
Stenscholl *Highld* 136 NG4767
Stenton *Loth* 118 NT6274
Stepaside *Dyfed* 31 SN1307
Stepney *Gt Lon* 27 TQ3581
Stepping Hill *Gt Man* 79 SJ9187
Steppingley *Beds* 38 TL0135
Stepps *Strath* 116 NS6568
Sternfield *Suffk* 55 TM3861
Sterridge *Devon* 19 SS5546
Stert *Wilts* 23 SU0259
Stetchworth *Cambs* 53 TL6459
Steven's Crouch *E Susx* 17 TQ7115
Stevenage *Herts* 39 TL2325
Stevenston *Strath* 106 NS2742
Steventon *Hants* 24 SU5447
Steventon *Oxon* 37 SU4691
Steventon End *Essex* 53 TL5942
Stevington *Beds* 51 SP9853
Stewartby *Beds* 38 TL0142
Stewarton *Strath* 105 NR6919
Stewarton *Strath* 115 NS4246
Stewkley *Bucks* 38 SP8525
Stewley *Somset* 10 ST3118
Stewton *Lincs* 77 TF3687
Steyne Cross *IOW* 13 SZ6487
Steyning *W Susx* 15 TQ1711
Steynton *Dyfed* 30 SM9108
Stibb *Cnwll* 18 SS2210
Stibb Cross *Devon* 18 SS4314
Stibb Green *Wilts* 23 SU2262
Stibbard *Norfk* 66 TF9828
Stibbington *Cambs* 51 TL0998
Stichill *Border* 110 NT7138
Sticker *Cnwll* 3 SW9750
Stickford *Lincs* 77 TF3560
Sticklepath *Devon* 8 SX6494
Sticklepath *Somset* 20 ST0435
Stickling Green *Essex* 39 TL4732
Stickney *Lincs* 77 TF3456
Stidd *Lancs* 81 SD6536
Stiff Green *Kent* 28 TQ8761
Stiffkey *Norfk* 66 TF9743
Stifford's Bridge *H & W* 47 SO7448
Stile Bridge *Kent* 28 TQ7547
Stileway *Somset* 21 ST4640
Stilligarry *W Isls* 154 NF7638
Stillingfleet *N York* 83 SE5940
Stillington *Cleve* 96 NZ3723
Stillington *N York* 90 SE5867
Stilton *Cambs* 52 TL1689
Stinchcombe *Gloucs* 35 ST7398
Stinsford *Dorset* 11 SY7191
Stirchley *Shrops* 60 SJ6906
Stirchley *W Mids* 61 SP0581
Stirling *Cent* 116 NS7993
Stirling *Gramp* 143 NK1242
Stirtloe *Cambs* 52 TL1966
Stirton *N York* 82 SD9753
Stisted *Essex* 40 TL8024
Stitchcombe *Wilts* 36 SU2369
Stithians *Cnwll* 3 SW7336
Stittal *Humb* 84 SE7652
Stittenham *N York* 90 SE6767
Stivichall *W Mids* 61 SP3376
Stixwould *Lincs* 76 TF1765
Stoak *Ches* 71 SJ4273
Stobo *Border* 109 NT1838
Stoborough *Dorset* 11 SY9286
Stoborough Green *Dorset* 11 SY9285
Stobs Castle *Border* 109 NT5008
Stobswood *Nthumb* 103 NZ2195
Stock *Avon* 21 ST4561
Stock *Essex* 40 TQ6999
Stock Gifford *Avon* 35 ST6279
Stock Green *H & W* 47 SO9859
Stock Wood *H & W* 47 SP0058
Stockbridge *Hants* 23 SU3535
Stockbriggs *Strath* 107 NS7936
Stockbury *Kent* 28 TQ8461
Stockcross *Berks* 24 SU4368
Stockdale *Cnwll* 3 SW7837
Stockdalewath *Cumb* 93 NY3845
Stocker's Hill *Kent* 28 TQ9650
Stockerston *Leics* 51 SP8397
Stocking *H & W* 47 SO6230
Stocking Green *Bucks* 38 SP8047
Stocking Pelham *Herts* 39 TL4529
Stockingford *Warwks* 61 SP3391
Stockland *Devon* 9 ST2404
Stockland Bristol *Somset* 20 ST2443
Stockland Green *Kent* 16 TQ5642
Stockleigh English *Devon* 8 SS8406
Stockleigh Pomeroy *Devon* 9 SS8703
Stockley *Wilts* 22 ST9967
Stockley Hill *H & W* 46 SO3738
Stocklinch *Somset* 10 ST3817
Stockmoor *H & W* 46 SO3954
Stockmoor *H & W* 46 SO3954
Stockport *Gt Man* 79 SJ8990
Stocksbridge *S York* 74 SK2698
Stocksfield *Nthumb* 103 NZ0561
Stockstreet *Essex* 40 TL8322
Stockton *H & W* 46 SO5261
Stockton *Norfk* 67 TM3894
Stockton *Shrops* 72 SJ7716
Stockton *Shrops* 60 SO7399
Stockton *Shrops* 58 SJ2601
Stockton *Shrops* 60 SO7299
Stockton *Warwks* 49 SP4364
Stockton *Wilts* 22 ST9738
Stockton Brook *Staffs* 72 SJ9152
Stockton Heath *Ches* 78 SJ6186
Stockton on Teme *H & W* 47 SO7167
Stockton on the Forest *N York* 83 SE6556
Stockton-on-Tees *Cleve* 96 NZ4419
Stockwell *Gloucs* 35 SO9414
Stockwell End *W Mids* 60 SJ8800


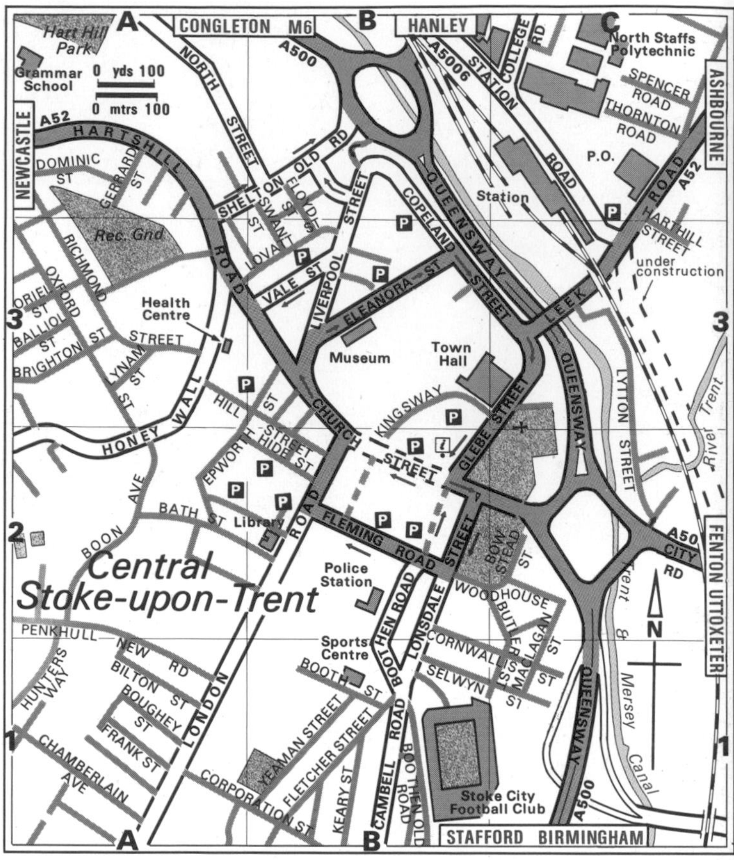

CONGLETON M6
HANLEY
North Staffs Polytechnic
Hart Hill Park
Grammar School
0 yds 100
0 mtrs 100
NEWCASTLE
ASHBOURNE
A500
A52
HARTSHILL
NORTH STREET
STATION ROAD
COLLEGE RD
SPENCER ROAD
THORNTON ROAD
P.O.
Station
DOMINIC ST
GERRARD ST
SHELTON OLD RD
FLOYD ST
SWAIN ST
OVAL
VALE ST
LIVERPOOL STREET
COPELAND STREET
QUEENSWAY
HARTHILL STREET
under construction
Rec. Gnd
RICHMOND
OXFORD
ORIEL ST
BALLIOL ST
BRIGHTON ST
Health Centre
STREET
ELEANORA ST
LEEK ROAD
LYNAM ST
Museum
Town Hall
HONEY WALL
HILL ST
KINGSWAY
CHURCH STREET
GLEBE STREET
LYTTON STREET
River Trent
EPWORTH STREET
HIDE ST
STREET
BOON AVE
BATH ST
Library
FLEMING ROAD
A50 CITY RD
Central Stoke-upon-Trent
Police Station
BOWSTEAD ST
WOODHOUSE
BUTLER ST
MACLAGAN ST
PENKHULL
NEW RD
BILTON ST
BOUGHEY
FRANK ST
LONDON ROAD
Sports Centre
BOOTH ST
BOOTHEN ROAD
LONSDALE STREET
CORNWALL ST
SELWYN ST
HUNTERS WAY
CHAMBERLAIN AVE
YEAMAN STREET
FLETCHER STREET
CORPORATION ST
KEARY ST
CAMPBELL ROAD
BOOTHEN OLD ROAD
Stoke City Football Club
Trent & Mersey Canal
FENTON UTTOXETER
N
STAFFORD BIRMINGHAM



Stockwell Heath *Staffs* 73 SK0521
Stockwood *Avon* 21 ST6268
Stockwood *Dorset* 10 ST5806
Stodday *Lancs* 87 SD4658
Stodmarsh *Kent* 29 TR2160
Stody *Norfk* 66 TG0535
Stoer *Highld* 148 NC0428
Stoford *Somset* 10 ST5613
Stoford *Wilts* 23 SU0835
Stogumber *Somset* 20 ST0937
Stogumber *Somset* 20 ST0936
Stogursey *Somset* 20 ST2042
Stogursey *Somset* 20 ST1942
Stoke *Devon* 18 SS2324
Stoke *Hants* 24 SU4051
Stoke *Hants* 13 SU7202
Stoke *Kent* 28 TQ8274
Stoke *W Mids* 61 SP3678
Stoke Abbott *Dorset* 10 ST4500
Stoke Albany *Nhants* 51 SP8088
Stoke Ash *Suffk* 54 TM1170
Stoke Bardolph *Notts* 63 SK6441
Stoke Bliss *H & W* 47 SO6563
Stoke Bruerne *Nhants* 49 SP7449
Stoke by Clare *Suffk* 53 TL7443
Stoke Canon *Devon* 9 SX9397
Stoke Charity *Hants* 24 SU4839
Stoke Climsland *Cnwll* 5 SX3574
Stoke Cross *H & W* 47 SO6250
Stoke D'Abernon *Surrey* 26 TQ1259
Stoke Doyle *Nhants* 51 TL0286
Stoke Dry *Leics* 51 SP8596
Stoke End *Warwks* 61 SP1696
Stoke Farthing *Wilts* 23 SU0525
Stoke Ferry *Norfk* 65 TF7000
Stoke Fleming *Devon* 7 SX8648
Stoke Gabriel *Devon* 7 SX8557
Stoke Gabriel *Devon* 7 SX8457
Stoke Golding *Leics* 61 SP3997
Stoke Goldington *Bucks* 38 SP8348
Stoke Green *Bucks* 26 SU9882
Stoke Hammond *Bucks* 38 SP8829
Stoke Heath *H & W* 47 SO9468
Stoke Heath *Shrops* 72 SJ6529
Stoke Heath *W Mids* 61 SP3580
Stoke Holy Cross *Norfk* 67 TG2301
Stoke Lacy *H & W* 46 SO6149
Stoke Lyne *Oxon* 49 SP5628
Stoke Mandeville *Bucks* 38 SP8310
Stoke Newington *Gt Lon* 27 TQ3386
Stoke Orchard *Gloucs* 47 SO9128
Stoke Poges *Bucks* 26 SU9783
Stoke Pound *H & W* 47 SO9667
Stoke Prior *H & W* 46 SO5256
Stoke Prior *H & W* 47 SO9467
Stoke Rivers *Devon* 19 SS6335
Stoke Rochford *Lincs* 63 SK9127
Stoke Row *Oxon* 37 SU6884
Stoke St. Gregory *Somset* 21 ST3426
Stoke St. Mary *Somset* 20 ST2622
Stoke St. Michael *Somset* 22 ST6646
Stoke St. Milborough *Shrops* 59 SO5682
Stoke sub Hamdon *Somset* 10 ST4717
Stoke Talmage *Oxon* 37 SU6799
Stoke Trister *Somset* 22 ST7328
Stoke upon Tern *Shrops* 59 SJ6328
Stoke Wake *Dorset* 11 ST7606
Stoke Wharf *H & W* 47 SO9567
Stoke-by-Nayland *Suffk* 54 TL9836
Stoke-on-Trent *Staffs* 72 SJ8745
Stoke-upon-Trent *Staffs* 72 SJ8745
Stokeford *Dorset* 11 SY8787
Stokeham *Notts* 75 SK7876
Stokeinteignhead *Devon* 7 SX9170
Stokenchurch *Bucks* 37 SU7696
Stokenham *Devon* 7 SX8042
Stokesay *Shrops* 59 SO4381
Stokesby *Norfk* 67 TG4310
Stokesley *N York* 90 NZ5208
Stolford *Somset* 20 ST2245
Stolford *Somset* 20 ST0332
Ston Easton *Somset* 21 ST6253
Stondon Massey *Essex* 27 TL5800
Stone *Bucks* 37 SP7812
Stone *Gloucs* 35 ST6895
Stone *H & W* 60 SO8675
Stone *Kent* 27 TQ5774
Stone *Kent* 17 TQ9427
Stone *S York* 75 SK5589
Stone *Somset* 21 ST5834
Stone *Staffs* 72 SJ9034
Stone Allerton *Somset* 21 ST3950
Stone Bridge Corner *Cambs* 64 TF2700
Stone Chair *W York* 82 SE1227
Stone Cross *E Susx* 16 TQ5128
Stone Cross *E Susx* 16 TQ6431
Stone Cross *E Susx* 16 TQ6104
Stone Cross *Kent* 16 TQ5239
Stone Cross *Kent* 28 TR0236
Stone Cross *Kent* 29 TR3257
Stone Hill *S York* 83 SE6809
Stone House *Cumb* 88 SD7785
Stone Rows *Leics* 61 SK3214
Stone Street *Kent* 27 TQ5754
Stone Street *Suffk* 55 TM3882
Stone Street *Suffk* 54 TM0143
Stone Street *Suffk* 54 TL9639
Stone-edge-Batch *Avon* 34 ST4671
Stonea *Cambs* 65 TL4693
Stonebridge *Avon* 21 ST3959
Stonebridge *Norfk* 54 TL9290
Stonebridge *W Mids* 61 SP2182
Stonebroom *Derbys* 74 SK4159
Stonebury *Herts* 39 TL3828
Stonechrubie *Highld* 145 NC2419
Stonecross Green *Suffk* 54 TL8257
Stonecrouch *Kent* 16 TQ7033
Stoneferry *Humb* 85 TA1231
Stonefield *Strath* 113 NR8671
Stonegarthside *Cumb* 101 NY4780
Stonegate *E Susx* 16 TQ6628
Stonegate *N York* 90 NZ7709
Stonegrave *N York* 90 SE6577
Stonehall *H & W* 47 SO8848
Stonehaugh *Nthumb* 102 NY7976
Stonehaven *Gramp* 135 NO8786
Stonehill Green *Gt Lon* 27 TQ4870
Stonehouse *Ches* 71 SJ5070
Stonehouse *D & G* 100 NX8268
Stonehouse *Devon* 6 SX4653
Stonehouse *Gloucs* 35 SO8005
Stonehouse *Nthumb* 94 NY6958
Stonehouse *Strath* 116 NS7546
Stoneleigh *Warwks* 61 SP3372
Stoneley Green *Ches* 71 SJ6151
Stonely *Cambs* 52 TL1167
Stoner Hill *Hants* 13 SU7225
Stones Green *Essex* 41 TM1626
Stonesby *Leics* 63 SK8224
Stonesfield *Oxon* 36 SP3917
Stonethwaite *Cumb* 93 NY2613
Stonetree Green *Kent* 29 TR0637
Stonewells *Gramp* 141 NJ2865
Stonewood *Kent* 27 TQ5972
Stoney Cross *Hants* 12 SU2511
Stoney Middleton *Derbys* 74 SK2275
Stoney Stanton *Leics* 50 SP4994
Stoney Stoke *Somset* 22 ST7032
Stoney Stratton *Somset* 21 ST6539
Stoney Stretton *Shrops* 59 SJ3809
Stoneybridge *W Isls* 154 NF7433
Stoneyburn *Loth* 117 NS9862
Stoneygate *Leics* 62 SK6002
Stoneyhills *Essex* 40 TQ9597
Stoneykirk *D & G* 98 NX0853
Stoneywood *Cent* 116 NS7982

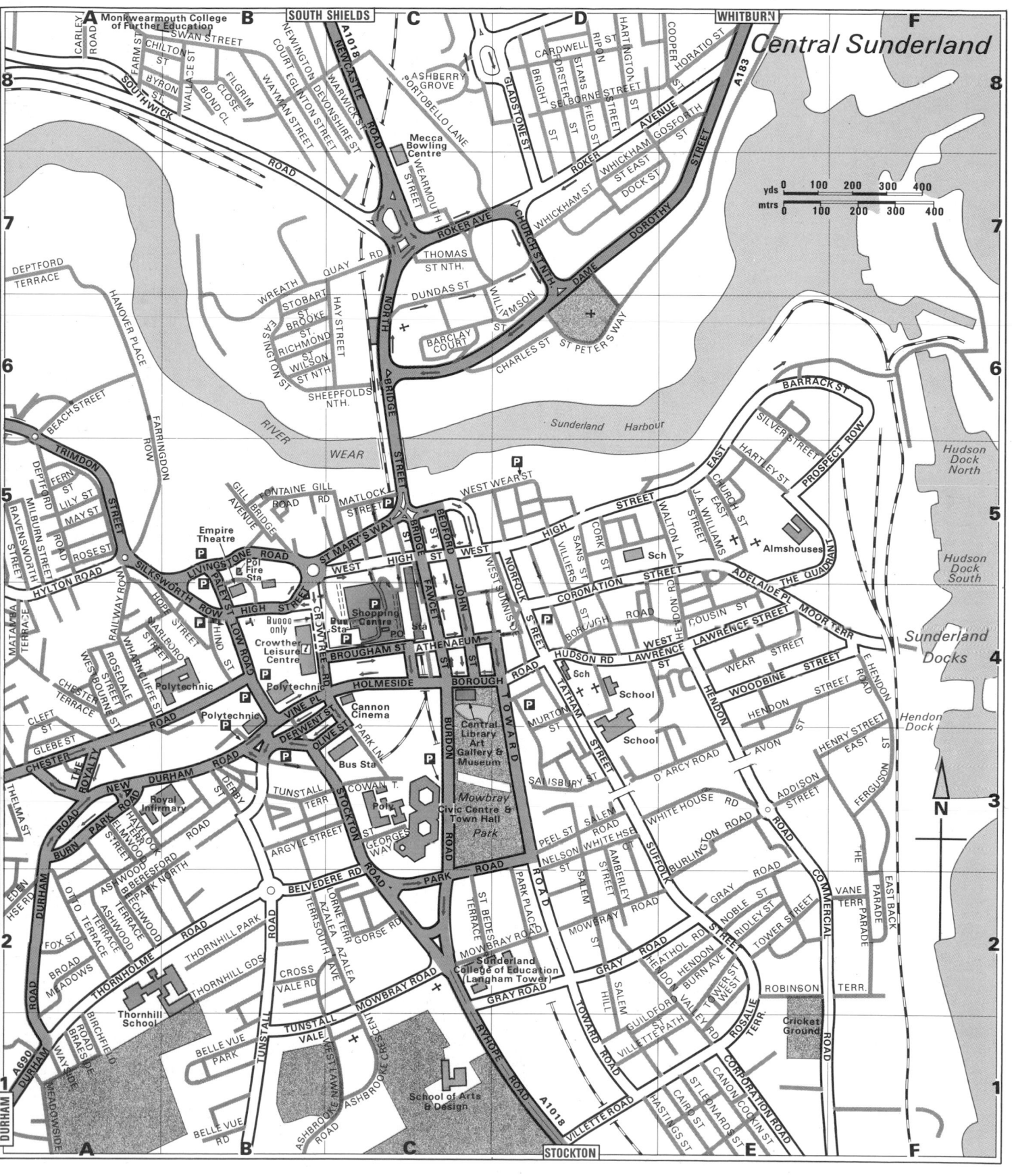

Central Sunderland

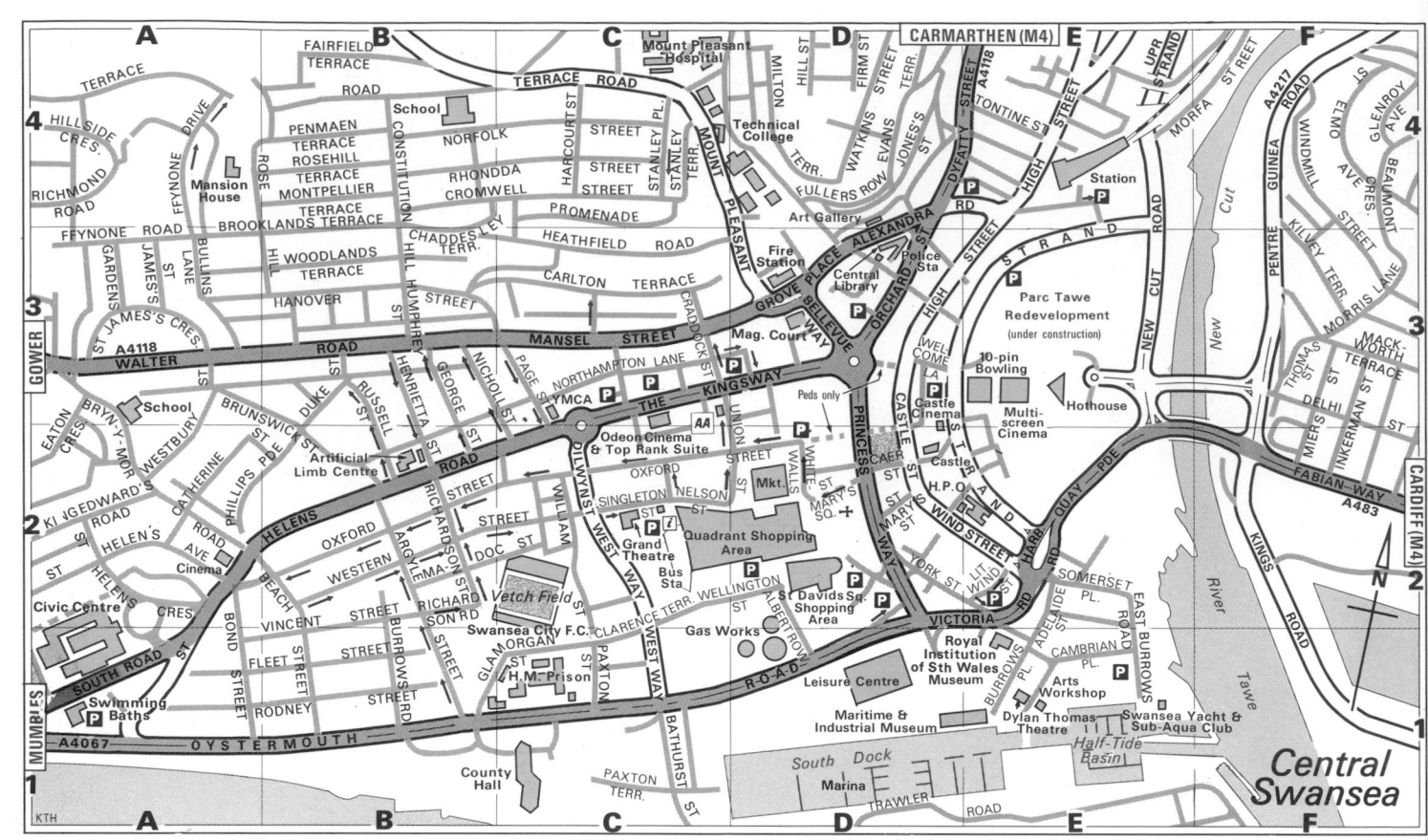

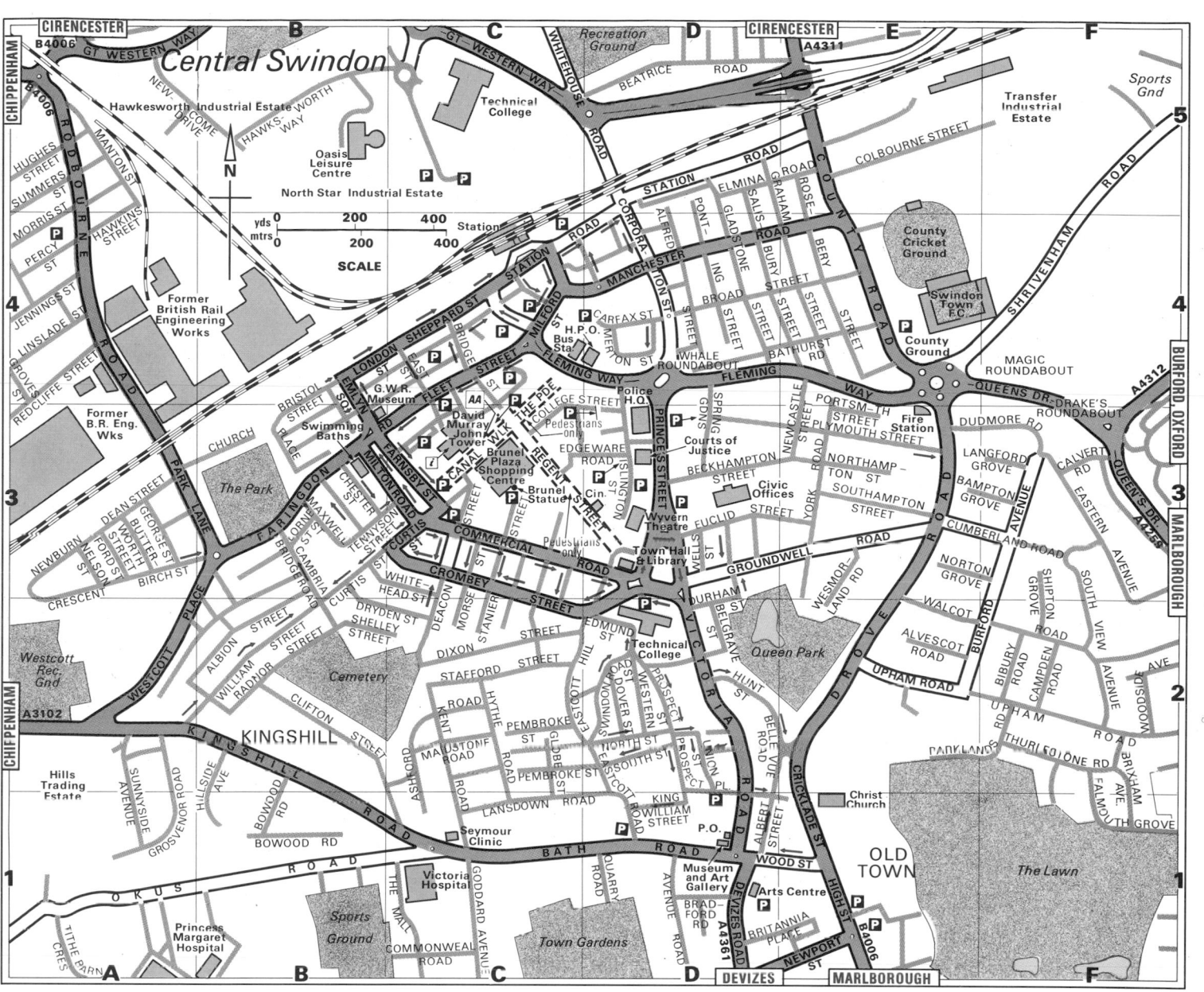

Central Swindon

Tabley Hill Threehammer Common

# T


Tabley Hill *Ches* 79 SJ7379
Tackley *Oxon* 37 SP4720
Tacolneston *Norfk* 66 TM1495
Tadcaster *N York* 83 SE4843
Taddington *Derbys* 74 SK1471
Taddiport *Devon* 18 SS4818
Tadley *Hants* 24 SU6061
Tadlow *Cambs* 52 TL2847
Tadmarton *Oxon* 48 SP3937
Tadwick *Avon* 35 ST7470
Tadworth *Surrey* 26 TQ2356
Tafarn-y-bwlch *Dyfed* 31 SN0834
Tafarn-y-Gelyn *Clwyd* 70 SJ1961
Tafarnaubach *Gwent* 33 SO1210
Tafarnaubach *M Glam* 33 SO1110
Taff Merthyr Garden Villa *M Glam* 33 ST1198
Taff's Well *M Glam* 33 ST1283
Tafolwern *Powys* 57 SH8902
Tai'n-lon *Gwynd* 68 SH4450
Tai'r Bull *Powys* 45 SN9926
Taibach *W Glam* 32 SS7788
Tain *Highld* 151 ND2266
Tain *Highld* 147 NH7781
Takeley *Essex* 40 TL5621
Takeley Street *Essex* 39 TL5421
Tal-y-Bont *Gwynd* 69 SH7668
Tal-y-Bont *Gwynd* 69 SH7668
Tal-y-bont *Gwynd* 57 SH5921
Tal-y-bont *Gwynd* 69 SH6070
Tal-y-cafn *Gwynd* 69 SH7971
Tal-y-coed *Gwent* 34 SO4115
Tal-y-garn *M Glam* 33 ST0379
Tal-y-llyn *Gwynd* 57 SH7109
Tal-y-Waun *Gwent* 34 SO2604
Talachddu *Powys* 45 SO0833
Talacre *Clwyd* 70 SJ1283
Talaton *Devon* 9 SY0699
Talbenny *Dyfed* 30 SM8412
Talbot Village *Dorset* 12 SZ0793
Taleford *Devon* 4 SX0996
Talerddig *Powys* 58 SH9300
Talgarreg *Dyfed* 42 SN4251
Talgarth *Gwynd* 57 SN6899
Talgarth *Powys* 45 SO1533
Taliesin *Dyfed* 43 SN6591
Talisker *Highld* 136 NG3230
Talke *Staffs* 72 SJ8253
Talke Pits *Staffs* 72 SJ8352
Talkin *Cumb* 94 NY5457
Talla Linnfoots *Border* 108 NT1320
Talladale *Highld* 144 NG9270
Tallaminnoc *Strath* 106 NX4098
Tallarn Green *Clwyd* 71 SJ4444
Tallentire *Cumb* 92 NY1045
Talley *Dyfed* 44 SN6332
Tallington *Lincs* 64 TF0908
Tallwrn *Clwyd* 71 SJ2947
Talmine *Highld* 149 NC5863
Talog *Dyfed* 31 SN3325
Talsarn *Dyfed* 44 SN5456
Talsarnau *Gwynd* 57 SH6135
Talskiddy *Cnwll* 4 SW9165
Talwrn *Clwyd* 71 SJ3847
Talwrn *Gwynd* 68 SH4877
Talybont *Dyfed* 43 SN6589
Talybont-on-Usk *Powys* 33 SO1122
Talysarn *Gwynd* 68 SH4852
Talywern *Powys* 57 SH8200
Tamer Lane End *Gt Man* 79 SD6401
Tamerton Foliot *Devon* 6 SX4761
Tamworth *Staffs* 61 SK2004
Tamworth Green *Lincs* 64 TF3842
Tan Hill *N York* 88 NY8907
Tan Office Green *Suffk* 53 TL7858
Tan-y-Bwlch *Gwynd* 57 SH6540
Tan-y-fron *Clwyd* 71 SJ2952
Tan-y-fron *Clwyd* 70 SH9664
Tan-y-groes *Dyfed* 42 SN2849
Tancred *N York* 89 SE4558
Tancredston *Dyfed* 30 SM8826
Tandlemuir *Strath* 115 NS3361
Tandridge *Surrey* 27 TQ3750
Tanfield *Dur* 96 NZ1855
Tanfield Lea *Dur* 96 NZ1854
Tangiers *Dyfed* 30 SM9518
Tangley *Hants* 23 SU3252
Tangmere *W Susx* 14 SU9006
Tangusdale *W Isls* 154 NF6500
Tankerness *Ork* 155 HY5108
Tankersley *S York* 74 SK3499
Tankerton *Kent* 29 TR1167
Tannach *Highld* 151 ND3247
Tannachie *Gramp* 135 NO7884
Tannadice *Tays* 134 NO4758
Tanner Green *H & W* 61 SP0874
Tannington *Suffk* 55 TM2467
Tannochside *Strath* 116 NS6962
Tansley *Derbys* 74 SK3259
Tansor *Nhants* 51 TL0590
Tantobie *Dur* 96 NZ1754
Tanton *N York* 90 NZ5210
Tanwood *H & W* 60 SO8974
Tanworth in Arden *Warwks* 61 SP1170
Tanygrisiau *Gwynd* 56 SH4945
Taplow *Bucks* 26 SU9182
Tarbert *Strath* 113 NR6182
Tarbert *Strath* 113 NR6551
Tarbert *Strath* 113 NR8668
Tarbert *W Isls* 154 NB1500
Tarbet *Highld* 148 NC1649
Tarbet *Highld* 129 NM7992
Tarbet *Strath* 123 NN3104
Tarbock Green *Mersyd* 78 SJ4687
Tarbolton *Strath* 107 NS4327
Tarbrax *Strath* 117 NT0255
Tardebigge *H & W* 47 SO9969
Tardy Gate *Lancs* 80 SD5426
Tarfside *Tays* 134 NO4979
Tarland *Gramp* 134 NJ4804
Tarleton *Lancs* 80 SD4520
Tarlscough *Lancs* 80 SD4314
Tarlton *Gloucs* 35 ST9599
Tarnock *Somset* 21 ST3852
Tarns *Cumb* 92 NY1247
Tarnside *Cumb* 87 SD4390
Tarporley *Ches* 71 SJ5562
Tarr *Somset* 20 ST1030
Tarr *Somset* 19 SS8632
Tarrant Crawford *Dorset* 11 ST9203
Tarrant Gunville *Dorset* 11 ST9212
Tarrant Hinton *Dorset* 11 ST9310
Tarrant Keynston *Dorset* 11 ST9204
Tarrant Launceston *Dorset* 11 ST9409
Tarrant Monkton *Dorset* 11 ST9408
Tarrant Rawston *Dorset* 11 ST9306
Tarrant Rushton *Dorset* 11 ST9305
Tarring Neville *E Susx* 16 TQ4404
Tarrington *H & W* 47 SO6240
Tarrylin *Strath* 105 NR9621
Tarskavaig *Highld* 129 NG5810
Tarves *Gramp* 143 NJ8631
Tarvie *Tays* 133 NO0164
Tarvin *Ches* 71 SJ4966
Tarvin Sands *Ches* 71 SJ4967
Tasburgh *Norfk* 67 TM2096
Tasley *Shrops* 60 SO6894
Taston *Oxon* 36 SP3621
Tatenhill *Staffs* 73 SK2022
Tathall End *Bucks* 38 SP8246
Tatham *Lancs* 87 SD6069
Tathwell *Lincs* 77 TF3281
Tatsfield *Surrey* 27 TQ4156
Tattenhall *Ches* 71 SJ4858
Tatterford *Norfk* 66 TF8628
Tattersett *Norfk* 66 TF8429
Tattershall *Lincs* 76 TF2157
Tattershall Bridge *Lincs* 76 TF1956
Tattershall Thorpe *Lincs* 76 TF2159
Tattingstone *Suffk* 54 TM1337
Tattingstone White Horse *Suffk* 54 TM1338
Tatworth *Somset* 10 ST3205
Tauchers *Gramp* 141 NJ3649
Taunton *Somset* 20 ST2324
Taverham *Norfk* 66 TG1614
Taverners Green *Essex* 40 TL5618
Tavernspite *Dyfed* 31 SN1812
Tavistock *Devon* 6 SX4774
Taw green *Devon* 8 SX6597
Tawstock *Devon* 19 SS5529
Taxal *Derbys* 79 SK0079
Taychreggan Hotel *Strath* 123 NN0421
Tayinloan *Strath* 105 NR7044
Taynish *Strath* 113 NR7282
Taynton *Gloucs* 35 SO7222
Taynton *Oxon* 36 SP2313
Taynuilt *Strath* 122 NN0031
Tayport *Fife* 127 NO4628
Tayvallich *Strath* 113 NR7487
Tealby *Lincs* 76 TF1590
Teangue *Highld* 129 NG6609
Teanord *Highld* 140 NH5964
Tebay *Cumb* 87 NY6104
Tebworth *Beds* 38 SP9926
Tedburn St. Mary *Devon* 8 SX8194
Teddington *Gloucs* 47 SO9632
Teddington *Gt Lon* 26 TQ1671
Tedstone Delamere *H & W* 47 SO6958
Tedstone Wafer *H & W* 47 SO6759
Teeton *Nhants* 50 SP6970
Teffont Evias *Wilts* 22 ST9831
Teffont Magna *Wilts* 22 ST9832
Tegryn *Dyfed* 31 SN2233
Teigh *Leics* 63 SK8615
Teign Village *Devon* 8 SX8381
Teigncombe *Devon* 8 SX6787
Teigngrace *Devon* 7 SX8474
Teignmouth *Devon* 7 SX9473
Telford *Shrops* 60 SJ6908
Tellisford *Somset* 22 ST8055
Telscombe *E Susx* 15 TQ4003
Telscombe Cliffs *E Susx* 15 TQ4001
Tempar *Tays* 124 NN6857
Templand *D & G* 100 NY0886
Temple *Cnwll* 4 SX1473
Temple *Loth* 117 NT3158
Temple *Strath* 115 NS5469
Temple Balsall *W Mids* 61 SP2076
Temple Bar *Dyfed* 44 SN5354
Temple Cloud *Avon* 21 ST6157
Temple End *Suffk* 53 TL6650
Temple Ewell *Kent* 29 TR2844
Temple Grafton *Warwks* 48 SP1255
Temple Guiting *Gloucs* 48 SP0928
Temple Hirst *N York* 83 SE6024
Temple Normanton *Derbys* 74 SK4167
Temple Pier *Highld* 139 NH5330
Temple Sowerby *Cumb* 94 NY6127
Templecombe *Somset* 22 ST7022
Templehall *Tays* 127 NO4936
Templeton *Devon* 19 SS8813
Templeton *Dyfed* 31 SN1111
Templeton Bridge *Devon* 19 SS8714
Templetown *Dur* 95 NZ1049
Tempsford *Beds* 52 TL1653
Ten Mile Bank *Norfk* 65 TL5996
Tenbury Wells *H & W* 46 SO5968
Tenby *Dyfed* 31 SN1300
Tendring *Essex* 41 TM1424
Tendring Green *Essex* 41 TM1326
Tendring Heath *Essex* 41 TM1326
Tenpenny Heath *Essex* 41 TM0820
Tenterden *Kent* 17 TQ8833
Terling *Essex* 40 TL7715
Tern *Shrops* 59 SJ6216
Ternhill *Shrops* 59 SJ6332
Terregles *D & G* 100 NX9377
Terrington *N York* 90 SE6670
Terrington St. Clement *Norfk* 65 TF5520
Terrington St. John *Norfk* 65 TF5314
Terry's Cross *W Susx* 15 TQ2314
Terry's Green *Warwks* 61 SP1073
Teston *Kent* 28 TQ7053
Testwood *Hants* 12 SU3514
Tetbury *Gloucs* 35 ST8993
Tetbury Upton *Gloucs* 35 ST8795
Tetchill *Shrops* 59 SJ3932
Tetcott *Devon* 5 SX3396
Tetford *Lincs* 77 TF3374
Tetney *Lincs* 77 TA3100
Tetney Lock *Lincs* 85 TA3402
Tetsworth *Oxon* 37 SP6801
Tettenhall *W Mids* 60 SJ8800
Tettenhall Wood *W Mids* 60 SO8799
Tetworth *Cambs* 52 TL2253
Teversal *Notts* 75 SK4861
Teversham *Cambs* 53 TL4958
Teviothead *Border* 109 NT4005
Tewel *Gramp* 135 NO8085
Tewinbury *Herts* 39 TL2714
Tewkesbury *Gloucs* 47 SO8933
Teynham *Kent* 28 TQ9562
Thackley *W York* 82 SE1739
Thackthwaite *Cumb* 93 NY4225
Thackthwaite *Cumb* 92 NY1423
Thakeham *W Susx* 14 TQ1017
Thame *Oxon* 37 SP7005
Thames Ditton *Surrey* 26 TQ1567
Thamesmead *Gt Lon* 27 TQ4780
Thanington *Kent* 29 TR1356
Thankerton *Strath* 108 NS9737
Tharston *Norfk* 66 TM1894
Thatcham *Berks* 24 SU5167
Thatto Heath *Mersyd* 78 SJ5093
Thaxted *Essex* 40 TL6131
The Abbey *Gwynd* 69 SH7865
The Bank *Ches* 72 SJ8457
The Bank *Shrops* 59 SO6199
The Beeches *Gloucs* 35 SP0201
The Biggins *Cambs* 53 TL4788
The Bourne *H & W* 47 SO9856
The Bratch *Staffs* 60 SO8693
The Broad *H & W* 46 SO4961
The Brunt *Loth* 118 NT6873
The Bryn *Gwent* 34 SO3309
The Bungalow *IOM* 153 SC3987
The Bush *Kent* 28 TQ6649
The Butts *Gloucs* 35 SO8916
The Chart *Surrey* 27 TQ4251
The Chequer *Clwyd* 71 SJ4840
The City *Beds* 52 TL1159
The City *Bucks* 37 SU7896
The Common *Oxon* 48 SP2927
The Common *Wilts* 35 SU0285
The Corner *Kent* 28 TQ7041
The Corner *Shrops* 59 SO4387
The Crossways *H & W* 46 SO3538
The Den *Strath* 115 NS3251
The Fence *Gloucs* 34 SO5405
The Forge *H & W* 46 SO3459
The Forstal *E Susx* 27 TQ5455
The Forstal *Kent* 28 TR0439
The Fouralls *Shrops* 72 SJ6831
The Green *Essex* 40 TL7719
The Grove *H & W* 47 SO8740
The Haven *W Susx* 14 TQ0830
The Haw *Gloucs* 47 SO8427
The Hirsel *Border* 110 NT8240
The Holt *Berks* 37 SU8078
The Horns *Kent* 17 TQ7429
The Howe *IOM* 153 SC1967
The Leacon *Kent* 17 TQ9833
The Lee *Bucks* 38 SP9004
The Lochs *Gramp* 141 NJ3020
The Marsh *Ches* 72 SJ8463
The Middles *Dur* 96 NZ2051
The Mound *Highld* 147 NH7798
The Mumbles *W Glam* 32 SS6187
The Mythe *Gloucs* 47 SO8934
The Nant *Clwyd* 70 SJ2850
The Narth *Gwent* 34 SO5206
The Neuk *Gramp* 135 NO7397
The Pill *Gwent* 34 ST4887
The Quarry *Gloucs* 35 ST7399
The Quarter *Kent* 28 TQ8844
The Reddings *Gloucs* 35 SO9021
The Rookery *Staffs* 72 SJ8555
The Rowe *Staffs* 72 SJ8238
The Sands *Surrey* 25 SU8846
The Shoe *Wilts* 35 ST8074
The Smithies *Shrops* 60 SO6897
The Spike *Cambs* 53 TL4848
The Spring *Warwks* 61 SP2873
The Square *Gwent* 34 ST2796
The Stair *Kent* 16 TQ6037
The Stocks *Kent* 17 TQ9127
The Straits *Hants* 25 SU7839
The Thrift *Herts* 39 TL3139
The Towans *Cnwll* 2 SW5538
The Vauld *H & W* 46 SO5349
The Wrythe *Gt Lon* 27 TQ2765
Thealby *Humb* 84 SE8917
Theale *Berks* 24 SU6471
Theale *Somset* 21 ST4646
Thearne *Humb* 85 TA0736
Theberton *Suffk* 55 TM4365
Thedden Grange *Hants* 24 SU6839
Theddingworth *Leics* 50 SP6685
Theddlethorpe All Saints *Lincs* 77 TF4688
Theddlethorpe St. Helen *Lincs* 77 TF4788
Thelbridge Barton *Devon* 19 SS7812
Thelbridge Cross *Devon* 19 SS7812
Thelnetham *Suffk* 54 TM0178
Thelveton *Norfk* 54 TM1681
Thelwall *Ches* 79 SJ6587
Themelthorpe *Norfk* 66 TG0524
Thenford *Nhants* 49 SP5241
Theobald's Green *Wilts* 23 SU0268
Therfield *Herts* 39 TL3337
Thetford *Norfk* 54 TL8783
Thetwaite *Cumb* 93 NY3744
Theydon Bois *Essex* 27 TQ4499
Thicket Prior *Humb* 83 SE6943
Thickwood *Wilts* 35 ST8272
Thimbleby *Lincs* 76 TF2369
Thimbleby *N York* 89 SE4495
Thingwall *Mersyd* 78 SJ2884
Thirkleby *N York* 89 SE4778
Thirlby *N York* 90 SE4883
Thirlestane *Border* 118 NT5647
Thirlspot *Cumb* 93 NY3118
Thirn *N York* 89 SE2185
Thirsk *N York* 89 SE4282
Thirtleby *Humb* 85 TA1634
Thistleton *Lancs* 80 SD4037
Thistleton *Leics* 63 SK9117
Thistley Green *Suffk* 53 TL6776
Thixendale *N York* 90 SE8461
Thockrington *Nthumb* 102 NY9578
Tholomas Drove *Cambs* 65 TF4006
Tholthorpe *N York* 89 SE4766
Thomas Chapel *Dyfed* 31 SN1008
Thomas Close *Cumb* 93 NY4340
Thomas Town *Warwks* 45 SO0763
Thomastown *Gramp* 142 NJ5737
Thompson *Norfk* 66 TL9296
Thomshill *Gramp* 141 NJ2157
Thong *Kent* 28 TQ6770
Thongsleigh *Devon* 9 SS9011
Thoralby *N York* 88 SE0086
Thoresby *Notts* 75 SK6371
Thoresthorpe *Lincs* 77 TF4578
Thoresway *Lincs* 76 TF1696
Thorganby *Lincs* 76 TF2097
Thorganby *N York* 83 SE6841
Thorgill *N York* 90 SE7096
Thorington *Suffk* 55 TM4174
Thorington Street *Suffk* 54 TM0135
Thorlby *N York* 82 SD9653
Thorley *Herts* 39 TL4719
Thorley *IOW* 12 SZ3688
Thorley Houses *Herts* 39 TL4620
Thorley Street *IOW* 12 SZ3788
Thormanby *N York* 90 SE4974
Thorn's Flush *Surrey* 14 TQ0440
Thornaby-on-Tees *Cleve* 97 NZ4518
Thornage *Norfk* 66 TG0536
Thornborough *Bucks* 49 SP7433
Thornborough *N York* 89 SE2979
Thornbury *Avon* 35 ST6490
Thornbury *Devon* 18 SS4008
Thornbury *H & W* 46 SO6159
Thornbury *W York* 82 SE1933
Thornby *Cumb* 93 NY2951
Thornby *Nhants* 50 SP6675
Thorncliff *Staffs* 73 SK0158
Thorncombe *Dorset* 10 ST3703
Thorncombe Street *Surrey* 25 TQ0042
Thorncott Green *Beds* 52 TL1547
Thorncross *IOW* 13 SZ4381
Thorndon *Suffk* 54 TM1469
Thorndon Cross *Devon* 5 SX5293
Thorne *S York* 83 SE6813
Thorne *Somset* 10 ST5217
Thorne St. Margaret *Somset* 20 ST0920
Thornecroft *Devon* 7 SX7767
Thornehillhead *Devon* 18 SS4116
Thorner *W York* 83 SE3740
Thornes *Staffs* 61 SK0703
Thornes *W York* 83 SE3219
Thorney *Bucks* 26 TQ0379
Thorney *Cambs* 64 TF2804
Thorney *Notts* 76 SK8572
Thorney *Somset* 21 ST4222
Thorney Hill *Hants* 12 SZ2099
Thorney Toll *Cambs* 64 TF3404
Thornfalcon *Somset* 20 ST2723
Thornford *Dorset* 10 ST6013
Thorngrafton *Nthumb* 102 NY7865
Thorngrove *Somset* 21 ST3632
Thorngumbald *Humb* 85 TA2026
Thornham *Norfk* 65 TF7343
Thornham Magna *Suffk* 54 TM1071
Thornham Parva *Suffk* 54 TM1072
Thornhaugh *Cambs* 64 TF0600
Thornhill *Cent* 116 NN6600
Thornhill *D & G* 100 NX8795
Thornhill *Derbys* 74 SK1983
Thornhill *Hants* 13 SU4612
Thornhill *M Glam* 33 ST1584
Thornhill *W York* 82 SE2418
Thornhill Lees *W York* 82 SE2419
Thornhills *W York* 82 SE1523
Thornholme *Humb* 91 TA1163
Thornicombe *Dorset* 11 ST8703
Thornington *Nthumb* 110 NT8833
Thornley *Dur* 95 NZ1137
Thornley *Dur* 96 NZ3639
Thornley Gate *Cumb* 95 NY8356
Thornliebank *Strath* 115 NS5459
Thorns *Suffk* 53 TL7455
Thorns Green *Gt Man* 79 SJ7984
Thornsett *Derbys* 79 SK0187
Thornthwaite *Cumb* 93 NY2225
Thornthwaite *N York* 83 SE5618
Thornthwaite *N York* 89 SE1758
Thornton *Bucks* 49 SP7435
Thornton *Cleve* 89 NZ4713
Thornton *Dyfed* 30 SM9007
Thornton *Fife* 117 NT2897
Thornton *Humb* 84 SE7545
Thornton *Lancs* 80 SD3342
Thornton *Leics* 62 SK4607
Thornton *Lincs* 77 TF2467
Thornton *Mersyd* 78 SD3301
Thornton *Nthumb* 111 NT9547
Thornton *Tays* 126 NO3946
Thornton *W York* 82 SE0932
Thornton Curtis *Humb* 85 TA0817
Thornton Dale *N York* 90 SE8383
Thornton Green *Ches* 71 SJ4473
Thornton Heath *Gt Lon* 27 TQ3168
Thornton Hough *Mersyd* 78 SJ3081
Thornton le Moor *Lincs* 76 TF0496
Thornton Rust *N York* 88 SD9689
Thornton Steward *N York* 89 SE1786
Thornton Watlass *N York* 89 SE2385
Thornton-in-Craven *N York* 81 SD9048
Thornton-in-Lonsdale *N York* 87 SD6879
Thornton-le-Beans *N York* 89 SE3990
Thornton-le-Clay *N York* 90 SE6875
Thornton-le-Moor *N York* 89 SE3988
Thornton-le-Moors *Ches* 71 SJ4474
Thornton-le-Street *N York* 89 SE4186
Thorntonhall *Strath* 115 NS5955
Thorntonloch *Loth* 119 NT7574
Thornwood Common *Essex* 39 TL4604
Thornydyes *Border* 110 NT6148
Thornythwaite *Cumb* 93 NY3922
Thoroton *Notts* 63 SK7642
Thorp Arch *W York* 83 SE4346
Thorpe *Derbys* 73 SK1550
Thorpe *Humb* 84 SE9946
Thorpe *Lincs* 77 TF4981
Thorpe *N York* 88 SE0161
Thorpe *Norfk* 67 TM4398
Thorpe *Notts* 75 SK7649
Thorpe *Surrey* 26 TQ0168
Thorpe Abbotts *Norfk* 55 TM1979
Thorpe Acre *Leics* 62 SK5120
Thorpe Arnold *Leics* 63 SK7720
Thorpe Audlin *W York* 83 SE4715
Thorpe Bassett *N York* 90 SE8673
Thorpe Bay *Essex* 40 TQ9185
Thorpe by Water *Leics* 51 SP8996
Thorpe Common *S York* 74 SK3895
Thorpe Constantine *Staffs* 61 SK2508
Thorpe End *Norfk* 67 TG2811
Thorpe Green *Essex* 41 TM1623
Thorpe Green *Lancs* 81 SD5823
Thorpe Green *Suffk* 54 TL9354
Thorpe Hesley *S York* 74 SK3796
Thorpe in Balne *S York* 83 SE5910
Thorpe in the Fallows *Lincs* 76 SK9180
Thorpe Langton *Leics* 50 SP7492
Thorpe Larches *Dur* 96 NZ3826
Thorpe Lea *Surrey* 26 TQ0270
Thorpe le Street *Humb* 84 SE8343
Thorpe Malsor *Nhants* 51 SP8378
Thorpe Mandeville *Nhants* 49 SP5344
Thorpe Market *Norfk* 67 TG2435
Thorpe Morieux *Suffk* 54 TL9453
Thorpe on the Hill *Lincs* 76 SK9065
Thorpe on the Hill *W York* 82 SE3125
Thorpe Perrow *N York* 89 SE2685
Thorpe Salvin *S York* 75 SK5281
Thorpe Satchville *Leics* 63 SK7311
Thorpe St. Andrew *Norfk* 67 TG2608
Thorpe St. Peter *Lincs* 77 TF4860
Thorpe Thewles *Cleve* 96 NZ4023
Thorpe Tilney *Lincs* 76 TF1257
Thorpe Underwood *N York* 89 SE4659
Thorpe Underwood *Nhants* 50 SP7880
Thorpe Waterville *Nhants* 51 TL0281
Thorpe Willoughby *N York* 83 SE5731
Thorpe-le-Soken *Essex* 41 TM1722
Thorpeness *Suffk* 55 TM4759
Thorpland *Norfk* 65 TF6108
Thorrington *Essex* 41 TM0920
Thorverton *Devon* 9 SS9202
Thrales End *Beds* 38 TL1116
Thrandeston *Suffk* 54 TM1176
Thrapston *Nhants* 51 SP9978
Threapland *Cumb* 92 NY1539
Threapland *N York* 88 SD9860
Threapwood *Ches* 71 SJ4344
Threapwood Head *Staffs* 73 SK0342
Threave *Strath* 106 NS3406
Threawood *Staffs* 73 SK1342
Three Ashes *H & W* 46 SO5123
Three Bridges *W Susx* 15 TQ2837
Three Burrows *Cnwll* 3 SW7446
Three Chimneys *Kent* 28 TQ8238
Three Cocks *Powys* 45 SO1737
Three Crosses *W Glam* 32 SS5794
Three Cups Corner *E Susx* 16 TQ6320
Three Gates *H & W* 47 SO6862
Three Hammers *Cnwll* 5 SX2387
Three Holes *Norfk* 65 TF5000
Three Lane Ends *Gt Man* 79 SD8309
Three Leg Cross *E Susx* 16 TQ6831
Three Legged Cross *Dorset* 12 SU0806
Three Mile Cross *Berks* 24 SU7167
Three Mile Stone *Cnwll* 3 SW7745
Three Miletown *Loth* 117 NT0675
Three Oaks *E Susx* 17 TQ8314
Threehammer Common *Norfk* 67 TG3419

Threekingham

Tregaswith

Threekingham *Lincs* 64 TF0836
Threepwood *Border* 109 NT5143
Threlkeld *Cumb* 93 NY3125
Threshfield *N York* 88 SD9963
Thrigby *Norfk* 67 TG4612
Thringarth *Dur* 95 NY9322
Thringstone *Leics* 62 SK4217
Thrintoft *N York* 89 SE3193
Thriplow *Cambs* 53 TL4346
Throapham *S York* 75 SK5387
Throckenhalt *Lincs* 64 TF3509
Throcking *Herts* 39 TL3330
Throckley *T & W* 103 NZ1566
Throckmorton *H & W* 47 SO9749
Throop *Dorset* 12 SZ1294
Throop *Dorset* 11 SY8292
Throphill *Nthumb* 103 NZ1386
Thropton *Nthumb* 103 NU0202
Througham *Gloucs* 35 SO9108
Throughgate *D & G* 100 NX8784
Throwleigh *Devon* 8 SX6690
Throwley *Kent* 28 TQ9955
Throwley Forstal *Kent* 28 TQ9854
Thrumpton *Notts* 75 SK7080
Thrumpton *Notts* 62 SK5131
Thrumster *Highld* 151 ND3345
Thrunscoe *Humb* 85 TA3001
Thrunton *Nthumb* 111 NU0810
Thrup *Oxon* 36 SU2998
Thrupp *Gloucs* 35 SO8603
Thrupp *Oxon* 37 SP4716
Thrushelton *Devon* 5 SX4487
Thrushesbush *Essex* 39 TL4909
Thrushgill *Lancs* 87 SD6462
Thrussington *Leics* 63 SK6515
Thruxton *H & W* 46 SO4334
Thruxton *Hants* 23 SU2845
Thruxton *Hants* 23 SU2845
Thrybergh *S York* 75 SK4695
Thulston *Derbys* 62 SK4031
Thundergarth Mains *D & G* 101 NY1780
Thundersley *Essex* 40 TQ7988
Thurcaston *Leics* 62 SK5610
Thurcroft *S York* 75 SK4988
Thurdistoft *Highld* 151 ND2167
Thurdon *Cnwll* 18 SS2811
Thurgarton *Norfk* 66 TG1835
Thurgarton *Notts* 75 SK6949
Thurgoland *S York* 82 SE2801
Thurlaston *Leics* 50 SP5099
Thurlaston *Warwks* 50 SP4671
Thurlbear *Somset* 20 ST2621
Thurlby *Lincs* 76 SK9061
Thurlby *Lincs* 77 TF4876
Thurlby *Lincs* 64 TF0916
Thurleigh *Beds* 51 TL0558
Thurlestone *Devon* 7 SX6742
Thurlow *Suffk* 53 TL6750
Thurloxton *Somset* 20 ST2730
Thurlstone *S York* 82 SE2303
Thurlton *Norfk* 67 TM4198
Thurlwood *Ches* 72 SJ8057
Thurmaston *Leics* 62 SK6109
Thurnby *Leics* 63 SK6403
Thurne *Norfk* 67 TG4015
Thurnham *Kent* 28 TQ8057
Thurning *Nhants* 51 TL0883
Thurning *Norfk* 66 TG0829
Thurnscoe *S York* 83 SE4605
Thursby *Cumb* 93 NY3250
Thursden *Lancs* 81 SD9035
Thursford *Norfk* 66 TF9833
Thursley *Surrey* 25 SU9039
Thurso *Highld* 151 ND1168
Thurstaston *Mersyd* 78 SJ2484
Thurston *Suffk* 54 TL9365
Thurston Clough *Gt Man* 82 SD9707
Thurston Planch *Suffk* 54 TL9364
Thurstonfield *Cumb* 93 NY3156
Thurstonland *W York* 82 SE1610
Thurton *Norfk* 67 TG3200
Thurvaston *Derbys* 73 SK2437
Thuxton *Norfk* 66 TG0307
Thwaite *N York* 88 SD8998
Thwaite *Suffk* 54 TM1168
Thwaite *Suffk* 54 TM1168
Thwaite Head *Cumb* 101 NY3490
Thwaite St. Mary *Norfk* 67 TM3395
Thwaites *W York* 82 SE0741
Thwaites Brow *W York* 82 SE0740
Thwing *Humb* 91 TA0570
Tibbermore *Tays* 125 NO0523
Tibbers *D & G* 100 NX8696
Tibberton *Gloucs* 35 SO7521
Tibberton *H & W* 47 SO9057
Tibberton *Shrops* 72 SJ6820
Tibbie Shiels Inn *Border* 109 NT2320
Tibenham *Norfk* 54 TM1389
Tibshelf *Derbys* 75 SK4361
Tibthorpe *Humb* 84 SE9555
Ticehurst *E Susx* 16 TQ6930
Tichborne *Hants* 24 SU5730
Tickencote *Leics* 63 SK9809
Tickenham *Avon* 34 ST4571
Tickford End *Bucks* 38 SP8843
Tickhill *S York* 75 SK5993
Ticklerton *Shrops* 59 SO4891
Ticknall *Derbys* 62 SK3524
Tickton *Humb* 84 TA0641
Tidbury Green *W Mids* 61 SP1075
Tidcombe *Wilts* 23 SU2858
Tidcombe *Wilts* 23 SU2858
Tiddington *Oxon* 37 SP6404
Tiddington *Warwks* 48 SP2255
Tidebrook *E Susx* 16 TQ6130
Tideford *Cnwll* 5 SX3459
Tideford Cross *Cnwll* 5 SX3461
Tidenham *Gloucs* 34 ST5595
Tideswell *Derbys* 74 SK1575
Tidmarsh *Berks* 24 SU6374
Tidmington *Warwks* 48 SP2538
Tidpit *Hants* 12 SU0718
Tiers Cross *Dyfed* 30 SM9010
Tiffield *Nhants* 49 SP6951
Tifty *Gramp* 142 NJ7740
Tigerton *Tays* 134 NO5364
Tigharry *W Isls* 154 NF7171
Tighnabruaich *Strath* 114 NR9873
Tighnafiline *Highld* 144 NG8789
Tigley *Devon* 7 SX7560
Tilbrook *Cambs* 51 TL0769
Tilbury *Essex* 27 TQ6476
Tilbury Green *Essex* 53 TL7441
Tile Cross *W Mids* 61 SP1687
Tile Hill *W Mids* 61 SP2777
Tilehouse Green *W Mids* 61 SP1777
Tilehurst *Berks* 24 SU6673
Tilford *Surrey* 25 SU8743
Tilgate *W Susx* 15 TQ2735
Tilgate Forest Row *W Susx* 15 TQ2632
Tilham Street *Somset* 21 ST5535
Tillicoultry *Cent* 116 NS9297
Tillingham *Essex* 41 TL9904
Tillington *H & W* 46 SO4644
Tillington *W Susx* 14 SU9621
Tillington Common *H & W* 46 SO4545
Tilly *Essex* 40 TL5926
Tillybirloch *Gramp* 135 NJ6807
Tillycairn *Gramp* 134 NO4697
Tillyfourie *Gramp* 135 NJ6412
Tillygreig *Gramp* 143 NJ8823
Tillyrie *Tays* 126 NO1006
Tilmanstone *Kent* 29 TR3051
Tiln *Notts* 75 SK7084
Tilney All Saints *Norfk* 65 TF5618
Tilney High End *Norfk* 65 TF5617
Tilney St. Lawrence *Norfk* 65 TF5414
Tilshead *Wilts* 23 SU0347
Tilstock *Shrops* 59 SJ5437
Tilston *Ches* 71 SJ4651
Tilstone Bank *Ches* 71 SJ5659
Tilstone Fearnall *Ches* 71 SJ5660
Tilsworth *Beds* 38 SP9724
Tilton on the Hill *Leics* 63 SK7405
Tiltups End *Gloucs* 35 ST8497
Timberland *Lincs* 76 TF1258
Timbersbrook *Ches* 72 SJ8962
Timberscombe *Somset* 20 SS9542
Timble *N York* 82 SE1753
Timewell *Devon* 20 SS9625
Timpanheck *D & G* 101 NY3274
Timperley *Gt Man* 79 SJ7888
Timsbury *Avon* 22 ST6658
Timsbury *Hants* 23 SU3424
Timsgarry *W Isls* 154 NB0634
Timworth *Suffk* 54 TL8669
Timworth Green *Suffk* 54 TL8669
Tincleton *Dorset* 11 SY7691
Tindale *Cumb* 94 NY6259
Tindale Crescent *Dur* 96 NZ2027
Tingewick *Bucks* 49 SP6532
Tingley *W York* 82 SE2826
Tingrith *Beds* 38 TL0032
Tinhay *Devon* 5 SX3985
Tinhay *Devon* 5 SX3985
Tinker's Hill *Hants* 23 SU3947
Tinkersley *Derbys* 74 SK2665
Tinsley *S York* 74 SK4090
Tinsley Green *W Susx* 15 TQ2839
Tintagel *Cnwll* 4 SX0588
Tintern Parva *Gwent* 34 SO5200
Tintinhull *Somset* 21 ST5019
Tintwistle *Derbys* 74 SK0297
Tinwald *D & G* 100 NY0081
Tinwald *D & G* 100 NY0081
Tinwell *Leics* 63 TF0006
Tipp's End *Norfk* 65 TL5095
Tippacott *Devon* 19 SS7646
Tiptoe *Hants* 12 SZ2597
Tipton *W Mids* 60 SO9592
Tipton Green *W Mids* 60 SO9492
Tipton St. John *Devon* 9 SY0991
Tiptree *Essex* 40 TL8916
Tiptree Heath *Essex* 40 TL8815
Tir-y-fron *Clwyd* 70 SJ2859
Tirabad *Powys* 45 SN8741
Tiretigan *Strath* 113 NR7262
Tirley *Gloucs* 47 SO8328
Tiroran *Strath* 121 NM4727
Tirphil *M Glam* 33 SO1303
Tirril *Cumb* 94 NY5026
Tisbury *Wilts* 22 ST9429
Tisman's Common *W Susx* 14 TQ0732
Tissington *Derbys* 73 SK1752
Titchberry *Devon* 18 SS2427
Titchfield *Hants* 13 SU5305
Titchfield Common *Hants* 13 SU5206
Titchmarsh *Nhants* 51 TL0279
Titchwell *Norfk* 65 TF7643
Tithby *Notts* 63 SK6936
Titley *H & W* 46 SO3360
Titlington *Nthumb* 111 NU0915
Titmore End *Herts* 39 TL2027
Titsey *Surrey* 27 TQ4054
Tittensor *Staffs* 72 SJ8738
Tittleshall *Norfk* 66 TF8921
Titton *H & W* 60 SO8270
Tiverton *Ches* 71 SJ5560
Tiverton *Devon* 9 SS9512
Tivetshall St. Margaret *Norfk* 54 TM1787
Tivetshall St. Mary *Norfk* 54 TM1686
Tivington *Somset* 20 SS9345
Tivy Dale *S York* 82 SE2707
Tixall *Staffs* 72 SJ9722
Tixover *Leics* 51 SK9700
Toab *Shet* 155 HU3811
Toadhole *Derbys* 74 SK3957
Toadmoor *Derbys* 74 SK3450
Toadmoor *Derbys* 74 SK3450
Tobermory *Strath* 121 NM5055
Toberonochy *Strath* 122 NM7408
Tobson *W Isls* 154 NB1438
Tocher *Gramp* 142 NJ6932
Tochieneal *Gramp* 142 NJ5165
Tochieneal *Gramp* 142 NJ5165
Tockenham *Wilts* 36 SU0379
Tockenham Wick *Wilts* 36 SU0381
Tocketts *Cleve* 97 NZ6117
Tockington *Avon* 34 ST6086
Tockwith *N York* 83 SE4652
Todber *Dorset* 22 ST7920
Todburn *Nthumb* 103 NZ1195
Toddington *Beds* 38 TL0128
Toddington *Gloucs* 48 SP0343
Todds Green *Herts* 39 TL2126
Todenham *Gloucs* 48 SP2436
Todhills *Cumb* 101 NY3663
Todhills *Dur* 96 NZ2133
Todhills *Tays* 127 NO4239
Todmorden *W York* 81 SD9324
Todwick *S York* 75 SK4984
Toft *Cambs* 52 TL3655
Toft *Ches* 79 SJ7676
Toft *Lincs* 64 TF0617
Toft *Shet* 155 HU4376
Toft *Warwks* 50 SP4870
Toft Hill *Dur* 96 NZ1428
Toft Monks *Norfk* 67 TM4295
Toft next Newton *Lincs* 76 TF0488
Toftrees *Norfk* 66 TF8927
Tofts *Highld* 151 ND3668
Toftwood *Norfk* 66 TF9911
Togston *Nthumb* 103 NU2402
Tokavaig *Highld* 129 NG6011
Tokers Green *Oxon* 37 SU7077
Toldavas *Cnwll* 2 SW4226
Toldish *Cnwll* 4 SW9259
Toll Bar *S York* 83 SE5507
Tolland *Somset* 20 ST1032
Tollard Farnham *Dorset* 11 ST9515
Tollard Royal *Wilts* 11 ST9417
Tollbar End *W Mids* 61 SP3675
Toller Fratrum *Dorset* 10 SY5797
Toller Porcorum *Dorset* 10 SY5697
Toller Whelme *Dorset* 10 ST5101
Tollerton *N York* 90 SE5164
Tollerton *Notts* 62 SK6134
Tollesbury *Essex* 40 TL9510
Tolleshunt D'Arcy *Essex* 40 TL9312
Tolleshunt Knight *Essex* 40 TL9114
Tolleshunt Major *Essex* 40 TL9011
Tolpuddle *Dorset* 11 SY7994
Tolsta *W Isls* 154 NB5446
Tolstachaolais *W Isls* 154 NB1938
Tolvan *Cnwll* 2 SW7028
Tolver *Cnwll* 2 SW4932
Tolworth *Gt Lon* 26 TQ1966
Tomaknock *Tays* 125 NN8821
Tomatin *Highld* 140 NH8028
Tomchrasky *Highld* 131 NH3512
Tomdoun *Highld* 131 NH1501
Tomich *Highld* 146 NC6005
Tomich *Highld* 139 NH3127
Tomich *Highld* 139 NH5348
Tomich *Highld* 146 NH6971
Tomintoul *Gramp* 141 NJ1618
Tomintoul *Gramp* 133 NO1490
Tomlow *Warwks* 49 SP4663
Tomnacross *Highld* 139 NH5141
Tomnavoulin *Gramp* 141 NJ2026
Tompkin *Staffs* 72 SJ9451
Ton *Gwent* 34 ST3695
Ton *Gwent* 34 SO3301
Ton Pentre *M Glam* 33 SS9795
Ton-teg *M Glam* 33 ST0986
Tonbridge *Kent* 16 TQ5846
Tondu *M Glam* 33 SS8984
Tonedale *Somset* 20 ST1221
Tonfanau *Gwynd* 57 SH5604
Tong *Kent* 28 TQ9556
Tong *Shrops* 60 SJ7907
Tong *W York* 82 SE2230
Tong Green *Kent* 28 TQ9853
Tong Norton *Shrops* 60 SJ7908
Tong Street *W York* 82 SE1901
Tonge *Leics* 62 SK4123
Tongham *Surrey* 25 SU8849
Tongland *D & G* 99 NX6954
Tongue *Highld* 149 NC5957
Tongue End *Lincs* 64 TF1518
Tongwynlais *S Glam* 33 ST1382
Tonmawr *W Glam* 32 SS8096
Tonna *W Glam* 32 SS7798
Tonwell *Herts* 39 TL3316
Tonypandy *M Glam* 33 SS9991
Tonyrefail *M Glam* 33 ST0188
Toot Baldon *Oxon* 37 SP5600
Toot Hill *Essex* 27 TL5102
Toot Hill *Hants* 12 SU3718
Toothill *Wilts* 36 SU1283
Tooting *Gt Lon* 27 TQ2771
Tooting Bec *Gt Lon* 27 TQ2872
Top of Hebers *Gt Man* 79 SD8607
Top-y-rhos *Clwyd* 70 SJ2558
Topcliffe *N York* 89 SE4076
Topcroft *Norfk* 67 TM2693
Topcroft Street *Norfk* 67 TM2692
Topham *S York* 83 SE6217
Toppesfield *Essex* 53 TL7437
Toppings *Gt Man* 81 SD7213
Toprow *Norfk* 66 TM1698
Topsham *Devon* 9 SX9788
Toravaig *Highld* 136 NG4944
Torbay *Devon* 7 SX8962
Torbeg *Strath* 105 NR8929
Torboll *Highld* 147 NH7599
Torbreck *Highld* 140 NH6440
Torbryan *Devon* 7 SX8266
Torcastle *Highld* 131 NN1378
Torcross *Devon* 7 SX8242
Tore *Highld* 140 NH6052
Torfrey *Cnwll* 3 SX1154
Torhousemuir *D & G* 99 NX3957
Torksey *Lincs* 76 SK8378
Torlum *W Isls* 154 NF7850
Tormarton *Avon* 35 ST7678
Tormitchell *Strath* 106 NX2394
Tormore *Strath* 105 NR8932
Tornagrain *Highld* 140 NH7649
Tornaveen *Gramp* 134 NJ6106
Torness *Highld* 139 NH5826
Torness *Strath* 121 NM6532
Tornewton *Devon* 7 SX8167
Toronto *Nthumb* 96 NZ1930
Torosay Castle *Strath* 122 NM7235
Torpenhow *Cumb* 93 NY2039
Torphichen *Loth* 117 NS9772
Torphins *Gramp* 134 NJ6202
Torpoint *Cnwll* 6 SX4355
Torquay *Devon* 7 SX9164
Torquhan *Border* 118 NT4447
Torr *Devon* 6 SX5751
Torran *Highld* 137 NG5949
Torrance *Strath* 116 NS6174
Torranyard *Strath* 115 NS3544
Torre *Somset* 20 ST0439
Torridon *Highld* 138 NG9055
Torridon House *Highld* 138 NG8657
Torrin *Highld* 129 NG5720
Torrisdale *Highld* 149 NC6761
Torrisdale Square *Strath* 105 NR7936
Torrish *Highld* 147 NC9718
Torrisholme *Lancs* 87 SD4563
Torrobull *Highld* 146 NC5904
Torry *Gramp* 135 NJ9405
Torryburn *Fife* 117 NT0386
Tortan *H & W* 60 SO8472
Torteval *Guern* 152 GN0000
Torthorwald *D & G* 100 NY0378
Tortington *W Susx* 14 TQ0005
Tortworth *Avon* 35 ST7093
Torver *Cumb* 86 SD2894
Torwood *Cent* 116 NS8384
Torwoodlee Mains *Border* 109 NT4738
Torworth *Notts* 75 SK6586
Toscaig *Highld* 137 NG7138
Toseland *Cambs* 52 TL2362
Tosside *Lancs* 81 SD7656
Tostock *Suffk* 54 TL9563
Totaig *Highld* 136 NG2050
Tote *Highld* 136 NG4149
Tote Hill *W Susx* 14 SU8624
Totegan *Highld* 150 NC8268
Tothill *Lincs* 77 TF4181
Totland *IOW* 12 SZ3286
Totley *S York* 74 SK3079
Totley Brook *S York* 74 SK3180
Totnes *Devon* 7 SX8060
Toton *Notts* 62 SK5034
Totronald *Strath* 120 NM1656
Totscore *Highld* 136 NG3866
Tottenham *Gt Lon* 27 TQ3390
Tottenhill *Norfk* 65 TF6411
Totteridge *Gt Lon* 26 TQ2494
Totternhoe *Beds* 38 SP9821
Tottington *Gt Man* 81 SD7712
Tottleworth *Lancs* 81 SD7331
Totton *Hants* 12 SU3513
Touchen End *Berks* 26 SU8776
Toulston *N York* 83 SE4543
Toulton *Somset* 20 ST1931
Toulvaddie *Highld* 147 NH8880
Toux *Gramp* 142 NJ5458
Tovil *Kent* 28 TQ7554
Tow Law *Dur* 95 NZ1139
Towan *Cnwll* 4 SW8774
Towan *Cnwll* 3 SX0148
Toward *Strath* 114 NS1367
Toward Quay *Strath* 114 NS1168
Towcester *Nhants* 49 SP6948
Towe End *Cumb* 94 NY6325
Towednack *Cnwll* 2 SW4838
Towersey *Oxon* 37 SP7305
Towie *Gramp* 134 NJ4412
Town End *Cambs* 65 TL4195
Town End *Cumb* 101 NY3687
Town End *Cumb* 87 SD4484
Town End *Lincs* 63 SK9943
Town Green *Lancs* 78 SD4005
Town Green *Norfk* 67 TG3612
Town Head *Cumb* 87 NY4103
Town Head *N York* 82 SE1648
Town Head *N York* 88 SD8258
Town Kelloe *Dur* 96 NZ3637
Town Lane *Gt Man* 79 SJ6999
Town Littleworth *E Susx* 15 TQ4111
Town Moor *T & W* 103 NZ2465
Town of Lowdon *Mersyd* 78 SJ6196
Town Row *E Susx* 16 TQ5630
Town Street *Suffk* 53 TL7786
Town Yetholm *Border* 110 NT8127
Townend Cumb *Cumb* 94 NY5246
Towngate *Cumb* 94 NY5246
Towngate *Lincs* 64 TF1310
Townhead *Cumb* 92 NY0736
Townhead *Cumb* 94 NY6334
Townhead *D & G* 100 NY0188
Townhead *D & G* 99 NX6946
Townhead *S York* 82 SE1602
Townhead of Greenlaw *D & G* 99 NX7465
Townhill *Loth* 117 NT1089
Townlake *Devon* 5 SX4074
Towns End *Hants* 24 SU5659
Townsend *Somset* 10 ST3714
Townshend *Cnwll* 2 SW5932
Townwell *Avon* 35 ST7090
Towthorpe *Humb* 91 SE9062
Towthorpe *N York* 90 SE6258
Towthorpe *N York* 90 SE6258
Towton *N York* 83 SE4839
Towyn *Clwyd* 70 SH9779
Toy's Hill *Kent* 27 TQ4751
Toynton All Saints *Lincs* 77 TF3963
Toynton Fen Side *Lincs* 77 TF3961
Toynton St. Peter *Lincs* 77 TF4063
Trabboch *Strath* 107 NS4321
Trabbochburn *Strath* 107 NS4621
Traboe *Cnwll* 3 SW7421
Tracewell *Somset* 20 ST0720
Tradespark *Highld* 140 NH8656
Traethsaith *Dyfed* 42 SN2751
Trafford Park *Gt Man* 79 SJ7896
Trallong *Powys* 45 SN9629
Tranent *Loth* 118 NT4072
Trannack *Cnwll* 2 SW5633
Trantelbeg *Highld* 150 NC8952
Trantlemore *Highld* 150 NC8953
Tranwell *Nthumb* 103 NZ1883
Trap's Green *Warwks* 48 SP1069
Trapp *Dyfed* 32 SN6519
Trapshill *Berks* 23 SU3763
Traquair *Border* 109 NT3334
Trash Green *Berks* 24 SU6569
Traveller's Rest *Devon* 19 SS6027
Trawden *Lancs* 81 SD9138
Trawscoed *Dyfed* 43 SN6672
Trawsfynydd *Gwynd* 57 SH7035
Tre Aubrey *S Glam* 33 ST0372
Tre'r-ddol *Dyfed* 43 SN6692
Tre-Gibbon *M Glam* 33 SN9905
Tre-gagle *Gwent* 34 SO5208
Tre-groes *Dyfed* 42 SN4044
Tre-mostyn *Clwyd* 70 SJ1479
Tre-Vaughan *Dyfed* 31 SN4021
Tre-wyn *Gwent* 34 SO3222
Trealaw *M Glam* 33 ST0092
Trealaw *M Glam* 33 SS9992
Treales *Lancs* 80 SD4332
Treamble *Cnwll* 3 SW7856
Trearddur Bay *Gwynd* 68 SH2478
Treaslane *Highld* 136 NG3953
Treator *Cnwll* 4 SW9075
Trebanos *W Glam* 32 SN7103
Trebartha *Cnwll* 5 SX2677
Trebarvah *Cnwll* 2 SW7130
Trebarwith *Cnwll* 4 SX0586
Trebeath *Cnwll* 5 SX2587
Trebehor *Cnwll* 2 SW3724
Trebelzue *Cnwll* 4 SW8464
Trebetherick *Cnwll* 4 SW9378
Trebudannon *Cnwll* 4 SW8961
Trebullett *Cnwll* 5 SX3278
Treburgett *Cnwll* 4 SX0579
Treburick *Cnwll* 4 SW8972
Treburley *Cnwll* 5 SX3477
Treburrick *Cnwll* 4 SW8670
Trebursye Oak *Cnwll* 5 SX3084
Trebyan *Cnwll* 4 SX0763
Trecastle *Powys* 45 SN8829
Trecogo *M Glam* 5 SX3080
Trecott *Devon* 8 SS6300
Trecwn *Dyfed* 30 SM9632
Trecynon *M Glam* 33 SN9903
Tredaule *Cnwll* 5 SX2381
Tredavoe *Cnwll* 2 SW4528
Tredegar *Gwent* 33 SO1408
Tredethy *Cnwll* 4 SX0672
Tredington *Gloucs* 47 SO9029
Tredington *Warwks* 48 SP2543
Tredinnick *Cnwll* 4 SX0459
Tredinnick *Cnwll* 4 SX1666
Tredinnick *Cnwll* 5 SX2957
Tredinnick *Cnwll* 5 SX2357
Tredinnick *Cnwll* 4 SW9270
Tredomen *Powys* 45 SO1231
Tredrissi *Dyfed* 31 SN0742
Tredrizzick *Cnwll* 4 SW9576
Tredunhock *Gwent* 34 ST3794
Tredustan *Powys* 45 SO1332
Treen *Cnwll* 2 SW4337
Treen *Cnwll* 2 SW3923
Treesmill *Cnwll* 3 SX0855
Treeton *S York* 75 SK4387
Trefacca *Powys* 45 SO1431
Trefasser *Dyfed* 30 SM8938
Trefdraeth *Gwynd* 68 SH4070
Trefeglwys *Powys* 58 SN9690
Trefenter *Dyfed* 43 SN6068
Treffgarne *Dyfed* 30 SM9523
Treffgarne Owen *Dyfed* 30 SM8625
Treffynnon *Dyfed* 30 SM8428
Trefil *Gwent* 33 SO1212
Trefilan *Dyfed* 44 SN5457
Treflach Wood *Shrops* 58 SJ2625
Trefnannau *Powys* 58 SJ2316
Trefnant *Clwyd* 70 SJ0570
Trefonen *Shrops* 58 SJ2526
Trefor *Gwynd* 68 SH3779
Treforda *Cnwll* 4 SX0988
Treforest *M Glam* 33 ST0888
Trefrew *Cnwll* 4 SX1084
Trefriw *Gwynd* 69 SH7863
Tregadillett *Cnwll* 5 SX2983
Tregaian *Gwynd* 68 SH4580
Tregare *Gwent* 34 SO4110
Tregarne *Cnwll* 3 SW7822
Tregaron *Dyfed* 44 SN6859
Tregarth *Gwynd* 69 SH6067
Tregaswith *Cnwll* 4 SW8962

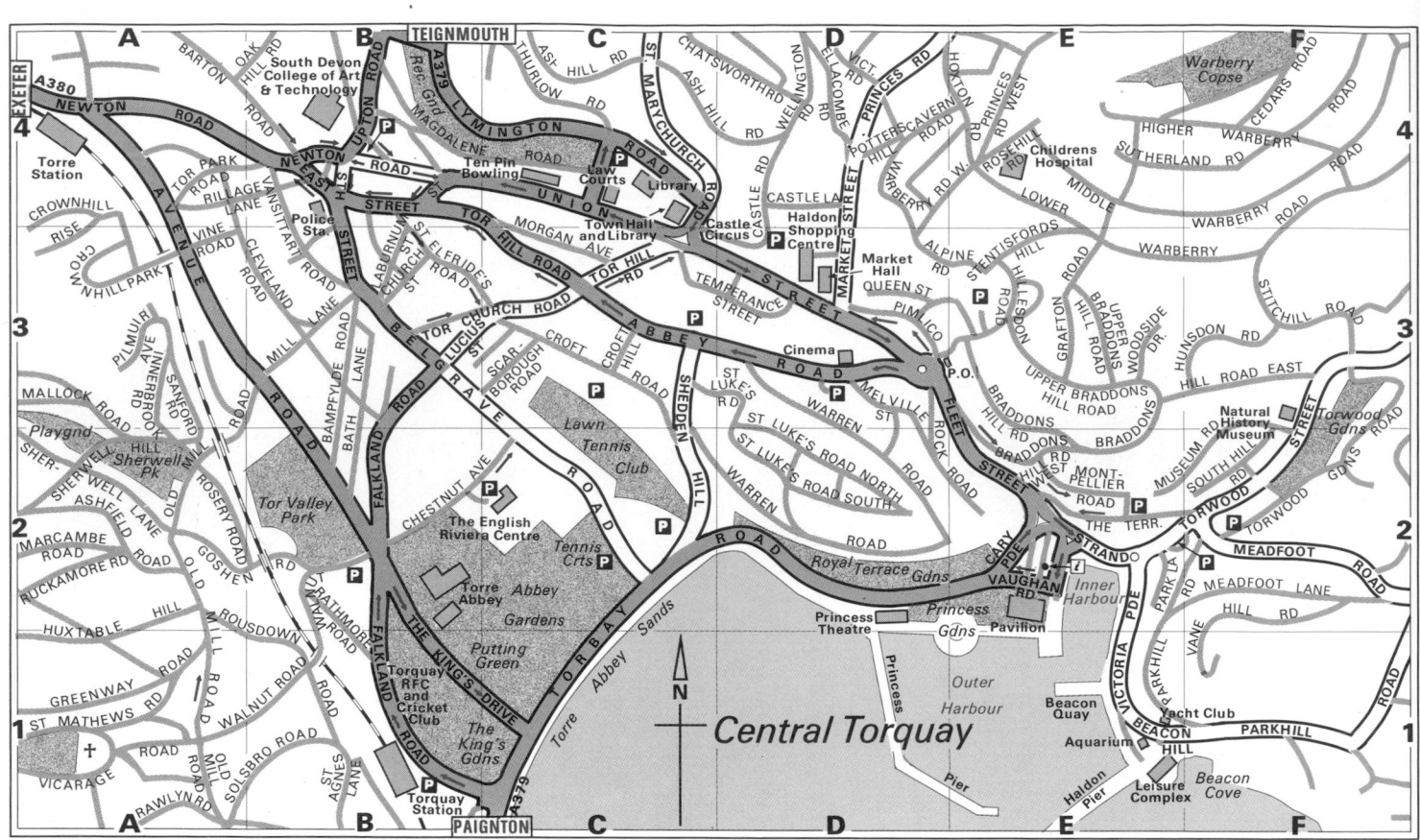

Central Torquay

| Name | № | Ref |
|---|---|---|
| Tregatta Cnwll | 4 | SX0587 |
| Tregawne Cnwll | 4 | SX0066 |
| Tregear Cnwll | 3 | SW8750 |
| Tregeare Cnwll | 5 | SX2486 |
| Tregeiriog Clwyd | 58 | SJ1733 |
| Tregele Gwynd | 68 | SH3592 |
| Tregellist Cnwll | 4 | SX0177 |
| Tregenna Cnwll | 3 | SW8743 |
| Tregenna Cnwll | 4 | SX0971 |
| Tregeseal Cnwll | 2 | SW3832 |
| Tregew Cnwll | 3 | SW8034 |
| Tregidden Cnwll | 3 | SW7523 |
| Tregiddle Cnwll | 2 | SW6723 |
| Tregidgeo Cnwll | 3 | SW9647 |
| Tregiskey Cnwll | 3 | SX0146 |
| Treglemais Dyfed | 30 | SM8229 |
| Tregole Cnwll | 5 | SX1998 |
| Tregolls Cnwll | 3 | SW7335 |
| Tregonce Cnwll | 4 | SW9373 |
| Tregonetha Cnwll | 4 | SW9563 |
| Tregony Cnwll | 3 | SW9244 |
| Tregoodwell Cnwll | 4 | SX1183 |
| Tregoose Cnwll | 2 | SW6823 |
| Tregoss Cnwll | 4 | SW9660 |
| Tregowris Cnwll | 3 | SW7523 |
| Tregoyd Powys | 45 | SO1937 |
| Tregrehan Mills Cnwll | 3 | SX0453 |
| Tregullon Cnwll | 4 | SX0664 |
| Tregunna Cnwll | 4 | SW9673 |
| Tregunnon Cnwll | 5 | SX2283 |
| Tregurrian Cnwll | 4 | SW8465 |
| Tregustick Cnwll | 4 | SW9966 |
| Tregynon Powys | 58 | SO1099 |
| Trehafod M Glam | 33 | ST0490 |
| Trehan Cnwll | 5 | SX4058 |
| Treharris M Glam | 33 | ST0996 |
| Treharrock Cnwll | 4 | SX0277 |
| Trehemborne Cnwll | 4 | SW8773 |
| Treherbert Dyfed | 44 | SN5847 |
| Treherbert M Glam | 33 | SS9498 |
| Treheveras Cnwll | 3 | SW8146 |
| Trehunist Cnwll | 5 | SX3163 |
| Trekelland M Glam | 5 | SX3480 |
| Trekenner Cnwll | 5 | SX3478 |
| Treknow Cnwll | 4 | SX0586 |
| Trelan Cnwll | 3 | SW7418 |
| Trelash Cnwll | 4 | SX1890 |
| Trelassick Cnwll | 3 | SW8752 |
| Trelawne Cnwll | 5 | SX2154 |
| Trelawnyd Clwyd | 70 | SJ0879 |
| Treleague Cnwll | 3 | SW7821 |
| Treleaver Cnwll | 3 | SW7716 |
| Trelech Dyfed | 31 | SN2830 |
| Trelech a'r Betws Dyfed | 31 | SN3026 |
| Treleddyd-fawr Dyfed | 30 | SM7528 |
| Trelew Cnwll | 3 | SW8035 |
| Trelewis M Glam | 33 | ST1096 |
| Treligga Cnwll | 4 | SX0584 |
| Trelights Cnwll | 4 | SW9979 |
| Trelill Cnwll | 4 | SX0478 |
| Trelion Cnwll | 3 | SW9252 |
| Trelissick Cnwll | 3 | SW8339 |
| Trelleck Gwent | 34 | SO5005 |
| Trelleck Grange Gwent | 34 | SO4901 |
| Trelminoe M Glam | 5 | SX3181 |
| Trelogan Clwyd | 70 | SJ1180 |
| Trelonk Cnwll | 3 | SW8941 |
| Trelow Cnwll | 4 | SW9269 |
| Trelowarren Cnwll | 2 | SW7124 |
| Trelowia Cnwll | 5 | SX2956 |
| Treluggan Cnwll | 3 | SW8838 |
| Trelystan Powys | 58 | SJ2503 |
| Tremadog Gwynd | 57 | SH5640 |
| Tremail Cnwll | 5 | SX1686 |
| Tremain Dyfed | 42 | SN2348 |
| Tremaine Cnwll | 5 | SX2388 |
| Tremar Cnwll | 5 | SX2568 |
| Trematon Cnwll | 5 | SX3959 |
| Trembraze Cnwll | 5 | SX2565 |
| Tremeirchion Clwyd | 70 | SJ0773 |
| Tremethick Cross Cnwll | 2 | SW4430 |
| Tremollett Cnwll | 5 | SX2975 |
| Tremore Cnwll | 4 | SX0165 |
| Trenance Cnwll | 2 | SW6718 |
| Trenance Cnwll | 3 | SW8022 |
| Trenance Cnwll | 4 | SW9270 |
| Trenarren Cnwll | 3 | SX0348 |
| Trenault Cnwll | 5 | SX2683 |
| Trench Shrops | 60 | SJ6913 |
| Trench Green Oxon | 37 | SU6877 |
| Trencreek Cnwll | 4 | SW8260 |
| Trencreek Cnwll | 4 | SX1896 |
| Trendeal Cnwll | 3 | SW8952 |
| Trendrine Cnwll | 2 | SW4739 |
| Treneague Cnwll | 4 | SW9851 |
| Trenear Cnwll | 2 | SW6831 |
| Treneglos Cnwll | 5 | SX2088 |
| Trenerth Cnwll | 2 | SW6035 |
| Trenewan Cnwll | 4 | SX1753 |
| Trenewth Cnwll | 4 | SX0778 |
| Trengothal Cnwll | 2 | SW3724 |
| Trengune Cnwll | 4 | SX1893 |
| Treninnick Cnwll | 4 | SW8160 |
| Trenowah Cnwll | 4 | SW7959 |
| Trenoweth Cnwll | 3 | SW7533 |
| Trent Dorset | 10 | ST5918 |
| Trent Lincs | 76 | SK8381 |
| Trent Vale Staffs | 72 | SJ8643 |
| Trentham Staffs | 72 | SJ8641 |
| Trentishoe Devon | 19 | SS6448 |
| Trentlock Derbys | 62 | SK4831 |
| Treoes S Glam | 33 | SS9478 |
| Treorchy M Glam | 33 | SS9597 |
| Trequite Cnwll | 4 | SX0277 |
| Trerhyngyll S Glam | 33 | ST0077 |
| Trerulefoot Cnwll | 5 | SX3258 |
| Tresahor Cnwll | 3 | SW7431 |
| Tresawle Cnwll | 3 | SW8946 |
| Trescott Staffs | 60 | SO8597 |
| Trescowe Cnwll | 2 | SW5731 |
| Tresean Cnwll | 4 | SW7858 |
| Tresham Avon | 35 | ST7991 |
| Tresillian Cnwll | 3 | SW8646 |
| Tresinney Cnwll | 4 | SX1081 |
| Treskinnick Cross Cnwll | 5 | SX2098 |
| Treslea Cnwll | 4 | SX1368 |
| Tresmeer Cnwll | 5 | SX2387 |
| Tresparrett Cnwll | 5 | SX1491 |
| Tressait Tays | 132 | NN8160 |
| Tresta Shet | 155 | HU3651 |
| Tresta Shet | 155 | HU6190 |
| Treswell Notts | 75 | SK7779 |
| Treswithian Cnwll | 2 | SW6241 |
| Trethawle Cnwll | 5 | SX2662 |
| Trethevey Cnwll | 4 | SX0789 |
| Trethewey Cnwll | 2 | SW3824 |
| Trethomas M Glam | 33 | ST1888 |
| Trethosa Cnwll | 3 | SW9454 |
| Trethurgy Cnwll | 3 | SX0355 |
| Tretio Dyfed | 30 | SM7828 |
| Tretire H & W | 46 | SO5123 |
| Tretower Powys | 33 | SO1821 |
| Tretower Powys | 33 | SO1821 |
| Treuddyn Clwyd | 70 | SJ2557 |
| Trevadlock Cnwll | 5 | SX2579 |
| Trevague Cnwll | 5 | SX2379 |
| Trevalyn Clwyd | 71 | SJ3856 |
| Trevanger Cnwll | 4 | SW9077 |
| Trevanson Cnwll | 4 | SW9772 |
| Trevarrack Cnwll | 2 | SW4831 |
| Trevarren Cnwll | 4 | SW9160 |
| Trevarrian Cnwll | 4 | SW8566 |
| Trevarrick Cnwll | 3 | SW9843 |
| Trevarth Cnwll | 3 | SW7240 |
| Trevaughan Dyfed | 31 | SN1915 |
| Treveal Cnwll | 2 | SW4740 |
| Treveal Cnwll | 4 | SW7850 |
| Treveale Cnwll | 3 | SW8751 |
| Treveighan Cnwll | 4 | SX0779 |
| Trevellas Cnwll | 3 | SW7452 |
| Trevelmond Cnwll | 5 | SX2063 |
| Trevempor Cnwll | 4 | SW8159 |
| Treveneague Cnwll | 2 | SW5432 |
| Treveor Cnwll | 3 | SW9841 |
| Treverbyn Cnwll | 3 | SW8849 |
| Treverbyn Cnwll | 4 | SX0157 |
| Treverva Cnwll | 3 | SW7531 |
| Trevescan Cnwll | 2 | SW3524 |
| Trevethin Gwent | 34 | SO2802 |
| Trevia Cnwll | 4 | SX0983 |
| Trevigro Cnwll | 5 | SX3369 |
| Trevilla Cnwll | 3 | SW8239 |
| Trevilledor Cnwll | 4 | SW8967 |
| Trevilson Cnwll | 3 | SW8455 |
| Trevine Dyfed | 30 | SM8432 |
| Treviscoe Cnwll | 3 | SW9455 |
| Treviskey Cnwll | 3 | SW9340 |
| Trevissick Cnwll | 3 | SX0248 |
| Trevithal Cnwll | 2 | SW4626 |
| Trevithick Cnwll | 4 | SW8862 |
| Trevithick Cnwll | 3 | SW9645 |
| Trevivian Cnwll | 4 | SX1785 |
| Trevoll Cnwll | 4 | SW8358 |
| Trevone Cnwll | 4 | SW8975 |
| Trevor Clwyd | 70 | SJ2642 |
| Trevor Gwynd | 56 | SH3746 |
| Trevorgans Cnwll | 2 | SW4025 |
| Trevorrick Cnwll | 4 | SW8672 |
| Trevorrick Cnwll | 4 | SW9273 |
| Trevose Cnwll | 4 | SW8675 |
| Trew Cnwll | 2 | SW6129 |
| Trewalder Cnwll | 4 | SX0782 |
| Trewalkin Powys | 45 | SO1531 |
| Trewarlett M Glam | 5 | SX3379 |
| Trewarmett Cnwll | 4 | SX0686 |
| Trewarthenick Cnwll | 3 | SW9044 |
| Trewassa Cnwll | 4 | SX1486 |
| Trewaves Cnwll | 2 | SW5926 |
| Treween Cnwll | 5 | SX2282 |
| Trewellard Cnwll | 2 | SW3733 |
| Trewen Cnwll | 4 | SX0577 |
| Trewennack Cnwll | 2 | SW6828 |
| Trewent Dyfed | 30 | SS0197 |
| Trewern Powys | 58 | SJ2811 |
| Trewetha Cnwll | 4 | SX0080 |
| Trewethern Cnwll | 4 | SX0076 |
| Trewidland Cnwll | 5 | SX2560 |
| Trewillis Cnwll | 3 | SW7717 |
| Trewince Cnwll | 3 | SW8633 |
| Trewint Cnwll | 4 | SX1072 |
| Trewint Cnwll | 5 | SX2180 |
| Trewint Cnwll | 5 | SX2983 |
| Trewirgie Cnwll | 3 | SW6739 |
| Trewithian Cnwll | 3 | SW8737 |
| Trewithick Cnwll | 3 | SW8737 |
| Trewoodloe M Glam | 5 | SX3271 |
| Trewoofe Cnwll | 2 | SW4425 |
| Trewoon Cnwll | 2 | SW6819 |
| Trewoon Cnwll | 3 | SW9952 |
| Treworgan Cnwll | 3 | SW8349 |
| Treworlas Cnwll | 3 | SW8938 |
| Treworld Cnwll | 4 | SX1190 |
| Treworthal Cnwll | 3 | SW8838 |
| Treyarnon Cnwll | 4 | SW8673 |
| Treyford W Susx | 14 | SU8218 |
| Triangle Glocs | 34 | SO5401 |
| Triangle W York | 82 | SE0422 |
| Trickett's Cross Dorset | 12 | SU0801 |
| Triermain Cumb | 102 | NY5967 |
| Triffleton Dyfed | 30 | SM9724 |
| Trillacott Cnwll | 5 | SX2689 |
| Trimdon Dur | 96 | NZ3634 |
| Trimdon Colliery Dur | 96 | NZ3835 |
| Trimdon Grange Dur | 96 | NZ3635 |
| Trimingham Norfk | 67 | TG2738 |
| Trimley Suffk | 55 | TM2737 |
| Trimley Heath Suffk | 55 | TM2738 |
| Trimley Lower Street Suffk | 55 | TM2636 |
| Trimpley H & W | 60 | SO7978 |
| Trimsaran Dyfed | 32 | SN4504 |
| Trimstone Devon | 19 | SS5043 |
| Trinafour Tays | 132 | NN7264 |
| Trinant Gwent | 33 | ST2099 |
| Trinant Gwent | 33 | SO2000 |
| Tring Herts | 38 | SP9211 |
| Tring Wharf Herts | 38 | SP9212 |
| Tringford Herts | 38 | SP9113 |
| Trinity Jersey | 152 | JS0000 |
| Trinity Tays | 134 | NO6061 |
| Trinity Gask Tays | 108 | NS9618 |
| Triscombe Somset | 20 | ST1535 |
| Triscombe Somset | 20 | SS9237 |
| Trislaig Highld | 130 | NN0874 |
| Trispen Cnwll | 3 | SW8450 |
| Tritlington Nthumb | 103 | NZ2092 |
| Troan Cnwll | 4 | SW8957 |
| Trochry Tays | 125 | NN9740 |
| Trodigal Strath | 104 | NR6420 |
| Troedrhiwfuwch M Glam | 33 | SO1204 |
| Troedyraur Dyfed | 42 | SN3245 |
| Troedyrhiw M Glam | 33 | SO0702 |
| Trofarth Clwyd | 69 | SH8571 |
| Trois Bois Jersey | 152 | JS0000 |
| Troon Cnwll | 2 | SW6638 |
| Troon Strath | 106 | NS3230 |
| Trossachs Hotel Cent | 99 | NX6879 |
| Troston Suffk | 54 | TL8972 |
| Troswell Cnwll | 5 | SX2592 |
| Trots Hill H & W | 47 | SO8856 |
| Trottiscliffe Kent | 27 | TQ6460 |
| Trotton W Susx | 14 | SU8322 |
| Trough Gate Lancs | 81 | SD8821 |
| Troughend Nthumb | 102 | NY8692 |
| Troutbeck Cumb | 87 | NY4002 |
| Troutbeck Bridge Cumb | 87 | NY4000 |
| Trow Green Glocs | 34 | SO5706 |
| Troway Derbys | 74 | SK3879 |
| Trowbridge Wilts | 22 | ST8557 |
| Trowell Notts | 62 | SK4839 |
| Trowle Common Wilts | 22 | ST8358 |
| Trowse Newton Norfk | 67 | TG2406 |
| Troy W York | 82 | SE2438 |
| Trudoxhill Somset | 22 | ST7443 |
| Trull Somset | 20 | ST2122 |
| Trumfleet S York | 83 | SE6012 |
| Trumisgarry W Isls | 154 | NF8674 |
| Trumpan Highld | 136 | NG2261 |
| Trumpet H & W | 47 | SO6539 |
| Trumpington Cambs | 53 | TL4456 |
| Trumpington Cambs | 53 | TL4754 |
| Trumpsgreen Surrey | 25 | SU9967 |
| Trunch Norfk | 67 | TG2834 |
| Trunnah Lancs | 80 | SD3442 |
| Truro Cnwll | 3 | SW8244 |
| Truscott Cnwll | 5 | SX2985 |
| Trusham Devon | 8 | SX8582 |
| Trusley Derbys | 73 | SK2535 |
| Trysull Staffs | 60 | SO8594 |
| Tubney Oxon | 36 | SU4398 |
| Tuckenhay Devon | 7 | SX8156 |
| Tuckhill Shrops | 60 | SO7888 |
| Tuckingmill Cnwll | 2 | SW6540 |
| Tuckingmill Wilts | 22 | ST9329 |
| Tuckton Dorset | 12 | SZ1492 |
| Tucoyse Cnwll | 3 | SW9646 |
| Tuddenham Suffk | 53 | TL7371 |
| Tuddenham Suffk | 55 | TM1948 |
| Tudeley Kent | 16 | TQ6245 |

Tudhoe
Usworth

Tudhoe *Dur* 96 NZ2535
Tudweiloig *Gwynd* 56 SH2336
Tuesley *Surrey* 25 SU9642
Tuffley *Gloucs* 35 SO8314
Tufton *Dyfed* 30 SN0428
Tufton *Hants* 24 SU4546
Tugby *Leics* 63 SK7601
Tugford *Shrops* 59 SO5687
Tughall *Nthumb* 111 NU2126
Tullibody *Cent* 116 NS8595
Tullich *Highld* 140 NH6328
Tullich *Highld* 147 NH8576
Tullich *Strath* 123 NN0815
Tullich Muir *Highld* 146 NH7273
Tulliemet *Tays* 125 NO0052
Tulloch *Cent* 124 NN5120
Tulloch *Gramp* 143 NJ7931
Tulloch *Gramp* 135 NO7671
Tulloch Station *Highld* 131 NN3580
Tullochgorm *Strath* 114 NR9695
Tullybeagles Lodge *Tays* 125 NO0136
Tullynessle *Gramp* 142 NJ5519
Tumble *Dyfed* 32 SN5411
Tumbler's Green *Essex* 40 TL8025
Tumby *Lincs* 76 TF2359
Tumby Woodside *Lincs* 77 TF2757
Tummel Bridge *Tays* 132 NN7659
Tungate *Norfk* 67 TG2629
Tunstall *Humb* 85 TA3031
Tunstall *Kent* 28 TQ8961
Tunstall *Lancs* 87 SD6073
Tunstall *N York* 89 SE2195
Tunstall *Norfk* 67 TG4108
Tunstall *Staffs* 72 SJ7727
Tunstall *Staffs* 72 SJ8551
Tunstall *Suffk* 55 TM3655
Tunstall *T & W* 96 NZ3953
Tunstead *Derbys* 74 SK1175
Tunstead *Norfk* 67 TG3022
Tunstead Milton *Derbys* 74 SK0280
Tunworth *Hants* 24 SU6748
Tupsley *H & W* 46 SO5340
Tur Langton *Leics* 50 SP7194
Turgis Green *Hants* 24 SU6959
Turin *Tays* 127 NO5352
Turkdean *Gloucs* 36 SP1017
Turleigh *Wilts* 22 ST8060
Turleygreen *Shrops* 60 SO7685
Turn *Lancs* 81 SD8118
Turnastone *H & W* 46 SO3536
Turnberry *Strath* 106 NS2005
Turnchapel *Devon* 6 SX4952
Turnditch *Derbys* 73 SK2946
Turner Green *Lancs* 81 SD6030
Turner's Green *E Susx* 16 TQ6218
Turner's Green *Warwks* 48 SP1969
Turner's Hill *W Susx* 15 TQ3435
Turners Puddle *Dorset* 11 SY8394
Turnworth *Dorset* 11 ST8107
Turriff *Gramp* 142 NJ7250
Turton Bottoms *Gt Man* 81 SD7315
Turvey *Beds* 38 SP9452
Turville *Bucks* 37 SU7691
Turville Heath *Bucks* 37 SU7490
Turweston *Bucks* 49 SP6037
Tushielaw Inn *Border* 109 NT3017
Tushingham cum Grindley *Ches* 71 SJ5246
Tutbury *Staffs* 73 SK2128
Tutnall *H & W* 60 SO9970
Tutshill *Gloucs* 34 ST5495
Tuttington *Norfk* 67 TG2227
Tutwell *M Glam* 5 SX3876
Tuxford *Notts* 75 SK7471
Twatt *Ork* 155 HY2624
Twatt *Shet* 155 HU3253
Twechar *Strath* 116 NS6975
Tweedmouth *Nthumb* 119 NT9952
Tweedsmuir *Border* 108 NT1024
Twelve Oaks *E Susx* 16 TQ6820
Twelveheads *Cnwll* 3 SW7642
Twemlow Green *Ches* 79 SJ7868
Twenty *Lincs* 64 TF1520
Twerton *Avon* 22 ST7264
Twickenham *Gt Lon* 26 TQ1673
Twigworth *Gloucs* 35 SO8422
Twineham *W Susx* 15 TQ2519
Twineham Green *W Susx* 15 TQ2520
Twinhoe *Avon* 22 ST7359
Twinstead *Essex* 54 TL8636
Twiss Green *Ches* 79 SJ6595
Twitchen *Devon* 19 SS7830
Twitchen *Shrops* 46 SO3779
Twitham *Kent* 29 TR2556
Two Bridges *Devon* 6 SX6075
Two Dales *Derbys* 74 SK2762
Two Gates *Staffs* 61 SK2101
Two Mile Oak Cross *Devon* 7 SX8467
Two Pots *Devon* 19 SS5344
Two Waters *Herts* 38 TL0505
Twycross *Leics* 62 SK3305
Twyford *Berks* 37 SU7976
Twyford *Bucks* 49 SP6626
Twyford *Derbys* 62 SK3228
Twyford *Hants* 13 SU4824
Twyford *Leics* 63 SK7210
Twyford *Lincs* 63 SK9323
Twyford *Norfk* 66 TG0124
Twyford Common *H & W* 46 SO5035
Twyn-carno *M Glam* 33 SO1108
Twyn-y-Sheriff *Gwent* 34 SO4005
Twyn-yr-Odyn *S Glam* 33 ST1173
Twynholm *D & G* 99 NX6654
Twyning *Gloucs* 47 SO8936
Twyning Green *Gloucs* 47 SO9036
Twynllanan *Dyfed* 44 SN7524
Twynmynydd *Dyfed* 32 SN6614
Twywell *Nhants* 51 SP9578
Ty Rhiw *M Glam* 33 ST1283
Ty'n-dwr *Clwyd* 70 SJ2341
Ty'n-y-bryn *M Glam* 30 SS0087
Ty'n-y-coedcae *M Glam* 33 ST1988
Ty'n-y-groes *Gwynd* 69 SH7771
Ty-nant *Clwyd* 70 SH9845
Ty-nant *Gwynd* 58 SH9026
Tyberton *H & W* 46 SO3839
Tyburn *W Mids* 61 SP1391
Tycroes *Dyfed* 32 SN6010
Tycrwyn *Powys* 58 SJ1018
Tydd Gote *Lincs* 65 TF4518
Tydd St. Giles *Cambs* 65 TF4216
Tydd St. Mary *Lincs* 65 TF4418
Tye *Hants* 13 SU7302
Tye Green *Essex* 39 TL5424
Tye Green *Essex* 40 TL7821
Tye Green *Essex* 53 TL5935
Tyersal *W York* 82 SE1932
Tyldesley *Gt Man* 79 SD6802
Tyler Hill *Kent* 29 TR1461
Tyler's Green *Essex* 39 TL5005
Tylers Green *Bucks* 26 SU9093
Tylers Green *Surrey* 27 TQ3552
Tylorstown *M Glam* 33 ST0095
Tylwch *Powys* 58 SN9780
Tyn-y-graig *Powys* 45 SO0149
Tyn-y-nant *M Glam* 33 ST0685
Tynant *M Glam* 33 ST0684
Tyndrum *Cent* 123 NN3330
Tyneham *Dorset* 11 SY8880
Tynemouth *T & W* 103 NZ3669
Tynewydd *M Glam* 33 SS9399
Tyninghame *Loth* 118 NT6179
Tynron *D & G* 100 NX8093
Tyntesfield *Avon* 34 ST5071
Tynygongl *Gwynd* 68 SH5082
Tynygongl *Gwynd* 68 SH5182
Tynygraig *Dyfed* 43 SN6969
Tyringham *Bucks* 38 SP8546
Tyseley *W Mids* 61 SP1184
Tythecott *Devon* 18 SS4117
Tythegston *M Glam* 33 SS8578
Tytherington *Avon* 35 ST6788
Tytherington *Ches* 79 SJ9175
Tytherington *Somset* 22 ST7744
Tytherington *Wilts* 22 ST9140
Tytherleigh *Devon* 10 ST3203
Tywardreath *Cnwll* 3 SX0854
Tywardreath Highway *Cnwll* 3 SX0755
Tywyn *Gwynd* 69 SH5790
Tywyn *Gwynd* 69 SH7978

# U

Uachdar *W Isls* 154 NF7955
Ubbeston Green *Suffk* 55 TM3272
Ubley *Avon* 21 ST5257
Uckerby *N York* 89 NZ2402
Uckfield *E Susx* 16 TQ4721
Uckinghall *H & W* 47 SO8637
Uckington *Gloucs* 47 SO9224
Uckington *Shrops* 59 SJ5709
Uddingston *Strath* 116 NS6960
Uddington *Strath* 108 NS8633
Udimore *E Susx* 17 TQ8719
Udny Green *Gramp* 143 NJ8726
Uffcott *Wilts* 36 SU1277
Uffculme *Devon* 20 ST0620
Uffculme *Devon* 9 ST0612
Uffington *Oxon* 36 SU3089
Uffington *Shrops* 59 SJ5314
Ufford *Cambs* 64 TF0904
Ufford *Suffk* 55 TM2952
Ufton *Warwks* 48 SP3762
Ufton Nervet *Berks* 24 SU6367
Ugadale *Strath* 105 NR7828
Ugborough *Devon* 7 SX6755
Uggeshall *Suffk* 55 TM4480
Ugglebarnby *N York* 90 NZ8807
Ughill *Derbys* 74 SK2590
Ugley *Essex* 39 TL5228
Ugley Green *Essex* 39 TL5227
Ugthorpe *N York* 90 NZ7911
Uig *Highld* 136 NG1952
Uig *Highld* 136 NG3963
Uig *Strath* 120 NM1754
Uig *W Isls* 154 NB0534
Uigshader *Highld* 136 NG4346
Uisken *Strath* 121 NM3919
Ulbster *Highld* 151 ND3241
Ulcat Row *Cumb* 93 NY4022
Ulceby *Humb* 85 TA1014
Ulceby *Lincs* 77 TF4272
Ulceby Skitter *Humb* 85 TA1014
Ulcombe *Kent* 28 TQ8448
Uldale *Cumb* 93 NY2437
Uley *Gloucs* 35 ST7898
Ulgham *Nthumb* 103 NZ2392
Ullapool *Highld* 145 NH1294
Ulleby Cross *Lincs* 77 TF4173
Ullenhall *Warwks* 48 SP1267
Ullenwood *Gloucs* 35 SO9416
Ulleskelf *N York* 83 SE5139
Ullesthorpe *Leics* 50 SP5087
Ulley *S York* 75 SK4687
Ullingswick *H & W* 46 SO5950
Ullinish *Highld* 136 NG3237
Ullock *Cumb* 92 NY0724
Ulpha *Cumb* 87 SD3581
Ulpha *Cumb* 86 SD1993
Ulrome *Humb* 85 TA1656
Ulsta *Shet* 155 HU4680
Ulting Wick *Essex* 40 TL8009
Ulverley Green *W Mids* 61 SP1381
Ulverston *Cumb* 86 SD2878
Ulwell *Dorset* 12 SZ0280
Umachan *Highld* 137 NG6150
Umberleigh *Devon* 19 SS6023
Under Burnmouth *D & G* 101 NY4783
Under River *Kent* 27 TQ5552
Underbarrow *Cumb* 87 SD4692
Undercliffe *W York* 82 SE1834
Underdale *Shrops* 59 SJ5013
Underley Hall *Cumb* 87 SD6179
Underling Green *Kent* 28 TQ7546
Underwood *Gwent* 34 ST3888
Underwood *Notts* 75 SK4750
Undley *Suffk* 53 TL6981
Undy *Gwent* 34 ST4386
Union Mills *IOM* 153 SC3578
Union Street *E Susx* 16 TQ7031
Unstone *Derbys* 74 SK3777
Unstone Green *Derbys* 74 SK3776
Unsworth *Gt Man* 79 SD8207
Unthank *Cumb* 93 NY3948
Unthank *Cumb* 94 NY6050
Unthank *Cumb* 93 NY3948
Unthank *Nthumb* 111 NT9848
Unthank End *Cumb* 93 NY4535
Up Cerne *Dorset* 11 ST6502
Up Exe *Devon* 9 SS9302
Up Holland *Lancs* 78 SD5105
Up Marden *W Susx* 14 SU7914
Up Mudford *Somset* 10 ST5718
Up Nately *Hants* 24 SU6951
Up Somborne *Hants* 23 SU3932
Up Sydling *Dorset* 10 ST6201
Upavon *Wilts* 23 SU1354
Upchurch *Kent* 28 TQ8467
Upcott *Devon* 19 SS5739
Upcott *Devon* 19 SS7529
Upcott *H & W* 46 SO3250
Upcott *Somset* 20 SS9025
Updown Hill *Surrey* 25 SU9363
Upend *Cambs* 53 TL7058
Upgate *Norfk* 66 TG1418
Upgate Street *Norfk* 66 TM0992
Upgate Street *Norfk* 67 TM2891
Uphall *Dorset* 10 ST5502
Uphall *Loth* 117 NT0671
Upham *Devon* 19 SS8808
Upham *Hants* 13 SU5320
Uphampton *H & W* 47 SO8364
Uphampton *H & W* 46 SO3963
Uphill *Avon* 21 ST3158
Uplawmoor *Strath* 115 NS4355
Upleadon *Gloucs* 47 SO7527
Upleatham *Cleve* 97 NZ6319
Uplees *Kent* 17 TR0004
Uploders *Dorset* 10 SY5093
Uplowman *Devon* 9 ST0115
Uplyme *Devon* 10 SY3293
Upminster *Gt Lon* 27 TQ5686
Upottery *Devon* 9 ST2007
Uppark *W Susx* 14 SU7717
Upparthong *W York* 82 SE1208
Uppat House *Highld* 147 NC8702
Uppaton *Devon* 5 SX4380
Upper Affcot *Shrops* 59 SO4486
Upper Ardchronie *Highld* 146 NH6188
Upper Arley *H & W* 60 SO7680
Upper Arncott *Oxon* 37 SP6017
Upper Astrop *Nhants* 49 SP5137
Upper Basildon *Berks* 37 SU5976
Upper Batley *W York* 82 SE2325
Upper Beeding *W Susx* 15 TQ1910
Upper Benefield *Nhants* 51 SP9789
Upper Bentley *H & W* 47 SO9966
Upper Bighouse *Highld* 150 NC8857
Upper Birchwood *Derbys* 75 SK4355
Upper Boat *M Glam* 33 ST1087
Upper Boddington *Nhants* 49 SP4853
Upper Borth *Dyfed* 43 SN6088
Upper Brailes *Warwks* 48 SP3040
Upper Breakish *Highld* 129 NG6823
Upper Breinton *H & W* 46 SO4640
Upper Broadheath *H & W* 47 SO8056
Upper Broughton *Notts* 63 SK6826
Upper Bucklebury *Berks* 24 SU5468
Upper Burgate *Hants* 12 SU1516
Upper Bush *Kent* 28 TQ6966
Upper Cairmie *Tays* 105 NS0319
Upper Cairn *D & G* 107 NS6912
Upper Caldecote *Beds* 52 TL1645
Upper Canada *Avon* 21 ST3658
Upper Canterton *Hants* 12 SU2612
Upper Catesby *Nhants* 49 SP5259
Upper Catshill *H & W* 60 SO9674
Upper Chapel *Powys* 45 SO0040
Upper Cheddon *Somset* 20 ST2328
Upper Chickgrove *Wilts* 22 ST9730
Upper Chute *Wilts* 23 SU2953
Upper Chute *Wilts* 23 SU2953
Upper Clapton *Gt Lon* 27 TQ3487
Upper Clatford *Hants* 23 SU3543
Upper Clynnog *Gwynd* 56 SH4746
Upper Coberley *Gloucs* 35 SO9815
Upper Cokeham *W Susx* 15 TQ1705
Upper Cotton *Staffs* 73 SK0547
Upper Cound *Shrops* 59 SJ5505
Upper Cudworth *S York* 83 SE3908
Upper Cumberworth *W York* 82 SE2008
Upper Cwmtwrch *Powys* 32 SN7611
Upper Dallachy *Gramp* 141 NJ3662
Upper Deal *Kent* 29 TR3651
Upper Dean *Beds* 51 TL0467
Upper Denby *W York* 82 SE2307
Upper Denton *Cumb* 102 NY6165
Upper Dicker *E Susx* 16 TQ5509
Upper Dinchope *Shrops* 59 SO4583
Upper Dovercourt *Essex* 41 TM2331
Upper Drumbane *Cent* 124 NN6606
Upper Dunsforth *N York* 89 SE4463
Upper Eashing *Surrey* 25 SU9543
Upper Egleton *H & W* 47 SO6345
Upper Elkstone *Staffs* 74 SK0559
Upper Ellastone *Staffs* 73 SK1143
Upper Elmers End *Gt Lon* 27 TQ3667
Upper End *Derbys* 74 SK0876
Upper Enham *Hants* 23 SU3649
Upper Ethrie *Highld* 140 NH7662
Upper Farmcote *Shrops* 60 SO7792
Upper Farringdon *Hants* 24 SU7135
Upper Framilode *Gloucs* 35 SO7510
Upper Froyle *Hants* 24 SU7542
Upper Godney *Somset* 21 ST4842
Upper Gravenhurst *Beds* 38 TL1136
Upper Green *Berks* 23 SU3763
Upper Green *Essex* 53 TL5935
Upper Green *Gwent* 34 SO3818
Upper Green *Suffk* 53 TL7464
Upper Grove Common *H & W* 46 SO5526
Upper Hackney *Derbys* 74 SK2861
Upper Hale *Surrey* 25 SU8449
Upper Halliford *Surrey* 26 TQ0968
Upper Halling *Kent* 28 TQ6964
Upper Hambleton *Leics* 63 SK9007
Upper Harbledown *Kent* 29 TR1158
Upper Hardres Court *Kent* 29 TR1550
Upper Hardwick *H & W* 46 SO4057
Upper Hartfield *E Susx* 16 TQ4634
Upper Hartshay *Derbys* 74 SK3850
Upper Hatherley *Gloucs* 35 SO9221
Upper Hatton *Staffs* 72 SJ8337
Upper Haugh *S York* 74 SK4297
Upper Hayton *Shrops* 59 SO5281
Upper Heaton *W York* 82 SE1719
Upper Helmsley *N York* 83 SE6956
Upper Hergest *H & W* 46 SO2654
Upper Heyford *Nhants* 49 SP6659
Upper Heyford *Oxon* 49 SP4925
Upper Hill *H & W* 46 SO4753
Upper Hockenden *Kent* 27 TQ5069
Upper Hopton *W York* 82 SE1918
Upper Howsell *H & W* 47 SO7748
Upper Hulme *Staffs* 73 SK0160
Upper Ifold *Surrey* 14 TQ0033
Upper Inglesham *Wilts* 36 SU2096
Upper Keith *Loth* 118 NT4562
Upper Kilcott *Avon* 35 ST7988
Upper Killay *W Glam* 32 SS5892
Upper Kinchrackine *Strath* 123 NN1627
Upper Lambourn *Berks* 36 SU3180
Upper Landywood *Staffs* 60 SJ9805
Upper Langford *Avon* 21 ST4659
Upper Langwith *Derbys* 75 SK5169
Upper Largo *Fife* 127 NO4203
Upper Leigh *Staffs* 73 SK0136
Upper Ley *Gloucs* 35 SO7217
Upper Littleton *Avon* 21 ST5564
Upper Lochton *Gramp* 135 NO6997
Upper Longdon *Staffs* 61 SK0614
Upper Ludstone *Shrops* 60 SO8095
Upper Lybster *Highld* 151 ND2537
Upper Lydbrook *Gloucs* 34 SO6015
Upper Lyde *H & W* 46 SO4944
Upper Lye *H & W* 46 SO3965
Upper Maes-coed *H & W* 46 SO3334
Upper Midhope *Derbys* 74 SK2199
Upper Milton *H & W* 60 SO8072
Upper Minety *Wilts* 35 SU0091
Upper Moor *H & W* 47 SO9747
Upper Mulben *Gramp* 141 NJ2551
Upper Nesbet *Border* 110 NT6727
Upper Netchwood *Shrops* 59 SO6192
Upper Nobut *Staffs* 73 SK0435
Upper Norwood *W Susx* 14 SU9317
Upper Ollach *Highld* 137 NG5137
Upper Padley *Derbys* 74 SK2478
Upper Pennington *Hants* 12 SZ3095
Upper Pickwick *Wilts* 35 ST8571
Upper Pollicott *Bucks* 37 SP7013
Upper Pond Street *Essex* 39 TL4536
Upper Poppleton *N York* 83 SE5554
Upper Pulley *Shrops* 59 SJ4808
Upper Quinton *Warwks* 48 SP1846
Upper Ratley *Hants* 23 SU3223
Upper Rochford *H & W* 47 SO6367
Upper Ruscoe *D & G* 99 NX5661
Upper Sapey *H & W* 47 SO6863
Upper Seagry *Wilts* 35 ST9480
Upper Shelton *Beds* 38 SP9843
Upper Sheringham *Norfk* 66 TG1441
Upper Shuckburgh *Warwks* 49 SP4961
Upper Slaughter *Gloucs* 48 SP1523
Upper Soudley *Gloucs* 35 SO6510
Upper Spond *H & W* 46 SO3153
Upper Standen *Kent* 29 TR2240
Upper Staploe *Beds* 52 TL1459
Upper Stepford *D & G* 100 NX8681
Upper Stoke *Norfk* 67 TG2502
Upper Stondon *Beds* 39 TL1535
Upper Stowe *Nhants* 49 SP6456
Upper Street *Hants* 12 SU1418
Upper Street *Norfk* 67 TG3217
Upper Street *Norfk* 67 TG3617
Upper Street *Norfk* 54 TM1779
Upper Street *Suffk* 53 TL7851
Upper Street *Suffk* 54 TM1434
Upper Street *Suffk* 54 TM1051
Upper Sundon *Beds* 38 TL0427
Upper Swell *Gloucs* 48 SP1726
Upper Tankersley *S York* 74 SK3399
Upper Tasburgh *Norfk* 67 TM2095
Upper Tean *Staffs* 73 SK0139
Upper Threapwood *Ches* 71 SJ4345
Upper Town *Avon* 21 ST5265
Upper Town *Derbys* 73 SK2351
Upper Town *Derbys* 74 SK2462
Upper Town *Dur* 95 NZ0737
Upper Town *H & W* 46 SO5848
Upper Town *Suffk* 54 TL9267
Upper Tysoe *Warwks* 48 SP3343
Upper Ufford *Suffk* 55 TM2953
Upper Upham *Wilts* 36 SU2277
Upper Upnor *Kent* 28 TQ7570
Upper Victoria *Tays* 127 NO5336
Upper Vobster *Somset* 22 ST7049
Upper Wardington *Oxon* 49 SP4945
Upper Weald *Bucks* 38 SP8037
Upper Weedon *Nhants* 49 SP6158
Upper Wellingham *E Susx* 16 TQ4313
Upper Weston *Avon* 22 ST7266
Upper Weybread *Suffk* 55 TM2379
Upper Whiston *S York* 75 SK4588
Upper Wick *H & W* 47 SO8252
Upper Wield *Hants* 24 SU6238
Upper Winchendon *Bucks* 37 SP7414
Upper Witton *W Mids* 61 SP0892
Upper Woodford *Wilts* 23 SU1237
Upper Wootton *Hants* 24 SU5854
Upper Wraxall *Wilts* 35 ST8074
Upper Wyche *H & W* 47 SO7643
Upperby *Cumb* 93 NY4153
Upperglen *Highld* 136 NG3151
Uppermill *Gt Man* 82 SD9905
Uppermoorside *W York* 82 SE2430
Upperthorpe *Derbys* 75 SK4580
Upperthorpe *Humb* 84 SE7426
Upperton *Derbys* 74 SK3264
Upperton *W Susx* 14 SU9522
Uppertown *Highld* 151 ND3576
Upperup *Gloucs* 36 SU0396
Upperwood *Derbys* 74 SK2957
Uppincott *Devon* 9 SS9106
Uppingham *Leics* 51 SP8699
Uppington *Dorset* 11 SU0106
Uppington *Shrops* 59 SJ5909
Upsall *N York* 89 SE4586
Upsettlington *Border* 110 NT8846
Upshire *Essex* 27 TL4100
Upstreet *Kent* 29 TR2263
Upthorpe *Suffk* 54 TL9772
Upton *Berks* 26 SU9779
Upton *Bucks* 37 SP7711
Upton *Cambs* 64 TF1000
Upton *Cambs* 52 TL1778
Upton *Ches* 78 SJ5087
Upton *Ches* 71 SJ4169
Upton *Cnwll* 18 SS2004
Upton *Cnwll* 5 SX2772
Upton *Cumb* 93 NY3139
Upton *Devon* 9 ST0902
Upton *Devon* 7 SX7043
Upton *Dorset* 11 SY7483
Upton *Dorset* 11 SY9893
Upton *Dyfed* 30 SN0204
Upton *Hants* 23 SU3555
Upton *Hants* 12 SU3717
Upton *Humb* 85 TA1454
Upton *Leics* 61 SP3699
Upton *Lincs* 76 SK8686
Upton *Mersyd* 78 SJ2788
Upton *Nhants* 49 SP7159
Upton *Norfk* 67 TG3912
Upton *Notts* 75 SK7354
Upton *Notts* 75 SK7476
Upton *Oxon* 36 SP2312
Upton *Oxon* 37 SU5186
Upton *Somset* 20 SS9928
Upton *Somset* 21 ST4526
Upton *W York* 83 SE4713
Upton *Warwks* 48 SP1257
Upton Bishop *H & W* 47 SO6527
Upton Cheyney *Avon* 35 ST6970
Upton Cressett *Shrops* 59 SO6592
Upton Crews *H & W* 47 SO6527
Upton Cross *Cnwll* 5 SX2872
Upton End *Beds* 38 TL1234
Upton Grey *Hants* 24 SU6948
Upton Heath *Ches* 71 SJ4169
Upton Hellions *Devon* 8 SS8303
Upton Lovell *Wilts* 22 ST9440
Upton Magna *Shrops* 59 SJ5512
Upton Noble *Somset* 22 ST7139
Upton Pyne *Devon* 9 SX9197
Upton Scudamore *Wilts* 22 ST8647
Upton Snodsbury *H & W* 47 SO9454
Upton St. Leonards *Gloucs* 35 SO8615
Upton Towans *Cnwll* 2 SW5740
Upton upon Severn *H & W* 47 SO8540
Upton Warren *H & W* 47 SO9367
Upton Wood *Kent* 29 TR2546
Upwaltham *W Susx* 14 SU9413
Upware *Cambs* 53 TL5470
Upwell *Norfk* 65 TF5002
Upwey *Dorset* 11 SY6684
Upwick Green *Herts* 39 TL4524
Upwood *Cambs* 52 TL2582
Urchany *Highld* 140 NH8849
Urchfont *Wilts* 23 SU0356
Urdimarsh *H & W* 46 SO5248
Ure Bank *N York* 89 SE3172
Urlay Nook *Cleve* 96 NZ3816
Urmston *Gt Man* 79 SJ7694
Urquhart *Gramp* 141 NJ2862
Urra *N York* 90 NZ5601
Urray *Highld* 139 NH5052
Ushaw Moor *Dur* 96 NZ2242
Usk *Gwent* 34 SO3700
Usselby *Lincs* 76 TF0993
Usworth *T & W* 96 NZ3058

Weetwood

Weston-in-Gordano


| | | |
|---|---|---|
| Weetwood *W York* | **82** | SE2737 |
| Weir *Lancs* | **81** | SD8625 |
| Weir Quay *Devon* | **6** | SX4365 |
| Weirbrook *Shrops* | **59** | SJ3524 |
| Welbeck Abbey *Notts* | **75** | SK5574 |
| Welborne *Norfk* | **66** | TG0610 |
| Welbourn *Lincs* | **76** | SK9654 |
| Welburn *N York* | **90** | SE7168 |
| Welbury *N York* | **89** | NZ3902 |
| Welby *Lincs* | **63** | SK9738 |
| Welches Dam *Cambs* | **53** | TL4786 |
| Welcombe *Devon* | **18** | SS2218 |
| Welford *Berks* | **24** | SU4072 |
| Welford *Nhants* | **50** | SP6480 |
| Welford-on-Avon *Warwks* | **48** | SP1442 |
| Welham *Leics* | **50** | SP7692 |
| Welham *Notts* | **75** | SK7382 |
| Welham Green *Herts* | **39** | TL2305 |
| Well *Hants* | **24** | SU7646 |
| Well *Lincs* | **77** | TF4473 |
| Well *N York* | **89** | SE2681 |
| Well End *Bucks* | **26** | SU8888 |
| Well End *Herts* | **26** | TQ2098 |
| Well Fold *W York* | **82** | SE2024 |
| Well Head *Herts* | **39** | TL1727 |
| Well Hill *Kent* | **27** | TQ4963 |
| Well Town *Devon* | **20** | SS9050 |
| Welland *H & W* | **47** | SO7940 |
| Wellbank *Tays* | **127** | NO4737 |
| Wellbury *Herts* | **38** | TL1328 |
| Wellesbourne *Warwks* | **48** | SP2755 |
| Wellesbourne Mountford *Warwks* | **48** | SP2855 |
| Wellfield *Dur* | **96** | NZ4137 |
| Wellhouse *Berks* | **24** | SU5272 |
| Welling *Gt Lon* | **27** | TQ4575 |
| Wellingborough *Nhants* | **51** | SP8968 |
| Wellingham *Norfk* | **66** | TF8722 |
| Wellingore *Lincs* | **76** | SK9856 |
| Wellington *Cumb* | **86** | NY0704 |
| Wellington *H & W* | **46** | SO4948 |
| Wellington *Shrops* | **59** | SJ6511 |
| Wellington *Somset* | **20** | ST1521 |
| Wellington *Somset* | **20** | ST1320 |
| Wellington Heath *H & W* | **47** | SO7140 |
| Wellington Marsh *H & W* | **46** | SO4946 |
| Wellow *Avon* | **22** | ST7358 |
| Wellow *IOW* | **12** | SZ3887 |
| Wellow *Notts* | **75** | SK6666 |
| Wellpond Green *Herts* | **39** | TL4122 |
| Wells *Somset* | **21** | ST5445 |
| Wells Green *Ches* | **72** | SJ6853 |
| Wells Head *W York* | **82** | SE0833 |
| Wells of Ythan *Gramp* | **142** | NJ6338 |
| Wells-Next-The-Sea *Norfk* | **66** | TF9143 |
| Wellsborough *Leics* | **62** | SK3602 |
| Wellstye Green *Essex* | **40** | TL6318 |
| Welltree *Tays* | **108** | NS9622 |
| Wellwood *Fife* | **117** | NT0988 |
| Welney *Norfk* | **65** | TL5294 |
| Welsh End *Shrops* | **59** | SJ5035 |
| Welsh Frankton *Shrops* | **59** | SJ3633 |
| Welsh Hook *Dyfed* | **30** | SM9327 |
| Welsh Newton *H & W* | **34** | SO4918 |
| Welsh St. Donats *S Glam* | **33** | ST0276 |
| Welshampton *Shrops* | **59** | SJ4335 |
| Welshpool *Powys* | **58** | SJ2207 |
| Welton *Cumb* | **93** | NY3544 |
| Welton *Humb* | **84** | SE9527 |
| Welton *Lincs* | **76** | TF0079 |
| Welton *Nhants* | **50** | SP5865 |
| Welton le Marsh *Lincs* | **77** | TF4768 |
| Welton le Wold *Lincs* | **77** | TF2787 |
| Welwick *Humb* | **85** | TA3421 |
| Welwyn *Herts* | **39** | TL2316 |
| Welwyn Garden City *Herts* | **39** | TL2312 |
| Wem *Shrops* | **59** | SJ5129 |
| Wembdon *Somset* | **20** | ST2837 |
| Wembley *Gt Lon* | **26** | TQ1885 |
| Wembury *Devon* | **6** | SX5148 |
| Wembworthy *Devon* | **19** | SS6609 |
| Wemyss Bay *Strath* | **114** | NS1969 |
| Wenallt *Dyfed* | **43** | SN6771 |
| Wendens Ambo *Essex* | **39** | TL5136 |
| Wendlebury *Oxon* | **37** | SP5519 |
| Wendling *Norfk* | **66** | TF9312 |
| Wendover *Bucks* | **38** | SP8607 |
| Wendron *Cnwll* | **2** | SW6731 |
| Wendy *Cambs* | **52** | TL3247 |
| Wenfordbridge *Cnwll* | **4** | SX0875 |
| Wenhaston *Suffk* | **55** | TM4275 |
| Wennington *Cambs* | **52** | TL2379 |
| Wennington *Gt Lon* | **27** | TQ5381 |
| Wennington *Lancs* | **87** | SD6169 |
| Wensley *Derbys* | **74** | SK2661 |
| Wensley *N York* | **89** | SE0989 |
| Wentbridge *W York* | **83** | SE4817 |
| Wentnor *Shrops* | **59** | SO3892 |
| Wentworth *Cambs* | **53** | TL4878 |
| Wentworth *S York* | **74** | SK3898 |
| Wentworth Castle *S York* | **82** | SE3102 |
| Wenvoe *S Glam* | **33** | ST1272 |
| Weobley *H & W* | **46** | SO4051 |
| Weobley Marsh *H & W* | **46** | SO4151 |
| Wepham *W Susx* | **14** | TQ0408 |
| Wereham *Norfk* | **65** | TF6801 |
| Wergs *Staffs* | **60** | SJ8701 |
| Wern *Powys* | **58** | SH9612 |
| Wern *Powys* | **58** | SJ2513 |
| Wern *Powys* | **33** | SO1217 |
| Wern *Shrops* | **58** | SJ2734 |
| Wern-y-gaer *Clwyd* | **70** | SJ2068 |
| Werneth Low *Gt Man* | **79** | SJ9592 |
| Wernffrwd *W Glam* | **32** | SS5194 |
| Wernrheolydd *Gwent* | **34** | SO3913 |
| Werrington *Cambs* | **64** | TF1603 |
| Werrington *Cnwll* | **5** | SX3287 |
| Werrington *Staffs* | **72** | SJ9447 |
| Wervin *Ches* | **71** | SJ4271 |
| Wesham *Lancs* | **80** | SD4133 |
| Wessington *Derbys* | **74** | SK3757 |
| West Aberthaw *S Glam* | **20** | ST0266 |
| West Acre *Norfk* | **65** | TF7715 |
| West Allerdean *Nthumb* | **111** | NT9646 |
| West Allotment *T & W* | **103** | NZ3170 |
| West Alvington *Devon* | **7** | SX7243 |
| West Amesbury *Wilts* | **23** | SU1341 |
| West Anstey *Devon* | **19** | SS8527 |
| West Appleton *N York* | **89** | SE2294 |
| West Ashby *Lincs* | **77** | TF2672 |
| West Ashling *W Susx* | **14** | SU8107 |
| West Ashton *Wilts* | **22** | ST8755 |
| West Auckland *Dur* | **96** | NZ1826 |
| West Ayton *N York* | **91** | SE9884 |
| West Bagborough *Somset* | **20** | ST1633 |
| West Balsdon *Cnwll* | **5** | SX2798 |
| West Bank *Ches* | **78** | SJ5184 |
| West Bank *Gwent* | **33** | SO2105 |
| West Barkwith *Lincs* | **76** | TF1580 |
| West Barnby *N York* | **90** | NZ8112 |
| West Barnham *W Susx* | **14** | SU9505 |
| West Barns *Loth* | **118** | NT6578 |
| West Barsham *Norfk* | **66** | TF9033 |
| West Bay *Dorset* | **10** | SY4690 |
| West Beckham *Norfk* | **66** | TG1439 |
| West Bedfont *Surrey* | **26** | TQ0674 |
| West Bergholt *Essex* | **40** | TL9527 |
| West Bexington *Dorset* | **10** | SY5386 |
| West Bilney *Norfk* | **65** | TF7115 |
| West Blatchington *E Susx* | **15** | TQ2706 |
| West Bolden *T & W* | **96** | NZ3462 |
| West Boldon *T & W* | **96** | NZ3443 |
| West Bourton *Dorset* | **22** | ST7629 |
| West Bowling *W York* | **82** | SE1630 |
| West Brabourne *Kent* | **29** | TR0742 |
| West Bradenham *Norfk* | **66** | TF9208 |
| West Bradford *Lancs* | **81** | SD7444 |
| West Bradley *Somset* | **21** | ST5536 |
| West Bretton *W York* | **82** | SE2813 |
| West Bridgford *Notts* | **62** | SK5837 |
| West Briscoe *Dur* | **95** | NY9619 |
| West Bromwich *W Mids* | **60** | SP0091 |
| West Buckland *Devon* | **19** | SS6531 |
| West Buckland *Somset* | **20** | ST1720 |
| West Burnside *Gramp* | **135** | NO7070 |
| West Burnside *Gramp* | **135** | NO7070 |
| West Burton *N York* | **88** | SE0186 |
| West Burton *W Susx* | **14** | TQ0014 |
| West Butsfiel *Dur* | **95** | NZ0945 |
| West Butterwick *Humb* | **84** | SE8305 |
| West Cairngaan *D & G* | **98** | NX1232 |
| West Caister *Norfk* | **67** | TG5111 |
| West Calder *Loth* | **117** | NT0163 |
| West Camel *Somset* | **21** | ST5724 |
| West Causeway-head *Cumb* | **92** | NY1253 |
| West Chaldon *Dorset* | **11** | SY7783 |
| West Challow *Oxon* | **36** | SU3688 |
| West Charleton *Devon* | **7** | SX7542 |
| West Chelborough *Dorset* | **10** | ST5405 |
| West Chevington *Nthumb* | **103** | NZ2297 |
| West Chiltington *W Susx* | **14** | TQ0918 |
| West Chinnock *Somset* | **10** | ST4613 |
| West Chisenbury *Wilts* | **23** | SU1352 |
| West Clandon *Surrey* | **26** | TQ0452 |
| West Cliffe *Kent* | **29** | TR3444 |
| West Coker *Somset* | **10** | ST5113 |
| West Combe *Devon* | **7** | SX7662 |
| West Compton *Dorset* | **10** | SY5694 |
| West Compton *Somset* | **21** | ST5942 |
| West Cottingwith *N York* | **83** | SE6942 |
| West Cowick *Humb* | **83** | SE6521 |
| West Craigneuk *Strath* | **116** | NS7765 |
| West Cross *W Glam* | **32** | SS6189 |
| West Curry *Cnwll* | **5** | SX2893 |
| West Curthwaite *Cumb* | **93** | NY3249 |
| West Dean *Hants* | **23** | SU2526 |
| West Dean *W Susx* | **14** | SU8512 |
| West Dean *Wilts* | **23** | SU2526 |
| West Deeping *Lincs* | **64** | TF1008 |
| West Derby *Mersyd* | **78** | SJ3993 |
| West Dereham *Norfk* | **65** | TF6500 |
| West Down *Devon* | **19** | SS5142 |
| West Drayton *Gt Lon* | **26** | TQ0679 |
| West Drayton *Notts* | **75** | SK7074 |
| West Dunnet *Highld* | **151** | ND2171 |
| West Ella *Humb* | **84** | TA0029 |
| West End *Avon* | **21** | ST4569 |
| West End *Avon* | **35** | ST7188 |
| West End *Beds* | **51** | SP9853 |
| West End *Berks* | **37** | SU8275 |
| West End *Cambs* | **52** | TL3168 |
| West End *Cumb* | **93** | NY3258 |
| West End *Gwent* | **33** | ST2195 |
| West End *Hants* | **24** | SU6335 |
| West End *Hants* | **13** | SU4614 |
| West End *Herts* | **39** | TL2608 |
| West End *Herts* | **39** | TL3306 |
| West End *Humb* | **84** | SE9131 |
| West End *Humb* | **85** | TA1830 |
| West End *Humb* | **85** | TA2627 |
| West End *Lancs* | **81** | SD7328 |
| West End *Lincs* | **77** | TF3598 |
| West End *N York* | **83** | SE5140 |
| West End *N York* | **89** | SE1457 |
| West End *Norfk* | **66** | TF9109 |
| West End *Norfk* | **67** | TG5011 |
| West End *Oxon* | **37** | SU5886 |
| West End *Somset* | **22** | ST6735 |
| West End *Surrey* | **26** | TQ1364 |
| West End *Surrey* | **25** | SU9461 |
| West End *W Susx* | **15** | TQ2016 |
| West End *W York* | **82** | SE2238 |
| West End *Wilts* | **22** | ST9123 |
| West End *Wilts* | **22** | ST9824 |
| West End *Wilts* | **35** | ST9777 |
| West End Green *Hants* | **24** | SU6661 |
| West Ewell *Surrey* | **26** | TQ2063 |
| West Farleigh *Kent* | **28** | TQ7152 |
| West Farndon *Nhants* | **49** | SP5251 |
| West Felton *Shrops* | **59** | SJ3425 |
| West Firle *E Susx* | **16** | TQ4707 |
| West Firsby *Lincs* | **76** | SK9784 |
| West Flotmanby *N York* | **91** | TA0779 |
| West Garforth *W York* | **83** | SE3833 |
| West Garforth *W York* | **83** | SE3932 |
| West Garty *Highld* | **147** | NC9912 |
| West Geirnish *W Isls* | **154** | NF7741 |
| West Ginge *Oxon* | **37** | SU4486 |
| West Grafton *Wilts* | **23** | SU2460 |
| West Green *Hants* | **24** | SU7456 |
| West Grimstead *Wilts* | **23** | SU2026 |
| West Grinstead *W Susx* | **15** | TQ1720 |
| West Haddlesey *N York* | **83** | SE5626 |
| West Haddon *Nhants* | **50** | SP6371 |
| West Hagbourne *Oxon* | **37** | SU5187 |
| West Hagley *H & W* | **60** | SO9080 |
| West Hallam *Derbys* | **62** | SK4341 |
| West Hallam Common *Derbys* | **62** | SK4241 |
| West Halton *Humb* | **84** | SE9020 |
| West Ham *Gt Lon* | **27** | TQ3983 |
| West Handley *Derbys* | **74** | SK3977 |
| West Hanney *Oxon* | **36** | SU4092 |
| West Hanningfield *Essex* | **17** | TQ7300 |
| West Harnham *Wilts* | **23** | SU1229 |
| West Harptree *Avon* | **21** | ST5556 |
| West Harting *W Susx* | **14** | SU7821 |
| West Hatch *Somset* | **20** | ST2820 |
| West Hatch *Wilts* | **22** | ST9228 |
| West Head *Norfk* | **65** | TF5705 |
| West Heath *Hants* | **24** | SU5858 |
| West Heath *W Mids* | **60** | SP0277 |
| West Helmsdale *Highld* | **147** | ND0115 |
| West Hendred *Oxon* | **37** | SU4488 |
| West Herrington *T & W* | **96** | NZ3352 |
| West Heslerton *N York* | **91** | SE9175 |
| West Hewish *Avon* | **21** | ST3964 |
| West Hill *Devon* | **9** | SY0694 |
| West Hoathly *W Susx* | **15** | TQ3632 |
| West Holme *Dorset* | **11** | SY8885 |
| West Holywell *T & W* | **103** | NZ3072 |
| West Horndon *Essex* | **40** | TQ6288 |
| West Horrington *Somset* | **21** | ST5747 |
| West Horsley *Surrey* | **26** | TQ0752 |
| West Horton *Nthumb* | **111** | NU0230 |
| West Hougham *Kent* | **29** | TR2640 |
| West Howe *Dorset* | **12** | SZ0595 |
| West Howetown *Somset* | **20** | SS9135 |
| West Huntspill *Somset* | **20** | ST3044 |
| West Hyde *Beds* | **38** | TL1117 |
| West Hyde *Herts* | **26** | TQ0391 |
| West Hythe *Kent* | **17** | TR1234 |
| West Ilkerton *Devon* | **19** | SS7046 |
| West Ilsley *Berks* | **37** | SU4782 |
| West Itchenor *W Susx* | **14** | SU7900 |
| West Keal *Lincs* | **77** | TF3663 |
| West Kennet *Wilts* | **23** | SU1168 |
| West Kilbride *Strath* | **114** | NS2048 |
| West Kingsdown *Kent* | **27** | TQ5763 |
| West Kington *Wilts* | **35** | ST8077 |
| West Kirby *Mersyd* | **78** | SJ2186 |
| West Knapton *N York* | **90** | SE8775 |
| West Knighton *Dorset* | **11** | SY7387 |
| West Knoyle *Wilts* | **22** | ST8532 |
| West Lambrook *Somset* | **10** | ST4110 |
| West Langdon *Kent* | **29** | TR3247 |
| West Langwell *Highld* | **146** | NC6909 |
| West Laroch *Highld* | **130** | NN0758 |
| West Lavington *W Susx* | **14** | SU8920 |
| West Lavington *Wilts* | **22** | SU0052 |
| West Layton *N York* | **89** | NZ1410 |
| West Leake *Notts* | **62** | SK5226 |
| West Learmouth *Nthumb* | **110** | NT8437 |
| West Lees *N York* | **89** | NZ4702 |
| West Leigh *Devon* | **8** | SS6805 |
| West Leigh *Devon* | **7** | SX7557 |
| West Leigh *Somset* | **20** | ST1231 |
| West Lexham *Norfk* | **66** | TF8417 |
| West Lilling *N York* | **90** | SE6465 |
| West Linton *Border* | **117** | NT1551 |
| West Littleton *Avon* | **35** | ST7675 |
| West Lockinge *Oxon* | **36** | SU4187 |
| West Luccombe *Somset* | **19** | SS8946 |
| West Lulworth *Dorset* | **11** | SY8280 |
| West Lutton *N York* | **91** | SE9369 |
| West Lydford *Somset* | **21** | ST5632 |
| West Lyn *Devon* | **19** | SS7248 |
| West Lyng *Somset* | **21** | ST3228 |
| West Lynn *Norfk* | **65** | TF6120 |
| West Malling *Kent* | **28** | TQ6857 |
| West Malvern *H & W* | **47** | SO7646 |
| West Marden *W Susx* | **14** | SU7713 |
| West Markham *Notts* | **75** | SK7272 |
| West Marsh *Humb* | **85** | TA2509 |
| West Marton *N York* | **81** | SD8950 |
| West Melta *S York* | **83** | SE4001 |
| West Meon *Hants* | **13** | SU6424 |
| West Meon Hut *Hants* | **13** | SU6526 |
| West Meon Woodlands *Hants* | **13** | SU6426 |
| West Mersea *Essex* | **41** | TM0112 |
| West Milton *Dorset* | **10** | SY5096 |
| West Minster *Kent* | **28** | TQ9073 |
| West Monkton *Somset* | **20** | ST2528 |
| West Moors *Dorset* | **12** | SU0802 |
| West Morden *Dorset* | **11** | SY9095 |
| West Morton *W York* | **82** | SE0942 |
| West Mudford *Somset* | **21** | ST5620 |
| West melbury *Dorset* | **22** | ST8720 |
| West Ness *N York* | **90** | SE6879 |
| West Newbiggin *Dur* | **96** | NZ3518 |
| West Newton *Humb* | **85** | TA2037 |
| West Newton *Norfk* | **65** | TF6928 |
| West Newton *Somset* | **20** | ST2829 |
| West Norwood *Gt Lon* | **27** | TQ3171 |
| West Ogwell *Devon* | **7** | SX8170 |
| West Orchard *Dorset* | **11** | ST8216 |
| West Overton *Wilts* | **23** | SU1267 |
| West Panson *Devon* | **5** | SX3491 |
| West Parley *Dorset* | **12** | SZ0997 |
| West Peckham *Kent* | **27** | TQ6452 |
| West Pelton *Dur* | **96** | NZ2352 |
| West Pennard *Somset* | **21** | ST5438 |
| West Pentire *Cnwll* | **4** | SW7760 |
| West Perry *Cambs* | **52** | TL1466 |
| West Porlock *Somset* | **33** | SS8797 |
| West Prawle *Devon* | **7** | SX7637 |
| West Preston *W Susx* | **14** | TQ0502 |
| West Pulham *Dorset* | **11** | ST7008 |
| West Putford *Devon* | **18** | SS3616 |
| West Quantoxhead *Somset* | **20** | ST1142 |
| West Raddon *Devon* | **9** | SS8902 |
| West Rainton *T & W* | **96** | NZ3246 |
| West Rasen *Lincs* | **76** | TF0589 |
| West Ravendale *Humb* | **76** | TF2299 |
| West Raynham *Norfk* | **66** | TF8725 |
| West Retford *Notts* | **75** | SK6981 |
| West Rounton *N York* | **89** | NZ4103 |
| West Row *Suffk* | **53** | TL6775 |
| West Rudham *Norfk* | **66** | TF8128 |
| West Runton *Norfk* | **66** | TG1842 |
| West Safford *Dorset* | **11** | SY7289 |
| West Saltoun *Loth* | **118** | NT4667 |
| West Sandford *Devon* | **8** | SS8102 |
| West Sandwick *Shet* | **155** | HU4588 |
| West Scrafton *N York* | **88** | SE0783 |
| West Sleekburn *Nthumb* | **103** | NZ2884 |
| West Somerton *Norfk* | **67** | TG4720 |
| West Stoke *W Susx* | **14** | SU8308 |
| West Stonesdale *N York* | **88** | NY8802 |
| West Stoughton *Somset* | **21** | ST4149 |
| West Stour *Dorset* | **22** | ST7822 |
| West Stourmouth *Kent* | **29** | TR2562 |
| West Stow *Suffk* | **54** | TL8171 |
| West Stowell *Wilts* | **23** | SU1362 |
| West Stratton *Hants* | **24** | SU5240 |
| West Street *Kent* | **28** | TQ7376 |
| West Street *Kent* | **29** | TR3254 |
| West Street *Kent* | **28** | TQ9054 |
| West Street *Suffk* | **54** | TL9871 |
| West Tanfield *N York* | **89** | SE2678 |
| West Taphouse *Cnwll* | **4** | SX1463 |
| West Tarbert *Strath* | **113** | NR8467 |
| West Tarring *W Susx* | **14** | TQ1203 |
| West Thorney *W Susx* | **14** | SU7602 |
| West Thorpe *Notts* | **62** | SK6225 |
| West Thurrock *Essex* | **27** | TQ5877 |
| West Tilbury *Essex* | **28** | TQ6677 |
| West Tisted *Hants* | **24** | SU6529 |
| West Torrington *Lincs* | **76** | TF1381 |
| West Town *Avon* | **21** | ST5160 |
| West Town *Avon* | **21** | ST4868 |
| West Town *Devon* | **18** | SS3221 |
| West Town *H & W* | **46** | SO4361 |
| West Town *Hants* | **13** | SZ7099 |
| West Town *Somset* | **22** | ST7041 |
| West Town *Somset* | **21** | ST5335 |
| West Tytherley *Hants* | **23** | SU2730 |
| West Tytherley *Hants* | **23** | SU2730 |
| West Tytherton *Wilts* | **35** | ST9474 |
| West Walton *Norfk* | **65** | TF4713 |
| West Walton Highway *Norfk* | **65** | TF4913 |
| West Weetwood *Nthumb* | **111** | NU0029 |
| West Wellow *Hants* | **12** | SU2918 |
| West Wellow *Hants* | **12** | SU2818 |
| West Wembury *Devon* | **6** | SX5249 |
| West Wemyss *Fife* | **118** | NT3294 |
| West Wick *Avon* | **21** | ST3762 |
| West Wickham *Cambs* | **53** | TL6149 |
| West Wickham *Gt Lon* | **27** | TQ3766 |
| West Williamston *Dyfed* | **30** | SN0305 |
| West Winch *Norfk* | **65** | TF6316 |
| West Winterslow *Wilts* | **23** | SU2232 |
| West Wittering *W Susx* | **14** | SZ7898 |
| West Witton *N York* | **88** | SE0588 |
| West Woodburn *Nthumb* | **102** | NY8986 |
| West Woodhay *Berks* | **23** | SU3962 |
| West Woodlands *Somset* | **22** | ST7743 |
| West Worldham *Hants* | **24** | SU7437 |
| West Worthing *W Susx* | **15** | TQ1302 |
| West Wratting *Essex* | **53** | TL6052 |
| West Wycombe *Bucks* | **37** | SU8294 |
| West Wylam *Nthumb* | **103** | NZ1063 |
| West Yatton *Wilts* | **35** | ST8575 |
| West Yoke *Kent* | **27** | TQ5965 |
| West Youlstone *Cnwll* | **18** | SS2615 |
| Westbere *Kent* | **29** | TR1961 |
| Westborough *Lincs* | **63** | SK8544 |
| Westbourne *W Susx* | **13** | SU7507 |
| Westbrook *Berks* | **24** | SU4272 |
| Westbrook *Kent* | **29** | TR3470 |
| Westbrook *Wilts* | **22** | ST9565 |
| Westbury *Bucks* | **49** | SP6235 |
| Westbury *Shrops* | **59** | SJ3509 |
| Westbury *Wilts* | **22** | ST8751 |
| Westbury Leigh *Wilts* | **22** | ST8649 |
| Westbury on Severn *Gloucs* | **35** | SO7114 |
| Westbury-on-Trym *Avon* | **34** | ST5777 |
| Westbury-on-trym *Avon* | **34** | ST5877 |
| Westbury-sub-Mendip *Somset* | **21** | ST5049 |
| Westby *Lancs* | **80** | SD3831 |
| Westcliff-on-Sea *Essex* | **40** | TQ8686 |
| Westcombe *Somset* | **22** | ST6739 |
| Westcote *Gloucs* | **36** | SP2120 |
| Westcott *Bucks* | **37** | SP7117 |
| Westcott *Devon* | **9** | ST0204 |
| Westcott *Somset* | **19** | SS8720 |
| Westcott *Surrey* | **15** | TQ1448 |
| Westcott Barton *Oxon* | **49** | SP4325 |
| Westcourt *Wilts* | **23** | SU2261 |
| Westdean *E Susx* | **16** | TV5299 |
| Westdown Camp *Wilts* | **23** | SU0447 |
| Westdowns *Cnwll* | **4** | SX0582 |
| Wested *Kent* | **27** | TQ5166 |
| Westend *Gloucs* | **35** | SO7807 |
| Westend Town *Nthumb* | **102** | NY7865 |
| Westenhanger *Kent* | **29** | TR1237 |
| Wester Causewayend *Loth* | **117** | NT0861 |
| Wester Drumashie *Highld* | **140** | NH6032 |
| Wester Ellister *Strath* | **112** | NR2053 |
| Wester Essenside *Border* | **109** | NT4320 |
| Wester Ochiltree *Loth* | **117** | NT0374 |
| Wester Pitkierie *Fife* | **127** | NO5505 |
| Wester Rarichie *Highld* | **147** | NH8374 |
| Westerdale *Highld* | **151** | ND1251 |
| Westerdale *N York* | **90** | NZ6605 |
| Westerfield *Suffk* | **54** | TM1747 |
| Westergate *W Susx* | **14** | SU9305 |
| Westerham *Kent* | **27** | TQ4454 |
| Westerhope *T & W* | **103** | NZ1966 |
| Westerland *Devon* | **7** | SX8662 |
| Westerleigh *Avon* | **35** | ST6979 |
| Westerloch *Highld* | **151** | ND3258 |
| Westerton *Tays* | **127** | NO6754 |
| Westfield *Avon* | **22** | ST6753 |
| Westfield *E Susx* | **17** | TQ8115 |
| Westfield *Loth* | **116** | NS9472 |
| Westfield *Norfk* | **66** | TF9909 |
| Westfield Sole *Kent* | **28** | TQ7761 |
| Westfields *Dorset* | **11** | ST7206 |
| Westfields *H & W* | **46** | SO4941 |
| Westfields of Rattray *Tays* | **126** | NO1846 |
| Westford *Somset* | **20** | ST1120 |
| Westgate *Dur* | **95** | NY9038 |
| Westgate *Humb* | **84** | SE7707 |
| Westgate *Norfk* | **66** | TF9740 |
| Westgate Hill *W York* | **82** | SE2029 |
| Westgate on Sea *Kent* | **29** | TR3270 |
| Westgate Street *Norfk* | **67** | TG1921 |
| Westhall *Gramp* | **142** | NJ6826 |
| Westhall *Suffk* | **55** | TM4280 |
| Westham *Dorset* | **11** | SY6579 |
| Westham *E Susx* | **16** | TQ6404 |
| Westham *Somset* | **21** | ST4046 |
| Westhampnett *W Susx* | **14** | SU8806 |
| Westhay *Somset* | **21** | ST4342 |
| Westhead *Lancs* | **78** | SD4407 |
| Westhide *H & W* | **46** | SO5843 |
| Westhill *Gramp* | **135** | NJ8307 |
| Westholme *Somset* | **21** | ST5642 |
| Westhope *H & W* | **46** | SO4651 |
| Westhope *Shrops* | **59** | SO4786 |
| Westhorp *Nhants* | **49** | SP5152 |
| Westhorpe *Lincs* | **64** | TF2231 |
| Westhorpe *Suffk* | **54** | TM0568 |
| Westhoughton *Gt Man* | **79** | SD6506 |
| Westhouse *N York* | **87** | SD6673 |
| Westhouses *Derbys* | **74** | SK4257 |
| Westhumble *Surrey* | **26** | TQ1651 |
| Westlake *Devon* | **6** | SX6253 |
| Westland Green *Herts* | **39** | TL4222 |
| Westleigh *Devon* | **18** | SS4728 |
| Westleigh *Devon* | **9** | ST0517 |
| Westleton *Suffk* | **55** | TM4469 |
| Westley *Shrops* | **59** | SJ3607 |
| Westley *Suffk* | **54** | TL8264 |
| Westley Heights *Essex* | **40** | TQ6887 |
| Westley Waterless *Cambs* | **53** | TL6156 |
| Westlington *Bucks* | **37** | SP7610 |
| Westlinton *Cumb* | **101** | NY3964 |
| Westmarsh *Kent* | **29** | TR2761 |
| Westmeston *E Susx* | **15** | TQ3313 |
| Westmill *Herts* | **39** | TL3627 |
| Westmoor *T & W* | **103** | NZ2670 |
| Westmuir *Tays* | **126** | NO3652 |
| Westnewton *Cumb* | **92** | NY1344 |
| Westoe *T & W* | **103** | NZ3765 |
| Weston *Avon* | **22** | ST7366 |
| Weston *Berks* | **36** | SU3973 |
| Weston *Ches* | **78** | SJ5080 |
| Weston *Ches* | **72** | SJ7252 |
| Weston *Devon* | **9** | ST1500 |
| Weston *Devon* | **9** | SY1688 |
| Weston *Dorset* | **11** | SY6871 |
| Weston *H & W* | **46** | SO3656 |
| Weston *Hants* | **13** | SU7221 |
| Weston *Herts* | **39** | TL2530 |
| Weston *Lincs* | **64** | TF2925 |
| Weston *Nhants* | **49** | SP5846 |
| Weston *Notts* | **75** | SK7767 |
| Weston *Shrops* | **46** | SO3373 |
| Weston *Shrops* | **59** | SJ2927 |
| Weston *Shrops* | **59** | SJ5629 |
| Weston *Staffs* | **72** | SJ9727 |
| Weston *W York* | **82** | SE1747 |
| Weston Beggard *H & W* | **46** | SO5841 |
| Weston by Welland *Nhants* | **50** | SP7791 |
| Weston Colley *Hants* | **24** | SU5039 |
| Weston Colville *Cambs* | **53** | TL6153 |
| Weston Corbett *Hants* | **24** | SU6846 |
| Weston Coyney *Staffs* | **72** | SJ9343 |
| Weston Favel *Nhants* | **50** | SP7962 |
| Weston Favell *Nhants* | **50** | SP7962 |
| Weston Green *Cambs* | **53** | TL6252 |
| Weston Heath *Shrops* | **60** | SJ7713 |
| Weston Hills *Lincs* | **64** | TF2720 |
| Weston in Arden *Warwks* | **61** | SP3886 |
| Weston Jones *Staffs* | **72** | SJ7624 |
| Weston Longville *Norfk* | **66** | TG1115 |
| Weston Lullingfields *Shrops* | **59** | SJ4224 |
| Weston Patrick *Hants* | **24** | SU6946 |
| Weston Rhyn *Shrops* | **58** | SJ2835 |
| Weston Subedge *Gloucs* | **48** | SP1240 |
| Weston Turville *Bucks* | **38** | SP8510 |
| Weston Underwood *Bucks* | **38** | SP8650 |
| Weston Underwood *Derbys* | **73** | SK2942 |
| Weston under Penyard *H & W* | **35** | SO6322 |
| Weston under Wetherley *Warwks* | **48** | SP3669 |
| Weston-in-Gordano *Avon* | **34** | ST4474 |

Weston-on-Trent Windmill


| | | |
|---|---|---|
| Weston-on-Trent *Derbys* | 62 | SK4028 |
| Weston-on-the-Green *Oxon* | 37 | SP5318 |
| Weston-Super-Mare *Avon* | 21 | ST3261 |
| Weston-under-Lizard *Staffs* | 60 | SJ8010 |
| Westonbirt *Gloucs* | 35 | ST8589 |
| Westoning *Beds* | 38 | TL0332 |
| Westoning Woodend *Beds* | 38 | TL0232 |
| Westonzoyland *Somset* | 21 | ST3534 |
| Westover *Hants* | 23 | SU3640 |
| Westow *N York* | 90 | SE7565 |
| Westpeek *Devon* | 5 | SX3493 |
| Westport *Somset* | 21 | ST3820 |
| Westport *Strath* | 104 | NR6526 |
| Westquarter *Cent* | 116 | NS9178 |
| Westra *S Glam* | 33 | ST1471 |
| Westridge Green *Berks* | 37 | SU5679 |
| Westrigg *Loth* | 116 | NS9067 |
| Westrop *Wilts* | 36 | SU1992 |
| Westruther *Border* | 110 | NT6349 |
| Westry *Cambs* | 65 | TL3998 |
| Westthope *Derbys* | 75 | SK4579 |
| Westward *Cumb* | 93 | NY2744 |
| Westward Ho *Devon* | 18 | SS4329 |
| Westwell *Kent* | 28 | TQ9847 |
| Westwell *Oxon* | 36 | SP2210 |
| Westwell Leacon *Kent* | 28 | TQ9547 |
| Westwick *Cambs* | 53 | TL4265 |
| Westwick *Dur* | 95 | NZ0715 |
| Westwick *Norfk* | 67 | TG2726 |
| Westwood *Devon* | 9 | SY0199 |
| Westwood *Kent* | 27 | TQ6070 |
| Westwood *Kent* | 29 | TR3667 |
| Westwood *Notts* | 75 | SK4551 |
| Westwood *Wilts* | 22 | ST8059 |
| Westwood Heath *W Mids* | 61 | SP2776 |
| Westwoodside *Humb* | 75 | SE7400 |
| Wetham Green *Kent* | 28 | TQ8467 |
| Wetheral *Cumb* | 93 | NY4654 |
| Wetherby *W York* | 83 | SE4048 |
| Wetherden *Suffk* | 54 | TM0062 |
| Wetheringsett *Suffk* | 54 | TM1266 |
| Wethersfield *Essex* | 40 | TL7131 |
| Wetherup Street *Suffk* | 54 | TM1464 |
| Wetley Rocks *Staffs* | 72 | SJ9649 |
| Wettenhall *Ches* | 71 | SJ6261 |
| Wetton *Staffs* | 73 | SK1055 |
| Wetwang *Humb* | 91 | SE9358 |
| Wetwood *Staffs* | 72 | SJ7733 |
| Wexcombe *Wilts* | 23 | SU2658 |
| Wexham *Bucks* | 26 | SU9882 |
| Wexham Street *Bucks* | 26 | SU9883 |
| Weybourne *Norfk* | 66 | TG1143 |
| Weybread *Suffk* | 55 | TM2480 |
| Weybread Street *Suffk* | 55 | TM2479 |
| Weybridge *Surrey* | 26 | TQ0764 |
| Weycroft *Devon* | 36 | SU3099 |
| Weydale *Highld* | 151 | ND1564 |
| Weyhill *Hants* | 23 | SU3146 |
| Weymouth *Dorset* | 11 | SY6778 |
| Whaddon *Bucks* | 38 | SP8034 |
| Whaddon *Cambs* | 52 | TL3546 |
| Whaddon *Gloucs* | 35 | SO8313 |
| Whaddon *Wilts* | 22 | ST8861 |
| Whaddon *Wilts* | 23 | SU1926 |
| Whale *Cumb* | 94 | NY5221 |
| Whaley *Derbys* | 75 | SK5171 |
| Whaley Bridge *Derbys* | 79 | SK0180 |
| Whaley Thorns *Notts* | 90 | SE5271 |
| Whaligoe *Highld* | 151 | ND3140 |
| Whalley *Lancs* | 81 | SD7336 |
| Whalley Banks *Lancs* | 81 | SD7335 |
| Whalton *Nthumb* | 103 | NZ1281 |
| Wham *N York* | 88 | SD7762 |
| Whamley *Nthumb* | 102 | NY8766 |
| Whaplode *Lincs* | 64 | TF3224 |
| Whaplode Drove *Lincs* | 64 | TF3113 |
| Wharf *Warwks* | 49 | SP4352 |
| Wharfe *N York* | 88 | SD7869 |
| Wharles *Lancs* | 80 | SD4435 |
| Wharley End *Beds* | 38 | SP9342 |
| Wharncliffe Side *S York* | 74 | SK2995 |
| Wharram le Street *N York* | 90 | SE8665 |
| Wharton *Ches* | 72 | SJ6666 |
| Wharton *H & W* | 46 | SO5055 |
| Whashton Green *N York* | 89 | NZ1405 |
| Whasset *Cumb* | 87 | SD5181 |
| Whaston *N York* | 89 | NZ1506 |
| Whatcote *Warwks* | 48 | SP2944 |
| Whateley *Warwks* | 61 | SP2299 |
| Whatfield *Suffk* | 54 | TM0246 |
| Whatley *Somset* | 10 | ST3607 |
| Whatley *Somset* | 22 | ST7347 |
| Whatley's End *Avon* | 35 | ST6581 |
| Whatlington *E Susx* | 17 | TQ7618 |
| Whatsole Street *Kent* | 29 | TR1144 |
| Whatstandwell *Derbys* | 74 | SK3354 |
| Whatton *Notts* | 63 | SK7439 |
| Whauphill *D & G* | 99 | NX4049 |
| Whaw *N York* | 88 | NY9804 |
| Wheal Rose *Cnwll* | 3 | SW7244 |
| Wheatacre *Norfk* | 67 | TM4694 |
| Wheatfield *Oxon* | 37 | SU6899 |
| Wheathampstead *Herts* | 39 | TL1714 |
| Wheathill *Shrops* | 59 | SO6282 |
| Wheathill *Somset* | 21 | ST5830 |
| Wheatley *Hants* | 25 | SU7840 |
| Wheatley *Oxon* | 37 | SP5905 |
| Wheatley *W York* | 82 | SE0726 |
| Wheatley Hill *Dur* | 96 | NZ3738 |
| Wheatley Hills *S York* | 83 | SE5905 |
| Wheatley Lane *Lancs* | 81 | SD8337 |
| Wheaton Aston *Staffs* | 60 | SJ8512 |
| Wheatsheaf *Clwyd* | 71 | SJ3253 |
| Wheddon Cross *Somset* | 20 | SS9238 |
| Wheel Inn *Cnwll* | 2 | SW6921 |
| Wheelbarrow Town *Kent* | 29 | TR1445 |
| Wheeler End Common *Bucks* | 37 | SU8093 |
| Wheeler's Green *Oxon* | 24 | SU7672 |
| Wheeler's Street *Kent* | 28 | TQ8444 |
| Wheelerstreet *Surrey* | 25 | SU9440 |
| Wheelock *Ches* | 72 | SJ7559 |
| Wheelock Heath *Ches* | 72 | SJ7457 |
| Wheelton *Lancs* | 81 | SD6021 |
| Wheldale *W York* | 83 | SE4426 |
| Wheldrake *N York* | 83 | SE6844 |
| Whelpley Hill *Bucks* | 38 | TL0004 |
| Whelpo *Cumb* | 93 | NY3139 |
| Whelston *Clwyd* | 70 | SJ2076 |
| Whemstead *Herts* | 39 | TL3121 |
| Whenby *N York* | 90 | SE6369 |
| Whepstead *Suffk* | 54 | TL8358 |
| Wherstead *Suffk* | 54 | TM1540 |
| Wherwell *Hants* | 23 | SU3941 |
| Wheston *Derbys* | 74 | SK1376 |
| Whetsted *Kent* | 28 | TQ6546 |
| Whetstone *Gt Lon* | 27 | TQ2693 |
| Whetstone *Leics* | 50 | SP5597 |
| Wheyrigg *Cumb* | 93 | NY1948 |
| Whicham *Cumb* | 86 | SD1382 |
| Whichford *Warwks* | 48 | SP3134 |
| Whickham *T & W* | 96 | NZ2061 |
| Whiddon *Devon* | 18 | SX4799 |
| Whiddon Down *Devon* | 8 | SX6992 |
| Whight's Corner *Suffk* | 54 | TM1242 |
| Whigstreet *Tays* | 127 | NO4844 |
| Whiligh *E Susx* | 16 | TQ6431 |
| Whilton *Nhants* | 49 | SP6364 |
| Whim *Border* | 117 | NT2153 |
| Whimble *Devon* | 18 | SS3403 |
| Whimple *Devon* | 9 | SY0497 |
| Whimpwell Green *Norfk* | 67 | TG3829 |
| Whin Lane End *Lancs* | 80 | SD3941 |
| Whinburgh *Norfk* | 66 | TG0009 |
| Whinnie Liggate *D & G* | 99 | NX7152 |
| Whinnow *Cumb* | 93 | NY3051 |
| Whinny Hill *Cleve* | 96 | NZ3818 |
| Whipcott *Devon* | 20 | ST0718 |
| Whippingham *IOW* | 13 | SZ5193 |
| Whipsnade *Beds* | 38 | TL0108 |
| Whipton *Devon* | 9 | SX9493 |
| Whisby *Lincs* | 76 | SK9067 |
| Whissendine *Leics* | 63 | SK8214 |
| Whissonsett *Norfk* | 66 | TF9123 |
| Whistley Green *Berks* | 25 | SU7974 |
| Whiston *Mersyd* | 78 | SJ4791 |
| Whiston *Nhants* | 51 | SP8460 |
| Whiston *S York* | 75 | SK4490 |
| Whiston *Staffs* | 73 | SK0347 |
| Whiston *Staffs* | 60 | SJ8914 |
| Whiston Cross *Shrops* | 60 | SJ7903 |
| Whiston Eaves *Staffs* | 73 | SK0446 |
| Whiston Lane End *Mersyd* | 78 | SJ4690 |
| Whitacre Fields *Warwks* | 61 | SP2592 |
| Whitbeck *Cumb* | 86 | SD1184 |
| Whitbourne *H & W* | 47 | SO7156 |
| Whitburn *Loth* | 116 | NS9464 |
| Whitburn *T & W* | 96 | NZ4062 |
| Whitby *Ches* | 71 | SJ3975 |
| Whitby *N York* | 91 | NZ8910 |
| Whitbyheath *Ches* | 71 | SJ3974 |
| Whitchurch *Avon* | 21 | ST6167 |
| Whitchurch *Bucks* | 38 | SP8020 |
| Whitchurch *Devon* | 6 | SX4972 |
| Whitchurch *Dyfed* | 30 | SM8025 |
| Whitchurch *H & W* | 34 | SO5417 |
| Whitchurch *Hants* | 24 | SU4648 |
| Whitchurch *Oxon* | 37 | SU6377 |
| Whitchurch *S Glam* | 33 | ST1579 |
| Whitchurch *Shrops* | 71 | SJ5441 |
| Whitchurch Canonicorum *Dorset* | 10 | SY3995 |
| Whitchurch Hill *Oxon* | 37 | SU6378 |
| Whitcombe *Dorset* | 11 | SY7188 |
| Whitcot *Shrops* | 59 | SO3791 |
| Whitcott Keysett *Shrops* | 58 | SO2782 |
| White Chapel *H & W* | 48 | SP0740 |
| White Chapel *Lancs* | 81 | SD5541 |
| White Colne *Essex* | 40 | TL8830 |
| White Coppice *Lancs* | 81 | SD6119 |
| White Cross *Cnwll* | 2 | SW6821 |
| White End *H & W* | 47 | SO7834 |
| White Kirkley *Dur* | 95 | NZ0255 |
| White Lackington *Dorset* | 11 | SY7198 |
| White Ladies Aston *H & W* | 47 | SO9252 |
| White Notley *Essex* | 40 | TL7818 |
| White Ox *Avon* | 22 | ST7258 |
| White Pit *Lincs* | 77 | TF3777 |
| White Roding *Essex* | 40 | TL5613 |
| White Stake *Lancs* | 80 | SD5125 |
| White Stone *H & W* | 46 | SO5642 |
| White Stone Cross *Devon* | 9 | SX8993 |
| White Waltham *Berks* | 26 | SU8577 |
| White-le-Head *Dur* | 96 | NZ1754 |
| Whiteacre *Kent* | 29 | TR1148 |
| Whiteacre Heath *Warwks* | 61 | SP2292 |
| Whiteash Green *Essex* | 40 | TL7931 |
| Whitebirk *Lancs* | 81 | SD7028 |
| Whitebridge *Highld* | 139 | NH4815 |
| Whitebrook *Gwent* | 34 | SO5306 |
| Whitecairns *Gramp* | 143 | NJ9218 |
| Whitechapel *Gt Lon* | 27 | TQ3381 |
| Whitechurch *Dyfed* | 31 | SN1536 |
| Whitecliffe *Gloucs* | 34 | SO5609 |
| Whitecraig *Loth* | 118 | NT3470 |
| Whitecroft *Gloucs* | 34 | SO6106 |
| Whitecrook *D & G* | 98 | NX1656 |
| Whitecross *Cnwll* | 2 | SW5234 |
| Whitecross *Cnwll* | 4 | SW9672 |
| Whiteface *Highld* | 146 | NH7088 |
| Whitefarland *Strath* | 105 | NR8642 |
| Whitefield *Devon* | 19 | SS7035 |
| Whitefield *Gt Man* | 79 | SD8006 |
| Whitefield Lane End *Mersyd* | 78 | SJ4589 |
| Whiteford *Gramp* | 142 | NJ7126 |
| Whitegate *Ches* | 71 | SJ6269 |
| Whitehall *Hants* | 24 | SU7452 |
| Whitehall *Ork* | 155 | HY6528 |
| Whitehall *W Susx* | 15 | TQ1321 |
| Whitehaven *Cumb* | 92 | NX9718 |
| Whitehill *Hants* | 14 | SU7934 |
| Whitehill *Kent* | 29 | TR0950 |
| Whitehills *Gramp* | 142 | NJ6565 |
| Whitehouse *Gramp* | 142 | NJ6114 |
| Whitehouse *Strath* | 113 | NR8161 |
| Whitehouse Common *W Mids* | 61 | SP1397 |
| Whitekirk *Loth* | 118 | NT5981 |
| Whitelackington *Somset* | 10 | ST3815 |
| Whiteley Bank *IOW* | 13 | SZ5581 |
| Whiteley Green *Ches* | 79 | SJ9278 |
| Whiteley Village *Surrey* | 26 | TQ0962 |
| Whitemans Green *W Susx* | 15 | TQ3025 |
| Whitemire *Gramp* | 140 | NH9854 |
| Whitemoor *Cnwll* | 4 | SW9757 |
| Whitemoor *Derbys* | 74 | SK3648 |
| Whitemoor *Notts* | 62 | SK5442 |
| Whitemoor *Staffs* | 72 | SJ8861 |
| Whitenap *Hants* | 12 | SU3721 |
| Whiteoak Green *Oxon* | 36 | SP3414 |
| Whiteparish *Wilts* | 23 | SU2423 |
| Whiterashes *Gramp* | 143 | NJ8523 |
| Whiterow *Gramp* | 141 | NJ0257 |
| Whiterow *Highld* | 151 | ND3648 |
| Whiteshill *Gloucs* | 35 | SO8407 |
| Whitesmith *E Susx* | 16 | TQ5214 |
| Whitestaunton *Somset* | 10 | ST2810 |
| Whitestone *Devon* | 9 | SX8694 |
| Whitestreet Green *Suffk* | 54 | TL9739 |
| Whitewall Corner *N York* | 90 | SE7969 |
| Whiteway *Avon* | 22 | ST7263 |
| Whitewell *Lancs* | 81 | SD6646 |
| Whitewell-on-the-Hill *N York* | 90 | SE7265 |
| Whiteworks *Devon* | 6 | SX6171 |
| Whitfield *Avon* | 35 | ST6791 |
| Whitfield *Kent* | 29 | TR3045 |
| Whitfield *Nhants* | 49 | SP6039 |
| Whitfield *Nthumb* | 94 | NY7758 |
| Whitfield Hall *Nthumb* | 94 | NY7756 |
| Whitford *Clwyd* | 70 | SJ1478 |
| Whitford *Devon* | 10 | SY2595 |
| Whitgift *Humb* | 84 | SE8122 |
| Whitgift *Humb* | 84 | SE8022 |
| Whitgreave *Staffs* | 72 | SJ8928 |
| Whithorn *D & G* | 99 | NX4440 |
| Whiting Bay *Strath* | 105 | NS0425 |
| Whitington *Norfk* | 65 | TL7199 |
| Whitkirk *W York* | 83 | SE3634 |
| Whitland *Dyfed* | 31 | SN1916 |
| Whitlaw *Border* | 109 | NT5012 |
| Whitletts *Strath* | 106 | NS3623 |
| Whitley *Berks* | 24 | SU7270 |
| Whitley *Ches* | 71 | SJ6178 |
| Whitley *N York* | 83 | SE5620 |
| Whitley *S York* | 74 | SK3494 |
| Whitley *Wilts* | 22 | ST8866 |
| Whitley Bay *T & W* | 103 | NZ3572 |
| Whitley Chapel *Nthumb* | 95 | NY9357 |
| Whitley Heath *Staffs* | 72 | SJ8126 |
| Whitley Lower *W York* | 82 | SE2217 |
| Whitley Row *Kent* | 27 | TQ4952 |
| Whitlieburn *Strath* | 114 | NS2163 |
| Whitlock's End *W Mids* | 61 | SP1076 |
| Whitlow *S York* | 74 | SK3182 |
| Whitminster *Gloucs* | 35 | SO7708 |
| Whitmore *Dorset* | 12 | SU0609 |
| Whitmore *Staffs* | 72 | SJ8041 |
| Whitnage *Devon* | 9 | ST0215 |
| Whitnash *Warwks* | 48 | SP3263 |
| Whitney *H & W* | 46 | SO2747 |
| Whitrigg *Cumb* | 93 | NY2038 |
| Whitrigg *Cumb* | 93 | NY2257 |
| Whitrigglees *Cumb* | 93 | NY2457 |
| Whitsbury *Hants* | 12 | SU1218 |
| Whitsford *Devon* | 19 | SS6633 |
| Whitsome *Border* | 119 | NT8650 |
| Whitson *Gwent* | 34 | ST3883 |
| Whitstable *Kent* | 29 | TR1066 |
| Whitstone *Cnwll* | 5 | SX2698 |
| Whittingham *Nthumb* | 111 | NU0612 |
| Whittingslow *Shrops* | 59 | SO4388 |
| Whittington *Derbys* | 74 | SK3875 |
| Whittington *Gloucs* | 35 | SP0120 |
| Whittington *H & W* | 47 | SO8752 |
| Whittington *Lancs* | 87 | SD5976 |
| Whittington *Shrops* | 59 | SJ3231 |
| Whittington *Staffs* | 61 | SK1508 |
| Whittington *Staffs* | 60 | SO8682 |
| Whittington *Warwks* | 61 | SP2999 |
| Whittle-le-Woods *Lancs* | 81 | SD5821 |
| Whittlebury *Nhants* | 49 | SP6943 |
| Whittlesey *Cambs* | 64 | TL2697 |
| Whittlesford *Cambs* | 53 | TL4748 |
| Whittlestone Head *Lancs* | 81 | SD7119 |
| Whitton *Cleve* | 96 | NZ3921 |
| Whitton *Humb* | 84 | SE9024 |
| Whitton *Powys* | 46 | SO2767 |
| Whitton *Shrops* | 46 | SO5772 |
| Whitton *Suffk* | 54 | TM1447 |
| Whittonditch *Wilts* | 36 | SU2872 |
| Whittonstall *Nthumb* | 95 | NZ0757 |
| Whitway *Hants* | 24 | SU4559 |
| Whitwell *Derbys* | 75 | SK5276 |
| Whitwell *Herts* | 39 | TL1820 |
| Whitwell *IOW* | 13 | SZ5277 |
| Whitwell *Leics* | 63 | SK9208 |
| Whitwell *N York* | 89 | SE2899 |
| Whitwell Street *Norfk* | 66 | TG1022 |
| Whitwick *Leics* | 62 | SK4316 |
| Whitwood *W York* | 83 | SE4124 |
| Whitworth *Lancs* | 81 | SD8818 |
| Whixall *Shrops* | 59 | SJ5134 |
| Whixley *N York* | 89 | SE4458 |
| Whorlton *Dur* | 95 | NZ1014 |
| Whorlton *N York* | 90 | NZ4802 |
| Whyle *H & W* | 46 | SO5561 |
| Whyteleafe *Surrey* | 27 | TQ3358 |
| Wibdon *Gloucs* | 34 | ST5797 |
| Wibsey *W York* | 82 | SE1430 |
| Wibtoft *Warwks* | 50 | SP4887 |
| Wichenford *H & W* | 47 | SO7860 |
| Wichling *Kent* | 28 | TQ9256 |
| Wick *Avon* | 35 | ST7072 |
| Wick *Devon* | 9 | ST1604 |
| Wick *Dorset* | 12 | SZ1591 |
| Wick *H & W* | 47 | SO9645 |
| Wick *Highld* | 151 | ND3650 |
| Wick *M Glam* | 33 | SS9272 |
| Wick *Somset* | 21 | ST4027 |
| Wick *Somset* | 20 | ST2144 |
| Wick *W Susx* | 14 | TQ0203 |
| Wick *Wilts* | 12 | SU1621 |
| Wick End *Beds* | 38 | SP9850 |
| Wick Rissington *Gloucs* | 36 | SP1821 |
| Wick St. Lawrence *Avon* | 21 | ST3665 |
| Wicken *Cambs* | 53 | TL5770 |
| Wicken *Nhants* | 49 | SP7439 |
| Wicken Bonhunt *Essex* | 39 | TL4933 |
| Wickenby *Lincs* | 76 | TF0882 |
| Wicker Street Green *Suffk* | 54 | TL9742 |
| Wickersley *S York* | 75 | SK4791 |
| Wickford *Essex* | 40 | TQ7593 |
| Wickham *Berks* | 36 | SU3971 |
| Wickham *Hants* | 13 | SU5711 |
| Wickham Bishops *Essex* | 40 | TL8412 |
| Wickham Green *Berks* | 24 | SU4072 |
| Wickham Green *Suffk* | 54 | TM0969 |
| Wickham Heath *Berks* | 24 | SU4169 |
| Wickham Market *Suffk* | 55 | TM3055 |
| Wickham Skeith *Suffk* | 54 | TM0969 |
| Wickham St. Paul *Essex* | 54 | TL8336 |
| Wickham Street *Suffk* | 53 | TL7654 |
| Wickham Street *Suffk* | 54 | TM0869 |
| Wickhambreaux *Kent* | 29 | TR2158 |
| Wickhambrook *Suffk* | 53 | TL7554 |
| Wickhamford *H & W* | 48 | SP0641 |
| Wickhampton *Norfk* | 67 | TG4205 |
| Wicklewood *Norfk* | 66 | TG0702 |
| Wickmere *Norfk* | 66 | TG1733 |
| Wickstreet *E Susx* | 16 | TQ5308 |
| Wickwar *Avon* | 35 | ST7288 |
| Widdington *Essex* | 39 | TL5331 |
| Widdop *Lancs* | 81 | SD9333 |
| Widdrington *T & W* | 103 | NZ2595 |
| Widdrington Station *T & W* | 103 | NZ2494 |
| Wide Open *T & W* | 103 | NZ2372 |
| Widecombe in the Moor *Devon* | 8 | SX7176 |
| Widegates *Cnwll* | 5 | SX2857 |
| Widemouth Bay *Cnwll* | 18 | SS2002 |
| Widford *Essex* | 40 | TL6905 |
| Widford *Herts* | 39 | TL4116 |
| Widford *Oxon* | 36 | SP2712 |
| Widham *Wilts* | 36 | SU0988 |
| Widmer End *Bucks* | 26 | SU8796 |
| Widmerpool *Notts* | 63 | SK6327 |
| Widmore *Gt Lon* | 27 | TQ4268 |
| Widnes *Ches* | 78 | SJ5184 |
| Widworthy *Devon* | 18 | SX2199 |
| Wigan *Gt Man* | 78 | SD5805 |
| Wigborough *Somset* | 10 | ST4415 |
| Wiggaton *Devon* | 9 | SY1093 |
| Wiggenhall St. Germans *Norfk* | 65 | TF5914 |
| Wiggenhall St. Mary Magda *Norfk* | 65 | TF5911 |
| Wiggenhall St. Mary the V *Norfk* | 65 | TF5814 |
| Wiggens Green *Essex* | 53 | TL6642 |
| Wiggenstall *Staffs* | 74 | SK0960 |
| Wiggington *Shrops* | 59 | SJ3335 |
| Wigginton *Herts* | 38 | SP9310 |
| Wigginton *N York* | 90 | SE5958 |
| Wigginton *Oxon* | 48 | SP3833 |
| Wigginton *Staffs* | 61 | SK2106 |
| Wigglesworth *N York* | 88 | SD8157 |
| Wiggold *Gloucs* | 36 | SP0404 |
| Wiggonby *Cumb* | 93 | NY2953 |
| Wiggonholt *W Susx* | 14 | TQ0616 |
| Wigham *Devon* | 19 | SS7508 |
| Wighill *N York* | 83 | SE4746 |
| Wighton *Norfk* | 66 | TF9439 |
| Wigley *Hants* | 12 | SU3217 |
| Wigmore *H & W* | 46 | SO4169 |
| Wigmore *Kent* | 28 | TQ7964 |
| Wigsley *Notts* | 76 | SK8570 |
| Wigsthorpe *Nhants* | 51 | TL0482 |
| Wigston *Leics* | 50 | SP6199 |
| Wigston Fields *Leics* | 50 | SK6000 |
| Wigston Parva *Leics* | 50 | SP4689 |
| Wigthorpe *Notts* | 75 | SK5983 |
| Wigtoft *Lincs* | 64 | TF2636 |
| Wigton *Cumb* | 93 | NY2548 |
| Wigtown *D & G* | 99 | NX4355 |
| Wigtwizzle *S York* | 74 | SK2495 |
| Wike *W York* | 83 | SE3342 |
| Wilbarston *Nhants* | 51 | SP8188 |
| Wilberfoss *Humb* | 84 | SE7350 |
| Wilburton *Cambs* | 53 | TL4785 |
| Wilby *Nhants* | 51 | SP8666 |
| Wilby *Norfk* | 54 | TM0389 |
| Wilby *Suffk* | 55 | TM2472 |
| Wilcot *Wilts* | 23 | SU1360 |
| Wilcrick *Gwent* | 34 | ST4088 |
| Wilday Green *Derbys* | 74 | SK2274 |
| Wildboarclough *Ches* | 79 | SJ9868 |
| Wilden *Beds* | 51 | TL0955 |
| Wilden *H & W* | 60 | SO8272 |
| Wildhern *Hants* | 23 | SU3550 |
| Wildhill *Herts* | 39 | TL2606 |
| Wildmanbridge *Strath* | 116 | NS8253 |
| Wildmoor *H & W* | 60 | SO9575 |
| Wildsworth *Lincs* | 75 | SK8097 |
| Wilford *Notts* | 62 | SK5637 |
| Wilkesley *Ches* | 71 | SJ6241 |
| Wilkhaven *Highld* | 147 | NH9486 |
| Wilkieston *Fife* | 117 | NT1268 |
| Wilkin's Green *Herts* | 39 | TL1907 |
| Wilksby *Lincs* | 77 | TF2862 |
| Willand *Devon* | 9 | ST0310 |
| Willards Hill *E Susx* | 17 | TQ7124 |
| Willaston *Ches* | 71 | SJ3377 |
| Willaston *Ches* | 72 | SJ6752 |
| Willcott *Shrops* | 59 | SJ3718 |
| Willen *Bucks* | 38 | SP8741 |
| Willenhall *W Mids* | 60 | SO9698 |
| Willenhall *W Mids* | 61 | SP3676 |
| Willerby *Humb* | 84 | TA0230 |
| Willerby *N York* | 91 | TA0079 |
| Willersey *Gloucs* | 48 | SP1039 |
| Willersley *H & W* | 46 | SO3147 |
| Willesborough *Kent* | 28 | TR0441 |
| Willesborough Lees *Kent* | 28 | TR0342 |
| Willesden *Gt Lon* | 26 | TQ2284 |
| Willesleigh *Devon* | 19 | SS6033 |
| Willesley *Wilts* | 35 | ST8588 |
| Willett *Somset* | 20 | ST1033 |
| Willey *Shrops* | 60 | SO6799 |
| Willey *Warwks* | 50 | SP4984 |
| Willey Green *Surrey* | 25 | SU9351 |
| Williamscot *Oxon* | 49 | SP4745 |
| Williamstown *M Glam* | 33 | ST0090 |
| Willian *Herts* | 39 | TL2230 |
| Willingale *Essex* | 40 | TL5907 |
| Willingdon *E Susx* | 16 | TQ5902 |
| Willingham *Cambs* | 52 | TL4070 |
| Willingham *Lincs* | 76 | SK8784 |
| Willingham Green *Cambs* | 53 | TL6254 |
| Willington *Beds* | 52 | TL1150 |
| Willington *Derbys* | 73 | SK2928 |
| Willington *Dur* | 96 | NZ1935 |
| Willington *Kent* | 28 | TQ7853 |
| Willington *Warwks* | 48 | SP2638 |
| Willington Corner *Ches* | 71 | SJ5366 |
| Willington Quay *T & W* | 103 | NZ3167 |
| Willitoft *Humb* | 84 | SE7434 |
| Williton *Somset* | 20 | ST0740 |
| Willoughbridge *Staffs* | 72 | SJ7440 |
| Willoughby *Lincs* | 64 | TF0537 |
| Willoughby *Lincs* | 77 | TF4771 |
| Willoughby *Warwks* | 50 | SP5167 |
| Willoughby Hills *Lincs* | 64 | TF3545 |
| Willoughby Waterleys *Leics* | 50 | SP5792 |
| Willoughby-on-the-Wolds *Notts* | 63 | SK6325 |
| Willoughton *Lincs* | 76 | SK9293 |
| Willow Green *Ches* | 71 | SJ6076 |
| Willows Green *Essex* | 40 | TL7219 |
| Willsbridge *Avon* | 35 | ST6670 |
| Willsworthy *Devon* | 8 | SX5381 |
| Willtown *Somset* | 21 | ST3924 |
| Wilmcote *Warwks* | 48 | SP1658 |
| Wilmington *Avon* | 22 | ST6962 |
| Wilmington *Devon* | 9 | SY2199 |
| Wilmington *E Susx* | 16 | TQ5404 |
| Wilmington *Kent* | 27 | TQ5371 |
| Wilmslow *Ches* | 79 | SJ8481 |
| Wilnecote *Staffs* | 61 | SK2201 |
| Wilpshire *Lancs* | 81 | SD6832 |
| Wilsden *W York* | 82 | SE0936 |
| Wilsford *Lincs* | 63 | TF0042 |
| Wilsford *Wilts* | 23 | SU1057 |
| Wilsford *Wilts* | 23 | SU1339 |
| Wilsham *Devon* | 19 | SS7548 |
| Wilshaw *W York* | 82 | SE1109 |
| Wilsill *N York* | 89 | SE1864 |
| Wilsley Green *Kent* | 28 | TQ7737 |
| Wilsley Pound *Kent* | 28 | TQ7837 |
| Wilson *H & W* | 46 | SO5523 |
| Wilson *Leics* | 62 | SK4024 |
| Wilsontown *Strath* | 116 | NS9455 |
| Wilstead *Beds* | 38 | TL0643 |
| Wilsthorpe *Lincs* | 64 | TF0913 |
| Wilstone *Herts* | 38 | SP9014 |
| Wilstone Green *Herts* | 38 | SP9013 |
| Wilton *Cleve* | 97 | NZ5819 |
| Wilton *Cleve* | 97 | NZ5819 |
| Wilton *Cumb* | 86 | NY0411 |
| Wilton *H & W* | 46 | SO5824 |
| Wilton *N York* | 90 | SE8582 |
| Wilton *Wilts* | 23 | SU0931 |
| Wilton *Wilts* | 23 | SU2661 |
| Wilton Dean *Border* | 109 | NT4914 |
| Wimbish *Essex* | 53 | TL5936 |
| Wimbish Green *Essex* | 53 | TL6035 |
| Wimblebury *Staffs* | 60 | SK0111 |
| Wimbledon *Gt Lon* | 26 | TQ2370 |
| Wimblington *Cambs* | 65 | TL4192 |
| Wimborne Minster *Dorset* | 11 | SZ0199 |
| Wimborne St. Giles *Dorset* | 12 | SU0212 |
| Wimbotsham *Norfk* | 65 | TF6205 |
| Wimpstone *Warwks* | 48 | SP2148 |
| Wincanton *Somset* | 22 | ST7128 |
| Winceby *Lincs* | 77 | TF3268 |
| Wincham *Ches* | 79 | SJ6775 |
| Winchburgh *Loth* | 117 | NT0974 |
| Winchcombe *Gloucs* | 48 | SP0228 |
| Winchelsea *E Susx* | 17 | TQ9017 |
| Winchelsea Beach *E Susx* | 17 | TQ9115 |
| Winchester *Hants* | 24 | SU4829 |
| Winchet Hill *Kent* | 28 | TQ7340 |
| Winchfield *Hants* | 24 | SU7654 |
| Winchmore Hill *Bucks* | 26 | SU9395 |
| Winchmore Hill *Gt Lon* | 27 | TQ3194 |
| Wincle *Ches* | 72 | SJ9666 |
| Wincobank *S York* | 74 | SK3891 |
| Winder *Cumb* | 92 | NY0417 |
| Windermere *Cumb* | 87 | SD4198 |
| Winderton *Warwks* | 48 | SP3240 |
| Windhill *Highld* | 139 | NH5348 |
| Windlehurst *Gt Man* | 79 | SJ9586 |
| Windlesham *Surrey* | 25 | SU9264 |
| Windmill *Cnwll* | 4 | SW8975 |
| Windmill *Derbys* | 74 | SK1677 |

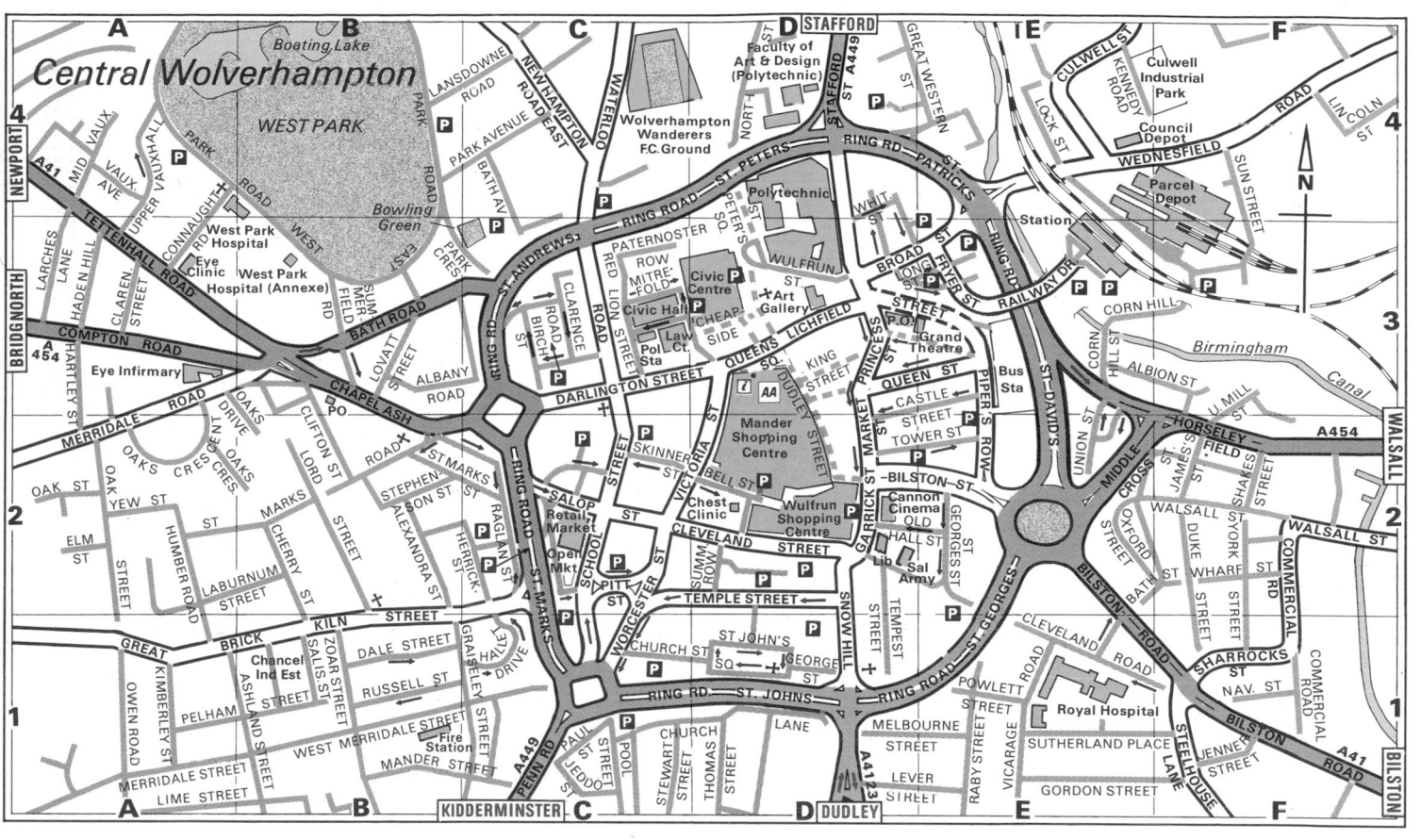

Woodend Ythsie


| | | |
|---|---|---|
| Woodend *Cumb* | 86 | SD1696 |
| Woodend *Highld* | 130 | NM7861 |
| Woodend *Loth* | 116 | NS9269 |
| Woodend *Nhants* | 49 | SP6149 |
| Woodend *Staffs* | 73 | SK1726 |
| Woodend *W Susx* | 14 | SU8108 |
| Woodend Green *Essex* | 39 | TL5528 |
| Woodfalls *Wilts* | 12 | SU1920 |
| Woodford *Devon* | 7 | SX7950 |
| Woodford *Gloucs* | 35 | ST6996 |
| Woodford *Gt Lon* | 27 | TQ4092 |
| Woodford *Gt Man* | 79 | SJ8882 |
| Woodford *Nhants* | 51 | SP9676 |
| Woodford Bridge *Gt Lon* | 27 | TQ4291 |
| Woodford End *Bucks* | 49 | SP6148 |
| Woodford Halse *Nhants* | 49 | SP5452 |
| Woodford Wells *Gt Lon* | 27 | TQ4093 |
| Woodgate *Devon* | 9 | ST1015 |
| Woodgate *H & W* | 47 | SO9666 |
| Woodgate *Norfk* | 66 | TF8915 |
| Woodgate *Norfk* | 66 | TG0216 |
| Woodgate *W Mids* | 60 | SO9982 |
| Woodgate *W Susx* | 14 | SU9304 |
| Woodgreen *Hants* | 12 | SU1717 |
| Woodgreen *Oxon* | 36 | SP3610 |
| Woodhall *N York* | 88 | SD9790 |
| Woodhall Hill *W York* | 82 | SE1935 |
| Woodhall Spa *Lincs* | 76 | TF1962 |
| Woodham *Bucks* | 37 | SP7018 |
| Woodham *Dur* | 96 | NZ2826 |
| Woodham *Lincs* | 76 | TF2367 |
| Woodham Ferrers *Essex* | 40 | TQ7999 |
| Woodham Mortimer *Essex* | 40 | TL8104 |
| Woodham Walter *Essex* | 40 | TL8107 |
| Woodhaven *Fife* | 126 | NO4126 |
| Woodhead *Gramp* | 143 | NJ7938 |
| Woodhill *Shrops* | 60 | SO7384 |
| Woodhill *Somset* | 21 | ST3527 |
| Woodhorn *Nthumb* | 103 | NZ2988 |
| Woodhorn Demesne *Nthumb* | 103 | NZ3088 |
| Woodhouse *Cumb* | 93 | NY3252 |
| Woodhouse *Leics* | 62 | SK5315 |
| Woodhouse *S York* | 74 | SK4284 |
| Woodhouse *W York* | 83 | SE3821 |
| Woodhouse *W York* | 82 | SE2932 |
| Woodhouse Eaves *Leics* | 62 | SK5214 |
| Woodhouse Green *Staffs* | 72 | SJ9162 |
| Woodhouse Mill *S York* | 75 | SK4385 |
| Woodhouselee *Fife* | 117 | NT2364 |
| Woodhouses *Gt Man* | 79 | SD9100 |
| Woodhouses *Staffs* | 61 | SK0809 |
| Woodhouses *Staffs* | 73 | SK1519 |
| Woodhuish *Devon* | 7 | SX9152 |
| Woodhurst *Cambs* | 52 | TL3176 |
| Woodingdean *E Susx* | 15 | TQ3505 |
| Woodkirk *W York* | 82 | SE2725 |
| Woodland *Devon* | 6 | SX6250 |
| Woodland *Devon* | 7 | SX7968 |
| Woodland *Dur* | 95 | NZ0726 |
| Woodland *Gramp* | 143 | NJ8723 |
| Woodland *Kent* | 29 | TR1441 |
| Woodland *Strath* | 106 | NX1795 |
| Woodland Head *Devon* | 8 | SX7796 |
| Woodland Street *Somset* | 21 | ST5437 |
| Woodland View *S York* | 74 | SK3188 |
| Woodlands *Dorset* | 12 | SU0508 |
| Woodlands *Gramp* | 135 | NO7895 |
| Woodlands *Hants* | 12 | SU3211 |
| Woodlands *Kent* | 27 | TQ5660 |
| Woodlands *N York* | 83 | SE3255 |
| Woodlands *S York* | 83 | SE5308 |
| Woodlands Park *Berks* | 26 | SU8678 |
| Woodlands St. Mary *Berks* | 36 | SU3375 |
| Woodlands St. Mary *Berks* | 36 | SU3375 |
| Woodleigh *Devon* | 7 | SX7348 |
| Woodlesford *W York* | 83 | SE3629 |
| Woodley *Berks* | 25 | SU7773 |
| Woodley *Gt Man* | 79 | SJ9492 |
| Woodley Green *Berks* | 26 | SU8480 |
| Woodlords *Strath* | 117 | NT0056 |
| Woodmancote *Gloucs* | 47 | SO9727 |
| Woodmancote *Gloucs* | 35 | SP0008 |
| Woodmancote *Gloucs* | 35 | ST7697 |
| Woodmancote *H & W* | 47 | SO9142 |
| Woodmancote *W Susx* | 14 | SU7707 |
| Woodmancote *W Susx* | 15 | TQ2314 |
| Woodmancott *Hants* | 24 | SU5642 |
| Woodmansey *Humb* | 84 | TA0538 |
| Woodmansgreen *W Susx* | 14 | SU8627 |
| Woodmansterne *Surrey* | 27 | TQ2759 |
| Woodmanton *Devon* | 4 | SX0185 |
| Woodmarsh *Wilts* | 22 | ST8555 |
| Woodmill *Staffs* | 73 | SK1321 |
| Woodminton *Wilts* | 22 | SU0122 |
| Woodnesborough *Kent* | 29 | TR3157 |
| Woodnewton *Nhants* | 51 | TL0394 |
| Woodnook *Notts* | 75 | SK4752 |
| Woodplumpton *Lancs* | 80 | SD5034 |
| Woodrising *Norfk* | 66 | TF9803 |
| Woodrow *H & W* | 60 | SO8875 |
| Woodseaves *Shrops* | 72 | SJ6831 |
| Woodseaves *Staffs* | 72 | SJ7925 |
| Woodsend *Wilts* | 36 | SU2275 |
| Woodsetts *S York* | 75 | SK5483 |
| Woodsford *Dorset* | 11 | SY7690 |
| Woodside *Berks* | 25 | SU9371 |
| Woodside *Cumb* | 92 | NY0434 |
| Woodside *D & G* | 100 | NY0475 |
| Woodside *Dyfed* | 31 | SN1406 |
| Woodside *Essex* | 39 | TL4704 |
| Woodside *Fife* | 127 | NO4207 |
| Woodside *Gt Lon* | 27 | TQ3467 |
| Woodside *Hants* | 12 | SZ3294 |
| Woodside *Herts* | 39 | TL2406 |
| Woodside *Tays* | 126 | NO2037 |
| Woodside Green *Kent* | 28 | TQ9053 |
| Woodstock *Dyfed* | 30 | SN0325 |
| Woodstock *Oxon* | 37 | SP4416 |
| Woodston *Cambs* | 64 | TL1897 |
| Woodthorpe *Derbys* | 75 | SK4574 |
| Woodthorpe *Leics* | 62 | SK5417 |
| Woodthorpe *Lincs* | 77 | TF4380 |
| Woodton *Norfk* | 67 | TM2994 |
| Woodtown *Devon* | 18 | SS4123 |
| Woodtown *Devon* | 18 | SS4926 |
| Woodvale *Mersyd* | 80 | SD3011 |
| Woodville *Derbys* | 62 | SK3119 |
| Woodwall Green *Staffs* | 72 | SJ7831 |
| Woody Bay *Devon* | 19 | SS6748 |
| Woodyates *Dorset* | 12 | SU0219 |
| Woofferton *Shrops* | 46 | SO5268 |
| Wookey *Somset* | 21 | ST5145 |
| Wookey Hole *Somset* | 21 | ST5347 |
| Wool *Dorset* | 11 | SY8486 |
| Woolacombe *Devon* | 18 | SS4643 |
| Woolage Green *Kent* | 29 | TR2349 |
| Woolage Village *Kent* | 26 | TQ2250 |
| Woolaston *Gloucs* | 34 | ST5899 |
| Woolaston Common *Gloucs* | 34 | SO5801 |
| Woolavington *Somset* | 21 | ST3441 |
| Woolbeding *W Susx* | 14 | SU8722 |
| Woolbrook *Devon* | 4 | SX1289 |
| Woolcotts *Somset* | 20 | SS9731 |
| Wooldale *W York* | 82 | SE1508 |
| Wooler *Nthumb* | 111 | NT9928 |
| Wooley Bridge *Derbys* | 79 | SK0195 |
| Woolfardisworthy *Devon* | 19 | SS8208 |
| Woolfardisworthy *Devon* | 18 | SS3321 |
| Woolfold *Gt Man* | 81 | SD7812 |
| Woolhampton *Berks* | 24 | SU5766 |
| Woolhanger *Devon* | 19 | SS6945 |
| Woolhope *H & W* | 46 | SO6135 |
| Woolland *Dorset* | 11 | ST7707 |
| Woollard *Avon* | 21 | ST6364 |
| Woollaton *Devon* | 18 | SS4712 |
| Woollensbrook *Herts* | 39 | TL3609 |
| Woolley *Avon* | 22 | ST7468 |
| Woolley *Cambs* | 52 | TL1474 |
| Woolley *Cnwll* | 18 | SS2516 |
| Woolley *Derbys* | 74 | SK3760 |
| Woolley *W York* | 82 | SE3113 |
| Woolmer Green *Herts* | 39 | TL2518 |
| Woolmere Green *H & W* | 47 | SO9663 |
| Woolmerston *Somset* | 20 | ST2533 |
| Woolminstone *Somset* | 10 | ST4008 |
| Woolpack *Kent* | 28 | TQ8537 |
| Woolpack Inn *Cumb* | 86 | NY1901 |
| Woolpit *Suffk* | 54 | TL9762 |
| Woolpit Green *Suffk* | 54 | TL9761 |
| Woolscott *Warwks* | 50 | SP4968 |
| Woolsgrove *Devon* | 8 | SS7902 |
| Woolsgrove *Devon* | 8 | SS7902 |
| Woolsington *T & W* | 103 | NZ1870 |
| Woolstaston *Shrops* | 59 | SO4598 |
| Woolsthorpe *Lincs* | 63 | SK8333 |
| Woolsthorpe *Lincs* | 63 | SK9224 |
| Woolston *Ches* | 79 | SJ6589 |
| Woolston *Devon* | 7 | SX7150 |
| Woolston *Devon* | 7 | SX7141 |
| Woolston *Hants* | 13 | SU4410 |
| Woolston *Shrops* | 59 | SJ3224 |
| Woolston *Shrops* | 59 | SO4287 |
| Woolston *Somset* | 20 | ST1139 |
| Woolston *Somset* | 21 | ST6528 |
| Woolston Green *Devon* | 7 | SX7765 |
| Woolstone *Bucks* | 38 | SP8738 |
| Woolstone *Gloucs* | 47 | SO9530 |
| Woolstone *Oxon* | 36 | SU2987 |
| Woolton *Mersyd* | 78 | SJ4286 |
| Woolton Hill *Hants* | 24 | SU4261 |
| Woolvers Hill *Avon* | 21 | ST3860 |
| Woolverstone *Suffk* | 54 | TM1838 |
| Woolverton *Somset* | 22 | ST7853 |
| Woolwich *Gt Lon* | 27 | TQ4478 |
| Woonton *H & W* | 46 | SO5562 |
| Woonton *H & W* | 46 | SO3552 |
| Wooperton *Nthumb* | 111 | NU0420 |
| Woore *Shrops* | 72 | SJ7342 |
| Wooston *Devon* | 8 | SX7689 |
| Wootten Breadmead *Beds* | 38 | TL0243 |
| Wootten Green *Suffk* | 55 | TM2373 |
| Wootton *Beds* | 38 | TL0045 |
| Wootton *H & W* | 46 | SO3252 |
| Wootton *Hants* | 12 | SZ2498 |
| Wootton *Humb* | 85 | TA0815 |
| Wootton *IOW* | 13 | SZ5492 |
| Wootton *Kent* | 29 | TR2246 |
| Wootton *Nhants* | 49 | SP7656 |
| Wootton *Oxon* | 36 | SP4319 |
| Wootton *Oxon* | 37 | SP4701 |
| Wootton *Shrops* | 59 | SJ3327 |
| Wootton *Staffs* | 72 | SJ8227 |
| Wootton *Staffs* | 73 | SK1045 |
| Wootton Bassett *Wilts* | 36 | SU0782 |
| Wootton Bridge *IOW* | 13 | SZ5492 |
| Wootton Common *IOW* | 13 | SZ5391 |
| Wootton Courtenay *Somset* | 20 | SS9343 |
| Wootton Fitzpaine *Dorset* | 10 | SY3695 |
| Wootton Rivers *Wilts* | 23 | SU1963 |
| Wootton St. Lawrence *Hants* | 24 | SU5953 |
| Wootton Wawen *Warwks* | 48 | SP1563 |
| Worbarrow *Dorset* | 11 | SY8779 |
| Worcester *H & W* | 47 | SO8555 |
| Worcester Park *Gt Lon* | 26 | TQ2165 |
| Wordsley *W Mids* | 60 | SO8987 |
| Worfield *Shrops* | 60 | SO7596 |
| Worgret *Dorset* | 11 | SY9087 |
| Workington *Cumb* | 92 | NX9928 |
| Worksop *Notts* | 75 | SK5879 |
| Worlaby *Humb* | 84 | TA0113 |
| Worlaby *Lincs* | 77 | TF3476 |
| World's End *Berks* | 37 | SU4876 |
| Worlds End *Bucks* | 38 | SP8509 |
| Worlds End *Hants* | 13 | SU6312 |
| Worlds End *W Susx* | 15 | TQ3220 |
| Worle *Avon* | 21 | ST3563 |
| Worleston *Ches* | 72 | SJ6556 |
| Worlingham *Suffk* | 55 | TM4489 |
| Worlington *Devon* | 19 | SS7713 |
| Worlington *Suffk* | 53 | TL6973 |
| Worlingworth *Suffk* | 55 | TM2368 |
| Wormald Green *N York* | 89 | SE3065 |
| Wormbridge *H & W* | 46 | SO4230 |
| Wormegay *Norfk* | 65 | TF6611 |
| Wormelow Tump *H & W* | 46 | SO4930 |
| Wormhill *Derbys* | 74 | SK1274 |
| Wormhill *H & W* | 46 | SO4239 |
| Wormingford *Essex* | 40 | TL9332 |
| Worminghall *Bucks* | 37 | SP6308 |
| Wormington *Gloucs* | 48 | SP0336 |
| Worminster *Somset* | 21 | ST5742 |
| Wormiston *Border* | 117 | NT2345 |
| Wormit *Fife* | 126 | NO3926 |
| Wormleighton *Warwks* | 49 | SP4453 |
| Wormley *Herts* | 39 | TL3605 |
| Wormley *Surrey* | 25 | SU9438 |
| Wormley Hill *S York* | 83 | SE6616 |
| Wormleybury *Herts* | 39 | TL3506 |
| Wormshill *Kent* | 28 | TQ8857 |
| Wormsley *H & W* | 46 | SO4247 |
| Worplesdon *Surrey* | 25 | SU9753 |
| Worrall *S York* | 74 | SK3092 |
| Worsbrough *S York* | 83 | SE3503 |
| Worsbrough Bridge *S York* | 83 | SE3403 |
| Worsbrough Dale *S York* | 83 | SE3402 |
| Worsley *Gt Man* | 79 | SD7500 |
| Worsley Mesnes *Gt Man* | 78 | SD5703 |
| Worstead *Norfk* | 67 | TG3026 |
| Worsthorne *Lancs* | 81 | SD8732 |
| Worston *Devon* | 6 | SX5952 |
| Worston *Lancs* | 81 | SD7742 |
| Worswell *Devon* | 6 | SX5447 |
| Worth *Kent* | 29 | TR3356 |
| Worth *Somset* | 21 | ST5145 |
| Worth *W Susx* | 15 | TQ3036 |
| Worth Abbey *Surrey* | 15 | TQ3134 |
| Worth Matravers *Dorset* | 11 | SY9777 |
| Wortham *Suffk* | 54 | TM0877 |
| Worthen *Shrops* | 59 | SJ3204 |
| Worthenbury *Clwyd* | 71 | SJ4246 |
| Worthing *Norfk* | 66 | TF9919 |
| Worthing *W Susx* | 15 | TQ1402 |
| Worthington *Leics* | 62 | SK4020 |
| Worthybrook *Gwent* | 34 | SO4711 |
| Worting *Hants* | 24 | SU5952 |
| Wortley *S York* | 74 | SK3099 |
| Wortley *W York* | 82 | SE2732 |
| Worton *N York* | 88 | SD9589 |
| Worton *Wilts* | 22 | ST9757 |
| Wortwell *Norfk* | 55 | TM2784 |
| Wotherton *Shrops* | 58 | SJ2800 |
| Wothorpe *Cambs* | 64 | TF0205 |
| Wotter *Devon* | 6 | SX5562 |
| Wotton *Surrey* | 14 | TQ1247 |
| Wotton Under Edge *Gloucs* | 35 | ST7593 |
| Wotton Underwood *Bucks* | 37 | SP6816 |
| Woughton on the Green *Bucks* | 38 | SP8737 |
| Wouldham *Kent* | 28 | TQ7164 |
| Woundale *Shrops* | 60 | SO7793 |
| Wrabness *Essex* | 41 | TM1731 |
| Wrafton *Devon* | 18 | SS4935 |
| Wragby *Lincs* | 76 | TF1378 |
| Wragby *W York* | 83 | SE4014 |
| Wramplingham *Norfk* | 66 | TG1106 |
| Wrangaton *Devon* | 7 | SX6757 |
| Wrangbrook *W York* | 83 | SE4013 |
| Wrangle *Lincs* | 77 | TF4250 |
| Wrangle Common *Lincs* | 77 | TF4253 |
| Wrangle Lowgate *Lincs* | 77 | TF4451 |
| Wrangway *Somset* | 9 | ST1217 |
| Wrantage *Somset* | 20 | ST3022 |
| Wrawby *Humb* | 84 | TA0108 |
| Wraxall *Avon* | 34 | ST4871 |
| Wraxall *Somset* | 21 | ST6036 |
| Wray *Lancs* | 87 | SD6067 |
| Wray Castle *Cumb* | 93 | NY3730 |
| Wraysbury *Berks* | 25 | TQ0074 |
| Wrayton *Lancs* | 87 | SD6172 |
| Wrea Green *Lancs* | 80 | SD3931 |
| Wreaks End *Cumb* | 101 | NY2186 |
| Wreay *Cumb* | 93 | NY4424 |
| Wreay *Cumb* | 93 | NY4348 |
| Wreay *Cumb* | 93 | NY4423 |
| Wrecclesham *Surrey* | 25 | SU8245 |
| Wrekenton *T & W* | 96 | NZ2758 |
| Wrelton *N York* | 90 | SE7686 |
| Wrenbury *Ches* | 71 | SJ5947 |
| Wrench Green *N York* | 91 | SE9689 |
| Wreningham *Norfk* | 66 | TM1699 |
| Wrentham *Suffk* | 55 | TM4982 |
| Wrentnall *Shrops* | 59 | SJ4203 |
| Wrentthorpe *W York* | 82 | SE3122 |
| Wressing *Devon* | 9 | ST0508 |
| Wressle *Humb* | 84 | SE9709 |
| Wressle *Humb* | 84 | SE7031 |
| Wrestlingworth *Beds* | 52 | TL2547 |
| Wretton *Norfk* | 65 | TF6900 |
| Wrexham *Clwyd* | 71 | SJ3350 |
| Wribbenhall *H & W* | 60 | SO7975 |
| Wrickton *Shrops* | 59 | SO6486 |
| Wright's Green *Essex* | 39 | TL5017 |
| Wrightington Bar *Lancs* | 80 | SD5313 |
| Wrinehill *Staffs* | 72 | SJ7547 |
| Wrington *Avon* | 21 | ST4762 |
| Wringworthy *Cnwll* | 5 | SX2658 |
| Writhlington *Somset* | 22 | ST7054 |
| Writtle *Essex* | 40 | TL6706 |
| Wrockwardine *Shrops* | 59 | SJ6212 |
| Wroot *Humb* | 84 | SE7103 |
| Wrose *W York* | 82 | SE1636 |
| Wrotham *Kent* | 27 | TQ6159 |
| Wrotham Green *Kent* | 27 | TQ6357 |
| Wrottesley *Staffs* | 60 | SJ8201 |
| Wroughton *Wilts* | 36 | SU1480 |
| Wroxall *IOW* | 13 | SZ5579 |
| Wroxall *Warwks* | 61 | SP2271 |
| Wroxeter *Shrops* | 59 | SJ5608 |
| Wroxham *Norfk* | 67 | TG3017 |
| Wroxton *Oxon* | 49 | SP4141 |
| Wyaston *Derbys* | 73 | SK1842 |
| Wyatt's Green *Essex* | 27 | TQ5999 |
| Wyberton *Lincs* | 64 | TF3240 |
| Wyboston *Beds* | 52 | TL1656 |
| Wybunbury *Ches* | 72 | SJ6949 |
| Wych *Dorset* | 10 | SY4791 |
| Wych Cross *E Susx* | 15 | TQ4131 |
| Wychbold *H & W* | 47 | SO9266 |
| Wychnor *Staffs* | 73 | SK1716 |
| Wyck *Hants* | 24 | SU7539 |
| Wycliffe *Dur* | 95 | NZ1114 |
| Wycoller *Lancs* | 81 | SD9339 |
| Wycomb *Leics* | 63 | SK7724 |
| Wycombe Marsh *Bucks* | 26 | SU8892 |
| Wyddial *Herts* | 39 | TL3731 |
| Wye *Kent* | 28 | TR0546 |
| Wyesham *Gwent* | 34 | SO5111 |
| Wyfordby *Leics* | 63 | SK7918 |
| Wyke *Devon* | 5 | SX2996 |
| Wyke *Devon* | 9 | SX8799 |
| Wyke *Dorset* | 22 | ST7926 |
| Wyke *Shrops* | 59 | SJ6402 |
| Wyke *Surrey* | 25 | SU9251 |
| Wyke *W York* | 82 | SE1526 |
| Wyke Champflower *Somset* | 22 | ST6634 |
| Wyke Regis *Dorset* | 11 | SY6677 |
| Wyke The *Shrops* | 60 | SJ7306 |
| Wykeham *N York* | 90 | SE8175 |
| Wykeham *N York* | 91 | SE9683 |
| Wyken *Shrops* | 60 | SO7695 |
| Wyken *W Mids* | 61 | SP3680 |
| Wykey *Shrops* | 59 | SJ3925 |
| Wykin *Leics* | 61 | SP4095 |
| Wylam *Nthumb* | 103 | NZ1164 |
| Wylde Green *W Mids* | 61 | SP1294 |
| Wyllie *Gwent* | 33 | ST1794 |
| Wylye *Wilts* | 22 | SU0037 |
| Wymeswold *Leics* | 62 | SK6023 |
| Wymington *Beds* | 51 | SP9564 |
| Wymondham *Leics* | 63 | SK8518 |
| Wymondham *Norfk* | 66 | TG1101 |
| Wyndham *M Glam* | 33 | SS9392 |
| Wynds Point *H & W* | 47 | SO7640 |
| Wynford Eagle *Dorset* | 10 | SY5895 |
| Wyre Piddle *H & W* | 47 | SO9647 |
| Wysall *Notts* | 62 | SK6027 |
| Wyson *H & W* | 46 | SO5267 |
| Wythall *H & W* | 61 | SP0774 |
| Wytham *Oxon* | 37 | SP4708 |
| Wythburn *Cumb* | 93 | NY3214 |
| Wythenshawe *Gt Man* | 79 | SJ8386 |
| Wythop Mill *Cumb* | 93 | NY1729 |
| Wyton *Cambs* | 52 | TL2772 |
| Wyton *Humb* | 85 | TA1733 |
| Wyverstone *Suffk* | 54 | TM0468 |
| Wyverstone Street *Suffk* | 54 | TM0367 |
| Wyville *Lincs* | 63 | SK8729 |
| Wyvis Lodge *Highld* | 146 | NH4873 |


# Y


| | | |
|---|---|---|
| Y Rhiw *Gwynd* | 56 | SH2227 |
| Y-Ffrith *Clwyd* | 70 | SJ0483 |
| Yaddlethorpe *Humb* | 84 | SE8806 |
| Yafford *IOW* | 13 | SZ4481 |
| Yafforth *N York* | 89 | SE3494 |
| Yalberton *Devon* | 7 | SX8658 |
| Yalding *Kent* | 28 | TQ7050 |
| Yalverton *Devon* | 6 | SX5267 |
| Yanworth *Gloucs* | 36 | SP0713 |
| Yapham *Humb* | 84 | SE7851 |
| Yapton *W Susx* | 14 | SU9703 |
| Yarborough *Avon* | 21 | ST3858 |
| Yarbridge *IOW* | 13 | SZ6086 |
| Yarburgh *Lincs* | 77 | TF3493 |
| Yarcombe *Devon* | 9 | ST2408 |
| Yard *Devon* | 19 | SS7721 |
| Yarde *Somset* | 20 | ST0538 |
| Yardley *W Mids* | 61 | SP1386 |
| Yardley Gobion *Nhants* | 49 | SP7644 |
| Yardley Hastings *Nhants* | 51 | SP8656 |
| Yardley Wood *W Mids* | 61 | SP1080 |
| Yardro *Powys* | 45 | SO2258 |
| Yarford *Somset* | 20 | ST2029 |
| Yarkhill *H & W* | 46 | SO6042 |
| Yarlet *Staffs* | 72 | SJ9129 |
| Yarley *Somset* | 21 | ST5045 |
| Yarlington *Somset* | 21 | ST6529 |
| Yarlsber *N York* | 87 | SD7072 |
| Yarm *Cleve* | 89 | NZ4111 |
| Yarmouth *IOW* | 12 | SZ3589 |
| Yarnacott *Devon* | 19 | SS6230 |
| Yarnbrook *Wilts* | 22 | ST8654 |
| Yarnfield *Staffs* | 72 | SJ8632 |
| Yarnscombe *Devon* | 19 | SS5523 |
| Yarnton *Oxon* | 37 | SP4712 |
| Yarpole *H & W* | 46 | SO4664 |
| Yarrow *Border* | 109 | NT3528 |
| Yarrow *Somset* | 21 | ST3747 |
| Yarrow Feus *Border* | 109 | NT3325 |
| Yarrowford *Border* | 109 | NT4030 |
| Yarsop *H & W* | 46 | SO4047 |
| Yarwell *Nhants* | 51 | TL0797 |
| Yate *Avon* | 35 | ST7082 |
| Yateley *Hants* | 25 | SU8260 |
| Yatesbury *Wilts* | 36 | SU0671 |
| Yattendon *Berks* | 24 | SU5574 |
| Yatton *Avon* | 21 | ST4365 |
| Yatton *H & W* | 46 | SO4367 |
| Yatton *H & W* | 47 | SO6330 |
| Yatton Keynell *Wilts* | 35 | ST8676 |
| Yaverland *IOW* | 13 | SZ6185 |
| Yawl *Devon* | 10 | SY3194 |
| Yawthorpe *Lincs* | 76 | SK8992 |
| Yaxham *Norfk* | 66 | TG0010 |
| Yaxley *Cambs* | 64 | TL1892 |
| Yaxley *Suffk* | 54 | TM1274 |
| Yazor *H & W* | 46 | SO4046 |
| Yeading *Gt Lon* | 26 | TQ1182 |
| Yeadon *W York* | 82 | SE2040 |
| Yealand Conyers *Lancs* | 87 | SD5074 |
| Yealand Redmayne *Lancs* | 87 | SD4975 |
| Yealand Redmayne *Lancs* | 87 | SD5075 |
| Yealand Stores *Lancs* | 87 | SD5075 |
| Yealmpton *Devon* | 6 | SX5751 |
| Yearby *Cleve* | 97 | NZ5921 |
| Yearngill *Cumb* | 92 | NY1343 |
| Yearsley *N York* | 90 | SE5874 |
| Yeaton *Shrops* | 59 | SJ4319 |
| Yeaveley *Derbys* | 73 | SK1840 |
| Yedingham *N York* | 91 | SE8979 |
| Yelford *Oxon* | 36 | SP3504 |
| Yelland *Devon* | 18 | SS4932 |
| Yelling *Cambs* | 52 | TL2662 |
| Yelvertoft *Nhants* | 50 | SP5975 |
| Yelvertoft *Nhants* | 50 | SP6075 |
| Yelverton *Norfk* | 67 | TG2902 |
| Yenston *Somset* | 22 | ST7120 |
| Yeo Mill *Somset* | 19 | SS8426 |
| Yeo Park *Devon* | 6 | SX5852 |
| Yeo Vale *Devon* | 18 | SS4223 |
| Yeoford *Devon* | 8 | SX7898 |
| Yeolmbridge *Cnwll* | 5 | SX3187 |
| Yeovil *Somset* | 10 | ST5515 |
| Yeovil Marsh *Somset* | 10 | ST5418 |
| Yeovilton *Somset* | 21 | ST5422 |
| Yerbeston *Dyfed* | 30 | SN0609 |
| Yesnaby *Ork* | 155 | HY2215 |
| Yetlington *Nthumb* | 111 | NU0209 |
| Yetminster *Dorset* | 10 | ST5910 |
| Yetson *Devon* | 7 | SX8056 |
| Yettington *Devon* | 9 | SY0585 |
| Yetts O'Muckhart *Cent* | 117 | NO0001 |
| Yew Green *Warwks* | 48 | SP2367 |
| Yews Green *W York* | 82 | SE1030 |
| Yielden *Beds* | 51 | TL0167 |
| Yieldingtree *H & W* | 60 | SO8977 |
| Yieldshields *Strath* | 116 | NS8750 |
| Yiewsley *Gt Lon* | 26 | TQ0680 |
| Ynysboeth *M Glam* | 33 | ST0695 |
| Ynysddu *Gwent* | 33 | ST1792 |
| Ynysforgan *W Glam* | 32 | SS6799 |
| Ynyshir *M Glam* | 33 | ST0292 |
| Ynyslas *Dyfed* | 43 | SN6293 |
| Ynysmaerdy *M Glam* | 33 | ST0383 |
| Ynysmeudwy *W Glam* | 32 | SN7305 |
| Ynyswen *M Glam* | 33 | SS9597 |
| Ynyswen *Powys* | 33 | SN8313 |
| Ynysybwl *M Glam* | 33 | ST0594 |
| Ynysymaengwyn *Gwynd* | 57 | SH5902 |
| Yockenthwaite *N York* | 88 | SD9078 |
| Yockleton *Shrops* | 59 | SJ3910 |
| Yokefleet *Humb* | 84 | SE8124 |
| Yoker *Strath* | 115 | NS5169 |
| Yonder Bognie *Gramp* | 142 | NJ6046 |
| Yondertown *Devon* | 6 | SX5958 |
| York *Lancs* | 81 | SD7133 |
| York *N York* | 83 | SE6052 |
| York Town *Hants* | 25 | SU8660 |
| Yorkletts *Kent* | 29 | TR0963 |
| Yorkley *Gloucs* | 35 | SO6307 |
| Yorton Heath *Shrops* | 59 | SJ5022 |
| Youlgreave *Derbys* | 74 | SK2164 |
| Youlthorpe *Humb* | 84 | SE7655 |
| Youlton *N York* | 90 | SE4963 |
| Young's End *Essex* | 40 | TL7419 |
| Youngsbury *Herts* | 39 | TL3618 |
| Yoxall *Staffs* | 73 | SK1418 |
| Yoxford *Suffk* | 55 | TM3968 |
| Yoxford Little Street *Suffk* | 55 | TM3869 |
| Ysbyty Cynfyn *Dyfed* | 43 | SN7578 |
| Ysbyty Ifan *Gwynd* | 69 | SH8448 |
| Ysbyty Ystwyth *Dyfed* | 43 | SN7371 |
| Ysceifiog *Clwyd* | 70 | SJ1571 |
| Ysgubor-y-Coed *Dyfed* | 43 | SN6895 |
| Ystalyfera *W Glam* | 32 | SN7708 |
| Ystrad *M Glam* | 33 | SS9895 |
| Ystrad Aeron *Dyfed* | 44 | SN5256 |
| Ystrad Meurig *Dyfed* | 43 | SN7067 |
| Ystrad Mynach *M Glam* | 33 | ST1494 |
| Ystrad-ffyn *Dyfed* | 44 | SN7846 |
| Ystradfellte *Powys* | 33 | SN9313 |
| Ystradgynlais *Powys* | 32 | SN7910 |
| Ystradowen *Dyfed* | 32 | SN7512 |
| Ystradowen *S Glam* | 33 | ST0177 |
| Ystumtuen *Dyfed* | 43 | SN7378 |
| Ythsie *Gramp* | 143 | NJ8830 |

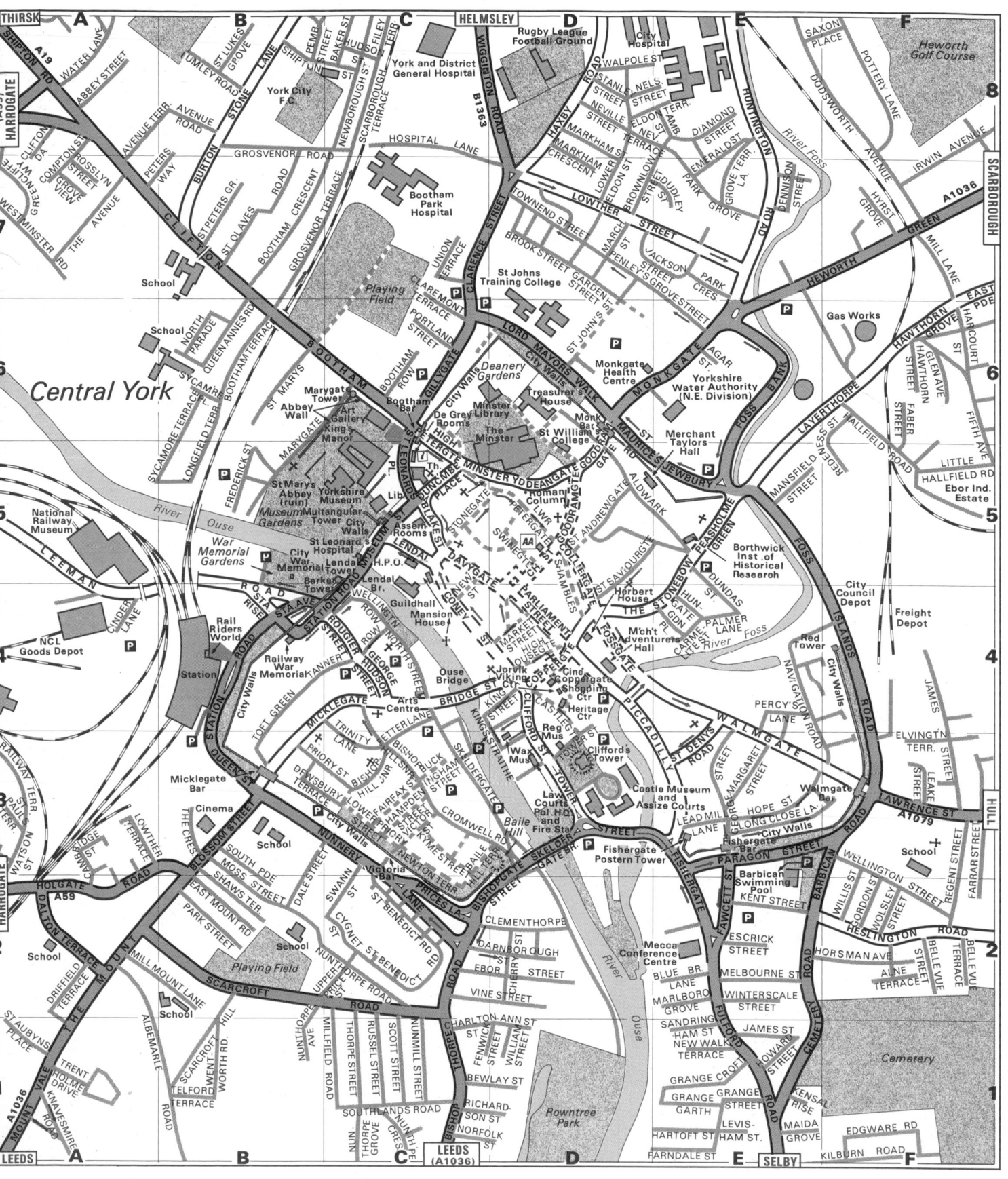

# Central York

**Z**

# London's Orbital Routes

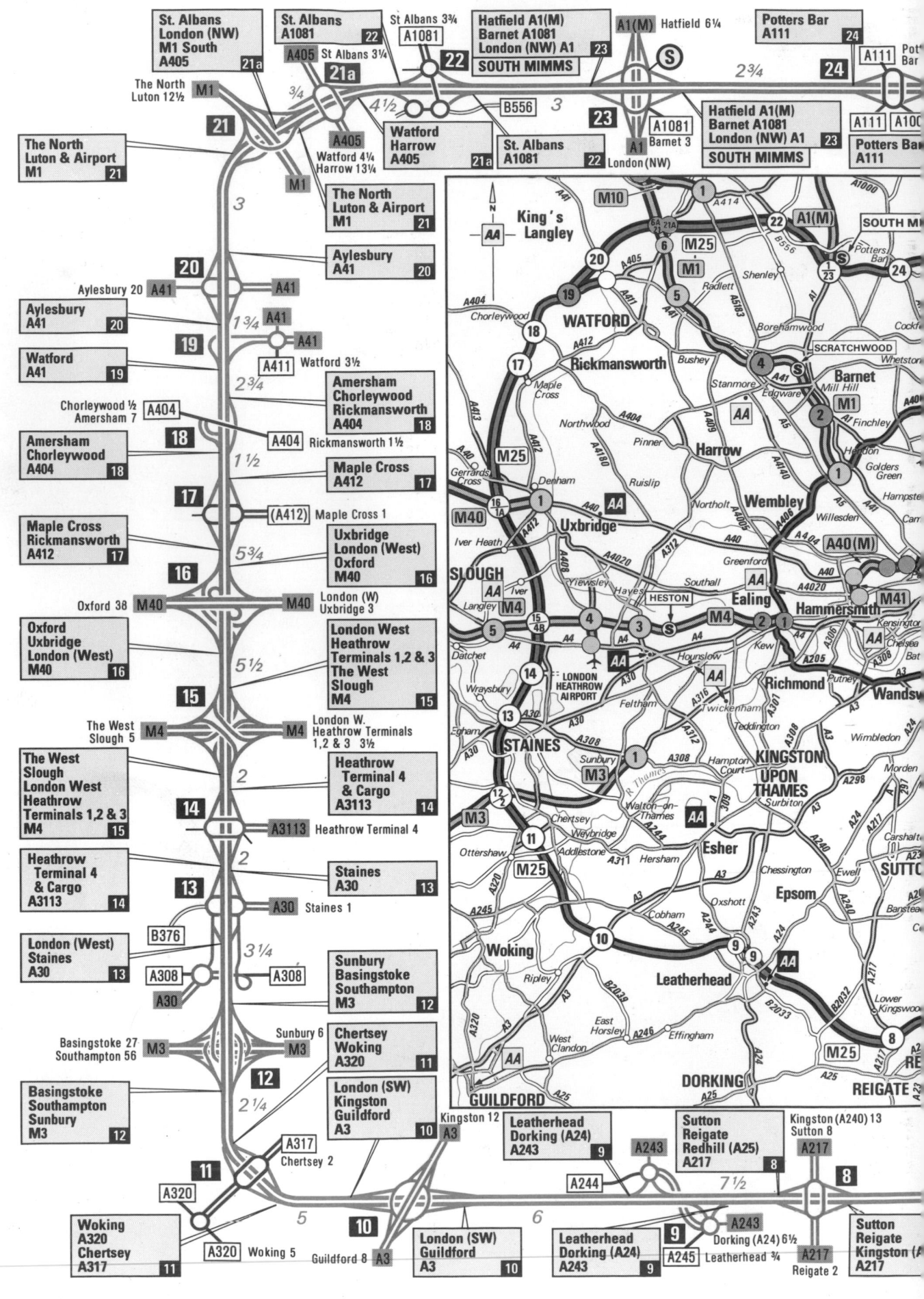